Special Edition
Using
SAP R/3

Third Edition

Special Edition
Using
SAP R/3

Third Edition

**Written by ASAP World Consultancy
and Jonathan Blain with**

Mark Denning, Jonathan Lingard, Bernard Dodd, Eric Matthews, Gray Elkington, Max Nyiri, Wendy Hewson, Jonathan R. Tate, Kate Hill, Philippa Worth

**Contributions by
Natasha Courtenay-Smith, Sarah Pritchard**

Prentice·Hall of India Private Limited
New Delhi - 110 001
1999

This Fifth Indian Reprint—Rs. 395.00
(Original U.S. Edition—Rs. 3278.00)

SPECIAL EDITION USING SAP R/3, 3rd Ed.
by ASAP World Consultancy and Jonathan Blain

This Eastern Economy Edition is the authorized, unabridged reprint published by Prentice-Hall of India Private Limited, © 1999 by special arrangement with Que Corporation, a division of Macmillan Computer Publishing, 201 W. 103rd Street, Indianapolis, Indiana 46290, U.S.A.

This edition is authorized for sale only in Bangladesh, India, Maldives, Nepal, Pakistan and Sri Lanka.

ISBN-81-203-1526-X

The export rights of this book are vested solely with the publisher.

Fifth Printing (Third Edition)   ...   ...   **January, 1999**

Published by Asoke K. Ghosh, Prentice-Hall of India Private Limited, M-97, Connaught Circus, New Delhi-110001 and Printed by Bhuvnesh Seth at Replika Press Private Limited, E-803, DSIDC, Narela Industrial Park, Delhi-110040.

Contents at a Glance

Contents

III Managing Complex Systems

8 Developing Businesses on a Continuous Basis   157

9 Building Global Business Systems   169

IV Steering the Corporation

12 Understanding the Financial Accounting Module   213

16 Understanding the R/3 Project System   373

V Manufacturing Applications

17 Understanding the Production Planning Module   387

18 Understanding the Production Planning for Process Industries Module 423

VI Supporting Applications

20 Understanding the Sales and Distribution Module   469

VII Considering Specialized Configurations

24 Pursuing a Vertical Market Initiative 625

VIII Maintaining and Enhancing the Implementation

IX Implementation Issues

32 Overview of SAP Implementations   725

X SAP Employment Market

Credits

EXECUTIVE EDITOR
Bryan Gambrel

ACQUISITIONS EDITOR
Angela C. Kozlowski

DEVELOPMENT EDITOR
Susan Shaw Dunn

MANAGING EDITOR
Patrick Kanouse

PROJECT EDITOR
Rebecca Mounts

COPY EDITOR
Fran Blauw

INDEXER
Joy Dean Lee

PROOFREADER
Kim Cofer

TECHNICAL EDITORS
Brian Bokanyi, senior consultant at CAP Gemini-PBS
David Knittle

INTERIOR DESIGN
Ruth Lewis

COVER DESIGN
Dan Armstrong

LAYOUT TECHNICIANS
Ayanna Lacey
Heather Hiatt Miller

I dedicate this book to my dear wife, Jennifer, and our beautiful daughter, Kezia, and to my parents, David and Neva Blain, who have been so supportive.
—*Jonathan Blain*

About the Authors

ASAP World Consultancy is an international SAP consulting company. It is in the business of selling high-quality products and services relating to SAP and other enterprise applications, computing systems, and implementations. ASAP World Consultancy is part of the ASAP group of companies, whose activities include the following:

- SAP Documentation Consultancy
- SAP Recruitment
- SAP Training
- SAP Access and Security Consultancy
- SAP Internal & External Communications Consultancy
- SAP System Testing Consultancy & Resourcing
- SAP Human Issues Consultancy
- SAP Resource Planning Consultancy
- Business Process Reengineering and Change Management Consultancy
- Hardware and Installation Consultancy
- Introductory SAP courses for corporate clients worldwide
- SAP Skills Transfer to Your Employees
- Development of SAP Complementary Solutions
- SAP Market Research
- SAP acquisitions, mergers, and joint ventures
- SAP Procurement Consultancy

ASAP World Consultancy is headquartered in Henley on Thames, England, but operates all over the world with virtual offices in the United States, Australia, South Africa, and mainland Europe. ASAP has a commitment to quality and is focused on meeting the business objectives of its clients through a number of highly specialized divisions and companies.

The company prides itself on the quality of its people. It uses a combination of its own employees and associates, who bring a wealth of experience and skills to meet the needs of its customers.

ASAP World Consultancy can be contacted at the following address:

ASAP World Consultancy
ASAP House
P.O. Box 4463
Henley on Thames, Oxfordshire, UK
RG9 6YW

Telephone: +44 (0) 1491 414411
Fax: +44 (0) 1491 414412
Email: **enquiry@asap-consultancy.co.uk**
Author comments: **author.comments@asap-consultancy.co.uk**
Web site: **http://www.asap-consultancy.co.uk**

ASAP 24-hour Virtual Offices
New York City, NY
Voice Mail: (212) 253-4180
Fax: (212) 253-4180

Sydney, Australia
Voice Mail: +61 (0)2 9475 0551
Fax: +61 (0)2 9475 0551

Brussels, Belgium
Voice Mail: +32 (0)2 706 50 04
Fax: +32 (0)2 706 50 04

See the advertisements at the back of this book for more details.

Jonathan Blain is the founder of the ASAP group of companies. He has been working with SAP products since 1991. He has a strong business background, having spent 10 years in the oil industry working in a variety of different roles in the downstream sector for Mobil Corporation. He has specialist knowledge of large-scale SAP implementations, project management, human issues, planning, communications, security, training, documentation, and SAP recruitment. He has benefited from professional business training with the Henley Management College and other institutions.

As a management consultant, he has specialized in matching corporate business strategies to IT strategies. He has a special interest in business engineering and the effective management of change when implementing large-scale IT systems.

Coming from a business rather than systems background, he is focused on providing business solutions. He believes that the implementation of SAP can improve the way that companies do business and that, provided common sense and logical thinking are applied, SAP implementations don't need to be daunting.

Jonathan is a keen yachtsman and is the vice chairman of the Yacht Owners Association in the UK. He has been instrumental in the development of the "Hy Tech Sprint" yacht, a revolutionary 43-foot light displacement, water-ballasted ocean cruiser.

After graduating from Liverpool University in mathematics with management, **Mark Denning** worked in line management before becoming a management consultant. During his time as a consultant, he has focused on the IT sector, including projects for clients such as ICL and Apple. He has also developed a specialty in analytical tools, including the development of an outlet analysis tool for retail chains and an in-depth study into the potential market for analytical marketing application. This has left him with an in-depth strategic understanding of IT systems and their impact on businesses as a whole.

After graduating in psychology at Aberdeen University, **Bernard Dodd** built and directed an industrial training research unit over a period of nine years at the Department of Psychology, University of Sheffield. Two years with an international business consultancy led to an open competition direct entry to the specialist Civil Service, where he served in the Royal Navy for 17 years to become the senior psychological advisor to the Second Sea Lord. Since 1990, he has specialized in technical interviewing of experts and the writing of system documentation and user handbooks for the computer-intensive industries.

Gray Elkington is managing director of Hambleden Consulting, a firm that helps its clients develop the customer-focused culture they need to become market leaders. From their base near Henley on Thames, Gray and his colleagues work in multidisciplinary teams on key performance issues, always placing the client company's internal relationships firmly at the top of the development agenda. After working for some years on the people issues involved with the reengineering of business and management processes, Gray can contribute valuable guidance to those tasked with implementing SAP, especially to those concerned with how the changes may affect employees and customers.

Wendy Hewson is a chartered accountant. Before becoming a teacher fellow at Cranfield School of Management, she was a management consultant with Arthur Andersen and vice president of Merrill Lynch. Wendy is a visiting lecturer at City University Business School in London and is an expert in business planning and lifetime values in the financial services sector.

Wendy is a partner in the Hewson Consulting Group, established in 1989, and has specialized in application of information technology to sales and marketing operations. The group is well known for its research reports and involvement in large systems implementations. Hewson Consulting Group also manages Mercatus, the Association for the Use of Information Technology in Sales and Marketing.

Kate Hill is a director of McHugh Hill Associates, an SAP consulting company specializing in training and project management. She has spent the last eight years working in the SAP training arena. Her work has covered R/2 and R/3 as a training team manager and "hands-on" trainer. Kate has designed and run courses across a broad spectrum of SAP modules—Sales and Distribution, Materials Management, Finance, and Controlling—for organizations such as Arjo Wiggins Fine Papers, Mobil, Tate and Lyle, IBM, and Siemens Nixdorf.

Jonathan Lingard is a freelance SAP consultant and manager. He has spent five years working on SAP implementation projects in Europe and the United States. His clients have been blue-chip multinational companies using SAP as part of business restructuring projects. His responsibilities have included the coordination, evaluation, and execution of SAP ABAP customization requests; the management of SAP authorization profiles; and the delivery of business process–oriented training. He has also been responsible for business and system process design structures. He received a bachelor's in economics and philosophy from the University of Oxford, England, in 1990.

Eric Matthews has been involved in the IT industry in the United Kingdom and southeast Asia since 1970, originally with UNIVAC mainframe computer systems, performing sales, marketing, and branch management roles, before becoming a country general manager. He has since operated as an independent consultant in the IT industry, advising on and performing international recruitment, systems implementations, management, marketing, acquisition, and venture capital-raising projects. He has in recent years been heavily involved in managing market research and has written many published reports as well as managing single-client research. Eric's work has taken him to five continents from his home base in England's Thames valley.

Max Nyiri, Ph.D psychology and Ph.D. computer science (Germany), is an IT business strategist, who has developed extensive experience in the determination and evaluation of enterprise application/management information requirements, and the recommendation and implementation of IT solutions for business. He uses project management and strategy implementation experience to ensure strategic alignment of information technology with business requirements. Max was a senior executive consultant to various multinational companies. He worked for the IT strategy division of Coopers & Lybrand Consulting. His success was marked by being the youngest IT senior executive worldwide for Volkswagen. He consulted for the business information technology division of Arthur Andersen Business Consulting as a senior executive and is now a senior executive of Standard Bank of South Africa.

Jonathan R. Tate is a senior manager at PriceWaterhouseCoopers, London, responsible for the firm's SAP control and security practice. Before this, he worked for five years in Mobil Corporation as the manager of the SAP Controls Group, providing controls advice to SAP installations worldwide. In 1995, Jonathan established the SAP Audit and Controls User Group, of which he is still chairman. He also is an executive member of the SAP (UK) User Group. He has spoken at numerous conferences on SAP controls and contributed regularly to SAP publications. He graduated from London University with a degree in economics and is an associate of the Chartered Institute of Management Accountants. He previously worked for Coopers & Lybrand and for Shell, performing a range of accounting, systems, and consulting roles.

A graduate of Sussex University and fluent in French, **Philippa Worth** has lived and worked in France and Denmark. Her career has encompassed most principal elements of the marketing mix, and she has experience in corporate management. Philippa is a consultant in the United Kingdom. Her practice provides marketing and corporate communications services to small- to medium-sized enterprises, and contributes to regional economic development initiatives in the UK and France. Her client base draws from both the public and private sectors. Philippa's skills include corporate publications and law, marketing support material, employee communications, business development, and inward investment.

Natasha Courtenay-Smith graduated from the University of Sussex in experimental psychology and now works for ASAP in the UK.

Sarah Pritchard graduated from Cambridge University.

Acknowledgments

In writing this book, we have benefited from the help and support of hundreds of people. There would not be enough space here to acknowledge everyone. They have each given their time and effort freely to make this book thorough, accurate, and useful to the readers. Equally, there are many companies who have given us much of their valuable time and shared their thoughts and opinions.

Our heartfelt thanks go to everyone who has helped. The writing of this book has been a team effort, and just praise should go to each and every team member.

Tell Us What You Think!

As the reader of this book, *you* are our most important critic and commentator. We value your opinion and want to know what we're doing right, what we could do better, what areas you'd like to see us publish in, and any other words of wisdom you're willing to pass our way.

As the Executive Editor for the Programming team at Macmillan Computer Publishing, I welcome your comments. You can fax, email, or write me directly to let me know what you did or didn't like about this book—as well as what we can do to make our books stronger.

Please note that I cannot help you with technical problems related to the topic of this book, and that due to the high volume of mail I receive, I might not be able to reply to every message.

When you write, please be sure to include this book's title and author as well as your name and phone or fax number. I will carefully review your comments and share them with the author and editors who worked on the book.

Fax: [317-817-7070]

E-mail: **cs_db@mcp.com**

Mail: Bryan Gambrel, Executive Editor
          Programming
          Macmillan Computer Publishing
          201 West 103rd Street
          Indianapolis, IN 46290 USA

Introduction

In this chapter

System Identification Codes

This book is about the products of one manufacturer: SAP AG, or SAP Aktiengesellschaft. SAP AG stands for Systems, Applications, Products in Data Processing.

There are two SAP system identification codes: R/2 and R/3. R/2 was developed as a mainframe system; R/3 was developed for the multilevel client/server environment. An SAP installation can include both R/2 and R/3 systems configured, for example, as central host and satellites.

Each R/2 and R/3 system includes a BASIS module to which application modules are added. A module can contain several components, and a component can include several functions. Although a module may be installed, it's not necessary for all its components to be configured to be active. Similarly, a component doesn't need to have all its functions available to users.

This book concentrates on the R/3 system and its applications. The function list used for reference is R/3 Release 3.1 Version G (which can be abbreviated as R/3 Rel.3.1G). Developments and enhancements to R/3 Release 3.1, which are discussed in this book, are available as R/3 Releases 4.0 and 4.5, which are fully compatible with Release 3.1. When the R/2 system is mentioned in this book, the reference is to R/2 Release 5.0, unless otherwise specified.

N O T E   This isn't a user handbook. It's not a glossy demonstration of how easy the system is to use. Very little of the specific information will be readily provided by the vendors and the implementers.

Although the authors are arguably the least reliable judges of this book's quality, it does attempt to distill the experience, good and bad, gathered in the authors' collective years of toil at the task of applying methods to what people do to make things better.

Some of this wisdom is quite definitely peculiar to the business computing realm. Other equally peculiar wisdom comes from older technologies that enjoyed the titles of "training," "mechanization," and even "automation." One excuse for including this know-how is that the progress of human evolution has virtually stopped, partly as a result of the very rapid evolution of machinery, especially of the information-manipulating kind.

The Scope of This Book

In this book, the authors intend to bridge the gap between hearsay and expertise. Many of you are aware of the dominant market position of the SAP enterprise, and you usually understand that considerable expertise has been invested in the products and the way they're implemented. You haven't been mislead. The SAP systems are indeed complex and sophisticated. This third edition of the book records additions to the complexity of the SAP range of products in terms of the business processes that can be carried by these systems. Much of the additions' sophistication is directed at making the business operations easier to implement and as resistant to human errors as possible. The most important developments may turn out to be the new programs to facilitate intranet and Internet communications. These programs enable enterprise-wide business processes and make them open for controlled use via the Internet to almost any terminal device that can respond to Java applets.

However, the process of implementing an SAP R/3 system is conducted by many people who aren't computer experts in each of the thousands of specialties—nor do they need to be. The systems come complete with the most advanced computer-assisted tools for guiding you through the implementation process from first analysis through customizing to performance evaluation of the working installation.

This book is partly technical, partly persuasive. The technical parts are intended to convince those of you interested in business process development and reengineering that the SAP standard software library is comprehensive in its use of new technologies and in its coverage of modern business activities in all sectors of industry and commerce, in private companies, and in public services. The persuasive aspects of this book focus on the long-lasting benefits of understanding your company's business so well that you can successfully implement R/3 and increase profitability.

The parts of this book follow:

- Part I, "Introducing SAP," encompasses the first two chapters, which introduce the company and give an indication of how users will react with the modules.

- Part II, "Reviewing the Technical Background," explains how the R/3 modules achieve their results and how to use the implementation tools. Part II encompasses Chapters 3 through 7.

- Part III, "Managing Complex Systems," shows how the multilevel client/server R/3 system can serve a global company. Chapters 8 through 11 comprise this part.

- Part IV, "Steering the Corporation," describes the Financial and Planning modules in Chapters 12 through 16.

- Part V, "Manufacturing Applications," details the modules designed for manufacturing and plant maintenance in Chapters 17 through 19.

- Part VI, "Supporting Applications," describes the modules for Sales and Distribution, Human Resources, and Materials Management, all of which can be accessed from the Internet. Part VI encompasses Chapters 20 through 23.

- Part VII, "Considering Specialized Configurations," introduces some preconfigured and enhanced R/3 installations designed for rapid implementation in specific industries. Chapters 24 and 25 make up this part of the book.

- Part VIII, "Maintaining and Enhancing the Implementation," considers documentation, online service, the development of company-specific programs, and business workflow management. You can find Chapters 26 through 31 in this part.

- Part IX, "Implementation Issues," surveys the methods of implementation and the management of the changes that new systems require. Chapters 32 through 38 encompass this part.

■ Part X, "SAP Employment Market," reviews the methods and prospects of finding a job as a consultant in the context of SAP and its global organization. You can find Chapters 39 through 44 in this part. Chapter 44, "The ASAP Institute and the ASAP Standards and Assessment Board," illustrates one recent development in selecting and training consultants to meet the acute shortage of SAP implementation skills.

■ The final section of the book contains Appendixes A through F, which provide reference information such as a glossary and information on the migration of systems from R/2 to R/3.

What Will Be Gained from This Book

This book isn't intended to be skimmed quickly. Apply a focused search to this book, and you will find a pointer to what you're looking for, if not the complete information. The most satisfied readers will find that they have acquired the concepts and the language with which to ask questions of the SAP specialists.

Thoughtful readers can expect to gain a thorough understanding of the changes that will need to take place in each department to implement its module. This book provides the explanations of why the changes have to take place and the benefits to be gained by having them done well.

It wouldn't be an unreasonable outcome if serious readers saved the cost of this book by deciding that the SAP system isn't what their particular company should have at the top of its shopping list.

If you are in the happy position of being a project sponsor, we would like to think that you have developed an eye for this subject—what to look at and what to look for, and when to exercise firm control, and on what issues.

Intended Readers

The authors have three groups of readers in mind:

■ Those close to an SAP system
■ Those who are thinking about an SAP system
■ Those who want to know what is entailed in running a modern, comprehensive business data processing system

Two aspects to the installation of any system deserve equal attention: the technical details of the system and the effects the system is likely to have on the staff and its conduct of your business. This book reflects these two concerns by offering technical and implementation sections.

Consultants and Advisory Staff

The intended readers close to an SAP system are consultants, programmers, launchers and managers, and emergency service providers in the data and personnel categories. They're likely to be

- People involved in an SAP implementation
- People interested in implementing an SAP system
- People interested in working with SAP

One task that could fall on anyone close to an SAP system is to explain why the programs are arranged as they are and why the users have to interact with a standard interface. Such explanations will be required at all levels—to the chief executive officer, as well as the input clerk. The content for such explanations is available in this book.

Similarly, the technical specialists in a company will want to know why their current methods won't be replicated exactly in the new SAP system.

Managers at all levels will find that this book can go into considerable detail about the data processing functions provided by the SAP programs so that they can recognize aspects of their own work that could be facilitated by having the system at their command. On the other hand, they will see that a complex system does require a disciplined approach to, for example, the maintenance of uniform data records in standard formats.

Consultants will see that SAP system designers have made provisions for them to build for their client a system that's unique yet assembled from standard business programs that have been thoroughly tested and refined. This book prepares consultants to ask clients the right questions and to make proper allowances for the work involved in customizing a system to fit the specific circumstances and requirements of the client.

If you want to become an SAP consultant, you will see that an extensive body of technical expertise is built into SAP programs because they have been developed in partnerships with specific industries. You will also recognize that the computer technology of the SAP systems is in continuous development in order to maintain a position in the forefront. Experienced consultants will have come to grips with the necessity of maintaining a continuous schedule of self-education in order to be in position for the next technical and perhaps geopolitical development.

Prospective SAP Users

If you're thinking about installing an SAP system or an extension to an existing SAP system, this book will be of interest because it maps out the various possibilities. You will see what's available and what it can achieve; you will also see what will have to be done if these kinds of results are to be realized in your own situation. You won't find the costs of SAP programs in this volume, but you will get a good idea of the magnitude of the work and expense entailed if you decide to go ahead with an installation.

As a person seriously thinking about an SAP installation, you may well find that this book draws your attention to the possibilities of achieving results that weren't at the top of your list of priorities but nevertheless would be well worthwhile in themselves and as investments in expertise for the future.

If you are a potential decision-maker in the matter of choosing a new computer installation, you should be careful about setting out the standards and parameters on which your decision will be made. You won't want to put your entire business in the hands of an unreliable and inflexible system. Yet you won't want to specify a grossly over-elaborate system for the job you want it to do. This book tells you what the SAP R/3 system and its applications can do; it may become the standard against which you judge competitors' proposals.

General Readers

You can consider yourself a general reader of this book if you're not a consultant or a manager about to purchase a computer system.

Perhaps you are familiar with computing but not with industry and business. You will find that this book gives you the key concepts used by the various departments of business, whether or not a computer is involved. The net result could be that you develop a way of thinking about computing in the context of business applications. This book will point you toward the business concepts that should be given the highest priority.

On the other hand, you might be a general reader who is familiar with one or more sectors of industry and yet not fully conversant with the way business computing is developing. In this book, you will recognize many business ideas. What might intrigue you is the way they're supported by standard business functions and a system of master data records, for example. Often, the best way of processing and storing business data is quite different from the way these operations are carried out in a people-and-paper system, where the main retrieval mechanism is in the mind of the person who put the data into storage.

If you are a general reader with no business experience and no computer experience, this book will still give you a comprehensive road map of the territory.

Intended Outcomes of Publishing

There will be a significant increase in the number of successful SAP implementations. In particular, this book is intended to increase the productivity and the reputation of the following groups of people:

- The implementation team, for delivering an effective system on time, within budget, and with good omens for successful operations
- The project research team, for preparing the decisions
- The sponsor, for making the decision
- SAP AG, for making available efficient tools to do the job

The first and second editions of this book are being used by those involved with SAP R/3 as a means of filling in gaps in their awareness of the various applications and modules available. These editions enable them to seek out more detailed information when they need it by looking under the appropriate module titles. The other use of the previous editions is as training courses for those who are preparing for a career as an SAP implementation specialist.

The Business Territory

Good businesspeople usually possess a thorough knowledge of the geographical and technical territory in which their business operates. They know a great deal about who buys what and how these purchases can be obtained or manufactured at a good price. They appreciate the needs of individual customers. They take into account the operating problems of the warehouses and manufacturing plants when making plans. All this is the business territory.

The territory of an SAP consultant and a manager who might want to employ a consultant is business process reengineering: installing new hardware and software, or making the transition from manual to mechanized business processing in some or all of the work of the company. Because SAP software can be set up to assist in any business process in any sector of commerce and industry, two complex decisions need to be made:

- What aspects of the business will be reengineered?
- Will the SAP software be the best choice?

Because SAP can handle any type of business structure, decisions have to be made as to how the company should be analyzed to yield the best structure for designing the application software that will drive the SAP standard software modules. For example, a simple manufacturing business can be viewed as two components—one looks after the product, the other looks after the money. Yet this model has a serious flaw in it. Who looks after the customers?

Mechanization of business processes has been controlled largely by the equipment available: its cost and its capabilities. As capabilities have increased, the cost of programming the equipment has become an ever-larger proportion of the total cost of reengineering. Complexity can be costly.

The decision-maker has to set out the pros and cons of providing office automation and communications to assist in each element of the business. Reengineering everything might be costly yet fruitful, although the time necessary to achieve this may entail an unacceptable risk of the market changing too much in the interim. What's needed is a software tool that allows the chosen design to be up and running quickly, yet enables that design to be easy to tune to new circumstances as they arise.

Making a complex decision isn't easy; some decision-makers may be prone to several errors.

Some Procedures for Using This Book

You could begin at the end or, if you must, at the beginning of this book. The table of contents might be a good place to start your reading.

Perhaps you prefer to see some illustrations before you begin studying the text. You might even flip through for some pictures before doing anything else. However, this book isn't a picture book, and there is no information in the illustrations that isn't also in the text.

A sensible approach to intensive study is to first make up your mind about what you want to find and then keep on looking until you find it. If you have a particular type of business in mind—your own or one you would like to be a part of—you might find it interesting to cull for information directly relevant to your business and deliberately skip anything that doesn't seem relevant at this stage.

The world of computing is paved with clusters of capital letters that mean something to those who use them as technical terms. If you know what the letters of the acronym stand for, you might be able to work out what the whole term refers to. A good way of sampling this book is to think of an acronym and see if this book mentions it.

If you already know how computers and other things go wrong, you might want to see whether SAP and the authors know this as well.

Delegation is a possibility. You could place a Post-it note in each part that seems difficult and ask a junior colleague to give you a report by the end of the work week.

Errors in Decision-Making

You might be under pressure to choose between making a high-quality decision or a fast one. More information might give you extra accuracy and confidence, but the response will be delayed if more input is required. There is a right moment for most decisions—maybe when costs are low, or maybe as a matter of cornering the market by spending now to profit later. Or the right moment might be when you know you can lay your hands on the expertise to get it right.

Reluctance is resistance to change. Timidity may be passed off as prudence, but it may also allow the best moment for a decision to pass by. The research team shouldn't be allowed to go on looking indefinitely. Lack of data isn't necessarily an excuse for avoiding a decision. If analysis takes too long, a slow movement in the problem might take place that renders the solution invalid.

Hunches may have to be the basis for impossible decisions. There may be no rational means of arriving at a choice under the circumstances. In diagnosis, there might not be enough information to come to a single conclusion. A decision may have to be based on a hunch, an unsupported prediction of what might be in the future. With luck, at least one course of action can be adapted to circumstances if they change as implementation proceeds. SAP is an example.

Extra information may be sought by decision-makers beyond what is necessary for a logical choice, particularly if a choice has been made and declared already. This isn't the same as finding out more about the option chosen to make better use of it. Although it might be comforting, redundant verification of a decision that has already been made can be costly in time and resources.

Tunnel vision or rigid thinking can afflict decision-makers. If no options or alternatives are presented, or if the variety of choices is too narrow, the risk of a bad decision can be high. And it's not good enough for researchers to dig out some options that are clearly out of the question. Genuine alternatives must be considered before making a choice. Despite what may be said about timidity, doing nothing should always be a carefully considered option.

A bad decision can occur if the dominant attribute is used without evidence to justify the choice. The sales force for a certain product might seem very knowledgeable because they're always displaying their knowledge. This knowledge could be erroneous, however, and the product might not be suitable for the job in mind.

Looking at the Business

One way to avoid some bad decisions is to deliberately look at the business of the company from more than one viewpoint. Some politicians are renowned for declaring that growth will come from the service industries rather than the manufacturing sectors. Every manufacturer knows, however, that his customers will judge him on the quality of his service as well as the quality of his product.

These are examples of viewpoints worth considering. Should business process reengineering adjust the emphasis within the company between manufacturing and service, between customer relations and supplier relations, between collecting debts and internal economies? The SAP modules can be used in an infinite variety of ways so that the finished system reflects and serves whatever business structure is appropriate.

Model 1: Material and Finance

The model (in your mind or on paper) that you have of your business represents how you think of it. It could be like a tunnel: Things and effort go in; profit and fatigue come out.

Perhaps you have an accounting view of your business. Valuable material is hanging about that needs to be managed, lest it be misused or wasted. And someone has to be in charge of the treasury; otherwise, there won't be enough cash to pay wages and bills. If that's the first image that comes to mind when you think about modeling your business, why not draw it out on very large paper so that you will have room to add pieces and elaborate on your concept?

Some more elements need to be added to your model if every person and job in your company will find a place in the scheme of things. For example, several departments, or at least work sections, probably aren't yet represented:

- Accounts Payable
- General Ledger
- Management Accounting
- Accounts Receivable
- Transport

The difficulty with this modeling is that not all the elements are of the same type (see Figure I.1). Who put the Transport section next to Accounts Receivable?

FIGURE I.1
A simple business might
seem to revolve around
material and finance.

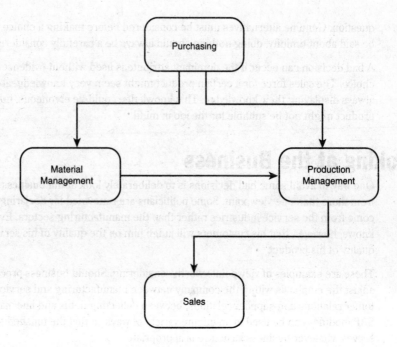

Model 2: Customers, Suppliers, and Internal Management

As you add elements to your company's model, sooner or later you will find that outsiders are getting included—such as suppliers and customers (see Figure I.2).

If you haven't already guessed, the purpose of this very elementary introduction to business modeling is to convince you that the SAP R/3 system not only provides a wealth of tested and working business software, but also includes the means by which you can build a model of your existing business under the guidance and support of the R/3 system. You can also use the system support modules to modify this model of the existing situation until it represents how you would like the business of the company to be conducted in the future. You will thus be guided into elaborating a target concept.

The SAP organization isn't just providing the means by which you can draw more elaborate models; there is more to it than that. If you take the trouble to describe your existing situation in the way suggested by the R/3 system, you will find that it's but a relatively small and not too difficult step to achieve a specification of exactly which SAP modules would be necessary to have your target concept running as a model in simulation mode. This would be followed very rapidly by the same system going live as the basis for the data processing of your business and its management.

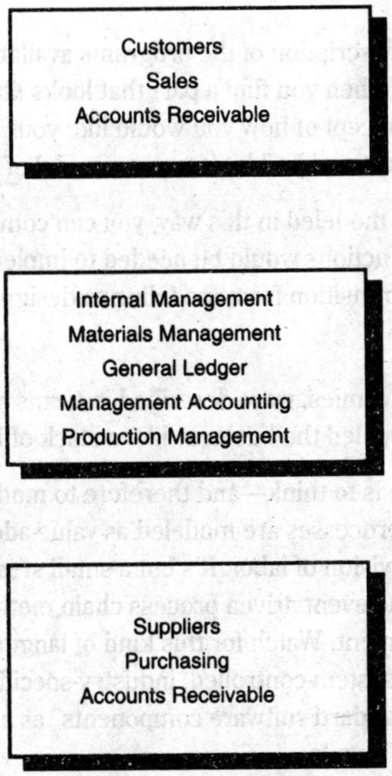

FIGURE I.2
Customers, suppliers, and internal management might appear to live in separate domains.

```
┌─────────────────────────┐
│      Customers          │
│       Sales             │
│   Accounts Receivable   │
└─────────────────────────┘
```

```
┌─────────────────────────┐
│   Internal Management    │
│   Materials Management   │
│     General Ledger       │
│  Management Accounting   │
│  Production Management   │
└─────────────────────────┘
```

```
┌─────────────────────────┐
│       Suppliers          │
│       Purchasing         │
│   Accounts Receivable    │
└─────────────────────────┘
```

The Orientation of the SAP R/3 System

SAP R/3's designers have worked with thousands of companies, making the transition from legacy data processing methods based on mechanization of traditional manual procedures. They have seen how difficult a process it can be if you start with the existing procedures and try to stitch on a computer.

So the designers have started at the other end. They have built and tested all the standard business programs needed to put together a modern system for just about every type and structure of business, whether the throughput is mainly material objects or mainly information, or even if the throughput is people in hospitals, for example. Each standard program has been specialized to perform to the highest possible level in the work for which it is designed. There are no compromises.

Because these standard programs are so highly polished, users aren't allowed to alter them in any way at all. They are sacrosanct.

These highly efficient programs are subject to only one form of control. They're designed to consult tables. Into these tables, you can place the words and numbers that will make each program your own. You can tell the programs what to do without tinkering with their internal mechanisms. The process is called *customizing* because it tailors the programs to suit customers.

The Enterprise Data Model

Inside the R/3 system is a complete description of the programs available. You can inspect this description from various viewpoints. When you find a part that looks like something in your existing company or in your target concept of how you would like your company to be, you can have the system save a copy of that part and build it into your model of your enterprise.

If you have a piece of your enterprise modeled in this way, you can command the system to show just which standard business functions would be needed to implement that part of your enterprise. There can be a seamless transition from modeling to designing the implementation.

Business Process Orientation

At one time, businesses, like military armies, were described in terms of the numbers of people at each rank in the hierarchy. You modeled the business like a stack of bricks.

A more modern and fruitful approach is to think—and therefore to model—in terms of processes. Particularly, the logistics processes are modeled as value-adding chains of subprocesses, not according to the division of labor. It's but a small step to think of the entire corporation as the subject to which the event-driven process chain method should be applied as part of business workflow management. Watch for this kind of language to acquire the status of technical terminology. Try "system-controlled, industry-specific, and company-specific modification procedures applied to standard software components" as a working definition of what the SAP implementation activity entails.

Because quantities and values are invariably posted simultaneously, synchronized logistics management and financial accounting is normal and results in improved quality through efficient logistics.

With the rapidly widening possibilities afforded by improved communications, including the Internet, the business model for the immediate future will take for granted an efficient logistics system and a closely coupled manufacturing organization. The SAP model looks toward customer-driven enterprises that take orders for and deliver goods and services globally.

The extensive array of SAP products includes many different examples of standard business programs that can be configured and customized to suit individual user corporations.

Since the first edition of this book, SAP R/3 has become easier to install and has established links with more third-party systems and products. It now provides reliable and secure components to conduct business worldwide through the Internet.

Introducing SAP

Reviewing the SAP Corporation

Introducing SAP

SAP was founded in 1972 and has grown to become the world's fifth largest software company.

SAP is the name of the company as well as the computer system. The SAP system consists of a number of fully integrated modules that cover virtually every aspect of business management. SAP meets the increasing needs of commercial and other organizations that are striving for greater efficiency and effectiveness. Information technology is now at the very core of major organizations around the world, and its importance is beyond question. Market forces and customer expectations continually pressure organizations to improve the performance of their systems. While many software companies have looked at areas of business and have developed systems to support those areas, SAP has looked toward the whole business. SAP offers a unique system that supports nearly all areas of business on a global scale. SAP provides the opportunity to replace large numbers of independent systems developed and implemented in established organizations with one single modular system. Each module performs a different function but is designed to work with other modules. SAP is fully integrated and offers true compatibility across business functions.

SAP is a German company but operates all over the world, with 28 subsidiaries and affiliates and six partner companies maintaining offices in 40 countries. The following is a partial list of countries with SAP installations:

Americas

Argentina	Brazil	Canada
Mexico	U.S.A.	

Europe

Austria	Belgium	Czech Republic
Denmark	France	Germany
Greece	Hungary	Italy
Netherlands	Norway	Poland
Portugal	Russia	Slovak Republic
Spain	Sweden	Switzerland
United Kingdom		

Pacific Rim

Australia	China	Hong Kong
India	Indonesia	Japan
Korea	Malaysia	New Zealand
Philippines	Singapore	Thailand

Africa/Middle East

Israel	Turkey	South Africa

The Executive Board

- Prof. Dr. H. C. Hasso Plattner, co-chairman AG
- Prof. Dr. Henning Kagermann, co-chairman
- Dr Claus E. Heinrich
- Gerhard Oswald
- Paul Wahl
- Dr. Peter Zencke

Supervisory Board

- Dietmar Hopp
- Dr. H.C. Klaus Tschira

The Name

SAP's name is derived from

Systems, Applications, Products in Data Processing

Corporate Headquarters

SAP Aktiengesellschaft
SAP AG
Neurottstraße 16
D-6909 Walldorf
Germany
06227 34-0

Corporate Goals

SAP has defined its corporate goals as the following:

- Customer satisfaction
- Profitability
- Growth
- Employee satisfaction

History

SAP was founded in 1972 by five people: Herbert Wellenreuther, Dietmar Hopp, Haas-Werner Hector, Hasso Plattner, and Klaus Tschira. Wellenreuther had, while employed by IBM, developed a financial accounting package running in batch for an IBM customer (Naturin). SAP bought the rights from Naturin and started to design and implement the real-time finance system as a standard package based on Wellenreuther's experience with the application. SAP sold the first copy of the standard system to Imperial Chemical Industries (ICI) for the same price as later customers. Simultaneously, they developed an MM-Materials Management system for ICI but reserved all property rights for SAP. From the cash flow of the MM system, SAP financed the development of the FI-Financial Accounting system. The MM system later was converted to a standard package, which in turn was financed by revenue from the FI Package. Both were the first modules of System R, which later was renamed R/1 to better distinguish it from its successors, R/2 and R/3.

SAP's Markets

SAP markets its products all over the world to almost every industry imaginable, as well as government and educational institutions and hospitals. Here are some of the industries served by SAP:

- Automotive
- Building and heavy construction
- Building materials, clay, and glass
- Chemicals
- Clothing and textiles
- Communications services and media
- Consulting and software
- Consumer packaged goods—food and nonfood
- Education institutions and research
- Electronic/optic and communications equipment
- Financial services, banks, and insurance
- Furniture
- Government, public administration, and utility services
- Healthcare and hospitals
- Industrial and commercial machinery
- Museums and associations
- Oil and gas
- Pharmaceuticals
- Primary metal, metal products, and steel
- Raw materials, mining, and agriculture
- Retail and wholesale
- Services, such as property and plant maintenance
- Ship, aerospace, and train construction

- Storage, distribution, and shipping
- Transportation services and tourism
- Utilities
- Wood and paper

The following is an incomplete list of SAP R/2 customers:

ABB	Eastman Kodak	Mobil
Adidas	Esso	Motorola
AEG	Exxon	Nissan Europe
AGIP	Fuji	Polygram
Allianz	General Electric	Schindler Elevator
Aral	Goodyear	SEAT
Coca-Cola	Hapag-Lloyd	Swissair
Compaq	Krupp-Hoesch	Tchibo
Danone	Lufthansa German Airlines	Texaco
Deutsche Bahn	Marriott	Toyota
Deutsche Bank	Miele	ZDF
Dow Chemical	Milupa	

The following is an incomplete list of SAP R/3 customers:

Dow Chemical	Milupa	
Airbus Industrie	DuPont	MIT
Akzo	Frankfurt Airport	Nestlé
Alcatel	Henkel	Petrofina
American Airlines	Hercules	Philips
Apple	Hewlett-Packard	Philip Morris
Autodesk	Hitachi	Pirelli
BASF	Hoechst	Procter & Gamble
Bayer	Hoffman-La Roche	Rhone Poulenc
Bertelsmann	IBM	Rolex
BMW	ICI	Rothmans
Bosch	Lego	Royal LePage
British Rail	Mannesmann	RTL
Carlsberg	Mercedes Benz	Sandoz
Chevron	Merck	SAT 1
Ciba Geigy	Metro International	Schlumberger

Digital Equipment	Micrografx	Shell
Siemens	Total Oil	Varta
Solvoy	Unilever	Vattenfall
Thyssen Stahl	University of Oxford	Wuerth

Figure 1.1 shows the makeup of SAP's group sales. SAP's primary business activity remains the sale of its software systems. ●

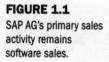

FIGURE 1.1
SAP AG's primary sales
activity remains
software sales.

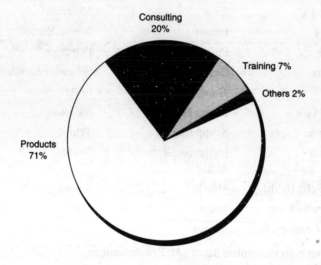

Interacting with the SAP Systems

Exploring the Interface Between System and User

The user interface of the SAP system presents users with attractive and informative displays and enables them to perform tasks easily and intuitively. It also allows users to streamline repetitive tasks if those tasks cannot be automated altogether.

The concept of the SAP user interface is based on its use in communications, where one system has to transfer data to and from another. The design of the screens and the logic used to process user entries are consistent across applications and hardware. In client/server networks, the presentation servers are assigned considerable computing resources.

Running Sessions

A session starts after you successfully log on. If one operation is taking some time to complete, or if you want to relate two items of information, you can open another session at the same time. The screen shows you a fresh window for your other session. You now have two sessions running at the same time. You can have up to nine sessions, each in its own window, and you can move the windows if you need to compare one with another.

Defining User Profiles

A *user* is a person who has permission to use the system and an identification code that tells the system which password to expect for that authorized user.

A *user profile* is established by the system supervisor to give the user permission to use certain functions. For example, a user who has learned only to enter purchase orders is not allowed to send them off to suppliers without supervisor authorization. The profile can also tell the system which language the user expects and which department he belongs to for administrative purposes. A user profile can be set up to display a certain part of the system as soon as the user logs on. The system supervisor can also specify that a profile set up more than one session for you, depending on what you were doing the last time you were working on the system.

Using Tables in SAP Applications

A *table* is a collection of data fields arranged in rows and columns, not all of which need to be onscreen at the same time. Each field has its own column.

However, a screen field might not be as large as the data field. When you type data in a screen field, the characters move to the left when you get near the end of the field. You can continue entering characters until the underlying data field is full.

Tables are used throughout the SAP systems to present data that fits into a rectangular pattern of rows and columns. A list of parts numbers, names, and prices would fit nicely in a table of three columns and could have as many rows as there are different parts, for example.

You can ask SAP to sort the table so that the most expensive parts come first, or you can have the list arranged in order according to part number. Your screen seldom is big enough to let you see the whole table, so you must have some way of selecting which items to look at.

Almost everything you do in a business system is based on tables, even if you ask for the graphical presentation system to convert the table to a picture for you. Some tables contain data, like the parts list; others contain control data that tells the system how things should be done. For example, you could have a list of screens in a table so that when you finish with one, the next one appears.

Tables have an important technical role in SAP software, because they enable you to make customizations without affecting SAP's reliability and integrity. This type of table contains system-control data and can be edited only by SAP or by users with special authorization.

Most functions consult a table of parameters with default values that can be edited as part of the customization process so that the functions work with the business requirements of the company in which the R/3 system is installed. These tables of basic commercial data contain information that might have to be maintained from time to time, such as ZIP codes, country keys, and wage types. Some aspects of the logic might have to be changed if a local legal situation develops or changes are made to the pricing policy for certain customer groups, for example.

Some tables contain information about your company structure and its particular locations, printer equipment, and authorizations. Although these tables initially contain sample values provided by SAP, you will need to change and maintain them.

Master data and transaction data specific to individual applications also are in these tables. These tables probably will be edited by the system during the normal course of business, such as when a new customer account is opened.

Understanding the Transaction Concept

A *business transaction* is an exchange between one part of a system and another. Suppose that a production plant takes delivery of some material from a warehouse in exchange for a delivery receipt. The warehouse uses the delivery receipt to reconcile the stock of material with the inventory. Meanwhile, the accounting department notes that the valuable material has moved from the warehouse to the production plant. It posts some financial transactions to record this exchange of value for material.

When a user is working at a terminal, a transaction with the system is not finished until the system is satisfied that the entry of information is correct. The system records the transaction automatically as a document that remains in the system as proof of who entered the information and when.

If the transaction involves a purchase order, for example, the details of that order are written on the document by the system whenever possible. The user already will have selected a supplier on the database, so the details can be entered by the system.

▶ **See** "The BASIS System," **p. 70**

Manual Invoice Entry   If you have to manually enter an invoice that has not been posted automatically, SAP R/3 provides all possible help. You can enter and post a check received and match the payment to specific open items in the customer account, for example, all in one operation.

The successful posting of a transaction does not occur until the necessary data is recorded as an SAP document and is complete and error-free. You can set aside a transaction document before it is ready for posting; the system validates any information you have entered and reports to you any discrepancies.

The SAP document has a document header showing the posting date, document date, document reference number, and currency key. The body of the document contains one or more line items showing the amount and identifying the product and terms of payment. The system generates certain line items, such as tax entries, cash discounts, and exchange rate differences, as applicable.

You can set up helping routines and use standard data-entry functions such as these:

- Recalling a previous screen for copying and editing
- Retaining data for individual users for several transactions
- Adapting a copy of a data-entry screen so that it is better suited to a set of transactions you are expecting
- Searching for an account number by using match codes to narrow the search

You can copy an SAP document that records a previous transaction and use it as a sample or model to be edited. This sample can be a regular document that has been set aside, perhaps as an incomplete transaction document. The posting date and new values might have to be entered—by you or the system—before posting.

Recurring Entries   If you expect to make a series of entries in which the amounts are always the same, you can set up a recurring entry. You might want to do this for monthly service fees, for example.

A *recurring entry* is a set of data that will not be used until the due dates. Until then, the entries will not update account balances.

You have to specify the first and last dates and the frequency or time interval between. The system automatically posts the required transaction on each due date.

Interpreting the Document Principle

A transaction of posting to any account does not succeed unless debits equal credits. The entries for such a posting are not accepted unless they pass the validation tests applied in the dynpro step of the dialog routine running at the point of data entry.

This successful posting to an account as a result of the transaction is regarded by SAP as a self-contained and coherent unit of data. It constitutes a meaningful business act. Information has to be given to the SAP system, and the system checks for all the errors that can be detected at this stage of the business process.

The unit is defined as an SAP document because evidence of this posting event and details of the transaction can be displayed in a standard document format. No posting can take place without leaving an SAP document ready to be used in the audit and in any processing or posting intended to control or analyze accounts.

A transaction of entry, checking, and posting data can take place directly with the FI-Financial Accounting system, where the results include posting to the GL-General Ledger and its subledgers. A transaction can also direct data to other SAP applications. For example, you might enter data from original documents, such as goods receipt notes and packing lists.

Every SAP application operates the method of transactions that create SAP documents. For example, the FI-FA Fixed Assets Management component can accept a transaction that records an investment in a fixed asset and, at the same time, the transaction can post the invoice for the investment. This automatically records the transaction in the following accounts:

- Fixed assets
- Vendor's account
- General ledger, Accounts Payable subledger
- Cost accounting: by order, by project, by fixed asset group or type

The *Generally Agreed Accounting Principles* (GAAP) are derived from the essence of a reliable accounting system: Any number in the system can be traced through the accounting procedures to the point of origin—either a calculation or an entry from outside the accounting system. The design of an SAP document meets and exceeds GAAP requirements.

Before a transaction can be successfully completed, the mandatory SAP document must be created. This occurs only after strict validation of the entries. Uniform data structures must be used, and the transaction must obey clear-cut rules about posting. The SAP document identifies the rules used for each line item.

A *data object* is a cluster of data items recorded as fields. Each field is allowed a maximum size and type of content according to the defined data domain specification assigned to it. A field cannot accept any value or other content unless it is in accord with this domain definition.

NOTE   An SAP document is a data object and must obey the rules of SAP objects.

Reading Header Fields

An SAP document is displayed first in overview format and then in more detail, depending on which line item is selected.

The header of an SAP document overview always includes organizational data and full identification of the document, including these items:

- Document number
- Company code

- Fiscal year
- Document date
- Intercompany number
- Reference document
- Debit/credit total
- Currency

Reading Line-Item Detail Fields

The body of an SAP document is displayed in overview format with one line of column titles and one or more line items to carry summary details of the entries.

You can find more details on these line items by using overlay windows at the display terminal:

- General Ledger account
- Company code
- Intercompany number
- Currency
- Transaction amount
- Debit/credit
- Tax amount
- Tax code
- Business area
- Cost center
- Order identification
- Project identification
- Asset identification
- Material code
- Personnel number
- Allocation code
- Reference document identification
- Document header text
- Document type (transaction type, journal type)
- Posting key (debit or credit, what type of account this line item is allowed to be posted to)

Using Flexible Numbering

Document Number is a mandatory field on an SAP document header and on each of the detail displays for the line item. SAP R/3 offers a choice of manual or automatic assignment.

You can specify various methods for automatic SAP document numbering. It can be quite useful, for example, to allocate ranges of code numbers (which can include letters) according to the type of transaction. You could do this to organize the listing of journal entries by type of document, such as the following:

- Customer invoices
- Customer payments
- Down payments
- Credit memos

Finding Optional Details

The line items on an SAP document display have to point to fields that contain the information required under GAAP to maintain a reliable accounting system. Each SAP client company, however, will want to use the system's flexibility to set up not only a chart of accounts to meet the mandatory requirements of company law regarding external accounting, but also additional accounts for the analysis, planning, and control of the business.

You might want to define a sort code to use for allocation and analysis, for example. You might need to customize the system to allow and validate entries that flag items such as special payment terms.

Whatever data is required or allowed in a particular transaction entry is recorded in the SAP document. Therefore, this information serves as the content for online accounting by SAP R/3 and is also available for subsequent processing.

Understanding the Set Concept

The logical concept of a set is used in the FI-GLX Extended General Ledger for reporting, planning, and ledger processing. A *set* refers to a data structure and its relationships with other data structures. You can define a set of numbers to serve as identification codes of bank accounts, for example. A list of cost centers also can specify a set.

You might not know the actual members of a set until you use the set definition. The "top three operating divisions for gaining new customers in the current month" is a set definition of this kind.

The definition of a set can include relationships between specific firms or companies in a group, not necessarily at the same level. They can be specified by their individual company codes.

A set can contain any data objects that meet the logical criteria of the definition for membership of that set.

Specific business functions can call on a set definition stored for use later. Assessment and distribution often take place under the control of sets.

The following chapters discuss the various document types associated with the R/3 applications:

Interpreting the SAP Style Guide to Screen Design

The SAP GUI is the *graphical user interface* common to all SAP modules in presentation style and general use. Specific uses of the special function keys may apply in some components.

The SAP Style Guide sets out the graphical appearance and use of the principal elements of the screen displays:

- Online help accesses the online documentation via hypertext references, which permit navigation between blocks of text and illustrative material.
- Control elements include check boxes, list boxes, pushbuttons, and radio buttons. Where necessary, scrollbars are provided to access material that does not fit on one screen or box.
- All SAP R/3 application functions can be accessed via menus, which are constructed consistently throughout the system. Menus can be constructed for specific groups of users.
- Toolbars are provided where necessary to supplement the standard toolbar, which provides the most frequently used navigation commands and tools for accessing online help.
- A function-key bar tells you the purpose of each function key; each key represents one the most important functions of the application.
- You can display entry values for fields with designated value domains and use those values as selection options. When the valid entries can be limited by other methods, the set of options is also displayed for selection.

Developing the Office Communications Interface

The SAP R/3 system uses *temporary sequential* (TEMSE) object files to manage text sent or received over the system's office communications interface.

The central communications interface can send any text generated within or received by the SAP R/3 system to any of the following destinations:

- Any user of the same SAP R/3 system
- Any user of another SAP R/3 system
- Any user of a non-SAP office communications system
- Users of telex, fax, or teletex services
- X.400 email subscribers
- A printer

The SAPcomm API is an *Application Programming Interface* that enables the connection of third-party communications products that set up links to external standard communications services.

Remote function call (RFC) techniques are used to implement a gateway to UNIX mail.

The *Messaging Application Programming Interface* (MAPI), a component of the Microsoft *Windows Open Service Architecture* (WOSA), is accessible via the SAPmail electronic mail component. This makes SAP R/3 services available to Microsoft Mail (MS-Mail) as a server; SAP R/3 also can act as a client for MS-Mail services.

These standard methods for linking different business processes are in rapid development to facilitate a seamless integration between an R/3 system and users who are communicating with it via a network.

Introducing New User Interface Facilities with R/3 Release 4.5

The successive releases of R/3 extend the scope of the available software and hence increase the potential complexity of the user interface systems needed to control it. However, new software has improved the quality of the GUI in many ways.

Application Link Enabling (ALE) technology enables you to manage a more complex organization from a single control point. You now can view the distribution of a system with the ALE Distribution Model Viewer, a Visio add-in. You can use ALE processing with more than 250 business objects; these are being developed in Microsoft Visual Studio, IBM Access Builder, and Inprise Delphi/Connect, all of which you can access through suitable BAPIs and business objects. Release 4.5 also includes an Interface Adviser component that enables R/3 systems to be integrated with non-SAP software.

Introducing the Self-Upgrading User Interface

As of Release 4.5, the user interface upgrades itself whenever the server detects that the desktop does not contain the latest software release.

Release 3.1 of R/3 introduced SAPforms, which enables you to create and use electronic forms. Release 4.5 supports Microsoft Outlook forms in SAPoffice and can synchronize the R/3 employee calendar with the Microsoft Outlook calendar. ●

Reviewing the Technical Background

Exploring R/3 Architecture

Reviewing Basic Principles

The SAP system contains a BASIS system to which applications can be added. Each application has several components that can be installed as required. A component includes a range of functions that may be mandatory or optional.

All functions, at whatever level, can be directed to perform in a variety of ways by parameters that can be adjusted by the user during the customizing process.

The standard business functions of the SAP R/3 system can execute the full range of business system processes used in almost every type of business enterprise. The scope of these functions extends from the conduct of controlled dialog with a user, through the processes required to maintain an integrated data system, up to the higher order statistical and control functions expected in an enterprise-controlling system.

The system extends not only in scope across the full range of data processing required by a complex corporate organization, but also through the implementation process by which the existing business system is described and developed into the target concept of what will be a new business supported by the SAP system.

The transactions with the system can range from data exchange to decision-making, from software development to display design, from automatic processing to extensive financial and other reporting.

Multitier Client/Server Architecture

The R/3 system operates by using the client/server principle applied across several levels. It is highly modular, and the principle is applied primarily through software so that the modes of interaction between the various clients and servers can be controlled.

Dedicated servers can be linked by communications networks and perform certain tasks without affecting the integrity of the data and processes of the central system network.

Open System Principles

An open system allows the interplay and portability of applications, data, and user interfaces by adhering to international standards for these elements.

This definition of an open system is based on the work of the POSIX 1003.0 Committee of the *Institute of Electrical and Electronics Engineers* (IEEE), which is devoted to the *Portable Operating System Interface for UNIX* (POSIX).

The following international open interface standards are embodied in the R/3 system:

- *Transfer Control Protocol/Internet Protocol* (TCP/IP), for the network communications protocol and other secure protocols
- *Remote procedure calls* (RPCs), implemented in ABAP/4 as *remote function calls* (RFCs), to enable other systems to call R/3 functions; constitutes the R/3 open programming interface

- *Common Programming Interface-Communication* (CPI-C), for program-to-program communications across multiple systems
- *Structured Query Language* (SQL) and *open database connectivity* (ODBC), the standards used for open data access to R/3 business data stored in relational databases
- *Object linking and embedding/dynamic data exchange* (OLE/DDE), the primary standard for integrating PC applications with R/3
- X.400/X.500, *Messaging Application Programming Interface* (MAPI), and *Electronic Data Interchange* (EDI), the standards for external communications

Open interfaces are also established to provide access to specialized applications.

The following specialized applications entail open-interface communications with R/3:

- *Computer-aided design* (CAD)
- Optical archiving
- Production-related technical subsystems, such as DASS, which provides for plant data collection

Production technical systems are discussed in Chapter 18, "Understanding the Production Planning for Process Industries Module."

Portability Across Operating Systems

In addition to running under all major UNIX operating systems, the R/3 system can run under the following operating systems:

- MPE/iX
- OpenVMS
- OS/400
- Windows NT

Portability Across Databases

The R/3 system is compatible with the database systems marketed by a variety of companies, including these:

- IBM (DB2)
- Informix
- Oracle
- Software AG
- Sybase

Portability Across Presentation Front Ends

The SAP *graphical user interface* (GUI) can display, in list or graphical format, all output from the R/3 standard functions on most front-end presentation systems, including the following:

- Macintosh
- OS/2PM
- OSF/Motif
- Windows

Integration with Distributed Applications

In many companies, application systems have been developed without online links to a central system. Even when an integrated system is designed for technical or economic reasons, some application systems have to be uncoupled so that they can be used on their own. Their databases may have to be isolated from the other systems.

Yet the SAP system depends on manipulating complex data objects that may have their constituent data elements located in a variety of databases, including some that are at least occasionally uncoupled.

Application Link Enabling (ALE) is the technology of integrating asynchronously coupled clusters of applications by using a method of message-based integration. It allows R/2 and R/3 systems to cooperate with each other and with third-party systems so that both data and business functions are consistent throughout the cluster. This is discussed in Chapter 8, "Developing Businesses on a Continuous Basis."

Uncoupling Applications, Front Ends, and Databases

Each component of an application—the software, the front-end system, and the database—is likely to be developed independently of the others. For instance, front-end presentation and user-interaction systems have changed from simple keyboards to slave terminals to intelligent PC-based user interface systems. Similarly, database hardware and software tend to be developed in cycles that are not attuned to developments in specific business software or user interface improvement.

Because the SAP modular system of standard business software has always been designed with this diversity of hardware recognized as a salient feature of the business environment, there is no particular difficulty in uncoupling the application logic from the presentation system and the database configuration.

Dedicated Database Servers   The central database can be serviced in a single processor, a multiprocessor, or a cluster of processors. The configuration of the database complex can be adjusted to suit the volume of data and the traffic on the system.

Dedicated Application Logic Servers   The advantage of having one or more applications running on dedicated servers is that purely local business can be conducted with the systems uncoupled. The central facility then can be updated at the most convenient time and by the most efficient channels.

As in the case of the dedicated database installation, a computer system assigned to one or more applications can be reconfigured to use different numbers and types of processors and interfaces according to the traffic demand and the complexity of the data items being processed.

Scaling the processor capacity does not affect the application logic.

Special Task Servers   You can integrate a variety of specialized computer systems with the R/3 system:

- Optical archiving
- X.400 messages
- Telex and fax
- Background processing of transaction data
- Control systems for complex production plants

Presentation Servers   In accord with the technical evolutionary principle, the range and variety of presentation devices are likely to increase as manufacturers seek cheaper production methods and specialized niche markets in which their products will flourish. For instance, because of the wide market for personal computers, these devices have become viable alternatives to dedicated and custom-built user interface equipment.

The SAP R/3 system supports the following types of presentation devices:

- Windows, based on the *Windows Style Guide* and directed by a dispatcher to control the different forms of communication
- OS/2 PCs
- Apple Macintosh
- OSF/Motif for X terminals
- OSF/Motif for workstations

The R/3 system tends to adopt the style and local functionality of the presentation platform so that you do not have to get used to a different look or operating-key configuration.

The interface between the user and an application is discussed in Chapter 2, "Interacting with the SAP Systems."

Provisions for Continuous Business Development

Business processes have always undergone change. New methods are invented to cope with new products or new customer requirements; old methods are adjusted to suit new circumstances. New people are recruited to replace those who are used to the old system of working.

Some of these changes are beneficial, some are not. For example, new people might be ready to learn the new ways but lack experience with the customers, the suppliers, and the products. Such wisdom might be needed, even under the new regime.

The SAP system expects a business to change. And the first big change to be expected is the installation of the SAP system itself.

What is needed is help in describing how things are done now, and help in arranging the system so that it will work well in the future. The last thing an implementer wants is a host of problems with computer code. The last thing a managing director wants is a wonderful system that does not do what is necessary to support the business.

Two methods and the tools to apply them are built in to the SAP systems:

- Enterprise data modeling, which helps you plot out where you are now and where you're going.
- Customizing, which allows you to adjust the standard business software so that it exactly fits your future way of doing business. This is done without modifying any source code.

Enterprise Data Models

Input is processed to become output. This is a verbal model of a company. It is an information model, even if it is not very informative.

Head office manages a purchasing department and a sales department. This is slightly more informative but not really useful.

But suppose that you name all the work units—the activity centers in your company—and then write down what each one does. Then you're on the way to assembling a useful information model of your enterprise.

Chapter 5, "Consulting the R/3 Reference Model," discusses how the system contains a complete information model of itself that you can inspect in list format or explore in graphical presentation. You can see how your model of your existing company's business processes compares with the model in the system.

Chapter 6, "Optimizing Business Processing," shows how this tool can guide you through the process of designing a new system for your company that will work the first time, because all the standard business functions you need to get started have been predefined and programmed so that they integrate with each other.

Tools for Adapting Software

Another tool that is a fundamental part of the SAP concept and the R/3 system is the customizing system. When you look at part of the R/3 Reference Model, you can recognize many business functions that you already have in your operating departments, such as Sales and Production.

With the advice and support of the R/3 Analyzer, you can select the functions of interest from the R/3 Reference Model and start to build a system that fits your own situation and your target concept of how you want things to be. This first edition of the target system could be run as it stands, because it is made up of predefined standard business functions that are fully working and properly integrated with each other.

But this system will not feel like your own tailor-made system. If you call for a list of your company's products, you will not see your specific products, because the system knows nothing about them. If you have one production plant and two warehouses, the R/3 Reference Model shows the plant as the owner of a warehouse, but it does not know that you have two warehouses until you tell it so.

The process of adjusting and particularizing your model system without altering any source code is discussed in Chapter 7, "Customizing."

Client/Server Multitier Architecture

SAP systems are designed for the medium-to-large corporate business entity with many worldwide locations and many data-processing facilities.

The size and complexity of such companies, and the increasing capability of computer systems to rapidly process large quantities of data, have combined to encourage the concept and physical construction of networks of servers providing support to a number of clients or users.

Most business systems have to provide three main functions:

- Database services to retain information—for example, on materials and methods used in manufacture and packaging
- Application data processing—for example, to ensure that materials required for production are delivered to the right place at the correct time and that the stock is replenished
- Presentation services—for example, to report the progress of production and the state of the inventory

The SAP R/3 software system provides the functionality to support all such businesses. It also allows the target system to be fine-tuned so that it reaches peak performance quickly and adapts rapidly and effectively to changes in circumstances.

Your SAP system can be configured to suit your size by allocating different processing systems to the three essential services of database management, application processing, and presentation services.

Central System Alone

A central system by itself can provide database, application processing, and presentation services.

Decentralized Presentation

The central system can encompass the database and the R/3 application software, but the presentation system is a decentralized network of user interfaces.

Client with Server to Database

The central host system may carry the R/3 BASIS and one or more applications. The database then has to be a separate system accessed via a server.

Three-Level Client/Server Configuration

The most versatile configuration employs three levels of client/server distributed processing.

In the core of the system is a high-speed network of R/3 database servers. The R/3 applications are networked around the database cluster and have independent access to it. The R/3 applications are fully integrated with each other.

User access to any of the applications—and hence to any of the database servers—is mediated by an outer network of presentation servers that form the R/3 front-end systems, where they can be integrated with PC tools and subsystems. Figure 3.1 shows a triple-level client/server configuration. There is not a strict interpretation of *level* in this context, which could be referred to as *multilevel* client/server configuration.

FIGURE 3.1

Triple client/server
configuration.

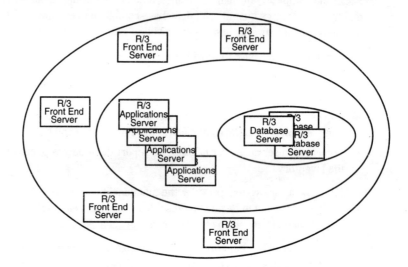

Even Loads

Any user can be in touch with several application servers at the same time. In some areas, you might need to balance the load by installing specialized application servers. The following areas, in particular, are often served by systems optimized for their differing requirements:

- SD-Sales and Distribution
- FI-Financial Accounting
- HR-Human Resources Management

Front-end and back-end computer systems are subject to different cost structures. The client/server architecture allows an economical deployment of computing resources by separating the three server levels.

The advantage is experienced by the user in the form of generous computing resources for the display and prompting services that make the work easier and more effective. This can be seen in contrast to older systems, which had to compromise between the costs of presentation support systems and the cost of providing adequate central system resources.

From the corporate point of view, the economy of providing specialized database servers allows a generous allocation of storage and processing resources to maintain extensive reference data and full historical information down to the business transaction detail level.

Heterogeneous Platforms

The SAP system has been designed to cope with change, including change in the hardware and operating systems. Therefore, the new SAP implementation must expect to integrate with the legacy of database and presentation platforms and operating systems that have been serving the company prior to the business process reengineering.

For example, an R/3 installation can consist of the following assembly of heterogeneous platforms, in any combination:

- Presentation by Windows 3.1, UNIX, Windows NT, OS/2, Windows 95
- Application by Windows NT, UNIX, Open VMS, MPE/iX
- Database by Windows NT, UNIX, Open VMS, MPE/iX, AS/400/DB2

Client/Server Communications

The architecture of R/3 allows various protocols for communication between the elements of the configuration. TCP/IP and *Open Systems Interconnect* (OSI) are examples.

The standard network protocol for open systems has become TCP/IP. It is supported by all operating systems relevant to R/3 systems.

Transfer Protocols

In accord with the SAP philosophy of choosing the most appropriate method for the task, different protocols have been adopted for each type of communication between the components of a multitiered client/server system:

- TCP/IP is used for handling communications within the client/server configurations of the R/3 system.
- The IBM network protocol LU6.2 is used for communication between the R/3 system and the mainframe host.
- Whatever transfer protocol is used, the interchange at the user interface is under the *Systems, Applications, Products* (SAP) presentation protocol.
- Data is transferred between an application and a database server using SQL, the fourth-generation language for manipulating data defined by *American National Standards Institute* (ANSI).

Data Transfer by WAN and LAN Linkage

The SAP presentation protocol is optimized for linking presentation servers directly to the R/3 system and via *wide-area networks* (WANs). When a large volume of data has to be transferred, a *local area network* (LAN) is needed—for example, between database servers and applications.

Program-to-Program Communications

Basic services for program-to-program communications at the ABAP/4 programming level are implemented by using functions from the *Common Programming Interface-Communication* (CPI-C) standard. The start set of CPI-C has been integrated into the ABAP/4 language.

When one program has to communicate with another program, an internal gateway is used to convert the CPI-C commands to the protocol used for external transfer, such as TCP/IP or LU6.2, according to whether the transfer is between applications or with a mainframe host.

Synchronous CPI-C   The transfer of the CPI-C commands and the management of transmission between applications or to a mainframe host takes place in a mutually dependent mode in a fixed-time relationship. This process is known as *synchronous communication.*

If it is not possible to use synchronous communication, the alternative is asynchronous communication, which may be necessary in these types of situations:

- Starting a process on a target system has to be carried out manually—for example, because particular media have to be loaded manually.
- The target computer temporarily can't accept or provide data.

Asynchronous Q-API   The R/3 system can maintain data in buffers that are queued and waiting for a suitable moment to be transferred to the receiving computer. This moment can be defined by a schedule or determined by the availability of the receiving computer. These queues can be freely integrated into any of the SAP application programs. The mechanism of choice is *Queue Application Programming Interface* (Q-API).

Two types of data format are supported under Q-API:

- The batch input format defined for accepting external data records into the R/3 system, which is directly recognized and entered into normal interactive transactions
- Data in a format that has been defined for the receiving program to suit the specific situation

RFC and RPC Protocols   The standard business functions of the R/3 system can be called and accessed freely without any special provision by the user apart from the normal business authorization procedures that may limit access of certain users to specific functions. However, your implementation may include some functions that were specially written in the ABAP/4 programming language to perform functions unique to your organization. The discussion in Chapter 29, "Developing ABAP/4 Programs with the R/3 Workbench," outlines the method of building these special-function modules.

The *Remote function call* (RFC) is the SAP ABAP/4 programming language implementation of the *remote procedure call* (RPC) protocol, which is the standard adopted for accessing special-function modules.

The following types of special functions can be accessed by using the RFC protocol:

- Functions residing in the R/3 system special-function library
- External programs called from within ABAP/4 applications
- Function modules that reside in other computers

RFC can be used by an R/3 application to communicate in both directions with other R/3 applications, with R/2 programs, and with external applications running on other systems.

The R/3 runtime system controls any communications with other computers initiated by RFC procedures. Environments in the C language typically use RFC methods.

Asynchronous RFC Features   RFC recognizes the syntax and usage for calling normal-function modules in the R/3 system. The user does not have to know that the function is using a remote computing resource. Calls can be dynamic and do not entail setting up static communications modules or stubs. A system table is used to recognize the destination name of a remote call and to set up a suitable type of connection with the partner. When the R/3 system is installed, the partners can be configured as logical target systems that the system specifies later in detail.

The RFC protocol is available in the TCP/IP and the *Systems Network Architecture* (SNA) LU6.2 network protocol.

An API for an external C language program can be set up by using an RFC. R/3 function modules can be called by external programs by the same mechanism. Error handling is done by a standard exception mechanism that allows remote debugging and troubleshooting across system boundaries.

The RFC protocol supports all ABAP/4 data types, such as single fields, data structures made from data objects, and tables. The protocol is fully integrated into the ABAP/4 R/3 Program Development Workbench. A *software development kit,* RFC-SDK, is available to support the creation of non-SAP programs that recognize remote function calls.

RFC's Delta Management Functions   The overhead cost of communication between programs can be reduced by RFC's Delta functions. The *Delta functions* concentrate on detecting and responding to small changes. A function typically needs to transfer a table of data as one of its parameters. The Delta method allows a first full transfer and then subsequently transfers only data elements that have changed. These changes are communicated by a transfer of log tables that carry details of the changes made by the transactions.

The RFC Delta management functions offer the following benefits:

- The target system executes the RFC calls in the same order and within the same program context as in the calling system.
- Each RFC is executed only once.

■ The status of an RFC call can be queried at any time to access the data in the log tables and ascertain the progress of the transaction.

■ A callback function can be activated to invoke further activities in the calling system.

Application Methodology

Between the network of database servers and the front-end or presentation servers of an SAP R/3 multitier client/server system is the network of business applications that control the logic of the business transactions. The extensive range of applications is illustrated by the list in Chapter 4, "Introducing R/3 Software Architecture." The programs of these business applications are interpreted by an R/3 runtime system installed on every application server.

▶ **See** "The SAP R/3 Applications," **p. 64**

Business Transactions

A *business transaction* is a unit of work that makes sense to those concerned with the activities of the business. The business transaction has to be carried on a computer system. The combined business requirements and computer constraints dictate the logical functions of a transaction.

Data Consistency   A business transaction must not corrupt data. For example, a value entered in one type of unit must not be interpreted as if it were something different unless the system can operate a conversion procedure from one to another, and back again, if necessary. A supplier's address must not appear in different forms if it refers to the same location. The delivery service might be able to recognize their equivalence, but the computer system tends to regard two differing addresses as references to separate locations.

While a transaction is taking place, a data object that is undergoing an update should be reserved exclusively for the user controlling the transaction. Until that transaction is complete, no other user should be allowed access to the critical data object. Furthermore, until the transaction is complete, it should be possible for the user to backtrack through all the steps and undo any of the data entries or changes he made. The database should be capable of returning to how it was before the transaction began.

Business Requirements   A computerized business transaction should be at least as subtle as the manual procedure it replaces. If you are creating an order for manufacturing, you should reserve the materials required at the same time. If you are posting items in financial accounting, it makes sense to post credit and debit items together.

Dynpros for Dialog Steps   The SAP mechanism for controlling the steps of a business transaction is the *dynamic program,* or *dynpro*. It presents the user with screens that make sense in the context of the work being done, and it makes sure that the logical data requirements of the business application are correctly met.

SAP Logical Units of Work

Modern database systems are fast. They cannot wait for a user to complete data entry. A database step has to be completed as a single operation so that the database can go on to process the next item, probably on behalf of a different user.

By contrast, the *logical unit of work* (LUW) of a typical SAP application involves many database operations, as well as a host of interactions with the user and perhaps other systems.

A SAP LUW is executed entirely or not at all—there is no interim stage. An SAP business transaction can consist of one or more logical units of work. An SAP LUW can span several dialog steps, each corresponding to a database transaction or LUW, which is the only way a database can be updated.

The end of an SAP LUW is marked by a COMMIT WORK instruction or by the completion of the corresponding database update.

Runtime Environment

The R/3 runtime system is written in the ANSI-C language, and the R/3 application programs are written in ABAP/4. Dynpros are interpreted, not compiled.

The runtime environment for R/3 applications is made up of the two processors necessary to interpret the dynpros.

User Sessions

A user logs on, calls on a series of transactions, and then logs off. During this session, you can perform more than one sequence of actions by opening additional sessions, which appear on separate windows in the user interface screen. Within each session, you can perform the actions in any suitable order and suspend and later resume processing.

This multiple-session arrangement allows you to work on other activities if you must wait for processing resources or data. If you know the transaction code, you can open a new session where the activity can be processed. Otherwise, you can open a session from the system menu and identify what work you want to perform there.

The Application Dispatcher

The R/3 runtime system appears to the operating system as an aggregate of parallel processes. Each application includes a central dispatcher that allocates work to a number of work processes. A work process can consist of one or more task handlers. Figure 3.2 illustrates this concept.

There are special work processes for the following types of activities:

- Interactive dialog processing
- Updating the database in response to changed documents

- Background batch processing
- Spooling
- Management of locks

FIGURE 3.2
Each R/3 application
has a dispatcher for its
work processes.

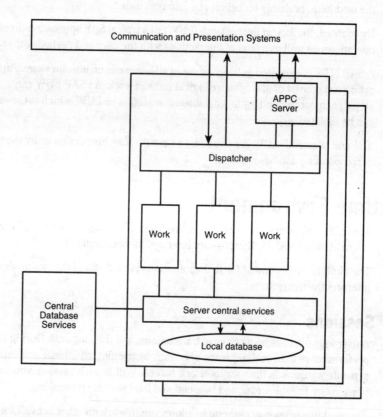

A work process can link directly to a database, which can be in another computer and can entail routing via shared communications services. All other data traffic, such as communications to the SAP GUI and to other programs, is routed through the dispatcher.

Advanced Program-to-Program Communications

An *Advanced Program-to-Program Communications* (APPC) server is built in to the dispatcher that can recognize and respond to communications requests submitted by the work processes. It relays these requests to the SAP gateway, which is also integrated into the dispatcher to serve as the R/3 system interface for the supported interface protocols, such as TCP/IP and LU6.2. In this role, it resembles a transaction monitor. Figure 3.3 summarizes these possibilities.

When user interaction with a dynpro needs to be processed, the dispatcher places it in a queue for the next available interactive work process. When one is available, it executes exactly one dialog step and then makes itself available to process the next item in the queue.

The processing of this one dialog step generates output messages that include a response screen that is sent back to the mode from which the user input originated. The user can work with several modes in separate windows (see Figure 3.4).

FIGURE 3.3

Communications and central database services.

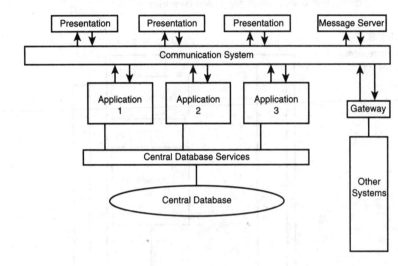

FIGURE 3.4

One or more batch work processes support the dynpros.

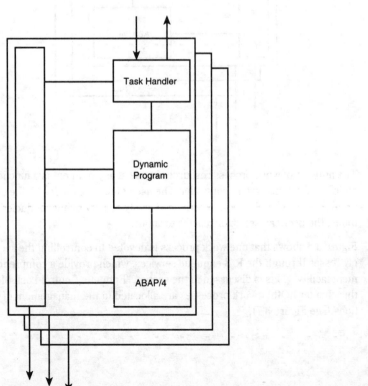

A work process can conduct more than one activity. Each activity within the work process is coordinated by a task handler that activates the dynpro processor or the ABAP/4 processor as necessary to service the request for application logic processing, such as dialogs, database updates, and background processes (see Figure 3.5).

FIGURE 3.5

One or more work processes supervise dialogs.

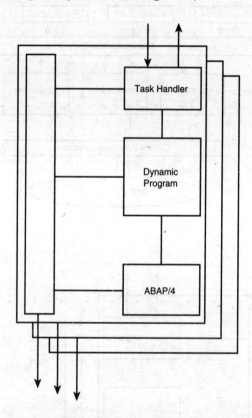

The number of work process resources in use at any moment is a function of the workload anticipated by the system controller. The use of multiple modes by the user allows work to progress. Even if delays are experienced in any activity being conducted on behalf of one mode, the user can set up or reactivate another.

Figure 3.6 shows that one work process is devoted to controlling the security of individual processes through the R/3 enqueue services, which provide a comprehensive lock-management facility. (This is discussed in the section "Enqueue Central Lock Management," later in this chapter.) Other work processes are allocated to the management of print spooling functions (see Figure 3.7).

FIGURE 3.6
One work process
handles enqueue lock
management.

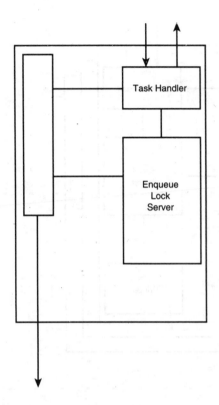

The ABAP/4 Data Dictionary

The R/3 runtime environment is based on two processors: one for ABAP/4 and one for the dynpros. Both continually refer to the ABAP/4 data dictionary, which stores definitions of all R/3 data structures. Semantic and technical information stored in the dictionary constitute the universe of data used by the R/3 system.

Figure 3.8 indicates that work processes have to be assigned the tasks of updating the database on which the ABAP/4 programs depend.

Database Updates from the Transaction Log Records   A dialog program can supervise many dialog steps. Each step generates a log record that is not processed until after the dialog part is complete. Therefore any database changes resulting from the dialog part of the transaction are not physically realized until the associated log records are processed. If the user interrupts a transaction during the dialog phase, or if the transaction fails for any other reason, there are no database changes to reverse because none were made.

Synchronous Updating   If the updating process is in synch with the dialog, the user has to wait for each update to be completed before committing the next. High throughput rates are possible if system resources can be made available.

FIGURE 3.7
One or more work
processes; each serves
a spool for a printer.

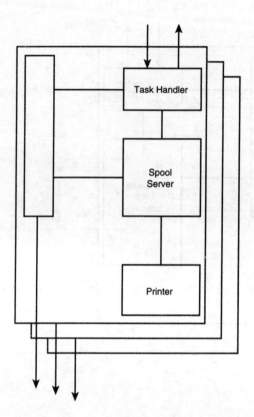

If you need fast interaction with users working under a heavy processing load, you should uncouple the dialogs from database updates to institute asynchronous updating.

Multiple Component Updating

If you want to use asynchronous updating, the dialog elements of transactions are separated from the actual updating of the database. This allows dialogs to proceed quickly, regardless of what has to happen in relation to the database. The accelerating effect is most noticeable when entering large volumes of data.

The work destined to be performed in updating the database is taken from the log of the transactions. Each log entry record carries all the data needed to perform the changes, along with the names of the update routines that have to be invoked. These entries are complete work elements in themselves and are referred to as *update components*. Each is treated as a separate data object and is assigned individually by the dispatcher to an update work process.

Primary Update Components (U1)   If a data element is declared as a U1 primary update component, it always is assigned by the dispatcher to a primary work process, where it is given high priority. Primary components take precedence over secondary components.

FIGURE 3.8
One or more work
processes specialize in
updating the database.

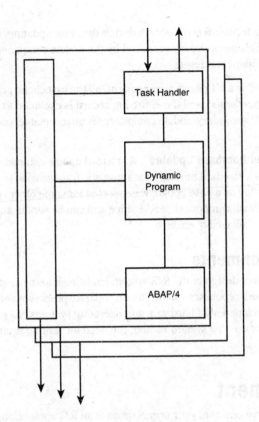

Primary update components are usually time-critical control data elements that must be recorded in the database as soon as possible. Seat reservations and changes to the records of material available for immediate production are examples.

The primary components of different log records can be assigned to different update processes and updated concurrently.

Secondary Update Components (U2)   The secondary components in a log record of a transaction have to wait until all the primary components are processed. The secondary components then can be dealt with in any order—if necessary, by different update processes, perhaps running on different computers.

U2 secondary components carry the data for results and statistical returns that do not need to be updated immediately. The dispatcher assigns these components in work packets for the work processes as these resources become available.

Error States During Updating   The dialog process under control of the dynamic programs catches errors—such as values outside the permitted range—before the transaction is accepted from the user. Problems in the updating process are more likely to occur for technical reasons, such as the overflow of a file or database buffer. These error conditions are routed automatically to the system administrator, who deals with these problems.

Data Consistency   If a technical error occurs during database updating, it cannot be corrected by the user. Any changes already proposed by the update component are rejected, and the entire update component is refused.

If the component refused is a U1 primary component, all the associated primary components in the same log record are reversed, and the entire log record is excluded from the update process. By contrast, if a U2 secondary update component is unacceptable, only that component is blocked.

Notification of Rejected Database Updates   A rejected update component is assigned an identifier that generates a standard message for automatic transmission to the user whose dialog caused the faulty log or whose update was rejected for some other reason. This message is processed by the SAPmail component of SAPoffice and can be sent to any user of an SAP application who has the mail facility enabled.

Multiprocessor Environments

The inherent client/server design of the R/3 system lends itself to the employment of multiprocessors. Different work processes can be run on separate processors and on processors of different types. The development of hardware and operating systems can provide enhancements to the operation of the R/3 system without the need for reprogramming or extensive reconfiguring.

System Management

If the backbone and nerve center of your organization is an R/3 application, you need and expect continuous operation, perhaps over a wide geographical complex working 24 hours a day. The CCMS-Computing Center Management System is discussed in Chapter 11, "Maintaining the Computer System."

In particular, you expect the system to do much of its work in the form of background processes from which you can demand reports at any time and in any convenient format. Several types of work can be done in the background, and each is given a system designed to optimize the activities.

Dialog-Free Background Processing

With a user in the loop, the R/3 system uses the online dialog programs to call for input and to check its validity before submitting it for further processing. Background processes frequently use the same programs that control the dialogs. Any number of background processes can be executed along with the online dialogs.

Spooling Control

The scope of spooling techniques includes all forms of buffered relay of information to media such as printers and fax devices. Many computers can be involved.

It is usual to designate one computer as the spool server through which all spooling jobs are routed to and from the spooling systems of the individual computers. If a new device is added to the network, it has to be defined only once to the server.

A central file is designated as *temporary sequential* (TEMSE) to buffer the information to be output to the spooling mechanism. For each TEMSE dataset, a separate order contains detailed instructions that include the logical name of the destination printer or other device.

Enqueue Central Lock Management

The locking mechanisms of many relational database systems are not adequate to control complex business data objects. To meet this need for controlling access from many users and applications to a complex data object, the parts of which may be distributed among any number of relational tables, the R/3 system uses an internal central lock manager installed on one of the database servers or on one of the application servers.

When a transaction consists of several dialog steps, the dispatcher can assign each step to a different work process. It is essential that no changes are made to any data object that has been locked until all the dialog steps are completed. The locks assigned have to be transferred when work processes are changed.

If a database operation is to be uncoupled from a dialog process, it is also essential that certain data elements are not changed by any other application in the period between the dialog operations and the consequent database updates. For example, an order accepted on the basis of material in stock relies on that material still being available when the database is updated to mark it as reserved for the specific order. Another ordering system cannot be allowed to reserve the same material in the interim.

The R/3 system alerts the user if there is going to be potential competition for access to the same record. The second request is refused until the first is satisfied.

When the log record generated by the dialog is used to update the database, the update program automatically removes all the locks that were put in place during the transaction.

Memory Management

There are two types of main memory:

- Reserved main memory areas exclusively at the disposal of a particular work process
- Shared main memory areas used jointly by all work processes

The reserved areas are used to store mode-specific data that needs to be retained for longer than a single work step. Before R/3 Release 3.0, two areas are distinguished by how they are used: *roll* and *paging*.

Roll Area of Reserved Memory   Data that is made available to a work process automatically at the beginning of a dialog step is rolled into a reserved area of memory. At the end of the dialog step, this data is rolled out to be returned to the database, if necessary. The memory released then is available for other processes.

The roll area of memory is reserved for the exclusive use of a specific work process while it is active. Some of the types of information that use roll memory follow:

- Data specific to the particular user, including access privileges and identification
- Entry data previously collected by steps of the dialog that have already been completed
- Management information required by the two processors for ABAP/4 and dynpro activities

Paging Area of Reserved Memory   The paging areas of reserved memory can be used by applications to store extensive collections of data that may vary greatly in length. The paging areas are accordingly organized into segments assigned to a work process when they are needed and withdrawn when they are needed elsewhere.

Managing the Roll and Page Memories   When each processing step is complete, the contents of the reserved roll and paging areas are buffered in two shared memory pools. The shared memory areas are used as buffers for database, program, and table operations. Both pools are within the system's virtual address space, and the memory manager can coordinate external paging through the operating system and internal paging through the dispatcher.

Extended Memory Management and R/3 User Session Contexts

R/3 Release 3.0 introduced an extended memory capability that permits a more intensive use of virtual memory. Reservations for roll and paging areas are no longer necessary and have been replaced by the R/3 user session context system.

When a work process is conducting activities as part of a step in a user dialog, it needs ready access to a set of data elements. These elements are the *user session context*.

If another work process is assigned to the next step in the dialog, the information now in some or all of the data elements of the first user session context must be made available to the second work process. The second user session context may also require additional information.

Before Release 3.0, user session context information was transferred by the roll-in, roll-out method of copying information. This took a great deal of time and many system resources.

In Release 3.0 and later releases, the data needed by subsequent user session contexts is accessed not by copying, but by mapping. The information transferred to the subsequent dialog step is not the actual data, but a set of pointers that indicate where that data can be found. Thus, a very complex data structure can be addressed or mapped for use by a work process by the transfer of a simple mapping pointer message.

N O T E   Data swapping is handled by the operating system.

Using mapping rather than copying in this context is expected to provide a much faster response time and, in certain installations, the possibility of handling larger loads without adding application servers.

Developments in virtual memory made possible by 64-bit architecture are expected to extend the benefits of the mapping concept.

Open Interfaces to Third-Party Products

Three types of interfaces are used:

- Collectors of data about the operating system performance, the database, and the network
- Service interfaces to supervise backup, recovery, spooling, and security
- Management interfaces for handling messages and events related to application monitoring and control

These systems are discussed in Part VIII, "Maintaining and Enhancing the Implementation."

Database Services

The design philosophy of R/3 is based on the open system concept, which stipulates that communications to and from an open system should be restricted only by the demands of the standards in force.

The standard adopted language for the definition of data and its manipulation is SQL. Any database that can interface according to this standard can be used by the R/3 system without the user needing to be aware of the detailed mechanisms of the database server. New products can be used as they become available without discarding the old and reprogramming the system.

However, not all database manufacturers offer the same range of SQL functions. The ABAP/4 Development Workbench, used to write all SAP R/3 business programs, has adopted two SQL standards: *Open* and *Native*.

Open SQL

ABAP/4 Open SQL is an extension of the ABAP/4 language, which ensures the success of any application that accesses a database using only the functions of the Open SQL. Any database that supports this set of functions can be used by an R/3 system.

Native SQL

Many vendors of database systems have enhanced their products by adding functions outside the set specified by the Open SQL standard. These improved functions cannot be used by a system limited to the Open SQL standard.

ABAP/4 Native SQL can call the enhanced functions of a specific database system whether all calls are encapsulated in a module specific to that database system. The module must also recognize the calls made in ABAP/4 Native SQL and respond to them by initiating the database commands specific to the particular system that will initiate the enhanced functions.

New database systems can be used by R/3 if the calling modules use ABAP/4 Native SQL and if the specific database system includes the special module to interpret the Native SQL commands.

SQL Set Operations

One of SQL's most useful facilities is its capability to recognize logical set operations and use them to manipulate sets of records, such as arrays. This feature helps accelerate network communications in client/server architectures.

Optimized SQL Instructions

If you are seeking a very small number of records from a database, it might take more effort to prepare an optimum search strategy than to seek the result directly. However, if the data volumes are large and diverse, there might be an advantage in using optimized SQL instructions.

Database vendors offer a range, from optimized instructions in fixed agendas to dynamic buffering of optimized instructions.

The R/3 approach is to encapsulate database-specific functions in a system interface that eliminates the need for applications programmers to construct their own for each database.

Multiple Database Access

Database vendors usually offer a range of gateways and transparent distribution mechanisms that can be used by R/3 to access these sources.

Open Data

The concept of an open database includes the notion that all data is stored in tables ready to be instantly inspected and used without any need for complex data-retrieval instructions in a language specific to the one vendor. There are at least two routes to achieving this facility: building a specific interface and using a standardized interface such as ODBC.

However, it is not enough for a system to be able to locate a specific data element in different types of databases. It is also necessary for the user to be able to work out what that data means.

Semantic openness refers to the capability that enables users to locate the data tables and elements that hold the information they need—data that will have the proper meaning when it is placed in the context of interest.

The SAP Enterprise Data Model

The intention of the Enterprise Data Model is to enable the user of a database network to assemble the data relevant to that enterprise and to attach the correct interpretation to it. This topic is discussed in Chapter 10, "Developing an SAP Open Information Warehouse."

Client Caching

The purpose of using client caches to buffer communications with databases is to optimize client/server operations. Every application server has an installed database service as part of the R/3 runtime environment. Client caches are located in main memory and hold the data most frequently used by that application. This reduces network traffic and the load on the database server. Typical contents of a client cache include such information as this:

- ABAP/4 programs
- Dynpros
- Information from the ABAP/4 data dictionary
- Business parameters that usually remain unchanged in a running system

Cache Content   The exact contents of a client cache are determined by the client company use profile. The cache is managed by the R/3 runtime system database services. Thus, individual applications just need to read from the cache buffers; they do not have to be concerned with their management. When a change is made to any data element in the client cache, the message servers respond immediately by declaring the update to the buffers of all the other applications.

Dynamic Management of Client Caches   When a client/server network is first installed and configured, it is not necessary to specify which application functions should be installed on which application servers. The first time a transaction is called, the corresponding module pool of programs is dynamically loaded from the database into the cache buffer of the next available application server, so this module pool is available to all users of this server.

The cache is maintained under the control of a *least recently used* (LRU) condition, which ensures that the memory is used to best effect.

Distributed Applications

In a client/server environment that can call upon a very large library of standard business functions and a correspondingly extensive system of databases, it's inevitable that large amounts of data will move between the distributed applications and their supporting servers. Efficient mechanisms have been developed to do this without the intervention of any user.

Dialog-Free Data Input to R/3

Probably the first large parcel of information to be input to your R/3 system without the intervention of a dialog with the user will be the legacy records of your business as it was before the R/3 system went live.

Although a user does not have to be involved, the R/3 system accepts mass imports of data as if they were generated by a series of transactions. Therefore, the system performs all the checks and updates it needs to ensure that the data is consistent and properly stored in the efficient data structures of the R/3 records. Exactly the same ABAP/4 programs are active as when the data is entered by a user.

Batch data communications (BDC) or *batch input* is a standard system that works along the same lines. The effect is to simulate a normal user dialog. The system automatically supplies the data for what would be user display screens from a special dataset, and any error situations that occur during the BDC session are logged.

The BDC dataset is created by a specific program written in a language such as C to accept the incoming data and store it in appropriate data formats selected from the standard data structures declared in the ABAP/4 data dictionary. This ensures that the new data is recognized by all R/3 applications and can be used by them when needed.

The preferred method of conditioning incoming data is to use a special ABAP/4 database interface that uses ABAP/4 Native SQL to access the legacy database.

Electronic Data Interchange Methods

Suppose that your company needs to exchange data with a business partner that is not fully integrated in your R/3 system and is using hardware and software that is not directly compatible with it. You can use the R/3 open EDI interface to exchange normal business documents and messages with specialized EDI subsystems from a variety of vendors.

R/3 offers two methods for handling EDI:

- A direct interface with the relevant R/3 application
- Messages passed for manual handling

IDocs (Intermediate EDI Documents)   The international standards EDIFACT and ANSI X12 are used to create fields for application data in IDoc intermediate documents, which also provide encoded fields using *International Standards Organization* (ISO) codes for data such as units of measurement.

Users can define how they want EDI to be applied. For example, a user can be informed by email, and certain situations can be monitored so that manual intervention can be mandated under specified conditions.

Application Link Enabling (ALE)   The IDoc (intermediate document) method is used in the ALE concept, which allows an R/3 system to grow by interacting with other systems through asynchronous links that exchange documents carrying messages and application data set out according to predefined business rules.

▶ **See** "Facilities Online," **p. 503**

Relationships with Production Technical Subsystems

Two elements are required to link R/3 with a production-related technical subsystem:

- A component of R/3
- An SAP component installed in the technical subsystem to perform the functions of a *transceiver,* which interprets the output of a control or monitoring device and transmits to it a signal to initiate some action, such as resetting a recording instrument or opening a valve

The two components are linked by standard communications channels that are predefined in the R/3 element. Conversations with technical subsystems are always controlled by R/3, which initiates and uncouples the linkage when it is no longer active. It ensures that the data read from the R/3 database and written to the technical subsystem interface is error-free and complete.

TCP/IP can be used to establish a link through other computers using the Internet Protocol. The flow of data can also be carried out using CPI-C.

Distributed Satellite Systems

The principle of establishing satellite systems that can operate locally and also integrate fully with a central R/2 or R/3 system offers the following advantages:

- The individual local systems can be implemented to best use the equipment and other resources available.
- The local system may be able to take advantage of low-cost computing power.
- By using SAP standard interfaces, the satellites do not have to be SAP systems or R/3 applications; they can be legacy systems already fully operational and responsible for storing specialized data.
- The local system can run without continuous reference to the central host system, which is thereby relieved of some workload that can be scheduled for more convenient times.

Applications as Satellites

Here are some applications that have successfully operated in the satellite manner:

- DASS production control station
- EIS-Executive Information System
- Treasury Workstation
- Components of the HR-Human Resources Management System
- LVS-Warehouse Management System

The international operation of distributed applications is discussed in Chapter 9, "Building Global Business Systems."

Reliability and Security

An R/3 implementation is in a critical role at the center of the management focus of your company. The applications integrated with the R/3 system must be reliable and available to users. The functions in all the applications must work correctly. The necessary data must be available when required.

In addition, the integrity of the data must be absolute.

> **CAUTION**
>
> The confidentiality of the data and the applications must be strictly maintained by a structure of authorizations. No data or software code must be altered or corrupted, either intentionally or by accident.

Functionality of the Software

The first consideration when assessing the capability of a piece of software to do the job intended, completely and exclusively, must be the methods used to design and build it.

However extensive the testing of software, it is unlikely that all problem situations are encountered, so there must be a degree of doubt as to the absolute reliability of the package. This degree of uncertainty can be made as small as possible by extending the scope of the prerelease testing. Many legacy computer programs have generated maintenance expenses many times their development cost, because they were not fully specified in the first instance and not thoroughly elaborated at the design stage. Several chapters in this book are devoted to the SAP tools for designing and developing reliable and efficient programs.

Security Levels and Confidentiality

The security of the data and software in the R/3 system and applications must be addressed at several levels:

- Desktop-presentation system level
- Application level
- Database level
- Operating system level
- Network level

The SAP approach to managing the security of a complex system across all these levels is to establish a set of internal and external security services:

- R/3 internal security services, which concern the desktop systems, application servers, database servers, and network communications at the application level
- Database security services, which are provided by the database computer
- System security services, which are assisted by the ease with which the R/3 system can be reconfigured without a loss of services if any subsystem comes offline
- Network security services

Reliability and Availability Through Support

The CCMS-Computing Center Management System, described in Chapter 11, "Maintaining the Computer System," operates a procedure of monitoring, controlling, and checking that covers the application's level R/3 activities, the database activities, the operating systems, and the network.

The SAP GUI maintains a system log at the desktop level. There is remote support at this level by the OSS-Online Service System, discussed in Chapter 28, "Using the Online Service System." Support is available online separately at each of these levels:

- Applications level
- Database level
- Operating system level
- Network level

Introducing R/3 Software Architecture

To ensure the success and efficient implementation of SAP systems, a comprehensive suite of mature standard business applications is available for introduction and customizing. Under the guidance of sophisticated tools, a procedure is provided for establishing an accurate model of the existing system and elaborating the target concept system. Various tools support an efficient process of design to make the transition.

In cases in which a standard business function has not been developed, a sophisticated programming language is available to create new programs that can be fully integrated with the standard SAP systems.

SAP's intention is to maintain and enhance the reputation of the R/2 and R/3 systems with respect to the following objectives:

- Provide a complete infrastructure for corporate information processing.
- Maintain a comprehensive repertoire of standard business functions that can be combined to model a wide range of business processes.
- Ensure that all SAP systems are usable worldwide.
- Retain a thoroughgoing open policy with respect to data access and functionality.
- Support distributed applications and interfaces to non-SAP systems.

A Method and a Means to Implement SAP

The extensive range of SAP standard software modules allows any model of business flow to be engineered. The precise details of each customized installation are set up as the application programs are installed, configured, and customized. There are three directions of development in the range of SAP products:

- Changes in the way companies do business are tracked and sometimes anticipated by SAP-improved software modules, such as R/3 workflow and control over it from the Internet to enable electronic commerce with business partners and potential customers.
- SAP R/3 is made available in preconfigured forms specifically designed for rapid implementation in a particular type of industry.
- Software systems are provided as tools to support the process of changing businesses to increase profitability by using computing and communications technologies.

The SAP R/3 Applications

All R/3 installations include a set of components that form the core of the system. This set is referred to as the *R/3 BASIS* or the *R/3 standard system*. R/3 BASIS provides you with the tools to build a suite of integrated programs that can be fitted exactly to the requirements of your company and changed as your company develops.

An SAP R/3 application or module is a set of programs designed for a specific type of business data processing. Each application is fully integrated with R/3 BASIS. This allows each application to communicate with any other application.

Some application modules depend on other applications. For example, the CO-Controlling module depends on the FI-Financial Accounting module. Some components of a module, as well as some functions within a component, are optional. As a result of this flexibility, each R/3 installation can be built to fit exactly the unique requirements of the client company.

An installation must include R/3 BASIS and usually includes one of the applications—the FI-Financial Accounting module is the obvious choice.

The SAP system of standard business programs is being developed in a number of directions. A function within a component can be enhanced so that it becomes a complex module. For example, the requirements of enterprise controlling can be met by the components of the CO-Controlling module. The EC-Enterprise Controlling product is available as a separate module and includes functions not available in the CO-Controlling module.

Another direction of development is to provide extra integrating functions that interact with a group of application modules. For example, the LO-Logistics General module is designed to provide integrating functions for the following applications:

- SD-Sales and Distribution
- PP-Production Planning
- MM-Materials Management
- PM-Plant Maintenance
- QM-Quality Management

A further direction of development of the SAP product range in one in which many companies in a particular sector of business share a specialized requirement. In such circumstances, an SAP partner company might develop a specialized enhancement of the R/3 system to be marketed as an "Industry Solution." As a result of these evolution types, the title of an application or a component might be changed to reflect the change of focus.

The following application modules are discussed in separate chapters:

- FI-Financial Accounting in Chapter 12, "Understanding the Financial Accounting Module"
- CO-Controlling in Chapter 13, "Understanding the Controlling Module"
- EC-Enterprise Controlling in Chapter 14, "Understanding the Enterprise Controlling Module"
- TR-Treasury in Chapter 15, "Understanding the Treasury Module"
- PS-Project System in Chapter 16, "Understanding the R/3 Project System"
- PP-Production Planning in Chapter 17, "Understanding the Production Planning Module"
- PP-PI Production Planning for the Process Industries in Chapter 18, "Understanding the Production Planning for Process Industries Module"
- PM-Plant Maintenance in Chapter 19, "Understanding the Plant Maintenance Module"

■ SD-Sales and Distribution in Chapter 20, "Understanding the Sales & Distribution Module"

■ HR-Human Resources in Chapter 22, "Understanding the Human Resources Module"

■ MM-Materials Management in Chapter 23, "Understanding the Materials Management Module"

Each application addresses a main sector of business activity, ranging from financial accounting to human resources. The modules most likely to be associated with the title of an application are grouped under that application. However, the fully integrated design of all SAP standard business programs allows great flexibility in the assembly of modules to form a specific implementation. For example, if you are installing the SD and FI modules and want to pay your salespeople bonuses through the R/3 system, you might be required to implement portions of HR as well.

Every implementation needs an SAP R/3 BASIS module that provides the elements of the SAP R/3 runtime system. It includes the fundamental tools and functions of the R/3 data dictionary, SAP R/3 Reference Model, ABAP/4 Development Workbench, and R/3 customizing component.

When designing an implementation, you use the R/3 Reference Model to select which module components are needed in the target system. This process is described in Chapters 5, "Consulting the R/3 Reference Model," and 6, "Optimizing Business Processing." Chapter 7, "Customizing," discusses the process that completes the installation process by making the integrated system exactly fit the host company.

Customizing Standard Software   SAP offers standard software that cannot be altered by the business user. What can, and usually must, be customized to suit the individual company is the type of data held in the computer system and the type of processing performed on the data. It is also necessary to arrange for the flow of data processing to match the needs of the particular company's procedures.

Application Integration   SAP software is available in a range of integrated application systems that allow the software to match the needs of the user community. For example, the Real Time Systems SAP R/2 and SAP R/3 are available with individual applications integrated to link the organizationally related areas of company activity, as described here:

■ Production planning and control is integrated with technical data processing to offer controlled inventory management.

■ Material requirements planning and procurement logistics are related to yield just-in-time supply.

■ Sales information and operating results analyses come together in marketing planning.

System Identification

An SAP product is a suite of standard software made up of individual programs that have been written to carry out computing tasks in the most efficient manner possible. None of these programs can be altered in any fundamental way by the user without SAP's approval. The OSS-Online Service System issues a code module for any modification required to accommodate errors remaining in the released version of a program.

SAP R/2 is a system for mainframes. The SAP R/3 system for open system architecture allows medium-size companies and affiliates of corporations to take advantage of the highly integrated SAP software. It applies the client/server concept across multiple levels.

The system identification of R/2 or R/3 is supplemented by the identification of the release and version, followed in some instances by an identification of the latest correction set. For example, R/2 4.3B signifies the R/2 system release 4 at development level 3 updated with corrections set B. The discussions in this book are based on the function list for System R/3 Release 3.0 Version 6.1 and include comments on the functional changes introduced in Releases 4.0 and 4.5.

Customizing

SAP standard programs are designed to be totally reliable and to work together as a coordinated suite of modules.

By itself, an SAP program is not very friendly to an individual user. It does not know what sort of business is to be conducted or exactly how the user company wants to invoice and conduct other transactions with its customers. If an SAP implementation is to look and behave as if it really understands the company it is working for, it must be configured and customized.

Naturally, the SAP software expects to be told how to behave in a specific company and has standard routines to help the company experts set out what has to be done in a format that SAP can accept. The experts who do this are referred to as *applications programmers* or *applications developers*.

Suppose that your company customizes an SAP application so that it insists that sales contacts are recorded as named individuals, with a title and preferred salutation, a job title, an informal first name, and then all the communications and address information divided into fields of characters. If a potential sales prospect telephones your company, the SAP application can fetch a screen that prompts you to enter this information.

When the user tells the system what type of transaction is to be conducted—a sales inquiry, for example—certain information might be essential, some might be displayed to prompt the user, and some might be required by the system but not shown onscreen. The inquiry number and department are examples of information the system can generate if it is configured to do so. You can decide during customization how much information to display, but the system will insist that you enter the mandatory information before it processes the transaction.

SAP includes a standard program for every conceivable business operation. The art and skill of the applications programmer is to make the work of future users as easy and error-free as possible by giving the correct operating instructions to these standard programs.

The ABAP/4 Data Dictionary

The *data dictionary* is a collection of data objects—such as tables, domain definitions, field specifications, screen formats, and report specifications—used in the standard business programs written in the ABAP/4 programming language.

The data dictionary ensures that SAP standard software always gets the data in a format it is designed to process. All communications to and from an SAP system use the standard formats set out in the data dictionary.

The ABAP/4 data dictionary specifies more than 7,000 domains associated with more than 80,000 fields and arranged in more than 8,000 tables.

Data-Storage Structures

Data organization is of vital importance to a system that is specialized to process it, and an SAP program is no exception. A consistent data-storage policy and terminology exist throughout the SAP products.

Fields   A *field* is a string of characters. A *character* is a letter, numeral, symbol, or space character that can be generated by the keyboard and recognized by the computer operating system.

A *text object* is a string of characters that usually stay together, such as a ZIP code or fax number.

A single character, a text object, and a field are examples of data elements. Information is recorded in a character field from which the user display element is derived. A field might contain just a single character, or it might hold more characters than the space on the screen would suggest. Characters previously entered scroll off to make room for new characters. The application developer can specify how many characters of a field are displayed.

Domains   To reduce the possibility of data error, a field used in an SAP program usually is subject to rules that constrain the scope of its contents. A date field has to be given characters that can be interpreted as a valid calendar date, for example. A Yes/No field admits only one of the following entries:

　　　　Y, N, y, n, Yes, No, YES, NO, blank

A field designated for the identification code of a permitted user refuses to accept anything that is not on the list of permitted user codes.

The set of permissible entries for a particular field is described as the *domain* of that field. Several fields can have the same domain if they are all allowed to have the same set of attributes, entries, or values.

A domain can identify one value as the default to be offered to the user for confirmation or amendment. The default value can be the one previously chosen by the user.

If an operator attempts to enter data into a field that is not acceptable to its domain, the entry is refused, and a specific error message appears as an explanation.

You might be able to ask for help in the form of a list of the values permitted in a domain. After you select one of these values, the system enters it in the field and shows it on the display. The value will be a member of the permitted entries defined by the domain, but it can be rejected as an invalid entry for some other reason.

Data Elements of Data Objects   Fields can be grouped together as data elements and handled as a unitary data object. For example, a customer name, address, and phone number are data elements in a data object that represent this customer in the system.

The user can choose which data elements are displayed after a particular data object is selected.

Records   A *record* is a set of fields. In most cases, the record is a set of data objects that can be accessed by their identification codes. The record usually can be selected by specifying one or more of its constituent data objects. For example, you can select the records of all customers and group them by ZIP code.

Tables   A *table* is a named set of fields that can be displayed in the rectangular format of rows and columns. There might be only one row or one column, or a table can have any number of rows; each row can also be referred to as a *record*. The names of the columns can correspond to fields of the records.

Filenames, text objects, and system parameters are examples of data stored in SAP tables. Each table contains one or more fields. A simple example is a list of codes, each with a brief description of what the code signifies. In this case, a line of the table, a record, contains two fields—one with a domain of, say, three alphanumeric characters, the other with, say, 30 characters for descriptive or explanatory matter.

You can use such a record like this: Set the screen to display the description as a confirmation after the user selects or enters a valid code. The user might realize that the wrong code has been entered when the description is displayed. If the table does not contain the code entered, an error message appears and the system waits for a correction.

Files   A *file* is a named set of records. It can be of unspecified length. It can also be free of any formatting constraints so that it accepts any input. In such instances, however, there must be some method of deciding how the entries in the file are to be interpreted when the time comes to attribute meaning to the data.

Master Data and Transaction Data   Data can be placed into two groups, depending on their functions:

- Master data that seldom changes, such as customer or vendor details and material technical records or part numbers
- Transaction data that the system uses during data processing, such as when receiving goods or when changing something in a master data record

Both data types must conform to the specifications of the data dictionary.

***Online Transaction Processing* (OLTP)**   A transaction is being processed online when the system waits for the user or operator to enter the next data object required.

Batch Transaction Processing   Batch transaction processing can take place when all the information required has been previously arranged on a file so that the system does not have to wait for the operator to enter each data element. A batch processing job can be scheduled to take place in the background whenever computing capacity is available, or it can be scheduled for a date and time. This time can be when spare capacity is likely to be available, or it can be at regular intervals so that transactions are not kept waiting. Backing up part of the database can be a timed batch job.

Creating New Data Objects

Files and text objects can be created by applications programmers or users, provided they conform to the SAP data dictionary. For example, new customer files must replicate the structure and domains of the existing customer files. The normal result of creating a new file includes adding a record to a table that lists similar files.

Database

A *database* is a collection of files shared by multiple applications. An SAP system can operate on more than one database. The collection of files can be managed by a database system on another computer. The *database system* refers to the management of any elements of online or batch transactions that entail making changes to the database. This can include directing the database management system to conduct a search and report its findings. Certainly, such applications as MM-Materials Management, PP-Production Planning, and FI-Financial Accounting will demand changes to the database.

The BASIS System

The SAP software provides methods for controlling the widest range of hardware. Each item of equipment has an operating system that can be as simple as an on/off signal or as complicated as a multitasking computer operating system.

The SAP BASIS system exercises control over whatever hardware configuration is in use and the applications running on it. In particular, it is responsible for the SAP R/3 runtime system.

The main services provided through the BASIS system follow:

- System administration, including the Computer Center Management System, authorizations, networking, printing, and memory management
- Database administration for Oracle, Informix, DB2/400, and DB2/AIX
- BASIS services and communications, such as word processing, style layout controls, archiving, office functions, and communications channels
- ABAP/4 Development Workbench, including tutorials, tools, and guidelines
- Business Engineering Workbench, including the Procedure Model, Reference Model, business workflow, and customization

The main method of interaction between the runtime system and a user is through a dynpro. A *mask* is a screen used to enter or view data. An *entry field* is a space on a mask in which the user can enter data. A series of such screen masks, together with the associated processing logic, can be treated as a unit. The SAP name for such a unit is *dynamic program* or *dynpro*. A *dialog program* is a series of transaction steps, each of which is controlled by a dynpro, that can be used to validate data being entered by a user or a communications channel (in which case the error messages are stored on file rather than shown to the user).

System Parameters

A *system parameter* is a value in a field in a table that can be used to control how a standard SAP program operates for a specific application. The system parameter can control the type of processing, the flow of processing, or both. There is no other way to change or customize the behavior of an SAP standard program; it must be done by changing the value in one or more system parameter fields.

System parameters can be altered by an application programmer or a user only within the constraints allowed by the SAP system version and release in use.

The Condition Technique

The SAP R/3 condition technique gets its name from the discipline of formal logic—in particular, from the conditional proposition form that can be expressed as the following:

> If {a certain set of conditions is in fact true}
> Then {certain other conditions will be true}

The logical If-Then condition technique is used extensively in the SAP R/3 system to enable the computer to carry out specified actions automatically—provided that the proper conditions are satisfied by the necessary data.

Data Principles

The user of a business computer must expect to be presented with a combination of menus and data forms. The spaces on data forms can accept entries from the operator, or they can be filled in by the system.

One key to effective application design is a respect for data:

- Data that is obviously wrong should be corrected as soon as the error can be detected.
- Data that is apparently correct should be held in one place only so that if changes have to be made, they can be effective immediately wherever this information is used.
- If the data to be entered can be anticipated or has been gathered previously, the user should be shown the data and invited to confirm the entry rather than to type it again.

SAP R/3 Software Architecture Advantages

The SAP architecture embraces a complete infrastructure of information processing, from the finest detail of a business transaction up to the corporate level of enterprise controlling. The

SAP R/3 system is based on a system of layers, each operating in a client/server manner, with interfaces as necessary to SAP R/2 systems and non-SAP systems. The international standards for open system interfaces are recognized. The SAP R/3 system is extremely portable across operating systems, databases, and presentation systems. Synchronous and asynchronous coupling between applications is supported.

Enterprise modeling is affected, with a provision for rapid response to the changing needs of evolving organizations.

The effects of these various software and hardware provisions add up to a powerful system that provides for the future:

- **Scalability in response to demand.** The multitier architecture based on the client/server paradigm allows fresh equipment to be installed at any level and to follow the load profiles and the requirement for additional processing created by adding applications.

- **Portable software.** Software usually remains in use longer than hardware. SAP software is exceptionally portable across hardware and operating systems, and across database systems.

- **Interoperability with PC applications.** *Object linking and embedding* (OLE) interfaces are provided, and *remote function call* (RFC) procedures allow the SAP systems to integrate both the data and the functions of the SAP R/3 system with those of PC applications and datasources.

- **Simple customizing without programming.** Not only are the SAP systems readily adjustable to fit exactly into the business requirement, but they come with customizing tools to ensure that this adaptation is carried out as easily and as accurately as possible without broaching the protected standard business software functions, which remain intact and efficiently integrated with the rest of the SAP systems.

- **New integrated software development.** The ABAP/4 business programming language is used for all SAP R/3 software. New functions can be developed in this language under the guidance of the ABAP/4 R/3 Workbench tool, which ensures that the resulting code is properly articulated with the rest of the standard software.

- **Ergonomic user interface in Windows format.** The SAP graphical user interface has adopted Windows conventions to make it readily operable by new users. Presentations of complex information and relationships are available in tabular list formats and graphical displays at the choice of the user, who can switch readily between formats. It is also standard for the user to be able to *drill down* to underlying data by selecting the graphical symbol of interest or its tabular list representation, and to call for even more detailed displays by using the special function keys. Immediate transfer of skills from previous Windows applications also is available.

Components of the Main SAP R/3 Applications

The applications and their components are discussed in their appropriate chapters. The titles used in the provisional function list for System R/3 Release 3.0 Version 6.1 are presented here to illustrate the type and scope of the SAP R/3 system of integrated standard business software.

CA-Cross Application

The R/3 Cross Application area contains a set of modules that can be used throughout the R/3 system:

- CA-BPT Business Process Technology
- CA-DM Document Management
- CA-CL Classification
- CA-CAD CAD integration

R/3 Release 3.0 includes cross-application components available in earlier releases and additional integrative modules that are coded without the CA prefix:

- SAP Office
- SAP Business Workflow
- R/3 Business Engineering Workbench, which includes the R/3 Reference Model and the R/3 Implementation Model
- R/3 Business Navigator, which includes the R/3 Process Model, the R/3 Data Model, and the R/3 Customizing System
- R/3 Analyzer, which is available online with the R/3 system or as a standalone PC-based system and is used to access the R/3 Reference Model

Two additional SAP products should be mentioned in the context of cross-application modules:

- OSS-Online Service System
- CCMS-Computing Center Management System

FI-Financial Accounting

The legal requirement for a company to publish financial documents is served by the FI application, which contains the following modules:

- FI-GL General Ledger
- FI-AR Accounts Receivable
- FI-AP Accounts Payable
- FI-LC Legal Consolidation
- FI-SL Special Purpose Ledger

CO-Controlling

The distinctive feature of SAP controlling functions is that the values represented there are planned or reported amounts and quantities that are not legal requirements. Nevertheless, they constitute important numerical data that can be used to better control a business. The following are optional modules that can be integrated with the FI modules from which they may derive their information:

- CO-OM Overhead Cost Control
- CO-PC Product Costing
- CO-ABC Activity-Based Costing
- CO-PA Sales and Profitability Analysis
- CO-PRO Project Control

IM-Capital Investment Management

The modules for managing fixed and financial assets are available as parts of an IM-Investment Management application that can be used by specialist companies, although they are often included in the implementations for manufacturing and distributing organizations. The IM modules follow:

- IM-FA Tangible Fixed Assets
- IM-FI Financial Investments

EC-Enterprise Controlling

The concept of an enterprise controller is supported by a group of modules that provide functionality in addition to the main applications used for operational activities. The EC modules follow:

- EC-EIS Executive Information System
- EC-BP Business Planning
- EC-MC Management Consolidation
- EC-PCA Profit Center Accounting

TR-Treasury

The Financial Accounting module provides fundamental software to manage the Treasury function, but the TR modules offer more extensive analysis and reporting facilities designed for their specialized tasks:

- TR-TM Treasury Management
- TR-FM Funds Management
- TR-CM Cash Management

PS-Project System

The project concept has been highly developed to accommodate all types of research and development projects. The components follow:

- PS-BD Basic Data
- PS-OS Operational Structures
- PS-PLN Project Planning
- PS-APP Approval
- PS-EXE Project Execution/Integration
- PS-IS Information System

LO-Logistics General

Logistics as a distinctive discipline integrates the manufacturing and distribution functions to promote management focused on the costs and profitability of the separate activities and their relationship with the overall profitability of the enterprise. The Logistics modules follow:

- LO-LIS Logistics Information System
- LO-MD Master Data
- LO-PR Forecast
- LO-VC Variant Configuration
- LO-ECH Engineering Change Management

HR-Human Resources

The HR-Human Resources application provides an integrated human resource management system by facilitating the use of the components of the PD-Personal Planning and Development module and the PA-Personnel Administration module:

- HR-PD Personal Planning and Development
- PD-OM Organizational Management
- PD-SCM Seminar and Convention Management
- PD-PD Personnel Development
- PD-WFP Workforce Planning
- PD-RPL Room Reservations Planning
- HR-PA Personnel Administration
- PA-EMP Employee Management
- PA-BEN Benefits
- PA-COM Compensation Administration
- PA-APP Applicant Management
- PA-TIM Time Management
- PA-INW Incentive Wages
- PA-TRV Travel Expenses
- PA-PAY Payroll

PP-Production Planning

Manufacturing is the natural province of the PP modules, which are extensively used in all kinds of production companies. The standard PP modules include a range of components specialized for continuous-processing companies, where the flow of materials and their quality control are central concerns. The PP components follow:

- PP-BD Basic Data
- PP-SOP Sales and Operations Planning
- PP-MP Master Planning
- PP-CRP Capacity Requirements Planning
- PP-MRP Material Requirements Planning
- PP-SFC Production Orders
- PP-PC Product Costing (which is also CO-PC Product Costing)
- PP-KAB Kanban/Just-in-Time Production
- PP-REM Repetitive Manufacturing
- PP-ATO Assembly Orders
- PP-PI Production Planning for Process Industries
- PP-PDC Plant Data Collection
- PP-IS Information System

MM-Materials Management

A *material* is represented by a master record and can, in fact, be a person or a service. Therefore the MM application is widely used in support of manufacturing, distribution, and service industries. The MM components follow:

- MM-MRP Material Requirements Planning
- MM-PUR Purchasing
- MM-IM Inventory Management
- MM-WM Warehouse Management
- MM-IV Invoice Verification
- MM-IS Information System
- MM-EDI Electronic Data Interchange

PM-Plant Maintenance

Plant maintenance is obviously crucial to the production industries. However, the PM application is also used by maintenance service industries, because the target of a maintenance task can be in any plant owned by any company. The PM components follow:

- PM-EQM Equipment and Technical Objects
- PM-PRM Preventive Maintenance

- PM-WOC Maintenance Order Management
- PM-PRO Maintenance Projects
- PM-SMA Service Management
- PM-IS Plant Maintenance Information System

QM-Quality Management

Although the quality-management functions originated in the PP-Production Planning application, they are available as a separate module that can be integrated with any of the applications. The QM components follow:

- QM-PT Planning Tools
- QM-IM Inspection Processing
- QM-QC Quality Control
- QM-CA Quality Certificates
- QM-QN Quality Notifications

SD-Sales and Distribution

The Sales and Distribution application integrated with the Financial application may well form the core data-processing resource of many companies. The components of the SD application follow:

- SD-MD Master Data
- SD-GF Basic Functions
- SD-SLS Sales
- SD-SHP Shipping
- SD-BIL Billing
- SD-CAS Sales Support
- SD-IS Information System
- SD-EDI Electronic Data Interchange

INT-International Development

The emergence of integrated global trading systems has created the need for a system to be able to recognize the features of commercial significance at each trading location. Currency, legal requirements, and commercial practice are featured in the components, which are consulted as required when the user profile is identified prior to each terminal session. The INT components follow:

- IN-APA Asian and Pacific Area
- IN-EUR Europe
- IN-NAM North America

▪ IN-AFM Africa/Middle East

▪ IN-SAM South America

IS-Industry Solutions

An IS-Industry Solution is an enhancement of the standard R/3 system and may include some or all components of any R/3 application, according to the sector of industry for which it was designed. The following are examples of Industry Solutions:

▪ IS-PS Public Sector

▪ IS-H Hospitals

▪ IS-B Banks

▪ IS-IS Real Estate Management

Future Developments in SAP Software

The SAP organization has always had a policy of continuous business development. The driving forces are the need to keep up with the marketplace in product and requirement details and also the need to meet the evolving legal obligations placed on companies. These obligations have been in connection with food or dangerous products but include legal requirements to track individual components in the aviation industry, for example. Additional obligations are imposed in connection with the disposal of waste products, including heat and light.

The need to prepare for natural human error and pernicious manipulations is no less urgent than in former times. Profit and business survival remain of interest. The software developments can be expected to follow the leads of the Industry Solution products, where some examples are given of specialized assemblies of modules targeted at a relatively narrow sector of industry.

The Internet as a news medium and presentation arena for SAP products can be accessed at the following address:

http://www.sap.com

The Internet as a medium for communications among business partners, customers, and suppliers is likely to develop on the basis of the EDI-Electronic Data Interchange components available in many of the current R/3 modules.

The EDI interface methodology uses a range of IDoc intermediate document types to exchange business documents between the SAP system and the EDI subsystem. These IDoc data objects can be developed by SAP or by the user organization, perhaps by adding a segment to a standard SAP IDoc type.

▷ **See** "Electronic Data Interchange Methods," **p. 58**

CHAPTER 3

Consulting the R/3 Reference Model

The Data Object Structure of the R/3 System

The Reference Model is a data structure that contains a complete description of the R/3 system and its business functions. The model can be accessed in different ways and for various purposes. In particular, you can use it to simulate your business as it could be carried on if the SAP R/3 system were installed and configured to suit your particular circumstances. Using the model to develop your business efficiently is described in Chapter 6, "Optimizing Business Processing"; this chapter, on the other hand, concentrates on the R/3 Reference Model, the basis of the R/3 Analyzer.

R/3 is object-oriented. The units that the SAP standard business functions are designed to handle are data objects that can be of any complexity. For example, a data object might consist of only an identification code number for the object and one field that contains the information of interest—a part number, for example.

Such an object is likely to be much more useful if it is permanently associated with other objects—in this example, the name of the part in each SAP-supported language. The bundle of data elements that make up the part number, part name, and any other information needed about this part is handled as a single object by the R/3 system. If you ask for this part by name or by number, the system will have available the rest of the information that goes to make up the data object. The user has control over which data elements appear on the display, but they are all there ready for immediate access.

There is no limit to the complexity of a data object, because the data elements themselves can be complex objects.

A purchase order is a data object. It includes many data elements in the header, and each order item represents a complex data object. When the purchase order is entered, it becomes a document that is posted to various processes. Each process examines it to see if it is carrying the information that triggers or signals that process to take action.

Every item of information processed by the R/3 system is treated as an object—a project plan is an object, a user password is an object, an arrow on a graph is an object.

An Enterprise Model for Reference

One class of data objects that R/3 recognizes is the Enterprise Model. The enterprise can be a department or the entire company, and the Enterprise Model is a way of specifying how the information and material move within the organization as it does business.

To help you specify the material and information flows of your company in a standard manner that can be used to develop the efficiency of your business, the SAP R/3 Reference Model is provided as part of the system. It is an information model stored in graphical form that can be displayed using a standard symbology.

The R/3 Reference Model contains all the common business process structures, linked in a completely integrated fashion that can be set to work without further adjustment. However, the standard R/3 Reference Model probably includes many functions and data structures not relevant to your organization. The process of customizing is provided in the R/3 system to enable you to adjust the R/3 Reference Model until it exactly fits the needs and structure of your specific organization.

When this match is complete, the model is referred to as an *Enterprise Data Model.*

This topic is also discussed in Chapter 10, "Developing an SAP Open Information Warehouse."

The Concept of an *Event-Driven Process Chain* (EPC)

The components of the R/3 Reference Model, and any Enterprise Data Models derived from it, are *event-driven process chains* (EPCs). The graphical representation of these models shows which events lead to which activities.

The designers of the SAP R/3 system found that no other method of specifying the requirements of a standard business software system was as fruitful and as easy to comprehend as the event-driven process chain. Where did the EPC come from? Why is it so useful?

Three Basic Design Principles

If you are trying to write down what goes on in a workplace or what has to be done to get a certain result, you will ask yourself three types of questions. You might not think about these issues at the right time, but if you omit any of them, you will discover that the work is not going as well as you expected, and that there is something missing from your job descriptions for the people involved.

What Should Be Done?   Perhaps it is obvious. Surely everyone knows that you should not be working at something if you do not know what has to be done. Yet there are people busy at work who have not stopped to think about the task they are tackling or the function they are supposed to be performing.

If you show someone performing the actions of a job without paying attention to what the purpose of the task is, you might well raise a laugh. They are just going through the motions, without understanding.

Who Should Do Something?   If you are looking at a team of people, a department, or a company, the second question is also obvious. Which member of the team should be the one to begin the task? Who is on the lookout for an occasion to set the team to work? Who is ready to notice an event of importance to the team if one occurs?

Even if you are working by yourself, this question must still be answered. Is this a job for me, or should I do nothing and let somebody else do something?

In the representation of your enterprise, it is clearly a matter of some importance to identify which organizational unit is responsible for action in response to the significant events. And this responsibility is not just a matter of having someone to blame if something goes wrong. The organizational unit responsible for an activity will need to be provided with the tools, time, and energy resources to do it.

What Information Is Needed?   To perform a function, the responsible organizational unit needs to know what the task is. How to carry out this task will be a question of certain knowledge or skill that can be called on in the organizational unit. The necessary information for a task can be defined as an information object, a set of instructions together with the essential data, or an indication of where it can be found.

Some tasks are performed only by virtue of a human skill that is not generally available. In such cases, the critical information must include a specification of who in the company can be called on to provide this skill or enlist the aid of an outside provider.

The Historical Sequence of Information Models

Perhaps the oldest information model is the family tree. It shows who the parents are and, therefore, who is most likely to have the most power and experience. This information model is not necessarily accurate in that sense, however; a child may be more capable than a parent or a grandparent.

The family tree may suggest how the people are grouped into families and thus into organizational units. A structure diagram with a specified directionality has arrows rather than plain lines, or has a definite up or down, before or after, which is in some way ordered. Such a structure can be drawn as a *digraph,* a directed graph.

The standard organization diagram is a digraph in which the ordering is from chief executive at the top to most junior worker at the bottom. Some companies have a dozen layers of seniority; some have only two or three.

The organizational digraph can indicate who is responsible to whom. What it does not show is who does what or how it is done.

Models of Units in an Organization   The family tree digraph leads to the organizational chart in easy stages. Groups of workpeople are associated as departments and represented as boxes or nodes on the digraph. Head Office is responsible for Purchasing and Sales.

The trouble with a simple organizational unit model is that it shows, by the arcs or arrows, who is in charge, but not what anyone does. In particular, there is no indication of, for example, how a sales order can cause the generation of a purchase order to replace the stock or commission work for the sales order. There is no flow of material shown and no indication of how information might flow. From looking at the organization chart, you could be led to believe that all information exchanges between Purchasing and Sales must be routed via Head Office. This is almost never the situation.

Task Models   A simple task model is a cooking recipe. Take the ingredients and carry out the cooking processes. If you saw this in graphical form, it would have an input block and an output block, with an arrow from input to output. One worker might perform the function of converting input to output. All the cook's skill or production worker's expertise is concealed by the arrow that links the input raw materials to the finished products.

Task models can get very complicated if there are many inputs and many outputs, including the finished product, some byproducts, and some wastes, for example. But these task models do not usually portray the fact that a great deal of knowledge and skill is needed for the inputs to be correctly and efficiently transformed into the outputs.

Information Models   The third type of formal model to be developed has to be a supplement to the others. It concentrates on the information needed to carry out a function.

How does the worker know which materials and tools to select? Where did he acquire the skills? What is he looking at and what is he looking for when he is monitoring the quality of his work?

Information is a difficult concept to define. If you know that a coin has two faces, and you know that it has fallen heads up, you have acquired one bit of information, which your computer could record as one binary digit.

The menu is the troublesome part. How can you possibly choose what to order for dinner until you know what the menu offers? If there are eight possibilities and you choose one, the chef will have acquired three binary digits of information from you that will be valuable to him because it means that he need not cook seven of the dishes on the menu, at least not for you. If your R/3 system can tell whether the document is a sales order or a purchase order, this will be information that can be used to narrow down the possibilities for subsequent action.

The concept of information is not relevant unless you know the menu. The R/3 system can recognize a large but limited number of document types. You can add to this list during customizing if you are prepared to tell the system how a new type of document is to be recognized, and what actions are to be taken when one is encountered.

A gardener might know the names of hundreds of plants and be able to recognize them. She could carry out the task of walking through a garden and speaking the names of most of the plants. She has a considerable amount of information. However, this does not mean she is a gardener capable of cultivating any of these plants.

The information model is good at specifying the size of the menu from which the skilled person can make a choice. The larger the menu of possible events that could occur, the greater the amount of information necessary to allocate the correct names.

Naming the parts is a good way to begin to acquire a skill, but it does not necessarily help you to do the right thing every time.

EPC Objects

If you are looking for some sort of analytical object as a standard building block for showing how a company does business, the EPC is the prime candidate. One process may lead to another and so on down a chain that is complete only when the result is achieved. But a set of process chains that do not have precisely specified events as their exclusive triggers is of no use. Each process chain must begin only when the specified event occurs. And if that event does occur, there must be no question as to whether the assigned process chain will begin. When the certain data elements in certain data objects match the conditions laid down when defining the event that will drive a chain, that chain and only that chain is initiated.

There is no limit to the complexity of an EPC, because each process in the chain can itself give rise to a complex data object that can take part in the initiation of other EPCs.

The Relationship Between Stimulus Response Theory and EPC Methods

If you are teaching a person or an animal to do something that does not come naturally to it, something that is not in its instinctual repertoire or in the knowledge and skills it has learned, you have to pay careful attention to the stimulus and the response.

Suppose that you want the user to press the F1 key. You could get this to happen in several ways:

- Take the user's finger and push it on the F1 key.
- Say to the user, "Press the F1 key."
- Say to the user, "Select PF1."

Have you taught the user anything useful? Perhaps the system will respond with a helpful message and the user will guess that the PF1 key is the key to use if he needs help. But not necessarily. The user might not associate what the system did with the key he pressed.

Try a different lesson. Say to the student user of the system something like this: "If you need help, and the screen is showing you a picture or other sign labeled HELP, try pressing the key marked F1 to call the special programmed function labeled PF1."

This lesson is not very exciting, but it does illustrate that we learn to do things, such as pressing a Help key, and we learn when this action is likely to be needed or appropriate. For example, we could all press key F6 without difficulty, but would we all know whether that would be a good idea and would help us accomplish what we are trying to do? The response of pressing a particular key is not much use to us if we have no idea when it should be carried out.

In the language of the psychologists, we have to associate a useful response with the stimulus for that response. If we manage to do this on a reliable basis, we are said to have acquired an *operant*—a *stimulus-response* (S-R) pair.

One stimulus triggering one response might not seem very momentous. The clever part comes when we can tell the difference between stimuli that might otherwise be confused. We might have names or labels for many of the significant stimuli in our private world. *Fire* is a word that carries a warning. System Error 1492 is a term for something that seems to be important for the computer. What we can do if we see this onscreen is to ask somebody what to do about it. That, at least, is an appropriate response. One day we might learn a better one.

Many errors made by people and machines occur because the response was not quite right for the stimulus situation at the time. There could be two types of fault here:

- The stimulus triggered the correct response, which was then executed badly—right but sloppy.

- The response was executed perfectly, but there was a subtle difference in the stimulus situation that should have triggered quite a different response—beautiful but inappropriate.

S-R Chains

The operant's stimulus-response model as a useful way of thinking about how people and machines carry out tasks can be extended to describe a sequence of actions. The first stimulus is the signal to begin the task with the first response. As this response is carried out, it should create the stimulus situation that triggers the next operant in the chain.

If the learning has been perfect, there will be no point at which the person doing the task asks, "What do I do next?" Every action serves as the trigger for the next. And with copious practice, the sequence speeds up and the task performer looks ahead and prepares for the upcoming steps. With even more practice, the whole chain may rattle along without the performer paying it any conscious attention. We might say it becomes instinctual. As soon as it is given the go-ahead, the next conscious event is the delivery of the finished result.

EPCs as System Responses to Events

The EPC can be regarded as a sequence of actions that has been developed to provide a stable and appropriate response to the event that is its trigger. There is a simple idea here, but one that can be used to build reliable software.

The Data Attributes of an Event

In the language of SAP system design, the data object recognized as an event can store an unlimited amount of data. However, this data cannot be readily accessed unless it is recorded systematically and uniformly across all events.

The data fields of an event master record are clustered as attributes. Each attribute cluster is assigned a set of standard data field titles, which can be extended and developed during customizing, if necessary.

Event Attribute 1

The following fields are located in attribute 1:

- Name of the event
- Identifier code
- Synonymous names (aliases) for this event
- Full designation of the event that places it in the software context
- Description or definition of the event
- Author of the event specification
- Origin of the event

The following data fields are available in the event master to indicate the originating source of the control and substantive information associated with the event:

- Outside of company
- In-house
- Outside of system
- Within system
- System interdependent

Event Attribute 2

Additional characteristics of the event are stored in attribute 2 to specify the type of event, the event's classification in terms of its logical function, and the event's function in the context of an EPC.

Type of Event   The assembly of critical information that constitutes an event can be generated in one of three ways that define the type of event:

- Interactively generated event
- Automatically generated event
- Manually generated event

Event Classification   The status of an event as part of an EPC is used to classify it:

- **Trigger** specifies that the event can initiate an EPC at any time if the specified data becomes critical.
- **Secondary condition** indicates that this event is not itself a trigger but an intermediate or secondary criterion cluster of data that might have to be satisfied or consulted for an EPC to reach its conclusion.
- **State** indicates that the event serves the purpose of holding the result of other processes that then can be used as required, perhaps by many other EPCs.

Functional Purpose of an Event   In the context of an EPC, the beginning and end items are clearly important because they enable input information and output results to be available to the rest of the system. Events are therefore categorized according to their function:

- Start event
- Finish event
- Start or finish event
- Internal process event, which may be subject to monitoring for special purposes but will not normally be apparent to the user of the system

Event Attribute 3

The third attribute cluster of an event carries the data concerned with time. It is consulted by the system on a routine basis to determine whether the event has to be set to trigger the associated EPC.

Time of Occurrence   The system needs to identify which events have been scheduled for a fixed time or a schedule of times. This attribute value can be known or unknown.

Frequency of Event   If the event is scheduled to recur, these details are recorded:

- Times per year
- Times per month
- Times per week
- Times per day

The Data Attributes of a Function

The standard structure of the data associated with a function is to cluster the data elements as three attributes.

Function Attribute 1

The following fields are located in function attribute 1:

- Name of the function
- Identifier code
- Synonymous names (aliases) for this function
- Full designation of the function that places it in the software context
- Description or definition of the function
- Author of the function specification
- Source information
- System attributes, including the transaction code and the release level

Function Attribute 2

The way the function is used and its classification as a standard business program or a function written specifically for the customer is recorded in function attribute 2.

Functional Assignment   The assignment of a function in terms of its functional use is categorized as this:

- Outside of company
- In-house
- Outside of system
- Within system
- Optional function
- Mandatory function

Classification of the Function   The system recognizes the following types of functions by a code in the function master record:

- Standard system function
- Customer-specific additional system function
- External system function

Function Attribute 3

The third function attribute cluster is devoted to data concerning the processing type and frequency. The function master records the time needed for the function to acquire the data and the time taken to actually process the data. The system costs of processing are accumulated in this attribute.

Function Processing Type   The type of processing entailed by the function determines the system resources to which it is assigned. The processing types are specified as the following:

- Interactive
- Automatic
- Manual
- Central
- Local

Frequency of Processing   The actual times of processing can be used to accumulate frequency data such as this:

- Times per year
- Times per month
- Times per week
- Times per day

Processing Duration   The learning time is recorded as a moving average to indicate the time taken for the function to acquire all the datasources and documents needed to perform the function.

The actual processing time is also recorded as a moving average of the time taken to process the data after it is assembled from its sources.

Processing Costs   The costs of calling this function can be accumulated on a moving-average basis and evaluated in financial terms, or on the basis of system processing costs expressed in resource-usage units.

The Data Attributes of a Process

A process taking part in an EPC can be assigned a very large number of data elements. They are clustered into two attributes.

Process Attribute 1

The following fields are located in process attribute 1:

- Name of the process
- Identifier code
- Synonymous names (aliases) for this process
- Full designation of the process that places it in the software context
- Description or definition of the process
- Author of the process specification

Process Assignment   A process can be assigned to a single organizational unit or to an entire system. The details are stored under the following headings:

- Organizational unit
- System assignment to application, module, transaction
- Required input information
- Generated output information
- Start event identification
- End event identification
- Process links

Processing Changes   There will be changes in the organization in which a process is carried on. The details of these processing changes are recorded in the process master record under the following headings:

- Organizations involved in the changes
- Frequency with which the organization is changed
- Systems and media affected by the changes
- Frequency with which the system or medium is changed

Information Statistics   The information storage requirements generated by the operation of a process can be a source of major costs. These requirements are recorded on the process master in terms of the following groups:

- Information storage within the system
- Information storage outside the system
- Information storage requirements not supported by information technology methods and equipment

Process Attribute 2

Additional information about the process is stored in the master in attribute cluster 2. The theme is processing statistics.

Process Duration The following data objects are stored in the process master:

- Learning time
- Processing time
- Transmission time
- Wait time
- Entry time
- Output time

Process Quantity Structures The process master stores data structures to record the quantities of material or information processed, and also the quantities transmitted.

Process Costs The following process costs are recorded:

- Overall costs
- Personnel costs
- Machine costs
- Material costs

Data Transmission Statistics are recorded for the following classes of data transmission entailed by the process:

- IT-supported, online
- IT-supported, batch
- Manual

Transmission Medium The distribution of data transmission across the following media and methods is recorded for the process:

- Network
- Data-processing list
- Written documents and forms
- Card file
- Oral data transmission

Views of an Information Model

It is apparent from the complexity of the data attribute structures that many data elements need to be stored in the system. Consistency of data structure and use is ensured by using, as a standard reference, a suite of data structures stored centrally in the SAP metadatabase and retrieved by the SAP R/3 Analyzer.

From the user's point of view, the system contains all the information available. What is more difficult to appreciate is the extent and variety of this information, and the infinite flexibility of the systems available to retrieve it.

The SAP approach is to offer the user five avenues by which the extensive SAP database can be approached. Each avenue of approach affords a different view of the data structures and their contents. The standard SAP object orientation is maintained throughout—it is essential to efficient internal program logic.

Because they all originate in the same database, these five views are dovetailed. They are overlapping partial views, each of which is logically consistent because of the shared basis and consistent use of data structures and processing disciplines.

- The **Process view** interprets the R/3 Reference Model as an integrated network of EPCs and thus relates directly to the operation of your R/3 system.

- The **Data view** sees the R/3 Reference Model as clusters of aggregated data structures that can be represented through the SAP R/3 Analyzer as data objects using their names and "header" data to navigate with the aid of graphical displays. These same data structures can also be viewed down to the detailed level required for in-house programming developments using the ABAP/4 programming language.

- The **Information-Flow view** concentrates on the necessary flow of information between EPCs. It can be used in the early stage of system design when the details of the functions have yet to be specified. In the Information-Flow view, it is not necessary to say how or when the information is captured and transmitted.

- The **Function view** provides a summary display or listing of the complete array of active functions in a specific implementation of the R/3 system.

- The **Organization view** shows the semantic relationships between the various organizational units that represent your company as a functioning enterprise supported by the R/3 system. A master organization view is held in the R/3 system that depicts the organizational structure of the system itself so that you can compare your specific organizational structure with the master to check that the hierarchical relationships correspond. If you want to establish an organizational structure that cannot be modeled by using the standard R/3 Reference Model components, you can add to these modeling components during customizing.

These views are discussed in more detail in subsequent sections, beginning with the Process view because of its emphasis on EPC logic. But first, you need to understand the graphical symbols used for all SAP displays and views of the R/3 Reference Model.

The Formal Components of EPC Modeling

The aim of the Reference Model is to be precise about the events to which the R/3 system responds and about the actions that take place as a consequence. Expressing this model entirely in the form of a spoken language runs the risk of losing much of this precision, not only in the process of translating the model for use in different countries of the world, but also in the interpretation by those who speak the language in which it is expressed. Each reader has a particular educational background that enables him or her to understand his or her native tongue by recognizing symbols, which are combined to become words or concept icons, which then are combined in groups to express actions, relationships, and ideas.

The computer will not accept this vagueness. It must be told when a number is to be treated as an amount, which currency is to be used, and so on. If the system is to issue a warning if a customer order exceeds the amount of credit allowed, the system must know what this amount is and which items in the order must be used to compute it.

So the system must work from defined events that it can recognize, and it must have the capability to carry out a series of processes, each of which may be a sequence that is or isn't triggered according to precise conditions detected when specific events occur.

And to enable programmers and system managers, consultants, and heads of departments to communicate with precision across national language barriers when necessary, there has to be a logically formal system of symbols and relationships for this purpose.

A convenient way of sharing ideas about this formal system of symbology is to present it in graphical format. The exact format or style of the symbols is obviously not critical, but the way they are used and interpreted do have to conform to the defined logic.

Event

The R/3 system defines an *event* as a set of values for which it has a predefined action that it initiates if this set of values occurs. The location of these values in the records of the system is part of the definition of the event, and so are the specific amounts or other data elements that are treated as significant if they occur in these defined locations.

For example, if the total amount on the sales order document that is being processed will be the cause of a warning message sent to the operator, the system must know that this customer's credit limit is recorded in a specific field in the master data records for this customer. The system has been set to check all sales orders against available credit.

In logical language, this example situation can be expressed as the following:

> IF the current document is a sales order,
>
> AND IF this current customer has a credit limit,
>
> AND IF the value of the sales order total is greater than the value of the customer's credit limit,
>
> THEN issue a warning to the user who is entering the sales order.

The warning is an action that happens when the system recognizes a significant event. In this example, the event is made up of three components:

- The document being entered has to be a sales order.
- The customer has to be subject to a credit limit.
- There has to be an arithmetic relationship between two numbers, namely the order total and the customer's credit limit.

The warning is an action that takes place because the appropriate triggering conditions occurred and because the system was provided with a warning function. This warning function has several constituent processes that probably include at least the following actions:

- The system logs and time-stamps the event to record that this customer placed an order that exceeded his credit limit.

- The system displays a standard text that includes fields to receive the actual values—in this case, the credit limit and the amount of the excess.

- A suggestion or proposal is provided to the operator concerning what should be done, if anything, to get authorization for the extra credit or to block the order pending further investigation.

Although this example is very simple, clearly many elements in the process chain are driven by the event of a customer about to exceed his credit limit.

The Standard Symbol for an Event   The trigger for an EPC is defined in terms of a set of specific data elements and the critical values or ranges of values that generate consequent activities on the part of the system. Figure 5.1 shows the shape used to depict an event on charts of EPCs.

FIGURE 5.1

The graphical symbol for an event.

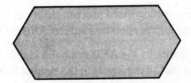

Generated Event   Each activity in an EPC results in a set of logical conditions that may include the set of values that constitute the critical triggering event for another EPC. This subsequent event is referred to as a *generated event*.

In the earlier example, the logging of the over-credit event is triggered by a generated event that includes the result of the arithmetic comparison. If the difference is one way, the warning function is triggered; if it is in the other direction, the warning function is not triggered.

Function

In mathematical or logical terms, a function brings about a transformation from an initial state to a target state. For example, an inverse function could be defined as one that changes a plus sign (+) into a minus sign (–). It would also be expected to transform a minus sign into a plus sign. Another example is a currency conversion function.

The transformation carried out by a function can be expressed in the conditional form. For example, the inverse function could be specified as the following:

If the sign is +, substitute the sign –.

If the sign is –, substitute the sign +.

In this example, the inverse function is followed by a chain of other processes if it is called in an accounting situation. And it is called only if one of certain events occurs that meets the conditions for triggering it.

The purpose of a function is to do something. It is activated by one of a set of events and can operate on information gathered from any sources. Which data items are processed can be determined by the function itself. Alternatively, the objects on which the function work can be indicated or passed to it in the function call, which is triggered by the significant event.

The symbol for a function is a rounded rectangle and may be connected by flow lines emanating from any convenient part of it (see Figure 5.2).

FIGURE 5.2
The graphical symbol for
a function.

Logical Operators

There has to be a convention for representing that a process chain can only be driven by a particular set of circumstances. Three logical operators suffice: AND, XOR, and OR.

AND   The conjunction of events is shown by the AND symbol, a circle containing an inverted V shape. It is interpreted as meaning that all the inputs to the symbol have to be TRUE for the output to occur. Figure 5.3 shows the symbol for AND (Conjunction).

FIGURE 5.3
The graphical symbol for
AND (Conjunction).

Exclusive OR (XOR)   The exclusive OR (XOR) is interpreted as requiring one but not both of its inputs to be TRUE for the output to occur. Figure 5.4 shows the XOR symbol.

FIGURE 5.4
The graphical symbol for
Exclusive OR.

Either or Both (Don't Care)   The Don't Care circled V symbol represents the situation where either input will suffice on its own, or both can be TRUE, to allow an output (see Figure 5.5).

FIGURE 5.5
The graphical symbol for
Either or Both (Don't
Care).

Control Flow

Control flow may be a matter of time or sequence ordering. The dotted line with an arrowhead shows how one event depends on a function, or one function depends on an event (see Figure 5.6).

FIGURE 5.6

The graphical symbol for control flow.

The dotted arrow is not used to represent the flow of information such as the details of a purchase order. The control arrow merely indicates that two elements of a graphical model are necessarily joined by a control connection that can carry one binary digit that can be interpreted as TRUE or FALSE, YES or NO.

This signal may, in fact, pass along a communications link that also carries large quantities of information. If so, this channel can appear on the Enterprise Model using the full-line arrow symbol.

Process Pointer

The process pointer shows where the next process in a chain is to be found (see Figure 5.7).

FIGURE 5.7

The graphical symbol for a process pointer.

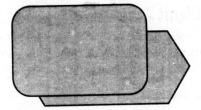

Organizational Unit

The ellipse is used for an organizational unit. It represents the element used in the company organizational structure. It may be a department, a section, or a person. You can also define organizational units in terms of the material groups they process or the markets they serve. Figure 5.8 shows the symbol for an organizational unit.

FIGURE 5.8

The graphical symbol for an organizational unit.

Information, Material, or Resource Object

Real-world objects such as information packages, materials, and resource objects such as energy or services may have to be represented in the EPC model. A plain rectangle with sharp corners is the standard symbol (see Figure 5.9).

FIGURE 5.9
The graphical symbol for information, material, or resource object.

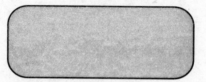

Information or Material Flow

The flow of information is usually to read, change, or write data. This arrow symbol can also be used to show the movement of material. Figure 5.10 depicts the type of arrows used for the flow of information or material.

FIGURE 5.10
Graphical symbols for information or material flow.

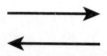

Resource or Organizational Unit Assignment

A solid line without arrowheads is used to indicate which unit or staff resource is processed by a function. Figure 5.11 illustrates how a plain line may have to make several right-angle turns to depict how a function is associated with a resource including personnel.

FIGURE 5.11
Graphical symbols for resource or organizational unit assignment or attachment.

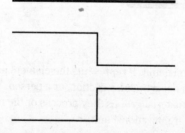

Combining Events and Functions

To draw a true and useful picture of how your company carries out its business operations, the graphical symbols have to be combined. An event is a combination of logic and data that has been defined as the trigger for the initiation of one or more functions. You can build a model of any complexity by combining a fairly small number of symbols in various ways.

Two Events Can Trigger a Function

A programmed business function can be designed to handle many different kinds of events. Some of these events may be exclusive; others may occur in conjunction with each other. These differences in the logic of the EPC are shown in the diagrams by the way the various symbols are arranged.

Either of Two Events Can Trigger the Function   Figure 5.12 shows the situation where either of two events is sufficient to trigger the function. In Figure 5.12, there's no possibility that both of the events could occur together.

FIGURE 5.12
Either of two events can trigger a function, but not both.

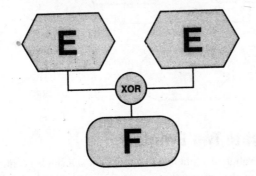

Both Events Are Needed to Trigger the Function   If a particular function needs several events to occur before it can start to run, there are two ways of setting it out in the graphical model:

- Define an event to include all the conditions and critical values of the data necessary for the function to be triggered.
- Define the trigger to be a combination of events already defined for other purposes.

Figure 5.13 shows the situation where two essential events have to occur in conjunction for the function to be initiated.

FIGURE 5.13
Both events must occur to trigger the function.

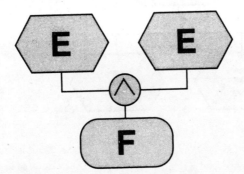

One or More of the Events Are Needed to Trigger the Function   If a function has been designed to cope with several events in any combination, the trigger can be defined as one or more events from a list or set of possibilities. The function runs if any event in the set occurs, regardless of how many others also occur. Figure 5.14 shows a simple illustration of this situation.

FIGURE 5.14
At least one event must occur to trigger the function.

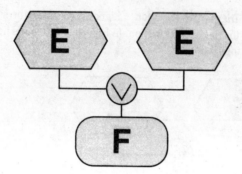

A Function Can Generate Two Events

It is very rare for the operation of a function to generate just a single event. At the very least, there is one event if the function operates successfully and another if a problem is encountered. However, an EPC has to be shown at a selected level of detail. The user can instruct the system to leave out details or include them to make the graphical display as helpful as possible.

Figure 5.15 shows part of a model where the function is depicted as being the generator of one of two events, but not both. Figure 5.16 shows a function that generates both events every time it runs. Figure 5.17 depicts a function that generates one or more events according to the results of the computation that goes on as part of the function.

FIGURE 5.15
The function generates either of two events, but not both.

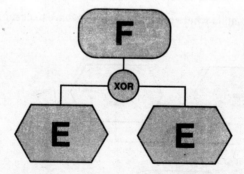

FIGURE 5.16
The function generates
both events.

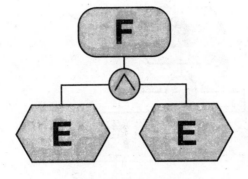

FIGURE 5.17
The function generates
one or more of the
events.

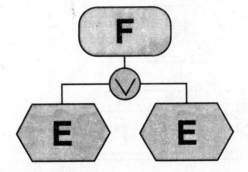

An Event Can Trigger More Than One Function

The interpretation of data according to predefined criteria defines an event in an SAP model of
your company. When the computer decides that a particular combination of data is a critical
event, several functions may be called into action automatically.

An Event Cannot Be Ambiguous   The SAP definition of an event is as the reliable trigger for
one or more events. There cannot be any doubt as to which event is triggered. Therefore, the
diagram in Figure 5.18 that uses the XOR symbol is not allowed, because it does not show how
each function has a distinct triggering event or combination of events. An EPC diagram cannot
include a symbol to show that either one or both events will occur, because this is equivalent to
saying that the event is ambiguous about which function to trigger.

An Event Can Trigger Two or More Functions   If your model needs to show that an event
causes the running of two or more functions, the AND symbol is used, as shown in Figure 5.19.

An Event Cannot Be Indecisive   The diagram in Figure 5.20 is not allowed, because it suggests that either of two functions could be triggered. An event is defined as the necessary and
sufficient collection of data for the triggering of a specific function. If several functions occur in
response to an event, they must all occur. An event cannot be indecisive in identifying which
business functions should be performed.

FIGURE 5.18
An event cannot trigger either of two or more events.

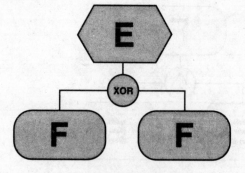

FIGURE 5.19
An event can initiate more than one function.

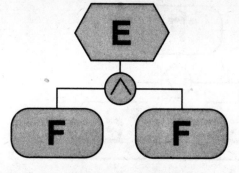

FIGURE 5.20
An event must select reliably which function to trigger.

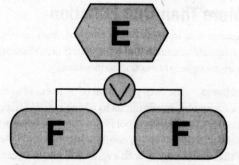

Two Functions Can Generate the Same Event

A critical arrangement of data can arise from more than one situation. There are three logical possibilities, all of which are legal in EPC modeling.

Only One Function Generates the Event   It might be the case that an event that is critical for something else can be caused by a variety of functions. The first of the two functions to operate generates this event in the situation shown in Figure 5.21.

FIGURE 5.21
Either of two functions
can generate the event,
but not both.

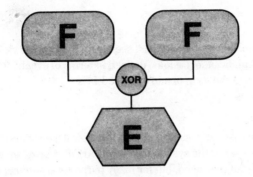

All Functions Must Operate to Generate the Event   One use of an event is to register the moment when a certain set of functions has operated successfully. Figure 5.22 shows the situation where two functions must finish before the event is generated.

FIGURE 5.22
Both functions have to
operate to generate the
event.

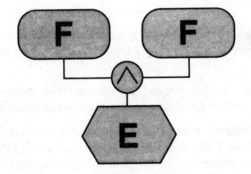

One or Both Functions Together Generate the Event   If any one or more than one of a group of functions will suffice to generate an event, you can depict the logic as in Figure 5.23.

FIGURE 5.23
One or more functions
have to operate to
generate the event.

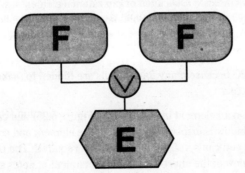

Process View

The dynamics of an information system are best seen from the Process view, because the objects of scrutiny are the significant occasions, defined in terms of events, that inevitably prompt the R/3 system into action in the form of one or more EPCs.

Lean EPCs

Too many events and processes are associated with the typical user transaction to make a useful presentation to the user or the system developer. ABAP/4 programmers know how to get down to the level of detail they need, but for many purposes, a summary format is more useful. This is provided as a system of lean or sparse displays of EPCs that show the essential relationships in each of the five views and offer a display of reasonable size and complexity to the user. Drilling down for extra detail is always possible by selecting the item of interest on the display and using the special function keys.

An EPC Example

To illustrate the semantics of EPC methods of specifying how business is recorded in order to be transferred to a computer support system, a simple scenario is described in text and in graphical terms.

Text Process Description   Goods arrive and are checked. If they are satisfactory, they are passed to production. If they are not, they are rejected or blocked pending further inspection.

Graphical Process Description   Each EPC has to begin with at least one event and be completed by at least one final or finish event. The main constituents of an EPC are passive components (events) and active components (the functions that do something). The control-flow connections between these events and functions are shown as dotted arrows, which may be branched at logical operators shown as circles bearing the appropriate logical symbol to signify AND, Exclusive OR, or Don't Care.

Solid lines without arrows indicate associated organizational elements, such as the department or work center responsible for the function. Solid-line arrows show the flow of information, documents, or material. Figure 5.24 shows part of a lean EPC that depicts only the main events and functions and their essential relationships.

The example is a lean EPC because many finer details are hidden to make the overall structure of the business function clear.

If you place your cursor on an element in an EPC (see Figure 5.25) and call for help by using a special function key, a window is displayed pointing to the element and containing the detailed reference document that you can scroll and bookmark as required. The reference document may be a more detailed view of the chart or a textual document of notes and procedural instructions. These documents are developed and annotated as the system implementation proceeds. The whole process of converting parts of the R/3 Reference Model to an *Enterprise Data Model* (EDM) of your particular company is discussed in Chapter 7, "Customizing."

FIGURE 5.24
A model of a lean EPC.

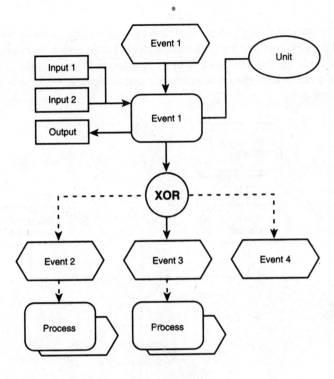

FIGURE 5.25
A specific EPC.

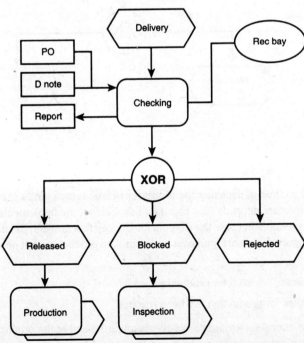

When the particular functions are identified by the graphical element labels, the generalized form of the EPC becomes particular and is stored by the system as a unique graphical object. This gradually builds up to the EDM of your company. Figure 5.26 illustrates how a fragment of this model might look when it takes into account the specific work centers and process flows in a target company.

FIGURE 5.26

Part of an EPC.

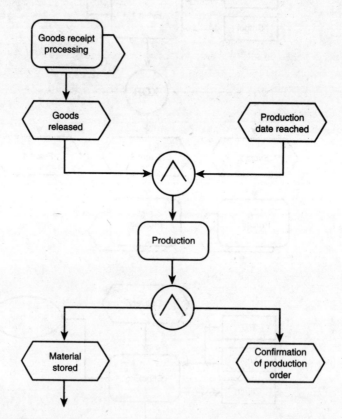

Choosing Key Events

The formal method of depicting the processes of business in terms of EPCs that can be supported by software depends very much on the ability of the implementers to choose the right significant events to become the triggers for the key functions. In the fragment of an EPC shown in Figure 5.26, two significant events initiate production, but only if they occur in conjunction:

- Goods are released for production
- The date for production has been reached

In the same example, two significant events mark the end of the production function: material is stored after production processing, and the financial system is informed by a confirmation of the production order. Both events should be depicted in the chart of the business process, because they each are needed for subsequent activities.

If the EPC is not initiated by a carefully chosen event set or does not terminate with events that will take part in another EPC, the power of the method is not fully realized.

Information-Flow View

Every EPC depends on information being input to the function through the data objects of the triggering events. There will be additional inputs of information if the chain is a complex one made up of a structure of EPCs, each with its own data held in the critical events.

Because the purposes of the function include the generation of events that carry items of information that cause other EPCs to activate, every function can be seen to generate output information.

If you had the full details of an EPC, you could work out the effective input and output information flow across the function. However, at the early stage of business system implementation, the exact details of the component EPCs may not be known. In such cases, it might be helpful to plot the structure of the business in terms of information flows, knowing that the SAP R/3 system will be able to provide the precise standard business software when the time comes to develop and elaborate the implementation.

The R/3 Reference Model provides a powerful facility to portray automatically the existing and necessary information flows between the standard business functions at the application and functional area levels. Figure 5.27 depicts the expected information flows between the functions and for which R/3 standard business programs have been developed.

FIGURE 5.27

The R/3 Reference Model suggests the necessary information flows.

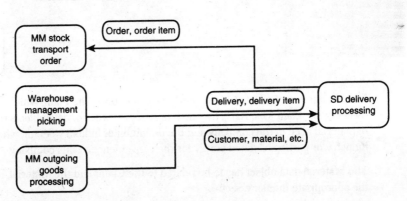

Data View

Although the operation of EPCs creates and changes the information stored in the individual data objects of the system as a result of the functions initiated, certain relationships also exist between data objects independently of any processing that occurs. For example, a plant may "own" a production capacity because it is responsible for the machinery and personnel that provides it. A warehouse, which is treated as a plant, can be assigned certain materials quite independently of any functional relationships that exist when this material is used for production or sales.

These operational relationships between the data objects of the system are stored in the form of information objects that can be seen by calling for the Data-Cluster view of the R/3 Reference Model. Figure 5.28 shows how the necessary data objects are clustered to form the data structure that represents a type of material located in a specific plant in your company.

FIGURE 5.28

Relationships between data clusters are shown in the Data view.

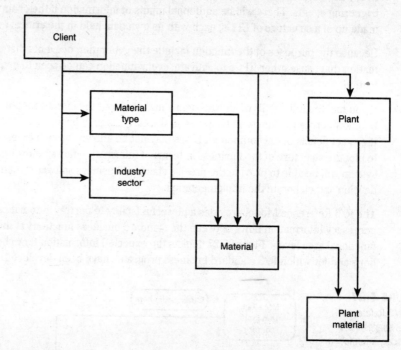

In this fragment of a Data-Cluster view, the Client owns the Plant, which is the responsible owner of the Plant Material. The Client is also the owner of data objects representing the types of material used in the company and the definition of Industry Sector, which is specific to the industry or perhaps defined purely for the convenience of this company.

The Material data object has to be related to the Client and the Material Type and be placed in the appropriate Industry Sector.

The Client may own several plants, each of which may hold stocks of the same material. Therefore, there has to be a data cluster of records in the database that represents the conjunction of plant and material, to be labeled in this example as Plant Material. An item of material from one plant is not necessarily treated as identical to the same item from another.

Of course, many other data input relationships will exist for each of the information blocks shown on this Data-Cluster view. There also will be many additional outgoing relationships to data structures that need to be represented—in this example, by the blocks labeled Material Type, Industry Sector, Material, Plant, and Plant Material.

The Data Cluster Concept

For the purposes of program development, the fine details of data objects have to be made available from the R/3 Reference Model. However, for the purposes of customizing and analyzing your business with the aid of the R/3 Reference Model and the SAP R/3 Analyzer, the most appropriate data level usually is an aggregated data structure in which the objects are displayed at the summary level, which is referred to as the *data cluster*.

A continuous range of data cluster levels is available from level 0, entry level, down to the level of the finest detail, as required for software development. These levels correspond to the Function view levels discussed in the next section.

At any stage, you can point to a charted element and use the special function keys to drill down for more detailed information.

Function View

The Function view of the R/3 Reference Model can show how the functions are subordinate to each other in the form of a function tree. The following levels are the most useful:

- **Level 0** describes an application, such as Sales and Distribution, as a single entity. The corporate enterprise usually has several in the form of an integrated business system.
- **Level 1** shows the functional areas covered by each application as blocks on the organization chart.
- **Level 2** portrays the principal functions needed to support each functional area, such as the preparation of quotations in the Sales area.
- **Level 3** displays the variations within each function that will be recognized by the user as needing a slightly different method of processing—in the way that third-party order processing is different from standard order processing, for example.
- **Level 4 and the levels below** usually are not regarded as part of the Functional view, because they are the province of the system development teams and are not of concern to the user or the implementer of a standard business software system.

Organization View

The R/3 Reference Model contains a model of the organizational system on which it is based. Although many variations of company organization can be replicated by using the components and relationships provided as standard in the R/3 system, it is also possible to design custom-built organizational structures if the standard elements are not sufficient.

Figure 5.29 shows part of the R/3 Reference Model. You can use this model to form the basis for the elaboration of your company organization view of the reference model by replicating the entities or "blocks" at each level until the model corresponds to the organizational structure of your company.

FIGURE 5.29

You can use the structure of the R/3 Reference Model as a pattern.

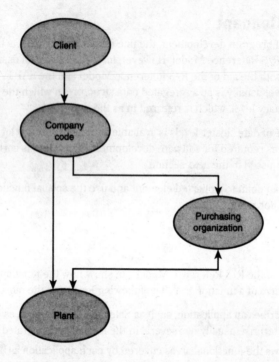

The graphical displays of the model offer a wide variety of presentation styles and annotation possibilities. Figure 5.30 shows the standard graphical presentation of part of the Reference Model as it is being elaborated by copying and editing graphical structures to build an EDM of your company as it is now, or as you want it to be when you complete the process of business process reengineering.

The main tool for using the R/3 Reference Model in the implementation of your company's business software support is the SAP R/3 Analyzer, which is described in Chapter 6, "Optimizing Business Processing."

FIGURE 5.30

The organizational structure of your company will be in accord with the R/3 model.

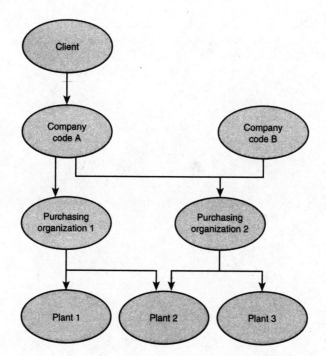

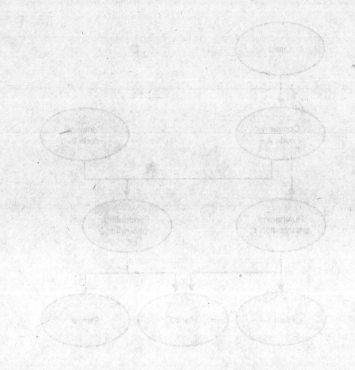

Optimizing Business Processing

Analyzing with the Reference Model

All businesses should be in the process of continuous development. They should be looking for ways to adjust to changing conditions, and they should be developing new perspectives on the long-term future.

Optimizing is the process of making things work better, not regardless of cost and other relevant factors, but *in relation to* these factors. The time available to make changes is often an important factor. The skills of the people making these changes and those who will have to live and work with them must also be considered.

Usually, several things ought to be changed to improve the situation. Which to tackle first and with how much effort are just two of the important decisions. Optimizing is much more than just trying to make changes piecemeal and without a method.

Some businesses require such radical surgery that the trauma of change is called *business process reengineering*. The intention of the designers of the R/3 Analyzer is to reduce the possible negative effects of this trauma without lessening the benefits of making sensible changes.

The purpose of the R/3 Analyzer is to provide a set of tools for selecting from the R/3 system of predefined software—just those standard business programs that will best serve your company. All the programs in the R/3 system and its applications are fully integrated with one another. Whatever selections you make, the resulting system is automatically integrated.

Your company might be a good fit for the predefined R/3 standard business functions as they stand. But if some modifications would improve the fit and make the system easier to use by your workforce, the customizing process (itself thoroughly supported by R/3 tools) can make the necessary adjustments without interfering with the highly developed and efficient standard software of the BASIS system and the associated applications. The objective is tool-supported optimization of business processes across all applications.

The R/3 Analyzer includes the following facilities:

- R/3 Reference Model
- SAP Introductory Method
- ARIS Toolset Navigation Component

The full ARIS Toolset BASIS Component is additional to the R/3 Analyzer module. It is required if the components of the R/3 Reference Model need to be copied, modified, or supplemented to create a nonstandard R/3 Reference Model for specific corporate modeling.

The R/3 Analyzer draws on the R/3 Reference Model as its knowledge base to provide the details of the standard business functions available in the R/3 system. Chapter 5, "Consulting the R/3 Reference Model," discusses this R/3 Reference Model and the five views it provides:

- Process view
- Function view
- Information-Flow view

■ Data view

■ Organization view

This chapter introduces the work of the R/3 Analyzer and shows you how to use it by selecting from the R/3 Reference Model the components needed for the target concept for your new system.

The Two Uses of the R/3 Analyzer

The R/3 Analyzer is optimized for two distinct types of work: research and implementation. The results of the first are available to facilitate the second. In particular, the investigation should result in a *technical concept*, the SAP term for an elaborate scheme of standard business functions that run as an integrated R/3 system and fit exactly the requirements of your company.

Research Studies with the R/3 Analyzer

First you need to become familiar with the R/3 system so that you can learn what is available and how you can access it. You can do this with the R/3 Analyzer, which supports the SAP Introductory Method of implementing R/3 for the first time in a client company.

There are four essential stages to a research study:

■ Description of the current situation

■ Identification of weaknesses and opportunities for improvement

■ Identification of possible SAP R/3 functions of interest

■ Explanation of possible alternative means to optimize the business processes of the company

You should base a management decision on the results of a research study that determines whether an SAP implementation exercise should move to the next stage—presenting the details of the standard business functions you need.

The Present Situation

One way you can describe how you currently do things is to use the current procedure documents and operational desk manuals. Another method is to ask the opinions of the people doing the work. Yet another source is the training staff that teaches newcomers.

The current company organizational chart might give you a picture of how responsibilities are delegated. And the troubleshooting specialists in the company will have a fund of information on how things could be improved.

Perhaps the most promising method of describing how things are done now is to set out the structures and the flows in the graphical and logical conventions of the R/3 Reference Model.

Here are the five views of how things are done now:

- The **Process view** gives you an integrated network of event-driven process chains and relates directly to the operation of your proposed R/3 system.

- The **Data view** requires you to be specific about the clusters of aggregated data structures that exist in order for your company to do business.

- The **Information-Flow view** concentrates on the necessary flows of information between event-driven process chains. It can be used in the early stage of system design when the details of the functions still have to be specified.

- The **Function view** can be developed to create a summary display or listing of the functions carried out now that would have to exist in a future implementation of the R/3 system as well.

- The **Organization view** shows the relationships between the organizational units you choose to represent your company as a functioning enterprise.

What to Look for in the Current Situation

The R/3 Analyzer is based on extensive experience in implementing business software. It is designed to apply this experience in preparation for new installations. It maps your current situation to a set of data elements that it can manipulate. For example, business entities (such as work centers) with relationships between them (such as the sequence in a production line) can be displayed graphically.

Shared, Divided, and Confused Lines of Responsibility   The flow of significant information should be directly related to the lines of responsibility. If two departments are responsible for the same activity, there is a very real possibility that neither of them will admit any fault. Nothing will get done. There is also a difficulty if the group or person closest to the customer, who knows what is wanted and what is lacking in your service, can't do anything about it. If the one who notices a blemish can put it right immediately and permanently, there will be more job satisfaction in the work and fewer complaints from the customers.

Does your organization separate too much the detection of a significant event from the execution of the proper chain of responses? Where are the event-driven process chains in the present situation? Do they cross and recross departmental boundaries unnecessarily?

Some organizations find that they can do without several layers of management hierarchy. Entire departments may lose their reason for existence if their functions are better performed elsewhere—perhaps automatically by the system, or perhaps by a person who enjoys an extended scope and range of work because the technical know-how is so readily available from up-to-date sources.

Disjointed Information Technological Support   Information technology should be focused to simplify tasks wherever possible. At a simple level, does the desk manual really tell you how to get the best out of your terminal? Does it help you use the help system? At a more complicated level, do you have to keep on typing the same phrases or—worse—the same part numbers and customer addresses?

Does your company include any places where data has to be read from a source document and written elsewhere? Are there any checks of its validity? Is anybody else doing the same thing for the same data in another part of the organization?

You might find that the data is presented onscreen. The viewer might have to highlight the relevant parts and pick them up for transfer to a form or other document. Could you have the system do this transfer in a fragment of the time it takes the operator, and with no errors?

If you are studying a work activity with the intention of implementing an SAP module, you will find that the standard business software has been designed to give the user all possible support. It would be a mistake to try to copy your existing procedures exactly if they contain operations that could be performed automatically by the R/3 system.

The integrated document concept is a standard feature of SAP systems. Each business transaction causes the generation of at least one standard document. And all the data elements needed at the next stage of the event-driven process chain are transferred to this document. The user of the system can intervene in this automatic transfer process, because the system often presents for approval the best proposal that can be assembled on the basis of the data available. For example, if one of your customers is speaking to you about a recent order, the system can show you the recent orders from this customer so that you can quickly determine which one is the subject of interest. After you find it, the system has all the supporting information handy that you could possibly need to discuss the topic in depth with the customer. And you can also have at hand the latest information from your company concerning the business area and the products likely to be of interest to your contact.

When you are describing the present situation, you must be careful to specify where the information comes from. How much depends on the knowledge in the head of the person doing the work? The Information-Flow view of the R/3 Reference Model is very useful here, because it suggests the information channels present in a well-tailored business. You might not find all of them in your own organization as it stands now.

If you use the R/3 Reference Model as the standard against which to judge the integrity and logical rigor of your present system, you will be well on your way to developing the judgment needed to best use the R/3 Analyzer.

Matching Requirements with SAP Functions

If a functional module of the R/3 system covers more than you need for a certain aspect of your company's business, you can easily prune it to remove unneeded elements. There is no reason why your users should see menus and lists of possibilities that contain items they will never need.

The R/3 Analyzer guides you through the process of picking out from the R/3 Reference Model only those standard business programs necessary to support the processes and functions you intend to reengineer. As this identification proceeds, the R/3 Analyzer stores the results and is ready to present them to you in graphical or list form at any stage for you to review the developing design and make changes.

After you finish the initial stage of sketching a rough model of the current state of your business, you are ready to use the more powerful facilities of the R/3 Analyzer to firm up a design.

Alternative Solutions

The SAP system sometimes presents several ways of achieving the same result. Some functions carry out the standard business processes expected in a wide range of industrial and commercial sectors. However, some modules are designed with a particular range of client organizations in mind. They might go into much more detail than you need. For example, SD-Sales and Distribution is an application that offers a wide scope of functionality in the sales area of work and in the arrangements for making deliveries and processing invoices. If you have few suppliers and few customers, all using a constant system of delivery, you might not need the same delivery management functions as a company supplying thousands of customers. On the other hand, inventory management might be important if your products have to be tracked in dated batches and stored in particular types of storage facilities. You might have a choice of modules.

One alternative a good consultant should always consider is to minimize the automation and computer support used for a business. What would be the consequences of doing everything manually? In some cases, you might be able to perform certain functions much more cheaply and flexibly if you don't have to go through a computerized intermediary. The deliberate attempt to draft a manual system might be a quick route to specifying a very effective computer support system.

Using the R/3 Analyzer Introductory Method to Implement R/3

The idea is to choose from the alternative business processes offered by R/3 and modify them:

1. You have to select from and add to the R/3 Reference Model functional structures.
2. The results have to be passed to the Customizing module for fine-tuning of the system components.
3. You will want to go live with your system under the control of the SAP Business Workflow Management system.

The R/3 Analyzer is a tool for carrying out the preparatory work most efficiently. It prompts users to carry out the necessary steps in the proper order, and it keeps track of the work done and the decisions made.

The Process Matrix

The current situation has to be captured in a formal system that can be processed and can take advantage of previous work to elaborate the *system concept* for your company. Three documents are required and may be very extensive:

■ A chart of the information inputs and outputs throughout the company

■ An organizational chart of the enterprise

■ A process matrix

The procedure for the current situation can be described by the methods used by the Analyzer. Figure 6.1 shows the first part of a chart of this process.

FIGURE 6.1

Describing the current situation.

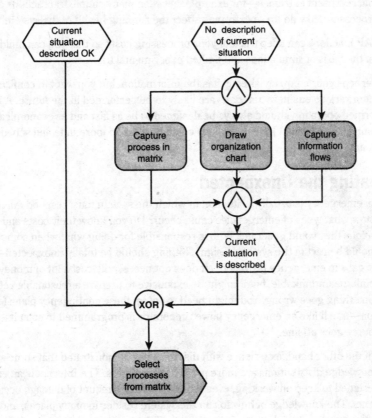

The process matrix is essentially a table that records the component processes that take place in your enterprise. The processes are displayed, with their names and identification taken from the R/3 Reference Model.

The chart or matrix is provided by the R/3 Analyzer as a display of the R/3 processes that have been preprogrammed in the form of standard business software using the ABAP/4 language. Against each item, you signify whether the particular function is required in your target system concept. For example, you might have to process requests for quotation documents. There is a standard business function for this. Will you need this only as part of standard order processing, or will you also need it in the context of contracts?

Collecting Trial Data

You might need to stage a trial operation—in part of a real plant or in a simulation—to see what type of statistical information you'll need when choosing possible enactments of your target system concept. You might have to gather data on the electronic storage and communications demands, for example. You might want to see what will happen in various worst-case scenarios that represent extremes—for example, between many simple transactions and a few elaborate processes. How do these extremes affect the running health of the system?

SAP functions can keep track of your processing costs so that you can build up reasonable data on the basis of simulations and limited experimental trials.

Perhaps your company already has the information, but you want to confirm estimates of how often various business functions are likely to be performed in the future. A frequently performed operation should always be designed to be as fast and as economical in system resources as possible. Rare operations could be allowed more time and scheduled for off-peak hours.

Anticipating the Unexpected

An emergency is usually a situation in which the system must respond quickly. But do you know what types of emergencies could occur? Do you know their costs and the types of complications they could generate? Who is responsible for doing what when something rare happens should be part of the system design. Nothing should be totally unexpected—there should be no gaps in emergency provisions. It does not necessarily cost a lot of money to get people to think the unthinkable, but it might be expensive to prepare a reasonable action plan on the day something goes wrong. You might need to set up these contingency plans for automatic initiation—much like an emergency power generator is programmed to start itself if the regular source goes off-line.

On the other hand, experience with disasters has demonstrated that some system designs and knowledge distributions are more prudent than others. The Internet is an example of a system designed to keep on working, even if a considerable amount of damage occurs to its components. The knowledge of how to run the system resides in many places, and there are many pathways along which this information can flow. An alternative approach is to consolidate the knowledge in a central location and defend it robustly.

Another example of a distributable system is medical knowledge. It might be a better strategy to have many people who can do simple medical procedures rather than rely solely on a few who can perform any procedure. The latter approach depends on being able to move the patient to the medical experts when necessary.

The target concept should include what has to be done in the normal course of business and at least a recognition of the types of emergencies that could arise.

Computing the Extent of Change

Change is costly. Paint the walls, and people spend time discussing the effect. Changing a procedure bit by bit, by the evolutionary method, is a common practice in all walks of life and places of work. Traumatic or at least discontinuous changes in the form of revolutionary work-place upheaval might have to be a consequence if you decide to go for a target system concept that is quite unlike anything current. The benefits of large-scale change must outweigh the inherent costs.

Changing the SAP standard business programs to make them better suited to what you want to do is much easier than it sounds, because the system has myriad supporting functions to help you see how things are progressing and to propose sensible additions and refinements to help you get everything right the first time. But you do have to arrive at a firm specification of where you are going and where you are starting from.

Selecting Functions from the R/3 Reference Model

As you work down the process matrix that shows what you are going to need in the way of programmed functions, the R/3 Reference Model shows you scenarios that you will recognize: sales order processing, physical inventory taking, personnel recruiting, and so on. Figure 6.2 shows the top level of the process-selection matrix. By selecting any item on the display and using the special function keys, you can see any level of detail about the item of interest. This is referred to as *drilling down*.

FIGURE 6.2
The process-selection matrix shows what is in the R/3 Reference Model.

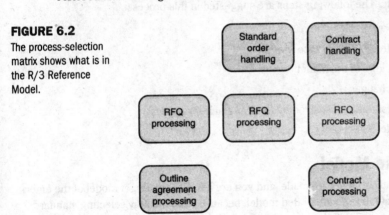

The R/3 Analyzer Determines Processes

As you refine the target concept for the system to support your new enterprise, you can approve it stage by stage. After the design of a component is approved, the R/3 Analyzer automatically selects the relevant underlying R/3 processes. Sometimes, certain aspects of your target concept might remain that are not available in a standard business function in the R/3 Reference Model. In this case, you must develop enterprise-specific scenarios from which the programmers can create enterprise-specific processes to add to your company's version of the standard R/3 Reference Model.

Assigning Responsible Organizational Units to Functions

The first stage of allocating functions to organizational units probably will focus on the names and the structure of departments and work sections that already exist or are anticipated for the new organization. You will probably want to assign jobs to the traditional teams that can best do them. However, it might become obvious from the R/3 Analyzer that there could be a different organizational structure based on the way the standard business functions of the R/3 Reference Model interact with one another and the activities you identified from your study of the current situation. For example, the R/3 Reference Model does not expect any gaps in the communications channels between departments. It also does not welcome any manual entry of data in documents that the standard R/3 system normally can complete automatically.

In particular, the system might recommend that you remove one or more layers of supervisory staff and management from your organizational chart. And as you determine the structure of your target organization, the information flows between the new units are installed automatically. The result is a better scheme of doing business. Indeed, it might be this suggestion that you have unnecessary information channels that prompts you to revamp your structure.

Under the guidance of the R/3 Analyzer, the continuous business process reengineering cycle is just about inevitable. The following steps are suggested in this process:

1. Describe the present situation.
2. Model it from the R/3 Reference Model.
3. Study the five views of the model.
4. Make needed changes.
5. See the new description displayed by the R/3 Analyzer system.
6. Repeat the cycle, if necessary.

The Target Enterprise Model

Eventually, no more adjustments are made, and you are left with the target model of the enterprise you want to create. It is an integrated model, because you built it by selecting standard business functions from the R/3 Reference Model. It should be close to what you want, because you started with a description of the current situation and followed the advice of the R/3 Analyzer. Then you accepted the information flows that it suggested as essential for the system to remain viable and integrated.

There could be two types of discrepancies between your target enterprise model and the ideal:

■ The R/3 Reference Model does not include a function that your particular business requires.

■ The target system doesn't exactly fit your requirements, and the user interface doesn't bear the unmistakable imprint of your business and your corporation.

The first discrepancy is a signal to look at the R/3 Reference Model more carefully. If something is still missing, it must be defined as a new program development project for work with the ABAP/4 programming language supported by the ABAP/4 Development Workbench (see Chapter 29, "Developing ABAP/4 Programs with the R/3 Workbench"). Meanwhile, your target enterprise model will have to be content with a definition of the information flows and functional specification for the new component until it is developed and tested.

The second discrepancy between the target enterprise model and what you really want is a matter for customizing.

The R/3 Analyzer Selects Predefined Customizing Activities

The SAP R/3 standard software is designed on the assumption that the client company will want to alter it. Yet the client company does not want to have the software rebuilt in its entirety. And at no stage in the modification process does the client want to have the system fail because of a programming error.

The SAP approach to customizing is to have all the software refer to parameters stored in tables in standard formats. The customizing module gives the implementing company access to these tables but not to the underlying software. Therefore, the client cannot do anything that will crash the R/3 system.

For example, a standard business program to conduct warehouse management refers to a table of the types of storage facilities that might be found in a warehouse. All the common types of bins, pallets, racks, marked floor space, and so on are in the table. If your company needs something different, you can add to the table; you are prompted to supply the details of how it is to be handled (its size and capacity, for example). If you will never need some items in the table, you can delete them.

With a minimum of manual effort, you can complete the customizing process, because the system proposes all the customizing activities needed according to the functions you specified in your target enterprise model.

Rough Survey Procedure

Although the procedure is referred to as *rough,* the method entails a precise formal process of capturing the system relationships of the current situation in a format that can readily be adjusted to correspond with the R/3 Reference Model. By doing so, the opportunities for improving the current situation become apparent, and the means to make the necessary changes are identified in the suite of standard business programs of the R/3 system.

The procedure for conducting a rough survey of the present situation begins with the identification and recording of the objectives of the organization and the units in the company responsible for these activities.

Objectives and the Organizational Units Responsible

By mapping the company's objectives and the departmental units responsible, it is possible to discern the following types of imperfections in business system design:

- Functions specific to the company—not because they are unique in the industry, but because they were developed piecemeal as the company found it necessary to elaborate its procedures to cope with new circumstances
- Functions performed redundantly by two or more work units, or without purpose by one
- Functions that lack information technological support and that could be improved if this support were provided
- Discontinuities in the flow of information or control caused by unnecessarily strict demarcation between unit responsibilities
- Data held in more than one place
- Information captured or entered manually that is already available in the system
- Data transcribed from one medium to another

Figure 6.3 suggests that each objective depends on the successful performance of certain functional areas. You can create similar objectives diagrams at any level of detail.

FIGURE 6.3

The objectives diagram shows the functional areas responsible.

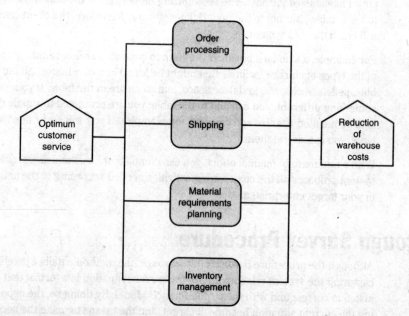

Existing Organizational Structure

You can use the traditional organization chart in the SAP R/3 system to depict the management relationships between the existing departments and work sections. Figure 6.4 is part of such a chart. The R/3 Reference Model includes typical chart sections that can be edited and articulated to create a graphical model of the current situation.

FIGURE 6.4
A current organizational
chart.

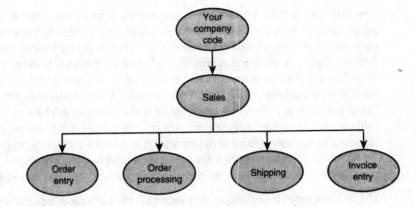

Function Trees

The complexity of business processes makes it necessary to use some form of hierarchical structure to show that each process is made up of a series of subprocesses of event-driven process chains, which in turn can entail lower levels of event-driven process chains.

The most informative way to describe the current processing structure of your company is by using *function trees*. You use the format and models of the R/3 Reference Model and adapt the elements until they accurately represent how you do business. Figure 6.5 shows part of a function tree.

FIGURE 6.5
The function tree
defines the scope of
the organizational unit.

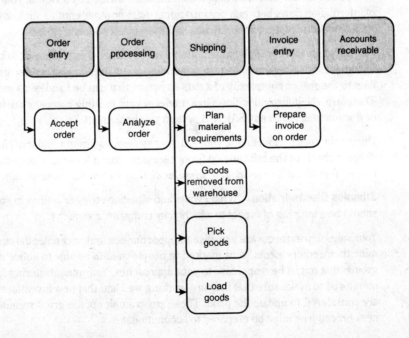

Your first edition of the function tree for a department might use terms and labels your company is familiar with. On the other hand, you might find that the R/3 Reference Model suggests names of functions that are somewhat different. In particular, you might define a certain function under a single function title. The R/3 Reference Model, however, might define that same function in terms of several subfunctions, which appears to increase the complexity of the work of the department. In Figure 6.5, for example, Accept Order is a subfunction of Order Entry, and Analyze Order is a subfunction of Order Processing. The organization of these subfunctions recognizes that the entry of a customer order should concentrate on efficiently capturing an accurate picture of exactly what it is the customer wants, whereas the analysis of the order takes into account how the customer requirements are to be met. The same person might perform both functions, but there are two points of view, two sets of priorities.

The R/3 Reference Model might offer a simplification of your existing procedures. Your target concept of how you will use the R/3 to run your new business design might have fewer elements than your model of the current situation. This can happen because the R/3 design takes it for granted that the computer system has access to a comprehensive database and sufficient speed of retrieval to use it effectively. As soon as you know what the customer wants, the system can tell you how to arrange for it to be provided. The same person can carry out several steps of the process with the support of the technology.

Information-Flow Mapping

In the process of capturing an accurate picture of how your business currently is conducted, your rough model should be supplemented and informed by a view of your company as a series of information flows between organizational units or other entities such as database records. An SAP document is a carrier of data and therefore a collector of data.

The definition of an SAP document allows for any form of data element to be handled as a document with a header of its own or as a document item in a larger document. There is no limit to the size or complexity of a data structure that can be handled as an SAP document. Therefore, the information flows in a model of your existing company are treated as documents or document items in any SAP R/3 system you implement.

During the rough modeling of your existing system, you might find it useful to develop very detailed charts of the information flows necessary to get business done efficiently. Two techniques should not be overlooked: *stimulus discrimination* and *response differentiation*.

Stimulus Discrimination   What events and situations trigger actions in your company? There should be a long list of events to which your company is sensitive.

Your sales departments are sensitive to opportunities to detect potential customers and determine their requirements. Your marketing people want to be able to notice changes in the target groups that might be responsive to your approaches. Your manufacturing facilities need to be monitored to make sure that they are working well and that new inventions and developments are considered to update the plant. These are examples of the gross stimulus types your business procedures must be prepared to accommodate.

At a finer-grain level, your sales department, for example, probably has different procedures for regular customers and one-time customers. So the detailed procedures have to include a data-capture operation that determines which type of customer is being processed. The data capture might be a simple matter of identifying an inquirer as a previous customer and confirming that no details have changed. Or a one-time new customer might be subjected to inquiry techniques to establish information such as name and address.

These trivial examples illustrate the technique of compiling a list of all the stimulus situations of importance: previous customer, regular customer, new customer or prospect, one-time customer, and so on. The outcome of this stimulus discrimination should be a set of elements that represent the occasions when a collection of data from outside the system is essential. The information required should be sufficient to determine precisely which stimulus of interest has occurred. Such an occasion is defined in the SAP system as an *event*. However, at the rough stage of system description, information-flow models may suffice with the graphical elements labeled with the stimulus of interest.

The method of information-flow mapping should show how each stimulus of interest leads to a different response. Certain stimuli might be grouped together; these events in the outside world are treated as equivalent by the system. The variants of a stimulus class usually retain their individual identity, though, because one or more data elements are carried through the processing sequences.

Response Differentiation   When you compile a list of the stimuli of interest, it is a good idea to also compile a list of the responses that occur in your company. For example, different customers might enjoy different terms and conditions of payment. Why is this? How does the system user know which terms should apply? How are new customers assigned to the more favorable terms?

If you know that your company has 11 different sets of credit conditions, for example, you should be prepared to find 11 sets of stimulus conditions you can use as guidelines to assign a new customer to the appropriate credit condition.

You might be unlucky. You might find that your company responds differently to different customers for no apparent reason. You have discovered an *information gap* where there should be an *information flow*.

Back-to-Front Information Mapping   When your auditor comes to inspect your annual accounts, he or she is entitled to select a value on the financial documents and see how it was computed. Which pieces of data were processed to arrive at this figure?

When your SAP system is fully implemented, you will be able to select any figure in the accounts and use the special function keys to trace back to the primary documents and the information they carry to see for yourself how the final total was compiled. You can drill down the value of the inventory, for example, until you are looking at the subtotals for each warehouse. Then for each warehouse, you can drill down on the total for a material, and so on until you are looking at the valuation given to each batch or each inventoried item of stock.

The *back-to-front method* of analyzing your current business system follows the same logic as your auditor. You list all the outputs from your company and keep asking to see how they were produced until you trace their history back to the input of the information and materials that took part in their production.

Of course, if you have already compiled a comprehensive list of the different responsive actions that constitute your business, and if you have also compiled a list of all situations and events that trigger an action from at least one part of your organization, you will have to hand over much of the information needed to conduct a back-to-front scrutiny of how your company's outputs came into being.

The way SAP systems describe stimuli and responses is designed to sit comfortably on the logic and mechanisms of computer programming. By and large, the systems do one thing at a time. Complicated things are done by processes chained together and triggered by a specific event.

Process Chains

Each process of your existing business system requires an input—such as a document, a person, or device—to recognize that it is significant and deserves a response. Your system also requires a further inflow of information and perhaps material as the process carries out its activities. Figure 6.6 shows some of the process chains associated with order handling.

FIGURE 6.6
Customer order handling is a process chain.

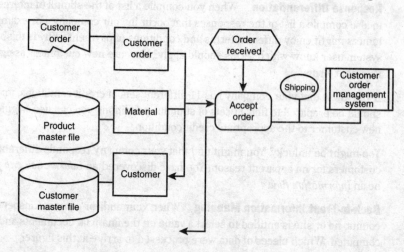

When the function of the first process runs its course, the next process in the chain is initiated by the passing on of information in the form of a document, and perhaps material. The more precise your knowledge of the process chains in your business, the better your models of the current and future systems will be.

Reviewing the Rough Survey

When making a rough survey of the existing situation in your company, you need to specify the following:

- Objectives
- Organizational chart with responsibilities assigned
- Function tree
- Information-flow diagram
- Event-driven process chains

To achieve this, you can call on the R/3 Reference Model to show models of typical structures. You can copy and modify these structures to reflect how you do business. You might want to call for lists of the significant stimulus events to which your company must respond, and you will need to identify all the forms these responses can take. You might even check the validity of your data by the back-to-front method of tracing how and why things are done as they are.

The next step is to convert your rough survey of the existing situation into the target concept—the enterprise model that will be the design for your future business system. The tool for achieving this is the R/3 Analyzer.

Technical Elaboration of a Target Concept

Technical elaboration is the process of specifying exactly which SAP standard business programs will be used to run your target business. You also have to make arrangements for these standard programs to interact to achieve exactly the result you require.

The Process-Selection Matrix

The first step in technical elaboration is the process-selection matrix. Each application has a comprehensive process-selection matrix you can use to identify the standard business functions you need in your target concept system. Below each item in the matrix is another process diagram at a more detailed modeling level. Figure 6.7 suggests how the process-selection matrix can handle the complexity of an integrated business application.

At any stage in a process diagram, the chart may use a process pointer symbol to indicate that the process chain continues. There might not be enough space to display the details. The connection might be to another series of event-driven process chains—perhaps to another application.

Company-Specific Functions   You might find that the R/3 Reference Model does not contain a standard business function that can be adapted to one or more of the functions in your chart of the current situation. In this case, you can assign a new function symbol to this function and add it to your model. The system is aware that you have created your own version of the R/3 Reference Model, and the whole process is treated as an engineering change management activity. The original R/3 Reference Model itself is not modified. You will have to subject the unique new function to program development work to establish the program to execute the new functions you require.

FIGURE 6.7
The SD-Sales and Distribution application has a comprehensive process-selection matrix.

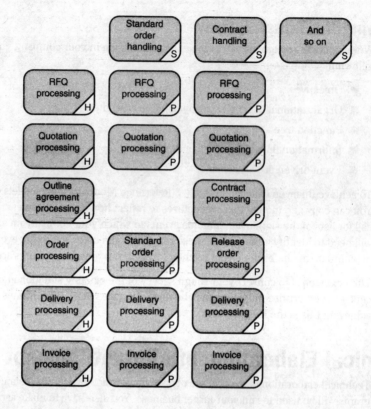

The R/3 Analyzer includes the navigation component of the ARIS Toolset. The other components can be added to this component if extensive program development work is necessary.

Deleting Functions   As you proceed through the selection process, you might come across unneeded functions. If you check the Functional Use attribute of one of these functions, you can discover whether it is optional or mandatory. If a function is marked as mandatory, it cannot be deleted from the process-selection matrix because it includes processing on which other functions depend. If a function is optional, you can delete it from the matrix so that it forms no part of your target concept.

Additional Standard Functionality   The process-selection matrix might indicate that you don't need certain functions in your target concept. These additional functions fall into two categories:

- Functions that are almost certainly of no benefit to the target concept system
- Functions not specified in the description of the current situation and not imagined as part of the new enterprise, but that would be very useful if included in the target concept

If a function is of no benefit and is optional, you can delete it. Mandatory functions cannot be deleted. Potentially useful functions should be retained, even if they are optional.

Input and Output Information Objects

Many functions need data. They must get this data from an information item. All functions create information items when they are activated, even if it is only the date and time when they were called. Standard SAP functions accessed from the R/3 Reference Model show which information items they need and which they will create. Figure 6.8 shows how information inputs and outputs are mapped in the Analyzer.

FIGURE 6.8

A function requires information input and creates output.

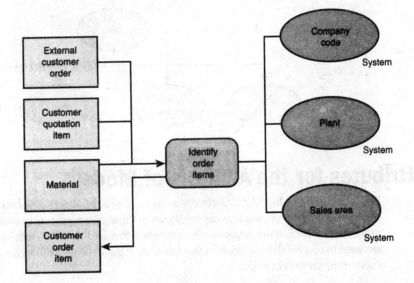

Your model of the existing situation might include information items that are not mentioned in the R/3 Reference Model standard version of the function you are considering. For example, you might have some data on a storage medium used in a system that will be rendered obsolete by your new implementation. The legacy data objects necessary to the functioning of your target system can be identified in the target model. The SAP support system provides the data-transfer mechanisms to integrate the legacy records with your target system.

Revisions of Organizational Structure

Client, Company Code, Plant, and Activity Center are examples of R/3 organizational units that can be associated with particular functions. If you examine the structure of the R/3 functions, you can see that the standard system of R/3 organizational units is applied. You can determine, for example, whether a particular function is normally executed at the Company Code level or at the Activity Center level.

If you adopt the standard R/3 organizational structure for your target concept, the various programs are automatically integrated, and authorization structures can be applied without difficulty.

The number of organizational units needed can be reduced if the standard functions already include the processes carried out in some of the units. Figure 6.9 illustrates such a reduction.

FIGURE 6.9
The target organization
has fewer units than the
current organization.

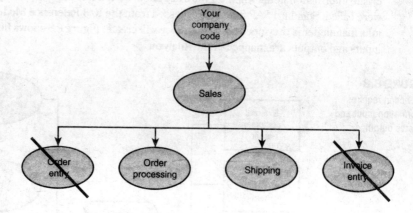

Attributes for the Analysis of Models

Each data object in the SAP R/3 system is made up of a set of data elements arranged in a structure. Values or parameters can be placed in these data elements to control the way the data object is used. If the data object represents a standard function, some of the data elements are used to control the operation of this function. If the data element is changed, the function operates in a different manner.

The symbols on the chart for your existing company and the symbols on the chart for your target concept are data objects. Some data elements control the visual display of a symbol when it appears in a chart. Some data elements contain information that can be used to perform quantitative and qualitative comparisons of different models of your existing or target system.

The following data objects are used to depict event-driven process chains:

- Events (hexagonal blocks)
- Functions (blocks with rounded corners)
- Control flows (dotted arrows)
- Logical operators (circles)
- Information objects or materials (rectangles)
- Organizational units (ovals)

Each object has a unique identification number for each example of its use. Your actual model symbols will have a different set of identification numbers for the objects depicted in the model of your target concept.

Types of Comparison Between Models

These comparisons show the types of results you can achieve by using the data elements of the data objects used to assemble the models:

- Comparing different variants of a target process
- Comparing a target process with the original R/3 Reference Model process
- Comparing the actual process now in operation with the corresponding target process
- Comparing the actual process with the corresponding process in the R/3 Reference Model

Dimensions of Model Comparison

Data attributes are edited to model your existing and target business processes in the R/3 Reference Model. Data attributes can be analyzed in various ways:

- Quantity-of-data and frequency-of-use statistics
- Time data to be used to compute throughput times, delay times, processing times, and transmission times within the process
- Statistics and time data aggregated to higher order processes
- Cost data assigned to various cost types to be used to derive indexes that reflect processing costs

Manner-of-Use Data

The functions include data elements to indicate how the function is performed according to the following categories:

- Online, interactively with the user
- In batch mode, without interacting with the user
- Automatically, without interacting with the user
- Manually, by the user without system support

The Quality of a Function

The data structure of a modeling element includes a provision to store the degree of user satisfaction with the function. This depends on the scope and content of the function. For example, a function performed online using interaction with the user might not offer all the choices required. The quality of satisfaction is expressed as good, satisfactory, or poor.

Future Information Flows

When the target model of your business is created under control of the R/3 Analyzer, the standard business functions identified from the R/3 Reference Model are transferred automatically to your model. If you call for an Information-Flow view of this model, you will see that the information flows between functional elements are depicted. Figure 6.10 suggests how the data flowing between functional elements is transcribed onto standard SAP documents as specific document items or updates to the header information.

FIGURE 6.10

Information flows become SAP document items.

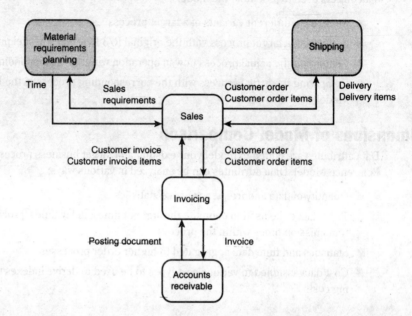

You can adopt the standard titles for the documents or use your own. From your survey of the existing situation, you can see how the information pathways suggested by the R/3 Reference Model relate to the information flows you have identified. In particular, the R/3 Reference Model indicates that each time a function receives a document, a transmission should be returned to the sending element of a document. This process confirms the receipt of the first transmission and provides a report on the current status of the process.

Suppose that a customer order document with details of the customer order items is sent to Shipping from Sales. When the shipping process is completed, the delivery document (with details of the delivery items) is sent from Shipping to Sales as confirmation that the shipping processes have done what they are supposed to do. If, for any reason, the delivery is incomplete, the details immediately become apparent to the Sales department, which will be prepared to discuss the facts of the delivery with the customer if a query arises.

A manual system might not be able to carry out this type of routine confirmation in detail for every function. Under the SAP discipline, it is standard practice.

The integrated functions of the R/3 system are predefined with the necessary information flows established through the system of SAP documents. This ensures that the detailed functioning of the system is logged in the form of electronic documents stored under the master record headings of the functions involved in the communications. The Sales department can look at the stored documents that record the activities of the Shipping section in connection with their customer orders. The materials requirements planners can see how they were kept informed of the sales requirements and how they transmitted their schedules back to the Sales department.

When you look at the Information-Flow views of your future organization, at the process chains, or at the responsibilities, you might get some ideas about changing the organizational structure of your company to better use your new system.

If your company is prepared to adjust to future changes, you will want to ensure that the information flows to and within your company are aligned to this objective. For example, you will want to check that there is a flow of information from Production to Purchasing to report on the suitability of the materials being delivered from the various suppliers. This flow ought to include all the factors that might have an impact on current production and any indicators of how things might change in the future.

Future Organizational Structure

Passing a pieceof work from one person to another is disruptive and inevitably takes time that might not result in significant added value to the product being handled. It is the same with information-processing work—the fewer changes of staff, the better. It is most important to minimize the number of transitions from one department to another. Your organization should be arranged so that the workflow crosses departmental boundaries only with good reason.

In the sample fragment of an enterprise model, the existing situation portrayed a work section devoted to data capture for the purpose of order entry. Another set of people entered the data needed to create invoices. Both sections might have been in the habit of typing the name and address of the customer. Why not combine the sections and have the computer type the details from existing records whenever possible?

Modeling Organizational Structure

The standard SAP organizational structure is used in the R/3 Reference Model to arrange the levels in the display of the organization and the associated functions. All the elements are assigned identification numbers that echo this structure.

In the R/3 applications, the standard organizational structure is replicated and also used to shape the display of the elements. Figure 6.11 shows part of the R/3 Reference Model. It contains only one definitive reference model for each element. Your model can freely replicate and rename these reference items.

When you take over a copy of the R/3 Reference Model to use as the basis for your target enterprise model, you can insert the oval symbols to represent the organizational units of your target company structure. Each unit can be assigned the title now in use, or the system can be left to assign names based on the R/3 Reference Model. Figure 6.12 depicts part of a target enterprise model. The oval symbols are attached by simple lines to depict the fact that certain functions in the model are the responsibility of specific named units in your company.

FIGURE 6.11

The R/3 Reference Model has the basic elements.

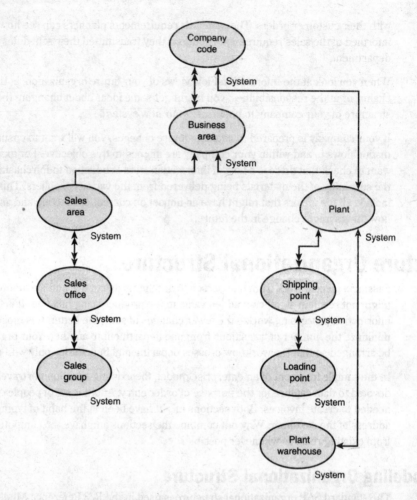

Because the system underlying the R/3 Reference Model is structured according to the standard SAP system of organizational structure using the Client, Company Code, Business Area, and Plant series of levels, the relationship between the organizational units of your target enterprise must follow the same hierarchical pattern. You might have to take this into consideration to harmonize your new structure with your new business support system.

Review of Required Organizational Changes

You will have been on the alert for signs of blemishes in the existing system that you want to avoid in the design of your new system. Organizational breaks, missing information technology, and discontinuities in the use of information media are the main snags.

FIGURE 6.12

The target concept organization adds to the R/3 Reference Model.

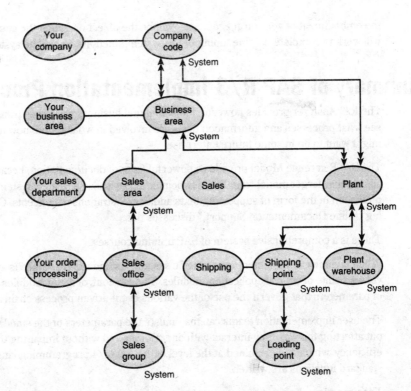

If major changes need to be made, you must present a case for these changes based on the details of the defects discovered and the possible consequences of leaving them untreated. On the benefits side of the account, you will want to draw attention to the time saved by having the system provide data and work procedure suggestions whenever possible. Improved service to the customer and better use of supplier resources will be noted as consequences of having fewer transfers of business across departmental boundaries.

Transfer of Results for Customizing

The Customizing module recognizes that more than 4,000 types of activity can take place to make improvements to the target model of an enterprise before it reaches its peak performance. The nature of these fine-tuning adjustments ranges from a subtle choice of batch sampling statistical techniques to the presentation of the date and time in the format customary in the user organization. The aim is to make sure that the steps of the event-driven process chains are carried out correctly and most efficiently. This process is discussed in Chapter 7, "Customizing."

The work of customizing does not normally proceed until the target concept is fully elaborated under the R/3 Analyzer using the R/3 Reference Model as its database. After the target concept is submitted and approved, your selection of functions from the R/3 Reference Model—

the embodiment of your target concept—will be the object on which the customizing module will work to complete the fine-tuning of the system functions before the system goes live.

Summary of SAP R/3 Implementation Procedure

The R/3 Analyzer provides powerful tools to model business processes transparently. You can see what processes and information flows are involved in what you do now and in what you might want to do in some future enterprise.

The R/3 Reference Model provides a powerful form of documentation, because it can display an actual or target model from five viewpoints. There is also a related system of online documentation in the form of supporting texts and demonstrations of concepts. Chapter 26, "Providing Online Documentation Support," discusses this.

There is a comprehensive system of SAP training courses.

When it comes to implementing a specific system, a standard procedure is available that involves a suite of central application modules. You can control these modules by adjusting tables of parameters that govern the use of the various event-driven process chains.

The user implementation teams can manipulate the parameters of the standard functions without affecting the way they interact with one another and without impairing their fundamental efficiency, which is determined at the level of the ABAP/4 programming language in which the standard functions are written.

The user client does not have access to the code of the standard business functions.

Unique customer-specific functions can be developed in the ABAP/4 language and integrated in the target system. Client companies also can add functions to form their own version of the standard R/3 Reference Model using the ARIS Toolset.

Future changes and adjustments to the target concept system can be modeled and simulated by the R/3 Reference Model before implementation. ●

Customizing

Taking a Broad View of Customizing

The SAP R/3 system contains a model of itself in the form of the SAP R/3 Reference Model, which records all standard business functions available in the system. These functions are shown in a neutral or paradigm form, which is later converted into an enterprise-specific organizational structure. The process of achieving this transition begins with analyzing your business, continues with selecting from the standard components, and ends with fine-tuning the whole system, which is called *customizing*.

Customizing is a fine-tuning activity carried out on a system already running in prototype form. Its design has already been through many processes, each of them guided and supported by a specialized SAP tool that can pass on its output to the next tool in the process.

The IMG-Implementation Management Guide is a tool that helps you with the process of customization; it prompts you to carry out the steps of the R/3 customizing procedure.

Two Model Companies

The SAP R/3 system is delivered complete with Client 000, which represents a neutral test company with the following attributes:

- A simple organizational structure
- Consistent parameters for all applications
- Country-specific accounting schemes
- Standard settings for account determination
- Configurations for control of standard transactions
- Sample profiles

The sample profiles included in Client 000 follow:

- Dunning and payment
- Material requirements, planning, and forecasting
- Pricing
- Message control
- Printout and form layouts
- Authorization structure

Client 000 is used by the delivering consultants to prove the integration of the various system components and the way they are controlled by the SAP *graphical user interface* (GUI).

Client 001 is reserved for production-related preparatory activities. It lacks master data and movement data. No company-specific parameters are defined. Standard settings are available for some functions. If your company uses workshop data-collecting devices, for example, you can use Client 001 to see whether these devices can be properly linked through the standard R/3 interfaces.

Analyzing the Existing Situation and the Target Concept

The SAP R/3 Reference Model is a data structure that can be consulted to determine which standard business functions are available in the SAP R/3 system as predefined integrated programs. One way to consult the model is by using the SAP R/3 Analyzer, which is discussed in Chapter 6, "Optimizing Business Processing." The Analyzer guides you through the process of describing your current system and the target concept of your business that you are aiming for. The Analyzer helps you look at your two companies, existing and target, from these points of view:

- The **Process view** depicts a company as a structure of event-driven process chains that carry out the necessary work when the right event conditions are in place.

- The **Information-Flow view** allows you to see how each activity gets the information it needs, and who is responsible for sending it and keeping it up-to-date.

- The **Data-Cluster view** sets out all items of information that have to be captured and stored in a systematic manner so that they can be found again when they are needed.

- The **Function view** shows how your company has high-level functions that depend on lower-level functions, and so on, down to the functions responsible for handling the information and materials passing through the company.

By looking at all these views of your present situation and the situation when your target concept has been implemented, you can progressively refine your target to make proper provisions for the market and manufacturing or purchasing conditions your company will have to confront during the long lifetime of the software you are designing for your target concept.

The user is guided on the basis of business criteria and objects to conduct the essential setting transactions. It is not necessary to know the names of any tables, table relationships, or transaction codes.

The IMG-Implementation Management Guide provides a plan of activities. Information on deadlines, resources, and status management can be stored. The IMG acts as a dedicated project management system. Project-specific documentation can be assigned to every element of the guide so that it becomes an effective record of how the customizing took place.

Entire organizational units can be copied, deleted, and provided with new parameters.

Selecting Functions for the Target Concept

Having drawn up various views of your target concept after inspecting similar views of the existing situation and consulting the long-term plans of your company, you are faced with the task of selecting functions from the many available in the SAP R/3 system. You will want to do this carefully, because you might decide that the SAP R/3 Reference Model does not include all the specialized functions necessary for your target concept.

Before you express a need to develop new software, you should use the SAP R/3 Analyzer to explore the possibilities of setting the control parameters of existing functions to achieve the results you want. If you are still unsatisfied, look at the most promising functions and see if you could add a *customer exit*. This interface, which is normally inactive in the function, can be activated as a way to launch out of the function in a controlled manner to execute a piece of program that you have developed to do that extra piece of work that is not part of the function's everyday repertoire.

If you cannot get a simulation of your target concept to perform as you want it to (even with extra customer exits), you can go over to the ABAP/4 Development Workbench, where you will find the tools necessary to carry out major surgery on copies of existing functions to build the functionality you want.

After you select the functions you need from a standard SAP R/3 Reference Model, and after you build any extra programs, you have to get the whole system customized. All the necessary routines are already in the SAP R/3 system and its applications.

Starting to Make Customizing Alterations to R/3

Fine-tuning your system begins with the approval for your target concept. You already have used the process-selection matrices to select just those functions directly needed for your enterprise, together with certain others suggested by the system because they are mandatory stepping stones to the results you want.

As the system becomes aware of the details of your target concept during the process of identifying functions from the process-selection matrix, it can select those customizing activities that it knows will have to be performed before the new system can go live and work properly from the start. There are some 5,000 customizing activities to choose from.

Reviewing the Objectives of Customizing

Customizing has to achieve certain objectives—economically in terms of cost and manpower, but reliably in terms of building a system that stands up to battering by real and sometimes erroneous data and real and sometimes careless users. SAP R/3 Customizing has three jobs to do:

- Introducing and extending SAP R/3 system applications smoothly and transparently
- Adapting the neutral reference functions to the company's target concept in detail
- Controlling and documenting the process of introducing the system

 TIP A summary of the procedural model recommended in the SAP IMG (implementation guide) is written and structured using hypertext techniques that enable the online reader to move quickly to information relevant to the task in hand.

Implementing Phase 1: Organization and Conceptual Design

A project team must be appointed, trained, and provided with suitable tools, such as the R/3 Reference Model in perhaps a standalone version. The team has to gather all the requirements from all the responsible departments concerning the new system and its purposes. Then there must be an organizational plan of the project activities. The standards to be achieved should be published, and tests must be defined that will prove the quality. These tests include setting up an R/3 test system and test clients that will be used to prove the validity and integrity of the target system before it goes live.

Arriving at a definition of the target concept and a plan for getting there entails both requirements analysis and conceptual design. The organization of the development project has to take place alongside the work on the target.

Defining the As-Is Situation

This operation can be one of the most difficult, because it requires those familiar with the company to describe how it operates. The precise details might be overlooked or taken for granted. This phase requires a determined detective to trace all the assumptions and customary practices in a complex organization.

It is useful to document the as-is situation in event-driven process chains as far as possible, because these chains will readily map to R/3 functional documentation. For the same reason, the to-be configuration of business processes is mapped as event-driven process chains.

Installing the R/3 System and Training the Project Team

The installation of the SAP R/3 system has to come early in a project, because the tools need it, although you can get a long way by using the PC versions of the SAP R/3 Analyzer and the R/3 Reference Model. Training must take place on the R/3 processes, and tools need to be provided to set up the system functions. Everyone on the project must learn SAP concepts and methods.

When the team is familiar with R/3 fundamentals, it needs to define existing business processes as far as possible in terms that comfortably map onto the R/3 functions and processes. If this functional requirement model is achieved by using the SAP concepts, the transition to the next stage—identifying the hardware requirements of these standard programs—will be a relatively easy. The outcome is perhaps a preliminary project plan that can serve to initiate the implementation project.

Setting Up a System Environment

The R/3 Customizing procedure defines the following steps to create the system environment:

1. Set up systems and clients.
2. Set up user master records for project team members.
3. Set up the client management and correction/transport service.
4. Build the system environment.

Most implementations also require these additional tasks:

- Set up remote services.
- Change country-specific settings.

- Create the Enterprise IMG.
- Create customizing projects for all elements and enhancements not encompassed by the main project.

Reaching Milestone 1: Concept and Plan

It is always possible to look back on a complex project and divide it into milestone stages identifying the significant events. What is much more difficult—and much more productive if done well—is setting out these stages beforehand. The first milestone is to specify the system in terms of concepts and plans, although very little might have been set up in software and hardware.

Project functions, interfaces, and system infrastructure should all be defined and specified. The functions, procedures, and responsibilities must be assigned to members of the project team. Then work should start on designing the interfaces required by the target system and the infrastructure it needs in terms of the physical facilities and resources that must be in place in addition to the software.

Implementing Phase 2: Detailed Design and System Setup

Global settings are the targets for phase 2. Parameter values must be selected that the system will use to control how the various functions interact. For example, functions that aren't needed in your company won't be offered in the menus. At this stage, the text and field labels for printouts and screen displays can be edited to suit your company.

The Procedure of the Customizing Menu

Each SAP application contributes a Customizing menu as an alternative to the implementation guide. The following information types *(infotypes)* are addressed in both the system-aided guides and the Customizing menus:

- Concept information
- Dependencies
- Standard settings
- Recommendations
- Activities
- Status management
- Documentation

The reason for using a standard set of infotypes is to ensure that all applications and their users can interpret the data stored in any of the databases. The infotype signals how the data is to be decoded and how it is used in business programs. Several thousand infotypes may be used in an implementation.

Posting Transactions for Setting Global Parameters

The global parameters that have to be particularized or taken as defaults are grouped according to the broad implementation functions to which they are crucial. The following headings refer to the prompts that appear in the Customizing menus:

- Enterprise Structure
- Cross-Application Components
- Document Management System
- Classification System
- CAD Integration
- Plant Data Collection
- General Task Functions
- Documentation Tools
- Distribution (ALE)
- IDoc Interface/Electronic Data Interchange
- Open Information Warehouse

The Customizing menu continues with prompts to establish company structure by selecting and adapting the standard R/3 system organization units. Then comes the establishment of master data according to the following procedure:

1. Determine master data fields and content.
2. Configure master data.
3. Test master data settings.
4. Detail master data transfer.

Each R/3 application that is to be installed and configured has to be supplied with the settings appropriate to its components, as noted in Table 7.1.

Table 7.1   Components of R/3

Financial Accounting

Financial Accounting Global Settings

General Ledger Accounting

Accounts Receivable and Accounts Payable

Legal Consolidation

Consolidation Preparation

Asset Accounting

Special Purpose Ledger

continues

Table 7.1   Continued

Treasury

Cash Management

Cash Budget Management and Financial Budgeting

Funds Management

Controlling

Controlling General

Overhead Cost Controlling

Cost and Revenue Element Accounting

Cost Center Accounting

Activity-Based Costing

Overhead Cost Orders

Product Cost Controlling

Profitability Analysis

Investment Management

Investment Programs

Investment Orders

Investment Projects

Enterprise Controlling

Profit Center Accounting

Executive Information System

Logistics - General

Logistics Basic Data: Material Master

Logistics Basic Data: Business Partners

Logistics Basic Data: Batch Management

Logistics Basic Data: Advertising Media

Environment Data

Variant Configuration

Engineering Change Management

Logistics Information System (LIS)

Sales and Distribution

Master Data

Basic Functions

Sales

Shipping

Transportation

Foreign Trade

Billing

Sales Support

Electronic Data Interchange

Data Transfer and Archiving

System Modification

Authorization Management

Materials Management

Consumption-Based Planning

Purchasing

Inventory Management

Valuation and Account Assignment

Warehouse Management

Invoice Verification

Quality Management

Quality Planning

Quality Inspection

Quality Certificates

Quality Notification

Information System

Basic Settings and Environment

Plant Maintenance

Equipment and Technical Objects

Preventive Maintenance

Maintenance Order Management

Information System

continues

Table 7.1 Continued

Production

Basic Data

Sales & Operations Planning

Master Planning

Demand Management

MPS

Production Optimization Interface

Capacity Planning

Material Requirements Planning

Production Orders

Kanban

Repetitive Manufacturing

Production Planning - Process Industries

Project System

Personnel Planning and Development

Global settings for Personnel Planning and Development

Organizational Management

Training and Event Management

Personnel Development

Workforce Planning

Shift Planning

Personnel Capacity Planning

Room Reservations Planning

Personnel Administration and Payroll Accounting

Personnel Administration

Benefits

Recruitment

Time Management

Incentive Wages

Business Trips

Personnel Planning and Development
Payroll: Germany
Payroll: Austria
Payroll: Switzerland
Payroll: France
Payroll: United Kingdom
Payroll: USA
Payroll: Australia
Payroll: Japan
Payroll: Singapore
Payroll: International

The next stage is to define and create the data-transfer programs and the interfaces that use them. Then they must be tested.

Next, the reporting functions must be assigned their detailed parameters, together with the procedures for archiving.

Authorizations also must be configured and tested.

Performing the Final Test

As each stage of design and customization takes place, thorough testing of the individual elements in isolation is also done. However, the final test must be of the integration of all standard and enhanced functions, using a realistic simulation of the processing demands expected. Thus, each aspect of the system must be technically challenged and confirmed with the intended user departments:

- Global system settings
- System organization units
- System settings
- Interfaces and enhancements
- Reporting
- Archive management
- Authorizations, profiles, and user master records

A formal test design sets out what processes and functions to verify, who's responsible, and what methods to use. The test plan also specifies what documentation should be produced as evidence that the test was correctly and successfully carried out.

Reaching Milestone 2: Documented Prototype

The plan arrived at by the foregoing procedures must be checked for quality before work begins on the prototype. Detailed designs must be completed and implemented for at least the interfaces and the most frequently called procedures. Organizational structures and basic data must be determined during this stage.

Printed forms, reporting, and authorization need attention next before the prototype can be subjected to proper quality checking.

Implementing Phase 3: Preparations for Going Live

Creating a "go-live plan" is a task that has to come before the following steps:

1. Finalize the production system configuration.
2. Procure system equipment.
3. Create master data for users.
4. Create a plan for data transfer.
5. Define structure, content, and presentation formats.
6. Prepare to create user documentation.
7. Create a change concept.
8. Create user documentation.

Setting Up the Production Environment

For some implementers, the conceptual and planning stages are the hardest parts. For others, the hardware and software represent the challenge. In this phase, you carry out these steps:

1. Install the network.
2. Install hardware and software for users.
3. Install R/3 on the production system.
4. Train users.
5. Create a training program.
6. Prepare and conduct training.
7. Define and establish system administration.
8. Train the System Administration staff.
9. Transfer data to the production system.
10. Transfer customizing settings and development objects.
11. Carry out data transfer.
12. Check the quality of the production system.
13. Verify user documentation.

14. Validate the productive environment.
15. Validate the user training delivered.
16. Validate the organization of system administration.
17. Validate data transfers.
18. Validate the project plan.
19. Create a validation report.
20. Agree to proceed to the next phase.

For each step, the Implementation Management Guide provides prompts and supporting documentation.

Reaching Milestone 3: Productive System Ready

With the prototype working and approved, the productive system enters its final planning phases. By now, your implementation team should have written user documentation.

The productive environment, peopled with trained users who can call on a competent system administration, is essential. The new organization should be in place, and archiving should be well under way.

Before the productive system can be given a quality check, you must analyze the likely loading on the system. The integration of the system components should be tested and the final manual entry of master data completed.

Implementing Phase 4: Productive Operation

Productive operation cannot be achieved without looking at the people and the systems. The start of live operation is obviously a critical moment at which the staff involved may need extra support. At the same time, a help-desk function should be established as a permanent support for users.

Optimizing System Performance

As the productive system starts to operate, it might become apparent that some computer system resources tend to overload, while others are underutilized. Not until the system is working at its full efficiency should the implementation project be formally closed.

The project will probably continue in some form as a means of correcting unwanted variances in the operating characteristics. There will be system maintenance and the release of some upgrades to various functions.

The implementation guide in its computer-assisted manifestation is at the core of customizing. It reminds you of what must be done and keeps track of what has been done. And it is tailored to your target as soon as you decide which applications you will be using.

Reaching Milestone 4: Optimization Completed

With the system operational, the remaining two tasks are to optimize the technical and organizational operations. Tools are available for measuring system component performance. The Computer-Aided Testing Tool (CATT) is an example.

Customizing the Enterprise

The milestones of the procedural model for customizing R/3 mark the stages of preparing an integrated business data processing system for a single company. Enterprises with a complex company structure can also be accommodated by the system by calling on the customizing functions.

The IMG is structured to provide views that lead the implementation team through the necessary steps of customizing:

- SAP Reference IMG view
- Enterprise IMG view
- Project(s) IMG view(s)
- Release-Specific IMG view
- Other IMG views defined for the user

The SAP Reference view contains all the procedural steps needed to implement all the functions R/3 offers. Each lower-level IMG view is a subset of the information held in the SAP Reference IMG view, which can be accessed online by the following sequence:

Choose Tools→Business Engineering→Customizing

Implementation Projects→SAP Reference IMG

If you specify the countries in which your enterprise will operate, the system generates an Enterprise IMG that contains only the steps you need to take to customize your system for those countries. If you change the scope of your enterprise, you can regenerate the Enterprise IMG, and it retains the project information relevant to the new circumstances.

A project in this context usually is focused on one or more countries and the applications that will operate in them. You can set up several projects, and appropriate project IMGs will be generated for them.

If you implement a new release or upgrade of R/3 or one of its applications, the issue of the release note will be the reference for the generation of a release IMG that suggests the steps needed to customize it.

Using the Structure of an IMG Activity

An IMG view is essentially a plan to customize activities associated with the information needed to carry out those activities successfully. Each activity in the IMG view is presented with the following structure:

- Conceptual information to set the activity in context and explain what is required
- A requirements document that records what has to be achieved that can be used to record progress on the status of each step
- Standard parameter settings for the software as supplied that will be the default values unless customized
- Recommendations by SAP as to how the function should be customized
- A suggested sequence of activities to carry out the customizing efficiently
- Additional reading that only some implementers will need, which is accessible by hyperlinks and as a glossary

Each element of this structure is stored as a separate document so that the user can be selective in accessing the information. Facilities exist to extend the IMG at any level by adding documents or structures of documents. However, it is not possible to delete any of the IMG elements that are provided by SAP as standard.

N O T E   An IMG is set up as a hypertext book with a dynamic bookmark and the capability to expand and contract the scope of the display.

Setting Up Additional Structures by Customizing Transactions

You can perform simple customizing transactions, such as the routine identification of a group of materials in MM-Materials Management. This type of customizing transaction is initiated from a specific view of the IMG. Complex business objects, such as a financial document type or a personnel structure, are created and maintained by a special customizing transaction or a View-Cluster transaction in which views and clusters of relevant documents can be conveniently displayed together.

Each customizing transaction can include a reference to a graphic item and a textual definition associated with the structure being maintained.

Each business object in each application has to be customized:

- Financial Accounting requires customizing activities to define, copy, delete, and check company codes and to similarly maintain master records for credit control area, business area, functional area, and consolidation business area.
- Treasury maintains the master records for the financial management area.
- Controlling maintains the master records for the controlling area and the operating concern.
- Logistics - General maintains the master records for valuation area, plant, location, and division.
- Sales and Distribution maintains the master records for sales organization, distribution channel, sales office, sales group, shipping point, loading point, and transportation planning point.

- Materials Management maintains the master records for storage location, purchasing organization, and warehouse number.
- Plant Maintenance maintains the master records for the maintenance planning plant.
- Human Resources maintains the master records for personnel area, personnel subarea, employee group, and employee subgroup.

Specifying Account Assignment in Customizing

The various applications require their data objects to be associated with the relevant accounts and other business objects. You do this by customizing within the relevant application modules:

- Financial Accounting assigns company code to company and to credit control area, and assigns business area to consolidation business area.
- Treasury assigns company code to financial management area and controlling area to financial management area.
- Controlling assigns company code to controlling area and controlling area to operating concern.
- Logistics - General assigns plant to company code and business area to plant/valuation area and division. It also specifies how data comparisons take place between sales plant or valuation area and division and business area.
- Sales and Distribution assigns sales organization to company code, distribution channel to sales organization, and division to sales organization. It sets up sales areas and assigns sales offices to sales areas, sales groups to sales offices, and plant to sales organization and distribution channel. Shipping points have to be assigned to plants. If business areas are in use, the appropriate accounts must be assigned to them. The Sales and Distribution customizing defines rules by sales area, assigns each business area to a plant and division, and defines business areas by sales areas.
- Materials Management assigns purchasing organization to company code, purchasing organization to plant, standard purchasing organization to plant, purchasing organization to reference purchasing organization, and warehouse number to plant/storage location.
- Plant Maintenance assigns maintenance planning plant to maintenance plant.
- Human Resources assigns personnel area to company code, and employee subgroup to employee group.

The final customizing activity will probably be a call of the Consistency Check function to scan the enterprise structure to determine whether any aspects might hinder the Sales and Distribution operations.

Customizing WebRFC Applications

Although the *Web remote function call* (WebRFC) functionality allows a standard Web browser to operate as a new kind of R/3 front end, the everchanging nature of Web presentation and interaction facilities tends to make any user interface design seem old-fashioned if the latest enhancements are not in evidence. No doubt your company has established a policy and style for presenting itself on the Internet. You could have this presentation controlled exclusively by ABAP/4 code. On the other hand, many of your requirements can be anticipated in general terms and formed into templates available to you for modification with your own details and graphic styles.

SAP Web reporting uses the same approach. The WebRFC template syntax defines a method of setting up templates containing HTML tags and placeholders that are replaced with your particular data at runtime. However, the user company is not totally free to rebuild these templates, because the HTML code that replaces the placeholders at runtime must be determined by the particular WebRFC application. An arrangement of template parameters is provided to extend the ways in which your designers can customize your Web pages that run R/3 applications.

The WebRFC templates and template parameters used in applications are stored in the database tables WWWDATA and WWWPARAMS. The following function modules are provided so that you can access these tables to modify standard SAP templates and create your own:

- WWW_HTML_MERGER
- WWW_LOAD_TEMPLATE_ATTRIBUTES
- WWW_LOAD_OBJECT_ATTRIBUTES

Many types of data can be stored in the database table WWWDATA, such as binary data for graphics and SAP Internet transaction server files.

Copying and Adjusting Web Objects

The ABAP/4 Development Workbench offers Transaction SMW0, which can modify or create an HTML template. This function allows you to choose one of these object types:

- HTML templates for WebRFC applications
- Binary data for WebRFC applications
- Objects for Internet applications

WebRFC applications require data objects that conform to the *Multiple Internet Mail Extension* (MIME) standard. MIME types include HTML templates, binary data such as graphics, and WinWord files. The MIME types and their file extensions are stored in the database table MIMETYPES, to which you can add new types or modified copies of existing entries.

Restricting Access to Web Objects

R/3 reports cannot be viewed on a Web browser unless you have designated them individually or as report trees for Web reporting. In this way, you can control which R/3 reports are available over the Internet. ●

P A R T III

Managing Complex Systems

CHAPTER 8

Developing Businesses on a Continuous Basis

In this chapter

Keeping a Business Actively Under Development

The context into which you'll introduce an SAP system will seldom be a green-field site for a business that is unique because nothing like it has ever been seen before.

The system will be part of a continuous business development. As the analysis proceeds, it will become clearer just where the business could be developed to provide some advantages. As the first modules of the system go live, a further flood of information will occur on how the business can be improved.

The decision to implement R/3 as an enterprise-controlling system will obviously be at the end of a long process of considering the benefits, the costs, and the alternative options. The *Implementation Management Guide* (IMG) and the R/3 Procedural Model are products designed to support the implementation team after the main decision is made. However, a company seldom decides to implement several R/3 applications at once—there is usually a gradual and progressive implementation.

Thus, the first-time R/3 user and the company adding a new application are in somewhat similar circumstances. They both have to justify reengineering part of their company's business data processing.

If you are in the advantageous position of being able to direct the analysis of the data that will inevitably be stored by the system, you will be able to prepare reports to show the best ways of continuing the development process. The SAP modules are designed to facilitate continuous development, not for the sake of running a more elaborate system, but for the purpose of making your business more effective and efficient.

Whether you are looking at an existing computer-supported business, a manual system, or a recent implementation of an SAP-integrated suite of applications, you ought to address certain issues before you take any further steps to develop your business processes.

Contemplating a Transition from Traditional Accounting

Auditors who are used to inspecting the financial documents of a company are sometimes very streetwise. They have seen it all before. They can teach the computer people a thing or two.

Recording Useful Data

In the days of handwritten ledgers, there was always a chance that the chief accountant would let you write a marginal note to explain an entry in the ledger. But a computer system will encapsulate the entry with the original annotations, never to be altered. The lesson to be learned from this is that the modern system must be very strict about enforcing a consistent input convention, a policy, a habit, and a set of rules obeyed by everyone so that it can be interpreted by and informative to a stranger—an auditor, for example—some months after entry. All users have to be as accurate in memorandum fields as they are in the fields that will be checked by the accounting procedures.

Following a Design Checklist

The SAP Design Checklist points to issues that have to be taken into account before beginning implementation or at an early stage. The Implementation Management Guide is a detailed support system for implementation and customizing.

The SAP R/3 Analyzer provides tools and prompts for eliciting the necessary preliminary information, but the customer management team will have to arrive at suitable conclusions and decisions.

The task of technical interviewing to determine how work currently progresses is an art form requiring talent and patience, not to mention an efficient and flexible recording method for which the usual surrogate is a secretary. The modern methods are described in Chapter 6, "Optimizing Business Processing."

Recording How Things Are Done Now

One obvious starting point for business process reengineering is a description of the current mechanisms, be they mediated by people or by machines. The three possible sources for this invaluable information usually won't correspond on all or even any points of detail.

These sources of a view on how things are done now are the management, the documentation, and the people who do the work.

Sampling Management's Views of the Current System

Obviously, some undocumented aspects of a business are known to some managers but not to the entire workforce. Then there are some aspects of the business that the management has initiated but not followed up in close enough detail to determine whether their intentions have been put into practice in the way they instructed.

Finally, some aspects of the business have developed through local initiatives, for good or for bad, and have not come to management's notice. Operational doctrine has been recognized as what happens as a matter of custom and practice in addition to or despite what instructions have been received from management or what is documented. Operational doctrine is not necessarily better or worse than the doctrine set out in the book—it is a neutral term.

Documenting the Current System

Rarely is a current system fully documented to the extent that a suitable person could do any job, albeit slowly, by following exactly the instructions in the book. What may be available is the specification drawn up when the system was being put out to tender or when the contractor confirmed what was being implemented. However, chances are the system developers and programmers were too busy designing and programming to find time to document everything. And any aspects of the business that were not captured by the software or paper system forms are not likely to be available for inspection by anyone seeking to reengineer the business process some time later.

Embarrassing as it might be to read, one of the most valuable documents pertaining to the current system is a log of the complaints and snags encountered by its users, including the customers and suppliers (who must be counted as prime users of any business system, even if they press none of its keys). The shrewd reader of such a log would also note all the problems that could be expected but did not seem to happen. Does the existing system have hidden merits? How does the system cope with stress, and how do the people working with it alter what they do to manage any difficulties that come their way?

The training staff members are good sources of information on the current system. They know their specialty well because they have explained it many times and coached many beginners in its subtle ways.

Trainers will also have a hidden agenda of ideas that they promote on top of or despite the official doctrine. They will know ways of using the current system to navigate problems not anticipated by the designers or not considered serious enough to warrant additional software or hardware investment. In the craft trades, some tools always exist that have been constructed or reshaped by the users to make them more effective.

Tapping Sources of Operational Doctrine

Operational doctrine is what you pass on unofficially to your fellow workers to make their tasks more successful. It might be a habit of taking a break even if the phone is ringing, or it might be the infamous device of the absent principal: "I'm sorry, but my boss has instructed me not to allow anyone a discount." You might pass on operational doctrine in a formal lecture to every newcomer, or you might not even realize that you are a role model for how to survive in the workplace. There might be some company or departmental jokes that in fact crystallize the good and the bad points about the way things are.

There might be an unofficial practice of entering data that is known to be faulty, so the difficult work item lands on the supervisor's screen and, with luck, is dealt with by someone on the next shift.

Not all operational doctrine is bad for business. The implementers of an SAP system have tremendous scope for building into the new system all the best elements of the operational doctrine that have evolved through experience with its ancestor, whether this was a computer system or a paper-and-people system.

Wisdom from operational doctrine does not come without effort. It's amazing how many experts on all subjects pronounce on what is happening, what has happened, or what is there without ever having visited the place.

A token visit to the site is better than no visit at all, but the more time spent with the people closest to the work, the better. In skills analysis work, it used to be considered only right and proper that the analyst should have a try at performing the skill. An expert would be on hand to give help and guidance, and if he were really kind, he would set up the job so that the poor old analyst would have a reasonable chance of not making too much of a fool of himself, or worse.

There are two reasons to justify trying the job for yourself. It might become apparent just what sort of job it is for the person doing it on a daily basis, and it might demonstrate to the expert that you think this job is important enough to spend a little time looking at it. If you are really lucky, you will be able to spend enough time on the spot to allow a little discourse on what really matters and what the challenging aspects are.

Listen very carefully to what is said when you have been on site for some time. So often the most valuable information does not come to light until the contact has matured to the extent that jokes may be exchanged. Listen with utmost care to the last few moments of your contact with the person who knows the most about the job and the system.

Seeking Out the Layers of Decision

As more and more business processes are mechanized and automated, and as more and more communications channels converge on each individual, it is clear that the responsibility for making decisions has moved down the management chain.

The modern telephone operator in touch with a client might not have to transfer the call to someone else for a decision, because the information and the logical basis for a decision are onscreen as soon as the client's needs are identified. Indeed, there might not be a telephone operator as such in a telesales organization. At the other extreme, there are call centers that handle the telephone business on behalf of several clients without the callers being aware that they are conducting business through an intermediate agency.

Because the system can make decisions on the basis of prearranged logical rules applied to the individual case, there is no need for a wise supervisor to take part in the interaction with the client. One layer of decision-making has been let go.

The SAP implementers have to be very careful to check out who makes what decision in practice, whatever the books might say. If the business process reengineering fails to use the speed and data access of the new systems, it falls into the trap of simply copying the existing mechanisms, instead of creating new methods based on experience of the old, coupled with the benefits of the new technologies. Will it still be necessary to do things in the old way when the new systems are in place?

The most significant of the benefits of the new systems is the ability to make decisions rapidly and reliably.

Appreciating that Many Good Ideas Have Already Been Suggested

People at work think a lot. They have ideas. They might not tell just anyone about these ideas for fear of ridicule. They might not allow their ideas to appear in written reports.

Essential reading for the SAP research team are the reports on the current system and the business conducted on it. Essential listening is what anyone says about the current practices, whether it is good or bad, whether said in earnest or in jest.

Suppose that a very large and critical data processing system is now years behind implementation and grossly over budget. Two contributory causes are embarrassingly obvious:

■ The designers did not consult with the current operators about what was required to make their work absolutely free from error, even at high workloads.

■ The software programmers found that the commissioning authorities often changed the specifications of what was required after work had begun.

Reading and listening are like brainstorming: Much is useless, but you cannot tell which is which until afterward. And a really good idea might be mentioned only once. With all this flow of written material and site visit anecdotes, the SAP researcher needs to be disciplined to look out for the soft spots, the opportunities for improvement.

Researching the Decision to Reengineer Business Processes

The cost and importance of this decision call for the most careful research and preparation so that the decision is taken on the basis of what really matters and with each of the options is given proper consideration. These research resources allocated to prepare the decision might go to waste; the actual benefits might vary in magnitude and direction and pop up in unexpected places. Nevertheless, the decision to reengineer should be given the best possible chances of being the correct one.

Considering Why Projects Fail

Although reengineering projects fail for many reasons, some obvious reasons should be considered by all concerned. Preparation might be ill-informed or totally absent; inadequate software or hardware might have been installed; application implementation might be incompetent and poorly resourced. Under each heading are a number of factors worth taking care of.

Using a Project Research Team

To prepare for the important decisions, a research team seems an obvious necessity. Yet it is not uncommon for this team to be built from a variety of experts who are so knowledgeable in their own specialties that they cannot be spared to devote any attention to the project. The team does need time to do its work. It also needs discretion, insulation from possible traumatic job turbulence, and out-of-the-ordinary expertise.

Who should be on the team? The contractor might have to mix with the in-house research and development people. Expertise; fresh eyes; and familiarity with the vendors, products, customers, competitors, and the marketplace as a whole are the qualities to be on the lookout for.

Tasking the Project Research Team

The purpose of establishing a project research team is to set up a good decision structure in which each option is supported by the relevant information. The team members need to know the scope of this decision structure: How wide or how narrow is their brief? Should they consider any relevant issue, whether it be related to business, personnel, hardware, or software in content?

Certain issues need to be raised before deciding to implement SAP: consistency between modules, terminology, programmed function keys, conventions in screen layouts, languages, currencies, legal requirements, pricing data on invoices, health and safety, reporting, tax management, and rounding.

It is indeed providential that the SAP designers have built a tool to monitor and prompt all these decisions before the system goes live. This tool, the *Implementation Management Guide* (IMG), is described in Chapter 7, "Customizing."

Using the ABAP/4 Development Organizer

The ABAP/4 Development Organizer is a component of the ABAP/4 Development Workbench. The Organizer is a support tool for the development and maintenance of large software systems developed in SAP R/3. The target users are teams of developers and individuals—centralized efforts and local. Members of a project group might work on one or several computers.

Development projects are best divided into various jobs, each of which is the responsibility of an individual or a project group leader. Any development object that is changed by a person or group assigned to a job is automatically logged and then reserved exclusively for that specific job. No other developer may alter that object until it's released by the job team that first changed it. Others can look at it, run it, or copy it under a different identification, but only the developer who "owns" it for the time being can make any alterations.

By adopting this principle of a developer owning an object until it is finished, individual jobs can be released independently of one another. Changes are managed.

In addition to being assigned a responsible developer, each object under development is associated with a development class that designates the application area of the object. This allows the object to be found and the knowledgeable people to be identified.

When the development of an object has reached a satisfactory stage, it is released. Current versions of this object then are stored automatically, and the newly released version becomes immediately available to all applications that use it.

Developmental changes are usually first confined to a family of separate test systems, where their effects can be evaluated before being combined and transferred to productive systems.

Each transfer of a changed object from a test system is automatically logged so that any problems arising can be attributed to the specific transfer responsible. It is usual to perform a simulation by using the changed objects before allowing them to be transferred to the target system.

Part of each development job is to arrange hierarchically organized documentation that covers the aims of the project, its status, and any special aspects. The result is that any changes can be tracked and related to the stored versions they have superseded.

Engineering Software Functions

The SAP approach to software development seeks to establish for each development project a structure of self-contained partial functions. They are *self-contained* in that an individual developer or a team may work on one of them, knowing that their efforts will lead to a programming component that will integrate with SAP R/3 and the work of other developers. A *partial function* is a method and a computerized mechanism that will work effectively within the scope defined for it, not necessarily a complete function that an end user might invoke.

Because the work units are self-contained, they can be tested and adjusted before being built into larger sequences.

Whatever the size and scope of a software engineering development, whether a partial function or a complete application module, four distinct phases should be resourced and documented for what they are.

Implementing Phase 1: Conceptual Design

The first phase of a development project should reach its conclusion with the production of a conceptual design for the new business program. Conceptual design seldom proceeds in an orderly sequence, but four elements should be recognized and documented: preliminary study, analysis, design, and presentation.

Identifying Value-Adding Pathways   The preliminary study is focused by an overall aim. Generally, this aim is to optimize performance and cost all along the pathways within the company where value is added, including the process of business process reengineering itself. The preliminary study should make a business case to justify the selection of business functions for development.

Identifying Standard Components in the R/3 Reference Model   The R/3 Reference Model, discussed in Chapter 5, "Consulting the R/3 Reference Model," is a part of the R/3 BASIS system that can be used to determine which standard R/3 applications and functions should be selected and customized to suit your company's requirements.

Designing from the EDM-Enterprise Data Model   *Design* is the explanation of the right system concept in sufficient detail for its worth to be judged.

The EDM-Enterprise Data Model is derived from the R/3 Reference Model. It provides the business processes of your company as you want them to be when the new development is completed: process, function, information flow, data, and organization. These views are discussed in Chapter 10, "Developing an SAP Open Information Warehouse."

Presenting the Preliminary Study   *Presentation* is the process of building consensus up to the highest management level for the direction and cost of the development. There will have been a considerable amount of interchange between those who have clear ideas about how the business processes should be developed and those who know what is achievable with the resources available in the existing system and the staff. Additions to either of these and the allocation of funds for this purpose must be approved on the basis of the presentation of the results of the preliminary study.

Implementing Phase 2: Defining the Application Structure

The second phase of a development project begins after a budget is allocated on the basis of the preliminary study for the purpose of elaborating the conceptual design to match the structure of the R/3 functions in detail. The main task is to define the data architecture and database organization, and to create a prototype of the intended system component. This should entail iterative early prototyping of components with end users.

Implementing Phase 3: Realization and Implementation

The third phase of a development project begins when the data object management policies begin to be implemented. For example, any data that will be accessed by the new business function being developed will have to be made available to it. If it is data that is already in an SAP application, it is in a format that is already compatible. If it is held in a legacy system for which there is a standard SAP interface, the data can be accessed online or transferred in a single operation before the new function goes online. If the data in the legacy system is not in a format for which a standard SAP interface exists, arrangements must be made to have an ABAP/4 interface program written or for an agency to convert the data.

The development team has to ensure that all fields specified in the Enterprise Data Model have been checked to confirm that they contain the proper data or can be accessed when needed.

Implementing Phase 4: Final Test and Installation

The fourth phase of a development project has to include user training, followed by a final test in which the new function is subjected to the demands it will meet when operational.

A new piece of program is an extension of the EDM, and it must be tested to ensure that it integrates properly. This entails an additional test that is carried out when the new components and the existing EDM are merged. A mass test and runtime analysis are needed to measure the effects of heavy system loads and to prove that the resource allocation provisions are working and can meet the demand. At this stage, it is normally necessary for the new function to be authorized for release, which allows it to be called by authorized users.

Making the Decision to Reengineer Business Processes

After all the research is done and the information is presented, it is time for a series of decision stages that entail weighing intangibles and estimating probabilities. Some well-known phenomena may appear under these conditions. Human beings are not always very clever when it comes to picking winners. It is best to be aware of how good intentions can be led astray when dealing with intangibles and uncertainties.

Office automation following on mechanization means the end of work for many people. If the human resources philosophy is applied thoroughly, there can be a minimization of disturbance to those who find themselves without work. The personnel managers who have a means to relocate their staff in new jobs are fortunate.

Beware the Pitfalls

Input errors can cause a lot of trouble if they are not detected at the time. Stress and anxiety can move a decimal point without being noticed, the person on the phone might not be the one you were expecting, and you might have called up the wrong screen. Modern business systems try to reduce the opportunities for input error by narrowing the possibilities and having the operator choose from a list rather than enter the identifier, although there might be speed advantages in allowing people who know what they are doing to anticipate and type ahead.

Misunderstanding what is being said might occur through language and technical communication difficulties. Having the operator paraphrase what was thought to be the requirement might help, and the system can suggest what might be a standard wording. These are techniques that some operators have evolved for themselves that can easily be supported by SAP and made available to all.

Misinterpretations of incidents and situations may give rise to operational problems. One tactic is to have the operator complete a checklist that is adjusted online in order to avoid asking for any information that is already known from the records or that can be inferred by answers to previous questions. For example, the staff at a bank that accepts telephone transactions used to ask how they might help; now they begin by asking for your ZIP code, name, and initials. This allows their system to offer your last-known address, which they recite for you to confirm before they move on down their list of questions. It is a quick procedure and seems friendly.

Misreading trends has caught many a businessperson unprepared. Something that changes only slowly or in subtle ways that are not thought important at the time can cause trouble. If you are reengineering a business process with an SAP system, having data analyzed to reveal any trends, however gradual, isn't difficult. But what is not possible is for SAP to infer a trend when no data has been collected that could have some bearing on it.

Are customers buying mobile phones because they are fashionable, because they save time or money, or because they might come in handy in the event of an accident or threat? In the absence of any pertinent data, the SAP system might be able to provide an analysis of customers over several parameters, one of which might suggest a possible explanation. Further data must come from talking to customers, so the SAP screen will have to be used to record free-text notes or perhaps a choice of keywords or an entry in an analysis field based on answers to some questions.

This example illustrates the use of modern technology to collect current data on what relevant people are thinking: what customers say, what suppliers say, and what inquirers are asking about. And the facilities of SAP support such research studies from the exploratory stages right through to the stage where hard data can be collected.

The system will be ready to discern trends in the data as soon as any basis for the analysis can be specified.

Waste has always been a soft spot, whether in time, material, energy, or personnel. Business process reengineering can be the opportunity to set up methods for monitoring the consumption of these resources and for comparing one situation with another, one accounting period with another.

Profit and loss have always been part of business monitoring. Nowadays few workers are totally out of contact with the computer, so there is the possibility of online assessment, in profit and loss terms, of the performance of managers, supervisors, operators, contractors, and even advisors.

N O T E One might argue that the sort of performance monitoring that can be carried out by the system is rather trivial: hours worked, calls made, expenses, sales, profits, staff turnover—a mixed bag indeed, some items more important than others, depending on the company and the person being monitored.

Monitoring the New Business

Is it too outrageous to claim that to reengineer a business by applying the SAP concept is to make it a new business? If it is indeed a new business, it is right and proper to consider how and in what ways it is to be monitored. But on what basis should it be declared a success?

Some favorite indexes of success aren't unimportant, such as profit. Nowadays, though, the success of a business is judged in part on its effect on the environment. The employees will have their own dimensions for judging company performance.

However, a project to reengineer some business processes should not get very far before setting out some criteria by which it can be judged. What are to be the indicators of project progress, success, and failure? Where are the critical places to look for telltale signs of whether a project is going well or badly? Which numbers or other indicators should be scrutinized? Where are the pressure points to stop the bleeding? Is there anywhere the stick could be applied?

These queries, which have to be answered in the context of a business process reengineering project if it is to be cost-effective, are not peculiar to the computer industry. They are matters that leaders of all workteams should give high priority. They apply with no less force to workteams of one, where the leader and the worker are the same person. You have to know where you are going in order to know whether you are progressing in the right direction. ●

Building Global Business Systems

Developing Multinational Accounting

You might have a global business that you run on the back of an envelope, or you might have a global computing system that does hardly any business at all. This chapter is about the enhancements of the SAP R/3 system designed to make productive worldwide business processing an everyday affair.

Three factors are important to multinational companies:

- Operating screens and reports must be available in the user's language.
- Amounts must appear in the local currency.
- The taxes, legal financial reports, and payment methods must be those acceptable to the host nation.

If the corporation has subsidiary companies trading in more than one nation, you might need an additional language and currency for use by the head office, plus methods of making adjustments for any differences between accounting or other business practices in the overseas host nations. The SAP system makes copious provisions for all three factors.

Language

SAP supports an increasing number of languages. Each language is designated by a code entered during the logon process or by defaults to the language defined in the user profile. Screens and online reports appear in the language of the person performing the logon function.

The method is based on a set of standard texts assigned to reports, screen displays, and printed documents. Each standard text is available in a variant that provides the local language translation. The system selects the variant to match the profile of the logged-on user.

Operational Currencies

The following currencies are defined for operational purposes. Their codes are assigned to each function by default, which you can alter:

- **Local currency** is also the reporting currency for the company code.
- **Document currency** is the one specified for entry on SAP documents.
- **Group currency** is an alternative to document currency for group reporting.
- **Updating currency** is defined for posting debits and credits to the GI-General Ledger in parallel with the local currency.
- **Credit-limit currency** is the currency chosen to maintain the credit limit.
- **Ledger currency** is an alternative to the updating currency for the ledger.

Additional currency assignments are available in the SAP Foreign Exchange Management component, which is part of TR-TM Treasury Management.

Currencies in Transactions

Each company code has a local currency for reporting. The system records the amounts in this local currency and also in a currency specified as the document currency, which is used on all documents in addition to the local currency. You can enter documents in any currency.

You have the following two options for converting currencies:

- Enter an exchange rate when you enter the transaction document.
- Allow the system to translate between document and local currencies by referring to a table of daily exchange rates.

The system can be customized in a couple of ways:

- A specific user must enter amounts in a particular currency, which can be the local currency or the document currency.
- A specific user may be permitted to enter amounts in either local or document currency.

Whatever the customizing arrangements, the system displays amounts in both local and document currencies. It rounds off minor differences by using rules established for this purpose. These differences can occur when several line items are converted and then added in both currencies.

Customer monthly debits and credits are kept by the system only in local currency. The reconciliation account for the Accounts Receivable subledger is kept in local currency and in all the other posted currencies.

Currency Exchange Differences

A line item may be expressed in a currency other than the local or document currency. You can enter payments to clear such foreign currency line items by using either local or document currency.

The payment expressed in the system document currency will have been converted from the local currency at an exchange rate adopted by the system according to the rules laid down for assigning the daily exchange rate. If this rate has changed from the rate that prevailed when the invoice was written, the payment amount might not match the open item amount. In such cases, the system automatically calculates and posts an exchange-difference entry to a separate account established for this purpose.

Currency Translation in Consolidation

Three basic currency conversion methods are used in the consolidation of group accounts:

- Reporting date method
- Modified reporting date method
- Temporal method

Groups of items in the balance sheet and profit-and-loss statement are converted at one of these exchange rates:

- Reporting date rate
- Average rate
- Historical rate

FI-LC Legal Consolidation can translate any items at any rates and use any of the methods for any of the individual companies. This program provides solutions for several problems:

- Exchange differences between the date of the transaction and the date of the currency conversion
- Rounding differences
- The Assets History sheet failing to use rates that were current on the reporting date
- Posting a transaction difference but failing to reverse the previous translation differences

The international law requires that all intercompany balances be eliminated before presenting the balance sheet and profit-and-loss statement. All possible pairs of individual companies must be investigated for evidence that they have been trading with each other.

If the individual companies have installed and configured SAP accounting applications, there will have been automatic dual currency accounting in which every transaction is documented at the time in both the local currency and the currency designated for all transactions in the group. The FI-LC Legal Component allows you to trace any currency-translation differences between the local currency at the prevailing rate of exchange and the transaction currency. An exchange rate difference correction then can be posted in the balance sheet account designated for currency translation gains and losses and thus brought into the consolidated financial statement.

Foreign Currency Valuations

At the end of each posting period and at the end of the year, you might have to value open items expressed in foreign currency. You might need to value by a method for local tax purposes that is different from the method stockholders in the parent company want to see in the balance sheet and profit-and-loss statement. The SAP method is to define two parallel valuation areas, each of which may assign a monetary value to open items by a different method.

When the time comes to post a foreign currency payment, the system clears any currency translation gain or loss that has already been recorded. The posting destination account might depend on the currency and the type of transaction. In any event, the system records on each open item the accumulated translation difference.

You then have the choice of displaying in your local currency either the historical original value of each open item or the current value.

When you clear an item such as this, the system automatically reverses this translation gain or loss. You thus can monitor the situation at any time, not only at the end of each period.

SAP Foreign Exchange Management System

The purpose of the Foreign Exchange Management system is to record, monitor, and settle foreign exchange contracts. Unlike most other foreign exchange systems, the SAP Foreign Exchange Management system is not targeted at banks. It is directly integrated with TR-CM Cash Management and automatically posts entries to FI-Financial Accounting.

The system has international functionality and supports the international communications standards. Its distinctive feature is that it links foreign exchange contracts to the specific open items being hedged.

The instruments of foreign exchange are constantly being developed and supplemented by new instruments. You can easily incorporate new means of foreign exchange trading. The instruments now recognized include the following:

- Various forward exchange transaction types
- Combination of hedging and use
- Global and individual hedging

The standard business functions of SAP R/3 are available to the Foreign Exchange Management system and integrate with it in the following ways:

- Cash management
- Automatic posting
- Automatic correspondence
- Document history
- Links to contracts, purchase orders, and invoices
- Control by internal checking
- Centralized foreign exchange management
- Introduction of new instruments, such as options and futures
- Flexible reporting
- Word processing and graphical presentation of reports

Foreign Exchange Business Types

A *business type* defines the business transaction as a program object and controls the processing logic in the system, including the data recorded by the system and how it is obtained. The business type can determine the following operational details:

- Sequence of screens for data entry
- Data fields to be mandatory, optional, or suppressed
- Manner in which TR-CM Cash Management and FI-Financial Accounting applications are updated by the Foreign Exchange Management system

The controlling functionality of business types can be adjusted online.

The system is provided with definitions for the most common business types covering the foreign exchange market instruments. You can define an internal business type and assign it to transactions by entering its code. You can use the codes to sort your business into the appropriate journals. You can use such internal business types to control foreign exchange trading within a group of companies and to support the concept of a centralized treasury department. SAP includes an extensive range of TM-Treasury Management components.

You can define a statistical business type for a special task. It will not update the TR-CM Cash Management system or any FI-GL General Ledger balances and, in this respect, is analogous to planning data.

Foreign Exchange Management Function Types

A *function type* defines the stage or milestone that a foreign exchange contract has reached in its life cycle when you post the transaction. You can decide which steps are relevant for your company. The following are examples:

- Initiating a transaction
- Modifying
- Prolonging
- Settling

Each transaction generates a document where the business type and function type are recorded, and hence the stage reached by a foreign exchange contract. The business type and function type together control the data entry and processing. The specific function type determines the following:

- What appears on the data-entry screen and which fields are suppressed
- Which fields require data and which are optional
- The control and release function
- The confirmation printout
- The integration of data into an account

The system automatically records all changes to a foreign exchange contract in the form of documents that log the changes of function type from initiation to settlement and archiving.

The INT-International Development Application

An established range of enhancements to the SAP R/3 system is designed to customize a global system according to the international trading communities in which it operates. These are presented as modules of the INT-International Development application:

- IN-APA Asian and Pacific Area
- IN-EUR Europe
- IN-NAM North America

- IN-AFM Africa and Middle East
- IN-SAM South America

Foreign Trade

The SD-Sales and Distribution application includes a module that specializes in the regulations governing foreign trade. The following functions are available in the SD-FT Foreign Trade module:

- FT-Processing
- FT-Declarations to Authorities
- FT-Export Control
- FT-Preference Agreements
- FT-Control

Export Data Records

When your company is operating in a business zone in which local export and import rules are in force, the SAP applications can be configured with the appropriate processing logic. For example, the European Community has imposed special rules on international business transactions since January 1993. The INTRASTAT procedure requires that reports be submitted periodically to the appropriate national authority for all export transactions within the community. The following export data items are relevant to INTRASTAT reporting, managed automatically by the SD-Sales and Distribution system and quoted in the delivery and billing documents:

- Community code, country, and region of origin of the product (stored in the master record)
- Route planned for delivery, which determines the customs office and mode of transport
- Business transaction type and export procedure

The customer master records include the value-added tax VAT REG NO field in which the company's VAT registration number is stored. It applies at the company code level of organization structure, and therefore to all structural elements below it.

Country-Specific Regulations

The business practices and legal requirements of specific countries extend over the following kinds of issues:

- Legal reporting
- Valuations
- Taxes
- Payment processing

The following examples illustrate the differences in national codes of practice that can be installed as integral components of a specific SAP R/3 system:

- Federal Republic of Germany: Check/Bill of Exchange
- Switzerland: POR Procedure
- France: LCR and LCC
- Italy: Ricevuta Bancaria

Special National Human Resources Features

A substantial part of the HR-Human Resources application is already defined to accept international operations as a normal part of business. However, some aspects require the integration of supplements programmed to recognize differences in the legal requirements and business practices of different nations and different business communities.

HR-Human Resources National Supplements

The national supplements provide dynpros and the associated screen designs that can take advantage of different language pools to conduct the human resources business functions according to the customs, terminology, and legal requirements of the country concerned. With globalized enterprises, the personnel administration does not have to be for the country in which the functions are being used.

Multilingual Capabilities

Applications and modules within applications can be presented in any of the supported languages. Alternatively, the application can be maintained in the language of the host installation, and then any of its constituent functions can be assigned a different language, according to the user profile of the person logging on to perform that function.

Language Text Pools for ABAP/4 Programs   When the code in an ABAP/4 program requires a text element to be displayed onscreen, it specifies the number of the text element to be used. The code does not have to be changed in order to access another element if the user's language changes. The language in which the text element is presented is determined by the language selected by the user profile.

Language text pools are used for screen layouts, online help, and online documentation.

Pictographic Languages   The DBCS is a *Double-Byte Character Set* system that can support the pictographic languages that have a large number of characters—Japanese and Chinese, for example.

Wide Character String Handling   The ABAP/4 language has been extended to recognize data type W, for wide character fields, and some other functions that permit double-byte characters to be mixed with normal, single-byte characters in the same field. ●

CHAPTER 10

Developing an SAP Open Information Warehouse

In this chapter

Exploring the *Open Information Warehouse* (OIW) Concept

An information warehouse provides technical, business, and statistical data for any part of the corporation that might need it. An *Enterprise Data Model* (EDM) provides a structure into which data can be fitted so that it makes sense to those who examine it. In other words, the warehouse provides the information; the enterprise model gives it business meaning.

The concept of an open database is that all data is stored in tables that are ready to be instantly inspected and used without any need for complex data-retrieval instructions in a specific language peculiar to one vendor.

An *Open Information Warehouse* (OIW) suggests that all the information is readily available in a form ready for use without the need for special access operations. There is also the implication that the inventory of the warehouse is comprehensive and up-to-date.

Datasources

SAP information systems are available for all the main applications and are an integral part of their operation. They are an obvious source of data concerning their specific areas of business activity. And they already cooperate with one another to share master data such as supplier details and materials master data. They are also integrated with the financial accounting modules.

If the OIW is to be developed in support of the EIS-Executive Information System, there will be a demand for information from the TM-Treasury Management module, which could include online information links to the financial and materials market information systems provided by non-SAP vendors.

The following SAP sources contribute to the OIW:

- *Financial Information System* (FIS), discussed in Chapter 12, "Understanding the Financial Accounting Module"
- *Controlling Information System* (CIS), discussed in Chapter 13, "Understanding the Controlling Module"
- *Purchasing Information System* (PURCHIS), discussed in Chapter 20, "Understanding the Sales & Distribution Module"
- *Materials Management Information System* (MMIS), discussed in Chapter 23, "Understanding the Materials Management Module"
- *Production Planning Information System* (PPIS), discussed in Chapter 17, "Understanding the Production Planning Module"
- *Shop Floor Information System* (SFIS), discussed in Chapter 17, "Understanding the Production Planning Module"
- *Plant Maintenance Information System* (PMIS), discussed in Chapter 19, "Understanding the Plant Maintenance Module"

- *Sales Information System* (SIS), discussed in Chapter 20, "Understanding the Sales & Distribution Module"
- *Human Resources Information System* (HIS), discussed in Chapter 22, "Understanding the Human Resources Module"

Designing a Specialized Business Information Warehouse

Chapter 14, "Understanding the Enterprise Controlling Module," includes a discussion of the EC-EIS component. This Executive Information System is designed to process information about your corporate business that is stored in the various applications that form your enterprise data processing system. You can see this as a specialized data-extraction system. However, the broader concept of an open business information store includes the notion that the information is deliberately arranged to provide the most versatile business resource. The mechanisms of building such data stores and the systems for retrieving the information needed to answer queries raised by the users are naturally technical matters. These matters cannot be resolved, however, unless the business management is clear as to how the company will improve profitability so that the cost of building an information warehouse is justified.

It is probably self-evident that a data warehouse has to be able to use existing information, even though this might be stored on a variety of database platforms. Access has to be rapid. The user must be able to massage data quickly into the form needed for the occasion. And many users should be able to call on it without creating bottlenecks.

You would also expect a database management system to be relatively easy to support and reconfigure—for example, if affiliated companies contribute their data and their supply chains. Naturally, the data has to be easy to back up online and secure from unauthorized access.

In most situations, the data arising from everyday transactions is needed to update any historical data. A balance may have to be struck between transaction processing and database management.

If you are thinking in terms of an enterprise-wide data warehouse, you might base your request for funding on the following potential benefits to management:

- Data held in a single place can be reliably checked for accuracy.
- Reporting is more accurate than attempting to reconcile and interpret reports from separate databases.
- Data mining and analysis can find trends that might not be obvious if the data were not aggregated.

You might set a target of being able to report the state of business throughout the corporate enterprise at the close of any day's trading for which the records exist. Hopefully this includes the day before the report is scheduled. A different type of business objective that can be served by a data warehouse is to report performance in terms of profit rather than volume of sales, for example.

From the point of view of a customer or business partner making contact with the company, a unified data warehouse could offer the benefits of an up-to-date folio of previous documents that demonstrates that the customer is recognized and valued. For example, a telephone inquiry can automatically initiate a contact report so that the representative has all the latest information on hand by the time the call is taken.

The experts agree that the most important preliminary to the building of a data warehouse is an agreement about the business objectives and their relative priorities. This entails a close scrutiny of the value chains in the business so that the data warehouse technologies can be focused where they will produce the most benefit.

Understanding Data Mining

The basic purpose of data mining is to look for patterns in data. The simplest pattern is one that satisfies a search query, such as all customers who have placed an order in the current financial year and live within a specific marketing region. This type of convergent search terminates when all examples that match the pattern are found, if there are any in the database.

Data mining usually refers to more intelligent searching, which falls into the categories of supervised and unsupervised machine learning. In each case, the machine is seeking to find which records in the database go together in some way because some aspects of their data can be related.

Supervision entails setting off the search by declaring some relationships in the data that have to be considered, at least to begin with. For example, records may be examined further only if they already reveal that the customer referred to has spent more than a certain amount during the period under consideration. Given this baseline, the supervised search can be told to look for patterns—for example, only in the types of goods purchased. You then may ask to find the purchasing patterns associated with the purchase of a particular item.

These data-mining operations can tell you only which data values are associated; they can say nothing about the reasons. On the other hand, you may reasonably infer that your chances of making a sale to a prospect who has already bought a product associated with your product will be higher than if there is no discernible relationship.

You might want to concentrate your objective on an area where the intelligent data-mining engine found a strong association, even if you cannot understand why some of the data values appear as part of the significant pattern. For example, one study found that prospective air combat pilots who could list a large number of sporting equipment items were more likely to become successful flyers than those who could name only a few. The explanations for this could be diverse. Sportsmen have better hand-eye coordination; team players are used to doing what they are told and putting up with discomfort.

If you use a pattern discerned by data mining to guide your future activities, you must expect some disappointments. Sometimes the prediction will turn out to be false for individual cases: Some of the rejected candidates would have been successful. This fallibility can be demonstrated by carrying out your pattern recognition and then paying no attention to it until a large sample of data has been accumulated. How good does your prediction look now? How many successes would you have lost if you had followed the policy suggested by the pattern mined from the data? Your accountant will be able to tell you how much money you might have saved by applying the policy compared to what you actually spent by ignoring it.

For example, an nonselective advertising campaign may reach some unexpected customers. And their unusual data then can be used to help discern yet more significant patterns.

Some data-mining products are set up to develop a range of data models that is then applied to fresh data competitively to see which variation is the best predictor. By this means, it is possible to determine the relative worth of each element in the model. This may be important if the cost of obtaining the data object is high. Having to conduct an interview, for example, may entail a very high cost, which may or may not be worthwhile in terms of the consequences of making a false positive prediction and the consequences of making a negative or rejection decision when this would not have been justified. More subtle computations of probabilities can be used to steer the data-mining engine in the direction most likely to be fruitful.

Applying Data-Mining Techniques

The difference between database querying and data mining is that the query typically defines the parameters within which the response must fall, whereas the mining operation tries to discern relationships in the data without regard to their significance. Thus, a mining operation may begin with a definition in very general terms of what is required, such as the characteristics shared by most of the customers who purchased a particular product line over a defined period. A multidimensional query could determine who they are, and you could refine the query to test out any hypotheses you form. A mining tool would let you know the significant relationships in the data without any suggestions from you.

Marketing should be one of the first business operations to benefit from a data warehouse with data-mining tools. This is based on the assumption that the past buying behavior of a defined group of customers is a good predictor of their future buying habits. The benefits of setting up a subtle data warehousing system might appear in the following key aspects of business:

- Retaining existing customers
- Measuring the success of marketing activities
- Compiling information about sales and customers for use in marketing

You might want to be on the lookout for attitudes in your company that focus on the need for fresh research and information gathering in contrast to the view that data already is available that could be better used.

Data warehouses for the retail sector have developed to the extent that it is possible to identify a sensible sequence for building them, along the following lines:

1. Determine the mix of objectives for which the database is to be assembled.
2. Extract the data needed for the analyses that will achieve the objectives.
3. Filter the data.
4. Clean the data.

5. Format the data into a common data structure.

6. Archive the clean, formatted data separately from the general archives of transaction data and master data.

The objectives considered, but not always implemented, in the retail sector will probably include the following:

- Develop and maintain customer profiles.
- Support customer relationship marketing.
- Analyze "market baskets" to determine items commonly purchased together by sectors of the customer base.
- Support micromerchandising to target particular customer sectors or even individual customers just before their predicted next purchase.
- Support specific product categories by providing particular management information.
- Anticipate seasonal variations by providing particular management information.
- Control product replenishment and the relationships with suppliers.
- Optimize stock control.

These matters of business justification for data warehouse operations and the sensible sequence for setting them up are probably common to projects large and small. Useful tools are available at the PC level, and some advisers will counsel beginning small and building out.

Designing Virtual Data Warehouses

One advantage of a very large and comprehensive data warehouse is that—in theory, at least—any query you might have can be answered from one location if the necessary data exists. There may have to be a great deal of deductive processing to filter the data and assemble it to illuminate your problem. The cost in time and processing power may be very large.

Another possibility is for each department to maintain just the database that it needs for its immediate purposes. Thus sales, marketing, and finance, for example, may each run a miniature datamart that can answer most queries reasonably efficiently from the data held locally.

The virtual data warehouse concept developed from the possibility of giving users all the search tools they may need for each datamart, and having the results processed into a "single-image" format so that the user is hardly aware that the data may have been assembled from diverse sources.

For the virtual warehouse concept to work really well, however, the query designers have to anticipate what sort of questions the various types of users may want to ask. This requires that they appreciate the pertinent business data structures and the way in which the data can be manipulated to business advantage. The quality of the data thus processed has to be seen in terms of the profitability arising.

The profitability of a data warehouse might well turn on the success with which the users are trained to use it effectively.

Reviewing the *Document Management System* (DMS)

The R/3 document management system can treat as a document any data-storage medium that contains information intended to be sent to a user or to another system. The medium handled as a document can contain any type of storable information that contains an object, such as a technical drawing, a graphic, a program, or a text document.

Each document managed by the DMS is associated with a document info record maintained in the SAP system to record the processing status, the storage location of the actual document, and administrative data. From the document info record, the DMS can locate and manage any object defined as a document.

N O T E   At the customizing stage, the Implementation Management Guide for the Document Management System offers various configuration options for the DMS under cross-application components.

Your system has to be informed of the various media types and the varieties of formats that will be recognized as documents by the R/3 system and its DMS. SAP ArchiveLink handles SAP documents, as does the CAD interface if customized to do so. The DMS is just one central function available from the Logistics menu.

Linking Document Objects

A document is recognized as an object and therefore can be linked through object links to other objects. These can be other documents or any process, such as a task defined in a workflow. By this means, a processing task can automatically assemble the relevant documents and copy them to the relevant destinations.

Another significant benefit of defining a data object as an SAP document, with its document info record, is that you can apply the Engineering Change Management Processing Options for Documents to it. This means, for example, that every editing change to a document is treated like an engineering change to a physical object. A change has to be documented and dated so that there can be no doubt as to the contents of any document that has been copied else-where—to form part of a legal contract, for example, or to control the processing in a manufacturing plant. You can arrange for certain document types to be sent only to particular workstations and to be subject to specific authorizations. You might arrange for project managers to be sent particular documents that are folders of the items relevant to the particular stage they are managing.

Using the DMS with an OIW

The resources of the DMS are at your disposal to help you find some of what you need when you are designing a data warehouse. The R/3 classification system offers many functions designed to help you locate information held in document form. You can search on the basis of subject matter and search for an item because you know it is linked with a data object, such as one of the following:

- Another document

- A material identified by its material number, its name, or part of its name

- An item of equipment where you have given its name or only the identification of the activity where it is used

- A project identified by its number, the person responsible, the purpose, and so on

- A quotation

- A sales order

- A customer or vendor identified by an attribute in the master records

Although the DMS and the various application information systems can provide all the information available in the system, the information they access is not specifically arranged for the specialized retrieval processes usually required to justify the costs of building and maintaining an OIW as a separate system. Thus, the SAP OIW is perhaps better conceived as a virtual data warehouse.

Exploring the *Enterprise Data Model* (EDM)

An EDM makes sense of and takes account of how the business uses the data structures defined in the active ABAP/4 data dictionary. The EDM is built from entity-relationship elements that portray the relevant information objects and their relationships from a business standpoint. For example, the following relationship is between data structures seen from a data-processing standpoint:

```
Value S = Value C + Value P
```

The same relationship has a different interpretation when seen from a business perspective:

Profit **is** Sales Revenue **less** Costs.

One view is a model for the computer to specify the calculation procedures; the other is a model of how the business can survive and flourish if the management can manipulate the values in a certain way. These examples are obviously a little sparse. Figure 10.1 shows part of a slightly more developed model.

Differentiating Object Types in an EDM

The following object types appear in the sample model fragment:

- The **Organizational Unit** is part of the R/3 Reference Model and is assigned the name of the operating company or department that the EDM is representing.

- The **Position** is modeled from the R/3 Reference Model and named to suit the specific company with a title such as Sales Representative.

FIGURE 10.1
Part of an Enterprise
Data Model.

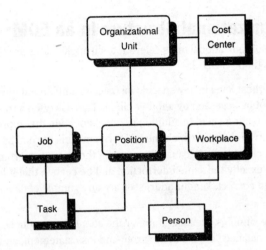

- Several **Workplaces** can be assigned the same position, each able to accommodate one person.
- The **Job** is a set of tasks based on a specific workplace but not necessarily the only set of tasks performed there.
- The **Task** is a component of a job and usually includes a fairly well-defined set of work input materials or messages for which appropriate work procedures exist.

NOTE   Two other object types, not part of the Human Resources Organization and Planning component, are necessarily addressed by relationships in this arena. They particularize any instance of the model by naming a person assigned to perform a job, who therefore is attached to a workplace that carries the responsibilities of a position, and a Cost Center such as a specific plant or department.

Illustrating Relationships in an EDM

The data model fragment in Figure 10.1 implies the following relationships:

- A named person *holds both* a Workplace and a Position.
- The Workplace *is part of* the Position.
- The Position *is part of* an Organizational Unit.
- The Organizational Unit *is allocated to* a particular Cost Center.
- The Position *describes* a Job.
- The Job describes one or more Tasks.
- A Task describes a special case of a Position.

Graphical symbols are used by the R/3 system to display different views of the EDM to emphasize the relationships between the objects of the model.

▶ **See** "The Formal Components of EPC Modeling," **p. 91**

Discerning the Organizational Structure in an EDM

The SAP R/3 general organizational units relevant to all applications are taken from the standard reference that is the R/3 EDM:

- **Client** is the highest level in any specific instance or implementation of R/3. The data of one client cannot be accessed by another client. There is often a training client and a development or testing client in addition to the client code that represents your group or corporate identity and under which the SAP system runs normal business. Some data is managed at the client level, because everyone in the corporate group of companies will want to refer to exactly the same information and be certain that it has been maintained, is up-to-date, and correct. Vendor addresses are an example of data managed at the client level.

- **Company code** signifies a legal unit under the client that produces its own financial documents, the balance sheet, and the profit-and-loss statement, and may well maintain them continuously reconciled.

- **Plant** is an organizational unit that is seen as central to the production planning concept. A plant can be a production site or a group of storage locations that shares materials. Plant is the unit for which MRP prepares plans and maintains the inventory. It is the focus of MM-Materials Management. Each plant is given planning and control elements such as material, inventory, operations, work centers, and so on.

The lower levels of organizational structure tend to be specific to the application. For example, the lower levels of a physical warehouse data structure reference warehouse areas and perhaps bin types and bin numbers, whereas the lowest level in a human resource personnel data structure is an individual person.

Using Application Information Systems as Components of the OIW

Each R/3 application has reporting functions that act as an information service that can select, collate, and summarize transaction data and master data held in the particular application, or reserved for it in a central store. For example, the following information systems can be called on if their parent applications have been installed and configured in your R/3 implementation:

- LIS-Logistics Information System
- FIS-Financial Information System
- HRIS-Human Resources Information System

The EIS-Executive Information System may also be installed and configured with the application information systems or as a cross-application system.

At the application level, the information services may be further subdivided for the convenience of users who want to maximize the profitability of their area of responsibility. For example, a Logistics Information System may be available as separate subsystems such as these:

- Purchasing Information System
- Sales Information System
- Inventory Controlling
- Shop Floor Information System
- Plant Maintenance Information System
- Quality Management Information System

The aim of the designer of an OIW is to make available a series of views of the data that is selective and pertinent to the viewer's business. The details of the source of the data usually are not relevant if the integrity and timeliness of the data are assured.

The OIW usually arranges for the most important information to be held in databases parallel to the Sales and Production operating systems. These parallel data stores contain key figures that have been computed to suit the associated business decision processes. The display of these key figures is supported by the standard graphical and tabular layouts for the convenience of the user.

You can see what is available from the system by consulting the OIW Catalog, which provides three related tables:

- A list of the info objects that can be accessed from the OIW
- A list of the datasources from which the info objects have been compiled or copied
- A list of *contains* relations telling you which info objects are available from each datasource

Exploring the Logistics Information System

The Logistics Information System maintains up-to-date information taken from the operating applications—such as Sales, Purchasing, Production, and Plant Maintenance—according to the configuration of your system. This technique is referred to as *online transaction processing* (OLTP). The LIS extracts statistical data from the OLTP to compile summary and periodic data that can be made available through the OIW using the information structures defined for it. Other applications provide similar information systems.

Online analytical processing (OLAP) is designed so that the user can call on analysis and reporting tools to evaluate data provided in the information system. A wide range of standard analysis procedures is available through OLAP, and you can specify how lists are presented and depicted graphically. Flexible planning, forecasting, and early-warning analysis for potential exceptional situations complement the facilities. A *Logistics Information Library* (LIL) is provided to catalog key figures.

Constructing an Information Structure

Although many information structures are provided as standard, you can also create variants of them to suit your business. An information structure has three parts:

- **Characteristics** are information items, such as the code for the plant or a material, that can be used to aggregate statistical information.

- **Key figures** are values that have particular business significance, such as the sales volume.

- **Period unit** is a time reference that can be used to determine when the values of the key figures are accumulated separately for each characteristic. The options are day, week, month, and posting period.

Standard information structures are provided for each application module, to which you can add customized variants to combine information structures and vary the updating rules. You can do this by using the Implementation Guide in the Business Engineering Tools menu.

The following structures are examples of the variety and complexity of the standard information displays available in the various applications:

S001	Customer
S002	Sales office
S003	Sales organization
S004	Material
S005	Shipping point
S006	Sales employee
S011	Purchasing group—for purchasing group analysis
S012	Purchasing—for the material groups, vendor, and material analysis
S013	Vendor evaluation—for the standard analysis of vendor evaluation, updated at goods receipt and purchase order postings
S015	Subsequent settlement—updated at the events invoice receipt for a purchase order (vendor business volume) or subsequent settlements of an arrangement (income) by credit memo/billing document
S031	Movements—for material movements of current valuated stock and vendor consignment stock
S033	Movements (individual records)—for daily material movement data also identified by document number
S034	Movements (batches)
S035	Stocks (batches)

The array of information structures used as standards extends through all the applications and can be used if the relevant modules are installed and configured.

Using Evaluation Structures

If your business health can be reflected in some way by a particular analysis or set of analyses of data that is available in your system or that can be calculated from this data, you can build an evaluation structure, test it, and set it up as a standard and perhaps automatic calculation to be performed at suitable intervals. Creating a business-health indicator is a matter of picking up the characteristics and key figures of interest and putting them together as a logical or arithmetic formula held in an evaluation structure. The report this structure generates when it is activated can be adjusted to suit your requirements. For example, you might prefer a list of the important results, or you might want to combine them in a standard graphical presentation.

Planning in an Information System

Any information systems that have been installed and configured in your system can be used to support a planning function. This leads to a significant analysis of the differences between the planned and actual values achieved for the entities in the plan. Thus you can define an evaluation structure that is particularly indicative for the health of a certain aspect of your business, define target or planned values for it over a time span, and then have the system report on the results.

With the introduction of Release 3.0, the planning functionalities of the information systems and the *Sales and Operations Planning* (SOP) components were integrated as one central planning and forecasting tool.

Calling Distributed Datasources with Application Link Enabling

You can call the following information systems through the ALE functionality:

- Purchasing Information System
- Sales Information System
- Inventory Controlling

The planning functions can also be applied across networks of these information systems using ALE technology.

Because you can readily call in or distribute information using the ALE functions, many organizations arrange their OIW facilities as a hub and periphery design in which a central R/3 system at the hub can communicate with local operating databases and other R/3 systems running in affiliated companies.

You can use the release mechanism to enable information distribution systems of any complexity. For example, you can define that a purchase order being saved is a significant event to which the integrated system will respond with these actions:

1. Scan the customer distribution model to identify which, if any, customers should be informed that a purchase order has been created.
2. If one or more message recipients are identified, call the Purchasing IDoc Interface, which generates a structured IDoc message containing the details of the purchase order, and place it in the distribution system so that copies reach the intended destinations.

The following menu path is probably available on your system to support these operations:

Logistics Data Warehouse→Data Basis

Tools→Distribution of Statistical Data

Calling Up the Information System Menus

The information systems of the applications installed and configured in your system can be accessed by a menu path such as the following:

Logistics→Logistics Controlling

Inventory Controlling→Sales Info System

You can also reach an information system from the parent application. You can use this path, for example:

Logistics→Materials Management

Purchasing→Outline Agreement

Reporting→Purch. Info System

When you reach the menu of an information system, you are offered a choice. You can initiate one of the standard analyses and store user-specific settings. If your system includes customized information structures, these may also be offered with the standard analyses. The flexible analysis option allows you to create information structures and process them in ways that you define or that have already been defined.

The Early Warning System is an arrangement where you target specific weak points in your logistics chains and have the system monitor them. You can also have the system alert you to any exceptional situations that might lead to problems if not dealt with immediately.

If you want to inspect the key figures available in the Logistics area, you can use the *Logistics Information Library* (LIL). Approximately 1,000 key figures are available as standard, plus any that have been added to suit your particular company. From the LIL facility, you can also create and classify key figures so that you later can identify them by the class name you assign to them in the LIL.

The Logistics Information System Environment menu offers a simple tool for combining key figures to create and change general hierarchies that are to be used for evaluations. The Environment option also gives you access to any documentation available in the application for any transaction you are interested in.

Finding Key Figures

There are three ways to locate a key figure in the Logistics Information Library:

■ Search by text strings or catchwords that are in the description field of the key figure master record, using any logical combination of and with or. You can use up to seven search terms, and each term can contain up to 20 characters.

■ Search by using attributes available in the R/3 Classification scheme, which can include terms defined specifically for your company.

■ Nominate info sets, which are key figures that are grouped together because of their logical or business relationships.

Whichever method of selection you use, the screen displays a list of key figures and hierarchy trees that meet your specification. You can select Back to add terms to the previous step in the retrieval sequence before repeating the search. Alternatively, you can choose Edit→Text Retrieval to add another term that refines the selection you have already assembled.

The following sequence brings you into the classification scheme to locate key figures:

> Select Info Library→Key figure retrieval→Via classification.

R/3 Classification is made up of 36 classifying attributes divided into four groups:

- **Information Object,** such as equipment, customer, vendor, material, material type, product group, and material group
- **Information Category,** such as deviation, proportion, number, rating figure, capacity, quantity, master data, date, value, and time
- **Functional Area,** such as purchasing, production, plant maintenance, stores, quality assurance, and sales
- **Organizational Unit,** such as work scheduler, work center, MRP controller, purchasing group, purchasing organization, business area, storage location, division, sales office, sales organization, shipping point, sales employee, and plant

If you mark attributes from the classification display, you get a list showing all the key figures that have been associated with these attributes.

You might want to build info sets containing references to certain key figures. One of the most useful info sets would contain all the key figures you ought to check on a regular basis. A single-level info set is made up of key figures. A multilevel info set contains members that are hierarchical references to other info sets.

Displaying Additional Information

It is possible to locate a key figure by a textual search in the documentation records associated with it. In fact, each key figure defined in your system has the following additional information:

- Documentation on the report, program, transaction, or table from which the key figure is copied or calculated
- The retrieval path to this source
- Technical information about the derivation of the key figure, such as the Logistics Information System, if this key figure is integrated in the LIS

You can inspect this additional information by marking the key figure of interest and selecting Details and the type of information you require.

Using the SAP OIW Module

The SAP OIW is effectively built from the information systems already available in the R/3 system, provided that these systems have been installed and configured in the particular *instance* or implementation. The contents of this data warehouse are defined and cataloged as info objects. They can be inspected individually or combined to respond to queries.

A warehouse has to have a list of its contents. This list is referred to in SAP as *the Catalog*. Although the OIW Catalog lists metadata structures such as tables, programs, reports, and specialized information systems, the OIW can be used without necessarily understanding how these structures work. Exactly which data structures appear in the OIW Catalog is determined at the stage of customizing the OIW, because in most implementations, the OIW does not hold its own data. It is therefore in the category of virtual data warehouse, because it depends on data maintained elsewhere in the various applications and possibly in external systems.

The SAP data warehouse is termed *open* because it has an interface that can be programmed to interact with external systems. For example, you can call up queries from Microsoft Excel worksheets that are answered from the OIW via the OIW front end for Microsoft Excel.

The OIW interface is an SAP Business API. The rules that control its operations are held in the *Business Object Repository* (BOR) as two methods objects that are called in turn to read the OIW Catalog and run an OIW query.

Their symbols and names appear on the SAP OIW toolbar and in the Microsoft Excel Data menu.

Working in the OIW Browser

You might already have all the queries you need in the system. However, you can edit a query and save a variant, because the OIW browser demonstrates exactly how it will display the data. The info objects to appear in the columns are shown, and those that contain units of measurement or currency are displayed as values and associated units.

You can also control whether a query is answered using the R/3 internal system of IDs or whether short texts in a specified language are displayed, when available. You can drag new info objects from the OIW Catalog display into your query design to become new columns or as entries in the Result area of the Excel worksheet. Similarly, you can drag info objects from the Catalog to the list of selections or directly to a cell in the worksheet.

The catalog shows the datasources available; you can double-click to indicate your requirement. If you do not choose, the system uses the most suitable sources for your query. For example, you might prefer to use a somewhat ancient datasource if it has already been assembled and can be accessed rapidly.

Controlling the OIW Browser

An info object appears in the browser only if it can be combined with the info objects already selected for the query. Info objects can appear only if they are available in one or more of the datasources in the OIW Catalog. Therefore, if you demand more data in your query, you might have less selectable objects that can supply that data. If you remove columns or selections from the query, there might be a wider offering of suitable info objects.

Defining SAP R/3 Business Objects

An object in the language of *object-oriented programming* (OOP) is an entity that carries a data element that signifies the state it is in, such as OFF or ON, and some method by which this state can be changed. There might be more than one method of changing an object's state, and it might have more than two states. What matters to the user is what else happens or could happen if an object changes its state. For example, an object that has the function of recognizing when a purchase order has arrived could also be given the functions of setting in motion other actions, such as checking the stock availability and the customer's credit status.

You could imagine a more complicated business object that has the function of finding not only the best supplier for the goods required but also other potential customers for these goods. Such a business object might behave very much like an astute manager. It could be allowed to search widely for both customers and suppliers. You might also want to endow it with rules for choosing the best buy in the context of the pool of customers available. You might want it to use the profitability of each potential trading activity as one of the factors to take into account when deciding on the best course of action. It might be prudent to set limits to the scope of this automatic manager business object and to have a human assessor called into the functionality when these limits are approached.

This example would not be out of place in many industrial contexts. A purchasing staff, marketing staff, and sales staff will be carrying out elements of this complex function. A standard business object could add the routine widening of search horizons, because the information-gathering process would not entail extra human time.

Now suppose the suppliers identified by your automatic manager business object are aware that a requirement for their type of product has been put out to competitive tender. They might well have a similar type of business object that could find the best way of meeting the requirement. And so the automatic manager business object could find itself being used over and over again, each reincarnation using different particular details but each using the standard business process that has been programmed to work as efficiently as possible as a business object.

The advantage of thinking in terms of business objects is that you can forget about the details once you know the purpose and manner of use for each of your objects of interest. The *interface* of a business object is a definition of what information is necessary to use and control the business object.

This technology is but an extension of the SAP standard process of building business software elements that can be customized to suit the circumstances of the user company. Limits are set so that the functional integrity of the program is not compromised. In particular, an SAP R/3 business object cannot be altered in such a way that it is no longer compatible with the rest of any R/3 implementation. It will always remain a fully integrated component. For example, a customer can be fully documented in a standard business object that is replicated or instantiated as needed until all existing customers are represented as business objects. In a similar way, a sales order can be defined to include all the necessary attributes and processing methods in a business object that can be *cloned* as needed to represent and process in a standard way each new sales order.

Understanding the SAP R/3 *Business Object Repository* (BOR)

One aid to appreciating what a business object can do for your business is an organized place or repository from which particular objects can be called as needed. The *Business Object Repository* (BOR) is a database that holds reusable standard business processes that can be called on to build a specific implementation quickly. The BOR can contribute as a central documentation of R/3, because it can be accessed via the Repository API, which can interface with system development and implementation systems. Thus the program developer can find out about the data definitions, screen designs, and program objects available in R/3.

So that you can access the contents of the R/3 Repository in an orderly and efficient manner, its contents are identified by their purpose.

Objects that are related directly to business concepts include the following:

- Customer
- Material
- Order
- Quotation
- Request for quotation
- Object variants defined specifically for the user company

Technical objects held in the BOR are also objects familiar to the business community and users of business computing. The technical objects include the following:

- Texts
- Notes
- Calendars
- Work items
- Archived documents
- Texts for display on the user interface screen
- Graphics
- Spreadsheets

The objects in the repository do not have to be completely specified in advance. There is a *Dynamic Invocation Interface* (DII) to allow the details to be supplied at runtime via the interface—for example, to establish the dimensions of a spreadsheet. This technique is referred to as *late binding*.

The location of an object and its coding can remain unknown to the user client because the system consults the object automatically and reports the requested information at runtime.

At runtime, the coding and location of the business object are identified by the registration element that is defined as part of the definition of object types in the BOR. The client never knows the registered location of the object. The client may be accessing the business object via a distributed system, perhaps using the Internet, but the business object merely receives a request via the BOR and reports the results back to the client along the same route.

Another opportunity afforded by the inclusion of the BOR is the facility to allow an individual client to create a company-specific business object that is created as a subtype of a standard SAP business object. It therefore inherits all the essential attributes, methods, and events if the object is to integrate with the rest of the R/3 implementation. The client then can edit the data definitions and store the company-specific business object under its own name. The runtime component of the BOR then is simply instructed to use the new business object in place of the master supplied with the system.

The BOR is equipped to respond to SAP *remote function calls* (RFCs) from outside R/3—perhaps from an R/2 or third-party system, for example. Interfaces are now available to comply with standards such as Object Management Group's CORBA and Microsoft's COM/DCOM.

Release 3.0 contained 170 SAP business objects in the BOR. Release 3.1 includes almost 1,000 different business objects designed to SAP standards. Release 4.0 contains many more.

The BOR and the general R/3 repository it is part of constitute a suite of integrated components from which the implementation engineer can build a system to meet the way you want to do business when the system goes live. During the design phase, the *Business Engineering Workbench* (BEW) can be set up to use the repository as a passive source of information and later as a resource for simulating parts of the intended business system.

The repository of standard business objects is a database. However, it includes not only data objects, but also processing methods that are handled as objects, and still more complex entities in the form of business objects that can include both data and the prescribed methods for processing new information.

Such a database has a search method and a query language such as SQL that can be called by a *Database SQL Library* (DBSL) agent. The library agent can be interfaced to proprietary database systems so that existing data can be called into use by an R/3 system.

N O T E   An OIW can be built as an interacting network of SAP R/3 and proprietary database systems. ▨

Detecting Patterns of Events

One key to designing useful business objects is the existence of recurring patterns that can be recognized by a system and have a business significance. The arrival of a purchase order is an event that can be detected in any of several ways and checked for validity. Your business will expect other purchase orders. Therefore, investment in business objects to cope with them may be worthwhile. There is a pattern to such events; purchase orders can be recognized.

If you are looking at a set of events that do not share any common features, you could be said to be a problem solver. You might have to create a new and unique procedure to deal with each event. But you still might find it convenient to use a database that contains business objects. If you are repairing a system and decide that a particular part needs replacing, it might be convenient to call up the maintenance object for that system and have it run not only system checks directly, or via keyed-in data, but also the stock control module to determine the best way of acquiring the part you need, its cost, and delivery information.

Updating Business Objects

This chapter has been illustrating the concept of business objects with examples of wide-ranging online functionality. An intermediate procedure is to have your data held as business objects that carry static information between formal updates. A price list or telephone book could be said to be business objects. But if you never make any updates when new information is available, your business objects are not as useful as ones that are updated according to the rules that have been programmed into them, whether or not you decide to update them manually.

Applying the Master Data Object Principle

It has always been fundamental to SAP standard business program design that each data object should reside in only one location where it is known to be the master data object. It can be copied but not altered without leaving a record of who altered it and when. Once a master object is updated, all subsequent calls to that object should encounter the new information.

SAP's standard date functions have always been business objects that carry information, such as the system date and time, and processes that could transform this value to express the date and time in various time zones and in appropriate languages and formats. If you try to enter a date that is not in one of the acceptable formats, an SAP system does its best to convert it. It does not let you enter the time or date in a format of your own invention, because this might not be understood by other users and the business processes they are running.

Using the Business Object Repository

The concept of a business object is central to the design philosophy of SAP software. Each SAP standard business process is programmed in ABAP/4 code. These highly reliable software components are not open to alteration by the user organization. However, the actions they take can be controlled by the information stored, perhaps dynamically, in the tables associated with them. Because the code of a business object can be altered only by SAP-authorized programmers, the system of business objects works reliably. What the implementation engineers have to do is to charge the control tables with the data required to service the client organization. Now these control tables are themselves made according to master data specifications that are business objects in their own right, because they can prevent unsuitable data from getting into their storage locations.

Thus the total collection of business objects—whether single data records or complex modules of data and procedures—constitutes the SAP R/3 system. If you examine any one of these objects, you will be made aware of the functions it performs and the controls that will be exercised over the information it accepts. The set of business objects is therefore a dynamic system documentation. Whatever you need to know is always available as part of the business object itself.

The way to access this documentation is by means of an API. For example, you could invoke an API that presents the application documentation on your graphical user interface. If you are working with Release 3.1 or 4.0, this GUI could be presented to you across the Internet and displayed on your portable PC or whatever terminal device can operate as a virtual machine for Java applets. If you have a business process modeling tool with a suitable API to your R/3 application, you can see the system documentation in the form of graphical and other displays according to how you configured your modeling tool. If you are operating with an SAP or third-party business process reengineering tool, you will probably have a suitable API to look at the structure of your SAP R/3 application. More than 1,000 business API components have been created. ●

CHAPTER 11

Maintaining the Computer System

In this chapter

Designing a Monitoring Strategy

The first concept of corrective maintenance is to try to avoid it by performing inspections, monitoring, and doing preventive maintenance. The second concept is to get the system running again as quickly as possible if it does break down.

When a system is as complicated as a distributed computer network, there is an additional aspect of maintenance that is obvious as soon as you see the task as maintaining a service instead of just keeping some machinery working. Interruptions to services can occur because parts of the system become overloaded. Bottlenecks reveal themselves. In this respect, there may be a serious difficulty in accessing a system such as SAP R/3 over the Internet, because not all the links and service providers that may be chained for a transaction need to have the same high-channel capacity that is more usual in an intranet where many fewer users are linked by channels of much higher bandwidth. For this reason, this chapter is primarily focused on the intranet scenario.

The task of monitoring all parts of a complex system will be all but incomprehensible unless some attempt is made to divide the target systems into groups. For example, some services are necessarily online, and others can comfortably be provided by resources that are not fully stretched. They may be elsewhere in a different time zone. They may be the same resources used in background mode when workloads permit.

A strategic decision will be made here. Just how much does the company's profitability depend on each service? Where should the monitoring effort be concentrated?

After the priorities are assigned across the target systems, the next task is to identify what problems could occur in each service. For example,

- Shortage of memory may be causing excessive page swapping and increasing system loading that seems unrelated to profitable work.
- Networks may be slowing down the rest of the system. Most authorities recommend that a line normally should not be operating at more than 40 percent of the capacity supported by the wire.
- Inadequate disks and input/output systems will be implicated if business processes are queuing for a CPU that is idle or can't be assigned to a CPU.
- A CPU that seems to be forever working at full stretch should be taken as a suggestion that perhaps the work should be shared or the CPU upgraded.

These ideas have to be firmed up into a set of hard monitoring rules that can trigger alarms for the system administrator. There might have to be a series of alarms, each reacting to a more serious violation of the specified threshold. A system is required that can take action comfortably before a bottleneck can occur so that there is virtually no possibility of interruption in a service crucial for the company's viability.

If a system of alarms is conditional on specified critical values, there can be logging of system performance using the same monitoring processes. And from the logs may come insight into further improvements to the maintenance of the computer and the services it supports.

Although there are several third-party suppliers of computer management systems, the next sections focus on the SAP CCMS product.

Introducing the CCMS-Computing Center Management System

The *Computing Center Management System* (CCMS) provides an efficient and flexible system for monitoring and controlling the SAP system and its application modules. It is required to manage the routine tasks of monitoring and controlling background processing and database backups. The design of the CCMS includes the best methods of discovering problems as early as possible.

Global business systems are complex. To monitor and manage them requires software and hardware specifically designed for the purpose:

- **Can the CCMS manage very large networks and global companies?** The CCMS combines with the various host and application system platforms to build an integrated large network manager.

- **Is the CCMS an open system?** SAP has developed *Simple Network Management Protocol* (SNMP) extensions to provide various *Management Information Bases* (MIBs). These are designed to interface with all types of systems and system platforms.

- **What happens if a component of a distant system breaks down?** A global alert monitor function displays this fact in the CCMS.

- **In a global system, where are the computing loads managed?** The CCMS can assign users to sufficient free capacity and oversee the time-controlled distribution of system resources.

- **How is the management of backing up data arranged in a global system?** The backup and recovery of data can be supervised through the CCMS with the associated security and authorization.

Examining CCMS Components

The components of the CCMS are included in the standard R/3 system.

The SAP GUI provides functions and control options that are easy to interpret by their graphics, and easy to use by selecting items onscreen and using the special function keys. Beginning with R/3 Release 3.0, the CCMS functions are supported by the SM-Service Management component, which is designed to enhance computer center management.

The CCMS receives notification of service requirements, which it can relate to its model of the equipment in the system. This model represents the hardware, software, network addresses, cables, and other items from which the network is built. Furthermore, each component, such as a local network server, is represented with all its dependent software and hardware, and the object networks such as *local area networks* (LANs) and *wide-area networks* (WANs).

Each item has been assigned standard partner activities so that appropriate service contractors can be identified if a fault arises. The accounting and pricing arrangements are also set up for each activity so that the administration of the service contracts can proceed efficiently and largely automatically.

The SM-Service Management component also responds to change notices to maintain the network models.

Integrating the CCMS

The SAP R/3 CCMS is integrated with the facilities of the various host platforms and operating environments. For the R/3 system to qualify as an open system, it must support the interaction of any of its applications with any other to the extent that any user interface can access any applications, which in turn can exchange data with each other. The interplay of applications depends on a shared system of international standards for interfaces, services, and data formats.

The following international standards are supported by R/3:

- *Transmission Control Protocol/Internet Protocol* (TCP/IP) is the standard network protocol for open systems and is supported by all R/3 applications.

- *Remote function call* (RFC) is the SAP ABAP/4 programming language adaptation of *remote procedure call* (RPC), which permits other systems to call R/3 applications.

- *Common Programming Interface-Communication* (CPI-C) is a set of standardized definitions for program-to-program communication across systems.

- *Structured Query Language* (SQL) is the ANSI fourth-generation language for manipulating data.

- *Open database connectivity* (ODBC) is a Microsoft standard for table-oriented data access based on SQL definitions.

- *Object linking and embedding* (OLE) is a Microsoft technology that permits objects to be connected and incorporated across multiple files and programs.

- X.400 is a series of recommendations for message-handling systems with extensive security options. These originate from the *International Telecommunications Union* (ITU) through its agency, CCITT *(International Telephone and Telegraph Consultative Committee)*.

- X.500 is a series of standards for directory services, also issued as *International Standards Organization* (ISO) 9594, drawn up by the CCITT. These standards require the use of directory user agents to control access to a directory information base.

- *Messaging Application Programming Interface* (MAPI) is part of the Microsoft *Windows Open Service Architecture* (WOSA).

- *Electronic Data Interchange* (EDI) is a standardized scheme for exchanging business data between different systems by means of defined business documents, such as invoices and orders.

- *Computer-assisted design* (CAD) is supported by a series of standards for the transmission and storage of technical documents, including drawings and textual materials.

- *Computer Output on Laser Disc* (COLD) is a method of writing image data for optical archiving. The SAP ArchiveLink uses COLD to store digitized bitmapped pixel data linked directly to coded documents and data; it therefore can be used to retrieve the stored image.
- Technical subsystems are company-specific devices that interact with plant controls and instruments through interfaces adapted for this purpose.

Managing Open Network Management Platforms

The overall management system for an association of large heterogeneous networks from various vendors may be considered to be a manager of the more local network managers of the network constituents. The difficulty is creating a system that gives the components sufficient flexibility to interact with each other without losing the advantages of control by a *supermanager.* The central controller must have intimate knowledge of the details of all the elements.

By contrast, an open network management platform is a product that allows all users direct management of the network technologies. Under these conditions, there is no need for each component network to have its own separate network manager.

This concept is also referred to as *enterprise management* and is discussed in Chapter 14, "Understanding the Enterprise Controlling Module."

Understanding Network Management Protocols and Application Interfaces

Although various management protocols have been developed, the formative standard for open management platforms has been SNMP.

The success of an open network management platform depends not only on a shared management protocol, but also on the availability of an *Application Programming Interface* (API) for each network application. An API should be a well-defined and thoroughly documented method of exchanging data and commands with the application, no matter which platform it is running on or which vendor provided it.

An SAP Management Information Base is the data interface between the R/3 system and additional services, not necessarily on SAP system platforms. The open systems philosophy is designed to provide seamless integration with all systems, whatever their origin and configuration.

The following sample open network management platforms have been accepted by a significant number of user organizations:

- SunConnect SunNet Manager
- Hewlett-Packard OpenView
- IBM NewView/6000

These products extend the CCMS facilities to the large network environment with the additional functionality needed to manage the network nodes and the operations centers.

From the R/3 CCMS, you can query the current configuration and status information of all internal and external systems. The status information from the integrated R/3 applications can be combined with alarms from other networks, other systems, and certain specialized applications. You are then in a position to use your central display to present the total system information necessary for global problem solving.

The way to global control of automated systems is opened up by this approach. The open network management product can be tailored to the requirements of your global integrated systems by means of a central specification of operator profiles and an integrated set of customizing specifications that can be extended to include all significant system components. The essential functions can be controlled through any combination of these systems to provide the following services:

- Event control
- Messaging
- Problem handling

Monitoring the System

The elements of system monitoring fall into two sections: *alarm services* and *system performance monitoring*. The focus of these activities is the global alert monitor function, which is supplemented with various other monitors for detailed analysis and record keeping.

Assigning Alarm Services

The status of each system component is tested and logged at frequent intervals, together with information on the queues waiting for service and, if any, error messages generated by the local controlling systems.

Monitoring Alerts Globally   The *global alert monitor* assembles in one integrated display system all the alarms and warning messages generated by the peripheral systems and their communications. This information can be displayed under the standard SAP GUI, which allows the user to select any item and drill down to see the documents that contributed to its calculation: the data and the calculation formulas and conditions.

Monitoring Databases   The *database monitor* keeps track of the free space available and the volume of traffic to and from each database. The system also logs the date and time of each transaction so that the database monitor can derive performance measures to assess all the significant dimensions of the operation of the database complexes.

Monitoring Operating Systems   The *operating system monitor* tracks the availability of main memory and disk space in order to assign processing workloads to those parts of the global system that can best handle them.

Again, the performance of the system under scrutiny is measured—for example, in terms of CPU task times and throughput capacity.

Monitoring Networks   The visual display of the *network monitor* is supplemented by listing displays to show the network's integrity and its load at all times. These utilization statistics are continuously logged and can be analyzed online.

Monitoring Job Scheduling   For the processing of background jobs and the allocation of system resources, the *job scheduling monitor* concentrates on the incoming requests and the reports of the status of the systems needed and available to meet them.

Monitoring Applications   The *application server statistics* compiled by the computer center are an important source of information needed for strategic and tactical planning at the global level. In addition, lists can be compiled for any data of interest and then subjected to whatever statistical analysis best reveals their significance.

Measuring Performance

The performance of an integrated system should be measured for two reasons:

- To determine the data that can be used in the future to balance workloads and prevent bottlenecks
- To identify the most frequently called functions so that they can be considered for technical improvement to increase their efficiency

The CCMS module includes tools to monitor the runtime performance of R/3 applications in, for example, the following respects:

- Response time of dialogs
- Number of dialog steps per hour
- CPU use and load factor

Controlling the System

The essence of computer network system control is to plan what data processing and storage requirements will be met by the system resources that will be available at the time. It is necessary to know which resources are available and what workloads have already been assigned to those resources. The endeavor is much like any process controlling—perhaps quicker, and certainly demanding in expertise and rapid decision making.

Optimizing the Load Distribution in the Client/Server Environment

The optimizing function is a development of resource planning, which has always been a combination of predicting future requirements and applying historical data about how operations consume resources.

The database has to include measurements of the performance of the system components. There must also be estimates of the loads that the planned requirements will place on those components.

Over and above the assigning of workloads to resources that will be available to handle them, there has always had to be an element of safety planning—keeping capacity in reserve in case a critical resource breaks down. As a result, a culture and discipline of safety stocks and reserves has developed, which becomes manifest in guidelines for the use of capacities. Workloads are shared so that no resource is overstretched while an equivalent capacity is underused.

In the context of a computer-based production system, there is an indispensable requirement for fast and accurate displays of the status of all the production resources and planned requirements. When the production resources are the computers and networks themselves, the same requirement exists. Processing loads and computing capacities have to be integrated with the database operating and capacity factors.

Assigning Users to Sufficient Free Capacity

Having a network with a central global planning and control capability can make it possible for the total productivity of the system to be much increased, because the CCMS will be aware of the requirements for data processing and the planned availability of the resources. The users can be assigned to the capacities that will be best able to cope.

The system functions for distributing loads can provide a load-balancing service for groups of users who share the same set of dialogs. When you sign on to work in a particular area, such as SD Order Entry or Accounts Payable in Financial Accounting, you will be assigned automatically to a server that is for the moment handling the smallest load.

Time-Controlled Distribution of System Resources

When there is a choice between background and online processing, system resource planners obviously have more degrees of freedom. If the network spans time zones, the daily load patterns can be used to plan a timetable of resource allocations.

The following operating modes are predefined:

- Online operations where most work processes are defined as dialog processes
- Nighttime operation where most work processes are defined as background processes
- Maintenance operations that are restricted to certain authorized users

Processing control for the operatorless nighttime mode is based on the following function types:

- Recognition of different job classes
- Responses to external events
- Starting and controlling external programs by using RFCs
- Reservation of processing resources according to the priority of background jobs

The Computing Center Management System also operates its own system of priorities to ensure the scheduling and monitoring of data backup and to recover tasks in conjunction with the application processing workloads.

Using Backup Services

The system services emanating from the CCMS in addition to the global alert monitoring function are essentially those entailed in looking after background processing and the safety functions of backup, recovery, and security.

Processing in the Background

The planning of system resources seeks to best use background processing whenever there is no absolute requirement for online immediate response. There are several methods of anticipating the online requirements so that the background processing can provide support in the form of data that has been selected and processed on the basis of the likely needs of the online user. For example, the user who habitually works with material masters of certain types will appreciate it if the central management system has already updated these masters before his daily work schedule begins.

Managing Backups

One key benefit of being linked to a system with a formal backup management system is the security of being able to recover much of earlier work in the event of a local system failure. Yet the costs of comprehensive and frequent backups can be considerable. A policy for backup management has to be in place; the ideal owner of this policy is the CCMS, which can also ensure that it is obeyed.

T I P   The HP OmniBack II system is an example of a backup system. It can reach 20GB per hour.

While this type of system is in operation, access to certain records must be blocked so that the records are available for backup. This is implemented in the R/3 system during transaction processing.

> **N O T E**   As the speed of available backup equipment increases, it becomes increasingly feasible to adopt a regime of online backup where the records are copied very frequently. The faster the rate of transactions in a system, the shorter the interval should be between backups to minimize data loss if any part of the system goes offline. Disk mirroring effectively maintains the backup continuously as a faithful replica of the operational storage medium.

Recovering

The tasks of recovering from a disruption and restoring backed up records are subject to the same developments as the backup operation itself. The frequency of operation and the resolution of possible conflicts between old and new records are matters of the utmost importance that have to be controlled by rigid rules programmed into the system.

Promoting Security

The measures taken for backing up and restoring data under controlled conditions after a disruption are clearly central to the maintenance of data security.

The invasion of a system by unauthorized users and unregistered programs has to be prevented at all levels. If the CCMS can indeed monitor the status and performance of all components in the global system, there will be the opportunity to alert the peripheral units of any unexplained irregularities and to measure the extent of the impairment.

A suite of authorization policies and security procedures is obviously essential. It is provided as an integral part of the R/3 system and therefore extends to all SAP applications integrated with it. However, the security, reliability, confidentiality, and integrity of data and programs held in non-SAP satellite systems have to be ensured by paying attention to the details of these specific components.

Exploring SNMP Applications

To report the configuration and status of any system component integrated with the R/3 system, use the SAP MIB system, which is based on the SNMP.

Collecting Data

The data collector interface currently monitors information from the following systems provided by the *Remote Network Monitoring Management Information Bases* (RMON-MIBs) maintained by special network analyzers:

- Ethernet
- Token ring
- FDDI
- ATM

These sources provide network information about the current segment loads and collision rates, for example.

Using EarlyWatch

The purpose of the EarlyWatch system is to monitor a system and detect the possibility of operating problems before they have had time to disrupt production. A team of experts is available to interpret the information gathered through the SAP MIB system using the SNMP. Chapter 28, "Using the Online Service System," discusses this further.

Supporting the Field Service Engineer

The FSSS-Field Service Support System is a notebook-based system that fully integrates with the R/3 system. It was developed by VSG Software with SAP to provide service technicians with critical information. In particular, the parent R/3 system automatically transfers to the notebooks the assigned daily tasks and reconciles the outcomes reported by the engineer.

The engineer has access to important information, such as the details of the reported problem and accurate notification of the hardware and software in use by the internal or external customer at the site to be visited. The notebook may also be downloaded with a technical opinion from a senior engineer as to the possible cause of the trouble and a recommended strategy for troubleshooting. ●

Supporting the Field Service Engineer

P A R T

IV

Steering the Corporation

Understanding the Financial Accounting Module

In this chapter

Introducing the SAP R/3 Financial Accounting Components

The SAP product module FI-Financial Accounting includes a number of components. They can be installed and configured in various combinations to suit the individual implementation.

The SAP FI-Financial Accounting components are discussed in the following sequence, along with some topics relevant to them all:

- FI-GL General Ledger
- FI-AR Accounts Receivable
- FI-AP Accounts Payable
- FI-AA Asset Accounting
- FI-LC Consolidation

Putting Accounting into Perspective

Accounting is a source of support for the people who do things. At its best, it sheds light on the value of what they are doing and the value of the materials they use and those they throw away. It should help them waste less and add more value by using information and skill. Those who have invested in the company will also want to see how things are going. They will want to look at the annual accounts, for a start.

At its worst, accounting is the painful process of collecting a confusing blanket of numbers to throw over an enterprise and is really a waste of time and resources. There is a legal requirement to publish the financial documents, but it might take an expert to figure out just which elements of the business are contributing to the value of the material and information passing through the company, and which aren't.

The possibility—indeed, the necessity for all but the tiniest of firms—of managing the accounts on a computer opens up the chance to make one of two mistakes at the design and implementation stage:

- The first mistake is to overlook the many ways in which the computer can add value to the information and material work items passing through the company. For example, the computer can make sure that the customer is provided with exactly what he needs and is properly billed so that he pays for it. Manual systems can be used to serve this purpose if the person in charge of them is diligent and energetic. By contrast, the computer can be diligent and energetic in business when everything is going according to plan, can detect slow responses on both sides, and can call attention to this imperfection—not simply by ringing an alarm bell, but by gathering the pertinent information and presenting it to a suitable person to make a decision.

- The second mistake in conceiving a computer-assisted accounting system is to assume that it is simply a matter of mechanized books.

The computer can be made to be good at what it does only if it is endowed with impeccable behavior. As far as possible, it must be incorruptible. Entry errors might occur that aren't detected at the time, for example. In such instances, it must be possible to trace the origin of the error, make corrections to the accounting, and perhaps take steps to make this type of error less likely in the future—or at least have it detected at the time. The SAP system takes this moral stand very seriously. Each time a transaction takes place between SAP and the outside world, an SAP document is created and stamped with the date and time. The terminal device signs the document, and the user is obliged to leave his or her identification there too. From this moment of formal entry launching the transaction, there is no further opportunity to annotate or adjust anything illegal; the time-stamped SAP document recording the entry event is locked. Therefore it is best if it is checked before it is launched, and it would be very helpful to append any annotations or explanatory remarks at this stage. There will usually be a choice of standard annotations to cope with most eventualities, plus the possibility of entering free text by way of explanation.

If the transaction is legal but in error, a correcting transaction must be enacted. This too leaves its mark on the audit trail by generating an SAP document.

Accruals are an essential part of modern online accounting. Costs, charges, and possibly profits are linked to the time period and cost or profit center to which they belong, rather than to any general fund. The aim is to reveal the true value to the company of whatever activity is using its resources.

Checking the Data

Checks are made at every stage where an automatic assessment can be made as to whether the information coming in is reasonable. Do the figures balance? Is this transaction legal? Has this decision-maker been authorized to make this choice?

SAP standard business software is built around the aim of providing continuous measurement of the profitability of everything that's going on. Each business function records how often it is used and how long it takes to do its work. And this kind of performance information is available to illuminate any scrutiny of how resources are used.

This sophistication in accounting performance measurement, provided as standard in the SAP systems, is additional to the *Generally Accepted Accounting Principles* (GAAP), but it may well make a very significant difference to the figures on the profit-and-loss account.

The ideal accounting system is able to re-create an unbroken audit trail from each and every transaction to the balance sheet and profit-and-loss account of the company. The auditor should be able to point to any number on the financial documents of the company and ask to see how it was computed, right back to the documents that came from the outside world carrying the information that found its way into the computer.

SAP FI-Financial Accounting can always deliver an unbroken audit trail, because every external and internal transaction creates a record in the form of an SAP document, which can be called to substantiate the audit and prove the credentials of the company's accounts. On this foundation it is possible to demonstrate just how the system is complying with the *Generally*

Accepted Accounting Principles (GAAP) tenets as applied to computerized accounting systems. The GAAP requirements arise from a set of statutory regulations, decrees, and ordinances that embody the experience of the accounting professions and serve as the basis on which each nation may develop additional accounting traditions and requirements.

Accounting Worldwide

SAP International Development is a set of models, one for each geographical area of the world, that enables the SAP system to take account of the rules and practices of the major trading communities.

The INT-International Development module includes the following components:

- IN-APA Asian and Pacific area
- IN-EUR Europe
- IN-NAM North America
- IN-AFM Africa and Middle East
- IN-SAM South America

These modules, fully integrated into the R/3 system during implementation, are additional to the standard R/3 provision for translating screen text and currency values to suit the local language, local currency, and reference languages of the group head office system.

FI-AP Accounts Payable and FI-AR Accounts Receivable are subledgers of the FI-GL General Ledger and are completely integrated with it. They are sometimes referred to as the *personal subledgers* because they contain information associated with customers and vendors and might be subject to rules or customs of privacy and nondisclosure.

The balance sheet has a Receivables account in which line items in customer accounts are subtotaled or totaled. The Payables account in the General Ledger subtotals or totals the line items from the vendor accounts.

Each customer transaction updates the balance of the Receivables account in the General Ledger, and each vendor transaction updates the balance of the Payables account in the General Ledger.

TR-CM Cash Management is concerned with bank balances and cash, usually on a daily basis. The associated subledgers will have accounts in the General Ledger and will therefore be integrated with it. The transactions of the various types of Cash Management include the following functions:

- Reconciling and sorting bank accounts
- Planning short- to medium-term cash requirements and cash investments
- Buying, managing, and selling securities, loans, and time deposits
- Managing foreign exchange

PA-PAY Payroll, FI-AA Asset Accounting, and MM-Materials Management also have subledgers and balance sheet accounts that enable them to integrate with the General Ledger in the same way as Payables and Receivables.

For each of these transactions in the subledgers and the FI-General Ledger, an SAP document is created that can be used to keep track of any element of the transaction details recorded in it. Material code number, asset number, personnel number of the entry clerk—these are all examples of transaction details that can be used to retrieve transactions for analysis.

The FI-General Ledger module also offers some of the facilities of an Extended General Ledger, even if the SAP Extended General Ledger system hasn't been installed. The extended facilities allow you to enter cost data such as cost center, cost unit, and project identification with each transaction.

After each transaction, because the General Ledger will have been updated, you can display or print lists of updates to the balance sheet and profit-and-loss statement. You can also print or display balance sheet reports and any other report of the financial system.

Configuring and Customizing Financial Accounting

The SAP R/3 system with the FI-Financial Accounting application installed will have been configured for a particular country. The features specific to the accounting laws and customs will have been configured to operate correctly.

The system will also have been configured to comply with GAAP.

A typical national chart of accounts will be in place (see Figure 12.1). If you have a multinational installation, the necessary additional charts of accounts will be installed.

If you install another SAP application, the system generates the FI-General Ledger accounts required automatically.

The parameter settings for specific countries will have been adjusted to suit a particular delivery client for your first installation. This is usually treated as your standard SAP client. It is assigned a client code, which ensures that all data and documents are identified as belonging to this client. If you install an application additional to the R/3 system, you can allow the specific parameter settings to be installed in your standard client account. Or you might prefer to create a set of separate client codes, one for each of your individual companies if you have a multinational group.

Exploring the General Ledger

A company's internal accounting system is designed to control costs. Investors in the company will want to know how the company's capital has been assigned in the external accounting system that includes the General Ledger.

FIGURE 12.1
The Client is the unique pinnacle of the enterprise.

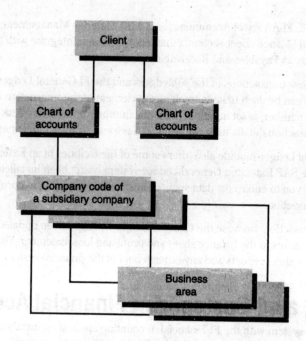

For convenience, the General Ledger is supported by a set of subledgers, including Accounts Receivable, Accounts Payable, Fixed Assets, Human Resources, and Materials (see Figure 12.2). The external accounting system should show what the company is worth.

Using a Chart of Accounts in Common

Following the principle that you should be able to analyze any number that appears on the external account documents by examining its components, the cost accounting system should be supplied with all the expense and revenue entries. Costing data allocated to period or product line also is posted to the General Ledger via a Common Chart of Accounts that is shared by both the financial (external) accounting system and the cost (internal) accounting system.

The General Ledger is a series of account balances. Modern online accounting maintains the General Ledger balances continuously. Data that has been entered and posted is posted immediately to the General Ledger and also to the CO-Controlling system if it has been installed. The balance sheet and the profit-and-loss account are based on the General Ledger.

The accounts named in the General Ledger are called—no surprise—*General Ledger accounts.* One or more General Ledger account balances can be derived from a corresponding subledger specified in the chart of accounts.

An Extended General Ledger uses accounts that are based on a range of subledgers that allow analyses from different points of view. For example, accounts might focus on cost centers, product costs, or activities. These options are provided by using the CO-Controlling system as an internal accounting system. Entered data posted to the General Ledger is posted to the CO system and its components as part of the Extended General Ledger.

FIGURE 12.2

The Enterprise Data Model can represent all the business objects and processes, and their interrelationships.

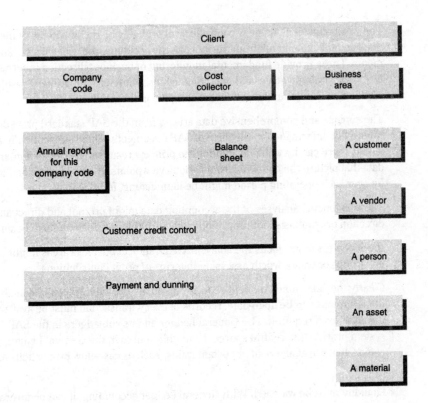

Integrating Accounting Through the General Ledger

The General Ledger is the source from which the external accounting documents, the balance sheet, and the profit-and-loss statement are built. Because this information is to be audited, it must be supported by audit trails that show how each summary total is computed. If a complete audit trail exists, there is also the possibility of using that information to make some decisions before the end-of-year results are computed.

Making interim decisions on the basis of accounting information is the province of business controlling, for which the SAP CO-Controlling module has been developed. This is examined at length in Chapter 13, "Understanding the Controlling Module."

Controlling depends on detailed record-keeping in which the individual transactions retain their identity, their date, their sources, and the identification of the users who worked on them. Only if the accounting information is retained in this fine detail can the controlling functions assemble it and manipulate it to find out what is happening in the business. If the decision-makers cannot establish what is happening, they will be prone to take no action when they should, take action when they shouldn't, or take with complete enthusiasm the wrong action.

The work units of a business controller will probably be the line items of the business transactions and the statements from the journal, the accounts, the trial balance, and the final statements. These provide fundamental monitoring of business direction in terms of movement and progress, strategic goals, and operating tactics. These are the primary results achieved as a result of investing human and financial capital in the company.

The copious and comprehensive data arising from the SAP standard procedure of capturing all transaction information in the form of SAP documents can be subsequently analyzed. For example, there can be valuable additions to primary results in the form of interpretations of the data that picture the company from various viewpoints. A look at profit and loss for each activity over each operating period might be illuminating, for example.

These additional analyses of the accounting data might prompt and direct an interim change of direction or emphasis, but they might also form the essential inputs to business planning.

Profit centers might focus the analysis. Geographical business areas might be of interest. Product groups often are worth assessing in terms of profit contributions.

Clearly the data should be held centrally if you are seeking widespread analyses. If you want the information to be up-to-date, records of every transaction must be available to contribute to the analyses if required. The General Ledger and its subledgers in the SAP online accounting system provide this central source. From this source in the General Ledger, you can extract comprehensive analyses of important ratios, such as cash-flow proportions and workload per person.

Liquidity must be watched. With General Ledger accounting, it can be forecast by looking at projected cash disbursements and receipts in the short and medium

Planning the Finance   If a business plan has been created in the SAP system and efficient tools are available to assist, the actual results can be compared to planned ones in whatever dimensions and ratios are of interest.

Planning that's integrated across an entire company must include plans for the balance sheet and the profit-and-loss (P&L) statements. Cash plans are required that include project receipts and payments.

Controls over the ongoing activities of the company will begin by comparing the balance sheet and the P&L statements year on year. Short-term cash management using projected cash payments and receipts and a daily financial statement may be essential. Control of ongoing business can also make good use of financial analyses, comparisons, and ratios based on the organization's structure in terms of business areas or units.

Interpreting Subledgers   Subledgers can be the means by which control is exercised over the entities they represent. Receivables and payables can be managed by inspecting analyses of due dates, amounts, selected customers, regions, and so on. Assets may attract the attention of controllers because of automatic reports of their ratios, depreciation, capitalized cost, and net book value. Inventory transactions, invoices, and personnel expenses are other examples of aspects of a business that can be made available to controllers, because the SAP system has the unbreakable habit of capturing all transactions from all system components in the form of SAP documents that can be collated and analyzed into whatever informative structure is logically feasible.

The logical qualification is an obvious reminder that data that hasn't been entered into the SAP system at some stage or other cannot take part in subsequent analyses. If, however, the necessary primary data is in the system, automatic profit-and-loss information can be computed. Overheads can be monitored and attributed to such headings as Cost Center and Order Settlement. Product cost accounting can shed light on the costs of ongoing jobs. Technical and commercial projects can be monitored, controlled, and brought into the plans. Profitability analyses will be possible on the basis of cost of sales and period accounting.

At any time it is possible to clear individual line items in business transactions and reconcile separate controlling units with the General Ledger.

Following the General Ledger Accounting Routine

Each business transaction creates a record in the format of an SAP document. The transaction might be part of a batch input or the result of a dialogue transaction at a terminal. The transaction is checked and validated as far as possible and returned for correction if necessary.

When the transaction is posted, it is stored on the Record log as an SAP document. The system updates the Daily Journal file and posts the transaction to the appropriate reconciliation account of the General Ledger. At that moment, the related account balances, trial balances, balance sheet, and P&L statement reports are accessible onscreen.

Special document types and posting keys provide access to particular types of transactions:

- Customer or vendor invoices
- Cash receipts and disbursements
- Inventory transactions
- Allocations or distributions for cost accounting
- Transactions involving two or more profit centers
- Transactions involving two or more company codes
- Statistical postings (noted items, guarantees, and so on)
- Special business transactions (down payments, bills of exchange, and so on)

Entering and posting a transaction document immediately updates both financial accounting and cost accounting. The General Ledger and its subledgers use the information, and so do the cost analyses that are elaborated from the data.

The Transaction log is available to feed the General Ledger and the subsystems managing asset accounting, inventory accounting, cost accounting, order and project accounting, product costing, profitability analysis, and the subledgers of Accounts Receivable and Payable. And from any or all of this, the finance and controlling information system can extract and present whatever primary or derived information is required.

Integrated real-time bookkeeping ensures that verified data is available for processing in all areas at once by automatically clearing cost accounting transactions in the General Ledger and its subledgers.

The financial and cost accounting systems are constantly reconciled at the level of the individual General Ledger accounts. These accounts are named in the Common Chart of Accounts.

Working with the Chart of Accounts

The Chart of Accounts is used to configure any account in the General Ledger so that it serves two purposes:

- Permits entry of transaction details required by the business
- Provides for any balance sheet or profit-and-loss statement required by law

The business will want to plan and operate some logistic processes—and exercise financial control. The law demands proper external accounting practice so that shareholders can value their holdings and see that taxes are paid.

The processes of the business can be classified broadly according to the focus of the activities and their managers. The first group of General Ledger accounts monitors activities concerned with building the productive resources of the company:

- Procurement of investment items such as fixed assets, current assets, and financial assets
- Extraordinary expenses or revenues

The next group of accounts deals with how the day-to-day production and processing activities affect the value of the company:

- Procurement of materials
- Consumption of company resources
- Valuation of finished or semifinished products

The third group is of activities with their own accounts in the General Ledger to show how sales of products are set against costs to yield the financial statements:

- Sales revenue or sales deductions
- Closing to balance sheet and profit-and-loss statement

Using Account Classes

External accounting balances are classified into account classes using the Chart of Accounts:

- Fixed assets and long-term capital
- Finances, current assets, short-term capital
- Nonoperating expense and revenue
- Materials or stock

- Primary cost elements
- Secondary cost elements
- Job order cost elements
- Stock of finished and semifinished products
- Yield or changes to stock or capitalized internal activity
- Closing balances

Using Internal Controlling Account Classes

Controlling balances arrived at by internal accounting fall into four categories according to their purpose. *Project cost settlement* or *job order costing* allows for purchases and allocations of resources that have to be made to carry out projects and complete specific job orders that might not yield any financial return during the current accounting period. These costs are therefore treated as investments.

Cost center accounting is used to gather specified types of cost under the heading, which is most useful for business purposes. These cost centers may correspond to departments or be used to associate costs with a specific plant or item of equipment that's considered as a focus for understanding and managing the enterprise.

Job order or *product costing* is the traditional process of associating costs with specific orders from customers or for internal production work—the manufacture of goods for inventory is a common example.

Profitability analysis is the process of relating the financial yield of part of the enterprise to the costs of owning and running it. There are no restrictions on how the parts to be analyzed are defined. The profitability of a work unit might be of interest, or the value of carrying out a change of procedure might be the target. The wisdom of all business decisions might have to be assessed in relation to the short- and long-term profitability of the consequences.

The Common Chart of Accounts can both record all the costs and revenues and also provide all the factors needed for financial control via internal accounting; this demonstrates the integration of accounting.

The Chart of Accounts installed in a specific implementation must comply with statutory requirements under company law as it is practiced in the host country. It must also embody the essential elements of GAAP, the accounting principles that set the standard for a reliable accounting system.

Differentiating the Two Primary Functions of the General Ledger

The FI-GL General Ledger component recognizes the two main reasons for asking for reports from a General Ledger.

Monitoring Financial Health   Shareholders might be very interested in the financial statements required by law—the balance sheet and the profit-and-loss statement. These two financial documents are the basis of external accounting, because they reveal the financial health of a company.

The profit-and-loss computations depend on closing the accounts in the General Ledger at the end of the financial year. One primary function of the General Ledger is to allow this year-end closing to take place orderly.

Reviewing the Results for the Year   The other primary function of the General Ledger is financial accounting for the current fiscal year.

The function of collecting and recording data from transactions is one part of financial accounting. Posting data and reconciling on a continuous basis make up the other part.

The SAP system creates a document for each transaction that can be used for a flexible reporting and analysis system, with the capability to establish a valid audit trail using these recorded transaction documents.

Reconciliation is performed at the transaction level before an entry is posted, but there has to be a closing of the reconciliation accounts at the end of the month and then at the end of the year. A facility exists in R/3 to call up daily or monthly reports at any time.

Posting Special General Ledger Transactions

The accounts in the Special General Ledger are reconciliation accounts for special subledger transactions that don't directly involve sales or purchases and may not be balanced with the receivables and payables. The Special General Ledger indicator is a single-character code to distinguish these transactions from sales to customers or purchases from vendors. The following transaction types are examples of Special General Ledger transactions:

Acquisitions	Down payments
Dispositions	Bills of exchange
Depreciation	Monthly payroll
Transfers	Period closing entries

Year-End Closing

The law for closing a fiscal year requires entries to closing accounts for the balance sheet and profit-and-loss statement. The SAP FI system ensures that year-end closing entries are transferred from subledgers such as Accounts Receivable, Accounts Payable, and Fixed Assets.

Provision is also made for closing entries manually and individually. You can close a fiscal year at any time. The flexible online reporting system offers separate formats of the financial documents for tax authorities, stockholders, legal consolidation of associated companies, and so on.

Forming Complex Organizations with the Chart of Accounts

The Chart of Accounts has to include all the General Ledger accounts in an accounting system. You can specify what transaction data goes where so that each account contains all the required details for closing. Internal accounting usually requires that certain types of data be sent to each account used in the controlling functions.

There are two possibilities for using a Common Chart of Accounts in a complex organization:

- You can have a centralized organization that has the maximum number of accounts at group level in a uniform Chart of Accounts that applies to all company codes in the group.
- You can be a decentralized organization in which each company code has its own chart of accounts.

In either case, it is possible to use sample accounts taken from the reference system with transfer rules for individual company codes. This allows each company to have some flexibility while operating to a Common Chart of Accounts.

Exploring International Taxation

The SAP system is international. The taxation functions commonly needed have been programmed as standard business functions with tables of parameters available for customization to the organization and to the specific operational features required.

When you use the SAP system, you will have signified the country where your company is located and, if prompted, the country where your vendor or customer is located. The system adopts the taxation regimes appropriate to each country.

The system calculates tax or adjusts it automatically. When you enter the transaction, you cause the system to create the SAP document containing all the details. Then it immediately posts the taxes as it updates the accounts. The required tax reports are generated automatically.

Calling Standard Taxation Functions   The FI-Financial Accounting module includes the following standard international taxation functions:

- Taxes on sales and purchases
- Bills of exchange tax
- Tax base for tax calculation
- Definitions of all required tax rates
- Methods for the determination of due dates for tax payment
- Tax-calculation procedures
- Tax base for cash discount
- Dependent taxes as surcharges or deductions
- European Community acquisition tax
- Division into deductible and nondeductible taxes

Withholding tax can be programmed to suit your requirements. The process uses the following functions:

- Tax base
- Definition of all required tax rates

- Flagging of all vendors affected
- Determination of due dates for tax payments

The system verifies withholding tax when you enter a vendor invoice and payment; you don't have to check the tax entries later. The necessary reports are prepared automatically.

Although the system adopts the appropriate standard tax regime as soon as you indicate the country, you can adjust parameters to meet your specific tax requirements. For example, you might have to make adjustments to the standard procedure because of a change in the national taxation regulations, or because you are working in a country that doesn't exactly follow any of the standard tax regimes programmed into the system.

Country-specific tax requirements are notified in the SAP INT-International component and may be used to customize your particular implementation.

Examining Country-Specific Taxation Requirements   Specific taxation rules for charging, disclosing, and paying tax are accommodated by customizing each company code operating in that country. Specific forms of payment and common payment media are prepared for each country.

The following examples illustrate the range of differences that can be handled by the system:

- German-speaking countries in Europe require a tax adjustment if the payment for an invoice is net of cash discount. Other countries calculate tax liability on the invoiced amount.
- Different countries have their own arrangements for tax exemptions and delay of liability.
- Withholding tax is subject to wide differences in scope and method.

Supporting Intercompany Accounting

A group containing two or more individual companies will have an organizational structure designed to facilitate day-to-day operations. For example, each company might buy material and manage a warehouse. Each might run a Sales and Distribution division. To increase the complexity of the organization somewhat, suppose that there is also a head office that functions as a separate company. The head office, as a company, might have oversight of two other companies. Each business unit will incur expenses and probably enjoy revenue.

For the sake of business convenience, two or even three of these units might combine to make a purchase, perhaps at a discount because of the size of the order. One payment to the vendor is made against one invoice.

Again for good business reasons, the units might join forces to provide a service to a customer. For example, Purchasing might provide the material goods, and Distribution might look after their delivery. Again, one payment from the customer is made against one invoice.

If each business unit is managed as an individual company, all intercompany transactions within the group and with customers and vendors must obey the rules of intercompany accounting. In particular, transactions must leave records that allow intercompany business to be legally audited to give a true picture of the group as a whole and of the individual companies when it comes to drawing up the financial documents.

With modern online computerized accounting systems, the balance sheets and the profit-and-loss statements of the group and each individual company are readily available at any time. The principles of intercompany accounting are applied when your company is part of a group; they also apply when your customer or your vendor is part of another group.

The SAP accounting system uses methods that support intercompany transactions and complies with GAAP.

Posting Intercompany Expense and Revenue   Two divisions of a group, each with a separate company code, may jointly make a purchase or issue goods. (The same principles apply if more than two company codes are involved.)

You have to enter and post the expense item in both company codes, but you post only one vendor account in one of the company codes (it doesn't matter which one). The system automatically calculates and posts the receivables and payables between company codes, just as if you were entering a regular transaction in one company code.

The system creates line items for receivables and payables between company codes. It also generates an SAP document in each company code. As it does so, it assigns a unique intercompany transaction number, which appears on all documents and vouchers.

The debits don't have to equal the credits in each company code. Only within the entire intercompany transaction do they have to balance.

Paying for Intercompany Purchases   Several companies in a group may purchase from the same vendor. You can pay for the purchase by making a single payment, with the vendor account number being the same in the vendor master record in each company in the group. One company has to keep a central bank account to be used to pay on behalf of the other companies.

Issuing Cash Receipts for Two or More Company Codes

Some companies in a group may have customers in common. If one of these customers offers payment for two or more company codes in the group, you can use this procedure:

1. Match open items to the amount of the payment.
2. Process the selected items, sharing the payments flexibly if necessary.
3. Apply cash discount calculations in each company.
4. Clear documents for each company.

The system automatically posts the required clearing account in each company.

Separating Head Office and Branch Accounts

Your supplier might be a branch with its own account, but its head office might want to receive your payment. In this case, you can enter its head office account number in the master record for the branch vendor. When you enter a transaction to the branch account, the system posts the transaction to the head office account, leaving a cleared entry on the branch account to show who supplied the goods or service.

The master includes data about the branch and a reference to another master to give details of the head office. By this means, dunning letters can be sent to the head office, the branch, or both for overdue refunds, for example.

Making Vendor Payments to an Alternative Recipient

Your supplier might not have to deal with its payments due. For example, it might have a head office that receives payment. You can record in its master data the account number of this alternative recipient. The system then processes return transfers and other vendor payment business through the banks to the alternative recipient.

If you do post vendor invoices to an affiliate, you have to record in the master data of the branch vendor a group-wide company account number that will be used during consolidation to eliminate the invoices that would otherwise appear twice in the company accounts. The system can look at the transaction documents bearing this group-wide company account number and identify any replicated entries, because the payment was made to an affiliate that was not the original vendor.

Recording Intercompany Payments

One vendor might have supplied several company codes in the same group. The payment system can make one payment and then settle the intercompany accounts by calculating and posting receivables and payables between company codes.

The transaction needs you to define one of the company codes and enter it as a normal paying company. The system assigns the document a unique intercompany identification number, which is used to ensure that the other members of the company code group pay their shares.

Eliminating Intercompany Payables and Receivables

FI-Financial Accounting eliminates intercompany balances by open item only if each trading partner is marked in the vendor master record. You must also ensure that the reporting procedures inform the consolidating department of the numbers of these trading partners, at least on the items relating to intercompany payables, receivables, revenues, and expenses.

The law requires that all intercompany balances be eliminated before presenting the balance sheet and profit-and-loss statement. All possible pairs of individual companies must be investigated for evidence that they have been trading with each other.

In practice, significant differences between the way individual companies keep their records may make complete elimination impractical. Here are the most frequent causes of discrepancies in elimination:

- Currency translation differences
- Differences in the timing of entries for goods in transit between individual companies
- Specific reserves set aside for doubtful accounts
- Liabilities that aren't acknowledged in the records

The most difficult-to-handle cause is currency translation; the others can usually be resolved by applying corporate policies in a thoroughgoing manner.

If the individual companies have installed and configured SAP accounting applications, there will be automatic dual currency accounting in which every transaction is documented, at the time it occurs, in both the local currency and the currency designated for all transactions in the group.

If the FI-LC Consolidation component has been installed and configured in your company, it allows you to trace any currency translation differences between the local currency, at the prevailing rate of exchange, and the transaction currency. An exchange rate difference correction then is posted automatically in the balance sheet account designated for this purpose, and thus brought into the consolidated financial statement.

Recognizing Language Differences

Because R/3 is an international system, the names of all General Ledger accounts can be translated if the language key is entered together with the name of the account in the target language. This process can be repeated for all languages in the group. This way, you may add or modify General Ledger account names in the language of the holding company, and later log on and call for the account balances in the language of your logon profile.

In a listing of the Charts of Accounts, each chart is annotated to show the main language and all alternatives available.

Manipulating Currencies

The following operational currencies have been defined, and their codes are assigned to each function by default (you can alter the default settings):

- Local currency is also the reporting currency for the company code.
- Document currency is that specified for entry on SAP documents.
- Group currency is an alternative to document currency for group reporting.
- Updating currency is defined for posting debits and credits to the General Ledger in parallel with the local currency.
- Credit limit currency is what is chosen to maintain the credit limit.
- Ledger currency is an alternative to the updating currency for that ledger.

Additional currency assignments are available in the SAP Foreign Exchange Management component.

Managing Currencies in Transactions

Each company code has a local currency for reporting. The system records amounts in this local currency and also in a currency specified as the document currency, which is used on all documents in addition to the local currency.

NOTE You can enter documents in any currency. ▉

You have two options for converting currencies:

- ▉ Enter an exchange rate when you enter the transaction document.
- ▉ The system translates between document and local currencies by referring to a table of daily exchange rates that is updated manually or maintained automatically by a link to a separate database.

The system can be customized in various ways:

- ▉ A specific user enters amounts in a particular currency, which can be the local currency or the document currency.
- ▉ A specific user can be permitted to enter amounts in either local or document currency.

Whatever the customizing arrangements, the system displays amounts in both local and document currencies. It rounds off minor differences, using rules established for this purpose. These differences can occur when several line items are converted and then added in both currencies.

Customer monthly debits and credits are kept by the system only in local currency. The reconciliation account for the Accounts Receivable subledger is kept in local currency and in all the other posted currencies.

Dealing with Currency Exchange Differences

A line item can be expressed in a currency other than the local or document currency. You can enter payments to clear such foreign currency line items by using either local or document currency.

The payment expressed in the document currency will have been converted from the local currency at an exchange rate adopted by the system according to the rules set for assigning the daily exchange rate. If this rate has changed from the rate prevailing when the invoice was written, the payment amount might not match the open item amount. In such cases, the system automatically calculates and posts an exchange-difference entry to a separate account established for this purpose.

Establishing General Ledger Master Data

General Ledger master data includes the data shown in Table 12.1.

Table 12.1   Account Identification Information
General Data About Each Account
Account number
Account name
Type of General Ledger account
Data for Each Company Code
Currency
Whether managed on an open item basis
Sort basis when line items are displayed

You can enter this master data through the FI system for each account separately or by groups of accounts. Your installation might have a configured SAP data interface to allow direct input of master data under certain conditions.

Maintaining General Ledger Master Data   Accounts can be added to the General Ledger, and certain parameters can be modified. You can block and delete accounts during the fiscal year. As in all SAP R/3 directories, match codes set up by the individual user can be used to find specific accounts by entering an easily remembered name or title.

Your activities with General Ledger accounts are logged, as are all transactions, so that all modifications can be traced.

Administering General Ledger Accounts   An *open item* is one can that can be partially settled; it remains open until the item is fully cleared. If an item isn't to be managed on an open-item basis, the settlement has to be in full or not at all. Rules can be established—for example, in the partial payment of accounts outstanding, to determine that the largest items should be settled first, or perhaps those that have been open the longest. Such manipulations might not be permitted in some General Ledger accounts, because that would destroy their informative nature.

By and large, if you have the authority to manipulate the General Ledger accounts, you won't have any restrictions—only obligations.

Some accounts are allowed to display to anyone the line items on which they are based—payroll usually isn't one of them.

Another example of instructions attaching to a data object representing a General Ledger account is how the line items are displayed—their sort order and perhaps any masks applied to conceal certain values.

Keeping Daily Journals and Interim Statements   When it is time for year-end closing, SAP programs are available to help you prepare your system to be closed. But daily and monthly closings have no special requirements and no extra entries to make, because the account balances are maintained all the time.

At the end of each day, you can see a report of the exact closing balances for the day. These are based on the line items and the total debits and credits entered.

For periods of a day or more, it is easy to ask for reports of data that have been posted over the period, sorted by date or by any of the fields that appear in the relevant SAP documents that were created for the transactions.

The practice of calling daily or short-period journals can be helpful. You can validate data entry soon after it occurs, so you can control it.

These journals can help you decide how to close posting periods and account for accruals. You might want to define two accounting periods that are open for this purpose.

Preparing Year-End Closing   Monthly and interim closings entail no technical requirements. Year-end closing, however, has to be anticipated by running a series of SAP programs. The operation of these year-end programs is automatic to a large extent. These year-end programs serve two main purposes: They reorganize SAP documents into more convenient groupings, and they reconcile summary records with the individual documents on which they are based.

Year-End Closing Tasks   The year-end closing sequence has to include the following steps:

1. Close posting periods.
2. Revalue all line items and General Ledger account balances to adjust for foreign currencies.
3. Sort open and closed receivables by their due dates.
4. Sort open and closed payables by their due dates.
5. Identify and adjust vendor accounts with debit.
6. Identify and adjust customer accounts with credit balances.
7. Post reevaluations.
8. Post adjustments.
9. Post accruals.
10. Print the balance sheet with the profit-and-loss statement.

Automatic Closing   Automatic closing programs compile a series of reports that will support you by preparing what you will need to close the year. These supporting reports include

▓ Reconciliations of documents with monthly debits and credits

▓ Posting totals

▓ Accumulated balance trail

▓ Balances carried forward from the balance sheet of the previous year

Reporting from the General Ledger   The main reports in the General Ledger are available online with a range of sorting and presentation options to help in year-end closing and final reporting:

- Account Statements
- Document Journal
- Balance Sheet with Profit-and-Loss Statement
- Balance Sheet Adjustments
- Reconciliation of Documents with Monthly Debits and Credits
- Posting Totals
- Customer Open Items
- Overdue Receivables
- Customer Open Items by General Ledger Indicator Code
- Line-Item Journal
- General Ledger
- Accumulated Balance Audit Trial
- Vendor Open Items
- Accounts Payable in Local Currency
- Open Checks
- Chart of Accounts
- Bill of Exchange Register

Using Financial Statement Report Formats   The balance sheet is always printed with the profit-and-loss statement. Together they satisfy the legal requirement for a company to publish an annual financial statement.

The essential components of the company financial statement are

- Fixed assets
- Current assets
- Equity
- Debt
- Profit-and-loss statement

These essential requirements relate to the basic elements of the Chart of Accounts from which the financial statement is constructed.

A complex company is required by law to present a financial statement for each of its components separately and a consolidated statement for the group or company as a whole.

There may be a different chart of accounts for each company in a group. SAP FI-GL General Ledger allows all these variations of organizational structure to be accommodated when preparing the financial statement.

The process of designing or customizing the format of the balance sheet and the profit-and-loss statement entails specifying the following details for each account:

- Levels of account detail
- Headings and subheadings
- Text
- Subtotaling and totaling

Separate formats can be designed according to the target readership of the financial documents:

- Stockholders and tax authorities
- Group requirements
- Profit centers

Balances on all accounts are always current. Therefore, a profit-and-loss statement can be prepared at any time, as can a balance sheet.

Extra facilities have been provided as extensions to the functions that allow financial statements to be drafted in a wide range of formats to suit all types of company organizations. These facilities have been integrated and placed under the control of a sophisticated user interface.

The EC-EIS Enterprise Controlling-Executive Information System is an SAP tool that's under continual development and improvement in order to give the SAP R/3 user a comprehensive, integrated, online reporting system that offers all the functions that can be exercised on the accounting system.

Understanding the Extended General Ledger Component

For historical and legal reasons, the General Ledger has been the primary means by which an auditor or an investor can see how well or badly a company has been managed. The results of this management are extracted to form the balance sheet, showing the end-of-year value of the company's assets and the trading report or profit-and-loss statement, revealing how the assets have been set to work for profit or have diminished through losses. The General Ledger is thus the basis for external accounting, but it won't show all the useful information that has been collected in the course of the trading year, such as who bought what.

The manager has to submit to the procedures of internal accounting to see more closely how resources may be better applied. Perhaps it is informative if the financial summaries contain breakdowns of activities by geographical business areas, type of business, product, and so on. These other ways of collating business information for the benefit of exercising better control of a company are provided with standard business functions and collected as the CO-Controlling module.

The FI-Financial module primarily serves the requirements of external accounting. The CO-Controlling module serves internal accounting. They both serve the same company by sharing a Common Chart of Accounts that includes accounts that aren't necessary to meet the legal requirements of the financial statement—those requirements that are met by the General Ledger, from which the balance sheet and the profit-and-loss statement are derived.

These extra accounts are there to improve the usefulness of the financial system in the matter of controlling the company.

The FI-GL General Ledger accounts plus these extra accounts and account subtotals comprise the FI-GLX Extended General Ledger.

The General Ledger is extended by being integrated with the Common Chart of Accounts in order to take advantage of the facilities offered by the CO-Controlling modules.

Although the Controlling system is specialized for internal accounting procedures, its effect is to maximize the favorable values and minimize the unfavorable values that are summarized in the formal legal documents of external accounting—namely, the balance sheet and the profit-and-loss statement. After all, the company's purpose is to make money from its activities and its use of the capital invested in it. The CO-Controlling module represents a comprehensive application of the SAP system to all the elements of a company's business.

Exploring the GLX Standalone Extended General Ledger

The Extended General Ledger is an SAP product that can stand alone and accept data from external systems using software from other suppliers. It can also be installed to integrate with the SAP R/3 system and interact with components of the FI-Financial module and the CO-Controlling module. Directly or via the CO-Controlling module, the Extended General Ledger module can link up with any SAP R/3 components.

The bridge between other applications and the Extended General Ledger consists of one or more ledgers. Not all transaction data from other applications will find a corresponding account in the Extended General Ledger. The system ensures that updates from another application correspond with at least one ledger. A standard program is supplied with the Extended General Ledger to check that this reconciliation is in fact taking place.

You can reconcile the Extended General Ledger with the transaction data at any time.

Planning in the FI-GLX Extended General Ledger

The plan consists of three operations and a reporting stage that can occur at any time and be repeated as often as required:

- **Specify planning objects.** The first step is to set out the planning cost objects or levels at which planning is to take place, such as business area, cost centers, General Ledger accounts, and months or other posting periods.

- **Assigning values.** Entering target values and budgets to be assigned to the planning cost objects can be done manually or with assistance from automatic-distribution functions.

■ **Collating data.** Collecting transaction data and collating it to match planning levels and objects is the most intensive operation in terms of information flow.

■ **Reporting.** The standard SAP R/3 flexible reporting functions show you, for any combinations of planning cost objects that you require, how actual values stand up against plans and targets.

Any or all of these procedures can be automated by setting parameters under control of the Extended General Ledger component.

Using the Extended General Ledger

The following actions can be carried out through the Extended General Ledger program:

■ Specify General Ledger account subtotals to collect data on chosen periods or another focus of interest.

■ Name the account subtotals.

■ Specify the criteria for posting entries to each subtotal.

■ Record and update account subtotals from the transaction information entered in SAP documents.

■ Accept data from other SAP applications.

■ Accept data from systems that don't use SAP software.

■ Enter financial plans in the form of planned values for each relevant account and account subtotal of the Extended General Ledger.

■ Report on the planned and actual account totals and subtotals for the period or other focus of interest.

■ Design reports based on flexible fiscal years.

■ Provide parallel reports in up to three currencies.

Specifying Inflow of Data to the Extended General Ledger

Data reaching the Extended General Ledger system will have arisen mainly by transactions in other systems, other SAP applications, or systems provided by other suppliers. SAP provides a comprehensive suite of standard interfaces.

The flow can take place immediately after a transaction is posted, at regular intervals, or via batch transfers. Validation can take place to ensure that the incoming data complies with the conditions imposed by the Extended General Ledger. Substitution of transaction data can take place so that what is retained can be further processed by the client systems using the facilities provided by the Extended General Ledger module.

Checking for consistency has to occur. For example, master data in the Extended General Ledger must have elements to name and specify all the data objects that will be needed and that will be used to store data incoming from the associated applications. Account identification, cost center, product identification, and any other attribute of interest will have to find a place in the Extended General Ledger from which it can be retrieved and identified—even though, in the case of non-SAP systems, it may no longer be easily traced in the system that first created it.

One solution is to have the Extended General Ledger acquire master data from the transferring system. This imposes the requirement that transactions in the transferring system include all the information of interest as either optional or required entries. Obviously, information that hasn't been collected by the transferring system cannot subsequently be accessed from the Extended General Ledger.

A set of master data shared by all applications ensures consistency of data across all systems using the Extended General Ledger.

From other SAP R/3 applications, the preliminaries to data transfer include establishing the following specifications:

- Which transactions will update the Extended General Ledger. Sources might include financial accounting, material management, or job order accounting.
- Which particular ledger is to be updated, and how.
- Whether each ledger is to be updated immediately or at regular intervals.

SAP R/3 provides guidance and prompting to enable you to set up the validation rules in each case, based on rules and combinations of fields that you can define. The system then validates transaction data, subtotals, or totals in the ledgers specified.

It is usual to have other SAP applications automatically transfer the data for the Extended General Ledger. A direct data-entry function is also provided to allow the entry of notes or consolidation entries, for example. As is normal practice, these entries create SAP documents, which can be flagged to show that they are records of direct entries to the Extended General Ledger and, if necessary, may be displayed separately.

Making Assessments in the Extended General Ledger

In this context, *assessment* refers to the process of gathering cost information from a number of sources. Consider freight charges across all warehouses for all products in a particular group, or on a particular list of products. Assessment is the process of seeking out the details and calculating the total of these charges.

This task is in the province of the Extended General Ledger. Needless to say, it won't succeed if the master data of the Extended General Ledger makes no mention of freight charges or any data field that could be used to make a proper substitution—delivery charges, for example.

Performing Distribution in the Extended General Ledger

Distribution is sharing. For example, the total of freight charges across the group may be distributed by sharing it as some kind of overhead charge imposed by the accounting system. Who should share this burden might be hotly debated, but in the end the Extended General Ledger will have to be told to divide this cost between various accounts.

There are two types of distribution:

- Single-dimension
- More than one dimension or level of detail

Single-dimension distribution takes place when a value is credited to the sender and debited to a single receiving account. For example, a cost center can be created to allow certain costs to be reported under the name of that center. Administration Costs might be the name of a cost center; Freight Costs might be another.

Distribution can also be directed at more than one receiving entity. The set of recipients might include all production departments. The costs can be distributed across specific products in a product group, for example.

Whether the distribution is to a single receiver (such as a cost center) or to a set of receivers, there are three methods of computing how much is attributed to each:

- **Fixed-amount method.** You decide how much to charge each individual recipient. A fixed amount is debited to each, and the sender is credited with the total.

- **Fixed-share method.** You decide what percentage share of the amount to be distributed is charged to each recipient. Each recipient is debited with the fixed share, and the sender is credited with the total of these shares, which doesn't need to equal 100 percent of the assessed charge. The sender may retain a share.

- **Dynamic method.** The amount to be distributed is calculated by the system on the basis of the subtotals already recorded in the Extended General Ledger.

Interpreting the Set Concept

The logical concept of a set is used in the Extended General Ledger for reporting, planning, and ledger processing. A *set* refers to a data structure and its relationships with other data structures. A set of numbers may be defined, where the numbers are the identification codes of bank accounts, for example. A list of cost centers may constitute a set.

The actual members of a set may not be known until the set definition is called into use. "The top three operating divisions for gaining new customers in the current month" is a set definition of this kind. The definition of a set may include relationships between specific firms or companies in a group, not necessarily at the same level. A set may contain any collection of data objects that meet the logical criteria forming the definition for membership of that set.

Specific business functions may call on a set definition that has been stored for use later. Assessment and distribution often take place under the control of sets.

Posting Planned Amounts in the Extended General Ledger

The basic concept is to set target values for account totals or subtotals for one or more periods. Actual values totaled from the transaction data then are compared with these planned targets.

The method is to enter a planned total and then have it allocated to periods by various standard functions. Flexible planning and controlling facilities are provided through special functions and tools in the Extended General Ledger.

In practice, the planning usually requires several iterations in which suggested budgets and target values are distributed in various ways until a proper distribution system is determined. The starting point for a plan is a set of plan parameters:

- Basic data and targets to be entered
- Planned currency for transactions, and the local and group currencies
- Planned types of main and additional quantities
- Standard period allocation keys
- Input units (hundreds, thousands, millions)
- Planned number of decimal places
- Plan version identification
- Data objects to be used

The plan parameters depend on the authorization profiles of the users. Not all users are allowed to alter certain parameters.

You can specify for display at any time sets of plan parameters to be used as the basis for planning and for suggesting more appropriate amounts to be set as targets.

Using Planning Perspectives

Centralized planning entails planning cost elements—for example, for all cost centers. Decentralized planning deals with each cost center individually.

The Extended General Ledger allows both perspectives, and you can switch between perspectives online.

The technique of setting up plan parameters allows the planning process to begin with a complete plan that can be used without altering anything. On the other hand, any of the parameter values can be changed if the user is so authorized. The distribution functions can be changed, as can the sets of account totals and subtotals on which they act. Individual amounts may be overwritten.

Each version of a plan can be stored for later comparison.

There are many standard ways of distributing planned amounts. Annual or quarterly input values are usually distributed to planning periods by using one or more distribution keys.

A *distribution key* is a tag or code that can be used simply as a label, or it can refer to a complex data object that serves as a distribution formula. There is a standard distribution key for allotting an amount equally to every working day in the current month, for example. SAP R/3 offers a wide variety of standard distribution keys, and the user can define unique keys available for use with other planning periods or other versions of the plan.

There are distribution keys for use with various planning objects such as sales, personnel expenses, and so on. There are standard keys for product groups and for product types such as "semifinished products." Such keys can be used to plan for production cost centers so that, in this example, the value of semifinished products appears in the Extended General Ledger reports under that heading and also attracts a designated share of the cost of warehousing or other assessments.

This system of distribution keys can be used with the suite of distribution functions and the logical concept of sets to arrange for a flexible and focused planning system that can be adjusted to suit changing business conditions.

Manipulating Reporting Dimensions

The reporting system of the Extended General Ledger is particularly flexible. You can use it to report by any field already defined for accumulating subtotals.

Installations of SAP R/3 vary according to customer needs, but there may be account subtotals for planned data and actual data, for product groups and business areas, for individual products, and for cost centers. Many permutations could make business sense for a particular user. Even the choice of time period may be an important matter for individual purposes. SAP R/3 can work with up to 365 time periods a year.

There are standard reports for the main tasks:

- Reconciling and controlling account subtotals
- Providing an audit trail for internal and external auditors

Report Design   Report design takes place with the aid of a menu-driven system that applies predefined system standards.

You can accept the details suggested by the system by copying from another report and changing some of the details individually onscreen. You can specify the content and layout in advance by changing the parameters of an existing customized report, or modify a standard report within the permitted domains.

You can specify or adjust these factors to design a customized report:

- Report layout
- Datasources
- Fields to appear in each row
- Level of detail—how data is subtotaled and totaled
- Which amounts will appear in the columns (actual, plan, day, month, quarter, total year)
- Which data is to be selected
- Whether and which ratios are to be calculated and their formulas
- Text to appear in the report

Report Output Media   Reports can be produced online or in batches. They can be stored for later analysis or printing, possibly by other users. The range of output routes available for reporting follows:

- Online screen listing with user control of format and content
- Printing in accord with ad hoc designs to replicate screen reports
- Printing to standard report formats
- Printing to customized report formats and selected destination printers
- Printing to sequential files in the system for subsequent processing or printing
- Printing to local PC files available to selected network users
- Sending graphic reports to screen or printers with SAP Business Graphics

Facilities of the Online Reporting System   The SAP system of using a parameter table to specify report design allows you to make the following changes online:

- Change the level of detailing.
- Change the subtotaling.
- Change the content of the columns.
- Output all or parts of the report to file or to printer.

Display controls enable you to change what you see:

- Switch to another report with another perspective.
- Select a row in the report and see the whole of the SAP document on which it is based.
- Select an area of the report—a group of row items and some of the columns—and call on SAP Business Graphics to present the data in one of a range of graphical styles that you can adjust and annotate before storing or consigning it to one or more of the output routes.

The reporting system of the Extended General Ledger gives you the capability to extract pertinent data and process it so that you can present it in ways that best serve the cause of effective decision-making.

Understanding the Accounts Receivable Component

Accounts Receivable is a subledger of the FI-GL General Ledger and is completely integrated with it at the following levels:

- Master data
- Transaction data
- Reporting system

The General Ledger and its subledgers share the Common Chart of Accounts with all applications, and also share all the details of master records. Reporting can draw from the General Ledger and the Accounts Receivable subledger.

The purpose of the Accounts Receivable subledger is to keep track of customers and the transactions that involve them. Its job is to collect money—to process cash receipts and dun customers who are late in paying. It shares the same accounting needs as the SD-Sales and Distribution module.

Transaction data is stored centrally in the document database, and the corresponding line items and details are stored in the subledgers as appropriate. The system automatically updates a subtotal of a balance sheet account for every business transaction and reconciles the account subtotals and the line items to ensure that the financial information is always correct and always current.

The system maintains account balances by debits and credits for up to 16 posting periods.

Every transaction creates an SAP document, and the data is immediately posted to the General Ledger. Hence, every business transaction recorded in this way automatically updates the balance sheet or the profit-and-loss statement. This is the defining characteristic of an up-to-date, networked accounting and controlling system.

Setting Up Master Records

The sales organization doesn't need to have the same organizational structure as the legal structure of the company. One sales department may handle products from two or more associated companies. The system of master records makes provisions for this. Master data is organized into three parts: general data, data applicable only for specific company codes, and sales data.

General data is the information of a general kind needed by all or some departments about each customer:

- Name, address, telephone, fax, modem number
- Customer registration number
- Line of business, business group
- Bank account data

For each separate company using the sales organization, there may be different entries against each company code to reflect its different methods of doing business with the customer:

- Standard payment terms
- Data for dunning overdue accounts
- Data for direct debit
- Data for correspondence, such as the account number, name, and salutation or title of the clerk responsible for purchasing

You may also have to specify a particular General Ledger reconciliation account for each company contributing products to the sales organization.

Processing Master Data Records

Access to customer master data records has to be controlled by limiting the staff allowed to modify certain data fields. The method is to use the system of authorizations to restrict the use of certain functions that can affect the critical fields of the customer master records. These restrictions then can be applied to accounting data, sales data, or both.

When a new or prospective customer is identified, a new master record is created and assigned to an account group. The account group determines whether you can assign account numbers within specified ranges, or whether this is done automatically by the system. You won't be allowed to assign the same account number more than once, but you can have both customers and vendors within the same range of numbers.

The account group also controls which fields are active in this master record. The fields offered by the account group can be chosen and assigned to one of three categories:

- Fields in which the user must make a valid entry.
- Fields the user can either leave blank or make an entry in.
- Fields that are suppressed so that they don't appear onscreen at all. You can suppress a whole screen of fields if you don't need them for a particular master record.

The FI-AR Accounts Receivable system makes it easy to create master records by offering various options:

- You can copy a master record from a reference record that has been established for the purpose. You have to make at least one alteration to it before you post it to become a new master record.
- You can copy the master record of an existing customer and edit the unwanted details to make it into a new master record.
- You can create the new customer master record by entering all the necessary details.

After you enter and store a customer master record, you can call it back again and change almost any of the fields. You have a choice of whether to go through all the fields or to work on only one set of fields—for example, the payment details. You can selectively display master records so that you see only those fields of interest to the task at hand.

Using One-Time Accounts

If you think a customer is probably not going to become a regular purchaser, you can set up a one-time account by selecting a special function. This creates a master record that contains only the essential control data, such as the number of the reconciliation account to which this sale will be posted. You can supply the address and the bank account data when you enter an invoice. This information then arrives in the one-time account master record, where the dunning and payment programs can find it when they need it.

Differentiating Head Office and Branch Accounts

Your customer might be a branch with its own account, but the head office might foot the bill. In this case, you can enter the head office account number in the master record for the branch customer. When you enter a transaction to the branch account, the system posts the transaction to the head office account, leaving a cleared entry on the branch account to show who received the goods or service.

The master includes data about the branch and a reference to another master to give details of the head office. This way, dunning letters can be sent to the head office, the branch, or both.

Accepting Payments from an Alternative Payer

Your customer might not have to deal with his own payments. You can record in his master data the account number of the alternative payer, and the system then processes direct debits, return transfers, and other customer payment business through the banks for the other payer.

If you post customer invoices to an affiliate, you have to record in the master data of the branch customer a group-wide company account number to be used during consolidation to eliminate the invoices that otherwise would appear twice in the company accounts. The system can look at the transaction documents bearing this group-wide company account number and identify any replicated entries because the payment was made by an affiliate who wasn't the original customer.

Posting Customer Transactions in Accounts Receivable

As soon as the master data is stored for a customer, a customer transaction can occur. If the master is for a one-time account, the data will be sparse.

If you have installed and configured SAP SD-Sales and Distribution with the SAP FI-Financial system, invoices entered in the SD system are automatically posted to General Ledger accounts in FI. If you have another invoicing system, the route to the FI-GL General Ledger accounts is through an SAP open interface, which automatically transfers and posts invoice data to General Ledger accounts. If you have to manually enter an invoice that hasn't been posted automatically, SAP R/3 provides all possible help. You can enter and post a check received and match the payment to specific open items in the customer account, all in one operation.

The successful posting of a transaction doesn't occur until the necessary data is recorded as an SAP document and is complete and error-free. You can set aside a transaction document before it is ready for posting, in which case the system validates any information you have already entered and reports any discrepancies to you.

The SAP document has to end up with a document header showing the posting date, document date, document reference number, and currency key. The body of the document contains one or more line items showing the amount and identifying the product and terms of payment. The system generates certain line items—such as tax entries, cash discounts, and exchange rate differences—as applicable.

You can set up helping routines and use standard data-entry functions such as these:

- Using default values that you can edit at the time of entry
- Recalling for copying and editing a previous screen
- Retaining data for individual users for several transactions
- Adapting a copy of a data-entry screen so that it is better suited to a set of transactions you are expecting
- Searching for an account number by using match codes to narrow the search

An SAP document that records a previous transaction can be copied to act as a sample or model to be edited. This sample can be a regular document that has been set aside, perhaps as an incomplete transaction document. The posting date and new values might have to be changed before posting.

Setting Up Recurring Entries

If you are expecting to make a series of entries where the amounts are always the same, you can set up a *recurring entry*. Monthly service fees are an example.

A recurring entry is a set of data that isn't used until the due dates. Until then, the entries don't update account balances.

You have to specify the first and last dates and the frequency or time interval. The system automatically posts the required transaction on each due date.

Performing Special Transactions in the FI-AR Accounts Receivable Subledger

The standard general-purpose data-entry function can be called from FI-AR Accounts Receivable to make special entries such as credit memos and adjustments. Down payments, bills of exchange, and security deposits are examples of special General Ledger transactions. Separate account balances are maintained for them.

Accepting Different Currencies

Each company code has a local currency for reporting. The system records amounts in this local currency and also in a currency that is specified as the document currency and is used on all documents in addition to the local currency.

You can enter documents in any currency. You have two options for converting currencies:

- Enter an exchange rate when you enter the transaction document.
- Allow the system to translate between document and local currencies by referring to a table of daily exchange rates.

Which method you use depends on the settings made in customizing, although there is a specific currency translation function that you can call if the default arrangement isn't acceptable.

You can customize the system in various ways:

- A specific user enters amounts in a particular currency, which can be the local currency or the system document currency.
- A specific user can be permitted to enter amounts in either local or document currency.

Whatever the customizing arrangements, the system displays amounts in both local and document currencies. It rounds off minor differences, using rules established for these purposes. These differences can occur when several line items are converted and then added in both currencies.

Customer monthly debits and credits are kept by the system only in local currency. The reconciliation account for the Accounts Receivable subledger is kept in local currency and in all the other posted currencies.

Posting Cash Receipts

When a customer is paying in the traditional manner, it is usual to find references to invoices or other documents with the check or other form of payment. You may find a document number written on the check, on a payment list, or in a payment advice note.

You have to enter four essential items of data:

- Account number for the bank
- Amount paid
- Bank fees
- Document numbers of the invoices being paid

The system has to total the open items for this customer and compare this total with the amount being paid, making allowances for any cash discount due for early payment or other reasons. If the total due equals the total paid, the system posts the payment and marks all the line items as cleared. The action of marking a line item as cleared includes recording for each line the clearing date and the identification number of the SAP document that is the stored evidence of the transaction—in this case, the payment document.

The audit trail might need to trace any amount to the point where it first appears in the system.

Searching for Open Items

If customers haven't told you which invoices are being paid by writing their numbers on the check or by including an advice note, you have to find out by using the system. For example, you can call for a search for open items for this customer. There might be too many items to decide which are being settled by this payment, so you can narrow the search by giving exact values or ranges of values for almost any header fields and line item fields that could appear on a transaction document.

It is recommended that you use no more than a handful of search fields. Here are the most useful fields for narrowing a search for open items for a customer:

- Document Reference Number
- Posting Date
- Invoice Amount
- Posting Key

For any of your searching criteria, you can accept a range of values: any document number between two given numbers, any posting date over a specified interval, any invoice amount greater than or less than a given amount, or any posting key out of a short list that you specify.

The system's first response to a search command is to display a summary screen showing the items it found. The summary totals the amounts. If this total equals your customer's payment, your search is over; if not, you must refine the search. You can select a few items from the summary screen and look at their details to find some better entries for a more focused search.

TIP   The summary screen layout might be more useful to you if you change its display format by moving or replacing some of the columns until you are looking at only the details that interest you. At any time, you can switch the display between showing the details of a line item and showing the entire document. This includes the entry offsetting this customer line item, if there is one.

If your search for open items is successful, you arrive at a list of invoices that add up to the same amount being offered as payment by the customer. Allowances for cash discounts have been calculated by the system, and you can see this from the display. There may also be differences because of the conversions between currencies.

When your system is being customized, you can specify the limits within which the system automatically posts minor payment differences. You can also establish special rules for each user so that any differences larger than a certain amount are referred to a user with the authorization to deal with them.

When the selected open items balance the payment, you can post the document.

Handling Partial Payments

If the open items don't balance the payment after cash discounts have been allowed, you have three options:

- You can post a payment on account.
- You can clear an open item and post a residual item.
- You can enter a partial payment with a reference to the open item that remains open.

If you cannot find any amounts at all to match with the payment, the only option is to post the payment on account. If you cannot completely match the payment to the open items, the best option again is to post the payment on account.

If you know the open item concerned and the payment is only partial, you can clear the full amount of the open item but open a residual item to cover the difference still unpaid. Alternatively, you can enter the payment with a note to refer to the open item for which the payment is a partial settlement.

If there are many possible open items, you can tell the system to choose open items without defining any search criteria. The system tries various combinations of open items in an attempt to match the amount paid. It suggests a set of items that together add up to an amount as close as possible to the amount paid.

Posting Bank Fees

If a bank charge is associated with a cash receipt, you can enter it at the same time. The system automatically generates and displays a line item for the bank fee.

Managing Currency Exchange Differences

A line item can be expressed in a currency other than the local or document currency. You can enter payments to clear such foreign currency line items with either local or document currency.

The payment expressed in the document currency will have been converted from the local currency at an exchange rate adopted by the system according to the rules laid down for assigning the daily exchange rate. If this rate has changed from the rate prevailing when the invoice was written, the payment amount might not match the open item amount. In such cases, the system calculates and posts an exchange-difference entry to a separate account established for this purpose.

Making Down Payment Entries

A payment that is the first of a series of partial payments can be identified as a down payment and recorded as such. The item remains open, and the amount is posted to an account established for the purpose of accumulating such payments until the full payment is received. Only then is the item cleared, and the holding account is cleared by the same amount.

Handling Vendor Open Items

Because the FI-GL General Ledger accounts are fully integrated, vendor open items can be cleared at the same time as customer payments.

Handling Open Items for Different Customers

The integrated FI-AR Accounts Receivable component accepts each item as an independent task, because each item has access to the complete set of data objects needed to process it. Therefore, open items can be found for several customers and cleared by the appropriate payments in the same session.

Handling Open Items with Different Company Codes

Open items bearing different company codes can be cleared at the same time. The system records a clearing document in each company code.

Automatic Clearing in Accounts Receivable

If your customer allows you to collect by direct debit, the FI-AR component offers you a payment program that collects all invoices when due.

Reimbursing customers with checks or by bank transfers follows the FI-AP Accounts Payable procedures for automatic payment.

If the FI-CM Cash Management component is installed, you can clear automatically. Your bank statement can be provided by file transfer, and the system posts the entries to the FI-GL General Ledger and also clears the matching open items in the customer accounts. You only have to intervene if the data from the transfer is incomplete.

Using Payment Procedures for Particular Countries

Variations in the legal payment procedures for different countries have been encapsulated in the standard business procedures of the FI-AR Accounts Receivable component. National payment procedures can be specified for your implementation during the customizing process.

Dunning Accounts Receivable

Each customer's master data includes a field to indicate what is to be done about overdue invoices. This dunning code identifies an established dunning procedure.

A dunning procedure is independent of company codes. It records the grace period, the dunning intervals, and the number of dunning levels.

The SAPscript word processing program is available to you to design and change the format of dunning letters. You are provided with some model letters at each dunning level during customization. You can change and edit the text of the letter and also the company logo, position of the address window, and footers. You also can give open items referred to in the letter a special format and content for this purpose.

A *dunning proposal* is a set of suggestions assembled by the system, which you can accept as it stands or alter in various ways. The system creates a dunning proposal by using due dates and a method of selecting which accounts are to be dunned. You may have defined this method previously.

You then process the dunning proposal online. You can target the dunning letters to particular clerks, or you might decide to assign particular dunning letters to the dunning levels and then designate a level to each of the individual open items. The dunning level of the whole account is changed automatically to the highest dunning level of any open item. You can release specific open items and accounts to be referenced in the dunning letters. The system records all changes to open items that are to be dunned.

Customizing Dunning Letters   You can use the same letter forms throughout the group, or you can use different forms for each company code. Certain text might appear only for particular company codes. You can decide for each company code whether an individual dunning letter is to be prepared for each dunning level. If this is to be the case, only the items with that dunning level appear on the dunning letter.

Individual accounts can have their own dunning letters. Customer items can be assigned to different dunning areas, each of which is given a separate dunning letter. If the SD-Sales and Distribution system has been installed and configured, the dunning areas can be made to correspond to the areas of the sales organization, the distribution channel, or the division.

Refunds overdue from a vendor can be dunned. You also can have the dunning program subtract vendor items from customer items when they concern the same company, if the master records specify that this is permitted.

Selecting the Route for Dunning Letters   The dunning program can direct dunning letters to the EDI-Electronic Document Interchange system on the basis of individual customer or vendor accounts, or in accord with a group or dunning area policy. You can also use the office system to send the letters by telex, messenger, or postal delivery.

Reports on Dunning   The system always prepares a standard Processing log. It can also offer the following reports pertaining to dunning:

- List of blocked items
- List of blocked accounts
- List of items with special dunning keys
- Dunning statistics

Posting Special General Ledger Transactions

Transactions posted to a customer's account automatically update the FI-AR General Ledger Accounts Receivable, which is a reconciliation account, if they are invoices, credit memos, or payments. Some transactions posted to the customer account may update FI-GL General Ledger accounts other than FI-AR Accounts Receivable. These accounts, a type of Special General Ledger account, are reconciliation accounts recording business that is neither a sale to a customer nor a purchase from a vendor.

Special General Ledger transactions include

- Down payments
- Bills of exchange
- Security deposits
- Guarantees

Down Payments   A *down payment* is a payment for a product or service not yet supplied or performed. Down payments have to be reported in the balance sheet separately from other receivables or payables.

Down payments made are reported as assets: down payments received are reported as liabilities.

A down payment request can be recorded as a note to the files that is displayed with other open items for each customer. As a note, it doesn't update account balances. However, like any other open item, you can dun the request for a down payment with the dunning program and collect the down payment by direct debit with the payment program.

You can enter and post a customer down payment gross; the tax is included in the down payment and offset in a tax clearing account. Or you can post the down payment net. The balance sheet reports it correctly either way.

When you post the final invoice, you can display all the down payments and apply them to the customer invoice. They may match the invoice in full or in part, but you cannot clear the invoice until you receive payment from the customer.

Bills of Exchange Receivable A *bill of exchange* is a document that promises to pay a certain amount on a certain date in exchange for a specific business transaction that has taken place. A *bill of exchange receivable* is a promise that payment can be collected from a customer on the expiration date on the bill. It is a form of IOU with a date set for payment.

When a customer submits a bill of exchange, you can use the search facilities to find open items to match it if there is any doubt regarding the invoice it belongs to.

A bill of exchange receivable is an open item until the bill itself is deposited at the bank and discounted there against your account. Alternatively, your customer could pay cash to the amount of a bill of exchange. Either method of concluding the payment permits you to close the open invoice item.

Because the bill of exchange receivable is a promise and not a payment, it is posted to a Special General Ledger account set up for this purpose and is called the Bills of Exchange Receivable account.

If the customer offers you a cash or check payment before the bill of exchange receivable expires, you can reverse the deposit in the Bills of Exchange Receivable account and post the cash against the open item in the normal way.

Bills of Exchange Discount Ledger *Discounting* is the process of depositing bills of exchange that aren't yet due. The system can prepare a deposit slip for bills of exchange. Discounting also refers to the process of depositing a postdated check and deducting interest on the amount (the discount) until the due date. Commission or collection fees can be charged on both bills of exchange and checks.

The system can prepare the Discount Ledger. This ledger is a journal in which all bills of exchange are entered. The following data fields are mandatory:

- Due Date
- Amount
- Name and Address of the Drawer
- Name and Address of the Previous Holder
- Place of Payment
- Name and Address of the Drawee
- Discount

You can specify default values for each company code for the following:

- Discount percentage
- Collection fees
- Bill of exchange tax

These charges have to be posted to separate accounts in the General Ledger. The system can prepare a bill for the customer that details these charges.

Bills of exchange deposits can be recorded and annotated as the following:

- Discounted before the due date
- Collected on the due date
- Factored—an exporter gets cash immediately from a bank or other financial institution that takes responsibility for collecting the receivable amounts or the amounts due on the bills of exchange

Making Security Deposits

A *security deposit* is a payment made in advance against the possibility of poor performance by one of the parties to a transaction—for example, the payment by the buyer or the performance of the seller. Security deposits are reported as noted items in the financial statements.

Managing Guarantees

A *guarantee* is a contract entered into by a third party to pay up to a specified limit if, on one hand, one of the parties to a transaction fails to deliver the contracted materials or service or, on the other hand, fails to pay the amount due.

Guarantees are reported as noted items in the financial statements.

Reporting in the Accounts Receivable Component

The online reporting facilities of the Accounts Receivable program can be supplemented by printed outputs in single or batch modes. These reports can be sent to a file or to a printer. There are three main classes of reports:

- Master Record reports
- Customer Account statements and Open Item reports
- Balance Audit Trail reports

Customers can be selected by various criteria, singly or in the form of logical expressions that isolate customers on the basis of one or more attributes of their master records combined with attributes computed from their accounts—for example, customers with a ZIP code beginning with 462 who haven't ordered in the previous six months.

The content of a report is under your control. You can mix master data and account data, subject to authorization.

If the items are still in the system, you can call for reports of customer open items that sort the items by ranges of due dates or by values, according to the report specification that you build or copy from a previous design.

Reporting the Audit Trail

A legally valid financial accounting system has to have a method of demonstrating all the transactions that contributed to each balance on the balance sheet. It has to show the balance at the beginning of the accounting period and all debits and credits applied to the account to reach the balance at the close of the period.

Every computer system has limits on the amount of storage space it can make available for any particular purpose. The SAP approach to the management of storage space is to archive all the line items in a balance audit trail separately from the document data that records the transactions. When a balance audit trail is required (usually at the end of the accounting period), the line item archive can be scanned without also having to read all the document data.

The Balance Audit Trail report contains a list of customer line items and a control total for each customer account. Reconciliation account totals are also shown so that the accounts can be matched with accounts in other parts of your accounting system.

The customer line items for accounts that aren't managed on an open item basis can be sorted in chronological order to assist in tracking them.

When open item accounting is in practice, the balance audit trail sorts the cleared (paid) line items to the beginning of each account, arranged in clearing date order and then by clearing document number. This helps you trace how and when an item was cleared. The uncleared open items are at the end of each account listing.

Understanding the Accounts Payable Component

The Accounts Payable component is a subledger of the General Ledger and is completely integrated with it at the following levels:

- Master data
- Transaction data
- Reporting system

The Accounts Payable subledger keeps track of the vendors of goods, materials, and services. Its job is to pay for them. It is an integral part of the purchasing system.

Master data entered or modified in one application is available to all others. Transaction data is accessible to all. Reporting can draw from the General Ledger and the Accounts Payable subledger.

Transaction data is stored centrally in the document database, and the corresponding line items and details are stored in the subledgers as appropriate. The system automatically updates a subtotal of a balance sheet account for every business transaction and reconciles the account subtotals and line items to ensure that the financial information is always correct and current.

Every transaction creates an SAP document, and the data is immediately posted to the General Ledger. Hence, every business transaction recorded in this way automatically updates the balance sheet or the profit-and-loss statement. This is the defining characteristic of an up-to-date networked accounting and controlling system.

Recognizing the Business Functions of Accounts Payable

Accounts Payable includes a program that records orders, deliveries, and invoices for each vendor. Operating transactions automatically update accounts in the FI-General Ledger system. When you post a vendor transaction, the system immediately updates the Accounts Payable account. Accounts Payable is directly integrated with Cash Management, which supports cash planning and dunning. An automatic payment program can be called from Accounts Payable.

N O T E   SAP Purchasing is a group of components from MM-Materials Management that can be installed and configured to integrate with Accounts Payable. The Purchasing functions are discussed in Chapter 23, "Understanding the Materials Management Module."

Reporting on matters concerned with FI-AP Accounts Payable follows the SAP standard business functions to yield the following reports, for example:

- List of due dates for accounts payable
- Currency lists
- Hit list

Correspondence concerning Accounts Payable can be set to provide automatic letters and messages for purposes such as these:

- Balance confirmation
- Information
- Interest calculation

Ensuring Compliance with GAAP

The methods used by SAP FI-AP Accounts Payable to adhere to GAAP are the methods used throughout the SAP system.

Vendor information is stored in vendor master data records that are the only source of this information and are kept up-to-date by all users and applications that have reason to interact with them. The master data is entered once and stays in one place only. Everyone knows where to find it and can discover when it was last updated.

Transactions concerning vendors automatically create SAP documents that can be used to keep track of the transactions and the actions that arise from them. These SAP documents can be used to compile a legal audit trail for each balance amount in the balance sheet. They can also be used to record other information that will be used by controlling systems with interests in vendor transactions.

SAP documents have to comply with GAAP in the matter of capturing the information essential to the proper and legal analysis and control of business. These documents, automatically created during vendor transactions under the Accounts Payable system, can be displayed and altered, in a controlled manner, using the SAP standard business functions for manipulating SAP documents.

The vendor accounts and others involved with the Accounts Payable system are updated in accord with GAAP recommendations, and the proper record must be created whenever any changes are made to the account balances or the SAP documents that record such activities.

Exploring Vendor Master Records

In accordance with the SAP principle of redundancy-free data storage, the standard practice is to use master records for the control of seldom-changed basic data. At the master record design stage, you have to ensure that a vendor master data object has a data field for every item of information needed to record and post business transactions with vendors.

If the information you require can be supplied by the system, you shouldn't have to enter it by hand every time you attempt to carry out a vendor transaction.

Information in a master record isn't necessarily available to anyone who is interested in it. Certain data objects may be closed to a user who doesn't have the authorization to access them. The vendor's bank balance is an example of data that's not available for scrutiny by just anyone.

The SAP MM-Materials Management and Purchasing components must be installed and configured to use information directed at a purchasing department. If the Purchasing components have been installed, both the purchasing department and the accounting department use the vendor master record from time to time. There have to be data fields to suit them both:

- General data concerning the vendor that everyone will need (address, telephone number, telex and modem codes, and so on).
- Data about the vendor that might be of interest to any of the various company codes representing the different legal entities into which the purchasing company may be divided. Accounting data is an example.
- Data about the vendor that might be important to any of the purchasing organizations that might buy from this vendor. These might not correspond to the divisions differentiated by the company codes.

The company code divides the company into legal divisions for accounting purposes. Master data for each company code includes the following:

- Payment terms
- Customer account number under that company code

- Reconciliation account number
- Payment methods
- How the vendor line items are to be sorted on displays under each company code

Creating and Maintaining Vendor Master Records

When a new or prospective vendor is identified, a new master record is created. It must be assigned to an account group.

The account group determines whether you can assign account numbers within specified ranges, or whether this will be done automatically by the system.

You aren't allowed to assign the same account number more than once, but you can have both customers and vendors within the same range of numbers.

The account group also controls which fields are active in this master record. The fields offered by the account group can be chosen and assigned to one of three categories:

- Fields in which the user must make a valid entry.
- Fields the user can either leave blank or make an entry in.
- Fields that are suppressed so that they don't appear onscreen at all. You can suppress a whole screen of fields if you don't need them for a particular master record.

The FI-AP Accounts Payable system makes it easy to create vendor master records by offering various options:

- You can copy a master record from a reference record that has been established for the purpose. You have to make at least one alteration to it before you post it in order for it to become a new vendor master record.
- You can copy the master record of an existing vendor and edit the unwanted details to make it into a new master record.
- You can create the new vendor master record by entering all the necessary details.

After you enter and store a vendor master record, you can call it back again and change almost any of the fields. You have a choice of whether to go through all the fields or to work on only one set of fields—for example, the product or service details. You can selectively display master vendor records so that you see only those fields of interest to the task at hand.

Using One-Time Accounts

If you think a vendor is probably not going to become a regular supplier, you can set up a one-time account by selecting a special function. This creates a master record that contains only the essential control data, such as the number of the reconciliation account to which this purchase will be posted. You can supply the address and the bank account data when you enter an invoice received. This information then arrives in the one-time account master record, where the dunning and payment programs can find it when they need it.

Differentiating Head Office and Branch Accounts

Your supplier might be a branch with its own account, but the head office might want to receive your payment. In this case, you can enter the head office account number in the master record for the branch vendor. When you enter a transaction to the branch account, the system posts the transaction to the head office account, leaving a cleared entry on the branch account to show who supplied the goods or service.

The master includes data about the branch and a reference to another master to give details of the head office. By this means, dunning letters can be sent to the head office, the branch, or both for overdue refunds, for example.

Making Vendor Payments to an Alternative Recipient

Your supplier might not have to deal with his payments due. You can record in his master data the account number of the alternative recipient. The system then processes return transfers and other vendor payment business through the banks to the alternative recipient.

If you do post vendor invoices to an affiliate, you have to record in the master data of the branch vendor a group-wide company account number that will be used during consolidation to eliminate invoices that otherwise would appear twice in the company accounts. The system can look at the transaction documents bearing this group-wide company account number and identify any replicated entries because the payment was made to an affiliate who wasn't the original vendor.

Posting Transactions in Accounts Payable

When you post a transaction to a vendor account, the reconciliation account for Accounts Payable is updated immediately in the General Ledger. The system updates a separate account for each type of vendor transaction:

- Purchases
- Down payments
- Bills of exchange payable
- Guarantees

Orders to and invoices from vendors also update financial planning and cash management data.

Posting Vendor Invoices

The SAP FI-Financial Accounting system is integrated with the MM-Materials Management system. An invoice with an order and delivery date can be entered and validated in MM-Materials Management. Validated invoices are posted automatically to the General Ledger accounts in the FI-Financial Accounting system, if the two systems are suitably configured.

Using Electronic Data Interchange

Vendor invoices can be received by *Electronic Data Interchange* (EDI). Data entry starts automatically, and the system converts it from EDI format to the online entry format for line items.

You are asked to correct and complete any erroneous or incomplete transactions. These are automatically saved for you during the EDI.

Making Manual Invoice Entries

If you have to manually enter an invoice that hasn't been posted automatically, SAP R/3 provides all possible help.

The successful posting of a transaction doesn't occur until the necessary data is recorded as an SAP document and is complete and error-free. You can set aside a transaction document before it is ready for posting, in which case the system validates any information you already entered and reports any discrepancies to you.

The SAP document has to end up with a document header showing the posting date, document date, document reference number, and currency key. The body of the document contains one or more line items showing the amount and identifying the product and terms of payment. The system generates certain line items such as tax entries, cash discounts, and exchange rate differences as applicable.

You can set up helping routines and use standard data-entry functions such as these:

- Using default values that you can edit at the time of entry
- Recalling for copying and editing a previous screen
- Retaining data for individual users for several transactions
- Adapting a copy of a data-entry screen so that it is better suited to a set of transactions that you are expecting
- Searching for an account number by using match codes to narrow the search

An SAP document that records a previous transaction can be copied to act as a sample or model to be edited. This sample can be a regular document that has been set aside, perhaps as an incomplete transaction document. The posting date and new values might have to be changed before posting.

Arranging Recurring Entries

If you are expecting to make a series of entries where the amounts are always the same, you can set up a recurring entry. Monthly service charges under contract are an example.

A *recurring entry* is a set of data that isn't used until the due dates. Until then, the entries don't update account balances. You have to specify the first and last dates and the frequency or time interval. The system automatically posts the required transaction on each of the due dates.

Posting Special Transactions in the Accounts Payable Subledger

The standard general-purpose data-entry function can be called from Accounts Payable to make Special General Ledger entries such as credit memos and adjustments. Down payments, bills of exchange, and security deposits are examples of Special General Ledger transactions. Separate account balances are maintained for them.

Entering Net Vendor Invoices   A *net vendor invoice* records the liability to the vendor after the cash discount is factored in. When you process a net vendor invoice, you have to enter the gross amount. The system calculates the net amount line by line.

When this type of invoice is posted, the General Ledger entries in the Accounts Payable subledger include the offsetting amounts net of the cash discount. The amount of the cash discount automatically is posted to a discount clearing account. It stays there until you pay the invoice and then is released.

The purchase of a fixed asset can be recorded as a net vendor invoice. This way, the amount representing the value of the fixed asset is net of the cash discount and can be depreciated in the normal way. The discount clearing account carries the amount of the cash discount, but it doesn't have to be cleared later because it is released when payment is made for the fixed asset.

Requests for Down Payments   If you enter a request to the payment program to generate a down payment to a vendor, the system makes the payment and stores the request without updating any account balances.

You have to support the request with all the necessary payment data and the due date for the payment to be completed. You can call for a display of all requests for down payment. You have the option to display down payments gross (including tax) or net (excluding tax). The net amount is reported in the balance sheet, and the tax appears in the tax account.

When the payment program carries out all the down payments and you receive the final invoice from the vendor, you can enter it. The system displays all the down payments made on this invoice, and you can apply them to offset the invoice in whole or in part. The payment program then pays any amount outstanding to the vendor.

Arranging Automatic Payment Functions

Manual entering of payments is necessary, for example, if a vendor is to collect from you by direct debits. But the most effective timesaver in Accounts Payable is the automatic payment program. The payment program proceeds in two stages:

- Generating and presenting for editing a payment proposal
- Executing the approved payment proposal

You can also execute a payment without considering a payment proposal.

Generating a Payment Proposal   The purpose of a payment proposal is to maximize a cash discount within the constraints set by certain data in the vendor master records and by the way the payment program is set up. Displaying vendor open items shows you who is yet unpaid; you must decide who to choose for payment.

There are various ways to select who to pay—on the basis of due dates, amounts in order of magnitude, and so on. The system checks the due dates of vendor open items and proposes a method of payment for each, depending on the master data and the requirement to maximize the cash discount. The system also chooses one of your banks to provide the funds for each payment.

The system can generate a form for a check or automatic payment medium such as disk or online electronic transfer. You have to assign a medium of this kind for each payment, either individually or based on the default values suggested by the system on the basis of data in the vendor master records. You can directly specify the choice of medium in advance of a batch of payment proposals.

Editing a Payment Proposal   You have several options regarding the payment proposal. For example, you might have the authorization allowing you to do the following:

- Change the proposed method of payment for an open item.
- Change the proposed bank.
- Block an open item to stop it from being paid.
- Add another open item to the payment proposal.
- Change the cash discount level of an open item to be paid.

Executing the Edited Payment Proposal   Execution of a valid payment proposal is largely automatic. The payment program generates SAP payment documents and posts payments to the appropriate General Ledger accounts. The vendor items in the payment proposal are marked as cleared and are given a reference number that links them to the SAP payment document.

Each country and payment method combination has a specific program to print the checks or payment forms in the language and style for that country and, if a disk or other electronic payment notification channel is used, in the format for that medium. The system compiles a log of each payment run and all payment methods applied so that you can see the effects and exercise control.

Maximizing Cash Discounts

Each vendor open item carries a base amount that is the payment due before applying cash discounts. Each vendor master record contains information about the payment terms a vendor has agreed to with the purchasing company. In the purchasing group, different payment terms may be negotiated with each business entity defined by the company codes.

The payment terms for each company code purchasing from a vendor include at least one cash discount term, expressed as a percentage discount, and a cash discount date related to the date of the invoice. For example, the following are cash discount payment terms:

- 3 percent if paid within 14 days of the date of the invoice
- 2.5 percent if paid on or before the 15th of the month following the date of the invoice

For each open item, you can enter one or two payment terms and a date for net payment. The system can calculate the discount due date by referring to the terms of payment and the invoice date. You might want to enter a date for net payment within a discount period on a date that suits your requirements.

You might find national differences in the practice of settling accounts. In France, for example, it is customary to pay an invoice with a bill of exchange immediately so that the due dates of the bill of exchange and the invoice are the same.

The SAP payment program can be set to pay, by bill of exchange, all invoices due within a specific time period. Many different payment methods are available in the system.

The payment program can also be used to make payments by check, bank transfer, postal check, and other methods specific to particular countries or trading areas.

Multinational accounting is supported by the SAP INT-International Development module:

- IN-APA Asian and Pacific Area
- IN-EUR Europe
- IN-NAM North America
- IN-AFM Africa and Middle East
- IN-SAM South America

Selecting Payment Methods

There are no limits to the number of different payment methods you can use for each country. Many forms are supplied via an SAP script that is then used to control the printing in the language of the destination country. You can edit the supplied forms so that they precisely suit your payment format.

You can ask the system to select the payment method from a list of up to 10 methods that have been nominated in the vendor master record. The automatic selection of payment method can be governed by such factors as these:

- Amount to be paid
- Number of open items paid
- Currency of the receiver
- Location of the vendor
- Amount available in the bank account

Open items can be grouped for payment, and individual items can be marked to be paid separately. You can nominate a specific open item to be paid in a particular way.

Your system might have been set up to choose one of the vendor's banks on the basis of the suitability of the bank to pay—for example, by bills of exchange. The choice might rest on your bank's capability to make a direct transfer to the vendor's bank. Banks are given group codes to indicate who can transfer to whom.

The payment system can be asked to choose one of your banks from which to make a payment. You can rank-order your banks and have the system work down the list looking for sufficient cash and the appropriate means of paying. You may have the system choose one of your banks because it has a branch near the vendor. You can also override the automatic selection by commanding it through an entry in the open line item or by changing the vendor master data.

Alternative Payment Recipient   If payment has to go to a recipient other than the vendor, you can arrange it in various ways:

- All payments in all company codes can be redirected by entering the new account number in the general data of the vendor master record.

- All payments in a specific company code can be redirected by entering the new account number in the company code section of the vendor master record.

- Payments for specific open items can be redirected by marking each open item by a code, but only if this is expressly permitted by an entry in the vendor master record specifying the alternative account number.

Recording Intercompany Payments

One vendor may have supplied several company codes in the same group. The payment system can make one payment and then settle the intercompany accounts by calculating and posting receivables and payables between company codes.

The transaction needs you to define one of the company codes and enter it as a normal paying company. The system assigns the document a unique intercompany identification number that is used to ensure that the other members of the company code group pay their shares.

Clearing Sales Contra Purchases

If a vendor is also a customer, you can clear vendor and customer open items against each other via a Contra account. The vendor and customer master records must be able to identify each other by holding the respective account numbers in the company code areas. This sort of dealing also must be explicitly permitted by the appropriate master data items.

Processing Credit and Debit Memos

A transaction that reduces amounts receivable from a customer—for example, if the customer returns damaged goods—is a *credit memo*. A *debit memo* is a transaction that reduces amounts payable to a vendor because, for example, you send damaged goods back to your vendor.

When you post credit memos, the payment program immediately processes them. If you post a debit memo to a vendor who is to reimburse the amount, you can apply a multilevel dunning program.

A credit memo can be offset with specific invoices. The payment program subtracts the credit memo amount from the amount due for the vendor open items.

Posting Reverse Documents

If you mistakenly post a transaction to the wrong vendor, you can reverse this transaction and the associated SAP document. The system generates a reversing entry for each item wrongly posted.

Understanding the Financial Controlling Component

Under the heading of Financial Controlling, it is convenient to place Cash Management, Financial Planning, Public Accounting, and Funds Management. SAP standard business functions support each of these areas, and they can be installed and implemented in various combinations.

Exploring FI-CM Cash Management

The Cash Management component plans, controls, and monitors the liquidity of the business and contributes to its profitability if possible. The key accounting distinction to be made is between cash accounts that record actual available liquid assets and clearing accounts that represent payments in transit.

The operational concept is to plan all transactions that have payment advice notes, control cash, and invest cash. The method entails using the SAP fully automatic payment routines to optimize short-term interest revenue and money market transactions.

The computer context is a closely integrated system containing SAP Cash Management, the payment program, and FI-AP Accounts Payable.

FI-CM Cash Management Procedure   The main steps needed to manage cash efficiently follow:

1. Store information in the form of payment advice notes until you receive the payments.
2. Prepare to clear open items by using the information held as payment advice notes.
3. Process partial payments, either by open items or by account.
4. Receive bank statements by file transfer, if available.
5. Clear open items by referring to bank statements or payment advice notes.
6. Update expected cash receipts.
7. Use the payment advice notes to plan cash flow in the short term—up to five days, for example.

Managing Cash Accounts and Clearing Accounts   Cash accounts record actual available liquidity; clearing accounts represent payments in transit. For each cash or clearing account, you can specify individually how it is to be managed. The SAP standard business functions ensure that all the items in these accounts are consistent with the balance sheet at all times.

You have five options for managing an account:

- Managed on an open-item basis
- Kept by value dates
- Kept with various currencies in parallel
- Posted automatically by the payment program
- Cleared automatically by using an electronic banking function

Cash Management Objects   The SAP system operates on objects that are either program objects designed to carry out a business process, or data objects providing information when it is needed by the programmed business processes. Cash management and short-term cash position forecasting depend on transaction information being made available to the various processes that will prepare data objects such as a daily cash report or plans to control the allocation of cash.

FI-CM Cash Management must be assigned transaction information from the following sources:

- FI-GL General Ledger
- FI-AR Accounts Receivable
- FI-AP Accounts Payable

If there is a schedule of funds to be made available, FI-CM Cash Management must be notified in order to use this information in the forecasting. If any of the ledgers has recurring entries, the Cash Management function should know about it.

Many of these relationships between the parts of the SAP system already are in place due to the integrated design of the various modules. However, the precise details may have to be configured and customized to make the best use of them in an individual implementation, depending on which components are installed and the interfaces to outside systems that are to be active.

Transactions for Processing Payments   The payment program makes available a wide range of options for payment of individual accounts and groupings of sets of accounts. The possibilities include the following:

- Enter bank statements quickly.
- Optionally clear open items automatically subject to specified controls, such as the availability of cash.
- Record payment advice notes and list them for display.
- Delete payment advice notes.
- Provide preliminary information about payment orders, checks received, bank statements, and discounted bills of exchange.
- Prepare check deposit slips by using default posting instructions.
- Manage checks outstanding.

- Control checks deposited.
- Manage bills of exchange receivable and payable.
- Calculate interest automatically.

Throughout all these transactions, the integrity of the FI-GL General Ledger is maintained by the automatic functions of FI-CM Cash Management, FI-AR Accounts Receivable, and FI-AP Accounts Payable.

Using Electronic Banking Facilities

Electronic banking reduces the time needed for entering data and supports the aim of timely cash management.

Electronic banking methods use data transfer by portable storage media such as tape or by direct communication line transfer of files. These files can contain general data or transaction data in the form of bank statements or transaction documents in the SAP document format or in formats provided by other systems.

The effects of rapid file transfer include the following contributions to the goal of more secure, quicker, and more efficient processing and clearing of payments:

- Bank statements can be posted automatically.
- Bank statements can be transferred, and clearing accounts can be processed automatically.
- Data can be transferred to FI-AR Accounts Receivable, and cash receipts can be processed automatically.
- Bank charges can be posted automatically.
- Exchange rate differences can be posted automatically, and foreign currency accounts can be managed more effectively.

Arranging Automatic Bank Account Clearing

The result of automatic bank account clearing is an improvement in your control of cash, because you can process payment advice notes and clear bank statements on a daily basis. This optimizes liquidity reserves and interest income.

You still have the option of intervening in the automatic processes and making manual corrections. You can arrange the FI-CM Cash Management position display, for example, to separate specific accounts or groups of accounts. You also can split the display to differentiate checks, bank transfers, payment advice notes, and so on. Amounts and dates can be used to rank-order or divide into sets the items to be displayed.

Intercompany transactions and the separation into multiple levels of accounts is facilitated. You have control over the processing of different payment methods and the minimum balance to be maintained in each bank account. The system can be primed to create all the necessary correspondence automatically.

Forecasting and Managing Medium-Term Cash Flow

The purpose of a cash management and financial controlling system is to maintain liquidity in order to fulfill payment obligations.

Short-term management consists of looking at the current liquidity position and what the situation might be in a few days, typically one working week. Medium-term cash management and forecasting has a horizon that extends to a year.

One product of medium-term financial planning is the annual cash plan. This plan must show how liquidity is to be secured over the period by exercising financial control. The annual plan can be set out at any level of detail and for any arrangement of the organizational structure the data will support.

Making an Annual Cash Flow Plan

With modern accounting systems, the financial planning period can be of any duration, since the information to be reported is assembled online when the design of the report is used to generate the presentation of the information. SAP FI-Financial Accounting supports comprehensive planning:

- The fiscal year can be flexible and can include any number of periods.
- The multilevel dependencies between totals and subtotals, departments and subdepartments, and so on are automatically taken into account when assessing and distributing planning data.
- Data transfer from and to other systems occurs through clearly defined data interfaces, which can serve the aims of financial planning in addition to their other traffic.

The information sources of most interest to the financial planner follow:

- Accounts receivable and payable
- Planned cash expenditures and receipts
- Open orders from customers
- Purchase orders to vendors

The financial planning report must address the following issues for each period of the plan for each group within the company that is to be part of the plan:

- Overall liquidity
- Committed funds
- Types of risk

Using Financial Controlling

The control process comes into prominence when values set out in the financial plan are compared with the actual values achieved by the business. A quick reaction demands a short planning and accounting period, so that actual and planned or budgeted amounts can be compared in time to make a correction. The SAP FI-Financial Controlling module can provide for cycles of monitoring and control that range upward from one day.

Managing Decentralized Funds

Public accounting is a form of financial controlling that focuses on a budget made available to cover expenses over the fiscal year or a shorter accounting period. Recent changes to the methods of financial controlling have made the concept of public accounting equivalent to funds accounting.

The SAP FI-Financial Accounting system provides comprehensive support for two tasks:

- Preparing a budget
- Monitoring the budget by tracking the achievement of targets in each of the divisions of the budget

Preparing a budget entails estimating or assigning target values for the following:

- Cash requirements for operations
- Cash requirements for capital investment projects
- Planned cash receipts

You can assign responsibility for providing, managing, and accounting for funds for each item separately, and then combine them in a total budget. Under this total, you then can prepare individual plans that make a division into administrative and capital budgets.

A budget can be stored with a version number, and the process can be repeated by using some or all parameters as a model from which a new version is created. If the proposed applications of funds exceed the funds available, you can identify the funding required to balance the budget.

Target Data   When a budget is translated into planned target amounts for each account subtotal that makes up the structure of the budget, each target represents the best estimate of the costs or revenues that will or should be realized.

As the period passes, fresh targets can arise as a result of operating costs, investments, and cash receipts that weren't anticipated exactly in the plan. Targets may have to alter if the budget isn't to be exceeded or underspent. The data for these adjustments may arise from any of the following causes:

- Funds released and allocated to operating areas additional to the original budget
- Amendments to the budget either in total or in allocation to subdivisions
- Internal transfers
- Commitment authorizations that can be anticipated to exceed the budget
- Unexpended balances
- Anticipated expenditures

Checking That Funds Are Available   The funds committed are revealed by the purchase orders. The system checks to make sure they don't exceed the funds available. The cash available is checked, and the vendor invoices may have to be reviewed by persons responsible for the budget.

Payment from Funds   When you post an invoice, the system updates the "actual" data. Cash payment orders are printed by the system to be signed and passed to the controller. The system can be set up to maintain a cash journal that records all cash transactions by date.

Ensuring Liquidity

Reports from the system allow you to plan liquidity, because you can analyze payment dates and methods for both commitments and invoices. Reports online enable you to compare targets, expenses, and receipts in accordance with the budget system. Down payments, invoice amounts, and final payments can be gathered into supplementary reports. An individual line item can be scrutinized, and the history of a commitment can be inspected in the form of the related transaction documents.

Controlling Funds

Public accounting and funds controlling activities tend to emphasize monitoring receipts and expenditures—the sources of funds and their applications. Public sector accounting is centered on monitoring payments. The main aim is to have actual expenses equal the budget.

In organizations that seek a return on investment in financial terms, the orientation is on budgeting for expenses. The cash-flow statement is prepared to safeguard liquidity, monitor financing, and analyze investments.

Aspects of Funds Controlling   The budget uses a plan to allocate funds to each function and organization unit over a period or succession of periods. The source of funds is an organizational unit, such as Area, Division, Department, or Individual. Each source can manage the application of part of the budget to activities intended to add value to the information or work items passing through the company. The funds can be applied to the following:

- Investments, such as stocks of materials, energy, or partially completed work
- Output-related expenses, such as raw materials, supplies, or maintenance
- Serviceability costs, such as depreciation, repairs, or capital investments that affect the value of the plant

The progress of the funds through the budget period is monitored by using the ongoing business transactions. Separate records are made of the details of receipts and expenditures, using the budget structure to allocate them to fund sources (fundholders) so that reports can be written showing how the funds were used in relation to the budgeted targets.

Because the structure of the budget does not have to coincide with the commercial or production structure of the company, the funds controlling system can provide a sophisticated monitoring and control mechanism that can be aligned to whatever decision-making activities will best serve the company.

Analyzing Liquidity (Available)

Cash is available money. It usually is in currency or is a credit balance in a bank. It is available to make payments immediately, in contrast to investments and fixed assets, which aren't available to pay debts until they are converted to liquid assets.

Liquidity (available) represents the estimated ability of a customer or vendor to settle outstanding debts promptly. Computing it entails two analytical tasks to build up credit and liquidity information about customers:

- Analyzing customer accounts, their credit limits, payment history up to their current account balance, and their dunning program
- Analyzing open items, both receivables and payables

Operating Credit Limit Control Areas

A *credit control area* is a set of one or more company codes and a currency for credit controlling that applies to all company codes in that area. This currency doesn't need to be the same as the currency of any company codes in the credit control area.

You can set a total amount as the credit limit for a group and a limit for each company in a credit control area. There may be several credit control areas under one group.

Different customers may be assigned a credit limit account that they share. Any order or invoice posted to any of these joint holders of a credit limit account causes the system to check whether the joint credit account limit has been exceeded. For example, different branches treated as separate customers may share a credit limit account held by the head office.

You can decide which transaction types affect a credit limit account balance. Bills of exchange receivable, for example, are often posted to the credit limit account.

NOTE   If your installation includes the SAP SD-Sales and Distribution application, the system automatically checks on the credit limit when you enter an order.

Online customer credit control is essential if you record payments and offset paid items promptly. You can review the credit situation and the liquidity of any customer at any time in terms of the following elements:

- Customer credit limit and current account balance
- Payments due
- Dunning program and dunning level in force
- Payment history

Recording Payment History

Under your direction, the system can automatically record a payment history for any or all customers for each month, going back 16 months, using the following factors:

- Number of payment transactions
- Payment amounts
- Average days in arrears for each of the 16 months

For the most recent period, the data is sorted by net payment and payment under each specific cash discount arrangement.

Merely as a simulation or what-if exercise, you can ask to see how the payment history would change if this customer paid immediately all the items open on a specified date. This way, you can simulate the payment history report, including the current open and overdue items.

The system also contributes to the payment history of a customer by recording totals of authorized and unauthorized deductions. The average discount rate is calculated, as is the interest amount based on the items paid after the due dates, including items still unpaid on the date you choose for making the calculation. A fictitious or nominal interest rate is used for these calculations, which you can set to give you a fair picture of how much interest has been lost to your company because of this customer's late payments.

You can total the amounts outstanding on open items and also on items paid in arrears. These are sorted by number of days in arrears of the due dates for net payment or days in excess of the time limits for payments to attract cash discounts.

Tracking Open Items   The financial control system relies on tracking uncleared items. You can identify one or more customers or vendors and sort their open items in whatever way is most informative for you. Similarly, you can specify how you want the columns of the report and what periods you are interested in. You can have the system choose open items that fall due within any range of dates.

When you have found an individual account that needs your attention, you can display all the open items for that account and use the flexible line item search facilities to focus on just those lines you require.

Preparing for Open Financial Accounting

The basis for Open FI is a network of information sources and business processes. One task of this network is to generate real-time data relevant to each decision in the commercial and financial processes. With global business being conducted between complex enterprises, it is not a simple matter to determine what data is relevant and how it should be processed. For example, you might need to assess the creditworthiness of a business partner. Your affiliated companies might have some relevant information, and there might be public information that can be accessed. SAP R/3's full computing resources may have to be used.

Developing Business on the Internet

The elaboration of network software is proceeding rapidly because the mechanisms are available and there are many advantages. The attractions—or at least the potentials—are distributed among consumer-to-business, business-to-business, and within-business applications.

Here are some of the advantages most often cited by companies making a business case for introducing Internet communications:

- The Internet is easy to use, around the world, at any time.
- It gives you selective and easy access to relevant information at a pace and complexity under the control of the reader.
- It can serve as a low-cost marketing channel with wide market exposure and considerable penetration.
- The same familiar interface can access a variety of services in depth, if required.
- Inquiries are answered immediately.
- The inquirer can be asked intelligent questions, because information previously collected can be taken into consideration, either automatically or by the operator.
- Moving images with sound can be under the viewer's control to demonstrate the product and to discover which aspects interest the prospective purchaser.
- Increased revenue may arise from a low cost of sales.
- The Internet may have become the preferred source of information on all matters for some sectors of the market.
- You can use simple cut-and-paste operations to compile email purchase orders and request other services.
- Standard tasks can be automated under the control of a suitable authorization profile system.

In practice, there has to be a considerable amount of system refinement to realize all the benefits. User training has to be thorough at all terminals in the network. There also has to be a truly supportive back office to ensure that promises made electronically are kept by timely responses from the logistics systems.

Recognizing the Possibilities of Electronic Commerce with R/3

The implementation of local networks based on mainframe computers and dedicated communications has a relatively long history. Client/server configurations allow distributed computing whereby the user at a workstation or simple terminal can be connected not only to databases, but also to additional computing power to process the data. In simple terms, the concept entails accessing a system through a terminal dedicated for this purpose. The extent and complexity of the system is often not apparent to individual users, and it doesn't need to be in most applications.

However, there are very real limitations on the number of terminals that can be operating at the same time. SAP R/3 and R/2 can adjust the allocation of computing resources to the workload on a dynamic basis, and the procedures to cope with equipment and communications channel malfunctions are well understood.

Apart from automated banking terminals, the direct conduct of commercial business by individual users isn't yet widespread. But the SAP R/3 range of standard business software is anticipating a change.

Developing Electronic Delivery Channels

The customers of banking and financial services are expecting reduced prices and improved services. The electronic delivery channel, in any of its various forms, can be an efficient provider of the services required by the customer. But it can also be the means by which the customer can access competing services, sample their offerings, and rapidly switch accounts to the most attractive provider.

One of the balances to be managed is the mix between low-cost self-service and high-cost personal contact with a banking or financial representative. Another problem is the rate to charge. Should some types of customers pay more than others?

One possibility is to arrange the networks to recognize the customer and then deliver a service and presentation package finely tuned to match the needs and preferences of individual customers. Clearly the technology of personalized display formats and controls is available to the computer user and could be made available to the customer at a public or private terminal to a financial service provider. One-to-one marketing is perhaps a useful concept in this connection.

Combining Components of Open FI

At each phase of a business process, support activities can add value to the sequence by applying information to control the process. The following sales sequence illustrates the way the SAP R/3 components can be configured:

- Marketing services
- Quotations
- Customer credit control using real-time scoring of this customer's payment history
- Order processing
- Monitoring export credit insurance
- Invoice processing
- Factoring
- Asset-backed securities
- Dunning
- Exporting credit insurance premium notifications and collections
- Payment
- Updating customer payment history

One way the financial systems can be made more efficient is by linking the processes into workflow sequences. A workflow sequence is initiated only by specified conditions and then proceeds automatically. The user can specify that an intermediate step cannot be taken until an authorized user inspects the relevant display and signifies approval for the next operation to take place. For example, SAP R/3 FI is used as the core application in an enhanced FI-AR Accounts Receivable module that is specialized to manage *asset-backed securities* (ABSs).

Cash flows expected from orders and revenues are essential components of short- and medium-term budgetary planning. Measures may have to be taken to protect your financial position against possible cash-flow contingencies. For example, a currency exposure cover, in the form of a microhedging transaction, can be put in place by allocating forward currency exchange dealings to the order or billing document from which they originate. The effect is to automatically protect the cash flow expected from the transaction.

Understanding the Financial Assets Management Component

Financial assets management is the process of valuing and controlling financial assets and liabilities with a view to securing the liquidity of the company and managing it. *Liabilities* are loans to the company. The main financial assets of a company include

- Securities
- Time deposits
- Loans granted—for example, from the company to employees

The FI-FA Financial Assets Management component is integrated with FI-Financial Accounting and Cash Management and closely linked to the SAP FI-FEM Foreign Exchange Management System so that you can hedge your business risks by investments in foreign currency. There is also an option to update Cash Management and Financial Accounting according to the results of foreign exchange contracts.

To effectively manage the full range of financial assets, it is necessary to pay proper attention to the following tasks:

- Record keeping
- Liquidity planning
- Financial asset analysis

The SAP system provides the programs to achieve good results in each of these tasks. The FI-CM Cash Management system provides the means to carry out liquidity planning, whereas FI-AR Accounts Receivable is specialized in managing overdue customer open items. All SAP systems automatically generate the transaction documents from which are drawn all the items of information used in subsequent accounting and analysis for planning and control.

The FI-FA Financial Assets Management system can be used by companies in all types of commerce and industry. There are additional applications for industries—like insurance, for example—that have special relationships between financial assets at different levels and between different classes of business, as well as complex interrelationships with other financial institutions.

Establishing Business Associate Master Data

A business associate is a company or institution that, in some way, shares the financial risks of your business by acting in one or more of the following roles:

- A borrower that owes you money
- A lender that expects money from you
- Banks that may hold some of your money like a borrower
- Banks that may have allowed you an overdraft or loan of some kind and are in the role of lender
- Issuers of financial instruments

The SAP system provides master data records where you can centrally hold the details of your dealings with each of your associates. You can record electronic notes, to whatever length you need, about telephone conversations and any other interchange that's not readily discerned from the operational business documents and transaction records stored automatically by the system. These records can extend back any number of years.

The following fields are standard in the business associate master records:

- Company name, address, and type of business
- Contact people by name, title, position, and department
- Validity checks set up for this business associate
- Links to other SAP and outside systems that concern this business associate
- Total current balance or exposure
- Financial ratios for the reviewing of creditworthiness

Differentiating Asset Types

SAP FI-FA Financial Assets Management expects you to divide your financial assets into asset types, which you use to differentiate how you conduct transactions. Here are some examples of standard asset types recognized by the system:

- Loans
- Securities
- Time deposits in the money market

The system is customized to suit the range of financial assets likely to be held by each company.

Types of Investments   Each type of asset includes a range of investment types, each of which can be provided with a customized transaction procedure adapted from the standard procedures supplied with the system. Bonds that are fixed-income securities, variable-income securities, zero-coupon bonds, and equities are examples of investment types with standard procedures. The different investment types are differentiated in this way because they can affect the company's liquidity and profitability in different ways. Financial asset transactions can be tracked by calling for reports that are sorted by status (such as offer, reservation, or agreement) or by type of business transaction (such as purchase of securities or prolongation of time deposits).

Loan Administration   The asset type *loans* is further differentiated by the type of investment to support more effective processing. The loan types follow:

- Loans receivable
- Loans payable
- Installment loans
- Annuity loans

Loans can benefit from the flexible business functions of the SAP system, because their administration is conducted by the FI-FA Financial Assets Management component, which uses the basic system along with any other applications installed and configured to interact with it, such as FI-CM Cash Management. The main business functions and data objects involved in the administration of loans follow:

- Basic contract
- Discount management
- Interest plan and amortization of principal
- Flexible value dates
- Automatic postings
- Cash management forecast
- Reporting
- Word processing and automatic correspondence

Planning Interest and the Amortization of Principal

Standard conditions of interest and amortization are made available by the system. You can call on them to be applied to a particular loan or group of loans for which you have established the amounts and the payment regime. This loan plan can be printed automatically as a letter. The plan of interest and amortization of principal sets out the following amounts and other features in a legal format acceptable in the country to which it applies:

- Fixed or variable interest rate
- Prepayment or additional payment

- Term of loan
- Calculation of effective date of interest based on payments, according to the loan-pricing regulations or other procedures in cases of international securities trading
- Calculation of annuities or principal amounts
- Commission due for origination of the transaction
- Currency arrangements

When a plan of interest and amortization of principal is approved and the details are established in the SAP system, there are several possibilities. The loan administrator can set up commands for automatic execution or initiate online any of the following activities to add value to the loan investment:

- Accrue interest to particular periods or other accounting subheadings
- Post interest automatically
- Plan amounts by posting them to the appropriate control accounts in the Extended General Ledger
- Revalue loans in one or more foreign currencies
- Report balances using a flexible formatting system
- Update the cash-flow plan for interest and amortization of principal
- Print account statements

If you have installed and configured the Cash Management system, your forecast of liquidity can include and display all the planned flows of payments of interest, repayments of principal, and payments on expenditures. When a change of your liquidity occurs, such as when a balloon payment or a payment of interest is received, the system updates the cash-flow plan and the Cash Management data when you post the transaction.

Administering Securities

Securities are bought by a purchase order and sold, fully or in part, by a sales order. These orders always refer to the securities master data records for the details so that data integrity can be maintained.

The master data records for securities can be updated from external data via an SAP standard interface. These records can also be created and updated online or in batches.

The master record of a security contains the following types of information:

- Name of the issuer and description of its business
- Conditions attaching to this security, such as interest rate and arrangements for amortization of principal
- Classification of this security in terms of types and groupings used by your company
- Technical characteristics of this security—for example, whether it is tax-free

The interest rate can be variable and linked to a key rate that is specified during customizing.

In your company, the asset type *securities* can be divided into these investment types:

- Bonds that are fixed-income securities
- Variable-income or floating-rate securities
- Zero-coupon bonds
- Equities

You may be authorized to add investment types to this list of security assets.

Securities Purchase Orders   From the securities master record, enter the relevant order data and the amount. Any currency can be selected to denominate securities; the fees, interest, and repayment of principal can also be expressed in any currency. The system calculates any partial-period interest and fees incurred in the form of commission, foreign exchange, or other charges.

When you purchase a security, the system takes up the plan for interest and amortization of principal and makes the data available to Cash Management, where it is part of liquidity planning. You can immediately view calculations of the effective yield and rate of return. The SAP system supports calculations by any of the common methods:

- AIBD
- Braess/Fangmeyer
- Moosmüller

Securities Sales Orders   From the securities master record, enter the relevant order data and the amount. Securities can be denominated in any currency. The fees, interest, and repayment of principal can also be expressed in any currency.

The system calculates any partial-period interest and fees incurred in the form of commission, foreign exchange, or other charges. The gain or loss is computed immediately.

When you sell a security denominated in a foreign currency, the system can calculate the gain or loss separately from the gain or loss resulting from the currency exchange. The system posts the currency exchange gains or losses to a profit-and-loss account designated specifically for that purpose.

 TIP   You can select individual valuation instead of total valuation. If you choose this option, you must match exactly sales to purchases. Gains and losses then are reported on the transactions individually.

Making Valuations

A separate price table is maintained for valuing securities. This table contains the so-called *book value* of each security. It can be updated from external sources.

There are two moments for valuing securities—before you print a balance sheet and when you sell. If you value your securities before you sell, the balance sheet doesn't take into account the unrealized profits and losses. You must define the valuation rules for each balance sheet account in the General Ledger. You can have the valuation rules applied to each security and control them by parameters you set. Or you can ask for the valuation of an individual security or for your entire portfolio. Capitalized fees are maintained as a separate item and can be released against subsequent trading.

Managing Money Market Transactions

Transactions on the money market are usually either time deposits or demand deposits. FI-FA Financial Assets Management distinguishes between these two types. The system is directly integrated with FI-CM Cash Management.

You can establish different procedures for each type of money market transaction. The status of a transaction and the approval procedures control what happens at each stage. You can determine which staff members are restricted to transactions in a particular currency and the fixed maximum amount they can post. Confirmation letters are printed automatically when transactions are recorded.

The flow of a money market transaction involves the following processes:

1. The bank publishes money market data transferred to your system, which joins the basic data you hold on your business associates and customers.

2. When a transaction is initiated, the basic data pertinent to the business associate and the money market product is accessed, and the decision on the amount to be bought or sold is recorded on the transaction document.

3. The transaction document passes through the control procedure for approval.

4. When the transaction is released from control, there is an exchange with the bank to confirm the details of the transaction.

5. The sale or purchase is fulfilled by an exchange of documents.

6. Posting the transaction generates internal documentation, which can be revised internally.

Using Standing Instructions Regarding Time Deposits and Demand Deposits

The SAP FI-FA Financial Assets Management system supports the common methods of paying interest. The financial data to complete the transaction is provided to the Cash Management system when the cash is available. If you want to prolong the period of a time deposit, the system offers a function to record the prolongation with all the data, including the amount invested and the terms.

Arrangements to make regular automatic accruals of the interest are straightforward. It is standard practice to set up regular foreign currency valuations of investments in the money market and to use the hedging system to cover business risks in foreign currency.

The value of demand deposits can be tracked by setting up a current account—one for each deposit, if necessary—into which you have the system enter the new interest rates daily. Sales or purchase orders for these demand deposits are posted to this account, and the system prints confirmation letters automatically.

Controlling Transactions in Financial Assets Management

Transactions in FI-FA Financial Assets Management are identified by the nature of the business transaction and by the status or milestone reached in its progress. For example, a transaction might be selected from a list because it concerns the purchase of securities. Another transaction might be a matter of prolonging a time deposit.

The status of a financial asset transaction can be expressed in different ways for various types of assets. A typical arrangement is to define status as one of a set of codes that signify some or all of the following logical and business milestones:

- New investment
- Inquiry
- Offer
- Reservation
- Agreement, conclusion of negotiations leading to a contract, and scheduling arrangement
- Partial payment
- Full payment
- Planned interest and amortization of capital
- Contract prolonged
- Contract ended

Each new form of investment can entail designing or adapting a sequence of data-entry screens. You might need to change some of the parameters that control what appears on the screens and how the entries are to be processed.

The SAP system offers a suite of business programs that supports an investment transaction from beginning to end. The processing routines are grouped as the following:

- Initiation, which includes inquiry and offer procedures, with internal controls as required
- Concluding establishment of the contract by reaching agreement with the associate and scheduling payments under internal control
- Payment control
- Planning interest and amortization of principal
- Ending a contract or prolonging it

Managing Internal Control and the Separation of Duties

You can choose to define your own methods of internal control over financial asset transactions. You can specify that an investment is reviewed by a minimum of two or even three persons, each of whom must carry, in his or her personal master data file, the authorization necessary to perform the role that has been designated for this type of investment approval. Limits for each employee who might use the system and each currency are important components of the automatic control procedures applied by the system.

You also will probably want to prevent the processing of an investment transaction from one status to another until the details are scrutinized and the transaction is marked for release to the next status and hence to subsequent activities.

Interacting with the Cash Management System

When you are setting up a new transaction in FI-FA Financial Assets Management, you can record the planned data in the FI-CM Cash Management system. For example, if you are granting a loan to an employee, you can have the amounts planned and the anticipated dates automatically transferred to the FI-Financial Accounting system and posted to the FI-GLX Extended General Ledger. In the case of granting a loan, for example, the stages of the entire transaction can be posted automatically:

- Disbursement
- Minimum deposit
- Amortization of principal
- Interest income

Arranging Automatic Correspondence

The standard business functions of the SAP system are available to generate correspondence on behalf of the FI-FA Financial Assets Management system in matters such as these:

- Cover letters
- Balance confirmations
- Account statements
- Interest payment plans

You can also automatically conduct correspondence by fax or telex. You might want to use SAPscript to customize your correspondence with individual business associates or groups of addressees. The functionality of SAPmail is on call to keep track of key dates and to monitor your investments.

Understanding the Consolidation Component

This SAP component is also referred to as FI-LC Legal Consolidation. *Legal consolidation* is the process of combining the financial statements of two or more individual companies to produce a consolidated financial statement that complies with legal requirements. The legal consolidated financial statement can also be supplemented and used for internal information purposes.

Consolidated financial statements are often required promptly, yet they often have to be assembled from incompatible data communications protocols in a software environment that is, to say the least, heterogeneous. Extra details can be required, and there can be a need to validate the data.

The purpose of the SAP FI-LC Consolidation module is to optimize and automate the consolidation process. The following additional functionality is offered by the module:

- Integration with the accounting software used by individual companies
- Automatic and reliable transfer of data from the individual financial statements
- Integration of internal and external group reporting
- Multinational accounting functions
- Standards for processing representations of organizational structures

The method of FI-LC Consolidation is first to prepare the financial data in each individual company and then to carry out computer integration.

Noting the Tasks of Consolidating

Preparation entails the following operations:

- Matching the individual company Chart of Accounts to the group Chart of Accounts
- Eliminating intercompany payables, receivables, revenue, and expenses that arise because individual companies in a group enjoy a variety of sender-recipient relationships
- Recording acquisition years for historical currency conversion
- Consolidating of investments

Computer integration is relatively straightforward if every individual company has installed and configured only SAP applications. In this case, they share a common environment of standard documents and data objects controlled by SAP standard business process software.

If one or more of the individual companies use a software system that can communicate with one of the interfaces supported by SAP, there are programs to facilitate the transfer of financial data. If one or more of the individual companies have been in the habit of using only paper forms and ledgers for accounting, there obviously has to be a stage of data input to at least a personal computer with a means of converting the data to a medium suitable for transfer to the SAP FI-LC Consolidation system. The alternative of last resort is probably a conventional mailing of the data to the head office of the host company, where an SAP R/3 workstation can be used to reenter the data.

Standardizing Entries

If the accounting practices of an individual company don't accord completely with the basis chosen for presenting the consolidated financial statements, it is possible to account for the differences in amounts by making a standardizing entry that is posted to a head office account designated for this purpose. These entries are stored in a separate file.

Translating Currencies in Consolidation

Three basic methods are used in the consolidation of group accounts:

- Reporting date method
- Modified reporting date method
- Temporal method

Groups of items in the balance sheet and profit-and-loss statement are converted at one of three exchange rates:

- Reporting date rate
- Average rate
- Historical rate

FI-LC Consolidation can translate any items at any rates and use any of the methods for any of the individual companies. This program provides solutions to several problems:

- Exchange differences between the date of the transaction and the date of the currency conversion
- Rounding differences
- The Assets History sheet using rates current on the reporting date
- Reversing the previous translation differences if a transaction difference is posted

Eliminating Intercompany Payables and Receivables

FI-Financial Accounting eliminates intercompany balances by open item only if each trading partner is marked in the vendor master record. You must also ensure that the reporting procedures inform the consolidating department of the numbers of these trading partners—at least on the items that relate to intercompany payables, receivables, revenues, and expenses.

The law requires that all intercompany balances be eliminated before presenting the balance sheet and profit-and-loss statement. All possible pairs of individual companies must be investigated for evidence that they have been trading with each other.

In practice, significant differences in the ways individual companies keep their records can make complete elimination impractical. Here are the most frequent causes of discrepancies in elimination:

- Currency translation differences
- Differences in the timing of entries for goods in transit between individual companies
- Specific reserves set aside for doubtful accounts
- Liabilities not acknowledged in the records

The cause that is most difficult to handle is currency translation; the others can usually be resolved by applying corporate policies in a thoroughgoing manner.

If the individual companies have installed and configured SAP accounting applications, there will have been automatic dual currency accounting, in which every transaction is documented at the time in both the local currency and the currency designated for all transactions in the group. The FI-LC component allows you to trace any currency translation differences between the local currency at the prevailing rate of exchange and the transaction currency. An exchange rate–difference correction then can be posted in the balance sheet account designated for this purpose and thus brought into the consolidated financial statement.

Consolidating Investments

When you use FI-LC Consolidation, you can specify which consolidation methods are used for subgroups of individual companies. For example, step consolidation first consolidates each accounting unit within every subgroup separately. Subgroups at the same level of the organization then are consolidated with each other, and so on until the final consolidation yields the financial information for the group as a whole—the top level.

Simultaneous consolidation treats all accounting units as equals under the head office and performs the whole consolidation in one step. You can specify what should happen if various methods yield differing results. Or you can use these methods and options together.

The system carries out simultaneous consolidation using each method chosen, applied to calculated equity shares that represent the values of the individual holdings. This is known as the *matrix method*.

Applying Investment Consolidation Procedures

FI-LC takes account of any minority interests in investments and any hidden reserves as it performs any of the following procedures—in most instances, automatically:

- First consolidation
- Subsequent consolidation
- Step acquisition and indirect changes in ownership
- Increase and decrease in capital
- Write-down of investment
- Complete divestiture or partial disposal
- Transfer of investment to a new owner

The balance sheet and the profit-and-loss accounts are corrected in parallel by the system. Goodwill and hidden reserves are amortized. Auxiliary records are updated. Every elimination entry is explained clearly—concisely or in detail—at your command.

The system meets the legal requirements for an Asset History sheet and the special situation of equity consolidations.

Consulting What-If Versions and Forecast Simulations of Consolidation

The system allows you to copy the consolidation data to a new version of the consolidated financial statement. You then can edit certain control tables for the new version so that a different method of consolidation is used. For example, you might want to see what would happen if valuation were done differently or if exchange rate differences were handled in another way.

You can also create a simulation of the consolidation process by using forecast data in place of actual data from financial statements. All the same manipulations can be carried out on plan data as on actual data.

Meeting the Annual Reporting Requirements of Complex Companies

The SAP FI-LC Consolidation component is the application of choice for analyzing and reporting for large and complex groups. The following types of reports usually are required at least annually, but often on an ad hoc basis at any time:

- Asset history sheet, reserves, and special items
- Summaries of payables and receivables
- Detailed information on selected items
- Group or parent company comparisons
- Sales by region or product line

SAP standard product FI-LC Consolidation includes predefined report specifications that serve most of these reporting needs.

Special Report Design   Small-volume reports can be generated to view online, print, or store by using the standard display control and item selection functions of the R/3 BASIS component. This flexible type of interactive reporting is a specific SAP technique.

Extensive consolidation reports and audit trails can be sent to a printer or a transfer medium. For example, preconsolidated financial statement data for a subgroup can be sent electronically or transferred to tape or disk for passing to the next-higher level in the group. Also, consolidated financial statement information can be directed to word processing and spreadsheet facilities, where it can be attached to letters and prepared for presentation.

Interactive Reporting   The process of interactive reporting starts with a display of data on your screen. It might be part of a warning or an advisory message from some other component of the system. The data might be there because you specifically asked for it by calling for a search based on a range of parameters. You might ask for items over a certain amount, for example.

When you see a data object onscreen that interests you, you can find out more about it by placing the cursor on it and pressing a function key to show you what you want to know. You might want to perform a what-if analysis using a value or other parameter of your choice in place of the actual value used to compute the item onscreen.

The following query types can be readily initiated:

- Details of specific items, going to ever-finer detail as you repeat your query action
- Comparisons
- Investments in companies
- Transaction types
- Standardizing and consolidating entries
- Graphical presentations of selected data

If your system is integrated with other SAP application modules, you can gain access to the data recorded by them. For example, you can inspect account balances and documents in the SAP FI-Financial Accounting system if your FI-LC Consolidation component is integrated with it. If your installation uses the SAP AM-Fixed Assets Management system, you can see and use in reports the information in the acquisition and retirement records. Your finished report can be readily drafted to show whatever combination of detail and summary information best serves your purpose.

Ratio Analysis   One important benefit of having an up-to-date accounting system with a flexible reporting facility on a powerful computer is the speed with which complex business calculations can be provided with the information necessary to ensure that they are valid. A frequently used outcome of business calculations is the ratio—a comparison between two numerical values obtained by dividing one by the other.

A ratio that compares one production period with another can be a useful indicator to guide internal management. The financial position of the company can be compared with that of a rival by means of one or more ratios. Ratios between individual company performance and consolidated financial statement amounts can be used to explain or amplify the annual report.

The FI-LC facilities allow you to define the same mathematical procedure for all these ratio calculations, but the actual variables and data depend on the purpose and the version number of the ratio calculation you specify when you call for the result.

Suppose that you define your ratio calculation in two stages:

- Specifying where the information is to come from
- Specifying how the information is to take part in the calculation

Suppose that you are interested in calculating the equity ratio, which you have agreed to define as the ratio of equity to total assets. The information could be gathered from three sources, but only one gives you exactly what you want:

- Equity (1) = Paid-in Capital + Reserves + Retained Earnings
- Equity (2) = Paid-in Capital + Required Adjustments + Pension Reserves
- Equity (3) = Total Assets – Total Liabilities

Equity (1) is in the language of a business report. Equity (2) appears by law on the balance sheet. Equity (3) is expressed in the terms used in cost accounting.

Your definition of the ratio you want corresponds to Equity (3). This is what the system uses to calculate the ratio for whatever time periods or organizational units you are interested in.

If you select an element on your display, the system shows you how it computed this element; it displays on a split screen the individual values that took part in the calculation. You can call for a 3D display of the information you isolated for your calculations.

Arranging Periodic Financial Statements

Unlike the annual consolidated financial statement, interim periodic financial statements can be selective in the information they report. You can flag each individual company to indicate its reporting category, and you can adopt the suggestions of the system based on ratio thresholds:

- The individual company information required is specified.
- Data will be derived from prior periods (as plan data).
- This company will be omitted from the periodic report.

Consolidation intervals have to be defined for each subgroup of companies:

- Yearly
- Half-yearly
- Quarterly
- Monthly

Different companies tend to post entries to accounts at different times of the accounting period. The system eliminates intercompany payables and receivables, which balances the unavoidable timing differences.

Intercompany profits and losses can be eliminated by using information from the previous year's financial statements. The system automatically posts the depreciation accrued during the periods of the periodic consolidated financial statement.

Using the Options for Consolidation

In the format for any account balance, external or internal, are two fields that can be used to eliminate intercompany balances. You can extend this format and use it to eliminate transactions between companies and business areas with sender-recipient relationships. You can also use this format for detailed internal group reporting. Because the SAP system uses central data administration, simple validation ensures that external and internal reports use the same data. ●

Understanding the Controlling Module

Introducing the Controlling Components

The Controlling system is integral to the SAP R/3 system. The concept of business controlling includes the planning of values, such as costs and revenues, that will appear in the financial documents. The company's performance has to be monitored and reported in relation to these planned values. Advice and information to management should be the outcomes.

Implementing the CO-Controlling system entails specifying the details of which quantities and values are to be subject to planning and therefore to the subsequent monitoring and reporting functions. The following components are included in the SAP CO-Controlling module, which is an integrated system for overhead cost controlling:

- CO-CCA Cost Center Accounting
- CO-ABC Activity-Based Costing
- CO-OPA Order and Project Accounting
- CO-PA Profitability Analysis
- CO-PCA Profit Center Accounting

The FI-GLX Extended General Ledger module and, as of Release 3.0, the FI-SL Special Purpose Ledger module use accounts based on a range of subledgers that allow overhead cost analyses from different points of view. For example, accounts may focus on cost centers, product costs, or activities. These facilities are provided by using the SAP CO-Controlling system as an internal accounting system.

N O T E   Beginning with Release 3.0, the name *Extended General Ledger* (FI-GLX) was changed to *Special Purpose Ledger,* and the FI-SL module took over the functions of the FI-GLX module.

The implementation of a controlling function in an organization is carried out in an SAP R/3 system in the following phases:

- Defining the structure of the organization in terms of units that can be controlled
- Setting up information flows that can monitor the performance of the controllable units
- Running the controlling system through cycles of the controlling tasks, which are repeated at a frequency suited to the type of business process

The R/3 system integrates all these phases by offering standard business programs that are fully integrated with each other. If you install the system in your company, the SAP Customizing procedures prompt you to select the functions that match your requirements. You also are invited to provide such details as the specific terms and names of work units so that the system as implemented is an accurate representation of your company.

The structure of a business organization can be seen from different points of view. One company will see itself as a group of complete and self-sufficient units reporting to a head office; another will think of the main functional areas, such as procurement, production, sales, and marketing.

To use a fully integrated system and exploit the value-adding functionalities available in a modern, computer-based installation, it is necessary to define an organization in terms of a detailed structure of cost centers with specified relationships between them. The CO-Controlling component provides the functionality you need to capture your company's structure in the form of a comprehensive cost center plan that clearly defines your company's responsibilities. When you have such a structure, the system uses it to run all the controlling functions.

This structure has to be rich enough in features to capture any type of organization and express it in a form that can be used by the computer system to carry out automatically as many of the necessary operations as possible. When automatic operation is not possible or not required, the system should be able to provide as much support and guidance as possible and make the work as efficient and effective as circumstances allow.

Business Planning and Control

In accord with the basic divide-and-measure approach to business control, it is useful to differentiate operational controlling systems from functional controlling systems. The operational controlling systems are provided with SAP R/3 components to support the four operational tasks:

- **Capital investment controlling** transfers activities to be capitalized and used to calculate depreciation and operating profits.
- **Financial controlling** monitors and plans scheduled payments from projects and orders.
- **Funds controlling** sees to the procurement, use, and creation of funds in all areas.
- **Cost and profit controlling** monitors the costs of all company activities.

Applying Alternative Cost Accounting Methods

The SAP R/3 standard business functions provide all the functionality needed to support most modern cost accounting systems.

The main differences between costing concepts arise in connection with the scope of the costs they include and the structure of these costs with respect to the organization structure. There are variations in the use of standard versus actual costs, and in the allocation of costs directly to the products or services, in contrast to allocating them to overhead. Methods may also vary in the relationships between cost center activities, such as in the use of primary costs, cost components, and secondary cost breakdown.

The SAP R/3 system can accommodate the following cost accounting methods:

- Actual costing
- Static and flexible normal costing
- Static and flexible standard costing
- Variable direct costing
- Activities and services costing
- Functional costing

You might want to take a step-by-step approach to the implementation of cost control by using actual costing, for example, and collecting the primary expenses in the cost centers by allocation and perhaps later automatically by direct posting.

Progressively Implementing Cost and Profit Controlling

The modular structure of SAP R/3 applications is designed to allow you to move progressively according to your company's developments and requirements. The application modules are discussed in a sequence in accord with this concept of progressive implementation.

Cost element accounting is a standard approach integral to the R/3 system. Functions are predefined to create and maintain cost element master data and calculate imputed cost elements. The R/3 system can mediate the importing and incorporation of posting data from external systems. There is full reporting on cost elements. Individual business transactions are structured, recorded, assigned, and reported by using the FI-GL General Ledger profit-and-loss account structure.

CO-CCA Cost Center Accounting has to plan, monitor, control, and settle all business activities and responsibilities. It has functions to create and maintain cost center master data and to accept or modify definitions of statistical ratios. Cost center postings and transfers have their specialized functions, as do distribution, assessment, and allocation between cost centers. Primary cost elements can be used in the planning functions for cost centers. The user can define the screen and printed report layout formats from the cost center reporting system. Planning functional dependencies and the detailed planning of cost centers are supported by the CO-CCA Cost Center Accounting component.

CO-ABC Activity Based Costing is used to cost the internal flow of activities with functions to plan, evaluate, and allocate. CO-OPA Order and Project Accounting is specialized in the tasks of planning, monitoring, and settling the activities, services, and processes that take place as the result of internal orders and projects.

CO-PA Profitability Analysis is required in order to report on complex sales organizations and complex product hierarchies. In SAP R/3, results analysis is conducted by using the cost-of-sales approach or by period accounting.

Installing the Controlling Area Concept

The starting point and method of navigating through the details of a controlling system form a structure made up of units and links. This structure is stored in the SAP R/3 system and can be inspected in various ways, including a graphical representation. The structure may be the same topological network as the management structure, with each level of managers responsible to more senior managers on the level above. Traditional business organizations tend to have a pyramid structure rising to the owner on the pinnacle. Government and military organizations are notorious for having very tall pyramids. Modern, small companies in the high-tech domain are notorious for having very flat structures, very few layers of management, and a boss who is ready to speak to anyone at almost any time.

The logical justification for any type of structure is based on the demands placed on it by external circumstances and by the need for the owner to exert some control over it.

The owner's controlling area is perhaps the managing director or the chief executive officer. This person has a controlling area of the whole company. The department heads have controlling areas defined by the territory of their departments—or perhaps their controlling areas are better specified by the activities for which they are responsible.

The SAP R/3 CO-Controlling module holds master data on the controlling areas that you have decided to establish for your company. These may correspond exactly with the departments that exist already, but if you are looking for a method of adding value to information and material as they pass through your company, it would be prudent at least to consider other ways of setting up controlling areas.

What you will be looking for are profit centers that can be controlled on the basis of the measured profit they contribute to the company. One or more of these profit centers constitute an area of responsibility that is a proper subject for the application of controlling area discipline.

The conceptual tools of area controlling include the following:

- **Cost center.** This is a place in which costs are incurred. It may be a unit within a company, distinguished by an area of responsibility, location, or accounting method.

- **Order.** An order is an instrument for planning and controlling costs. In a business environment, it is a document. In the SAP environment it is an SAP document, which has a standard set of constituent parts and is subjected to strict internal control by the computer system so that it can take part in the legal requirements of an audit trail.

- **Project.** The defining characteristic of a project is that it has to achieve a certain result in a specified time without exceeding the budget allocated to it. There are many types of projects—for example, capital-spending, research and development, engineer-to-order manufacturing, investment program, data processing, and customer project.

- **Cost object.** Whatever work is undertaken, whether planning, controlling, informing, and so on, there are features that can be used to focus the computation of costs. The cost object does not have to be a real object, and it doesn't really have to engage in any activity that consumes resources or generates revenue. The cost object is a convenient conceptual destination that can appear in the accounts with accrued costs or revenues.

- **Market or business segment structure.** The control of a business may be improved if information is collected about part of it—for example, the sale of certain products in a specified market area over a range of accounting periods. Another example of a segment is the value of raw materials in each possible location where the capacity for additional production exists.

In logical terms, a *controlling area* consists of accounting units within an organization that all use the same cost accounting configuration. Normally the controlling area is coextensive with the company code, which usually stands for an individual company in a corporate structure. For cross-company cost accounting, one controlling area may be assigned to cover the areas of responsibility of more than one company code.

These conceptual tools have been efficiently programmed into the SAP standard business processes in the most useful of forms, the generic form, which you can customize to fit your particular circumstance. For example, you can record in the master data how you want to define the business segments and how you want to select the cost objects to monitor. You also can specify how orders and projects are assigned to cost centers.

The CO-Controlling module accepts your requirements and delivers a flexible controlling system that fits your company.

Connecting Financial Accounting with Controlling

At the heart of every accounting system must be the general ledger, and the SAP system is no exception. The FI-Financial Accounting module serves the FI-GL General Ledger.

The Common Chart of Accounts contains all the accounts available to a company. Every company—and, therefore, every unit identified by a company code—must be assigned to the Common Chart of Accounts.

The concept of the controlling area is integral to the internal controlling functions. Each controlling area is assigned to the Common Chart of Accounts. This ensures that every transaction in each area is posted to an account in the Common Chart of Accounts and therefore will be reconciled and take part in the financial accounting that provides the balance sheet and profit-and-loss accounts required by law.

The CO-Controlling system uses the FI-GL General Ledger accounts directly. In particular, it uses the FI-GL General Ledger profit-and-loss accounts as primary cost and revenue elements.

With certain exceptions, the CO-Controlling system needs no separate reconciliation with the FI-GL General Ledger and its subledger accounting systems. The exceptions arise if you use the special feature of CO-Controlling that manages imputed costs or accruals. CO-Controlling allows you to create imputed costs at a level of detail other than that used in financial accounting: You can record costs that have no equivalent in the accounts of financial accounting. These intentional differences can be reconciled and cleared by using the CO-Controlling functions provided for this purpose.

Secondary cost elements are maintained by CO-Controlling in addition to the primary accounts of the FI-GL General Ledger. This constitutes a two-level system of accounts; each level records accounting data using a different degree of detail.

However, the extra details maintained by CO-Controlling in the secondary cost elements are integrated with FI-GL General Ledger accounts by means of the controlling areas, which are represented in the Common Chart of Accounts. In accordance with *Generally Accepted Accounting Principles* (GAAP), it is possible to trace any transaction posted on the General Ledger down through the controlling area and to the cost center, which holds all the details of the cost elements used to compute it.

The value flow in the subledgers of the FI-GL General Ledger is always reconciled via special reconciliation accounts. You can always analyze data into summaries by using these accounts, which give you reports such as monthly debits and credits, account balances, and so on, and you can inspect individual business transactions. With this kind of functionality, you can substantiate any of the values shown in your trial balance.

If you have installed and configured an SAP application such as CO-Controlling, you have an additional and parallel way of looking at the value flows in your organization. But because the system is fully integrated, you will know that the values and value flows revealed by the external accounting documents, the balance sheet, and the profit-and-loss statement are fully reconciled with the value flows that are uncovered by your parallel internal accounting system, implemented using the standard business functions of the SAP CO-Controlling module.

You will have a fresh way of looking at how the values change by doing business.

Using Cost Objects to Track Added Value

In simple terms, a *cost object* is something that incurs costs: two of them cost twice as much; 10 of them cost 10 times as much.

A particular cost object can be declared to be in a market segment by entering it in the master record of that segment. This cost object could also be identified in the processes of inventory accounting.

A cost center is charged overhead, because that is where the costs originate. Overhead posted to that cost center then is transferred to the cost objects that are the responsibility of that cost center. The proportion of the overhead allocated is determined by the quantities of cost objects or by some other rule. In this way, the cost object has to bear a share of the overhead.

Revenues and sales deductions are reported in the relevant market segments and profit centers.

You can use period accounting at the profit center level, incorporating changes to the inventory in the period. You can also use cost-of-sales accounting at the market segment level. The cost object method enables an accurate system of accounting that helps you control the value-adding business processes of your company.

Integrating Planning and Decision Support

One important decision to be made is often the product mix. You want to make sure that you optimize the contribution of each product line to the profit margin. Your methods will include tentative variations in the planned production costs, which the system develops through your organization's work flows to arrive at the planned values in each area of interest. You can display any combination of planned values for any cost object or set of objects, right up to the planned figures for the entire company.

This is *integrated planning,* and it depends on the following functions, which are programmed in the CO-Controlling system:

- Planned assessment, distribution, and accruals of imputed costs
- Planned allocation of internal activities
- Planned assessment of costs on orders and projects

These functions cannot succeed unless you provide the data or tell the system how to find them. The system supports you in this preparation by guiding you through these essential tasks and performing the necessary calculations automatically whenever possible:

- Planning of cost centers
- Planning of internal orders and projects
- Determining standard costs of products for stock production and for unit costing of customer orders
- Planning contribution margins and profits in sales management

Again, the system needs information to help you in the development of your plans. CO-Controlling provides the programs to support the following preliminaries:

- Creating the activity plan by using the activities for each work center and cost center
- Integrating detailed planned sales quantities for the individual reference objects, including assigned costs and revenue
- Developing automatic standard cost estimates based on bills of materials and routings

Reporting in Controlling

The SAP *Executive Information System* (EIS) and the reporting facilities of CO-Controlling are fully integrated. Within the SAP R/3 computer system, the reporting facilities are highly flexible. Reports are easy to define for ad hoc purposes and to maintain as needs change. The content and format are virtually unlimited and can be differentiated by user groups. Reports can be stored, recalled, and processed by the SAP graphics presentation component.

Online navigation facilities make it easy for you to switch between report formats without losing the focus of your inquiry. For example, you can select an item on a list and use the function keys to call up a more detailed report on the item selected.

Reports designed in the CO-Controlling module are applicable to all its components. Standard predefined reports are available for the following purposes:

- Comparing actual values with the planned entries
- Comparing the performance of different cost objects, such as cost centers, orders, and projects
- Assembling balance lists and balances of activities
- Inspecting individual line items

You can select a cost center and call up all the settlement objects linked to it. You can also trace the costs on each object back to the individual business transactions that caused them.

Integrating Controlling with R/3 Applications

All the information in all the R/3 applications that have been installed and configured is available directly. Any information output of the system, from the annual sales and production plan to the individual planning steps and down to the planning and processing details of individual orders, may be called on by the CO-Controlling system. For example, standard business functions are available for the following tasks:

- Using bills of material and routings to prepare cost estimates for products and orders
- Updating a costing as production progresses by transferring times and material valuations automatically as they become available
- Evaluating quantities used of supplies and raw materials
- Evaluating semifinished and finished products in stock
- Using cost-of-sales accounting to provide an ongoing analysis of profitability based on invoiced sales quantities

The success of a controlling function depends on the integration of planned and actual data at all stages and levels of the production process.

Integrating Controlling with Human Resources Management

Cost centers can be given time factors for each of their activities by applying the methods of activity-based cost accounting. The SAP HR-Human Resources Management system can transfer the planned personnel costs to the FI-Financial Accounting and CO-Controlling modules. The actual confirmed monthly personnel costs are updated simultaneously in both FI-Financial Accounting and the cost accounting components in CO-Controlling.

The personnel data used for salaries and wage payments is the same as the data used to allocate personnel costs to orders and projects. HR-Human Resources provides both.

Reviewing Cost Element Accounting Principles

A *cost element* is a classification code. It is a mandatory data field on transactions that involve costs arising in a company code. It is used to label and differentiate the following cost types:

- Direct cost elements for goods and services procured externally
- Indirect (internal activity) cost elements

There may be several cost element types, based on a classification of cost elements by use or origin:

- Material cost element
- Settlement cost elements for orders
- Cost elements for internal cost allocations

A cost element is also used to maintain a collection of information—in particular, the transaction documents that bear the code of the cost element and have been selected, for example, for a specific accounting period.

Direct cost elements are maintained in the FI-GL General Ledger master records. Indirect cost elements have no counterpart in the financial accounts and are maintained exclusively in cost accounting.

The cost element concept ensures that each business transaction posted under a particular cost element in the CO-Controlling system is properly assigned to the relevant cost centers, orders, projects, cost objects, and so on.

Each material issue in MM-Materials Management, each invoice recorded in SD-Sales and Distribution, each external invoice in SD-IV Invoice Verification—these flow via the FI-GL General Ledger account to the appropriate cost or profit object.

The expense accounts of the FI-GL General Ledger Chart of Accounts are automatically adopted by the CO-Controlling system as primary cost elements. Additional primary cost elements have to be added to the financial Chart of Accounts to accommodate accruals and imputed costs. The aim is to ensure that all the costs incurred in a particular accounting period and documented in the CO-Controlling system are properly reconciled with the General Ledger. The method of establishing a default coding block cost element is also used to support this aim.

Secondary cost elements are created and managed only in CO-Controlling. They represent value flows such as these:

- Internal cost allocation
- Surcharge allocation
- Settlement transactions

Adopting Cost Elements

The CO-Controlling system carries an extensive set of standard cost elements, which you can adopt and edit for your own installation. There is a match code search facility to locate the one you want on the basis of a specific name or label that you have assigned. The match code search can also include values such as order number ranges and dates that you define to narrow the field of your search. You can block out those you are unlikely to need.

The standard cost elements begin with certain parameters established, such as these:

- Default coding block element assignment to the balance sheet accounts
- Whether quantities are recorded
- How costs are displayed in reports

The system logs any changes you make to the cost element masters.

A *cost element group* is a set of cost elements used with select records to define lines and columns in reports. These elements can be used for planning purposes. There are no constraints on how you can combine and arrange cost elements into cost element groups. You can display the cost element groups in the form of a tree diagram.

Applying Accrual Methods

The accounting period most useful when controlling a business is seldom the same period used for financial accounting. To produce a reconciliation, you need to use accruals that assign imputed costs to the financial accounting periods under an account heading that indicates their cause. There are three methods:

- **Percentage method.** If you know the cost elements, you can build up a database from which to calculate the imputed costs for each financial period by allocating a percentage to each period. You can do this for both planned data and actual costs, by period and by cause.

- **Plan/actual method.** If no relevant historical values or quantities are available to enter into your base cost elements, you can make a plan or estimate of them across the relevant time periods and by cause. Then you can have the system post the planned values as imputed costs and later make an adjustment when the actual cost data becomes available.

- **Target/actual method.** If you expect your costs to be directly related to the operating output, you can use the techniques of activity-based cost accounting to arrive at target values, which the system posts as imputed costs to the relevant financial accounting periods and causes. Again, you must have the system make an adjustment when the actual values are obtained.

There are other ways of accounting for imputed costs that entail simultaneous posting of accrued costs to both FI-Financial Accounting and CO-Controlling. Alternatively, you can establish imputed cost objects, which can be reconciliation cost centers or reconciliation orders.

Revealing Price Variances

The CO-Controlling system can calculate the influence of price fluctuations for each posting transaction. The difference is displayed as a variance in the SAP document recording the transaction.

The SAP MM-Materials Management application can provide the difference between the standard price of a material and the moving average price.

Differences can also be computed between the actual cost to the cost center and the value posted to it from FI-Financial Accounting as a percentage share of the actual value distributed across a number of cost centers.

Reporting in Cost Element Accounting

The flexible SAP R/3 reporting system allows you to analyze cost elements from any point of view:

- By individual cost elements, cost element groups, or subgroups
- By other cost objects, such as cost centers, orders, and projects

Cost Center Accounting with CO-CCA

A *cost center* is a place in which costs are incurred because at least one activity originates there. It does not have to correspond to a real place in the geographical sense—it can be a functional unit that makes business sense. If one person does two different types of work, you might find it helpful to place one type in one cost center and the rest in another. The cost center is a unit within a company distinguished by area of responsibility, location or special accounting method, and by activity-related aspects.

All cost centers have to belong to a controlling area. If more than one FI-Financial Accounting company is in the area, you also have to specify which cost center belongs to which company by assigning a company code to the master record for each cost center.

Each cost center has a defined validity period, and all changes to the master record are related to this validity period. You decide when cost center changes are to take effect.

The cost center master record indicates by parameters which functions can be active:

- Will the cost center master record accept planning data?
- Is posting allowed to this cost center?
- Will the cost center maintain open items?
- Can quantities be entered on the cost center master record?
- What blocking logic applies?
- What is the type of this cost center?
- What is the cost center currency? This defaults to the area currency but can be changed.

The cost center concept allows transaction data to be validated against cost center masters as soon as they are established, even if CO-CCA Cost Center Accounting is still being implemented.

Cost centers can be grouped in alternative configurations that can be changed at any time. The transaction data itself is always assigned to the relevant cost center. Alternative cost center groups may correspond to organizational or functional distinctions related to decision-making, departmental, or controlling requirements.

Actual Costing

When primary costs are entered, you specify a cost center as the destination in the cost accounting system. SAP R/3 automatically creates an SAP document to record the transaction and post it to the appropriate subledger of the FI-GL General Ledger. At the same time, CO-Controlling creates a second copy for itself. Thus CO-Controlling can be self-contained, yet the audit trail is still intact.

The following SAP applications are fully integrated with CO-CCA Cost Center Accounting and may act as feeder systems sending actual cost data to it:

- FI-Financial Accounting
- FI-AM Asset Management

- MM-Materials Management
- PP-Production Planning
- HR-Human Resources Management
- SD-Sales and Distribution

The data from these feeder systems can be used to calculate statistical ratios for the purpose of internal cost allocation and ratio analysis. The data can be formed into groups and used in the same way as cost elements and cost centers.

External data from non-SAP systems can be automatically transferred through SAP standard interfaces, and there is a flexible and supportive interface for the manual input of data. Every transaction is recorded in the standard form of a CO document, which is additional to the standard SAP document created by every transaction.

Costs are transferred between cost centers, but the original cost element data remains unchanged. CO-CCA Cost Center Accounting sponsors two types of cost distribution:

- Periodic transfer of primary cost totals from FI-Financial Accounting to a temporary clearing cost center in CO-Controlling
- Distribution of primary and secondary costs within CO-Controlling

Distributing Costs Within CO-CCA

The distribution method of CO-CCA Cost Center Accounting is totally flexible and under your control. The sender is a cost center that has access to rules for distributing the cost elements to the receivers, which are also cost centers. You have control over the allocation structures, so distribution can be made to suit the needs of your company. The identity of the sender is preserved in all distribution postings, and the system keeps a log of all the relevant data.

You can simulate distribution to test out the effects of the rules before you post the values. These examples illustrate the variety of available distribution rules:

- Fixed specific amounts or values calculated at the time and based on shared portions or percentages
- Actual data or planned data
- Allocation across a pattern of cost centers determined at the time by the system

 TIP Generally, it is advisable to group sender and receiver cost centers in the same controlling area in order to give them identical distribution rules; you then can combine distribution rules. For example, you could allocate 70 percent of a cost arising from sales evenly to the cost centers for individual sales representatives and split 20 percent between the central sales organizations in proportion to the number of sales representatives working in them. This example illustrates that you do not have to distribute all the costs; the sender cost center still has 10 percent.

You can immediately see the effects of a distribution by calling for a standard online report available through the special functions keys. You can repeat the distribution procedures at any time.

Applying the Assessment Procedure

The processing logic is similar for assessment and distribution. The cost center sending cost data is credited with the total of the accounts assigned to it, and the receiver cost center is debited by using special cost elements that signify that the transaction is part of an assessment procedure.

By looking at the appropriate secondary cost elements, you can analyze the results of the assessment.

Calculating Surcharges

A cost-allocation method that is additional to assessment and available in CO-Controlling is the surcharge-calculation function. This calculates a supplement, usually as a percentage, that is used to apply overhead in absorption costing—for example, when a service receiver is charged for overhead incurred by the service provider on an individual business transaction basis.

You can call on CO-CCA Cost Center Accounting to calculate a surcharge at a percentage rate based on one or more cost elements. The system simultaneously credits and debits the relevant cost centers with the calculated surcharge, which is posted under a predefined surcharge cost element.

Cost Center Planning Procedures

Cost center planning anticipates the volume of costs for a particular period at each cost center you have identified in your company. You can plan for one fiscal year ahead or for several. You can have the year divided into parts, up to 365, or you can use a rolling system of planning.

Within your overall period of choice—the fiscal year, perhaps—the system reallocates any planned values according to your selection from the predefined distribution keys, to which you can add your own.

One thing you have to decide is the planning level, which defines the cost center where you set out your plan. If the plan is to be applied across the entire enterprise, the planning level is the SAP Client, which subsumes all subordinate companies. If the plan is for a single subsidiary, the level is Company Code, which appears on all master records associated with this plan.

The plan specifies details such as these:

- Quantity-based activities
- Value-based primary and secondary cost elements
- Statistical ratios

After you settle on the planning level, the system provides you with detailed planning support in the form of standard texts for documenting the plan and formulas for calculating all the standard statistical ratios. The SAP product costing system can supply information to your plan in the form of quantity and value details of particular cost elements. Although you can change and correct the cost center plan at any time by repeating individual sections of the overall planning sequence, you can also block your plan, version by version, to prevent any changes. You can also use the standard R/3 authorization functions to control changes to your plan.

Suppose that your cost center plan contains a planned value for a particular cost element that should really be subjected to more detailed attention. The system allows you to define individual items to separate what you regard as the important factors that should be subjected to detailed planning. These influencing factors illustrate the concept:

- A material may be subject to wide fluctuations in cost due to an unstable market. Your plan could specify the code number of this material, and the SAP MM-Materials Management application would keep your plan up-to-date by posting the current price of this material to your plan.
- Some cost centers in your plan may be sensitive to employee-related wages and salaries. You could have this influencing factor evaluated by using price tables and cost rates by employee group or individual employee, if necessary.
- Some cost centers may be sensitive to the costs associated with individual activities and external services. You might want to highlight these as influencing factors to be actively and automatically taken into your plan.
- There may be risks or overheads that ought to attract surcharges at some cost centers. You can factor these into your plan.

SAP standard business functions are also available to support the concept of having cost centers working to a cost center budget.

Activity-Based Costing with CO-ABC

In cost accounting terms, an *activity* is a process that can be counted and that attracts costs. In business terms, a production process is achieved by a network of activities. If you want to find out the cost of a process, you have to know the activities and the quantities of work done by each.

The purpose of the CO-ABC Activity-Based Costing component of the SAP R/3 CO-Controlling module is to help you plan, monitor, and settle activity types in the accounts of cost centers. Activity types serve as allocation bases and are used as cost drivers to determine and send incurred costs to receivers.

The CO-ABC Activity-Based Costing system allows you to develop fully integrated activity costing in a controlled, step-by-step fashion. There is an inevitable logical sequence:

1. Define the activity types that are of interest to your company because they add value, attract costs, or both.
2. Specify how each activity type will be measured and the units to be used.
3. Create a plan using your activity types and their quantities.
4. Extend the plan to include the costs that depend on activities and the rates to be applied.
5. Allocate, or set up rules to allocate, activity costs for both planned and actual data.

6. Predistribute the fixed costs and attach a value to each activity type that cannot be measured.

7. Determine the variances over the period and allocate them to activities or cost centers.

Assigning Activity Types and Allocation Bases

The measurement of productivity has to start with a measurement, or at least a quantitative assessment of activity. A production cost center has measurements of time required, number, weight or volume of each product, and units finished and semifinished. The service cost centers have records of jobs, hours worked by each skilled trade, and energy and materials used.

Sales and administrative tasks are also becoming subject to measurement of a nominal kind, where something that can be counted—such as the number of calls made—is used as an index of activity. Each call entails an amount of work that can be assessed and evaluated, at least in average terms. Data on an activity typically, depending on the type, includes information on the planned activity quantity, the capacity, and the output quantity. Activities can be assigned to activity groups so that you can carry out some operations on all members of the group simultaneously. This might be useful as you change your controlling task from planning to allocation, to determination of cost rates, and so on. There is no limit in CO-Controlling to the number and scope of the activity groups you use.

The master record of an activity group contains parameters you can use to define how the group is handled. There are parameters to define settlement cost elements to be used in the direct allocation of planned and actual values. You can flag particular activities as statistical, which ensures that the system adopts a standard procedure for calculations according to the needs of the moment, including assessment, distribution, and computing ratios for use in reporting.

Planning the Flow of Activities

For each cost center, you have to arrive at a planned value for each activity. And you must reconcile this amount of activity with the amount of activity planned in the Logistics system. The system assists you with this.

The CO-ABC Activity-Based Costing module differentiates three types of planning:

- Statistical ratios
- Activity quantities
- Primary and secondary cost elements

A statistical ratio in planning can be simply a number for each posting period, or it can be a cumulative number computed for each period on the basis of data. If the cost center produces quantified activities, the planned or actual quantity of output can be the basis for planning the primary and secondary cost elements, because the output quantity of the cost center can be converted to values.

Given the input of primary and secondary costs to a cost center and the output in terms of evaluated quantities of activities, you can have the system compute the efficiency of the cost center in each of its activities. The same method is used to plan the activities to be produced and consumed in the flow of internal activities. You then have the basis for planning secondary costs.

Simulating and Reconciling Activities

The logistics plan and the controlling plan may be inconsistent. Bottlenecks and idle production capacity may be foreseen.

Interactive activity analysis allows you to look at several activities at once to see which will have spare capacity and which are destined to be subjected to demands that are beyond their capacity. You might be able to indicate a displacement of work or resources, or replace one activity with another. The system immediately simulates the cost effects of your tentative change of plan, which you can confirm when you are satisfied or store as a separate version of the plan.

Starting at any cost center, you can command a display of the activity types received from or sent to an adjacent cost center level. This allows you to trace the functional dependencies between individual activity types.

Activity-Based Cost Planning

Each activity type and each cost center can be given as many cost elements as necessary. You can enter the planned cost elements as values, or as values to be computed at the time on the basis of quantities and prevailing rates. The cost element can be given a planned overall value or a planned quantity.

Both procedures can be carried out as full or marginal costs and can direct a split into fixed and variable components. The system provides formulas, formal specifications, texts, and report characteristics.

The CO-Controlling system distributes the planned values for the variable primary cost elements for the year. You can see the effects on costs of any fluctuations in planned activity levels. You can call for the fixed costs to be distributed by using standard rules or your own rules.

The internal exchange of activities also causes secondary costs to be incurred. These are computed by taking the amounts of the allocated activity quantities and valuing them at the appropriate standard rates defined in the sender cost centers. Receivers of internal activity costs include the following:

- Cost centers
- Orders for cost centers that are overhead cost orders
- Production orders for semifinished and finished products
- Capital spending orders for fixed assets
- Sales orders or sales cost objects

After planning values for internal orders, you might want to allocate the planned costs to the receiver cost centers. The original producing cost centers retain the information.

Using Political Prices

Standard prices and standard rates at which cost center activities should be charged are among the important results to come out of any planning exercise. The total cost is divided by the total quantity in each case. You might be in a business that prefers not to use the actual or historical standard price computed as an average based on total cost and total quantity.

You might have to set rates that are determined by political factors rather than by computation. You have to enter political rates manually. You then can use these rates to evaluate planned and actual quantities. The system thus retains an accurate representation of internal activity cost flows and cost allocations, even if the rates are not the strictly determined product of formal business planning.

Allocating Indirect Costs to Nonmeasurable Activities

The system has indirect cost-allocation functions you can use to allocate costs accurately to the objects that caused them. You may be able to apply standard methods if you can derive an index of activity that can serve as a quantity to which you can apply a rate. But the indirect allocation functions are available for when the most reasonable method is to assess costs and allocate them to their causes.

Observing Cost Center Variances

Variance analysis is a method of monitoring business activity.

A variance is defined as the computed difference between actual costs and planned costs, using the following formula:

Actual Cost = Planned Cost +/– Variance

Variances can be calculated at any level:

- Cost center
- Cost element
- Activity type

Four variance factors explain why actual costs can vary from planned costs:

- **Price variance** is caused by differences between the actual and planned prices of the goods and services used.

- **Usage variance** is generated by uneconomical working practices in the production process.

- **Volume variance** occurs when the planned volume is not reached or is exceeded, which causes the fixed costs to be under- or overabsorbed by the actual product volume.

- **Cost center over- or underabsorption of fixed costs** results from using different standard rates in the plan from those applied in the posting of actual activities—the so-called political rates. The same effects may occur if the cost center plans have not been reconciled.

The total of these variances for all cost elements and activity types within a cost center provides the overall variance for that cost center.

For each combination of cost element and activity type on each cost center, the CO-ABC Activity-Based Costing system maintains a value structure for controlling. Each value is split into fixed part and variable part:

- Planned costs
- Target costs
- Variance types
- Actual costs
- Planned/actual use

You can have the variances calculated and included as part of the cost components:

- Actual Cost = Planned Cost +/– Cost Variance
- Actual Price = Planned Price +/– Price Variance
- Target Costs = Actual Volume × Planned Rates
- Usage Variance = Actual Costs – Target Costs – Price Variance
- Volume Variance = Target Costs – Actual Activity × Planned Price
- Over-/Underabsorption = Target Costs – Allocated Costs – Volume Variance

Charging Variances

The CO-Controlling system evaluates each activity by applying the planned rate to the activity quantity. If you have the historical variances or your system can get them for you, you might be able to use them in a fresh version of your plan. Similarly, if you have some way of anticipating future variances or want to conduct a what-if simulation exercise, you can create a fresh plan version.

You might want to use anticipated variances in the cost-allocation process. To accurately represent the value flow in your company, it is essential to allocate cost center variances periodically. You can specify whether to use historical, standard, or anticipated variances for the subsequent charging process. In this way, you can transfer all variances directly to your profitability analysis system.

An alternative approach is to pass on usage variances to the receivers but to keep as a charge on the producing cost center the variances resulting from too little output. They go to the profitability analysis system from there.

You can charge variances periodically to the following receiver types:

- Individual cost centers
- Internal orders or projects
- Production orders—and therefore to the finished and semifinished product inventory

- Cost objects in profitability analysis
- Fixed assets

If you arrange for actual variances to be charged to cost objects in CO-PA Profitability Analysis, you will be on the way toward the creation of the detailed cost structures necessary to a system of contribution margin accounting.

Variances are posted under the CO-ABC Activity-Based Costing system using the rules and procedures of direct cost allocation. The system specifies the allocation cost element by its identification code and by whether the value is fixed or variable on the sender or receiver object. It also ensures that identical variance types are used.

The effect of all these procedures is to accurately allocate all actual costs to the precise area of the company where they originated. This serves the legal requirement of external accounting and the need for comprehensive internal reporting as a basis for controlling the company.

Holding Alternative Activity Rates in Parallel

The method of attributing costs to the workplaces where they were incurred can be regarded as an imputed allocation approach; cost centers accrue costs because of the activities they undertake and the overheads they incur. The CO-Controlling system also operates a system of parallel activity rates that can provide alternative evaluations relevant to various accounting purposes.

At the cost element level, you can put together a cost portfolio to be included in an alternative activity rate for each cost element. If these rates are used when calculating internal activity flows, you can produce cost estimates that conform to all legal and tax regulations for which your portfolio is correct.

These calculations lead to the derivation of the balance sheet and profitability analysis. You can compare estimated sales costs and total costs of production as they appear in the external financial documents—the balance sheet and profit-and-loss statement.

Costing Activities and Services

By looking more and more closely at the way they produce their goods and services, companies have been able to make extensive improvements. The need is for a system of structured overhead costing.

The first thing to do is to identify and define the *cost drivers*—the allocation bases that influence how activity costs are allocated to the cost centers that generate them. The *cost driver* is a subprocess that can be measured for individual cost center activities, as in these examples:

- Number of purchase order items successfully processed
- Number of quotation items
- Delivery items in sales
- Dunning operations and payment differences handled

Subprocesses are grouped together into primary processes that can be addressed by the product costing system to determine the costs of administrative and service activities.

You will discover what each subprocess costs. You are on the way to an activity-based profitability analysis.

Planning and Simulating the Subprocesses

The basic disciplines of activity-based accounting have to be applied to ensure that the activities at a cost center are integrated with the accounting and controlling systems. However, there is a further level of detail to be considered if activities are to be analyzed into their constituent subprocesses.

A business process can be represented by a chain of activities and products or a network of such chains. In the SAP R/3 system, this chain or network is managed by a process sequence structure, which can be of any complexity.

The process sequence structure can be used to simulate the flow of material through a sequence of activities that create, for example, a series of semifinished products and terminate with the finished product. The SAP PP-Production Planning module is specialized in this work.

For the purpose of analyzing overhead activities and services, the CO-ABC Activity-Based Costing module provides full supporting functions.

The system of costing based on a process sequence structure requires that all processes and subprocesses be quantified in terms of quantity and value flow. This allows analysis and reporting to be carried out to a level of detail that yields a list of activities. This list documents the ways in which the activity levels of the parent cost centers exert influence on the costs of the primary processes and their subprocesses. How do support costs alter when business gets better or worse?

Using Process Cost Rates

The purpose of applying the methods of activity-based costing to the detailed processes and subprocesses of a production company is to compute process cost rates. How much does it cost to put one invoice item through the office? How much to move one pallet from production to the warehouse?

If you have process cost rates at this level of detail, you can take a standard costing based on a bill of materials and routings, for example, and cost each of the processes entailed. Or you can have the SAP system do it for you.

If you have these process cost rates for all subprocesses in each activity type, you can transfer the process costs from CO-CCA Cost Center Accounting directly to CO-PA Profitability Analysis. Because you have the process costs associated with each activity contained by CO-CCA Cost Center Accounting, you can have these process costs included in the value flow patterns identified by both product costing and period costing.

Order and Project Accounting with CO-OPA

The purpose of the CO-OPA Order and Project Accounting module is to analyze and settle the costs arising from internal orders and projects.

The purpose of internal orders is to monitor costs to assist in decision-making and to manage the allocation and settlement of activity costs to target objects, including FI-GL General Ledger accounts. Projects can also be used for these purposes. Complex projects are more properly the province of the SAP R/3 PS-Project System, which is discussed in Chapter 16, "Understanding the R/3 Project System."

Internal orders are usually defined for a particular task, event, or internal change measure that has to be planned, monitored, and settled in great detail. These orders are distinguished by their origin and by the time allocated for their completion. They vary in their settlement arrangements and in how they appear in the reporting functions.

SAP R/3 classifies internal orders as shown here:

- Production-related orders used in Logistics
- Sales orders used in SD-Sales and Distribution
- Internal orders used in CO-Controlling

Although the internal orders of the Logistics modules and the SD-Sales and Distribution component serve mainly to monitor resources used and sales achieved, they also document estimated costs, actual costs, and revenues. In the PP-Production Planning and Control modules, the order has the job of annexing information on the latest estimate of costs until the actual costs replace them when the order is complete.

Sales orders that document costs and revenues are accessed by the CO-PA Profitability Analysis system. They also carry the information needed by CO-Controlling and PP-Production Planning and Control, for example. The orders for processing and settling internal costs usually support the integration of different business systems with the ways the particular company likes to do business and settle the costs.

Internal orders in CO-Controlling are differentiated by the following characteristics:

- Whether logistical, controlling, or settlement in main function
- Content of the order, such as product or project
- Whether an individual order or a standing order
- The significance of the values on the order, such as plan costs, actual costs, or variances
- Settlement receiver for the order, such as fixed asset account, cost center, cost object, project, stock, business segment, sales order, or FI-GL General Ledger account

An important feature of the CO-OPA Order and Project Accounting component is that you can assign the relevant costs on each order and project to the various receivers, split by period and allocated accurately by cause. They can be used for controlling overhead costs and production.

If you want to have an internal exercise that is a simple single-level project used only in the CO-Controlling system, you can specify how you want to monitor it and settle the costs incurred.

Interpreting Order Data Formats

The master data record for an order contains the order number and the parameters for controlling the business and technical system functions that deal with it. You will have been authorized to use a certain range of order numbers; otherwise, the system assigns the number.

The order master includes control data that specifies the transaction groups in which the order can take part. For example, an order type of Planning allows the entry for planning purposes only of information such as primary costs and overhead costs.

The order master also includes parameter fields to organize overhead components and to control the settlement functions. Some orders have the function of monitoring all open purchase orders, for example; others are intended for the detailed settlement of individual cost items.

This system of order parameters set into the master records enables you to establish a suite of order types. You can use these order types to specify how each order directs the value flow in your company. This flow conforms to your organizational structure and the way in which your company groups its business functions.

Managing the Status of Orders

The status of an order is the stage it has reached in its life cycle. The SAP CO-OPA Order and Project Accounting system is particularly flexible in the way it allows you to decide what should happen at each stage and through which stages a particular type of order should proceed on its way to completion. For example, you can choose where to have the system plan primary or secondary costs for each order.

This is the typical status sequence for an order:

- Order opened, basic data identified
- Planning primary and secondary costs
- Released for posting
- Execution
- Technical completion
- Accounting completion

Some of these business functions can be allowed to operate across more than one status. Planning information can be allowed to be added to an order while it is being executed, for example.

Classifying Orders by Content

Because they are treated differently, orders are classified by their content and controlling objectives into various types.

■ **Job orders** collect and analyze the planned and actual costs for a commodity or operational event that won't be capitalized, such as minor repairs or staff training. These orders are settled on the objects that caused them by means of the periodic cost center accounting procedures.

■ **Capital spending orders** on the fixed assets produced in-house and on maintenance costs serve to manage the planning and allocation of costs over the lifetime of the order, which can be an open order.

■ **Production orders** are used to set up costing sheets by gathering primary costs from FI-Financial Accounting and secondary costs from overhead assessment. Activity costs come from internal allocation. Issues of raw materials and semifinished materials are notified from MM-Materials Management. Production orders in Logistics use bills of materials, routings, and cost centers. They are fully integrated into the overall capacity planning and monitoring functions.

■ **Sales orders** can have posted to them any type of cost and revenue items taken directly from SD-Sales and Distribution. These can be transferred directly to the appropriate business segments in CO-PA Profitability Analysis.

■ An **individual order** is typically unique and of long duration. The quantity structures are seldom fully known at the start, so planning is carried out in stages. Where an individual order entails multilevel production processing and a complex web of activities, partial orders may be created. The SAP R/3 Project System is specialized for this kind of work in make-to-order production.

■ **Standing orders** are used when cost centers have to be split into smaller activity units, such as small repairs, minor maintenance, or individual vehicles in a company fleet.

■ **Statistical orders** are used to receive additional account assignments in order to summarize, sort, and display cost objects according to specific criteria. The amount posted appears under the original cost element heading on the appropriate account, and again on the statistical order. Revenues can also be collated by a statistical order.

Planning Orders

You can plan an order's overall value. You can also plan according to the cost elements and activity types, either on the specific order or by transferring the values from a unit you have already costed. The following cost elements and activity types can be planned on orders:

■ Primary costs by cost element or cost element group, in values or in quantities to which the system will apply cost rates at the time

■ Cost center activities as the secondary costs, planned down to the level of individual operations if necessary

■ Overhead, planned with the overhead application functions

■ Statistical ratios, to be used to form business ratios when reporting

Distribution keys provide a choice between planning orders annually with a standard distribution across months, and planning for each month separately. Order groups can be assembled for overhead calculation, planning, and reporting.

The functionality and screens used in CO-CCA Cost Center Accounting are available to give planning views of your flexible combinations of planning objects and planning content. For example, you can call for planning views on all or any of the following situations:

- Many cost elements on a single order
- Many cost element groups on a single order
- Many cost elements on an order group
- Many cost element groups on an order group

Whatever planning steps you take, you can store in the system a choice of standard explanatory texts with additional information to document your decisions.

If the order takes a long time to execute, the assumptions on which the plan was built may become out of date. Each plan is noted as a new version whenever you change something, so that subsequent analysis arrives at an accurate picture. If a plan has already been released and changes have to be made, you can have the system document the entry of the modified order plan and the changes made to it in the form of a copy of the plan line items that have been altered.

Unit Costing

You might have a cost element plan that is too global for certain requirements—perhaps you want to assign only some of the costs to an order. You can create the order by using cost elements and have the system make out a unit cost plan later, when the actual values or quantities are transferred to the order.

Holding Open Items

If you want to place a reservation on a certain quantity of material or still have a commitment to pay for an external service on a specific order, you enter an open item. In the display, open items appear as values and quantities under the appropriate cost element heading, in the correct fiscal year and in the period that includes the planned supply date.

Open items can arise through purchasing in the MM-Materials Management system. If the invoice has been received, the open item can be evaluated from the actual prices; if not, the anticipated price must be used. Delivery costs are displayed separately so that they can be evaluated in the appropriate currency for the place where each cost element was incurred.

Material reservation in MM-IM Inventory Management creates an open item that is evaluated at the carrying price.

You can also generate an open item manually in the form of a funds reservation.

As you reduce an open item, the system helps you manage it by using the original currency. Analysis and posting can take place under the system rules for foreign currency and its exchange. The aim is to replace each open item on an order with the corresponding actual costs. If an open item concerns external services, the system reduces the purchase order by value, using the invoiced amount, whether full or partial. The system identifies any price differences by account and by order.

If an open item is a goods purchase order, as soon as the goods are received, the system automatically reduces the quantity and the value for the open purchase item. If the invoice is received before the goods, the system adjusts the open purchase order by adopting the invoice value in place of the purchase order value. If any amounts on the invoice or on the services received remain unsettled, the order stays open until they are finally cleared completely.

The order number and the posting details are retained when an order progresses from one business transaction to the next. The system can thus document the purchase order history, which enables you to trace a partial delivery or a partial invoice to the purchase order and then back to the original purchase requisition.

Open item management illustrates the close integration of logistics and accounting in the SAP system.

Actual Cost Accounting Transactions

Every SAP transaction generates an SAP document. If the document contains a posting to an order number, the CO-OPA Order and Project Accounting system charges the amount to the order under the relevant cost element heading and with that order number. You can trace the history of origin of each line item throughout the lifetime of the order.

Activities must take place so that production orders, maintenance orders, and job orders can be fulfilled. These activities are the responsibility of one or more cost centers. For each activity, the responsible cost center demands payment in the form of an internal cost allocation.

The CO-Controlling system evaluates the activity quantity at the appropriate rate. At the same time, line items are created to document the flow of value from the producing sender objects to the receiving objects. These take the form of a credit to the sending cost center and a debit to the receiving order. This is the process of direct internal cost allocation.

If the activity is not suited to quantification (if you can't say exactly how much of the item is needed for the order), you have to use indirect cost allocation, in which a periodic total is shared in some way between the receiving cost centers or orders.

Overhead is a charge that should be allocated as accurately as possible to the items that have to share its burden.

Settling Orders

Order settlement is the process of passing costs from the originating order to other cost objects. There are two groups of these target objects: internal postings within CO-Controlling and external postings to the accounts managed by FI-Financial Accounting and other applications.

Internal postings settle orders automatically using CO-CEA Cost Element Accounting. This component creates the necessary credit and debit line items in any of the following objects:

- Cost centers
- Internal orders
- Projects

- Business segments
- Sales orders

Orders can be settled by postings to external objects by using these functions:

- FI-AA Asset Accounting is for assets under construction or capitalized assets.
- MM-Materials Management settles any product manufactured in-house to inventory under the material number for a warehouse.
- FI-Financial Accounting can settle orders to the appropriate FI-GL General Ledger account.

Settlement Rules   Each order master includes a data element that determines the settlement rule to be applied to that order. The rule includes the following control parameters:

- Period of validity for the settlement rule.
- Target object or objects to which the costs are to be sent—for example, if part of the costs of the order will be capitalized and the rest distributed between certain cost centers.
- The cost element or elements under which the order value is to be credited. (Using cost element groups results in a debit to the receiver under each element.)
- Settlement of costs to a cost element within the CO-Controlling system.

The settlement rule may be a defined debit to the receiver. Several receivers may be targeted in proportions calculated from equivalence numbers or percentages. Absolute amounts may be settled, or costs may be based on quantity; the system uses the current rate when the settlement is performed.

If the order includes information on a suitable target object for settlement, such as a responsible cost center or related project identification, the system operates a default distribution rule generated on the basis of this information.

Orders that allocate costs to cost centers tend to be settled periodically; capital spending orders are settled at period end after the project is completed. Orders to be settled can be grouped according to the following criteria:

- Order type
- Date when settlement is to be performed
- Receiver of the settlement
- Corporate or company code
- Settlement to internal or external accounting system

You can create a settlement simulation list in the CO-OPA Order and Project Accounting system by using the allocation groups to check that the orders are both correct and complete. When the simulation is correct, you can use the list to execute the settlement. You can reverse a settlement made previously or repeat it at any time.

The system calculates the total settlement and the individual amounts debited to each receiver in the controlling area currency, from which you can convert if necessary. The settlement function differentiates debiting an order with full costs from debiting only direct costs. You might have previously distributed fixed costs in CO-CCA Cost Center Accounting, in which case this is allowed for in the value flow.

The order reporting system shows you the settlement history, which includes the dates and details of the amounts already settled, any reversals performed, and the balance remaining on the order.

Performing Order Summary Evaluations

If you want to compare two or more orders in detail, you might find it helpful to have the system classify orders by using a hierarchy. The CO-Controlling system allows you to put any criterion at the top of your hierarchy and any other criteria at each level below. You might ask these sorts of questions:

- How do the various companies in this group compare across these functions: repairs, advertising special campaigns, and so on?
- How do the various companies in this group compare for all departments and all production orders?

These criteria create a hierarchy over which the system can collate the data—in this example, for all production orders. The SAP R/3 flexible reporting functions allow you to view this data at any of these levels of your hierarchy and to switch readily from one viewpoint to another.

In fact, the system offers a complete method of order reporting from line item up to order, cost center, controlling area, and company. The online reporting techniques allow you to take any summary and drill down to the details of the order items that contribute to it.

Using Capital Spending Orders

The main objective of a capital spending order is to monitor the costs of producing assets and commodities in-house. Maintenance projects can be controlled and accounted in the same way.

The distinguishing feature of the SAP module CO-OPA Order and Project Accounting is its capability to settle in detail the actual costs according to individual rules for each item. You must specify the following:

- Target object(s) defined as one or more fixed assets in FI-AA Asset Accounting
- Date of settlement
- Scope of costs to be settled
- Settlement cost element heading
- Supplementary information

In addition to this capability to settle capital spending orders in precise detail, the system has the following important features:

- Planning is available for all resources and costs required, in quantity and value.
- Charges can be computed from prices at the time, with imputed allocations of overhead and actual costs.
- Open items for purchase requisitions, purchase orders, and material reservations are closely monitored.
- Display is possible of all cash-related procedures, such as down-payment requests and down payments.
- Concurrent evaluation and analysis of order reports can be performed.

Integrating Order and Project Accounting with Asset Accounting

If you are managing fixed assets such as buildings and machines, the settlement of capital spending orders is of crucial importance. The SAP R/3 system offers detailed settlement rules and a close integration with the FI-AA Asset Accounting component to yield the following advantages:

- Settlement of costs to the appropriate balance sheet accounts under the heading Assets Under Construction, while the capital spending order is ongoing
- Order-based display of special depreciations for Assets Under Construction
- Recognition of subsidies, grants, and down payments
- Settlement of partial orders over a hierarchy of orders

Because all costs are based on unified posting and settlement rules in the SAP R/3 system, you can allocate costs from orders and projects to the various target objects by using the same rules or rules you specified separately. You can keep track of complex overhead costs with maintenance and capital spending orders; this gives you the chance to take effective action immediately.

Creating Planned Cost Schedules

Costs and deadlines on orders and projects that take a long time to complete have to recognize the financial facts of life. Money is not always available when you need it. Financial and liquidity planning requires that you know what costs are expected on the orders and projects. It helps to have some idea of how the costs are likely to be incurred in detail over the first few accounting periods and in broader terms up to the date of completion.

A cost schedule is a plan extending the length of an order or project showing the values expected to be allocated to costs. The schedule has a key date. Until this date is known and entered on the plan, the forecast of costs has to be moved ahead to the best estimated date.

The SAP R/3 system provides support in the following ways:

- The system automatically determines the tasks from the planned start and finish dates for the order.
- Cost distribution across the schedule can be suited to the specific order.
- Graphical representations of the data model are readily available online and in print.

These manipulations of the cost schedules and the task plans are automatically available:

- Shifting the start date, retaining the duration
- Compressing the duration, retaining the finish date
- Expanding the duration

If you have carried out cost element planning or created a unit costing for the order, the system can use this information to develop a cost schedule.

Product Cost Accounting

The purpose of product cost accounting is to determine the unit cost of whatever product units your company does business in. These units are referred to as *cost objects,* with one cost object for each product or each distribution package for each product. The context is a technical production system that is customized to a particular company; the outcome is a company-specific costing system that integrates the flow of cost information from its origins.

A core technical discipline is based on the principle that costs should be accurately allocated to the processes that incur them. Several costing systems embody this principle in the particular circumstances of a certain type of business.

Product cost accounting addresses two types of costing:

- Production order costing
- Inventory costing

Four types of cost object controlling are differentiated, because they offer different benefits according to the type of business they are located in:

- Make-to-stock production
- Process manufacturing
- Make-to-order production
- Plant construction

All these types of product cost accounting are supported by the CO-Controlling module by the flexible use of cost objects.

Costing Requirements of Different Types of Companies

Modern controlling methods have developed to support technical manufacturing processes and service industries. The methods have to match the needs of the individual company. The SAP approach establishes a core of standard business functions that can be controlled by the implementer with parameters to yield a customized system finely tuned to the requirements of the user classes in the specific company.

Manufacturers require a costing system that shows where and by how much their manufacturing processes add value to their raw materials. They vary in their style of manufacturing according to whether they make to a production order or make to replace stock in their inventory. Their processes vary over a range, from discrete one-off production to repetitive production to continuous-flow production.

Trading companies need a method of costing to enable them to apply overhead and surcharges to the cost prices of their goods, which they often have to keep to set or agreed final selling prices.

Service companies tend to adopt the principles of process costing, which revolves around the concept of cost drivers—in this case, service activities. These companies need to be able to define, measure, plan, and pass on costs incurred by their cost drivers, service calls, and other activities.

Make-to-Order, Make-to-Stock, Continuous Flow   The manufacturing industry has a polished costing method based on routings taken by work units and bills of materials. They need to know what processes the product has to undergo, the costs of materials and resources, and the quantities. This information is the *quantity structure* for this product. If you have this information, you can begin to cost the product by assembling the costing components.

In the make-to-order company, the customer order sets off costing. Because each order is unique, there may be a shortage of routings and bills of materials that can be applied without editing. Yet it is of the utmost importance to be able to arrive quickly at a cost prediction for this one-off product so that the company can issue a quotation and take part in competitive tendering for the work. An effective costing system for this sort of company must give this approach to one-off tendering a high priority, because all future business may depend on its speed and accuracy.

Manufacturers who make to stock apply standard bills of materials and routings about which they may have copious actual data. Products and orders can be costed from this database.

If the manufacturing process is continuous, it is probably not well-suited to a great deal of variation. It will probably only work at its best if the rate of flow is within narrow limits. Nevertheless, the contribution of the various cost components to the cost of the finished product will be of interest to the management and shareholders. It is important to understand how and why costs vary if the flow rate and quality are allowed to move out of the normal operating ranges. This might happen because of variations in the raw materials or in the environmental conditions at the manufacturing plant.

Product-Costing Techniques   A costing system uses a set of costing objects, which are the different products, production and other orders, resources, and so on. The only qualification for a costing object is that it can be allocated costs that mean something when they are totaled under that costing object. The costing objects can be conceptual or tangible, organizational or geographical.

The pivotal concept in costing is the structure of cost drivers—cost objects onto which the actual costs are settled according to how they were incurred. SAP R/3 CO-Controlling provides a range of model structures on which you can base a structure specific to the needs of your company.

Three types of costing values might be settled on a cost structure:

- Planned values
- Target values
- Actual costs

You can apply cost data to arrive at a specific costing in two ways:

- Allocate the full costing to the cost objects
- Allocate only the variable costs to the cost objects, and apply overhead or surcharge

An integrated costing system has to have at least the following capabilities:

- Calculate alternative cost plans using different versions and timings.
- Control the activities and the value added by each operation.
- Settle actual costs, according to how they occurred, on a specific cost structure.

Unit Costing   If your company makes unique products only to customer orders, you need unit costing. You have very little choice but to cost each individual order by deciding which unitary components you will have to put together. You will have to find out what other costs will be incurred as you do so.

The relevant database is a set of reference unit cost estimates. CO-PC Product Costing helps you locate which elements you need, and you can transfer them in blocks to the relevant quotes and sales order items or to the cost accounting objects that will be orders and projects.

This builds the planned costs of the quote, which can be compared to the actual costs as the order proceeds toward completion. Materials are consumed, and these materials all have their quantities or values assigned to the accounts under the correct cost element headings as data is collected on the activities that consume them. Overhead is applied, and charges for external activities add to the cost.

The sales order is documented with a continuous comparison between planned and actual costs for the whole of its life. From this data, a simultaneous calculation of the contribution margin can be carried out and the results recorded on the sales order document.

Order Costing   In make-to-stock production, combining order and unit costing methods is useful because order lots and batches of product are usually produced in response to production orders. Different cost estimates are prepared as alternative versions that take part in simultaneous costing to ensure exact control of the actual costs incurred by the relevant cost elements, sender cost centers and their activities, materials used, and so on.

The system supports settlement of some or all costs to stock and automatic calculation to support inventory control over finished and semifinished products. The value of stocks of unfinished goods and work in process can be calculated automatically.

Process manufacturing includes production processes that have a step-by-step structure and those that entail a cyclic input of materials.

Continuous-flow production is characterized by long processing runs of a single basic material. The control document for continuous-flow processing is the period production order. Comparisons are made between target and actual costs, planned output for a period and actual output, including cost usages from backflushing surplus material or summarized confirmations of production. The costs are charged to individual cost elements of the production structure in relation to the quantities produced.

Backflushing occurs in the chemical industry—for example, where some of the output can be returned to the process as semifinished product. There may be byproducts and co-products with alternative uses to the main product, and some product may bypass some of the production stages in the process cycle. The production order documents these variations.

Trading companies need a costing system that can provide accurate valuations of the costs and the prices, taking into account the individual costing and pricing structures that prevail in the type of business and under the market conditions at the time. The basic method is to apply overhead to cost prices. Costing the overhead allows you to apply the overhead according to cost elements or in relation to overhead you have already calculated. The system allows you to use different levels of sales prices, such as net sales price or gross sales price, to compute additional overhead or surcharge, such as discounts or cash discounts. These factors vary in wholesaling and retailing.

Service companies use the functions and elements of process costing. The service operations have to be defined in terms of individual activities that can be measured. If these activities can each be measured, they can be subject to planning. When the work is done, the actual amount of each activity component can be entered in quantitative terms; the measured activity is the cost driver. This allows the valuation process to cost each activity using predetermined rates, and thus allocate the costs to the service cost structure under the appropriate cost element headings. From this point on, the flexible reporting system of SAP R/3 can be used to collate the information and present it to the decision-makers in your company.

Assigning Accounts with R/3 Cost Objects

A cost object exists for SAP R/3 if there is a master record for it. The function of a cost object is to control the allocation, analysis, and settlement of costs related to the object it represents. It may relate directly to a production unit; it may be an organizational structure component that is useful in reporting value flows. In essence, a cost object is an identification number and a set of master record data fields that can be accessed in connection with that number.

Unit costs of all cost objects are the basis for arriving at all costing values. The cost object could be an entity that is quite independent of any particular SAP application—a convenient peg on which to hang information relevant to the specific costing procedures of your company. A cost object may collect the cost of two or more other cost objects. This constitutes a cost object hierarchy, which can branch down any number of layers and extend to any number of cost objects on each level. Most cost structures are in the form of cost object hierarchies of this inverted tree shape if plotted, for example, through the SAP R/3 online reporting system using the graphical interface.

If you run projects or production lines, you might find it informative to have certain cost information gathered by cost objects, along with the normal product costing. One way to achieve this is to define unique cost objects for each project or production line of interest.

If your installation has other SAP modules installed and configured, you will find it convenient to use the cost objects from these applications to define your own unique cost objects by copying some or all data structures from these predefined SAP cost objects. For example, these cost object types are used in the following application modules:

- PS-Project System network, project item
- CO-Controlling internal order
- SD-Sales and Distribution sales order
- MM-Materials Management material number
- PP-Production Planning production order, routing
- PM-Plant Maintenance maintenance order

If you have the unit costs for all your cost objects, you can display inventory costings and call for profitability analyses by using the full set of fixed and variable costs. You can use any combination of the current costing systems in your company.

The SAP R/3 system carries the definitions, in the form of master data, for all the cost object controlling functions of the SAP integrated system. Any transaction with data relevant to costing is processed according to these definitions.

Results from Costing a Cost Object   Costing results are stored by version so that different methods and periods can be compared. Each assembly is itemized in a costing created from a cost object. The data used can be planned or actual, and it can be as valuations or as quantities to which standard rates can be applied by the system at the time. A costing produces information on each of 40 cost components for each cost object, itemized for each assembly, and the whole is replicated for each version of the costing structure, if required.

Legal analysis demands that the origins of cost estimates be identifiable. This, in turn, requires that details be kept for the cost origins of all the contributors to the values recorded as cost object components. A cost origin has to be a document that identifies a transaction by means such as these:

- The vendor number for external procurement and the provision of external activities
- The operation number, the identification of the sender cost center, and the activity type for each internal activity
- The material number or material group code, if there were stock movements or the consumption of goods
- The cost center for charging overhead

The SAP R/3 system running CO-PC Product Costing can carry out the following procedures using cost origins to associate posted movements with cost elements:

- Conduct valuation using individual cost structures or cost rates.
- Assign costs to standard cost elements.
- Establish the costing basis for overhead.
- Accept planning and account assignment directives at any level of the costing structures.
- Prepare reports at any analysis level to display planned or actual resource-usage variances.

Reviewing Valuation Methods

The following costing systems are available in the CO-Controlling module of the SAP R/3 system and can be used in any combination:

- Unit costing
- Product costing
- Production order costing
- Cost object controlling for make-to-stock production
- Cost object controlling for process manufacturing
- Cost object controlling for make-to-order production
- Cost object controlling for plant construction

The valuation of input factors and the presentation of this data for costing analysis are carried out by a uniform valuation method across all costing systems. The source of the data differentiates the methods; different methods are required for costing when technical quantities are involved, such as when using bills of materials and routings. Variations also occur when existing cost estimates have to be copied or referenced. Manual entry of cost estimates is supported, and the R/3 system suggests default values whenever possible for editing as necessary.

The valuation process extends to the following calculations:

- Planned input quantities with planned allocation rates and planned prices
- Actual input quantities with standard prices and standard activity prices
- Actual input quantities with actual prices and actual activity prices
- Partial or total output quantities
- Scrap quantities
- Order-specific cost settlement according to the quantities delivered
- Calculation of all types of variance
- Profitability analyses to different layout formats

Input quantities can be evaluated by any of a range of methods. The method chosen is recorded as the valuation variant. These variants follow:

- Standard prices, current prices, future or previous
- Moving average prices

- Tax-based and commercial or "political" prices
- Standard activity prices
- Actual activity prices
- Applying variances on standard or actual prices adjusted to match changes in planning or historical amounts

In the service sector, it is possible to have the system split the costs into fixed and variable components; this enables you to carry out marginal and absorption costing together. You can choose any viewpoint of output to evaluate services rendered.

By having the required functionality available online, the system offers a modern control system covering products and the analysis of results. The following outcomes are supported:

- The cost of goods manufactured and the cost of goods sold are displayed on efficient and informative cost structures. These structures are understandable from a business viewpoint and accurate from a product cost accounting perspective.

- You can see the effects on the financial accounts and year-end closing of using different valuation techniques. This enables you to make choices on the basis of correct information.

- Not all divisions of a corporate group have to use the same valuation methods; each can use the methods most suitable to the division.

- Detailed costing records can be made available for each alternative or parallel valuation of variances between planned and actual costs for each business segment.

- The costing methods throughout the group don't necessarily depend on the costing documentation requirements of the logistics operations.

Reporting in Product Cost Accounting

You can adjust the structure of a report to suit your requirements. The standard system contains many predefined standard reports that you can modify and extend, often in online mode. Both the format and the data are under your control.

Orders can be grouped by order type, for example, and then line items can be selected on the basis of their connection to a specific cost object. Summaries and graphical representations are available at all stages of analysis and reporting.

Cost objects can be compared and the variances computed by using any dimensions for comparison: between orders, between periods, between similar cost objects, and between cost objects of different types.

Planning and Simulating from Unit Costing

You can apply unit costing regardless of the status of an order, because it is based on a quantity structure that you define manually. Here are some uses of a comprehensive system of unit costing:

- Price determination
- Costing to make quotes and tenders
- Costing to support the processing of orders
- Planning of costs and resources to prepare order and project cost estimates
- Making sample cost estimates for new or existing products using an existing estimate as a reference model to be edited and updated
- Defining sales prices for sales orders
- Preparing, planning, controlling, and settling investments by means of orders and projects
- Preparing cost estimates for base planning objects, which can range from a single-level assembly to a multilevel structure that includes other base planning objects. A base planning object can also be an instrument for integrating information from other, non-SAP applications.

You can display the costing information before, during, and after production or project activities and before, during, and after sales activities.

In the activities of sales and distribution, you can use unit costing in a couple of ways:

- To transfer unit cost estimates at any time to reference objects such as orders, projects, and sales orders
- To cost and check quickly the feasibility of extra sales orders, alternative or modified product components or characteristics, and any changes in the activities involved

Analyzing Profitability with CO-PA

CO-PCA Profit Center Accounting is closely associated with CO-PA Profitability Analysis. However, there is an important distinction between the following aspects of profitability analysis:

- **Profitability analysis** is the periodic analysis of the profit and loss made by the strategic units or the entire company.
- **Cost-of-sales accounting** is also a form of profitability analysis. It is used in the management of market-oriented activities.

Both types of profitability analysis call on the same costing information but treat it in different ways. Sales managers need to be able to estimate profits in the short term by using interim reports. These reports are based on standard values and imputed costs derived from standard manufacturing costs with cash discounts and rebates. Sales managers use these interim reports because the actual data is not available at the time the billing document has to be issued. Periodic profitability analysis can wait for the actual values to be collated.

The SAP R/3 CO-PA Profitability Analysis component provides the full range of analyses covering the following requirements:

- Current sales data valued with standard costs and prices at the level of the individual product and for individual customers
- Calculation of actual cost variances for summarized business segments on a periodic basis
- Proportional assignment of fixed costs to measure net profit at the divisional level
- Application of period profit center accounting in situations involving large fluctuations in stock levels

Both the periodic profit-and-loss statement and the interim sales report must provide the answers to similar questions, even though their answers may take different forms:

- What is the relationship between gross sales and net sales revenue?
- How were the sales deductions calculated for each market segment?
- What was the profit on this specific order?
- Which products or market segments show the greatest increases in sales revenue?
- Which products or market segments made the highest contribution margin?
- What are the shifts, if any, between the main business segments?
- What are the planned contribution margins for each product?

The cost-of-sales accounting method uses standard costs to produce interim reports. This method enables you to look at any market segment immediately, without waiting for the actual data to arrive.

Accounting the Cost of Sales Using Standard Costs (Interim Reports)

The market-driven needs of sales management dictate the requirement to be able to estimate profits in the short term by using interim reports based on standard values and imputed costs. These interim values are derived from standard manufacturing costs with cash discounts and rebates, because the actual data is not available at the time the billing document must be issued.

When the actual data arrives, the interim reports are usually reconciled with it on a period basis to yield the Cost of Sales Accounting Using Actual Costs (reconciled) reports. Because of the lag in time, these reports are not as useful for managing the sales activities; their function is more to document and summarize.

Accounting By Fixed-Cost Absorption

Profitability accounting requires that profit and loss be calculated on the basis of both full costs and marginal costs using contribution margin accounting.

The actual costs can be assigned to the business segments collectively or in proportion to sales. Therefore, the fixed costs can be absorbed across several levels of the organization for each period.

When costs are assigned to user-defined business segments, they have usually been gathered from one or more cost centers. However, costs may have been assigned to orders so that they can be collected from the customers; these costs can also be taken into account. Direct costs can be assigned to any level of a business segment.

Using the SAP R/3 Organizational Structure

The structure of an organization from an accounting viewpoint must be formally defined if will be used by a computing system. SAP R/3 defines a multilevel structure in terms of nested classifications, which are known as the *Enterprise Data Model* (EDM):

- **Client** is the name of a dataset that cannot overlap any other client dataset. For example, TEST and MYCOMPANY could be clients with separate datasets. SAP R/3 works with only one client at a time.

- **Company code** is the identification number of an independent accounting unit that can generate its own financial statements. It is a legal requirement that a group that operates in several countries must establish a separate company code unit for each country.

- **Business area** is a company code that further subdivides the figures posted to the General Ledger of the parent company code but has to be reconciled with it. The business area is not an independent business unit, although it manages the transaction information and the financial results shown in the company code balance sheet and the profit-and-loss statement as they concern its business area.

- **Controlling area** takes into cost accounting both the accounting units, such as company codes and business areas, and the logistics units, such as plant and sales organization. A controlling area may encompass several company codes, providing they all share a Common Chart of Accounts.

- **Operating concern** is a unit used in CO-PA Profitability Analysis to focus on the market and sales of a business, in order to set off costs against revenue. An operating concern can encompass several controlling areas, provided they all use the same Chart of Accounts. The operating concern can also be selective in its zone of interest by defining specific segments of the market—in terms of a product range for a certain customer group in a sales area, for example.

- **Profit center** is a subsection of the business responsible for its own profit or loss. It must be assigned to only one controlling area.

Under the CO-Controlling system, any profit-related activity, such as sales or the internal exchange of goods and services, is documented in at least one of the controlling cost objects, such as orders, materials, assets, and cost centers. Each cost object must be assigned to the corresponding profit center.

To calculate a result from profitability analysis, all profit-related activities are copied to CO-PCA Profit Center Accounting, where they can be associated with their profit centers.

Exploring the Routes of Control Data Flow

CO-Controlling uses transaction data from the FI-GL General Ledger accounts to maintain its own set of records. Overhead costs are posted to one of the cost centers according to their source of origin. The CO-Controlling system uses additional postings to assign the direct costs to other cost objects, such as orders, processes, and business segments.

The overhead costs posted to the cost centers according to their origins are also reassigned by allocation rules to the other assignment objects, according to their use of the overhead.

CO-Controlling shares direct costs and overhead costs among the assignment objects according to their use. It also allocates the values to other cost objects for the purpose of control and analysis.

Revenue and sales deductions are posted directly to the relevant business segment or profit center. The cost objects either remain in inventory or are posted through to profitability analysis.

You can thus carry out period accounting at the profit center level, taking into account changes in inventory. You also can call for cost-of-sales accounting in each business segment.

CO-Controlling operates a system that is parallel to the FI-Financial Accounting system but separate from it. You can display a business-oriented profit-and-loss analysis, because all the data objects that have a bearing on the computation of value added are represented in the analysis and can therefore be scrutinized down to the details of the individual transactions from which the data is drawn. The cost data is allocated according to rules that are under your control; this helps you avoid any misunderstandings when interpreting your analysis reports.

Customer quotations and sales orders provide the information that CO-PA Profitability Analysis needs:

- Billing documents
- Sales quantities
- Revenues
- Sales deductions

Issued, received, or manufactured goods produce the information that helps calculate the following items, for example:

- Manufacturing costs
- Standard costs
- Moving average price
- Transfer prices

External activities carried out by contractors, for example, are either posted directly to CO-PA Profitability Analysis from FI-Financial Accounting or are settled from the orders and projects that also contribute to CO-PA Profitability Analysis.

You also can analyze separate business segments, because you can post cost and revenue data directly to a business segment, just as you can post the data to any cost center. Any of the following systems can carry out direct postings automatically:

- FI-Financial Accounting
- CO-Controlling
- SD-Sales and Distribution

By contrast, a profit center is not a separate account assignment object. The values held by it are derived from the master data assignments of the cost objects in the CO-Controlling system. Posting these values to a profit center occurs automatically in the background under the supervision of the CO-PCA Profit Center Accounting standard business functions.

Accounting with Revenue Elements

The *Generally Accepted Accounting Principles* (GAAP) require that the values recorded in the accounts of a company are in a permanent state of reconciliation. To comply with this requirement, an online accounting system has to maintain a journal, a set of account balances, and all the documents to support them. SAP R/3 meets these conditions and, in some respects, exceeds them. In particular, revenue data transferred to CO-PA Profitability Analysis can be reconciled with the posted revenue in FI-Financial Accounting.

The SD-Sales and Distribution system posts revenue data originating in the invoiced sales orders to the relevant FI-GL General Ledger accounts for revenue accounting. These accounts have to be specified in the Common Chart of Accounts belonging to the company code. This chart defines the usual revenue accounts that have been structured to suit the company code, and there will be accounts that contain sales deductions, return deliveries, rebates, credit memos, and any other noted financial instruments used by that company code.

To allow reconciliation between the two systems, the revenue elements defined in FI-Financial Accounting must be in accord with the revenue elements used by the CO-PA Profitability Analysis system. This shared set of revenue elements must reflect not only the financial accounting structure of the Chart of Accounts, but also the structures developed to provide a sensitive and timely mechanism for cost controlling and profitability analysis.

The billing data from the SD-Sales and Distribution system or from an individual user interface has to be directed simultaneously toward two accounting processes:

- FI-Financial Accounting has to identify the destination in terms of the revenue accounts in the Chart of Accounts.
- CO-PA Profitability Analysis has to identify the destination in terms of the revenue elements of that system, which are usually derived from the revenue account structure that appears in the Chart of Accounts.

Sometimes the sources of revenue in company codes are not readily matched to the revenue elements of the CO-PA Profitability Analysis system. In these cases, you can use the FI-GLX Extended General Ledger to associate the revenue sources with the appropriate items from the lists of origins recognized by this component. The additional subdivisions of revenue accounts supported by the Extended General Ledger remain reconciled with the General Ledger revenue accounts. Calling on the extra analysis information available through the Extended General Ledger enables accurate reconciliation with the revenue elements of the CO-PA Profitability Analysis component.

Using Estimate Revenue Elements

Sometimes you might find that the billing data transferred to CO-PA Profitability Analysis is not accurate. Revenue elements may have to be estimated. For example, a sales deduction could be estimated as 10 percent of domestic sales revenue on the grounds that previous analyses support this as a reasonable prediction. The CO-PA Profitability Analysis system can provide a complete and up-to-date estimate of gross and net revenues as soon as the billing takes place.

Such estimated sales deductions are usually posted and transferred to FI-Financial Accounting, where they can be balanced with the actual sales deductions when they are available. If necessary, the CO-PA Profitability Analysis system then adjusts the calculation for future estimates.

A typical report structure for an estimated revenue element includes the following display fields:

- Gross revenue
- Freight and packing
- Discount
- Estimate rebate or cash discount
- Estimate warranty
- Net revenue

Calculating Profitability

Profitability is calculated for a business segment. The SAP R/3 system is supplied with a set of criteria from which the definition of a business segment can be assembled. The most commonly used criteria are provided as lists of proposals that can be adopted or ignored when you set up your own CO-PA Profitability Analysis system. You can define unique criteria to suit your own circumstances.

These are some ways you can specify how you want to define the business segments to be used in your company code:

- From the customer masters, define some customer groups on the basis of their shared location, line of business, value of past transactions, and so on.
- From the material masters, define a range of products that will be included in a business segment.
- From the required business classification code you have defined for entry on each sales order, select certain values to be included in a business segment.

Data that will be used to specify criteria can be taken from any of the integrated SAP applications. Complex criteria can be built up by using the objects that appear only in the CO-Controlling module or only in the CO-PA Profitability Analysis system itself.

You can combine criteria across dimensions and levels to make a business segment specification that will give you the profitability analysis for exactly what it is you want to take a look at. Here's an example:

> *Segment A is defined as any transaction that involves any member of Customer Group CG1 that is in Industry I6 and deals with any product in Product Group P4 and has been authorized by Sales Consultant SC26. And it might be that Sales Consultant SC26 is defined as any member of Department G who has been temporarily assigned to Department S and is working from Office O7.*

In summary, a business segment is a portion of your business that you have defined in terms of products, customers, activities, and organization, combined in any way you want.

Unlike cost centers and order data structures, for example, the business segments do not have to exist in the form of master records. When a segment is needed, the transaction data is assembled according to the definition of the segment. When a document is automatically transferred from another integrated application—SD-Sales and Distribution, for example—all the information about the customer and the products that is needed to meet the criteria for the business segments is copied from the relevant customer and product master records to the sales order or the billing document. When this data is transferred to the CO-PA Profitability Analysis system, the remaining criteria for building the business segment are applied to determine where the item is posted in the CO-PA Profitability Analysis system.

Manual entry of line items is supported, along with the use of planned values. In these circumstances, the CO-PA Profitability Analysis system derives the information necessary to place the entries or planning date in the appropriate business segments.

A business segment is an account assignment object to which an entry may be posted, provided that all the segment criteria are met by valid data in the entry. This proviso ensures that subsequent analyses will be possible, using different subselections from the business segment criteria if necessary.

Establishing Key Figures

The R/3 CO-PA Profitability Analysis system uses the concept of key figures to define the lowest level at which it is possible to display the quantities, revenue, sales deductions, and costs when you are carrying out a contribution margin calculation for a business segment. The system offers lists of commonly used key figures as proposals for you to adopt or supplement by key figures of your own specification.

These key figures can be set at any level of detail. Revenue, for example, can be displayed across a revenue element structure consisting of revenue from external customers and partner companies. Revenue alterations, such as credit memos, rebates, and sales deductions can be displayed as separate revenue elements.

Costs are stored as value fields; the details depend on the specific SAP R/3 applications that are installed and configured. For example, the following costs could be displayed in the CO-PA Profitability Analysis system:

- From CO-PC Product Cost Accounting, the manufacturing costs from product cost estimates

- From CO-OPA Order and Project Accounting, the manufacturing costs, or the cost of the goods sold as documented on sales orders

- From CO-OPA Order and Project Accounting or from the SAP R/3 PS-Project System, the manufacturing costs or the cost of purchases, as documented by projects

- From CO-OPA Order and Project Accounting, or from the SAP R/3 PS-Project System, the costs of overhead projects or orders

- From PP-Production Planning, the variances from production orders

- From CO-CCA Cost Center Accounting, the fixed costs

- From CO-CCA Cost Center Accounting, the variances

- From FI-Financial Accounting, the direct postings

- From CO-PA Profitability Analysis, the estimated costs

Planning Sales, Revenue, and Profit

The planning of sales quantities, revenue, and profit in the context of corporate planning is the exclusive province of the SAP R/3 CO-PA Profitability Analysis system. The business segment is the focus of this planning.

The possibilities of business segment planning include the following:

- Planning the sales quantity for a business segment

- Using the planned sales quantity and the values available to the system for revenue, discounts, rebates, and so on to compute the planned gross revenue and planned net revenue

- Transferring the planned costs, such as manufacturing cost and cost center overheads, from the CO-Controlling system, and calculating the planned profit for a business segment

- Planning all fixed cost allocations at different levels of the segment

The CO-PA Profitability Analysis system allows you to plan sales quantity data for any number of business segments, defined as you want. So there is no need to specify a permanent level at which planned values and quantities will be entered. Each business can operate sales and profit planning in the most informative way. And the SAP R/3 graphical interface is available to assist you.

Profit Center Accounting with CO-PCA

A profit center is not an independent account assignment object. It derives its information from existing account assignment objects. The master record of each account assignment object includes a field that identifies the responsible profit center. The profit center is defined by an organizational master record in the system and can therefore store descriptive information—in particular, the criteria that define which account assignment objects it is responsible for.

Profit centers can be summarized and their results combined on any number of hierarchical levels and across different hierarchies. The profit center is a way of looking at a particular selection of transaction data assigned to various accounts to see how it affects the operating profit of that portion of the business the profit center represents.

Ledger-Based Period Accounting at the Profit Center Level

Profit centers allow you to collate all profit-related posting information under the divisions of your organizational structure. Every posting is saved simultaneously as a line item, and totals are recorded in the FI-GLX Financial Accounting Extended General Ledger. As a consequence, CO-PCA Profit Center Accounting is functionally separate from the cost-of-sales accounting used in CO-PA Profitability Analysis.

When you place an original account assignment object in the domain of a profit center, you are setting up separate data flows under control of the posting rules that will be obeyed by the CO-PCA Profit Center Accounting system. Transaction data is transferred in real time. When it comes into existence in the FI-Financial Accounting system, the CO-Controlling system sets up a copy in parallel, and the CO-PCA Profit Center Accounting system reflects this copy.

Primary cost information is reflected from

- Cost centers
- Orders
- Projects
- Product planning orders

Secondary costs may be reflected in profit centers as a result of

- Cost allocation
- Cost assessment
- Cost distribution
- Transfer postings
- Order settlement
- Accruals
- Surcharges

Revenues can appear in profit centers as the result of

- Direct account assignment from FI-Financial Accounting
- Billing documents via the interface with SD-Sales and Distribution

Values attributable to changes in inventory and work in process can also be reflected in profit centers.

The Structure of a Ledger-Based Period Accounting Profitability Report

The line item of a period accounting profitability report represents an FI-GL General Ledger account number and its name. The line items can be selected and organized by hierarchies of profit centers.

There is continuous reconciliation at the company code level between the FI-Financial Accounting system and the CO-PCA Profit Center Accounting system. Thus the inputs to each profit center can be any combination of the following sources of information:

- Customer orders and projects
- Cost objects
- Fixed assets
- Materials management
- Internal orders and projects
- Manufacturing orders
- Cost centers

Transaction data from any external system or SAP application can be integrated with the R/3 system.

The benefits of this integrated system include the following insights:

- The flow of the value of goods from one profit center to another is displayed, having eliminated internal transactions.
- The profitability report reveals the origins of all profit-relevant data.

CHAPTER 14

Understanding the Enterprise Controlling Module

In this chapter

Consulting the Executive Information System

The essence of enterprise controlling is the translation of management objectives into planned target performances, usually expressed as monetary values, for the parts of the enterprise, and perhaps also for the links between them. These planned values are frequently compared to the actual values, and steps are taken to adjust the plan for the next period and the resources allocated to achieve it.

The basis of this endeavor must be reliable and timely information. The realm of the enterprise controller has to include the business data-processing system. In terms of the SAP R/3 system, the data of interest resides—at least conceptually—in the Open Information Warehouse (discussed in Chapter 10, "Developing an SAP Open Information Warehouse"), along with the EDM-Enterprise Data Model that helps make business sense of the stored information.

The SAP product at the center of enterprise controlling is the SAP-EIS Executive Information System.

The Executive Information System provides flexible access to the *Open Information Warehouse* (OIW) for the purpose of reporting the following to the enterprise controller:

- The financial status of the company
- The results of corporate planning and controlling
- Investment in the resources of the company
- Maintenance of the assets of the company
- Acquisition and development of the company's human resources
- Market factors related to decision-making, including supply markets, market segment performance, and competitor performance
- Structural factors in the business processes, such as production structure, cost structure, financial accounting structure, and profitability analysis procedures

The originating sources for the data needed for this type of reporting are located within the company and in the external environment. For example, the performance of the various markets and the competitors in them need subtle data collection if the results are to be meaningful to the enterprise controller.

By design, the data generated by the SAP systems in the company always is available in a form that can be immediately processed and interpreted in terms of the EDM-Enterprise Data Model of the company and its various views.

Each SAP R/3 system application has a suite of information system functions that can be integrated to provide the necessary flow of data about the internal systems of the company and, to a certain extent, about some of the market factors.

Each R/3 application installed and configured in your installation is set up to provide information for the SAP EIS. The enterprise controllers can use the *drill-down* procedure on any item that appears on their user interface screens. This allows them to work down the hierarchy of data objects until they reach the individual item of interest, or until they call functions to collate the data in summary form.

The SAP EIS also can report on exceptions. This allows the enterprise controller to define the trends or specific values used as indexes of the health of the enterprise. Acceptable ranges of these indicator variables can be defined so that the EIS reports only when the specified indicator is found to be out of the acceptable range. The system performs calculations of any complexity to arrive at a value that indicates the enterprise parameter that has been selected as one of the indexes for exception reporting to the enterprise controller.

Accessing the Logistics Information System

The integrated Logistics module essentially focuses on managing production from purchasing through to sales and distribution. It encompasses many profit-generating activities of your company and therefore is of vital interest to the enterprise controllers.

The LO-LIS Logistics Information System includes components that collate information from each application installed in your implementation, such as SD-Sales and Distribution, PP-Production Planning, MM-Materials Management, PM-Plant Maintenance, and QM-Quality Management.

Accessing the Financial Information System

The scope of the FIS-Financial Information System includes information on customers and vendors, including prospects and alternative suppliers.

Accessing the Human Resources Information System

The HRIS-Human Resources Information System can maintain detailed information on the skills and qualifications not only of the people now on the payroll, but also of those who have left and might be considered for reemployment. Furthermore, the system can maintain personnel profiles for all the work positions in the company using the same system of classification used to record the staff's capabilities.

As training takes place and work experience accumulates, the value of the company's human resource assets increases. This information is recorded in the Human Resources Information System and is available at any moment to the enterprise controller. If part of the enterprise is controlled automatically—the assignment of sales representatives to callers, for example—the system can determine which members of the staff are available at that moment, and the call can be routed to the person best qualified to take it.

The same logical approach to the distribution of enterprise controlling is ready to be applied at many levels and aspects of the business of your company. If the information in the system is complete and accurate, and if a good set of rules can be applied to it to arrive at a valid decision, there may be a good case for having the system carry out the decision-making process automatically. Depending on the importance of the decision, you might decide to have the system merely propose a course of action for the approval of a human decision-maker. On the other hand, you might want to take advantage of the speed and timeliness offered by the system, and rely on an automatic logging of the events and perhaps a scheduled report to keep you aware of what enterprise controlling decisions the system is making on your behalf.

Using Standard Business Management Programs

Most components of the Financial and Controlling modules needed for enterprise controlling are normally integrated in an SAP R/3 system. Their functionality therefore is part of the EIS Executive Information System and is available to the EC-Enterprise Controlling module.

The following standard components are obviously relevant:

- EC-BP Business Planning
- EC-MC Management Consolidation
- EC-PCA Profit Center Accounting

Using Additional Components for Enterprise Controlling

The wide variety of enterprises using the SAP R/3 system demonstrates how versatile the system can be. In particular, the relative importance of the different types of business accounting will not be the same for each enterprise. Different combinations of the following components from the CO-Controlling module can be configured in support of the EC-Enterprise Controlling module:

- CO-CCA Cost Center Accounting
- CO-OPA Order and Project Accounting
- CO-PC Product Cost Accounting
- CO-PA Profitability Analysis

Using Cost Center Accounting

The distribution method of CO-CCA is totally flexible and under your control. You can simulate distribution to test the effects of the rules before you post the values. You can see the effects of a distribution immediately by calling for an online report, and you can repeat the distribution procedures at any time.

Using Order and Project Accounting

The distinguishing feature of the SAP module CO-OPA Order and Project Accounting is its capability to settle in detail the actual costs according to rules particular to each item. In addition to this capability to settle capital spending orders in precise detail, CO-OPA offers these benefits:

- Planning is available for all resources and costs required, in quantity and value.
- Charges can be computed from prices at the time, with imputed allocations of overhead and actual costs.
- Open items for purchase requisitions, purchase orders, and material reservations are closely monitored.

- All cash-related procedures such as down-payment requests and down payments are displayed.
- Order reports are evaluated and analyzed concurrently.

Integration of Order and Project Accounting with Asset Accounting If you are managing fixed assets such as buildings and machines, the settlement of capital spending orders is of crucial importance. The system offers detailed settlement rules and a close integration with the FI-AA Asset Accounting system to offer these advantages:

- Settlement of costs to the appropriate balance sheet accounts under the heading Assets Under Construction while the capital spending order is ongoing
- Order-based display of special depreciation for *assets under construction* (AuCs)
- Recognition of subsidies, grants, and down payments
- Settlement of partial orders over a hierarchy of orders

Because all costs are based on unified posting and settlement rules in the SAP R/3 system, you can allocate costs from orders and projects to the various target objects using the same rules or rules that you have specified separately. You can keep track of complex overhead costs with maintenance and capital spending orders; this gives you the chance to take effective action as soon as possible.

Capital Spending Orders When a company is capable of producing some assets and commodities in-house, the main objective of a capital spending order is to monitor the costs of doing so. Maintenance projects can be controlled and accounted in the same way.

Planned Cost Schedules Costs and deadlines on orders and projects that take a long time to complete are constrained by the financial facts of life. Money is not always available when you need it. You need to know what costs are expected on the orders and projects in order to perform financial and liquidity planning. It helps to have some idea of how the costs are likely to be incurred in detail over the first few accounting periods and in broader terms thereafter up to the date of completion.

A cost schedule is a plan, extending the length of an order or a project, showing the values expected to be allocated to costs. The schedule has a key date. Until this date is known and entered on the plan, the forecast of costs has to be moved ahead to the best estimated date.

The SAP R/3 system supports the EC-Enterprise Controller in the following ways:

- The system automatically determines the tasks from the planned start and finish dates for the order.
- Cost distribution across the schedule can be suited to the specific order.
- Graphical representations of the data model are readily available online and in print.

If you have carried out cost element planning or created a unit costing for the order, the system can use this information to develop a cost schedule.

A costing system uses a set of *costing objects*, which are the different products, production orders and other orders, resources, and so on. The only qualification for a costing object is that it can be allocated costs that mean something when they are totaled under the heading of that costing object. The costing objects can be conceptual or tangible, organizational or geographical.

The pivotal concept in costing is the structure of *cost drivers,* or cost objects on which the actual costs are settled, according to how they were incurred. SAP R/3 CO-Controlling provides a range of model structures on which you can base a structure specific to the needs of your company.

Using Product Cost Accounting

The purpose of the CO-PC Product Cost Accounting module is to determine the unit cost of the product units your company does business in. These units are referred to as *cost objects.* One cost object exists for each product or each distribution package for each product. A cost object is an entity in the R/3 system that can be used as the reference for a cost estimate. You can use any of the following types of business entities as cost objects:

- Materials
- Cost object IDs
- Production orders
- Sales document items (inquiry, quotation, sales order)
- Projects—*work breakdown structure* (WBS) elements
- Internal orders
- Primary cost elements

SAP is an integrated system. The CO-PC Product Cost Accounting module is directly linked to the results from the Logistics modules. CO-PC passes data to the SD-Sales and Distribution module for sales orders. And, it passes data to the CO-OPA Order and Project Accounting component and the SAP R/3 Project System for internal cost control.

The CO-PC Product Cost Accounting component addresses the following costing types:

- **Production order costing,** in which the costs of producing a batch or run from the production line are computed and associated with the production order that initiated the production run.
- **Inventory costing,** which computes the cost of each item in the inventory of stock and semifinished products.

These costing procedures are discussed in Chapter 13, "Understanding the Controlling Module."

Four types of cost object controlling are differentiated because they offer different benefits according to the type of business they are located in:

- Make-to-stock production
- Process manufacturing

■ Make-to-order production

■ Plant construction

Costing Requirements of Different Company Types   Modern controlling methods have developed to support technical manufacturing processes and service industries. The methods have to match the needs of the individual company. The SAP approach is to establish an extensive library of standard business functions that can be controlled by the implementers by parameters to yield a customized system finely tuned to the requirements of the different classes of users in a specific company.

Manufacturers require a costing system that shows where and by how much their manufacturing processes add value to their raw materials. They differ in their style of manufacturing according to whether they make to a production order or to replace stock in their inventory. Their processes differ over a range from discrete one-off production to repetitive production to continuous-flow production.

Trading companies need a method of costing that enables them to apply overhead and surcharges to the cost prices of their goods, which they often have to keep to set or agreed-on final selling prices.

Service companies tend to adopt the principles of process costing, which revolves around the concept of cost drivers—in this case, the service activities. These companies need to be able to define, measure, plan, and pass on the costs incurred by their cost drivers, service calls, and other activities.

Make-to-Order, Make-to-Stock, Continuous Flow   The manufacturing industry has a polished costing method based on routings taken by work units and bills of materials. Manufacturing companies need to know what processes the product has to undergo, the costs of materials and resources, and the quantities. This is referred to as the *quantity structure* for this product. If you have this information, you can begin to cost the product by assembling the costing components.

The customer order sets off costing in the make-to-order company. Because each order is unique, very few routings and bills of materials can be applied without editing. Yet it is of the utmost importance to be able to arrive quickly at a cost prediction for this one-off product in order to be able to issue a quotation and take part in competitive tendering for the work. An effective costing system for this sort of company must give this approach to one-off tendering a high priority, because its future business may depend on its speed and accuracy.

Manufacturers who make to stock apply standard bills of materials and routings that may contain great amounts of actual data. Products and orders for quantities of products can be costed from this database.

If the manufacturing process is continuous, it is probably not prone to much variation. It probably works at its best only if the rate of flow is within narrow limits. Nevertheless, the contribution of the various cost components to the cost of the finished product is of interest to the management and shareholders. It is important to understand how and why costs vary if the flow rate and quality are allowed to move out of the normal operating ranges. This might happen because of variations in the raw materials or in the environmental conditions at the manufacturing plant.

The SAP R/3 Cost Object as an Account Assignment Device   A cost object exists for SAP R/3 if there is a master record for it. The function of a cost object is to control the allocation, analysis, and settlement of costs related to the object it represents. It may relate directly to a production unit, or it may be an organizational structure component that is useful in reporting value flows. In essence, a cost object is an identification number and a set of master record data fields that can be accessed in connection with that number.

Unit costs of each cost object are the basis for arriving at all costing values. If your installation has other SAP modules installed and configured, you will find it convenient to use the cost objects from these applications to define your own unique cost objects by copying some or all data structures from these predefined SAP cost objects. For example, these cost object types are used in the following application modules:

- PS-Project System—network, project item
- CO-Controlling—internal order
- SD-Sales and Distribution—sales order
- MM-Materials Management—material number
- PP-Production Planning—production order, routing
- PM-Plant Maintenance—maintenance order

If you have the unit costs for all your cost objects, you can display inventory costs and call for profitability analyses using the full set of fixed and variable costs. You can use any combination of the costing systems currently used in your company.

The CO-PC Product Cost Accounting component of the SAP R/3 system carries the definitions, in the form of master data, for all the cost object controlling functions of the SAP integrated system. Any transaction that contains data relevant to costing is processed according to these definitions.

Valuation Methods in Product Costing   The following costing systems are available in the CO-PC Product Cost Accounting component of the SAP R/3 system and can be used in any combination:

- Unit costing
- Product costing
- Production order costing
- Cost object controlling for make-to-stock production
- Cost object controlling for process manufacturing
- Cost object controlling for make-to-order production
- Cost object controlling for plant construction

The valuation process extends to the following calculations:

- Planned input quantities with planned allocation rates and planned prices
- Actual input quantities with standard prices and standard activity prices
- Actual input quantities with actual prices and actual activity prices
- Partial or total output quantities
- Scrap quantities .
- Order-specific cost settlement according to the quantities delivered
- Calculation of all variance types
- Profitability analyses

The EC-Enterprise Controlling module can report the effects of using different valuation techniques on the financial accounts and year-end closing. You then can make choices on the basis of correct information.

Using Profitability Analysis

CO-PCA Profit Center Accounting is closely associated with CO-PA Profitability Analysis. An important distinction should be made between the following aspects of profitability analysis:

- Periodic analysis of the profit and loss generated by the strategic units, or by the entire company, is usually referred to as **profitability analysis**.
- **Cost-of-sales accounting** is also a form of profitability analysis, which is used in the management of market-oriented activities.

Both types of analyses call on the same costing information but treat it in different ways. Sales managers need to be able to estimate profits in the short term by using interim reports based on standard values and imputed costs derived from standard manufacturing costs with cash discounts and rebates, because the actual data is not available at the time the billing document has to be issued. Periodic profitability analysis can wait for the actual cost values to be collected and collated.

The CO-PA Profitability Analysis component offers the full range of analyses covering the following requirements:

- Current sales data valued with standard costs and prices at the level of the individual product and for individual customers
- Calculation of actual cost variances for summarized business segments on a periodic basis
- Proportional assignment of fixed costs to measure net profit at the divisional level
- Application of period profit center accounting in situations with large fluctuations in stock levels

Challenging the Enterprise Controller

You could define a successful enterprise analyst as a person who could quickly assemble accurate answers to the following types of questions:

- What is the relationship between gross sales and net sales revenue?
- How were the sales deductions calculated for each market segment?
- What was the profit on this specific order?
- Which products or market segments are showing the greatest increases in sales revenue?
- Which products or market segments are making the highest contribution margin?
- What are the differences over time, if any, among the main business segments?
- What are the planned contribution margins for each product?

If your successful enterprise analyst also had the ear of the appropriate managers, you could be on the way to having a successful enterprise controller.

Applying Cost-of-Sales Accounting Using Standard Costs (Interim Reports)

The cost-of-sales accounting method, using standard costs to produce interim reports, allows you to look at any market segment immediately without waiting for the actual data to arrive.

The market-driven needs of sales management dictate the requirement to be able to estimate profits in the short term by using interim reports based on standard values and imputed costs. These interim values are derived from standard manufacturing costs with cash discounts and rebates, because the actual data is not available at the time the billing document has to be issued.

When the actual data arrives, the interim reports are usually reconciled with it periodically to yield the cost-of-sales accounting using actual costs (reconciled reports). Because of the lag time, these reports are not so useful for managing the sales activities—their function is more to document and summarize.

Representing the Company Organizational Structure

The structure of an organization from an accounting viewpoint must be formally defined if it is to be used by a computing system. SAP R/3 defines a multilevel structure in terms of nested classifications that comprise the EDM-Enterprise Data Model. The EDM consists of these elements:

- **Client** is a name attached to a dataset that cannot overlap any other client dataset. SAP R/3 works with only one client at a time.
- **Company code** is the identification number of an independent accounting unit that can generate its own financial statements. It is a legal requirement that a group that operates in several countries must establish a separate company code unit for each country.

- **Business area** is a subdivision of a company code that further divides the figures posted to the General Ledger of the parent company code but has to be reconciled with it. The business area is not an independent business unit, although it manages the transaction information and the financial results shown in the company code balance sheet and profit-and-loss statement as it relates to that business area.

- **Controlling area** takes into cost accounting both the accounting units (such as company codes and business areas) and the logistics units (such as plant and sales organization). A controlling area may encompass several company codes, as long as they all share a Common Chart of Accounts.

- **Operating concern** is a unit used in CO-PA Profitability Analysis to focus on the market and sales of a business in order to set off costs against revenue. An operating concern can encompass several controlling areas, as long as they all use a Common Chart of Accounts. The operating concern can also be selective in its zone of interest by defining specific segments of the market—in terms, for example, of a product range—in a sales area for a certain customer group.

- **Profit center** is a subsection of the business responsible for its own profit or loss. It must be assigned to only one controlling area.

Under the CO-Controlling system, any profit-related activity—such as sales or the internal exchange of goods and services—is documented in at least one of the controlling cost objects, such as orders, materials, assets, and cost centers. Each cost object must be assigned to the corresponding profit center.

To calculate a result from profitability analysis, all profit-related activities are copied to CO-PCA Profit Center Accounting, where they can be associated with their profit centers.

Revenue Element Accounting

The *Generally Accepted Accounting Principles* (GAAP) require that the values recorded in the accounts of a company be in a permanent state of reconciliation. To comply with this requirement, an online accounting system has to maintain a journal, a set of account balances, and all the documents to support them. The SAP R/3 system meets these conditions and, in some respects, exceeds them.

In particular, revenue data transferred to CO-PA Profitability Analysis can be reconciled with the posted revenue in FI-Financial Accounting.

In company codes where the sources of revenue are not readily matched to the revenue elements of the CO-PA Profitability Analysis system, the facilities of the FI-GLX Extended General Ledger generally are used to associate the revenue sources with the appropriate items chosen from the lists of origins recognized by this component. The additional subdivisions of revenue accounts supported by the Extended General Ledger and, as of Release 3.0, the FI-SL Special Purpose Ledger remain reconciled with the General Ledger revenue accounts. The advantage of calling on the extra analysis information available through the Extended General Ledger is that it enables accurate reconciliation with the revenue elements of the CO-PA Profitability Analysis component.

Estimating Revenue Elements

Occasionally, the billing data transferred to CO-PA Profitability Analysis may not be accurate. Revenue elements may have to be estimated. For example, a sales deduction could be estimated as 10 percent of domestic sales revenue on the grounds that previous analyses support this as a reasonable prediction.

The benefit is that the CO-PA Profitability Analysis system can provide a complete and up-to-date estimate of gross and net revenues as soon as the billing takes place.

Such estimated sales deductions are usually posted and transferred to FI-Financial Accounting, where they can be balanced with the actual sales deductions when they become available. If necessary, the CO-PA Profitability Analysis system then adjusts the calculation for future estimates.

Calculating Profitability

Profitability is calculated for a business segment. The SAP R/3 system offers a set of criteria from which you can assemble the definition of a business segment. The most commonly used criteria are provided as lists of proposals that can be . dopted or ignored when you set up your own CO-PA Profitability Analysis system. You can define fresh criteria to suit your own circumstances.

Planning Sales, Revenue, and Profit

The planning of sales quantities, revenue, and profit in the context of corporate planning is the exclusive province of the SAP R/3 CO-PA Profitability Analysis system. The business segment is the focus of this planning.

The possibilities of business segment planning follow:

■ Plan the sales quantity for a business segment.

■ Use the planned sales quantity and the values available to the system for revenue, discounts, rebates, and so on to compute the planned gross revenue and the planned net revenue.

■ Transfer the planned costs, such as manufacturing costs and cost center overheads, from the CO-Controlling system, and calculate the planned profit for a business segment.

■ Plan all fixed-cost allocations at different levels of the segment.

The CO-PA Profitability Analysis system allows you to plan sales quantity data for any number of business segments, defined as you want. So there is no need to specify a corporate level at which planned values and quantities are entered. Each business can operate sales and profit planning in the most informative way, and the SAP R/3 graphical interface is available to assist.

Profit Center Accounting Using the EC-PCA Module

A profit center is not an independent account assignment object; it gets its information from existing account assignment objects. The master record of each account assignment object includes a field that identifies the responsible profit center. The profit center is defined by an organizational master record in the system and therefore can store descriptive information—in particular, the criteria that define which account assignment objects it is responsible for.

Profit centers can be summarized and their results combined on any number of hierarchical levels and across different hierarchies.

The profit center is a way of looking at a particular selection of transaction data assigned to various accounts to see how it affects the operating profit of that portion of the business the profit center represents.

Ledger-Based Period Accounting at the Profit Center Level

Profit centers allow you to collate all profit-related posting information under the divisions of your organizational structure. Every posting is saved simultaneously as a line item and a totals record in the FI-GLX Extended General Ledger.

As a consequence, CO-PCA Profit Center Accounting is functionally separated from the cost-of-sales accounting used in CO-PA Profitability Analysis.

Revenues can appear in profit centers as the result of these actions:

- Direct account assignment from FI-Financial Accounting
- Billing documents via the interface with SD-Sales and Distribution

Values attributable to changes in inventory and work in progress can also be reflected in profit centers.

The Structure of a Ledger-Based Period Accounting Profitability Report

The line item of a period accounting profitability report represents an FI-GL General Ledger account number and its name. The line items can be selected and organized by hierarchies of profit centers.

There is continuous reconciliation at the company-code level between the FI-Financial Accounting system and the CO-PCA Profit Center Accounting system.

Thus, the inputs to each profit center can be any combination of the following sources of information:

- Customer orders and projects
- Cost objects
- Fixed assets

- Materials management
- Internal orders and projects
- Manufacturing orders
- Cost centers
- Transaction data from the FI-Financial Accounting, Logistics, and external systems

Some of the benefits of this integrated system follow:

- The flow of the value of goods from one profit center to another is displayed, having eliminated internal transactions.
- The profitability report reveals the origins of all profit-relevant data.

Accessing Early-Warning Information about Business Partners

One way you can set up a network to improve profitability is to arrange an early-warning system that discreetly but continuously updates information on specific business partners—perhaps all of them. For example, the important information for the management of outstanding debts, the *receivables,* may be centered on corporate customers and business transactions carried out with them and with their affiliated companies.

The normal source of this kind of information is an integrated online network of external information suppliers, such as credit reporting agencies and credit sales insurance firms. The Dun and Bradstreet database, for example, carries up-to-date information on more than 17 million companies. The information is available in 26 data elements, which can be culled selectively from the database.

Introducing the Strategic Enterprise Management Application

The SEM, due to be delivered in 1998, is an integrated suite of four component applications focused on cost-based and profit-based value management. The objective of this package is to provide information to senior management that can be used to increase the value of the enterprise for stakeholders such as employees, investors, and business partners.

The package is based on SAP R/3 and features the SAP Business Framework with *Business Application Programming Interface* (BAPI) technology. Implementations can be rapid, and new business designs can be set to work by using open, object-oriented technologies that allow R/3 to integrate with non-SAP applications without losing the integrity and reliability of unified SAP R/3 systems.

The *SAP Business Framework* is an integrated architecture standard that allows R/3 applications to work with third-party products and technologies. The *Business Framework* (BF) offers simplified upgrading and maintenance of links with legacy and R/2 systems, and with systems that are specific to an individual user company. The BF component includes more than 400 BAPIs, which allow integration with more than 1,000 third-party products and systems identified as members of the "BAPI Network." Any systems connecting through the SAP Business Framework can be upgraded independently of the main R/3 system.

The SAP SEM provides advanced developments of the fundamental R/3 applications and can support, for example, the following kinds of activities, each encapsulated in its own module:

- **Business Planning and Simulation** includes advanced simulation and scenario modeling with Business Risk Management facilities.

- **Stakeholder Relationship Management** provides communications channels with stakeholders such as employees, investors, analysts, customers, and suppliers.

- **Business Consolidation and Sourcing** includes a Web-based Editorial Workbench for gathering external information; a Corporate Performance Monitor, which includes *key performance indicators* (KPIs); and the optional Management Cockpit.

From the enterprise perspective, SAP R/3 offers planning, executing, and controlling business activities *horizontally* along the value chain, no matter how complex the corporate structure. The intention of SAP Strategic Enterprise Management is to add a *vertical* dimension by integrating the value-chain activities with value-based management processes such as strategic planning, risk management, and value communication to the people involved.

There are close connections with the operational execution systems for supply-chain activities and also to the extended financial planning and control components so that corporate strategies can be immediately applied to the processes that will implement them.

The key resource for SEM is the SAP Business Information Warehouse, which can readily respond to requests for complex information retrieval and analysis. ●

Understanding the Treasury Module

Relating Treasury and Capital Investment Management

The scope of TR-Treasury includes liquidity, market risk, planning, and portfolio management. The areas of application include all businesses that care about their cash flow and assets. The TR-TM Treasury Management component is shared with the IM-Capital Investment Management module (which is also discussed in this chapter).

The Treasury module is the part of your organization concerned with medium- and long-term financial planning, along with the medium-term management and control of revenues and expenditures. The focus is on the financial state of the company in the future. These objectives can be met to some degree by using the FI-Financial Accounting module, but the TR-Treasury module provides some enhanced functions additional to FI-IM Investment Management and FI-AM Fixed Assets Management.

Introducing the Treasury Module

The TR-Treasury module includes these components:

- TR-CM Cash Management
- TR-FM Funds Management
- TR-TM Treasury Management

The IM-Investment Management module includes these components:

- IM-FA Tangible Fixed Assets
- IM-FI Financial Investments

N O T E   The TR and IM modules overlap because the functions of IM-FI Financial Investments are the same as those of TR-TM Treasury Management. ■

The TR-Treasury module integrates cash management and cash forecasting with your company's logistics activities and financial transactions. For example, TR enables you to apply cash budgeting tools and commitment accounting methods that take into consideration the allocation of responsibilities. These methods also consider the current budget positions and the sources of the relevant funds to allow very subtle monitoring and control.

The TR module, as of Release 3.0, includes tools to analyze the money market, securities, and derivatives. The functions also presented as the SAP Foreign Exchange Management component are included in TR-Treasury to enable the analysis of foreign exchange risk online with electronic banking features to enhance the integration with FI-GL General Ledger and FI-AR Accounts Receivable components.

Cash Management

The day-to-day management of short-term and long-term cash flows is integrated with the CO-Controlling module and its planning capabilities to allow you to ensure that fund reservations are not likely to compromise future liquidity.

Electronic banking functions are associated with payment advice note processing so that you can specify automatic adjustment of standard algorithms or your own interpretation algorithms for clearing payments. You can also carry out a post-processing transaction to gain access to line items that cannot be posted automatically.

Funds Management

At the center of the TR-FM Funds Management component is the twin concept of budget objects and budget commitment funds centers. The structured budget data objects can be maintained and assigned to the budget commitment funds centers to provide a flexible system that clearly displays the way in which budgets are allocated to the hierarchy.

The allocation of budgets can be carried out from the bottom up so that subordinate items can be committed, even if the higher-level budgets have not been allocated. Different versions of budgets can be maintained separately, and different sources of funds can be designated for each financial management area.

Treasury Management

The Treasury Management component supports business transactions from the trading stage to back-office processing and then to eventual posting in the financial accounting system.

The scope of TR-TM includes these types of activities:

- Short-term cash management
- Long-term cash management
- Long-term financial budgeting
- Money market dealings
- Foreign exchange dealings, including spot dealing, forward exchange, and swap dealing
- Derivative financial instruments, including hedging transactions, swaps, caps, floors, options, and futures
- Securities management, including buying and selling, maintaining deposits and portfolios, acquiring and exercising conversions, and subscription and option rights
- Loan management, including fixed-term and at-notice deposits and loans (both loans granted and loans obtained)
- Collateral security management, including encumbrances on real estate and guarantees

Functionality   The displays and functions provided by the component include the following:

- Up-to-the-minute liquidity, currency, and risk position data for your company and its assets
- Portfolio updates and valuations
- Option prices
- Cross rates
- Transaction data monitoring
- What-if scenario simulations in association with IS-IS, the SAP Industry Solution for insurance companies

Risk management functions include the monitoring of changes in market prices, interest rates, and exchange rates.

Shared Functions and Tools   The central functions and tools that can be accessed from all TR-TM components include the following:

- Partner and address administration
- Investment mathematics
- Flexible instrument generator
- Status-controlled transaction processing
- Correspondence processing
- Limit monitoring
- Real-time reporting

Integrating with the SAP Industry Solution for Insurance

The TR-TM application is integrated with the IS-IS Industry Solution for Insurance and Real Estate Management, through which it can support the following functional areas:

- Extended management of loans
- Extended treasury management
- Real estate management
- Premium reserve funds and statutory reporting for insurance companies

Integrating with the SAP Industry Solution for Banks

The TR-TM application is also integrated with the IS-B Industry Solution for Banks, through which it can support the following functional areas:

- Back-office data pooling
- Single transaction costing
- Bank profitability analysis
- Risk management
- Statutory reporting

Relating to Tangible Fixed Assets

The IM-FA Tangible Fixed Assets component analyzes capital investments and supports their management. The principal functions of the component follow:

- Preinvestment analysis
- Capital investment master data, planning, budgeting, and allocation
- Measurement of capital investment performance and integration with the CO-Controlling module and CO-OPA Order and Project Accounting component
- Valuation and settlement
- Depreciation simulation
- Asset controlling
- Information system and connection to the EIS-Executive Information System

The IM-FA component shares functionality with the FI-AM Assets Management component.

Relating to Financial Investments

The IM-FI component carries out the functions of TR-TM Treasury Management.

Managing Investments Actively

This section develops the ideas of investing in financial assets and the strategies for managing their acquisition and disposal.

If you are in the business of making clothes last a long time by sewing them to make repairs, you will appreciate the advice that *A stitch in time saves nine.* If you are in the business of making sure that your company will last a long time, you will agree that it is often cheaper in the long run to make a deliberate and positive investment rather than to wait for a disaster to occur and plunge you into more expensive damage limitation.

In financial matters, the notion of *control* is synonymous with planning, monitoring, and analyzing results so that future plans will be more effective. The following precautionary questions are pertinent:

- How should existing assets be managed to maximize my company's return on the investment?
- How should new capital investment projects be planned and controlled?
- What should be the mix of manual and automatic processing in the management of investments?

The standard activities of an investment department are based on the need to purchase new assets and operating equipment. The daily decision matrix includes perhaps hundreds of decisions of the following types:

■ Should we repair or replace this faulty asset?

■ Should we buy this improved equipment or stay with the existing plant, which is working well, although it is not as advanced as the latest designs?

■ Should we snap up this resource now because it is available at bargain prices, or should we wait until there is a clearly defined need for it?

■ How long will this plant last at the present rate of use?

■ Should we invest in more repair facilities to alleviate the problems with the existing equipment, or should we invest in new and possibly unknown equipment in the hope that it will prove more effective?

You can use some common-sense measures to reduce the uncertainty that is characteristic of investment decision-making. You have to be prepared to search for information from sources such as these:

■ Competitors who have faced similar decisions

■ Scientific disciplines that have research evidence that could illuminate at least parts of your investment decision space

■ In-company technical resources that may be aware of information relevant to your proposed investment

■ Lessons learned from errors and equipment failures in similar activities

■ Commercial knowledge arrived at by analyzing business activities and results in similar situations

Although the big decision might seem to be the one that initiates an investment, it might be much more difficult to abandon a project or relinquish an investment if it turns out to be a failure. Worse still, it might be very difficult to cut off a project in its prime, when all is going well, just because it looks like it might fail sometime in the future. But there is nothing in the investment manager's job specification that says that the work will be easy or enjoyable. What good data processing can do, however, is help you avoid the kind of mistakes that are made because the right information is not extracted and highlighted when it could be used to improve the decision-making.

With complex and expensive investments, there is no chance to sit back and let the investment earn profit. Investment control is for the life of the asset—both its useful life and its economical disposal.

The depreciation of an asset is a function of its use and other factors that affect its value. It might become obsolete, for example. One important lesson to be learned from managing buildings, for example, is that the cost of repairs and maintenance may soon accumulate to more than the cost of acquisition. Similarly, an inexpensive item of production machinery may cost more to run than a more expensive one.

The moral from this kind of experience is to set out a plan of the expected life of each investment and annotate it with all the costs of owning and operating it. Include both preventive maintenance and the best estimate you can make of the likely cost of repairs and replacements. You could set up a key figure report element that lets you see just how much is spent on maintenance for each asset and how this works out as a percentage of its procurement costs.

Managing Investments in a Corporate Group

A multinational company will contain several individual company codes that are independent organizational units and render their own financial documents in the form of the balance sheet and the profit-and-loss statement. These units tend to operate in different currencies, for which the SAP R/3 system can maintain accounting data in parallel. Procedures exist for conducting a legal consolidation of these separate accounting structures.

Investments in a multinational corporation are represented by many records held on local computer systems. The SAP R/3 system can integrate these distributed systems by the *Application Link Enabling* (ALE) technology. This allows object data structures to be posted and reported. In particular, the capital investment programs of the affiliated companies can be reported to a central client database in R/3, even if some of the sending companies are using other systems. External software and standard systems such as Microsoft Access can be used as sources by accessing them through the *remote function call* (RFC) technique.

The ALE technique is applied to filter the investment documents of the distributed companies according to the requirements of the head office. For example, some options have investment reports at the summary level and at the level of individual investment measures and projects.

These are the standard reporting levels applicable to capital investment management:

- Company code
- Business area
- Profit center
- Plant
- Balance sheet item
- Capital investment program per approval year
- Capital investment program position

The reporting dimensions for capital investment programs and related capital investment measures include the following as options:

- Total and annual planned values
- Total and annual approved budget values
- Actual values
- Open item values

The data collated at the remote systems is summarized by period as directed before it is consolidated at the head office.

Using the Investment Management Functions

The Treasury is the part of your organization concerned with medium- and long-term financial planning, as well as the medium-term management and control of revenues and expenditures. The focus is on the financial state of the company in the future.

These objectives can be met to some degree by using the FI-Financial Accounting application. The modules of Financial Accounting specifically concerned with investments follow:

- FI-IM Investment Management
- FI-AM Assets Management

The functions used by FI-IM are also available to the FI-AA Asset Accounting module, although the continuity does not extend beyond year-end closing unless the IM application is installed and configured. The IM application supports the following investment-management processes:

- Capital spending requests
- Capital investment measures
- Capital investment programs
- Simulation and depreciation forecasting

The investment modules can be installed in SAP R/3 as a standalone system known as the IM-Investment Management application.

Financial Investments   IM-FI Financial Investments carries out the functions of TR-TM Treasury Management when the IM application is configured for investment management as a specialization.

Separating the Treasury Functions

As of R/3 Release 3.0, the long-term financial management functions are available in two separate but overlapping modules that can be installed independently of each other:

- TR-Treasury
- IM-Investment Management

Individual components from these modules can be installed and configured to integrate with the FI-Financial Accounting module. They are also available as integrated enhancements of R/3 designed for specific sectors of business and industry and prefixed with IS to designate an industry solution.

Organizing Investment Data

The essence of complex system management is to divide business activities into tasks and to divide data into units that can be readily retrieved and applied to the tasks as necessary. There are two target readership groups for financial documents:

- Shareholders and legal authorities who demand the external accounts in the prescribed formats

- Internal management, which must be able to freely select data in order to discover opportunities for improving the company

Investment control has to operate with a flexible data structure that can be called on to satisfy both types of scrutinizers.

Defining an Investment Program

The highest level of investment information held in a master record is the capital investment program structure. An investment program is defined in SAP R/3 by a master record that specifies a hierarchical structure for all the planned and budgeted investment costs of a company for a specific period. How you define this hierarchy is up to you. You can use the existing organizational units and separate the reasons for the investments or the balance sheet items. If you need to, you can define investment program types that specify the objects to which investment funds can be assigned.

Defining Capital Investment Program Types

The capital investment program types indicate the reasons for making capital investments. Here are some typical examples:

- Asset expansion to include new products
- Modernization
- Asset replacement measures
- Environmental protection

Specifying Capital Investment Program Positions

A *capital investment program position* is a data object that represents a reference point within a capital investment program. It refers to an organizational unit that is responsible for a well-defined stage of the project. The program position can have additional user-definable classifying characteristics (for example, investment type). It carries planned and budget values for the investment in one of the following reporting structures:

- Controlling area
- Company code
- Business area
- Profit center
- Plant

A capital investment program position can also be defined by additional characteristics, such as the investment type or reason. For example, a capital investment program position may be defined as an asset replacement investment type targeted at a specific plant belonging to a particular company code. The transaction data associated with this position is classified and posted accordingly.

A capital investment program is defined within a single controlling area, but there can be more than one capital investment program position element at any level. For example, a refurbishment project may involve several plant locations. In each plant, you can designate a technical site or another type of investment position to serve as the focal point for allocating budgets and recording costs and progress.

Each active capital investment program position element is represented as a capital investment project or element in a project. This needs a budget and therefore a company code responsible for this finance and also perhaps a controlling area that can summarize the programs across more than one company code.

Any particular capital investment order is assigned to a specific plant, to a profit center, and perhaps to a business area. The accounting of this capital investment order makes sure that the costs are assigned to specific cost centers as appropriate.

Using Capital Investment Measures

A capital investment measure is a project or an internal order used to carry out an asset investment. It is classified as a capital investment because it cannot be posted to fixed assets as direct capitalization. The usual reasons are that the project budget is very large and it includes a considerable internal activity component.

Two types of data are stored in master records of a capital investment measure, such as a project or an internal order. One set of data includes the controlling information; the other is the actual data of an *asset under construction* (AuC). This data is used to identify the following components:

- The investment components that need to be capitalized on the balance sheet
- Special depreciations that have to be reported
- Capital investment support measures needed during the construction phase

The capital investment measure can be accessed from both the Financial Accounting system and the Controlling system.

Analyzing Investment Proposals

Suppose that a requirement for a capital-intensive investment project is submitted for your consideration. How can you decide whether it is wise to go ahead?

What you need to know is the profitability of the project at each accounting period throughout its expected life and as far as its final disposal. You can apply static business mathematics and compute the values invested less the depreciation to arrive at a trajectory of costs and revenues that will provide the data for a graph of profitability over the project's life cycle.

Dynamic mathematics would provide a similar projection into the future if you could define some assumptions about the interest rates and market values over the lifetime period. For example, you could allow for predicted fluctuations by defining an internal interest rate. Alternatively, or in addition, you could compute the predicted capitalized value of your investment at each period in its life cycle.

If you have been able to carry out similar preinvestment analyses for each capital investment program you are evaluating, you might be able to come to a rational decision about which program to choose.

Your system might be able to provide actual data from previous investment projects that you can refer to as the basis for a numerical model for your proposed project. You then can use your assumptions about future interest rates and market values to refine and update the model.

As an additional facility, you could develop several versions of a preinvestment plan and associated analyses, with each variant using different parameters to represent, for example, optimistic and pessimistic views of your markets and the effectiveness of your resources.

In summary, the preinvestment analysis process can be set up using data processing to allow the decision-maker to choose between fully elaborated and costed plans that genuinely represent viable business alternatives. Any proposal that cannot be shown to be profitable at the planning stage, even if the assumptions are favorable, will not be considered as an option in the decision.

In practice, it might turn out to be a matter of how investment resources are to be distributed among the competing claimants. Everyone can compile a wish list, but not all wishes can be made to come true.

In accord with the common-sense procedure of subdividing complex items into a structure of components, the SAP R/3 investment functions work with three types of values distributed across as many units as needed to map your investment programs to your company cost centers. Planned values, budgeted values, and distributed values are stored for the company or controlling area. Each value is computed by adding the corresponding values from each business area. These business areas are defined on any convenient basis and represent the budget-holding authority at a particular level under the control of a business area manager. Each business area can be further subdivided and allocated a budget in a similar fashion.

If you already have organizational units that are convenient for capital investment budgets, you can direct the system to use those units to form a suitable distribution structure. You then can edit this structure manually if it does not correspond to the most convenient arrangement.

Cost Planning Capital Investment Programs

The costing of an investment program—and, hence, the cost planning—takes place from the bottom up. You can assign the actual capital investment measures planned for each year to the company codes that will be responsible for them.

The intended activities associated with a capital investment program must be included in the process of budgeting across the company. The controlling instruments that can be used automatically with capital investment programs follow:

- A project managed by the SAP R/3 Project System
- An SAP internal order
- An SAP maintenance order

For each preinvestment analysis you conduct, one of these instruments can be specified. The planned and actual values that represent internal activities, external activities, down payments, and overhead are posted to the instrument you choose.

If you cannot clearly assign a certain capital investment measure to one company code in the investment program, you can arrange a percentage distribution of a capital investment measure among several program positions. If necessary, you can enter and maintain the planned values directly in the investment program structure at any level of the hierarchy. The system checks that your manual alterations to the plan do not cause an excess in the value of the next level in the hierarchy.

Early Depreciation Forecasting and Cost Planning

A *depreciation forecast* is a set of values distributed across a series of time periods. These amounts represent the best estimates of how the value of the company's assets will move as a result of depreciation. You can define a depreciation area that takes a different viewpoint from the actual depreciation calculated by one of the standard methods. For example, you could define a depreciation area that calculates the depreciation of fixed assets for a tax-based balance sheet. Another area may be designed to support your cost accounting analyses by expressing the depreciation of the fixed assets slightly differently.

You can include the cost plans of a capital investment program in your depreciation forecast. Each program position value that has been planned but not yet distributed to lower levels of the investment hierarchy can be treated as an object to be processed by a specific depreciation procedure.

This means that you can compare different depreciation calculations and capitalization programs and obtain a long-term overview of the progression of your fixed assets and the possible effects of taxes on your investments.

The R/3 line item settlement facility allows you to use the balance sheet to trace the costing differences generated by special investment postings and to discern the variance between book depreciation and tax-based depreciation. Each line of every asset in your balance sheet that pertains to a capital investment measure includes a reference to its origin.

Your depreciation forecast can be regarded as a simulation of depreciation effects over a series of reporting periods. The values calculated can be transferred to your system of cost center planning.

Budgeting in the Capital Investment Program

A budget is distributed to the capital investment program positions. An individual capital investment measure can derive the budget directly from one of these positions. You can control just how strictly the system manages the availability of the budget funds. For example, you can prevent any individual capital investment budget for a measure associated with a capital investment program position from being assigned a value that would cause the position to exceed its allocation. On the other hand, if you do not want to exercise strict availability control, you can monitor the situation by using current period reports.

The annual expenditure budget represents the funds that have to be made available for particular investments in a given year. The IM can derive this pattern of expenditure in either of two ways:

- Aggregate the values budgeted for all the capital investment measures in a given year.
- Use the values specified directly in the capital investment program.

Each capital investment measure will have an individual approved budget that will be the total budget for this measure, regardless of how many years the measure may take.

The recommended procedure is to maintain approved budgets for capital investment programs to represent the upper limit of funds, and then to maintain in addition a continuous monitoring of the pattern of commitments that have been made for future years of the capital investment program. The IM module enables you to control the format when displaying these values.

It is usually a good idea to further subdivide budgets so that you can distinguish budget components that have to be capitalized from those that can be accounted for in pure cost items. You might also need to display budgets split in terms of internal and external activities.

Displaying the Budget Approval History

Each capital investment program position can be displayed as the original approved budget, along with these types of changes:

- Supplementary budget entries that allow extra funds to be applied in a top-down procedure from higher-level program positions to lower-level positions and, hence, individual capital investment measures, if needed
- Returns of surplus funds that are entered at the lowest level; from there, they are passed to a higher-level program position

Using the Research Reporting Tool

To evaluate a capital investment program, the Capital Investment Program Information System can be customized by using the standard Research reporting tool. For example, you can customize these standard reports:

- Capital investment program structures, plan values, budget values, and availability
- Investment projects
- Investment orders master data, order lists, and order selection
- Investment order summarization
- Depreciation simulation

Linking with the Executive Information System

The Capital Investment Program Information System is integrated with the EIS-Executive Information System. From there, reports can be compiled automatically using the established key figures. Reports then can be sorted by the existing organizational units, such as company codes, business areas, profit centers, plants, and so on.

Multinational corporations are served by the standard SAP R/3 system of maintaining currencies in parallel. The values of a capital investment program can be converted to the currency of the company code at the time of reporting and also to a currency defined as the standard for corporate capital investment program reporting.

The EIS can interface with non-SAP systems that are carrying capital investment program information needed for corporate reporting.

Capitalizing Assets Directly

A large capital investment measure normally is budgeted. However, some assets are capitalized directly by applying the flat-rate investment procedure. For example, a general resource such as local computers and vehicle fleets are likely to be capitalized directly and then subject to standard depreciation procedures.

If you allocate a budget for assets that will be directly capitalized, you can plan and monitor how these asset acquisitions are contributing to your capital investment program. If you do not allocate a budget for directly capitalized assets, there is a danger that your company will be allocating resources that are not attributed to capital investment and recognized as such.

Using the Flat-Rate Investment Procedure

The flat-rate investment procedure can be used as an alternative to the capital investment program technique. It can also be applied to individual elements in a program.

To fund assets that are to be capitalized directly, you can use the standard cost object *asset under construction* (AuC), the SAP internal order, or an SAP project. However, these instruments are not entirely satisfactory for this type of purchase, because there would have to be an intermediate step of debiting the order or project and subsequently settling it. The alternative is to record asset acquisitions by using the SAP R/3 IM flat-rate budget object as a special program item in a capital investment program. All the orders or projects that represent budgets for individual assets can be linked to a special program item that represents the flat-rate budget object for purchased assets.

Referencing a Capitalization Structure

A capitalization structure allows you to specify the cost component percentages of a capital investment measure that do not need to be capitalized for each cost element or cost element group, and for each activity type or group of activity types. If necessary, different versions can be defined in the capitalization structure for the various depreciation areas of fixed assets. The capitalization structure is defined for each controlling area and identified by using a capitalization key, which can be maintained in the master data of capitalization investment measures.

Linking Budgets and Fixed Asset Masters

The FI-AA Asset Accounting module provides master records to represent the fixed assets and to store all the transactions associated with them. The fixed asset master includes a data object that records the investment account assignment to be used for any associated order or project. If you have many assets to be assigned in this way to investment accounts, you can define general replacement rules to enable your system to automatically assign assets to the appropriate investment account. For example, you could specify a logical condition that assigns to a designated account any asset that satisfies all the following conditions:

- Assets of a particular class—say, vehicles
- Acquired in a specific business area, such as retail distribution in the southwest region
- Procured for an identified distribution center, such as Plant 53

Updating Open Items

An *open item* is a contractual or scheduled commitment that is not yet reflected in financial accounting but leads to actual expenditures in the future. A fixed asset can be conveniently handled by using open item management. All business transactions connected with procurement of the asset are directly linked to the asset master. Purchase orders, for example, are assigned directly to the asset number for which they are intended. The goods receipt and invoice are similarly assigned to the asset master.

When a purchase order for an asset is entered in the purchasing system, its value is used to debit the project or order to which the asset is assigned with a liability of the same amount. The liability is converted to an actual value when the goods are received or the invoice is posted. If you do not want the order or project to be posted with the actual cost elements, you can specify it as a receiver for statistical values only, rather than actual amounts.

Individual assets can be acquired without going through the purchasing system. You can route them through the FI-AP Accounts Payable module to be posted directly to an existing asset portfolio. The additional value then is posted statistically to the order or project.

You can control the availability of additional assets by allowing them to be released to an order or project only if the corresponding budget is still available and has not been depleted for any reason.

Using the Capital Investment Information System with Flat-Rate Budgets

When the capital investment is being conducted with flat-rate budgets, the asset acquisitions are represented by investment program items and orders or projects. You can display the actual values of your asset portfolio and call for breakdowns by asset. You can readily switch between program items and their component orders and individual asset items. You can have a combined display of the total planned investment, the budgets for selected areas, and the investments that have already been implemented and have generated fixed assets.

Creating Assets Internally by Capital Investment Measures

A *capital investment measure* is an SAP internal order or SAP project. It is used to control an AuC within a company that is using the same functions that are used when an AuC is procured primarily from external sources and therefore is subject to external accounting rules.

There are two classes of capital investment measure:

- Capital investment order
- Capital investment project

A project includes a *project structure plan* (PSP) and therefore PSP elements, some of which can be orders.

Both classes of capital investment measures have the task of managing the operational implementation of the investment plan. This includes the following activities:

- Recording primary and secondary costs
- Calculating overhead rates and interest
- Managing down payments
- Managing open purchase orders

By these means, the capital investment order or project can provide a single data object that has collected all the costs for a capital investment measure—both those already charged to fixed assets and those held in the controlling system, which are the elements of the capital investment program that have yet to be implemented.

There are several reasons to use a capital investment order or project instead of a series of standard orders or projects. These are probably the most significant advantages:

- Program items that have been so designated are automatically capitalized to the balance sheet account item *asset under construction* (AuC).
- Convenient arrangements can be made to settle the capital investment measure at month-end closing and period closing.
- The cost of goods manufactured and the cost of acquired assets can be valued simultaneously by each of the depreciation procedures.

The depreciation procedures are identified in asset accounting as depreciation areas because they are conducted for slightly different purposes. They include the following variations of the depreciation technique:

- Commercial balance sheet depreciation
- Taxed-based balance sheet depreciation
- Depreciation calculated for the consolidated balance sheet

The management of investments by using the technique of capital investment measures and their associated master record structures can be advantageous for companies that need to plan and control large individual investments or for companies that use their own resources to create the assets.

Selecting the Type of Capital Investment Measure

Four types of cost assignment objects can be useful in a capital investment program:

- Capital investment project
- Capital investment order
- Job shop order
- *Asset under construction* (AuC)

Making a Capital Investment Project Structure Plan

A *project structure plan* (PSP) relates a set of activities in the form of a hierarchy in which the PSP elements are arranged in levels. A capital investment PSP element is represented by a master data record that includes information on the following items:

- Identification of the project leader
- Requesting cost center
- Cost center responsible for implementing the capital investment measure
- User-defined data fields

A PSP element can be divided into lower-level elements, each of which can be subdivided, and so on. The subdivision can take place at any stage—from planning to implementation of a project.

The role of a PSP is to form the basis of the planning and control of a project. In particular, the PSP is specialized for the following functions:

- Displaying labor, time, and cost required for a project
- Controlling the integration of any subsequent project-planning activities
- Planning project costs
- Distributing the project budget

In all these functions, the controlling activities extend to each level of the PSP architecture under control of the user.

A project is intended to be a structured set of activities in which the costs and time management are planned, controlled, and monitored in as much detail as you require. The following logistics functions are integral to project management:

- Scheduling
- Resource and capacity management
- Network planning and cost distribution to individual activities

- Analysis of the interdependencies between activities
- Planning of optimum procedures within the project
- Scheduling of external resources
- Management of contingencies, such as resource bottlenecks and changes of requirements

Understanding a Capital Investment Order

Unlike a project structure, a capital investment order is not divided into subtasks because it is a single-level structure. Most logistics functions that characterize project management are not needed for capital investment orders.

An order can be assigned to a PSP element in the master data records. An internal job shop order, for example, can be placed in the context of a large capital investment measure. If this work needs to be viewed or analyzed as a separate subtask, even though it is part of a large project structure plan, you can call for the order itself from the order processing system and see the progress and settlement situation. The individual order is identified in the PSP and therefore takes part in the reporting and settlement procedures of the project as a whole.

Managing an Asset Under Construction

The AuC data object is used to identify assets that have to be reported as capitalized assets in the balance sheet. When an order or a project structure plan is released for planning and posting, the system automatically sets up an AuC item in the balance sheet accounts. It is the normal practice to set up a separate AuC balance sheet account item for each order or project structure plan element. The alternative is to identify cost elements and assign them to different AuC balance sheet account items according to their type. The system automatically creates a separate AuC record for each cost element, according to its origin. Each project AuC item then is assigned to an appropriate balance sheet account AuC item.

Every capital investment measure is associated with an AuC item in the balance sheet that represents the balance sheet value of an order or project structure plan element. This value change is reported in asset accounting, in the balance sheet reports, and in the Asset History sheet. However, the system will not let you post any value directly to the AuC before the primary cost objects (the order or the project) are settled.

Cost Planning and Budgeting for Capital Investment Programs

There are several approaches to planning for capital investments, whether by orders or through projects. For example, you can draw up general plans in the form of annual amounts that take no account of cost elements or cost element planning. You could have these annual totals broken down into individual reporting periods.

If you apply unit costing techniques, you can plan the expected consumption of materials, constituent base objects, and materials. It might be useful to maintain a set of statistical key figures in this connection. These plans could be differentiated by organizational unit.

Using Account Determination Keys

The primary costs of a capital investment measure can be planned by cost element estimated by value or quantity. If a cost element is to be reported according to several account determination keys, you can apply detailed planning by using these as the primary cost elements. You can specify the account determination key in order to combine quantity and value measurements. The system recognizes the following account determination factors:

- Material items recognized by their material numbers as defining members of an overhead area, such as the supplies overhead area
- Cost components generated as personnel-related wage and salary amounts valued by using costing tables and cost rates
- Activities required in support of planned external or internal activities
- Surcharges applied as percentage rates—using various base quantities to compute risk surcharges and price surcharges, for example

If you have systems of cost centers and overhead rates, you can use them to plan internal activities for the capital investment measures in your program.

From the price of activities calculated by cost center accounting, you can work out the quantities of internal activities of the types that could be performed for each capital investment measure. You have to find some way of determining the quantities you will probably need and applying the activity costs to arrive at the value that must be debited to the capital investment measure as secondary cost elements.

After values are determined for primary and secondary costs, overhead costing techniques are applied to compute flat-rate overhead surcharges for each cost element. You have control over how much surcharge is applied and the cost element to which it is assigned.

The result of these stages is a set of planned total costs for the capital investment measure. These planned costs then are transferred directly to the capital investment program cost planning. You can carry out this transfer automatically by associating an order or project with a particular capital investment program position or measure.

You can view the associations between program positions and orders or projects through the availability control reports, where you can inspect the planned, actual, and assigned amounts for each capital investment program or individual capital investment measure.

The source and distribution of a budget for a capital investment program is copied from the plan. You might want to apply discounts to the planned amounts before you allow them to become budget amounts.

If a new capital investment measure begins in the current year, you can approve its total budget directly from the capital investment program. This total covers the entire measure, however many years it may last. Distribution across the expected years of the program is carried out later and gives you the annual expenditure budgets—the *annual slices*—for each capital investment measure in each year.

Controlling Availability of Funding

The approved total budget and the annual expenditure budgets may be subject to passive or active availability control. The passive control mode simply reports the availability of funds. Active control can be carried out directly for each activity. If your project exceeds the budget for any one item, the person responsible can be informed automatically by mail through the SAP R/3 Business Workflow application. The manager can also respond through the workflow—for example, by electing to provide a budget supplement.

Goods and services required in conjunction with a capital investment measure can be procured through the SAP R/3 Purchasing System and FI-FA Financial Accounting. When an order for goods or services is posted, an open item is created automatically to document the commitment of funds from a capital investment measure or program. This document effectively plans the future costs of the capital investment measure. When the goods or services are delivered or an invoice is received, the open item is removed if the delivery is complete. If there is only a partial delivery, the open item is reduced by a proportionate amount.

The relevant capital investment measure is automatically debited with the purchase order value as actual costs when the goods or services are received or by the invoice amount when the invoice is received. An invoice can be directly posted by Financial Accounting without reference to a purchase order. In these circumstances, the capital investment measure is directly updated by an additional account assignment annotated as `Capital Investment Order` or `Capital Investment Project`, as appropriate.

Documenting Internal Value Flows

Cost centers provide activities to capital investment measures. Each of these activities is specified by quantity and by value. The flow of these internal activities is recorded as direct internal activity allocation. The controlling system converts the activity quantity to a monetary value by referring to the price arrived at through cost center accounting. An individual item consisting of a certain quantity of a particular activity is recorded as a credit memo at the sending cost center and as a corresponding debit memo in the capital investment measure record, which is the receiving object.

Allocating Activity Costs Indirectly

If an activity cannot be quantified for each transaction, an indirect allocation can be set up. This is done by periodic transfer posting of a proportion of the costs of providing the activity. This method allows the transfer of costs between cost centers and orders.

Allocating Overhead as Surcharges on a Capital Investment Measure

In the procedures of planned cost accounting, the computation of overhead rates is used to arrive at a method of distributing costs. In a similar way, overhead surcharges can be applied to capital investment measures. The overhead surcharges are not usually included in the cost rates for the various activities provided by cost centers. Therefore an amount representing a proportion of the overhead surcharges has to be debited to the capital investment measure in accord with the *cost by cause* principle.

Capitalizing Internal Activities

A percentage of internal activities can be capitalized under fixed assets. You can choose different valuation types as a basis for computing a percentage. For example, you might be allowed to capitalize all internal activities to fixed assets when using commercial valuation. However, for tax purposes, you might have to value your company by capitalizing only 80 percent of internal activities. For corporate reporting of the consolidated accounts, you might have to capitalize no more than 70 percent.

Accounting for Down Payments

It is usual for a long capital investment project to be subject to the requirement for installments or down payments as the work proceeds. When the external activity is completed, the invoice quotes the total invoice amount, which must be posted in full. However, if you have been making down payments during the course of the construction of the asset, your final payment will be much less than the full invoice amount.

Furthermore, there is a legal requirement to balance the accounts of AuC so that the down payments already made are assigned as fixed assets.

The SAP R/3 solution to this complex posting requirement is to have a down payment posted as such by the FI-AP Accounts Payable module. At the same time, an additional account assignment is made to the purchase order under which the down payment is made. The amount of the down payment is automatically updated in the records of the capital investment measure, where it is assigned to a specific cost element created for the purpose of recording down payments. At the end of the accounting period, the down payment on behalf of a capital investment measure is automatically prepared for capitalization by being transferred to the Fixed Assets account.

 If your system does not have a purchase order as a reference for a down payment, you can post the down payment directly to the capital investment measure without affecting the value flow documentation.

Capitalizing Interest During the Construction Phase

A long construction phase for an asset represents capital lockup, because there is value in the partially completed asset that cannot be applied elsewhere in the company. The laws governing the region in which your company is located may permit account balancing in which the interest on capital investment projects is allowed to be capitalized under fixed assets. In any circumstance, you might find it useful to compare the interest calculated on book depreciation versus tax-based depreciation, for example.

The system enables you to consult an interest table and to determine the cost elements for which interest is to be computed. You can also specify which depreciation areas will apply an interest computation, and which rate of interest is used. Compound interest can be calculated with a user-defined time period. The system calculates the interest at the end of the defined periods and debits the capital investment measure with these values.

Within a capital investment project, the interest on capital invested is treated as a normal cost element that can be charged to fixed assets or to the normal receivers of cost accounting assignments, which are the cost centers.

Assigning Investment Support During the Construction Phase

If your capital investment measure attracts investment support from you host country during the construction phase, you have various ways of accounting for it. For example, you can apply any of these techniques:

■ Deduct the value of the investment support from the balance sheet values of the AuC and thereby reduce the acquisition value of it.

■ Treat the investment support as a revenue from the asset, which will not affect its acquisition value.

■ Apply the investment support as a reserve for special depreciation on the liabilities side.

If you create a special depreciation reserve for investment support subsidies, you might have to dissolve this reserve on the asset side over the useful life of the asset.

The system offers you proposal lists at each stage of planning the use and subsequent posting of investment support measures. These documents are presented in formats suitable for submitting to the supporting authorities.

When a capital investment project is completed, the system transfers capital investment measures to fixed assets on the asset side with due allowance for depreciation. If the capital investment measure has been receiving capital investment subsidies, the system makes a transfer posting for the total subsidy amount.

Using Settlement Functions for Capital Investment Measures

There are many ways of arranging settlements for capital investment measures and many tools to assist in this process. The settlement rules to be applied are stored in the master records of each capital investment order or capital investment project.

The display of a capital investment measure that includes a number of items can be settled one line at a time if you want to assign a settlement rule to each line item individually. You can assign settlement rules according to cost element so that the settlement receivers are assigned according to their origin groups. For example, external activities usually are charged to fixed assets. Internal activities are distributed on a percentage basis between fixed assets and certain cost centers.

Most items created for a capital investment measure are settled to an AuC account at the end of the period. However, this leads to their being capitalized, which might not be appropriate or legal for items that should be accounted, wholly or partially, as costs. The costs should not be capitalized as fixed assets; instead, they should be settled on cost objects, including cost centers, internal orders, project structure plan elements, and profitability segments.

These cost assignments to the Controlling module allow you to generate the following reports each month:

- Settlement by period to the cost accounting receivers
- Balance sheet display of AuC
- Asset History sheet

Customizing Final Settlement to Fixed Assets

A capital investment creates a resource that is intended to be used when it is completed but may come into productive use before all the work on it is done. These matters must be resolved before final settlement can take place:

- Will the capital investment measure be represented as a single fixed asset or as several fixed assets?
- Which cost center(s) will be assigned responsibility for the new assets?
- How will the new assets be depreciated?

After you resolve these issues, you can create master data sets for the new fixed assets and assign them to the correct asset classes. From a list of the new assets, you can select line items for individual assignment, or you can settle by groups based on original cost element postings. You can also distribute a line item among several fixed asset receivers.

You might decide to settle some of the new asset items to cost centers in the controlling application. In this case, you have to settle by line item so that you will have detailed proof of origin on the settlement receivers where needed for controlling purposes and to comply with the legal requirements for rendering the external accounts.

The final settlement process credits the AuC account with the corresponding amount. Items from previous years are shown automatically as transfer postings, and items from the current year appear as acquisitions in the final fixed assets accounts.

Reporting Internal Accounting for Capital Investment Measures

The SAP R/3 system includes a standard reporting system for capital investment measures that is used for both orders and projects. You can modify the standard reporting system to create exactly the reports you require for your individual circumstances. You then can change the reports as necessary without losing the efficient collation procedures that are integral to the standard report.

These are the main presentation options:

- Ongoing profitability control by budget/actual comparison
- Cost development displays extending over several reporting periods
- Interactive drill-down report control of analyses from controlling area down to line item level

Reporting External Accounting for Capital Investment Measures

Legal external accounting requires that capital investment measures show legally valid proofs of origin for the values recorded in the fixed assets accounts. An AuC automatically generates an Asset History sheet and appears in the Asset list and any standard asset report. To inspect this data, the following capabilities are available:

- Asset History sheets flexibly defined and selective in their displays of columns and lines
- Reports that can implement the widest range of sorting procedures
- Comparison reports that display the effects of using different depreciation area formulas

Positive Auditing with the SAP R/3 Auditor Workstation

The workstation module can operate with individual companies and on a global enterprise basis. It can operate as a standalone module and interface with datasources through standard SAP interfaces. It normally operates online with the SAP R/3 system. The auditors work in the operational system and must be authorized to read the current dataset.

The focus of this workstation is on more positive auditing activities and consulting, although the standard processes of compiling evaluation documents and reports are fully supported. The *Generally Accepted Accounting Principles* (GAAP) remain the guiding standards, but the workstation is optimized for the benefit of internal and external auditors, system auditors, and cost accounting personnel. The module was first developed for the German auditing environment and is being given the capability to recognize other auditing conventions.

The R/3 Audit Information System is also available to the auditor workstation. This information system can construct an audit report tree from which users can call individual reports and evaluation programs that can work with preclosing interim lists such as Assets, Receivables, Balance Confirmation, Balance List, Domestic Customers, and so on. ●

CHAPTER 16

Understanding the R/3 Project System

In this chapter

Recognizing a Project

The concept of a project has developed to mean a task with most, if not all, of the following characteristics:

- Complex, one-off, and high-risk
- Probably of strategic significance to the sponsor
- Precise goals that have been negotiated and agreed on between the project management and the internal or external customer
- Limited in duration
- Entails high costs
- Requires intensive commitment of resource capacities
- Subject to strict quality requirements

These stringent requirements are met only if a unified project management structure can be set up that can control all task elements, whatever the range of departments involved.

The purpose of the R/3 PS-Project System module is to efficiently manage the stages of a project from planning to completion. The system is fully integrated with all other SAP modules. Four types of projects help define the functionality required of a Project System that is not specific to any one industry or field of business:

- Research and development
- Engineer-to-order development
- Investment programs
- Data-processing projects

Each project proceeds along a trajectory—a path of activities that consume resources—until the purpose of the project is achieved and reported. At each stage, SAP R/3 standard business functions are organized as support by the R/3 Project System.

Setting the Project Trajectory

Although some stages of a project may be abbreviated or extended according to the nature and complexity of the endeavor, it is usually possible to discern the following groups of tasks, especially if the R/3 Project System is at work:

- Rough-cut planning with times and values set against a work breakdown structure or at least a listing of what has to be done
- Fine planning that may use cost element planning or unit costing methods and entails the manual entry of critical dates, detailing of activities, automatic R/3 scheduling, and highlighting of critical activities
- Coordination of resources through automatic purchase requisitions and materials reservation plans; inventory management; and network planning of people, capacities, materials, operating resources, and services

■ Monitoring of materials, capacities, and funds as the project is approved and executed using budget management of approved and released project budgets; funds commitments and assignment to projects; and checking availability of funds, materials, and capacities with an overrun alarm to the project manager

■ Project closing with results analysis and settlement

Understanding the SAP Enterprise Data Model

The R/3 BASIS system offers a comprehensive suite of data structures that enables you to map in detail the structure of your company. This feature is available no matter what business or industry you operate in and no matter how individual your organizational structure is.

To help you become aware of the data architecture of the R/3 system, an information model is provided showing the information objects of all the integrated application software. This is discussed in Chapter 5, "Consulting the R/3 Reference Model." This model not only shows you what data objects are available in the R/3 system, it also reveals clearly how these data objects relate to each other. You will see how your specific business can be accurately represented in the R/3 data objects. If you choose to decide which functions will be required, the R/3 BASIS system annotates a copy of the Reference Model so that you can see what you selected. This copy then is referred to as the EDM-Enterprise Data Model of your implementation and is the principal instrument for controlling how your system is built. After you identify the processes and business control instruments of your company in the Reference Model, you can be certain that they will be fully integrated when the time comes to run the finished system.

Understanding the R/3 Standard Project System

The PS-Project System is delivered ready to be configured and customized to fit your particular situation. It includes an *Implementation Management Guide* (IMG), which introduces the business functions and a customizing menu to access the standard settings and technical recommendations. You can set up the R/3 Project System in the IMG itself.

The R/3 Project System extensively uses the SAP Enterprise Data Model to support you in the definition and management of your projects. For example, the standard organizational structures in the FI-Financial Accounting module have a strict logical form. *Client* in an SAP system refers to the highest level of the organizational structure. The owner of the entire corporation is identified as the client and is assigned a client code, such as 000. Client 001 will probably be a client created for testing purposes. The data associated with one client cannot be transferred to the records of another client.

Although the R/3 Reference Model contains only one definitive example of each data structure, your company can build any number of replications into its Enterprise Data Model to represent all the working elements that exist.

Logistics organizational structures, for example, follow strict logical definitions. The modules in the Logistics group follow:

- SD-Sales and Distribution
- PP-Production Planning
- MM-Materials Management
- PM-Plant Maintenance
- QM-Quality Management

Because all applications are integrated with the FI-Financial Accounting module, the logistics structures have to map onto the financial structures. The financial statements must be prepared up to the client level. In the applications modules, the data structures must extend to a great depth of detail in order to encompass the operational entities that add value to the business through the activities in which they engage. If managers care about it, the system has a place for it.

A client can have any number of

- Controlling areas
- Business areas

A controlling area can have any number of

- Profit centers
- Cost centers
- Company codes, which is how subsidiary companies are identified

A company code can have any number of

- Purchasing organizations
- Plants

A purchasing organization can have any number of

- Purchasing groups

A plant can have any number of

- Functional locations or pieces of equipment
- Storage locations
- Work centers

A work center can have any number of

- Activities
- Machines
- People

A project can be concerned with any combination of entities in the company. It may even cover the entire corporation from the client level downward.

Assigning Organizational Structures in the Project System

The Project System illustrates how the data objects of the R/3 system are used to monitor and control the costs and revenues of the work done in your company. Each element points to the responsible organizational unit, which will be represented by a data object. These data objects can attract not only the costs and revenues information, but also any technical information relevant to the operations of the accounting system or the other functions of your company.

This illustration of the relationships between project elements and organizational entities is an example of the application of the SAP Enterprise Data Model and could be a model for part or all of your company's activities.

The master data records used by the Project System are formally structured. Thus a *project* is represented by a master record that has a predefined structure of data fields. One field contains the unique identification code of the project, which then is associated with all the elements attached to this data structure, such as work breakdown structure elements, profit centers, and so on.

A project has

- One project definition
- One or more work breakdown structure elements
- One or more networks or subnetworks

A project definition has

- One project identification
- One or more controlling areas
- One or more company codes
- One or more cost centers

A work breakdown structure element has

- One or more profit centers
- One or more business areas
- One or more cost centers
- One or more plants
- One or more activities
- One or more functional locations or pieces of equipment

A network has

- One or more profit centers
- One or more business areas
- One or more plants
- One or more activities

An activity has

- One or more activity types
- One or more material components

An activity type is one of the following:

- An activity processed internally at a specified work center
- An activity processed externally, via a purchasing organization and a purchasing group
- A general costs activity assigned to a company code

A material component has

- A purchasing organization
- A purchasing group
- A plant
- A storage location

Setting the Project Definition

A *project definition* is a data object requiring certain fields to contain valid entries—to relate it to the company organization, for example. The definition also includes text to describe the project goals or mission. You can also add a reference to the settlement rule that covers all the objects in the project.

It is not necessary to define any activities or networks in order to establish a project definition. You can add these later.

Assigning the Work Breakdown Structure

The *work breakdown structure* (WBS) can be used to track costs incurred in an activity network. It includes a hierarchy of tasks and subtasks to any number of levels and can be represented by a tree diagram.

The individual tasks have to be described by a member of the project team by selecting activity types and entering the details to generate valid WBS elements. You can increase the level of detail at any stage of a project. The WBS elements must contain all the data necessary to carry out the work of the project, as well as the time and costs.

You can also use the WBS elements to plan dates, costs, and budgets before and during a project. Each element is assigned an operative indicator that determines its properties for the duration of the project:

- Planning elements for actual costs
- Account assignment elements to which you want to post costs
- Billing elements to which you want to post revenues

WBS structures already in existence can be referenced during data entry, as can portions of the hierarchy from other projects.

Defining Networks

In general terms, a *network* is a connected structure of nodes and links that signifies relationships between the nodes, such as *Must be completed before....* The nodes in a network may also be networks. A subnetwork is part of a network. In the R/3 system, a network is defined formally as an activity-on-node structure containing instructions on how to carry out activities in a specific way, in a specific order, and in a specific time period.

A complex project uses both a WBS and an activity network. The R/3 Network Library contains neutral network structures for commonly used processes, which you can copy into your project. The network type distinguishes networks by their use. The network type controls these elements:

- Costing variants for plan, target, and actual costs
- Order type
- Number ranges permitted—for example, for activity numbers
- Open items into which the user can insert information
- Status profile
- Authorizations

Understanding Project Time Planning

The R/3 system recognizes the following calendar types, which can be used in project planning:

- Gregorian
- Factory calendars (any number)
- Work center–specific operating calendars, with shifts if appropriate

The following types of dates are accepted:

- Basic dates manually entered for the WBS valid at the time of entry
- Forecast dates entered manually
- Actual dates showing the progress of the project
- System-calculated dates created during network scheduling

Planning dates can be entered on the lists and overviews, in the hierarchy display, or in the Gantt chart. Three methods or forms are available for planning:

- **Top down,** beginning with the dates for the highest WBS element in the project hierarchy
- **Bottom up,** starting with the subordinate WBS elements
- **Free,** in which you plan without reference to hierarchical dependencies

The R/3 Project System automatically carries out all possible checking and updating.

Understanding Project Cost Planning

At the conceptual and rough-cut planning stage, the planning of costs will suggest the costs you expect the project to incur. At the approval stage, planning indicates the way ahead for budget allocation. During project execution, the role of the planned dates and costs is to monitor variances between planned and actual values.

The system offers the following forms of cost planning:

- Structural planning that is independent of cost elements
- Detailed planning of direct costs by quantity and value
- Detailed planning of secondary costs using planned activity quantity and the standard CO-Controlling rate for the sender activity
- Unit costing using data and methods from CO-CEA Cost Element Accounting and purchasing in MM-Materials Management, if required
- Cost planning in the network, in which the network activities are used as cost elements in the unit costing technique

You can copy WBSs and parts of WBSs when projects will use the same processes. Different versions of a project plan can be saved and maintained simultaneously—for example, in best-case and worst-case scenarios.

Understanding Capacity Requirement Planning

For internal activities in each work center, you define available capacities and specify formulas for calculating them. As you enter the quantity of work to be performed, you indicate the required capacity units. This information is used by the system when scheduling capacity requirements.

You can plan external activities by referencing a purchasing information record for a contractor that shows the prices and delivery times. The Project System creates a purchase requisition from this information, which it then converts to a purchase order when the activity is released.

Maintaining Documents, Production Resources, and Tools

Project documents can include drawings, technical specifications, and other items from word processing sources. You can manage project documents along with *production resources and tools* (PRTs). Alternatively, you can allocate documents directly to WBS elements from a document management system, even if it is not the one installed in R/3.

The R/3 Project System recognizes and maintains three categories of PRTs:

- PRTs with a material master record that are stock items on inventory
- PRTs with a document info record that are part of the R/3 document management system
- PRTs with their own PRT master record that can be allocated in network activities

Document management under R/3 for WBS elements maintains the following information about each document:

- Storage location of the document, such as CAD system, PC file, filing cabinet
- Object status
- Location of original data
- Person responsible

Availability checks by the R/3 Project System cover capacities, materials, production resources, and tools. When you're customizing your R/3 Project System, you tell the system whether and how checks are to be made on material availability, and whether scheduled receipts or only on-hand inventory should be scanned.

A complete workflow for missing parts is provided to manage the shortage through to goods receipt and backorder updating.

The system determines whether each PRT is available according to its status and refers to the PS information system to compare the available capacity with the capacity load per work center. It then calculates the capacity utilization.

Capacity leveling is available and simulations can be performed to see how the capacity available might be affected by measures and events such as these:

- Orders
- Midpoint scheduling
- Rescheduling
- Outsourcing
- Work-center changes

Understanding Project Budgeting

A budget for a project is created when planning is completed and approval is granted. A *cost plan* is an estimate. A *budget* is a fixed amount that has to be allocated to the WBS elements, either by adopting the values arrived at by detailed planning or by distributing the budget manually by entering the values directly into the WBS elements.

Your finance director might not actually release all the funds for your approved budget. The R/3 Project System is being extended to control the release of funds in relation to specific WBS elements.

Changes in a budget can be accommodated by the following instruments, all of which are reversible:

- Supplements that you can process from the top down in the WBS
- Returns of excess funds that you can process from the bottom up in the WBS
- Transfers of funds that you can process from one WBS element with a budget to another element, which also must have a budget, although it does not have to belong to the same project

The following functions are being developed by SAP:

■ Logging all budget updates in an approval history

■ Copying a WBS with its planned values and budgets in order to budget a comparable project

■ Reassigning individual WBS elements or project branches, along with their budget values

Executing a Project

Execution begins with project release. For business processes to be assigned to a project, you must signify an account assignment to a network activity or a WBS element. As the project is executed, funds assignments appear in the project as open items and actual values.

Variances will occur between planned and actual values. These variances require that you supply planning updates in the form of fresh information to be used in planning subsequent activities.

Each activity appears on a completion confirmation slip when it is finished. These slips update the capacity load of the work center and record the actual costs. The remaining duration and work to finish the network also are updated by these confirmations. A confirmation can be canceled.

You will have to enter the following information either manually or automatically into your activity and network completion confirmations:

■ Degree of processing

■ Work center

■ Dates

■ Duration

■ Forecast values

The network and the WBS remain in accord. Changes in one are reflected in the other.

The system provides for passive funds availability control, which monitors the funds assigned, and active funds availability control, which can stop any funds commitment to prevent it from going into excess. You can influence the configuration of availability control by determining the following:

■ Whether funds are checked against the total project budget or the allocation for the current year

■ Which activities, such as purchase orders or postings in CO-CEA Cost Element Accounting, will be subject to availability control

■ Whether a percentage tolerance or an absolute tolerance will be allowed on an activity

■ Which action will be taken if a tolerance limit for an activity is approached or exceeded— for example, a warning, a message to the project manager, or a rejection of the posting with a tolerance error message

The settlement of costs incurred in a project on one or more receivers is automatically accompanied by corresponding credit postings to the project itself. The costs settled are recorded in the relevant receiver. Debit postings assigned to the project remain on display even after settlement.

The following types of assignment account objects can accept the settlement as receivers:

- Cost center
- Project
- Asset
- General Ledger account
- Business segment

The project or the WBS element master must include a specification of the settlement rule. This specification may consist of several distribution rules (each defining the settlement receiver), the distribution of costs, and the settlement type.

The settlement structure determines how the process is controlled. It specifies the settlement cost elements or the value fields from an operating concern that will be assigned to cost elements and cost element groups.

A separate structure is available for use by CO-PA Profitability Analysis, which is known as the *PA Settlement Structure*.

Calling on Different Project Views

Within an organization, each area looks at a project from a different viewpoint. Each department needs a different selection of information:

- **Sales** focuses on the customer order and the sales cycle from inquiry to quotation to sales order, billing, and delivery notes.
- **Manufacturing** operates with planned orders and production orders, as well as with bills of materials, plants, work-center hierarchies, and production schedules.
- **Materials Management** manages vendors and inventory.
- **Financial Accounting** ensures cash flow and makes sure that interest is managed properly.
- **Cost Accounting** views a project from the point of the cost controller.
- **Capital Spending** depends on effective planning, and the Project System discipline is central.
- **Asset Accounting** can be used with capital spending projects to provide accurate forecasting, even before the asset is commissioned.
- **Profitability Analysis** on a periodic basis is essential for long-term customer projects that need accurate controlling and account balancing.

Because of its capability to adopt any or all of these viewpoints, the R/3 Project System is an embodiment of integrated business accounting. Not only can a specific project take advantage of the functions of the separate applications, but the Project System itself can also be the main executive controller for the business as a whole.

The PS-IS Information System is an efficient project-analysis tool, which is undergoing continuous program development to increase the depth of its analytical penetration as well as the clarity and pertinence of its presentation methods. The following additional functions are in development to enable you to better assess the progress of a project:

- **Portfolio graphics** will represent dates and costs of several projects at once.
- **Milestone trend analysis** will detect and compare schedule deviations and trends.
- **Earned value calculation** will provide another internal progress check and an activity confirmation for the customer by comparing various methods of measuring earned value during the progress of an activity.

Support for good business practice is available in the R/3 Project System.

Optimizing Projects Across Business Networks

Because each company naturally tends to concentrate on the things it does best, projects at the enterprise level need to extend across many partners, perhaps on a multinational basis. The need to exploit the benefits of cooperation gives high priority to efficient project management.

The SAP *Application Link Enabling* (ALE) mechanism allows both information and business systems to be widely distributed so that all partners in a project can have the same software functions as well as the same project plan, along with the master and control data they require. As an example, a networked project can refer to a material using a shared name and supporting master records. If required, the global sales and contribution margin of this product can be reported through the same network.

Through the ALE linkage, individual companies can distribute their transaction workloads—for example, if data or products are distributed but a common service is offered throughout the network. In research and development projects, individual tasks often are distributed across locations. A networked Project System can ensure that the contributory parts are put together on time to produce the composite result intended. The logistics, documentation, and finance of the contributing agencies can also be managed through the same networked Project System.

N O T E The Project System is for critical, costly, intensive tasks that will make a strategic improvement to the sponsoring company. It has to cross departmental boundaries and meet strict budgets within deadlines. ■

Manufacturing Applications

Understanding the Production Planning Module

Introducing the Production Planning Module

Versatility is the distinctive feature of the PP-Production Planning and Control module. It is designed to be used in any sector of industry. The scope of this module includes groups of functions in the following components:

- PP-BD Basic Data for Production
- PP-SOP Sales and Operations Planning
- PP-MP Master Planning
- PP-MRP Material Requirements Planning
- PP-CRP Capacity Requirements Planning
- PP-SFC Production Orders (formerly Shop Floor Control)
- PP-PC Product Costing
- PP-PI Production Planning for the Process Industries (see Chapter 18, "Understanding the Production Planning for Process Industries Module")

Integrating Supply Chain Management

The classic *Material Requirements Planning* approach (MRP II) takes as its starting point a plan of the operations to be carried out, whether in sales or orders and projects. From this stage, the system offers accepted methods of planning and control of materials through to delivery of the products.

Now that online management of all aspects of business is becoming the norm, and not only in medium-sized and large companies, it has become essential for a company to link the MRP II disciplines to the sales and controlling functions. In the context of the SAP standard business functions and integrated applications, the linking of MRP II and SAP takes place in three stages that are linked seamlessly together:

1. Customer order details are passed automatically to the SD-IS Sales Information System and to the CO-PA Profitability Analysis system.

2. The PP-SOP Sales and Operations Planning system selects the necessary information from the SD-IS Sales Information System and the CO-PA Profitability Analysis component.

3. The sales and operations plan is passed to the demand management functions. From here, the PP-MRP Material Requirements Planning component can initiate the MRP II Planning Chain, which ends with the generation of the necessary order proposals.

New customer orders are offset with the orders previously planned, and the next cycle of the optimized planning run can begin. The integrated quality control provided by the SAP R/3 QM-Quality Management system is applied to all the operations of the PP-Production Planning and Control module.

Defining Basic Data for Production in the PP-BD Component

The objects of interest to production planning are obviously the products and the methods by which they are produced and managed. The SAP R/3 system is designed for medium-sized and large organizations. The same products and production processes might appear in different divisions, so the organizational structure must be defined and then referenced in the basic data records for production and production planning.

Assigning Data to Organizational Units

The SAP R/3 general organizational units relevant to production planning are taken from the SAP R/3 Enterprise Data Model:

- **Author instance** is the highest level in R/3 and is identified by the code sysid. It's at this level that some data is managed because it can be set up for all lower levels. Currencies and units of measure are examples.

- **Client** is the second-highest level. The data of one client may not interact with another client. There are often a training client and a testing client, in addition to the client code that represents your group or corporate identity and under which the SAP system runs normal business. Some data is managed at the client level because everyone in the corporate group of companies will want to refer to exactly the same information and be certain that it has been maintained as up-to-date and correct. Vendor addresses are an example of data managed at the client level.

- **Company code** signifies a legal unit under the client that produces its own financial documents, the balance sheet, and the profit-and-loss statement, and may well maintain them continuously reconciled.

- **Plant** is an organizational unit that is seen as central to the production planning concept. A plant can be a production site or a group of storage locations that share materials. Plant is the unit for which MRP prepares plans and maintains the inventory. It is the focus of MM-Materials Management. Each plant is given planning and control elements such as material, inventory, operations, work centers, and so on.

Planning can take place across plants. For example, products manufactured in different plants can be combined for planning purposes into a product group. Manufacturing can also take place and be controlled on a cross-plant basis.

The stocks held in individual storage locations within a plant can also be managed separately with respect to inventory, and planned using MRP.

You may have defined other organizational units to suit your own planning and production needs. These user-defined organizational units can be used to focus material requirements planning:

- **Planning Plant** is the one plant chosen as the central unit when you are engaging in cross-plant material requirements planning.

■ **Work Center** is the central planning element to use when you are applying shop floor control and capacity planning. The system allows you to build work center hierarchies and use them for MRP.

■ **Planner Group** is a definition of people who are chosen, not by name necessarily, but by their personnel group, which is assigned by the Human Resources functions. This way, the members of a planning group can be selected from those who are available on the day they are needed and who have the necessary experience and qualifications. You can define other planning groups. Three planner groups are commonly assigned materials, resources, and production tools.

■ **MRP Controller Group** is an identification for those who are experienced at material requirements planning.

■ **Work Scheduler Group** is an identification of those with experience in scheduling work resources, including people.

■ **Shop Floor Controller Group** is an identification of those with experience in the detailed management of shop floor personnel and the places they work.

Defining a Material

It is standard throughout the SAP R/3 system to define *material* to include whatever is used in the production process. The following are examples of material in the SAP R/3 system:

■ Finished products
■ Intermediate assemblies
■ Unfinished products
■ Raw materials
■ Part-processed materials
■ Resources such as energy, air, and water
■ Packaging
■ Services

Storing Information as a Material Data Structure

Two principles apply to the storage of data in the SAP R/3 system:

■ Information that is expected to remain constant for a long time is entered in one place only, and any changes to it are logged.

■ Local information is stored at the level encompassing all the operational units for which it is pertinent but can be made available elsewhere.

You have the following range of options:

■ At the level of the client or the company code, maintain general data valid for the whole organization—for example, material code numbers, multilingual text concerning each material code, and classification rules applicable to material.

- At the plant level, maintain the data for material requirements planning and production planning and control and also valid bills of material and routings.
- Maintain inventories at the level of the individual storage location, of which a plant may have more than one.
- Maintain the sales data at the level of each purchasing organization and distribution channel.

You can define individual access authorizations as create, change, or display only. These can be specific to each user and each organizational level. If you are authorized to create transaction data, you can display and change it unless the item is reserved as read-only. If you are authorized at the intermediate level, you can alter a record but not generate a new one. For example, a sales representative might be allowed to change the address of a supplier, but not to create new suppliers or delete existing addresses.

Confining Materials to User Departments

Sections of the information on a material master can be allocated to different user departments, such as the MRP department, the work-scheduling department, and so on. By doing this, you can give each department access to just the information it needs about a specific material.

Establishing Material Types

Material data is maintained centrally. You can call for different views of the master records by referring to the material type. For example, you can maintain data for work scheduling in the case of a material of the type "semifinished goods," but you cannot schedule raw materials.

The material type determines certain other control parameters:

- Which user departments can maintain the data for a material of this type
- Procurement type, which indicates how this material is procured: in-house manufacturing or external procurement
- Type of inventory control to be used—for example, whether by quantity, value, or both

You can create and configure material types to suit your business.

Recognizing Industry Sectors

If a material is used in more than one industry, you may decide to create industry sectors in which the material type is configured in a special way for each sector.

Managing Batches and Special Stock

Batches of a material are managed at the storage-location level, but you might want to differentiate between, for example, special stock and batches:

- A **batch** is a partial quantity of material. The material in the batch is managed separately in the inventory. It might be a production lot or a delivery lot, for example.

- **Special stock** may be designated as vendor special stock, for example, because it is a consignment from a particular vendor.
- **Customer special stock** might be the designation of, for example, packaging materials returnable by the customer.
- **Activity-related special stock** might be identified because it is going to a particular customer on a make-to-order product, for example.

Using Departmental Profiles for Materials

You can use an existing material master record as a reference when creating a new material master. The data necessary on the user departments of your company can be maintained in the form of user department profiles, which contain no reference to any specific material, but you can reference them when creating a new material master. Each user department can set individual options to control how this data is applied.

Creating Bills of Material

The *bill of material* (BoM) is an instrument for describing the structure of a product for any of the following production types:

- Repetitive manufacturing
- Manufacturing products with variants
- Process manufacturing
- Make-to-order production

You can also maintain bills of material for sales orders, projects, equipment, and documents.

The BoM is used in central planning functions, such as material requirements planning and product costing. Five forms of the basic BoM are supported in PP-Production Planning and Control. You can create them at any time by extending a simple BoM:

- **Simple BoM.** One rigidly defined bill of material is associated with one material.
- **Variant BoM.** Several similar materials are associated with one bill of material.
- **Multiple BoM.** A set of bills of material describing each of several different production processes, constituents, or relative quantities of components, all of which produce the same material. There are several ways of making the same thing.
- **One-time BoM.** A bill of material for a specific sales order that is used in make-to-order production.
- **Configurable BoM.** A bill of material that is configured automatically on the basis of logical links. It is used for complex variant structures or process-dependent BoM configuration in continuous-flow production.

Exploring the BoM Data Structure

The BoM has a header and one or more items. The header indicates that the BoM is assigned to one or more plants and specifies its validity period. The header also carries its status indicator, which determines whether the BoM is released for production in its current form.

The BoM items each describe a component of the assembly in terms of the following categories, which you can subdivide as the need arises:

- **Stock items** are components kept in stock.
- **Nonstock items** may have purchasing data that you have maintained and that can be used to link with MM-Purchasing.
- **Variable-size items** must have the quantity to be used calculated automatically from the sizes entered.
- **Document items** include drawings or safety instructions integrated into the BoM.
- **Text items** are available for you to store all types of text in association with the BoM.

Byproducts and scrap can be represented on the BoM by negative quantities that will be processed in PP-MRP Material Requirements Planning and CO-PC Product Costing.

Parts of a BoM can be marked for the attention of a particular department, or a separate BoM can be used for each department.

Maintaining a BoM

You can update a BoM from the CAD system or directly in PP-Production Planning and Control. Copying and editing functions are available. The standard SAP R/3 classification system can search for suitable materials quickly.

Engineering change management is facilitated by mass changes to bills of material. The integrated engineering change management functions allow you to track the complete history of changes to a BoM.

Using BoM Explosion Numbers

A *BoM explosion number* is a method of making extra information available to the users of a BoM in a controlled manner. The BoM is given a master record that indicates whether it applies specifically to one product or to many. The BoM explosion number may go through several revision levels, each of which carries the *fixed key date* (the date on which that particular version of a BoM explosion should come into force). From that date, the content of the BoM explosion number has to be taken into account by the production scheduling and routing functions.

▶ **See** "Initiating a BoM Explosion," **p. 574**

The BoM explosion number is a reference to a technical document that can serve a range of functions, such as these:

- Notifying the details of product liability obligations
- Referencing ISO standards for quality assurance
- Documenting an engineering change made during the production process
- Referencing the relevant technical drawings and pointing out the salient features
- Documenting the technical status according to which a product is manufactured for all BoM levels
- Ensuring that the correct BoM and the corresponding routing are used in orders for spare parts

Directing the Materials

The BoM can be used to control production in several different plants, if they have the necessary resources. The R/3 system documents production resources in terms of work centers through which the material is routed. Thus, different plants can use different work centers and therefore need individual routing instructions.

Defining Work Centers

A *work center* is both a place where a process is carried on by means of activities and a technical concept in the PP-Production Planning and Control system. The real work center has people, machines, production lines, assembly lines, and all the paraphernalia of industry. The work center in SAP R/3 is a data object.

In the data object of the type "work center," you can specify the data for the scheduling, costing, and capacity planning of operations. Formulas held there can compute execution times, costs, capacity requirements, and so on.

The SAP Customizing module allows you to specify the data at your work centers in order to serve your company's needs. The system supplies default values for a work center to simplify and speed up work scheduling, or you can copy or reference from one source to another. The work center has standard texts to assist you in maintaining the correct operation descriptions in routings. Any parameter unit held at a work center can be given up to six standard values to speed up complex costing or duration calculations, for example. You just specify by a key the value to be used on each occasion.

Work centers are assigned to a cost center during work center data maintenance. This provides the link to the CO-Controlling system.

Every aspect of activity at a work center can be assigned a capacity value, which then takes part in capacity planning, production control, and the scheduling of routings. Not only can you define capacities for machines and labor, but you can also set up capacity parameters to define virtually any resource you might need to improve the value added by each work center. Here are some examples:

- Energy consumption
- Emissions
- Reserve capacities for rush orders

Documenting Routings

A *routing* is the industrial equivalent of a cooking recipe—what you need and the sequence of what has to be done to it, including advice on how you will know when the process has reached a satisfactory conclusion. The SAP R/3 PP-Production Planning and Control system uses a routing to document all aspects of a production process:

- The individual manufacturing steps or stages
- Material
- Capacities
- Production facilities
- Tools and plant fixtures
- Inspection procedures and quality standards on all aspects of the production processes in the routing

You can portray a routing as a *digraph*—a directed graph showing activities linked by arrows that show you which activities have to be completed or partially completed before the next activity begins. A complex production process that can cope with a range of products and variants needs a complex digraph to portray it. You can display a digraph in tabular or network form. You can represent the activities by arrows—perhaps to a scale where the length of the arrow is in proportion to the length of time taken by the activity. However, SAP R/3 always adopts another convention that represents the activities as nodes, often drawn as rectangular boxes, with the arrows showing the logical relationships between the activities. How long the arrows are or how many changes of direction they take on your digraph is of no significance.

SAP R/3 pathways or network routes are made up of a combination of the following subnetworks:

- **Linear** routings have the form of a chain of activities, each one beginning when, but not until, the previous activity finishes.
- **Parallel** routings have sections where two or more linear routing subsections start and end at shared junction points.
- **Split** routings contain steps where two or more activities all start and finish.
- **Overlapped** routings have sections where one activity begins before the previous one fully completes its work.

The conventional routing shows, in digraph format, the progress of materials or workpieces through the production sequence. If you have some operational sequences repeatedly used in a routing, you can assign them to a named reference operation set maintained by the work scheduler. The routing then can simply refer to this reference operation set when the operational sequence is needed as part of the production process.

Routings are maintained separately for each plant, but you can have the same routing applied to the same material at other plants and at other work centers. This is how the SAP R/3 system would represent cross-plant manufacturing. Here are some options:

- Allocate one material to one routing.
- Allow several routings to show different ways of producing the same material.
- Allocate several materials to the same routing—for example, to document the production of very similar variants.

Work Scheduling Operations and Sequences

The work scheduler provides an overview function that allows you to maintain all the essential information in one step. The work center contributes default values that you can amend if necessary:

- Identification of the work center at which the operation will take place is mandatory.
- You must confirm or change the control key. This enables the work scheduler to determine the following matters:
  - Whether the operation is to be costed
  - Whether capacity loads are to be computed for it
  - Whether and how the operation is to be confirmed
  - Whether time tickets are to be printed if this operation is to be used in an order
- You can accept the default description of the operation, or you can enter a different one from the work scheduler by choosing standard text from a list of options. Alternatively, you can create unique text by using the SAPscript word processing tool.
- You can accept default standard values for the technical aspects of the operation, or you can enter fresh standard values manually. Alternatively, values can be calculated automatically by the CAPP-Computer Aided Process Planning module.

External processing is signaled by operations marked with an external processing control key that ensures integration with MM-Materials Management purchasing functions. For example, a goods receipt, given in acknowledgment of external processing of this operation carried out by a vendor, is confirmed in the order.

You can specify work data in detail down to the level of suboperations; the standard values in the suboperations cumulate automatically in the operation. You might want to do this if, for example, it is better to have costing and capacity planning done on each suboperation, even though scheduling is carried out at the level of the operation. If several work centers will be cooperating in an operation, you might again usefully employ the concept of suboperations. The functions are provided for you to specify which parts of operations are to be carried out by specific manufacturing cells.

You can use the operational sequences of a routing in a variety of ways:

- A fully linear standard routing sequence might be all you need if there is only one way to do the job—only one production sequence is feasible.

■ You might want to create parallel sequences to portray and manage a situation in which you have two or more essentially similar production sequences with nothing to choose between them.

■ The third possibility is a set of two or more alternative sequences. In this case, you might be able to carry out parts of your standard routing sequence using some other operations or even other work centers. You might want to use these alternative sequences if you think that your standard routing might become overloaded unless you divert some of the work.

The display functions available to the work scheduler include many standard functions that can be customized for your own company.

You can inspect any of the data objects in the SAP R/3 system by calling for an intelligent listing. To do this, you specify something that identifies a group of data objects that you think will interest you the most. You might select on the basis of work centers, orders, production resources and tools, or any combination of these search factors. With the list in front of you, the intelligence becomes apparent when you select a line item that interests you and press one of the function keys. You then see the line item displayed in more detail, according to which drilling-down function you chose.

You can call a scheduling overview by choosing routings. A Gantt chart, for example, might be your display of choice. It gives you a quick overview of the durations of overlapped or parallel sequences of production processes, as well as the information you need to get to the required controlling functions. You also have the option of going deeper into the information available on any data object onscreen.

Yet another source of information is the where-used listing, which focuses on a particular tool or other production resource and shows you every operation in which it takes part. This way, you can carry out a mass change—for example, to replace one tool by another wherever it is used.

The PRT maintenance component is provided as a source of information on all *production resources and tools* (PRTs) used throughout the company. The PRTs are classified so that you can rapidly find a tool for whatever job you have in mind, or you can find all the jobs for which a certain tool or other resource has been used in the past. Three types of master records are relevant to production planning:

■ **Material** master records are used if purchasing and inventory functions are needed in relation to a PRT.

■ **PRT** master records carry the minimal amount of information needed simply to document that a specific production resource is needed in a routing.

■ **Document** master records are used if the resource needed for production has the status of a document, such as a drawing or a program for a numerically controlled machine.

The resources of the SAP R/3 DMS-Document Management System and the CAD system are at your disposal.

Locating Information with SAP R/3 Classification

No matter where you are working in the various application modules, you can access the SAP R/3 Classification system. It offers many functions to help you locate information held in document form. You can search on the basis of subject matter or for an item that is linked with a data object, such as these:

- Another document
- A routing
- A material identified by its material number, its name, or part of its name
- A material because it is similar to one you have already identified that may be out of stock, for example
- An item of equipment for which you have given the name or only the identification of the activity where it is used
- A project identified by its number, the person responsible, the purpose, and so on
- A quotation
- A sales order
- A customer or a vendor identified by an attribute in the master records

The SAP R/3 Classification system allows you to give classes (of products, for example) catch-words, or local names that help you locate what is wanted. Each class of objects in the system has a set of characteristics, some unique to that object, some shared by other objects—variants, for example. If you establish a class hierarchy with classes, subclasses, and so on, the characteristics of the class are passed on to members of the subclasses lower down the hierarchy. When you are entering the data for an individual item, you do not have to repeat all the data, because some of it is inherited from the parent class, the grandparent class, and so on. If you have to generate a master record for a new object—a new routing, for example—the system prompts you to supply the data required, depending on the level at which you are creating something. In this example, the standard characteristics of a routing are offered as defaults, and you are prompted to carry on from there.

Searching with the SAP R/3 Classification system proceeds in two stages:

- Find the class that contains the object of your search by means of its name, by catch-words you have assigned to your classes, by viewing a graphical display of the class hierarchy and stepping through it until you find what you want, or by searching with a match code.
- Use object characteristics to narrow down the search until you have the object you require. Characteristics may be identified by constant values or value ranges.

You might want to define different lists of characteristics for each department in your company. Then you can be sure that the objects you find will be only those relevant to the area you are working in. Because of the hierarchical structure of the classes of objects in the Classification system, you can find anything you are looking for rapidly and with the specification of only the minimum of search data.

Introducing the User's Interface to the CAD System

Many production environments are developing with this fact of life at the forefront of their design philosophy: Very few products remain the same for very long. No step in the production cycle can afford to stand still in the search for speed and relevance when it comes to making changes. *Computer-assisted design* (CAD) and *engineering databases* (EDBs) have to be integrated with the PP-Production Planning and Control system.

The SAP CAD user interface with the SAP R/3 system offers the design engineer the following functionality:

- You can use the SAP R/3 Classification system to search for suitable parts and avoid duplication of design work.
- The SAP R/3 DMS-Document Management System is available to manage documents and drawings and to integrate information from EDBs.
- All the basic data held in material masters, bills of material, and documents in the PP-Production Planning and Control system are accessible.
- An assembly drawing created in the CAD system and containing the basic design and engineering data can be designated as a bill of material in the PP-Production Planning and Control system, which maintains the BoM during work scheduling.
- From the CAD system, the functional locations and the equipment data objects used by the PM-Plant Maintenance system can be maintained.
- The CAD user interface has access to a library of functions containing subroutines that enable data exchange with any CAD system; EDB; technical information system; non-SAP application; and workstation, PC, or host system on which the data resides.

Allocating Resources for Production

When you or the SAP R/3 system and its applications have assigned a work center for a particular task, the capacity of this work center to carry out the required activities will already be known, and the calculation can proceed to ensure that sufficient capacity will be available when it is needed. However, the materials, the workpieces, and the resources needed for production—including the tools, jigs, and fixtures—have to be allocated to the work center.

The work scheduler looks for the specifications of the materials in the bill of materials and selects what is needed. If there is no bill of materials, or if it lacks some of the necessary information, the scheduler has to seek this information from the unit responsible for maintaining bills of material.

Managing Engineering Change

Using change numbers is standard practice throughout SAP R/3 and its applications. If a bill of materials or a routing is to be changed, the engineering change management system in your company signals this change by publishing a change number and a date when it will be released. Alterations in the work scheduling have to take this into account and ensure that the new routings, for example, take effect from that date and have been anticipated in the planning processes.

Each engineering change master document is given a unique change number by using a system determined by the user organization. The document is dated and contains a note explaining the reason for the change. You can define its status to block it and prevent it from being released until, for example, all the items to be changed are specified. The change master also carries a valid-from date.

The object list in the change master records identifies all the data objects to be affected, such as these:

- Materials
- Bills of material
- Task lists, such as routings
- Documents

Any number of objects may be included in the same change number master. All changes are stored according to date and the reason for making the change. The following change history information is stored in the list of changes:

- Old and new status of the changed data
- Change date
- Person who made the change
- Date from which the change is valid
- Type of change or reason, such as "item deleted" or "new item"
- Old and new values for what was changed

Managing Quality with the QM Module

The standard business functions that support the SAP system of quality management are an integral part of the PP-Production Planning application. They are also available as a separate module, QM-Quality Management, which can be installed and configured when the PP-Production Planning module is not part of your R/3 system.

Inspecting for Quality Control

It has become standard business practice to address the issue of quality at every level. The bills of material and the routings describe what has to be done, so they have to include the operation of inspection. The task of quality inspection takes time and resources, which means that it has to take its place in the marketplace for time and other resources under the PP-Production Planning and Control system.

Unspecialized inspection has its place, but when there are known possibilities of variations in material, processing operations, and personal skills, the inspection has to be given very clear direction in terms of the following factors:

- At which stages in the sequence of production processes will inspections take place?
- Will the workflow be sampled or inspected in its entirety?

- Who will be responsible for each inspection?
- What processing has to take place to prepare the product for inspection?
- Which parts or attributes will the inspector look at, measure or test with a gauge, or send off a sample of for analysis by the laboratory at each inspection stage?
- What will the inspector see if everything is fine, if further testing is needed, or if one of the known faults is present in the piece of work?

In summary, the production documentation must formally specify to the inspector what to look at, what to look for, and what action to take in every case. And a fresh pair of eyes available to look at the quality of work is not a bad idea.

In accord with the master data philosophy of the SAP R/3 system, frequently used data is written in one place where it can be updated and used in exactly the same form by everybody who needs it. This principle applies to production data. The quantitative and qualitative aspects of inspection, sampling parameters, target values, and tolerances are created as independent basic data elements. The components of a specification that will be used to inspect and test quality are all data elements that can be used in other inspection specifications. They will also be used in production and can be printed on the order to show which standards are in force.

Integrating Inspection Plans with Routings

Overall, modern quality management requires inspection at every operation. The routing is a plan of operations. The inspection planner can use the same functions as the routings. And the inspections can be integrated with the production routings. If the inspection has to take place outside production, as in the case of goods received or goods to be issued, the inspection planner can use the inspection criteria to create a special inspection plan. Better than that, the inspector can call on predefined reference operation sets and master inspection characteristics as the starting point from which a customized plan can be created.

Inspection plans fall into logical groupings:

- **Material** inspection plans concentrate on what might be, in some cases, a very specialized method of inspection specific to that one material.
- **Individual** inspection plans are usually intended to be used for a material in relation to a specific customer or vendor, for example.
- **Family** inspection plans determine the inspection scope of a family of parts. This family can be defined in terms of materials, sources, or destinations. Or it can be defined in terms of a combination of certain materials from certain vendors, and so on.

When the inspection planner assigns a material to a plan, it is usual to define at the same time the target values and tolerances to be applied across the scope of the plan.

The scope and details of an inspection plan can be reassigned at any time. *Dynamic modification* refers to the process of adjusting the inspection plan according to the most recent inspection results.

Calling on Computer Aided Process Planning

The SAP R/3 Configurator database interface provides a wide range of functions for automatic generation of routings from a knowledge base. The CAPP-Computer Aided Process Planning module automatically calculates standard values, such as setup times and machine times, and applies them to the routings generated by the SAP R/3 Configurator to provide the following facilities:

- Generation of operation sequences
- Selection of work centers
- Selection and allocation of production resources and tools
- Allocation of material components to operations

A knowledge base is required to be set up in the form of tables and formulas that must include, for example, the following types of information for all operations:

- Calculation rules for standard work center operating values as stipulated in a labor union contract
- Company-specific tables of planned times for operations
- Materials
- Weights
- Tolerances
- Feeds and so on

SAP R/3 provides functions to check this knowledge base for consistency and for maintenance of the data.

The knowledge base must also contain methods that describe how particular tables and formulas are to be linked to arrive at a result—for example, a calculated setup time for a particular process. The calculation of a standard value can be split into subcalculations—for each step in an operation, for example. Existing data can be used to reduce the amount of fresh calculations entailed.

The methods have to be combined in sequence into the sets of calculations that provide all the results needed to plan each particular process. The process has to be assigned to a work center.

When you consider creating or changing a routing, you might find that several alternative processes could occur at a certain point in the routing. You have to select the one to be used. Then you must look at the methods to be used in the process you have selected; there may be several options. Again, you have to select which methods will form the basis of the process.

After you select the methods to be used in a process at a work center, the PP-Production Planning and Control system calculates the standard values.

Controlling Output in the Production Planning Module

Corporate financial viability may well depend on the accuracy and timeliness of the information flows in your company. The SAP R/3 output control functions offer flexible management of workflow across all SAP applications.

The following examples of user-defined events illustrate the variety of services offered:

- Delivery notes generated and sent automatically to the ship-to party via a medium of your choice
- Invoices sent at a time you specify
- Automatic mail to the work scheduler if a bill of material is changed
- Formulation of production output proposals and their conditions
- Generation of an output proposal during transaction processing
- Generation of an output document
- Editing of outputs
- Sending outputs at a time you specify
- Status reports generated automatically on the processing stage of an output
- Output proposals generated when a specified set of conditions (a data constellation) is detected

When you are offered an output proposal, it includes details such as these:

- Time when the output is to be sent
- Recipient of the output
- Medium to be used for sending, such as printout, telex, R/Mail, teletext, telefax, and Electronic Data Interchange

You can accept the output proposal or edit any of the details.

Planning Sales and Operations in the PP-SOP Component

If you want to set targets for long- and medium-term sales quantities and to roughly plan the production activities necessary to achieve these targets, use the PP-SOP Sales and Operations Planning system. At a later stage, the detailed planning through BoM explosion and scheduling via the routing will take place under the direction of the SAP PP-MP Master Planning standard programs.

Using Levels in Sales and Operations Planning

The broad-brush planning carried out by PP-SOP Sales and Operations Planning can be done at the level of the finished product or at the product group level. Any combination of materials and products can be designed as a product group and planned together as a unit. This is the method of choice if there are too many products to justify planning at an individual level.

After you decide on the level of planning, products, or product groups, you must set up the sales quantities for each of the future periods you are planning. There are various ways of arriving at these values or quantities of the products or product groups:

■ Manually enter sales quantities or values for each period.

■ Have the system use historical values to forecast automatically.

■ Copy the values from CO-PA Profitability Analysis.

■ Copy the sales quantities from the SD-IS Sales Information System.

■ Copy the sales quantities from a non-SAP system.

From the sales forecast, you must next generate production plans that can meet your planned sales. The system helps ensure that you make the best use of your existing resources as you put together your production plan.

The last stage of this rough planning process is *disaggregation*, which entails taking apart any product groups you have aggregated for rough planning purposes. In the end, you must pass on to PP-MP Master Planning only individual product plans.

Defining Product Groups

The purpose of establishing a product group is to be able to conduct in one operation the sales and operations planning for many individual products. A product group can be made up of any materials or product groups arranged in product group hierarchies. Thus, for example, product group A may be defined by listing any combination of products or product types.

A material can be assigned to several product groups; you can have alternative product hierarchies. You can also define and plan product groups that span some or all of your plants.

The product group hierarchy concept illustrates the general principle, used throughout SAP R/3, of data objects inheriting the characteristics of their parents in the hierarchy. In this case, the inheritance consists of the planning data assigned by the processing conducted by PP-SOP Sales and Operations Planning.

The measurement units might vary at different levels of a product group structure. Simple arithmetic calculation may have to be carried out to make the conversion, or it may be a matter of converting a rough plan forecast of weight or bulk into a target in terms of individual workpieces. If more than one product shares a planned total, you have to specify the proportional factors needed to disaggregate the total into the relative percentage and to the planned numbers of each product.

You can ask the system to calculate proportional factors on the basis of historical data, or you can enter the factors manually.

Eliciting Forecasts

A graphical display of forecast results is standard across all SAP applications. In the case of PP-Production Planning and Control, the main tasks of the forecast follow:

- Forecasting product groups and finished products
- Forecasting material requirements in support of consumption-based planning
- Determining the data used to calculate safety stock and reorder levels

Although any data can be accessed in the SAP R/3 system, a standard interface has been programmed between the PP-Production Planning and Control system and the following SAP applications:

- LIS-Logistics Information System, which includes the SD-IS Sales Information System and the PIS-Purchasing Information System
- MM-Materials Management, for the materials consumption data

The forecasting process takes place in the background for several materials at once until all the objects in the plan have received attention. If you are not satisfied with any of the forecast values or quantities arrived at automatically, you can make any adjustment manually at the online display.

The historical data may point to trends and patterns that can be used to make better forecasts. You can find out what those are by having the system carry out model analysis on the data. The system determines which of its model profiles best fits the historical data, and it continues to check to make sure that the profile chosen is the best. It changes models automatically if you allow it. Alternatively, you can specify which model you want to use. The models now available for analyzing the historical time series of data for any variables you specify follow:

- A **constant value** model determines a steady forecast amount or a moving average.
- A **trend model** determines an equation to plot the future trend of values.
- A **seasonal model** plots a cyclical pattern.
- **Trend and seasonal** models combined predict a shifting cyclical pattern.

The models are recorded as forecast profiles that are not tied to any one material. The material master record contains a reference to the forecast profile that is associated with it. In this way, data entry is minimized and the forecast can be generated for any material over any time line.

Fine-Tuning the Sales Plan

You can change sales quantities at any time in the PP-SOP Sales and Operations Planning system. This gives you a continuous planning horizon.

Your sales forecast might use product groups. If so, the system automatically accumulates the historical values for all members of the product group.

You can add new parameters to the forecast simulation on a what-if basis. Each run can be stored as an alternative version of your forecast. In this interactive process, you can adjust the figures taken from historical values if you think this will improve your forecast.

When you are viewing a graphical display of your forecast and plan, you can make permanent adjustments to it simply by moving the graph points with your mouse.

If your installation can give you values from CO-PA Profitability Analysis, your PP-Production Planning and Control module can aggregate the detailed data automatically, ready for you to add it to your sales plan. Similarly, the SD-IS Sales Information System or any non-SAP system can send you data for your product group or material-level sales plan. Of course, you can redistribute the data over different production plants in your plan and make refinements to your forecast data manually.

Developing a Production Plan from a Sales Plan

The starting production plan is usually one that exactly matches your sales plan. The system copies quantities and dates directly from your sales plan to make the production plan.

You can also specify a target in terms of the number of days the stock of each product is expected to last—a measure of the stock on hand related to the expected consumption of the stock. The system then calculates the production quantities needed to maintain this amount of stock, referred to as the *target days' supply.*

Using various distribution tools if necessary, you can also manually enter the stock levels required.

Versions of your production plan can be simulated and stored separately.

Disaggregating a Plan

After the PP-SOP Sales and Operations Planning system develops sales and production plans using product groups as the working units, the plan values have to be disaggregated into plan elements that apply to the individual members of the product groups.

There are two methods for automatically disaggregating a product group:

■ Group members can be finished products or product groups that are split according to the proportional factors assigned to them.

■ Product group members can be distributed over time by using a splitting key to choose between calendar months, weeks, calendar days, and working days.

Integrating Corporate Planning

The detailed actual planning takes place under the control of the PP-MP Master Planning functions. The data moves to this system from the PP-SOP Sales and Operations Planning system along two routes:

■ Direct passing of independent requirements for each finished product as indicated in the sales plan or production plan

■ Copying for reference only, in which the data on the independent requirements for finished products may be altered by the PP-MP Master Planning system

Master Planning in the PP-MP Component

The master plan has to settle on master schedule items, the resources they will require, and their start and finish times. A *master schedule item* is a finished product or an important assembly that will make a big difference to total turnover or profit or will dominate the production process because of its complexity.

The planning for these important master schedule items has to make the key decisions for your company on how production resources are to be used. Three things have to be done:

1. Select the planning and production strategy.
2. Determine the quantities required and their delivery dates.
3. Assemble the master plan for the master schedule items.

Managing Demand

Demand management has to serve three functions:

- Determine the quantities and dates for the finished products and important assemblies that are being made in anticipation of future orders.
- Specify the strategy to be used for planning and producing or procuring a product.
- Define the planning strategy to be used for order-oriented production and the planning for preproduction of assemblies for future make-to-order production.

There are three production strategies and three planning strategies, and each has several variations:

- **Make to stock** in anticipation of sales, net, or gross.
- **Make to order** using sales orders copied from SD-Sales and Distribution or orders created directly in PP-Production Planning and Control, keeping all information on requirements and costs attached to each separate order.
- **Make in lots** in response to one or more sales orders and internal stock replenishment orders.

You also need to decide how you will offset planned values with sales orders when they occur.

Planning With and Without Final Assembly

Sometimes you cannot afford to wait for sales orders before you start to produce or procure certain assemblies, semifinished products, or raw materials. What you can do is set up independent requirements that trigger planning and production for stock. When orders arrive, you then can offer faster delivery.

You can take the independent requirements to the final assembly level, or you can stop production before this stage and carry out the rest of the assembly only when you have an order. This creates a dependent requirement that you can meet partially from stock, offsetting this against your planned independent requirement.

Applying the Planning Material Concept

When several products start out looking the same and sharing the same preliminary production processes, you can establish a planning material to represent the product up to the point when it is treated differently to make the distinct products. A planning material can be treated exactly like any other material and can be subjected to the various planning strategies.

Using Assemblies to Focus Planning

If you use assemblies to produce a large number of variants according to customer requirements, it might be easier to focus the planning on these assemblies. You can plan assembly requirements that are independent of orders and later offset them when the customer orders specify which variants are needed and therefore which assemblies.

Consulting Reference Figures when Maintaining Independent Requirements

Risks are attached to planning and producing products that have not been confirmed as orders. The following reference figures are available to help if you'are in the role of material requirements planner:

- A sales plan for the product
- A forecast for the product calculated automatically from sales planning information
- A rough-cut production plan for the product from PP-SOP Sales and Operations Planning
- Independent requirements that already have been planned and perhaps already produced for the product and perhaps for specific customers

The MRP controller is warned automatically if any of these reference figures are changed.

The independent requirements can be split across any planning periods: near future in weeks, for example, or far future in months. A complete change history may be mandated for each independent requirement. Like other planning instruments, an independent requirements plan can be given a version number and therefore can exist in alternative versions.

Scheduling Master Item Production

Extra attention is given to planning and scheduling those items that take up critical resources or that can have a big influence on profits. Items marked as master schedule items can be finished products, assemblies, or raw materials.

In a master planning run, only the master schedule items are considered. For each item, a *bill of material* (BoM) is used to generate the dependent requirements. Further levels of detail below this—the BoM explosion data—are not processed at this stage. Thus, the MRP controller can manipulate the master plan before any extensive processing takes place on the various BoM explosion detail levels.

You can protect the master plan from automatic changes by using a planning time fence created for each material. This prevents the MRP run from altering any order proposal within the time fence unless authorized.

The master plan can be adjusted online, and simulation can be used to check the results. A series of standard evaluations is available to the MRP controller through various display presentations. *Available-to-promise* (ATP) quantities can be displayed to show stocks and receipts that have not yet been reserved by planning against any particular sales order.

Master planning across several sites is supported by full information flows and, for example, by distributing production quantities among various sites according to quotas that may also be applied to the procurement of materials from various plants.

Using the Distribution Warehouse Concept

A *distribution warehouse* is a plant that is the supplier for several companies, for several countries, or for several companies that are each in a different country. Such a warehouse is a unit that should be subject to planning.

One advantage of the warehouse concept is that you can use various planning strategies for the same product, depending on the warehouse through which it is to be distributed. One warehouse might use consumption-based planning; another might be better planned using an MRP procedure. Forecasting and evaluation can be carried out with and across the distribution warehouses.

The supply of goods from the production plants to the distribution warehouses is handled by the purchasing and distribution functions in the MM-Materials Management and SD-Sales and Distribution systems.

Material Requirements Planning in the PP-MRP Component

The PP-MRP Material Requirements Planning component and the MRP II Planning Chain propose orders for materials so that they will be in the right place, at the right time, and in the right quantity. The method is based on the principle of exception reporting. Material requirements planning is generally a matter of planning only those materials that have changed in stock or those that have anticipated demands that have changed since the previous computation.

An MRP net change planning run is a limited exercise that can be repeated at short intervals so that you can always be up-to-date. Furthermore, you can limit the planning horizon to match your current priorities. You can replan a single item if you want—daily, if necessary.

An MRP run generates exception messages for the controller in situations such as these:

- If material is ordered but not delivered on time
- If stock is below safety level

If a planned purchase order or production order is not required, the system automatically creates a proposal to cancel or reschedule the order—whichever makes better sense—to avoid having something that is not likely to be needed at the time scheduled.

The controller can call for an MRP list per material, or for an overview per material of the stock or requirements situation—this is similar to the MRP list, except that the current situation is portrayed in the form of changes. If you have several MRP controllers, you can allocate certain groups of materials to each.

The controller can display receipts and issues on the time axis in any time period and can call up more detailed information on any item. From the list, you can make any kind of change to an order. Multilevel pegging enables you to locate the original source of each receipt or issue, so that in the case of a delay, for example, you can identify the requirements that generated the order and therefore will be affected by the delay. *Available-to-promise* (ATP) quantities can be displayed by the MRP controller.

The controller has two procedures to use in planning material requirements:

- Consumption-based planning, including reorder point planning and forecast-based planning
- Material requirements planning for each production plant or procurement plant

Consumption-Based Planning

Reorder point planning depends on specifying a safety stock level below which the stock should not be allowed to fall, bearing in mind the possibility of unexpected requirements. The reorder point makes allowance for stock predicted to fall while the replacement stock is being delivered. When stock reaches the reorder point, the system generates an order proposal to replenish the stock.

You can enter both the reorder point and the safety stock level, or the system can call on forecasts to calculate both, depending on the service level and the replenishment lead time. The SAP R/3 regular forecast program ensures that the reorder and safety stock levels are automatically adapted to the current delivery and consumption situation.

Material Requirements Planning

Sales orders and planned independent requirements, along with the dependent requirements arising from BoM explosion, define the material requirements. The availability calculation is precise down to the nearest day. The system can also cope with additional unplanned withdrawals on the basis of previous consumption patterns.

Any material requirement that will greatly influence the overall planning result can be designated as a master schedule item. It then receives extra planning attention, including a check on resources before the BoM explosion is carried out, which might otherwise initiate an automatic change of the complete master plan. Net planning has to have stock levels checked; gross planning does not.

Lot-Sizing

If the net requirements calculation anticipates a shortage on a specific date, the system determines the exact quantity to be procured or produced. There is a choice open to the MRP controller of lot-sizing procedure: static, period, optimum, or user-defined. The controller also specifies the minimum and maximum lot size, and a rounding value to allow the lot size to cover an exact multiple of the order unit. Production or assembly scrap is predefined and also taken into account in the lot size.

Static lot-sizing covers three procedures:

- Lot for lot uses the shortage quantity as the order quantity.
- Fixed-lot size is defined in the material master; several orders are generated if necessary to cover the shortage.
- Replenishment takes place up to the maximum stock level specified in the material master.

Period lot-sizing takes the requirement quantities for a certain period of time as the lot. The period can be daily, weekly, or monthly, or an individual planning calendar can be maintained for this purpose.

Optimum lot-sizing notes the storage costs per unit of material compared with the costs independent of lot size. The optimum lot size is when the sum of both cost factors is at a minimum. The MRP controller has a choice of optimum lot-sizing procedures:

- Least unit cost
- Part period balancing
- Groff reorder procedure
- Dynamic lot-size creation

For materials to be produced in-house, order proposals have to be converted to production orders within user-defined planning horizons. For parts to be purchased, the MRP controller can specify which of the following the system should create:

- Planned order, which must be converted to a purchase requisition at the appropriate time
- Purchase requisition, which is converted by the purchasing department to a purchase order, a release order (from stock), or a delivery schedule
- Delivery schedule, which is an agreement that comes into force when the requirements are needed; a valid delivery agreement will have been specified via the material source list

The relevant BoM explosion has to be initiated for in-house production and also for purchase requisitions and delivery schedules used for subcontracting.

Order Proposal Scheduling in MRP

Backward scheduling applies to material requirements planning and forecast planning, because the requirement date in the future is known in both cases. The start date is found from the replenishment lead time. If the system finds that the material cannot be delivered on time, the controller is informed of the expected delay and the system automatically begins forward scheduling.

Reorder point planning requires that stock replenishment begin as soon as the shortage becomes imminent—that is, when it is unlikely to be covered by the normal reordering provision. The system then determines when the stock will be available again. If goods have to go through quality control, an allowance can be made for goods receipt processing time.

Capacity Requirements Planning in the PP-CRP Component

The purpose of capacity planning is to provide planners with a flexible system of overviews of the capacity utilization at all the work centers at a plant, and also of the planning instruments used to achieve capacity leveling.

The capacities available at a work center can be defined in various ways that allow you to create requirements for different types of orders and to monitor how the capacity is used. Capacity planning deals with the capacity categories at a work center, and the amounts of these capacities available to meet the loads accumulating for them. The following types of capacities illustrate the wide-ranging uses of the concept:

■ Labor
■ Pooled capacity shared with certain other work centers
■ Machine capacity
■ Energy consumption
■ Wastes from a process
■ Reserves set aside for rush orders

Every type of capacity available at a work center can be plotted on the time axis to show how much of it is available at any moment. The system provides a graphical display of each availability through time. Work center hierarchies can be subjected to a choice of capacity-cumulating calculations.

Shift sequences are defined and maintained centrally in SAP R/3 and can be applied to work centers to have the necessary adjustments made automatically by the system.

Scheduling in Capacity Planning

The scheduling process can be carried out at the rough-cut level using internal production time per operation, for example. To control production activities accurately, you may need to establish time elements to cover the details. Consider these examples:

- Floats, order floats before and after production, and queue times
- Setup and tear-down times to take account of the time costs of changing from one activity to another
- Interoperation times where a minimum wait time is required, or a time to move the piece from one place to another

Basic planning data has to be maintained as entered values and as tables or formulas from which the necessary values can be calculated.

Calculating Capacity Requirements

Planned orders are the basis for rough-cut and medium-term planning. The capacity requirements will have been calculated for these planned orders, and a detailed picture will be available of the way the critical work centers will be occupied by the various activities.

Production orders are the instruments for detailed planning and control. The capacity requirements for production orders are the basis of shop floor control of work centers.

Maintenance orders derived from the PM-Plant Maintenance system include capacity requirements so that systematic capacity leveling can be carried out in that system or in the PP-Production Planning and Control module.

Networks are used in project management and in the SAP R/3 PS-Project System. Every activity in a network can have its capacity requirements planned.

Quality inspection orders are available in SAP R/3. They also generate capacity requirements that can be subjected to planning calculations.

An operation can impose more than one type of capacity load on a work center, and it is possible to calculate more complex capacity requirements—as in operations that require more than one machine, for example.

Evaluating the Capacity Load Situation

The *capacity load* refers to the capacity requirements in relation to the capacity available. However, particular users will want to have this sort of information processed differently according to their interests. Customizing allows you to have a custom-made and pertinent display of the capacity situation and its significance for your work. For example, the following tools are provided to individualize the presentation of load evaluations in the form of overview lists or graphics:

- **Profiles** define the period under consideration by the planner, the work centers and capacities to be evaluated, and the orders and operations to be analyzed.
- **Groupings** allow evaluations to summarize any set of capacities, regardless of where they are drawn from and from which time period.
- **Sortings** allow user-defined data to be arranged according to the most informative scheme.

■ **Cumulation** allows capacity load data to be combined by work center hierarchies, by level, and across time periods.

You can select a data object in a presentation and press a special function key to get further information on that object; this capability is standard across SAP R/3.

Capacity Leveling

Simulation is available to the planner at every level. You can make changes to the available capacity and adjust the lot size. Deadline movements and changes of work center can be tried out in the simulation. Plan versions can be stored until the optimum plan is released for production.

Simple lead time scheduling can result in a loading of infinity for one or more work center capacities—in other words, a bottleneck. On the other hand, capacity scheduling takes into consideration the orders already dispatched when it calculates the operation dates for an order; overloads are thus avoided.

Because the dispatching sequence reflects the priority attached to work items, it is crucial to successful capacity scheduling. Optimization of the production sequence is often combined with capacity leveling. There are programs to conduct sequencing to optimize setup time, which can be adjusted automatically according to user-defined criteria.

Manual capacity leveling is carried out by resource planning, which dispatches only as many orders to a work center as can be processed there. A graphic planning table is provided so that you can easily see the orders already dispatched to a work center and the orders or operations waiting to be dispatched. The system supports you with detailed information on the availability of material and capacity, the stage reached by preceding operations, and the dispatching rules offered as guidance to simplify the planning of resources.

Capacity Availability Checking

A bottleneck occurs when the required capacity is not available. Availability checking ensures that the capacity is available. It is possible to check, at every planning phase, that the required capacity will be available at the particular work center when it is required, either for an individual order or for an entire order structure.

If the required capacity won't be available, the system proposes a date by which the order can be produced without bottlenecks. You can also make this sort of capacity decision on the basis of a simulation of an order structure created on behalf of a customer inquiry. This helps you avoid promising delivery dates that cannot be realistically met according to the current capacity use in your work centers.

At the time of order release, after detailed planning has already taken place, you can again carry out an availability check to make sure that the capacities you need will actually be available at the work centers.

Controlling Production Orders in the PP-SFC Component

This PP-Production Planning component, also referred to as *Shop Floor Control*, converts the planning specifications of the PP-MRP Material Requirements Planning component into actual production orders to be carried out. It then coordinates all aspects of the production process and resource use.

The benefits of close control of production activity include minimization of costs and inventory, best use of available capacities, adherence to delivery dates, and elevation of quality standards.

Controlling Production Activity

Production activity is controlled mainly by the production order, which describes all planned and actual elements related to production. The production order informs the shop floor controller of the following matters:

- What is to be produced
- Production deadlines to be met
- Resources needed, such as materials, documents, capacities, production resources and tools, and so on
- Which costs are to be incurred
- How costs are to be settled

The production order passes through four phases, each receiving a slightly different emphasis in the matter of production control:

- Order creation, including the conversion from planned orders, routing selection, scheduling of capacities, job order costing, and creation of requisitions
- Order processing, including order release, material issues, completion confirmations, and receipt to stock
- Order completion, including technical order completion with the deletion of outstanding capacity loads and reservations
- Order settlement

Converting Planned Orders

Although you can always manually create and enter a production order for a rush order or another special order, most production orders are created by converting planned orders that have been generated automatically by the PP-MRP Material Requirements Planning system. This conversion is carried out automatically by the system. Manual intervention is necessary only when a problem is foreseen. For example, the user must make a choice if no suitable routing can be found. The user must also intervene if there is a choice of alternative routings, and no selection criteria is available to allow MRP to make the decision automatically.

By identifying the relevant opening period, the MRP controller can select the planned orders that are due for conversion into production orders. If so customized, the conversion process carries out the following tasks in the background:

- Transfer general data from the planned order to the production order.
- Transfer details of the material to be produced.
- Transfer the bill of material components.
- Transfer the order quantity.
- Transfer the basic dates.
- Assign to the production order the component requirements created by PP-MRP Material Requirements Planning.
- Create requisitions automatically for BoM components that won't be produced in-house, and initiate purchasing action by the MM-Materials Management system.
- Create material reservations automatically for BoM components manufactured in-house.
- Select routings.
- Select bills of material in special cases and carry out BoM explosions.
- Transfer the results, if they are available, of the rough-cut planning of planned orders.
- Schedule the production order according to the dates calculated in PP-MRP Material Requirements Planning.
- Calculate capacity loads and dispatch them to the work centers.
- Carry out job order costing on the basis of planned material consumption, prevailing cost rates for internal labor, and costs of external processing, as appropriate.
- Update on the production order the actual costs when completion confirmations and material issues are carried out.
- Delete the planned order if the conversion to a production order has been successful.

Processing Orders

The work scheduler offers the following support functions from the PP-SFC Production Orders component:

- Order release to the shop floor, with the printing of shop papers for the specific operations of an order, for an order as a whole, or for all the orders released for that period
- Material issues
- Completion confirmations
- Receipt to stock

You also have a Status Management function, which displays an overview of the current status of an order at any given time, using a status sequence that you can define to suit the methods of your company. The details of all orders on hand are available when required.

The following shop papers can be printed:

- Operation control ticket and job tickets
- Pick lists
- Material issue slips
- Lists of production resources and tools
- Time tickets
- Completion confirmation slips

The shop papers can carry bar codes, and you have control over the selection of the information to be printed. The papers can be formatted in a company-specific layout and directed to the outlets of choice.

Material issues can be carried out for an entire order or against individual reservations. The issue of material components automatically updates the actual costs on the production order. Backflushing of material issues can take place, in which the confirmation of an operation automatically creates a withdrawal posting of the material components allocated to that operation.

Completion confirmations allow you to document the quantities produced, the scrap, and the production times for an operation. This way, you can monitor production capacity use and incurred manufacturing costs. The actual quantities, attendance times, and actual costs are automatically updated in order as each completion confirmation is posted at a *Plant Data Collection* (PDC) station or through the online functions of the PP-Production Planning and Control system. The system will have assigned a completion confirmation number to each operation that can be entered by presenting the bar code on the system-printed confirmation slip.

Various completion confirmation arrangements are available:

- **Normal** confirmation confirms each operation individually.
- **Standard** confirmation uses target values as actual values to minimize the number of entries required.
- **Collective** confirmation allows several completion confirmations for different orders to be confirmed against a list.
- **Milestone** confirmation confirms an operation that has been marked as a milestone. This automatically confirms all preceding operations that are not themselves milestones.

Receipts to stock from production orders can occur for partial lots or for the entire production lot. The receipt is posted, according to the job control, to an individual customer stock or as stock that is not related to an order. The valuation strategy specifies in the material master whether to use planned costs, planned prices, or standard prices, for example.

The work scheduler can call on reports that use the extensive capacity planning functions. You can select the following orders for your report:

- Orders for a particular material
- Orders under a particular MRP controller

■ Orders for a particular shop floor controller

■ Orders that use particular production resources and tools

Integrating Production Activity Control with Technical Subsystems

Because the PP-Production Planning and Control system is an open system, there is no reason why you should not connect it to any technical subsystem. You could use a variety of channels:

■ **Plant Data Collection/Machine Data Collection (PDC/MDC).** You can arrange plant data, machine data, and attendance time data collection through this channel to link with the PP-Production Planning and Control system and the HR-Human Resources system.

■ **Digital or numerical control (DNC).** You can transfer information on required production resources and tools to a subordinate DNC or PRT management function.

■ **Transfer control.** You can send requests to move material from one activity to another in the production area.

■ **Process visualization.** Use this channel to exchange master data and movement data with process engineering and process visualization systems.

■ **Quality data collection.** This channel transfers information on the specified checking procedures to automatic measurement data-entry systems that return the results to the QM-Quality Management system.

■ **Technical optimization.** You can link scrap minimization and setup time optimization systems at work centers to the PP-Production Planning and Control system.

Completing an Order

An order is technically completed when it is marked using the Status Management function. This causes the deletion of outstanding capacity loads and reservations. Further postings to this order are prohibited.

Settling an Order

When delivery is completed, an order can be settled. The system calculates the balance between debit postings to the order and credit postings. The order account then is debited or credited accordingly. Only after an order is technically completed and settled is it archived.

Debit postings to an order may include material issues, external labor, and completion confirmations debited to the order. Credit postings to an order can be caused by receipts to stock.

Controlling Production

Production controlling achieves a balance among the following factors:

■ Product quality

■ Short delivery times

■ Highly reliable delivery dates

- Minimum costs
- Low stocks
- High utilization of work center capacities

The LIS-Logistics Information System has a subset of functions that serve the PP-SFC Shop Floor Control and Information System, which are being developed into the CAPISCE *(Computer Architecture for Production Information Systems in a Competitive Environment)* for the European Community. This is a flexible tool for consolidating, summarizing, and analyzing data gathered from production activity control. It offers two types of analyses:

- **Standard analyses** use statistical databases, which are information structures to which important performance measures are written automatically.
- **Flexible analyses** are based on one or more of the SAP database structures and can include data selected using criteria you have defined.

The data for a standard analysis can be consolidated at levels of your choosing. For example, your report can collate information from the following levels:

- Plant
- Work scheduler group
- MRP controller group
- Work center hierarchy
- Material

With the report onscreen, you can select any value and press a special function key to drill down and see the data used to compile the value of your choice. Switching between tabular and graphical displays of your data is always an option.

You can call input and output diagrams for any work centers of interest. These diagrams show the incoming and outgoing production orders cumulatively along the time axis. You can display the scheduled activity values for these orders and the capacity available at the work center for them. Operating hours at the work center can also be displayed on a time axis.

If you want a particular analysis, you can select onscreen the data objects and performance measures you need. The system then devises and presents an evaluation report using these measures on these data objects.

Inventory controlling is an integral part of production controlling. It concentrates on the receipt and issue of goods from various points of view, including these:

- Inventory turnover
- Range of coverage
- Dead stock
- Stock value
- Number of goods receipts and issues

The MM-Materials Management system specializes in the management of inventory.

Product Costing in the PP-PC Component

The SAP R/3 system guarantees a detailed costing procedure for all common production types. Cost objects are defined and maintained by using manually entered data or via the CO-Controlling and PP-Production Planning and Control modules.

The link between logistics and managerial accounting is the discipline of cost object controlling, which seeks to determine the planned costs and target production costs, or costs of sales, of a product or an order. For each product or order, a value structure determined by internal accounting is applied to evaluate the corresponding quantity structure. This process is replicated for plan, target, and actual values.

The information units for cost object controlling are the work center and the order; or, if there is no order, the units are the work center and the bill of material and routing. Unit costing is also possible.

The results of costing in general are used to arrive at the following analyses:

- Price formation and pricing policy
- Valuation
- Control of costs of goods manufactured
- Profitability analysis

Product Costing

Repetitive manufacturing and standard manufacturing from production orders both depend on product costing. Planning and calculating the manufacturing costs are of central importance. In these examples of nonorder-related costing, you use the BoMs and routings to plan and control manufacturing costs. Some costing variants can be adapted to your situation:

- Standard costing at the beginning of the fiscal year for each cost object
- Monthly modified standard cost estimates
- Current costing
- Inventory costing

Costing results are divided up into a selection of 40 standard cost components recognized by SAP R/3. The same classification is used for both standard cost estimates and the cost elements used to control manufacturing costs. Each cost estimate can be stored in itemized form, and you can identify control objects for each estimate.

Bills of material and routings can be fully exploded into their constituents over all stages of production. So if you want to define a particular cost split, the results are automatically rolled up over all levels. Each level is displayed using the same selection from the 40 cost components.

Every costing variant used in product costing can be associated with a corresponding valuation variant or strategy, which you can define as a rank-ordered sequence of prices, as in this example:

- Planned price
- Moving average price
- Price relevant to a specific tax or trade law
- Price determined from standard cost rates

Thus, you can establish costing strategies for the following purposes:

- Inventory stock valuation
- Inventory accounting
- Order accounting
- Profitability analysis

Planning Special Types of Production

The SAP R/3 system provides functions developed specifically to serve the following types of manufacturing:

- Make-to-order manufacturing is particularly well served by the PP-Production Planning and Control system and the SAP R/3 PS-Project System.
- Make-to-stock repetitive and continuous-flow manufacturing types are supported by the PP-Production Planning and Control system, which offers production controllers a versatile and flexible system of assessing the master production schedule from different points of view—for example, by individual order, by all activities concerning a specified material or set of materials, and so on.
- Process manufacturing makes good use of the resource management, recipe management, and warehouse management functions. The specialized SAP R/3 module is PP-PI Production Planning for Process Industries.

There are two variants of repetitive manufacturing:

- One variant uses run schedule headers to group independent planned orders or production orders to form a run. This run is managed as a single production order.
- The other variant assigns the costs to specific cost collectors. For example, a run may be assigned to a single cost collector. Alternatively, particular materials can be assigned to individual cost collectors.

These variants of repetitive manufacturing have been extensively developed for the automotive industry.

▶ **See** "Introducing SAP R/3 Automotive Industry," **p. 628**

CHAPTER 18

Understanding the Production Planning for Process Industries Module

In this chapter

Recognizing the Process Industry as a Specialist Area

The following features mark a company as a candidate for the application of the PP-PI Production Planning for Process Industries module:

- Discontinuous forms of manufacturing take place in batches grouped together as production campaigns characterized by an unchanging basic recipe throughout the campaign.

- The plant itself can be used in various ways to produce a range of related products.

- Unnecessary clean-out operations and changeovers are to be avoided.

- Process control is active because the quality of the ingredients and the environmental conditions may vary.

- The control of product quality depends on close coordination with a dedicated laboratory.

- The production plant is only partially automated, so some of the process control instructions have to be in natural language and some in a machine-readable language.

- The recipe and production order must be archived for each batch, along with the actual data on the process.

- All messages, whether in machine or natural language, must be archived for subsequent analysis.

The following industries have effectively applied the methods programmed in the PP-PI module:

- Chemical
- Pharmaceutical
- Food
- Beverages
- Parts of the electronics industry where process manufacturing is prevalent

Reviewing the PP-PI Functions

The following groups of functions are provided in Production Planning for Process Industries:

- Material master data
- Resources master data
- Master recipes
- Process order planning
- Campaign and process capacity planning
- Process management
- Process data documentation and evaluation
- Integration with a *Laboratory Information Management System* (LIMS)

- Integration with SAP R/3 QM-Quality Management
- Integration with higher-level systems, SAP R/2, non-SAP, SAP R/3 MM, and SAP R/3 MRP

Establishing Material Master Data

The concept of resources includes the SAP concept of materials. The MM-Materials Management system has a well-established system of standard business programs to manage the following in a uniform manner as examples of materials that can be identified from the material master records:

- Raw materials
- Semifinished products
- Finished products
- Assemblies and component subassemblies
- Batches of products or resources
- Services

Specifying Resources Master Data

In addition to the type of resource already identified by the MM-Materials Management system, a class of user-defined resources has been established in the PP-PI Production Planning for Process Industries module. The following are examples of the types of resources recognized by PP-PI:

- Production plant and equipment
- Production staff
- Waste disposal facilities
- Recycling facilities
- Employees working in waste disposal and recycling facilities
- Energy sources
- Transport
- Storage facilities

The concept of a resource is used as an organizational unit on which to focus not only the control of the production processes, but also the calculations associated with requirement and output planning, capacity planning, and the analysis and evaluation of the use of these resources.

Defining Resource Hierarchies and Categories

Users can form resource hierarchies to allow capacity aggregation and the simulation of resource activities, using several different resource structures in parallel, if required.

Resources can be assigned to categories formally defined by users or selected from the suggestions offered by the PP-PI component. You have a variety of possibilities with the resource category concept:

- **Line** is a route through the production plant passing through one or more processing units that can be used in more than one way to produce complete batches of product, recycled materials remaining, or disposed wastes. NAMUR and ISA/SP88 are references that include definitions of the concept of line. A line may be regarded as the root of a resource hierarchy that includes one or more processing units. A plant may consist of one or more lines or resource hierarchies.

- A **processing unit** is the smallest logistic unit at which a batch can be manufactured. It may be a vessel in which several process operations can be performed.

- **Labor** can consist of the resource of a single person, or it can be specified as a group of people with the same qualifications.

- **Transport** is a resource that can carry material between warehouse and plant lines. Pipes and transporting tanks can be used for this purpose in addition to conventional vehicles.

- **In-process storage** refers to the facilities for holding material between production steps.

If you assign a resource to a resource category, you can display the resource in screens and fields common to all resources of that category. A default resource is a user-defined master resource record created during customizing to set up values that can be accessed and edited when creating a new instance of that resource in that plant.

Separating Primary and Secondary Resources

The *primary resource,* from the viewpoint of planning and control, is the space and equipment in the plant that must be regarded as occupied or committed exclusively to the operation while it is taking place. All the phases within this operation are scheduled to last for the entire time period, because nothing else can happen in this primary resource until all phases of the operation are finished.

If some resources are needed for only some phases of an operation and are the kind of resources that could be used elsewhere if they were free, these flexible resources are called *secondary resources.* You can specify when they start and finish in relation to the start or the finish time of the primary resource operation or the phase in which they are required. For example, a line operator may be required for only one or two critical phases of an operation.

You might have several resources that can be called on to do the same thing during an operation. You don't have to choose which one to use until you are ready to release the process order for that batch. These equivalent resources can be assigned to a resource class, which is identified in the master recipe for that operation. Before you make the actual selection, the system checks that the characteristics of the resource make it suitable for the intended purpose.

Resources have to be aggregated up through their hierarchies to carry out rough-cut capacity planning and medium-term planning. You might want to add resources to a hierarchy. The SAP

R/3 graphic editor enables you to maintain any resource hierarchy by editing the symbols. The resource records are updated automatically after you finish making adjustments.

Using Resource Networks

Processing units and the other resources that serve them are inevitably constrained by the demands of the production processes and the interrelationships between resources. A material cannot flow from one unit to another unless a route or pipeline connects the two, and that channel has to be free to accept the traffic. The picture is best displayed as a network that can change automatically to report the situation and can be changed by the controller to make an improvement. SAP R/3 provides a graphical convention to express the predecessor-successor relationships as blocks connected by lines. The blocks contain data fields. You can readily navigate throughout the network.

Links can be shown as lines on a network or as a data object in a field. You can link resources with any of these objects:

- Cost center
- A named person
- A position defined in the HR-PA Human Resources Personnel Administration system
- A specific qualification or suitability assessment (the SAP R/3 Classification system helps you identify this)
- A profile that specifies a set of qualifications or other personnel requirements, such as experience

Every resource has to be allocated to a cost center. This association is used when the CO-PC Product Costing or CO-OPA Order and Project Accounting module is computing costs. The link to a person tells you who is working at a resource.

Defining Resources and Capacity Categories

Capacity is the availability and capability of a resource to perform a task within a particular period of time. The capacity may remain idle if the people and equipment have no work to do. Resources can be assigned to resource categories, and capacities can be assigned to corresponding capacity categories. If a resource is available, it automatically is assigned the proper capacity categories.

Process orders are scheduled to capacities. Shop floor control and capacity planning are likewise focused on capacities.

Although a capacity is typically measured and maintained in time units (usually hours), conversion factors can be applied to allow the system to manipulate a capacity in other units—of volume or energy, for example. A pooled capacity can be provided by a clean-out team, for example, that can be called to work on several different plant lines.

An *exclusive capacity* commitment indicates that the resource can't make available any spare capacity—for example, when it is processing a part load. A *nonexclusive capacity* can be committed to several orders or to several operations that take place in the one resource.

If you need to go into finer detail for resource planning, you can subdivide capacities and maintain availability data on each part separately. Similarly, you can divide a resource consisting of a work team into individual persons who have different qualifications that you want to schedule and cost in a particular manner.

Applying Resource Data Functions

Default values can be associated with a resource to simplify the maintenance of operations in recipes. For example, standard texts can be assigned to a resource so that they can be referenced when compiling the operation texts in a recipe that uses this resource. The wage group of employees at the resource may be another useful default that depends on the resource master data. Standard values for the time taken and the energy requirements can be referenced in a similar way, with the choice of having them used automatically or only in the form of proposals to be confirmed by an operator or planner.

Formulas assigned to a resource can help you calculate execution times and costs. Every capacity defined for a specific resource can be given a formula to be used when the system is computing the capacity requirements of a particular process order assigned to it.

Where a resource is used in a recipe, standard values for the activity types can be entered. For each activity type assigned to this resource, you also can specify how these standard values are to be costed. In-house activities use the cost rates defined in the cost center to which each resource is assigned.

Analyzing Capacity Loadings

Each operation master carries data on the standard values of each capacity associated with that operation and the quantities needed. This information comes via the formulas stored for the resources.

During capacity load analysis, the system works out how much of each capacity is required to carry out the operations entailed in completing the process order. This is compared to the quantities available of all the necessary capacities.

If you call up the interactive graphic planning table, you can dispatch operations to resources and carry out capacity leveling. You can also send the load analysis through the interface to Microsoft Excel or a word processing system.

At any stage of planning, you can ask that the capacity availability be checked for an order or for an entire order structure. If the system sees a bottleneck ahead, it proposes a date to the planner for a revised schedule for this order to avoid the bottleneck.

Here are some of the questions the system can answer immediately:

- What are my available resources?
- Which cost centers are assigned to these resources?
- What are the capacities at these resources?

■ Which resources are currently using this specific capacity?

■ What is the hierarchical structure of my resources?

■ Which materials are being used at this specific resource?

■ Which recipes are using this particular resource?

Consulting Master Recipes

A *master recipe* documents all the specifications of a process and describes in detail how a particular plant is to be used to produce one or more materials in a production run.

The SAP R/3 module PP-PI Production Planning for Process Industries conforms with the norms and guidelines published by the following institutions:

■ Instrument Society of America, ISA Norm SP88

■ NAMUR, a multinational norms working committee for measuring and control techniques in the chemical industry

■ European Batch Forum, which coordinates ISA and European multinational committees such as NAMUR

■ Food and Drug Administration Good Manufacturing Practice guidelines for documenting process specifications

Changes are documented separately by the PP-PI system for each recipe and for each data object in it, both material and process. Change numbers can be used to control the time period of validity for a change.

The master recipe is used in PP-MRP Material Requirements Planning and in campaign planning under the PP-PI system. Links are maintained with the PP-Production Planning and Control module and the functionality offered by it.

Reviewing Master Recipe Functions

The steps of the production, the resources and materials to be used, the process instructions, and the data necessary for control—these are the constituents of a master recipe. It is much like a routing, an inspection plan, or a maintenance task list; all can be usefully represented by a network and handled by the SAP R/3 Network Library.

The recipe has to show the time sequence of the operations and phases. An *operation* is an independent part of a recipe that is carried out at a primary processing unit, perhaps in phases, and perhaps with secondary resources allocated to it for some or all of the time it spends at the resource.

A *process instruction* is a structure stored in the master recipe that transfers data or instructions from process planning to process control—in particular, to the phases of a recipe. After a process order containing a recipe is released for production, the operations and their phases are combined to form control recipes.

Assigning Control Recipe Destinations

A *control recipe destination* is defined in the master recipe. It specifies which operations and phases are to be made into control recipes for that destination. The destination for a control recipe can be a line operator, or it can be a process control system, in which case you can specify the technical address and whether the data transfer is to be triggered by the SAP R/3 system or by the process controller.

Interpreting the Master Recipe Material List

The *bill of material* (BoM) specifies the materials that make up a finished product. The master recipe material list used in the PP-PI Production Planning for Process Industries module specifies all the materials associated with a process—inputs as well as the products. For example, a catalyst or part of the output product can be recycled through the process. There may be more than one output product.

The material list shows the following:

■ Planned values for each input material
■ Mixing ratios
■ Yields of each product
■ Substances remaining, which may be considered byproducts or waste

You have to establish a definition of all of these materials, the finished products, the input materials, and the materials remaining in the material master records of the MM-Materials Management system.

Defining Intramaterials

Some processes create substances that are sampled, measured, and controlled but are then consumed in the process and do not appear as output materials. These are *intramaterials,* and they don't have to be defined in the material master records of the MM-Materials Management system. The intramaterial may be simply a charge load that is made up in some preliminary operation before being passed to the main process. However, it may be a material that is substantially different in physical or chemical properties from the input material because it has passed through one or more operations.

Intramaterials have to be defined in process orders because they need to be part of the material requirements calculations and they usually have to be inspected.

Because an intramaterial may have to be handled during inspections and the plant carrying it may be subject to failure, the intramaterial may have to be defined in the substance master records of one or more of the components that are under continuous development in the business areas of safety, health, and environmental protection. For example, an R/3 solution called *Safety, Health, and Environment* (SH&E) is being tested with the following functions as an Occupational Health component:

- Planning medical examinations
- Performance and documentation of examinations
- Follow-up actions, evaluations, and statistics

The Environmental Management component already includes product safety and dangerous goods functions.

Understanding Nonmanufacturing Master Recipes

The manufacturing master recipes control the production of a batch. Other recipe types are supported by the PP-PI Production Planning for Process Industries system:

- Clean-out recipes are inserted between two operations, if required.
- Changeover recipes specify what has to be done and the resources and substances needed to change from one production campaign to another.
- Equipment-testing recipes specify the process instructions that have to be followed to carry out and document the periodic functional testing of a plant line.

Planning in Process Orders

A *process order* is an SAP R/3 transaction that describes the actual production of one or several lots or batches, giving dates and quantities. Before a process order can be released for production, it has to be built up from the master recipe by adding dates, floats, specific resources, and so on.

Planning for these process orders takes up data from PP-MRP Material Requirements Planning or from campaign planning runs and generates process orders for batches within a plan that coordinates all resources. Because the process order contains all the planned and actual data related to production, it's the prime control instrument.

The master recipe data provides the information necessary to generate control recipes for all required operations and phases. If you do not select a master recipe, the system creates a process order with one token operation, on which you can later elaborate.

The system will not allow you to release an order unless the material components are available. It then reserves the materials. The MRP run will have already carried out availability checks based on planned data, but this second check informs the controllers if any unplanned circumstance has upset the plans.

With the basic order dates from the MRP run and rough-cut capacity plans (if available), the scheduling function can determine the start and finish dates for the order and its operations.

Order release initiates the following actions:

1. Material reservations made for available and reserved stock are updated in the corresponding material master record in MM-Materials Management.
2. The availability of the material is checked automatically.

3. Individual resources can be selected to replace the previous specification. The customer may have requested the alteration, or the process controller may have placed restrictions on the allocation of resources.

4. The controller can allocate an inspection lot record to receive the inspection results.

5. Shop floor papers can be printed.

6. Permission is granted for the controller to carry out movements to and from the warehouse for this order.

7. Permission is granted for the controller to carry out confirmations for this order.

Several types of evaluations and analyses are available to the planners and controllers, such as these displays:

■ All process orders for a material—for example, for a particular MRP controller or shop floor controller

■ A list of missing materials

■ A list of pegged elements

■ Orders in backlog

Planners and controllers can also display output from shop floor information systems and comments from line operators. Here are some examples of potentially important evaluations:

■ Resources

■ Materials

■ Operations

■ Orders

■ Material consumption

■ Product costs

Controlling with Cost Objects

Cost objects are used to allocate costs according to how they were incurred—as an order, a material, a network of cost centers, and so on.

Costing of process orders proceeds from planned material consumption and the charge rates established for in-house production activities on the basis of actual production costs. You can use these functions on process orders:

■ Calculate planned costs

■ Calculate actual costs

■ Transfer actual costs to other objects in the SAP R/3 system, such as materials or customer orders

■ Analyze planned and actual costs

You can use the CO-Controlling system to collate cost element data and focus on your total costs. Chapter 13, "Understanding the Controlling Module," discusses this system in more detail.

It is also possible to determine the costs of process orders yet to be settled, and to transfer the value of work in progress to the FI-Financial Accounting system. Schedule dates are important because the planned costs have to be distributed over the scheduled periods, according to the dates when the operation or phase is actually carried out. Chapter 12, "Understanding the Financial Accounting Module," discusses the FI system in more detail.

You can display the following cost element analyses:

- Primary cost elements corresponding to FI-GL General Ledger accounts, such as raw materials and semifinished goods
- Secondary cost elements derived from the CO-Controlling system, such as internal activity allocation and overhead costs
- Cost itemization using cost element groups and origin groups, or according to costing items previously calculated for individual materials and activities
- A cost component split into individual cost elements defined during customizing and used in material valuation and profitability analysis

Planning Production Campaigns and Process Capacities

A *campaign* is an extended run of production that may involve a train or line of processes intended to run continuously or by producing a series of batches to what is essentially the same master recipe.

Campaign planning is rough-cut or long-term planning; process planning is detailed or short-term planning. New functionality for campaign planning is under development.

Production plant planning tends to be initiated by publishing planned requirements in the form of a production plan or campaign. Waste or recycling plants usually receive input from many other production plants in the form of remaining materials that have to be processed. These ingredients and their expected scheduling initiate planning for waste and recycling operations.

Capacity Leveling

The object of capacity leveling across company-wide process chains is to schedule required resources to make the best use of limited capacities available. By "best use," you probably mean some blend of contradictory goals, such as short lead times, low inventory, adherence to delivery dates, optimum order mix, and so on. Capacity leveling is an art that takes different forms depending on where you work, but SAP R/3 provides some very powerful tools to assist you.

During customizing, you can define an overall profile for capacity leveling and several subprofiles for displays and list formation. For example, you can choose to have a planning table display something like the following over a range of time periods:

- Capacity requirements per capacity category
- Capacity requirements listed by planned and process orders
- Capacity requirements per process order and/or operation

You have the freedom to set up your displays over a wide range and to select and filter the data to suit your needs. In particular, you might find it helpful to display a planning window that you can move forward and backward across the planning schedule, and that shows a few time periods on either side of the central time period. You can customize the colors and add extra symbols to make the display more informative.

Objects of direct planning relevance, such as capacities and dates, can be changed onscreen and the consequences simulated before confirming the alterations. You can dispatch planned and process orders from the planning table, and you can deallocate operations or reschedule them. You can manipulate phases and secondary resources in similar ways.

Applying Planning Strategies

There is no one optimum strategy for planning complex work processes to best use resources and yet have short lead times, for example. But several techniques and guidelines have been developed in the process industries and should be considered by anyone in the position of work scheduler or process planner.

You have to dispatch jobs to resources at the right moment, so you need to know how long they are going to take and what resources to send them to. The system offers parameters and indicators to build your planning strategy:

- **Planning Direction.** The system schedules operations forward from the next start date or backward from the required completion date.
- **Dispatch Soonest.** You can mark an operation with this indicator to ensure that it is scheduled as early as possible in the planning period.
- **Insert.** One or more operations can be inserted on a particular date. The system shifts other resource commitments to make room for the insert and reschedules them around the insert using the planning direction you specify.
- **Close Gaps.** Marking an operation with this indicator tells the system that it can bring forward other actions if you decide to deallocate the marked operation.
- **Terminate Planning if Error.** This indicator on an order signals that all planning activity is to cease if an error condition is reported by another function—if material is not available, for example.
- **ATP Period Logic.** This indicator takes its name from the available-to-promise sales concept, which reminds the sales planner that material is available to sell only if it has not already been promised elsewhere. In the process industry, for example, if the plan is for each period to process the same amount, and if the planned production for one period

is exceeded by 100 percent (perhaps because it makes no sense to interrupt the process), the next period should contribute no production at all. From the planner's viewpoint, this brings the actual production back to the planned production. In this example, however, the result of overproduction may leave the stock situation in critical condition, and additional rush orders might have to be turned away.

- **Dispatching Sort Key.** You can define a sort key to arrange process orders selected for dispatch in a particular sequence. Alternatively, you can arrange for a tailor-made program written in the SAP ABAP/4 programming language to be called to carry out a sorting to your requirements. Each SAP application is supplied with a range of *user exits*, which can be set up during customizing to pass data to and from other software programs. If these programs have been installed and configured, their user exits appear as options in the relevant menu screens of the user interface.

- **Planning Log.** As a planning run is taking place, the system generates log messages for the operations according to the activated functions. The messages may signal warnings or errors, or just extract information. You can have these messages analyzed to see whether the planning strategy can be improved.

Operations can be dispatched in ways that influence the data assigned to them and how they are executed. For example, if you dispatch an operation that is only part of an order to a vacant float that is not large enough to accommodate the rest of the order, there may be a long delay before suitable capacity becomes available to complete the order.

The following functions can be deactivated if necessary:

- Sorting of operations to be dispatched
- Checking dates—for example, of the order dispatch against the basic order date recorded on the planned order, or against previous or following dates of items from the same order
- Checking material availability on the planned date
- Immediate midpoint scheduling of the order

Capacity requirements can be split across resources, including individual resources, such as people.

Selecting Resources from the Resource Network

The master recipe is the place where you define how resources are to be selected. The SAP R/3 Classification system uses these selection criteria when preparing a list of possible resources that can be committed for a particular order, either by manual selection or automatically. If several operations are dispatched automatically, the characteristics of the operations defined in the master recipes are compared with those available in order to make the appropriate choices.

If a planning strategy is in force, it may constrain the automatic dispatching tactics. The system always checks that the network of resources includes a link from the preceding resource before dispatching the next operation.

Managing Processes

The aim of process management is to coordinate process control and quality assurance for each process order. The process order includes the process instructions in the form of control recipes, which are sent to the people who will control the process or the SAP LIMS-Laboratory Information Management System.

Process management, in turn, gets back process messages containing the actual data generated from the execution of the operations, the quantities and qualities, which it passes on to various destinations. The details are established during customizing.

Assigning Process Instructions

The *process order* defines the phases of an order to which the process instructions are assigned. These instructions are expressed as characteristics such as material number or quantity. For each characteristic, a value is assigned, such as the code number of the material or the number of quantity units.

These instructions are user-defined to suit the specific installations on the plant line. You can have instructions in natural language just as the line operators have machine instructions for automatic process control equipment. This list indicates the range of process instruction variables you can specify:

- **Process parameter.** A machine instruction or text.
- **Process data request.** Addressed to process control to send actual process data to PP-PI.
- **Process message subscription.** A list of the unplanned event types to be reported, such as alarms and the exceeding of limits.
- **Process data calculation formula.** Specifies the calculation that must be recorded on the Process Instruction sheet and sends its value to specified destinations using a process message.
- **Inspection results request.** Specifies that one or more operations or phases are to be subject to inspections and have the results recorded.
- **Dynamic function call.** Enables the line operator to call a user-defined function module from within the PI sheet procedure. For example, this function module can conduct dialogs with the line operator or automatically retrieve data from internal or external applications. The dynamic function call is the line operator's connection with the rest of the SAP R/3 system and its interfaces to SAP and non-SAP applications.

Assigning Control Recipe Destinations

The control systems or line operators who need to know the process instructions are defined during customizing as the *control recipe destinations*. They are assigned to a process order at the level of the phase of an operation so that the controller of that phase receives the process instruction, regardless of who or what is getting instructions about the other phases. This assignment can therefore take account of the resource network and its links, as well as detailed interactions between controllers and processing resources as the operations pass through their respective phases.

Using the PI Sheet

The *Process Instruction* (PI) sheet procedure can be conducted by a handwritten sheet, a computer-printed document, or a screen available to the line operator. In the electronic format, there is the added advantage that the operator can enter information and initiate calls to function modules to send or receive information. The following functions are supported by the online PI sheet procedure:

- Display of control instructions in natural language
- Operator input fields that are immediately validated and sent to the predefined destinations in the form of process messages
- Quantity calculations using entered data and predefined formulas from the control recipe, which are sent to predefined destinations as process messages
- Direct connection to the SAP R/3 QM-Quality Management module for the purpose of entering the results of in-process control or inspection tasks
- Direct calls of user-defined functions to conduct dialogs or call data from internal or external applications

Defining Process Messages

Message categories for transferring data to SAP components are predefined. These types of SAP R/3 objects are predefined SAP message destinations:

- SAP R/3 function modules
- External functions
- Users of the SAPoffice mail system
- ABAP/4 tables used by company-specific programs written in the SAP ABAP/4 programming language

You can define company-specific message categories during customizing. You can use these categories, for example, to call non-SAP external functions or to access user-defined ABAP/4 tables in which the contents of a message can be stored for subsequent evaluation.

These examples of process messages to SAP R/3 modules illustrate their use:

- The process control system sends a process message on the amount of ingredients charged into the process vessel. This is a change of stock that is automatically posted to the Inventory Control module of MM-Materials Management.
- The status of an operation is sent for display on the planning table.
- Product quality is reported and transferred to the batch record for archiving.

Monitoring Control Recipe and Process Messages

The *control recipe monitor* is a display screen showing the current status of each control recipe as it passes from generation to completion. The overview of control recipes can be supplemented by logs containing detailed information of the history of each control recipe, including all time-stamped changes and malfunctions.

Similarly, the *process message monitor* displays the status of process messages from the moment they are received by process management until they are sent to their destinations. A message is stored if the destination does not exist or is temporarily inaccessible. Incomplete or incorrect process messages can be edited at the monitor and dispatched to their proper destinations.

Managing Quality

The SAP R/3 QM-Quality Management system is linked to the PP-PI Production Planning for Process Industries system, whether or not an additional link exists to an SAP LIMS-Laboratory Information Management System.

One function of QM-Quality Management is to maintain the master data necessary to comply with the recommendations of the ISO9000 international standard on quality control, which includes the complete documentation of all activities and procedures. In particular, it is essential to document the information necessary to measure and assess the quality of any product at any stage in its production, from raw materials to finished product. The inspection operations require resources that can be preplanned and costed from the beginning of product development only if this kind of information is available.

When an inspection lot is generated from a process order, its first function is to document that an inspection is to be conducted. Several partial production lots can be allocated to an inspection lot. Available inspection results are stored under the inspection lot number in the QM-Quality Management database. Access to these results has to be via this inspection lot number.

There is an important distinction between in-process control or inspection, and post-process control or inspection. The attraction of in-process control is that the inspection results can be used as feedback to change the control recipe and thus control the current processing. If a laboratory facility is involved, the production order can include the provision of an inspection lot for the purpose of analysis, as well as the specification of the quality standards that must be met.

If batch inspection is the practice, the MM-Materials Management system manages the material in stocks of batch size, and the SAP R/3 Classification system contains a specification of the attributes of a batch of each material to be handled in this way. Each batch retains its individual identity and quality information.

The capacity of the laboratory to carry out these analyses of inspection lots can be made the subject of capacity planning and scheduling, an important consideration if the laboratory working hours do not extend to cover the production hours.

Communication to a laboratory can be carried out by the QM-IDI Inspection Data Interface.

Integrating with Associated Systems

There are various ways of linking the PP-PI Production Planning for Process Industries system with the many and varied MPR-Material Requirements Planning systems found in this industry. The linking is differentiated as vertical or horizontal. *Vertical linking* is where the PP-PI system is subordinate to a higher-level MRP system. *Horizontal linking* refers to a PP-PI system and an MRP system that have a common network linking their rough-cut or campaign planning systems and their detailed planning systems. Neither is subordinate to the other. Currently, no cross-system linking logic is available for this horizontal configuration.

SAP R/3 enables you to link the MRP level of any higher-level system with the detailed planning system of PP-PI Production Planning for Process Industries.

There are three types of integration:

- Linking one SAP R/3.3 installation to SAP R/3.3 system is possible in both the vertical and the horizontal forms, because each system has its own database. This arrangement is not supported for SAP R/3 Release 3.0, because of the limitations imposed on a system with more than one central database.

- An SAP R/2 mainframe system can be linked to a client/server system that uses SAP R/3 Release 3.0. The SAP R/2 system can be vertically integrated with several subordinate SAP R/3 systems. This arrangement is carried out via CPI-C/LU 6.2.

- Linking between an external host system and the SAP R/3 system is supported as a vertical integration by Release 3.0, using file-transfer tools. Releases of R/3 from 3.1 onward use other methods.

Vertical Linking in SAP R/3 Release 3.0

The requirements of a logic that will integrate the MRP level of any system with the detailed planning system of PP-PI include the following:

- Transfer material master data using file-transfer methodology as part of the migration project.

- Transfer material requirements by reading them into the list of external requirements of the PP-PI component. If the higher-level system is an SAP R/2 system, the requirements can be transferred from the production order with quantities and dates; otherwise, the requirements have to be first converted to a UNIX file.

- Transfer inventory records via the batch input interface for goods receipts.

- Allocate requirements to process orders using the copying techniques established during customizing.

- Confirm material consumption for the process order by reading this into a UNIX file after the order is processed, and return the file to the SAP R/2 or other higher-level system.

- Confirm processed material requirements by posting order confirmations back to the SAP R/2 or other higher-level system.

Logging and Evaluating Process Data

It is becoming increasingly important for manufacturers to maintain detailed records of process data in the form of planned values for recipes and actual values for executed process orders. There may be a legal requirement to hold proof of the correct execution of production runs and a commercial requirement to discern opportunities to improve the efficiency of the plant and its associated activities.

For example, the U.S. *Food and Drug Administration* (FDA) advises that the following information should be documented for each batch produced:

- Process order number and batch number
- Charging and yield information
- Process Instruction sheet
- Equipment and resources used
- Laboratory analysis values for quality inspections
- Errors and malfunctions during batch operations
- Location and identification of finished products
- Confirmation by line operator

In accordance with the FDA *Good Manufacturing Practice* (GMP) guidelines, the electronic batch record contains all the preceding information, which is written under a time stamp for each item and event from the moment the order is released until it is located in the warehouse.

The process order is the main focus of the electronic batch record, which is formatted as print lists. The following objects also contribute data in the same format:

- Process Instruction sheets with comments and notes listed at the end
- Inspection lot data records
- Process messages from the Process Message log
- User-defined lists generated by the user and archived

Introducing the EH&S-Environment, Health, & Safety Management Module

The EH&S-Environment, Health, & Safety Management module is completely integrated with the PP-PI Production Planning for Process Industries module. The EH&S module provides environmental, occupational health, and product stewardship management all through the logistics chain.

The R/3 Substance Management component is available in the standard R/3 system as of Release 3.0F. It differentiates pure substances, mixtures, and preparations; and it provides the basis for EH&S. Some components follow:

- Substance database with predefined attributes
- Product database with predefined attributes
- Substance database with user-defined attributes
- Product database with user-defined attributes
- Risk and Safety Phrases catalog with management of translated phrases
- Distribution of substance database over organization structures
- Material safety data sheet for reporting and evaluation
- Accident procedures for reporting and evaluation

The EH&S module is also completely integrated with these SAP applications:

- SD-Sales and Distribution
- MM-Materials Management
- WM-Workplace Management
- PM-Plant Maintenance

This allows companies to monitor and control EH&S factors through all business processes and for the full life cycle of substances and products. EH&S also monitors compliance with the directives and regulations currently in force in the locations of the entire supply chain.

The Substance Management component supports textual descriptions and substance characteristics as language phrases that are handled as standard texts that can be used to create reporting documents on substance-related issues.

A Hazardous Materials Management component is available as of R/3 Release 4.0.

Introducing the Advanced Planner and Optimizer

The SAP APO-Advanced Planner and Optimizer is an element of the SAP SCOPE strategy, which addresses the supply chain and methods of improving it.

The APO-Advanced Planner and Optimizer includes the following components for planning the supply chain:

- Supply Chain Cockpit
- Forecasting
- Advanced Planning and Scheduling
- Available-to-Promise Server

The SAP APO uses SAP LiveCache technology, which processes data objects that are resident in memory. This allows APO to carry out its functions in real time. It integrates with R/3 and non-R/3 systems simultaneously.

The focal operation in supply chain management is the monitoring of possible exception conditions. The SCC-Supply Chain Cockpit presents collated information from all parts of a supply chain to a graphical interface from which action can be taken as necessary.

The components of the SCC follow:

■ **Supply Chain Engineer.** Allows graphical maintenance of extended supply chain models, which may include details of plants, distribution centers, and constraints; as well as factory layouts with associated machinery, storage locations, and constraints.

■ **Supply Chain Alert Monitor.** Provides reviews, forecasts, plans, and schedules derived from status data collected live from the system, plus performance figures and any exceptions or problems detected.

The Supply Chain Cockpit can be configured to suit a wide range of industries and business structures. One task will be to logically aggregate the condition records across the entire supply chain so that the decisions presented to the controller are as simple as possible.

The SCC has an interface that enables users to consult and use it for control actions from anywhere over the supply chain via the Internet. ●

CHAPTER 19

Understanding the Plant Maintenance Module

In this chapter

Building a System to Manage Plant Maintenance

The increasing application of mechanization and the use of power-assisted tools in modern industry have emphasized the importance of plant maintenance. Automation and the attendant instrumentation and control technologies also have continued to extend. Variations in the quality of output and the unscheduled interruption of output flow continue to be of the utmost significance to the profitability of an enterprise.

Plant maintenance is clearly essential, and the cost of doing it badly can be high. In addition to the owners and shareholders in an enterprise, members of the public are rightly concerned that industrial plants should not be allowed to malfunction. There are too many instances of serious outcomes arising from lapses in preventive maintenance and inadequate performance in corrective maintenance.

The SAP approach of developing standard business software customized to suit a particular installation has been applied to the management of plant maintenance. In 1986, the SAP R/2 mainframe system began to provide plant maintenance support by using the RM-INST software, which was subsequently migrated to R/3 as a client/server module and developed into the PM-Plant Maintenance module.

The system is based on a rigorous specification of data objects and the processing with which they are associated. Flexible user interface systems make the PM-Plant Maintenance module easy to operate, and it is fully integrated with the other SAP R/3 modules that have been installed and configured.

The SAP R/3 PM-Plant Maintenance module includes standard business programs, grouped into the following components:

- PM-EQM Equipment and Technical Objects
- PM-PRM Preventive Maintenance
- PM-WOC Maintenance Order Management
- PM-PRO Maintenance Projects
- PM-SMA Service Management
- PMIS-Plant Maintenance Information System

Organizing the Data for Plant Maintenance

The operational units of interest to PM-Plant Maintenance are your company's production and storage facilities and those of any of your customers for whom you manage plant maintenance. In accordance with the data management philosophy pervading all SAP products, the operational systems of interest have to be defined in terms of a common organizational structure that, if called on, can take the smallest item and trace its owners up through the organizational chart to the very top, which in SAP R/3 terms is the *client*. The PM-Plant Maintenance module introduces several layers of organizational structure for managing plant maintenance, but they have to be placed in the common organizational hierarchy that will eventually link them to the client.

Applying the SAP Organizational Units

The SAP R/3 general organizational units relevant to PM-Plant Maintenance are taken from the SAP R/3 Enterprise Data Model:

- **Client.** The highest level in SAP R/3. The data of one client cannot be accessed by another client. There is often a training client and a testing client, in addition to the client code that represents your group or corporate identity and under which the SAP system runs normal business. Some data is managed at the client level, because everyone in the corporate group of companies will want to refer to exactly the same information and be certain that it is up-to-date and correct. Vendor addresses are an example of data managed at the client level.

- **Company code.** A legal unit under the client that produces its own financial documents, the balance sheet, and the profit-and-loss statement; and may well maintain them as continuously reconciled.

- **Plant.** An organizational unit that is clearly central to maintenance management. A plant can be a production site or a group of storage locations that share materials. Plant is the unit for which MRP-Material Requirements Planning prepares plans and maintains the inventory. It is the focus of MM-Materials Management. Each plant will have been assigned planning and control elements, such as material, inventory, operations, work centers, and so on. Under PM-Plant Maintenance, a plant is where operational systems are located and where they have to be maintained.

Using Plant Maintenance Organizational Units

As an extension of the SAP R/3 structure of organizational units, the PM-Plant Maintenance system uses some units primarily related to physical locations, and some created mainly for the purposes of planning.

The following location-related organizational units are recognized and have their own master records:

- **Maintenance Plant.** Where the operational systems of a company are installed, and where their maintenance is most likely to take place.

- **Application Area Part.** A part of a production plant that can be designated as an application area and assigned to a particular contact person responsible for coordination between the production and maintenance departments.

- **Piece of Equipment.** The data object that represents the resource used to carry out a maintenance task can be a piece of equipment, a production resource, a tool, a test instrument, and so on. It can be a resource in a production line or a suite of implemented software. A piece of equipment cannot be allocated to more than one plant at a time.

- **Functional Area.** Where a task is carried out; a functional unit in an operational system. A functional area cannot be allocated to more than one plant at a time.

The following planning-related organizational units are recognized and have their own master records:

■ **PM Planning Plant.** Several maintenance plants can be associated for planning purposes, and one of the group is given the status of the PM Planning Plant. If a plant undertakes its own planning, it is treated as the PM Planning Plant. Maintenance requirements may arise from the PM Planning Plant, which are directed there from other maintenance plants.

■ **PM Planner Group.** A large company may have a central work scheduling department that constitutes a PM Planner Group. At the workshop level, the planner group may consist of just one foreperson or perhaps a group of shop floor area supervisors.

■ **PM Work Center.** The capacity unit for maintenance work is the work center, usually allocated to the PM Planning Plant. The PM Work Center may be a mobile capacity that can be deployed to other plants or loaned to the PM Planning Plant.

Describing the Structure of Plant Systems

The part of an operational system that appears on the inventory—the *inventoried object*—is known for maintenance purposes as a piece of equipment. It lives, at least conceptually, in a functional location. It can be dismantled from this functional location and installed in another functional location. An area of a plant that is designated as a functional area for maintenance purposes may contain one or many functional locations, depending on the number of pieces of equipment located in it.

The PM-Plant Maintenance system allows an unlimited number of levels in a structure—as many as you need to properly represent the piece of equipment you are going to maintain. Variable systems structuring is supported. The system allows you to define the depth and type of structure you are going to use for numbering pieces of equipment. You indicate which numbering structure you are going to use by means of a *structure indicator.*

A piece of equipment may constitute an individual technical system, or a technical system may include one or more pieces of equipment. The piece of equipment may need to be subdivided into materials of type Assembly and of type Spare. The assemblies and spares that make up a piece of equipment can be specified in an equipment or PM bill of material.

The data structures used by the PM-Plant Maintenance module follow the data object conventions used throughout SAP systems. Any field in a master record can be assigned data, which is used by the application. The field may be assigned the name of a data object, in which case the system can access that named object and use the data it contains. Indeed, the named object may contain the names of yet other objects that can be accessed in the same way. The structure is hierarchical, which enables you to drill down the linked data objects to find any required data item. Functional locations, pieces of equipment, and assemblies can all be hierarchical structures themselves, and so on, without limits to depth.

Referring to Functional Locations

All processing required by PM-Plant Maintenance can be carried out in relation to functional locations. If additional information about operational systems is required, you can refer to the equipment management data held in these functional locations.

You can decide how to allocate operational systems to the functional locations used by PM-Plant Maintenance. The structure may correspond to the structure of the manufacturing process, to the operational function, or to the plant area in which the maintenance work will take place. Indeed, the business may have no physical space that could be recognized as the plant.

Here is an example of a maintenance numbering structure with four levels and no punctuation symbols:

Production area	1234
System	1234123
Subarea	123412312
Functional unit	1234123121234

This next example of a user-defined systems structure in PM-Plant Maintenance has six levels and uses alphanumeric coding with some punctuation:

System	an	B6
Area	an-n	B6-3
Subarea	an-n-aann	B6-3-SA26
Function	an-n-aanna	B6-3-SA26Z
Subfunction	an-n-aanna/a	B6-3-SA26Z/G
Item	an-n-aanna/a/nnn	B6-3-SA26Z/G/123

You can graphically display the structures with which your maintenance operations are working. By selecting an item on your display and using the special function buttons, you can call up additional information on the item you selected and make changes to it. Alternatively, you can move the display up and down the levels of your hierarchy.

Each functional location has associated master data, which identifies its place in the maintenance structure and locates it in the plant. The master data also points to the PM-Plant Maintenance accounting and planning data. The information can be supplemented by references to word processing documents and drawings, and the SAP R/3 Classification system. Multilingual texts and access to the equipment usage information complete the data catalog associated with a functional location.

Copying from Reference Functional Locations

If several individual systems belong to the same category and therefore will likely have data in common, you can set up a reference functional location, which contains all the data except the actual location information. When you create a new instance of this system, all the reference data is copied to your new master for you to edit (if necessary) and supplement with the information particular to the new system.

Changes to a reference functional location may be allowed to propagate to all the functional locations of the same category.

Defining Pieces of Equipment

Pieces of equipment are defined as the tangible objects in a company subject to the PM-Plant Maintenance system. They fall into categories, which can be defined during user customization. The following types of serialized objects are likely to be in the list of objects that require maintenance:

- Production equipment
- Production resources and tools
- Test and measurement equipment
- Transport equipment
- Customer equipment maintained under contract

The following guidelines suggest when it is worth creating an equipment master record in the PM-Plant Maintenance system:

- The object will require individual data management.
- The object will require maintenance, whether planned, regular, or as repairs.
- Maintenance has to be recorded—for example, for insurance, safety, annual checks.
- Technical data on the object will have to be collected and evaluated over a long time.
- Maintenance costs for the object are to be monitored.
- Records are to be kept of the usage time at functional locations.

A piece of equipment retains its individual identity through its master data records, no matter where it is being used. It has its usage time segments cumulated from purchase to disposal. By this means, the person responsible for planning is identified and the account assignment data is documented, whether the equipment is being used in production, is in storage, or is in the inventory of a customer.

The equipment master usage time segment also documents the status changes of a piece of equipment according to a status structure, which can be user-defined, as in the following examples:

- Planned
- Undergoing testing
- In productive use
- Broken down
- Scrapped

The main data attribute clusters of an equipment master are structured as the following:

- Identification, general data, location data
- SD-Sales and Distribution data

- PM-Plant Maintenance data
- Documents and drawings
- Multilingual texts
- Internal remarks and notes
- SAP R/3 multiple classification and supplementary technical characteristics
- Equipment usage records

Using the Install and Dismantle Functions

You can give equipment the installed status by accessing the appropriate master record and applying the install function to assign it to a functional location, having perhaps first dismantled the item it is to replace.

You can achieve the same result by first accessing the functional location master record and then dismantling and installing as required. The usage records are updated automatically by these functions, and a new time segment begins every time a change of functional location occurs.

If the equipment is main equipment at the head of an equipment hierarchy, the entire structure below the equipment selected is given the installed or dismantled status. The equipment master records are assigned a numbering system during customizing, which is followed when the details of your company's plant are defined for maintenance purposes. At any stage, you can see where an individual piece of equipment is located in relation to the hierarchy—to which higher-order equipment it belongs, and which pieces of equipment come below it and therefore are subject to the same maintenance planning procedures.

Defining Maintenance Assemblies and PM *Bills of Material* (BoMs)

An *assembly,* in the engineering context of the PM-Plant Maintenance system, is not an individual object like a piece of equipment; it represents a category useful for directing attention to parts or aspects of a piece of equipment. Assemblies in the PM system are managed as material master records. Only the engineering data needs to be maintained. Assemblies can be used across plants. However, assemblies also used in the MM-Materials Management system for procurement and as stock items for storage will have to be assigned to a plant, because they will have to have comprehensive data maintenance.

A *bill of material* (BoM) for plant maintenance displays the structural elements of a technical object, such as an operational system, as a list of the material items marked as maintenance assemblies. A PM BoM can be created for an individual piece of equipment or for a functional location. A PM BoM can also be valid for a list of technical objects.

If all technical objects assigned to a BoM are identical, they can share the BoM. If only some attributes are in common, the differences can be managed as variants on the common BoM. If you have many identical pieces of equipment, you might find it useful to define a category for them by assigning a category name to a material master and having it adopt the BoM that applies to all present and future examples of that category.

When a technical object such as a functional location or a piece of equipment is considered from the point of view of a higher-level structure of which it is a part, the system automatically takes account of all the details in the BoM. You can keep track of the usage of materials and assemblies, even when you are working at higher levels, by calling up a "where-used" list. If you highlight on the user display a material or an assembly, you are offered a choice of special function keys. If you select a material used in various places in the plant, the "where-used" function provides you with a list of these places and the pieces of equipment involved. If your display includes a technical maintenance procedure, for example, you can ask for a list of all the situations in which this procedure is used in your plant.

The validity of a BoM is specified by a starting date from which any changes are valid. An ending date can also be specified. You can use this information to identify which BoM was used on previous maintenance schedules, for example.

The BoM has a header in which the planner assigns the BoM to one or more plants, specifies the validity, and sets the status management key to indicate whether the BoM is released for maintenance purposes in its current form.

The object parts itemized in the BoM can be assemblies for engineering maintenance or spares, or documents or drawings. The parts are differentiated by item category:

- **Stock items** are automatically reserved when used in a PM-Plant Maintenance order.
- **Nonstock items** automatically create a purchase requisition and therefore an order-specific material procurement via SD-Sales and Distribution, Purchasing. A material master does not necessarily have to be present in MM-Materials Management.
- **Variable-sized items** can be entered in the size required, because the system automatically converts them to the stockable sizes and quantities to draft the purchase requisition.
- **Document items** include drawings and safety regulations.
- **Text items** are free-format text added for user-defined reasons.

Recognizing Engineering Change Management

The SAP R/3 system manages engineering changes as a central basic data function, which is used on the following data objects:

- Materials
- Documents
- Bills of material
- Task lists

Each change is dated and assigned a standard reason. Changes can be sorted by number, date, or reason. Any number of basic objects can be changed with one change number.

Defining Networks in Plant Maintenance

The functional locations and pieces of equipment in one operational system can be connected in various ways with other systems. The PM-Plant Maintenance system must take account of these connections when planning and executing maintenance.

The SAP R/3 standard ways of representing operational systems are the *work breakdown structure* (WBS) and the network. Both are described in Chapter 31, "Managing R/3 Business Workflow."

The essence of a network is the link between objects. In the context of the PM-Plant Maintenance system, the object is often a functional location or a piece of equipment. The link can be in terms of workflow, energy flow, control, and so on. The linked objects can be in different systems.

In the SAP R/3 system, an object link master record includes the following types of information:

- Descriptive information on the type of link
- Whether the link is directional or nondirectional
- The technical, not necessarily tangible, objects at each end of the link

Technical links can be classified and evaluated using specific criteria by the SAP R/3 Classification system. Through the PM-Plant Maintenance system, the network of links can be used to plan and notify the connected systems of maintenance activities and also to analyze the consequences of any malfunction that may occur.

Locating Objects with the Classification System

The R/3 Classification system is a central function available to all applications. It is particularly relevant to maintenance because of the large numbers of different objects that fall into the scope of a PM-Plant Maintenance system.

Here are some of the various object types:

- Pieces of equipment
- Functional locations
- Assemblies
- Spares
- Materials
- Task lists

For each object type, you may need to maintain data on many instances and many variations of class-specific data.

The SAP R/3 Classification system recognizes the following structural elements:

- Classes, each with a catchword assigned to it
- Multilevel class hierarchies

■ Classifiable objects

■ Characteristics that describe the properties of classifiable objects

■ Values that particularize a characteristic and can be expressed in user-defined or standard formats, with value ranges also user-defined or standard

Descriptions of the characteristics and the values that can be assigned to them are available in all SAP-supported languages.

When you create a new object using the SAP R/3 Classification system, you can copy data fields from the master records, including the extensive descriptive information often stored there.

You can also copy from external storage media any data that has been stored in standard formats, such as DIN 4001. This is an example of a data format used in several plant maintenance record systems. The classes and characteristics of the equipment recorded on a DIN 4001 database are generated automatically if the data is transferred to the PM-Plant Maintenance application module.

You can also classify a material directly from the *computer-aided design* (CAD) system or search there for materials.

To search using the Classification system, you first select an object class. Then you search within the class using characteristics and their values. If your search yields a dataset instead of a single item, you can call on an extensive range of standard evaluation functions and perform a systematic analysis of your dataset.

Notifying Unplanned Maintenance Requirements

A *maintenance notification* describes a technical state of exception in a reference object. It may be a malfunction or other exceptional circumstance that requires prompt action in addition to the regular activities of preventive maintenance.

If you know the reference object, you can define the functional location and the affected piece of equipment or the malfunctioning assembly. You can document this in the maintenance notification.

However, you might not know exactly what has gone wrong—only the production area or the approximate position within a technical system where the problem lies. In this situation, the hierarchy data structures of the PM module help. You select the name of the area in which you think the problem has arisen. The special function keys offer you a variety of options for refining your search until you identify the suspect unit. At any stage in your search, you can call for technical information, such as the relevant BoM, which might help you narrow your focus to identify an appropriate target for a maintenance procedure.

After work is technically complete, the maintenance notification can be used to document the completion confirmation. This technical explanation can result in further maintenance notifications.

Using the Structure of a Maintenance Notification

A flexible maintenance catalog system based on location-specific or equipment-specific data is used for allocating types and causes of damage and the effects on the objects and the tasks to be performed. Catalogs are structured in the following manner:

- **By type,** such as damage catalog, tasks catalog, and causes catalog
- **By code groups,** such as vehicles, pumps, and instruments
- **By code group task codes,** such as vehicle brakes tested

You can use the SAP R/3 Classification system to classify maintenance notifications and amplify them with specific data.

When you create a functional location or a piece of equipment master, you can assign the maintenance catalog that would be appropriate in the event of a malfunction or unusual event.

Adding Tasks to a Maintenance Notification

An extra task may be required in addition to carrying out maintenance. For example, it might be necessary to document an incident and collect evidence at the location. Tasks of this kind can be specified in the maintenance notification. Activities to carry out the repair can be allocated from the task catalog, which is based on experience. New tasks can be specified and documented through the SAP word processing system.

Maintenance notifications already in the PM-Plant Maintenance system can be selected for processing by using a search criterion. This may entail specifying time parameters; organizational parameters, such as cost centers; or functional parameters, such as downtime or damage description. After you refine your selection of maintenance notifications, you can assign one or more of them to an order, in which case the data in the notifications is copied to the order, where it can eventually be evaluated in the maintenance order history.

The PM notifications can be controlled by a flexible status management system to which you can add status processing steps such as the following:

- Create a maintenance notification.
- Confirm a technical explanation.
- Begin processing a maintenance order.
- Confirm completion of a maintenance order.
- Process completion of notification.

You can use this status management system to select maintenance notifications for further processing, which may enable them to graduate to the next status. For example, you can call for a piece of equipment to be dismantled far enough to determine whether it failed in the way suggested from previous maintenance histories of this type of assembly in each location where it is installed in your plant. This investigation may give you the information you need in order to decide whether to replace this item or have it repaired.

N O T E   Withdrawing a piece of equipment from production may have serious consequences for the
production schedule until the equipment can be replaced. On the other hand, the
interruption might give you the opportunity to schedule other items for maintenance at the same
time. ▪

Carrying Out Maintenance Orders

The execution of a maintenance task is initiated and controlled by a maintenance order, which
specifies the following details:

- Type of maintenance order
- Scope of the order
- Dates for starting and finishing the entire maintenance order and its stages, if any
- Resources to be used to carry out the order

Maintenance orders are of three types, which vary by the extent of available previous planning:

- **Regular PM-Plant Maintenance orders** released by maintenance schedules at due
  dates with their scope prescribed
- **Planned PM-Plant Maintenance orders** arising from maintenance notifications, from
  which they can be directly converted into maintenance orders to ensure that foreseen
  repair tasks are carried out
- **Unplanned PM-Plant Maintenance orders,** which tend to be rush orders created
  with a minimum of information in response to an unforeseen machine breakdown or
  malfunction, or as immediate action after an accident

One of the essentials of a maintenance order is a precise reference to one or more technical
objects. The period of validity of a maintenance order is differentiated between individual orders and standing orders, which are valid for a longer period but have to be confirmed on each
occasion they are scheduled.

On either basis, an order is created for each maintenance task so that the costs of maintenance
and the history of maintenance tasks can be documented for each technical object in the order.

A maintenance order can be processed internally through your own maintenance workshops,
or externally by service companies if, for example, the cost-effectiveness is superior, the specialized knowledge is unavailable in-house, or temporary bottlenecks would otherwise occur.

Interpreting Maintenance Order Elements

The structure of a PM order includes the following elements:

- Order header
- PM order object list

- Operations and suboperations within the scope of this order
- Material list for the order
- *Production resources and tools* (PRTs)

The order header has general information and precise data on the following essentials:

- Order type
- The person responsible
- Dates
- Priorities
- The PM order reference object list

A reference object can be specified as a whole system or as a subsystem. The PM-Plant Maintenance module amplifies the reference object by also listing the individual functional locations, pieces of equipment, and maintenance assemblies.

The scope of a maintenance order is expressed in terms of the operations and suboperations that make up the individual work steps needed to complete the maintenance task. The specification of each operation has to include the following information:

- Description of operation or suboperation
- Work center to perform the operation
- Amount of work required
- Duration of the work
- Whether the operation is to be processed internally or externally by a third party

The numbered order of the list of operations normally is the sequence in which the operations are to be performed. SAP is developing a facility to specify a network structure in which the maintenance task can benefit from the parallel working of some of its suboperations. Major maintenance operations can take advantage of the functionality of the SAP Workflow and the SAP R/3 Project System modules, which are designed to support networked activities.

Materials listed for a maintenance order can be allocated directly to each operation, or they can be assigned by including the relevant PM-Plant Maintenance bill of material. Either way, the material number, quantity, and prices have to be documented in each instance.

The material list can include stock and nonstock materials, which may or may not have master records already established. If they do not, you have to enter the details instead of copying them from the master records. The stock materials generate stock reservations automatically; the other materials are passed to MM-Materials Management, Purchasing, under the control of purchase requisitions, again generated automatically.

All the resources—such as tools, measuring equipment, and documents or drawings—needed for the maintenance operations are managed in the system as PRTs. They can be assigned to the operations in any quantity. The types of tangible objects that can be managed as PRTs include the following:

- Sets of instructions
- Hand tools
- Portable power tools
- Machine tools established in the plant for maintenance purposes
- Machine tools established in the plant with capacity available for maintenance purposes
- Measuring and calibration equipment
- Programs for numerically controlled machine tools
- Drawings
- Jigs and fixtures

Processing Maintenance Orders

Regular maintenance entails planning ahead. How far ahead to plan—the *call horizon*—depends on the anticipated equipment loads and equipment maintenance requirements. Regular maintenance orders are created by scheduling maintenance plans containing the maintenance strategy and the scheduling parameters. When the orders are released, they are complete and ready to be carried out.

If you are entering a maintenance order directly, or if the order has been converted from a maintenance notification, the details of the order may have to be elaborated as the result of subsequent planning or processing.

When the origin is a maintenance notification, an individual maintenance order is complete as far as the list of reference objects, the scope and purpose of the task, and the required execution dates. All that remains to be added is the execution data. You might have a bundle of maintenance notifications that are all to be covered by a single maintenance order. In such a case, you can refer to a main object, such as a technical system, a subsystem, a piece of equipment, a cost center, or a location. When you see the object list the SAP R/3 system will produce, you can link the individual maintenance notifications with the reference objects to which they should be directed.

A maintenance order is subject to status control, which can be user-defined, as it traverses the main documented steps in the order cycle, as this example shows:

Order creation→Order release→Order printing→Order confirmation→
Order completion

Each status defines the processing forms that are permitted and forbidden, and also the automatic documentation that will occur. For example, you cannot have an order printed until its status has reached the "Released" level. When printing has occurred, the status automatically shifts to "Printed" if this is what you decreed should happen when you customized your system.

In some circumstances, you might need to interrupt the maintenance order processing. In these instances, the system can document the exceptional status according to its cause. For example, a maintenance order might have to be held up because a wrong component has been delivered. You can also manually interrupt a maintenance task because there is a more urgent demand on the resources allocated to it, and you want to alter the priority. This intrusion is documented automatically, although you are invited to record an explanation by selecting a reason from a list offered by the PM system, or by entering free text.

Settling Maintenance Orders

The estimated costs for a maintenance order are calculated at the planning stage, and the actual costs are computed when the order completion can provide the information necessary in the form of the times of the capacity loads at the internal workshops or the loads on the external services.

All the costs are displayed by a cost element, selected as appropriate from the list of 40 standard cost elements recognized by the CO-Controlling module. The accounting period is assigned on the basis of the activity dates, and the amounts are debited to the appropriate target account.

Managing Maintenance Resources

The capacity available at a maintenance workshop is defined in terms of work centers. A *work center* is a data object that represents any of the following kinds of resources:

- A group of people—in a maintenance workshop, for example
- An individual person
- An individual machine or machine tool

The SAP R/3 functions devoted to work center costing have a list of standard formulas that can be assigned to a maintenance work center in order to determine the execution time, costs, and capacity requirements of any work that can be sent there. You can supplement and adapt these formulas to suit your own company maintenance methods.

The work center is the focus for maintenance planning. When an order is placed, the system automatically checks that the necessary capacities will be available at the times required and that the spares and reserve parts or operating supplies will be on hand when the order is released for execution. Production resources and tools, such as special devices and lifting gear, may be assigned permanently to reference objects, or they may be available for more general use.

A work center may have been assigned default values that can be copied to any maintenance order allocated to it. There will be a link to a cost center and to an activity type in the CO-Controlling module, so that internal activities can be costed and cleared on the basis of the maintenance activities allocated to the cost center.

Budgets for maintenance projects are monitored by the SAP R/3 Project System.

Defining Maintenance Work Center Capacities

The units for measuring capacity at a maintenance work center can be defined to suit the circumstance, and any amount can be allocated. The capacity available can be defined as a standard available capacity, which is governed by the following factors:

- Capacity rate per unit time of the available people and their machines
- Number of shifts
- Usage time per shift
- Degree of utilization authorized

The available capacity might not be evenly distributed over time; it may have to be defined as a profile or distribution function.

The capacity requirements entailed by the maintenance order are based on the operations, the suboperations, and the time required. The activity capacity requirements may have to be allocated to more than one work center to provide the range and quantities of the various capacities necessary. Not every work center is omnipotent; some are specialized, whereas some are too heavily committed elsewhere.

The maintenance planner will call up a capacity load situation display for each work center to see how the capacity requirements allocated to this resource in each planning period match up to the capacities available. If the work center can provide a range of maintenance capabilities, the planner will have the display show how the capacity requirements are loaded on the capacities available in each activity category.

If you are carrying out estimate planning, you might find it useful to build a work center hierarchy specifically for the estimate. You can have this evaluated and analyzed to make your estimate more precise.

Planning and Scheduling Regular Maintenance Tasks

Quality control depends on reliable processing to make sure that the planned adjustments are accurately sustained. An unreliable plant produces unreliable products. Unreliable production lines can become the target of legal and market reaction because the consumers of the product—and the neighbors of the plant—lose faith in the company.

A worn plant is unreliable; an unreliable plant can malfunction catastrophically. Regular maintenance should identify sources of unreliability and accidents waiting to happen. These are not new arguments, but they are becoming salient. Companies are seeking better maintenance management; prevention costs less than cure.

A *maintenance strategy* is a data object that represents the scheduling rules for regular maintenance tasks and describes the maintenance packages that specify the maintenance activities prescribed for particular technical systems or categories of systems. The details are established during customizing.

Maintenance scheduling rules fall into various groups, such as the following:

- Calendar scheduling
- Factory calendar scheduling
- Fixed key date scheduling on a monthly or yearly basis
- Activity-based scheduling that arranges maintenance according to the work done by the technical system or functional location to be maintained

A *maintenance package* is a data object that gathers the details required to schedule planned maintenance orders. It includes the following data:

- Package number
- Frequency of package
- Unit of time or activity
- Package hierarchy relationships
- Description of operations and suboperations
- Package start offset
- Float periods

Interpreting Maintenance Items

A *maintenance item* specifies the activities to be carried out on an object and their frequency. The objects can be specified as an object list of unlimited length specifying equipment numbers and functional location numbers, or the uppermost item of a structure of objects in the form of an object hierarchy. General maintenance task lists or equipment-specific task lists are the sources of the activities specified in the maintenance item in the form of short or long texts.

The maintenance item also determines the account assignment data for settling the maintenance task.

Consulting the Maintenance History

The maintenance history consists of the following components:

- Location history of the piece of equipment installed at functional locations
- Notification history and completion confirmation documentation
- Task history of completed maintenance orders, including the resources used

Parts of the maintenance history are generated automatically in the PM-Plant Maintenance module whenever any of the following types of processing occur:

- Maintaining master data
- Creating maintenance notifications
- Processing maintenance notifications

> ▓ Scheduling maintenance plans
>
> ▓ Processing maintenance orders

You can use the maintenance history to analyze by object, by function, or by task-specific criteria, in any combination. Here are some examples of the questions that can be answered by this method:

> ▓ Where has this particular pump been used over recent years?
>
> ▓ Which pieces of equipment have been installed at this particular functional location over the past few years? Is it possible to discern any differences in the suitability of the equipment supplied by different manufacturers at this functional location over this time?
>
> ▓ Which functional locations have suffered damage over the past few years? Which of them improved once they started using the new material?

Specifying the Usage History

Usage histories can be compiled for pieces of equipment and for functional locations. When you carry out customizing, you can define the changes of status or other events to be used to mark out usage periods. For example, the following changes initiate a new usage period marker in a usage history:

> ▓ Change in the location of the equipment, such as functional location, actual location, and area
>
> ▓ Change in the assignment account data for cost center or asset
>
> ▓ Change in planning structure data—for example, the responsible work center is changed
>
> ▓ Status changes—for example, among freely available, undergoing testing, in production, and canceled

You can also trace changes under the ECM-Engineering Change Management system.

Building the Notification History

When maintenance notifications are completed, they become historical notifications. These are linked with the maintenance tasks they initiated to form the notification history of the particular technical system or piece of equipment.

Building the Task History in the Maintenance Order

A maintenance order acquires the documentation of all materials issued and the internal or external services used in the course of its completion, as well as what was done and how much it cost. On completion, this information is transferred to the maintenance task history, where it is available for analysis. You can archive completed maintenance orders in addition to using the standard provision for storing completed orders only for a limited period.

Consulting the Plant Maintenance Information System

The PMIS-Plant Maintenance Information System is an SAP module and a component of the LIS-Logistics Information System. Therefore, PMIS has access to the LIL-Logistics Information Library and a statistical database.

PMIS can provide two types of analysis:

- **Standard analysis.** The system maintains statistical information structures that are updated automatically from the SAP R/3 application—in this case, the PM-Plant Maintenance application.
- **Flexible analysis.** You can call on any SAP data structures and perform analyses for the purpose at hand.

The PMIS allows you to perform analyses of actual data using the information structures. You can also enter planning data into these structures for the purposes of comparison and simulation.

A PM-Plant Maintenance statistical information structure in the PM Information System includes the following types of information dimensions:

- **Objects.** The entities to provide the focal points for the consolidation of actual data, such as functional location, piece of equipment, manufacturer, location, and maintenance plant.
- **Performance measures.** Statistical compilations of data that could be particularly significant for plant maintenance, such as the number of notifications, number of damage incidents, and length of downtime.
- **Time unit.** Day, week, month, and posting period.

Thus, the PMIS can report the value accumulated in a particular performance measure for a particular object over a specified period.

Reporting with Standard Information Structures

The PMIS-Plant Maintenance Information System offers five standard information structures, which contain the important performance measures for the effective analysis and control of a plant maintenance facility. These measures are grouped according to the following theme clusters:

- Location and planning
- Object class and manufacturer
- Damage analysis
- Object statistics
- Breakdown statistics

When you call for an analysis under the PMIS, the system applies formulas to calculate summary values as necessary—for example, Mean Time to Repair. More than 20 performance measures are available, based on up-to-date information collected automatically from the PM-Plant Maintenance system.

During customizing, you can create additional information structures to suit the requirements of your plant maintenance enterprise.

Standard analyses are available through the normal SAP R/3 system, which offers numerous standard business programs to perform various types of calculations and statistical summations over the following objects, using a scope you define with various selection options to focus on the data to be used:

- Object class
- Manufacturer
- Location
- Planner group
- Damage
- Object statistics
- Breakdown

When you have a data object onscreen, you can select a special function key to perform a drill-down function to inspect the analysis at various levels. You can also apply a predefined analysis path, which is referred to as the *standard drill-down sequence*.

For each level of analysis, the following types of functions are provided to analyze and display the data in graphical form:

- Cumulative curve
- Correlation
- ABC analysis
- Classification
- Dual classification
- Rankings

Providing Plant Maintenance to a Customer

Functions in the plant maintenance sector are undergoing continuous development. The increasing significance of manufacturer liability and the complexity of products are both factors that press for the development of more effective ways of managing and executing maintenance activities as a service to the customer.

The PM-Plant Maintenance system provides most of the functionality needed to support a business in providing maintenance as a customer service. SAP R/3 Release 3.0 will provide some enhancements.

Documenting a Customer's Equipment

The tangible objects to be maintained on behalf of a customer can be categorized by PM-Plant Maintenance in the same way as pieces of equipment. These maintenance objects might include the following categories:

- Equipment and instruments that are standardized to a large extent, such as medical instruments, forklift trucks, and photocopiers
- Special machines
- Buildings
- Computer systems, both hardware and software

The master record system of PM-Plant Maintenance is perfectly suited to the task of keeping track of such objects. The enhancements of Release 3.0 will include, in the equipment master records, data fields for the people in the customer company who will be the contacts for executing maintenance tasks, and for mailings and queries. These fields will be titled Customer, End Customer, and Operator.

Your company will probably have internal employees who are assigned to support particular customers. If maintenance service is to be provided, more than one person from your company may be assigned to support the customer. You can link one or more personnel records to a customer master equipment record for this purpose.

A piece of equipment can be assigned to a customer sales area to assist in managing the maintenance service. The equipment can also be assigned to a customer functional location.

Interpreting Customer Maintenance Service Contracts

A contract is represented by a data structure that differentiates maintenance contracts on the following bases:

- **Contract items** refer to pieces of equipment, functional locations, and their PM-Plant Maintenance assemblies. Several objects can be linked as an object list.
- **Contract types** may be leasing or rental, with or without maintenance services.
- **Validity** refers to the period of validity of the maintenance contract for each item separately and the validity of the contract as a whole.
- **Status** is the contract for each item that is subject to status maintenance, which can be set to locked, inactive, or straightforward, and any user-defined status indicator.
- **Deletion** can occur only through subsequent contract file reorganization in response to the setting of a deletion indicator for the contract or individual contract items.
- **Employees,** internal and customer, can be allocated to the contract header in the same way as pieces of equipment.
- **Commercial aspects** include price, conditions, and payment methods.
- **Termination conditions** are specified from a system-provided list by a key.
- **Settlement procedure** is specified at the contract level, although inactive items will not be invoiced.

- **Response time,** the contracted callout time, depends on the contracted service window, the time the notification was made, the type of damage, and the equipment assembly affected.

- **Maintenance,** as the periodic or activity-dependent service contract, can be represented by including planned maintenance items in the contract.

- **Services** are usually directed at an object or object category. Continuous services, such as a hot line, can be included in the service master records.

- **Control** is the control object to which all costs and revenue affecting the maintenance contract can be specified to facilitate the monitoring of the cost-effectiveness of the maintenance contract.

Responding to a Customer's Malfunction Notification

Speed is of the essence when a customer calls for service in response to a malfunction. The PM procedure can begin with the absolute minimum of manual data entry:

- Functional location or equipment number
- Damage
- Customer contact
- Repair date required

The system displays the customer number for control purposes, and your customer service representative can check over the telephone the type of contract the customer has. This can determine whether he is entitled to use a hot-line service.

The customer representative might need to use a help system to find relevant information. The PM-Plant Maintenance system then can provide the information normally available for in-house maintenance:

- Long texts on equipment category–specific damage symptoms
- Access to the equipment history

The system monitors response time, and a warning is issued if the order dates arising from the notification will exceed the response times permitted in the contract.

Differentiating Responses in Customer Service Orders

There can be a wide variation in the types of response to a customer's call for service under contract:

- There is no planning, the order is entered during or after the service task is performed, the resources used are entered on the customer order, and only brief documentation is entered for the maintenance history. The whole operation, including contract and warranty checking, can take place within SD-Sales and Distribution.

- The customer calls, a maintenance notification is generated, and the repair is made at his premises. The service technician records the times and materials, and billing proceeds after contract and warranty checks.

- Maintenance processing occurs with a quotation, which is referenced in a customer order if it is accepted.
- The maintenance task is extensive and warrants the use of the SAP R/3 PS-Project System.
- The maintenance task is part of a regular maintenance contract.
- The piece of equipment to be maintained is collected and returned after maintenance. A goods receipt has to be posted to the customer's special stock account and balanced by a corresponding goods issue when the repaired item is returned under a delivery note.
- The maintenance entails travel expenses accounted for in the HR-Human Resources module and as one resource used, copied to the PM order, and then to the SD-Sales and Distribution order.

If your company is providing a maintenance service to other companies in your group or to outside customers, you will want to be able to integrate any or all of the preceding requirements into a single system. When a call arrives at the customer service desk, there should be no hesitation in calling on the required information and processing the inquiry or request for maintenance. The PM-Plant Maintenance module can be configured to provide this facility through its seamless integration with the other R/3 modules.

Anticipating Developments in Plant Maintenance Software

The following component function groups have been identified by SAP as under development or in the process of pilot testing:

- Manually created maintenance order histories can be added to the PM system and collated with related order histories for evaluation. Various portable computers have been approved for interfacing with R/3 for this purpose.
- Materials and assemblies legally required to be individually monitored can be identified by their serial numbers and their maintenance conducted on this basis. Serialized parts can be traced by calling on "where-used" reporting if they are likely to be parts of larger assemblies or located in plant items contracted for maintenance.
- Technical systems can be associated with specific activity counters and measurement points from which usage data can be culled for the purposes of initiating routine maintenance activities and interpreting fault reports. Condition records can be used to set up logical combinations of elapsed time and usage criteria for automatically creating maintenance orders.
- Technical permits are issued to control access to pieces of equipment, and activity permits may be required to allow certain activities in sensitive locations. These permits can be identified in order processing and in the orders for managing external work teams.

■ Activity planning facilities are available for optimizing the deployment of internal and external maintenance teams.

■ Capacity and resource planning is available for capacity leveling and redistribution across available resources.

The management and efficient deployment of maintenance resources have attracted attention because of the inherent reliability of much electronic equipment and because of the relative ease with which a faulty component can be replaced by another while it is being repaired. Third-party maintenance companies are tending to acquire large portfolios of maintenance contracts with the intention of deploying their repair teams and subcontractors across a wide span of customers.

The possibility of contracting an online help desk and consequent remote maintenance has been supported by SAP developments in the form of networking facilities for managing plant maintenance that are compatible with the Internet as well as the high-bandwidth lines of the typical corporate intranet. ●

Supporting Applications

IV

Supporting Applications

Understanding the Sales and Distribution Module

In this chapter

Understanding the Module's Design

The design of the Sales and Distribution module puts the emphasis on using a sales strategy that is sensitive to the market. A priority of customizing should be to set up a data structure that can record, analyze, and control the activities that will satisfy your customers and yield adequate profit over the next accounting period and into the future.

The SD-Sales and Distribution system provides a set of master data records and a system of documented business transactions. The standard business programs of the module are organized around the following five functions:

- SD-MD Master Data
- SD-CAS Sales Support
- SD-SLS Sales
- SD-SHP Shipping
- SD-BIL Billing

You will know that these activities represent value-adding processes because your company will lose value in terms of reputation and in financial terms if any of them is allowed to perform badly.

Two other functions are available from the R/3 system and are used by the SD-Sales and Distribution module. They are important because they control the flow of information between the parts of a Sales and Distribution organization and the other SAP applications in the R/3 system. They also provide the links between the system itself and its users, wherever they might be:

- SAP EDI-Electronic Data Interchange
- SD-IS Sales and Distribution Information System

Electronic Data Interchange (EDI) refers to the electronic channels of communication that, in modern business practice, have replaced the messenger systems carrying printed documents. The term *document* is used for both an electronic record and a paper one. Similarly, *printing* may in fact refer to the transmission by electronic means of information that could be printed if required.

The SD-IS Sales Information System allows you to gain insight on all matters concerning prospecting, sales, and delivery. This system of displays and analytical processes is provided to flexibly access the master records and the transaction data that allows you to conduct statistical analyses and evaluations in support of decision-making and strategic planning.

Establishing Organizational Structures

The SAP R/3 general organizational units relevant to SD-Sales and Distribution are taken from the SAP R/3 *Enterprise Data Model* (EDM):

- **Client** is the highest level in SAP R/3. The data of one client cannot be accessed from another client. There is often a training client and a testing client, in addition to the client code that represents your group or corporate identity and under which the SAP system runs normal business. Some data is managed at the client level, because everyone in the corporate group of companies will want to refer to exactly the same information and be certain that it has been maintained as up-to-date and correct. Vendor addresses are an example of data managed at the client level.

- **Company code** signifies a legal unit under the client level that produces its own financial documents, balance sheet, and profit-and-loss statement, and may well maintain them as continuously reconciled.

- **Plant** can be a production facility or a group of storage locations where stock is kept. This term is also used in the context of *transportation plant* in the SD-Sales and Distribution system. The vehicle is treated as a temporary storage location. Planning and inventory management take place at the plant level and are the focus of materials management. A plant can supply its material stock to more than one sales organization.

- **Sales organization** has a legal connotation in that it represents the unit responsible for selling and, therefore, is responsible for product liability and rights of legal recourse. All business transactions in SD-Sales and Distribution have to be processed financially within a sales organization. A sales organization can draw its materials from more than one plant.

- **Distribution channel** defines how different materials reach the consumer—directly, or through a materials wholesaler, for example.

- **Sales division** is a subdivision of a distribution channel. The division might have been assigned only some of the total product range, and there might be customer-specific agreements for each division.

- **Sales area** defines a combination of not more than one division, distribution channel, and sales organization. Thus, if two divisions are using the same distribution channel, each division will be considered to belong to a different sales area. An individual customer can be assigned to more than one sales area if differing requirements and agreements must be considered. Prices, minimum order, and delivery quantities are the sort of factors that might have to be recognized by creating unique sales areas for them, always in the SAP R/3 structural context of a sales organization and perhaps a sales division and distribution channel as well.

- **Sales office** is a method of representing the internal organization. It's a division under the client level.

- **Sales group** is a further internal subdivision of the people in a particular sales office.

- **Salesperson** is the subject of a unique personnel master record.

- **Shipping point** is a location within a plant where deliveries are processed. Each delivery is assigned to and processed by only one shipping point.

- **Loading point** is a part of a shipping point that can offer a capacity to handle deliveries. Several similar loading points might exist, and there might be different equipment at some loading points that makes them more suitable for particular types of deliveries—forklifts for pallets, for example.

The flexibility of the SAP R/3 system to represent complex and company-specific shipping structures depends on the technique of combining the various types of organizational units.

Specifying Master Data in the SD-MD Component

In an SAP system, information that is needed in several places or at different times is entered only once. It resides in master records, where it can be kept up-to-date so that all who access it are given the most accurate and recent information available to the system.

Each master data record has a unique number, and you can arrange to confine certain ranges of these numbers to specific sales areas. The Sales Department will use this master information in its business transactions. Here are some of the uses the Sales Department will find for the master data record:

- General details about business partners
- Information specific to particular customers
- Materials, including services as well as objects and assemblies
- Texts about materials and sales conditions
- Prices from cost data collected, from standard calculations, from direct entries, and from planning processes
- Surcharges and discounts
- Taxes applied according to local rules
- New product proposals to be offered during the sales processing

It's clearly important to have accurate information available to those who need it. It's fundamental to the design of all SAP systems that a database of master records is held and maintained under strict conditions that ensure that any user who calls on this information can be informed of the date when it was entered or last amended, and of the identification of the person responsible for the change. It's also a design principle that any automatic function operating in support of the user will also use the master records. If a sales representative is compiling an order for a customer, for example, the address of that customer will be accessed from the master record. If the customer changes his address, the master will be changed—not a local record held by the person who was first informed of the change.

Such a strict system of data maintenance can succeed only if it's also flexible in the ways in which the stored information can be presented to users and applied to the business processes. This section illustrates the range of options open to users in relation to the master data records.

Processing Master Data Records

You can copy master records and change them, using a variety of standard functions to do so; the system records and time-stamps every change. To find a master record speedily, you can use any part of any data field as a match code.

Identifying Business Partners

A *business partner* is any person or organization that is involved in some way with a business transaction in SD-Sales and Distribution. For example, the customer, your sales representative, and the carrier are all represented by business partner functions in the system.

Documenting Customers

Each person or company that has bought from you in the past—or is accorded the status of a prospective customer, because you have a reasonable expectation that the person or company will purchase from you in the future—is represented by a master record. The customer master record stores the following data types:

- General data about the customer and the contact person
- Sales-specific data about pricing, deliveries, and output documents
- Company code data, which includes banking and posting details or payment data for that part of the customer corporation that is trading with you

If a customer is unlikely to deal with you more than once, you don't need to create a full master record. Such a transaction can be recorded on a one-time customer record or *Contra Pro Diverse* (CPD) customer record.

Assigning Account Groups

Your customer might have a complex organizational structure that prevents you from entering a simple sold-to party record for the requirement. The customer master record can be used to represent any of these account groups:

- Sold-to party
- Ship-to party
- Bill-to party
- Payer

Each account group can be assigned a specific selection from the available transaction data. Its documents then will be automatically tailor-made for it by the system. The SD-Sales and Distribution module is provided with definitions and models for the common types of customer relationships. You can also define your own account groups and specify which elements of transaction data are to be included in documents assigned to these groups.

Documenting the Contact Person

All the information you need to carry out sales support is held in the contact person records that are part of the customer master.

Documenting Carriers and Suppliers

A business partner that is also a carrier and supplier would have a master record maintained in the MM-Materials Management and FI-Financial Accounting modules. If the supplier is also an occasional customer, you can enter its supplier number in its customer record in the SD-Sales and Distribution system, which automatically creates a link so that the two records always share exactly the same data in all the fields they have in common.

Working with the HR-Human Resources Records

If you create a personnel record (for one of your customer sales representatives, for example), the master will be managed by the HR-Human Resources module. You therefore can refer to a member of your staff by entering his or her personnel master record number. This makes available to you any other details that you are authorized to see about the person.

Using MM-Materials Management Masters

The products and services represented and managed by the MM-Materials Management system can also be created and referred to from the SD-Sales and Distribution module. For example, a sales representative might acquire information about a new supplier of a material that is already represented by a material master record. The details can be posted to the MM-Materials Management system, where they are verified and incorporated into the database. If a prospective customer inquires about a material that he hasn't previously purchased from your company, the details available in the material masters can be used to provide up-to-date, accurate information. If there is no relevant material master, the MM-Materials Management system records this inquiry and alerts the material controller.

Assigning Material Type   The material type created in customizing is assigned to a material when the material master data is created. This ensures that the data fields irrelevant to a specific type of material are suppressed when the record is onscreen.

Allocating Industry Sectors   The industry sectors you find in your business that should be given differential treatment in one or more aspects of SD-Sales and Distribution can be defined during customizing. You then can make sure that products for each industry sector are assigned the corresponding type of master data structures, which allows the system to maintain particular information and use it to be responsive to that sector's needs. For example, the difference between one industry sector and another might be in the matter of distribution lot size or in the way billing takes place. In this instance, you might decide that some of your products will be sold and packaged in two or more ways: single units for the retail industry sector and pallets for the wholesale industry sector. Each sector has a different costing and billing procedure.

Four attributes serve to format the material master data into clusters: general data, data specific to a particular sales area, plant-specific data, and storage location and inventory management data. The SAP term for a cluster of associated data elements is an *attribute*.

Recording General Data   Any characteristic of a material that will always be the same is stored in the general data attribute and is made available every time the material takes part in a transaction. For example, a specific type of steel will have a unique material number and a particular description or specification. The units of measurement might be a function of the method of manufacture, such as a roll of spring steel, or they might be decided on the basis of the most economical unit for procuring this material, such as a pallet.

The following data types can be stored as general data because they are constant across all sources and uses of this material: material number, description, units of measure, weight, volume, material division, and so on.

Locating Data Specific to a Sales Area   Each sales area may be supplied from a particular warehouse or manufacturing plant. Although the material number is the same, the division of the supply between delivery plants will entail a relevant record on the material master. If, for example, the same material can be obtained from another sales area, if necessary, the material master records should show this, even though each sales area normally uses a separate source.

The following are examples of data that can be specific to each sales area:

- Delivering plant
- Sales texts
- Units of measure
- Product hierarchy information
- Shipping data

Storing Plant-Specific Data   Whether the supplying plant is a warehouse or a manufacturing unit, the costs of storing a material there, and the MRP-Materials Requirements Planning procedures, will need to be known to plan, cost, and schedule a sales order. This information also finds its place in the appropriate attribute of the material master from which it can be accessed by the SD-Sales and Distribution module.

The following are examples of data that may be specific to each plant:

- MRP profile
- Production costs
- Export data

Keeping Storage Location and Inventory Management Data   A warehouse may have storage locations designed specifically for particular materials. If a material has to be stored in such a location, this information is stored in the material master records.

The following examples illustrate the material data that may have to be stored in the storage location and inventory management attribute:

- Temperature conditions
- No other material to be stored in the location reserved for this material
- Storage conditions, such as dust and humidity control
- Special handling facilities essential for this material

Relationships to the particular sales organizations and distribution channels may affect some or all entries. Any particulars determined by the master records of a superior level in the organizational structure are inherited by a data object in a lower level, unless the record at the lower level carries specific instructions to the contrary. For example, a material that has to be stored in a cooled warehouse will show this requirement in its material master data record. If a particular method of packaging has been determined for a whole class of materials, any material belonging to this class will be packed in this way unless the individual material master record carries contrary instructions.

Working with a Bill of Material

When a product is made up of several components, the details are documented in a *bill of material* (BoM). If additional information is required about any of these components, a BoM explosion may be used to call in the extra documentation. If several products vary by only a few components, the technique of BoM variants may be used. These topics are discussed in Chapter 17, "Understanding the Production Planning Module."

Controlling Material Status

You can adopt the standard status indicators of the MM-Materials Management system or define indicators of your own to control sales activities. For example, you might want to block the taking of orders for a batch of defective material but permit inquiries about the product in anticipation that a future batch will not be defective. A discontinued product can be the subject of status control so that future orders will be blocked, even though the product is still being shipped to satisfy existing orders.

Initiating Stock and Inventory Inquiries

Flexible display facilities permit you to assess the various plant stocks and summarize them in the form of overviews. Special stock can be identified for different treatments—for example, special stock destined for only one customer.

Understanding Customer Material Info Records

If a customer needs special sales and delivery requirements that aren't met by the information stored in the customer master or the relevant material masters, you can set up a customer material info record that takes precedence over the rules established elsewhere. The info record contains information such as customer, sales organization, and distribution channel; your material number and description; the customer's material number and description; shipping data; partial delivery arrangements; and so on. The system uses the customer material info record to prepare a sales proposal ready to be placed in the sales order if you approve it. The system also uses the customer material info records when using EDI to complete sales orders. Customers primarily send EDI requirements using their own product numbers, not the supplier product numbers.

The SD-Sales and Distribution module will operate material determination and material substitution procedures if they have been established. For example, you can define a set of criteria to select a suitable material automatically. You may also have set up the criteria for a material to be substituted automatically in orders for a particular customer. The material listing and material exclusion rules are valid for a certain time period and restrict the choice of options presented by the system when preparing a sales proposal.

Using the Condition Technique

The SAP R/3 *condition technique* gets its name from the discipline of formal logic and, in particular, from the conditional proposition form, which can be expressed as the following:

If (all conditions in a certain set of conditions are true)
Then (certain actions can be taken)

The logical if-then technique is used extensively in the SAP R/3 system to enable the computer to carry out specified actions automatically only if the proper conditions are satisfied by the necessary data.

The choice of price information and the imposition of discounts or surcharges are matters that vary from business to business. You can use any data in a document as the condition or trigger for the application of your pricing structure.

Price lists can be standard, based on the material used, customer-specific, and so on. Discounts or surcharges can be allocated by customer, material, price group, material group, and any combinations of such criteria.

Each condition master record has a specified time validity, and you can specify whether it permits or forbids manual changes during this period.

Conditions can also define the circumstances under which the system is allowed to handle sales taxes as surcharges. The standard SD-Sales and Distribution system is provided with sales tax formulas for most parts of the world, and you can add your own.

Understanding SD Transactions

Every business transaction is documented automatically by the SAP R/3 system. The SD-Sales and Distribution module provides for a separate document type to be created for every stage of the sales and distribution chain of processes. Changes to a document, such as revisions of prices or quantities, are stored in the change history associated with each document. Standard business programs are available for executing and displaying the results of all the usual sales and distribution functions, to which you can add your own variants during customizing.

Using a Sales and Distribution Document

The SAP business transaction document is a versatile instrument, created automatically and always subject to the rule that changes must be documented and time-stamped. These are some of the day-to-day uses of the SAP Document in the SD-Sales and Distribution system:

- Pricing
- Availability checks
- Transfer of requirements
- Sales or distribution document printing medium and formatting
- Management of short standard texts or long texts and drawings
- Delivery management and document printing
- Billing management and document printing
- Provision of data to the SD-IS Sales and Distribution Information System

Tracing Document Flow

Each sales and distribution transaction generates a document adapted to the business at hand. If a certain type of transaction doesn't require some of the many possible functions, the resulting document doesn't need to contain any reference to them. If you or the system has reason to carry out additional functions on the document, the new activities leave evidence in the usual way.

The typical flow of activities in a Sales Department is reflected in the flow and development of the corresponding SD-Sales and Distribution documents, as shown in this example:

1. A sales representative makes a series of calls to a potential customer, and information is collected in sales activity documents.

2. If the potential customer makes an inquiry, a quotation can be created and assigned a limited validity period. An inquiry document can be created for the same purpose. This can subsequently lead to a quotation.

3. If the potential customer accepts the quotation, a sales order has to be delivered by a specified date.

4. The system must confirm that the material will be available.

5. Scheduling of the necessary transport for the required date has to be arranged.

6. A picking control document may be necessary to collate the parts of the order.

7. When the goods are about to leave the plant, there has to be a series of stock and value adjustments in the MM-Materials Management and FI-Financial Accounting departmental systems. If the relevant delivery document hasn't been received when goods are issued, a goods issue document has to be created to initiate the same processes.

8. The billing document may be sent, emailed, faxed, or transferred via EDI to the customer, and the event is recorded with a transfer of data to the FI-Financial Accounting department.

At any stage in the document flow, you can find out what is in the previous document, and so on, right back to the first contact between your company and the customer. If the flow you are scrutinizing has been completed, you can inspect the delivery document and the invoice. Whatever your query, the automatically generated process documentation will be readily available to show you what you want to know.

Monitoring Processing Status   Progress along this document flow and the transaction processing that it represents are documented automatically and can be controlled by a system of status indicators to signal the stage reached in the transaction. You can call for information by using the status indicator, which causes the system to respond with information to answer the following kinds of questions:

■ Has the customer accepted all the quotation items, and have the items been copied to a sales order?

■ Is the sales order complete?

- Which items haven't yet been delivered?
- Has this transaction reached the stage of being fully invoiced?

You can issue commands to block the progress of a transaction if, for example, you see a problem with the quality of the stock that might be assigned to this order.

Locating a Document   You can always access a document by entering its document number. The standard SAP R/3 system is applied in SD-Sales and Distribution of using match codes to initiate a search that narrows down the list from which you have to select the document you require. Match codes can be customized to meet any requirements. The following match codes are standard:

- Sales activities selected by specifying one or more of the short texts that may have been copied to the document
- Sales documents by customer purchase order number
- Credit and debit memos that have been released for further processing
- Deliveries from a specific shipping point according to a range of goods issue dates
- Billing documents that haven't yet passed on to the FI-Financial Accounting system

Interpreting Document Structure and Datasources

The documents created by the SD-Sales and Distribution system follow the standard SAP R/3 convention of including a header plus one or more items. The system differentiates between SD-CAS Sales Support activities carried on without any specific reference to individual customers, and activities that deal with sales and distribution to individual customers. The sales and distribution activities for specified customers are discussed in the following subsections.

Referring to Document Header Contents   The general data in the header applies to the whole document, unless specifically countermanded by a particular line item. The data includes information and references to standard documents or master records concerning the following matters:

- Sold-to party
- Sales area as defined during customizing
- Terms of payment
- Technical and legal texts
- Purchasing data
- Ship-to party
- Carrier
- Other business partners

Reading Sales Document Items   The items in a Sales and Distribution document consist of data about the goods and services ordered by the customer. One or more subitems may be attached to each document item, each of which is followed by one or more schedule lines. The document items and their subitems include the following data:

- Material number
- Quantity
- Alternative shipping addresses
- Prices
- Business data, if different from the header information

Each of the schedule lines applicable to document items or their subitems can include the following types of data:

- Delivery date
- Quantity
- Shipping data
- Procurement data
- Partial delivery information in the form of an initial delivery schedule line, followed by the subsequent and final delivery schedule line

Using Item Categories   You can set up your system to differentiate between item categories by applying rules determined during customizing. For example, you can adopt the following item category scheme:

- Sales order document items
- Delivery and billing document items
- Text document items
- Value document items

In this case, you can establish from the category type whether an availability check is required, whether the item has to be priced, and whether the item is deliverable.

Applying Data-Creation Techniques   In addition to entering data manually, you can use the SD-Sales and Distribution system to make extensive use of copying. You can copy data from master records and information from the preceding document when processing an order. By these means, you can rapidly and accurately assemble documents. For example, you can copy the details of the sold-to party and any business partners from the relevant master records. You might be able to reference previous customer material info records or product proposals; the system can do this for you if it is suitably armed with the logical conditions to control the copying.

Before you release any stage of document in a sales transaction, you can amend any of the standard or proposal data if you have made a special arrangement with the customer. You can copy the sales order to create a delivery note, for example, and then edit it if the customer requires a different destination for this particular delivery.

If you do decide to use a document as a reference, the system checks that it can be released for this purpose, and you can have it checked to see whether it's still valid before you copy from it.

Using Texts in SD Documents   You can use the SAPscript word processing system for preparing text. You can store text at the header level, where it is applicable to all document items and subitems and remains if you create another Sales and Distribution document using this header. Shipping regulations and terms of payment are examples of the kind of text that might be usefully stored at the header level.

Alternatively, you can store text at the level of an individual item. In this case, it applies only to this item, but again, if you decide to use this item elsewhere, your text is available there also, because it still is attached to the item. Material short texts and packaging instructions are examples of the type of written material that can remain with the item.

The SAPscript module can provide these texts in any of the supported languages. The SAPscript component of the R/3 system generates texts for storage as data elements for reuse and one-off messages to other users and customers or suppliers. SAPscript is discussed in Chapter 2, "Interacting with the SAP Systems."

Differentiating Types of Business Transactions

The standard version of the SD-Sales and Distribution system can recognize and support the most frequently used types of business transactions. You can refine or modify these functions to suit your company and create new business transaction types with the pertinent business functionality.

Handling Inquiries and Quotations   Inquiries and quotations are standard SAP Documents that are created before a sales order is taken and are limited to a specific validity period. They should be customized to gather information on the reasons for the inquiry and the reasons for rejection if a sales order doesn't result.

By accessing one of the overview screens, you can find out whether the materials or services in the inquiry or quotation will be available on the date required. Although little information is recorded as the result of an inquiry, you can use it to begin to plan a sales strategy for this potential customer. As you seek further clarification of the customer's requirements, you can build a better relationship and have the results of your prospecting endeavors stored in the documents and customer master records.

Processing Sales Orders   Even if you haven't offered a quotation, you can still enter a sales order to check availability and carry out a credit limit check. You will want to carry out pricing at this stage, if you haven't already done so. The required delivery date may well affect the price.

Managing Scheduling Agreements and Contracts   This type of business transaction is an outline agreement with a customer to supply goods and services over a specified period of time. The quantities and dates are specified in the *scheduling agreement*. A *contract* is also an outline agreement to supply goods and services in the future, but the delivery date isn't specified until later, when it's published in a release order.

Placing a Rush Order   You can create a sales order and initiate a delivery at the same time. This rush order causes the system to create the delivery for you as soon as you enter the order. It checks availability and carries out scheduling for both the order and the delivery documents at the same time.

Arranging Production to Order   If you have elected to enter this type of order, a production requirement is created to produce the material directly as a result of the customer order. When the material reaches the finished product stage, it is treated as special stock.

The individual customer requirement is passed to material requirements planning, and the availability is checked against the customer special stock. When production and external purchase order processing are completed, the appropriate inward goods movement for the customer special stock is posted. This records that goods have been produced specifically for the individual customer and assigned to his or her special stock. Delivery takes place from this stock.

Using Customer Consignment Stock   If you have set aside some goods that one of your customers can call on at any time, and you haven't yet been paid for these goods, they are treated as *consignment goods*. If you are the vendor, you still own the consignment.

The warehouse holding these consignment goods notifies the vendor if the customer picks up or is issued with any of the goods. The vendor charges the customer for them. If any of the consignment goods are not required by the customer, they can be returned to the vendor.

In the SD-Sales and Distribution system, customer consignment stock is managed separately by generating consignment fill-up orders for the customer, consignment issues from the stock, billing documents, and consignment pickup documents.

Accounting for Returnable Packaging   The system maintains a separate stock of returnable packaging or transportation material for each customer. This material has to be returned within a specified time period. The vendor still owns it. The SD-Sales and Distribution system offers functions for the dispatch and pickup of returnable packaging, so that you can enter it in deliveries and bill the customer for any packaging not returned within the set time.

Taking Complaints   If a customer complains of damage during transportation or isn't satisfied with the goods or services, you can call on special SAP R/3 functions to process these complaints. A *return* is a transaction that arranges for the faulty goods to be picked up or for replacements to be delivered free of charge. If you find that you have overcharged or undercharged a customer, you can create a credit or debit memo request document that sets in motion the appropriate financial procedure.

Setting Up Third-Party Deals   If you are the contractor in a third-party deal, you will commission a third-party vendor to deliver the goods directly to the customer or to the destination specified as the customer's ship-to party. In these cases, the SD-Sales and Distribution system automatically creates purchase requisitions for the sales order that specify the delivery dates and quantities. The Purchasing Department, using the MM-Materials Management system, processes these purchasing requirements and creates purchase orders for them. If the vendor notifies the system that the quantities or the dates have to be changed, the system automatically corrects the sales document.

The third-party vendor will send you an invoice as soon as the goods have been delivered to the customer. You then can carry out billing for the third-party deal by having the system copy the quantity delivered from the invoice document to the billing document that goes to the customer.

Posting Stock Transfers   A requisition for stock to be transferred can be created automatically by PP-MRP Material Requirements Planning. The requisition can also be initiated from a purchase requisition entered manually.

When such a requisition is converted to a purchase order, the plant that is to deliver the material is informed of the stock transfer requirement, and the purchase order appears in the Delivery Due list on the SD-Sales and Distribution system display. All the shipping functions then can be applied to the stock transfer. The FI-Financial Accounting system of the delivering plant will get a goods issue posting, and the receiving plant will be posted a goods receipt.

Managing Cross-Company Sales   When one company needs products and services from other parts of the group, the cross-company sales function of the SD-Sales and Distribution system can be invoked. A sales organization can sell for plants in a different company code. Legally, this means that more than one company is involved in the processing of a sales order. It's necessary to apply intercompany invoicing between the company codes to adjust the value flow after the sales order is completed.

Working with the SD-CAS Sales Support Component

Here are some possible purposes of a sales support function:

- Promote business development
- Improve customer service
- Provide a mechanism through which all in-house and external sales personnel can contribute any useful information to a central facility, from which they can also draw freely in order to further their own sales activities
- Support sales promotion by individuals
- Improve communication throughout the sales force
- Provide methods for evaluating competitors and their products

A computer-based sales support function would also be expected to automate as many of the routine tasks of the sales department as possible. Master data and the documented evidence of business transaction processing are the prime sources of direct information of use to sales support. The SD-IS Sales and Distribution Information System is a further source of analyses based on sales summaries and the statistics of sales orders. The sales support activities also provide inputs to the SD-IS Information System.

Documenting Partners and Personnel

Because they represent your company in the market, each sales and sales support person is given a master record in the SD-Sales and Distribution system. *Sales personnel* is defined as people who are documented in the HR-Human Resources system as direct employees of your company, and who also are recognized by the SD-Sales and Distribution module because of the roles they may be called on to play in the sales and distribution activities. *Sales partners* are recognized and documented in the SD-Sales and Distribution system as consultancy partners or sales agents, but they aren't direct employees of your company and don't necessarily have personnel records in your HR-Human Resources system.

Maintaining Customers, Prospects, and Contacts

The management of customers and sales prospects constitutes a major part of the SD-CAS Sales Support software component. The customer master record holds most of the information in the standard SAP format of attributes, which are clusters of thematically related data fields.

A customer master has records for general details as well as the following:

■ Company organizational structure, annual sales, number of employees, status as a customer of your organization, and market areas of goods and services

■ Contact persons by name and position

■ Contact-person details, such as first name, form of salutation, birth date, marital status, buying habits, sales strategy to use, visiting hours, home address, business address, interests, and pastimes

A prospect is handled by the SD-Sales and Distribution module as a customer without a record of past purchases. The records and processing functions are the same.

If you are looking for a particular contact person, you can search for the company by name or number. Alternatively, you can search for the person's details, which enable you to keep track of that person if he or she moves from one of your customers to another. You may have a very large database of potential customers on which you are maintaining a watching brief and a diligent data-collecting effort.

There are no restrictions on the definition and number of attributes maintained in your master records for customers, sales prospects, and contact persons.

Tracking Competitors and Their Products

New markets and new market segments are often detected by closely observing what your competitors are and are not doing. You can store this kind of data systematically in the SD-Sales and Distribution system.

Recording Competitor Companies   You can use the system of master records to store data on your competitor companies, using the same structure as you use for customers, but with some important additions:

■ Industry classifications

■ Annual sales

■ Employees

■ Other information about the competitor stored in a structured format that allows you to conduct searches and compile statistical summaries

Recording Competitive Products   You need a database that includes all the important details for your own products, but if you want a comparison, you will also need to enter your competitors' products on the same set of master attributes. You can also have structured texts to locate critical information by classification and search techniques. Like your own products, competitive products will be assigned to product hierarchies on which a comparison can be based.

Managing Sales Activities and Promotions

The outcomes of previous sales activities have to be stored to become an input to the design of the next sales campaign. The method used by SD-Sales and Distribution is to store all interactions with the potential customer population in the data structures referred to as *sales activities*. The following are examples of activities by SD-CAS Sales Support that are documented by recording the outcomes of sales activities in such records:

- Sales calls in person
- Telemarketing calls
- Brochure mailings
- Calls received from potential customers
- Presentations
- Conferences
- Promotions

The standard SD-Sales and Distribution system recognizes three activity types:

- Sales call
- Sales letter
- Telephone call

You can define other sales activity types to add to this list during customizing.

Processing a Sales Activity   The basic information on the SAP Document generated as a result of a sales activity will include the following data elements:

- Customer number.
- Contact person at the customer company.
- Your sales organization or sales group conducting the sales activity.
- Date and time of the sales activity.
- Type of sales activity carried out.
- The reason for the activity, which can be entered using standard keys.
- The outcome of the activity, which can be entered by using standard keys and can have additional standard short text or freeform text. For example, "sales order" and "invitation to give a presentation" are standard activity outcomes that the system offers as options from which you can choose.

Authorization may be required to change or display a sales activity document.

When an authorized salesperson is processing a sales activity, the data from the SD-IS Sales and Distribution Information System can be accessed to show, for example, sales trends for this market segment or for this customer.

You can amplify the information carried by a sales activity master record by defining a set of standard texts that specify how a set of keys is to be interpreted. For example, you can set up codes for preparation notes, reports, and reactions to sales promotions. If you attach one of these codes to a free-text note or a standard short-text phrase, you can store the data in a way that will make it easy to access, classify, and use in the future.

Your sales activities will often have specific follow-up actions that can be predefined and permanently associated with the sales activity. These actions can be scheduled by elapsed time or given a firm date for completion. When you are planning your sales support work, you can call for a display of the planned sales activities and outstanding follow-up actions. The system will also give you complete histories of previous sales activities.

Conducting Direct Mailing   The standard SAP R/3 direct mailing function requires you to provide the following data elements:

- Address list for direct mailing
- Content and layout for the correspondence
- Enclosures for each addressee

This information will be stored in a direct mailing master record, so you can use it again or take it as a reference model when creating a new mailing.

You can use selection variants or search specifications to cull addresses from customers, sales prospects, and contact persons. Editing and all variants of customized texts can be used to make each mailing specific to each company in your group and to each unit in your customer's company, if necessary.

If you buy address lists, the system will automatically check that the new addresses of potential customers are in accord with the information you already have about them. The person responsible for each mailing can be identified in the mailing master record.

Managing Sales with the SD-SLS Component

The functionality of the SD-SLS Sales component of the SD-Sales and Distribution system is concentrated on the processing of sales transaction data in the wide variety of modes and contexts characteristic of the sales and distribution sector of business. There are many varieties of sales orders and many uses to which the resulting documents can be put. This section concentrates on some of the unique functional enhancements provided by the SAP R/3 system.

Handling Inquiries and Quotations

The inquiry or quotation will be handled by the system as the beginning of a sales order into which it will be converted if a sale is forthcoming. The quotation will carry a date marking the end of its validity period, which you can use to monitor the inquiries and quotations and to determine the order in which they should receive your attention.

You will have identified the material required by the inquirer, perhaps by its material number, or perhaps because you have used a previous quotation or order for this customer. You can also enter the material in text form, which the system interprets using the SAP R/3 Classification system. It then finds a material number for you to consider entering at a later date or for the system to enter automatically.

Several alternative materials could possibly interest the customer. You can quote for these as well as for the material requested. If the customer places an order, the system will work on the material the customer chose from your quotation.

Using the SD-SLS Sales Component

The philosophy behind the functionality of the SD-SLS Sales component is to minimize the work you have to do to complete an order. The standard approach is to find what is required and propose it to the user for adjustment and confirmation. So if you simply enter a list of items, the system will try to find these items in a previous order for this customer. If none of these items exist in those orders, it looks for the items in the master records and offers you the default values it finds there. For example, it will suggest business partners to deliver the material if that has happened before. It will propose that you use the lot size and packaging customary for this material, and so on. Much of the information will be in material and customer master records:

- Pricing
- Tax determination
- Weight and volume determination
- Delivery scheduling
- Payment methods

The system will offer textual materials to be included in the sales order if this is customary, and it will have detailed proposals for creating the commercial papers.

If you have to save a sales document before it's fully serviced with appropriate and valid information, the system accords it the status of an incomplete document and reminds you with a list of the missing items. When you return to the work, the system can show you all the incomplete documents in your task list, with lists of defects for each.

Processing Outline Agreements

There are two types of outline agreements with a customer to supply goods and services over a specified period of time: contracts and scheduling agreements.

A *contract* is an outline agreement to supply goods and services in the future, but the delivery date and shipping arrangements aren't specified until the customer requests delivery of the goods in the contract. At this time, a release order is issued and processed in the same way as a sales order. The quantities and general data of each release order are noted in the contract, and the quantities remaining to be delivered are updated there accordingly.

The quantities and dates are specified from the beginning in a *scheduling agreement,* which is otherwise processed much like a series of contracts, using the dates and quantities specified in the outline schedule.

Updating Back Orders

If you call for a list of back orders, you will see the order items that couldn't be confirmed because something wasn't available. The availability will be checked again automatically, and you will see the current situation. If some orders can now be satisfied, you can use the update functions to have the sales orders confirmed directly.

Pricing

The SD-Sales and Distribution system will carry out pricing automatically by using predefined prices, surcharges, and discounts. You can change the data proposed by the system for computing the prices, and you can change the price for a particular business transaction. This pricing method is applied to quotations, sales orders, and billing documents. At any time, you can call for pricing analysis so that you can inspect the figures and the procedures used to arrive at the price proposal.

The system must find the price to be charged for each particular material. It first looks for a customer-specific material price and uses that if it finds one. If it doesn't, it seeks a price-list price valid for a business segment or some other sector of the market that includes this customer. Only if there is no valid price list does the system use the basic price for the material.

This logical sequence of methods for determining a price for a material is set out in the form of a condition stored as a condition master record. There is no limit to the complexity of a condition, because it has the task of controlling how the system assembles the cost data and other factors that go into the calculation of a price.

For example, a material might have a base price and a price for the duration of a sales promotion. The material might be a member of a price group that specifies that it is subject to a certain surcharge or discount. There might be a surcharge if less than a specified minimum quantity is ordered. Some materials have to be priced to reflect the changes in the currency-exchange rate between its country of origin and its point of sale. A certain customer might be allowed a particular price discount, and the quantity ordered might attract further discounts. If the customer agrees to pay in advance, a rebate might be included in the price calculation.

Any factors that can affect pricing can be computed according to specific formulas and logical conditions that control when and how each contributing element is taken into the calculation. Although the calculation is automatic, the user and the customer can see the details of the calculation under certain conditions; these details appear as data in the relevant condition master. Sales taxes are handled similarly, using logical conditions and formulas appropriate to the pertinent legal system in force.

After the system arrives at a price to charge for the specific material, it looks to see whether a discount has been defined for this material, this customer, or this material only if bought by this customer. Thus, the system ends up with a price to charge for each item in the sales order.

A further check then is made to see whether the total value or total quantity should attract further surcharges or discounts. Only after the system arrives at an appropriate material price for each item, applies the discounts and surcharges, and reviews the totals for further surcharges and discounts, does it copy the price into the quotation, sales order or billing document.

These pricing processes are discussed further in Chapter 12, "Understanding the Financial Accounting Module," and Chapter 13, "Understanding the Controlling Module."

Controlling Shipping with the SD-SHP Component

All the data required to arrange a prompt delivery can be determined in the sales order. By having the system display all the orders due for delivery, you can manage the deadlines. Bottlenecks will be foreseen and the remedies will be at hand. These are the main activities supported by the SD-SHP Shipping functions:

- Monitoring the deadlines of orders due for delivery
- Creating and processing deliveries
- Monitoring the availability of goods
- Supporting the picking operations
- Supporting packing and loading
- Managing transportation
- Creating shipping output documents and transmitting them
- Managing decentralized shipping
- Posting the goods issue document to FI-Financial Accounting at the time of delivery

Compiling Shipping Work Lists

For every shipping point under the control of the Shipping Department, there can be a work list of sales orders due for delivery. How frequently these work lists are processed will be determined by the management and operating staff—all things being equal, the sooner the better.

A *shipping point* is a facility that offers a separate shipping capacity. It might be one of several identical loading bays, for example, or it might have a special handling capacity (such as a forklift) that is larger than the other shipping points. The shipping point might owe its individuality to its dedication to the orders for one particular customer. The appropriate shipping point is determined automatically by the system or is entered manually during order creation. The criteria for automatic shipping point determination follow:

- Shipping conditions specified for the sold-to party—for example, "as soon as possible" or "normal shipping conditions"

■ Loading group of the material—for example, "by crane," "by forklift truck," or "by special staff loading team"

■ Delivering plant—for example, "road truck," "rail wagon," or "dedicated transporter"

Each order item has to be assigned a route. The route chosen depends on the following criteria:

■ Shipping conditions specified for the sold-to party

■ Delivery weight of the order item

■ Geographical relationship of the destination to the shipping point

Each route imposes certain restrictions on the choice of transport and the number and nature of the legs of the journey. If the order item has to change delivery plant en route, there will be extra costs and delays. However, executing the whole route by one particular means of transport might be unacceptable for other reasons: It might take too long, the atmospheric pollution by the vehicle might be damaging to the reputation of your company, or the vehicle might have to make the return journey without a payload.

You can call up a list at any time to see which deliveries are scheduled to use a particular route or shipping point over a selected time interval. You might be able to improve the planning of loading and transportation activities by manually changing one or more of the parameters assigned by the system.

Creating and Processing Deliveries

To the SAP R/3 system, a delivery is a document. It has to carry all the data necessary for preparing and delivering the material in the sales order.

Creating a Delivery for a Particular Sales Order   The goods specified by material number and quantity can be copied from the sales order to the delivery document. The shipping point can be selected automatically by using the shipping conditions that will be available from the customer master records. If the shipping conditions have changed, or if there has been no previous specification of the customer shipping conditions, you can correct matters manually before you post the delivery to have it executed.

Creating All Deliveries Due   From your display of all sales orders due for delivery, you can select on the basis of a specific shipping point, a particular material, a single ship-to party, and so on in any combination that leaves you with the selection of deliveries due that you intend to create. You might also want to refine your list by imposing other restrictions, such as the maximum gross weight your vehicle can carry or the maximum overall dimensions.

The sales orders due, perhaps refined by your selection procedures, then can be processed simultaneously to become delivery documents. The system logs for your attention any incorrect sales order documents or ones that lack a needed data element. You might be able to return to these documents later to enter the missing data.

Creating Deliveries That Don't Refer to a Sales Order   It's possible to enter manually all the relevant information needed to create a delivery. You might want to do this if the central system cannot provide access to the sales order or if the information you require isn't there.

The section "Distribution of Functions under Decentralized Shipping," later in this chapter, discusses deliveries in the context of decentralized shipping, in which the relevant data is entered from a separate source, rather than copied directly at the time from the relevant sales order document.

Using Automatic Checks in Delivery Creation

The system carries out checks to help ensure that the delivery data is complete and correct. When you see the display of the delivery due list in detail, you might find that you have to change some data entered by the PP-MRP Material Requirements Planning function because the situation has changed since that planning operation was performed.

The specifications in the material master records in MM-Materials Management provide the data for automatically calculating the weights and volumes of the individual delivery items and the totals for the delivery as a whole. The same MM system is the source of stock data the system uses to determine whether the material intended for the delivery is available for this purpose.

At this moment, just before a delivery is created, the system looks again at the scheduling specifications in the sales order: the customer's required delivery date or the standard delivery conditions assigned in the customer's master records. You will see a warning and a proposal if a change in scheduling is called for.

Managing the Delivery Situation of an Item

A *delivery situation* is the result of evaluating the goods availability position and the agreements in place with the customer or the sold-to party concerning partial deliveries. Here are some examples of delivery situations:

- If the sold-to party will not accept partial deliveries, you have to ensure that all the items in the sales order are collected in one delivery group, which then becomes the focus. The availability check and the transfer of requirements have to be adjusted to fit the earliest delivery date possible for the delivery group.

- If the sold-to party has agreed to accept partial deliveries, you can, if necessary, create several deliveries from the one sales order. This might suit the availability situation, both of goods and of shipping facilities.

- It might make sense to combine several sales orders into one delivery group, if the customer has agreed to such an arrangement.

In all these procedures for effectively managing delivery situations as they arise and planning to smooth their passage before the time comes, you can allow the SAP R/3 system to act automatically by setting up the appropriate logical conditions and data elements.

Producing a Delivery Status Update   The creation of a delivery document, when it's posted and proved to be valid, tells the system to automatically update the materials stock and the work list of the Shipping Department, where a display of the delivery situation for the sales order will show the Updated status key.

Producing Shipping Output Documents   After the delivery is posted, the system asks whether you want to print or send by electronic mail the shipping output documents mandated during customizing.

Managing Shipping Elements   A *shipping element* is an item of material that is managed separately in the SD-Sales and Distribution system, because it's used in shipping and is necessary for handling and protecting the goods in transit. It might be on loan to the customer for a specified period, and a charge might be assessed if it's not returned within that period. Boxes, cartons, pallets, trucks, trailers, and supporting travel rigs can be managed as shipping elements.

To protect and handle a particular delivery, it might be necessary to have the item first packed in cartons. A group of cartons, perhaps, is protected by a box, and several boxes are loaded into a freight container. All these shipping elements can be treated as a hierarchy of shipping elements recognized by the system and specified for use for one or more types of material or one or more customers.

The shipping elements don't need to be specified as a hierarchical structure; they can be referenced simply as a packing list, which is also recognized by the system as a data object and can be altered by the procedures of change management.

Picking

A *picking list,* or *pick list,* is a document that ensures that the goods in the warehouse arrive at the shipping point at the right moment to become part of a delivery. Clearly, only the right goods and the right quantities will do. And it's no use getting the goods to the shipping point just before the transport is due to leave if some work has to be done to prepare the goods and protect them with the specified shipping elements. If the goods need special storage conditions, picking will have to make allowances for this.

The typical picking sequence follows:

1. A picking location or loading zone is automatically determined for a delivery, using data on the sales order delivery document that indicates the shipping point and storage conditions to be observed.

2. A picking list is printed for each delivery when the delivery is created or later. The picking list can be sent electronically.

3. After the picking operation assembles the available quantities at the picking location, the quantities are confirmed to the system. If they are insufficient but stock is available, picking is carried out again for the shortfall, using the same loading zone. If the quantities required cannot be picked to the picking zone for whatever reason, the delivery quantity is reduced. The system makes the appropriate adjustments to the order, shipping, and billing documents.

In some circumstances, you might have to enter the batch specification or the valuation type after picking is completed, because only at that stage will the necessary data be accurate. For example, some process industries have to expect a variation in the makeup of the finished product, because variables in the input materials and the environmental conditions affect the product.

Linking with the MM-WM Warehouse Management System

If you have installed and configured the MM-WM Warehouse Management system, the initiation of picking can take place through this system. The system maintains material master data that indicates the fixed storage bin or specified storage area in which the material can be found during picking. If the warehouse doesn't use fixed-bin storage, it's treated as a random warehouse. The MM-WM Warehouse Management system makes sure that a transfer order is created for each delivery item. When the goods arrive at the picking area, the transfer order is confirmed and the system enters the picked quantities directly into the delivery items on the delivery document.

Understanding the Formalities of Goods Issue

From the point of view of the shipping function, the business transaction is complete when the goods leave your company. In the SD-Sales and Distribution system, this event is represented by the posting of a goods issue corresponding to the delivery. Stock values are updated in the FI-Financial Accounting module as the stock level of material is reduced by the quantity of the goods issued.

The goods issue brings to an end the delivery processing. The information on the goods issue is stored in the sales order from which the delivery was initiated. The billing due list now shows the details of the delivery, so that it can be invoiced.

Operating Decentralized Shipping

When the SD-Sales and Distribution system reaches the point where it can specify a delivery, it might be convenient to pass this delivery document to another system. For example, there could be several satellite systems working on a decentralized shipping basis, each receiving a subset of the deliveries due from the central system.

Some advantages are recognized by companies that adopt the decentralized shipping approach:

- Shipping processing can be carried out continuously, even when the main computing system is unavailable.
- The SD-SHP Shipping module can be used on a satellite computer with another sales order processing system—for example, from the SAP R/2 system.
- The system load can be distributed over various computers by relieving the main system of the shipping functions.

The effect of decentralizing shipping in this manner is to minimize delivery times and improve customer service.

Distribution of Functions Under Decentralized Shipping   The sales order is entered on the central host computer system where the stocks are managed. The availability of the order items is checked there, and the scheduling takes place there for the shipping activities of perhaps all the satellite shipping subsystems.

When the due date arrives for a delivery, the satellite initiates the shipping activities and transfers the delivery data from the host. Data relevant to the materials handled by the satellite will already be held there in the form of copies of the material master records. A transfer of customer data takes place for every business transaction so that the information is up-to-date.

Picking at the satellite can be linked to an MM-WM Warehouse Management system there or on the host. As the batches and quantities are gathered to the picking location, the specifications are confirmed in the delivery document. You can add packaging and other shipping elements at the same time, as well as the weights and volumes for the loading data that will appear on the shipping output documents to be generated locally.

When the delivery is completed, the goods issue for the delivery is automatically confirmed. The data is transferred back to the host, where the status of the sales order is updated.

The satellite system doesn't post quantities or values to the FI-Financial Accounting system; this is done centrally when the delivery confirmation is returned.

As soon as the delivery is confirmed, the central host system releases the delivery for billing, and it appears on the billing due list.

Defining a Transportation Chain   One inevitable complexity of trading at a distance is that the goods might have to be carried to the customer along a chain of transportation modes, each of which will probably require its own paperwork and therefore will be looked after by a separate department at the location designated as the transportation planning point. Thus, the overland section might have a shipping document separate from a section across the sea.

A *transportation chain* can be defined as an SD master record that allows each leg or mode of transport to maintain separate output documents, texts, and status controls. Each transportation mode might entail a different pattern of shipping units, so the goods might have to be remarshaled at the intermediate loading points. Unless you create a transportation chain, this type of delivery has to be managed as a set of small shipments that are separated and combined as the transportation processes take place.

The transportation chain concept is applied by creating a journey consisting of a main leg, with preliminary legs and subsequent legs to complete the route. Within each leg, the standard automatic facilities are available. The transportation chain master record ensures that related data is copied as appropriate across the various legs.

Billing with the SD-BIL Component

The task of billing is to create the billing document and transfer the data to FI-Financial Accounting and profitability analysis.

SD-SLS Sales and SD-SHP Shipping are the source systems that provide the information used by SD-BIL Billing in the form of, for example, quantity and price data from the reference documents of the inquiry, quote, or sales order. In their turn, these documents will have called on, for example, the MM-Materials Management system to supply materials data.

SD-BIL Billing supports the following operations:

- Create invoices for deliveries or services rendered.
- Respond to debit memo requests by creating debit memos.
- Respond to credit memo requests by creating credit memos.
- Cancel billing document.
- Transfer posting data to FI-Financial Accounting.

Creating Billing Documents

A billing document can be created for a single delivery or sales order by entering the number of the delivery or sales order. If several deliveries or sales orders are awaiting billing, you have to direct your attention to the items on the billing due list.

Processing the Billing Due List   The work list of documents due for billing can be processed as a collective. You might prefer to restrict the items on this billing due list by defining selection criteria, such as the billing date for a particular sold-to party.

As the system collects the details of the documents due for billing, it compiles a log showing the defects of any that are incorrect or incomplete—as much as the system can check on these matters. You can examine this log and perhaps supply the information needed to correct the defective or incomplete items.

For all correct items in the billing due list or the subset that you have defined, the system automatically generates the billing documents and carries out the posting necessary to the accounts of the FI-Financial Accounting system.

Controlling Pricing and Tax   When you are about to create a billing document, you have to decide whether to carry out pricing and tax determination again by using the latest figures, or whether to instead copy the prices, surcharges, and discounts from the sales order on which the billing document is based. You can also change the price manually right up until the document is forwarded to the FI-Financial Accounting system by posting the completed billing document.

Canceling Billing Documents

The way to cancel a billing document is to create a cancellation document that cites the original billing document. When you post a cancellation document, the system creates the necessary reversal documents in FI-Financial Accounting. You can cancel credit memos and invoices.

Choosing a Billing Method

You can choose which billing method to use by looking at the calendar that contains the billing schedule for the particular customer. There are three main options:

- A separate invoice is created for each delivery.
- All deliveries within a particular user-defined period are combined to form a collective invoice.

■ Several invoices are created for different parts of a delivery according to the criteria defined by the customer, such as material pricing group.

Building an Invoice List   If one payer is responsible for several invoices, the invoices can be combined in an invoice list. This list can be compiled by a collective run and can include both single and collective invoices.

There might be an advantage to the payer in this, because you can total the invoices on the list and apply discounts on the total value. You might grant factoring commissions, for example.

The individual invoices on the invoice list or the total of the list can be posted to FI-Financial Accounting.

Applying Billing Method Rules   You can define the rules used to decide how to combine deliveries in a collective invoice or invoice list. You also can control the rules about splitting invoices for each customer or each type of business transaction. Here are two examples of billing method rules:

■ The sales order has to be completely delivered, and the goods issue has to be posted, before a delivery can be invoiced.

■ Deliveries or invoices cannot be combined if there is more than one payer.

Processing Complaints

There are two ways to process complaints: One can generate a credit memo, the other a debit memo.

Managing Returns   If a customer complains about the quality or type of goods involved in a delivery, you can pick up the goods free of charge from the customer location and generate a returns order in the Sales Department. This leads to a credit memo request and eventually a credit memo posted to the customer's account in FI-Financial Accounting. The returns order carries information about the complaint in short texts and perhaps free text, both of which can be analyzed later.

Recognizing Credit Memo Requests   A credit memo request may also occur in the Sales Department because the customer has complained about a late delivery. This request is blocked for billing until the amount of the credit is decided; then the request can be released, and a credit memo can be created. The credit memo is posted to the customer's account in the FI-Financial Accounting system.

Dealing with Debit Memo Requests   If a debit memo request is created in the Sales Department (perhaps because a customer has been undercharged), a similar procedure is followed. This time, the result is a debit memo amount, which is posted to Accounts Receivable in FI-Financial Accounting.

Linking with FI-Financial Accounting

The integration of SD-BIL Billing with the FI-Financial Accounting module allows the system to carry out posting automatically when a billing document is created.

Payments from the customer are monitored from the FI-Financial Accounting system, and any dunning of overdue payments originates from this system. The dunning key that determines the dunning procedure to be applied is first recorded in the sales order—either on the basis of customer master records or because you have made a manual entry of a dunning key or canceled the default key placed there by the system. This enables you to exclude the dunning of a customer for particular invoices.

Although the procedure is automatic, you can place a posting block on the transfer of invoices and credit or debit memos by an entry on the billing document. The posting will not take place until you release this block. Your display facilities enable you to list blocked billing documents so that you can easily attend to them.

Assigning a Revenue Account with the Condition Technique   When you post a billing document to the FI-Financial Accounting system, the appropriate revenue accounts and sales deduction accounts are determined by the system, using the condition technique.

A *condition* is a set of criteria used to make a decision. The standard account determination condition is to use defined ranges of values over the following criteria to determine the appropriate accounts for posting:

- Material
- Payer
- Business transaction type
- Condition type of the prices, surcharges, and discounts in the billing document

You control the critical values in each criterion, and you might want to define other criteria and their critical values during customizing.

Analyzing Revenue Account Determinations   During the processing of a billing, you can call for *revenue account determination analysis,* which shows you a listing of the FI-GL General Ledger accounts being used for prices, surcharges, and discounts for the particular business transaction on which you are working.

Processing Business Areas   The Revenue and Sales Deductions accounts in FI-Financial Accounting can be segmented according to user-defined business areas to provide a more structured analysis of profit and loss. When you are posting as a result of billing processing, the system takes the data on the deliveries or sales orders to determine the business area segments of the accounts to which posting should take place.

Assigning a CO-Controlling Account   Costs and revenues can be distributed among profit centers, business segments, or projects. These values are used for profitability analysis in the CO-Controlling module. This control account determination is specified in the CO system and in the SAP R/3 PS-Project System, both of which use the FI-GLX Extended General Ledger or the FI-SL Special Purpose Ledger.

Costs can also be assigned to the cost centers where they originated, as well as to orders, such as production orders. The cost centers are defined and maintained in the CO-Controlling module; see Chapter 13.

Applying Volume-Based Rebates

After a specified period of time passes, the sales to a specific customer in that period may qualify for the grant of a volume-based rebate. The rebate is a payment subsequent to the settlement of all the individual orders, and is arranged in the form of a credit memo posted to the account of the customer to whom it has been granted.

Defining Rebate Conditions   In the SD-Sales and Distribution system, the rules for automatically granting volume-based rebates are set up in the form of logical conditions that have to be met. During customizing, you can define the criteria and the critical values making up the conditions for a rebate agreement. For example, you might agree to grant a rebate rate based on the overall volume of sales to a specific customer in a certain period. You could offer an additional rebate for sales in a defined product group. And you could offer yet another additional rebate if the volume of sales of certain specific materials reaches a predefined value.

Any bill-to party can enjoy a rebate. This facility allows you to use rebate agreements to control the payment of licensing fees or commission payments.

Accruals in FI-Financial Accounting for volume-based rebate processing are created automatically. In every invoice, the rebate rate is recognized as an accruals rate, and the amount is posted to the appropriate account.

Calculating Rebates   Rebate settlement begins with a run to compile a list of credit memo requests. This will be based on the sales and accruals. You might want to edit this list manually.

When the credit memo request list is released, you can create the credit memos to reverse the accruals in the FI-Financial Accounting system. You thus credit the customers for the rebates you have granted.

Anticipating SD Enhancements in R/3 Releases 4.0 and 4.5

SAP R/3 Release 4.0 has a much-improved user interface and two marketing themes to differentiate it from earlier releases:

- Improving value chain management
- Reducing the time taken by its users to develop their products

There are additional features, such as full support for companies that want to deal in the Euro, including automatically reconciling differences caused by rounding up values after currency conversion. Dual currency displays are configurable.

Two industrial sectors have received special attention from the Release 4.0 software developers—hazardous goods management for chemical companies and flow processing support for the automotive industry.

Users of the Sales and Distribution application can expect to be able to implement additional functions if they update to SAP R/3 Release 4.0. Here are some examples of those functions:

- **Rebates in kind.** Manages those occasions when additional "on-top" goods are delivered free of charge or when part of the quantity sold is omitted from the invoice.

- **Automated Export System (AES).** A central medium for holding the foreign trade data needed by the different authorities and sending it electronically to customs authorities in the United States. A corresponding Automated Import System is under development in the form of a variety of independent modules that can be controlled over the Internet.

- **Documentary credits.** Used to control foreign trade transactions, because they are handed over only against proof of payment or acceptance. Letters of credit are managed as a form of payment.

- **Cancel goods issue for deliveries.** Allows you to release stock in transit by reversing the goods issue if, for example, a mistake has been made in the delivery.

- **Delivery interface.** Rationalizes the movement of EDI and ALE messages, such as shipping notifications between internal and external departments.

- **Down payments in customer orders.** These are to be incorporated as part of the customer agreement and stored in the sales order.

- **Value contracts.** Outline agreements in which materials will be released during a specified time period up to a certain total value.

- **MAIS-Material Information System.** Being used as a replacement for rolling *just-in-time* (JIT) delivery schedules. The quantities and dates are fixed in an MAIS pickup sheet.

- **Freight charge processing.** An enhancement of the Release 3.1 Transportation Planning and Optimizing functions for inbound and outbound shipments.

- **Payment card processing.** In SD, extends the range of acceptable payment cards and increases the number of partners in the payment card process. Card data is included in the sales order and carried through to Financial Accounting. Procurement card processing is included in this function.

- **Material service numbers as reference objects in service management.** Allows you to refer to serial numbers in services, such as preventive maintenance contracts.

A major innovation in R/3 Release 4.5 is the *Available-to-Promise* (ATP) Server. This provides the most accurate picture of the materials and resources likely to be available to a prospective customer at the time delivery is required. It's optimized to handle high volumes of orders, and the orders themselves can include line items of high volume. The ATP Server can assimilate reports on situations across the entire logistics supply chain.

The results from the ATP Server can be derived from logical and numerical rules or based on optimized availability checks. Delivery expectations can be published at the moment an order or inquiry is posted, and these expectations can be used to drive the logistics chain. ●

Developing Electronic Commerce

Preparing for New Business Methods

The implementation of local networks based on mainframe computers and dedicated communications has a relatively long history. Client/server configurations allowed distributed computing whereby the user at a workstation or simple terminal could be connected, not only to databases, but also to additional computing power to process the data. In simple terms, the concept entailed accessing a system through a terminal dedicated for this purpose. The extent and complexity of the system is often not apparent to the individual user, and it doesn't need to be in most applications.

However, there are very real limitations on the number of terminals that can be operating at the same time. SAP R/3 and R/2 can dynamically adjust the allocation of computing resources to the workload, and procedures to cope with equipment and communication channel malfunctions is well understood.

Apart from automated banking terminals, the direct conduct of commercial business by individual users is not yet widespread. But the SAP R/3 range of standard business software is anticipating a change.

The next generation of Internet servers will run at many times the speed of the current devices, but there will be much more traffic on the net. Several developments are at the research stage that, if adopted as standards, will facilitate systems that can accommodate literally millions of users online at the same instant.

SAP R/3 Components for Electronic Commerce

The work unit of SAP systems is the *transaction,* just as it is for electronic commerce. The components available for electronic commerce are software units that can operate in a range of operating systems and hardware devices. The concept is to make these units available for use by any system that receives SAP certification. Fundamental to R/3 Release 3.1 and 4.0 is the R/3 Internet Architecture, which allows the system to be scaled up to serve very large numbers of users via the SAP *Internet Transaction Server* (ITS), which runs on Windows NT 4.0.

BAPI and IAC

Business Application Programming Interfaces (BAPIs) are standards that can be used to design ways of controlling how a business application responds to a transaction. In essence, the application receives a message through a BAPI, which sets up the procedures for dealing with the data that also arrives at the BAPI. For example, a BAPI to a Human Resources database server may be configured to recognize a request for a person who has particular qualifications and is also available to carry out a task, such as processing a sales order. The server finds such a person, if possible, and returns the details to the system or person who initiated the request.

An *Internet Application Component* (IAC) is a standard business interface specifically designed to operate with the Internet or with an intranet. It is a characteristic of SAP R/3 IACs that they are isolated from the kernel of the R/3 system. They can be seen as separate components that can be developed and adapted without requiring any change in the main R/3 system.

In particular, the way an IAC reacts is determined when the Internet Web page is designed. Full multimedia facilities can be available, and the very style of the interchange between user and system is to build on the idea that the whole supply chain is responding without delay to the requests and requirements of the user. Goods and information are handled in the style of a production process in which the customer is the source of the prime information.

Facilities Online

The following titles indicate the range of services that have been rapidly elaborated using the SAP R/3 IACs and their supporting BAPIs. Some of them are available as loosely coupled systems using the *Application Link Enabling* (ALE) protocol.

- Product Catalog with facilities to service Interactive Requests
- Employment Opportunities with reporting to users on their Application Status
- KANBAN stock control logic and reporting from the SAP Available-to-Promise server
- Service Notification
- Sales Order Creation with reporting on Sales Order Status
- Measurement and Counter Readings from production plant and laboratory systems
- Quality Notification and Quality Certificates
- Consignment Stocks Status
- Project Data Confirmation
- Collective Release of Purchase Requisitions and Purchase Orders
- Who is Who staff listing and Integrated Inbox
- Internal Activity Allocation and Workflow Status
- Internal Price List, Requirement Request, and Requirement Request Status
- Asset Management

Electronic Commerce and Security

The variety of processes and the very large numbers of users who will have access to a networked electric commerce system inevitably raise questions about the privacy of personal data and the restriction of commercially sensitive information. Malicious damage to databases and other forms of hacking are real threats.

Firewalls are interfaces that allow the transmission of only authorized information and commands that have their sources verified. *Encryption* is the process of transforming a message into coded text so that it looks like gibberish to anyone who accesses it without authorization. A user who has the *key* to this encryption (because he is authorized to read this data) can *decrypt* the data to restore it to its original structure. The complexity of encryption procedures increases as codebreakers acquire the ability to decode private data.

The SAP R/3 BAPIs and IACs can implement the *Secure Electronic Transaction* (SET) standard, which is under continuous development by the Internet Engineering Task Force.

SAP R/3 Year-2000 Compliance

All releases of R/3 are compliant. No migration or upgrade is required for R/3 users. All date fields are 4 bytes, as are all related record layouts, screen layouts, match codes (secondary indexes), and data dictionary definitions.

Certification Tests   Year-2000 certification tests have been conducted on fields, transactions, and reports by hundreds of consultants and developers who entered predefined and arbitrary data to verify software quality. By using the SAP R/3 *Computer-Aided Testing Tool* (CATT), many of these tests were repeated with various system dates in the range of years from several years before to several years after 2000.

Data Interfaces   Third-party data interfaces may present dates in two-digit format, but the SAP system automatically converts a two-digit year into the proper four-digit number, so there is no impact. The input of data simulates data entry from a keyboard, so existing programs that process keyboard data entry correctly interpret and automatically convert two-digit year dates to the proper four-digit number.

Using Electronic Commerce

For a business to best use electronic commerce, it is essential that the workflow through business processes can be adjusted in order to benefit from any change or anticipated change in the market conditions. An installed and configured SAP R/3 implementation must be capable of improvement without disruption.

Continuous Process Improvement Capabilities

The Business Framework Architecture includes two BAPI types. The earlier type is used to access SAP and third-party applications from the R/3 BASIS core.

The most recent type of BAPI resides in the application, where it can process instructions that, in effect, reconfigure the complex of business processes. The BAPI enables customer organizations to apply new process-control logic and to change the presentation logic to correspond. This is achieved without disrupting business but, of course, under the strict discipline of change management. All adjustments are suspended until the release date, when their introduction is recorded in the change management documentation. For example, a production company might adjust its logic from an emphasis on process control to a distribution logic if the production plant becomes part of a different enterprise.

SAP R/3 Release 3.1 Java User Interface

The Java Virtual Machine can be deployed into virtually any presentation device. The SAP R/3 Java User Interface then can be transmitted to any of these devices, which then can be allowed access to R/3. In particular, this process can take advantage of low-cost devices, such as the Network Computer and the NetPC, which hold very little functionality locally because they are continuously in touch with the parent system over an intranet or the Internet.

The essential feature of the SAP Java BAPIs is that they use standard business objects and therefore provide a way of operating with standardized business content and logic without reference to the specific terminal device used for access.

SAP R/3 Unified Modeling Language Repository

The SAP R/3 Reference Model is held in the Business Repository, from which each function and data object can be drawn as needed. To raise the standards of business programming, cooperative work is in progress to define a *Unified Modeling Language* (UML), which uses high-level modeling to organize and refine the components, which then can take part in specific workflow sequences.

Business processes defined to the UML standard can be transferred to any UML-compliant repository. The Microsoft Repository has been populated from SAP R/3, so the programmers and tool developers who use Visual Basic can call on the SAP standard business processes to use them in their own environments.

SAPoffice

Although the SAPoffice electronic mail system has been available from SAP R/3 Release 3.0, it illustrates how a standard SAP system can be related to a variety of third-party systems. R/3 applications use SAPoffice to automatically generate electronic messages that inform users of critical business process events. Electronic messages from SAPoffice can start application processes and are integrated with SAP Business Workflow to provide automatic messaging services for workflow processes.

SAPoffice can send and receive electronic mail messages over the Internet by means of a *Simple Mail Transfer Protocol* (SMTP) interface. There is an interface to X.500 directories, and you can send external messages from SAPoffice by using SMTP, facsimile, or X.400 interfaces. SAPoffice can receive, process, and archive incoming faxes. You can upload and download files between SAPoffice and desktop applications such as Microsoft Word, Excel, PowerPoint, Microsoft Project, AmiPro, and WordPerfect.

The Documentum R/3 Interface

Documentum has built on standard *Document Management Systems* (DMS) and ArchiveLink technologies to develop a technology to handle most formats, such as images, word processing documents, spreadsheets, HTML Web pages, archives, and CAD drawings. The capability to access both SAP and non-SAP Documents is included.

The Attractions of Business on the Internet

The development of network software is proceeding rapidly because the mechanisms are available and there are many advantages. The attractions—or at least the potentials—are distributed among consumer-to-business, business-to-business, and within-business applications. The potential advantages follow:

- The Internet is easy to use around the world at any time.

- It provides selective and easy access to relevant information at a pace and complexity under the reader's control.

- It is a low-cost marketing channel with wide market exposure and considerable penetration.

- The same familiar interface can access a variety of services in-depth, if required.

- Inquiries are answered immediately.

- The inquirer can be asked intelligent questions, because previously collected information can be taken into consideration, either automatically or by the operator.

- Moving images with sound can be under the control of the viewer to demonstrate the product and discover which aspects interest her.

- Increased revenue may arise from a low cost of sales.

- The Internet may be the preferred source of information on all matters for some sectors of the market.

- Simple cut-and-paste operations can be used to compile email purchase orders and to request other services.

Electronic Commerce Partner Applications

SAP has always used development partners to accelerate the introduction of products that meet SAP certification standards. Some of the more recent partner applications illustrate the widening range of business applications as the potential market is opened by the introduction of reliable network standards.

R/3 PP-CBP Constraint-Based Planner

If two systems are linked by reciprocal messaging interfaces, there is the potential for conflict and circular processes in which the demand for action is passed back and forth. The R/3 PP-CBP Constraint-Based Planner carries out planning and scheduling material requirements and capacity requirements in real time. The application includes a real-time Due Date Quoting capability as an option within the ATP (Available-to-Promise) server.

Intelligent planning and scheduling for global supply chain management across both interenterprise and intraenterprise supply chains are embedded in SAP R/3 Release 4.0 to give fast warning of impending constraints in their supply chain plan. These potential trouble spots can be published to the relevant part of the company or network of business partners. The intelligent planner automatically suggests ways of removing the constraints.

Networked Workflow

Standard Web browsers, Microsoft Exchange, Lotus Notes, and custom applications can use R/3 Workflow Wizards to automate workflow design and thus control the workflow via a network. Workflow status reports are available in HTML format. The *Workflow Management Coalition* (WfMC) is an integrated implementation that includes the 52 published Workflow Application Programming Interfaces and the following components:

- Session Manager
- Distribution Architect
- Reference Model
- CATTesting
- Organization Architect
- IMG-Implementation Management Guide

Workflow Templates

Workflow templates can be executed and may serve as a guide for a company's own development. The individual steps of workflow templates are predefined as standard tasks. They contain a task description, linkage to the application logic through business objects, and prepared linkage to the company organization structure.

The *Business Object Repository* (BOR) delivered in R/3 includes predefined key fields, attributes, and methods. The events associated with the business objects' workflow definitions made from standard tasks can easily be combined and changed at any time with the graphical editor.

The IDES-International Demonstration and Education System

Workflow templates have been integrated into the IDES-International Demonstration and Education System. This can "play through" the operational sequences of a sample company. The preconfigured workflow scenarios can be executed and analyzed for learning and planning purposes.

Open Finance

The essence of Open FI is the notion of a network of information sources and business processes that can be called on in real time to generate the relevant data for each decision in the commercial and financial processes. With global business being conducted between complex enterprises, it is not a simple matter to determine creditworthiness, for example. You might have to use the full computing resources of SAP R/3.

SAP R/3 Components for Open FI

Each phase of a business process can have support activities that can be managed to add value to the sequence by applying information to control the process. The SAP components are designed to do this. The following sales sequence illustrates the way the components can be configured:

- Quotation, Marketing Services
- Customer Credit Control, Real Time Scoring
- Order, Monitor Export Credit Insurance
- Invoice, Factoring, Asset-Backed Securities
- Dunning Notice, Export Credit Insurance Premium Notification, Collection
- Payment, Payment History
- Asset-Backed Securities

An example of the way SAP R/3 FI is used as a core application is in the enhanced FI-AR Accounts Receivable component available to manage *asset-backed securities* (ABSs). Expected cash flows from orders and revenues are at the heart of short- and medium-term budgetary planning. You can provide currency exposure cover, in the form of a microhedging transaction, by allocating forward exchange dealings to the order or billing document from which the cash flows originate. The Internet and intranets will change the way you deal with receivables.

Business Partner Networking

Dun and Bradstreet's D&B Access program is an example of how the network can be used to improve profitability by enabling early-warning information to drive an efficient system of managing receivables. Its task is to monitor business partners discreetly but continuously. The important information concerns corporate customers, as well as business transactions carried out with them and their affiliated companies.

The source of this information is an integrated online network of external information suppliers, such as credit reporting agencies and credit sales insurance firms. The D&B database carries up-to-date information on more than 17 million companies. The information is available in 26 data elements that can be culled selectively from the database.

The Dun and Bradstreet data elements follow:

- Identification, D-U-N-S Number, Balance sheet filing date
- Rating (Risk grading), D&B Rating, Recommended credit limit, Loan recommendation
- Payment history, D&B payment index, Mean payment history
- Size, Capital shares issued, Shareholders' equity
- Revenues, Employees
- Financial analyses (Financial position at a glance)
- Quick Ratio, Current Ratio
- Working Capital, Profit/Loss
- Business activity, SIC 1 (Industry branch), SIC 2, Fields of activity
- Year founded, Ownership structure
- Parent company name, Parent company D-U-N-S number

■ Holding company name, Holding company D-U-N-S number

■ Negative information, Negative data indicator

Using *Internet Application Components* (IACs)

R/3 Internet Application Components link an R/3 implementation with the Internet. The IACs available now are being supplemented by additional software components as new developments in communications and presentation technology are released for general use.

Three IACs are discussed to illustrate the concepts:

■ Sales Order Creation

■ Sales Order Status

■ Available to Promise

These IACs are now in use in the Sales and Distribution business area of many companies. The IACs can be used by your staff and your business partners. They work equally well on the Internet or on a company intranet.

An IAC connects SAP R/3 to a Web browser, which becomes the user interface to the SAP R/3 system. IACs are handled by a standard software program known as the *Internet Transaction Server* (ITS).

A Web browser is a user interface that can interpret and respond to dialog boxes written in the *Hypertext Markup Language* (HTML). This is a standard language for creating document pages that can be processed on the Web. The language syntax is based on a set of tags or markers, usually arranged in matching pairs like opening and closing brackets. These tags can be recognized as commands to display the intervening text in a particular format. Tags have been defined to carry out almost all operations necessary for a user to receive messages from a host computer system and respond to the host as appropriate. As new media are brought into the scope of HTML, extra tags have to be defined that most computers can recognize through their Web browsers so that they can take the appropriate action. For example, there are HTML tags to change the format and color of the text included within the matched tags. If your computer does not have a color display, you still can read the text in the default color of your display.

The *Hypertext Transfer Protocol* (HTTP) defines how files are passed across systems if they are written in HTML. HTTP allows Web communication, with very little restriction on the type of hardware devices that can take part. However, the HTTP protocol is limited in its scope and can be inefficient.

HTML functions are provided within SAP Internet technology, which is distributed as the CA-ALW Cross Application module. The SAP R/3 *Internet Transaction Server* (ITS) is a program that improves the effectiveness of the connections between R/3 and the Internet. The software is available as of R/3 Release 3.1G and runs under Windows NT 4.0 (server version).

Although the HTML protocol is conceptually simple and easy to generate on any word processing system, it demands strict adherence to the language conventions. For example, the tag to begin a message has to be matched with exactly one tag that signals the end of the message. A complicated display, such as an input form, can be difficult to proofread and troubleshoot if an error has been introduced. SAP has developed IACs for important business applications to provide a stock of standard HTML files that can be used either directly or as a templates that you can edit to suit your particular requirements.

N O T E   The HTML syntax has become useful for creating help documentation, because it allows readers to jump from a highlighted item in a document to another page in the same document or in another document, perhaps on another computer if a suitable network connection has been established. *Internet* is the term used to include all kinds of systems that can be accessed by an HTML link, including other files in your own computer. *Intranet* is used when the network referred to is limited to a specified set of users such as your company and its business partners. The Web is, by definition, excluded from the scope of an intranet.

The number of users on the Internet is doubling each year. One service these users call on is the World Wide Web (or just the Web), which was first developed as a mechanism for exchanging texts and performing controlled searches to locate textual strings within them. Typically, a company offers a catalog that potential customers can search for information of interest. There will be a few HTML links to promote efficient navigation through the catalog and a `mailto` link through which customers can place orders or email queries.

SAP R/3 IACs increase the variety of modes of interaction available to Internet contacts of all kinds. Now the advantages recognized by customers who have used the Internet follow:

- The Internet provides low communications costs to many possible suppliers.
- Easy procedures are offered using a Web browser that may well be the standard desktop presentation for the user's operating system.
- The Internet offers continuous availability worldwide.
- Outgoing and incoming messages can be dealt with when convenient, in contrast to phone calls, which are difficult to stack.

As a provider of goods and services, you probably recognize the following additional advantages of Internet business:

- Many business stages can be conducted at a low cost over the Internet.
- Business processes can overlap and be integrated when the buyer sends product data directly to the warehouse, which is readily interrogated to determine the availability of stock.
- The customer can enter order and delivery data directly to accelerate the purchasing processes and reduce costs.

One benefit recognized by all Web browser users is the rapid acquisition of skill by the users, because they are manipulating the same browser for all their transactions. This will probably be the same system they use for personal Internet access. Companies that seriously extend their use of a browser for business transactions and general communications may be able to substantially reduce their staff training costs.

Exploring the Mechanisms of an IAC

SAP R/3 uses two different methods for communicating with the ITS:

- IACs based on Web transactions
- IACs based on the WebRFC gateway interface

Understanding IACs Based on Web Transactions   SAP R/3 Internet Application Components (IACs) based on Web transactions use the DIAG, a dialog exchange interface, to exchange screens and the contents of their fields. You will find that they provide most of the services of the SAP-GUI user interface by using HTML pages and forms.

SAP R/3 standard transactions are conducted by programs written in the ABAP/4 business processing language. The ITS does not accept ABAP/4 commands directly, because it has to comply with the specifications of the BAPI. This requires that screen design and user authorization procedures be consistent across all SAP R/3 BAPIs.

What the ITS does is use a service name, which you can assign, to stand for each IAC you need for your business. When you are using an IAC, the ITS holds copies of the technical information that might be required. For example, the ITS holds information so that the service name you have assigned for the IAC is associated with all the necessary transactions that might be called for on the SAP R/3 applications installed and configured in your implementation. The ITS manages these configuration files along with language resources and templates that you might need in order to build Web pages in the HTML format.

Understanding IACs Based on the WebRFC Gateway Interface   SAP R/3 can call on associated systems to perform tasks by using *remote function calls* (RFCs). In particular, R/3 can be linked to the ITS by the RFC methodology. Any IAC based on the WebRFC can use this linkage to exchange data between the ITS and an R/3 system. When requested by a Web user, the ITS calls a special function module in the R/3 system. From this module, the WebRFC gateway interface, any program can be called and any report can be initiated. The output results then are translated into HTML format and passed to the ITS for transmission to the Internet. Generally, the user has various opportunities to intervene in this process to make manual adjustments if necessary.

Building System Scenarios with IACs

In the course of your business activities, you will seldom want to operate just a single business function on its own. Your work will take place in a specific context, as part of a more or less routine workflow sequence. SAP has recognized these familiar sequences and prepared scenarios of IACs to conduct Web transactions between customers and your business, and between one business partner and another. Table 21.1 suggests how these scenarios of IACs are grouped and identified.

Table 21.1   IACs for Developing Business Scenarios

Logistics, General

Product Catalog

Sales and Distribution

Sales Order Creation

Sales Order Status

Available to Promise

Financial Accounting

Customer Account Information

Asset Information

Controlling

Internal Activity Allocation

Internal Price List

Project System

Project Data Confirmation

Human Resources Management

Employment Opportunities

Application Status

Who Is Who

Calendar of Events

Booked Events (R/3 Users)

Booked Events (Web Users)

Materials Management

Vendor-Managed Inventory,* as of Release 4.5

Consignment Stocks Status

Quality Management

Quality Certificates

Quality Notifications

Plant Maintenance and Service Management

Service Notifications

Measurement and Counter Readings

Production Planning and Control

KANBAN

Intranet

Materials Management

Requirement Requests

Requirement Request Status

Collective Release of Purchase Requisitions

Collective Release of Purchase Orders

BASIS

Integrated Inbox

*Vendor-Managed Inventory uses reports of sales and stocks from retail outlets to forecast sales and replenish stock in anticipation.

Developing an IAC

A Web transaction is usually defined from an executable R/3 transaction by adjusting a copy to make it compatible with the ITS. The Web Studio support tool is designed to facilitate this process.

 N O T E   Web Studio runs outside the R/3 system under Windows NT 4.0 and is included in the standard version of the ITS. ▨

For each Web transaction, a service description must exist in the file system of the computer on which the ITS is running. The service description is a file that contains all the information the ITS needs to call the R/3 transaction. These files can be created with Web Studio and later edited by a standard text editor.

If an Internet transaction uses only the language-specific graphics, filenames, or texts that are supplied directly from the R/3 system, no separate language resources need to be created. However, if you want to refer to graphics or texts that are specific to your particular implementation, you have to identify the language resource files. An HTML template should contain placeholders that can be associated at runtime with the language resources of the logon language. The ITS consults these language resources to locate suitable entries for the placeholders.

Each screen of an R/3 transaction needs a corresponding HTML template that uses business instructions to identify the fields onscreen. These templates can be created from a screen description using Web Studio, which automatically generates the corresponding placeholders and control instructions. The HTML pages usually require manual editing after changes are made. Some screen techniques such as the use of frames cannot be applied automatically by Web Studio.

Web Studio has the following functionality:

- Generates HTML templates that include a remote call of an R/3 function
- Generates service descriptions
- Edits all external text-based objects
- Communicates with the R/3 correction and transport system
- Communicates with the CheckIn/CheckOut functionality for Web objects

An important service provided by Web Studio is support of activities executed outside the R/3 system. For example, Web Studio places all files in the directory structure required by the ITS and makes sure that all objects are stored in the R/3 system. Any file required by an IAC based on Web transactions can be edited in Web Studio. Service descriptions can be generated by Web Studio under the control of dialog boxes and do not require manual editing.

The Debugger is an ITS operating mode for testing an IAC. You also can call for status information by specifying special parameters in the *universal resource locator* (URL) that calls the IAC.

Understanding How the ITS Works

You cannot access the R/3 system directly from a Web browser or via an HTML server because the two systems use different protocols and data formats. The ITS acts as an interface. When an SAP user sends a request to the HTML server, it prompts the ITS program to set up a connection to an R/3 system.

The user then can use the SAP system screen to send information to the ITS and the R/3 system to which it is connected. The R/3 system does not have to know that the user is working on a terminal through the ITS. It converts the screen data supplied by the SAP system into an HTML document. The HTML document is passed via the HTML server to the Web browser where it is displayed. In the opposite direction, field contents in HTML forms can be converted to screen data. The user's browser acts as a standard SAP GUI.

In practice, the ITS is an extremely complex application. Various components are resident, whereas others are loaded only when required. The ITS manages the various Web users, their different Internet transactions, and the system resources they need.

Understanding R/3 Development Objects for the Internet

Data exchange to and from the Internet is carried out by using SAP R/3 transactions and function modules. Various software development objects are needed to create and transmit service messages. They normally are configured during customizing. For example, the material availability service provided over the Internet is defined as the following:

- Development class: MDW1
- Transaction: CKAV
- Function group for the screens: W61V
- Function modules: BAPI_MATERIAL_AVAILABILITY

The ITS controls data output by inserting data in the appropriate fields of specified output forms that are presented to the Internet or to your company's intranet in the HTML format so that they can be read by the various browsers that serve the users.

The ITS is linked in two directions: to the HTTP server and to the R/3 system. Special certification services, such as Kerberos or SecuDe, are under development to provide extra security for the links between the ITS and your R/3 system. SAP recommends that the HTTP-S protocol be used between the Web browser and the HTTP server. This protocol is based on Secure Socket Layer 3.0, an enhancement of the HTTP protocol.

Exploring Internet Scenarios for Sales and Distribution

SAP has preconfigured a set of IACs to support the main business scenarios being managed over the Internet in addition to the normal operating systems. The next few sections indicate how these IACs fit into a business background and illustrate how they are operated in the Sales and Distribution context.

Using the SD-SLS-SO Sales Order Creation IAC

This consumer-to-business IAC is responsible for receiving orders from customers through the Internet and forwarding them as sales orders to an R/3 system. The most attractive situation is where a catalog is available or where the customers know exactly what they want and are primarily interested in a price comparison and a quick delivery offer.

The following customer benefits are offered:

- Customers can submit orders around the clock.
- Your customers can enter their orders directly by using your screen layout on your Web server without using the telephone or fax.
- Your response can be quick, with up-to-date price data and delivery times.
- Your customers can trace the progress of their orders at any time.

The advantages to the supplier business are based on the speed of the transactions:

- You can design the screen layout to help your customer enter data quickly and easily.
- You receive the sales order very soon after it is entered and therefore can deliver it that much sooner.
- You can prepare for the peak times for sales order entry and therefore improve performance.

The SD-SLS-SO Sales Order Creation IAC normally operates in the following sequence:

1. You offer your customers a product catalog from which they choose. They assign their selection to a "shopping basket."

2. If they ask for a quotation for the article in the shopping basket, they are given a customer-specific price and delivery date.

3. If they accept the quotation, a sales order is created automatically in your R/3 system, where it can be processed without delay.

4. The customer gets the order number, which can be used to inquire about the status of the order.

5. Your company now has a choice of either placing the Internet orders on a work list waiting to be checked, or immediately generating a work list from the orders outstanding.

You have to arrange authorizations and security before a customer can enter a sales order over the Internet. You have to assign each customer an SAP customer number and an initial password. Customers then should replace the initial password with their own. The system asks for the SAP number and password when the customer first assigns an article from the catalog to her shopping basket.

Using the SD-SLS-GF Sales Order Status IAC

If a customer wants to find out what has happened to his purchase orders, he can access your Sales Order Status IAC from the Internet. He can determine whether shipping is in progress for each purchase order and whether the goods are already on their way.

The Sales Order Status IAC operates in this way:

1. You give your customer the option to view the status of his purchase orders that exist in your SAP system.

2. The customer will have used an SAP customer number and password when logging on. The existing sales orders for this customer number can be selected and displayed.

Filtering can take place like this:

- Order data from
- Order data to
- Order number
- Purchase order number
- Material number

Your system then transmits to the customer a list of one or more sales orders containing the following information:

- Quantity of a material that has already been assigned to deliveries because the shipping department has started picking the goods and preparing for transportation
- Quantity of a material that is already on the way to a customer

N O T E Additional information on the shipment may be available over the Internet by clicking a hyperlink that connects to the transportation agent.

Using the SD-BF-AC Available-to-Promise IAC

The Available-to-Promise IAC allows an authorized person to check the availability of the necessary resources before making critical decisions or commitments. If your company focuses primarily on customers, you need unrestricted access to reliable information on the availability of resources at all times. Your salespeople need to be able to quote reliable delivery dates.

The standard R/3 system availability check provides a service to many logistics operations at all organizational levels. You can call for information at plant level, storage location level, and batch level.

The Available-to-Promise IAC screen shows the results of the material availability check as an overview.

Customer-oriented companies in the high-tech and consumer goods industries are likely to be interested in this IAC, particularly in Production Planning and in Sales and Distribution. Their customers may be invited to use the Available-to-Promise IAC for the following reasons:

- Available-to-Promise is available to users all over the world around the clock.
- The application is simple and easy to use, because customers can identify the product lines in the display to specify the products they are interested in.
- The Internet availability check doesn't need to entail communicating with the Sales department if a customer master record has been created for the material of interest.
- Vendors can use the IAC to find out which products and how many are still available. They can therefore anticipate deliveries.

After logging on to select material, you receive a graphical overview of the range of products. As a salesperson, MRP controller, or customer, you can check to see whether sufficient quantities of a product are available on the required date directly through the Internet. You can select the item of interest in any of the following ways:

- Navigating in the product tree
- Using the text search function
- Directly entering the material number
- Directly entering the material short description

You have to enter the desired delivery date and the quantity you require. The system then ascertains the quantity of the particular material that will be available to meet the delivery date you specified. The system checks to see how much of this material is already promised to meet the requirements already confirmed. Your display shows the available-to-promise quantity for each material at the material provision date, separately for each plant that can supply it. The provision date takes no account of any additional delays caused by delivery scheduling.

You can opt to have the end of the replenishment lead time reported for any material that is not available in the required quantity for the required date.

The browser you use to access the Available-to-Promise IAC must be Java-enabled and set so that Java programs can run. Netscape Navigator from Version 3.0 and Microsoft Internet Explorer from Version 3.0 are suitable. ●

CHAPTER 22

Understanding the Human Resources Module

In this chapter

Integrating HR Management

The SAP R/3 HR-Human Resources application brings together an extensive family of components that is fully integrated with the SAP R/3 system. These components are divided between two personnel modules:

- PA-Personnel Administration
- PD-Personnel Planning and Development

Most of the components of the HR-Human Resources application can be progressively implemented as required. Some of them can be configured as standalone systems, perhaps in a transitional stage in the progress toward a fully integrated SAP installation.

The constituent modules of the HR-Human Resources application are designed to serve two themes—one financial, one concerned with the skill of the workers:

- PA-Personnel Administration has an emphasis on payroll and associated procedures.
- PD-Personnel Planning and Development seeks to add value to the personnel resource by career management, beginning at first recruitment and with continuity across extended absences.

The HR-Human Resources system can stand alone or be fully integrated with the following SAP applications:

- FI-AM Asset Management, to reference the fixed-asset master records—for example, the asset of a specific company car
- FI-Financial Accounting—for example, to relate to payroll accounting and posting
- CO-Controlling and CO-OM Overhead Cost Control—for example, to analyze wages and salary costs
- PM-Plant Maintenance—for example, to transfer completion confirmations to the plants concerned and subsequently release the employees for other work
- PP-Production Planning and Control—for example, to transfer completion confirmations to the production departments and to assign employees to other activities

The comprehensive system of access protection is applied to all interactions of the HR-Human Resources application with any other SAP or non-SAP application.

Introducing the HR-Human Resources Application

The functions of the HR-Human Resources application are allocated to the constituent modules—PA-Personnel Administration and PD-Personnel Planning and Development (see Table 22.1). All the functions are fully integrated with each other and with the rest of the R/3 system.

Table 22.1 HR-Human Resources Components

HR-PA Personnel Administration	HR-PD Personnel Planning and Development
PA-EMP Employee Management	PD-OM Organizational Management
PA-BEN Benefits Administration	PD-SCM Seminar and Convention Management
PA-COM Compensation Administration	PD-PD Personnel Development
PA-APP Applicant Management	PD-WFP Workforce Planning
PA-TIM Time Management	PD-RPL Room Reservations Planning
PA-INW Incentive Wages	
PA-TRV Travel Expenses	
PA-PAY Payroll	

Understanding the Fundamentals of the HR-Human Resources Application

Certain concepts and procedures are part of the SAP R/3 system and available for all applications integrated with it. However, nine operational concepts have been particularly developed and exploited to good effect by many users of the HR-Human Resources application:

- Real-time operation of personnel functions
- The use of business areas to define the parts of the HR-Human Resources application and direct the user to the functions required
- Infotypes to manage and control access to sensitive areas of personnel data
- Personnel events, which are occasions when several infotypes are presented on the same screen, information is entered, and the system is called on to update the relevant infotypes automatically
- Dynamic events, which are initiated by the system when the user starts to enter the information that indicates what he wants to achieve
- Fast entry screens that allow you to deal with many individual personnel records and transactions at once
- Automatic date monitoring, which is continuous for all dates of significance to the personnel functions
- *Interactive Voice Response* (IVR), which can be used in personnel departments to deal with the typically large volume of routine inquiries
- Automatic sifting of résumé submissions in preparation for a recruiting or job reassignment interview

Real-Time Personnel Administration   The SAP R/3 HR-Human Resources application is designed to run in real time and to use the database in real time. This method has many important advantages; here are just a few:

- Although all processing can be performed online under the control of dialogs, it is also possible to set up batch processing, which is the normal procedure for writing to storage media and for reorganizing the database.

- If you have installed and configured the CO-CCA Cost Center Accounting component, checks can be made against the cost center master data when an employee is assigned to a cost center. If this installation has not been carried out, the HR-Human Resources application checks with its own table of records.

- When fresh data is entered, the system checks it for validity without delay, and there is less risk of making errors.

- Valid data is stored directly, with a time and date stamp, on a uniform database that is available immediately to all authorized users and is automatically subject to change control management that will cause all modifications to be logged.

Business Areas   The particular aspect of human resources management that is being addressed by a specific program is known as a *business area*. The following are examples of HR business areas that are serviced by the PA-Personnel Administration suite of standard business software:

- HR master data maintenance
- Payroll
- Time management
- Applicant administration
- Travel expenses

The following are examples of HR business operations that are serviced by the PD-Personnel Planning and Development suite of standard business software:

- Organization and planning
- Workplace and job description
- Qualifications and requirements
- Career planning
- Succession planning
- Personnel costs planning
- Seminar and convention management
- Workforce planning
- Shift planning

HR Infotypes   Personnel data is stored in information groups, each of which can be controlled for scope and access authorization. These information groups are referred to as *infotypes*. Not every personnel record must be assigned every infotype. The particular use of infotypes in your implementation will be specified during customizing.

The SAP R/3 HR-Human Resources application provides more than 100 standard infotypes. The following are examples of standard HR infotypes:

- Organizational assignment—for example, position, organizational unit, job
- Personnel data—for example, current name, name at birth
- Payroll status—for example, last payroll, date for recalculation
- Disability—categories used in this infotype can be subject to specific national regulation
- Leave entitlement—for example, negotiated leave, disability leave, additional leave
- Leave compensation
- Address—for example, permanent residence, temporary residence, home address
- Work schedule—for example, shift, time recording, work hours
- Contract elements—for example, hourly paid terms, fixed-price terms, chargeable expenses
- Base pay—for example, change in classification, pay scale increase, change in pay
- Garnishment of wages—for example, child support or alimony, garnishment of property, cession of wages
- Bank connection—for example, main bank connection, additional bank connection
- External transfer
- Recurring benefits and deductions—for example, commuter's allowance, rent withheld, company housing
- Additional payments—for example, Christmas bonus, service anniversary

Personnel Events   The infotypes used to manage personnel data in the HR-Human Resources system can be combined to form data-entry screens. Within the scope of your authorization, you can display any infotypes together. When the screen data is entered, the system automatically updates all the relevant infotypes. This sequence is referred to as a *personnel event*.

Dynamic Events   After you respond to a personnel event by entering some data, the system evaluates that data and responds accordingly to generate a dynamic event. If you take on a new employee, for example, the system creates a new personnel master record. At the same time, it calculates the end date of the probationary period and creates an appointment record. This dynamic event, in turn, generates another personnel event, because you will have to confirm that you accept the proposed appointment for someone to interview the new employee at the end of the probationary period.

A standard consequence of a personnel event is the generation by the system of a series of electronic mail messages informing all those who should be told what changes have been made as a result of the personnel event.

Fast Entry Screens   If you need to deal with several employees in the same way—the staff of a particular cost center, for example—the system selects the employees for you and displays their relevant records on your screen, where you can make individual or group adjustments before you commit the screen for processing.

If you are unfamiliar with any field on any screen, you can point to it and call for online help. This first displays the name of the field and then, if you require it, a longer explanation of how you can use it.

Automatic Date Monitoring   It is characteristic of personnel departments that many events recur on a calendar basis—for example, renewal of work permits and scheduled performance appraisals. The HR-Human Resources system monitors all such dates and lets everybody concerned know the details. And if necessary, the system updates their appointment books automatically.

Interactive Voice Response in Personnel Departments   For the staff of personnel departments, a large amount of time is taken up by answering routine inquiries from employees, such as "How many days can I have for my vacation this year?"

SAP has set up a system of digitized recordings of all the phrases commonly used in answering personnel queries. These phrases guide the caller through an automated telephone response system with a recorded message.

Employee Self Service (ESS) is a system that lets employees view and change personal information via the Internet or intranet.

Resumix   The Resumix System of Resumix Inc. is integrated with the SAP HR-Human Resources application to provide a completely automatic method of handling résumés. Applicants for an advertised position, or people who might be suitable for a job that is expected to become vacant, can be identified through the HR-Human Resources application.

If the job specification has been written using a standard vocabulary of terms that accurately express the attributes needed for the position, and if the applicants have drafted their résumés using the same vocabulary, a rank ordering of the applicants can be generated on the basis of a comparison between the job specification and the résumés. A more precise matching is possible if an application form is used.

If the suitability of an existing employee is being considered, facilities are available for building up a profile of qualifications on the basis of existing data in the HR-Human Resources application. This includes job history, assessment reports, and textual material written by the employee and the management.

Administering Benefits

The SAP R/3 system of benefits and salary administration is supported by the following components from the PA-Personnel Administration module of the HR-Human Resources system:

- PA-EMP Employee Management
- PA-BEN Benefits Administration
- PA-COM Compensation Administration

The system is driven by a series of tables that you can alter to provide for whatever system of benefits and salary your company uses.

Enrolling for Benefits and Insurance Coverage

A standard screen is provided to manage the enrollment of each employee individually. The PA-BEN Benefits Administration component recognizes the following types of benefits and insurance coverage:

- Welfare, including medical, dental, vision, and so on
- Spending and dependent care accounts
- Insurance, including life, AD&D, and dependent life
- Defined benefits and pensions
- Defined contributions, 401(k), RRSP, ESOP, and so on

Insurance coverages are specified by a system of tables that allows you to set out the method of calculation of premiums and benefits, and also how the associated costs are to be settled. There are facilities for employees to purchase additional coverage.

A flexible system is provided to enable you to particularize deferred compensation plans as part of a benefits package. The following details can be specified in this process:

- Eligibility requirements
- Contribution levels by employee
- Contribution levels by employer
- Vesting schedules
- Investment options
- Stock purchases and options

Administering Salaries

The aim of salary administration is to relate the salary structure of the organization to the goals of providing rewards for good performance identified during the review process and removing any imbalances from the current salary structure.

Facilities are provided by the PA-COM Compensation Administration functions to achieve the following results:

- Apply standard pay changes across organizational units.
- Override the standard pay change for any individual as an exception.
- Analyze the impact of any proposed salary changes on the organizational units and subunits.
- Automatically assign future salary records and calculations to the changed structure.

One method used to assign salary changes to employees is to use matrices to compare performance appraisal information and current salaries across employees in similar jobs.

Using National Supplements to the International HR-Human Resources System

The variations in the tax and benefit systems of different nations are accommodated in the SAP R/3 HR-Human Resources system by appending the appropriate national supplements during customizing.

Each special national supplement has the effect of adding to the suite of HR infotypes, which can be referenced when configuring the PA-BEN Benefits Administration module.

The following special national supplements are being complemented by new supplements under development.

Establishing Benefits for Austria

- Tax—for example, previous year, current year, subsequent year
- Commuter lump sums
- Social insurance
- Family allowance
- Sick certificates—for example, main person insured, insured spouse, insured child
- Previous employer

Establishing Benefits for Belgium

- Social Insurance—for example, category, registration of substitute employee, pension number, Social Insurance number
- Tax—for example, spouse, children, other persons in the same household, tax rule indicator
- Personal data—for example, Personal Registration number, Royal Service number, Pension Insurance number, Work Permit number, Social Security number
- Work schedule—for example, RSZ category, RSZ code, RSZ number, work regimen, work rhythm, work regulation, employee type (part-time/full-time), country indicator, work interruption, pay period
- Contract elements—for example, "Paritair Kommitee," Compensation Fund number, meal coupons, CAO/pension data

Establishing Benefits for Canada

- Residence status—for example, citizen/alien, passport data, work permit
- Additional personal data—for example, ethnic origin, military status
- Benefits—for example, employee welfare plans, medical, dental, vision, legal
- Insurance—for example, life, AD&D, dependent
- Deferred compensation and savings plans—for example, ESOP, RRSP, RRP, pension

- Tax—for example, federal, provincial
- Bond purchases—for example, denomination, recipient
- Injury and illness—for example, extended accident or illness tracking, accident data
- Workers' compensation—for example, entitlement, contribution, record-keeping, reporting
- Union—for example, job title, seniority
- Grievance tracking—for example, status, disciplinary action

Establishing Benefits for Denmark

- Tax
- Private pension
- Vacation or statutory holidays—for example, previous year, current year, subsequent year
- ATP pension

Establishing Benefits for France

- Social Insurance—for example, Social Insurance number, fund model
- Capital formation—for example, profit-sharing
- Leave processing
- Maternity protection

Establishing Benefits for Germany

- Tax—for example, previous year, current year, subsequent year
- Social Insurance—for example, obligatory, voluntary, Retirees' Health Insurance
- SI Supplementary Insurance
- Capital formation—for example, Saving Through B&L Association, Saving by Installments, life insurance
- DÜVO—for example, registration, interruption
- RWH/BWP
- BAT benefits
- Company pension plans
- Wage maintenance
- Direct insurance
- Previous employer—for example, tax, Social Insurance

Establishing Benefits for the United Kingdom

■ Income tax

■ National Insurance—employee and employer contributions, arrears

■ Court orders, payments, protected earnings, administration fees

■ Pensions

■ Statutory sick pay

■ Statutory maternity pay

Establishing Benefits for Netherlands

The following functions are handled by the standard HR functions:

■ Maternity protection cutoff dates

■ Options for capital formation

■ Travel expenses for trips between home and business

The special National Features extension offers the following extensions to the general functions included in the International HR-Human Resources system:

■ Employee taxes—for example, tax class, Sofi number, tax code indicator, deduction items, OT annual salary

■ Social Insurance—for example, person-related data such as the codes WW, ZW, WAO, ABP, VUT, BPF

■ Health Insurance funds—for example, private HI funds, compulsory HI funds

■ Social funds—for example, application types, decisions, appeals, payment options

■ Additional absence data—for example, data for tracking illnesses, dates for multiple treatment appointments, dates for work restrictions

■ Accident data—for example, accident status, accident class, type of injury

Establishing Benefits for Spain

■ Tax—for example, recipient key, annual gross

■ Social Insurance—for example, Social Insurance number, multiple work percentage

■ Various payees—for example, payee key, gross amount

■ Union—for example, union function, contribution

■ Seniority

Establishing Benefits for Switzerland

■ Tax—for example, canton, municipality, tax liability

■ Social Insurance—for example, AHV number, FAK, ALV

■ Pension fund—for example, fund, insurance type, premium

- Residence status—for example, status, expiry date
- Family—for example, Child Allowance

Establishing Benefits for the United States

- Residence status—for example, citizen/alien, passport data, work permit
- Additional personal data—for example, ethnic origin, military status
- Benefits—for example, medical, dental, vision, legal
- Insurance—for example, life insurance, AD&D, dependent insurance
- Savings plans and deferred compensation—for example, pension, 401(k), ESOP
- Tax—for example, federal, state, local
- Bond purchases—for example, denomination, recipient
- Injury and illness—for example, illness tracking, accident data, OSHA, workers compensation data
- Workers' compensation—for example, entitlement, contribution
- Union—for example, job title, seniority
- Grievances—for example, status, disciplinary action, grievance tracking
- US I-9 compliance

Managing Time with the PA-TIM Component

The purpose of the PA-TIM Time Management component of the Personnel Administration module is to provide the standard software for recording, assigning values, and evaluating all employee data relevant to time management.

Since the topic is often associated with time management, the PA-INW Incentive Wages component is also relevant.

The instrumentation and hardware of time measurement and recording is under continuous development, and SAP can update the standard interface modules to provide a comprehensive interface support system.

Understanding the Concepts Underpinning Time Management

To take advantage of the benefits of an integrated business system, it is necessary to translate many of the concepts and working practices of business into precise yet flexible operational definitions that can, in turn, be represented in a computer program.

Plant Calendar   The calendar that shows the possible working days of a particular plant is the *plant calendar.* This calendar must show the days of the working week, along with the days observed as general and regional holidays.

Day Program   The way in which one day is treated from the point of view of measuring the time at work is referred to as the *day program*. A series or pattern of day programs can repeat itself over the course of a plant calendar, taking into account only the working days in that calendar.

Time Model   The pattern of day programs that repeats in a plant calendar is called a *time model*. You can define as many different time models as you require, and they can have any duration you want.

Shift Scheduling   If you roll a time model over the plant calendar, you get a *shift schedule*. You can intervene, for example, to allow extra days before and after a planned plant shutdown; but common features, such as reduced working hours before holidays, can be taken into the time model in the form of special day programs that have shorter working hours.

Work Time   If your company works flexible work times or allows *flex time,* you have to specify the components of a working day in terms of a time frame and core times. Tolerance zones in the working day are usually designated to account for the short periods of irrelevant time before work officially begins and after it officially ends. You might want to allow a tolerance zone for people coming late to work.

The system allows you to define as many breaks in the day as you like. You can designate them as paid, unpaid, or paid at a special rate. Breaks can be defined as fixed, variable, or dynamic, in which case the length of the break depends on how much time has been worked or how much work has been completed.

You can allocate part of the day for orientation or "warming up," and you can record whether people are working extra hours to save up for time off later.

Any decisions you make on the rules attached to time measurement have to be given a period of validity, and the system automatically records the time and date of any changes you make to the tables that store this information. If necessary, the system can be called on to deliver a history of the changes that have been made to a set of master data records.

Time-Recording Variants   There are two common variants and several hybrid forms:

- Negative time recording
- Positive time recording

The base assumption of negative time recording is that everyone is at work all the time unless recorded as absent. You can ignore brief absences of a few minutes, and you will have a range of good reasons for deviating from the official work schedule:

- Absence, such as vacation, work incapacity, or stipulated day off
- Special work attendance, such as attending a seminar
- On-call duty
- Overtime
- Work time substitution

The recording methods at your disposal follow:

- Enter data on an individual record.
- Enter data for a group of people on a fast entry screen, such as overtime for the whole work center.
- Enter data using a special recording screen, such as an absence calendar.

Positive time recording entails recording the deviations from the work schedule and the actual times of work. This method is becoming more prevalent as a result of the following factors:

- Flexibility of work time is increasing, using formal and informal methods of time management.
- Flex time using time recording is more widespread.
- Workers more often determine their own work times.

As a consequence, the role of the shift schedule may often be restricted to providing a time frame and serving as the basis for the valuation of absences.

Linking to Recording Equipment

The so-called front-end time recording systems are installed with the purpose of establishing the time facts and collecting the data. These systems should not be treated as the method of evaluating the time data. This is the province of the HR-TIM Time Management system.

The usual method is for the central system to dispatch to the front-end time recording system a record known as a *minimaster data record*. This carries just enough data to accomplish what is required: to collect the time data for a given individual at a specified work center in relation to the time schedule that has been assigned.

Some companies combine time recording with admittance control. Depending on the equipment fitted in the workplace, the people admitted to a particular work center can be defined in terms of their assignment to that work center and perhaps also their authorization to enter locations elsewhere in the plant.

Maintaining Time Data

The standard SAP system of infotypes is used to organize the time data of the HR-Human Resources system. The following infotypes are recognized:

- Absences—for example, vacation, illness, temporary layoff
- Special work attendance—for example, different work center, errand, business trip, seminar
- Overtime—for example, overtime compensated by payment, overtime compensated by time off
- Substitutions—for example, shift substitution, workplace substitution
- On-call duty—for example, on-call duty, standby duty

- Absence quotas—for example, sabbatical, time off
- Attendance approvals—for example, overtime approval
- Actual work times—for example, with additional account assignment, differing payment, premium work time
- Time events—for example, clock-in/clock-out messages, work order confirmations
- Balance corrections—for example, rebooking overtime to flex time, paying out time-off credits

Time data can be managed directly by the PA-TIM Time Management system or through the technique of assigning people to time data agents, which can be cost centers, departments, or some other organizational entity that you have created for this purpose. The time data agent is assigned only some personnel infotypes—just the ones that are needed to manage time locally. In the central system, a second person will be responsible for unlocking time data collected by the time data agent only when the central "personnel clerk" authorizes its release.

Distributing Work Attendance Times to Cost Objects

The attendance times, however entered, can be subsequently distributed to cost objects such as cost centers, orders, or projects. Facilities are provided for you to make manual adjustments to the data before or after distribution to cost objects. If the data has already been posted, only the differences will be transferred.

There is full integration with CO-CCA Cost Center Accounting and PA-PAY Payroll.

Assigning Time Valuation

The PA-TIM Time Management module stores all its control logic in tables that you can adjust to yield a precisely tailored system suited to your requirements.

Each day, for each employee, the attendance or absence time is analyzed in relation to the preset values of the relevant shift schedule. The first result is a series of time pairs that signal when something began and when it finished—work, absence, and so on. Each time pair then is classified. By referring to the rules for overtime and so on, the system can refine the classification until each unit of time is identified by its type, which will be used to choose the wage type and eventually to compute the compensation.

All the logical rules for performing this classification and calculation procedure are stored in the form of tables, to which you can have access if you want to change the way the process is performed or any of the rates or base values.

If a new type of work time or absence category comes into being, you can set up the logic for identifying it and computing the appropriate compensation.

All time management data is stored in the form of time pairs and time types. When these are evaluated, it may be discovered that there has been an error in time recording or the way in which the time types were generated based on the work schedule and plant calendar.

If you decide to make a change in retrospect—a retroactive change—and you have the authority to do so, you can alter the original data; the system then recalculates the time data automatically and hence the consequent compensation due.

For example, you might decide that a new scheme should be backdated. As you redefine the dates for the validity of the scheme, the system recognizes that a recalculation is needed and carries it out automatically.

Using the PA-INW Component for Incentive Wages

It is customary to associate the collection of data for incentive wages with the same organization that manages time data. By integrating the collection of individual incentive wage data with group data, it is possible to achieve the following kinds of results:

- Recording group-relevant incentive wages data
- Determining evaluation factors such as the duration of group membership or the percentage of distribution

Premium rates are calculated by reference to tables to which you have access.

The standard system recognizes the following types of time ticket:

- Premium time tickets in individually computed incentive wages
- Time tickets for work times to be paid on average
- Quantity time tickets for planned times in group incentive wages
- Personnel time tickets for actual times in group incentive wage schemes
- Supervisor time tickets for individual piecework with relevance to a reference workgroup

You can readily add other types of time tickets.

Personnel Planning and Development

The purpose of personnel planning is to determine who will be required and when. The purpose of personnel development is to make sure that the aspirations of the personnel planners can be realized by selecting suitable applicants and giving them the broad educational qualifications and specific training requirements to ensure that sufficient suitable employees are available to do the jobs when they are required.

The functionality of the PD-Personnel Planning and Development module is embodied in the follow standard business program components:

- PD-OM Organizational Management
- PD-WFP Workforce Planning
- PD-PD Personnel Development
- PD-RPL Room Reservations Planning
- PD-SCM Seminar and Convention Management

The SAP standard business software in the Human Resources domain is under continuous development as this aspect of business grows in complexity and becomes ever more critical as the productivity of individual workers is increased by technological improvements in production and communication methods.

Specifying Business Areas

The business areas addressed by the PD-Personnel Planning and Development module include the following:

- Organization and Planning—the basic component
- Workplace and Job Description
- Applicant Data Administration
- Applicant Screening
- Qualifications and Requirements
- Career and Succession Planning
- Workplace and Job Grading
- External Training Administration
- Education and Training Administration
- Education and Training Planning
- Manpower Planning I (Long-Term)
- Manpower Planning II (Short-Term)
- Cost Planning
- Personnel Assessment and Trend Procedures

Developing the Data Model for Human Resources Management

It became apparent during the research and development phases for R/3 that the SAP standard business software approach could be extended to the data-manipulation areas associated with human resources management. The most significant technical development requirement was in the matter of handling more complex data structures concerning, for example, qualifications and job requirements. In particular, it is obviously essential to be able to store information about the positions in a company that its personnel might occupy.

If a person doing a job is to be replaced—by a substitute during the employee's absence, for example—the knowledge and skill needed for that job should be specified so that the replacement can be chosen and prepared by training to do that job with the absolute minimum loss of performance due to the changeover.

You might assume that the replacement person knows nothing and has to be trained in everything. If that person is already working in your company or in a similar job, though, you will be wrong in your assumption. Furthermore, you will be wasting resources and probably squandering the goodwill of the trainee if you make him or her take a full course of training.

It therefore is necessary to specify the starting qualifications and experience of anyone about to undergo training or about to take over a job that he has not done before. This is true for fresh applicants from outside your company as well as internal applicants.

SAP has adopted an extension of its data model approach to cope with this requirement to record the jobs and skills of the staff. The standard system of information types *(infotypes)* is still in operation. More than 100 infotypes have been defined in the SAP R/3 system. The standard models of organizational structure still apply.

But several additional data models have been introduced to cope with the complexities of personnel data. The result is an extensive object-oriented data scheme.

The scheme requires a clear distinction to be recognized between methods of representing structural relationships among planning data objects and other information about them. You can allocate several workplace positions to a cost center, the master records will show this "ownership" as a relation, and your graphical display can draw an arrow to represent it.

The accountants need to know who will pay for work done in a workplace, and they might want to analyze this in relation to a system of cost centers. But this kind of information does not help the Personnel department when it comes to filling positions with people. This is the kind of "other" information that has to be associated with positions and people, and it must be done in a very flexible manner if it is to be of any use.

The standard system of infotypes is used to associate sets of data elements with the attributes of data objects. During customizing, you can define which infotypes are required for each attribute of each type of data object, and how they should be displayed on the user interface screens. Infotypes can be assigned directly to planning objects independently of the object type.

The benefits of this approach stem from the fact that the standard methodology can be used to identify and link objects and to evaluate them. It also means that planning can be installed step by step, because a set of planning objects is no longer defined during system design, but instead during the actual installation and customizing of the system. The set can be extended later.

The method is used to establish extra data models in HR-Human Resources.

Using the Data Model in the PD-OM Organizational Management Component

The following object types are used:

- Organizational unit
- Position
- Workplace
- Job
- Task

Two anchor object types are accessed by the PD-OM Organizational Management component:

- Person as defined in the HR-Human Resources, PA-Personnel Administration module
- Cost center as defined in the CO-CCA Cost Center Accounting component

These anchor object types are not managed in the PD-OM Organizational Management component. Their data can be accessed via relationships that are master records that record the permanent association of a data element of a record in one database with a data element of a record in another database.

A cost center specified in CO-CCA Cost Center Accounting has allocated to it one or more organizational units, which can be all on the same level in a flat structure, or arranged into hierarchies, parts of which may be flat structures.

A person defined in the HR-Human Resources, PA-Personnel Administration system holds or occupies both a position and a workplace. The position is attached to a particular workplace, and the workplace is defined as having room for only one person. For example, a machine operator is a position. A position may be unoccupied, in which case it takes up no space in the workplace. Several positions could occupy a workplace, each held by different people but not at the same time. They would have to be shift workers or those engaged in job sharing. In addition, one person can have positions in more than one workplace, but again, not at the same time.

The position is part of an organizational unit.

A *job* is a description of what is entailed by a position—what the person holding that position has to achieve. There may be more work than one person can do, in which case there will be more than one position for the same job.

A *task* is what has to be done to carry out part of a job. One job might entail several different tasks, or separate tasks may be repetitions of a basic task, perhaps with minor variations from time to time caused by variations in the material being processed or in environmental conditions. The distinction between *task* and *job* is a matter to be established to suit the individual company.

A position may entail a specific personnel requirement, as may a specific workplace or one or more of the tasks entailed by the job to be performed there. For example, to be a high tower crane driver requires a person who is reliable and patient. This particular workplace cannot be occupied by a person who is afraid of heights. The task of controlling the swing of the load on the crane as it is being moved needs to be done by somebody who has both the knowledge and the eyesight to judge the situation. The crane driver also has to have a very special skill with hands and feet to operate the crane precisely and quickly to cancel the tendency for the load to swing on past the point where it is required to be placed. Each crane comprises one workplace. A person in the position of crane driver could be qualified to occupy any of these workplaces.

A person appointed to a position may have some requirements, but not all, in which case there is a requirement for a training program and, certainly in the case of the crane driver, a period of personal supervision by an experienced operator, perhaps leading to a formal certification of competence. The SAP R/3 system needs the object type Qualification to be recognized in order to support the Qualification and Requirements component of the PD-OM Organizational Management module.

Using the Data Model in the PA-APP Applicant Management Component

The PA-APP Applicant Management component adds the data object type Vacancy to the objects in the data model for PD-OM Organizational Management.

Creating a Data Model for Education and Training Administration

Each element in this data model is supported by standard infotypes. For example, a training course will need a data structure with data elements to represent the start date, finish date, location, account settlement arrangements, and so on—all of which can be assigned standard infotypes that can be used to build data-entry and display screens using the standard SAP R/3 methodology.

For example, a system of infotypes to contain the data necessary to administer education and training courses has to include the logical relationships and the structure to contain the details of the elements.

A *training program* is the sequence of course types needed by one person to qualify for a specific position within a stated time period. Each course of the same type is assumed to be equally effective and to cover the same content, even though the venue and the teachers might be different.

A *course type* requires one or more resource types, such as teachers, premises, and equipment. It may impart one or more qualifications, which are defined in terms of the positions for which they are preparation.

A course type may impart one or more task requirements, which may exceed the skills necessary for qualification or fall short of those skills.

A course type is defined by an entry in the catalog of course types. The course type is therefore a very flexible planning entity.

A *course* is a specific instance of a course type and uses one or more resources of one or more resource types. A *course group* is a set of courses. A course needs one or more instructors and one or more attendees. An *instructor* is a person internal to the company or an external person. An *attendee* is an internal person or an external person.

Building a Catalog of Course Types

The definition of a course type or other training event type is specified in a catalog of course types maintained by the HR-Human Resources application. The data attributes and elements of this catalog follow:

- Courses or other qualifications that are prerequisites for attendance at this event
- Qualifications provided by this course
- Contents of the training event
- Methods of this training event
- Dates and time patterns of this event
- Planned internal costs of this event, including currency, hours, and persons absent from normal work
- Minimum or maximum critical numbers for this event
- Technical resources of equipment and instructors required
- Course description in text form for use in brochures

Planning Human Resources

An organization is made up of organizational units, such as departments, teams, groups, and projects. It is displayed as an organizational chart.

Organizational units have jobs, and there is one job for each job title in the SAP R/3 Classification. For example, Secretary, Programmer, and Clerk are job titles for jobs. A job may have too much work for one person; there may be several positions for a job. There may be shift working, which increases the number of positions that have to be filled for the same job, and there may be several equivalent positions for that job in each shift.

The arrangement of positions is represented by an organization diagram. It shows the conventional hierarchical organization chart with the added feature of representing the number of positions at each job—usually graphically.

The scope of the HR-PD Personnel Planning and Development functions is illustrated by the following structures to which the planning procedures can be applied:

- Multiple reporting paths up and down the company hierarchy from any position selected on a display of an organization chart or organigram
- Organizational structure of any specific project
- Diversified responsibility organizations represented by the matrix methodology

Using HR Plan Versions and Status Control

When you allocate values to a structure of planning objects, you may be testing or simulating a tentative plan that you do not want to release for the moment, so you can store it as a plan version and retain control over its status. Changes can be made only in a planning object with the status of "planned." Every planning object has to pass through the following status stages:

- Active (in use)
- Planned
- Submitted
- Approved or rejected

Rejected data can be returned to the planned status for revision. You can also introduce other status control stages during customizing.

Creating Job Charts and Staffing Schedules

A *job chart,* in the context of the SAP R/3 PD-Personnel Planning and Development module, is created online by the system in response to the entry of a search specification determining the scope of the items to be included in the chart. The items can be tasks, jobs, or positions. Any of the items displayed can be selected as the subject for a drill-down operation in which you use the special function keys to display particular attributes of the item selected. In this manner, you can access and alter any of the job data records, to the extent that you have the authority to do so.

A *staffing schedule* is an attribute of a job or, if the job entails several different positions, of a position. The following types of staffing schedules are recognized and supported by the SAP R/3 PD-Personnel Planning and Development module:

- The position can be held by two or more persons.
- The position can be held by one person or a substitute.
- The position can be held by two people simultaneously for a fixed period.

The first type of staffing schedule is for a situation in which a job is planned to exist at a position only if there is work to be done. The position can be vacant because no suitable person is available. If there is more work than one person can do, there can be more than one identical position planned for the same job. If the work is not enough for the number of positions occupied at the workplace, there can be work sharing on the basis of percentage of material or by the number of hours worked.

If a person at a position is expected to be absent for a long period, a substitute person can be assigned to that position for the anticipated length of the absence. The substitute does not replace the person who is on the long leave of absence.

Having two people occupying the same position may occur when one of them is seconded to the other for training. The trainee may be intended as the successor, or the intention may be to create a second identical position for the same job when the training is completed. This form of simultaneous occupancy is usually of fixed duration, although the end of training may be dependent on the trainee reaching a defined standard for a formal qualification or for an internal award that is recorded as some kind of "authority to operate unsupervised."

The staffing schedule data for the jobs you have selected for display is generated automatically. The persons allocated to the positions on your display are identified from the master records, and their personal details, where relevant, are available from the personnel master records.

If one position on your display is determined to be vacant, you can call for the system to suggest suitable people on the basis of their qualifications and personal profiles. The system will attempt to match the people available with the personnel requirements specified for the vacant position. The system will operate with any set of personnel attributes you have defined: formal qualifications, experience, geographical location, and so on.

This process is a planning activity and, as such, can take place within any time frame. You can ask for a person to fill a vacancy as soon as possible. For example, you might have an overload in a telephone sales function and be looking for someone who is in the building or on the computer network, and who can be diverted from other work until the overload situation passes or at least until an extra position is created and filled on a permanent basis.

On the other hand, you might be looking at the staffing schedule for a planning period in the future. In such cases, the system offers you people who are suitable for the position and likely to be available when you plan to use them.

If the system cannot locate any existing personnel who could be assigned to a position that you plan to have filled by some specified date in the future, the HR-Human Resources system creates a vacancy specification based on the information it has about the job. The process of filling this vacancy from external sources or recruiting activities then can go ahead after this course of action is submitted for and granted approval.

All this automatic action depends absolutely on your having assembled an accurate job description.

Describing Jobs and Workplaces

The system accepts various conventions regarding the use of the concepts of jobs, tasks, and positions. This discussion does not seek to draw any firm distinctions among them.

SAP R/3 has a defined data object type designated as Task.

An SAP task is made up of any number of tasks and task complexes in any arrangement. The elements of this structure are either task structures themselves or individual tasks. A task structure may consist of a block of tasks with no particular interrelationship except the fact that they may have to be time shared by the person holding the position. For example, the receptionist might have to operate the security procedures, the telephone switchboard, and the visitors' coffee machine. Only the last task would be regarded as a single task rather than a task structure.

For some workplace positions, there may be good reasons for the job description to specify quantities or percentages allocated to the different tasks.

During the elaboration of a system of job descriptions for a newly designed work complex, it might be convenient to begin with a rather general job description that becomes progressively more detailed as the necessary information becomes available. During this process, it might become apparent where and on what basis one job should be allocated to more than one position. This is a reasonable approach, and the SAP R/3 PD-Personnel Planning and Development module supports it in a very flexible manner.

The task descriptions at the lowest level of detail of a task structure may be merely titles that serve as references to a job procedure manual, or they may be rough descriptions of an element of a job that is going to be taught by an instructor or by someone who is doing the job already. In other cases, it may be legally required that the details of a task element be formally documented. The system supports all varieties of job descriptions.

Workforce Planning with the PD-WFP Component

The PD-WFP Workforce Planning component is available to manage the details in installations where a very large volume of processing is entailed in job and workplace specification. Where this component has been installed and configured, your displays of job charts and staffing schedules will indicate how you can evaluate the supplementary job information as and when you need it.

The component makes available a wide range of data and evaluative processing that can be initiated in the context of the PD-Personnel Planning and Development module. This area of human resources management is under continuous research and development as the nature of work undergoes evolutionary and sometimes revolutionary changes. Methods of job evaluation have to be elaborate to track these developments.

The sections that follow give illustrative descriptions of some additional functions provided by the PD-WFP Workforce Planning component.

Planning Compensation

Pay scale groupings or absolute amounts can be stored—precisely or as ranges of values—to be the planned compensation for any of the following job description elements:

- Workplace
- Job
- Position
- Task

Standard evaluations can be called to provide the following results:

- Planned monthly costs for each organizational unit
- Comparison of planned payments with actual costs

Using Job Description Supplements

Information can be stored on any of the job description elements regarding the following matters:

- Authorizations necessary to perform the task element or to change its specified task description
- Auxiliary elements of the job description not detailed in the main description of the job or task—for example, whether a specific qualification is required by law to do the job, or whether special equipment is used at a workplace

Maintaining Healthcare Data

Medical histories can be entered against particular workplaces where, for example, follow-up data has been collected on previous incumbents of jobs dealing with hazardous materials or processes.

A workplace can be marked to indicate the requirement for preventive medical examinations at prescribed time intervals.

Applying Restrictions

Some jobs and workplaces require special protective clothing to be worn and therefore might not be suitable for persons who might have difficulty wearing those clothes. The place of work might be inaccessible or difficult to access by persons with certain disabilities. Some positions might be unsuitable for particular persons because of the hours worked or the types of activities performed. If a workplace has difficult emergency exits or hazardous emergency procedures, it might be unsuitable for certain persons. These matters have to be raised at some stage in the recruitment and appointment process.

Consulting Location Data

Although the location of a job in a workplace and the identification of the position or positions held there are matters documented in the central organization master data records, the supplementary records of the Workplace and Job Description component can be used to store additional information of importance, such as the following:

- Building identification
- Room number
- Telephone number
- Fax number
- Network address
- Complete postal address

This location data is used to compile telephone and organization directories, for example.

Planning Working Hours

The planned working time, to any level of accuracy, can be stored as data attached to an individual workplace or position. If the position is filled, the PD-Personnel Planning and Development system can compare the planned working hours with the contractual working hours of the person appointed. And when positions are summarized up to higher levels of the organizational structure, evaluations can be conducted not only on the basis of positions filled but also on the planned or actual working hours.

Assigning Persons to Groups

You can use certain personnel indicators to establish person subgroup types into which individuals can be classified. Certain positions or workplaces can be reserved for persons in a specific person subgroup.

Some companies, for example, reserve certain positions for hourly paid employees and others for those paid on a monthly basis. In some cases, certain positions are reserved for members of a particular trade union or for persons who are accredited members of a particular professional organization.

Assignment of a person to a person subgroup type can be determined by an SAP R/3 condition that specifies the logical relationships between two or more personal attributes, such as "Within a given age range" and "Chartered member of the XYZ Institute."

Building Task Structures

The information stored on a task can be in the nature of a comment on the duties involved rather than a description of the steps or technical stages. For example, the task can be characterized in terms of the main function of the person holding the position:

- To plan the work of the section
- To check the work of other people in the section
- To perform the task personally

The overall function of the task can be documented in the task structure record, as shown here:

- The purpose of this position is to provide a pleasant and efficient welcome to strangers visiting the plant for the first time.
- The function of this position is to make sure that no object or person enters the premises without leaving an adequate record of identity, purpose, and destination.
- The purpose of this position is to ensure that adequate records are kept securely of all materials of interest to the U.S. Customs Service that enter or leave the bonded warehouse.

Personnel Development   If the aim is to provide a comprehensive human resources service to your company and the people in it, the place to start is with a set of clear job descriptions. These descriptions must not only portray what is done, but must also show how these results are to be achieved. In some form or another, the necessary knowledge and skills have to be identified. There are two obvious methods:

- Identify people who can do the job, and then find out how their knowledge and skills are different from people who have just been recruited.
- Identify people who can do the job, and find out how they came to be in that happy position.

Neither method solves all the problems of getting good people into jobs they do well. The approach of personnel development is to assume that you have recruited at least some good people who will want to stay in your company, and then to provide them with a trajectory of jobs that gives them the opportunities to acquire not only the necessary knowledge and skills, but also the confidence in their abilities that is so essential to good performance.

Requirement and Qualification Profiles   The logic is simple. A person is suitable for a position if his qualifications match up with the requirements of all the jobs that will be his responsibility if he takes the appointment.

So a person can be more or less suitable. And he can be suitable in some respects and not in others. Put this data on a scale, and you have a suitability profile.

Some requirements of the job can be documented, and some can be set up in the form of admission tests. Some requirements can be described in general terms, such as "resourceful" or "sociable." The difficulty with using these types of words to describe the appropriate response to an unknown future situation is that, by definition, there is no way of knowing whether a specific individual can cope. For some personnel selection assignments, it might be best to concentrate on the negative side. For example, a person who has had no practice at first aid should not be placed in a position where it might be needed. A person who has shown no signs of being friendly to strangers should not be in charge of crowd control in cases of emergency.

Where you can define what is needed in terms of the amount or weighting of each of several characteristics, you can draw a job requirement profile. Some requirements will be absolute, with no room for leniency, whereas some will be desirable but not essential. In some positions, the lack of one good quality can be compensated for by an abundance of another. For example, a very good memory can serve as well as intelligence in some circumstances.

If you have a personnel selection procedure, even if it is just an interview, you might arrive at a measurement of the capability of each applicant in each dimension of the job that you can use to build a job requirement profile.

Put this data on a scale, and you have a qualification profile.

If you are bold enough to compare the qualification profile of a person against the job requirement profile, you can formulate the data to yield a suitability profile of this applicant for this job. And if you were to carry out this profile matching for all your applicants for all your vacancies, you would arrive at a list of people in rank order of suitability for each vacancy. This function is available through the PD-WFP Workforce Planning component.

These are the main functions:

- Manage the requirements for jobs, positions, workplaces, and tasks, and set priorities and weightings if required.
- Manage the qualifications of applicants and the quality or level of these qualifications.
- Mediate the substitution of qualifications in relation to job requirements when compiling a short list of suitable people.
- Create job requirement profiles.
- Create applicant qualification profiles.
- Compare requirement and qualification profiles and produce suitability profiles.
- Maintain a catalog of model qualifications and requirements.

This catalog of qualifications and requirements is supplied as standard in the PD-WFP Workforce Planning component. You can attach items from it to persons and positions or workplaces, and you can extend or adapt the catalog to suit the type of work carried out in your company.

The quality of a qualification can be expressed in terms of the level of proficiency attained by the person holding it. If this same qualification is associated with a position, the level will perhaps indicate what is regarded as an acceptable proficiency for that position.

Some qualifications represent knowledge and skills that can deteriorate over time, either by disuse or by becoming out-of-date. The PD-Personnel Planning and Development module provides the capability to enter a half-life value for a qualification, which is the period of time it takes for the skill to deteriorate to half its proficiency if it is not required by the job and if it is not kept up to standards by refresher training. The system will compute the exact degree of deterioration to be assumed for any other period under consideration if you have specified a value for the half-life.

If you are looking at a person who has been in a job that demands the exercise of the skill or other requirement corresponding to the qualifications he possessed on appointment, there is no reason to suppose that his proficiency has deteriorated at all.

Career Models   A *career model* is an ordered list of the types of opportunities open to a person in your company or a person you would like to recruit. Clearly, each step in the career model will be taken only if the person is suitable and willing to move, and if there is a vacancy in the target position.

The same approach is used for new recruits, selection of suitable successors for existing positions, and management of career paths.

The HR-Human Resources, PD-Personnel Planning and Development module provides the following functionality:

- Representation of careers
- Association of the career potential assessments taken from the selection procedure with the steps of potential career models
- Determination and representation of further training needs of individuals embarked on career paths
- Representation of further training programs
- Graphical editing of profiles and profile comparisons

Career Planning   The planning of an individual career begins with a discussion with the person concerned and the identification of one or more positions for which this person wants to be considered. This data is entered under the organizational structures established in the PD-OM Organizational Management component and the suitability profile of this candidate as computed.

The integrated PD-Personnel Planning and Development module offers a list of all the positions for which the candidate would be suitable and a sublist of those that are vacancies or are likely to be so on a future date suggested to the system.

The system can be run in simulation mode to analyze any domino effects. If the career candidate elects to accept an offer of a change of position, a vacancy will be created elsewhere, and so on. When the transfer or recruitment actually takes place, the system suggests all the vacant positions in succession so that the planner can be sure that the subsequent transfers are processed.

Representation of Human Resource Potentials   The first potentials of a candidate are derived from the assessment procedure, whether it be formal or informal. For every position for which the candidate is likely to be considered, his or her assessed potential is stored.

As time passes and experience is accumulated, these potentials can be adjusted on the basis of the new information coming to light. Alternatively, the assessed potentials can be stored with their original values intact and a set of current potentials maintained separately.

Succession Planning   Whereas career planning is looking from the employee's viewpoint, the function of *succession planning* is to be concerned with who will maintain the work of the company by succeeding to a specific position if and when it becomes vacant.

There may well be several candidates who would be suitable successors. This is a matter that can be illuminated by considering their qualification profiles in relation to the requirements profile of the position. Even so, there might be no real differences in the suitability profiles of several of the candidates. Other factors must be considered, for example:

- Time with the company
- Time served in the present position
- Staff association membership
- Educational background as a potential for further career development

Further Training Needs   It can easily happen that no candidate can match qualifications with the requirements for recruitment or career progression, as the case may be. Your company will have to weigh the costs and other considerations to decide whether to look again, perhaps elsewhere, for a person with the right qualifications, or whether to accept one candidate and make up the difference by having that person trained.

The system will tell you which qualifications are lacking, and to what level of proficiency they are required by the vacancy. If the training course database is accurate, the system will also tell you where and by what method the additional qualifications can be obtained.

This functionality enables you to create an education and training plan for an individual by reference to the qualification deficits discovered by the career planning activities. You can also modify these plans before they are released for processing.

The following functions are available through the PD-Personnel Development component:

- Manage internal and external training events.
- Manage and plan all the resources required for internal and external training events, such as rooms, instructors, course materials, and equipment.
- Process all correspondence in connection with training events.
- Check the prerequisite courses or other qualifications of the employees or external people who intend to enroll.

■ Automatically update the qualification master records of those who pass the course standards.

The component also can manage the booking of internal and external participants with the following facilities:

■ Automatic creation of waiting lists
■ Automatic sequential processing of waiting lists
■ Booking with priorities
■ Booking from lists
■ Canceling from lists

It is a feature of the component that all training events can be processed without regard to their time dependency, if necessary. For example, you can ask the component to create a complete catalog of all the further training events scheduled throughout the company.

The system ensures that a participant is not booked on the same course twice and is not destined for two courses that overlap in time. If you have installed the PA-TIM Time Management component, employees identified automatically by the system as suitable to act as instructors on a course will not be assigned to it if, for example, their vacations will make them unavailable.

Events can be linked to specific locations if this is necessary—for example, if a particular resource is available nowhere else. A specific language for the conduct of a course can be dealt with in a similar fashion.

Different calendars can be invoked to ensure that the courses are not planned for statutory holidays, for example.

Prebooking for a general course topic or theme, delimited by a range of dates, can be confirmed later by the release of firm booking for specific training events. Booking priority is covered by the following standard schemes:

■ Essential for the good of the company.
■ Normal, first come, first served.
■ Waiting list for places not filled by participants with higher priority. The system proposes a redistribution to subsequent courses of those remaining on the waiting list after the event takes place.

Education and Training Planning   Included in the HR-PD Personnel Planning and Development, PD-PD Personnel Development component is a suite of functions to carry out quantitative planning of education and training events and to make optimum use of time.

A requirement for planning arises in the form of data on the estimated number of courses made up from the requirements per subject and per calendar quarter. Alternatively, the requirements can be expressed as prebookings for each course type that specifies the subject or theme of interest. There are career and succession planning functions in the PD-OM Organizational Management component that provide a source of prebookings. These functions identify the needs for further training in connection with career planning and the preparation of successors for those who are moving on.

The education and training requirements are serviced by the following functions:

- Scheduling of numbers of different training events
- Optimizing of event schedules with respect to the resources available
- Scheduling sequences of training events for individuals or groups of participants

Overall scheduling depends on the following factors:

- Preset limits on the number of events each year
- Number and timing of events according to the prebookings
- Education and training budget
- Demands from career and succession planning

Optimized event scheduling has to take account of the resources required and their availability—for example,

- Suitable rooms according to the PD-RPL Room Reservations Planning component
- Instructors available according to the PA-TIM Time Management component
- Course materials and equipment

Applications for Personnel Recruitment   The PD-Personnel Planning and Development module is used in the recruitment situation with the PA-APP Applicant Management component, which includes applicant screening support functions.

A separate applicant database is maintained in the PA-APP Applicant Management component to which all the functions of the PA-Personnel Administration module can be applied. The data on any applicant who is accepted and hired is automatically transferred to the HR-Human Resources database, which is controlled by the PA-EMP Employee Management component.

Applicant Data Administration   The following services are provided by the integrated HR-Human Resources system:

- Managing internal and external applicant data
- Recognizing multiple, repeated, and duplicate applications
- Determining vacancies automatically from the HR planning components
- Triggering job advertisements automatically from the HR planning components, using job description text and a detailed breakdown of media and recruitment instruments in each
- Assigning applicants to advertisements to check cost-effectiveness
- Processing correspondence
- Applying the PA-TRV Travel Expenses component to process job interview costs and to reimburse interviewees
- Providing automatic data transfer to PA-EMP Employee Management

Applicant Screening   A position can be marked as vacant, which allows it to be released for filling. If an unoccupied position is not so marked, it will be ignored. If a position is subject to a long notice period, it can be marked as vacant although still occupied.

The applicant screening process can be used to find all applicants who are suited by their qualifications for any set of positions. You can screen for all positions in the company, for those on a particular set of career paths, or for those marked as vacant.

The ensuing hit list for each position contains those applicants whose qualification profiles most closely match the requirements profile for the position. There will be an automatic estimation of the possible training needs of any applicant who does not have each requirement to the degree required by the position.

Planning Personnel Costs

One function provided by the PD-WFP Workforce Planning component is the capability to estimate the wage and salary elements for a specified period. Simulations can be conducted that take into account various factors:

- Collective agreements
- Modified tax contributions
- Modified Social Insurance contributions
- Work schedules that attract special pay rates

The scope of the cost planning functions follows:

- Annual preview and budget planning
- User-defined estimation of individual elements from wages and salaries, as direct data entries, by transfer from the CO-CCA Cost Center Accounting or PA-PAY Payroll module
- Integration into the planning of facts, such as negotiated pay rates, that have already been dated and that affect the personnel costs
- Support for different simulations
- Graphical editing of the results and the target versus actual comparisons

Evaluating Jobs and Workplaces

This component is under development. It is intended to determine suitable compensations for individuals holding particular jobs. The values will be designed to reflect the importance of the job to the organization, as indexed by the type and skill needed to do the job, and the responsibility for budget and personnel. Analytic work evaluation and various other schemes of assigning monetary values to different kinds of work are being considered for inclusion in the component.

Using the Manpower Planning I Component

The long-term planning of manpower requirements of the company includes the distribution of planned amounts to each workplace on the basis of guideline figures that you enter, such as these:

- Planned turnover per product
- Planned output per product
- Planned turnover per location

The employees and their qualifications are taken into account, along with the number of employee hours available in the planning period.

The hours available are first distributed to take account of shift schedules and overtime planning. A second operation adjusts these hours to take account of the nonproductive hours arising from a range of causes.

Using the Manpower Planning II Component

The purpose of Manpower Planning II is to improve short-term planning by ensuring that business needs are covered by sufficient personnel.

The SAP R/3 BASIS system provides full integration of your system so that logistics data relating to the workplace and time data from PA-TIM Time Management are normally available to PD-Personnel Planning and Development. Your company might elect to keep the PD-Personnel Planning and Development system separate from the integrated logistics application modules, which are listed here:

- SD-Sales and Distribution
- PP-Production Planning
- MM-Materials Management
- PM-Plant Maintenance
- QM-Quality Management

The manufacturing data transferred from the logistics modules will be concerned with the following aspects of short-term manpower planning:

- General amounts of work planned and in progress
- General data from the work plans of your company, including the plant locations in relation to the addresses of the personnel who might be employed there
- Patterns of qualifications, formal and in terms of experience, needed throughout the planning period

It is necessary for the Manpower Planning II component to call on the PA-TIM Time Management component for the following types of information:

- Company time models
- Shift schedules

- Personal calendars of individual employees, which will yield information on employee hours that cannot be planned for normal work activities because they have been already assigned to activities such as vacations, education, training, or business trips

The PA-TIM Time Management component is also important in this context because it initiates manpower planning, and hence possibly redeployment or recruitment, if the number of suitable employees at a workplace at any time falls below the minimum required or is forecast to do so.

The Manpower Planning II component requires certain PD-Personnel Planning and Development components to be installed and configured, whether or not there is direct transfer from the logistics modules. PD-OM Organizational Management and PD-WFP Workforce Planning are required to provide the data on workplaces, the activities that need to be performed, and the employees assigned to them on specific dates and times throughout the planning period. These components are also needed to supply the job specifications of workplaces and the qualifications held by the employees in these positions, along with their suitability profiles.

The HR-Human Resources, PA-Personnel Administration module will also have to be installed, because it contains the employee master file required to gain access to the personnel data.

The emergency role of the Manpower Planning II component is to enable you to deal effectively and swiftly with unplanned staff shortages. You will want to locate the right people to fill the gaps.

The right person is one with all the requirements of the vacancy and no disadvantages. This is a true statement of the aim but is difficult to realize in practice.

The approach taken by this component is to assemble and make readily available all the information that might help you cover the staff shortage. For example, you might want to have records of the following types of information about employees:

- Whether a person is incompatible with another and should not be assigned to work with him or her
- How a particular work team should be made up from a specific mixture of personality types and capabilities
- Which persons have registered preferences or requested limitations on the working hours or working days of the week assigned to them

Workplaces should be assigned master records carrying data on factors that could help or hinder your efforts to fill an unplanned vacancy there:

- Minimum number of positions that should be occupied at the workplace
- Maximum number of positions that could be accommodated at the workplace
- Optimum number of people to be located at this workplace
- Preferred staffing arrangements for the different shifts or other working patterns that sometimes or regularly occur at the workplace

The solutions the Manpower Planning II component proposes to you will have to include the schemes and arrangements your company has discovered or developed over the years, plus any new possibilities that can be conceived now that you have a flexible integrated manpower planning system in operation. The list will probably include tactics such as these:

- Assigning a person to be on call in case his or her expertise or work capacity is needed at a workplace suffering a staff shortage

- Assigning standby duty

- Temporarily transferring an employee from another workplace or from another section of the plant

- Engaging outside personnel through a placement agency

- Engaging a person who was previously an employee

- Engaging a freelance worker

- Engaging a seasonal worker directly or via a seasonal worker agency

The component makes extensive use of the standard SAP graphical display facilities to make the operation of the functions easy for inexperienced users. As of R/3 Release 3.0, these facilities are controllable over the Internet.

Administering Travel Expenses with the PA-TRV Component

The purpose of the PA-TRV Travel Expenses component is to provide a seamless software system for managing a business-related trip—from application, through approval, to update and correction—by retroactive accounting. The scope of the component includes domestic and business trips, in the home country and abroad, for individuals and groups.

The approach is standard SAP: Maximize the integration between modules and components of the SAP R/3 system and any non-SAP connections; minimize the redundant storing of data.

The component is intended to be integrated with the SAP R/3 system in an open system architecture—UNIX, for example. It can also be used as part of the SAP R/2 systems on mainframe hosts. The PA-TRV Travel Expenses component can also be used as an output interface to external systems.

The following SAP R/3 modules and components will normally be installed and configured before the PA-TRV Travel Expenses component is set to work:

- FI-Financial Accounting

- CO-Controlling, CO-OM Overhead Cost Control

- HR-Human Resources

Maintaining the Structure of HR-TRV Travel Expenses

The component offers three groups of functions:

- **Basic version.** Provides the transactions, forms, and evaluation tables needed to carry out travel expense accounting in accord with the tax law of the country in which the R/3 system is installed.

- **Cost distribution.** Allows the component to redistribute travel costs from the employee level to cost objects such as trip, receipt or cost type, or stopover.

- **International supplements.** Allow variations of the basic evaluation procedure according to the requirements of other nations.

The supplements for tax calculations and country-specific payroll calculations are organized according to the divisions of the INT-International Development module:

IN-APA	Asian and Pacific Area
IN-EUR	Europe
IN-NAM	North America
IN-AFM	Africa/Middle East
IN-SAM	South America

Using Basic Version Functionality

The functions of the component can be grouped like this:

- Lump-sum accounting, where the amounts are taken from standard rates regardless of the expenditure actually incurred
- Representation of company regulations
- Procedures and administration

Applying Lump-Sum Accounting   The following functionality addresses the requirements of lump-sum accounting:

- Lump-sum accounting for accommodations, meals, and commuting costs
- Itemizing per invoice as accommodations, meals, commuting costs, business entertainment, or incidental costs
- Trip itemization and lump-sum accounting
- Reduction of lump sums and maximum amounts by predefined adjustments for active or passive business entertainment events

Representing Company Regulations   The PA-TRV Travel Expenses component affords flexible arrangements to record and automatically apply the rules and customs of the individual company:

- Definition of permitted circumstances via table entries
- Reduction of the daily rate for meals if a trip lasts less than one day

- Statutory trip types, errands or business trips
- Trips with stopovers
- Round trips
- Special business trips with day excursions to different customer sites
- Company-specific regulations that apply to trips representing the company and that can apply different rates according to the status of the employee and the nature of the trip or the territory in which it is made
- Company-internal event trips, such as attending a seminar or course, or a customer advisory service trip
- Trip-specific account assignment to company code, plant, cost center, order, or project
- Employee-specific overall proportional cost distribution to company code, plant, or cost center

Handling Trips Worldwide   The essential functions for managing overseas trips follow:

- Automatic currency conversion
- Border crossing
- Foreign trips worldwide

Procedures and Administration   The component supports a number of essential administrative procedures and facilities, such as the following:

- Application and approval procedures, trip approval notification at the planning stage, approval notification immediately prior to departure, advance of travel expenses, cancellation of a trip
- Internal or external number range assignment for trip number
- Model trip plans that can be edited
- Table-controlled statement per employee
- Interfaces to other SAP applications
- Day-specific accounting
- Special function keys to control fast entry of data
- Short form of travel expense accounting procedures for external services

Interfaces to other SAP applications will be established if the following applications have been installed and configured:

- FI-Financial Accounting
- CO-Controlling, CO-OM Overhead Cost Control
- HR-Human Resources, PA-PAY Payroll

Day-specific accounting is achieved by storing tax-free and company-internal refund rates in tables, which are also accessed to determine additional amounts or income-related expenses.

Applying Cost Distribution Functionality

The source of costs to be distributed can be an individual employee or a trip.

If several employees go together on a trip, the total costs associated with the trip can be distributed, in equal shares for each employee, to the company code, plant, or cost center with which that employee is associated.

Another cost distribution variant available in this component is to allocate to each cost center, project, or order the deviation account value representing the difference between planned and actual costs of the trip.

You can also enter a percentage distribution structure for each trip, and have it applied to the following item types to distribute the amounts to the appropriate company code, plant, cost center, order, or project:

- Total costs of the trip
- Costs pertaining to individual stopovers
- Individual travel expense receipts

You can also assign an individual expense receipt to a specific cost object and prevent it from being distributed with the other expenses of the trip.

Each employee master record will include an infotype for cost distribution and an infotype subtype for travel expenses. Therefore, you can call for a display of the proportional overall cost distribution of an individual employee over a range of trips. You can see if he or she tends to spend more money on one thing than another, and how these priorities change over a succession of trips.

It might make sense to allocate a percentage distribution for planning purposes to the overall costs of a trip, which then can be assigned to cost centers, for example. You can also separate the expenses of the individual stopovers and distribute one or more of them according to a percentage scheme.

Individual receipts can be distributed in proportion or in absolute amounts to the cost objects specified in your distribution plan.

Applying Functionality Empowered by International Supplements

International requirements for travel expense accounting may require additional information to be recorded.

Mileage distribution can be recorded for specific dates and the number of passengers, and luggage can be recorded on the basis of distance. Company lump sums can also be attributed on the basis of distance. Vehicle characteristics such as horsepower, engine capacity, and price might have to be recorded and taken into the valuations.

Mileage rates by country of destination can be applied. Cumulative miles covered by each employee can be recorded on a flexible time basis. The user can define mileage ranges over which lump-sum payments per mile can be specified.

The INT-International Development module can provide lump-sum accounting for additional expenditures on meals under the following circumstances:

- Border crossing for inward and outward legs of trips
- Trip duration can be calibrated in calendar days, 24-hour periods, or by times of day
- Days on which an employee is traveling for less than 24 hours can be evaluated according to the number of hours in transit or the time of day
- Lump sums and maximum amounts can be reduced on account of lunch coupons given out monthly

Certain trip activities can each attract a fixed lump sum, and all employee-specific travel expense regulations controlling travel privileges can be altered for each trip.

Cash advances are deducted from subsequent payments.

Consulting Personnel Master Data

The following employee personnel data is required by the PA-TRV Travel Expenses component:

- Name of employee
- Organizational assignment—for example, to plant, cost center, or person in charge
- Travel privileges—for example, authorization to run an expense account and the particular internal regulations under which it may be operated
- Banking connection for direct payment

Reviewing Travel Expenses Procedures

Central data recording can be used, or the travel expense procedures can be managed on a decentralized basis. Travel expense data recording without the submission of a prior application occurs in the following sequence:

- Employee submits a travel expense claim form.
- Data on the trip is checked and recorded.
- Trip claim is approved.
- Travel expense accounting action takes place in the PA-TRV Travel Expenses component.
- Data is transferred to the FI-Financial Accounting module and to the CO-Controlling, CCA-Cost Center Accounting component.
- Marked claim document is returned to employee.

Your company might require prior approval of a trip and use this occasion to provide help with booking travel tickets and accommodations. The benefits of advanced travel expense planning may include the following opportunities:

- Coordination of the means of transport for several employees making trips
- Overview of travel- and hotel-use patterns

- Discount negotiations on means of travel and hotel bookings
- Advance payments through the FI-Financial Accounting component credited to the employee's bank account or paid directly in cash or foreign currency

If the employee has to obtain prior approval, the following sequence is enacted:

1. The employee submits a travel expense claim form with a request for an advance.
2. Data on the trip is checked and recorded.
3. The trip advance payment is approved.
4. Travel expense planning action takes place in the PA-TRV Travel Expenses component.
5. Data is transferred to the FI-Financial Accounting module and to the CO-Controlling, CO-OM Overhead Cost Control component.
6. The trip advance is paid to the employee.
7. After the trip, the employee submits a record of the trip and the expenses incurred.
8. Data on the trip is checked, and the records are supplemented and updated.
9. The trip claim is approved.
10. Travel expense accounting action takes place in the PA-TRV Travel Expenses component.
11. Data is transferred to the FI-Financial Accounting module and the CO-Controlling, CO-OM Overhead Cost Control component.
12. The marked claim document is returned to the employee.

A development of this travel expense procedure is to have the employee enter the data; then the central facility applies the checking and financial actions.

Processing Trip Data

A single trip—from a short-distance errand, to a long-distance business trip, to a complex trip abroad—can be processed for an individual employee.

The following choices are offered if you want to review the documents on previous trips:

- Trip period
- Trip destination
- Customer
- Processing status of the trip

You can use any of these search specifications to locate a previous trip to copy as the basis for a new trip.

Creating a Trip   The system will require your personnel number and a trip schema, unless you opt to copy a previous trip. A *trip schema* is an instrument for controlling the sequence of screens. You can create a new trip schema or edit the table containing one of the standard trip schemas.

Data entry is required under the following headings:

- Beginning and ending time and date of trip
- Trip destination
- Number of domestic and foreign miles driven
- Number of passengers for calculating the passenger lump sum
- Lump-sum accounting for meals
- Number of overnight stays with lump-sum accounting
- Cost center for travel expense account posting if this is not to be the master cost center for the employee
- Trip activity types, such as seminar, customer visit, and so on
- Border crossing on return trip

Entering Individual Receipts   Trip receipts relevant to accounting are recorded. Each is assigned an expense-type key that determines the FI-GL General Ledger account to which expense receipts are to be posted. The keys and their associated FI-GL General Ledger accounts can be established to suit your company. This normally takes place during customizing.

These keys can also be used for statistical summaries of the travel expense types, both standard and user-defined.

Foreign currency can be entered on the trip receipt along with the exchange rate. The system can provide a default exchange rate and, if necessary, a default currency identifier based on the trip destination.

Recording Business Entertainment   If an employee is invited to a meal for business reasons, the lump sum payable for meals on that day is reduced by an amount determined by a predefined table. The maximum travel expense amount is also reduced.

The default entry for every day assumes that there is to be no deduction of travel expenses for business entertainment received.

Documenting Advances   Entries on a trip with the status "Travel Expense Application" that concern advances are evaluated by the PA-PAY Payroll program and the FI-Financial Accounting system. If the advance is approved, the employee receives it in the next payment run.

If an advance is approved for payment in cash, that amount has to be posted to a specific vendor or customer account. This might be a company to be visited by the person making the trip. In this instance, the advance claim serves as documentation for this posting.

The exchange rate is entered automatically when the currency is identified. The rate can be changed manually at any time, which leaves a change record in the system.

Advances can be refunded in the same manner.

Noting Stopovers   In addition to the main destination, one or more stopovers can be entered with their exact times of entry and departure.

Maximum amounts for travel expense claims and the lump-sum or blanket allowances for meals and accommodations are determined from predefined tables for each country. The 24-hour rule is applied: Standard rates and individual receipts are assigned for each day of a trip according to the last country the person was in before midnight, local time.

Determining Mileage Distribution   Passenger allowance to an employee is payable on the miles actually traveled by the passenger. The function allows this to be recorded in preparation for distribution to the cost objects. Mileage per employee is cumulated in this function.

Assigning Trip Texts   Text can be assembled from standard text elements or written freeform through the SAPscript word processing facility. It can be used for two-way communication between the travel expenses accounting office and the employee, and as additional documentation for trip activities. The format and printing destination will depend on the purpose of the text.

Maintaining Trip Status   The trip status maintenance screen offers a choice of status indicators. Which indicators can be altered depends on the authorizations of the user and the stage reached in the trip travel expenses transaction sequence. The following menu of possibilities is offered as standard:

- **Approval status.** Application, Application Approved, Trip Occurred, Trip Approved
- **Accounting status.** Open, For Accounting—To Be Settled, Canceled

You use function keys to control the recording of trip status data. If the accounting status is Open, there will be no accounting action, but changes to the documented will be stored.

If the status combination is Approved and For Accounting—To Be Settled, the trip is settled on the next billing run.

Using Fast Entry   You can use fast entry to enter several domestic trips for one employee in the same transaction.

Each trip in a multitrip fast entry is assigned an internal trip schema that controls the trip number allocated and marks the trip as domestic. For a trip lasting more than one day, you must enter the starting and finishing dates and times. All other trip data is entered on the line for the beginning date. The following fields are filled by the system with default values:

- **Area.** The area to which the employee is normally assigned
- **Errand or Business Trip.** The distance of the destination
- **Status.** Defaults on entry or when a detail is changed to Trip Approved—To Be Settled on the assumption that the travel expense claim is being submitted after the trip takes place

To postpone a trip, you can change the date fields.

You can use the copy function to quickly enter several one-day trips for the same employee.

The system will print for each employee a list of the trips that have been validated and settled.

Trip Accounting   The accounting period for travel expenses can be defined by the user. The normal choices are weekly, every two weeks, or monthly.

If an error is detected during a travel expense accounting run, the cause of the error is logged, and corrections must be made by the user travel accounting department.

Settlement is carried out only if the status of the trip document indicates that the travel expense application is approved and the trip is to be settled, or in the case of a planned trip, the trip is approved and is to be settled, for example, by paying an advance to the employee.

The settlement action normally includes the following processes:

- Conditions are accessed to determine the calculation procedures to be followed according to the country of destination, the area, the refund class or group, and any deductions to be made.
- Lump-sum charges and maximum charges are determined.
- The refund, tax-free, and additional amounts are calculated.
- Adjustments are made to take into account the duration of the first and last days of the trip.

Using Standard Forms   Two standard forms are provided as suggestions for printing the results of a trip settlement transaction for the benefit of the employee:

- Detailed statement
- Condensed statement

You can control the printing of the standard forms by referring to the SAP R/3 tables; you have access to these in order to manipulate the form and content of the printed statements.

Each day for which meals were taken is evaluated separately. The lump-sum accounting for accommodations, meals, and commuting expenses for each main destination or stopover are displayed first. Then the accounting data for the individual receipts follows.

The condensed statement is particularly useful for external service employees who make the same trip every day, because it allows you to present the accounting results of many standard trips in compact form.

Effecting Payment

There are several methods of effecting payment for travel expenses. It may take place along the channels of the SAP R/3 integrated system, or via a standard interface to a non-SAP system.

Paying via the FI-Financial Accounting System   Transfer of trip data to vendors or customer accounts for settlement of the travel expenses of an employee making a trip to their plant, or elsewhere on their behalf, can take place at varying time intervals.

If a trip that has been posted is subsequently changed, the differences are posted. If additional amounts occur, they have to be transferred to PA-PAY Payroll.

Paying via PA-PAY Payroll   All travel expenses relating to trips that have been fully entered and evaluated are paid out on the next payroll run.

Paying via External Non-SAP Financial Accounting or Payroll Accounting Systems   The programs to make a transfer will have been configured to access the external systems, so that you can directly access the travel expense accounting results database or a predefined sequential dataset, depending on the system.

Paying via the DME-Data Medium Exchange   The DME provides a fully configured means of paying from the PA-TRV Travel Expenses component.

Evaluating Trip Data

Three points of view have to be taken into consideration when evaluating trip data:

- Maximum tax-free lump sum and maximum amounts legally refundable by the employer
- Travel expense regulations and practices established in your company
- Amounts to be billed

There are three significant amounts to be billed:

- Amount that can be refunded tax-exempt to the employee under the legal regulations in force at the time
- Amount actually refunded by the company to the employee
- Amount that can be debited to other accounts

An additional amount is defined as an amount that is paid to an employee over and above what is legally refundable free of tax. This additional amount is included in payroll accounting and may attract tax deductions in the normal way.

If the amount refunded is less than the amount that can be refunded tax-exempt, the difference can be taken into account when claiming income-related expenses in the annual wage tax adjustment.

The tables used to evaluate trip expenses contain the dates when regulations come into force. If such a change takes place during a trip, the differences can be computed automatically.

The PA-TRV Travel Expenses component offers the following evaluation variants:

- Lump-sum amounts valid on the first day of a trip are valid throughout the trip.
- Lump-sum amounts valid on the last day of a trip are applied throughout the trip.
- The evaluation refers to the lump-sum amounts valid for each day of the trip.

Representing Company-Specific Regulations

Trip travel expense data can be evaluated by a combination of two standard methods available in the PA-TRV Travel Expenses component:

- Employees are assigned to refund levels valid for all their trips.
- Each trip is assigned to an area, which is an accounting instrument defined to suit the requirements of your company.

For example, employee-specific lump sums and maximum amounts are defined according to the refund level to which the employee has been assigned. The refund class or refund group can define the level at which the accommodations and meals are refunded. Vehicle regulations specific to your company can be specified by the refund class or group.

The area method of representing company-specific regulations can be used to apply differential rates in the following circumstances, for example:

- Additional allowance for trips to capital cities
- Trips between different company sites
- Seminar attendance

If an employee works for several company codes or plants, there will be an indicator in the specification of his travel privileges so that his travel expenses can be distributed and posted appropriately.

Area and Vehicle Regulations   Tables are used to set up area and vehicle regulations that specify the amounts refundable for different vehicle classes and travel expense areas. The effect is to impose logical conditions, as in the following examples:

- If an employee is entitled to refunds under regulation A, the basic mileage rate is $x, and under regulation B, it is $y.
- The regulation A exception mileage rate for trips to area 1 is $x + 10%, and for trips to area 2, it is $x + 5%.
- The regulation B exception mileage rate for trips to area 1 is $y + 8%, and for trips to area 2, it is $y + 4%.

Accommodations and Meals   Tables are also used to specify the allowances for accommodations and meals in order to award different amounts according to the regulation associated with the employee's refund group. Again, there can be any number of exceptions to the basic rates to be applied if the trip destination is in an area that attracts different accommodation- and meal-refund lump sums. ●

CHAPTER 23

Understanding the Materials Management Module

Introducing the MM Components

The MM-Materials Management module provides detailed support for the day-to-day activities of every type of business that entails the consumption of materials, including energy and services. The word *material* is given the widest connotation. The module includes the following components:

- MM-MRP Material Requirements Planning
- MM-PUR Purchasing
- MM-IM Inventory Management
- MM-WM Warehouse Management
- MM-IV Invoice Verification
- MM-IS Information System
- MM-EDI Electronic Data Interchange

Exploring the Organizational Structures

An essential characteristic of the SAP R/3 standard business programs is the strict adherence to a formal structure of data, regardless of the data's meaning or complexity. In no other way is it possible to build and maintain the very large systems of databases and transactional processing routines that a modern integrated system demands.

The structure of SAP R/3 data is designed to be adaptable to the structure of all the common configurations of head office and subsidiary operating units and work teams found or imagined in the context of modern business. The standard software isn't itself altered when it is implemented in your particular company—only the tables of parameters that control the software in order to fit your specific organization and its data-processing requirements. A set of definitions of terms must exist to make sure that everyone understands what the titles of the organizational units represent.

Defining the Client

The owner of the entire SAP R/3 system is the client, as far as the computer programs are concerned. The client has access to all the data. Some data may be stored and maintained for accuracy and timeliness at the client level because other parts of the organization may need it. The details of a vendor of a product used by some or all departments of a company is one type of data that should be stored at the client level.

The client is assigned a client code so that a data record maintained at this level can be recognized; the code prefixes the record number.

The system has only one genuine client for the purpose of assigning real data needed for the running of the corporate group of companies. A training client can be set up so that the staff can carry out exercises on the system using "for practice" data records prefixed by the training client code. The training client cannot gain access to the data owned by the real client.

Similarly, the implementing team can set up a testing client, which is used to verify that all standard business programs are producing the results and effects they have been designed to produce. Again, there is no way of confusing the testing data or the training client data with the real client data, because the testing client records carry the testing client code, which triggers various protective routines.

Defining the Company Code

When a corporate group consists of one or more separate companies, each legally allowed to maintain its separate balance sheet and profit-and-loss statement, the SAP R/3 system requires that the head office be recognized by the client code and that each subsidiary company be assigned a separate company code.

The structured data principle is applied. Data not required by an organizational unit belonging to a different part of the corporate organization can be confined to the company that uses it by storing it under its own company code. For example, the information necessary to manage the maintenance of a particular plant that one company uses may be of no interest to another part of the group. Personnel records may have to be stored at the client level, because people may be asked to move from one company code to another.

Naturally, the SAP R/3 system has provided for the situation where a set of records belonging to one company code can be copied for reference to another.

Defining the Purchasing Organization

A purchasing organization must be assigned to only one company code. This is a legal requirement that stems from the purchasing organization being assigned the responsibility of negotiating terms and conditions with vendors of the materials and services needed by this company code. When a purchasing transaction takes place, this company is responsible for the payments, not its purchasing organization. *Company code* is SAP shorthand for a company that is a subsidiary of the client code enterprise.

Defining the Purchasing Group

Most purchasing organizations have more than one buyer. Even if there is only one person in it, this purchasing organization can be divided, for purchasing accounting convenience, into purchasing groups according to any criteria you find helpful. Very often, specialist buyers are required who are knowledgeable in particular materials, and they may constitute the purchasing groups within the purchasing organization.

Defining the Plant

The SAP R/3 system recognizes a plant as a data object belonging to a specific company code. In fact, the plant doesn't need to be a production plant as such—it could be a warehouse or even part of a warehouse. What distinguishes a plant is that it is the site at which value can be added by production activities or at which valuable stock is held in an orderly fashion, as represented by an inventory in which the items are identified with their bin or other storage location. Their value is enhanced if you know they are there and can find them quickly when they are required for a production order or you need to know something about them to respond to a customer's inquiry.

Defining the Storage Location

The *storage location* is a data object that SAP R/3 treats as a collective label for a set of storage bins or other units in which material is held. A single bin may be a storage location. Any number of bins can be managed together as a single storage location, in which case the system can't select material from one bin rather than another unless special steps are taken to tell the system which bin is which. This facility is provided in the MM-WM Warehouse Management component.

Maintaining Basic Data Master Records

The information needed to manage materials and services is stored as basic data master records. The fundamental method of entering such data is by using an existing master record as a reference or model to be copied and modified to correspond to the data that has to be stored.

If you change any master record, you can be sure that the system will have logged this event. You can look back over the history of such changes for any record you select.

You can attach text to material master records for whatever purpose is relevant to your company.

The standard display facilities enable you to select a specific material master or set of masters by a wide range of methods. When you find what you need, you can drill down to see all the data associated with the material of interest.

Holding Vendor Records

The main purchasing functions served by the set of vendor master records follow:

- Requests for quotations
- Processing quotations
- Ordering

The main financial accounting activities supported by the vendor masters follow:

- Data entry during processing
- Verification of invoices from the vendors
- Payment of invoices to the vendors

Both groups of activities call on the same common set of vendor masters when processing transactions.

Using Once-Only Vendor Records
The system offers a master record on which you can store the basic transaction data for all vendors who aren't expected to supply your materials or services on a recurring basis.

Maintaining User Department Views of a Vendor Record   Suppose that the purchasing department needs the vendor information for ordering and checking deliveries. But the financial department is also interested in the vendors because payments have to be made. The sales function may also have an interest if the vendors are also to be customers. Each different user department in your company has a particular set of data fields in the vendor records that it needs. These fields are formally recorded as *views*. The system provides for these views by a series of tables. Each user department can specify which data elements of the vendor master records to access for their particular operations. Not everyone has to look at everything.

Adapting the Structure of Vendor Master Records   The level of the organizational structure at which the master records of a vendor are stored depends on who normally uses that vendor. For example, if your company has two purchasing organizations, Office and Plant, vendors of office supplies will have their records associated with the Office purchasing organization code, and the materials needed by the manufacturing and storage facilities will be supplied from vendors with their master records stored under the Plant purchasing organization code.

Each vendor master has the same data structure, which can be adjusted to suit your company during customizing. The attributes of this data object include data clusters such as the following:

- General data, such as the address and details of the communications channels to be used for email and fax.
- Purchasing data concerning prices and delivery, with the conditions and agreements made with this particular vendor.
- Accounting data, which includes details of the vendor's bank for direct payment and any agreed-on arrangements for payment. This data is managed and maintained at the company code level.

Using the Vendor Data Object   When an invoice or a purchasing transaction is being verified, the vendor details of this particular document are checked, as well as any calculations or authorization restrictions.

The vendor company may have a complex structure in which its sales organization is separate from the parent company. The vendor head office may bill you for goods supplied by the sales department, for example. So the vendor master record might have attributes or clusters of data fields to manage the monthly debits and credits, as well as an attribute for purchasing data concerning the purchasing organization, such as the currency used on orders and the defined trading conditions that specify how intercompany transactions are to be conducted. Data attributes for the accounting information are also under the company code, such as control account identification, terms of payment, and bank details.

Assigning Vendor Account Groups   Vendor accounts are assigned to account groups on the basis of their similarity according to criteria you define during customizing.

One group is for one-time vendors; you won't want to store more data than needed to complete the current transaction, because you don't expect to use them again. The structure of their master records is truncated as soon as you identify them as one-time or once-only vendors by assigning them to this account group.

The system also suggests specific master data structures for account groups confined to banking connections, head office business, and so on. You can adjust the account group master data structures to suit your company.

Displaying by Account Group   The main reason for assigning a vendor to an account group is to allow the system to filter out data fields that aren't required for transactions with members of that group so that those fields don't appear onscreen when you are doing business with that group. For example, if you are building a purchase order, you don't normally need to process the screens that deal with bank data.

Each vendor account group is allocated a specific range of vendor master record numbers. You can tell by looking at the vendor account number which vendor account group you are dealing with. If the company code appears, you also know that this record is maintained at the company-code level.

In general, the concept of *vendor* represents a source from which material can be procured. The nature of this material as a tangible object or in the form of a service and how it is bought and handled are matters documented in the material master records.

Understanding Material Masters

To implement an integrated system of production planning and materials management, you must have a central database where anyone in your company can find out all there is to know about any material passing through the plant. Everyone must use the same rules and data structures when they enter data about part numbers and descriptions of these parts. All finished and semifinished products, as well as all raw materials, must be subject to exactly the same information discipline.

The SAP R/3 system expects you to use a system based on the organizational structure you defined during customizing, but the system is flexible, and you can construct whatever arrangement best suits your company. For example, you will probably want to maintain data at the company-code level if it is to be used throughout the company. Accuracy and uniformity are ensured by this arrangement, but there is also a very compelling additional benefit: If you want to change any detail—a change of address of the expert on this material or a change of raw material specification, for example—you only have to alter the material master at the company-code level for the new information to be immediately in place on every screen that needs it.

Material requirements planning data is kept at the plant level, where it is needed from moment to moment. Purchasing data is needed at the plant level to maintain the inventory and anticipate potential shortfalls in the materials used in production. The economical batch size is an example of a purchasing data element that can be used to minimize the costs of production.

Stock data, product details and quantities, quality inspection reports, and so on are maintained at the storage-location level, because they can be planned into the production process with full cognizance of the inventory, handling, and transport implications. These factors may affect which storage location is chosen as the source.

Thus, a typical material master may have data attributes such as these:

- **General data,** such as material number, description, units of measure, and technical data
- **Plant-specific data,** such as material requirements planning type, planned delivery time, purchasing group, and batch indicator
- **Evaluation data,** such as evaluation price, evaluation procedure, and evaluation quantity
- **Warehouse management data,** such as unit of measure, palletization instructions, and directions to place in or remove from stock
- **Sales-specific data,** such as delivering plant and sales texts

Any of these data clusters can be further subdivided. For example, the plant-specific data might be extended to include the following types of data:

- Storage location data, such as the permitted period of storage, the individual stock field, or the storage area within a storage location where the material is kept
- Forecast data for this material
- Consumption data for this material

The R/3 system includes a Customizing component as standard. It allows the implementers of the R/3 system and its applications to select the functions relevant to the client company from the full array of SAP standard business programs. The Customizing component requires that you select or enter all the details that will appear when the standard programs are in use. The process is discussed in Chapter 7, "Customizing."

The format of a material master record is defined by a template. This is suggested by the system after you identify your requirements by selections from the materials management sections of the Customizing menu. At this time, you can also specify how long you want your material numbers to be, as well as the format to be used to separate data elements such as the company code and the purchasing organization identifier.

You will probably prefer to have each user department see only those elements of the material master it needs, according to the type of transaction it undertakes. The system prompts you to identify the user departments during customizing.

Assigning Material Type

The type to which you assign each material is a matter you decide according to the custom and practice in your company. For example, you may establish the following material types:

- Raw materials
- Semifinished products
- Finished products
- Services
- Trading goods
- Internally owned empty containers or transit rigs
- Externally owned containers

Using the Control Functions of a Material Type   The consequences of assigning one of your materials to a particular material type include a variety of constraints and restrictions that make the system easier to use and less likely to generate errors. For example, the material type master record may contain data elements that control the following activities in relation to each material assigned this material type:

- Which user departments can maintain the material, in the sense of making alterations to the data in the material master records
- The procurement type of this material
- How the FI-Financial Accounting module assigns a stock account automatically
- Whether quantities of the material on inventory, the financial values, or both are updated

The Materials Management System offers you a choice of all the standard material types, to which you can add your own by establishing new material type master records and specifying how you want the system to respond.

Assigning Materials to an Industry Sector   If your company, or one or more of the companies in your group, has to deal with a material that must be treated differently according to some criteria you specify for your own convenience, the concept of an industry sector can be applied. In the material master, there will be a data element that can hold an industry sector indicator, which then can be consulted to control how this material is used.

You might want to differentiate between products sold directly to the public and those going to other manufacturers to be incorporated into their products, for example. You could use the industry sector to identify where the transaction processing methods should be adjusted for the different customers. You could use the same industry sector to identify important differences in how you deal with various types of vendors supplying your company with goods and services. It might be convenient to define some industry sectors purely on the basis of one data element, such as the unit of measure—for example, European pallets, bags, or truckloads.

Applying Units of Measure   You can handle the management of material by using the individual piece or smallest indivisible entity. On the other hand, some materials have to be handled in groups defined by their packaging or their containers to be manipulated by the transport equipment.

If your company has a variety of units of measure for the same material, you can define conversion factors to be applied to the base unit. These factors can work either way. You can set up the system to compute the size and weight of a single piece from a pallet that has been weighed and carries a specified number of base units. Or you can have the system use a factor to compute the size of a quantity of base units, assuming that they are to be packed on the standard pallets, and so on. You can define these calculations for each material individually.

Identifying Batches   A *batch* is a partial stock of material that should be managed separately from other partial stocks of the same material. This partial stock will usually be given a batch number and other documented characteristics, such as the day it was produced and the quality inspection report.

A batch or lot may be distinguished as a production lot because it was all made from the same constituents in the same production campaign. This tracking of lots may be a legal requirement (in the food processing industry, for example), or it may be a recognition that, although the circumstances of production may not be wholly controllable, the quality of the material can be monitored and the information related to the individual batch while it remains in the plant. The weather and the composition of the raw materials are two factors that can affect a production process. Knowing a batch's identity and the laboratory analysis to which the batch was subjected can be very important when it is time to use the lot in further production processes or when it is to be sold to a customer.

A batch may also be identified because the quantities of materials in it arrived together from the delivery route. A delivery lot may have been subjected to influences during its transportation, which could be important for its users. If one item from a delivery lot is found to be unusual, the other items from the same delivery may have to be set aside for a quality control inspection.

Assigning to Special Stocks   A batch or a single item can be assigned as a special stock for a number of reasons that you might want to redefine during customizing. The standard special stock definitions fall into these groups:

- **Vendor special stocks.** Materials that arrive on consignment from a particular vendor and for which there may be a deferred payment arrangement whereby the user of these special stocks doesn't pay for them until they are used. Chapter 18, "Understanding the Production Planning for Process Industries Module," explains more about this use.

- **Customer special stocks.** Containers or other transportation equipment that still belongs to your company but is temporarily with your customer because it was used to hold your products. The customer may have to incur a special charge if this packing material isn't returned before the due date.

- **Event-related stocks.** Materials that have been ordered specifically because they will be needed for a planned event—for example, the building of a make-to-order product for which the customer has placed a firm order.

Altering a Material Master   A standard feature of the SAP R/3 system and its application modules is that every transaction that makes a change in the master data records is recorded in a log that stores the change management history for the records. The date and reference of the update are recorded on the master.

Material masters can be maintained and corrected centrally or in each user department, where the relevant information is at hand. The records still are held under the company code so that other departments can use them.

N O T E   There are several security levels to protect a master from unauthorized access. You may be prevented from looking at a data object or from changing it. You may also be prevented from creating new data objects by copying a master or generating one from the beginning.

Consulting Purchasing Info Records

If you want to find out which vendors have supplied a particular material in the past, or which materials can be obtained from a specific vendor, look in the purchasing info records. These master records contain information on the relationships between vendors and the materials and services they offer.

Interpreting Info Record Types   There are two types of purchasing info records, depending on whether a material master record is associated with the vendor. If there is a material master record, the relationship established by the purchasing info record is between this material master record and a vendor master record. This vendor can supply this material.

If there is no material master record but there is a vendor master record, the purchasing info master record carries the information needed to relate the vendor with one or more materials that are members of a material group. The relationship established by the purchasing info record is between a vendor master and a material group master. This vendor can supply some materials of this material group.

Accessing Data from a Purchasing Info Record   If you have located a particular purchasing info record, you can use it to gain access to the rest of the material data environment. The following types of information are available to you by pointing to the appropriate parts of the screen and using the special function keys:

- Current and future prices and purchasing conditions
- The identification number of the most recent purchase order that includes one of the materials on the purchasing info record, which helps you compare prices and packaging requirements, for example
- The number of the most recent purchase order involving the vendor on the purchasing info record
- Descriptive text concerning the material that is normally printed on the purchase order
- How much of this material has been ordered from this vendor to date
- Other ordering statistics regarding this material or vendor
- The price history of this material as ordered or quoted by different vendors
- The rating assigned to this vendor by the vendor evaluation system

Copying Data from a Central Source   The process of creating a purchase order causes the system to look for purchasing info records that might be relevant. If an info record is found, the system copies the data into the new purchase order for your approval. By this means, the important information, such as the price and the vendor details, can be determined centrally and maintained there for use by all who need it. This information appears without error on the purchasing documents.

Interpreting the Info Record Structure   The header of the info record contains general information relevant to all organizational levels of the purchasing info record. These levels carry the data applicable to the individual purchasing organizations or plants that will use the material when it arrives.

By using this structured-level approach, the purchasing info record can show where there are different purchasing conditions for the various purchasing organizations in the company. When the purchaser accesses a material, for example, the purchasing conditions applicable at his or her level of the company also are accessed through the purchasing info record.

You could expect the following types of information to be in the purchasing info record:

- Certificate of inspection data
- Text to be used on purchase orders
- Reminders
- Unit of measure
- Purchasing conditions
- Purchase order history
- Assignment to stock or consumable material

You can use any data fields on a purchasing info record as search specifications to retrieve all the info records that have the same data field value or a logical or mathematical function of it. For example, you can seek all info records that concern a specific material type or all info records that don't.

Creating Purchasing Info Records   A purchasing info record is created or changed automatically when a quotation is entered, a purchase order is entered, or a long-term purchasing agreement is created. You can also create or edit a purchasing info record manually.

Simulating the Net Price   Buyers will want to know who is the best supplier. You can use the purchasing info record system to set up simulations, as in these examples:

- Comparing the prices of various vendors for a material or material group
- Comparing the sales conditions of various vendors for a material or material group
- Showing the vendor's prices for all its materials
- Reviewing the net price of a range of vendors for various order quantities and other order data, such as delivery times and conditions attached to late deliveries

You can ask the system to determine the best source on the basis of the quantity required, the date required, and the vendor net price. It can do this for any number of plan versions you set up to explore the shape of the purchasing decision environment. You can also use the flexible display functions to present the results in graphical form.

Computing Vendor Net Price   The net price simulation can operate with any order quantities and other order data. It takes into account any incidental costs of delivery. If there is a cash discount for prompt payment, it factors this into the simulated price. In the same way, the system recognizes whether any price breaks are applicable because of the quantity required or the expected total price of the order. It also determines whether part of the order qualifies for such special purchasing conditions. Because the order information includes the date by which delivery is required, the system also can check that the net price has been computed using conditions that will be valid at that time.

Consulting a Bill of Material

In essence, a *bill of material* (BoM) is a list of the constituents of a composite product. It may be a list of the component subassemblies or a list of the parts to be included in a conglomerate—for example, products and a set of compact discs and documents on how to assemble these products and get them to work. The BoM is a flexible instrument now that it has made the transition from a list on a piece of paper to a data object in a computerized, integrated business system.

You can attach to the BoM other data objects, such as technical drawings and reports, that aren't themselves components of the product but are vital for its well-being while it is being processed or stored in your plant.

▶ **See** "Creating Bills of Material," **p. 392**

Working from the BoM   The list of components that make up a product is obviously an important document. These areas of activity depend on the BoM:

- Production planning and control
- Material requirements planning
- Costing
- Procurement
- Inventory management
- Warehouse management

Exploring the Structure of a BoM   A product is regarded as an assembly in the SAP R/3 system. Each assembly can be made from many parts that are themselves assemblies, and so on. The SAP R/3 system avoids data redundancy by following the convention that an assembly can be represented by any number of components. That some or all components are themselves complex assemblies isn't taken into account at the top level of the BoM.

If you want to see a list of all the constituent parts that make up a BoM, you have to initiate a *BoM explosion.*

Initiating a BoM Explosion   The notion of exploding a BoM is easy to understand if you start to do it. For each part of an assembly, list the constituent parts. For each of these constituent parts, list the constituent parts, and so on until every item on your list is a material that has a master record of its own, rather than a BoM telling you that the item is an assembly made from other parts.

This exploding procedure is precisely what has to be done if you want to calculate the weight of a complex product before it is assembled. This is also what you have to do if you are going to calculate the cost of producing this item. You cannot get away from the task of listing all the separate constituents and finding out what they will cost to purchase and what you will have to pay for the activities necessary to put them all together.

The BoM can obviously be a very complicated document. The SAP R/3 approach is to treat it as a hierarchy, in which the product identification code is at the pinnacle and the first-level

BoM specifies the components at this level. Each component can have its own BoM, which extends the hierarchy down one layer, and so on.

Using the BoM Explosion   Because the BoM is a list of component parts, it has a wide variety of uses:

- When you are creating an order for a subcontract, the mention of a BoM initiates the opening of all the subassemblies down to the level of materials that have their own material master records and can therefore be regarded as the lowest level of the BoM explosion hierarchy.

- If you want to reserve items from stock against a planned order, the exploded BoM for the ordered product generates the automatic reservation of all necessary materials.

- If you have to issue materials from stock to the production or delivery functions, the exploded BoM generates a full listing of materials, edited appropriately for the quantities needed.

Consulting the R/3 Classification

The SAP R/3 system supports a general classification system that can be applied to any master data records in the system or in the integrated applications. If master data records exist, they can be classified as materials, routings, documents, customers, vendors, batches, plants, storage locations, accounts, passwords, and authorizations.

If you know the classification of what you are looking for, the system shows you a list of all items that are assigned that classification. Then you can refine your search specification by going deeper down the classification hierarchy until you see the master record you need.

It might happen that the material you need is out of stock. In such a case, the system can tell you which other materials are in the same group according to the classification system. One of them might be suitable.

The classes in the classification can be single-level or multilevel. You can assign match codes freely. *Match codes* are names of your own choosing that represent particular levels in a multilevel classification scheme. A classification scheme managed by the computer purely in terms of class-code identifiers can also be understood by users in terms of more familiar titles, assigned as match codes. Here is part of a multilevel classification scheme that might appear in a marine insurance document:

- Vessels include marine vessels and objects being towed by marine vessels.
- Marine vessels include ships, boats, and floating objects.
- Floating objects include flotsam, jetsam, floating seabirds, undersea objects temporarily on the surface, and marine vessels apparently without any means of propulsion or steerage.

Any data object being processed by SAP R/3 that is identified by the classification system can be used to call up a list of objects with the same classification. You can move up or down the classification scheme to see details of the objects by selecting the item of interest and using the special function keys to perform the drill-down search operation.

The ways in which objects vary are defined as their *characteristics*. You can set up a scheme to describe your company's products and the materials used to make them. You need enough characteristics to specify each material and product uniquely. Each characteristic may have a limited range of possible values. For example, color may be assigned one of these values: blue or red. You can choose any color, as long as it is blue or red.

Text descriptions or definitions of the characteristics of the classification scheme and their possible values can be maintained in several languages. You can search for classified objects in any of the supported languages.

It might be useful to define one or more fields in a master record as characteristics to be used for classification purposes. If your material masters have data in the DIN 4001 format copied from an external storage system, the SAP R/3 system generates the required classes and characteristics.

An object can be assigned to more than one class.

Referring to Conditions

The SAP R/3 system supports a mechanism for establishing conditions in the form of condition master record. They can refer to any subject-matter domain or any SAP R/3 application. The logical interpretation of a condition is illustrated by the if-then format:

- If X is true, then Y becomes true.
- If the sales quantity is equal to or greater than the first price break, then the order attracts a discount of 3 percent.

The conditions most commonly met in materials management are provided by the system in predefined standard form. You can also add to this list by creating your own conditions.

Consulting Predefined Conditions   An important application of the condition technique is specific price determination based on these types of considerations:

- Discounts
- Surcharges by percentage and absolute amounts
- Delivery costs
- Cash discounts for prompt payment
- Taxes

Editing Price Determination   Users can define the sequence in which price determination conditions are applied during the pricing process. The system proposes a set of default values in the purchasing document, which you can amend and supplement with additional charges.

Each purchasing organization in a company can have its own pricing procedure. Each vendor or vendor group also can be assigned an individual pricing procedure.

Interpreting Master Price Determination Conditions   The pricing of purchase orders takes place automatically on the basis of the conditions established in the price determination master records. The conditions set out in purchase info records are master conditions to be applied to all purchase orders issued to that vendor. If a purchasing contract is in force with a vendor, the master conditions are stored in the contract document.

Starting with the master pricing conditions, there are various factors you might need to take into account before determining the final price:

- The purchasing organization
- Whether the individual vendor is subject to specific pricing conditions or modifications of the master conditions
- Whether the invoicing party varies from the actual supplier of the materials or services
- Whether certain items are subject to special conditions—such as on the basis of the material, the material group, the material type, or the plant
- Whether a contract item is involved that attracts special conditions

Controlling the Validity of Master Pricing Conditions   A set of pricing conditions stored in a master record is given a validity defined by a starting date and a validity period. If the starting date is in the future, the purchasing conditions aren't applied until that date. When the validity period is reached, the new base prices, discounts, and surcharges are automatically used in price determination.

Limiting Manual Alteration of Default Prices   In the central purchasing conditions master records, the purchasing manager can specify upper and lower limits on the adjustments that users at various levels of authorization are allowed to make. These limits can be defined in percentage terms and as absolute amounts.

Declaring Central Master Conditions   When a purchasing master conditions record is changed, the alterations are made automatically through all the purchase orders and contracts affected. This way, you can quickly check the effects of any changes in a vendor's price strategy.

If a vendor is prepared to offer your company a global discount using a percentage or absolute discount on all purchase orders you have placed, your prices are affected by a temporary alteration in the master purchasing conditions for this vendor. You can see the effect by viewing a listing of all your purchase orders for this vendor and comparing the total under the new and old purchasing conditions.

Planning Material Requirements

In the context of materials management, the main function of material requirements planning is to monitor stock at the end of each day and automatically generate purchase order proposals to be forwarded to the purchasing department. Material requirements planning is normally carried out at the plant level, so all the stock available in the plant is recognized by the planning run, whatever its storage location. However, you can also carry out material requirements planning runs at the level of individual storage locations, or at the plant level, with certain storage locations excluded.

Applying Net Change Planning

The material requirements planning run usually applies the net change planning procedure, in which the only materials subject to planning are those for which stocks have changed. If the planned requirements have also changed, a corresponding alteration must be made in the purchasing proposal. The material requirements planning run can be further shortened by predefining a planning horizon. These procedures give the material requirements planner a current view of planning results. The planner then can append information about important parts or assemblies and warnings of exceptional situations.

Applying Consumption-Based Planning

A simple and easy-to-use planning method is available for companies that don't have their own production plant. It works on the assumption that stock promised by a planned order is no longer *available to promise* (ATP) and should be replaced by initiating a material planning procedure.

There are two procedures for consumption-based planning:

- Reorder point planning
- Forecast-based planning

Using Reorder Point Planning   The *reorder point* is also known as the *reorder level.* If the warehouse stock of a material falls below the reorder level, the system automatically creates a purchase order proposal, unless the purchasing department has already created a purchase order for the required quantity.

Replenishing stock takes time. Therefore, the reorder point must be calculated on an assumption about how the remaining stock might be used while awaiting a delivery. The expected average consumption is a reasonable value, for example.

Previous consumption values over a comparable period under similar trading conditions would be a refinement, and a knowledge of future requirements would complement the picture. Prudence would counsel you to add a little safety stock in case the delivery is held up for any reason. These key parameters—the reorder point and the safety stock—can be entered manually, or they can be proposed by the system on the basis of past data and extrapolation rules that you specified for this purpose.

Using Inventory Management and Automatic Reorder Point Planning   It is important for you to keep stock levels low. Having the system automatically reorder stock based on evidence it has collected regarding consumption and delivery enables you to do this.

The Inventory Management function ensures that every time a material is taken from the warehouse, the stock level is checked to see whether it has fallen below the reorder level. If this is the situation, an entry is made in the material requirements planning file to generate a purchase order on the next material requirements planning run.

Using Forecast-Based Planning

The forecast-based planning method uses a forecast value or forecast quantity of stock instead of a stock reorder level as the starting point for the plan to replenish inventory.

The material requirements planning controller performs a material requirements forecast at regular intervals for each material needed over a period. For this purpose, the period can be defined as day, week, month, posting period, or split periods within this period. The planning horizon can be set in terms of the number of planning periods to be included in the calculations.

The basis for the forecast calculation includes a provision for safety stock and an assessment of the historical consumption data.

As material is reserved to be withdrawn from the warehouse in each planning period, the forecast requirement for that period is reduced by the corresponding amount. The remainder of the original forecast requirement for the period then is entered for the material requirements planning run and is subject to a purchase order. Stock that was planned and has been used isn't reordered, because purchase orders for the planned values already have been created.

N O T E   The calculation of net requirements compares the forecast quantities of each material for each period with the quantities that are expected to be available. Some of this stock may be in the warehouse now, and some of it may be scheduled for delivery in time to meet the requirement. If a deficit is foreseen, a purchase order proposal is generated.

Choosing Lot-Sizing Procedures

When a material requirements shortage is anticipated as the consequence of a planning run, the lot size for reordering is taken from the material master record, where it has been specified by the material requirements planning controller. The way it is determined and used depends on the choice of lot-sizing procedure. The SAP R/3 system supports an extensive set of lot-sizing procedures, to which you can add user-specific procedures as required. There are three basic procedures: static lot-sizing, periodic lot-sizing, and optimum lot-sizing.

Static Lot-Sizing   The lot size is calculated from the quantity specifications in the material master record. Three criteria can be used:

- Lot-for-lot order quantity
- Fixed-lot size
- Replenishment up to the maximum stock level

Periodic Lot-Sizing   The size of the lot to be reordered can be determined from the requirement quantities of one or more planning periods added together to form a purchase order proposal. You can choose the time period over which the requirements should be totaled:

- Daily lot size
- Weekly lot size

        ▓ Monthly lot size

        ▓ Lot size based on flexible period lengths within the accounting periods

        ▓ Freely definable periods according to a planning calendar used to determine lot size

Optimum Lot-Sizing   The cost of a large lot of material may yield a low unit cost, but there will be associated costs independent of lot size, as well as storage costs, which are usually related to lot size. There are several methods of working out an optimum ratio between the lot size and the independent and storage costs. SAP R/3 supports the following optimization procedures:

        ▓ Part-period balancing

        ▓ Least-unit costing

        ▓ Dynamic lot-size creation

        ▓ Groff reordering

Adding Restrictions on Lot Size   The material master records allow you to impose additional restrictions on the reorder lot size. The following types of restrictions are supported:

        ▓ **Minimum lot size** causes the system to round up the quantity reordered to meet the minimum lot size.

        ▓ **Maximum lot size** ensures that the system doesn't group period requirements that will generate a quantity larger than the maximum lot size.

        ▓ **Rounding adjustment** specifies that the lot size is rounded up or down to arrive at an exact multiple of the order unit. This method avoids the need to split a packaging unit, for example, or to ensure that the delivery transportation vehicle is used efficiently.

Arranging Quotas   You might get some of your supplies from several vendors, each of which operates its own delivery schedule. You can have the system take this into consideration by specifying quotas across vendors, across schedules, or both. This restriction is built in at the stage of the material requirements planning run using the specification you establish.

Interpreting a Material Requirements Planning Result

The output results from a material requirements planning run are summarized in two lists that you can display in various ways:

        ▓ **Material requirements planning list.** Shows the stock and requirements at the time of the last planning run.

        ▓ **Stock and requirements list.** Shows the current situation, including goods receipts, goods issues, and any other events relevant to planning the material requirements.

The following display formats are available for the material requirements planning results, and you can readily change from one to another:

        ▓ Days

        ▓ Weeks

- Months
- Posting period
- Planning calendar
- User-defined flexible period split

During a material requirements planning run, the system generates exception messages to alert the controller if any of the following events occur:

- Scheduling delay
- Rescheduling and cancellation
- Material stock level falling below the safety stock level

The controller may decide to group exception messages so that they can be displayed together. This is done by specifying the structure in an exception group master record.

Generating a Material Forecast

The material forecast is used to determine requirements and to compute the safety stock and reorder level—for individual materials, if necessary, but normally in batch mode. The material forecast depends on historical data, and its validity therefore depends on the accuracy of this data. The other crucial assumption is that material consumption patterns that are likely to continue into the future can be detected from examining the data.

To represent a pattern of material consumption, the system has four basic models. It chooses the model that best fits the historical data, or you can specify that a certain model be used:

- **Constant model** finds a single value that best fits the varying consumption values for the material as recorded in the historical data. It represents the average value—slightly refined, if you want—to play down the effects of occasional very high or very low values.

- **Trend model** finds a steady increase or decrease in the quantity of a material consumed.

- **Seasonal model** finds a regular pattern that repeats itself every year, with the peaks and troughs occurring at the same time of year and reaching to about the same value each cycle of the pattern.

- **Seasonal trend model** finds the data that best fits a seasonal pattern imposed on a steadily increasing or decreasing central value.

You can use the model to predict the value or quantity of material likely to be required at any time in the future. The assumption is that the pattern discerned in the data, or mandated by the material requirements planning controller, will continue to be applicable. You have to take it for granted that there will be no discontinuity in the pattern of consumption of this material.

Your assumption that nothing is going to change may be an error!

The only real comfort offered by the system in this matter is its capability to recalculate the parameters of the models at any time and to rebuild its forecasts using the latest data available.

▶ **See** "Business Planning and Control," **p. 289**

Purchasing by Exception

The aim of the MM-PUR Purchasing component is to automate the purchasing function of your company as much as possible so that the buyer only has to deal with exceptional circumstances, thus avoiding routine paperwork.

Almost all the data needed to create a purchase order should be in the system already. It should be copied automatically to reduce errors and speed up the task. A purchase order may start life as a purchase requisition originating in one of the user departments, or it may be created as a result of material requirements planning.

A source of supply of the material or service has to be identified by the system, by the user who needs the material, or by the purchasing department—perhaps after soliciting quotations from a number of potential suppliers.

The most common method of generating a purchase order is by copying one prepared for a previous purchase and updating it as necessary.

Reviewing the Purchasing Documents

The traditional paper documents associated with purchasing in a large organization have been reengineered to take advantage of the benefits of a fully integrated system in which almost all the information required to complete the documents can be found in the master records of the system, where they are kept up-to-date.

The following documents are used in purchasing:

- Purchase requisition
- Request for quotation
- Quotation
- Purchase order
- Contract
- Delivery scheduling agreement

Using the Purchasing Document Structure

The header of a purchasing document contains the document number and vendor details. The remainder of the document consists of one or more items that refer to specific materials or services to be procured and the quantities required.

Each item in a document can refer to one or more supplements. For example, an item in a purchasing document could refer to a supplement that details the order history of this item from the supplier.

Tracking a Purchase Requisition

A *requisition* is a request for a service to be rendered by another department. In the case of a purchase requisition, the request is for the purchasing department to procure a certain quantity of a material or service and to have it delivered to the originator of the request by a specific date.

The purchasing organization responds to the requisition by going through a series of steps to determine a source of supply, perhaps after a request for quotation submitted to several potential suppliers. After the purchase requisition is checked and a supplier is chosen, the requisition is released to be converted to a purchase order, which is checked again and released to the vendor for purchasing action, with the obligation to pay for it when the time comes.

Generating a Purchase Requisition   There are two ways to create a purchase requisition:

- Use a reference document as a model and edit a copy of it on behalf of the requesting department.
- Have the purchase requisition generated automatically by the material requirements planning process.

Finding Sources of Supply   If the system is aware of a suitable source of supply, it uses it to create a purchase requisition. The following sources of supply are recognized and used to generate the purchasing document if they are relevant:

- A fixed vendor as specified in the material master record
- An outline purchase agreement that has a validity period that includes the required delivery date
- A purchasing info record that identifies a possible vendor of the material or service required

Releasing Purchase Requisitions   Whether a purchase requisition is approved for release as a purchase order depends on the conditions imposed by the release strategy, which usually is a chain of release points. These release points are the individuals or the organizational units assigned the responsibility of approving requisitions after they are assigned a particular release strategy.

The release strategy is assigned automatically when the purchase requisition is entered. The strategy chosen depends on factors such as the value of the requisition and the material type of the requested items.

Allocating Sources to Purchase Requisitions   Given a list of the items awaiting purchasing action, the buyers will probably want to generate the purchase requisitions that fall into their individual areas of responsibility, because they will know where to obtain the particular materials.

If no approved sources can be identified, a list of possible suppliers must be created in order to distribute a request for quotation document.

Responding to a Request for Quotation

After a *request for quotation* (RFQ) to a vendor elicits a quotation, it is returned in the form of a list of the vendor's prices for the material, along with the purchase conditions and perhaps some additional information. This data is entered on the original RFQ document, which then becomes a source of all the information necessary to make an informed choice among the vendors who have responded to the RFQ.

After all the quotations are entered, the buyers can access the price comparison list and use it to have the system conduct a comparative analysis of the quoted prices and conditions, with a view to determining the most favorable quotation. The analysis data then can be automatically stored in a purchasing info record and the unsuccessful bidders automatically sent rejection letters.

Streamlining Purchase Order Processing

The aim of the automated purchase order component is to reduce the time taken to process purchase orders and minimize the chances of error. The method is to use data already in the system as much as possible.

Using References to Minimize Data-Entry Work   The buyer can use any of the following methods of finding an existing document to provide the data for a new purchase order:

- Select from a list of current requisitions.
- Select from a list of previous purchase orders.
- Call up an existing longer-term buying contract for the material and create a release order for the required amount of material to be delivered on the date specified. This causes the text, prices, and conditions to be copied from the contract to the release order.

Referencing a Purchasing Info Record   The purchasing info record performs some of the functions of a contract, in that it contains details of the vendor's prices and conditions for specific materials. When you create a purchase order, you can initiate the creation of a purchasing info record or the updating of one that exists already. When you call up a purchasing info record as a reference for a purchase order, you only have to enter the material number, the order quantity, and the delivery date required.

Generating Purchasing Documents Automatically   The place most often used to begin generating purchasing documents is the Purchase Order Item Overview screen, which displays the most important information you will need to create a new purchase order, an RFQ, or a delivery schedule. The information you can identify and copy from this screen follows:

- Material number
- Purchase order quantity
- Purchase order price
- Plant
- Storage location

Creating a Purchase Order   At this stage, you have a range of options to continue with the creation of the purchasing document:

- **Vendor Known** is the preferred choice if you know who will be the supplier.

■ **Vendor Unknown** tells the system to try to find suitable vendors on the basis of the purchase order items that have been entered up to that point in the creation of the purchase order. You might have to allocate particular orders among the proposed vendors if more than one is suggested by the system.

■ **Allocated Purchase Requisitions Exist** lets you call up a list of all purchase requisitions that have been placed with supply sources from the purchasing group to which you belong. From this historical data, you can choose a vendor, if one is suitable. The system then copies the relevant data to the new purchase order.

Assigning Accounts   The account to which the amount is to be posted when the goods are delivered has to be determined during the creation of the purchase order. You select the type or name of the account, and the system carries out an internal check and proposes an account number that will be entered on the purchase order if it is accepted.

Several accounts may have to be posted when the goods ordered by a purchase order are delivered. The net order value can be apportioned on a percentage basis or in terms of specified amounts to any number of individual cost objects, such as projects or cost centers.

▶ **See** "Cost Center Accounting with CO-CCA," **p. 298**

The allocation of a net order value to cost objects and the posting of the value to an account in the FI-Financial Accounting system are initiated by data copied automatically from purchase requisitions or contracts and replicated on any other documents that are generated using them as references.

Creating Outline Purchase Agreements

If your company frequently uses the same supplier for one or more materials or services, each subject to specified conditions that are likely to remain essentially the same for a period of time, it might be useful to set out a purchase agreement in outline form. This outline purchase agreement has a period of validity during which the conditions of the agreement remain valid, and it has a limit set to the quantity or value of the goods that can be supplied under this agreement during this period of validity.

The agreement is in outline form because it doesn't make any reference to the date required or the actual quantity or value of the material or service that is to be delivered. This information has to be supplied by a subsequent issue of a release order or a delivery schedule, which refers to the outline purchase agreement in order to define the conditions and other details of the contract to supply.

Recognizing Types of Outline Purchase Agreements   Many terms are used to refer to an outline purchase agreement. This discussion treats all these names as equivalent to an outline purchase agreement:

■ Blanket order

■ Blanket contract

■ Period contract

■ Bulk contract

■ Master agreement

■ Master contract

The contract to which an outline purchase agreement is the preliminary, and that is the source of data for generating documents, may be a value contract or a quantity contract, according to how the upper limit is defined. The value or quantity specified in the outline purchase agreement is the limit for the period of validity.

Working with Scheduling Agreements In many industries, the price of materials may be affected a great deal by the uncertainties of supply and demand. Your company might want to introduce a degree of stabilization into such a situation by setting up an arrangement for a schedule of material deliveries over a defined period of validity, during which the prices and conditions are to be kept constant.

The scheduling agreement usually specifies a total or target quantity for the period and a particular type of vendor scheduling of the constituent deliveries. Each material or service in the agreement may have its own vendor schedule. The details of the schedule within the validity period are regularly updated as the requirements of the purchasing company become known.

Working with Vendor Delivery Schedules The vendor trying to supply according to a schedule doesn't receive a purchase order or a release order. When the scheduling agreement validity period begins, the vendor works according to a vendor delivery schedule, which is regularly updated. Each line of the vendor delivery schedule represents an individual delivery shipment consisting of a specified quantity of the particular material, delivered to a precise storage or holding location in your plant on a particular date, and perhaps also at a particular time on that date if you are operating in a just-in-time or KANBAN environment.

Benefiting from Vendor Delivery Scheduling If vendor scheduling agreements are in place for all the component parts of a product assembly, your company can add considerable value to its products and gain a competitive edge over its rivals. You'll see these benefits:

■ A vendor delivery schedule can reduce the processing time and the amount of paper or electronic transmissions compared to an equivalent series of individual purchase orders or release orders.

■ Production at a plant can take place with a minimum of waiting stock—perhaps none.

■ The vendor does not have to hold up shipments to amass the quantity needed for a large delivery, because the order is dispatched to the schedule. From the vendor's viewpoint, the schedule provides a steadier basis on which to plan production.

Maintaining Sources of Supply

You need a list of sources for each material and service of interest to your purchasing group within the purchasing organization. This list is usually maintained manually, because the details change frequently. Also, sometimes new entries as fresh vendors come into the market, and the products of the purchasing company undergo development and thus require new sources of materials.

The source list for a material can also be maintained automatically by the following techniques:

- Adopting an existing source list as a first proposal for manual editing
- Copying from outline purchase agreements that refer to this material
- Copying from purchasing info records used to generate purchase orders in the past

The source list data maintenance functions enable you to assign dates and time periods to sources so that they are used only during the periods defined. These sources aren't allowed to supply goods out of season.

A quota system can be set up so that two or more vendors or internal sources share the requirement. The time-dependent condition can be applied with the quota system. This is figured into the calculation when a choice of sources is evaluated automatically.

Evaluating Vendors

If you are an experienced buyer, you might be able to make a wise choice of sources from the vendors and any internal production plant or storage location that has material available to meet your requirements. However, it might be difficult to build this experience in a changing market and with a changing labor force made up of people who share many tasks rather than specialize in one. If this scenario is even remotely like parts of your organization, you should seriously consider using the automatic vendor evaluation function.

Every vendor (including internal providers) for a particular material is awarded a score out of 100 by the vendor evaluation system. These are the main criteria used by the system:

- Price
- Quality
- Delivery
- Service

Users can define up to 99 main criteria, and the contribution of each criterion to the total score can be weighted to emphasize the factors your company feels are most important.

The system provides five subcriteria for each main criterion. You can define up to 20 subcriteria. The scores for subcriteria can be calculated in different ways, according to the type of data or other input made available:

- Automatic calculation uses data that already exists in the system.
- Semiautomatic calculation relies on values entered by the buyers, from which the system then calculates the score for the subcriteria.
- Manual input occurs when you enter a vendor's score for a subcriterion and cut out any assessment of other data for this part of the evaluation.

You can use the option of manual entry or one of the varieties of automatic evaluation, according to the importance of the material or the other attributes of the pool of possible suppliers. If any change is made to the data or the formulas used by the vendor evaluation system, a log entry is made and the event is recorded.

You can display the results of vendor evaluations in many ways. You can view a rank ordering of all vendors on the basis of all their scores on the materials they supply. Or you can view a rank ordering of suppliers for a specific material or service.

Reporting

Purchasing managers have to keep track of all their purchase orders and all their purchasing organizations. They must also be continually aware of their vendor population and newcomers to it that they haven't yet used.

If there are trends in the requirements of their own company, they must notice them in time to plan their purchasing schedules.

Analyzing Purchasing Documents   The following inquiries can be answered by calling for the relevant report:

- Which purchase orders were placed with a certain vendor over a specific period?
- Which purchase orders have been processed as far as delivery?
- Has this vendor delivered all or only part of this purchase order?
- Does this vendor have a good record for delivering on time?
- How many orders from this vendor have been received and found to be invoiced correctly?
- What is the average value of purchase orders handled by this purchasing organization or this buyer group?
- What are the total values of orders placed by each purchasing organization in this company?

Using Standard Analyses of Purchase Order Values   You can apply the standard SAP R/3 analysis functions to the historical data found in the purchase orders and the associated purchasing documents. Here are some examples:

- **Totals analysis** lets you see the number and total value of existing purchase orders.
- **ABC analysis** shows the distribution of vendors across three groups, defined as
  - A   Vendors that account for the highest value of material purchases
  - B   Vendors that account for an average value of purchases
  - C   Vendors from which the value of purchase is the lowest
- **Analysis in comparison with a reference period** shows how a composite value has changed over time or across data objects, such as a comparison between this period last year and the current period for the total value purchased by each purchasing organization in the company.
- **Frequency analysis** shows which order values occur most often in each purchasing organization. An example of its use is negotiating a better discount based on an immediate discount for large orders instead of an end-of-year volume rebate.

Considering Purchase Document Listing Options   The large volume of purchase documents and master records in most systems running the MM-Materials Management module necessitates a powerful yet flexible suite of functions to display to users just what is wanted for the immediate purpose, and to leave out what isn't wanted. The following search specifications are typical of the needs of the purchasing management departments (many of them are, or could be, initiated by special function keys):

- List all purchase orders issued by this particular purchasing group during this specific time period.
- List the requisitions for this material from any or all of the following group of vendors.
- List all archived purchasing info records for this material for this plant.
- Display the purchase order history of the selected item.

Managing Inventory

The inventory is a list as well as a physical collection of material items. Inventory management entails the planning and control of material stocks by quantity and value. It has also come to include the planning, data entry, and documentation of all goods movements to, from, and within the storage locations in the warehouses used by the company.

Managing Material Stocks by Quantity

Any transaction that causes a change of stock is entered in real time, and the consequent update of the stock situation takes place immediately. This gives the user an overview that is always current of the stock level of any material.

Anyone else in the company who is thinking of placing some kind of reservation on this stock immediately knows whether it is available. The material requirements planning file receives an entry for this material if the reorder level is reached.

Managing Material Stocks by Value

When you post a movement of goods, the value of this stock is also updated. A chain of consequent postings occurs:

- There is an automatic posting of the value change to the GI-General Ledger account in the FI-Financial Accounting module.
- Line items are created for the account assignments needed in the CO-Controlling module, such as cost centers, orders, projects, and assets.

The system works out the amounts to be posted by using the actual quantity of material to be moved, which you have to enter, and the value of this amount of material, which it computes by using the data in the order and the master records for this material.

It is also possible to post goods receipts for which the prices haven't been ascertained. The values are calculated when the invoices are received and entered.

Each movement of material causes the system to create a document recording the amounts and values, as well as the time and date of the movement. This document serves as proof that the goods were dispatched. When the goods arrive at their destination, the entry of the goods receipt completes the proof of the movement.

Inventory movements can be planned by using reservations identifying the material that has been allocated to a particular customer or production order, or perhaps assigned to some kind of special stock.

The physical movement of the stock within the warehouse can be controlled by means of printed goods, receipts, and goods issue slips, which can carry the appropriate bar code to speed data entry.

Several standard methods are available in the system that support the comparison of the physical stocks with the book inventory balances:

- Periodic inventory
- Continuous inventory
- Sample-based inventory

These methods can be supplemented by installing and configuring the MM-WM Warehouse Management module, which enables the detailed oversight and control of warehouses with complex systems of storage bins and storage areas. This system is discussed in more detail in Chapter 17, "Understanding the Production Planning Module."

Generating Goods Receipts for Purchase Orders

When goods are delivered that were ordered by a purchase order, the system locates this purchase order document and proposes default data from it to form the goods receipt documentation. If there has been no overdelivery or underdelivery, the goods receipt is documented on the purchase order, which then is given an updated status. The goods receipt data is used to update both the purchase order and the vendor evaluation record.

If the purchase order shows no goods receipt by the required delivery date, the purchasing department can begin the reminder procedure. Because the goods receipt data is recorded on the purchase order, there can be a follow-up of the purchase order history to judge how reliable the vendor has been with respect to delivery dates and the correctness of the quantities and specification of the goods or services supplied.

When the vendor invoice arrives and is entered, the system again refers to the purchase order to verify that the material and the quantity are in accord with what was ordered. After the system determines that the purchase order and invoice are in agreement, it can value the goods receipt by applying the price to the quantity.

The system allows you to enter goods receipts for several purchase orders in one transaction.

Managing Contingencies in Goods Receipts for Purchase Orders   If a delivery note arrives with no reference to a purchase order, you can look up the possible purchase orders under the material code number or the vendor number. Entering a purchase order number causes the system to display a collective entry screen showing all the open purchase order items separately. The scope of this display can be the plant under the user's company code or all plants in the group.

If there is still no reconciliation of the delivery note or goods receipt with an open purchase order, you can ask to see detailed information about the order item and make notes against the item in the document by selecting a standard short text or by using freeform text from a word processing system.

You might have to enter a goods receipt using a different unit of measure from that given in the purchase order. The system tolerates this and makes the conversion. The storage location and the quality inspection indicator default to the values in the purchase order item, and these can be overridden by manual entries. The delivery costs determined by the planning procedures also are transferred automatically. If tolerances are allowed for underdelivery or overdelivery, these are checked automatically.

One purchase order item can be assigned to several storage locations by creating several goods receipt items—one for each of the separate destinations. For example, a partial quantity can be posted to quality inspection and the remainder to goods receipt blocked stock, where it stays until a favorable quality inspection report allows it to be released for production.

Assigning a Goods Receipt to Consumption   Some goods are destined for immediate consumption rather than storage. In such cases, the system picks up the account assignment—to a cost center or order, for example—from the purchase order data. Even if such just-in-time purchases are to be allocated to several control accounts, this can be done by the system after the delivery occurs and the goods receipt is entered. The person in the procurement department who deals with purchase orders that go directly to consumption is notified of the arrival of the goods by an automatic letter via the SAPmail system.

Reserving Materials

A material that will be required in the future obviously must be subject to planning. A quantity and therefore a provisional value is computed for each planning period that stretches from the current period to the planning horizon. The planning department will have decided, based on past data or orders for products that are already on the books, that a certain requirement for this material will exist for each planning period. A wise purchasing department will have prepared the purchase order, the outline purchasing agreement, or the contract, which makes it very likely that the required material will arrive at the production line on the due date, and perhaps at the due time of day, in order to be ready for incorporation into the product.

A *reservation* is an instrument for making sure that this material is moved from stock to consumption at the correct moment. It assumes that the stock will be on inventory to enable this to happen, and it assumes that no other production order or customer order has already been promised this quantity of this material.

The system automatically checks that the material mentioned in a material reservation hasn't already been assigned elsewhere. If it is free (*available to promise*, or ATP), the system shows this amount of stock under the heading of Reserved Stock for this material. The quantity of stock available for other purposes is reduced by the same amount so that double-booking of the material doesn't occur.

The following data is included in the entry to initiate a reservation:

- Material number
- Batch number, if applicable
- Planned quantity
- Scheduled delivery date
- Intended use of the reserved material, such as the production or customer order number for which it is to be reserved

After the reserved material is approved for release to production or another destiny, the actual quantity is substituted for the planned quantity in the calculation of the costs and values.

Understanding Goods Issues

When goods are moved from a warehouse, there has to be a posting of material withdrawal. This triggers the posting of a reduction in the quantity and value of the warehouse stock of this material.

Every transaction concerning a withdrawal from a warehouse can be treated as a planned withdrawal or an unplanned withdrawal. The consumption statistics show each type separately.

If you begin to create a goods issue for material that is reserved, the system assumes that you need the quantity stated in the material reservation and that you will also want to post the withdrawal to the account assigned in that document.

Before you can complete the goods issue, you must specify the destination of the withdrawn material in the Ship-To Party field. This location is printed on the withdrawal slip.

If you are running a complex warehouse system under the MM-WM Warehouse Management component, the system can show you all the storage locations holding the type of goods you require. If the materials are shipped and inspected in batches, the batch identification is part of the reservation procedure. You can specify rules for the use of batches.

Using Transfer Postings and Stock Transfers

A simple system is for the goods to be received to a warehouse and then withdrawn to be sold or consumed by the production processes. The arrangements are more complex if there is more than one warehouse and more than one production plant, particularly if some or all cost centers belong to different parts of the company and have their own company code, which signifies that they are legally obligated to publish their own separate financial documents—that is, the balance sheet and profit-and-loss statement.

If some material stock is transferred from one warehouse to another, and if these warehouses belong to different company codes, the Financial Accounting systems of both company codes must be coordinated to reflect that something of value has moved from one to the other.

Using One-Step and Two-Step Stock Transfers   A transfer of stock in one step entails two posting operations in the transaction:

1. Withdraw the stock from the warehouse and credit the sender.
2. Deliver the stock and debit the receiver.

An interim receiver may have to be introduced with the title of *transfer stock* if the stock will spend a long time in transit, as in this example:

1. Withdraw the stock from the warehouse and credit the sender.
2. Assign the stock as transfer stock and debit the transfer stock account.
3. Transport the stock to the new location.
4. Release the stock and credit the transfer stock account.
5. Deliver the stock and debit the receiver.

The important feature of the transfer stock is that it is not unrestricted stock. It cannot be used until it is received in the storage location and in the accounts of the receiving cost object—the production plant, for example.

Making Stock Transfer Reservations   A classic example of transfer stock is the goods in a cargo vessel on the high seas. The stock has value but cannot be used until it is delivered. However, quantities of the stock can be reserved for specific orders and also traded on the commodities market. Therefore, value is added or taken away from the stock while it still has the status of being transfer stock.

Tracing Goods Movements for Production Orders

Material components for production are received into the warehouse, and their receipt is posted in inventory management. Any components that have been planned for production will have been automatically reserved for consumption by the production process on a specific date. Unforeseen circumstances may arise, necessitating the withdrawal from the warehouse of components that weren't part of the reservation because they didn't figure in the plan. Nevertheless, if they are used to complete a customer order or a production order, they have to be costed with the planned materials and documented on the order.

If the order being completed is a production order using bulk materials, the quantity needed might not be known exactly until the completion confirmation document for the production order is posted. At this stage, the adjustment of inventory is confirmed by supplying the actual quantities in place of the planned estimates.

Many processes generate byproducts, co-products, and waste materials. The differences among these product types is in their cost consequences. Some yield sales revenues; some incur costs of disposal. The quantities and sometimes the values can be planned and recognized in the accounting procedures.

Reserving Stock for Quality Inspection

The process of inventory management makes allowances for the temporary or permanent absence of part of the stock for the purpose of quality inspection. A partial delivery quantity—perhaps a selection of batches or a sample of items taken from them—becomes a transfer batch, which is transferred immediately to stock in quality inspection.

If the quality is acceptable, the remainder of the stock in quality inspection is transferred to unrestricted-use stock, where it can be reserved against future orders or withdrawn to consumption when required.

The quality inspection may also take place after the material has been received into the warehouse and planned for issue. In such cases, the material is transferred to quality inspection stock on its way to the consumption location.

Conserving Batch Data

Certain materials have to be permanently associated with the batch identification they received when they were first manufactured and inspected. Pharmaceutical products and some foodstuffs fall into this category.

Even if the material can be repackaged, it still might have to be managed with batch numbers.

The system maintains a unique batch number master record, where it stores the data pertaining to that batch, including these items:

- Country of origin
- Date-of-goods receipt
- Storage location and conditions of storage
- Batch quantity, weight, and dimensions
- Shelf life expiry date
- Status as warehouse stock or quality inspection stock

The use of a material that is managed in batches is scheduled on a batch number basis so that the material is selected for withdrawal in order of its date of manufacture. However, you can enter a different priority manually or choose batches from a list. All movements of the material must identify the batches by number.

Managing Special Stock

The essential characteristic of a special stock of a material is that it is owned by a company or a person different from the owner of the storage location in which it is on inventory. For example, your company might rent storage space in another company. Your stock is listed on that company's inventory as special stock. Similarly, you might have special stock on your inventory because it is owned outside your organization. The point is that special stock must be managed separately.

Two types of special stock are recognized by the system and managed separately:

- Vendor special stock
- Customer special stock

Managing Vendor Special Stock   Three types of special stock are held on behalf of a vendor:

- Consignment material belonging to the vendor but stored on your premises
- Returnable packaging material belonging to the vendor but stored on your premises
- Material provided by you to the vendor who is a contractor to you

Managing Customer Special Stock   Three types of special stock are held on behalf of a customer:

- Consignment material that is yours but is still at the customer's location, awaiting your decision as to its disposal
- Returnable packaging material of yours that is at the customer's location
- Sales order stock that hasn't been settled and is therefore still owned by you

Data entry for special stock movements must include the identification of the vendor, the customer, or the sales order. Special stock is discussed in more detail in Chapter 20, "Understanding the Sales and Distribution Module."

Conducting a Physical Inventory

It is a legal requirement that every company perform a physical check of the inventory at least once in the course of a business year. SAP R/3 standard business programs are available to carry out these physical inventory procedures:

- Periodic inventory
- Continuous inventory
- Inventory sampling

The system takes stock of the following types of material:

- Unrestricted-use stock
- Stock in quality inspection
- Special stock

Reviewing Inventory Functionality   Many functions support the taking of a physical inventory:

- Physical inventory documents can be created.
- Warehouse inventory lists can be printed.
- A block can be placed on stock movements of materials being inventoried.
- Data entry of the results of physically counting the stock is automatically related to the entries on the physical inventory documents.
- Differences between the physical inventory and the book inventory are presented in list format.

- Differences are posted by using the items of the physical inventory documents for reference.

- Large differences prompt the creation of documents to support a recount of the items that show a discrepancy.

- Every physical inventory is recorded for each material and retained indefinitely so that the history of any stock item can be traced over any number of years for which data was collected.

Sampling the Physical Inventory   When a warehouse contains a very large number of stock management units, it is possible to manage them and conduct a physical inventory of them on the basis of samples. Because the relationship between the sampled items and the rest of the warehouse can be determined automatically, it is possible to infer the full warehouse inventory from the results of physically counting the selected sample. The goods receipts and issues at the warehouse can be managed by using the same technique.

Evaluating Material

The standard approach of the SAP system is to assign values automatically to materials on an ongoing basis. The data is stored in material master records and can be adjusted manually.

When you need to value materials for balance sheet purposes, the system offers the *last-in-first-out* (LIFO) evaluation procedure, to which you can apply the lowest value determination procedure.

Assigning Evaluation Control Structures

You can control the scope of an evaluation exercise by choosing a company code or plant to specify the level of the separate evaluation areas. If the evaluation area is a company code, all the stocks in each company code area are evaluated on the same basis, and the results are accumulated over the company code. If the evaluation area is a plant, each plant in the company has its stocks evaluated separately.

Using Evaluation Classes   Materials with similar characteristics can be grouped to form an evaluation class. The FI-GL General Ledger stock account to which the evaluation is posted depends on the evaluation classes assigned to it.

Using Evaluation Categories   Different sets of material evaluation criteria can be associated with particular evaluation categories. For example, you might want to use different evaluation criteria because the material has a net value that partially depends on where it came from, the amount of work already done on it, and perhaps, the taxes or surcharges it has attracted.

Here are some examples of evaluation categories:

- Procurement
- Origin
- Status

You also can use the evaluation category system to represent differences in the condition or makeup of a material. You can split a material stock into separate lots for evaluation purposes according to an evaluation category scheme based on factors such as these:

- Quality
- Batch purity
- Batch quality control results, such as the variance in the critical dimensions
- Batch specification
- Batch history

Using Evaluation Types   *Evaluation types* are nominal values specified for each evaluation category. You might decide that your stock of a particular material should be evaluated according to the formula specified for each evaluation type to which it could be assigned. You can specify a different evaluation formula for each country of origin, for example, according to the following set of evaluation types from the Origin material evaluation category:

- Domestic, which may be the country of the plant or the company code
- European Community
- USA
- Other country

The lists of possible evaluation types and evaluation classes depend on your company's requirements as established during customizing.

Relating Evaluation to Price Control   The price control strategy enforced determines how a material stock is valued:

- **Standard price** requires all the stock of a material to be valued at the same standard price, regardless of the costs of any fresh postings to the inventory.
- **Moving average price** computes the price to be used to value the entire stock of a material by averaging the prices of all postings held in the inventory.

Applying LIFO Evaluation   Each material can be selected individually or on the basis of membership of a material group subject to *last-in-first-out* (LIFO) evaluation. The material can also be allocated to a LIFO pool and valued in this context.

Tracing Changes to Stock Values   The transactions that can be expected to alter the material stock quantities and stock values include those posted in connection with the following events:

- Goods receipts
- Transfer posting
- Goods issues
- Invoices
- Detection of stock differences between book inventory and physical inventory results
- Reevaluation of material stocks

The amounts arrived at from these transactions depend on the price control strategy in operation for each material involved.

Reviewing Evaluation Procedures

The basic evaluation procedure entails applying prices to inventory and posting the total to the General Ledger. The aim is to have the system continuously monitor the inventory situation so that reports can be generated at any time. The choice of price control method for a material affects the posting procedure at the goods receipt and invoice receipt levels.

Applying Standard Price Control   The standard price control technique uses prices derived from historical data, with various adjustments made to arrive at values that can be used throughout the planning period. All inventory postings are carried out by using the standard prices for the materials. If there are variances between the standard prices and the amounts charged on invoices or goods receipts, these differences are posted to price difference accounts. These differences provide a method of monitoring price changes and comparing them to the *moving average prices* (MAPs), which are displayed for each material.

The moving average price control technique requires that all goods receipts are posted with the goods receipt actual values, instead of standard prices. These acquisition prices are used to update the material master records automatically. There are very few circumstances in which a price variance can arise. This might occur if there are stock shortages. You can make manual changes to the acquisition price in the material master, but this is seldom necessary.

Posting a Goods Receipt   When you post a goods receipt, the system multiplies the net order price by the quantity and posts the resulting value to the goods receipt and invoice receipt clearing account in the FI-GL General Ledger. If the price control technique in use is standard price, the quantity entered is valued at the standard price. Any difference between the net order price and the standard price for the order is posted to the price difference account.

When the corresponding invoice is received and entered, the goods receipt and invoice receipt clearing account is cleared if there is no difference in the prices. Otherwise, the difference is posted to the price difference account, where it should clear the amount previously posted there when the goods were received and found by the system to be priced at a set of rates different from the standard.

If the *moving average price* (MAP) control technique is used, the difference is posted to the stock account, where it contributes to the average price the next time it is computed.

Handling Delivery Costs   The planned delivery costs are entered in the purchase order. The actual delivery costs are included in the goods receipt posting, which is to a freight or customs clearing account.

If the standard price control is in operation, any difference between the actual delivery costs and the planned delivery costs is posted to the price difference account. If the MAP control is being applied, the difference between the planned delivery costs of the material and the actual delivery costs is posted as an offsetting entry to the stock account of the material concerned, where it may affect the moving average acquisition price held on the material master.

Offsetting a Cash Discount   If a cash discount is part of the agreed-on terms for a purchase order, you can make a net posting for the goods receipt and the invoice receipt. The MAP of materials being priced on this basis is reduced as a result of the stock posting of the relevant discount amount. An offsetting entry is automatically made to a cash discount clearing account, where it remains until it is cleared at payment.

Managing Stocks with Split Evaluation   If a material is to be split for evaluation, the different stocks of the same material are treated independently. Each substock is valued according to the evaluation category assigned to it. An evaluation category master record has a header record in which each corresponding evaluation type is represented by the quantities of the material of that evaluation type, including the substock, and their values computed according to the price formula defined for that evaluation type.

Reevaluating Stock   A stock of material is revalued if there is a price change or if there is a credit or debit posting to its stock account. Changes can be entered manually under the following functions:

- **Material price change.** This can be effective immediately or from a specified date.
- **Material debit or credit posting.** This affects the evaluation of the stock only if the price control method decrees that the evaluation is based on the MAP of the stock.

Conducting Balance Sheet Evaluations

When you need to value an inventory in order to draw up a legal balance sheet, two standard computing functions are available in the SAP R/3 Materials Management component:

- LIFO evaluation
- Lowest value price determination

The results of these evaluations are used to compute evaluation adjustment postings to the FI-GL General Ledger for tax purposes and for commercial reasons concerning financial management.

Applying *Last-In-First-Out* (LIFO) Evaluation   If inflation is raising the market price of a material, the value of the company may appear to increase merely because the stock held in inventory is increasing in acquisition price. On the other hand, if it is assumed that the material most recently acquired, which is at the higher price, is the first material to be taken out of the warehouse into consumption, the value of the remaining stock is based on the lower acquisition price of the older stock. This is the LIFO stock evaluation used for balance sheet purposes.

If there is no difference in the important attributes of the old and the new stock, either can be released to consumption. If a limited shelf life is specified, the older stock is released first. For inventory purposes, however, the evaluation applies the acquisition price of the older stock to the total quantity on inventory.

Similar materials and materials with similar functions can be aggregated into pools that are valued together. The system provides two procedures for LIFO evaluation:

- Quantity LIFO procedure
- Index LIFO procedure

Applying the Quantity LIFO Procedure   If the stock at the end of a fiscal year is greater than the stock at the end of a previous year, the system creates a layer, which is a data object. The layer contains the following data elements:

- Identification of the fiscal year to which it is assigned
- The material number or material pool number to which it refers
- The quantity of the material in stock at the end of the year
- The quantity of the material in stock at the end of the previous year
- The computed difference in stock of this material between the reference year and the previous year

The increase in stock of this material in the year is defined as the *layer,* and the value of this layer is calculated by using the price for this year. The layer defined by the stock of this material carried over from the previous year still is on inventory and is valued at the price used when the inventory was valued for balance sheet purposes at the end of the previous fiscal year.

When the time comes to value the stock of this material at the end of this financial year, the quantity may be less than the previous year because the quantities issued exceeded the quantities received. In such cases, the balance sheet evaluation procedure must decide which layer of stock is to be regarded as the source of the stock consumed: Should it be the older layer or the newer layer?

If the LIFO procedure is in operation, evaluation starts valuing the stock consumed as if the most recently acquired layer is the source, regardless of whether goods issue has actually been on the basis of batch production date, delivery batch date, or some other criterion. The price of the goods consumed from inventory is taken from the stock layer for the current year until all the quantity in this layer is assigned to the consumption account. If yet further quantities of this stock must be considered to reach the quantity consumed in the year, the price is taken from the stock layer for the previous year in accord with the LIFO rule.

Applying Stock Layer Evaluation Methods   The SAP R/3 system provides various methods for valuing a stock layer of a material or material pool:

- **Evaluation** is based on the current value of the MAP maintained in the material master record.
- **Price for the total year** carries out evaluation on the basis of the MAP for all goods receipts in the reporting year.
- **Price for the partial year** values the stock of each material on the basis of the MAP for goods receipts in part of the reporting year, specified in terms of the number of months, starting with the first month in the reporting year.
- **Price by quantity** applies the MAP for each period separately, starting at the beginning of the year and stopping when the quantity of stock that has been valued is equal to the quantity recorded in the stock layer master.

The differences among these methods can be expressed as a difference in the assumptions made about the value of the stock in a layer:

- Evaluation of the whole layer at the current MAP assumes that the value of the stock has kept in step with the MAP. Therefore, the balance sheet shows what it is worth by applying the MAP as it is at the time of the report, which may be some months after the end of the fiscal year being reported.

- A price for the total year evaluation assigns to the whole layer the MAP current at the end of the reporting year.

- A price for the partial year evaluation assumes that the most reasonable price to use for the balance sheet is the MAP taken over the beginning few months of the reporting year.

- A price by quantity evaluation assumes that the balance sheet is best served by valuing a layer at the MAP determined monthly, which is more closely in tune with the cash flows of the company at the time.

Applying the Index LIFO Procedure   An *index procedure* refers to a price index for the material or material pool, and manages it by value alone. The value of a layer of a material or a material pool at the end of a fiscal year is calculated by using a price index and is recorded as the base year value of the layer.

At the end of the year, the value of the pool is recalculated using the price index applied to the base year value of the previous year. If the pool includes various layers from previous years, their separate values using their own base year prices are added together. If the value of the pool is greater than the total of the values of the separate layers, a new layer is created for the reporting year and is valued by the amount of this increase. If the value of the whole pool using the current base price is less than the total of the values of the separate parts, the LIFO rule is applied, and the most recent layer is diminished in value until the pool is valued at the amount calculated on the basis of the price index applied to the base year.

Differentiating Lowest Value Determinations

When drawing up a balance sheet, the inventory can be evaluated in accordance with either of the following principles:

- **Strict lowest value principle.** Specifies that where the price of a material can be determined by more than one method, the lowest value *must* be used.

- **Moderate lowest value principle.** Specifies that where the price of a material can be determined by more than one method, the lowest value *can* be used.

For example, the value of a stock layer can be calculated on the basis of the acquisition costs of the raw materials or other components, to which you add the production costs. The alternative might be to value the layer at the price quoted on the appropriate commodity exchange or other market price listing. The SAP R/3 system can support a range of procedures for automatically computing the lowest value that can be applied to stocks of material procured externally.

Accepting Lowest Value by Market Prices   The value for a material on inventory at the end of the fiscal year can be determined automatically by specifying the following sources of information:

- Purchase orders
- Contracts
- Purchasing info records
- Receipts of goods for purchase orders

Accepting Lowest Value by Range of Coverage   The *range of coverage* represents the time that the inventory stock of a material will last according to an estimate of its rate of consumption. The range of coverage can be based on past consumption data or on the values forecast.

The lowest value for a stock layer can be determined according to the range of coverage, calculated in months. A percentage discount then is applied, depending on the number of months.

Accepting Lowest Value by Movement Rate   The *movement rate* of a material is an index of the relation between goods receipts and goods issues of the material. It is calculated as a percentage.

If a material is classified as slow-moving or nonmoving, a devaluation indicator is set for it that causes the system to apply a percentage reduction in value according to the calculation rule specified for the devaluation indicator.

Accepting Linked Procedures   The system allows you to link evaluation procedures in sequence. For example, you can have the system determine the lowest price of a material according to market prices and then apply a reduction to allow for range of coverage or movement rate.

Interpreting Results   The outcome of material evaluation using the lowest value determination procedure can be used to update the Commercial Price field and the Tax field in the material master record. You then can call at any time for a list covering all your materials on inventory. This list includes proposals by the system on how you could transfer postings to devalue your individual stock accounts.

Verifying Invoices

When an invoice receipt is posted in the MM-Materials Management component, the system verifies it with the data in the purchasing and goods receipt functions, and then transmits the information to the accounting modules:

- FI-Financial Accounting
- CO-Controlling
- FI-AM Assets Management

When the invoice receipt is posted, an open item is generated in the vendor account that isn't cleared until the FI-Financial Accounting component confirms that payment has taken place. To do this, the invoice receipt must reference a purchase order or goods receipt in order to have access to the details of the materials and quantities.

The maximum amount each user is permitted to post during invoice verification is determined during MM-Materials Management customizing.

Entering Invoices with Order Reference

If you are entering an invoice receipt that references a purchase order, you just have to enter or confirm the order number. The system proposes the vendor and the following data:

- Tax rate
- Terms of cash discount
- Individual quantities and values of each material

When you post this entry, the system sends you messages to inform you of any variances between the invoice data and the purchase order data. You are allowed to define tolerance limits for the individual invoice items so that you won't be subjected to unimportant system messages. If the lower limit is exceeded, you are informed that the lower limit should be corrected. If the upper limit is exceeded, the system allows you to post the invoice receipt document, but it is blocked for payment.

N O T E To release a blocked document for payment by FI-Financial Accounting, you must enter a separate release transaction to document how you resolved the discrepancy.

Assuming that the system has accepted any variances between the purchase order and the invoice receipt, the act of posting the invoice creates a document to record the event and post the amounts to the relevant accounts, which are determined automatically. At the same time, the price history is updated if the invoice refers to a purchase order.

If the material in an invoice item is marked to be valued by the MAP method, the relevant material master record is updated at this time with the price and value of the material.

Entering Order Receipt References   If the invoice arrives with a reference to a goods receipt, the accounts payable clerk enters the document number for the goods receipt or the delivery slip number. The system locates the required data and proposes it for inclusion in the document that records the receipt of the invoice. Alternatively, users can enter the purchase order number to elicit the same information.

An individual delivery can be settled by entering the invoice receipt with a reference to the delivery note or goods receipt document.

If you enter a purchase order number during the invoice receipt entry, the system creates an invoice item for each item on the order for each goods receipt. This enables you to relate each particular goods receipt item to the order item to which it belongs.

Entering Invoices Without Order Reference   A bill for expenses—at a hotel, for example—doesn't necessarily have any reference item in the system from which the details can be retrieved so that the system can propose the details for invoice receipt entry. In such cases of purchases without purchase orders, you first create a vendor item and then create a document item corresponding to each item on the invoice you have received in order to record all details of the material or service for which payment must be made. The resulting document can be posted to a Materials account, a General Ledger account, or a Fixed Assets account, as appropriate.

Reviewing Invoice Entry Functions

The wide range of standard SAP R/3 display and data-entry functions is available for use in the invoice verification process. Some of the functions are particularly relevant:

- **Search for an open purchase order** can be initiated after identifying either a vendor or a material.

- **Search for a group of open purchase orders** finds all purchase orders relevant to an invoice that contains items from different orders.

- **Document editing** allows you to adjust an invoice receipt document as many times as you need to before you post it.

- **Document simulation** displays the balance for the document and shows you how the accounts would change if you were to actually post this particular invoice at this moment or at some future date.

- **Retrieve related information** enables you to access additional information not only on accounting matters—such as purchase order details, order history, or vendor data—but also material data, which could include the technical documents linked to the material master records.

Applying National Taxes

The system can be provided with the INT-International module, from which you can obtain automatic access to the valid deductible and nondeductible tax types for your own country and any other countries for which the module is configured.

As the invoice receipt is entered, the tax record and the tax amount also are entered, if they are part of the invoice. The system checks the correctness of the invoice amount, the tax record or code, and the tax amount. If there are any variances, the system informs you via system messages, but you still are allowed to post the invoice receipt.

If the invoice receipt doesn't include a tax amount, the tax can be calculated by the system by using the local tax module. If the invoice items have different tax records or codes, the tax is calculated for each item separately.

When you post an invoice receipt, the appropriate tax items are created automatically.

Applying Gross and Net Posting

During the process of entering an invoice receipt, you can specify the terms of payment. The system proposes the conditions from the purchase order or suggests the standard conditions as specified in the vendor master record. The standard terms of payment are expressed in the following manner, for example:

- A 3 percent cash discount applies if payment is made within 10 days.
- A 2 percent cash discount applies if payment is made within 20 days.
- Net payment is required within 30 days.

You can specify that the cash discount be cleared as a gross posting or as a net posting.

Gross Posting   The effect of specifying clearance by gross posting is to have the system ignore any cash discount amounts until the invoice is cleared for payment, when the discount amount is posted to a separate account assigned for the purpose of recording cash discounts. The advantage of this procedure is that the balances in the stock account and the cost accounts aren't affected by the cash discount.

Net Posting   If the posting is to be cleared net, the cash discount amount is credited directly to the account to which the costs detailed on the invoice receipt are posted. The cost center, for example, receives only the net amount from the invoice.

Excluding Items from Cash Discount   If an item on an invoice isn't going to attract a cash discount for early payment, it can be so marked on the invoice receipt document and thereby excluded from any discount calculations.

Reviewing Other Pricing Functions

In support of the invoice verification functions, the system conducts a wide range of automatic business processes. They are all fully integrated with the MM-Materials Management module and therefore with the other modules of the SAP R/3 system.

Foreign Currency   It is the practice in SAP R/3 systems that invoices are posted only in local currency. If you want to enter the invoice receipts in another currency, the system converts the amounts to the local currency and records both types in the invoice receipt document.

The method of establishing the exchange rate to use in currency conversion can be any of the following:

- A fixed exchange rate is stated on the purchase order.
- The exchange rate to be used is stored in the system.
- The exchange rate to be used is entered directly during invoice verification.

Account Assignments   Any materials not procured for stock and services must identify the accounts to which the amounts are to be assigned. An amount can be distributed to more than one account on a percentage basis or in terms of fixed amounts.

If an account has been assigned in a purchase order, that account cannot be changed if a goods receipt that has been subjected to evaluation is entered during invoice verification. If the goods receipt hasn't been valued, the accounts payable clerk can change the account assignment.

Subsequent Debits   If a transaction has already been cleared and additional costs are incurred, it is necessary to make a subsequent adjustment in the form of a debit. The adjustment is posted directly to the material or cost account, where the system updates the order history with respect to the value, although the quantity remains the same.

Credit Memos   If it becomes apparent after invoice verification is completed that a credit has to be posted, the credit memo function can be called from the invoice verification program. If the system encounters a credit memo document that refers to a purchase order or a goods receipt, it is treated as a cancellation of the corresponding invoice receipt document.

Down Payments   A vendor may have agreed to conditions that stipulate a down payment for all purchase orders. Alternatively, the terms for a down payment can be agreed on with the vendor in a particular purchase order. The down payment agreement can be made for the order as a whole or for individual order items.

If a down payment arrangement has been made, you receive a system message to this effect when the invoice verification function becomes aware that you are about to enter an invoice receipt for that order or for that vendor, if a standing arrangement for a down payment is in force.

The down payment must be the subject of a separate transfer posting to a vendor account established for this purpose, where it remains until the transaction is closed by the final payment.

Correspondence   The standard communications channels for internal mail are available to the invoice verification component, along with the standard interface to external systems. You can use the SAP R/3 word processing system to provide text for automatic entry into an invoice receipt document or to copy parts of the invoice itself into this document.

Planned Delivery Costs   The delivery costs can be planned and divided into a range of delivery cost types:

- Freight costs
- Customs duty
- Insurance
- Packaging labor, materials, and so on

Each type can be related to a method of calculation, such as the following:

- Fixed costs per delivery
- Delivery costs proportional to the quantity
- Delivery costs proportional to the number of shipping units or transportation plant units required
- Delivery costs to be computed as a fixed percentage of the total value or weight of goods delivered

The planned delivery costs are recorded on the purchase order for each order item, and the relevant amount for planned delivery costs is posted to the material account or to the cost account when the goods receipt is entered. At the same time, an offsetting entry is posted to a special clearing account, such as a freight clearing account.

When the invoice receipt document is being created, you can list all the delivery costs for a specific purchase order, for a particular vendor, or for a delivery note. You then can decide how you want the system to allocate the total delivery costs recorded in the invoice you have received. When you do so, the planned delivery costs are updated in the order history to take account of the actual delivery costs.

Unplanned Delivery Costs   The first time you get any information on unplanned delivery costs may be when you catch sight of the invoice. There will have been no previous entry of planned delivery costs.

The unplanned costs have to be taken from the invoice during invoice verification and entered in the invoice receipt document. The system distributes the total delivery costs among the individual items in proportion to their contribution to the value of the entire value invoiced. You can override this proportional distribution by a series of manual entries; rapid data-entry functions are provided where relevant. Unplanned delivery costs are posted directly to the materials account or to the appropriate costs account.

Managing Blocked Invoices

If you receive a system message informing you that there is some variance between the planned amounts and the actual amounts, or if you are aware of this anyway, you must write the new values over the proposed quantities and values. The following causes of variance may exist, perhaps at the same time:

- Quantity variance
- Quality variance
- Price variance
- Schedule variance
- Project budget overrun

Establishing Tolerances   To protect your users from excessive outpourings of system messages, you can define tolerances for individual variances by establishing upper and lower limits within which the system will accept the discrepancy. Outside these limits (above or below), users see a message.

You can always post an invoice receipt that includes a variance. However, if the value exceeds the upper limit, the invoice is blocked for payment.

Releasing Block Invoices   When an invoice item is found to have a discrepancy that exceeds the upper tolerance limit, the item is marked with a key indicating the reason, and the whole invoice is blocked. An item can be assigned several blocking reasons at the same time.

If you call up a list of all blocked invoices, you can deal with each invoice in two ways:

- Cancel one or more of the individual item-blocking reason keys if further investigation uncovers a good reason for the discrepancy—for example, a price variance is justified but there is still a discrepancy in the quantity.
- Release the invoice for payment, perhaps after changing the date from when the terms of payment are valid, so that the financial accounting department can pay the invoice without waiting for the outcome of an investigation into the reason for the variance.

Sometimes the reason for blocking an invoice is no longer valid. Perhaps the shortage in delivery quantity has been rectified, or perhaps the critical date in a schedule has passed. You can release an invoice yourself, or the system automatically releases all blocked invoices for which the reasons are no longer valid.

Managing Warehouses

The MM-Warehouse Management component supports the efficient and effective processing of logistics requirements within a company. In particular, the following logistics operations are provided with standard business functions:

- Managing complex warehouse structures
- Defining and managing storage bins
- Managing storage types
- Creating transfer orders
- Monitoring stock movements
- Executing stock placement and removal strategies
- Processing differences
- Managing hazardous materials
- Taking inventory at the storage-bin level
- Using bar codes
- Using warehouse reports

The MM-WM Warehouse Management system supports the processing of all movements, including goods receipts and goods issues initiated by the Inventory Management system, as well as goods issues from the Sales and Distribution system. The Warehouse Management system provides control over the movements within a warehouse, including stock transfers for replenishment orders.

Transactions in the Inventory Management system or in the Sales and Distribution system automatically trigger the Warehouse Management system to generate transfer requirements such as material movements, staging of materials for production orders, and shipping of goods for sales orders.

Specifying the Warehouse Structure

The representation of the warehouse structure in the SAP R/3 system follows the standard system of hierarchical levels stored in master records, starting with the client code, which is unique. Below this, there may be one or more company codes, each of which may operate one or more plants and warehouses.

Tables of logical and numerical values are provided so that you can adjust the system to make it represent the detailed structure and relationships within your configuration of warehouses and storage locations.

Warehouse Number   The physical warehouse complex is represented as a single number identifying that warehouse and a warehouse master record where a data structure may be stored. Each warehouse includes various types of storage locations.

Storage Type   A storage type can be differentiated by its physical location, its technical characteristics, and its place in the organizational structure of operational units and cost centers. A storage type is divided into subareas that may use different storage techniques and serve different functions or parts of the organization. The subareas of a storage type are divided into storage bins.

Storage Bin   A *storage bin* is the smallest part of a storage area within a storage type. It can be addressed for the purpose of directing material there or withdrawing material from it. All products in a storage bin, or in a space that is treated as a storage bin, are treated as exactly the same type. Any one of the products can be withdrawn for assignment to an order or transfer; there is no effective difference between the products.

Storage Section   A *storage section* is a grouping of storage bins represented as a section in the system according to criteria defined by the user. Storage sections have certain characteristics in common but not necessarily a shared location in a warehouse.

Storage Bin Type   The size of a storage bin is used to assign that bin to a storage bin type. The type is used in storage bin searches to build up the quantity of material required for a transfer.

Generating Transfer Requirement Documents

When a movement of stock has been planned in the MM-Materials Management system and needs to be executed by the MM-WM Warehouse Management system, a transfer requirement document must be created. This can be done manually in the Warehouse Management system or generated automatically in response to a goods movement posting in the MM-Materials Management system.

The transfer requirement can be used to plan for the following operations:

- Placing goods into stock
- Removing goods from stock
- Preparing for other goods transfers by moving stock within the warehouse

The transfer requirement doesn't execute the stock movement. A movement is executed only if a transfer order is created and confirmed.

If you want to know what should be moved and how much, the creation of a transfer requirement will provide the answers. If a movement has already been started by the confirmation of a transfer order and you try to create a transfer requirement for the same goods, you will discover whether the order was created automatically or manually, and whether an amount of the transfer has already been moved.

Creating Transfer Orders

Stock movements are controlled by transfer orders specifying the material number, the quantity, and the storage bins from which the stock is to be removed. A transfer order is also used to release goods from quality inspection, even if no physical movement occurs.

Confirming a Transfer   Some stock movements may have to be confirmed. The system provides a confirmation function that executes a confirmation automatically as soon as the physical transfer takes place. If the planned quantity isn't the same as the actual quantity transferred, you can record the difference before confirming the transfer order.

Tracing Events in Goods Receipt   A typical delivery of goods to a warehouse follows this series of tasks:

1. A delivery vehicle arrives, and the supervisor has the system create a material movement document.

2. The system generates a transfer requirement and a quantity posting to the goods receipt area.

3. The goods are unloaded to the goods receipt area.

4. The system creates a transfer order for the goods to assign them to destination storage bins, which then are reserved for these goods.

5. The transfer order is printed or electronically displayed to the goods movement section.

6. The goods are transferred to the storage bins reserved for them.

7. The quantities in the storage bins are checked and confirmed to the system.

8. The system prints the confirmation from the storage bin–checking operation on the transfer order document, which then is confirmed.

9. The system updates the inventory so that the goods are available for consumption or further movement.

The transfer order can support the following types of goods receipts:

- Based on a purchase order
- Without a reference purchase order
- Destined for an in-house production order
- For a batch reserved for inspection
- From a customer who is returning goods that are unwanted for any reason

Using a Transfer Order for Goods Issue   The transfer order function can also support goods issues for the following purposes:

- Goods issues to a cost center
- Goods issues to a project
- Staging of materials for production
- Delivery of goods to customers

Choosing Goods for a Delivery Note or Transfer Order   If the SAP R/3 SD-Sales and Distribution module has been installed and configured, the MM-WM Warehouse Management system can begin to automatically choose goods as soon as the delivery note is posted. If goods are to be chosen through the fixed bin-picking procedure, the bin to be used is determined from the material master, updated by goods receipts and withdrawals.

If the warehouse is organized randomly, a transfer order is created for each delivery item. When the transfer order is confirmed in the system, each delivery item is updated by the quantities picked, which may not be the same as the quantities planned. In such instances, a difference is documented.

Posting Changes and Stock Transfers   If a transaction doesn't involve the physical movement of goods, such as the receipt of goods, their issue, or their movement from one storage location to another within the warehouse, the system offers the following choices of posting changes and stock transfer functions:

- Release stock from quality inspection.
- Convert stock from consignment stock to company stock.
- Make a posting change from one batch to another.
- Change a material number of a quantity of stock.
- Accept the return of goods and complete the necessary processing.
- Make a posting change for a stock replenishment warehouse.

Registering Confirmation   If certain stock movements require confirmation, the system doesn't recognize any change in the relevant storage bins until the confirmation process is completed. You have to inform the system that the processing for the transfer order is finished. If only some of the transfer order items are subject to confirmation, you can register the confirmation on an individual item basis.

Notifying Differences   If the processing of a transfer order reveals that some of the goods were damaged during transit, or the quantities in the storage bins were insufficient or of the wrong material or batch specification, the system must be informed in the transfer order confirmation. This automatically generates a difference posting to Inventory Management.

Setting the Control Parameters for Transfer Order Processing   You can determine which functions can be executed automatically and which must be held up until a valid manual input is entered. The control functions also direct the warehouse documents to the appropriate printer or other output channel. The output can include bar codes.

Interpreting Search Strategies

The method used by the system to find the storage bins to be used for the placement or withdrawal of stock is defined as a *strategy*. When the system has used a strategy to find a suitable set of storage bins, it proposes this strategy for your approval or for you to change by manual entry.

The advantages of applying predefined search strategies are that the warehouse can be managed optimally for stock placements, and the system can quickly find the materials specified for stock removals. This approach can be applied to all types of warehouse configurations and placement methods.

Searching by Storage Type   You can specify that a particular material is to be stored in a specific type of storage. You can also assign classes of material to specific storage types—for example, subassemblies to be stored in high rack storage area number 1, finished assemblies in protected area 6.

Searching by Storage Section   Each material can be assigned to a particular area within the storage type for that material group—for example, fast-moving items in the front area F, slow-moving items in the back area B.

Searching by Bin Type   Certain bin types can be assigned to specific storage unit types so that the goods placed there can be accommodated in the best possible bin type. For example, bin types can be defined as pallets, wire baskets, or warehouse floor areas. Each bin of each type is identified by number and, through the bin master record, by storage type and location. Restrictions on the types of materials to be stored in a bin type can also be established in the bin type master record.

Searching by Storage Bin   The search for a specific storage bin can be conducted by using a similar strategy for both stock placement, which looks for unoccupied bins, and stock removal, which looks for bins occupied by the material required, subject to other constraints depending on the stock removal strategy used.

Specifying Stock Placement Strategies

The following stock placement strategies can be specified to enable the system to generate proposals for the placement of any stock arriving at a warehouse:

- The material is placed in the next suitable empty bin.
- The material is always assigned to the same fixed bin.
- The system doesn't make any proposal for placing the stock, but instead waits for the user to enter a destination.
- The system finds a bin that already contains this material and attempts to place the stock there, unless this would exceed the capacity of the bin, in which case it begins a search for another suitable bin. If no space can be found in an occupied bin, a suitable empty bin is used.
- Block storage is specified for materials that are to be stored in large quantities without taking up too much storage space.
- Shelf section storage is used when the storage area can take a different number of delivery units, depending on the size of the unit. For example, three European standard pallets can be stored in the space taken by two pallets of the size previously common in that industry.

Specifying Stock Removal Strategies

The choice of stock removal strategy is constrained by the placement of the goods in storage bins according to the placement strategies. The system knows where everything is located, down to the bin identification.

Two main stock removal strategies can be assigned to a specific material:

- *First-in-first-out* (FIFO) requires that the materials to be removed first are those that have been in the warehouse the longest. These materials have the earliest goods receipt date.

■ *Last-in-first-out* (**LIFO**) identifies for first removal those goods with the most recent goods receipt date.

Selecting Partial Quantities   If the system finds that a material has been placed in a storage type that includes storage areas that aren't all completely full to capacity, it seeks to fulfill the transfer order by selecting a combination of full and partly full storage areas that will exactly match the quantity required. This tends to optimize the use of storage facilities and material-handling activities.

Selecting for Large and Small Quantities   A warehouse may contain two types of storage areas for the same material—one for large delivery units containing a large quantity of the material, and the other for single assemblies or small deliverable units.

You can define a search strategy parameter that tells the system which removal source to use on the basis of a set quantity of the material required. You can also allow the splitting of large delivery units.

Reviewing the Inventory Functions

The legal requirement for conducting a physical inventory is that every storage bin must be checked at least once each fiscal year for quantity and the identity of the material it contains.

The SAP R/3 system allows you to define the physical inventory procedure individually for each storage type. This facility allows you to take account of any special technical or organizational factors concerning the materials or the storage arrangements that should be documented with the inventory. The following inventory procedures are provided as standard programs that can be controlled by parameters established during customizing:

■ Annual inventory count
■ Continuous inventory
■ Continuous inventory during stock placement
■ Continuous inventory based on zero-stock check
■ Inventory based on sampling procedure

Reading the Inventory Indicator   When a storage bin is inventoried, the corresponding storage bin master record is updated with an inventory indicator showing the date and which inventory procedure was used on it. This indicator also serves as legal proof that the physical inventory was carried out.

Detecting Differences   If any difference is detected between the recorded inventory and the physical inventory, the details are posted automatically to an interim storage area record for differences. The MM-IM Inventory Management component has access to this interim storage record, and the inventory manager can authorize the clearing of these differences by difference postings to the appropriate stock accounts.

Logging the Inventory History   A History log is maintained by the system to document the inventory history of every storage bin over a very long time period. This can be accessed in dialog mode.

Consulting System Inventory Records

The task of conducting the annual physical inventory is assisted by the system inventory records that are automatically generated when required, and by their associated functions:

- Printed warehouse inventory list
- Entry functions to post the counting results to the corresponding warehouse inventory list items
- Initiation of a recount if serious discrepancies are detected
- Investigation support to establish the reasons for discrepancies
- Clearing of differences with the creation of explanatory documents

Managing Storage Units

The storage unit management function in the MM-WM Warehouse Management component can maintain storage unit number records that include indicators of the type of storage unit, such as pallet, wire basket, and so on. Under this storage unit number, it is possible to group material quantities in logical units of a homogeneous or mixed quantity of materials. The storage unit number master record also stores data about the single material or combination of materials contained in the storage unit, such as the following:

- The material number
- The quantity of material
- Which operations have been performed on this material
- When this storage unit was last subjected to physical inventory

The following functions can be initiated from the storage unit management component:

- Create a transfer order for one or more storage units.
- Confirm a stock movement.
- Add stock to existing storage units.
- Print documents to accompany the storage unit.

One use for a storage unit system is to assemble a set of constituents or component parts that are thereafter documented and marshaled to the production or sales processes as a single composite object.

Managing a Decentralized Warehouse with an SAP R/2 Host System

An asynchronous program-to-program communications interface can be installed to integrate the SAP R/3 MM-WM Warehouse Management system with the SAP R/2 applications for Materials Management and Sales and Distribution.

Stock movements in the SAP R/2 Materials Management system initiate quantity postings in the SAP R/3 MM-WM Warehouse Management system as required. Delivery orders are transmitted to a decentralized warehouse unit for shipping. When picking is completed and confirmed, the actual quantities are ready for transmitting to the SAP R/2 host computer. If the host isn't available at the time, any differences on the delivery orders and any goods receipts taken from the production department are entered in the terminal of the decentralized SAP R/3 warehouse unit. When the host becomes available again, the SAP R/2 central Inventory Management system is updated from the SAP R/3 decentralized unit.

Using Special Functions

The MM-Materials Management module provides a range of flexible special functions that can operate in any of the constituent components, such as these:

- MM-MRP Material Requirements Planning
- MM-IM Inventory Management
- MM-IV Invoice Verification

The MM-Materials Management special functions offer the following program elements:

- Consignment material
- Special stocks of consignment material
- Material movements
- Subcontracting
- Vendor special stocks
- Goods receipt from a subcontractor
- Physical stock transfers by stock transport orders

Valuing Consignment Material

If you buy material from a vendor and pay for it, this material is valued on your balance sheet. However, the vendor may have delivered to your company a stock of material that you don't have to pay for unless and until you need it. Such material is treated as consignment material, and it isn't valued on your balance sheet even though it is on your inventory. You may return the consignment material, or part of it, when you no longer expect to need it.

If you do withdraw for consumption a partial quantity of consignment stores or transfer it to your own stock, the quantity you move is valued at the vendor's defined selling price, and you have to pay for it. Settlement of consignment material is usually conducted on a monthly or quarterly basis.

Managing Special Stocks of Consignment Material   You can manage consignment material by using the normal material number, and you therefore can call on the associated data from the material master records. However, these special stocks of consignment material are managed in separate areas of the storage location, according to vendor. Purchase prices of consignment stocks withdrawn are recorded according to vendor, and a MAP is maintained on the vendor master records for evaluation purposes.

Initiating Material Movements   When a goods receipt is processed for a consignment order item or a consignment scheduling agreement, the value and quantity are posted, according to the special stock indicator, to one of the following stock master record data fields:

- Unrestricted-use stock
- General goods receipt blocked stock
- Stock in quality inspection

The same actions can be carried out on batches of consignment material if the system has been preset to apply the batch status management facility. Consignment materials can also be withdrawn in a random sample for quality inspection. All the movements are posted under the control of the special stock indicator so that the pricing and evaluation procedures are alerted to the special circumstances.

There may be a contract in force stipulating that consignment stock remaining at the end of the fiscal year is to be transferred to the company's own stock. Such a transfer may be conducted at other times as a periodic replenishment of company stock according to consumption or planned requirements.

You can reserve consignment stock as a method of planning the withdrawal of material to consumption or in replenishment of company stock.

Subcontracting

The *subcontract order* is a method of outsourcing a business process. The subcontracting function in the MM-Materials Management module offers support for the following operations:

- Placing an outside contract for production activities and services
- Providing material components to the subcontractor for the production or assembly processes
- Issuing material such as equipment to the subcontractor from the ordering company's own stock or plant
- Posting as goods receipts the services performed and the goods produced by the subcontractor
- Posting the consumption or use of the issued material in the same transaction as the services and goods receipts

Holding Vendor Special Stocks   It may be convenient to maintain a stock of your materials on a subcontractor's premises. These materials are represented as *vendor special stocks,* because they aren't available for other purposes, but they still belong to your company because you engaged the subcontractor as a vendor.

If the material to be provided to a subcontractor has to be drawn from several batches, the identity of these batches is recorded in the delivery documents in case they are returned from the subcontractor or are subject to reversal because, for example, they are damaged or faulty.

Valuing a Goods Receipt from a Subcontractor   When goods that have been produced or assembled by a subcontractor are received at the contracting company, the quantities of the materials supplied are valued at their evaluation price taken from the material master records. The quantity and value are posted out of the stock for each material, and the quantities are included in the consumption statistics.

The value of the material received from the subcontractor is computed as the net purchase order value plus the evaluation cost of the material posted out of stock for this subcontract.

If the material is managed in batches, a separate goods issue item is created for each batch from which materials have been provided to the subcontractor.

If some of the material used was already being held by the subcontractor as vendor special stock, this amount appears as default values in the ratio of goods receipt quantity to purchase order quantity, which users can correct.

When the invoice is received from the subcontractor, the quantity of each material, which will have already been posted to consumption, can be corrected to account for any differences between planned use and actual use.

Making Physical Stock Transfers by Stock Transport Orders

If there are two or more plants in your company (and a plant can be a warehouse), you can transfer stock by means of a stock transport order. This can make sense if the costs of transporting stock are significant and the time in transit is considerable.

The acquisition price of this material for the receiving plant is computed as the evaluation of it in the issuing plant plus the costs of delivery. If the material is subject to MAP control, the MAP may change after each delivery.

The receiver plant orders the material from the issuing plant and plans the delivery costs, such as packaging, freight, transport insurance, customs duty, unloading, and so on. The planned delivery costs are recorded in the specific item of the order.

The source of the material posts a goods issue referring to the stock transport order. The quantity withdrawn from stock at this issuing plant is listed as stock in transit at the receiving plant.

When the goods arrive at the receiving plant, the system is posted with the goods receipt document referring to the goods transport order. This event effectively reduces the quantity and value of the stock in transit account and the value of the total of the purchase orders still open at the receiving plant.

Consulting the MM-IS Information System

The information systems are clearly central to efficient controlling of materials management. Particular display functions are optimized for the purchasing functions as the PURCHIS-Purchasing Information System, and for the Inventory Management system under the title of MM-IC Inventory Controlling.

Reviewing the Purchasing Information System

The goal of an information system is to select only the pertinent information and then to present it in ways that increase the probability of correct decisions being taken by those who view it. Two types of errors are associated with information presented to users for a decision:

- Error one offers users a choice of items that don't mean anything, or that mean something to viewers that was unintended by the system designer.
- Error two omits from the list of options some of the important possibilities, which can include such options as Do Nothing and None of the Above.

The PURCHIS-Purchasing Information System maintains its own database and can perform several important analysis procedures on it. For example, it can produce an analysis of vendors and of purchasing group activities. It can publish its results in terms of some 30 performance measures, such as the number of purchase orders in the period.

Not only can PURCHIS present data in a wide variety of list and graphical formats, but it can also assemble the data using the widest range of search strategies.

PURCHIS is part of the LO-LIS Logistics Information System and shares many of its routines with the SD-IS Sales & Distribution Information System. The Inventory Controlling system, which is also part of the Logistics Information system, is designed to reduce the information held in the Inventory Management system to a few informative performance measures that show which areas offer opportunities for improvement.

Initiating Standard Analyses   The basis of analyses using the PURCHIS methodology is the information structure, which includes data objects and performance measures associated with a time unit or period. For example, an information structure can be defined for a weekly period with these data objects:

- Purchasing group
- Vendor

The performance measures to be gathered on this information structure may include invoice value, net order value, number of order items, number of deliveries, and so on.

Using Standard Information Structures   The standard PURCHIS component is provided with three information structures containing more than 30 meaningful performance measures for all the analyses relevant to purchasing, grouped in thematic clusters. You can also define your own information structures by selecting objects and performance measures from lists and using the pickup technique to copy them to a display or printing format of your own design.

Update rules are predefined for every field in the information structures, and you can change the rules if you want. The updating of these statistical files can take place simultaneously with interactive processing or as a separate update processing run.

The standard analyses cover the statistical information you might need for the following organizational entities:

- Purchasing groups
- Vendors
- Material groups
- Materials

The scope of the data used for these compilations can be restricted interactively by applying selection criteria. You can select any item of interest in the display of results and use the drill-down technique to find information about the selected object at each layer down the information hierarchy that was used to compile the value in the report you selected in the first instance. At every level of a drill-down search, you can call for graphical and list displays, including the following functions:

- ABC analysis
- Dual classification
- Classification to the SAP R/3 scheme
- Ranking lists
- Planned versus actual comparisons

You can find detailed information at any level from the associated vendor master records, material master records, and purchasing documents.

Performing ABC Analysis   The *ABC analysis* concept refers to groupings of data objects according to the relative importance of one of the values held in a specified data element of all of these objects. For example, you can rank order all vendors in terms of their contribution to the total order value in the period of scrutiny. You then can specify that the A vendors will be those who together account for the first 70 percent of the order value, the B vendors will be those who together contribute the next 20 percent of the total order value, and the C vendors will be the remainder in the rank-ordered list, because they have individually contributed least and together contribute only 10 percent of the total order value for the period. The number of vendors in each of the A, B, and C groups will be in itself an interesting result of the ABC analysis.

Four different strategies of this kind are available for structuring ABC analysis, and the analysis can be conducted by using planned or actual values of the performance measure in question. The four standard sets of percentage values for the ABC analyses can be modified at customizing.

Conducting R/3 Classification   The classification function, which is an integral part of the R/3 system, provides a standard method for grouping together several data objects specified by a range of one of their values—for example, all production cost centers with company codes A to D and F. The members of this group then are examined with regard to one or more of the other performance data elements in their records, such as the number of work calendar days lost to production and the total value of output in the period.

Dual classification can be applied to reveal the relationship between the two performance measures and to demonstrate it in graphical or list format, using any of the materials or vendor data fields.

The PURCHIS component can be primed to execute user-defined analyses specified by settings on the following dimensions:

- Number of periods to be analyzed
- Performance measures to be displayed
- Standard structure to be followed when the user calls for a drill-down sequence
- Format and layout of the displayed or printed reports

Using Flexible Analysis and Evaluation Structures   You can use SAP R/3 standard business programs to tailor reports to suit the needs of the viewers. For example, those who need detail can see it and those who need an overview can get that, both from the same analysis.

The method uses a set of standard evaluation structures, which users can supplement on the basis of edited copies of the standards, if convenient. A data dictionary has to be identified, on which the evaluation structure will call to assemble the data it needs. A system document file containing purchasing documents would be a convenient type of data dictionary for many purposes.

An evaluation structure can be created by using standard performance measures in an appropriate formula.

Planning   It is often helpful to see how planned values compare to actual results. The same information structures accept planned and actual values, with the full facilities of the flexible display functions on hand to make clear the relationships in the data.

In this context, you can simulate future possibilities by using copies of the analyses, each conducted on a different set of hypothetical parameters. The simulation with the best outcome then can be designated as the official plan.

Inventory Controlling

The essence of inventory controlling is to make a plan that anticipates the requirements for all materials for the planning periods out to the extent of the planning horizon, to compare the planned with the actual, and to make effective and timely adjustments to the replenishment arrangements so that no shortages occur. This assignment is difficult, and there are some rules of thumb about keeping safety stocks on hand in case of unforeseen material requirements or unscheduled late deliveries.

If your company has a large inventory with many different materials, the problem is one of sampling the data. Here the MM-Materials Management system can help a great deal through its MM-IC Inventory Controlling component. First, it can demonstrate to you which materials and subassemblies ought to be monitored for reasons such as the following:

- High capital lockup occurs while in storage or production.
- Materials needed are purchased or stored in quantities that aren't efficient purchasing or storage units.

- Materials are stocked in excess of a reasonable coverage requirement, bearing in mind their expected consumption.
- Materials are seldom withdrawn from inventory and might be better purchased only for specific orders.

Optimizing The inventory controller may be authorized to adjust the safety stock levels and may be able to influence the purchasing lot size. The MM-IC Inventory Controlling component enables you to reduce stock by a specific amount through the automatic distribution of the target savings to the material stocks that are most sensitive on account of their values or the costs of storing and handling them. You could also learn some worthwhile lessons from a study of fluctuations in inventory that you could use to improve the synchronization of goods issues and receipts.

Measuring Performance The MM-IC Inventory Controlling component concentrates the most important analysis data into six composite performance measures:

- Consumption value using ABC analysis
- Stock value
- Dead stock
- Range of coverage
- Slow-moving items
- Inventory turnover

You can study the results of these compilations in two- and three-dimensional graphics and replicate the results in detailed checklists for closer examination. You can also use the drill-down procedure on any displayed aggregate value to view the data elements used to compute it.

Using Data Objects for Analysis

The standard data structures of the SAP R/3 system are designed to be analyzed at any level. Every materials analysis can be carried out by using the data aggregated to any particular level down to the plant level, which is the lowest level used for material master records. This means that you can see what is happening at any of the following levels in the organizational hierarchy:

- All plants, cumulated in a specified sequence
- Sales organization level
- Purchasing organization level
- Plant by plant

There are two types of analysis:

- **Total analysis** enables you to specify a completely flexible definition of the way the data records are to be collated and the measures that are to be computed. You also have complete control over how the results will be related to operational units and materials.

■ **Ranking list analysis** prepares the data in the form of rank orderings of the records according to values you specify. The records may be grouped, as in ABC analysis, or narrowed by the exclusion of very high and very low values. The scope is flexible with respect to the accounting periods.

P A R T VII

Considering Specialized Configurations

VII

Considering Specialized Configurations

Pursuing a Vertical Market Initiative

Providing R/3 for Specific Industries

The difference between *horizontal* and *vertical* in the context of SAP product marketing has developed in step with the evolution of the software packages. Earlier enhancements addressed the need to connect increasing numbers and types of peripheral systems. As the overall complexity increased, the need was recognized for a range of products essentially assembled and configured with a specific type of industry in mind. Many of these variants of standard R/3 were designated as IS-Industry Solutions. Some of them went on to develop into products under the vertical marketing initiative where they were designated as independent systems, such as SAP Retail.

The extending range of SAP Industry Solutions includes enhancements of the R/3 system, extensively developed to suit the needs of a particular type of industry or enterprise. Several have evolved from standard applications, because the users and the system developers have found ways in which the logic and software methodology of the SAP programs could be extended to suit the particular type of business.

Some industry-specific implementations of SAP R/3 are identified by the IS series of codes. For example, IS-Aviation was developed from the MM-Materials Management module to be optimized for the aircraft production and maintenance sectors. Where there was a need for additional integration of preconfigured SAP R/3 modules, as in the case of the aerospace industry, the specialized system would be identified by a title such as SAP R/3 Aerospace and Defense.

The process of configuring R/3 to suit a specific industry is controlled, in the first phase, by applying a standard business process configuration template. This prepares the R/3 system and its applications for the second phase, in which the system is quickly implemented and customized in any enterprise in the particular industry.

Each industry that receives the special attention of the SAP research teams can refer to an Industry Center of Expertise (ICOE) for its particular industry. This is where the collective wisdom of user groups and professional associations can be shared with the group of client companies who are using and extending the industry solution.

For example, the banking industry has shifted from managing money as a service for a particular community to income and risk management. The profitability of a banking product in a limited sector of the market has become a common calculation.

To respond to this requirement, the SAP ISB-Industry Solution for Banks has been developed as an enhancement of the standard R/3 system, which includes a system for determining market risks quantified on the basis of the money-at-risk calculation. This particular Industry Solution also provides the reporting structures, which are needed to meet the statutory obligations of the country in which the system is operating. The shared information is collated in the Banking Industry Center of Expertise.

If your industry has not yet been targeted for an Industry Solution, you need to apply the disciplines of the SAP Business Engineer to accelerate an implementation for your situation. This consists of a set of tools that plot out what you need and identify how these needs can be met from standard R/3 components. This chapter illustrates how various industries can accelerate the implementation of SAP R/3 by adopting a version of R/3 already customized for their requirement type, so that only relatively minor adjustments to fine-tune the customizing are necessary.

Introducing SAP R/3 Aerospace and Defense

The aerospace and defense industry is becoming smaller yet more globally distributed. In general, defense spending has been reduced. Quality standards remain high, however, and diverse governmental regulations demand compliance. The technology continues to add new elements that have to be incorporated into production cost-effectively. Commercial aircraft continue to be required as replacements and to meet increased demand.

Many requirements of the aerospace and defense sectors have been met by using the standard SAP R/3 components; and some aspects will be best served by the IS-Aviation Industry Solution described in a later section. The highest quality control and absolute tracking of all objects and documents throughout their production, use, and disposal are features of this sector.

IS-Aviation, the SAP R/2 mainframe system, has been used in the aviation industry for the following purposes:

- Production planning and control
- Materials management
- Maintenance planning and processing
- Sales, dispatch, and invoicing
- Financial accounting
- Assets accounting
- Human resources administration and payroll accounting
- Cost accounting and profitability analysis with order accounting
- Project management and control

The SAP R/3 IS-Aviation Industry Solution provides a client/server configuration to cover the same areas. It includes the following enhancements:

- Spec2000 communication standard applied to real-time logistics modules
- Serialized parts management
- Manufacturer part number management

R/3 Release 4.0 has developed the tracing functions by providing for a unique identifier permanently associated with each serially numbered part. This allows any individual part to be traced, no matter how many times it is dismantled and reassembled or reused elsewhere after maintenance.

Introducing SAP R/3 Automotive Industry

In this sector, the customer-driven supply chain has received a great deal of emphasis. Products are constantly under development, and there are many variants. Surplus production of an out-of-fashion variant can be very costly.

The following are elements in the SAP Automotive Industry Solution:

- Product features and options that can be easily configured and ordered over various communication channels, such as the Internet
- Release accounting inbound and outbound, with complete Electronic Data Interchange (EDI) to enable just-in-time (JIT) scheduling
- Retro-billing and evaluated receipt settlement, which can be used to provide paperless invoicing or third-party consignee functions
- Electronic KANBAN Engineering change management, which can be accomplished through direct computer-aided design (CAD) and Product Data Management (PDM)
- Standard integration warranty, service management functions, and equipment maintenance control

There is also complementary software for the automotive industry. The interfaces for CAD and PDM facilitate the integration of R/3 with specialized and legacy data systems where the required SAP certification has been achieved.

Developments and extensions of the basic functionality have been directed toward improving the production data processing in Release 4.5, particularly for the automotive industry.

Using a Material Requirements Planning Area

Release 4.5 recognizes a new entity known as the *Material Requirements Planning* (MRP) area. This entity allows a more refined method of MRP within a plant. The MRP area represents an organizational unit, for which Material Requirements Planning can be performed individually, and the results of the plant planning run can be displayed separately for each MRP area.

An MRP area can include one or several storage locations of a plant or a subcontractor for the materials planning of the parts to be provided. You can also assign a material to multiple MRP areas.

Making a Summarized *Just-in-Time* (JIT) Call

Requirements can be promulgated following an MRP run. However, you can now initiate a just-in-time call based on a specific delivery that is part of a scheduling agreement. The JIT call can be administered and transmitted as a separate document. When a material is required in production, you set the appropriate KANBAN to "empty." The system then generates a grouped JIT call.

Introducing SAP R/3 Banking

The banking industry is passing through a period of change because customers will not hesitate to change banks. Boundaries are disappearing to allow cross-border business, but not without introducing another set of regulatory requirements. There are more products and lines of business, and management needs more precise information.

The ISB-Industry Specific Banking Solution is suitable for various types of financial institutions. It can also be used by companies in commerce and industry. Additional applications for industries, such as insurance, have special relationships between financial assets, such as securities, loans, and real estate. Provisions have been made for complex relationships with other financial institutions.

N O T E   ISB is fully compatible with existing R/2 and R/3 installations and all the R/2 and R/3 product ranges. A global data pool can be used to create a banking data warehouse for external regulatory reporting integrated into the R/3 system.

Enhanced Profitability and Market-Risk Analysis components have been released to launch the ISB-Industry Specific Banking Solution. These new components integrate with elements of the banking and business management modules:

- Financial Accounting
- Purchasing
- Fixed Assets Management
- Real Estate Management
- HR-Human Resources
- PS-Project System

The intention of this industry-specific banking solution is to support in-depth analyses of performance across the enterprise. The client enterprise can call up customized date views that have been dynamically created from the most recent data. Standard profitability analysis views are offered as templates from which user views can be defined:

- Multilevel organization
- Customer
- Customer group
- Product
- Channel

The Risk Management component is designed to yield comprehensive and reliable views of the business risk, in detail, throughout the enterprise. The following evaluation techniques are offered as standard:

- **Market risk.** Computed according to the JP Morgan Risk Metrics specifications. Users can define the parameters to be used for market risk and the bases for data correlation.

- **Credit risk.** Evaluated and measured for all credit risks and exposures.
- **Asset and liability management.** Based on balance-sheet planning and simulation across the enterprise. Simulation can be conducted at macro and micro levels. Trends are computed for interest rates, transaction volumes, and the value of future business.

Introducing SAP R/3 Consumer Products

The concept of this Industry Solution is based on global brand management by integrating control over the extended supply chain from forecasting, via procurement and production, through to delivery to retailers. Brand promotion and marketing or pricing life-cycle management are treated to the proven SAP expertise in the production processes to encourage faster product innovation and improved time-to-market. The SAP Business Workflow and R/3 Project System are applied to coordinate product and packaging development activities.

Comprehensive sales and marketing tools are combined with efficient consumer response mechanisms to enable a faster exchange of point-of-sale data between production and retailers. The outcome is real-time information on consumption and consumer preferences.

Standard cost accounting capabilities allow enterprise-wide product and customer profitability analysis, and the integration of R/3 with Laboratory Information Management Systems (LIMS) provides the link between the laboratory and business supply chain processes.

The consumer products industry is subject to continuous change in products and the ways in which they reach their customers. Speedy response to inquiries is essential, so a 24-hour availability of product information and deliveries will probably be necessary. New products have to be launched quickly.

One guideline in this business area is *efficient consumer response*. This implies that a retailer will enjoy efficient replenishment of stock, hold an efficient assortment of stock items, and be supported by efficient introduction and promotion campaigns. All these objectives are to be directed at the consumer.

The company must know where and how profits are generated and lost along the supply chain so that corrective steps can be taken. The configuration of R/3 Consumer Products is directed toward this purpose by an integration of standard software components.

Offering Vendor-Managed Inventory

Vendor-managed inventory is a service that manufacturers offer retailers, where the manufacturer takes on the task of replenishing products at retail outlets. This strategy can be implemented only if the manufacturer has access to retailer sales figures and current stock levels. The manufacturer can forecast future sales and replenish the retailer's inventory more effectively. Release 4.5 now provides the corresponding functionality.

Presenting Catalogs with PRICAT Outbound Processing

A vendor can use the logical message type PRICAT to transfer data on prices and catalogs for goods and services to a customer. The message can contain all the vendor's products or just announce certain changes.

Updating with Mass Maintenance

Mass maintenance makes it easier to enter large amounts of data. To meet this requirement, SAP has developed a central tool that the various applications can use. The following types of master records can be updated by the mass maintenance functions:

- Material master
- Article master
- Customer master
- Vendor master

Introducing SAP R/3 Chemical

At the center of this Industry Solution are the standard SAP R/3 modules to support process manufacturing, quality management, process costing, and batch/lot management. The first SAP customer was a chemical company, and there are more than 600 chemical installations worldwide. There is a long-established Chemical Industry Center of Expertise. Customer expectations are high, not only with respect to price and delivery, but also concerning the control of potentially dangerous substances. Many products are competing in each niche, and the time-to-market of a new product may well be crucial. Flexible workflow control can adapt the processing to meet requirements and conditions, if necessary, through remote links directed by the Internet.

Introducing SAP R/3 High-Tech and Electronics

Decreased time-to-market and increased manufacturing productivity have to be reconciled in high technology industries where products become obsolete rapidly. Fewer people have to achieve more. In particular, each person may have to manage the entire business process for the order in hand rather than have it pass from department to department. To do this, the relevant information has to be accessed without delay. The technology to do this has to be seen as an asset rather than an expense.

Integrating purchasing, inventory management, sales, and distribution is configured to implement engineer to order (ETO) and configure to order (CTO) from the sales-order stage by using available to promise (ATP) information on the components. Extremely flexible production facilities can be engineered to support make-to-order (MTO), discrete, and repetitive manufacturing along with just-in-time (JIT) and KANBAN reordering logic.

Engineering change management (ECM) can be accomplished through direct integration of CAD and Product Data Management (PDM). Coherent quality management across the supply chain is essential to ensure consistent product, service, and process standards.

Customer loyalty may depend on the quality of after-sales service. The SAP Service Management component is available for integrated product support.

Introducing SAP R/3 Insurance

Insurance companies are increasingly looking to expand beyond their traditional markets, opening up to new risks and opportunities. Often, expense ratios will be high, and the revenue from premiums may be under pressure from competitors as national growth levels start to plateau. The risks in the form of claim liabilities ought to be tracked and controlled, because not all business lines are equally profitable. The investment holdings must be fluid and flexible.

Some insurance companies use separate systems for General Ledger accounting, regulatory compliance, policies, claims, and expense administration. Some form of business information warehouse has to be arranged so that these systems can efficiently contribute to a consolidated base of information from which both profitability and risk can be calculated. The results ought to be available to agents and administrators as well as managers. Decisions have to be quick and accurate.

SAP Insurance is built in the Business Framework, which allows the user organization to monitor and control the key performance measures so that a competitive advantage can be gained and held. The SAP Financial Services Group in the USA and the Industry Center of Expertise in Europe are available for consultation in this business area.

Introducing SAP R/3 Construction

The construction and engineering sector is characterized by shifting production sites and joint undertakings in which several building contractors work together on a project. It is common to order design services, materials, and equipment from internal departments as if they were outside companies. Subcontracting and complex payroll and human resources management are common in construction companies. There are complex warranties, suretyships, security deposits of varying duration, and advance and partial payments. There may be legal constraints on joint ventures that require special documentation.

Adding Functionality with Release 3.0

SAP R/3 Release 3.0 is designed for distributed installation in geographically separate units such as branch offices and subsidiaries. New functionality has been added as ABAP/4 enhancements to carry the specific procedures and terminology of the industry. Equipment control and maintenance at distant sites have received special emphasis.

The R/3 Project System has been customized for the construction industry. Project-based information views are provided. Settlement of all incurred costs and activities and periodic analysis by construction site are examples of project evaluation procedures. Allowances can be made for partial inspections, impending losses, and stock corrections. There is a comprehensive cross-application reporting system for construction companies.

These business applications also form part of a complete enterprise solution for the construction industry available from HOCHTIEF Software GmbH under the brand name of ARISTOTELES.

Introducing PDM with Release 4.0

The PDM-Engineering and Construction Product Data Management component is available with R/3 Release 4.0. It was designed specifically for the engineering and construction industry and is integrated with the ECM-Engineering Change Management components of R/3.

The standard R/3 system allows product data to be managed by linking external objects such as drawings, documents, and scanned images. These linkages are recorded in R/3 and are subjected to engineering change management so that all alterations can be traced and versions are released only under status control.

Some newer developments are directed as forging reliable links with third-party product data management systems, documentation systems, and CAD systems. All these linkages have to be subject to engineering change management.

The effectiveness of a part, a document, or a complex structure of parts and documents can be monitored if it can be tracked and associated with reports of its performance. Where parts are always identified by a unique serial number, such tracking entails more elaborate record keeping. This is available as of Release 4.0.

Cash-flow management has not always been of interest to engineers and constructors. However, forecasts of earned value analysis and profit analysis are now available to supplement traditional project reports. This leads on to project simulation as an aid to decision making. An effective means of generating a what-if report may be of great help when a project is well on its way and the sponsor changes the requirements.

Workforce planning and recording is a function developed specifically for the engineering and construction industry. A Cross-Application Time Sheet (CATS) function is provided in which actual work is recorded across applications. Intranet document viewing and communication is a standard facility.

Introducing SAP R/3 Education

The SAP R/3 HR-Human Resources application includes modules to manage the selection and booking of students in courses. Several third-party document management systems (DMSs) have received SAP certification because they can be seamlessly integrated with R/3 and its applications. A document can be any unit of text, sound, vision, animation, video, or any product of computer-assisted design.

> **N O T E**   It is expected that further assistance with the design and structure of tuition sequences will be available as the SAP development teams address the process of education with the concepts elaborated in physical manufacturing.

Introducing SAP R/3 Healthcare

It is apparent that the healthcare industry is faced with legal requirements, increasing competition, and cost pressures. These factors combine with patient demands for better service, less waiting, and treatment that is as rapid and painless as possible. All activities are increasingly scrutinized because the public is interested. Private and public funds are always less than the requirement, so cost management at all levels of the organization is essential. Financial and asset accounting has to be efficient and provide an up-to-the-minute picture of a hospital's status.

The disciplines of production planning and control in which SAP is so well practiced are clearly relevant. Materials management for efficient purchasing, inventory control, consumption analyses, and preventive maintenance are some obvious parallels. Human resource management has to be of the highest priority.

Complementary software for the healthcare industry is also available. The R/3 business applications can by extended by integration with clinical subsystems for laboratory, radiology, or surgery scheduling.

Introducing IS-H SAP Industry Solution for Hospitals

This SAP Industry Solution has been developed in the context of the type of hospital environment where a not-for-profit organization is required by law to carry out modern cost accounting and controlling. At the same time, there is a recognition of the benefits of bringing online supporting facilities such as laboratories, patient communications, and staff administration.

The IS-H Hospital Administration application includes the following components:

- IS-HPM Patient Management
- IS-HPA Patient Accounting
- IS-HCM Communications
- IS-HCO Hospital Controlling

The IS-H Hospital Administration application can be installed as a hospital information system. It will normally be integrated in stages with the following R/3 modules:

- TR-AM Asset Management
- FI-Financial Accounting
- MM-Materials Management
- CO-Controlling

Reviewing the Benefits of Integrating IS-H and SAP R/3

The benefits of an integrated combination of standard R/3 applications and the specialized IS-H components are seen by hospital authorities in contrast to the separate, previously installed standalone systems. Of particular value is the precise support of professional patient management in the context of strict legal requirements for cost control. The standard R/3 system of access authorizations is important in the hospital environment.

The wide variety of medical databases and technical instrumentation components can be accessed through the R/3 standard interfaces, and the SAP GUI can be used to communicate with medical and administrative staff.

Individual reporting programs can be developed from the models provided in IS-H, and new technical systems can be accommodated by developing ABAP/4 interface programs where necessary. The extension of medical databases and communications between hospitals is considered a prime requirement for future developments.

Introducing SAP R/3 Media

As opportunities have increased for customers to choose between media items and across media channels, the media industries have had to think in terms of media-neutral contents. Publishing may often have to be across several media. The fully digitized "document" has become the data object of interest.

The industry's response has been the development of fully integrated systems and workflow solutions for all business and production processes along the value chain of media production. SAP Media offers an integrated combination of standard business software and the interfaces necessary to link to complementary software associated with the media. The following tasks are supported by the application:

- Sales
- Handling of advertising orders
- Billing of advertisers
- Order processing of subscription and single-copy sales
- Logistics for circulation planning, shipping, and delivery

IS-P Publishing is a related Industry Solution optimized for a business sector in which tasks tend to be outsourced and where the lean management philosophy is seeking ways of moving decision making down the organizational structure.

Introducing SAP R/3 Metal

The SAP Industry Center of Expertise for the metal industry has been at the heart of research to determine the special software requirements of the aluminum and steel industry, both on the production side in the metal trades. Developments are expected in applications of constraint-based planning technology.

Industry-specific templates have been configured to customize the SAP R/3 standard business modules to be ready to run in the metal industry. The material management functions allow the user company to store data on the particular sizes and shapes in use, for example. The metal industry has many common standards, which can be set up as master records before the system is installed. Similarly, the operations of selecting and handling metal items are common throughout the industry. The configuration template can thus include both material data and many of the operations and tasks that will be required.

Introducing SAP R/3 Oil

The needs of the oil and gas industry are focused on exploration, transportation, and distribution. It is global and becoming deregulated. Eastern markets are opening, but new competitors have appeared, such as the superstore outlets in the United Kingdom and France. Differentiation is necessary, and the industry must react in different ways to specific markets. The SAP R/3 Industry Solution for the oil and gas industry links the entire value chain, from crude supply to commercial and retail customers.

Some of the features of IS-Oil follow:

- A comprehensive accounting system can handle multiple ledgers—legal and regulatory—as well as accounts payable, accounts receivable, sales, and expense processing.
- The association of cost drivers with business processes facilitates decisions based on the most up-to-date operational cost data without having to retrieve information from other systems.
- A human resources system enables the control of labor costs and skills availability.
- Integration with Plant Maintenance yields accurate labor costs for internal and external workers.
- Critical EDI transactions are supported.
- Exchange transactions are monitored to yield real-time exchange balance information. This component deals with complex fees and differentials.
- SAP Business Workflow allows the automation of business processes.

The oil and gas industry solution combines the core R/3 system with two industry-specific modules:

- The IS-Oil Upstream module was developed specifically for joint venture accounting. It integrates the complex accounting requirements of joint venture accounting while reducing staff overhead and data redundancy.
- The IS-Oil Downstream module offers an open, scalable, integrated solution that enables oil companies to support most of their information processing requirements with one integrated package that provides numerous functions unique to oil and gas marketing and refining.

Automating Order Fulfillment

The order process can be streamlined by automating the selection of supply location and allowing changes of product volume and temperature throughout the delivery. All types of packages and containers are managed.

Planning Bulk Distribution Requirements   This feature uses data within SAP to automate the entire order process. The system also handles complex international taxation, pricing, and exchange rate issues.

Managing the Hydrocarbon Inventory   This component amends existing core SAP inventory functionality to meet the standards of the American Society for Testing Material (ASTM) and the American Petroleum Institute (API) with respect to temperature correction, density, and specific gravity calculations. Ambient volumes, temperatures, and product densities are converted to standard volumes and weights corrected for temperature so that they can be used in calculations for material movements and measurements.

Retailing Oil   This component of IS-Oil provides a comprehensive picture at the service-station level by consolidating data from numerous sources into a single, virtual database. This facilitates various functions, ranging from distribution planning to profitability analysis.

Anticipating Developments in Exploration Management

Agreements are in place between SAP and the PriceWaterhouse World Energy Group to extend the SAP Oil & Gas solution to meet customers' upstream needs for exploration and production capabilities. If the agreements are approved by the industry regulatory authorities, the partners will consult a wide range of customers and develop systems for the upstream exploration and production market.

Introducing SAP R/3 Pharmaceuticals

The specialized modules of SAP R/3 are ideally suited to the pharmaceutical industry, with its emphasis on tight control over documentation and quality through a wide range of production and distribution processes.

A pharmaceutical customer can place an order against up-to-date inventory and production planning data while retaining close control over the detailed specification. Production will take place exclusively by approved processes under supervision of the production planner and to controlled recipes. Certificates of analysis will be generated and checked against production data and customer specifications. Real-time profit analysis will be available.

Introducing SAP R/3 Public Sector

Budget administration and fiscal accounting are the themes of this SAP Industry Solution, which can be fully integrated with other R/3 system applications. It has been developed as an enhancement of the TR-FM Treasury Funds Management component to suit the needs of public sector administration and not-for-profit organizations. The components provide an efficient workflow-supported facility, which enables you to distribute a budget across the various authorization levels. IS-PS meets requirements for complete accountability to governing bodies and legal authorities who might want to scrutinize the conduct of business from several different viewpoints that might not be easy to anticipate. The flexible reporting methods are seen as important in this connection.

SAP R/3 Public Sector manages administrative and budgeting processes commonly performed by agencies and organizations in national and state governments, universities, and not-for-profit organizations.

Introducing SAP R/3 Real Estate

The data objects controlled by this Industry Solution are real estate, buildings, rental units, and rooms. The target user is a manager of a large property portfolio who manages contractors and tenants. The system is sensitive to the due dates for payments and receipts by virtue of its links with the CO-Controlling module. It also performs the functions of project management for property maintenance and can be integrated with components of the PM-Plant Maintenance application. Earlier releases of the real estate software appeared with the code IS-IS.

Developments in the industry include the setting up of premises for specific purposes for a limited period, but with a wide variety of furniture and plants to be managed with the property.

Introducing SAP R/3 Retail

The R/3 Retail solution includes the Retail Industry (IS-R) component and supports retailers' core business processes, such as sourcing, planning, and tracking merchandise movement along the entire value chain. More than 200 new retail-specific business processes have been formed as templates or models, from which a particular retail business can assemble an integrated system. The leading retail point-of-sale systems have received SAP certification.

Online Purchasing and Banking

Supermarket and superstore companies are competing to build customer-driven services that make the best use of information technology. SAP R/3 Retail is being extended to facilitate Internet connections for the purpose of goods and services purchasing, including the provision of banking.

The standard retail management tasks are supported:

- Merchandising
- Assortment planning
- Price and promotion management
- Stock accounting

- Finance
- Distribution
- Store management information

Some users of R/3 Retail are developing their systems to provide full store replenishment.

Continuous-Flow Logistics

Efficient consumer response (ECR) is the notion of linking consumer product companies with retailers and wholesalers to share data on store assortment, replenishment, promotions, and product introductions. Implementation of this concept depends on establishing effective communications for which the Internet may prove to be suitable.

Applying Cross-Docking in the Distribution Center

If you procure merchandise for a distribution center and then immediately deliver this merchandise to a customer, you could operate cross-docking. You buy in exactly what you plan to sell and transfer it, without any unpacking, from one vehicle to another. The accounting has to recognize that the goods are not placed in stock.

Allocating Apparel Stock

The fashion industry needs software functions that include value and quota scales, so that the system can automatically allocate appropriate quantities of a generic article to each of its variants. This function is of particular relevance to the apparel and footwear industry.

Integrating Shelf Space Management

SAP Retail links with third-party software packages for planning and optimizing shelf space more effectively. The interface handles business process integration and data interchange.

Connecting with SAP SCOPE

The SAP supply-chain optimization, planning, and execution initiative is referred to as *SAP SCOPE*. It combines the SAP R/3 enterprise resource planning (ERP) solution with the R/3 Advanced Planner & Optimizer products and technologies, the SAP Sales Force Automation, SAP Business to Business Commerce, and a comprehensive business intelligence solution known as the SAP Business Information Warehouse.

Operating Vendor-Managed Inventory

Vendor-managed inventory is a service that manufacturers offer retailers, where the manufacturer takes on the task of replenishing products at retail outlets. This strategy can be implemented only if the manufacturer has access to retailer sales figures and current stock levels. The manufacturer can forecast future sales and replenish the retailer's inventory more effectively. Release 4.5 now offers the corresponding functionality.

Sending Catalogs with PRICAT Outbound Processing

A vendor can use the logical message type PRICAT to transfer data on prices and catalogs for goods and services to a customer. The message can contain all of a vendor's products, or just announce certain changes.

Updating with Mass Maintenance

Mass maintenance is a facility to keep large quantities of master records up-to-date. It can maintain the following record types:

- Material master
- Article master
- Customer master
- Vendor master

Introducing SAP R/3 Service Provider

The scope of services that can be supported by this Industry Solution includes all varieties of the following activities:

- Technical services
- Professional services
- Consulting
- Personnel management
- Recruiting
- Personnel selection
- Process outsourcing
- Research and development

What these activities have in common is their high dependence on personal skills and the difficulty of providing these services in the absence of suitable service providers. Each service order is associated with the resources needed and supported as necessary with ancillary activities. The target industry sector in which the service provider is operating will normally be reflected in the structures customized when this application is implemented.

Introducing SAP R/3 Transportation

Transportation occupies a special place in the supply chain of many industries and is well-served by elements from the various applications. However, it is recognized that some parts of the industry have developed effective solutions to their particular problems. Shipment optimization and shipment tracking have been identified as specialized skills for which it is appropriate to call on the existing solutions via a suitable Business Application Programming Interface (BAPI). Shipment papers and shipment cost calculation also fall into this category.

Bulk transportation has already been addressed in SAP IS-Oil, so the relevant parts of this application have been built in to the transportation system.

The safety and regulatory constraints on the transport of dangerous goods demand the use of specialized equipment and service agencies, which have to be brought in to the planning and costing computations.

Future developments will include automatic intelligent planning of routes and handling facilities to enhance the value-added chain, as well as the monitoring and control of all aspects of the quality of the transportation processes.

Introducing SAP R/3 IS-T Telecom

The IS-T Industry Solution for the telecommunications industry can be preconfigured to include any SAP R/3 applications. The communications industry is experiencing intense competition across its scope of work, which can range from constructing facilities for the company and its network, to providing repairs, upgrades, and modifications to the equipment owned by telecom customers. Cost control of processes and staff is being managed over the complete work order cycle, from a customer request to resource scheduling, execution, and history analysis. Regulations entail accurate service and control of the installed base of customer equipment and warranties, for which comprehensive reporting capabilities must exist.

Introducing SAP R/3 IS-U Utilities

IS-U is focused on the RIVA real-time customer information and billing system developed for utility and service companies. The industry is characterized by a shift from monopolies in a regulated market to a competition-based energy and service industry. There are restrictions; security of supply to the customer and the protection of the environment are recognized as onerous. Yet many of the legacy industrial enterprises cannot meet these kinds of conditions without considerable business process reengineering. In particular, it is necessary to adapt quickly and efficiently to changing circumstances of whatever nature.

When the concept of a business process is applied to the various utilities, it becomes possible to build and operate a composite system that operates among business partners across several sectors. Some business partner categories follow:

- Residential
- Nonresidential
- Customer
- Prospect
- Owner
- Bill recipient
- Installer

- Uninstaller
- Disposal agent

Here are some utilities sectors:

- Electricity
- Gas
- Water
- Waste water (sewage)
- District heating
- Home heating
- Waste disposal
- Cable TV
- Telephone
- Service order
- Service contract
- Goods
- Charges
- Taxes
- Fees and licenses

The application has facilities for extending the business partner types and utility categories. ●

Accelerating Implementation

Integrating R/3 with Existing Business Systems

Before a computer installation is delivered, several SAP business partners can build a system that will serve the customer's requirements, and then set up the software in it and prove that it works properly for the intended business before the system leaves the factory. This service minimizes on-site time and disruption to normal business and promotes higher uniform standards across processes and vendor technologies. It is also an example of a way to decrease the time and cost of implementing a complex SAP R/3 system.

Although SAP R/3 is a global enterprise system of great versatility and scope, it can take a great deal of time and expensive effort to install and configure. One way to accelerate implementation is to use your existing systems and look at systems available from third parties. This chapter presents some implementation examples.

Linking with HP OpenView OmniBack II

You can monitor and solve problems centrally from a graphical control station. You can also restore data to multiple disks simultaneously by using HP9000 UNIX system servers, Windows NT NetServer systems, and HP digital linear-tape libraries.

Linking to an IBM System 390 Mainframe with DB2

The IBM S/390 and OS/390 can support SAP R/3 in the role of DB2 database server. Because System 390 is scalable, many more users can access the database. In this way, both R/2 and R/3 users can work with their existing data and production systems in an R/3 enterprise management environment.

Using R/3 on an IBM Advanced System 400

The availability of R/3 on AS/400 systems is seen as important for mid-sized companies. For example, wholesalers, distribution specialists, and publishers may find the AS/400 hosting R/3 an attractive configuration, enabling them to integrate the sophisticated R/3 modules with their existing databases and specialized business processes.

Using the MVS Mainframe Version of R/3

Many very large databases, particularly in the banking and insurance business, are held on secure mainframes. The MVS mainframe version of SAP R/3 allows you to run the application portion of R/3 on a UNIX or Windows NT Server and access the MVS mainframe where the secure data is held.

Migrating Rapidly from R/2 to R/3

Versions of an SAP R/2 to R/3 migration package are available with R/2 Releases 4.3, 5.0, and 6.0. These packages are simple to operate. They also recognize that the migration of data objects must be reliable and thorough because of the high value of this information to the company. The disciplines of change management are applied so that a complete record is generated of what came from where. The newly placed data then can be properly interpreted.

The migration package includes program generators to build customer-specific export and import programs. Archives that must remain available (for legal reasons) in an acceptable alternative form are not migrated. A method for copying data that has been archived in R/2 directly to an R/3 archive is available nevertheless. The migration package processes the data to be migrated with the generated program logic, interprets the field assignments, and then writes the data to the R/3 System database.

Migration objects like material master records, accounting documents, and purchase orders have the physical structure of one or more chains of ABAP/4 data statements that specify field headers. These field headers, as well as all export and import programs, are generated individually in the customer system. This procedure enables your modifications to the record layout (such as added fields, changed field lengths, and changed field types) to be taken into account during migration.

This technique enables you to save a substantial amount of time compared to standard R/3 batch input. A data-transfer rate of at least 2Mbps is necessary for transfer to a nearby installation. If a specialized migration package isn't available, the recommended method for data transport is via 3480/3490 cassettes using the SCSI port. This step includes decompression of the dataset and the necessary code conversion from EBCDIC to ASCII.

Using the Migration Enterprise IMG

A procedure model guides you through all the phases of migration, from the conceptual phase to productive operation of the R/3 system. External help should not be necessary.

The *Implementation Management Guide* (IMG) for the migration enterprise is presented in *Hypertext Markup Language* (HTML). It offers the same structure for all migration objects, which are displayed with the ticked icon to be processed in the prescribed order. Double-clicking any icon reveals extra text and help. There is a display of migration sequence reminders and facilities for cross-application migration customizing so that the finished system has a uniform appearance and functionality.

A migration environment is available as a CD-ROM with a comprehensive installation guide for R/2 customers.

Integrating R/2 and R/3 Without Migration

By the year 2000, there will be about 1,000 productive R/2 installations, many of them very large. Releases 4.3 and 4.4 of R/2 will continue to be supported by the SAP hotline, although they were not maintained after 1996. SAP will continue to support R/2. For example, a body of accurate problem descriptions allows the *Online Software Service* (OSS) to access more than 40,000 solution notes with fast processing for customer queries. SAP R/2 Release 6.0 includes a number of interface configurations to cooperate with R/3. The Internet components of SAP R/3 Releases 3.1 and 4.0 will be available to the large R/2 installations that have integrated with an R/3 system.

Implementing the SAP Business Framework

The Business Framework allows configurable software modules to collaborate via standard interfaces in an architecture that is open to components from SAP and third parties. Client companies can add elements incrementally. The Business Framework allows SAP to deliver new capabilities, components, and technology to its customers on a continuous basis, independent of conventional upgrade release cycles.

Reviewing Business Framework Components

Some Business Framework building blocks follow:

- **HR-Human Resources** is a widely used component with a dedicated database and independent release cycle. Customers will be able to quickly and easily deploy new HR functionality as it is released. The HR component is integrated into R/3 Release 4.0, where it includes workflow and human resources management enhancements. There are new country-specific versions. Internet and intranet components are shipped with this release.

- **PDM-Product Data Management** combines its own engineering database with the workflow integration of the R/3 Manufacturing and Logistics modules.

- **TM-Treasury Management** manages financial transactions and portfolios. The integration of this Treasury component enables you to streamline financial cash flow, liquidity, portfolio, and risk-management operations.

- **ATP-Available to Promise** is an advanced global server for order processing and decision support. R/3 users with systems and sources distributed worldwide can perform sophisticated product availability checks across corporate networks or the Internet.

Another Business Framework building block is a dedicated reporting server that offers high-performance, cross-corporate reporting and decision support. It can take data from active R/3 components, from SAP's distributed Open Information Warehouse component, and from third-party database servers through corporate intranets or the Internet.

Collaborating with Open Interfaces

Business components collaborate within the Business Framework through *Business Application Programming Interfaces* (BAPIs). BAPIs provide a stable, standardized method for third-party applications and components to integrate into the Business Framework. These interfaces are being specified as part of SAP's initiative with customers, partners, Microsoft Corporation, and leading standards organizations.

Using Templates to Accelerate Configuration and Customizing

A newspaper turned in a record time for implementing an SAP R/3 system: 88 days from start to productive running. This rapid implementation was facilitated by using an industry-specific template that preconfigured and customized R/3 so that the master data and the associated processing routines were exactly what was required in the newspaper industry. Preconfigured newspaper business processes were set up to accept copy from reporters. Sales and Distribution modules were set up to handle advertising and the distribution of printed papers to the various transportation facilities. The inquiry section was ready to receive telephone, email, and fax inputs.

A template can specify how the whole system will work when the default settings are used. If the defaults are very close to the finished requirement, it is possible to set up training schemes for users. Therefore, on the day the system is delivered, users can handle routine business and probably take in stride any changes made during the final customizing of the template to make it exactly fit the target company.

More than 200 templates are available for most of the main industry sectors. Each is as comprehensive as it is possible to be without knowing the details of a specific user enterprise.

Simulating R/3 with the IntelliCorp Live Model

The Live Model software uses the R/3 Reference Model and the IMG to simulate the execution behavior of a proposed R/3 implementation. This allows the system to be checked and configured before acquisition.

The simulation of an intended R/3 system may have an important function in building the confidence of the staff, which has to operate the system and live with the consequences if anything fails to work as intended. But a simulation can also provide benchmark information to show you how the system will behave under high-load conditions. It might be wise to have a simulation of a mix of work that is not likely to occur but would have serious implications for the company if the system could not cope with it. The Internet has provided examples of service providers reducing their prices only to find their networks swamped with customers who then become disenchanted and leave, never to return.

Using Versions of R/3 for Particular Language Communities

If you are in a particular language community, the availability of a version of SAP R/3 in your language could be a big advantage in terms of the speed of your implementation. For example, the core modules FI, CO, MM, SD, and PP are available in Finnish with SAP R/3 Release 3.0; and all modules except HR support Finnish with Release 3.1. Some details are localized for the Finnish market. This Finnish version includes the following features:

- Outgoing and incoming payments
- Bank account number validation
- Intrastat reporting
- Finnish tax calculation procedures and tax codes
- Chart of depreciation
- Finnish calendar
- Chart of accounts

The development of SAP applications for specific language communities is expected to take a number of different directions. In some instances, the visual layout and symbol system of a language community will be related to the conventions of countries already using SAP applications. The standard business software can be translated or converted in such cases.

If the SAP designers are unfamiliar with the legal system of a target language community, specialists in that culture can install and configure a package of processing logic and reference data. But if the target community is not comfortable with the notion of symbolic transactions with a machine, a radical approach might be necessary. The SAP research teams are looking at various input and output devices that can be served by the Internet and may be a route to potential users who cannot yet use the conventional terminals.

Reviewing Componentization and Business Solutions

The SAP componentization initiative is focused on R/3 Release 4.0, in which many new business components were introduced, along with a wider range of complementary software products to which these components can be linked. A number of configurations of R/3 have been offered using these elements to provide business solutions. Here are a few examples:

- SAP Retail
- SAP Public Sector
- SAP Utilities

One defining characteristic of a business solution based on Release 4.0 is the emphasis on being able to engineer full business processing support throughout an extended supply chain from product design to the point of product delivery or consumption. The *componentization* concept emphasizes that the components can be added one at a time to an existing R/3 implementation with a minimum of disruption.

The components used in a business solution are recognized as parts of the SAP Business Framework, in which the capability to integrate with the rest of the R/3 applications throughout the enterprise is integral to the software design. Third-party software and hardware has always been associated with SAP systems, and the business components include features that extend the range of suppliers and the types of input and output equipment available for rapid integration with R/3. Two types of linkage are supported by standard interfaces: *loosely coupled* and *tightly coupled*. Loose coupling is exemplified by the *remote function call* (RFC) technique. Tight coupling refers to the full online integration typical of R/3 networked applications.

One essential component of a system is the database, and the componentization initiative recognizes that a shared common database is an integral part of an integrated system. There are several approved suppliers of database systems as components.

Another characteristic of a Release 4.0 business component is that it can be developed and released in improved or extended variants independently of the release of R/3. As a consequence, the project teams may be deployed on one component at a time instead of in large-scale simultaneous implementations. Before Release 3.0, systems needed a common database, and the entire system had to be upgraded as a whole. Loose coupling was introduced with Release 3.0 and was used primarily for supporting geographically remote sites.

Using Core Applications as Business Components

As of Release 4.0 of the Business Framework, the HR-Human Resources core application is available as a tightly coupled business component. This allows it to maintain its own database yet remain fully in touch with the other core applications, Financial and Logistics, through *Application Link Enabling* (ALE).

Future releases will include Financial and Logistics as independent business components that can also maintain their own databases yet couple tightly with the rest of the implementation.

As with other business components, the core applications that have evolved into business components can be upgraded independently of releases of R/3.

Accelerating Implementation with Active Help

You might be prepared to accept that accelerating the implementation of R/3 is a shorthand way of defining the goal of setting to work a cost-effective system based on R/3. The target system is an earner, not just an expense.

Release 4.0 includes new releases of all core R/3 components that add to their scope. They all now evoke the Active Help facility, which refines the help information by automatically referring to the process from which you called the help.

From the user's viewpoint, an improved help facility inevitably lessens operating delays and therefore brings forward the stage where the business processing system is repaying the costs of its installation and maintenance.

Introducing ASAP™ Methodology

AcceleratedSAP (ASAP) has become the standard methodology for SAP R/3 rapid implementation for the larger companies. With Release 4.0, the new Business Engineer provides a more efficient, comprehensive, and knowledge-based configuration process tool for applying standard business templates. It can be controlled by the Internet and, like other business components, has a separate release cycle. ASAP is intended for use by implementation and development project managers, business process consultants, and technical project managers.

Accelerating Upgrades and Migration

As of Release 4.5 of ASAP, customers can upgrade to R/3 4.x from correction levels in R/3 Releases 2.2, 3.0, or 3.1. The necessary software is delivered as business components that make it easier and faster to upgrade from Release 3.0 to Release 4.x.

The Legacy System Migration Workbench is a standard support tool that allows you to migrate from any legacy system to R/3. It requires a minimum of programmer expertise, because it includes procedures that ensure consistency, flexibility, and reusability of all migration programs generated on the workbench.

Using ASAP Roadmap, Tools, and Services

The ASAP Roadmap is a project plan with detailed descriptions of what, why, and how certain activities are performed. Examples, checklists, templates, questionnaires, and technical guides are included to take over the role of the Implementation Management Guide used with earlier releases.

The technical guides and technical accelerators of the ASAP Roadmap follow:

- Interface Adviser, which can run as a standalone Internet-enabled information source for using standard BAPIs and for creating interfaces between all SAP and approved third-party components
- Data conversion
- Authorization
- Printer setup

Configuration is guided by the Business Engineer and assisted by a range of industry-specific templates. The ASAP package arranges standard consulting and support tasks where specialist input is essential.

The ASAP package provides a project plan and a checklist that covers the entire implementation. The plan adopts the continuous system engineering approach, which begins by looking for SAP R/3 components that will meet future business requirements. This is in contrast to a more traditional approach, which begins with extensive documentation of the business situation as it is before the implementation begins.

As the business requirements are identified in what is called the *business blueprint,* the ASAP system makes recommendations and suggestions based on the best business practices and the SAP R/3 components available to support them. The outcome is identified as the *baseline* system.

By using these techniques, a working baseline system can be implemented in a matter of weeks. The fine-tuning and final preparation activities are carried out by iterations of the customizing and configuring process.

Personalizing the R/3 Interface

R/3 personalization has progressed since Release 3.0 in its task of making an implemented R/3 system rapidly adjustable to individual users to help accelerate the implementation of a successful and accepted family of work centers.

The application administrator takes the full menu of functions as implemented at the company level and progressively identifies functions at each menu level that are not needed by a specific group of work centers. When an employee signs on at such a work center, or when the workgroup is identified from a remote terminal, the system automatically refers to the reduced menu system so that users are never offered an option or a data-entry field they are unlikely to use. This simplified navigation may omit whole screens, particular functions, or only the unwanted fields of a screen table. Also, you can specify personalized field defaults so that repetitive tasks can be streamlined.

Another mechanism used by the personalization initiative is to provide fast processing of the functions and tasks needed at a workplace by consulting special registers that cache the data and software components most likely to be needed.

The application administrator can define personalization for groups of employees or for individual users by specifying a typical work center in terms of its personalized characteristics. One or more individuals are associated with the typical work center. The system automatically generates the authorization profiles and builds the personal user menus, which are presented when the named person logs on.

The administrator also specifies typical business cases and customizes them to exactly fit the circumstances. Again, the system generates specific user transactions when these typical business cases are encountered. The overall effect of personalization is to make the user interface a better place to work.

Introducing RRR, Ready-to-Run R/3

The Ready-to-Run R/3 package is an example of technical preconfiguration and is therefore in the category of accelerators for R/3 implementation. However, RRR is not integrated into the AcceleratedSAP method.

The normal R/3 implementation includes a stage where consultants technically configure the R/3 system in anticipation of the resources the client will need to carry out the business operations specified in the design. With the R/3 system up and running, the next stage is to customize the system to match it exactly to the client's requirements, down to the screen contents seen by users. These operations will be comparatively expensive for mid-range companies and prohibitive for small ones.

Ready-to-Run R/3 is a standard system that has been installed on a hardware platform chosen by the customer. When the hardware is running with R/3 Release 3.1 installed, it is shipped to the customer as RRR, Ready-to-Run R/3, where the customizing processes are completed.

RRR is aimed at companies that expect to have between 15 and 200 concurrent users on the system. Therefore it is directed at small and medium-sized companies instead of the very large enterprises in which SAP R/3 is normally implemented. The Ready-to-Run R/3 Quick Sizer tool can be run beforehand to collate the factors that will determine which one of the seven available RRR packages is most cost-effective.

The components of the RRR package follow:

- Preinstalled, preconfigured R/3 system
- Complete hardware, software, and network infrastructure
- Comprehensive operations and support concept

SAP carries out the technical setting-up operations with the most advanced methods and the best engineers. At the same time, the system is set up to offer the best practices so that customers will benefit from an efficient and comprehensive system from the beginning, even if the receiving staff is new to SAP enterprise software.

Maximizing Capabilities

The preconfiguring operations can ensure the most reliable and powerful system possible with the resources specified. The technical system parameters are set for the servers and the network configuration is specified for the customer before the hardware leaves the SAP partner laboratory.

The administration of a computer system includes deciding priorities for the allocation of system resources to serve the background and interactive processing modes, as well as to maximize the availability of the whole system. Again, these technical decisions can be made by SAP experts who deliver a fully optimized system because the use patterns have been accurately anticipated. The user company will no doubt want to fine-tune the system as it becomes more apparent how the business can best be served.

Sizing RRR

Ready-to-Run R/3 is available in packages according to the maximum number of active users expected. The smallest package handles up to 25 users; the largest handles 200 active users.

All packages use the Microsoft Windows NT operating system with a Microsoft SQL Server, Informix, Oracle, Dynamic Server, DB2/UDB, or DB/2 relational database management system. An AS/400 system using the DB2/400 database is also available. A standard printer is included in the package, along with front-end PCs, all preconfigured. An RRR implementation can be upgraded without restriction by adding suitable hardware and software.

RRR packages are available from the following SAP partners:

- Compaq
- Digital Equipment
- Hewlett-Packard
- IBM
- Bull
- Sun Microsystems
- NCR
- Siemens-Nixdorf

Reviewing RRR System Components

A typical RRR implementation offers the following types of system components:

- Production system with associated database server
- Application server with one or more applications
- Test system with associated database server
- Client PC as administrative control center
- LAN server for specified number of terminals

- Switch to existing network
- Router to SAP Remote Support

The precise configuration clearly depends on the customer's requirements and the nature of the existing business data processing arrangements.

Administering RRR

A key RRR component is the *System Administration Assistant* (SAA), which includes the capability to initiate administrative tasks with a single button click. The SAA also presents checklists and tasklists that should be performed on a daily, weekly, monthly, or yearly basis. For example, there are predefined batch jobs and associated job schedules for backup and month-end close.

As part of the RRR package, the designated system administrator is given a four-day training course in the use of SAA and the system as a whole. ●

PART VIII

Maintaining and Enhancing the Implementation

CHAPTER 26

Providing Online Documentation Support

In this chapter

Working with Online Documentation

If you need previously stored business information when you are online to the R/3 system, you can access it via the R/3 Classification system or by using the DMS-Document Management System (if it has been installed and configured). If you need information about the R/3 system itself, you must refer to the R/3 System Documentation Library. This is available on CD-ROM and can be installed on a server on your network. You can also read it from any PC equipped with a CD-ROM drive. The System Documentation Library is also available in book form.

As of Release 2.2, the R/3 Documentation Library can be accessed online using the Microsoft Windows help system. This entails installing a CD-ROM on a network server, which then provides context-sensitive access from R/3 transactions.

The intention of the SAP system designers was to make all relevant information, whether from transactions or from reference sources, easily accessible to users. It was also their prime objective to make sure that the presentation of this information is focused as much as possible on the user's immediate needs, and that it is offered in a format that is directly meaningful in its layout.

The *Document Management System* (DMS)

The DMS-Document Management System describes, manages, and displays documents of all types, independently of the application from which the documents were generated or from which they are most frequently accessed.

The following types of documents are included:

- Drawings
- Graphics
- Contracts
- Patents
- Business transaction documents

NOTE You can create additional document types through customizing.

Document Linking

Documents can be linked to objects in other R/3 applications and retrieved from elsewhere. You can use the online message control system to control the documents and manage workflow strategies. A document can be linked to one or more of the following kinds of data objects:

- Another document
- Materials
- Pieces of equipment

- Projects
- Quotations
- Sales orders
- Customer master records
- Vendor master records

For example, a drawing can be linked to material. The online message control system then informs work scheduling and production control of any changes to that drawing, which you can view from production work centers.

Classification of Data Objects

The R/3 Classification system, central to the retrieval procedure of the DMS, offers many functions to help you locate information held in records that can be retrieved in document form. You can search on the basis of subject matter, and you can search for an item because you know it is linked with a data object such as these:

- Another document
- Material identified by its material number or by its name, or part of its name
- An item of equipment where you have given its name or only the identification of the activity where it is used
- A project identified by its number, the person responsible, the purpose, and so on
- A quotation
- A sales order
- A customer or a vendor identified by an attribute in the master records

Any document can be located and displayed by using the retrieval functions of the Classification system or by conducting searches based on document info records.

Document Info Records

Information about a document can be stored in a document info record, which can include text in several languages. It also stores the name and department of the person responsible for the document, the place of the document in the case of hierarchical documents, and the authorization group necessary to view the main document.

Additional details of the document can be inserted in the document info record with a wide range of functions offered by the R/3 Classification system.

Document Change Control

You can establish your own sequence of status conditions to represent a document's life cycle. You can specify that the message control system inform certain users when the document changes status.

You can maintain document info records from the R/3 CAD user interface.

Changes to a document are associated with change numbers, which allows them to be integrated with the engineering change management system and therefore with the production system.

Language Text Pools

Language text pools are used for screen layouts, online help, and online documentation. When the code in an ABAP/4 program requires a text element to be displayed onscreen, it specifies the number of the text element to be used. The code does not have to be changed in order to access another element if the language of the user is changed. The language in which the text element is presented is determined by the language selected by the user profile.

R/3 System Documentation

The R/3 Documentation Library is available on CD-ROM, which can be read from any PC equipped with a CD-ROM drive. The Documentation Library is also available in book form.

As of Release 2.2, you can access the R/3 Documentation Library online by using the Microsoft Windows help system, which provides context-sensitive access from R/3 transactions.

Context-Sensitive Help

The help system requires the R/3 documentation to be installed from a CD-ROM on a network server. The following options are available during transaction processing from the user interface:

- **R/3 extended help.** Automatically links you to the documentation relevant to the current active transaction.
- **R/3 Library Manager.** Allows you to browse the documentation by selecting graphical icons and hierarchical menus.
- **Search dialog box.** Enables you to enter a keyword before choosing a topic so that your search is focused.

You can copy files from the R/3 Documentation CD-ROM to a hard disk drive for faster access—for example, on a laptop computer.

Independent Documentation Servers

A separate Windows help file is provided for each application. The R/3 online documentation can be arranged selectively on several documentation servers, which are independent of the application servers and can be configured to provide the optimal response times for a group of users and to conserve system resources.

You can get even faster retrieval by selectively copying files from the R/3 Documentation Library to individual machines.

R/3 Documentation from the OSS-Online Service System

If you encounter a problem that cannot be solved by referring to the online documentation, and if your installation is a registered user of the OSS-Online Service System, you also have access to the fullest advisory services and receive system information directly relevant to your problem. The OSS-Online Service System provides the following facilities, which are further discussed in Chapter 28, "Using the Online Service System":

- Orders for specific documentation
- An error notes database, which contains information about known problems and the methods for circumventing them
- HotNews, which notifies you of system developments
- HelpDesk, which provides personal advice, including suggestions for pertinent documentation

Other Documentation

A wide range of documentation is available directly from SAP and through the online services. The following types of documentation exist:

- SAP consulting services
- Product guidelines
- Marketing information and brochures
- R/3 handbooks
- Upgrading and installation instructions
- Release information
- SAPVisual CD-ROM Presentations

Internet Information Sources

The SAP sites on the World Wide Web are at

http://www.sap.com in Philadelphia

http://www.sap-ag.de in Walldorf, Germany

This site gives you access to the promotional material that is freely available to the public. This material supplements the CD-ROM and document forms of SAP information. The range of SAP information sources is discussed in Chapter 27, "Access Knowledge Products." ●

Access Knowledge Products

In this chapter

Reviewing the Implementation Management Guide

The IMG is delivered as part of R/3. It can support users in the following activities:

- Follow the recommended sequence for configuring and customizing a new system as a managed project.
- Switch readily between studying the documentation and carrying out system configuration.
- Generate an implementation guide specific to the current project.
- Document the project.
- Manage the progress of the project.

Chapter 7, "Customizing," discusses what is involved in configuring a system.

Learning from the R/3 Reference Model

The R/3 Reference Model is a model of all business processes and functions the R/3 system supports. It can be displayed and manipulated in graphical form. The format of the Reference Model is a network of *event-driven process chains* (EPCs), in which the relationships between the events and processes are shown with respect to timing and logical dependence. The way the EPCs are delivered as system components and applications is also apparent in the Reference Model.

The Business Navigator is a tool for displaying the R/3 Reference Model in either of the following views:

- Component view
- Process-Flow view

The Reference Model is an integral part of the R/3 system, and the Business Navigator appears as an option in the Tools menu. The Reference Model is discussed in Chapter 5, "Consulting the R/3 Reference Model."

Reviewing the International Demonstration and Education System

The IDES-International Demonstration and Education System is not strictly classified as a knowledge product, although it can provide a working model of a typical company and its transactions with customers and its overseas subsidiaries. There is a version of IDES to correspond with each release of R/3 in order to accurately demonstrate the transactions of the release throughout the full range of its functionality. IDES is distributed as a separate client in the standard R/3 system for which authorized logon is required.

The IDES Help facility includes an overview of each business scenario, sample data, and step-by-step instructions for carrying out the business processes. The following application areas and activities are demonstrated in the model company:

- Logistics
- Financial Accounting
- Human Resources
- Profit Center Accounting
- Product Costing
- Profitability Analysis

Preconfigured workflow scenarios can be executed and analyzed for instructional and planning purposes. You can move freely through the database of the IDES.

Within the confines of the model, screen displays can respond to user interaction, including display editing. You can also use the system to prototype a demonstration system by simulating design decisions.

Demonstrating with the IDES Notebook

The IDES Notebook is a version of the International Demonstration and Education System delivered in a portable notebook computer. The system components are installed on a 9.1GB external hard drive and include a selection of SAP Level 1 courses based on the R/3 Information Database and the iXOS archive functionality. The following components in the local language are preinstalled:

- The current SAP GUI
- R/3 Session Manager
- An ASAP demo version
- Beta version of the SAP Java GUI

The portable IDES system is updated by exchanging the external hard drive. Convenient customizing functions are included to simulate design decisions directly in the notebook.

Enrolling in SAP R/3 Training

Formally structured courses are available for all SAP products according to the following schemes:

- Introductory
- Intermediate, to acquire application skills
- Advanced, to acquire expertise for the unique implementation of each participant
- Delta, to impart the information needed to take advantage of the new functionality available in each release

Examples from the IDES can be used in the training courses.

Displaying R/3 Knowledge Products

An R/3 Knowledge Product is a source of information that includes self-study units and reference material. A Knowledge Product normally is confined to one application area or cross-application product. The presentation media may include online help files, screen cams, and videos.

Each Knowledge Product normally includes the following types of functional elements:

- Introduction and overview
- Self-study guided learning units
- Key topics to use for searching the Knowledge Product

The Knowledge Products are distributed as encrypted CD units. A key is required from an SAP authorized source for registered SAP customers.

Titles available as CD Knowledge Products are in two groups:

- Expert Competence CD Set
- Single R/3 Knowledge Product CDs

An additional type of CD Knowledge Product is becoming available to support the Vertical Market Initiative. The Downstream Oil Knowledge Product is a typical example.

Consulting the R/3 IS-Oil Downstream Knowledge Product

The IS-Oil Downstream Knowledge Product CD contains *all* the information and materials needed to learn about the SAP Oil & Gas solution, including the newly introduced R/3 IS-Oil Downstream component. The following types of components are included:

- Overview
- Multimedia presentations
- Marketing materials
- Tools
- Product details
- Customer examples
- Success stories

The IS-Oil Downstream Knowledge Product is presented as the following:

- An introduction, including two videos and a marketing brochure
- A guided-learning tour with drill-down facilities to the details, training slides, function brochure, and Reference Model
- Key topics, with implementation information for R/3 IS-Oil Downstream

CHAPTER 28

Using the Online Service System

In this chapter

Introducing the Online Service System

During implementation of the R/3 system, the OSS-Online Service System is used to solve problems found in a test system before they get to production. After the production system is live, the usual purpose of the OSS is to solve an existing problem thought to be a bug in the software, for which there is a known SAP solution. If you do have any areas of uncertainty, the components of the OSS-Online Service System are available in your installation to help you identify the reason and to see how to clear up the difficulty. There is also a remote connection to the OSS library of error notes organized so that you can search for a question that corresponds to your query. Further questions may be posed to you to clarify what it is you want to know. When the system is clear about this, it offers some solution proposals. And as a fallback position, the Online Service System facilitates a direct communications link to the SAP service team that will solve your problem.

The OSS-Online Service System also takes a proactive role by alerting users to any changes in SAP product releases and by providing notices of selected training courses that will likely be relevant.

The full OSS-Online Service System can be installed at a client site in the form of the Customer Competence Center, which specializes in solving the SAP R/3 system problems of a particular company.

It is necessary to register individual employees as users of the OSS-Online Service System. Forms are provided with new installations, and an online registration function is predefined so that you can start the OSS directly from your SAP R/3 system.

The system operates by processing problem messages entered by users. By interacting with users, the OSS determines the nature of the query or other type of message.

Before submitting problem messages, search the Error Notes database to see whether the topic has previously been encountered. You can search the Error Notes database according to any combination of these characteristics:

- Hardware specification
- Operating system
- Database
- R/3 release number

This search, even if not directly fruitful, might suggest how the problem situation can be presented as a message to the OSS. You can index problem messages to optimize the search procedure.

The OSS looks through your logged problem messages and sends you the error-note solutions, which might be relevant because of the keywords that have been recognized. From this set of notes, you can further select according to any combination of the following characteristics:

- Language of the notes
- SAP release
- Topic
- Application
- Error-note number
- Last-change date
- Words or phrases appearing in the text strings of the error notes

If you want to be kept up-to-date on a particular topic, you can set up a periodic error-note search over a specified time span by using the same search specification.

If you log a message that is not a problem but a request for some other type of interaction with the OSS, there will be an appropriate exchange of information and perhaps some follow-up action, such as the booking of a training course location.

Tracing a Problem

The following sequence of activities is typical of a problem-solving interaction between a customer and the OSS:

1. You create a problem message in the OSS.
2. You log the message in the OSS.
3. The OSS indexes the problem message and identifies the keywords in it.
4. The OSS assigns one or more specific category types to each keyword it recognizes.
5. You can see the colored highlights on the keywords to which the OSS will respond, and you can revise the message if necessary.
6. The OSS searches the Error Notes database for any notes relevant to each keyword in the problem message.
7. You call up a display of the error notes that have been found and classified by the system.

If any elements of the problem have not been solved by the system administrator using the selected error notes, you can send a message directly to the SAP R/3 First Level Customer Service.

Creating a Problem Message   When you log on to the OSS, the following details are automatically copied into the problem message document header as soon as you enter your user ID:

- Name of the reporting employee
- Customer installation hardware type and operating system release number
- Customer database type and release number
- SAP R/3 release number installed—for example, R/3 2.2, R/3 3.0, R/3 3.0A, R/3 3.0B
- System status at the time of logon

A customer data verification function is available to help you keep this information up-to-date.

The problem message content has to be formed by entering or selecting data elements for the following problem message fields:

- SAP R/3 application (App.), such as MM, HR, FI, PP, SD
- Problem priority (Prio), such as High and Normal
- A description of the problem in free text, using the standard keywords, if they are known, and with a system-generated problem number and default language code
- Short text (STxt), which is standard system text such as an error identification code reported by your system

Classifying a Problem Message   After your problem message is entered and validated, a pop-up menu invites you to classify it under one of the following message types:

- Error message
- Application consulting
- Technical consulting
- HelpDesk query
- Message for your SAP R/3 consultant or SAP partner
- Message for an SAP employee worldwide who will use the Reply function

Indexing Keywords   The system uses its internal indexing function to identify and color-code the keywords by category type if it recognizes any keywords in your message. You will obviously get a better response from the system if you make sure that your message refers to the appropriate keywords—as much as you can determine what they should be for your problem. The colors appear on your message as soon as you save it, so you can ensure that your message contains a useful range of keywords, used with precision, before you transmit it for processing.

The following category types are used to color-code the keywords in your problem message:

- Object names, such as SAP transaction codes, program names, and table names
- System message codes—for example, ORA1547, S0999, ERROR 1155
- System-specific terminology, such as tablespace, GUI, administrator, and menu

Processing Problem Messages

You can view the error notes that are selected by the system as being possibly relevant to your problem by selecting the problem message again. The system allows you to filter out error notes that are not relevant to your situation, so you can quickly arrive at the best information that can be assembled automatically.

The OSS allows you to download the error notes so that you can print them and direct them electronically to other users.

If the error notes presented on your problem message document are not applicable to your problem, you can submit the document for the attention of the First Level Customer Service. If the staff there cannot find the answer, the SAP development team continues to work with you until a satisfactory solution is found.

Each time you log on to the OSS, you see a status display of what has happened to all your problem messages. The left side of the problem message status screen shows how many messages are in each status at your company and the date of the most recent status change:

- **Entered** shows the number of messages not yet processed.
- **For your action** indicates how many messages are awaiting further data from you or are waiting for you to do something requested by SAP.
- **For confirmation** indicates how many problem messages have been returned from SAP with a set of error notes for you to accept and confirm to complete the problem, or to resubmit to First Level Customer Service for additional work.
- **Completed** shows how many problem messages were returned to your company and confirmed by you as satisfactory solutions to your problem.

The right side of the problem message status screen shows how many messages are in each status at SAP and the date of the most recent status change:

- **Received** indicates how many problem messages have been received by the SAP First Level Customer Service but have not been processed.
- **In process** shows how many problem messages are now being processed.
- **Completed** shows how many problem messages have been processed to the stage of submitting error notes but have not been confirmed by you as having reached a satisfactory state of resolution by your solving the problem or passing it to the First Level Customer Service.

Consulting a Database of Error Notes

The error notes in the database are written by SAP staff as detailed solutions to the problems posed by customers through the OSS and the First Level Customer Service.

Describing Error Note Content   The typical error note includes the following information:

- Problem symptoms to which this note is relevant.
- A short description of the cause of the problem.
- Detailed information on how to solve the problem.
- Corrections to your system that can be made in advance to forestall a problem or the recurrence of your current problem. These may take the form of a set of patch updates that will correct the system bugs concerned in the problem.

The error note also specifies the system platform information needed to identify the configurations to which the error note is applicable—for example,

- SAP R/3 release number
- Applications affected
- Operating system
- Database
- Graphical user interface front ends used

Searching for Specific Error Notes   In addition to the selection of error notes that will be made for you by the OSS staff, you can also search for specific error notes on the basis of any of the following search criteria, used in any logical combination of AND and OR:

- Language
- SAP R/3 release number
- Topic or keyword
- Application
- Error-note number
- Last-change date
- Error-note text strings

After you define a search specification to find the error notes that are likely to be relevant to your particular situation, you can store the profile and have the search carried out on a daily, weekly, or monthly basis over a specified period.

Interpreting the Error Note Status Overview Display

When you log on to the OSS, you see the error-note status overview display, in which the error notes are shown. The display of the number of notes and date of the most recent change is divided into the following fields:

- **Notes assigned to you** shows the number of previous notes and the number of new version notes.
- **New info from SAP** is divided into HotNews, Release Planning, and Installation and Upgrade.

Listing Previous Notes   This part of the problem message overview shows the total number of error notes that have been assigned to you in response to all your previous problem messages.

Locating New Versions   If any of the previous notes have been updated since they were first sent to you, they are counted in the New Versions field so that you are alerted that some of the information you might have applied to the solution of your problem might now be out of date and perhaps overtaken by better information.

Receiving HotNews   The latest high-priority information concerning the SAP R/3 system and its error alarm messages is carried in HotNews messages, so that you can prevent problems. These messages are not necessarily relevant to the problems you have previously reported through your problem messages. The number of HotNews messages is shown in the New Info from SAP section of the display.

Learning About Release Planning   Messages in this category are counted and displayed in the New Information from SAP section. They concern new developments in certain operating systems and database environments and the dates when the updated versions will be released.

Getting Installation and Upgrade Messages   If there have been any messages concerning the installation or upgrading of your SAP R/3 system, they are counted in this section of the display. It is important to read them before upgrading your SAP R/3 system.

Differentiating HotNews Messages

The characteristic of HotNews is that it is received directly through the OSS. The main category of HotNews is Alarm Alerts, which present error descriptions and their solutions, which must be implemented to avoid serious problems with your SAP R/3 system.

Training courses and company-specific events such as the startup of a production plant under SAP R/3 will be topics to be promulgated via HotNews messages.

After you signify that you have read a HotNews message, a confirmation is sent to SAP. If the message requires some action on your part, it generates the appropriate checklists, which are transmitted back to SAP to confirm that you have seen the information about what you should do.

The following categories of HotNews are used to differentiate topics:

- **Special-interest topics** include changes in release strategy and scheduling.
- **News and recommendations** suggest ways of improving your SAP R/3 system.

Receiving OSS Messages Through the HelpDesk

The OSS conveys a direct message to the SAP R/3 HelpDesk if you have not been able to get the information you require through the problem message procedure or by directly accessing error notes.

When you call or fax an SAP HelpDesk, the staff there enters your problem into the OSS. If the local HelpDesk is not immediately available, your inquiry is passed on to the appropriate contact person in one of the SAP worldwide service centers. You can still use the OSS to monitor how your inquiry is progressing.

Exploring R/3 Online Services

The main elements of the online services follow:

- SAP OSS-Online Service System
- Customer Competence Center with own OSS updated from the SAP OSS
- Local SAP HelpDesk

- SAP R/3 HelpDesk
- EarlyWatch
- Remote Consulting
- The HotNews and Upgrade Services
- SAP Error Notes database
- Online Error Correction
- Upgrade Support on Weekends

Meeting the Technical Requirements of the SAP Online Services

You must have a network connection to your nearest SAP Service Center, which establishes your official IP network address to allow your system to be accessed worldwide, if necessary. You need the SAP GUI software version 2.1J or higher.

A suitable network connection can be established over one of the following links in coordination with your SAP Service Center:

- **X.25.** A system available worldwide through the local telephone companies or via private network providers. It might be wise to refuse it permission to initiate incoming connections so that you have control over access.
- **Integrated Services Digital Network (ISDN).** Now being tested and gaining in acceptance. A gateway is required to enable the connection between the ISDN network and the provider network.
- **Frame Relay.** A system of connections offered by telephone companies such as AT&T, MCI, Sprint, WilTel, BT, VIAQ, INTERCOM, Deutsche Telekom, and Info AG.

Your company must have at least one unique IP address to connect to SAP if you are using the SAProuter software. If you are not using this software, your entire network must have a unique IP address to avoid collisions with other networks.

Ensuring Data Protection

Any network with an outside line is vulnerable to security breaches. The recommended security measures include the following:

- Configure the remote connection so that it cannot be opened by incoming connection requests.
- Use routers that can be configured to allow access only to certain business partners and SAP partners.
- Use passwords to protect accounts on computers accessible from the outside.
- Use access lists to limit the traffic over routers to certain specified software programs.
- Install the SAProuter software.

The SAProuter software forms a "firewall" security stage intermediate between the SAP gateway and the network, such as Frame Relay, X.25, or ISDN. It imposes a password check to allow access to the network IP addresses. The same system is used again between the network and the customer SAP R/3 system.

The movement of all messages is under the control of route transmission tables and SAP passwords, giving the system administrator an additional means of control over the access allowed to sensitive data or restricted systems.

Only the IP address of your computer is known to the SAProuter, and your network knows only the IP address of the SAP system using the SAProuter. This ensures that unauthorized access is not possible from one network to another.

Registering for Services Through OSS

You can register for the following SAP services through the OSS-Online Service System:

- EarlyWatch sessions
- Consulting sessions
- Customer Data Verification Service
- First Customer Shipment of prerelease versions of software

Making Suggestions for Developments via the OSS

It has long been a tradition in the SAP organization that users are considered one of the most important contributor communities for the purpose of developing the product range. If you have a suggestion for improving or enhancing the SAP R/3 functionality, a developmental message sent through the OSS is a convenient way to make it known. You have the advantage of being able to monitor its progress and see what becomes of it.

It is important to classify your message as a *problem message* if you discover that an existing function in an application does not work properly, and as a *development request* if you would like an existing function to be improved or a new one added.

Planning and Registering for Training Courses

The planning, selection of content, and registration of SAP training courses are all supported by the OSS-Online Service System. The following information systems are provided:

- Overviews of selected courses
- Assistance in choosing the right courses
- Details of prices and dates
- Enrollment information and joining instructions
- General information about SAP training courses and their methods

The OSS allows you to register online for a selected course. You can retrieve an area hotel list and directions to the SAP Training Center. You can review the information on all training courses for which employees in your organization have been registered, and you can select the format to show individual employees or time periods.

Reviewing the Benefits of OSS

If you have installed and configured the full range of the OSS-Online Service System and the SAP Remote Services software and communications equipment, you have a comprehensive and powerful support system at your disposal. The characteristic feature of this complex of functions is that you can ask for as much or as little assistance as you require: an automatic fault-location service up to a consulting visit, with information provided selectively and automatically at every level.

The list of benefits for your specific company depends on your circumstances. However, some of the following might be important:

- Continuous problem processing worldwide
- Immediate first-level customer service
- Direct access to the Error Notes database
- Problem prevention
- Review of the progress and history of a problem solution process
- Access to SAP staff and SAP partners
- Communication with other SAP R/3 users
- Latest information on SAP R/3 products

Using the SAP EarlyWatch System

The EarlyWatch system provides a proactive method of monitoring customer SAP R/3 systems by conducting regular analyses. Teams of experts at SAP carry out remote diagnosis of customer SAP R/3 installations worldwide.

Monitoring

The following elements can fall within the scope of EarlyWatch remote diagnosis:

- Network components
- Operating system
- Database
- SAP applications and configurations

The operation of the SAP R/3 system is monitored by evaluating statistical data collected by the individual system components. For example, the current status of the system and its resource use are available to EarlyWatch at all times. This information provides the basis for the regular performance and error analyses. Experts carry out these studies with a thorough knowledge of the platforms, databases, networks, and applications.

Calling on EarlyWatch Support During Implementation

The expertise of the EarlyWatch specialists can best be put to productive use when you are installing a new system or adding a new module. These are the times of greatest change, and it is under these conditions that deep knowledge and experience can be applied to make sure the new configuration performs to its top specification right from the start. You will see benefits not only in the rapid improvements in your company's methods of doing business, but also in the reduction of stress on the staff over what is always a difficult period when they are not sure just how much of their previous know-how will be useful under the changed circumstances. In some cases, their ingrained habits will not be recognized as such until the new method of working demands that they change.

The teams of experts are available to assist in the planning of master data transfer prior to going live and will advise you on the setting up of test runs for the new system. For example, the EarlyWatch team can carry out the following tasks:

- Dimensioning the free space of the table spaces
- Dimensioning SAP buffers
- Transferring the master data
- Transferring the transaction data
- Monitoring the disk space requirements for live operating
- Checking the free space of the tablespaces

When the system is approaching live operation, the EarlyWatch team can provide planning support and execution assistance for system testing under near-productive conditions. They will monitor the tests and evaluate the results. It will be their judgment that governs the fine-tuning of the system components to give the best results. And they will advise and set in motion the data backup provisions.

After the system begins live operation, EarlyWatch experts analyze the significant response times and carry out further component tuning, if necessary.

Reporting from the EarlyWatch Service

The focus of the EarlyWatch reporting methods is on the client/server load distribution and any foreseeable bottlenecks in the system components.

The findings of the reports are demonstrated by using visual methods such as charts, tables, and diagrams, which are also used to give an overview of the effects of any changes recommended by the EarlyWatch team.

Where there are areas of doubt, the reports describe the implications and suggest methods of collecting additional data, if necessary. These reports also suggest taking other steps to address the uncertainties and to make provisions to control the system if problems develop.

The standard methods of providing data security when networks are connected are used in the remote diagnosis operations of EarlyWatch. Every operation performed by an EarlyWatch specialist can be monitored from the customer's system.

The operation of the EarlyWatch system depends on a data link to one of the SAP service centers where teams of specialists are located. The details of this technical requirement are the same as for the other SAP Remote Services described earlier.

N O T E An additional requirement for the provision of the EarlyWatch service is that your system must be equipped with a Computing Center Management System that provides the graphics monitors on which the EarlyWatch system depends.

Specific customer problems are analyzed and remedial actions suggested as a result of EarlyWatch reports. If there is a case for developing new functionality to meet the needs of the customer, this is undertaken where appropriate.

If a customer indicates through the OSS-Online Service System that a consultation with an SAP partner is required, the Remote Services can be used to establish the background to the request before a consultation takes place. By using any combination of communications media, including online monitoring of the customer's system, the consultation can proceed with all parties sharing the same data—namely, the customer's system and the reports of its performance prepared in advance or called up at the time.

Using the SAP R/3 Information Database

The SAP R/3 Information database provides you with the latest information about SAP R/3 products and releases. In particular, the database carries the following types of data:

- SAP R/3 development strategy and product planning
- System development and delivery dates
- Duration of the maintenance period of new releases
- SAP R/3 services and certified SAP partners
- Training course enrollment calendar
- Available documents and publications in other media
- Technical information concerning remote connections and network products

The OSS-Online Service System supports searches over the SAP R/3 Information database using any of the following types of criteria:

- Key attributes, such as the release status of a specific application module
- A particular date for new information
- Keywords taken from the controlled index used on problem messages

If any of this information changes, the user is alerted after logging on to the OSS when a key appears onscreen labeled News on OSS. This key appears only if the particular user has not already seen the new or changed messages.

Any of the information you receive from the OSS and the SAP R/3 Information database can be downloaded to your own computer for later reference.

Accessing Information Resources

As part of the OSS-Online Service System, the following products can be ordered:

- **Service guidelines.** Descriptions of the SAP R/3 services.
- **Product guidelines.** Marketing information and brochures.
- **Documentation.** Includes SAP R/3 handbooks, upgrade and installation instructions, and release information.
- **Presentations.** Include the SAPvisual CD-ROM programs.

Installing the Customer Competence Center Product

It might be advantageous to install a *Customer Competence Center* (CCC) at your main site to build up knowledge specific to the type of business you conduct. Special SAP training for the staff of the center can be provided.

The OSS can be installed in your Competence Center and will automatically receive updates from the latest SAP R/3 system information maintained in the central SAP Online Service System.

The following servers provide the SAP Service Network to the third level, Development Support, and therefore can tackle the most difficult problems:

- Sapserv3, in Walldorf, Germany
- Sapserv4, in Foster City, California
- Sapserv5, in Tokyo
- Sapserv6, in Sydney, Australia
- Sapserv7, in Singapore
- Sapserv8, in Dublin, Ireland

CHAPTER 29

Developing ABAP/4 Programs with the R/3 Workbench

In this chapter

Introducing the ABAP/4 Development Workbench

The SAP software is written in ABAP/4, SAP's fourth-generation Advanced Business Programming Language. The ABAP/4 Development Workbench is a complete environment for creating business applications in this language to run in client/server installations.

A wide range of tools can be used on the Workbench. The workpieces can be absolutely new software, for which there is no existing SAP standard business program, that can be customized to suit your company. You can also work on copies of existing components that you have decided to extend to meet your requirements.

In either case, the strict control disciplines exercised by the ABAP/4 Development Workbench will ensure that the resulting software will run immediately on all computer types and all database systems supported by SAP. Because ABAP/4 is an interpreted language, each call on a function causes the code to be reinterpreted, complete with any modifications released after development work.

The developer working in the SAP R/3 environment does not have to be concerned with the complexities of client/server networking. Developed application modules can be run locally or on central host computers and can use any of the existing servers. All supported graphical user interfaces will run the products of the Workbench without requiring any changes or modifications.

Updating the Workbench

SAP software was and is designed mainly through the ABAP/4 Development Workbench. It has a long pedigree and a proven performance record. The exceptions are those portions of the BASIS system that have to be designed for the particular hardware platform on which R/3 is to run.

New concepts and products that come under SAP support are built in to the support systems of the ABAP/4 Development Workbench with each release of R/3. The application developer can be assured that the suggestions and advice offered by the Workbench are up-to-date with new technology, and that the detailed proposals will actually work when integrated with the existing SAP R/3 implementation.

Transiting Developmental Phases and Levels

Program development has to go through phases and cycles to prove that the software destined to go live will indeed do what it was intended to do and not do anything that it should not. The ABAP/4 Development Workbench expects program developers to need help and support throughout this process. It is also assumed that any developed application will itself undergo business maintenance sooner or later. The Workbench can store its working materials for later consultation.

Any new system or component added to an existing implementation will have to communicate with the rest of the system and use all the hardware and software facilities efficiently. The standard guidelines still apply:

- Data consistency must be achieved by maintaining master data in only one location.

- There should be no breaks in technological communication channels, and suitable defaults should be presented for confirmation whenever possible to avoid extensive manual data entry.

- Software components should be designed to be transported to new platforms as the equipment manufacturers make better devices from which to assemble complex systems.

The application developer using the ABAP/4 Development Workbench will find all the support needed to work at any level of detail:

- Metadata for the development of applications

- Proposals and standards for interfacing with databases

- Standard interfaces for linking to any networks already established—for example, to communicate with SAP R/2 systems and with database services provided for specific sectors of industry

- Procedures for detailed design of graphical user interfaces to suit both the requirements of the new application and the ergonomic needs of future users

Organizing the Workbench

Don't be surprised to find that the ABAP/4 Development Workbench is itself thoroughly and consistently organized with the structure of other SAP R/3 products. Software objects under new construction or development from standard SAP R/3 components are recognized as development objects and are attributed to an appropriate data structure.

A version of a software component is maintained as a data object separate from its predecessor or reference model. Strict control is exercised to ensure that software under development does not get tangled with the software of the SAP R/3 system itself, on which the ABAP/4 Development Workbench tool is being presented.

Locating the ABAP/4 Repository

All development objects being handled on the ABAP/4 Development Workbench are stored in the ABAP/4 Repository. The following types of objects may be under development:

- Dictionary objects

- ABAP/4 programs

- ABAP/4 objects, including dynpros, function modules, and other programs

- Documentation

- Help texts

The ABAP/4 Data Dictionary is located in the ABAP/4 Repository.

Consulting the ABAP/4 Repository Information System

The contents of the ABAP/4 Repository can be studied and selected by a comprehensive facility to create object lists, menus, and multiple windows for viewing and evaluating the information and objects in the Repository. This helps application developers and their managers maintain order during what can be a complex process.

Listing Data Objects   The ABAP/4 Repository Information System can list data objects available from the Repository, such as the following:

- Programs
- Tables
- Fields
- Data elements
- Field domains

These lists can be selective and can be sorted using attributes of the data objects, by the date of the last change, by the name of the team responsible for making the changes, and so on.

Investigating Relationships   Developmental programmers working with an existing system need to know what exists already. It is essential to work out what is related to what.

The ABAP/4 Repository Information System can focus on a table and its fields and report where they are used in existing dynpros and ABAP/4 programs. Report programs are also available to reveal the foreign-key relationships between different tables.

Navigating the ABAP/4 Repository   In accord with the standard SAP drill-down facility, any Repository object selected from a display from the ABAP/4 Repository Information System can be investigated further by using special function keys. Any semantically meaningful change of direction can be made. For example, from a list of data elements, the Information System can be asked to compile a list of all table fields in which these data elements appear. From this list of table fields, the system can create a list of where they are used in programs.

Locating Software Tools

The maintenance of software during development is supported by a full range of editing and debugging tools so that the processes of testing and tuning can proceed. These tools reside in the ABAP/4 Repository.

Consulting the Predefined Business Function Library

Most good ideas have already been thought of before, and this is no less true in software development. Very often, the best place to start from is not the beginning. The ABAP/4 Development Workbench offers a comprehensive repertoire of predefined standard business programs that are already fully operational and will integrate immediately with the rest of the SAP R/3 system.

Consulting the Active Data Dictionary

When a function is required to execute as part of a program or a dynpro, the SAP R/3 runtime system checks the time and date stamp on the program object code and compares it with the time stamp on the corresponding parts of the active Data Dictionary. If the Data Dictionary has been updated since the program object was generated, the SAP R/3 runtime system reinterprets the program and uses the latest Data Dictionary to regenerate the program object.

By this means, any changes in the active Data Dictionary are immediately promulgated to all parts of the SAP R/3 system and its applications. For example, if the domain of a particular field in a data object is increased by the addition of another acceptable option, the new domain list immediately appears on all screens that refer to this data object, to present users with the list of valid alternatives.

There is only one ABAP/4 Data Dictionary. It is actively integrated. However, application developers can save a version of this dictionary and declare it to be inactive, so that new items can be added as new program development proceeds. When everything is working correctly and the new component is ready to go live, the inactive Data Dictionary can be declared active and replaces the old one. You will need high-level authority to release a development object and promote it to the production system. The ABAP/4 Development Workbench is provided with a promotion utility function to manage the transition of a program from a development object to a standard business program that can be called on by any integrated applications for which users have the necessary authorization.

Understanding Metadata

If you think of a program as data, *metadata* is information about that program. In particular, an account of what a program does and how it should be used to improve your business is classified as metadata.

The SAP system is more precise. Metadata consists of descriptions of the data structures used in the programs. Therefore, metadata includes table and field definitions, and the specification of the domain of acceptable values for each field. The relationships between tables are also stored using foreign key tables as metadata in the active ABAP/4 Data Dictionary.

Understanding Internal Program Structure Metadata

The interrelationships between the parts and objects of a program in the context of a complex system are necessarily intricate. For example, program metadata has to include definitions for fields that can occur only in a dynpro and not in a database table. Temporary tables in a dynpro must be differentiated from tables permanently available to all.

Interfaces between programmed functions are concerned with passing parameters and control data. They have to be specified in the metadata.

Online help and checking services are available for the metadata as well as for data normally residing in a database.

The SAP R/3 system automatically generates metadata definitions for table and view functions for all supported database systems, so that any use of them by SAP R/3 is assured a consistent and reliable service based on the specifications in the active ABAP/4 Data Dictionary.

Defining Tables   A table includes fields. The functions performed by the data stored in these fields depend on the purpose of the table. For example, at least one type of table will be specified in order to be able to hold data received from a database system, which may be on another computer. By contrast, an internal table associated with a dynpro may serve the purpose of exchanging data with an ABAP/4 program.

Every field used in generated database tables, dynpros, and ABAP/4 programs is specified in the active ABAP/4 Data Dictionary by means of its attributes, which include format, length, and whether this field is used in the table's indexing key. Relationships with other tables are also part of a table's attributes.

A field has a *domain,* which is the specification or listing of the set of values that are accepted as valid entries for this field. The domain also includes the data type and length in terms of characters. How this field should be displayed onscreen is also part of the field domain. Domains exist as data elements, with their own identification code that can be used to refer to them.

A field also has a *data element* associated with it. The data element of a field describes its business meaning. The element can specify keywords that place the field in a specific technical or business context. Headings or labels for the field can be included in the data element. A documentation text for use by the online help system resides in the data element of a field. The domain of the field is identified by a code name in its data element.

The data element associated with a field can also be associated with other fields. It exists as a separate data object with its own identification code. It can be replaced automatically by its equivalent in the language of the user.

Embedding Data Structures in Tables   A field in a table can use an `include` function to represent an embedded data structure. This way, a data structure of any complexity can be built from a starting table, and this structure can itself be included in a larger structure.

If any element in a complex data structure is changed, all the related structures are updated accordingly.

Calculating with Data Structures   If a calculation is required within a program or for transferring data between programs, a calculation data structure can be defined and maintained centrally in the active ABAP/4 Data Dictionary. The calculation structure can call on the same domain definitions and explanatory data elements that are used with database structures.

Consulting Foreign Keys   If you try to enter incorrect data, an SAP dynpro intervenes and points out the nature of your error. Suppose that you specify that your corporation consists of a head office, code 01, and two separate company codes, 011 and 012, to represent two independent cost centers, each with a single plant with its own warehouse, codes W1 and W2. If you try to place some material for company code 012 in warehouse W1, which belongs to the other company code, the system will object because it has consulted a check table revealing that company code 011 owns warehouse W1 and company code 012 owns warehouse W2.

The table of who owns which warehouse is a foreign key source for checking entries to the materials list. Because you have defined the foreign key relationships in the active ABAP/4 Data Dictionary, the dynpro can validate the entry data before the transaction is posted. Much unnecessary processing is thereby obviated.

Creating Virtual Tables   A *data view* is an arrangement of data for a particular purpose. An application may require certain data to be gathered from various tables residing, perhaps, in other systems. This data will have to be arranged and presented in table form to the application user.

If the application programmer specifies a *virtual table,* which includes the fields needed in the most useful format, the system can assemble the necessary data elements by declaring the foreign key tables that will form the stepping stones to the desired data.

At the presentation stage, the fields obtained via the foreign keys can be assigned more appropriate titles if necessary. It is also possible to specify filtering functions that suppress from view any unwanted lines of the virtual table.

Placing Match Codes   A *match code* is an index pointing to original data. It is linked with a database index or with a view that effectively narrows the search target. A match code can also appear as a table entry, which is updated in response to certain predefined trigger situations. The match code can hold pointers to fields from more than one table, and criteria can be stipulated to limit the data records targeted.

Using Automatic Functions for Screen Fields   The way in which a field is displayed on a user's screen usually is determined by the *dictionary tables*, which define the length and data type of the screen field, and the *text elements,* which describe the significance of the content of the field in the Enterprise Data Model of the business.

If your application must import or output the contents of a field, the system looks in the dictionary for routines to convert between the internal and external representations. Fields for amounts or quantities can be displayed according to the parameters defined for certain reference fields in the dictionary, which include the currency or unit of measure appropriate to the installation.

Pressing the F1 special function key always displays documentation on the field indicated by the cursor, giving the business description of the field and the technical attributes from the corresponding domain. For certain fields, pressing the F4 key reveals possible entry values, from which one or more can be selected. This facility always is active when a match code, a check table, or fixed values are defined for the field.

Entries to a field are automatically checked at the moment of entry against the range defined in the dictionary. If foreign keys have been identified, they are taken into account and the check table procedure is applied.

Generating Database Definitions   The ABAP/4 Data Dictionary effectively defines a relational database independent of the database systems of individual vendors. The tables in the dictionary are mapped on the underlying database system to generate catalog definitions and catalog changes for all supported database systems.

The application developer does not need to be aware of the mechanisms of an individual database system. For example, if a system does not have an ALTER TABLE operation, the SAP R/3 system automatically creates programs to unload the data and write it back in the new structure. If the database system does recognize INSERT FIELD and similar functions to alter a table, SAP R/3 uses them.

Interpreting the Enterprise Data Model   The table definitions in the ABAP/4 Data Dictionary are designed to optimize data processing. The Enterprise Data Model is there to make business sense of what is going on.

The model is built from entity-relationship units that refer to the real objects in business, such as documents, messages, and materials. Staff members are also included in this use of the concept of *object*. The relationships stand for concepts such as ownership and membership. For example, a purchase order, when it is complete, will have a header and one or more documented line items representing the items to be purchased and their prices. This works as follows:

- A purchase order line is part of a purchase order.
- A purchase order header owns one or more purchase order lines.

If you call for help by pressing F1 from a purchase order display screen, you will see what the business significance is thought to be of the item your cursor has selected. This is an indirect reference to the *Enterprise Data Model* (EDM).

You can choose how to view the Enterprise Data Model. The first selection offered is based on the application from which the model is called, but you can inspect any section of the model at any level of detail. Figure 29.1 illustrates part of an EDM in list-display format.

You can also choose between a list display and a graphical presentation; you can suppress certain types of entities to make the picture clearer for the purpose you have in mind. Figure 29.2 shows part of a graphical display of an EDM.

The elements of most interest to business users might not all be available in the host application. For this reason, a system of data views is available in which the tables of interest are assembled automatically by accessing other sources of data, if necessary, to create virtual tables that include the fields of interest. These views can be used to program at the business level and to display the EDM with the level of detail and content that is most suitable for your purpose. Because all the data elements used to build views and virtual tables are defined in the ABAP/4 Data Dictionary, the user is assured of consistency of data and formatting.

FIGURE 29.1
Part of a list display of
the Enterprise Data
Model.

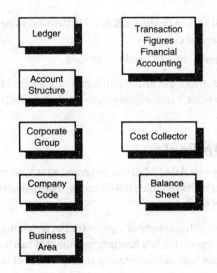

FIGURE 29.2
Part of a graphical
display of the
Enterprise Data Model.

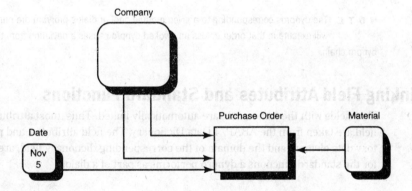

Programming Dialogs with Dynpro Technology

Every user dialog box is controlled by *dynamic programs* (dynpros) that include a screen and
its processing logic, along with validation procedures for checking entries.

Each dynpro controls exactly one dialog step. Even if there is no user to view them, the appropriate screen displays are available, and any error messages are sent to file.

The system works with more dialog steps than the user would imagine. Each dialog step consists of a *process before* output (PBO) and a *process after input* (PAI).

The commands and data of the dynpro have three objectives:

■ Present the screen layout that defines the positions of input and output fields, selection
   fields, graphical controls, texts, and so on.

- Define the attributes of all screen fields, such as their formats, value range checks, justification, leading zeros, and colors.
- Specify what has to happen in the PBO and PAI phases.

The dynpro might also have to activate the SAP multilingual capabilities and language-dependent documentation, help texts, error messages, and screen formats for large or pictographic character displays.

Referencing Dialog Module Pools

Each dynpro is based on exactly one ABAP/4 dialog program, which is organized into modules and can therefore be referenced by its module pool identifier. The dialog program handles calls to the constituent modules in its pool.

The dynpros likely to be invoked in the course of a given transaction must share the same common module pool. The only exception is a function module that has its own dynpros; this can be called from within a transaction without sharing the module pool of the rest of the dynpros of that transaction.

N O T E   The dynpros corresponding to a given module pool or dialog program are numbered, and will execute in that order unless an invoked dynpro causes a deviation from this static dynpro chain.

Linking Field Attributes and Standard Functions

Two fields with the same name are automatically linked. Thus, most attributes of the dynpro field are taken from the ABAP/4 Data Dictionary. The field attributes, and possibly the explanatory data element and the domain of the corresponding dictionary field, are used as the basis for the standard functions a dynpro performs as part of a dialog.

Understanding the Standard Functions of a Dynpro

The following activities are standard and performed by the dynpro itself for the one step of a dialog that is its scope:

- Automatic format checks for the screen fields.
- Automatic value range checks using the fixed range of the domain or the check table of the dictionary field.
- Online help, including searches in the glossary and the presentation of help texts from the data elements of the fields.
- Conversion of user entries into internal representations made available to the dialog program for which this dynpro is managing a step. The converse process is conducted for output to the user.
- Presentation of default values as directed, or acceptance of values to assign to specific user parameters.

▓ Operation of match code search if it has been declared as an attribute for the field concerned.

Interpreting Processing Logic

As mentioned earlier, the two halves of the dynpro processing logic are PBO and PAI. The syntactic structures of the ABAP/4 language are used in the PBO to initialize the screen in ways that are sensitive to context, and in the PAI to validate entries and invoke appropriate subsequent dialog steps, including the updating of the database.

Understanding Error Dialogs

The dynpro is autonomous in its execution of error detection and its presentation of context-sensitive error dialogs. In particular, the dynpro offers for correction only those fields logically related to the error that might therefore include the erroneous entry.

Revalidation and interchange with users continues until the dynpro is satisfied that the step has been properly completed.

Programming Advanced Business Applications

The ABAP/4 language is distinctive for the following reasons:

▓ ABAP/4—with the SAP R/3 Repository and the individual development tools—provides an integrated architecture for the development of new programs and the modification of existing SAP R/3 components.

▓ The developer does not have to be familiar with the technical details of the system environment, such as the operating system, database, network, or client/server communications.

▓ Structured programming is supported, with all the requirements for modularizing programs.

▓ The language is portable because the programs are translated into optimal internal representation, which is interpreted at runtime. The data is controlled by the ABAP/4 Data Dictionary, which can be altered independently of the programs because the data is regenerated automatically under the control of the dictionary.

▓ The scope of the language is tailored to the context of business information systems.

Prototyping

A preliminary version of the program can be prepared as a prototype that can be run. Because the language is interpreted at runtime, modifications and additions to the prototype can be tested until it becomes the final version and is released for business use. During prototyping, ABAP/4 programs can access all the SAP R/3 external channels.

Exploring the ABAP/4 Language Structure

The language in which all SAP R/3 programs are written is interpreted at runtime. It is made up of four types of program elements:

- **Declarative elements** specify the structure of the data to be processed in a program, such as tables that will be formed using field definitions specified in the ABAP/4 Data Dictionary.
- **Operational elements** initiate basic data manipulation—for example, MOVE and ADD.
- **Control elements** implement sequence structures (such as loops, branches, and subroutines) under the control of operators (such as DO, IF, CASE, and PERFORM).
- **Trigger elements** link program parts to events that can occur while a program is being executed—for example, TOP-OF-PAGE or AT USER-COMMAND.

Providing Multilingual Capabilities

The demands of global system development include requirements to ensure that different language communities can be integrated with a common business system.

Using Language Text Pools   A *text element* is a word or phrase that can be associated with any data field. The text element tells you what the data means in terms of its business significance.

When the code in an ABAP/4 program requires a text element to be displayed onscreen, it specifies the number of the text element to be used. The code does not have to be changed in order to access another element if the language of the user is changed. The language text pool from which the element is drawn is governed by the language selected in the user profile.

Pictographic Languages   The *Double-Byte Character Set* (DBCS) system can support the pictographic languages that have a large number of characters—Japanese and Chinese, for example.

Handling Wide Character Strings   The ABAP/4 language has been extended to recognize data type W for wide character fields and some other functions that permit double-byte characters to be mixed with normal single-byte characters in the same field.

Reviewing Elementary Business Data Types and Operations

In addition to the string-processing facilities common to all computer languages, the ABAP/4 functions include some operations that are ubiquitous in business. For example, special data types are defined for dates and times. In mixed expressions, numbers are interpreted as time intervals, depending on context. For example, a number added to a date shifts that date by that number of calendar days. Subtracting two time values yields their difference in seconds. The most-used business functions have been streamlined.

Processing Tables and SQL Elements

Tables in SAP systems are the most important data structure. The advanced business language offers many functions for handling tables.

In particular, the ABAP/4 Data Dictionary defines logical tables that can be matched to Open *Structured Query Language* (SQL) elements. The SAP R/3 database interface uses a high-performance buffering method, which it can use on all supported database systems. The application programmers can declare special work areas for these database exchanges.

Furthermore, the ABAP/4 Editor can directly check the syntax of Open SQL statements embedded in ABAP/4 code.

Internal tables can be used that exist only as long as a program is running. Many ABAP/4 functions are available to operate on these tables. These tables also can be dynamically enlarged. This method of using internal tables promotes an efficient use of memory and helps optimize runtime performance.

Building Modules

Simple subroutines can become modules, or function modules can be established for this purpose.

Subroutines of ABAP/4 and other programs can be called, and the name of the programs in which they are located can be dynamically determined when the call is made. Parameters can be passed by value or by reference.

Maintaining Function Modules

Function modules are fundamental to the organization and integration of applications in the SAP R/3 system. Function modules have these essential characteristics:

- The data interface of a function module can be extended in an upward-compatible manner, and it uses the definitions of the ABAP/4 Data Dictionary.
- Function modules can be validated in their own separate test environment by supplying input data and collecting the results for subsequent analysis by the SAP R/3 system itself through the *computer-aided testing tool* (CATT).
- Function modules can be managed in a function library.
- A function module can handle exceptions by itself.
- A function module can be called across system boundaries by a *Remote Function Call* (RFC).

Defining Customer or User Exits

The functionality of a standard SAP R/3 system component can be extended by using the customer exit facility without affecting the core logic. This method is cheaper than developing a new function. For example, the following standard customer exit calls are already in the system but will not have any effect until the customer logic is associated with them:

▓ CALL CUSTOMER_FUNCTION

▓ CALL CUSTOMER_SUBSCREEN

All potential customer requirements not already catered to by the existing standard business programs are implemented in the software as predefined interfaces that can be used as needed to insert customer-specific logic. The standard logic has the calls, but they are disabled until explicitly activated.

A clear division exists between SAP logic and customer logic, which is maintained by explicitly assigning each customer exit to an individual customer system. When SAP installs a new release of the standard software, the customer logic modules remain untouched; SAP guarantees that the customer exit calls will still be there in the new release.

Using the Development Tools

The tools of the ABAP/4 Development Workbench are easy to use. They employ dialogs to guide and advise the application developer in creating and combining development objects. One tool manages these objects and provides general functions, such as list, display, create, copy, test, and show where used. If you select an object, the function and the appropriate tool function are automatically called.

Calling the Screen Painter

To create, modify, display, or delete a dynpro, use the screen painter. It has three specialties:

▓ Arranging and positioning field designations and templates in the full-screen editor

▓ Specifying the display attributes of each field in the layout

▓ Entering processing logic

The screen painter also accepts general specifications for language and records the number of the next dynpro in the series for a static dynpro chain. You can specify the display type as a dialog box, selection screen, pop-up menu, and so on.

Support is provided for creating foreign-language versions of a dynpro that already exists.

Using Dialog Boxes A *secondary* or *modal dialog box* can be used to supplement or simplify a dialog box being conducted in a primary window. Additional work steps can be carried out there, as well as error-handling routines. A plan is being developed to extend dialog boxes to allow *parallel* or *nonmodal windows* in which two related activities can be conducted in tandem. This facility is demonstrated in the ABAP/4 Editor Development tool.

Using Graphics   A graphics editor is provided through the screen painter in addition to the text editor. It can insert graphical control elements such as the following:

- Pushbuttons
- Radio buttons, which offer the user a selection of one of several choices
- Check boxes, which allow the selection of more than one of the options
- List boxes, which facilitate work with very long lists
- Frames, which can have a built-in header field and encompass several related dynpro fields in a visual unit that accommodates automatically to variable amounts of field data

Any dictionary table can be displayed and used in a cut-and-paste mode to transfer fields to the screen layout. Multiple table fields can be placed by using this technique. When a field is selected, all the relevant attributes are also displayed for the developer to inspect.

Using the Menu Painter

In a central window, the application developer can see how the menus and graphical control elements, such as pushbuttons, are structured. The functions implemented in a program can be assigned to certain menus, function keys, and pushbuttons in a consistent way throughout the application.

The *SAP Style Guide* is a set of ergonomic standard designs for the visual elements. You can use your own designs or modify the standard assignments, and have the system generate lists of where you have violated the standards of the SAP Style Guide.

The language to be used is stipulated when creating a program. It is the same for text elements, the screen painter, and the menu painter. Other languages can be accommodated at runtime by referencing other language pools for the text elements.

A menu can be copied as a unit. Individual functions on a menu can be disabled, in which case they are dimmed. A main menu can consist of up to three nested levels of up to 15 items each.

Editing ABAP/4 Programs

Programs are entered and modified by using the ABAP/4 Editor. Standard text operations are available, as well as a number of special functions for easy program development:

- System-wide navigation and display of development objects
- A list of where development objects are used
- Calling of ABAP/4 report programs
- Elimination of programs embedded by an `include` instruction
- Display of syntax rules and permitted keywords
- Syntax checking of programs under development
- Insertion of program sections and routing control logic prepared in advance

▨ Structuring of source code using the Pretty Printer to reveal the structure of the code to make it easier to inspect

▨ Comparison of two programs using a split-screen editor

Browsing in the Editor   The editor's browsing functions start with object lists, from which a cascading navigation mode is possible, extending over many definition levels, to identify where the focal object is used throughout the system. The following operations, for example, are possible under the browser:

▨ Jumping from a subroutine call to the subroutine definition while still in the editor

▨ Branching from a table declaration in an ABAP/4 program to the corresponding table definition in the ABAP/4 Data Dictionary

▨ Branching from a table field in the ABAP/4 Data Dictionary to the corresponding data element and, from there, to its domain

▨ From the control logic of a dynpro, jumping directly into the program editor, opening the corresponding ABAP/4 modules

Your route while navigating is tracked, so you can always retrace your steps back to where you started.

Consulting Where-Used Lists   A search can be performed at any time on any development object to determine where it is currently being used within the system as a whole. For example, functions, fields, or tables can be identified wherever they are referenced throughout the system.

Debugging

Errors in ABAP/4 programs and dynpros can be detected. The debugger can switch between dynpro and module pool levels.

Interruption of the program by the debugger can occur after every command, at defined breakpoints, after a runtime error, or directly from the process monitor. Details of the objects involved in the error are displayed, and changes can be made before operation is resumed. Remote debugging across system boundaries can be done via *Remote Function Calls* (RFCs).

Measuring Software Performance Through Runtime Analysis

The consumption of computing resources can be measured and attributed to causes such as the following:

▨ Modular units, such as subroutines

▨ Database operations

▨ Operations involving internal tables in ABAP/4 programs

Performance statistics can be aggregated at various levels and separated into breakdowns for individual consumer processes.

Using the *Computer-Aided Testing Tool* (CATT)

The CATT is designed to support the description, combination, and automation of recurring business procedures for the purpose of setting up test runs. It can automatically simulate input dialogs and insert data from a background process. The tests are standardized and systematized, so they can be repeated precisely and as often as desired.

Reporting

A *report program* reads and processes part of a database. This can be a specialized database system accessed via the vendor's software or an SAP system. A possible method is to operate through a logical database.

Creating Logical Databases

A *logical database* is an ABAP/4 program and the data tables that are generated by it from the source database.

The fields required for a particular question or problem arising from an application can be declared and filled—perhaps by using foreign key relationships—to yield a validated hierarchical data structure that can be interactively searched and printed.

A similar method is used to assemble virtual tables from diverse sources for immediate use by an application.

As each line of a logical database is transferred from the source, the "running-through" process allows that line to be processed by a part of the program selected according to the source table for the data. In this way, ABAP/4 logic can influence the assembly of the logical database according to the outcome of processing parts of the data being transferred.

 There can be an efficiency benefit to the logical database technique: Each logical database serves more than one report. The access paths from the source databases only need to be coded once, the validity and authorization checks are performed only once, and provisions are made only once for navigating the data records.

N O T E The logical database technique depends on the query being phrased in the logical units assigned to the system. If the answer cannot be assembled by using the logical units, the logical database technique isn't appropriate. For example, a search for a file by its name illustrates the use of a logical database—the list of filenames. By contrast, a search for information by looking for words or character sequences in the content of the same files will perhaps locate information that's not apparent by using the classified filenames. However, the detailed search will take much longer.

Building Strategic Indexes

A *strategic index*—for example, of the company's 100 biggest customers—is a type of report that demands a great deal of computing power, but not necessarily daily. The index can be updated at a frequency that is in accord with the expected rate of change of the data. If your company normally sells to the same set of customers who are relatively unchanging in their requirements, the strategic index of sales in this example doesn't need to be calculated very often. If you operate in a volatile market, you might have to accept the computing overhead and call for a strategic index at frequent intervals.

Reporting

ABAP/4 reports are started from a special report menu. Each choice typically initiates a special dynpro, called a *selection screen,* that requires users to define or recall a search specification to limit the scope of the report. A report can also be called from within other ABAP/4 programs—a capability that is needed to support interactive reporting.

Using ABAP/4 Query

For users who are not familiar with ABAP/4 programming, the ABAP/4 Query application can generate reports automatically if they are not already included in the standard SAP R/3 system.

The sophistication of ABAP/4 Query reports is limited to ranking lists and statistics, but users can select a functional area, go to the pertinent tables, and locate the fields to be included in the report. The source is usually a subset of a logical database, and users can choose between report layout and sequence. The application can supply explanatory texts from the ABAP/4 Data Dictionary.

Organizing Development Work

An integral component of the ABAP/4 Development Workbench is the ABAP/4 Workbench Organizer. It is suitable for projects small and large. In many respects, the Workbench Organizer performs the functions of the Project System module (see Chapter 16, "Understanding the R/3 Project System"). The Project System methodology can be applied to software development.

However, particular care has to be taken when the R/3 system is being used to prototype new components, or to test new components before their incorporation into the production data-processing system of your company. The ABAP/4 Development Organizer controls the software development process through the functions of change management, which depend on the management of software classes and release versions.

Managing Changes

A development project typically requires several programmers or programming teams, each working on part of the program. Each job automatically logs every development object that has been a candidate for change. That development object then is reserved exclusively for that programmer or team. Others can inspect, but not alter it, until it is released by the team that first took on the job of developing it. Another team then can work on that development object under the same exclusive arrangement. There is no possibility of having two teams working on the same development object at the same time.

Assigning Objects to Development Classes

Each object under development can be freely assigned to a responsible developer and will be necessarily assigned a development class that indicates the type of expertise needed to understand it.

Managing Development Object Versions

When an object is released, the current versions of all the involved development objects are automatically stored, and the new objects become current. The changes are logged so that it is possible to determine or reconstruct the state of affairs before the release of the new version. Performance measurement may well ensue.

Ensuring Revision Security

The developers are responsible for creating hierarchical documentation of their objects, which is referenced in the change management records.

Using the Correction and Transport Utility

Development usually takes place in a system separate from the productive system. A testing client code can be declared so that an object undergoing correction in the development environment does not interfere with business.

The Transport or "promotion" utility is so named because it supervises the promotion of a program from the development environment to the production system. It is responsible for transferring objects, having carried out a simulation if necessary. The objects are locked in the production system to prevent direct changes to the code. Customizing then takes place.

The Transport utility carries out complete documentation of the process, and the SAP R/3 Repository Information System can be consulted to determine which developmental objects still reside there.

Introducing the ABAP Objects Language

The ABAP/4 language has evolved into a fully object-oriented language referred to as *ABAP Objects*. The software products of ABAP Objects can run in the secure transaction-based environment of SAP R/3, yet the development facility can support and take advantage of full object orientation.

Each ABAP Object is held as an object model that is locked as a single master, from which copies can inherit properties. This single inheritance source can therefore be controlled, and versions can be released only when they have been proved. Object persistence is maintained by relational database mechanisms.

ABAP Objects is a full object language and therefore supports the following features:

- Encapsulation of one structure in an "envelope" by which it can be called and manipulated

- Polymorphism, which allows various forms of an object to be recognized as belonging to the same class

- Interfaces, which are special classes that don't need to include an implementation piece of code that defines their actions, so that they can provide a channel of communication to another process without consulting a definition of that process or class of objects

The ABAP Objects package includes a set of individual and team development tools for managing the processes of creating new software.

As a contribution to rapid development of business applications, ABAP Objects has a suite of standard mechanisms that can provide the following types of preconfigured service:

- **Publish** can manage the preparation of multimedia items and software modules for transmission on a defined range of channel types.

- **Subscribe** allows users to access published items.

- **Event Trigger** allows published items to be "pushed" by automatically generating a subscription when a logical condition is satisfied as the triggering event.

The details of these services are supplied from separate tables of data provided by the users, so the integrity of the software cannot be compromised.

The ABAP Objects language can create an extended virtual machine that can be copied to almost any system, where it will rebuild the capability to interpret the commands of the language. This means that the software developed in this language can run on many different types of platforms. ●

Working with the Business Engineer

Exploring Business Engineering

The concept of business engineering has been refined from earlier ideas that have their roots in the natural process of learning a skill. Because a human or an animal acquires an important skill by repeated attempts, it is obvious that the skill develops in various ways. The sequence of moves becomes streamlined as wrong moves are eliminated. There is a concentration of force and effort only where it is needed, and the learner saves energy where possible. And if the learning process is successful, the skilled operation will be quick and effective.

In business and industry, the measurement of the time taken by each process became more important as machines were introduced and production engineering became a specialized discipline. In computer processing, the concept of *business process reengineering* (BPR) came to mean the fundamental investigation of all aspects of business, with the aim of locating opportunities to improve cost-effectiveness and also to direct attention to those avenues that promise the best profitability.

BPR has thus become the refinement of business processing by adopting the best methods and eliminating superfluous steps, stages, and even departments from workflow sequences. For example, the notion of "customer-driven production" has been implemented in some companies that previously built up stocks in anticipation of future orders.

Understanding Object-Oriented Information Engineering

Object-Oriented Information Engineering (OOIE) is a language for specifying object types, associations between object types, subtyping, and partitioning. This logically formal language extends the concept and usefulness of an *event-driven process chain* (EPC) as the fundamental unit for designing business processes. OOIE adds to the EPC elements the concept of an operation that is defined in terms of a request to achieve a certain goal. The operation is complete when all the state variables in it have been transformed to the values that will constitute a satisfactory result. "Find me a person who is available now to perform this task," could be regarded as a shorthand description of an object operation that could be used to yield a set of values in the form of a Human Resources data object holding a person's name, qualifications, and availability.

▶ **See** "The Concept of an *Event-Driven Process Chain* (EPC)," **p. 81**

The *trigger* for an operation or set of operations is defined as a set of specific values in a particular data object. Also, control conditions can apply logical operators to model processes of any complexity. IntelliCorp ModelStore Repository is a multiuser capability for the LiveModel SAP R/3 Edition that integrates a number of business modeling tools to support the OOIE discipline and, for example, allows a business process graphical diagram to be executed to test its validity.

Consulting Unified Modeling Language Repositories

Unified Modeling Language (UML) is an emerging standard for component-based software systems in which you have to specify your business processes in a particular formal language. This UML format can be interpreted by a range of high-level modeling tools and gives you a simulation of the process. You can also modify the model of your process and retest it. When the model is working perfectly, you can send it to whatever systems are supported by the particular modeling tool you are using.

A *UML repository* is a storehouse of reusable software that can be set to work in a wide variety of system environments. One of the first UML-compliant repositories, the Microsoft Repository, was first populated via the UML facility in SAP R/3.

Using the Business Engineer

The SAP R/3 Business Engineer helps you configure an implementation by providing an interface through which you can select the parts you need and put them all together quickly to yield a robust, flexible, and efficient business system.

The Business Engineer serves as a business system implementation assistant. You can see which elements of R/3 you will need by consulting the R/3 Reference Model. This shows you how event-driven process chains can be used to build a map of your business using only the standard R/3 components. The Implementation Management Guide shows you how to put the EPCs to work by using your data and your way of doing business.

You can use the graphical modeling displays to control the Business Engineer, or you can work with tabular data if you prefer. You can use any editor to insert your particular terminology and other information. You then reload the changed information to the R/3 Repository. Advanced assistants such as the ARIS Toolset, IntelliCorp's LiveModel for R/3, and Visio's Business Modeler can be used.

Using Configure-to-Order Methodology

The Business Engineer supports the SAP Configure-to-Order initiative and some automatic custom R/3 configurations. For example, R/3 can be customized on the basis of components and procedures, and specific user interfaces can be generated from standard settings—for example, to create transaction dialogs for a particular industry solution.

Tracking Continuous Customization

Interactive process optimization and the addition of new processes or components to live R/3 applications are examples of continuous customization. The Business Engineer keeps track of the changes and allows testing and simulation before releasing any newly customized element.

Preconfiguring

A particular advantage of the Business Engineer programming interface lies in R/3 processes being used and tested before you install an R/3 system. Typical transaction data can be processed and displayed on screens customized for your specific situation. You can make alterations before implementation. You can also use the same interface to make alterations to the processing and reporting after the system goes live.

By controlling your processing sequences with the SAP Business Workflow (perhaps via an intuitive graphical display), you can automate and timetable the execution of related activities across application boundaries, components, and organizational units.

The Business Engineer has become the recommended mode of designing and building a focused implementation of the R/3 system. When the system is in productive operation, the same interface handles system maintenance, because it can select and deselect R/3 applications and modules and authorize settings and formats specific to the user—all this at the graphical flow diagram level, if required.

Selecting Components from the Business Framework

The Business Engineer is a development from the R/3 Analyzer that uses the R/3 Reference Model to give you a full toolkit to exploit the open Business Framework architecture.

The key addition to the functionality is the facility with which components and subsystems can be integrated with the core SAP R/3 system as they become available after SAP certification. It is not necessary to adhere to the formalities of the release cycle in which the entire system is converted to the updated software. Nor is it necessary to limit the system to applications supported by SAP.

This important contribution to flexibility and rapid implementation is made possible because of a wide range of robust messaging technologies that can bridge the communication and control gaps between systems and installations that might otherwise be incompatible. SAP *Application Link Enabling* (ALE) and SAP Business Workflow are examples. The widespread use of business objects containing data and processing components is another reason contemporary business systems can be quickly implemented in spite of their complexity.

For example, your company might want to choose the following SAP applications to be preconfigured and customized by the Business Engineer, thus becoming components of your Business Framework:

- HR-Human Resources
- PDM-Product Data Management
- Treasury
- *Available-to-Promise* (ATP) Server
- Reporting Server

Introducing Internet Facilities in R/3 Releases 3.1, 4.0, and 4.5

SAP R/3 has always been thought of as a layered system. Outside is the presentation and user interface, inside this resides the application layer in which the processing takes place, and in the core is the database and its processors. The layered concept is implemented to allow as much processing power and data storage capacity to be assigned to each layer as the volume and type of traffic demand. New processors can be brought in as the load increases. This dynamic and largely automatic control allows the system to be scaled up to handle larger numbers of users and also to execute more complicated processing when this is required.

There has been a steady evolution of the Business Engineer from Release 3.1, which allowed the R/3 Reference Model to be restructured to provide a business-oriented approach to the R/3 processes and functions. Release 4.0 offers a method of responding to questions in order to configure the R/3 system interactively. What you have to do is specify the aspects of your enterprise that you want to involve in an R/3 implementation project. For example, you could specify Production, Product Development and Marketing, and Sales. In each of these areas, you can find the particular business scenarios of interest and select the processes and functions you need in each. The outcome is an Enterprise Model that directly relates to the R/3 functions and can therefore be used to configure your system, because the Enterprise Model contains the data needed to carry out a consistent configuration.

Release 4.5 has improved the scope of the Business Engineer in the following ways:

- ALE has been extended to accept an increasing number of business components.
- The ALE Distribution Model Viewer is shipped as a Visio add-in.
- A thousand *Business Application Programming Interfaces* (BAPIs) are provided to execute standard data-processing methods using more than 250 business objects invoked from COM/DCOM and CORBA.
- The Interface Adviser for Release 4.5 explains how to integrate the BAPIs with non-SAP software.

Evoking Thin Clients

If your processor does not have the code to do what you require, it can be made to download this code from a central repository. You may not be allowed to alter it, and when you next download it, some updates may have been carried out centrally. This thin client working is standard in SAP installations.

If your processor is a *Network Computer* (NC) or perhaps a NetPC, you may be operating from a screen that is entirely driven by code that has come to you from afar. The Java language is designed to run on almost any kind of computing device. It builds a Java Virtual Machine that responds appropriately to Java application elements *(applets)*, which present you with items such as display windows and active forms. You can enter data in these windows and forms or choose an option.

The attraction of the thin client is the small bandwidth it needs to communicate with its host. An intranet within a company or the Internet worldwide could be the link, even if a tone-modulated stage using an analog telephone line is necessary.

Not enough high-performance workstations and advanced PC devices are available to provide terminals for all the people who would like to communicate over the Internet. Thin-client technology enables these people to use whatever computing devices can be made available. The user console may be just a television display and a set of response buttons.

N O T E   As of Release 4.5, the GUI can upgrade itself automatically. When it communicates with a central server, the system automatically detects that a software upgrade of the user interface on the desktop is required, and the necessary software then is downloaded without user intervention. This ensures that all users can benefit from upgrades immediately.

Reviewing Components for Internet and Intranet Use

There are two ways of developing your business system via a network. You can open links to a public or private network and then restrict certain operations to users identified as authorized individuals. Sales orders might be acceptable from those with sufficient credit, and information inquiries might be limited to representatives of registered companies. The other way of developing your business is to initiate coded messages on a network that are understood only by their intended recipient. A command to a warehouse to dispatch an item would have to be coded. Several different types of components are needed to do business over the networks.

Using Browsers

Netscape Navigator and Microsoft Internet Explorer are two browsers that can be used to present screens and transmit data to a user at the end of a low-bandwidth Internet channel. If you "open a location," you see a display maintained by a distant computer that selects the display according to the details you entered when you specified the "location." If your terminal is connected to a computer that does not have the location you are seeking, it tries another computer and so on until the searching is fruitful, exhausted, or timed out.

The job of a browser is to put together the responses from the location so that the user is not aware of the complexity of the selection and delivery processes, although the delay in response might suggest that the mechanism is by no means straightforward.

Using a Web Server

A Web server is a computing resource assigned to the job of connecting Web clients, whether thin or thick, with the database or other service that has been requested. The server can be a standard software package such as the Microsoft Internet Information Server or the Netscape Enterprise Server.

Using an *Internet Transaction Server* (ITS)

An *Internet Transaction Server* (ITS) connects Internet application components and the Web server. It presents information in Web page format that can be accessed by employees, customers, and other users via a browser. The ITS manages network transactions and supports Java.

Using the SAP Automation Interface

SAP Automation is a programming interface that allows Internet application components and other third-party application components to automate the interaction with R/3. It also integrates R/3 with new technologies such as COM/DCOM, OMG CORBA, and Java, as well as with external applications such as *Interactive Voice Response* (IVR) applications and forms-based interfaces.

A SAP Automation Integration Toolkit is provided as a function of the Business Engineer.

Using Internet Application Components

SAP *Internet Application Components* (IACs) are easy-to-use software modules that customers can use to perform specific business tasks and operations across the Internet and intranets. SAP has 25 IACs and 10 employee self-service application components for human resources.

Using Business Application Programming Interfaces

BAPIs are open object-oriented interfaces based on SAP business objects. Several hundred BAPIs have been defined across all R/3 business application areas. They integrate IACs and core R/3 system functions and reside in the application server layer. SAP and independent developers can use the BAPIs to build Internet and intranet solutions by using R/3 and other business applications. BAPIs are Microsoft COM/DCOM-compliant and OMG CORBA-compatible.

Applying SAP Business Framework Architecture

Each release of the Business Engineer includes new R/3 release and system upgrades, as well as the IACs. These components can be linked in various ways, referred to as *scenarios*.

Evolving Intranet Applications

When enterprise solutions are extended to a corporate intranet, you can expect to have a large number of users who may be unfamiliar with R/3. Help and training advice systems must be carefully tailored, because traditional application training may not be cost-effective for such a group. Intuitive interaction and familiar browsers may allow data entry and maintenance to be reliably moved from the back office to the points at which the data originates.

Deploying Business-to-Business Applications

R/3 allows integrated business systems to cooperate across the Internet by using open standards for business transactions, such as the BAPI standard. Business components can interact with many different business systems. For example, fully electronic extended supply chain management may become feasible.

Deploying Consumer-to-Business Applications

Consumers anywhere in the world can use their standard Web browser to access authorized portions of the corporation's R/3 system to gain information and transact real-time business securely.

Providing Employee Self-Service Applications

In an installation with an open framework extending right through a complex of business applications, you may well find that you can apply for jobs and get an answer without leaving your terminal. Similarly, you might be able to look at, but not alter, your remuneration package or your leave entitlement. These examples illustrate the self-service Internet application components now available that can make significant additions to the added value chains of your company.

Selecting from the SAP Automation Integration Toolkit

To facilitate the automation (not only of the office but also of the laboratory and the links to the production and storage facilities of a worldwide network of business partners), SAP R/3 is delivered with an Automation Integration Toolkit that includes the following packages:

- **GUI Library** of display and interaction functions that can be assembled to deliver a particular working environment that will integrate with SAP R/3

- **GUI Component,** a framework for building a user interface

- **SAP-GUI in Java** to execute any SAP GUI component at any terminal that can run a Java Virtual Machine

- **SAP Business Object Repository,** which contains all the data objects used in SAP R/3, along with the associated processing components

- **BAPI Component,** one of several hundred available BAPIs that enable you to link with and control most business systems

- **RFC Library,** which contains the Remote Function Calls needed by most business systems where a BAPI is not available or not necessary

- **RFC Component,** the SAP open programmable interface to enable Remote Function Calls to external applications, tools, and ABAP/4 programming language routines

- **Transaction Component,** a programmable interface to set up the control parameters for transaction processing

- **SAP Assistant,** which performs the functions of workflow manager and documentation assistant for the work of the Business Engineer

Managing R/3 Business Workflow

Relating Business Workflow to R/3

The organization of work has a long history with two branches:

- The craft tradition, with the emphasis on one skilled person doing all the work
- The work-sharing tradition, where several people share the work, each doing only part of the process and perhaps, as a consequence, not being fully aware of how his or her part fits in with the rest

The R/3 Business Workflow is a concept as well as a cluster of program components that finds its place between the standard business software of R/3 and the Enterprise Data Model on which the customer application depends.

It's obvious that people at work need certain information and often can provide information that can be used elsewhere for the benefit of the business. *Workflow* refers to the movement of work items through a series of operations that add value to these items. It also refers to the flows of information that must take place if this added value is to be optimized. Thus a workflow is a combination of steps, events, and conditions for making decisions.

SAP Business Workflow is a concept that permeates the R/3 system and is devoted to developing and managing the flows of work and information that will make a business as effective and efficient as possible. The programs necessary to do this are an integral part of R/3.

SAP Business Workflow is part of R/3 BASIS and is integrated in the SAP development environment as a function within the BPT-Business Process Technology component of the CA-Cross Application module. The SAP process model provides the basis for the methodology and graphical representation. The R/3 Analyzer and the ABAP/4 Development Workbench can provide powerful supporting tools for establishing a Business Workflow Management System.

SAP Business Workflow is closely integrated with the R/3 HR-Human Resources module. It is this close connection between SAP components that allows the organizational structure, the operational structure, and the workflow model to be related to each other without redundancy and without repeated entering of the significant data objects, such as job titles and responsibilities. If the jobs are to be associated with named individuals in the model, changes in these names and other particulars are made automatically from the Human Resources components.

Targeting Areas for Business Workflow

All customers with R/3, whether or not other SAP components have been installed, can use SAP Business Workflow. The following sample workflow models can be customized and integrated as subworkflows in larger structures:

- Release of budgets
- Release of invoices
- Engineering change management
- Availability checks
- Project management

- System-controlled document management
- End-of-period settlement
- Processing of customer inquiries and orders that affect other departments
- Support for automatic escalation
- Purchase requisitions
- Purchase order releases
- Requests for leave or vacation
- Travel expense accounting
- Workflow management of applications developed by ABAP/4 Workbench

Managing Business Workflow

A workflow management system is intended to manage business processes automatically or semiautomatically by controlling the sequence of activities. It should ensure that the appropriate steps are carried out at the right moment by specific people or groups, or by particular data-processing programs and the machinery they control.

The simplest workflow system is a sequence of operations carried out on a work item. The workflow begins when the worker takes up the workpiece, and each operation begins when the previous operation has been completed. The worker will take time off; there may be delays in order to give some operations time—for the workpiece to cool off, for example; there may be delays in order to await a missing component or because the customer has to be asked for more information about his requirements. The workflow ends when the final inspection shows the job to be finished to the standard required.

Should the workflow include delivery and payment? What about after-sales service?

Traditional legacy workflow management was the supervisor's task. Spare sets of materials were kept ready so that no worker had idle time because there was nothing to do. Anyone slacking or going slow would be cautioned. Work study loomed large.

Task definition is a matter of dividing work into units that make sense. Here is a simple job with three tasks: Get the tools and materials ready, do the work, and check the work before passing it on.

You might prefer to look at work from back to front. The task is not finished until the work is checked and found to be up to standards. It will not be up to standards unless you have done some work on it. And you can't do any work unless you have the materials and the tools.

Another sort of task does not have any elements that directly alter the work item. This might be an inspection task that diverts some work items along one workflow path because they are up to standards, and sends other items along a different route as rejects that are to be scrapped or repaired. This task may add a lot of value to the business by making sure that bad products are not offered for sale.

If a person is doing the inspection task, there is a clear relationship with the people who are upstream in the workflow, those who are responsible for making or changing the work items. The inspector or the creator of the workpiece may be a machine; both may be automated. If they are also linked by a feedback loop, the faults detected by the inspector can be used to alter the task carried out by the creator.

In this context, the historical approach to workflow management was considered to be a matter of dividing the jobs into tasks that could be done repetitively by workers who needed almost no training and very little inflow of information because each job item was the same. Managers had most of the information.

Skilled craftspeople demonstrated a different style of workflow, however. One sign of a high level of skill is the ability and habit of anticipating what should come next. The skilled person is using information to manage the details of the workflow. Waiting times are used to prepare for the future and to tidy up from the past. And the craftsperson is not above telling management to order fresh stocks and tools in anticipation.

Because there may be a mix of people and automatic processes in the workflow, such a system can form bridges, not only between process chains from different SAP applications, but also between SAP processes and activities that are being carried out on other systems or by essentially manual procedures.

Automating Information and Process Flows

The principle of information flow depends on data being collected directly or entered manually at one or more places and then being selectively distributed to wherever it can usefully take part in a decision process. By itself, data isn't actually informative: You have to know what it means. This usually boils down to knowing when this item of data could make a difference in how a task is being performed. *Automation of information flows* refers to the design and implementation of systems so that all the information required to make each decision in the best possible way is made available to the program or the person responsible for making the decision. The data has to be accurate and timely. It may have to be summarized or interpreted.

The *automation of process flows* refers to the methodology of using information about a process to adjust or initiate some control over this process. A thermostat senses temperature and switches a heater or cooler on or off to control the process of supplying energy. The thermostat is obeying rules about what information to use and what to do with this information. The thermostat is an automated control system in which both the information flows and the process flow controls are automated—even the decision-making is automated.

A human operator standing by to react to a pointer on a dial is an example of a partially automated system. The information flow to the dial is automated, but the task of reacting to this information is left to the human operator. In some watch-keeping tasks, the operator is given strict instructions about when to react; in others, the operator has to build up experience and take into account many other factors before deciding when and how to react.

The advantage of automating both information flows and process flows, if this is feasible, is that the system can be run according to decision rules that are applied continuously and reliably. If a fine adjustment has to be made, it can be put into effect immediately. The results of this adjustment can be monitored through the automated information system. If the need for an adjustment is a complicated matter of weighing the pros and cons of changing things, an automated information system has access to a process-modeling facility you can use to simulate the process and try out the effects of any adjustment you are contemplating.

The adjustment might be a matter of small changes to the operating parameters, or the proposal might be to reroute part of the process or rebuild part of the workflow model. The SAP Workflow Management System facilitates both.

Linking Work Steps Actively

Waiting consumes time, one of the most costly business expenses. As soon as one task has been completed, the next one in the workflow should begin. Expensive processes, like talking to a medical consultant, may well work out cheaper in the long run if there is a queue of work items, or patients, in the waiting room. Since the medical consultant cannot say how long each consultation will take, it is customary to work with a pool of jobs from which work can be drawn. Partial automation in this field enables the doctor's receptionist to access medical records and patient information so that appointments can be arranged and queuing in the waiting room can be made as discreet and efficient as possible. The SAP IS-H Industry Solution for Hospitals is an industry-specific application specifically directed at the processes and information flows of the hospital and medical arena.

Under the SAP Business Workflow regime, users are actively informed about jobs that need to be carried out, and automatic execution of work steps and subprocesses occurs wherever possible.

Designing a Workflow

SAP Business Workflow controls the flow of work through a network of SAP applications, key workstations, and external systems. It is applicable to companies of all sizes and industries.

SAP Business Workflow includes a set of workflow definition tools you can use to create a runtime business management system. These tools are included in R/3, from Release 2.1.

You must specify an organization model in order to generate a workflow pattern exactly suited to the requirements of your business. R/3 offers a range of workflow templates that you can use as samples for the basis of a customized workflow.

SAP HR-Human Resources components are integrated with Business Workflow so that workers can be chosen for any task according to their skills, authorization, availability on site at the moment the task is to be performed, and the role definition for it.

A range of issues has to be taken into account before beginning implementation or at an early stage. SAP Business Workflow provides tools and prompts, but the customer management team has to arrive at suitable conclusions and decisions.

Task definitions must be established for each element of the business processes. In some cases, it may be decided that individuals should define their own tasks in the first instance; SAP Business Workflow allows this.

Workflow has to be specified as a set of linked processes that are either standard business processes or processes to be developed to meet the specification determined by R/3 on the grounds that everything must integrate. You must use the R/3 Reference Model to select templates for the processes as the starting points for customizing.

Role definitions may be needed for responsibilities that may affect several tasks and for tasks that can be carried out by a range of personnel.

Object interfaces are required if the attributes of an information object can be inspected or copied automatically. Event interfaces must be defined if a sensing device, a data link, or a person can change the information that is stored as part of an information object. User interfaces to a work list client are usually terminals at which an end user or operator can see which work items remain on the work list and make a decision on which item to tackle next. These interfaces provide a flexible means of presenting the activities of the R/3 application and influencing them.

Runtime systems are controlling programs through which R/3 can direct a set of workflows and provide monitoring information about its progress. Automatic execution of work steps may be possible. Its scope and functions must be established.

Deadline monitoring can be specified, with appropriate dunning.

Escalation procedures can be arranged to automatically increase the resources for work steps that have been revealed as critical by the online monitoring. Design decisions must be made regarding the scope and supervision of these procedures.

Using Workflow Definition Tools

You can use standard R/3 business process tasks to establish a workflow, or you can define tasks and object types to suit your company. You can also define specialized document types and documents not native to R/3.

Differentiating Task Types

SAP Business Workflow supports a range of task types:

- Standard tasks that are part of R/3.
- Customer-defined tasks created by calling object methods that ensure that the tasks so defined will be fully integrated with the rest of the R/3 application.
- Manual tasks that are at the discretion of the person assigned. These manual tasks need inputs and staffing, and they create outputs. Therefore, these tasks must be defined in the task catalog of your organization model so that they will be integrated with the rest of the R/3 application.

Consulting the R/3 Reference Model

R/3 includes a Reference Model (discussed in Chapter 5, "Consulting the R/3 Reference Model") that shows how all the standard business processes fit together, with all the information flows and supporting services in place. The R/3 Repository contains a very large library of successful work process models compiled in the R/3 system. The SAP Business Navigator can present these models as seen from different viewpoints:

- Process view
- Function view
- Communication view
- Information-Flow view
- Organization view

The Process view variants of these successful work process models are available in graphical form as event-driven process chains, which can be inspected in order to select a suitable Reference Model for a particular implementation of R/3.

▶ **See** "The Concept of an *Event-Driven Process Chain* (EPC)," **p. 81**

 TIP The R/3 Analyzer is a standalone PC tool for establishing how the R/3 models may be used in the elaboration of an enterprise model for a new implementation.

Adopting Workflow Templates

The following are examples of workflow templates provided in R/3:

- The Malfunction Report
- Preliminary Invoice Posting
- Budget Release Management
- Engineering Change Management

These are fully elaborated model examples that you can copy and then modify to suit your needs.

NOTE R/3 customizing is a standard process that offers default settings and recommendations to help custom build a process to suit your situation, especially when business process reengineering has been initiated. It often is quicker to modify a Reference Model than to design a new system from scratch. The R/3 Customizing module includes a model company with project management and documentation for training and testing purposes, along with the IMG-Implementation Management Guide.

Analyzing with Event-Driven Process Chains

The concept of workflow entails a sequence of steps that progress a work item through tasks performed on it that add value to it. This flow of work items usually passes via several people and processes; some of these people may take on different roles according to the progress of a work item along the workflow.

A workflow definition may be like a simple chain, with a beginning and an end, in which no variation is allowed or expected in the order in which the steps (the links of the chain) are carried out. If the flow is not a chain, it is vital to set out the conditions that have to be evaluated at each option point. What are the signs or symptoms that should cause the workflow to take a side turning? How will the program or the person know when to switch the process from one track to another?

One central idea of SAP programming is to define business in terms of *event-driven process chains* (EPCs), which are workflows, each attached inexorably to an event that constitutes the signal for it to begin. It is no use having a procedural chain of tasks if you do not know when to use it.

Whatever the shape or complexity of the workflow, there will be flows of information between some steps and events. The design team has to consider whether any other information flows ought to be established. The team must also consider which information flows are not necessary and which should be formalized as essential requirements. Traditional information flows are not always a good guide as to which information pathways really add value to the business and which are just wasteful.

The starting point of a formal workflow definition in R/3 must be a workflow task stored in the task catalog of the organization model being used as the Reference Model during implementation and being adjusted toward the model that will be used on startup.

Within the definition of this starting point task already stored in the task catalog, there must be a stored parameter value. If this value changes in a certain way, this will be the event that signals for the workflow to begin.

Under control of the SAP Graphical Workflow Editor, a workflow is defined by specific types of steps:

- Activity
- User decision
- Wait
- Subworkflow

These workflow steps may be defined for concurrent execution or for serial execution under the runtime environment.

Conditions that control alternative branches in the workflow can be based on selected characteristics or attributes of the processed business objects, or on attributes of the workflow itself such as wait times or associated costs. Conditions may be in logical or numerical form, beginning with If, or they may be Case conditions that are to be interpreted as "If this is a case of ..., then ..."

If a task can be performed by a program or a subworkflow of tasks that is already implemented and available for work at the moment required, this task may be released for automatic performance, and no human intervention is necessary. If no automatic procedure is available for the task, for whatever reason, the SAP Business Workflow calls on the HR-Human Resources application to supply the name of a person suitable for this responsibility, by virtue of his position or experience. Anyone who is not at work at the time will not be assigned this task. If no one can be found, the task defaults to the person responsible for this section of the workflow.

Static assignment refers to the process of deciding who should perform a task by reference to the task catalog in the organization model, where the person is defined by name, position, organization unit; or as the responsible user. *Dynamic assignment* takes place at runtime by reference to a defined role that must be discharged at this point in the business process. For example, the task of inspection by a specialist cannot be assigned to a named person until a specific work item is being processed, so that the nature of the work item can be used to select an appropriate specialist.

When a suitable person takes up the task, the workflow object supplies a text for guidance—a definition of what constitutes a satisfactory termination of events for this task—and a reference to the object method that can be used to solicit online help or documentation that shows everything needed to perform and check this task.

Using Workflows with Objects

An *object* in R/3 is a named set of information items that are grouped together because it is convenient to move them about as a group. Some objects are defined in order to improve computer activities; some are defined because they make good business sense. The information items belonging to an object can represent any of the following:

- Attributes of the object
- Methods that are operations performed on objects
- Events that are changes in the state of certain objects; in particular, changes in the value of one or more parameters held in specific data fields of an object

One guideline for using object-oriented programming is to try to ensure that each item of information is held in only one place. For example, a customer object has places to hold an address and telephone number. If the number is changed, only one data location has to be altered. Every process or person who needs this number looks in the same place for it, so as soon as it is changed, all the users of it will be up-to-date.

SAP standard business processes are objects. All who use them find them in the same place, which is the R/3 Reference Model. If these processes are altered, it will have been by the central in-house development team, and everyone will know as soon as they next use the process. If an implementer customizes a standard process, it will be a copy under a new name that is altered, not the master.

The organization structure of a company is stored as an object. Each position contains a reference to the person currently filling it; a new face in that job means a new reference in the organization object. But the particulars of each employee are held in employee objects, not in the organization object. Master data is entered only once.

Applying Object Methods

An object can perform one or more tasks by invoking *object methods*. For example, object Export1 includes four items:

- Invoice document
- Order
- Material
- Archived document

The sample object Export1 invokes three object methods concerned with processing the invoice in three steps:

1. Export1: Create invoice document
2. Export1: Edit invoice document
3. Export1: Display invoice document

Each step of invoice processing for object Export1 entails a task recognized by R/3 as a component of the organization model. Each task is assigned to a role that can be performed by a person with suitable qualifications and experience—perhaps an export invoice clerk in this example.

Exploring Object Interfaces

The R/3 system operates on units of information that are carried as computer documents to wherever they are needed. These units can be combined in various ways to form larger units.

When information is entered into R/3, it becomes a data object and is passed about just like a tangible object.

An *object interface* is a device or a process running on a programmed device that can extract the information needed to build the data object required by the workflow at a particular stage.

This object interface may get the information it requires from a sensing device, such as a barcode reader, for example, or it may have to collect a great deal of information from many sources and carry out some data processing on this information before it can create the object it requires. For example, there may be an object interface that has been given the job of finding out whether there are any bottlenecks in a production process. The required object is a parcel of information that specifies which processes are being held up, if any. The object interface usually will be able to say one of two things: Yes, here is the information; or No, the required information is not available.

Defining Events

An *event* is a change of state in one or more attributes of an object. Therefore, the event belongs to and is a characteristic of an object. An event invokes a *method,* which is a specified procedure or process that is only waiting for a signal to begin.

Events belonging to two or more objects may be linked. For example, an event occurring in one SAP application may elicit a defined response in another, perhaps causing the transport of data from one application to the other.

An event may prompt a workflow to start. Events may also terminate or abort a task, even if the events originate outside the workflow to which the task belongs.

A change of state in one object, an event, may be used to direct the flow of information or processing, not necessarily in the same workflow.

An *event interface* is a method of allowing events from other workflows to have some influence on how this process proceeds. For example, there is usually an event interface between a production process and a materials management system. Shortage of a material may well shut down the production process; early warning of the shortage may cause just a prudent slowing down.

Setting Up the Workflow Manager Runtime Environment

If a workflow is properly defined in terms of the tasks, roles, objects, and interfaces, it often is possible to set up a runtime system that can control and progress work items through the steps of their appropriate workflow. If the decision is to install an automated runtime system when a workflow is designed by using the R/3 tools, it is possible to call on the Workflow Manager, which is a runtime environment, to progress the event-driven process chains that constitute the workflow.

For testing purposes, a model client company can be engaged and simulations of the workflow carried out. The same runtime environment can be used to manage the workflow when the application runs with the customer company as client.

The Work Item Manager has the role of assigning work items to places defined in the organization model where they may be progressed to the next stage of the workflow. Items of a similar type are sent to a work list client, which receives work items from the Work Item Manager according to the range of work types for which it is suitable. The work list client may serve one or more terminals where people who are suitable for the role are likely to be working. The products of their work are returned to the work list client on their way to the next step in the workflow.

Defining Roles

Role definition is a process of recording who is responsible for what. In particular, a role definition should specify what information and experience are needed for a particular task. One type of role is the inspector who has to decide what happens next in a region of the workflow where there can be a choice. A role definition may also include an obligation to ensure that the process does not come to a halt or change its rate outside specified limits.

Dynamic role assignment can take place at runtime if the process can furnish the required information. For example, a role may be designated as "responsible for material." In this case, it may be necessary to know what material is identified on the invoice document before a suitable person can be selected to discharge this role. Dynamic role assignment may also have to take place to provide stand-ins, deputies, or proxies if the designated person or position holder is unavailable.

Consulting the Runtime Information System

Retrieval of workflow information can be based on the volume or costs of work items, or on any other data available in the fields of the objects in the system. For example, it is possible to retrieve the number of times a function has been called in a period of time.

Full analysis facilities are accessible online during workflow management, and statistics can also be compiled for subsequent scrutiny. For example, in a processing plant, the Work Item Manager component can find the yield of each process and the time each job is taking. This component then can suggest speeding up or slowing down particular operations. It can also be configured to issue the necessary commands automatically.

Several related workflows may have been defined through the Workflow Editor, in which case the Workflow Manager is responsible for control and coordination.

The results from the Workflow Item Manager are one or more work lists directed at the work list client, which services one or more users through a user interface. Dynamic allocation of staff to work items may be one responsibility of the work list client. If two or more users have signed on with the same role, they will see identical work lists, but items cleared by one will be deleted from the lists of all the others.

Users can customize their work list client interfaces to sort and display work items conveniently. The interface includes an inbox to the SAPoffice component. The SAPoffice function is distributed in the CA-Cross Application module as a part of the CA-BPT Business Process Technology component.

The work list client may also have access to SAP email, Internet, X.400, and SoftSwitch interfaces to non-SAP email systems. Sources that use the *Electronic Data Interchange* (EDI) protocol can be accessed via the SAP ArchiveLink and SAP Intermediate Document interfaces. These routes allow images of original documents to be accessed if required.

Using Application Interfaces

Work lists can be exported completely out of the R/3 system via the Microsoft *Messaging Application Programming Interface* (MAPI), if necessary. Workflow interfaces are available to allow the conduct of workflows on other SAP applications or on systems external to SAP.

N O T E   Communications and the controlled exchange of data between an R/3 system and other applications, including workflow systems, are matters that are in rapid evolution.

Linking

Event linking entails establishing relationships between events and therefore between the process chains driven by them. The following possibilities are examples of workflow connections that may have to be established in a specific workflow network:

- External systems may have to trigger R/3 events or workflows.
- R/3 events may have to elicit responses in external systems.
- Links between events must be established for generating and processing work items and workflows.
- Links between events must be established to work list clients that are managing the work lists of different user groups and their user interfaces.

Noting R/3 Standard Interfaces

R/3 supports the following standard interfaces:

- ANSI-SQL *(American National Standards Institute-Structured Query Language)*
- CPI-C *(Common Programming Interface-Communications)*
- EDI *(Electronic Data Interchange)*
- ODBC *(open database connectivity)*
- OLE *(object linking and embedding)*
- TCP/IP *(Transfer Control Protocol/Internet Protocol)*
- X.400

These standard interfaces can implement communications and the controlled exchange of data between R/3 and other applications, including workflow systems from other vendors. However, for the effective implementation of distributed application systems, an object-oriented approach with open integration between the modules is required. R/3 Release 3.0 includes business and workflow APIs to meet this requirement.

The concept of coupling is relevant. *Tight coupling* uses a central database to ensure guaranteed data consistency and business integration. *Loose coupling* allows master data to be held on more than one database. In this case, the way in which applications exchange messages must be controlled carefully, whether synchronously or asynchronously.

Loose coupling has advantages—for starters, each application is autonomous. For example, different releases of the SAP R/2 and R/3 systems can be in use in separate satellite systems without conflict. Also, one or more applications can be permitted temporary standalone operation. Another advantage of loose coupling is that SAP applications can easily communicate with third-party applications, and business processes can be integrated across multiple systems.

SAP Business Workflow can support such heterogeneous systems by use of its wide variety of messaging interfaces.

R/3 Release 3.0 offers two types of interfaces:

- Open integration modules as application interfaces (Business APIs)
- Interfaces for SAP Business Workflow (Workflow APIs)

Introducing BAPIs

SAP supports loose coupling using open integration modules as application interfaces within the scope of *Application Link Enabling* (ALE). In particular, SAP recognizes a requirement for external systems to be able to invoke R/3 applications. This is implemented as a series of *Business Application Programming Interfaces* (BAPIs), which can manipulate consistent data objects between R/3 and third-party systems.

Introducing Workflow APIs

Pending the development of a standard for workflow interfaces, SAP has developed a number of interfaces for specific workflow systems. Their capabilities are likely to be shared with whatever standard is established. ●

Implementation Issues

XI

Implementation Issues

Overview of SAP Implementations

Understanding the Scale of SAP Projects

If you're considering or actually implementing SAP, you're joining an ever-increasing number of the world's largest and most respected companies. The rise of the R/3 system has been nothing less than sensational. Since its launch in December 1992, the number of R/3 installations has increased to more than 14,000 in 1998. SAP has some excellent tools that significantly improve implementation quality and speed. Systems implementations in general are rarely easy, but SAP offers among the best tools and support in the industry.

Companies implementing SAP must be focused, and the whole project must be broken into small, manageable chunks. There must be a strong management team and strong support from the highest levels in the company.

Good preparation, planning, and control are vital. You will inevitably need external advice and support, and you should aim to get the very best.

One great difficulty of any computing project lies in quantifying the project's scale, and SAP is no different. In choosing to implement an SAP system, however, you're also choosing a ready-made and proven application that needs only to be configured to meet your business requirements.

This choice would appear to offer great advantages over building a custom application, and in most cases, it does. You should be aware, however, that SAP might not meet all your business requirements, and for reasons of efficiency, you might have to change your business practices to work within SAP's capabilities. In the relatively few instances in which SAP cannot meet your business requirements, you might be faced with changes to the core system. This can involve expensive development, and because SAP might not support this development, you might have problems when you need to upgrade.

It's difficult to know in advance whether SAP can meet all your business requirements, because the full business requirements frequently don't come to light until the project is well established. With SAP's phenomenal growth, most of your business requirements have probably already been encountered by other users and accommodated in SAP. Your company's business requirements are likely to be similar to those of other companies in your industry, and you should be able to benefit from industry solutions having already been developed for major industries. However, you should also be prepared to find business requirements that cannot be accommodated by the system.

Management quite rightly will want to know

- How long it will take to implement SAP
- What resources will be needed, human and other
- How much it will cost

These questions have no easy answers, because so many variables must be taken into account. The best management can do is consider every aspect very carefully, take professional advice from as many different sources as possible, and make a calculated guess. SAP itself, or a reputable and experienced SAP implementation specialist company, might be able to give you a reasonable estimate. However, they don't know your business and might be influenced by their desire to sell you their products or services.

If you intend to implement a number of the major modules, be prepared for a major project that will need a great many resources, careful planning, and quality management over a long period of time—anywhere from a few months to a number of years. A decision to implement SAP shouldn't be taken lightly. It's best to consider all the implications carefully before making any decisions.

Starting an SAP Project for the Right Reasons

SAP is causing so much excitement globally that it's easy to get caught up in the tidal wave of enthusiasm and rely too much on the confidence with which so many of the world's major companies are using it. Be certain that you are choosing SAP for the right reasons. This section discusses some of those reasons.

Business Process Reengineering

SAP and *business process reengineering* (BPR) go hand in hand. In fact, the latest concept from SAP is that of using SAP as a means of "continuous business engineering." You can use SAP's flexibility to continually reengineer your business, instead of going through a single reengineering process. You can hardly argue with the sense of this concept.

Staff Reduction

SAP is frequently seen as a means of reducing headcount by streamlining organizations and making systems more efficient. This is hardly the message companies want as common knowledge when every employee's cooperation is required for implementation. A worried workforce isn't good for business and can cause all sorts of motivational problems. When you take employees out of their line jobs and put them into a project team, they will naturally question what they are going to do when the project is completed.

Although you might be able to achieve headcount reductions in line jobs after SAP implementations, you have to consider the personnel requirements to support the system after the implementation. Companies working hard at reducing their head count might want to consider training key users well so that they can support their organization, thus avoiding the need for specialist support teams.

Organizational Change

You need a very thorough knowledge of SAP and your own organization and business to be able to predict what future organization you will require after implementation. Frequently, the postimplementation organization isn't properly considered until the project is reaching its advanced stages. The organizational change is linked closely to the business process reengineering, which is to a great extent controlled by the nature of the system.

Integrated System/Module Software

A well-integrated system can be a great aid in helping the company run efficiently. One of SAP's greatest advantages is its full integration, yet surprisingly some companies implement only one or a few modules.

Although the performance and functionality of the individual SAP modules undoubtedly rivals—and in most cases exceeds—that of other companies' standalone applications, SAP's integrated nature has to be one of the greatest reasons for choosing it. The benefits of the system handling complete processes seamlessly are difficult to ignore. You can forget problems of interfaces, system mismatches, duplicated data, and complex reporting problems.

The modular nature of the SAP software is a distinct advantage. You can purchase modules to meet your business requirements now, and add more modules to them whenever required.

Integration with Other Systems and Distribution Across Multiple Platforms

In large companies, many different systems are inevitably used. SAP R/3 offers great flexibility in terms of hardware, operating systems, databases, and graphical user interfaces.

Client/server technology is generally regarded as reliable, efficient, flexible, and cost-effective. SAP offers the best advantages of relational database and client/server technologies.

Corporate Standard

Most major corporations want to standardize their business operations to improve efficiency and increase their flexibility in responding to market conditions. Expectations of customer service levels are continually rising, competition is fierce, and managers are under pressure to deliver good results for shareholders.

The argument is compelling for doing away with a mish-mash of old systems that operate independently and require different skills and training requirements, and replacing them with a standard system that can be implemented worldwide. At a sweep, training and system support can be rationalized, and more important, management gains flexibility and access to information.

The issues of business globalization are at the forefront of boardroom strategies in most major corporations. As communications improve and world trade increases, companies not only have to look to exploiting world markets but also to trading globally. Historically corporate affiliates worldwide have tended to operate independently, but nowadays companies need to operate more as one global entity. A single, fully integrated business system such as SAP makes good business sense.

Capacity to Manage High Volumes of Processing

There can be nothing worse than investing huge sums of money in new systems and technologies only to find business growth and expansion stretching them to their limits in a short time.

With SAP you can sleep at night with the reassurance that 120 of the world's top 500 companies use the systems. SAP's huge R&D effort and testing of existing SAP systems in operation guarantees the system's capability to meet the large volumes of processing required by major corporations. You should be aware, however, that the software is only as good as the platform it's running on and the communications hardware.

New Startup Operations

SAP offers new businesses the opportunity to get up and running within a very short period of time. The tools the system offers are perfect for developing new organizations and efficiently engineering the business.

Reducing Processing Costs

Depending on the type of systems and hardware already being used, you might be able to reduce processing costs with SAP. Research and analysis are required individually to show the effect of an SAP implementation on processing costs.

Real-Time Processing

Real-time processing is the technology of today and is a key feature of SAP. The combination of a fully integrated and real-time system can offer businesses a competitive edge and contribute significantly to high efficiency and good customer service.

Standardizing the Skill Requirements of the Staff

The nature of the working world seems to be changing globally. An increasing number of companies are requiring a flexible workforce that can readily adapt to changing roles and circumstances. By adopting SAP systems and standardizing, companies can benefit from the resulting more standardized skill requirements. The great thing about working with SAP is that although the functions change throughout the system, the user interface is very similar across the modules. It's therefore much easier for users to gain skills on different parts of the system than it would be if each part were an independently purchased component.

Industry Standard Solutions

The old saying "Why reinvent the wheel?" applies to SAP's industry solutions, which are essentially modules configured and enhanced to meet the requirements of particular types of industries. It's very much a question of buying a shoe that fits instead of buying a kit of parts that you need to put together and modify.

Fast Development with Good Prototyping

SAP offers fast development and good prototyping capabilities, which are good reasons to choose the system. The cost of any systems development is linked to the time the development takes. Equally, the faster the system can be developed, the earlier the benefits can be realized.

Powerful Development Tools

SAP's development tools have made a significant impact on the speed and quality of SAP configuration. An impressive and comprehensive range of tools has been designed to handle almost every aspect of development and implementation, bringing real cost and project quality benefits.

Multilanguage Capabilities

SAP's multilanguage capabilities are awe-inspiring. The system can be run in 15 different languages, including Mandarin Chinese, and allows for the global adoption of SAP as a corporate standard.

Creating Your Own Vision for the Future

Whatever the reasons for choosing SAP, companies should develop their vision for the future early on. It's only by clearly knowing what you want to achieve that you can direct your project to take you to that future.

Two companies implementing exactly the same module may have very different objectives and may receive very different benefits. Companies need to make the system work for them to enable them to achieve their business goals.

After you define your vision for the future, you must publicize it well internally so that all employees are aware of what they are working toward.

Creating a Cash-Flow Forecast for SAP Systems

At some stage in the decision-making process, you must create a cash-flow forecast to support the proposal. This task presents many challenges, because 70 percent of the figures in the forecast will probably be assumptions, with the remaining 30 percent representing reasonably accurate known costs.

In the simplest analysis, you have two areas to consider: the software and hardware itself; and the cost of installing, configuring, training, and implementing. The second area presents the greatest difficulty, because you will undoubtedly have to make some uncomfortable assumptions. So many factors influence the costs that it is impractical to cover them all in this book. Systems projects in general are prone to budget and cost overruns, and even some of the most well-respected SAP implementers have had problems keeping costs and schedules under control.

Putting more effort and care into the planning and preparation before the project starts can lessen the risk and make predictions more accurate. The success of the project lies as much in the approach taken by the company buying the system as it does in the skills of contracted implementers.

When you perform an evaluation of an SAP project using discounted cash-flow techniques, you need to take six basic steps:

1. **Determine the economic life of the SAP investment.** The economic life of the SAP system is the number of years the system will be in use—taking into account system upgrades and enhancements. It's likely to be around five to 10 years.

2. **Identify the relevant cash flows.** The relevant cash flows should be those cash flows in and out of the business that occur only as a result of the decision to undertake the SAP project. It's important to ignore accounting adjustments for depreciation and central overheads, and to consider carefully the real cost of data processing/information technology support instead of the costs generated by arbitrary cost allocations.

   Two conceptual decisions affect the relevant cash flows: the treatment of tax and the treatment of inflation. Whatever the decision, it needs to be documented and applied consistently throughout the investment appraisal.

   Apart from the decision to include or exclude tax cash flows, only one other type of cash flow may be ignored—the payment or receipt of interest. In general, interest is taken care of in the discounting process, so to include it would give rise to double counting. The only exception might be projects for which a special financing deal is set up to finance hardware or software.

3. **Establish the discount rate to be used.** The discount rate should be the minimum rate of return required for a capital investment. Most companies use a version of their historical average cost of capital, adjusted to reflect forecast inflation. Some adjust the discount rate to reflect any significant risks associated with the investment. If the relevant cash flows exclude the effects of inflation, the discount rate used should also be adjusted to exclude inflation. If the project will likely be specifically funded by subsidized loans, grants, or even venture capital, the specific forecast funding costs can be used as the discount rate.

4. **Specify the compounding frequency.** The dates of incoming and outgoing cash flows determine when those cash flows are available to be reinvested (and so earn interest) and to be financed (and so incur interest). Therefore, in theory, cash flows should be dated as accurately as possible, and the compounding time interval should be set to reflect the frequency with which the cash is financed or reinvested. In practice, most companies assume that the cash flows occur at the year end, on the assumption that they are likely to be spread more or less evenly over the life of the investment.

5. **Perform the net present value calculations.** The next step is to calculate the value (in today's currency) of each SAP investment's cash flows. The *net present value* (NPV) of the investment is the sum of today's values. The easiest way to do the calculations is to use a spreadsheet.

6. **Evaluate the investment NPV against the base case.** The NPV of a capital investment proposal indicates the net wealth to be earned, after financing costs, from adopting the proposal. The implication is that there are only two alternatives: continue operations as they are, or adopt the proposal. However, in many cases, there are better competing alternatives or versions of the same proposal that can be compared and contrasted.

Although looking at discounted cash flow is one of the best ways of evaluating the financial viability of an SAP project, it's important to remember that IT project financial appraisals often contain subjective elements. Assumptions about inflation, funding costs, markets, competition, and the softer costs and benefits mean that the output of the appraisal, an estimated NPV, is only an estimate.

The decisions that managers make concerning the structure and strategy for their companies' information technology assets need to be tempered by many considerations that cannot be easily quantified and assimilated into a discounted cash flow model.

Difficulties of Quantifying Benefits and Assessing Risks

Most company directors have experienced the effort and pain involved in obtaining board-level approval for capital equipment purchases. Justifying investments in computer systems can be even more time-consuming and painful. One reason is that many benefits—particularly those relating to improved effectiveness—may be difficult to identify and quantify up front. For example, how can costs savings from new business processes be identified when the outcome of an SAP-centric process reengineering project is itself unknown?

Another reason why cost-justification can be so painful is that although the costs of the system are often borne by the Sales, Finance, or IT departments, some benefits, such as improved sales forecasting, may be companywide, spanning Marketing, Production, and even Customer Service.

Finally, accountants with little understanding of marketing or sales functions often produce cost-benefit analyses. The accountants may be reluctant to include estimates of benefits produced on a "best-guess" basis.

The following sections are set up to help companies prepare better information on costs and benefits—before the purchase decision and during SAP implementation. First you'll explore the real reasons that underpin the cost-benefit analyses that companies undertake. It's all too easy for managers to be naive in this complex and politically charged area. You'll then see how managers might change the focus and presentation of their cost-benefit analyses to better meet the real objectives of the exercise. You'll examine the types of risks an SAP project might involve and some techniques for evaluating the likely impact of risk and uncertainty. Finally, you'll learn how to recognize the real costs and benefits and provide a brief checklist of possible costs and benefits associated with SAP.

Why Companies Undertake Cost-Benefit Appraisals

In theory, the aim of a cost-benefit evaluation is to make sure that scarce resources (such as cash) are channeled into the areas that will make the organization more profitable. Yet in practice, the reasons that managers in companies put considerable effort into cost-benefit appraisals aren't as straightforward as they might seem.

In 1994, Hewson Consulting Group (HCG) conducted detailed research into how companies evaluate their investment in sales-driven and marketing-driven IT systems. The results are thought to be representative of most IT systems. HCG found that although 55 percent of systems appear to require a fully worked cost-benefit justification to obtain funds, the informal realities are quite different. In reality, this research showed that the numbers that companies produce on the benefits side are frequently there to make the official justification look good. Many managers have already made up their minds that the IT investment is worthwhile, and they need to invent the numbers to sell the idea to the board. In this case, the evaluation takes on a political role.

Other organizations undertake formal cost-benefit analyses because they believe that "whatever gets measured gets done." For these companies, the aim of the benefit appraisal isn't to control the allocation of resources to different IT projects, but instead to help set targets to control the project itself and to drive through the realization of the planned benefits. Finally, some organizations will identify the system costs and benefits retrospectively, as part of a postproject appraisal aimed at improving their capital investment processes.

It seems obvious, therefore, to conclude that in the complex world of business decision-making, not all cost-benefit evaluation exercises are as they seem. The secret of success is to understand exactly why the cost-benefit evaluation exercise is really needed in your company. The reason may be any of the following:

- **Economic.** An objective assessment of the options open to the company to establish whether investment in SAP will add value to the organization and whether it represents the best use of company resources.

- **Political.** A sales exercise to convince the budget holders that the investment is worthwhile, using whatever means necessary.

- **Control.** An exercise to identify, quantify, and communicate the target benefits and costs to drive through their realization.

- **Retrospective.** A review of how the investment decision was made, to learn from experience.

Although this section concentrates on the first use of cost-benefit evaluations, which is to decide whether an SAP project makes economic sense, Figure 32.1 outlines how the focus of the exercise might change if the evaluation is considered to be more political than economic, for example.

When to Do a Cost-Benefit Analysis

Most organizations analyze costs and benefits before deciding to acquire a system. They generally incorporate some form of cost-benefit analysis into the organization's capital approval process. However, if your SAP investment is considered high-cost and high-risk, you should also review the costs and benefits at the end of each stage of the project before proceeding to the next stage. This helps ensure that, if market conditions change or the original estimates of costs and benefits were wrong, the project plan can be modified appropriately.

FIGURE 32.1

Types of cost-benefit evaluations.

	Aims		Focus on
Economic	is the system worthwhile - will it increase profits? will it add value to the company? does the system represent one of the best uses of company capital?	The aim of an 'economic' evaluation is to establish if investment in the system will add value to the organization. Here the emphasis is on an objective assessment of the alternatives with a view to selecting the project that maximizes the return on company capital or other scarce resources. For example, will the use of a client relationship system increase profits or earnings per share? Furthermore, if your organization has limited access to funds or other scarce resources, such as key management time and skills, would other projects competing for those same resources offer a better return?	1 the state of your customer markets - how your system will support sales and market strategies. 2 the 'real' costs and benefits - the difference between the impact of the system and that of the next best alternative. This means focusing on the changes arising from the system and their likely associated cash flow, not central allocations of unchanging overheads or costs that have already been incurred. 3 the impact of risk (financial, market, operational, technical) on the estimated/most likely cash flows.
Political	can the budget holders be convinced that the system is worthwhile?	The aim of a 'procedural' evaluation is to get the funds and resources to finance and complete the project. Here the emphasis is on understanding the real procedures, both formal and informal, that control the use of capital and other resources.	1 understanding what drives the availability of capital funds. Are capital budgets available for all worthwhile projects or constrained to a total maximum amount. 2 demonstrating the way in which the system will support your business' mission and strategy. 3 thinking through the power implications. In particular the political dimension; information is power? 4 tilling the soil. Working on the social dimension. 5 meeting corporate hurdle rates. Typically this means adjusting project assumptions, in particular concerning the base case, next best alternative, and valuation and timing of benefits or changing the treatment of overheads, in particular indirect costs and cost allocations.
Control	to set targets to help drive through system benefits and plan and control the costs.	The aim of a 'control' evaluation is to identify, quantify and communicate the target benefits and costs of the system. Doing this up front will help ensure that the system is perceived and developed as benefit-oriented and the costs and risks are controlled.	1 measurable, objective and acceptable key performance indicators. 2 linking targets to company rewards systems and culture. 3 setting targets and control framework by reference to change management issues and techniques.
Retrospective	how effectively do we select and manage the implementation of projects? how can project management be improved next time? is the system being used effectively now? If not, what should we do next?	The air of a 'retrospective' evaluation is to learn from experience. If a sales management system has been successfully implemented in one division, the other group divisions could benefit from a similar system. Alternatively, a retrospective cost benefit analysis could indicate that significant further benefits might be achieved by continuing to develop the use and application of the system within the same division.	1 the accuracy of the forecast costs and benefits. 2 the procedures and controls used to design and implement the system. 3 the ongoing costs and benefits. 4 other companies use of sales and marketing systems - benchmarking.

© Hewson Consulting Group

Linking Systems Objectives to Corporate Strategies

Much has been written about the potential mismatch between corporate business strategies and IT strategies. HCG's research indicates that managers believe that many sales and marketing systems don't fully support their business's sales and marketing objectives.

Now that the use of personal computers and open systems architecture has reduced the time it takes to get systems operational, in principle it's easier to link systems objectives to business strategies. This means that systems strategies can now follow, rather than precede, business strategies.

Your investment in SAP will likely earn you money only if it enables you to achieve your business objectives more quickly, less expensively, or at less risk. The first step in producing a cost-benefit evaluation is to set out clearly how SAP might best support your business strategies.

Although it's relatively simple to demonstrate how SAP might help companies reduce overhead costs, it's considerably harder to explore how SAP might help improve an organization's competitive position in terms of improved customer service and better product development. Yet many business practitioners have emphasized IT's importance in changing marketing processes and improving competitive position and customer management.

SAP is such a vast system that you must consider it module by module. Depending on how many SAP modules you will implement, you might find that SAP can support many different business strategies across a wide cross-section of your company's operations. Because of the system's integrated nature, it's frequently at the center of a company's entire business. Linking the system processes to your corporate strategies is a large undertaking that is best achieved by creating frameworks to enable the analysis. It's well worth considering using a suitable expert to help you do this.

For example, HCG uses three frameworks to attempt to identify sales- and marketing-based IT investments that best support business strategies: *critical success factors* (CSFs), product market life-cycle analysis, and customer needs and opportunities analysis.

Critical success factor analysis applies equally well to all potential IS projects, whether their focus is on cost reduction or on some form of improved market positioning. The other two approaches are an extension of the critical (or key) success factor method of aligning IT investment to business strategy. Effective business strategy must forge a strong link between looking outward to the market and looking inward to the firm's assets and capabilities. Looking outward to the market means paying attention to the complex requirements and dynamics of carefully delineated customer market segments.

Therefore, in addition to traditional CSF analysis, which tends to be conducted on a top-down basis, organizations seeking to use IT to exploit an externally driven and market-focused business strategy need to use frameworks that help them develop bottom-up IS strategies through a detailed market analysis.

Critical Success Factors   *Critical success factors* (CSFs) are the limited number of areas in which results will ensure successful competitive performance for the organization—in simple terms, the few things an organization has to do well to survive. Whereas an organization's business objectives state what needs to be achieved and by what deadline, the CSFs indicate how the objective will be achieved. For example, a business objective might be to increase market share by 5 percent over the next three years. The associated CSFs might be

- We must provide a more efficient distribution system.
- We must better identify high-volume customers.
- We must make it easier for customers to do business with us.

Every CSF should be viewed as beginning with the words "We need…" or "We must…" Each CSF must be necessary to the goal and sufficient to achieve it. Typically, a business unit might have between five and 15 business objectives, and two to six critical success factors for each objective. Not all CSFs will be best met through an IT/IS project or solution, and some SAP projects may help an organization to achieve more than one CSF.

The advantage of using a CSF approach is that it can lead to a consensus view among managers as to where the greatest opportunities for IT investment lie—especially if done in a workshop setting. The disadvantage is that this approach can be too introspective and subjective and is too easily affected by strongly held views of individual vociferous managers.

Product Market Analyses   For product-focused companies with clearly articulated product market strategies, Figure 32.2 illustrates some appropriate systems objectives for each stage of the product life cycle. For products marked with a question mark (?), primary system objectives might be collection of information on potential products and markets to facilitate new product development. Organizations with many people and significant costs in this area might use groupware to enhance internal coordination among *new product development* (NPD), sales, and marketing, breaking down traditional functional barriers. The objectives are reduced communications costs, enhanced likelihood of successful NPD, and a significantly quicker product development cycle.

For products marked with the star in Figure 32.2, a primary market objective might be to build market share as cheaply and quickly as possible. Systems might be used to get rapid feedback on the effectiveness of sales and marketing campaigns. Because building market share in growing markets is often cheaper, valid system objectives might be to obtain new customers, increase market share, improve decision-making about marketing campaign effectiveness, and understand the market. For example, a high-technology products company might use SAP order entry to record market segment information at the time of entry, such as how the products will be used, so that better information on the effectiveness of marketing strategies can be obtained.

Strategically inclined companies with aspirations of large market shares use systems at this stage to build entry barriers through blocking distribution, creating significant product differentiation, locking new customers into long-term loyalty programs, or building switching costs.

Systems used to support "cash cow" products tend to have more defensive objectives. As the rate of market growth declines, building market share becomes more expensive. Also, as competition intensifies, products become less differentiated and prices fall. You might also find that the market is flooded with too much product, because competitors have continued to plan for product expansion without sufficiently anticipating the slowdown in market growth.

FIGURE 32.2

The market objectives for SAP projects can be identified by reference to product portfolios and product life cycles.

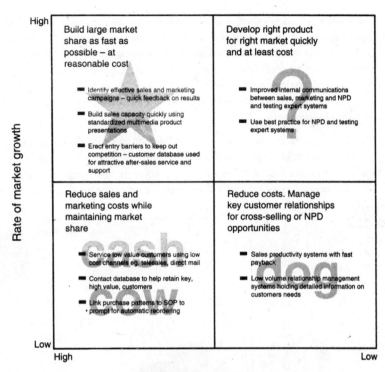

Relative market share

© Hewson Consulting Group

Cash cow system objectives might include reducing costs, making better use of existing resources, increasing customer service (as a way of maintaining product differentiation for as long as possible), and retaining customers. At this stage, a cash cow's market might be subsegmented into customers by future profit potential, for example. Computer-aided techniques, such as direct marketing, can be used to service low-profit–potential customers more cost-effectively. Relationship management (or key account management) systems might be used to increase the quality of service provided to high-potential customers. Economies of scale might be achieved by using marketing databases to cross-sell.

More strategic uses of systems might be to build entry barriers to keep out new, low-cost competition and thereby maintain the status quo for as long as possible.

For dogs in declining product markets, a company might want to reduce sales and marketing costs, increase operating efficiencies, eliminate competitors, or even, if sufficiently committed to the market, put off new entrants. Frequently, companies with declining products—but high customer knowledge and loyalty—use relationship management systems to cross-sell new products to a loyal customer base and identify opportunities for new product development.

Customer Needs and Opportunities Analysis   Customer-focused companies will want to use a customer life-cycle analysis to review the link between their systems and sales and marketing strategies. This analysis classifies customers according to their business potential and the compatibility of their needs with an organization's product offerings. The goal is to identify key customers and then to analyze how well in relation to the competition your products and services meet their requirements. It's a variation of the directional policy matrix traditionally used for product markets, which seeks to establish and present, as the basis of future action, how well in comparison to the competition an organization's existing products and services fit customer requirements.

It's important to assess compatibility relative to the competition and from the customers' point of view. Customers are classified into *agnostics, seeds, allies,* and *dogs* (see Figure 32.3). Customer strategies can be developed for each group, and sales and marketing systems' objectives can be focused more precisely on the areas of greatest profit potential.

FIGURE 32.3
Segmenting customers
and developing
customer strategies.

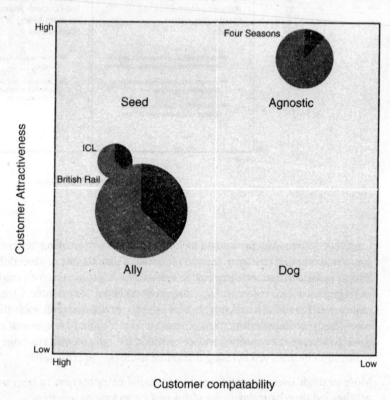

© Hewson Consulting Group

After you fine-tune your customer strategies, the next step is to ensure that the planned systems expenditure delivers benefits that closely support those strategies. For example, if you intend for your investment in SAP to support a customer retention strategy by improving customer service, you should justify it on the basis of a customer needs survey.

The critical areas for action revealed by customer needs surveys should be reflected in sales and marketing strategies and should be linked to sales and marketing system features. Figures 32.4 and 32.5 show how you can relate customer needs to customer retention strategies and cascade them down to IS objectives. The systems implications for each objective can be made explicit at this stage.

FIGURE 32.4

Using a customer needs survey to make systems more customer-focused.

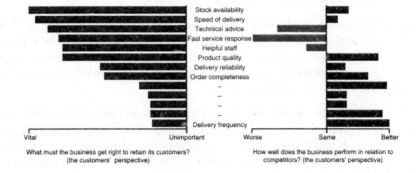

© Hewson Consulting Group

FIGURE 32.5

An example of linking sales and marketing systems' features to strategies.

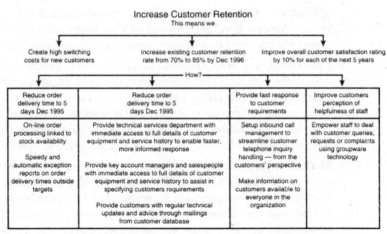

© Hewson Consulting Group

Using these formal techniques makes explicit the relationship between proposed sales and marketing systems and an organization's marketing and sales strategies. Unsupported assertions that "the system is essential to our strategies" typically indicate that benefits haven't been properly thought through. Systems proposals that don't support sales and marketing strategies should be rejected, or the strategies themselves should be reexamined. Only after the system is related to acceptable sales and marketing strategies should the most appropriate evaluation methods—financial or otherwise—be considered.

Assess the Impact of Risk

All large gains arise from a bet against poor odds. Do they? HCG's research shows that most respondents perceive the use of sales and marketing systems as low risk. The riskiness of any system is important, because the amount of risk determines the likelihood that planned benefits won't be achieved or that the budgeted costs will be exceeded. In this sense, from a practical viewpoint, risk is the same as uncertainty.

For example, the types of risks that may affect sales and marketing systems fall into three categories: technical, user, and market. The first two risks could be applied to any SAP module. Other risks may pertain to other SAP modules, too, such as legislative requirements imposed by governments (for example, new taxes to be applied to particular types of goods). You need to address each of these risks:

- **Technical risk.** Will the software, hardware, and communications actually work? This applies to any system, regardless of function. A system that works too slowly, crashes, or fails to accept or output information can seriously decrease user acceptance and enthusiasm. You can minimize technical risks by using proven combinations of software, hardware, and communications. This is particularly critical for systems that use distributed databases, support remote users on a WAN, or require file transfers to and from portable computers. Technical risks can also be minimized, at a cost, by using pilot studies and extensive testing before the system is implemented.

  SAP software itself probably offers the lowest possible risk in terms of software performance. However, it will perform only as it has been configured to, and it depends on the proper functioning of its hardware platform and communications equipment.

- **User risk.** Users take longer than planned to benefit from the system. How will users react to the system? Will they feel threatened, coerced, or resentful? How will the system change their existing status, job satisfaction, workflow, processes, or daily routine? Is their existing compensation package still appropriate? Therefore, how long will users likely take to learn how to use the system and to start to obtain the benefits? All these risks are manageable, providing that each is properly addressed.

- **Market risk.** Customers or markets change, making the current sales and marketing strategies invalid. This is the risk that, having installed your sales and marketing system, something dramatic happens in the marketplace that invalidates your current strategy. For example, the success of a low-cost foreign competitor might make the market economically unfeasible to pursue, particularly if your costs are highly geared (high fixed cost, low avoidable cost). Other factors might include government legislation affecting permitted sales and distribution channels, rapid changes in consumer preferences, technological advances or breakthroughs leading to product obsolescence, or industrywide decisions affecting many customers.

  The importance of assessing the likelihood of changes in your markets is key for major sales and marketing systems with long development time scales, large fixed costs, and long payback periods.

Project Risks (User and Market)   Project risks are the most likely type of risk to cause a project to fail. Here are some project risks and advice to overcome them:

- **Lack of top management commitment.** Provide full information on project costs and benefits, and ensure that you get the buy-in of senior management.

- **Failure of senior people to understand the solution.** Hold walk throughs explaining the way things will be when the new system is implemented.

- **Fear of cost levels.** Don't consider the costs in isolation from the benefits.

- **Inadequate budget set.** Use a conservative cost/benefit analysis to create the budget, while expecting to spend less.

- **Doubts as to whether benefits will be achieved.** Produce a rigorous cost/benefit analysis and get buy-in from senior management, who should take responsibility for the benefits to be realized.

- **Lack of interest by end users.** Run a "sales campaign" for the systems.

- **Lack of commitment from first-line management.** Focus on distinct benefits for managers.

- **Inability to define requirements.** Use prototyping to obtain sufficient user involvement.

- **Inexperience in projects of this scale.** Learn from other people's experience.

- **Poor use of systems in the field** (and thus underachievement of benefit levels). Change business processes to make an element of system use mandatory.

- **System falling into disuse after initial euphoria.** Plan for continual updating of systems, and budget for them.

- **Project failing due to inertia.** Buy the right level of external assistance. Give someone experienced an incentive to make it work. Don't buy external assistance as a commodity.

Steps to Minimize General Technical Risks   Here are some technical risks and advice on overcoming them:

- **Use of new, unproved technology.** Buy external expertise.

- **Use of old technology (in packaged solution).** Don't go only for solutions that have worked—they probably use old technology and are narrow in scope.

- **Inadequate current internal skill levels.** Accept that it will always be impossible to keep up with all new advances, and provide a skills transfer program on the technology chosen.

- **Fear of technological cul-de-sac given the current pace of change.** Appropriate technical architecture can "future-proof" developments by making them reusable alongside later applications.

- **Inability of current technical architecture to support new developments.** Develop new, flexible technical architecture using modern methodology.

- **Inability of data architecture to support distributed systems.** Rigorous data analysis is the key to avoiding integrity problems. You can buy experience by employing an experienced person or contracting another company to provide the expertise.

- **A human/computer interface that is too complex.** Prototype during development using a range of users, and test for usability.

- **Lack of experience in GUI systems design.** Take the best ideas from the market.

- **Problems changing old mainframe systems.** "Ring fence" old systems as far as possible, providing the flexibility to replace them later.

- **Inability to support applications after initial development** (for example, package implementation, turnkey solution). Ensure that mixed teams of in-house and external staff complete development.

- **Difficulty supporting distributed users.** Beginning early in the project, consider what might be an appropriate level of outsourcing or resource support.

- **Late delivery of software.** Set expectations carefully, and plan phased implementation, allowing applications slippage.

- **Hardware delivery problems.** Plan a contingency for each item.

- **Impact on core product processing systems.** "Ring fence" old systems with new and control interfaces. For example, you might "drip feed" data into old systems.

- **Implementing a number of partial solutions that don't work when integrated.** Verify system/application design end-to-end.

- **Central system development too large.** Phase functionality implementation with "quick wins," concentrating on areas of key business benefit.

Techniques for Evaluating Risks and Uncertainty

In cases where the intangible costs or benefits are significant but can be quantified only on a "best-guess" basis, you can use one or several of the following techniques to get a better fix on the intangibles.

Analyze Costs and Benefits Twice, Using the Most Optimistic/Most Pessimistic Estimates   The aim here is to identify how sensitive the cost-benefit analysis is to your assumptions on the monetary value of, for example, improved customer loyalty. You might find that the system can be cost-justified on a best- and worst-case basis, a best-case basis only, or on neither a best- nor a worst-case basis.

Use Probability to Estimate Expected Value of Costs and Benefits   If you're unsure about the extent of future costs and benefits but a number of possible outcomes are likely, you can use probability theory to calculate their value on a weighted average basis. A weighted average is best used in cases where a number of possible outcomes cover a continuum of benefits.

Suppose that you're unsure about the impact of the system on levels of sales and the sales mix. You can estimate the probability or likelihood of increased sales across various product lines or customer groups. You consider it highly probable that sales will increase by $15 million to $20 million, but the increase could actually be as great as $40 million. You set out these probabilities:

A. 40 percent chance of increased sales of $20 million

B. 40 percent chance of increased sales of $15 million

C. 10 percent chance of increased sales of $40 million

D. 10 percent chance of increased sales of $7 million

You then estimate the benefit that would be gained from each increased level of sales—in this case, the gross margin/contribution:

A. Benefit: $3,250,000

B. Benefit: $2,200,000

C. Benefit: $6,800,000

D. Benefit: $1,050,000

The expected benefit then is calculated by multiplying the estimated benefit of each increase in sales by the estimated probability of the increase being achieved. The expected benefit is the sum of the benefit of each outcome times the probability that the outcome will occur. In this example, the expected value of the sales forecasts is $2,965,000.

Benefit of Outcome	Probability of Outcome	Expected Benefit
A. $3,250,000	40%	$1,300,000–40% ×$3,250,000
B. $2,200,000	40%	$880,000–40% ×$2,200,000
C. $6,800,000	10%	$680,000–10% ×$6,800,000
D. $1,050,000	10%	$105,000–10% ×$1,050,000
Total Expected Value of Benefit:		**$2,965,000**

You can expand the expected value technique to allow for multiple probabilistic conditions linking—for example, the probabilities of initial and repeat sales. You can also use it with decision trees to model the expected value of the likely outcomes of several alternative scenarios over the life of the system.

You wouldn't use probability to calculate the weighted average of two very dissimilar outcomes, because the concept of a weighted average would be meaningless. For example, if you place a bet on the toss of a coin, $1 million each way, the weighted average outcome for you is zero—a 50 percent chance of winning $1 million and a 50 percent chance of losing the same amount. In this case, that the bet is worth zero on a weighted average basis is clearly not very helpful.

Identify Cost of Achieving Intangible Benefits   This method works back from the known costs and benefits to identify the residual level of cost that cannot be justified by the quantified benefits. For example, if the total cost of the system (including the cost of capital and inflation) is $1.25 million, but only $1 million worth of other (hard) benefits can be identified, to break even, the system has to generate an extra profit of $250,000 through increased sales or cost reductions. As a matter of business judgment, does your organization consider that resulting (but as yet unknown) increased levels in sales or cost reductions can justify the extra cost of $250,000? How much are you prepared to risk, and what does the $250,000 extra mean in terms of the extra turnover required? Is it a large or small increase on existing sales trends?

Use High Cost of Capital to Compensate for Risk   This method is the least preferable, although it's often used by large corporations to set project hurdle rates of return and business unit *return on investment* (ROI). The argument for the method is that the cost of capital for a project should take account of inflation and the risk premium required by investors. Therefore, high-risk projects have higher costs of capital. However, HCG has two objections to this method: it assumes that all the project's cash flows are equally risky, and it doesn't encourage management to investigate in detail the particular risks of a project.

Identify the "Real" Costs and Benefits

The system's real costs and benefits are the difference between the impact of the system and that of the next-best alternative. HCG always suggests that the systems investment should be compared to the next-best alternative. Companies tend to evaluate systems investments by using two scenarios: business with the system and business as it is now. They forget that the real decision is between the investment in SAP and the investment in the alternative system.

The choice of the base case or next-best alternative is also important but difficult. To decide whether the system is worthwhile and will add value to your company, you need to ask, "Add value in relation to what?" Other projects competing for resources may offer a better return. One of the best ways of getting board approval for a favored but not necessarily profitable project is to choose the "right" base case.

The real costs and benefits are the likely cash flows associated with the changes arising from the system. Notice that the emphasis is on cash, not profit. It's important to ignore accounting adjustments for depreciation and central overheads. Focus instead on how the system will change the cash going in and out of your organization. Carefully consider allocations of the costs of DP/IT department support. Do they have real cost implications? Consider also the cost of line management staff, particularly your sales and marketing staff's time. What does it cost in terms of lost business opportunities elsewhere? The opportunity costs of redirecting productive or creative employees from their front-line tasks are, almost without exception, ignored by organizations.

Estimating the monetary value of costs and benefits has been described as more of an art than a science. For sales and marketing-focused implementations of SAP in particular, costs and benefits are particularly difficult to estimate for two reasons:

- The extent and nature of the system's potential impact. Introducing a system may change how you advertise, promote, or sell your products.

- The intangible (or intermediate) nature of some benefits and the uncertainty as to the final outcome.

Table 32.1 shows a checklist of costs and benefits.

Table 32.1   A Checklist of Costs and Benefits

Type	Comment
Hardware	Initial purchase cost plus maintenance
Software, networks, and communications	Initial purchase cost plus maintenance, support, upgrades, and organization-specific work
Project management and use of IT or support departments	If you get charged for the use of, for example, your IT department, you might be inclined to include the charges as a consulting cost. If your organization doesn't have guidelines as to how you should treat the costs of other internal departments, you should consider the impact your system will have on those departments. Include only costs that will be incurred by internal departments as a result of their contribution toward your proposed system.
Publicizing the system/training	Cost of training courses, lost time of staff, manuals, and so on
Data transfer to new system	Cost of transferring data on customers, prospects, and so on to the new system
Productivity lag	Cost of the time spent by your staff being trained, understanding the system, changing the way they do things, and overcoming the learning curve. The costs will be a mixture of reduced administrative efficiency (overtime payments) and possible reductions or delays in achieving forecast sales.
Revenues/savings	Before you start to identify areas where savings can be made, you need to estimate the change between how you do things now and how you plan to do things in the future.
Increased sales	There are two ways of calculating the benefit. If sales could be increased another way (through employing more salespeople or increased advertising, for example), the benefit is the costs saved by not increasing sales through the best viable alternative method. If there is no viable alternative, the benefit is the contribution the increased sales will make to your bottom line (normally, sales revenues less direct costs).
Better sales mix	*Better sales mix* means increasing the sales of higher-margin or key strategic products.
Better customer mix	*Better customer mix* means selling to your most profitable or key strategic customers. This might mean customers who buy high-margin products with a high probability of repeat or additional sales.
Greater customer loyalty	The benefit, as with increased sales, can be calculated as the costs saved through not adopting the best viable alternative. Or, you can calculate the value of the sales contribution.

continues

Table 32.1   Continued

Type	Comment
Direct response advertising	Cost savings will depend on the goals of the system. Is it to increase the number of leads for the same expenditure, to reduce expenditure to obtain the same number of leads, or to obtain better-quality leads (in which case the costs savings will be later in the sales cycle)? If the reasons for advertising are mixed (for example, direct response plus market presence), reducing advertising expenditure might have a hidden cost.
People costs savings	People costs will be saved if the activities that cause costs are reduced in number (for example, reducing the number of backorders), or the administration process is improved. For all people costs savings, you should include salaries, pensions, National Insurance contributions (in the UK), bonuses, car costs (but not necessarily gas/travel), recruitment and nonproductive time of new hires, training, travel, and so on. However, for small or incremental headcount reductions, it's generally inappropriate to also include savings in office overhead, payroll administration, and so on, because none of these savings is likely in practice to occur. The same logic applies to salespeople's costs savings.
Staff motivation and loyalty	For all types of staff, increased motivation and loyalty should lead to reduced staff turnover. The benefits are savings in recruitment and training costs, as well as the ability to avoid initial low productivity as new employees work through the learning curve. For administrative staff, increased motivation should, over time, contribute to efficiency gains. Even if you can't identify specific future headcount reductions resulting from efficiency improvements, it generally is realistic to assume that if efficiency improves by, say, 10% over the life of the system, your headcount-related costs will be reduced by an equivalent amount.
More accurate sales forecasting	The benefits will depend on the way you produce your goods and services. For some organizations, better sales forecasting enables reductions in inventory (which provide savings on stockholding costs), production to be scheduled more efficiently (at lower unit cost), and the risk of stock obsolescence to be reduced.
Reduced sales lead time	Reducing your sales lead time tends to result in a one-off benefit of accelerating revenue collection.
Potential for cross-selling	As with increases in sales, there are two ways of calculating the benefit: the costs saved by not cross-selling using the best viable alternative method; or, if there is no viable alternative, the benefit of the contribution the increased sales will make to your bottom line (normally sales revenues less direct costs).

Type	Comment
Ability to respond to competition or changes in the marketplace	Very difficult to quantify! The benefit depends on the strength and style of your existing and future competition. In highly competitive and volatile markets, it's worth more to be able to notify customers of price and product changes and to be able to adapt your sales techniques quickly than it is in less competitive and less volatile markets. The benefits can be assessed in a number of ways: the costs of the best viable alternative, the reduced identified risks, or the expected value of the cost of not being able to respond to market or competitive risks.

Project Initiation

There is often a blur between the concept of SAP being implemented and an SAP project being initiated. It's possible for an SAP project to be initiated and for the conclusion to be that it will not be implemented, although I have never heard of this happening. *SAP project initiation* is the time at which a formal management decision is made to start a project.

Who Should Initiate the Project?

The first question that arises is whether business or systems people should initiate the SAP project. The people running the business use SAP systems. It's therefore logical that these same people should initiate the project. Unfortunately, the people running the business aren't always systems experts and aren't necessarily aware of the benefits that SAP could bring to their business.

The key question, therefore, is "Who will initiate the project, and why?" It would be more obvious if existing systems didn't meet the business requirements, because it would naturally become an issue that needs to be resolved. However, in most companies where SAP has been implemented, previous systems were in place that generally could meet the existing business requirements. Why, therefore, should anyone consider implementing SAP?

The answer probably lies in strategy. Good managers are continually looking at ways to improve their company, and consider the short-, medium-, and long-term future of the business. Considerations of products, plants and equipment, markets, and sales will probably be higher on the manager's agenda than systems, which are often regarded as costly overheads.

No doubt SAP can contribute enormously to the success of major companies, yet it's very difficult to actually quantify that contribution. Senior managers who ultimately will have to make the decision to move to SAP are going to have to read SAP literature and articles in their management magazines or attend specialist conferences and seminars to understand what SAP could do for their company.

IT employees are much more likely to know about SAP and to have a greater understanding of the technical and operating benefits than the businesspeople. The logical conclusion is that business managers and systems people should work together to initiate the project.

Difficulties Management Faces in Understanding the Issues

Managers face a very difficult task in understanding the important issues relating to the implementation of SAP, in advance and during the project itself. The demand on managers' time is the greatest limiting factor in their understanding of the issues that arise. They are paid to do the very demanding job of running the business, yet are faced with an additional workload that could arguably justify a full-time job in itself.

In this imperfect situation, managers are in a difficult position. They choose to educate themselves in SAP so that they can understand most of the issues themselves, or pay someone to advise them. Most often, they choose the latter, but with this comes the risk of bearing the cost of bad advice. Also, the advisors will probably not know as much about the individual business requirements as the managers themselves know.

TIP   My advice to managers is to get some training on SAP and use a variety of independent advisors to get as balanced a view as possible. You should be concerned if you're receiving conflicting advice, and you should avoid making any decisions until you fully understand the issues.

Impact of Project Development Policy

Many issues arise out of SAP project development, and it's advisable to develop a formal policy to give guidance to everyone concerned. The first issue is whether the project should be secret or open at the feasibility stage.

SAP projects invariably start with some sort of feasibility assessment. The initial investigations into the possibilities of using SAP frequently form part of a wider strategy study. Because these types of studies frequently look at the possibility of radical changes, discussions often take place behind closed doors. These simple brainstorming exercises can easily lead to rumors of massive job cuts or reorganizations spreading through the company grapevine, which can be very damaging to staff morale.

When ideas considered by many to be negative are bounced around organizations, there is an understandable rallying call by the opposition, which uses all the tools in its armory to defeat or knock new plans off-course. Some of the many tactics used include lobbying senior.management, trying to discredit plans, and talking about ruin and disaster. Management plans become twisted in the rumor mill and stories get changed in the telling, all of which is completely unproductive.

However, the case for secrecy in the feasibility stage has some advantages. You should consider using confidentiality agreements with project team members. The management team has a choice of announcing that a feasibility study is going on and stating when the results will be available, or keeping the whole thing completely hush-hush and announcing the plans when they are ready. Each choice has its own merits and disadvantages that have to be weighed by the executive management team. The greatest danger is that a secret study will become common knowledge, which could lead to a feeling of conspiracy.

Early Consideration of Control and Security

Control and security are very important and should be considered from the earliest stages of a project. It's well worth forming a special advisory team to investigate and advise you on the relevant issues. Such a team should include the internal audit manager, the system security manager, and representative line managers from the user community. It's well worth involving an SAP security and controls consultant to advise you from the earliest planning stages through to implementation and beyond.

There probably will not be any security or control issues that cannot be resolved. However, the integrated nature of SAP can give rise to security problems if not properly addressed. The overall system can be adequately controlled and security maintained in many ways. Job segregation, authorizations for particular system transactions, and control reports can all be used. Third-party access to the system must also be considered, for customers and suppliers.

Simply configuring the system properly can resolve many issues. In many cases, the move to SAP involves going back to the drawing board to develop security and control policies and procedures. You will be most vulnerable to security breaches at the time of implementation, when there might be uncertainty, many temporary employees, and heavy workloads for everyone. Possible redundancies and uncertainties might cause loyal employees to become unsettled, and the remote chance of system sabotage or fraud should never be taken lightly. Those who work closely with the system will be well aware of any holes in security.

Project Methodology

To stand any chance of successfully implementing SAP on time, within budget, and to a good standard, you must adopt a formal project methodology. You will receive useful guidance from SAP and its business partners, and you will find plenty of independent consultants with a wide variety of offerings. There isn't one correct implementation method; you must judge each on its merits.

The project methodology can be split into two parts. The first area deals with the system configuration and implementation, and the second deals with every other aspect of the project and change.

The first area has been addressed so comprehensively by SAP that you need to look no further. The experience gained by more than 4,500 SAP installations has been channeled into the development of specialist tools that provide an unbeatable framework to model business processes and configure the system. The SAP Procedure Model offers project and implementation management guidance. It provides a detailed guide of every stage of the project from the earliest planning stages through postinstallation operation.

Procedure Model   The Procedure Model is now an integral component of R/3. It provides guidance on the entire implementation process, including organizational and concept design, detailed design and system setup, preparations needed for going live, and production operation. It covers the following processes:

- **Organization and conceptual design.** Project preparation, setting up system environments, training the project team, defining functions and processes, designing interfaces and enhancements, project management

- **Detailed design and system setup.** Conceptual design, including quality checks; establishing global settings, company structures, master data, and functions and processes; creating interfaces and enhancements; establishing reporting, archiving management, and authorization management; system testing; developing application systems

- **Preparations for going live.** Creating the going-live plan and user documentation, setting up the production environment, training users, establishing system administration, transferring data to the production system, supporting quality systems

- **Production operation.** Supporting production operation, maximizing production operation, system maintenance and release upgrades

The Procedure Model uses these items:

- **IMG (Implementation Management Guide).** Documents system settings during configuration.

- **SAPoffice.** Stores and edits text and graphical information created during the course of project work. It offers links to PC packages such as Microsoft Word, Excel, PowerPoint, and Lotus Screen Cam.

- **Business Navigator.** Displays graphical models of business processes and functions.

R/3 Business Engineering Workbench   Chapter 29, "Developing ABAP/4 Programs with the R/3 Workbench," describes the R/3 Business Engineering Workbench, which is designed to do the following:

- Dramatically reduce implementation times by focusing on the most essential elements.

- Facilitate postconfiguration and change management across releases throughout the entire life cycle of R/3.

- Supply a complete business repository in the form of active business reference models, along with their configuration options.

- Demonstrate how process-driven configuration can be used to control the customizing process.

Procuring SAP Services

The blistering speed of change within the technological arena implies that many critical decisions are made on obsolete data (yesterday's facts). To be presumptuous in the IT environment today suggests ignorance. Never has information been so readily available to anybody interested in being at the cutting edge (real-time/online) of technology.

The problem shouldn't be the "best-fit" selection of hardware and software for a business, but instead the evolution of the selection. Thus, a successful SAP implementation isn't complete without an adequate technical SAP R/3 infrastructure. To create an alliance with the best supplier of computer services, you need a plan that predicts your long-term expenditure. This plan should look into the implications of a *request for quotation* (RFQ). The following areas illustrate the breadth of the exercise:

- Risk reduction
- Cost implications
- Rental cost versus purchasing
- Installation cost
- Service implications
- Warranty versus guarantee
- Service response times
- Legal implications
- Ownership of customization
- Nondelivered goods/services
- Technical implications
- Technical system changes
- Backup procedures
- Replacement services
- Supplier profile
- Organizational capabilities
- Financial strengths
- Future growth planning purposes
- Staffing requirements
- Training requirements
- Technical support structure
- Software patches
- Hardware fixes
- Installation plan
- Servers and software PC rollout plan

The mammoth sizing, scoping, and planning work for SAP in determining the options of various solutions must finally be crystallized—that is, you must find the hardware and software platform.

Project managers have often used a tender process for various requests and find themselves comfortable with this inquiry tool. Experience has shown that SAP R/3 platform tenders had left some questions open, particularly when you discuss the comparative analysis processes. As a tender strategist, you can develop many methods to achieve structured responses. The RFQ in Appendix B, "Example Request for Quotation of SAP Services," is an example that has been used very successfully by various management consultants and companies to provide a structured and reliable response from the service supplier.

What Type of Tenders Exist?

In many countries, you have to consider the legal implications of using words such as *tender,* *quotation,* or *proposal.* The tendering process is often a governmental request to get pricing of services or goods, whereby not only quantitative but also qualitative information is taken into account. The legal terms for each country are different but are mostly handled by a tender committee, which is governed by the tender board rules. A more commercial version is the *request for proposal* (RFP), whereby implicit in the statement is that you receive an offer of services or goods.

A much more deterministic approach would be the RFQ, whereby you, the requester, provide and define the boundaries of the expected solution. This approach seems to be more exacting, because you already know the product (SAP R/3).

It is not sufficient to express that you will be implementing SAP R/3; instead you should build a framework for the supplier with rules of how to deliver these services. The framework and the rules are the ABCs of a comprehensive RFQ. It eliminates all vague expectations of the deliverables required by all parties involved.

In a complex systems plan, there are some imperatives, such as a correct mix of specialist resources and a careful consideration of each task's duration.

The RFQ Differentiater

The need for practical guidelines in an RFQ is based on the required predictability of an implementation plan. Often, companies provide the supplier with some questions, not knowing or being aware of the supplier having only a vague understanding of the requests related to the product serviced by the supplier.

Tender responses often answer the possible fit of a client's profile rather than his or her actual needs. Thus, an unclear picture is painted that results in disputes and potential litigation.

Managing the Tendering Process

Clarity of thought and professional help are the major success factors in this area. Like so many things in life, a little bit of effort up front pays huge dividends over time. Given that SAP implementations require considerable investment, there can be considerable cost implications when choosing a consulting partner.

Using the RFQ example in Appendix B should be a starting point. ASAP World Consultancy is one of relatively few companies that offer specialist consulting services in this area. The firm's procurement consultancy practice manager says, "We believe that three areas of expertise are required: legal, accounting, and implementation knowledge. We provide a team bringing together the highest caliber people with these areas of expertise. Our service might be expensive, but it must surely be a wise investment." Unfortunately, it's difficult for companies to keep control of costs and to differentiate between the many offerings of SAP consulting companies who are all trying very hard to differentiate themselves from each other.

Building a Project Team

Every project has a beginning, middle, and end. Therefore, a team that you bring together to pursue a project is "on board" for only a finite period of time. For many, their place on a project is a temporary position where they are on loan from their existing job, and they might still owe allegiance to another role and another taskmaster. As such, many team members have half of their thoughts still on the job they have come from and the other half on what will become of them when the project is over. This leaves the project manager with the challenge of enlisting the team members' best efforts in service of the project—a job that can be likened to herding cats.

Of all the skills a project manager must master, therefore, the ability to build a strong and cohesive team must be at the top of the list. But the pursuit of this Holy Grail has left many otherwise highfliers exhausted and confused on the wayside.

So what is it that makes a team? What are the basic ingredients of the recipe for teamwork? And in what order should they be added to the mix? The following list of ingredients should be considered and added to the pot in sequential order:

1. Determine the requirements of a project manager.
2. Choose a project manager.
3. Determine the requirements of a project advisor.
4. Devise roles of project team members.
5. Draw up project team organization charts.
6. Determine how projects fit within the traditional organizational structure.
7. Determine how projects fit within the new organizational structure.
8. Recruit/assemble the right team.

Choosing a Project Manager

Step one is to choose a project manager. The sooner in the planning process you do so, the better. Few things are more motivating to a person than to have the opportunity to oversee and contribute to the plan that they will later be expected to carry out. Therefore, it's important to select the person for the job and to brief him or her as early in the process as possible.

But where do you find the person with the "right stuff?" The project manager is the person responsible for a project being completed on time, within budget, and to the agreed-on specifications. It's a demanding task, and successful project managers have much to be proud of. In fact, anyone who shows they can successfully run a project is usually so highly thought of that they are soon promoted to a line management post worthy of their proven organizational skills. Unfortunately, the flip side of the project manager's red carpet to corporate stardom is a dearth of experienced project managers ready and willing to take on the next project.

To compound the problem, the lifestyle of a project manager in these days of globalization is rarely conducive to a happy family life. Project managers are expected to spend many nights away from home and at the very least will spend many a late evening at the office. This makes it difficult to find experienced people who are truly content to be at the beck and call of a project.

What should you do? Appoint an experienced hand despite his or her family commitments, or some young "flier" whose enthusiasm and lack of family ties is in inverse proportion to work experience? The answer might lie somewhere between the two extremes. Combine one's experience with the other's flexibility. Consider appointing youth to the role of project manager and experience to the role of resident advisor. If they can work hand in hand (admittedly, this is no small "if"), you might just have a recipe for success and a project management template that could have many applications within your organization.

The project manager's role is "hands on" regardless of time or place, whereas the advisor's role can be mainly confined to being "in residence" and available during normal working hours. Moreover, world time differences are dissolved these days through voice mail and email, and shouldn't hinder the parties maintaining a valuable working relationship.

What Should You Require of a Project Manager?   From the project manager, you will want at least minimal competence and abilities in several areas.

Corporate Standing   The project manager must command influence within the organization commensurate with the importance of the project entrusted to him or her. Project managers must draw on corporate resources and will often need to scavenge these resources with at least the connivance of those "in charge."

Interpersonal Skills   These skills are needed to recruit and lead a diverse group of people—many who will likely be strangers to each other and to the project manager, regardless of the time they have spent working in the same company. This person has the important job of enlisting hearts, heads, and hands 100 percent in service of the project.

Cultural Sensitivity   You will also expect someone who is at least aware of the importance of cultural differences, even if they need to brush up on the particular cultures they will likely face in bringing a project to term.

Energy and Drive   Some people have the kind of life force that others may call *charisma*. This quality is especially important in creating the kind of tight coalition of minds that project management requires.

Business Savvy   Project managers must be aware of the business case. They must know where the project fits into overall business strategy. The more comprehensive the implementation of SAP, the more the demands in this respect and the more senior this person will need to be.

Technical Know-How   To earn respect from the team and to competently assess the risk factors associated with the project, project managers must be able to show a full grasp of the major issues, even though many details will be outside their experience.

Project Management   You will need someone who has worked in a project environment and who is aware of the phases that a project goes through, particularly the importance of controlling and reducing the time taken to navigate the critical path. Add to this an ability to keep costs under control.

What Should You Require of a Project Advisor?   Your project advisor should be a person of rank and someone who dominates their subject. They are at the center of your organization's claim to be a "learning organization." They should exhibit the following qualities.

Project Management   A project advisor will have a number of successful projects tucked under his or her belt.

Mentoring Skills   Advisors will also be people of "character"—people project managers actively seek to consult because of the way they listen and offer advice.

Well-Networked   If advisors cannot offer help from their own experience, they should know and be able to seek out other experienced hands to whom they can refer the project manager.

Devising Roles of Project Team Members

Team members should be enrolled as early in the project process as possible so that they can participate at an early stage in the planning phase. But the desire to populate the project must give way to the need to build the project team correctly. The flow chart on the left side of Figure 32.6 shows the traditional way that organizations and project teams tend to be constructed. That is, you look at who is available, invite them to join, assign roles, and then turn to the task to see what exactly needs to be done and what skills will be demanded of those present.

FIGURE 32.6
The traditional approach versus the process approach.

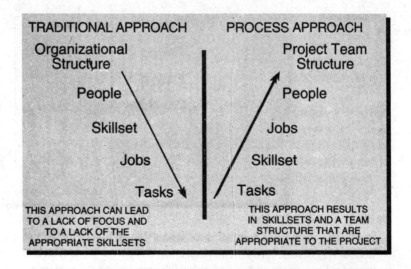

A more appropriate way of approaching this aspect of team building is illustrated on the right side of Figure 32.6, where the structure of the project team is designed as an outcome of processes, roles, and skills. This methodology is generated from the ideas developed by CSC Index, the management consultants that brought us process reengineering.

The flow chart on the right achieves a strong fit between the demands of the project and what the team members have to offer. This can only be motivating for team members and good for the project's outcome.

Drawing Up Project Team Organization Charts

As a result of planning roles, you will develop a firm idea of who does what and how each team member interrelates with the others. In SAP projects, traditional hierarchical organizational diagrams are inappropriate for faithfully representing the flow of information and the direction of project reporting lines. Roles tend to be varied, with people frequently reporting to different managers for different parts of their work.

What you need is a new way of thinking about and graphically displaying the interrelationships to help people change the way in which they view project management.

How Projects Fit Within Organizational Structures   In the past, project management in traditional stovepipe companies would cut across the pipes, drawing out their needs as and when required (see Figure 32.7). But this model leaves project managers without the most important traditional management tool—hierarchical position. Many projects owe their premature demise to the project manager's lack of corporate clout.

FIGURE 32.7

In a stovepipe structure, power lies with the functions; projects are a side issue.

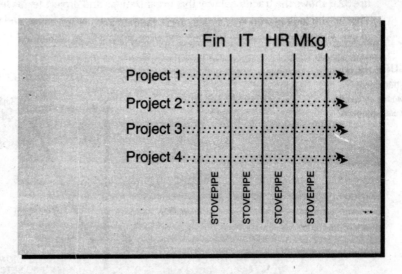

So what happens when you can't base leadership on hierarchy? In a project team that cuts horizontally across departmental functions, there is no top and no bottom; the membership is organized in a circle, and the group's willingness to put the project manager at the center of it will determine the team's success. Such willingness can come only from respect and trust, and these two forces combine to glue the team together (see Figure 32.8).

FIGURE 32.8
In the absence of hierarchy, the team's willingness to put the project manager at the center is critical.

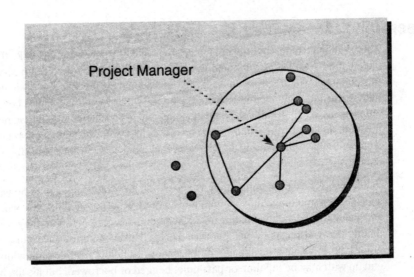

Project Manager

How Do Projects Fit Within the New Organizational Structure?
The changing market and industry conditions are leading to a slow breakdown of the stovepipe model of organization. Departmental empires are being toppled and are rising from the ashes in service to projects (see Figure 32.9).

FIGURE 32.9
Independent departments are being replaced with project-oriented teams.

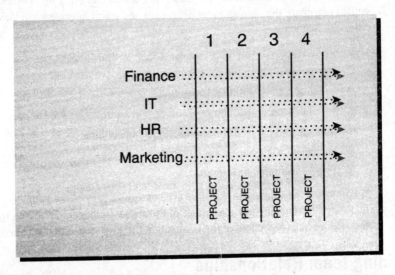

As the departments rise from the ashes, they are unrecognizable in their new incarnation. Instead of being well-entrenched baronies, they are now loose affiliations and networks of people whose main allegiance is to a project but who have common (often professional) interests, be they in human resources, information systems, or safety at work.

Recruiting/Assembling the Right Team

After you determine the roles that need to be filled by analyzing the tasks that need to be completed and the skills they demand (see "Devising Roles of Project Team Members" earlier in this chapter), you are ready to seek the right people for the job. Each role demands a particular mix of attributes and competencies. If your HR department maintains a central register of employees that shows the package of competencies each one has, all you need to do is browse through and select the people you need. More likely, however, no such register exists in your company, and you must rely on people's reputations within the organization to guide your choices.

In any event, resist the temptation to select only the people you get along with. Such a narrow specification might exclude talented newcomers or forgotten old-timers who might have the exact skills you need. No matter who you end up bringing together, they will need some help finding the best ways to work together. This is true even if they have worked alongside each other before (as covered shortly in the section "Building Team Relationships"). The team you end up with may be full-time or part-time, begged or borrowed, but it's likely in any event that you will have a mixture of the following types of team players.

Employees   Employees are directly employed members of your company, chosen above all for their technical and administrative skills.

Consultants   Consultants are outside experts who can bring in technical skills and others you enlist to facilitate the management processes and teach interpersonal skills. They might include the following:

- SAP business partners
- Independent SAP contractors
- Documentation/training consultants
- Human issues consultants
- Internal and external communications consultants
- Specialist SAP security consultants
- Project planning consultants

Customers   Customers in this case are representatives of the people the project is designed to serve. This may include a member of the senior management team if the project is internally focused, or an actual client of the company if the project is externally focused.

Building Team Relationships

If anyone knows about building relationships, it must be the military. In a profession where lives hang on teamwork, team spirit is a top priority. If someone is charged with watching your back, you want to be able to rely on that person 100 percent. Therefore, when not actively engaged in defending the country, the military works on building team spirit. The result is a regimental pride that stays with its members forever. It's not achieved by accident. The officers—people who know how to mold a disparate group into a team—carefully craft it. The result is a fitness for purpose and a readiness to go into action.

So much for the military—what about "real" life? How do you build the kind of relationships you can depend on in civilian life, relationships that work outside the hierarchy that are strong enough to survive the rough and tumble of life outside the secure walls of the departmental edifices? How, in other words, do you ensure that you have a real "relationship" and not just a "relation-dinghy?"

This is the concern of every organization that has realized the importance of basing its future on trust and camaraderie rather than fear and autocracy. These companies are beginning to appreciate that if they want to emulate the military's exceptional teamwork, they must put a similar emphasis on instilling the necessary behaviors—preferably before the rubber hits the ground and the team scatters in all directions in pursuit of their various tasks. Here are some concrete steps you can take to create strong teamwork:

1. Appoint team-building specialists to manage the process, emphasizing self-awareness and communications skills. If outdoor adventure training or yachting is part of the package, fine, but the kernel of this work should be to intensively investigate each team member's preferred way of operating. The team must learn what communications methods can overcome their stylistic differences and get everyone working well together.

2. Agree on a strategy that covers not only team building, but also team maintenance during the term of the project. You might want to schedule team-maintenance interventions far ahead on the calendar; otherwise, such maintenance will likely be overlooked in the heat of battle.

3. Brief the entire team, including consultants and customers, on the way in which teamwork is to be developed and maintained. Ensure that each participant has a personal reason for taking part, so that individual advantage is the basis for team advantage.

4. Assemble all team members at an off-site location (to minimize office distractions). This kind of work typically takes a number of days—not necessarily all at once, but it usually involves a night or two in residence at the conference site. Select a hotel that reflects the importance you feel should be given to the issue of teamwork.

Adopting Effective Working Practices

If you've been assigned as project manager, how do you go about instilling effective working practices in your team? This is especially important when your team members are on board because of their proficiency in areas of which you have minimal knowledge. Indeed, some projects can involve a multitude of different skill sets.

And yet as project manager, you must guide the team in the right direction, and in doing so instill effective working practices. How can you do this? The answer is to shape the culture in which your team operates. The culture then helps to influence the behavior of the team.

Although management by objectives tells managers what they ought to do, and the proper organization of their job enables them to do it, it's the culture of the organization that determines whether they *will* do it. It's the culture that motivates, that calls on a person's reserves of dedication and effort, that decides whether that person gives of their best or just does enough to get by.

In running a project, you have an opportunity to shape the kind of culture you need. Even though you must do so within the context of the larger organizational culture, your team will look to you to set the tone for this particular project. Your ability to do so, and do it well, will seriously affect your success at completing the project on time, within budget, and to specifications.

Shaping culture entails a straightforward process of describing the behaviors you want and ensuring that they are displayed. But why would anyone want to change his or her behavior and perhaps have to act "out of character" just because it suits your ideal of the perfect culture? The answer can only be that it is in his or her best interest to do so. They must want to be involved for their own ends, whatever they may be. So your job as project manager is to find out your team members' agendas and to remain aware of them as they develop through the life of the project. The extent to which the project acts as a vehicle for the team members' own aspirations will determine the degree of effort you can expect from them. In simple terms, you must put out the bait. Remember, though, whereas all cats like fish, your team members will have a variety of reasons for enlisting on the project team.

So now you have a project to complete and a number of prospective team members. How can you shape a culture appropriate to the demands of the project? Here is a step-by-step guide:

1. Meet all team members individually. Brief them on the purpose of the project. Explain the roles you have in mind for them. Ask them to tell you the reasons they might accept the role—for example, how will the project further their own ambitions?

2. Articulate the project purpose to the team as a whole. Underscore the aspects of particular importance to the client. These are likely to include cost, time frame, and certain technical specifications. In some cases, where the final payback is likely to dwarf the development costs (as is typical in the pharmaceutical industry), cost of development might not be a critical issue, but the time taken to bring the product to the market is. Be clear about what actually counts.

3. Take time out to begin the task of building strong teamwork (see the preceding section, "Building Team Relationships").

4. Armed with the knowledge of each individual's goals, synthesize a vision for the project that encompasses their aspirations as well as those of your client. Your team can help you do this. *Synthesizing a vision* merely means describing, in as much detail as possible, what the project's outcome will look like, even what it will feel like. Add in the consequences of completing it on time, within budget, ahead of the competition, or whatever else raises the energy level of those present.

Now that you know what you want to achieve, how do you want to achieve it? You don't have to have a detailed plan at this point, but what overall means are you prepared to use to achieve your ends? This is about the values you hold important, the standards you want to underpin the operations of the team. This isn't a "would be nice if we had them" list, but instead a list of values that, if lived out, would definitely make a difference to the smooth running of the project and the achievement of your vision. Again, use your team to distill the core values.

Next, begin the process of underpinning the values by translating them into specific behaviors that you deem important. For example, if respect for others is a value that should govern the way things are done, what specific behaviors will show such respect in the workplace? Some examples might be keeping abreast of team members' ambitions, ensuring a balanced lifestyle for team members, and starting and ending meetings on time.

Put in place support structures to ensure that the agreed-on behaviors are adhered to. The extent to which each behavior is already entrenched will determine what kind of support structure will be needed to encourage its adoption. Some examples of support structures for the preceding behaviors might be introducing a periodic career review, locking the parking lot at 6 p.m., and starting promptly without waiting for latecomers. Of course, the team must agree on such structures for them to be acceptable, and they need to be maintained only up to the point that the desired behavior becomes the norm. Remember in all of this that people in general want to do their best, and if you've selected your team well, this will particularly apply to them. The emphasis of the structures you introduce isn't so much to penalize unproductive behavior but to make it very plain to all what *best* means in the context of your project.

Ensure that everyone is properly briefed on their part in the project and invited to take on certain responsibilities by the person or people from whom they take instruction. The word *invited* is used deliberately. Peter Drucker, doyen of management gurus, would have us think of the people who work for us as "volunteers" and treat them as such. If it makes sense to do so within the command and control structures of companies, it must definitely make sense to do so when enrolling people on a project outside the system, given that they often have a "day job" to return to.

Use the tried-and-tested (and computerized) project management tools where appropriate, such as these:

- **PERT and critical path management.** Focus attention on those activities that, if foreshortened, will advance completion of the project.
- **Gantt chart.** Preferred by many because of its ease of use.

Experienced project players might feel comfortable without these graphical aids. It really depends on the size of your project and the amount of resources you need to use and keep tabs on. One advantage of using these aids is that they are said to steepen the "worry curve," and thereby minimize the risk of leaving too much to the end of the project.

Provide timely and crystal-clear feedback to individuals on their performance and the contribution their behavior makes to the project culture as a whole.

Keys to Success

Most people want to have a successful project and implementation, but in such a complex area with so many different aspects to consider, it can be difficult to achieve. When complex details are removed, a number of key areas significantly affect the project's likely success. If these areas are dealt with well, there is a good likelihood that the project will be successful. These main keys to success are described in this section.

Know Your Business

To implement SAP, you need to know your business. Although you might think this seems obvious, and it can appear to be one of the easiest tasks to perform, it is in fact extremely difficult when you start to look closely at this area.

If you're considering implementing SAP, your company is probably fairly large, with lots of employees, departments, plants, locations, processes, and procedures that all have to interact with each other. When you start an SAP project, the issue of knowing your business appears to be relatively straightforward. You've probably worked in your business for many years and have a very wide experience of your company's operations.

For the purposes of implementing SAP, however, your knowledge must be at a very low, basic level. You need to know the smallest details. You need to know absolutely everything that goes on—every person's role, every procedure, every policy, and every detail on every subject you can possibly think about. You need to understand not only what's going on now, but also what things are in the process of changing.

Few businesses remain static, and markets and business requirements invariably change. Only by consulting everybody in the business—with no exceptions—can you begin to really know your business at the lowest level. You must not only understand your business in its current form, but you must also be aware of the direction in which it's moving. An example of this might be the knowledge of some governmental legislative changes with which your company will have to comply at some known date in the future.

It's highly unlikely that any one person, or indeed group of people, will know your business well enough for the purposes of implementation. The detailed knowledge of your business that you need is held by every employee, every temporary worker, every contract staff member, and perhaps even by another company that you've contracted to handle a particular side of your business, such as transport. An analogy of a huge jigsaw puzzle can demonstrate the situation. There are tens of thousands of tiny pieces, each holding unique information that's difficult to make sense of. Yet by bringing each tiny piece together, you can see the whole picture. If even a few small pieces are missing, the image is spoiled.

At the start of the project, it's common for people to find it hard to look at a low enough level. The detail is everything. If the detail is ignored at the beginning of the project, the problems that occur later on will multiply tenfold. If you don't really get to know your business early on in the project, in every likelihood your project will end up over budget and behind schedule.

However, the job of really getting to know your business is an awesome one. Be relentless in your search. Leave no stone unturned.

T I P   You can use the following practical ideas to get to know your business in the detail required for an SAP project:

- Involve everyone, including all employees, temporary staff, contractors, third-party companies, and possibly even customers.
- Find an effective way of documenting the business.

■ Divide up the areas of business that will likely be affected, and allocate responsibility to trusted
  ⸱ personnel. When people know they are accountable, they are likely to take the task very
    seriously.

Know Your Existing Systems

There is an obvious link between knowing your systems and knowing your business. However,
it will help you considerably if you catalog all your existing systems. Include mainframes, PCs,
and all other platforms in use by any person in the company, whether they are employees,
temporary staff, contractors, third-party companies, or even customers. You will need to get a
very thorough picture of your existing systems to be able to move toward implementing SAP.
For each system, you will need to record the system name, a description of its function, the
person in charge of it, the platform, interfaces, and comments.

Know Your Organization

One major company moving into a massive office designed and built to its exact specifications
was embarrassed to find that the building wasn't big enough to accommodate all the staff. The
reason for the situation was that each department had many temporary employees—some who
were administered by the HR department and others who were administered independently.
When the HR department was asked to provide details on the number of employees and temporary staff, they did so diligently, but they were simply not aware of all the other temporary
staff being used.

When implementing SAP, information must be checked and double-checked. Not only do you
need to know your own organization well, but you also need to know how it interrelates with
the environment in which you operate. For example, you might have temporary staff, contractors, customers, and suppliers involved in your business processes—all who may affect your
SAP development and planning. By knowing your organization, you are in a better position to
develop your vision for the future and implement SAP in a way that enables you to realize your
vision. For each person, you need to record the job title, job description, location, ID number of
the person now filling the position, department, status (contractor/temporary/supplier/cus-
tomer), direct supervisor, and who reports to him/her.

Know Your Objectives

Defining objectives can be particularly hard because there are invariably many of them. Defining clear objectives will help everybody: management, employees, and members of the project
team. It's very easy as the project progresses for everybody to forget the objectives that were
defined originally as the objective of simply implementing the system takes over and becomes
the main focus. If throughout the duration of the project everyone stays focused on the defined
objectives, you stand a much greater chance of achieving them.

 TIP   Write down the objectives, laminate them, and distribute them to all employees in the company and
members of the project team. They can pin up these objectives all around the work area so that
everyone is absolutely clear on the overall goals.

System Testing Overview

System testing is an integral part of the system development process. You must carry out the testing function by function, process by process, and then expand it to fully integrated tests. After you successfully complete the fully integrated tests, you must carry out the testing using as close to full live system volumes of processing as possible.

Testing is a vital part of project development and provides an excellent progress indicator. Tests must be well-planned and well-executed, and you must accurately record the results.

Planning and preparing for the tests is a major task and comes at times of maximum workload and pressure for system developers. It's only by splitting the tasks into small, manageable chunks and allocating responsibility for each task to a particular individual that you can hope to complete the planning and tests themselves. During formal testing, system development invariably slows down, because resources have to be allocated to the tests.

Testing is the greatest indicator of readiness to go live, yet it's a tremendously difficult thing to manage. You might consider bringing in specialist teams to help prepare and run the tests.

Functionality Testing

Functionality testing is a daily task of system developers. They model, configure, and test as a routine. The difficulty is the dependency between different teams or different team members. These dependencies might be the shared use of master file information that needs to be set up or the reliance on others to process transactional data. Even on the development systems, there has to be system control and authorization so that particular parts of the system are closed to all except the people who need to work with them.

Integrated Testing

Integrated testing requires great cooperation among project team members, and confusion can arise if roles and responsibilities aren't clearly defined and understood. For example, the integrated testing of a number of processes across a number of SAP modules can involve many different teams. Financial modules rely on data from the sales module. Testing a customer placing a simple order can involve these processes:

- Customer establishment
- Order placement, with credit checks at the time of placement
- Delivery note creation
- Picking list creation
- Shipment creation
- Delivery and goods issue creation
- Invoice and statement creation
- Accounts receivable collection
- Financial postings
- Payment allocation

The correct entries have to be made in the General Ledger, the warehouse management systems have to deal with the order, and the production systems need to make or replenish the stock. This may trigger the purchasing systems to order the materials to make the stock, and so on. At the end of these processes, the reporting has to be tested.

Integrated testing relies on the creation of clearly defined scenarios that have defined purposes. To make them work, responsibility for performing the test has to be allocated to teams or individuals. It's equally important to review the results of the tests and to be able to take the appropriate action and retest the scenario.

Even in a company of modest size, the number of integrated test scenarios can run into thousands, becoming completely impractical and unmanageable. It's difficult to establish who should be driving the integrated tests. Each area of the project team needs to test its own area, and yet the people who have to use that area can best evaluate the system performance acceptability.

Each project area should be able to define a series of tests to carry out. If you were to look at each test, you would probably find that each team's requirements could be combined into a single scenario. Such analysis is immensely time-consuming, however, and it still leaves the problem of whose test it is and who is judging whether the test was a success. It could well be that six or eight people are judging the success of a single scenario.

For tests to work, the system has to be set up, the environment has to be clean of rubbish data that could spoil the test, and strict controls on system activity must be in place. Testing weekly or monthly reports, rebate schemes that apply in arrears, and so on is more difficult because these tests rely on a time interval that's difficult to re-create.

If you've documented your business requirements well, you can use these documents as a source for developing test scenarios.

Volume Testing

Volume tests are the same as integrated tests, but on a larger scale. The objective is to simulate the system activity as if the system was live and the business was being run on it.

If integrated tests are hard, it's not difficult to imagine the difficulties that can be encountered with volume testing. Undertaking volume testing requires, by its very nature, huge quantities of human resources. The question of where these resources come from is difficult to answer. There are probably not enough people on the project team, so you must involve users or others. Managed well, volume testing can function as a valuable part of the user training program, because it enables users to become familiar with the system.

The great difficulty, of course, is how companies manage to take users away from their jobs of running the business. Night sessions, weekend working, and canceled holidays are all options. None of these will likely be good for morale, however, and everyone will probably be under immense pressure as it is. You could hire in a team of testers, but that comes at a heavy price, because the testers need some training to enable them to carry out the tests.

Evaluating Test Results

Testing is a waste of time unless results are properly documented and evaluated. Every test that fails any aspect has to generate a task to put right the failure, and the fix itself has to be retested.

The difficulty with so much system development going on at the same time is that the testing process has to be continual. What worked today might not work tomorrow if someone has altered a setting.

There is a huge risk in going live without completing successful volume integrated tests, because you discover that things don't work only when it really matters. Small problems that can be overcome quickly are manageable, but as is often the case, some problems take time to fix, and if you can't service your customers or run your business, the costs can be massive. Disasters with SAP implementations may be very rare, but they have happened. You should take testing very seriously and allocate sufficient resources.

Going Live

At the start of a project, the thought of going live seems a long way off, yet the time soon comes when the fruits of everyone's labor make it a possibility. Before going live, you must ensure that you have, as a minimum, done all the following:

- Configured the system to meet your business requirements
- Thoroughly tested the system, not only function by function but also in a fully integrated environment
- Trained all the users
- Put in place new internal organizations
- Installed and tested all the necessary hardware
- Printed new stationery, if required
- Developed all interfaces with other systems
- Transferred master data and relevant transactional data from old systems, including customer master, material master, open orders, and accounts receivable and payable data
- Put in place a support structure for the new system

Even the smallest implementation requires a huge amount of effort and planning. The best way to plan an implementation is to create a critical path of tasks that need to be completed before you can go live. The critical path list needs to be developed by all key team leaders and project managers, along with the business managers. The best way of building a critical path is to get everyone involved, including users, to create their own lists. If managers in each area combine the tasks that need to be achieved, those tasks can be further combined with the tasks of other managers to produce a definitive plan.

It makes sense to dedicate somebody to the job of managing the planning. By using a project management system, project managers can know how the implementation is progressing and decide when it's realistic to go live.

Planning is more an art than a science, and you will need to get used to making assumptions and calculated guesses. It's easy to become a slave to the planning systems; you have to be careful that you don't spend half your time recording what everyone has done and inputting data to produce meaningless reports.

It's also easy for managers to feel out of control, and for good reason. It's very difficult to estimate how long a task will take when you haven't done it before and will probably never do it again. Even the most skilled and respected consultants can make mistakes when trying to estimate when companies will be ready to go live. You have to accept that in any systems implementation, most companies are embarking on a journey without knowing exactly when or where they will arrive.

By having direct control over as many factors as possible, you minimize the chance of the unknown throwing you violently off course. It's difficult to describe the pressures senior managers are under to complete the project on time and within budget. The pressure to go live on time is immense, yet the consequences of trying to do so before you are ready can be catastrophic. The pressures are inevitably and quite rightly passed down the line, for it takes total commitment, superhuman effort, and gritty determination to implement on time. SAP implementations are no place for weak-minded or second-rate people—the project team and users need to be hard-working, flexible, and determined.

If you are a senior manager making the go/no-go decision, you have my sympathy. If all your team leaders and users are confident that they are ready, you are a very lucky person, but in most cases the reality is that not all the items on your critical path are completed. You are now in a situation of compromise, and you start to ask the question, "What would happen if we went live without these particular tasks being completed?" If the answer is inconvenience or a little extra work internally, you might be able to live with it, but if you can't invoice your customers or your warehouse management system doesn't work properly, the situation is very different. More often than not, the issues aren't black and white but shades of gray, making the decision all the more difficult.

If you're implementing a financial module, you might need to go live at a month end or year end. You might need to take the opportunity of a national holiday when the company isn't open for business, or you might need the cooperation of your customers and suppliers, all of which require advance notice and planning. Whatever the issues, if you are responsible for making or recommending the decision to go live, you need to be well aware of all the factors that influence that decision.

Big Bang Versus Phased Approach

Depending on how many modules are being implemented, two approaches to implementation are possible: the Big Bang and the phased approach.

Big Bang   This approach takes courage. On a particular day, you stop using your old systems and start using SAP. The advantages of the Big Bang approach follow:

- Implementation is quicker, so employees and expensive project costs can be released earlier to save money.

- New system benefits can be realized sooner.

- Duplication of file maintenance in new and old systems can be minimized.

- Fewer interfaces to old systems are required.

Some of the disadvantages of this approach follow:

- The risk of catastrophic disaster is greater than with phased implementation—if something goes wrong, it could affect your whole business.

- More preparation is needed. If you aren't careful, implementation can slip.

- All users need training at the same time, which puts a huge strain on the training organization.

- The support groups need to be larger to cope with problems after implementation.

Phased Approach   With this approach, you implement module by module over a period of time. The advantages follow:

- The risk factor is lower.

- Support teams have a more manageable workload.

- The workload of the project team is more manageable, because team members can concentrate on a smaller area at a time instead of on everything all at once.

The disadvantages of the phased approach follow:

- You will have far more interface issues. You will need to write and test interfaces to and from existing systems that will be required only until you replace them with other SAP modules.

- The project will last longer.

- The full benefits of using SAP will be gained later.

- It will cost considerably more than the Big Bang approach (even assuming that it goes according to plan).

- Extended projects can be more mentally and physically wearing for users and project team members.

Disaster Recovery Plan

Most major companies have a disaster recovery plan that can be pulled into force if anything goes wrong with their computing systems. However, during times of change when the workload is at its greatest, uncertainty is commonplace and companies are at their most vulnerable if something goes wrong. It's easy to forget to update your disaster recovery plans before an implementation, but it's well worth the investment of bringing in additional help if necessary to create and rehearse a plan for your new systems before you go live.

Accounting Implications

Project managers should make sure that they are aware of all the accounting implications at the beginning of the project. It's well worth ensuring that a senior manager from the Accounting Department is involved in the early stages of the project. Some issues to consider follow:

- The need to implement at month end or year end versus a quieter time of year
- Tax reporting periods and reconciliations
- Setting up the General Ledger
- Managing open items from other systems when going live
- Transferring receivables and outstanding balances
- Establishing controls and audit procedures

Open Transactions in Old Systems

When going live, you can choose to process open transactions completely in an old system or transfer them to a new system. The decision as to how to manage each situation will depend on which modules are being implemented and what old systems are in place.

A multitude of issues can arise, and all need to be addressed. For example, if orders are taken in an old system, should they be re-created in SAP? If they are, how do you prevent duplicating them? If they aren't re-created in SAP, how do you manage the picking lists, dispatch notes, goods issues, and receivables? If the transaction goes through outside SAP, how do you get the inventory to balance and how do you cope with the impact on the production forecasting? There are lots of questions and no easy answers. The only way to deal with the issues of open transactions in old systems is to identify what they are and to decide how each one will be administered. If you close down for a few days, perhaps using a weekend and a national holiday, you might be able to clear all the outstanding orders in the old system and transfer just the financial balances.

Interfaces

Depending on which SAP modules you're implementing, you will need to consider the question of interfaces at an early stage. More than likely, you will need a number of interfaces in and out of SAP. You will need to create specifications, write the appropriate codes, and test them. You will also need to schedule when the interface programs will run. You should consider the control and security implications of accessing and amending master files and transactional data in SAP.

Dual Maintenance of Data

As you get closer to implementation, you will need to build and maintain your master files. The prospect of maintaining old systems along with SAP doesn't sound like much trouble until you actually have to do it. Invariably, users have this task, which provides a good opportunity for gaining system familiarity before going live. However, the timing is very important—if you do it too early, the workload for users can be immense, and if implementation is delayed, the dual maintenance can collapse and the whole process will have to be started again nearer to the date of going live.

Working with SAP Systems After Implementation

When SAP is successfully implemented, project team members feel relief, managers can sit back in their chairs again, and life for everyone can begin to return to normal. Going live might give everyone the feeling that it's all over, but normally a multitude of tasks must be performed, including these:

- Fixing system bugs in the configuration
- Supporting users with a help desk and additional training
- Making required system developments that weren't ready at the time of going live
- Organizing the system operation
- Operating control and security procedures
- Correcting errors in transactional and master data
- Ensuring that reporting functions are operating correctly

In many cases, you have to wait for the first of particular activities to take place before you can assess how each function works. Examples include orders, delivery notes, picking lists, shipments, goods issues, invoices, statements, payments allocations, accounting entries, work orders, and production planning.

SAP as an integrated system deals with entire business processes, and it's not until these entire business processes are completed that you can assess whether the system is functioning properly. You might need to wait until your first month end to establish whether the accounting functions are working as they should, or you might need to wait until orders have been processed to check your sales reporting. It therefore can be some time before you can determine how successful the implementation was. In the same way that it's easy for runners to slow down as they near the finish line, it's easy for project teams to slow down after implementation. But remember, "It ain't over till it's over."

Despite who officially owns the system before going live, it's the project team that feels most comfortable with it. However, on going live, the emphasis shifts immediately to the users. The project team had the opportunity to build confidence with the system without the pressure of running the company on it. The users, even though they received some training, probably feel as though they have been thrown in at the deep end of the pool and are expected to swim.

A new system always has teething problems (usually minor issues), but an infrastructure must be in place to deal with them quickly and efficiently. There is a natural settling-down period immediately after going live, which should quickly give way to normal working.

Supporting Systems and Users After Implementation

When SAP is implemented, the effective support of the system and users becomes essential. The use of the system is now an integral part of the organization's operation; any failure in the system or the way it's operated becomes a failure in the organization itself.

Careful planning is needed to ensure that the necessary support is in place. In most cases, the support structure that was in place during system development can be adapted. However, the number of users will likely increase, and many problems will be urgent. The system itself will likely respond differently with the large volume of processing created by a live system. Interfaces that worked in testing will have to work in the live environment, and there will be an inevitable settling-down period during which problems will arise that need to be resolved.

Most companies will develop their own support organization and procedures. An internal help desk is a necessity and provides a focal contact point for users as well as a central area where system performance can be monitored. Follow-up system training for users should be considered, as well as preparing training for new employees.

SAP Services

R/3 Services is the collective name for the comprehensive range of support services offered by SAP. These services include Problem Solving, Remote Support, Information, Customer Support, Product Design, and Certification.

Problem Solving   Four problem-solving services are designed to resolve technical problems and questions that result from the everyday use of SAP:

- First-level service is offered by one of two different media: telephone support or the *Online Service System* (OSS). Experts who can help with all types of system problems provide quick assistance. A 24-hour emergency service is available.

- The Error Notes Q&A Service support requires online connection to SAP and enables access to the Error Notes database through the OSS. This database holds information based on experience with SAP installations and stores notes to help resolve problems that other clients encountered before you. The system offers a context-sensitive search facility to help you find information.

- The Online Correction Service facility enables SAP's consultants to assign available solutions to problems that have been submitted. Corrections will be continuously updated and maintained.

- SAPNET is SAP's Internet-based online service. To gain entry, customers need their OSS user ID and password. SAPNET can also be accessed by direct remote connection for extra security. SAPNET supports all languages now supported by the R/3 system. The OSS is due to be integrated into SAPNET. R/3 notes, online corrections, and hot packages can be downloaded. Training course schedules are available, with seat availability and reservation options.

Remote Support   The following services identify and prevent potential system errors and optimize system performance:

- The Early Watch service enables SAP experts to access SAP installations remotely and optimize system performance by identifying system problems and eliminating resource and system bottlenecks. The customer regulates the online connection, and the service is offered on a by-request basis.

- The Remote Consulting Service enables customers to make an appointment with a skilled SAP consultant to discuss problems, analyze solutions, or discuss general issues. This service uses video-supported communications, which reduces consultant travel time and expenses.

- SAP's Information Services enable customers to access information on a wide variety of subjects, including the R/3 product itself.
- Information is available online through the *Online Service System* (OSS). You can access information on a variety of subjects, including training courses and SAP publications.
- The Hot News Service provides online information about the latest high-priority R/3 system information, including error alarm messages, release strategy information, system enhancement information, and service event schedules. Information is transmitted electronically to customer mailboxes, and the system is audited to ensure that customers receive the information sent.
- SAP produces a number of different CD-ROMs that contain a wide range of R/3 system information.

Customer Support   SAP's Customer Support services are aimed at quick problem solving and up-to-date information transfer.

Customer Competence Centers (CCC)   This service is available to large organizations that have purchased the R/3 system. It offers on-site support by providing the entire R/3 services within a customer's organization. Customers have direct access to SAP tools, information, and communications systems. The CCC is run by the customer's own staff, which is given training and is certified at regular intervals.

Active Customer Relationship   SAP offers a central contact point for customers and partners that provides "personal intensive support for customer concerns and integration of customer development requests and implementation of these requests in SAP and partners' services." *(Source: SAP Services brochure)*

Product Design   SAP has long relied on customer feedback to develop its systems. The company has developed a number of channels through which customers can influence future product design.

Customer Verification Shipment   Customers are encouraged to submit requests for new features and enhancements directly to SAP. If these requests are incorporated into the standard product, customers have the option of testing the relevant systems. During this time, customers receive intensive support and preferential query handling.

First Customer Shipment   This facility allows customers to test new releases in advance and to influence the development of future upgrades.

Development Request Service   SAP system development requests can be sent to SAP directly or through the Online Services System. On receipt, requests go to a product planning committee that considers the requests for inclusion in the standard product.

Certification   SAP's R/3 services are aimed at achieving high-quality standards by constant improvement to services. To ensure that SAP's partners maintain these same standards, a certification scheme is in place. SAP's certification scheme integrates its partners into its own quality assurance procedures. This offers customers a guarantee of a high standard of service. ●

through your problem messages. The number of HotNews messages is shown in the New Info from SAP section of the display.

Learning About Release Planning   Messages in this category are counted and displayed in the New Information from SAP section. They concern new developments in certain operating systems and database environments and the dates when the updated versions will be released.

Getting Installation and Upgrade Messages   If there have been any messages concerning the installation or upgrading of your SAP R/3 system, they are counted in this section of the display. It is important to read them before upgrading your SAP R/3 system.

Differentiating HotNews Messages

The characteristic of HotNews is that it is received directly through the OSS. The main category of HotNews is Alarm Alerts, which present error descriptions and their solutions, which must be implemented to avoid serious problems with your SAP R/3 system.

Training courses and company-specific events such as the startup of a production plant under SAP R/3 will be topics to be promulgated via HotNews messages.

After you signify that you have read a HotNews message, a confirmation is sent to SAP. If the message requires some action on your part, it generates the appropriate checklists, which are transmitted back to SAP to confirm that you have seen the information about what you should do.

The following categories of HotNews are used to differentiate topics:

- **Special-interest topics** include changes in release strategy and scheduling.
- **News and recommendations** suggest ways of improving your SAP R/3 system.

Receiving OSS Messages Through the HelpDesk

The OSS conveys a direct message to the SAP R/3 HelpDesk if you have not been able to get the information you require through the problem message procedure or by directly accessing error notes.

When you call or fax an SAP HelpDesk, the staff there enters your problem into the OSS. If the local HelpDesk is not immediately available, your inquiry is passed on to the appropriate contact person in one of the SAP worldwide service centers. You can still use the OSS to monitor how your inquiry is progressing.

Exploring R/3 Online Services

The main elements of the online services follow:

- SAP OSS-Online Service System
- Customer Competence Center with own OSS updated from the SAP OSS
- Local SAP HelpDesk

Optimization of the SAP Implementation

Business systems have evolved to the point where they can closely model a business's internal processes. This means that companies can save significantly on internal administration costs by automating standard business procedures.

The role of the employee is moving away from basic business administrator to a more challenging operator role. In particular, new working practices concentrate on three areas:

- Setup and configuration of business entities
- Management of business databases
- Exception handling

SAP, a very advanced business systems package, aims to maximize the automation of standard processes within a company. It allows a very high level of internal automation, which gives it a great advantage over its competitors. To achieve the maximum gains from these processes, users must learn to become computer confident and literate. The radical changes taking place in the workplace with the arrival of more sophisticated business software require companies to make a significant investment in time and money.

You will have gathered by now that SAP is not just another software package. No Plug-and-Play technology is involved, so SAP cannot simply be left to the IT department to "get on with it." Implementing SAP involves most of the people in an organization, and many of them will have had only limited exposure to a computer.

Experience has shown that the best way to take a company through the specifics of SAP implementation is with a business process-oriented approach. First, look at some problems that would be encountered if SAP were implemented using a traditional business change management methodology.

The Traditional "As-Is" and "To-Be" Approaches

The traditional business change management scenario, shown in Figure 33.1, takes a three-stage approach to business change implementation:

1. Define where the company is at the moment ("as-is").
2. Decide where the company will be in five years' time ("to-be").
3. Decide how the company will get from step 1 to step 2.

This approach has a number of problems, some relating to SAP specifically:

- Most companies (even those with ISO9000~1 accreditation) do not have a clear idea of all their internal business processes, and the idea of mapping them out can appear to be an expensive luxury.
- Many companies feel they cannot afford the expense of setting up working groups to debate the company's possible position in years to come.

■ SAP offers a particular philosophy about the way businesses should be structured, and despite its flexibility, implementing SAP would necessarily force particular procedural changes. Consequently, any proposed business strategy that does not acknowledge the implementation of the SAP way of business is likely to require substantial revision.

FIGURE 33.1
The three phases of the traditional business change management approach.

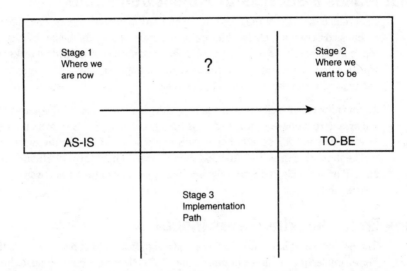

An SAP-Oriented Approach

SAP's success is due in part to the highly efficient business solution that it provides. If a company decides to go with SAP software, it must also accept that the millions of hours of development effort put into the system have come up with some pretty nifty solutions. In cases where a business and SAP disagree on the business approach to a particular problem, any business should seriously think about changing its approach to match that of SAP. Provided that a company is prepared to do this, following SAP-oriented business methodology will maximize the benefit of the changes, minimize the cost, and maximize the return of the whole exercise. There are four stages to the methodology:

1. Map the company onto a business hierarchy. Include all company functions. The business hierarchy must match SAP business structures.

2. Identify where SAP business processes fit in at the bottom of the hierarchy, and include them in the mapping.

3. Divide all tasks at the bottom of the hierarchy into one of three types:

   Automated   Tasks that SAP will do

   Manual   Tasks that a person will do

   Transactions   Tasks that a person working on SAP will do

4. Define the extent and limits of all tasks, including the frequency and resource usage.

NOTE An SAP implementation methodology has many possible variations. This methodology picks out the basic elements. ▪

What Makes a Successful Project Definition?

Experience shows that the most successful SAP implementations have been done with a map of business processes. This is a hierarchical picture of how the business is to be designed. At the top of the hierarchy is the company; at the bottom are the individual tasks performed by individuals minute by minute. This map explains what everyone in the company is doing and how each task fits into the overall corporate plan.

To maximize the efficiency gains achieved by implementing SAP, you must define—and more important, redefine—a company's business processes. The SAP system provides a Reference Model that you can use to help you with this process. However, the most successful companies will be those that drive the business model development through their own experience. When an SAP project fails, it is generally because the scope of the project wasn't fully mapped out beforehand.

Early Error-Checking Saves Money

The quality of the initial design work has a significant effect on the cost of the implementation. For example, one client spent more than $100,000 extra simply because the company implemented a poorly thought-out mechanism for recording sales costs (two or three fields on the order-entry screens).

The stages of an SAP project follow this pattern:

1. Requirements
2. Design
3. Configuration
4. Unit testing
5. Acceptance testing
6. Maintenance

The later an error is detected in this process, the more costly it is to correct. Errors detected at the maintenance stage are generally more than 100 times more expensive to fix than those detected at the requirements stage.

Users First, Computer Scientists Second

When you implement SAP, you must get early user involvement. In the "old days," we just let computer experts get on with it, and then there was this rather boring phase called "user acceptance," during which the users examined the system and said what they thought of it. Those old methods worked for the smaller, less complicated systems of days gone by. Today, however, SAP has more than 1 million lines of code, in addition to all those table settings, so early user involvement is essential. The first part of the SAP implementation defines exactly how users will use SAP.

Building the Function Hierarchy

When building the function hierarchy, use SAP's functional (and modular) structure to map your business. You will find that this leads to a cleaner solution and more efficient results than using other analyses, such as product-based structures.

Map Company onto Business Hierarchy

To build a model of the new business structure, you must assemble a hierarchical model of the business. The very act of putting this model together enables you and your company to assess the efficiency of your company's business processes. Ordinarily you do not have the time to assess the efficiency of the work you do, because you are too busy doing it!

Level 1: Top of Hierarchy   The top of the hierarchy is a single box, the company itself (see Figure 33.2). This includes all activities that affect a company's balance sheet and profit-and-loss statement.

FIGURE 33.2

Top of the business process hierarchy.

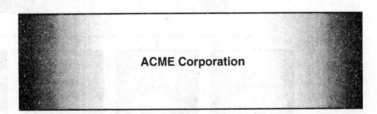

ACME Corporation

Level 2: Division by Business Group or SAP Module   One key issue is how the SAP implementation must reflect the system's most efficient use. To do this, a company must be prepared to adopt SAP's own business philosophy.

A common method of viewing a company is to divide the company into product groups, because this very often reflects a company's organization. This is especially true when the company has been formed through mergers and takeovers of competing companies. This also reflects the "marketing department's view of the universe."

For example, imagine a company with four basic product groups (see Figure 33.3):

- Consumer Product Group 1
- Consumer Product Group 2
- Medical Products
- Industrial Products

This way of viewing the company makes sense from a business viewpoint. It reflects the structure required to report on activities for the purposes of product costing and profitability analysis. However, it is not necessarily the best way of viewing the SAP implementation. Similar business functions are carried out for each product. You should instead consider planning by SAP module (see Figure 33.4).

FIGURE 33.3

The hierarchy by product group.

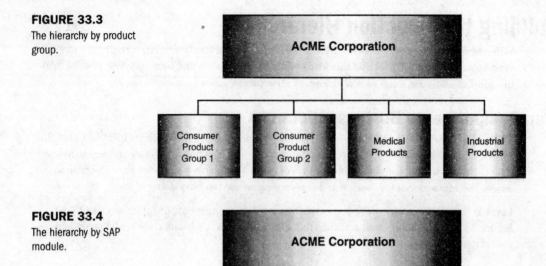

FIGURE 33.4

The hierarchy by SAP module.

Try to make as many similar cross-company business processes as possible. This is a new version of the old Adam Smith principle of specialization, in which companies' efficiency gains are made by breaking tasks into their smallest parts and allocating individuals to those parts.

Level 3: Division by SAP Submodules   Within each SAP module, split up the sections by those parts of the submodules that your company is planning to use. Although a company might think that it is implementing, for example, CO-Controlling, in reality the company is probably going to be implementing only part of that module. Therefore, it must be clear what component parts of each module are being used. The example in this chapter implements three parts of the FI-Finance module and two parts of the CO-CCA Cost Center Accounting module (see Figure 33.5).

Submodule as Core Business Unit

The submodules of the basic SAP modules represent a whole suite of functions around a single SAP business entity. Each submodule is based around an entity that mirrors a real-world business concept. Here are a few examples:

- **CO-CCA Cost Center Accounting.** The basic entity is the cost center. Cost centers are used to measure the costs incurred by individual departments.
- **MM-Materials Management.** The basic entity is the material, which represents a single product. Materials identify the nature and characteristics of the products held by a company.

FIGURE 33.5
The hierarchy down to
SAP submodule.

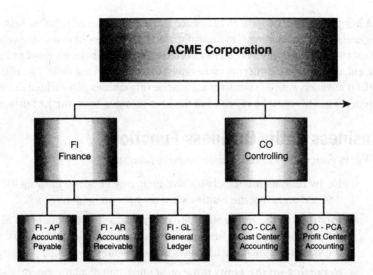

This entity is reflected in SAP by the underlying database structure, so it is worthwhile to use these entities—not only to form the basis of the task groups that the users will be given, but also to define the scope of the database administrator's work.

N O T E If you are familiar with object-oriented programming, you will see similarities between objects and the way in which SAP models business entities. ▪

Table 33.1 shows the core SAP business entities around which the SAP business systems operate. In larger projects, for each entity used, the definition of the characteristics (such as fields) can be a task assigned to a task force.

Table 33.1   Common SAP Business Entities

Submodule	Entity
FI-AP Accounts Payable	Vendor
FI-AR Accounts Receivable	Customer
FI-GL General Ledger	G/L Account
CO-CCA Cost Center Accounting	Cost Center
CO-PCA Profit Center Accounting	Profit Center
CO-OPA Order Process Accounting	Internal Order
MM-Materials Management	Material
MM-Purchasing	Supplier
SD-Sales and Distribution	Customer

A key part of SAP's approach to finance is the distinction SAP makes between financial and management accounting. Traditionally, many companies have a single set of financial accounts that covers a company's requirements to report on the balance sheet and profit-and-loss statement, and to provide internal management cost monitoring tools. The use of a set of controlling (CO) business entities distinct from finance (FI) entities gives added flexibility in financial reporting. This must be reflected in the breakdown in tasks on the business process hierarchy.

SAP Business Entity Business Functions

Within each entity are three basic business functions:

- **Entity management** includes setting up new entities, changing the entities' characteristics, and archiving the entities when they are no longer needed.
- **Postings to the entity** affect the entity's values. In the Materials Management modules, those values represent the quantities of stock held. In the Financial modules, FI and CO, the values are the financial values of the postings.
- **Reporting on the entity** is the most important of all the functions—the capability to examine the first two functions' progress.

SAP Business Entities Basic Model

The basic model you must follow puts your tasks in a hierarchy as shown here:

- Entity
- Entity management
- Postings to entity
- Reporting on entity

The following shows an example of how this applies to Cost Center Accounting, whereas Figure 33.6 shows how this fits into the hierarchy.

Entity	Function
Cost Center Accounting	Cost Center Management
	Cost Center Postings
	Cost Center Reporting

Each task in Table 33.2 is represented by an SAP transaction.

Table 33.2 Division of Functions into Task Groups

Function	Task Groups
Entity management	Create a cost center.
	Display a cost center.
	Change a cost center.
	Make cost center postings.
	Maintain cost center hierarchies.

Function	Task Groups
Postings to the entity	Post cost adjustments. Reallocate costs across cost centers.
Reporting on the entity	Display a list of the cost centers. Display cost center master records. Display costs per period. Display costs per quarter. Display planned versus actual costs. Display planned versus forecast costs. Display actual versus forecast costs.

FIGURE 33.6

Division of submodule by process types.

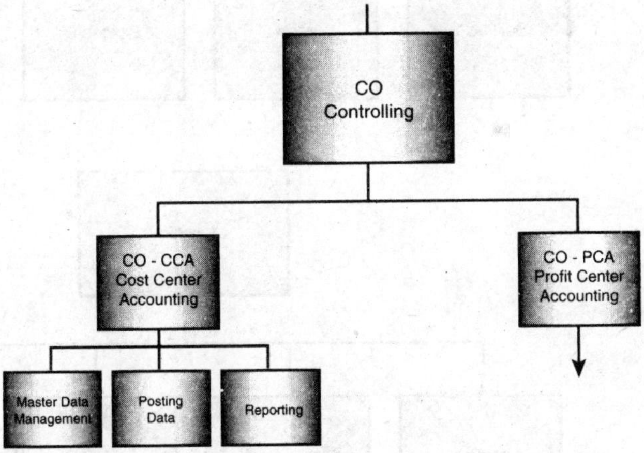

Tasks and the SAP Transaction Concept

The tasks at the bottom of the hierarchy are individual units of work. These units are done by a person or a computer, or in some cases by both.

- Humans perform manual tasks. You must plan for them. Their development is outside the scope of this book.

- Automated tasks are planned and programmed by system designers. When in place, they require relatively little maintenance.

User transactions are the key to the whole process. They require the coordination of human and machine. User transactions form the bulk of the information traffic flowing into and out of your databases. Transactions enable you to set up, examine, and modify SAP databases. These user transactions are the basic units around which you must plan, design, and build your system.

SAP uses transactions as the basic system process. You access these transactions through the menu structures, which try to model the hierarchical patterns into which business functions fit.

A *transaction* is a single business task carried out by a user. It consists of a set of screens that users pass through to complete the task (see Figure 33.7). A screen contains a number of fields (see Figure 33.8). A field relates to the contents of a part of a database.

FIGURE 33.7
Transactions are made up of a number of screens.

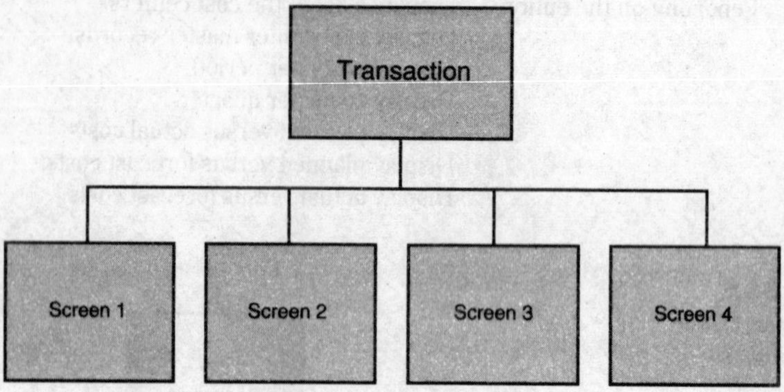

FIGURE 33.8
Each screen has a number of fields.

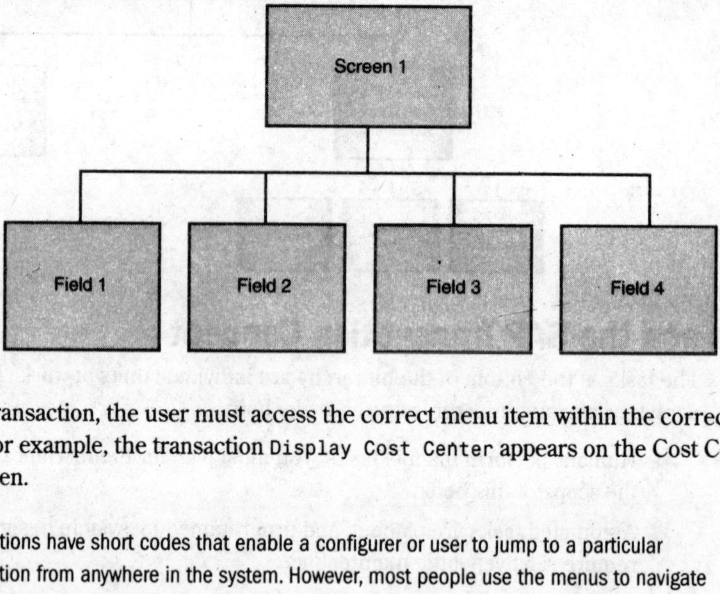

To carry out a transaction, the user must access the correct menu item within the correct menu screen. For example, the transaction Display Cost Center appears on the Cost Center Accounting screen.

N O T E Transactions have short codes that enable a configurer or user to jump to a particular transaction from anywhere in the system. However, most people use the menus to navigate the system. ▒

Building the Business Processes

Business processes are core concepts for implementing your SAP system. Figure 33.9 shows how a single business process is composed of a series of tasks that link together. The business process provides the context into which individual tasks fit.

FIGURE 33.9

The business process is a sequence of tasks.

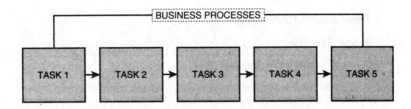

A task may be carried out manually (such as filling out a form), or it may be a transaction carried out by the system. Each task must have a named profile of the employee who will carry out the task (see Figure 33.10). For example, setting up a new cost center isn't something that happens in isolation from other events in business administration. Usually, there is a sign-off mechanism in which named individuals take responsibility for spending against the cost center. You must work these authorizations and forms into the system design before implementation activities take place.

FIGURE 33.10

Tasks must be linked to job profiles.

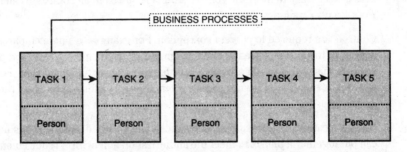

Take an example from the accounts payable function. On the SAP Accounts Payable screens, you will find a set of processes that you can use, no matter what business you are involved in. That is because paying a vendor who has sold you a photocopier and paying a vendor who has sold you a machine tool are very similar processes.

Table 33.3 shows the steps in the accounts payable process.

Table 33.3   Steps of the FI-Accounts Payable Process

Stage	Function
1	Receive the invoice.
2	Enter the invoice into the SAP system ("receive invoice" function).
3	The invoice is matched with the purchase order.
4	The invoice is matched with the goods receipt note.
5	The invoice is cleared for payment.
6	A payment proposal is run.
7	The payment proposal is authorized.

continues

Table 33.3 Continued	
Stage	**Function**
8	The payment program runs.
9	A check is printed, or an automatic bank transfer credit occurs.

Some processes are manual, and others are computer-based. It is this flow of tasks that provides your company with the foundation for meeting international quality standards such as ISO9000~1.

Job Function Matrix

You need to allocate the list of SAP tasks defined within the scope of the project to job profiles. This is necessary to meet the control criteria required in all companies and to provide a framework for user training.

Controls are required to prevent corruption. For example, a single employee is not given access to all the features needed to create an order, dispatch the goods, and process an invoice, because this power would provide a very tempting opportunity for theft. For the same reason, warehouse employees are not usually given access to information about the value of the goods on invoices.

Having created a business process hierarchy and grouped tasks into business processes, you can put together a matrix to meet the authorization and control requirements of your project. The matrix should list job titles. For each job title, list the system tasks that will be carried out. One copy of this matrix should be passed in front of the Accounting Department for review from a controls perspective. The other copy can be used by the Basis team to set up user authorization profiles.

Table 33.4 shows an example of a task listing.

Table 33.4 Example of a Task Listing	
Job	**Task**
Accounts Payable clerk	Enter the invoice.
	Match the invoice.
	Execute the check payment run.
	Execute the electronic payment run.
	Display a list of vendors.
Accounts Payable manager	Display a list of vendors.
	Display outstanding payments.
	Display payments made per month.
	Display payment per business area.

This mapping then is used by the Training Department to determine the contents of training courses that need to be given, and by the system administrator to set up user profiles.

Issues Around Business Process Modeling

So far, you have been examining a formal method for mapping business process requirements. Now it's time to look at some strategic and tactical issues that arise before, during, and after the business process definition that may affect the optimal approach.

What Portion of the Company Is Moving to SAP?

If 100 percent of the business is moving to SAP, the business process modeling includes all parts of the company. This simplifies the whole process, because it means that no time needs to be spent on defining project limits.

If less than 100 percent of the business is being transferred to SAP (for example, you are implementing for a division of the company), you need an extra step. Make a clear statement on the scope of the implementation. Make sure that all relevant managers have seen, digested, and approved of the scope of the document. You can use the business process hierarchy to clearly define the required processes.

Contracts with Outside Agencies

A common area of dispute between companies and outside IT consultants is the scope of work covered by the implementation. You can use the business hierarchy to precisely define the limits and extent of the contracted work.

Internal Contracts

Even for internal budget allocation, politics raises its ugly head. Within a company, the scope of a project must be clearly defined, too. Internal political processes will result in ambitious managers underquoting estimates for total project costs, often when the whole project's scope is not yet clearly defined. You can use the business process hierarchy to precisely define the limit and extent of the implementation.

The Inclusion of System Maintenance Functions

SAP maintenance brings with it a number of maintenance functions that must be factored in as business processes. These processes fall into four categories:

- **Hardware maintenance.** The provision and support of all required pieces of hardware, including printers, cables, and portable PCs.
- **Help desk.** Handles any unexpected problems that users have.
- **Database archiving.** The removal and storage of database records no longer required for immediate online processing. Over time, SAP databases will grow beyond the size necessary to run the business, so archiving will save disk space and improve system processing times.

■ **User authorization management.** The setup and maintenance of user-specific authorization profiles that dictate what specified users can do on the system. Security profiles must be set up and managed to allow all users to carry out the system tasks necessary to do their jobs.

Iterative Development of Business Processes

As your SAP system development continues, you might find it necessary to adjust this hierarchy. For example, as the Accounts Payable function develops, you might decide to include electronic banking alongside your manual check clearing and distribution. In that case, you must add an additional business process to the part of the hierarchy that includes the payment methods:

Business Process	Description
Before	
Vendor payment	Payment of a vendor by check
	Payment of a vendor by cash
After	
Vendor payment	Payment of a vendor by check
	Payment of a vendor by cash
	Payment of a vendor by electronic banking

Adding to the hierarchy will mean higher project costs. Consequently, you must build a contingency into the project resources up front for additional business processes being added. Some new business processes will be the result of additional requirements that your business will have to meet; others may be due to improvements in technology.

Reduction of Project Costs

One of the most common ways to reduce project costs is to reduce the number of business processes covered. In the preceding example, the scope of the original project was extended to include electronic banking. When unforeseen circumstances lead to delays in reaching target dates, or when a budget reduction is enforced on a project, cutting out single business processes is often a much more efficient way forward than delaying the whole project. So, in the example, waiting until after the live date to install the electronic banking part of accounts payable would mean that all other parts of the project could progress on time.

Keep It Simple

SAP is a complex package, and efficiency improvements can be made where the defined processes are made or kept simple.

It is likely that some business process variations within your company are not easily reproducible on the SAP systems. Before deciding to automate these functions, a cost-benefit analysis of the effect of implementing the variations would be worthwhile. The benefit is the extra functionality that the system provides. This can be calculated in terms of the number of work hours saved per year as a result of automating the extra processes.

From user managers, you can establish estimates for time saved weekly or monthly due to the extra functionality. You then can convert this into a yearly figure. The costs are the implementation, training, and change management costs associated with the additional functionality. This, too, can be calculated in number of work hours required to implement it. A hidden cost of adding complexity to the system is that it tends to increase the overall cost of maintaining it, because "bugs" are harder to track down.

The following is an example of a cost-benefit analysis (adding extra order types to handle a specialist product):

> Estimated number of work hours saved per week: 2

Therefore,

> Estimated number of work hours saved per year: 104

Number of work hours to add the changes:

Design	24
Changes	24
Testing	40
Training	44
Total cost	132 hours

If the SAP system will be used for one year or less, the changes are not worthwhile. If the changes will be operating for more than two years, it might be worthwhile to consider adding the changes.

Developing Nonstandard SAP Functions

SAP provides a full set of development tools for clients to use to develop their own transactions, screens, and even databases. Although these tools are available, you should keep the following points in mind before deciding to develop nonstandard SAP functions:

- The high cost of the license fees that SAP users pay reflects the amount of development work that has gone into the package over the last 20 years.

- Any problem that you have come across has almost certainly already occurred with some other client somewhere else.

- When a number of SAP clients have come up with a business requirement, SAP has incorporated the requirement into the basic system.

- Your company is unlikely to have many unique processes.

In general, try to avoid modifying the basic package as much as possible. ●

CHAPTER 34

SAP Control and Security

In this chapter

Understanding the SAP Control Environment

Where SAP is implemented as an integrated application (as it's most commonly seen), some considerable risks are involved. Apart from the exposure of holding all of an organization's key business data and processing most of its transactions within one application, SAP typically replaces a host of legacy systems where cross-application security and data integrity aren't significant issues. A user in the accounts payable function will have access to the accounts payable system and nothing more. With SAP, you face a situation where a user will have access to SAP; the functions he can perform and the mitigating controls must be defined during system configuration and implementation. Also, the broad and detailed functionality offered by SAP means that the operation of such control and security mechanisms is very complex and requires dedicated expert resources.

Controls and security usually appear somewhere on a project plan. However, in priority terms they are generally fairly low and, in the pressure of meeting an impending implementation deadline, are often pushed aside. This can lead to major problems after implementation, although the costs of any associated losses are difficult to quantify because a lack of control, as well as the increased likelihood of problems occurring, can mean that those problems go undetected.

N O T E   At this early stage, controls aren't owned by the project, by an IT security function, or by internal or external audit. Instead, think of controls as an integral part of each and every business process. As such, they should be accepted, in terms of the costs of operating controls as well as any residual risks, by the business owner.

As with any implementation issue, it's useful to work within a framework to address control issues so that they can be considered in a structured fashion. The model used here is fairly standard and can be applied to the implementation of any application system. Controls are essentially viewed in the following categories:

- **Access security controls.** Technical controls within an application that allow functions (business and technical) to be restricted to appropriate personnel. Controls in the various operating system and database technologies that can be used by the system aren't covered in detail here.

- **System integrity controls.** Technical mechanisms within a system that allow the management of change control within its internal framework.

- **Processing controls.** Technical controls within a system that allow for data integrity, both within the application and with regard to data interfaced from other systems.

- **Application controls.** Required by the business, these controls form an integral step in each business process. These are discussed only in general terms—the requirements in this area vary greatly between installations and are implemented through the normal business process mapping and system customization processes.

- **Data-entry controls.** Ensure the integrity of data at the point of user interface. These controls can be in the form of error/warning messaging, validation against master- or table-held data, and so on.

■ **Detect/compensating controls.** "Backstop controls" that can be relied on as a last resort if controls in any of the other categories fail. These are typically in the form of automatically generated reports that require post-facto user validation/approval.

Like any system, SAP is stronger in some of these areas than in others. As an overview, the system can be characterized within this framework:

■ **Access security controls.** Despite some identified weaknesses, this is generally a strong area of functionality in SAP. However, it's extremely complex to understand and implement correctly.

■ **System integrity controls.** SAP R/3 has developed an integral change management system whereby any program or table changes can be amended and recorded in a development environment and then promoted to a productive environment. This system has some significant weaknesses, however.

■ **Processing controls.** As an integrated system, SAP should have fewer data integrity problems than the architecture typically represented by legacy system environments with multiple interfaces that require control. However, the promotion of programs, tables, and other Data Dictionary objects between systems is critical, and again, the setup of SAP's systems to achieve this is very complex.

■ **Application controls.** SAP offers, through the customization of internal tables, the opportunity to implement a whole range of application controls. When implemented, such controls are reliable, although they might not always be flexible enough to meet the requirements of individual users. Extra development or reliance on post-facto control is often necessary in this area.

■ **Data-entry controls.** Generally, because SAP is an integrated application, controls here are very powerful. Master files can be looked up across modules to select the appropriate record, and data entry is checked in real time against information held elsewhere in the system. A user's ability to override key fields defaulted into transactions from other parts of the system, however, is a key weakness.

■ **Detect/compensating controls.** This is probably SAP's weakest area. Very few usable post-facto reports are delivered as standard, and reports that are available are notoriously hard to find. If control reporting is required, you are generally on your own, and reports will have to be coded before implementation.

Access Control

As discussed in the preceding section, SAP security (or the *authorization concept,* as it's termed by SAP) is a relatively strong area of control functionality. Because of SAP's integrated nature, its implementation is critical to the success of an SAP project. This section provides a general overview of SAP functionality in this area, with an explanation of some important weaknesses to keep in mind while implementing the system.

General Security Guidelines

In general terms, there is essentially nothing special about the management of access security in an SAP environment. Various frameworks are available for the evaluation of information systems security—for example, the following system:

- Security policy
- Security organization
- Assets classification and control
- Personnel security
- Physical and environmental security
- Computer and network management
- System access control
- System development and maintenance
- Business continuity planning
- Compliance

Examples of documents containing guidance of this nature are the "Orange Books" published by the U.S. Department of Defense and "A Code of Practice for Information Security Management," published by the U.K. Department of Trade and Industry.

As yet, no computer security certification is generally available. In the UK, a standard, BS7799, is now under review by the Department of Trade and Industry but is generally thought to be some way from formal endorsement. Again, it can serve as a useful guideline.

Operating System, Database, and Network Security

Unlike some platforms and applications, the greatest degree of functional control in SAP is exercised from within the application itself. If managed properly, there should be few concerns and minimum administration required in the operating system and database environments. The benchmark SAP architecture of a UNIX operating system and Oracle database requires only a handful of users. Apart from the SAP application itself (which needs to be established as a user in UNIX and Oracle) and system administrators, there should be few if any other users. There is certainly no need to establish SAP users in these environments for them to be able to access the application.

This scenario, of course, assumes that no applications other than SAP R/3 are running in the environment. If, for example, other UNIX-based applications are running on the same server as SAP R/3, there are likely to be other control considerations.

The area of network security, however, is one that requires careful consideration. For a start, each SAP user must be established as a user on the network. Also, network security in a client/server environment should be viewed as very much an emerging and unproved technology. There is not the degree of comfort that you can draw, for example, from years of working with products such as RACF and ACF2 in a mainframe environment.

CAUTION

It's possible to drop from SAP into UNIX and to execute certain, limited commands. This can be done through the use of the ABAP SAPMSOS0 transaction.

Overview of the SAP Authorization Concept

The authorization concept in SAP R/3 is based on the logical relationship between a user ID and the range of system authorizations with which it can be associated (see Figure 34.1). The user ID provides a gateway through which users can enter the system; when logon is achieved, the authorizations determine which system resources can be accessed by each user ID.

FIGURE 34.1

SAP R/3 authorization entity relationship.

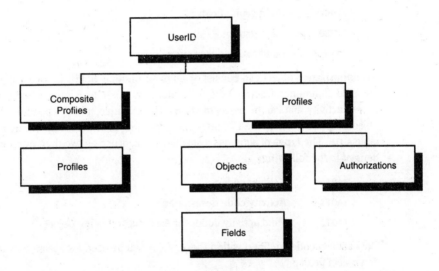

The architecture of the authorization system is based on the use of several individual but related logical components: profiles, objects, fields, and authorizations.

Within the system, the user ID refers exclusively to *profiles* when defining access privileges, instead of to individual authorization values. Every profile grants a set of specific system access authorities to a user, and a virtually unlimited number of profiles can be assigned to a user ID. Composite profiles can be defined, consisting of several concatenated single profiles.

An *object* is a logical entity used to group one or more related fields that require authority checking within the system. Objects themselves contain no values; instead, the *fields* contain values for authority checking, and the combination of field values for an object constitutes an *authorization*. Therefore, a profile references any number of authorizations that in themselves define the system resources that can be accessed.

Every object and profile must be uniquely named. Authorizations, however, can be identically named but must hold different values for their constituent object fields. This is because they are linked to an object name and are therefore physically and logically separate from each other.

Authorization Objects

All objects are defined in table TOBJ, which lists each object name and the individual field names associated with each object. Table TOBJT provides a separate list of objects, each accompanied by a textual description.

Objects can be grouped generically into object classes via transaction SU21. Classes provide a means of readily identifying functionally related groups of authorization objects (for example, Basis Administration, Financial Accounting, and so on).

Because the values of an object field can contain multiple (or a range of) values, it's often convenient to define a *field group* for an object. A field group contains the relevant values required for an authorization and can be shared across objects. Field groups are defined in the following:

T055	Field group fields
T055G	Field groups
T055T	Field group descriptions

An authorization object can consist of single or multiple fields. In the case of two-field objects, one field commonly describes the field value (for example, company code), and the other, the type of activity that can be performed on it (for example, add or change). This is most typical in objects associated with the FI-Financial Accounting module. Fields are defined in the internal table AUTH. The types of activities available are recorded as two-digit numeric values and are defined in the following:

TACT	Activity codes
TACTT	Activity code descriptions
TACTZ	Valid activity codes for each authorization object

Only activity codes defined within these tables can be used for assigning values for authorization object fields.

Authorization checking is performed when users request access to system resources. This is performed by a dedicated subroutine known as AUTHORITY-CHECK. This routine interrogates the system and returns a message indicating whether users have the required authorization values for the relevant object in their profiles. An error message appears if a user has insufficient authority.

This routine can be called directly from coding embedded in user-developed ABAP programs using the AUTHORIZATION-CHECK statement. In these cases, the object name and all fields of the object (with submitted values) must be coded; otherwise, the authorization check fails. If the AUTHORIZATION-CHECK statement isn't coded within ABAP programs, the relevant authorization checks are not performed.

As explained earlier, each SAP transaction, during processing, checks online the values (or the profiles) assigned to a specified authorization object in the user's master record. The authorization objects checked during transaction processing are hard coded into the ABAP code for that transaction and aren't easily accessible. This presents a problem when establishing user profiles—you might know which transactions need to be accessed, but the authorization objects that need to be granted for them to be successfully executed might be difficult to obtain.

SAP provides what can only be described as a partial solution to this problem: the trace function. Executing transaction SE30 (ABAP/IV Run-Time Analysis) allows a trace to be started, a transaction to be processed, and then a button to be selected that displays, in theory, all the authorization objects accessed through the execution of the transaction. For example, if the trace were run against transaction FB01 (post document), it might be expected to show General Ledger account authorizations, company code authorizations, and so on. The trace function has a few drawbacks, though:

- It's very time-consuming. Performing it for each transaction required in a large implementation would be very resource-intensive.
- It's not comprehensive; some authorizations simply aren't picked up and displayed with the trace function.
- Some transactions have so many options and so many data fields that it's almost impossible to ensure that every potential authorization check is invoked.

One large accounting firm has even gone to the lengths of rewriting the SE30 trace function in-house to ensure that more authorization objects are picked up. Some light is at the end of the tunnel, however. The SAP profile generator functionality available as of Release 4.0 of SAP R/3 provides a direct link between transactions and the authorization objects checked by them.

Another feature provided by SAP is in transaction SU53, which provides details of a transaction that hasn't been executed due to authorization check failure and displays the authorization objects missing from a user's profile. For this transaction to work, the system parameter Auth/check value write on must be set to a value greater than 1.

User Profiles

Most SAP implementation projects will develop user profiles specific to the job functions performed by individuals within the organization. For example, accounts payable clerks will need access to certain authorization objects, so a profile containing the objects with the appropriate values assigned to them will be created. This is often done by using the trace function, as described previously.

SAP as delivered, however, contains several hundred "standard" profiles, and some project managers pressed for time might be tempted to use these rather than go through the pain of defining their own. It's generally advisable to develop site-specific user profiles, though, because these are more likely to match the business requirements of a particular SAP implementation.

Some of the more sensitive standard profiles delivered with the system are in the BASIS (BC) area, particularly for use by security officers in assigning user authorizations. These profiles range in the level of system access they provide but generally are powerful—particularly profiles that offer blanket access to related authorization objects (see Table 34.1). Use of these profiles is optional, but because of their sensitivity, they should be reviewed before implementation to ensure that only authorized users have them assigned.

Table 34.1   BASIS System Standard Profiles

Profile Name	Description
S_ABAP_ALL	All ABAP/IV authorizations
S_ADMI_ALL	All system administrative functions
S_BDC_ALL	All batch input activities
S_BTCH_ALL	All batch processing authorizations
S_DDIC_ALL	DDIC, all authorizations
S_DDIC_SU	Data Dictionary, all authorizations
S_NUMBER	Number range maintenance, all authorizations
S_SCD0_ALL	Change documents, all authorizations
S_SCRP_ALL	All SAP script texts, styles, layout sets maintenance
S_SPOOL_ALL	All spool authorizations
S_SYST_ALL	All system authorizations
S_TABU_ALL	Standard table maintenance, all authorizations
S_TSKH_ALL	All system administrative authorizations
S_USER_ALL	User maintenance, all authorizations
SAP_ALL	All authorizations
SAP_ANWEND	All SAP R/3 (excluding system) application authorizations
Z_ANWEND	All user authorizations (excluding BC system)

N O T E   If you intend to use standard BASIS or application system profiles, you should ideally copy and rename the profiles. This will prevent problems in conversion during future upgrades of the SAP R/3 system.

Profiles and authorizations exist in maintenance and active versions. This configuration provides a means of amending profile and authorization data without affecting the online use of user IDs that reference the profiles and authorizations. All changes are performed on maintenance versions. A separate step is required to activate any changes; when this is done, the existing active version is supplanted by the maintenance version as the new active version. This also offers the advantage of segregating the maintenance and activation functions between different security officers, if required.

Security officers can grant access to functional authorizations for which they themselves don't have access—for example, a security officer can grant a user access to create a customer without requiring those authorizations himself. This feature of SAP R/3 means that security officer activities can be restricted through profiles to only the system resources they need to perform security activities. Profiles are altered and activated by using transaction SU02; for authorizations, use transaction SU03.

Password and User ID Parameters

Each SAP R/3 user must enter a unique user ID and password when logging on to the system. The user ID is assigned by a system administrator using transaction SU0, and that ID belongs to a single user for the duration of his or her required system access. This transaction is used for assigning profiles to the user ID and for defining basic user-ID–specific parameters.

N O T E   Although SU01 offers the facility to add or delete profiles from user IDs on an individual basis, transaction SU10 can be used to achieve the same end for a specified range of users.

Each user must be assigned to a user type. This indicates the type of processing the user ID can perform. The following choices are available for user type:

Online	Normal dialog user
BDC	Batch input session user
Batch	Batch job processing user
CPIC	CPIC (external system) user IDs

Batch and CPIC user IDs cannot be used for online system logon and are excluded from regular password change requirements. No feature exists in SAP R/3 to allow a user read-only access.

A user can optionally be assigned to a user group, which provides a means of functionally and logically grouping user IDs. User groups can be employed to limit the user IDs that can be updated by system administrators. User IDs not assigned to a user group are available for update by all system administrators. The user group can be entered in free textual format; no edit checking of the entered user group occurs. Typing errors can therefore result in the mismatch of values for user group on the user's record and the related authorization.

A user ID can optionally have a validity period defined, outside of which the user ID cannot be used. Similarly, a user ID can be locked or unlocked, which determines whether it can be used for logging on to the system.

CAUTION

User IDs can be deleted individually by using SU01. Alternatively, you can use transaction SU12 to delete all users defined on the system. The SU12 transaction is very powerful and should be used with extreme caution because it doesn't offer the capability to exclude user IDs from the mass-deletion process. SAP recommends that defunct user IDs be blocked rather than deleted from the system in order to preserve an audit trail, although this approach could potentially affect efficient user ID administration.

The system administrator assigns an initial password to a user ID, which the system requires to be altered at the logon screen when the user ID is used for the first time. Users can change their own passwords on the initial screen during any subsequent logon. A system administrator with access to transaction SU01 can alter the password of any user at any time.

A number of rules govern the format of passwords. Passwords must not

- Be less than three characters
- Begin with ! or ?
- Begin with any sequence of three characters contained in the user ID
- Begin with three identical characters
- Be any of the previous five passwords used
- Be pass or SAP*
- Include spaces as the first three characters

Additional organization-specific password checks can be coded for user ID logon processing. This is achieved through modification of the standard ABAP program SAPMS01R. Any edit checks added to this program are automatically executed during logon for every user ID. Because this program is delivered only once (at the initial installation of SAP R/3 in an organization), it will not require repetitive modification during subsequent system version upgrades. From Release 3.0 onward, custom password checks are added to table USR40 instead of through SAPMS01R.

System technical administrators who determine the logon validation procedure for all users can set global system parameters, as described in Table 34.2.

Table 34.2   System Parameters for Configuring User Logon

Parameter Name	Description
Login/min_password_lng	Minimum password length. The default is 3 and can be altered to 4 to 8 characters.
Login/password_expiration_time	Number of days after which a password must be changed.
Login/fails_to_session_end	Number of unsuccessful logon attempts before the system ends the logon procedure.
Login/fails_to_user_lock	Number of unsuccessful logon attempts before the system locks out the user.
Auth/check_value_write_on	Capture the last security check failure.
Rdisp/gui_auto_logout	SAP-GUI timeout.

These parameters can be viewed via transaction TU02. Access to view these parameters is controlled through the setting of user authorizations for object S_TOOLS_EX. These parameters cannot be set using SAP transactions; instead, they can be amended via one of the following methods:

- Run SAP-supplied ABAP RSPROFIL, which gives the option of viewing or amending system profile data.

- Set the parameters manually within the UNIX operating system, in the UNIX file `<systemid><instance>`.

- In Release 3.0 onward, you can choose Tools→Administration→Computing Centre→Management System and the Configuration→Profile Maintenance to set these parameters.

N O T E   As of Release 3.0 of SAP R/3, you can maintain an additional parameter that allows blocking of user IDs that have been inactive in the system for a specified number of days.

Segregating User, Profile, and Authorization Maintenance

SAP R/3 offers the facility to divide responsibility for maintenance of user IDs, profiles, and authorizations. Also, responsibility for maintaining and activating profiles and authorizations can be segregated. The advantages of segregating such access follow:

- By dividing the authority of security officers, a situation is prevented whereby a single security officer can create a user, define profiles and authorizations, and then activate them without any independent review. Because profiles and authorizations can be shared by many users, any changes to them should be reviewed before activation.

- The administration workload can be divided by cost center, department, or any other relevant criteria.

- User administration can be moved into the line where more timely information regarding the status of employees is likely to reside.

N O T E   SAP technical consultants have indicated that dividing maintenance responsibility in this way might not be suitable for small or medium-size installations involving only a moderate number of users, because by its nature it requires multiple security officers to administer, thereby involving a potentially unacceptable cost overhead. For other than large installations, it might be more effective only to partially implement the concept (for example, splitting update from activation administration, but allowing a single security officer to define user IDs, profiles, and authorizations). Alternatively, because user IDs can be assigned predefined profiles, it might be advantageous to rely on the business line functions to create users as required, and restrict security officer activities to profile/authorization maintenance (which requires activation). This decision is at the discretion of the individual organization.

Three objects are used to define security officer authorizations. All activity codes are numeric, and permissible values are defined in tables TACT and TACTT. Activity codes aren't limited to user master objects and are used extensively in other SAP R/3 authorizations.

Object S_USER_GRP determines which user groups can be administered and, consequently, all users assigned to those groups (see Table 34.3). Individual user IDs cannot be specified. Users not assigned to a user group are unprotected from update by any user who has the SU01 transaction.

Table 34.3 User Master Maintenance for User Groups (S_USER_GRP)

Field Name	Comment
ACTIV_AUTH	Activity
XUCLASS	User groups that can be accessed

Object S_USER_PRO determines which authorization profiles can be administered (see Table 34.4). Specific or generic profile names can be entered, because profiles aren't assigned to groups.

Table 34.4 User Master Maintenance for Authorization Profiles (S_USER_PRO)

Field Name	Comment
ACTIV_AUTH	Activity
XUPROFNAME	Profile names that be accessed

Object S_USER_AUT determines the authorizations that can be administered (see Table 34.5). Specific or generic authorization names can be entered. Also, it's possible to limit access to authorizations relating to a limited number of authorization objects.

Table 34.5 User Master Maintenance for Authorizations (S_USER_AUT)

Field Name	Comment
ACTIV_AUTH	Activity
XUAUTH	Authorization name that can be accessed
XUOBJECT	Object names for which authorizations can be accessed

Table 34.6 shows an example of the settings of security officer authorization objects.

Table 34.6 Security Officer Authorization Objects with Examples

Object/Field	Value	Comment
S_USER_GRP		
ACTIV_AUTH	2–3	Change and display
XUCLASS	TECH	All users assigned to class TECH
S_USER_PRO		
ACTIV_AUTH	7	Activate
XUPROFNAME	S_TABU*	All profiles with name beginning with S_TABU

Table 34.8   ABAP Authorization Objects with Examples

Object/Field	Value	Comment
S_PROGRAM		
P_GROUP	Any	Program group (for example, TEST).
P_ACTION	SUBMIT	Execute program.
EDIT		Maintain program attributes and texts.
VARIANT		Start and maintain variants.
BTCSUBMIT		Submit programs for background execution.
S_EDITOR		
P_GROUP	Any	Program group (for example, TEST).
EDT_ACTION	SHOW	Display program source.
EDIT		Amend program source.

Programs can be assigned to authorization groups for access protection. To obtain access to an ABAP program, the user's profile settings must match the program group to which the ABAP belongs. Those ABAPs not assigned to a group are available to all users. There is no edit checking against tables of the entry of program authorization group data, thereby increasing the possibility of error and gaps in program authorization protection.

ABAP programs aren't assigned to authorization groups at the time of system installation. Programs are assigned to functional classes, however, through entries in the following:

TRCL   Program classes

TRCLT   Program class descriptions

Although program classes offer no access protection (as opposed to authorization groups), they do provide a means of functionally identifying programs.

System Administration Functions

The authorization object S_ADMI_FCD provides access control over a number of diverse sensitive system functions. One of these objects is ABAP/IV debugging. Table 34.9 displays all possible values for this object and, where possible, it groups functionally similar values.

N O T E   The system requires that the object name not include numbers. Therefore, the object is named ABAP/IV rather than ABAP/4, which is the name of the programming language.

Table 34.9   System Authorization Functions Object (S_ADMI_FCD) and Possible Values

Value	Comment
TRAC	ABAP/IV trace authorization
STOP	ABAP/IV program debugging mode
REPL	Altering values in debugging mode
KERN	Examining the system kernel from within the ABAP/IV debugger
CUAD	SE41 GUI interface maintenance
DDIC	Data Dictionary maintenance
TCOD	Transaction code maintenance
SE01	Transport system transaction
EVNT	Maintaining system event IDs
SPAD	Cross-client spool administration
SPAR	Client-specific spool administration
SPTD	Cross-client TemSe* administration
SPTR	Client-specific TemSe* administration
SP01	Cross-user spool transaction handling
FONT	SAPscript font maintenance
STOM	Changing system trace switches
STOR	Evaluating traces
SM21	Evaluating System logs
UNIX	Issuing UNIX commands via SM52

TemSe is a data structure that is used to refer local times to a reference time held in the BASIS system.

Most available settings of S_ADMI_FCD are extremely sensitive; consequently, their allocation to anyone other than a highly restricted number of users constitutes a control risk. For example, having UNIX in a user authorization for this object allows the user to issue any UNIX operating system commands from within the SAP application. Also, users with STOP and REPL can run ABAP programs line by line and change the values of program variables while doing so.

N O T E   Transaction SM52 might not be available in some installations. However, the SAP-supplied ABAP program SAPMSOS0 generally is available, thus offering the capability to issue UNIX commands independent of SM52. This program therefore should be controlled through user settings of the authorization object S_PROGRAM.

The SAP Super User

A default super user, SAP*, is supplied in the form of a user master record with every SAP R/3 installation. This user ID has special properties, including unlimited access privileges that can be used to define access privileges for all other system users.

The SAP* user ID is also programmed into the system, so that if the SAP* user master record is deleted, the system-programmed SAP* user ID automatically replaces it as the super user. This ensures that an SAP* user ID exists in the system as the super user at all times.

> **CAUTION**
>
> It's at the discretion of the installer whether to create a user master record version for this ID or to leave the system version of SAP* in the system. However, because the system version of SAP* has unlimited authorizations and an unchangeable password, PASS, it's highly recommended that an SAP* user ID be created using SU01, so that normal user ID authorization and password checks can be instituted.
>
> The SAP* user ID can also be protected by hiding its global authorizations in another (secret) user ID, and giving the visible SAP* user ID read-only access. This provides some protection from unauthorized use of SAP* by someone with some SAP knowledge who might hack into the system and attempt to use SAP*.

SAP supplies a special user group, SUPER, and a number of profiles for use with the SAP* super user ID. Use of the SUPER user group ensures that the SAP* user ID cannot be deleted by any other user.

Special profiles are also available for assigning to the SAP* user ID (see Table 34.10).

Table 34.10   SAP Standard and Super User Profiles

Profile	Description
S_A.SYSTEM	Unlimited access to all users, profiles, and authorizations (as offered by S_USER_ALL)
S_A.ADMIN	Authorizations for SAP system administration. This includes all authorizations except for ■ Maintenance of users in user group SUPER ■ Maintenance of profiles and authorizations with names beginning with S_A.
S_A.CUSTOMIZ	Authorizations for use in the SAP Customizing system
S_A.DEVELOP	Authorizations for use in the SAP development environment (excludes any user or profile authorizations)
S_A.USER	BASIS system authorizations for end users (for example, S_PROGRAM and S_BDC_MONI)

S_A.SYSTEM and S_A.ADMIN operate similarly to the profiles S_USER_ALL and SAP_ALL.

Other Key Authorization Objects

This section describes some other key authorization areas/objects that were not covered in detail earlier but still require careful attention and implementation.

Batch Input Authorization   A single object is available to control access to batch input sessions: S_BDC_MONI. Table 34.11 shows the fields and range of valid values for this object.

Table 34.11   Batch Input Session Authorization Object (S_BDC_MONI)

Object/Field	Value(s)	Comment
BDCGROUPID	Any	Name of batch sessions for which a user is authorized (for example, FRED).
BDCAKTI	ABTC	Submit sessions for execution.
	AONL	Run sessions in interactive mode.
	ANAL	Analyze sessions, log, and queue.
	FREE	Release sessions.
	LOCK	Lock/unlock sessions.
	DELE	Delete sessions.

When a session is generated, a user ID and client number must be associated with it. When the session is processed in the background by the system batch input utility, ABAP RSBDCSUB, the profile settings of this user ID are used for authorization checking. If the session is released interactively (that is, manually by a user), the profile settings of the online user are used for authorization checking. No special authorizations are required to submit a batch session—it's only the management (such as release, deletion, or change) of sessions to which authorization objects are applied.

Each batch session writes entries to a log when it runs. This log contains details of error messages generated and general summary statistics, and it can be interrogated online to check the status of batch sessions.

Number Range Authorization   Authority to maintain number ranges is controlled via authorizations for the object S_NUMBER (see Table 34.12). This object defines the activities that can be performed on number range objects.

Table 34.12   Number Range Authorizations (S_NUMBER)

Object/Field	Value(s)	Comment
NROBJ	Any	Number range object name (for example, KREDITOR for vendors)
ACTVT	02	Change number range intervals
	03	Display number range intervals
	11	Change the last-used number in a number range interval

Object/Field	Value(s)	Comment
	13	Initialize the last-used number when transporting ranges between clients
	17	Maintain number range objects (pre-3.0c only)

Number range objects are used to define number range data within the system. These objects contain number range numbers, type, and other reference data specific to each business entity in the system that requires numbering. A uniquely named number range object exists for each entity requiring numbering; for example, objects KREDITOR and DEBITOR are, respectively, the number range objects associated with the vendor and customer number ranges.

Number ranges can be assigned internally or externally, depending on the configuration of the installation. Multiple number ranges can exist for the same number range object. Tables TNRO and TNROT define number range objects and number range object descriptions, respectively. Number ranges can be maintained via transaction SNRO or directly from within an application.

Change Document Authorization   Access to change documents is achieved through authorizations relating to the object S_SCD0. Table 34.13 describes valid authorization values for this object.

Table 34.13   Change Document Authorization Object (S_SCDO)

Field	Value	Description
ACTVT	02	Maintain and display change documents
	06	Delete change documents
	08	Display change documents
	12	Maintain change document objects

Segregation of Duties   In an integrated system, segregation of duties among related business functions, as represented by SAP transactions, is critical. For example, the procurement cycle from requisition to vendor payment is all contained within one application. The risks of broad access are obvious—if a user can create a fictitious vendor, generate purchase orders, receive goods, and generate payment, the risks of fraud are significant.

For this type of risk to be mitigated, it's necessary to identify these incompatible functions, or *conflicts,* and attempt to ensure that user profiles are established accordingly. A useful approach in doing this is to follow these steps:

1. Group SAP transactions identified as required by the business into generic areas—for example, vendor master maintenance, goods receipt, and general ledger postings.
2. Put these transactions into a matrix, as shown in Table 34.14.
3. Identify conflicts appropriately.

The matrix in Table 34.14 would be used as a tool during the implementation of SAP—all user profiles developed would be validated against it before activation. Some large SAP users have developed tables and ABAP reports within SAP to automate this process.

Table 34.14 Segregation of Duties Matrix

	01	02	03	04	05	06	07	08	09	10
01 Maintain Vendor					×	×				×
02 Vendor Evaluation		×			×					×
03 Requisitioning		×			×	×				
04 Request for Quotation		×								
05 Purchase Orders	×	×	×				×	×	×	×
06 Agreements/ Info. Records	×						×			
07 Materials						×	×		×	×
08 Goods Receipt					×		×		×	×
09 Material Movements					×		×	×		
10 Invoice Posting		×	×				×		×	

Reporting Tools

Generally speaking, the amount of information about access security available within SAP R/3 is very limited. Simple basic query tools aren't provided—for example, a report of which users have access to a given authorization isn't available. An SAP information system is provided from within the user administration menus, which provide a few standard queries, such as these:

- Lists of authorizations, profiles, users, and objects in the system
- Values assigned to a given profile or a given user
- Change documents for authorizations, profiles, and users

Several potentially useful ABAP reports are also available, as listed in Table 34.15.

Table 34.15 Standard Reports for Use in Control and Audit

Report	Description
RSAVGL00	Table comparison across clients
RSDECOMP	Comparing tables across two systems

Report	Description
RSDELSAP	Delete SAP* from client 066 (Early Watch client)
RSKEYS00	Tables comparison, system versus sequential file
RSTABL00	As for RSKEYS00
RSSTAT92	Table changes for a selected month
RSSTAT95	Table access statistics
RSPARAM	Display system parameter settings
RSUSER01	Test SAP_ALL
RSUSR000	List all active users

However, it's anticipated that each organization would need to construct its own dedicated reports to be able to perform effective audits and control reviews. It's important to set aside time and resources for this during the development and implementation phases of an SAP project.

Access Control in SAP R/2

In SAP R/2 (Release 5.0 and later), access security is essentially handled—internally to SAP, at least—in the same way as SAP R/3. The concepts of user master records, profiles (composite and simple), and authorization objects are still valid. As in SAP R/3, an authorization object contains fields to which values are assigned—in SAP R/2, this entity is known as a *value set*, whereas in SAP R/3, it's known as an *authorization*. The following is an example:

Object	BUK	Transactions authorized in a company code
Fields	BUK	Company code
	TCD	Transaction code
Value Set	BUK01	

Fields	Values
BUK	01
TCD	TS01

In this example, a user who has a profile containing the value set BUK01 can execute transaction TS01 in Company 01.

Another key difference between SAP R/2 and SAP R/3 is in the transactions used to manage access security. Table 34.16 lists the key transactions. These transactions should be split among user administrators, authorization administrators, and activation administrators to avoid segregation-of-duty problems in the access security administration area.

Table 34.16   SAP R/2 Access Security Transactions

Transaction	Description
TMU1	Specify user authorizations
TMU2	Maintain authorization profiles
TMU3	Maintain value sets
TMU4	Display user master and authorization information
TMU5	Maintain user parameters
TMU6	Activate profiles
TMU7	Activate value sets
USER	A menu of the previous transactions

Table 34.17 lists some of the more critical authorization objects provided to control access to ABAP programs and tables in SAP R/2.

Table 34.17   SAP R/2 Critical Authorization Objects

Object	Description
PROGRAM	Executes ABAP programs, maintaining variants, attributes, and texts
SAP-SQL	Executes programs that contain SQL instructions
EDITOR	Executes programs that don't contain SQL instructions
DBS	Accesses logical databases
RSTABLE	Modifies and displays table contents and table headers

As in SAP R/3, SAP R/2 has few useful standard reports. Most audit and control-type reports will have to be developed in-house during implementation or before that. Table 34.18 lists potentially useful reports.

Table 34.18   Potentially Useful SAP R/2 Reports

Report	Description
RSBLOG00	Reports the contents of the SAP System log (TRAC file). Must be run in batch mode.
RSSLOG00	Reports the contents of the SAP System log. The online version of RSBLOG00.

Report	Description
RSCLOG00	Reports the contents of the SAP System log, showing additional error references.
RSAQUSGR	Creates a list of all users, including the user groups to which each user is assigned.
RSTAPROT	Reports table changes made online.
RSACDI00	Reports table updates made online and in batch. Must be run in batch mode.

System Integrity Controls (Correction and Transport System)

The key mechanism for maintaining effective change control within SAP is the *Correction and Transport System* (CTS). This section explains the key features and control implications of the associated mechanisms.

Overview

The Correction and Transport System is used to migrate different elements from one SAP R/3 system to another. The CTS can apply corrections to more than one client at a time. The following elements can be migrated:

- ABAP programs
- SAP table structures (and other Data Dictionary objects)
- SAP table entries
- Data elements
- Domains

To process a change in one of these objects to a target system, follow this procedure:

1. Set up a correction for each change required. This can be automatically requested for some appropriate objects (for example, ABAP programs). Or you might have to set this up manually as the object is changed in the source environment.

2. Release a correction to a transport request. A number of corrections can be included in a transport request.

3. Release the transport request. It then is automatically copied to a UNIX file.

4. Initiate an import from UNIX to import the request and update the target system.

Each step is described in more detail in the following sections.

The Correction System

The correction system ensures that formal development work on objects is registered and documented, and that parallel, uncoordinated changes to objects are not possible, even in different SAP systems. SAP maintains a log of all corrections to ABAP programs and tables.

Creation of or changes to objects can be carried out only when a correction is opened. Corrections can be opened while editing an object (for example, in transaction SE38 for an ABAP program) or directly through the correction system (transaction SE01) before editing or creating an object. Opening a correction in advance allows all objects to be maintained as locked from maintenance by other users. Corrections can also be linked. Multiple environment objects can be linked to the same correction.

Corrections can be opened only in the system where the original copy of an object is located. The original location of an object can be defined as one of two systems:

- The system in which the object was created (usually the development system)
- The system "SAP" for objects delivered by SAP

A correction name is assigned when an ABAP program is created or changed. The format follows:

Correction	C11K9000115	
Where	C11	System name
	K	Transport request type
	9000115	Number

The sequential correction number is generated by SAP but can be changed (to allow a previous correction to be worked with), so correction sequence might not be complete. It's preferable to keep the number of corrections in each transport request as low as possible, in case a decision is made not to process a correction through to production.

As soon as an item is included in a correction list, you can review the details by using Tools→CASE→Maintenance→Corrections (which is the SE01 Transport and Correction System). Use the Editor button to see entries and tables.

The PROTECT button within the transaction prevents users from putting items in your correction but doesn't stop them from changing the base table or data. It's best, therefore, to transport corrections as soon as possible after they are set up.

Transport Requests

The transport system is used for moving objects from a development SAP system to a production system or, in fact, between any systems. The transport system can be used to do the following:

- Overwrite components and data in a target system.
- Delete and replace objects.

- Insert objects without overwriting existing ones.
- Delete objects.

The CTS mechanism operates with reference to a number of systems, as shown in Table 34.19.

Table 34.19   CTS Definitions

System	Description
Integration	The "original" system, where software is delivered from SAP, and where development work is carried out.
Consolidation	The primary production system and target of all integration system releases.
Recipient	Additional production systems. Releases to the consolidation system are automatically forwarded to the recipient systems.
Development	Optional systems that can be used to develop objects separately from the integration system (for example, third-party development). Originals are still located in the integration system.

Transports must be done by opening a transport request. Objects in corrections then are assigned to the transport request. All *transport requests* (TRs) are logged. They are applied chronologically and replace the existing object in the target client. This applies to client-dependent and client-independent data and tables. The default is to import the TR into the same client number the TR is being exported from—although this default can be overwritten.

The number of TRs should be minimized to mitigate administration effort. The TR's releaser has to be the TR's owner (that is, the raiser). However, the TR owner can be changed to another user—by someone other than the TR owner—via the CHANGE USER NAME option in the Edit menu option in SE01. This maneuver sometimes is needed for operational flexibility by programmers. This can also be done for corrections in the same way.

Procedures should require sign-off on all TRs being migrated into the production system to verify that the programmers are satisfied that this is a valid update.

A copy should always be transported—that is, transportation code K should normally be used. If code C is used, SAP will think the original now resides in the target system, not the source system, which can cause problems with upgrades and so on. Transportation code C isn't applicable for tables, but it is for ABAPs.

You can see information on the success of an export by using transaction SE01—choose Utilities→Transport Utilities. You can display a multilevel System log that provides information on imports (in the consolidation system) and exports (in the integration system). An exit code of 0 indicates a successful result.

It's possible to get a list of TRs that have been released from the source system and a list of TRs imported into the target system, but not a list of TRs released but not yet imported. You can keep a manual comparison and list, or you can write an ABAP to perform this comparison.

Repairs

Urgent corrections to objects are sometimes required in a nonoriginal system, where time or other factors preclude the creation of a correction and the execution of a transport. These corrections can be made by a *repair.* Any objects altered via a repair cannot be altered via a normal correction until the repair is closed. Repairs must be used for any objects where the original system is defined as SAP (that is, SAP-delivered). Repairs cannot be added to TRs and moved between systems.

Systemwide Parameters

Certain system parameters are maintained in tables that define the migration path between SAP environments. The examples in Table 34.20 assume that a three-tier (production, preproduction, development) architecture is implemented.

Table 34.20   Key CTS Tables

Table	Description
TSYST	Defines the system names in SAP in relation to the operating system and the Oracle database names. The system names are denoted by a three-character name, and SAP always appears as one of these—this is to enable the identification of the receipt of corrections from SAP Walldorf.
TASYS	Defines the relationship between the consolidation system and one or more recipient systems to which transports can be "auto-forwarded." The system SAP again appears in this table.
TDEVC	Lists all the development classes of development objects within the system. Related objects can be grouped in these classes. For all standard classes (for example, those assigned to delivered SAP objects), this will read SAP. For development classes assigned to user-developed objects, this defines the preproduction and development systems.
TADIR	Defines the available development environment objects in a system. The level of development allowed in each environment is also defined in a system parameter contained in this table—Program ID HEAD, Object Type SYST. The field can be edited can be set to A Any change allowed R Urgent repairs allowed _ No changes allowed During a development phase, this field can be set to R, but in a productive system, it should always be set to _. A should never be used.

Development Classes

Development classes are defined for each object in table TADIR. These classes must be assigned to ABAP programs on creation as part of the object attributes. The development class is used to group interdependent objects logically. All delivered SAP objects are predefined in development classes, and all user-defined development classes should be prefixed with a z.

ABAP Programs

When an ABAP program is changed, it is not necessary to identify included modules, *Common User Access* (CUA) definition, screens, texts, or documentation along with the source code.

When an ABAP in a development system is being changed by using transaction SE38, a correction is requested. The details of a new or existing correction then must be entered. A numeric version number of each ABAP program is assigned by the system. The correction then can be released and assigned to a TR from the same screen.

SAP Tables

The use of CTS in the maintenance of SAP tables is rather patchy, certainly in versions before Release 3.0. Tables can be maintained through the customization process or by using transaction SM31 to update the transaction directly.

If a table is being maintained through the customization process, an option generally is available to assign the changes to the table contents made to a correction. This is usually under the menu option Table View→Transport, although it's sometimes hidden under another option. Using this sets up a correction that then can be released and assigned to a TR in the normal manner.

For tables not maintained through the customization process, transaction SM31 must be used. For some tables predefined to the CTS, a correction automatically is generated, the details of which must be completed before the maintenance can take place. For other tables, a correction must be set up directly within transaction SE01, and the table arguments to be transported must be defined manually in a correction.

There is no simple means of establishing which tables

- Are updated only through the customization process
- Have been predefined to the CTS

In both cases, only the table data that has changed will be included in the correction.

Generally, tables aren't assigned a development class, so the target system needs to be defined when the correction is set up. This is defaulted from parameters contained in files in the UNIX directories shown in Table 34.21.

Table 34.21   CTS UNIX Directories

Directory	Description
/usr/sap/trans/log	Logs
/usr/sap/trans/buffer	Information on which transports are to be imported
/usr/sap/trans/cofiles	Information on TRs
/usr/sap/trans/sapnames	Information for users on TR status
/usr/sap/trans/tmp	Temporary data

Tables can be set with the flag Table Maintenance Allowed, which is set with transaction SE11. This means that online maintenance using transaction SM31 can be disallowed, so that only updates by TRs are permitted.

The table entries *at the time the transport takes place* are transported—not those at the time the correction is set up. It's possible to change a table that has been set up to be transported if the particular table isn't locked. This is common to many SAP tables.

Authorizations

UNIX security over the TR file in SAP is a critical issue and must be addressed.

Within SAP R/3, it's important to ensure that check objects are assigned to the CTS transactions. This might not be a major concern, because all these transactions do is copy data out into the UNIX area, and they don't actually import the data into any client—that is, no updates are performed. However, because the command to import the TR into the target client is done via UNIX, this will be done by technical support employees, who probably will not know the contents of the TR and so might just import any and all TRs they are asked to import.

Accordingly, even if SAP doesn't consider it necessary to put an authorization check on the CTS process, such authorization access should at least be in place over the release of TRs. This will prevent unauthorized users from releasing (potentially dangerous or fraudulent) TRs to be imported in the next import due.

Transaction SE01 (Transport and Correction System) is protected by the check object S_ADMI_FCD with a value of SE01. However, an unprotected transaction, STAR, is also provided in the system.

Processing Controls

This section discusses some key processing or technical controls. The correct and controlled implementation of these controls is essential to data integrity within an SAP system.

Dialog and Update Tasks

A key element of SAP R/3 processing is the way in which database update tasks are performed. There are essentially two steps to an SAP transaction: the dialog task and the update tasks.

The dialog task involves user terminal input being accepted by the SAP front-end software through a series of SAP GUI display screens. Following this, conversion to SAP's proprietary format takes place, and resulting processing requests are placed in an SAP request queue. These conversion and enqueue processes are performed by the SAP Dispatcher.

A log of all updates waiting to be passed on to the database is maintained in the file VBLOG. Cases can occur in which a dialog task has been completed—that is, as far as the user is concerned, his/her transaction has been posted—but the update task fails, so the database isn't updated with the relevant information. Such cases have serious implications for system database integrity. The record on VBLOG is set with an error flag and remains (successful updates are deleted from VBLOG). It's also possible to configure the system so that an express mail message is sent to a certain database administrator if this occurs.

Managing Batch Sessions

Batch (BTC) sessions can be created in SAP to do the following:

- Use a validation step when interfacing data from an external system
- Pass data from one part of an SAP system to another

Effective batch session management is critical to ensure that data is passed on to its target on a timely basis. The way BTC sessions are managed in SAP typically means that they have to be manually released so that a data update can be performed. A number of inherent risks are associated with this process:

- Access security must be effectively established to allow only authorized users to manage, release, and delete batch sessions. Authorization objects are provided for this purpose.
- If a batch session fails to be released successfully (through a processing error), the data within the session can be manually amended from within the batch session maintenance transactions. Unfortunately, there is an audit trail of any changes to data made in this manner, but nothing can be done about that.
- If batch sessions are not cleared on a timely basis, this can lead to confusion for users, such as releasing the wrong batch session. Or it can lead to errors in the original batch session if related records are changed or deleted from the database in the interim.

Unfortunately (but not surprisingly), there is a lack of helpful reporting tools within SAP in this area. It's therefore likely that some custom ABAP reports may have to be developed in this area—to list aged BTC sessions, for example.

Interface Controls

Automated interfaces into and out of SAP are typically managed through BTC sessions. The following control guidelines should be used when dealing with inbound and outbound interfaces:

- Control reports should be automatically produced from the source/receiving system and SAP to show the following for records input, accepted, and rejected: record count, total number of customers/vendors processed (where applicable), total value Cr (where applicable), total value Dr (where applicable), total amount (where applicable), and total volume (where applicable).

- Control reports should also list all input parameters entered when an ABAP report is run.

- Controls should be established over erroneous transactions, which can be held in suspense files so that they are nonamendable before reinput.

- For certain interfaces, it should be possible to run a nonupdating version of an interface program before a live run, so that inputs can be checked before transactions are actually created.

- All interface files produced by SAP or an external system should be uniquely identifiable by the use of interface type, creation date, creation time, and run number to ensure that files aren't confused or processed twice.

- All interface programs should be thoroughly tested, documented, and subjected to user acceptance before implementation.

- Users must be assigned responsibility for each interface and must be trained in the methods of controlling the interface.

For certain interfaces, you might want to load data direct from a PC environment (for example, Excel spreadsheet) into SAP. This is particularly common when you need to upload journal voucher information into the SAP FI-Financial Accounting General Ledger. In this case, the spreadsheet is used merely to perform a complex calculation to arrive at the value of a journal or series of journals that would otherwise be input manually into SAP. It's not data from a controlled application; therefore, it does not have to be subject to all the previous controls. However, the data should be subject to the same controls as it would be if it were input manually—for example, online validation, post-facto reporting, and supervisory review.

Application Controls

Application controls are, by definition, determined by the requirements of the business, and thus cannot be discussed in as specific terms as access security functionality, for example. The functionality available to build application controls is discussed in detail in the relevant chapters of this book; however, a few general points can be made in this area.

Application controls in SAP are typically table-driven and are established through the customization process during implementation. These types of controls are generally rather rigid—after they're implemented, it's difficult to switch them on and off dynamically. A couple of the more critical areas of application are discussed in this section by way of example:

value-based limit of authority controls in the procurement cycle and online customer credit checking in the sales cycle.

Limits of Authority

SAP-provided functionality over the release of purchase requisitions relies on the definition of the following:

- **Release strategy.** Defines the process of approval of purchase requisitions, based on their total value and the level(s) and order in which they must be approved online within the organization. Release values are determined at line-item level; up to eight release points can be defined for each release strategy.

- **Release condition.** Determines which release strategy is applied to a requisition, and depends on the account type, material group, plant, and value.

- **Release indicator.** Indicates the status of a requisition and determines, for example, whether the item can be ordered and whether the quantity or delivery date can be changed.

All these parameters are defined in tables during the customization process and must be established and agreed on with management before their implementation.

Online Credit Checking

SAP provides sales functionality centered around the use of sales order types. The type of credit check performed can be defined relative to specific order types—for example, an intercompany sales order can be processed with no credit check, whereas a standard order can be defined as having a credit check that does one of the following if it fails:

- Display a warning message.
- Prevent the order from being posted.
- Accept the order but block it from delivery.

Also, it's possible to define the values taken into account when the credit check is performed— that is, whether the following sales are included:

- Ordered but undelivered
- Delivered but uninvoiced
- Invoiced but unpaid

Each order type would have to be configured for these and a host of other parameters. This would be undertaken at preimplementation during the customization process.

Data-Entry Controls

Data entry into SAP is critical. One of the system's most appealing selling points is that data needs to be entered into the system only once. The downside of this is that data entered inaccurately will have serious ramifications throughout the system in terms of processing, particularly in the case of master file data that is referred to on numerous occasions throughout transaction input.

SAP has some important features that assist in the accurate entry of data into the system:

- **Match codes.** Used to look up relevant data (generally master files) when entering a transaction. For example, when a sales order is entered, match codes are used to select the correct customer record and material. This can be done without knowing the record number and without leaving the transaction. A customer can be identified by knowing the postal code and a material by knowing the product name it represents. Using match codes therefore assists in the accurate cross-referencing of other system data when processing a transaction.

- **Data tables.** Used to hold commonly accessed data elements and prevent the need for them to be entered continuously. For example, bookkeeping exchange rates are held in an SAP table and automatically default into the relevant fields when processing foreign currency General Ledger postings, sales orders, purchasing transactions, and so on.

A significant area of exposure exists, however, in the override of default data entered into SAP. For example, when a sales order is raised, certain data can be defaulted into the document:

- Delivery address (from the customer master)
- Terms of delivery (from the customer master)
- Sales tax rates (from a combination of customer master and tables)
- Payment terms (from a combination of customer master and tables)
- Exchange rates (from data tables)
- Sales prices (from the pricing file)

Depending on the system's configuration, any or all fields can be changed or overridden by the user entering the sales order into SAP. An implementation team configuring the system faces the paradox of wanting to maintain flexibility by allowing users to change defaulted data, while needing to retain a degree of functional control.

During the system design phase, it's therefore critical to correctly configure the complex tables that lie behind the control of dynpro field selection. Of course, all this work should be discussed with the relevant functional system owner to determine the degree of freedom that will be allowed and the degree of control that will be released.

Compensating Controls

Because of the problems associated with inflexible application controls and the potential capability to amend and override previously validated data, in an environment where tight supervisory control has been the norm, there might be some problems in managing expectations about the effectiveness and nature of the control environment following the implementation of SAP. Although many companies are moving away from the traditional hierarchical organization and direct supervisor-subordinate reporting relationships and toward flatter organizations and more empowered cultures, they might be unwilling to sacrifice controls they have always viewed as sacred.

The implementation of such controls likely will rely heavily on the use of system-generated post-facto control reports. Such reports can be broadly divided into a number of categories:

- **Master data creation/change authorization reports.** Customer master creations/ changes, vendor master creations/changes, material master creations/changes, GL account master creations/changes.
- **Master data validation reports.** Potential duplicate vendors, customers also established as vendors, customers with unlimited credit.
- **Transaction default override reports.** Critical fields overwritten on sales orders/ invoices, on purchase orders, on GL posting documents.
- **Authorization reports.** Purchase orders in excess of commitment authority; sales orders blocked, having failed credit check.
- **Backlog monitoring.** Customers' orders unfulfilled, purchase orders not printed/ issued, quality inspection stock levels.
- **Account reconciliation.** Accounts Payable to General Ledger reconciliation, Accounts Receivable to General Ledger reconciliation, General Ledger postings (can be restricted by certain value and account parameters—for example, postings with a P&L impact only).

It should not come as any surprise that SAP delivers very little in this area by way of standard reports. A significant amount of specification, programming, and testing is required. It's not uncommon to see more than 100 post-facto control reports developed in some large SAP implementations, especially with a more traditional culture and control environment.

When coding control reports, it's important to keep the following things in mind:

- Reports should always have pages numbered.
- The message End of Report should always appear on the last page.
- Report distribution should be automated wherever possible. This might involve setting up an internal table of users listing supervisor/department relationships. Page breaks should be inserted before each new user is listed.
- All reports should list user ID and name, user department, time/date stamp, and before and after images, when appropriate.

It's also important that retention periods for control reports are agreed on in advance with internal and external auditors, as well as any relevant tax or other government authorities.

In an SAP implementation project where controls are specified at a level that requires the development of a large number of post-facto control reports, it's always a struggle to get users to accept those reports. SAP often replaces legacy systems where controls have been developed within the system and a minimum of reports is necessary. Facing the arduous task of reviewing what might seem like mountains of paper will not be a popular prospect. It's therefore important to ensure that these reports are kept to a minimum. And, when required, full endorsement from owners should be given. Also, the business risks associated with not using the reports should be explained.

Addressing Control Issues During an SAP Implementation

Most organizations have enough to think about during an SAP implementation project without having to worry about the control issue. However, if this issue is not addressed at this stage, serious problems are inevitable later, and it's almost impossible to retrofit controls into an SAP environment. This section provides a few key pointers for project managers, controllers, and internal audit managers that should be considered before embarking on such a project.

Using Dedicated Controls Resources

Control issues don't generally come at the top—or even close to it—of an SAP implementation project's list of priorities. Basic business processes might still need to be designed, tested, and implemented; users trained; and data converted. Even if controls are considered important at the outset, they are often pushed back in the implementation schedule or are not addressed at all. This can have disastrous results following implementation; attempting to retrofit controls is almost impossible in some areas of SAP, and moreover, any exposure to the business is quantifiable during this period. Thus, it's strongly recommended that dedicated controls specialists be used on any SAP implementation project. Such individuals can be taken from a number of areas to ensure that the right people with relevant expertise are used:

- **Internal audit.** This is a common source of controls staff on SAP projects. Using members of this staff has the advantage of retaining any specialist controls knowledge within the organization. Also, assuming that a reporting line to audit is maintained, these employees retain independence from the project, and their diversion to activities not related to control can hopefully be prevented. The main disadvantage of using internal audit staff is that there is a very steep and expensive learning curve in getting up to speed on SAP. Also, a staff of at least three is required to become sufficiently expert in the control environment of the various modules. Assigning one individual from audit to work part-time on an SAP project, as often happens, is fairly worthless in terms of performing a detailed control evaluation of the system.

- **Project team members.** These people can be assigned to address control issues during implementation. Although this has the advantage of keeping the work within the project, it invariably results in the individuals concerned being taken off controls work and assigned to tasks perceived at the time as more pressing. Very rarely is this strategy successful.

- **External consultants.** Consultants are now available who can provide specialist advice in the area of security and controls. The most common place to look for such advice is from the Big Six accounting companies. The quality of service and depth of specialist knowledge now varies within such organizations but is improving. Also, many individual experts in the field are available to provide advice in this area. As with all stages of an SAP implementation, the use of consultants has to be carefully managed. Terms of reference must be tightly defined and the expertise of the consultants proposed must be fully examined.

Control Issues

Addressing control issues on an SAP project should be viewed in the context of two major phases: system development and configuration, and system implementation.

System Development and Configuration   The main tasks of the controls advisor in the development phase of an SAP implementation follow:

- Review the functionality of each business process to determine whether there are any associated SAP weaknesses. This can be done only through a detailed review of all dynpros and related master file information, as well as all customized table entries behind each transaction. This is a very lengthy process and requires a considerable degree of expertise to perform.

- Develop potential solutions to the control weaknesses identified. These solutions commonly come in the form of changes to table settings through the customization process or the development of post-facto control reports. It's generally best to avoid any source code changes unless a control issue is very high profile and there is no other acceptable solution.

- Meet with functional owners of the system and agree on controls.

System Implementation   During the system implementation phase of the project, a number of important control issues should be addressed:

- Access security
- Data conversion
- Automated interfaces
- Change control
- Development of procedures and implementation of control reports

Access Security   Key tasks are involved in a preimplementation review of access security. With regard to the establishment of users, it's essential to ensure the following:

- All access privileges are consistent with individuals' job responsibilities.
- Transaction access is reviewed for adequate segregation of duties.
- Transaction access is reviewed for particularly sensitive transactions, and access to these is kept to an absolute minimum.
- Third-party access is controlled in accordance with the company guidelines.
- All relevant details are completed on the user master (for example, some fields, such as Department, can be used to sort reports).
- Appropriate naming conventions are used for all users and authorizations.

Also, procedures should be developed to ensure the following:

- User IDs that haven't been recently used are identified and suspended.
- Users who leave the company or are transferred can be identified, and access is deleted and re-created as appropriate.
- Each change to a user ID is supported by a formally documented and authorized change request.
- Ownership of system transactions/authorizations is established, and the owners approve all requests for access to those transactions.

The broad access generally given to support and development users must also be properly controlled. This access should be subject to review and approval before implementation. It's quite common to agree on a period of grace (say, 30 days), during which team members continue to have broad access for immediate support requirements.

Data Conversion   Data conversion controls should be established to encompass the following:

- Conversion planning and the identification of dependencies
- A data cleanup exercise prior to conversion, to ensure that all data to be converted is accurate, valid, and current
- Procedures for the reconciliation and validation of all data
- Procedures for the parallel maintenance of master files
- Ownership of converted SAP files to enable user acceptance and sign-off procedures to be established
- Keeping the involvement of noncompany (that is, contract) personnel to a minimum, and subjecting all data input by temporary staff members to extra validation

Automated conversions require extra considerations to ensure adequate control:

- Control reports should be automatically produced from the input, interim, and final files.
- Control reports should include record counts and control totals on key fields.
- Listings of records not transferred to SAP due to error should be automatically produced (including record counts and control totals), and procedures should be developed for error handling.
- Records in error in batch sessions should be amended with care.
- SAP tables might need to be set up to be referenced during the automated conversion. The conversion procedure should include the maintenance of these tables.
- All conversion programs should be fully tested with user involvement and the test results documented.

Manual conversions also require specific controls to ensure accuracy and completeness:

- Input forms should be developed to collate data in a form suitable for entry to SAP.
- If any fields have been changed or were not included in previous files, they should be suitably approved and verified online to input forms.

Automated Interfaces   A checklist of key interface controls is provided in the Implementation Management Guide. It's important that for each interface identified, adequate control mechanisms are in place before implementation, as well as properly documented procedures for use in the operation of the interfaces.

Change Control   The correct establishment and implementation of change control is critical to the integrity of any SAP system. Relevant tables must be customized, and access to critical transactions must be restricted and segregated. Also, procedures for the operation of change requests should be developed, documented, and circulated to all development staff members.

Procedures and Control Reports   A list of all post-facto control reports developed to compensate for weaknesses in the SAP system should be used as the basis for inclusion in local procedures. Each report should be reviewed by users and relevant implementation team members to determine the following:

- Is the report applicable to the particular business unit in question?
- Is the report in a format and sort sequence that meets user requirements?
- Will the report be run online or in batch?
- What will be the frequency and scheduling of the report in batch?
- Who will be the recipient(s) of the report? The recipient must be independent of the activity being reported.

The method of report distribution is also critical. The most efficient and secure method of distribution is to ensure that reports automatically reach the intended recipient.

In many cases, the control reports are required before the official implementation date. Maintaining converted data and inputting transactions before implementation—for example, customer orders—require a review of the control reports.

Business procedures should be developed to cover all areas in which the system operates. Existing company policy/procedure guides should be used as the basis for developing new SAP-relevant procedures. From a control point of view, particular attention should be paid to ensure the following:

- Manual procedures compensate for all control weaknesses of SAP.
- All control weaknesses arising as a result of noncore or nonstandard functionality are addressed.
- Procedures are included for the use of all control reports.
- Procedures are included for the authorized update of all user tables.
- Procedures are included for the update and addition of master records and the relevant approval.

Auditing SAP

Following the implementation of SAP, the organization's auditors face a serious challenge, internal and external, in modifying and developing their audit approach and ensuring that their staff members have the right skills and tools to do this work. This section provides some useful tips on addressing this challenge.

Developing SAP Skills in the Audit Function

The best way to develop SAP skills within the audit function is to involve the audit staff in the development and implementation phases of the project. A rough estimate of the learning curve associated with SAP in this area is that it can take 12 to 18 months of full-time effort for an experienced system auditor to become fully conversant with the control functionality of one SAP module. If a system-based audit approach in which SAP is intensively evaluated and interrogated is to be used, this level of expertise will be necessary.

For some organizations, however, this is an expensive luxury and not a practical route to auditing SAP. Alternative audit approaches are discussed shortly.

More recently, several training courses have been developed—largely by the Big Six accounting firms—that specifically address audit and control issues. These courses tend to focus mainly on the technical areas of control within SAP; access security and change control feature prominently. The courses generally avoid looking at application controls within the modules in any great detail, aside perhaps from a cursory review of the FI-Financial Accounting module.

A SAP Auditor Workstation is now available specifically for use by auditors working online to an R/3 system.

Audit Approaches

Depending on an organization's size and the prevalence of SAP within it, several audit approaches are possible:

- **Dedicated SAP controls group (the "Rolls Royce" approach).** Some large companies have established groups of dedicated SAP experts within their audit function. Such groups are responsible for providing controls advice to any SAP implementation project, and for developing and maintaining any tools for use in auditing the system postimplementation. Such a group can also be given the responsibility of actually performing audits of the system, although it might be desirable for reasons of independence to keep this separate. It's perhaps difficult to rely on the objectivity of an auditor reviewing an SAP system that he/she helped design and implement.

- **Dedicated SAP expert auditors.** Smaller companies will likely assign the responsibilities of SAP review, project involvement, and audit to certain specialist auditors in the audit function, often to be performed in tandem with other responsibilities. This approach obviously doesn't provide the same level of SAP expertise, but it is quite common in smaller organizations. SAP audit tools are likely to be developed on an ongoing basis during audits and not maintained in the interim.

- **Auditing around the system.** If a system-based audit approach isn't used, a more traditional approach of validating the input and output of a computer system can be used. This approach doesn't rely at all on an understanding of how the application functions. Instead, the application is viewed as a "black box," and the approach relies on statistically generated samples of what are viewed as key documents. This approach isn't really recommended unless SAP represents a small part of an organization's business or an audit department is very small.

■ **Outsourcing the review of SAP.** The outsourcing of internal audit is a growth area, and because most big accounting firms are large enough to have developed at least some SAP expertise, this is an option. However, unless the whole internal audit function is outsourced, this approach can generate some communications problems.

Documenting Control Concerns

A key part of any SAP audit approach is how to document control features identified during evaluation of the application. Suggested audit steps could also be provided where specific weaknesses have been documented. A possible approach to documentation could be based on control objectives that some organizations have already documented—for example,

■ Control objective

■ SAP-related strength

■ SAP-related weakness

■ Associated audit step

The audit step could be running a computer audit program, verifying that a control report is produced and reviewed, or performing a test of a manual procedure in cases where the control objective isn't addressed by SAP functionality.

Audit Software

Developing *computer-assisted audit techniques* (CAATs) is an important part of developing an SAP audit approach. Any computer audit programs developed can do the following:

■ Test users' access to key system resources.

■ Read data files and report exceptions.

■ Review system settings (that is, customized table entries).

■ Look at other system-held information.

Several choices are available in the use of software.

ABAP/4   ABAP/4 is SAP's proprietary programming language and has been used to write most of the program code making up the SAP application modules. ABAP programming is undertaken from within the SAP application using standard menu/transaction options.

A number of important advantages and disadvantages are associated with using ABAP/4. The advantages follow:

■ ABAP/4 is fully integrated with the SAP application. Programs can be run from alternate sessions within SAP—toggling, for example, between a display transaction and report output.

- Any user with basic SAP navigational skills can start ABAP/4 programs. You don't need to become familiar with an external query package.

- Because ABAP/4 is a part of the SAP application, it will always read the most up-to-date data. It runs directly against the same Oracle (or other database) tables as the application.

- ABAP/4 takes advantage of the links between SAP data elements and Oracle table and field names. Therefore, the SAP Data Dictionary can be used to ensure that the correct field descriptor, for example, is output on reports.

- A wide range of selection options can be specified in the report screen. This enables users to reduce the quantity of data read by the program.

- Options are available to download ABAP/4 output to Excel spreadsheets, if required.

- Certain SAP elements (for example, user master and security information) are held in SAP pool tables and can be read only by using the ABAP/4 language.

- Several copies of standard SAP ABAP/4 are delivered with the application, which—although they aren't audit-specific—can be amended to serve as audit tools.

Here are some disadvantages of using ABAP/4:

- ABAP/4 is not a true fourth-generation language. Programmers require a high level of training to become expert and can demand high remuneration. The current demand for ABAP/4 programmers is high, and continuity of staff members is a problem.

- ABAP/4 doesn't provide flexible options to manipulate data onscreen. After the program output is produced, data can be manipulated onscreen only by using a download option.

- Changes to reports require a change in a development environment and promotion to production. This can be a time-consuming process.

Downloading Data   It's possible to write a single ABAP/4 program that downloads data to a flat file external to SAP. This data then can be interrogated using any number of data query/analysis packages. The advantages of such an approach follow:

- The cost of employing expensive ABAP/4 programmers is avoided; only the download ABAP/4 needs to be written.

- Audit staff members can write audit queries.

- Programs are easily amended and flexible.

- Programs are highly transportable.

Downloading data also has its disadvantages:

- Downloaded data isn't always reviewed on a timely basis; it soon becomes out-of-date.

- Because they are not using an integrated solution, users have to learn to use two systems. They will likely still have to log on to SAP to execute display transactions and perform other tasks.

- It's not possible to run a query that interrogates data and tables concurrently.

- It's not possible to download certain information—for example, user master records and authorizations.

Alternative Software   Several packages are available that can directly interrogate SAP R/3 data—for example, as held within the Oracle database. These packages allow direct and real-time access to the data, but there is a problem in this area: The SAP data is held in Oracle tables, and the names of these tables and the fields in them aren't represented by business-relevant text. Therefore, it's extremely difficult to construct a query with one of these packages because it's not possible to determine the data being analyzed. The link between SAP field names and their equivalents in the Oracle database is held within the SAP Data Dictionary, but it's not easily accessible. Some software companies are looking at establishing files that provide 'this mapping within their own package, but as yet these are very much in the formative stage.

Audit User Groups

An excellent means of sharing information, exchanging ideas, and jointly developing control and audit-relevant information is through the user group network. Audit-specific groups have been established and are very active in the United Kingdom and the United States. Active participation by all audit departments in organizations where SAP has been implemented is to be encouraged. ●

Managing Internal and External Communications

In this chapter

Overview of SAP Project Communications Issues

The formation of project teams frequently takes people away from their normal jobs, leaving a workload that needs to be covered by others. SAP projects are typified by the union of business and IT staff members from the company, with a variety of external employees brought in to support the project. The working environment is probably new, and many people do not know each other, let alone their positions and what is expected of them. The business personnel probably does not know too much about SAP, and the systems personnel probably does not know too much about the business. For the project to succeed, there has to be a huge volume of knowledge transfer and tremendous cooperation between team members and users. Effective communication therefore is vital and needs to be addressed before the project even begins.

Time is the most valuable asset on an SAP project. The second the project starts, the costs start rising; with senior consultants costing upward of $2,000 a day, you cannot afford to waste time, yet it is remarkably easy to do. Unnecessary meetings, meetings with no framework, and floods of email are the worst culprits. Information overload is as serious a problem as lack of information.

If you want your project to succeed, you must take communications seriously. Ideally, project management should seek some professional help from communications consultants to plan and monitor an effective communications policy. Undertaking an SAP project in a large company is a significant task that may well affect every person in the organization.

The following items need to be considered and communicated to those who need to know:

- Implications of SAP implementation
- Progress of SAP implementation
- Benefits of the SAP system—for example, the streamlining of business processes and resulting ease of operation
- Training requirements (a necessary corollary of the successful implementation of SAP) and details of the relevant course(s)

Do not leave these matters to the corporate grapevine—it is vital that the facts about SAP are not left to the often-fertile imaginations of employees, especially those likely to react adversely to the perceived effects of technological advance and change. Remember that corporate grapevines can operate at extraordinary speed—you need to avoid and, at best, preempt this.

Remember, as with project management, the timing of communications—as much as their clarity—is of the essence. You also will need to identify and focus on your audiences.

Subsequently, you will need to advise your customers about your organization's adoption of the SAP system. It is important to relay this information positively. After all, SAP will make an enormous and quantifiable difference to your service levels and, as a direct consequence, to your level of client satisfaction. Your organization's resulting increase in skills base, efficiency, and speed of response is good news; it is worth putting in some effort to get the message across.

Of course, you will also need to provide for the transmission of your messages to a wider external audience—the trade and national/international press, your shareholders (if any), and your suppliers.

The Importance of Effective Communication in SAP Projects

Good communications are not simply important, they are essential—they can improve working conditions and relationships within an organization; and promote internal and external confidence, growth, and success. Good communications enhance areas such as productivity, innovation, harmonious teamwork, good media relations, and optimum shareholder relations.

Good communications should form part of an organization's strategy and be adhered to at all corporate levels.

Nobody likes to think that he or she is a poor communicator, but however high your rating may be, there is always room for improvement. The same, of course, applies to organizations and corporate entities. The acid test of communication is always the vital, three-part question: Has the message been understood, registered, and accepted?

A great deal of research has been carried out on basic communication during the past 10 years. The results may give you pause for thought. Consider the following:

- Of oral instructions given, only about 50 percent were received and retained.
- Retention of information delivered at a lecture series drops from an upper limit of only 52 percent down to an unsatisfactory 25 percent.
- Of information passed one-to-one from boss to subordinate, only between 20 percent and 60 percent is absorbed.

Think about the matter in more depth, and you will find plenty of useful examples from your experience. You might find the following familiar:

- As the recipient of information, you can edit out unwelcome news, remembering only the positive elements.
- Everyone switches off if given too much information at once.
- We all tend to restrict information sharing by, for example, passing it on to a small, selected audience or even restricting it to an individual.
- The fewer links in the chain of communication, the easier it is to convey the message.
- Information conveyed orally is better understood and accepted if accompanied by open questions, including hostile ones.

Of course, entire chapters could be devoted to the ramifications of each of these examples. They are all fruitful and useful points for discussion, especially within the context of brainstorming sessions (one of the most useful management tools before determining strategy, because their informal context enables all imaginable points arising from a set of issues to be raised and dealt with creatively before practical testing).

Developing an SAP Project Communications Strategy

Before you formulate your communications strategy, look at how your organization now conducts communications. Are any channels already working well? This means, in effect, that messages are conveyed clearly and quickly, the channel operates as a two-way conveyor of information, and the efficiency of the process can be measured. If you already have efficient systems in place, you might simply need to update and upgrade them.

First Steps: The Communications Audit

Whatever the state of your organization's existing communications, your first step should be to conduct a communications audit. This combines desk research (involving, for example, a review of your corporate identity and information and support literature, along with press coverage files) and active research (surveying the attitudes of receivers of corporate messages transmitted internally and externally).

An audit might appear to be tedious and a waste of time. After all, you know all about your communications—but experience demonstrates that it is more likely that you only *think* you do. It is surprising how frequently communications, both external and internal (especially the latter), are ignored. Managers often assume that the channels are open and operating, without necessarily paying attention to whether messages are properly conveyed. Deficient communications can mean reduced efficiency and morale and, ultimately, the corollaries of reduced productivity and sales.

In any case, an audit saves you a great deal of time when you reach the stage of determining your communications strategy. Indeed, you will find that many elements of your strategy have been identified for you by the audit results.

If your budget allows you to commission independent communications consultants to conduct the audit on your behalf, do so. You will achieve a truly independent perspective on your existing communications channels and effectiveness, plus the bonus of expert recommendations. If you are operating under budgetary constraints, it is still possible to get an efficient audit. Remember, it must be as comprehensive, thorough, and objective as possible.

You can use a number of research techniques—typically, questionnaires (including a feedback section and allowing for anonymity), group discussions, and in-depth interviews. Always run a pilot study first; it is essential to keep you on track in your lines of questioning and may reveal areas of concern to your audiences that you had overlooked.

Whichever option you choose, you will almost certainly find that your respondents will readily make suggestions for improvements. In many cases, such suggestions will be especially valid because of their source: People who are actually carrying out or overseeing a process or those on the receiving end can normally be relied on to produce good ideas for its improvement. This is as true of communications as it is of any other industrial and commercial practice.

After you complete your audit, you will find that the results are an invaluable aid to formulating strategy. The extent and nature of your strategy are governed in other respects by two main factors: the size of your communications budget and the availability of trained staff to drive the strategy through the organization.

Ideally, your trained staff should be in a position to train others, as communications are an all-embracing corporate discipline. Communications involves everybody in your organization; it is not the sole preserve of one department or senior manager. For example, consider that the receptionist is often a client's first contact with an organization. This person can deal with a client in a way that facilitates or loses a sales/promotional opportunity.

Determine Strategy

When you are formulating your communications strategy, you need to ask questions such as these:

- With the help of SAP, where will the organization be in X years' time?
- How do you propose using SAP to get there?
- What external factors will affect corporate development? What systems, for example, do your competitors have in place; and will SAP offer quicker deliveries, fewer errors, or better customer service? Positive benefits must be transmitted to employees and customers—both present and potential.
- How will the SAP system itself help streamline and speed up communications channels?

When these questions are satisfactorily answered, you will need to define your objectives.

Define Objectives

What are the principal aims of your strategy? What do you need them to achieve for your organization? Agree on the answers to these questions, and then go on to identify your target audiences.

Identify Your Audiences

With whom should you be communicating? Segment your audience, which might break down like this:

Employees	Shareholders
Customers	Suppliers
Media	Project team
External contractors and consultants	

Try to be as specific as possible in defining the different groups your strategy must reach; this will help you to agree on your priorities.

Agree on Priorities

Which objectives are the most important or urgent? Agree on these so that resources can be allocated accordingly. You will probably find that there is insufficient funding to allow you to do everything at once.

Set Targets

You will need to monitor the implementation of your strategy at various key points. If you have set targets at this stage, the procedure will be easier; it will also help you to decide later whether to continue with certain activities, depending on their success rates.

Draw Up a Time Scale

At the risk of stating the obvious, your time scale must be realistic. The resources available to you should give you an indication of time scales. Remember, though, to build some slack into your time scales; allow extra time for interruption by urgent tasks, for example, and for surprise developments (they do happen—see the following section, "Plan For Contingencies"). It helps to map the time scale on a chart, which leads to your next task.

Plan Your Communications Campaign

You must be meticulous about planning your communications campaign, but do not forget that all-important element of creativity—good ideas. When realized, they often produce remarkably good results.

Be alert to opportunities; you will need to respond to them quickly. Here are a few examples:

- A well-known journalist wants to do a story about the effects on your organization of SAP implementation. You should have all the information he or she needs at hand, and a representative of your organization adept at explaining SAP should be available to offer a detailed briefing and, time permitting, a tour of the premises.

- A member of your staff suggests a further application for your SAP system that seems likely to enhance productivity. If you think this is the case, act on it—and make sure that the activity, its originator, and its results are publicized within the organization (and externally, if appropriate). A reward to the originator of the concept is good practice, too; it encourages further constructive suggestions from within your organization. You might even consider setting up a reward system.

Plan For Contingencies

As stated previously, you should always be prepared for the unexpected when planning and budgeting. Some communications projects may cost more if they are well-received. For example, that journalist previously cited could turn out to have colleagues in the same or other media, domestically or overseas, who require similar services from you. Or demand for a brochure could exceed the specifications of your print run.

Measure Results

Allowing for contingencies will enable you to measure your results. After your strategy has been in place for around six months, further research will be necessary to make sure that you can monitor changes in knowledge, perception, and attitudes. The results will give you a clear indication of what your strategy has achieved and what, if necessary, you need to do to enhance your continuing communications program.

Remember, your communications program is not just a one-off. You must keep the momentum going (see Figure 35.1).

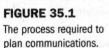

FIGURE 35.1
The process required to plan communications.

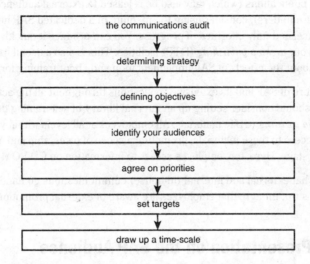

The Elements of Communications

Some elements were already touched on in the preceding sections. The bases are, of course, good written and oral skills. And it cannot be overemphasized how important these are. You might need to look at the possibility of further in-house training in presentation skills, for example, because these are crucial to the success of communication.

Your organization's essential style may have changed as a result of SAP, along with a number of practices. You might need to redesign your logo to symbolize these changes and overhaul your corporate identity accordingly. This is often the case at times of major change. Always examine these elements in detail before launching your program—you might need to obtain further budget allocation for design work.

Because you will almost certainly now be engaged in raising your profile in the marketplace, you must make sure that the image you convey is right for your organization. The image of your organization conveyed by your corporate identity must reflect your positioning in the marketplace, as well as the style and nature of your organization.

As for addressing your external and internal audiences, you will find that the nature of your audience will determine the mode of communication. After you identify your audiences, you will have a clear idea of the medium to use for addressing them. If not, you will need to seek expert advice from a communications consulting firm or public relations agency.

You will address your audiences in a number of ways. Your message may be transmitted via press releases along with a conference; via CD-ROM; or by a series of lectures given to relevant staff members, followed by an informal question-and-answer session.

If you have a corporate newsletter or paper, you will need to ensure that a series of features on your system migration to SAP gives positive and interesting information. If you do not have such internal publications (which may also be released to external audiences, such as trade press and shareholders), consider using the medium of a dedicated SAP newsletter to keep everyone concerned fully informed of progress. You can produce it quickly and cheaply in-house using your *desktop publishing* (DTP) facilities. This is also a useful medium for relaying information about the effects of SAP implementation and about training for its use.

Given the nature of SAP and its extensive applications throughout all the activities of your organization, you should consider setting up an internal library of self-training desk- and *computer-based training* (CBT) materials. All employees at all levels within your organization would have access to these materials, promoting a sense of ownership and self-determination from an early stage. Here, too, employee access to information on CD-ROM can be very helpful.

You will find that external and internal (in-house) communications go hand in hand to a great extent. Make sure, though, that employees are aware of external promotional initiatives before these happen.

Conducting a Presentation on the SAP Audience

Whatever your audience, whether internal (employees) or external (the press, customers, or shareholders), you should consider several points before opting for an open address.

The manner of a speaker is very important. First, you will be more effective if you seem to be an expert on your subject. Second, you must appear well-intentioned toward your audience. These factors apply whether you are seeking to convey information, change attitudes, or influence behavior. Although these factors might strike you as self-evident, it is surprising how often they are ignored. Many a crucial presentation has been ruined because the speaker is inaudible, boring, unconvincing, nervous, cannot handle an audience, or merely presents good material badly (with delivery working against content).

You should have a friendly, agreeable, and lively manner and seek to make the presentation interesting and enjoyable throughout. Your aim is to convey confidence and enthusiasm, and you should therefore be in constant contact with and in control of your audience.

If you have any doubts on these scores, seek help. You might need to take on further training. But whatever you decide, it is always a good idea to rehearse a presentation in front of a colleague or group of colleagues you know will give you constructive criticism and sound advice.

If it is possible, inspect the venue beforehand. Everyone should be able to see and hear you, and see your visual aids. Make sure that the room is arranged appropriately and will comfortably accommodate the expected attendees.

Oral presentations can vary enormously. However, for the purposes of presenting information about your SAP system, the following guidelines will prove useful.

TIP   Some companies in North America allow Toastmasters meetings, an organization that helps people become better speakers. Of course, attending such meetings is purely voluntary.

Opening   The *opening* is when you make contact with the audience, securing their attention. In doing so, you should make sure that you put them at ease and ensure receptivity by mentioning your links to them or related self-presenting, and explaining what you are going to talk about and why.

Remember, what you are going to talk about is important and interesting; SAP will help your organization solve important problems. These thoughts will help you focus on capturing and maintaining the interest of your audience.

Using Positive Statements and Arguments   Make sure that your statements and arguments are sound, with supporting evidence, good illustrations, and clear visual aids.

Structure your arguments. Make sure that the materials you use in support are inherently interesting. When you are explaining unfamiliar ideas or procedures, try using striking examples. These will help change audience attitudes.

Drawing Conclusions   You must not overlook your conclusion; otherwise, your presentation is left hanging and is not fully received by your audience.

Dealing with Discussions   You should indicate in advance that the floor will be open for discussion.

You should take audience contributions seriously and sympathetically—make an effort to understand the viewpoints put forward. You should not only deal with the points raised, but also try to work out the best solutions, preferably enlisting audience assistance, because this promotes understanding and acceptance.

Avoid any form of confrontation with the audience or individual members. Remember, your aim is to inform, persuade, and motivate.

Dealing with Objections   Always deal with objections honestly, addressing the objector directly but keeping an eye on the rest of the audience so that your answers apply to all those present. Use examples to illustrate your themes, and make sure that your replies are full and factual.

A useful exercise is to try to anticipate objections in advance and consider how you will address them. Remember, the better you know or have researched your audience, the better position you will be in to deal with any of their objections.

Retaining Audience Interest   At all times, you must retain your audience's interest. Here are a few tips to help you do so:

- Speak clearly! This often means loudly and distinctly. Try projecting your voice to all corners of the room, while keeping the quality of your voice—timber and pitch—under control. Unless you are an experienced speaker, you may need help with this.
- Avoid the major pitfalls of public speaking: sounding nervous, acting superior, and being boring.
- You should be able to vary the tone and pitch of your voice to make your delivery more interesting.

Using Visual Aids   Visual aids should be of high quality. Try to avoid cramming too much information onto them; your audience probably will not be able to decipher it all and take it in. One to three points may be covered in a single slide, for example, depending on the amount of information you need to convey. Remember, the visual aids act as a summary and focus; you will be outlining in more detail the statements, proposals, or arguments.

You should make sure that visual aids are legible, comprehensible, and in color.

Seminars/Lectures and Conferences   Seminars, lectures, and conferences for teams, groups, and departments are also important. Make sure that whoever addresses these audiences can do so clearly, confidently, and positively. The speakers(s) must inform, build loyalty, and motivate the audience.

Here are some other factors to consider:

- The audience may be resistant.
- The audience will definitely be asking themselves, "What's in it for me?" and "How will this affect my job?"

  Make sure that these questions are anticipated and answered as fully as possible—evasion does not work. However complex or antagonistic the question, always answer it. Evade a question, and your audience will lose faith in you, just as most of us do when watching a politician deliver a series of nonanswers to an interviewer on our television screens. Be calm, honest, and positive.

Things to avoid in this context might seem obvious, but they are always worth stating:

- Do not patronize your audience.
- Do not treat an audience as a homogeneous mass; they are individuals.
- Do not be impersonal—if you know the names of questioners, address them by name when replying.
- Do not be irrelevant.

Use humor by all means, and always match the style of humor to the type of audience.

Always stress that the successful implementation of SAP depends on teamwork and relationship building—and these involve everybody. The key phrases here are "how we are going to succeed together" and "how this will benefit you." These gain force if you look at your audience when you express them.

Lastly, keep an eye on the clock; try not to overrun your scheduled time.

Internal Promotion: Meetings

We all know that a major part of business is conducted at meetings. We all know, too, that not everybody enjoys meetings, whether they are chairing or participating. This is normally because meetings can frequently prove unproductive at best and counterproductive at worst.

To avoid such outcomes, do the following before the meeting:

- Start by considering your approach. What do you need to achieve? How much progress can you hope for? What decisions do you want to see made, and what actions do you want your audience to agree to?

- You usually have a major advantage, because you will already know the other attendees—and their concerns and attitudes. Try, therefore, to anticipate any opposition to your plans. And develop arguments to deal with this effectively.

- Rehearse your arguments as though you were going to present them on stage. Break them down into key points and know them so well that you can present them in any verbal form.

- Be ready to negotiate—and to listen. With each argument, there should be one key point on which you are prepared to compromise, within reason.

- Discuss proposals with team members and other allies to elicit their views and support.

- Make contact with your potential opponents. Be friendly, and try to find some common ground.

At the meeting, you should do the following:

- Arrive on time—make sure that you do not miss anything (or put yourself in the position of being discounted due to an absence, however brief).

- Greet everyone. Try to create an informal and cooperative atmosphere. People who are relaxed are more receptive.

- Make sure that everybody can hear you, and that you have captured their attention.

- If your proposal is complex, say it twice using different phraseology. For example, you can simplify "The SAP system will save us xxx dollars on distribution channels," by then saying, "In other words, we'll save x percent of our operating budget."

- Keep it short. When you finish making a point, especially a complicated one, there will probably be a few seconds of silence. Do not be tempted to fill it; your colleagues are engaged in absorbing what you have just said. Remember that extra words can dilute the force of an argument—and even fuel opposition.

- Concentrate on contributing to the important issues of the meeting. Do not feel that you have to participate in every discussion; some may be trivial and, if so, joining puts you at risk of being perceived as petty and tiresome.

- Always deal with objections competently. Consider them carefully, and address objectors in a friendly fashion. Look your critic in the eye as you respond, and make your points brief and hard-hitting while keeping your voice friendly.

The notice in Figure 35.2 was pinned to a notice board of an SAP project, bringing a few smiles to the faces of stressed project team members. Sadly, it seemed to apply perfectly to a great many of the meetings.

It is inevitable that meetings are a major part of SAP projects. Used well, they contribute enormously to a project's overall success. By following a structured approach, it is possible to greatly increase a meeting's efficiency:

FIGURE 35.2

A notice that appeared on the notice board of an SAP project.

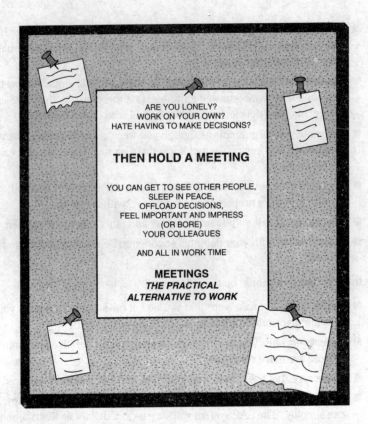

ARE YOU LONELY?
WORK ON YOUR OWN?
HATE HAVING TO MAKE DECISIONS?

THEN HOLD A MEETING

YOU CAN GET TO SEE OTHER PEOPLE,
SLEEP IN PEACE,
OFFLOAD DECISIONS,
FEEL IMPORTANT AND IMPRESS
(OR BORE)
YOUR COLLEAGUES

AND ALL IN WORK TIME

MEETINGS
THE PRACTICAL
ALTERNATIVE TO WORK

1. *Ensure ownership of the meeting.* Whoever arranges the meeting should take ownership of it.

2. *Create an agenda.* The meeting owner should issue a written agenda that clearly defines

    - Where the meeting is to be held
    - When the meeting starts and how long it will take
    - Who is attending the meeting
    - The purpose of the meeting
    - What is expected of those attending
    - The expected outcome of the meeting

3. *Use a facilitator.* A facilitator is an independent person who is not the owner. His or her purpose is to control the meeting, ensure that it meets its objectives, keep it from getting sidetracked, and ensure that certain points are raised and issues are captured.

    Typically, a facilitator introduces the meeting and asks all those attending what they would like to achieve by the end of the meeting. He or she then writes up on flip charts what everyone wants to achieve. As the meeting progresses, the facilitator captures on paper the issues as they arise. Toward the end of the meeting, the facilitator establishes how the meeting has met the expectations of the members and pulls together the next steps with details of who should do what and by when.

4. *Issue minutes.* The meeting owner's minutes summarize the results of the meeting and list who should do what and by when.

By controlling meetings in this way, everyone's intentions are focused on what the meeting is trying to achieve. Issues raised in the meeting are not lost, and a clear way forward is identified, with individuals knowing exactly what they have to do and by when.

Internal Promotion: Training

You will save time and effort if your internal communications program is drawn up in tandem with a training program. You will need to communicate closely with trainers on materials, actions, and progress.

First you need to plan your program with care to ensure that nobody is excluded and priority groups are established before implementing the program. Aspects you need to cover include career progression and the overall market perspective. Your organization has become more dynamic because of your adoption of SAP; this overall effect will demonstrate itself, but it needs to be promoted.

Always ensure that your trainees can comment on their training, when completed. There may have been gaps; there may be areas that need further expansion or illumination—all these need to be amended as the program progresses.

Remember:

- Plan
- Implement
- Monitor
- Measure
- Proceed on the basis of your findings

You and your organization will not be standing still. With the SAP system, you will always be going forward.

Internal Communications: User Groups

When training is completed, user groups are a useful channel for quality initiatives, internal promotion, and further training (often of the self-determined variety). Encourage teams to set up such groups whenever possible. You should make sure that these groups are not operating in a vacuum. Informal liaisons between different teams can iron out problems of comprehension, speed up adoption of new procedures, and reinforce a sense of involvement in SAP throughout the organization. Such lines of communication also facilitate quality control.

Set up a series of efficient and easy-to-use reporting lines. For example, email and groupware can be effectively exploited to these ends. Trainers and IT management should be actively examining the application of SAP to the communications arena.

External and Internal Promotion: Publications

Again, a dedicated newsletter can be useful. Always invite questions, comments, and contributions from your audience(s). Much of this feedback will prove helpful in, for example, identifying areas where further communication is required or where training must be focused.

Articles must be factual, but they must not be dry—you want people to read them, after all. If you have access to professional corporate writers, use them.

External Communications: Advertising

You don't need to be told that advertising is expensive. Before instructing an agency, try to see how much precampaign work you can do in-house. Study your competitors; look at the trade/business and national press, and advertising in other media. Determine what resources you need to devote to advertising your new message or messages.

Try to decide which media are most suitable for your organization. Exploiting a combination of trade press and billboards might be a winner for you. Of course, your agency can advise you on this. But, as ever, the more informed you are at the beginning, the more quickly you will achieve the desired results.

External Communications: PR and Media Relations

If you do not have in-house professionals, it is time to consult the experts. Remember, they are not cheap, but they can save your organization money; for example, editorial coverage can raise your organization's profile more precisely and more cheaply than advertising. Public relations is one of the most cost-effective promotional media.

You should maintain a close working relationship with your consultants; you will need to know what they are doing for you and what the results are likely to be. You should be in a position to monitor the results. Even though the consultants will be doing this, too, it is always worthwhile to double-check. After all, the results your consultants achieve are usually measurable. These may be in increased trade or national/international press coverage, increased sales, and an encouragingly favorable shift in customer attitudes. Always ensure that any results are measured according to the correct criteria for the action involved.

Do not forget to publicize encouraging results throughout the organization and its relationship network (where appropriate). You can do this via correspondence circulation, notice boards, or your newsletter or publications—even a combination of all three.

Targeting a Large Audience

The conference is your optimum method for reaching a large audience in the shortest possible time. If you lack in-house resources to plan and organize such events, you will have to look further afield.

Many PR agencies are expert in conference planning and organization. There are also specialist conference organizers. In a busy organizational environment, subcontracting such services can make sense; it saves your organization time and resources, and a really well-run conference is enormously valuable.

The experts in this field have a track record in ensuring that conference delegates are amused as well as informed—and the increased motivation this gives to a sales force, for example, will literally pay dividends.

Again, do your homework before selecting your consulting firm. Know your own messages and the audiences you want to reach. Speak to several different agencies, taking care to ensure that the ones you interview are experts in your own field and entirely sympathetic to your organization's activities and aims.

Remember, the most successful conferences are those based on a strong overall theme to which attendees can relate. The most common thematic examples in the industrial and commercial conference world are drawn from sports or war. But the field is wide open, and you can devise your own suitable concept. You are free to exercise your imagination, but bear in mind that what you are doing is informing, promoting loyalty, and motivating by means of enthusiasm.

External and Internal Communications: Writing Skills

Many academics, teachers, and authors believe that someone who cannot express his or her beliefs, thoughts, or feelings clearly in writing cannot think cogently. Although this opinion might seem rather damning, it does have a great deal of validity in the corporate environment. How many times have you wasted precious time working out what that memo writer really meant in paragraph 3, only to find that he or she repeats the same ideas in paragraph 12 (clouded, if possible, by even greater opacity)?

Examples of bad writing in business and professional life, if systematically collected, would fill another book. However, the rules for good writing—that is, clarity of expression—are very straightforward and easy to adhere to.

One of the most helpful guides to good writing is George Orwell's essay "Politics and the English Language." Orwell says that before you start writing, you should ask yourself four primary questions:

- What am I trying to say?
- What words will express it?
- What image or idiom will make it clearer?
- Is this image fresh enough to have an effect?

While writing and editing, you should also pose the following questions:

- Can I put it more succinctly?
- Have I said anything that is unavoidably ugly?

Most of Orwell's essential rules that apply in this context follow:

- Never use a metaphor, simile, or other figure of speech that you are used to seeing in print. Today's popular catch phrases date rapidly; an overused metaphor loses its force. Using such terms makes you sound lazy and unoriginal.

▓ Never use a long word when a short one will do. Try replacing *with regard to* with *on, in respect of* with *about*. Your sentences will be shorter and sharper.

▓ If it is possible to cut out a word, always cut it out.

▓ Never use the passive voice when you can use the active. It sounds more immediate (and closer to your speaking voice).

A useful rule is to cover one point per paragraph. Long paragraphs have a tendency to tire the eye of the reader, whose attention you really need to attract. Also, long paragraphs containing several tangled arguments tend to reduce the effectiveness and lucidity of those arguments.

N O T E   As you know, jargon can save time and effort. But when using jargon, beware. Unless you are addressing fellow specialists, remember to think about your audience; they might not have a clue what you are talking about when you use strictly technical terms. Do not use jargon or technical language unless you are sure that it will be fully understood or you have sufficient space in your document to explain your terminology. If you take this course, the same rules apply: Keep your explanations brief and make them as clear as possible. ▓

If you follow these rules, you will find it easier to organize your writing. There will be the additional benefit of producing written work that is fresh, attractive, and concise. It is therefore far more likely to be read and absorbed.

External and Internal Communications: Body Language

Whatever message you are putting across in person you can contradict by your body language. It is no good to stand on a platform and boldly deliver a brave new message if your posture is hunched and defensive.

Body language doesn't need to be the preserve of social anthropologists and zoologists. Anybody can learn about body language. You already possess the principal qualifications for engaging in such a study: your eyes and your powers of observation and recall. Watch groups at work and at play. Who is dominating? How? Who is resistant? How can you tell?

It is surprising how illuminating this unspoken language can be. Observe for yourself, and adopt practices that suit you, your style, and your comfort level. If you feel that you need further help, plenty of publications are available on the subject—in your public library, for example.

Using Groupware in SAP Implementations

If your company doesn't already use groupware, it should be seriously considered for your SAP project and implementation. Regardless of the brand of software you choose, groupware offers a tremendous tool to manage communications. The capability to look into anyone's planner and schedule a meeting, book a meeting room, and issue agendas and minutes is invaluable. You can raise issues, get people's comments, and come to speedy resolutions with the greatest efficiency. ●

CHAPTER 36

Training for SAP

In this chapter

Training for Success

The delivery of training is usually subject to severe time restraints. Frequently, large numbers of personnel need to be trained within a short period of time. Training schedules need to be flexible, to allow for the real world of people not being available, courses being missed, holidays, and the system not being available.

Training material has to be relevant to the users and well-written to ensure that it is easily understood. Usually there are tight time constraints on the preparation of material. Whether training material is computer-based or documentation written for guides or courses, it should be created with care.

You need to create an environment within the SAP system to use for training, without disturbing the development or production system. You also need a physical training area with training rooms, computer terminals, and other equipment.

Before training starts, an education and communications program should generate commitment among the staff to the introduction of SAP and an understanding of the real issues. This is particularly important if the project involves significant business process reengineering.

Having spent hours working on your training schedule, you will want to monitor each individual's attendance, to keep a record of nonattendance, and to adjust the plan accordingly.

Regardless of the methods of training or the organization or facilities in place, the most important thing is the effectiveness of the training given. An important aspect of the training process is to monitor effectiveness at every stage. If what you have planned and prepared is not effective, you need to change it quickly.

The training requirement carries on well beyond implementation. People not involved in the original training, such as new recruits and users, will require training in the future and will need to learn about changes to the system. You need to devise a long-term training strategy to deal with all future training requirements.

Project Team Training

More and more commercial companies will be offering SAP project team training in the future as the SAP market continues to grow, but now the most reliable training is offered by SAP itself. SAP offers approximately 400 courses, although availability varies around the world. In the UK, SAP has a brand-new training center at Heathrow. Project teams will need to be trained in the project methods being used, project policies and procedures, and many other things.

Defining Training Requirements

Defining who needs training in what skills is a lot easier if you have already defined the organization's business processes in an earlier phase of the project. Chapter 32, "Overview of SAP Implementations," looks at the importance of knowing your business and your organization. Because this amounts to a prerequisite to a successful SAP implementation, assume that this has been done. Your first step, therefore, is to match particular business processes to specific job functions—it is normally preferable to use job titles rather than named individuals—and to establish which modules and transactions each job needs to perform each process.

You also will need to make sure that nothing has been overlooked. When a process is initiated in one department and then passed to another for completion or authorization, it can fall between the cracks. Neither department considers the process its responsibility, and therefore, neither department manager identifies it as a process. Suppose that sales users make a contract with an overseas customer. The business requires that the Treasury sector safeguard against fluctuations in exchange rates. A bank fixes an exchange rate for transactions that will take place in the future. A mechanism is needed in the system to create a system message advising the Finance department that a new sales contract number has been created. Only by this electronic system message does Finance know to set up a new currency contract correctly in SAP. Until this is done, the Sales department cannot place orders against its sales contract.

Given SAP's integrated nature, picking up these things is obviously very important. There are two approaches to gathering all the information you require:

- **Interviews with key users.** Conduct structured interviews with key users and senior management who have a special interest in SAP's successful implementation.
- **Questionnaires.** Design a questionnaire for key users to complete to capture their thoughts on training requirements. Interviews can form a useful backup on completion.

After you gather the data, enter it into some form of matrix; the details obviously will vary according to your organization's particular requirements. However, the matrix should show the relationship between business processes and functional work groups (for example, Accounts Receivable, Warehouse X, Retail Sales). You now should be able to answer this question with some confidence: "Who needs training on what aspects of SAP's functionality, so that SAP's introduction into our organization will be as efficient and effective as possible?" However, do not expect this first pass to be your last—you will need to be flexible to accommodate changes as the implementation progresses.

You will also need to address other questions, such as these:

- What training methods will be most effective?
- What resources will I require to develop and deliver the training?
- Where should users receive their training (centrally or at local sites)?
- At what stage before "going live" should the users be trained?

Identifying Suitable Training Methods

You should carefully consider the method of delivering your training, because your decision will have a huge impact on the project budget. In this respect, there is nothing unique about an SAP implementation; the same options are open to you as with the implementation of any other computer system:

▨ Traditional classroom training, in which one trainer trains a homogenous group of users in a room set up for that purpose

▨ Individual coaching, where the user is trained one-on-one at his or her workplace or in the classroom

▨ Computer-based training packages

The method or combination of methods you use will depend on your own organization's particular circumstances, your budget, and (to some extent) your personal preferences.

Classroom Training

You may or may not already have a training room set up. If not, a cost will be involved in setting one up. The number of users you train at any one time will depend on various factors. How many PCs are in your training room? How many people can the trainer "control?" How many people can be pulled away from their jobs at the same time? Obviously, the more people you can process at a time, the cheaper your training will become, but experience shows that a group of more than about 8 to 10 people is difficult to handle.

Individual Coaching

Unless you have a very small implementation, the individual-coaching method probably will not be cost-effective. However, coaching might be necessary to scoop up any individuals who have missed the main training program or have fallen behind and have not learned enough in their classroom training.

Computer-Based Training (CBT)

A number of computer-based packages are on the market. Some require skilled programmers to tailor them, whereas others are less complex and can be used by an ordinary trainer. However, certain advantages and disadvantages are shared across the board.

Advantages   Here are some of the advantages of using CBT:

▨ Trainees can train themselves at a time suitable to them and acceptable to the business.

▨ Other than explaining how to load the package and get started, trainers do not play much of a role. This greatly reduces ongoing costs.

▨ Any decent package includes a feature that monitors the trainees' progress, preventing trainees from going on to the next step if they have failed to grasp the principles of the current stage.

▨ Most packages have a function that records trainees' scores. You can use these scores to identify people who need extra help, so that a human trainer can provide extra coaching.

▨ Training is consistent for each individual across the business.

▨ Training is available to new people coming in after implementation and for refresher courses.

Disadvantages   Here are some of the disadvantages of using CBT:

- The up-front purchase cost can be significant.
- A large development effort may be required, depending on the package and the complexity of your implementation. One supplier quoted a ratio of 150 development hours to one hour's training.
- Lack of human contact means that questions may go unanswered and business issues unresolved.
- A CBT package is less "fun" than a warm, friendly human trainer.

Developing the Training Team

Having chosen your method of training, you can now go on to build the team that will develop and deliver the training.

The makeup of this team will vary depending on the method you choose. For example, if you chose the CBT route, you will need a large number of developers and very few deliverers. If you chose mainly classroom training, you may want to have the people who develop the training materials deliver the training, or you may have a centralized development team that sends out the material for delivery by local trainers.

A further consideration is what type of people you want on the team. Do you want users co-opted on to the project team, information systems people on the project team, or external consultants? Obviously, there are no hard-and-fast rules here—just some points for you to consider.

Appointing Users

The advantages of using key business users include the following:

- They know how the business operates.
- They know their audience.
- They are cheaper than external consultants.
- They will be an immediately accessible source of help for other users after SAP is implemented.
- The skills they will have to develop will be kept in-house.

However, there are some disadvantages as well:

- Learning SAP requires a significant learning curve, which can be expensive in terms of time and money if they are sent on SAP's own courses, for example.
- Users will need skills in training and possibly some training on managing change if the implementation will result in a major change of business practice.
- Management must be totally committed to releasing users onto the project. Otherwise, users will be impossibly stretched between the training demands and the demands of their "real" jobs.
- To retain their skills in-house, users and their managers should consider and make explicit plans for career progression after implementation.

Using Information Systems Team Members

Here are some of the advantages of using your own *information systems* (IS) people as developers and deliverers of training:

- They are already familiar with SAP.
- They are already familiar with the business's use (or planned use) of SAP.
- It is cheaper than using external consultants.
- The skills IS people develop when learning the skills themselves before training will be useful to them personally in their careers within the company.
- Making this choice leaves the users free to run the business.

However, there are also some disadvantages to using IS people:

- The people chosen as trainers will need to acquire training skills.
- Their time must be carefully managed, and you must get a commitment from the project manager not to pull them off training development when problems arise in other IS areas.
- Training IS people in SAP gives them a highly-marketable skill. To avoid having your IS people lured away into the SAP contract market, give serious consideration to their career progression after the implementation.

Using External Consultants

The advantage of using external consultants is that they already have the SAP skills and the training skills to develop and deliver your SAP training. (If a consultant doesn't already have these skills, why use him?) However, there are a number of considerations:

- External consultants are expensive.
- They will not know your business, and thus will need to spend some time with your key users to understand it before they can start to be productive.
- Users may be distrustful of outsiders telling them how to do their jobs.
- Some external consultants might have ideas that do not suit the project.

Whatever approach you choose, remember that to gain the most benefit from your training program, you should identify and begin to involve the trainer(s) from a very early stage of the project. It is unrealistic to wheel someone in the last few weeks before going live and expect him to deliver effective training.

Preparing the Training Plan

You should incorporate training in the project plan and budget from the inception of the project. Costs that some companies overlook include the hidden costs of releasing personnel for training: documentation costs, overtime, and the cost of finding other people to cover the users' jobs while they are at the training.

A key decision is when to start. Starting early minimizes the overall project elapsed time (by overlapping the development of the training environment and materials with system testing) but may well generate substantial rework as system changes are made. Starting early also complicates the coordination of system build and training activities for individual project team members.

Starting later reduces the need to rework the material, but unless resources are available for very intensive course development and delivery, you might need to extend overall project time scales to allow for training time. As a rough guideline, you should not release parts of the system into training development until they are at least 80 percent correct and complete. You can build decisions on the readiness of particular modules of functionality for training development into quality assurance points—for example, at the end of build work or before system testing starts.

Given the dependency of the progress of systems build work and testing on the development of training materials, there should be open communication between the project manager and the training manager throughout the project's life. You cannot develop training material when the system is being built, because you don't know how it will work. Training development and delivery should be formally linked via precedence relationships in the project plan to agreed project milestones. For example, you could specify that training is not to start until system testing is completed. Therefore, if project milestones move, the impact on training schedules is apparent immediately.

You should also draw up a full training plan using the same planning tool and standards as the overall project plan. You must identify your own specific task lists, including these aspects:

- Course specification and design
- Quality assurance
- Creation of a training environment populated with valid data
- Production of training materials and user documentation (if a distinction is being made between these)
- Delivery (including delivery scheduling)

Preparing the Training Schedule

In the section "Defining Training Requirements," earlier in this chapter, you saw an approach to analyzing training needs and answering the question "Who needs training in what?" Now that you have identified your training course requirements, you need to specify the contents of each course and design it.

After you go through that process, you should be able to estimate how long each course will take to deliver. You then can do the simple calculation of dividing the number of users who need to take part in each course by the number of individuals you have decided is optimal, and then multiplying that result by the number of days of the course's duration. This gives you the number of training days you need to schedule.

This sounds simple, but scheduling can become extremely complicated. The business will impose limitations on your plans, so you will need to work around the following:

■ Business needs—for example, customer orders still need to be met during the training period

■ Particularly busy periods for certain departments—for example, period ends for Accounting

■ Holidays, vacations, and planned shutdowns

■ Shift patterns

■ Sickness

Some specialist software tools on the market can help you schedule, but you will need to remain flexible. Not allowing people to be ill when they should be attending an SAP training course unfortunately does not work. You also might find it helpful to have a local site contact to advise you on the best times to schedule courses. Personnel departments may take on this role and may also help in monitoring attendance and following up on nonattendance.

Preparing the Training Material

The physical appearance of the training documentation will vary from organization to organization. If you choose the CBT route, paper-based documentation may consist only of a guide to getting started on the package and maybe some quick reference help cards. Other organizations will choose classroom training backed up by screen illustrations and explanation. Still others might want to draw a distinction between *training materials* and *user guides*.

Generally, users tend *not* to reach for their training documentation when they have a problem. They usually ask a colleague. If your training budget is tight, keeping your training documentation short and simple could help keep costs down.

Ideally, the development team should generate some training documentation. At the very least, they should supply a series of flow diagrams or "route maps" that break down each business process into a series of steps and link each step to an individual SAP transaction. Some system development approaches could provide even more material—for example, detailed business cases developed for acceptance testing could be recycled as training aids.

You can choose your training materials from the following list, putting greatest emphasis on the areas most important to your organization:

■ Business processes and flow diagrams describing the processes

■ Screen illustrations with text descriptions of key fields

■ Introduction to basics of SAP (match codes, icons, and so on)

■ Trainer demonstrations

■ Trainee exercises and case histories

■ Help (quick reference) cards

Other considerations include the following:

- Do you want to differentiate between business training (explanations of how SAP will affect procedures, responsibilities, organizational structures, and so on) and systems training (hands-on operation of SAP)?

- Regardless of the form of documentation you use, spend some time deciding on standards so that it is consistent.

- It will take longer than you think for the documenter(s) to produce the materials.

- Don't forget to factor into your schedule the lead times required from external service suppliers, such as printers, reproduction shops, laminators, and so on.

- You might need to follow BS5750/ISO9000 procedures.

TIP Many programs enable you to capture screen illustrations. Lotus ScreenCam, for example, offers two very useful features. It captures still screens for inclusion in paper documentation, in file formats that you can import into nearly any word processor. It also can record a minivideo by capturing each keystroke in a process. With this feature, you can "film" any SAP process and then play it back as often as required.

ScreenCam is not a CBT program, and its capabilities are too limited for you to consider using it to generate full-scale CBT instruction packages. However, its recording feature can be invaluable for passing along information from highly skilled developers to documenters who have very little knowledge of SAP. For example, the IS team can use ScreenCam to capture each process after it goes through quality assurance and then pass it on to the documentation development team in this format. The documenter playing it back can see the process flow without needing to know how to use SAP.

Whatever form your training materials take, do not assume that they will remain static (see "Developing a Long-Term Training Strategy," later in this chapter); build in a system of maintaining version numbers before you start.

Creating the Right Training Environment

The right training environment consists of two factors: technical and human.

SAP Training Environment

You need to set up a separate training client or systems environment that represents the latest development work and can be refreshed regularly. It needs to be populated with sufficient data to make the training demonstrations and exercises realistic, including tables, master data, and documents. You should agree on a procedure for updating and controlling the system with the system manager as early in the project as you can.

Physical Training Environment

Although you are running an in-house training program, it will be more effective if you treat the trainees as though they are volunteers attending an external course. The training room should be made as comfortable as your budget allows, with sufficient (and sufficiently comfortable) chairs and tables to make the experience enjoyable. Some organizations prefer to have two trainees on each PC, so that they can work together and learn from each other. Having more than two trainees per PC is not practical.

If you are setting up a room from scratch, remember to specify plenty of power connection points and communications connection points for the computers. Also pay attention to the lighting; avoid direct sunlight on monitors and exclude natural daylight altogether if using *liquid crystal display* (LCD) tablets.

There are, broadly speaking, two methods of presenting trainer demonstrations to a large audience:

- Something that projects the image from the trainer's screen onto a large screen that everyone can see. Examples include LCD tablets with overhead projectors and dedicated computer projectors.

- A mechanism that allows the trainer to control all the trainees' screens by switching them so that they see what is on his or her screen. This is commonly referred to as *slaving;* once under the "master's" control, trainees' keyboards become inoperable, thus removing the temptation for them to "explore" rather than work on the topic currently under discussion.

Communication, Education, and Training

Communication, education, and training are three different activities, all of which have their places within a project's life cycle. Before training starts, a program of education and communication should be conducted to gain commitment to the introduction of SAP and an understanding of the real issues. This is particularly important if the project involves significant business process reengineering.

You will need different approaches to communicate the impact that SAP will (or may) have on different management levels. These two approaches have been successful in helping to gain commitment from the organization's most senior people at the inception of the project:

- Illustrate how SAP will support your industry's accepted "best practices." A number of courses cover best practice (entirely independent of SAP). If you can find a course appropriate to your board members, you can follow it up with an in-house presentation and discussion of how SAP will support them.

- Bring in a business "guru" to facilitate a discussion about the impact and benefits of introducing a fully integrated system.

After all the major decisions are made, you must make all employees aware of what the impact will be. It is best to plan an ongoing communications program to ensure that employees have a chance to ask all the questions they want and receive answers to those questions as the project progresses. Tried-and-tested approaches include the following:

- In-house overviews emphasizing the need for change
- Road shows/demonstrations of SAP functionality specific to the jobs of particular groups or departments
- Regular newsletters
- Online bulletins

Without effective education and communication, effective training is impossible. Instead of having a receptive audience willing to learn the functionality of SAP and knowing why they have to learn it, the trainer may be faced with a group of employees who are apprehensive about their futures and resistant to learning.

Controlling the Training Program

Having spent hours working on your training schedule, you will want to monitor each individual's attendance and keep a record of nonattendance. Another benefit of a successful education and communication program is that everyone will be aware of the importance of showing up for training when scheduled, and managers will think twice before pulling people out of training for business "emergencies." However, sometimes the business must take priority, or people (or even the trainer) are too ill to attend. Therefore, it is important to keep records regarding who receives training so that additional training can be run if necessary.

Quality control is also an issue. You should create a postcourse questionnaire to get feedback that is as objective as possible after each course. If a particular aspect is consistently criticized, this can be fixed at an early stage of the program. Other considerations follow:

- Although ideally, training should take place after testing is completed, "bugs" and other problems may manifest themselves during training. You should devise a formal method of capturing these problems and feeding them back to the development team before further training continues.
- If users consistently find an area difficult to master, you should plan to spend more time on that skill in class or develop a help card or similar tool to distribute.
- Experience shows that in order for people to refer to their manuals when they are using the system in a live environment, they need to have worked with manuals in the training course. Therefore, your training should include manual use.

Analyzing the Effectiveness of Your Training

Asking trainees to complete questionnaires after each course can provide some quality-control feedback about the efficiency of the delivery method and the content of the course. However, the effectiveness of training—that is, how well it prepares trainees to do their jobs using SAP—is hard to gauge before going live. Trainers have a useful role here in feeding back their observations of skill acquisition during the courses themselves.

Analyzing calls to the help desk in the first few weeks of implementation is one way of monitoring the effectiveness of training. Better still is one-to-one discussion with end users and their managers to get their feedback. This information is useful for the following:

- Establishing whether extra workshops/training sessions are required
- Improving training for further phases of the project (if applicable)
- Improving training for new users

Developing a Long-Term Training Strategy

In the euphoria of having successfully implemented SAP in your organization, don't forget to put a long-term SAP training strategy in place. There are two main areas to look at:

- People not on the original training program who will require training in the future
- Changes to the system that need to be relayed to all users

Newcomers joining the company obviously will require training, and the most appropriate way to provide this may be to build it into the standard induction program. Promotions and internal movement of employees may result in existing employees also requiring training. Also, employees who originally thought they did not need to know about SAP might change their minds some time after implementation. This may be through a gap in the training-needs analysis or through the individual feeling that it would be "nice to know." Your response to the latter requests will doubtless depend on the training resources you have available.

System changes may occur as a result of bug fixing or from requested and approved enhancements. You will need to communicate with the system maintenance team to pick up any changes, and having documented them, you will need to relay the changes to your users. You might choose to do this by distributing updates periodically, but to ensure that they do not simply get shoved in a drawer, you could run workshops to back up the updating procedure. Ideally, you should appoint a full-time training maintenance person, although your resources might not be sufficient to allow this.

Computer-Based Training with SAP's Simulation CBT Tool

Siemens Business Services and SAP (UK) have teamed up to create new and totally unique software-based training for SAP R/3.

VR Three is a revolutionary training system that claims to help cut costs and time scales for implementation of SAP R/3. Training is delivered on-site to users who can learn at their desks by running simulations of R/3. Customized CBT can be created quickly and simply in a way that was impossible before. VR Three is suited to each and every business's unique SAP configurations.

VR Three has been on the market since late 1997. Robert Taal, education support services manager of SAP (UK), states that customer response has been incredibly positive, and the benefits of this particular training pathway are very clear.

The Benefits of VR Three

VR Three has many benefits, as explained in the following sections.

Customized Training   It takes three days to learn to use VR Three to create customized training courses. CBT can subsequently be designed and created in a fraction of the time required with other systems. It is unnecessary to involve an SAP consultant in designing training material; an understanding of training needs is all that is required.

There's no limit to how unique and varied the training programs created with VR Three can be. At a basic level, any SAP configuration can be simulated. Building on this simulation allows creation of an even more dynamic training program that meets personal requirements exactly.

The possibilities for variations on this system are endless. More important, any settings made can quickly and easily be altered without the need for a programmer. Totally customized lessons can be created quickly and simply.

Live Simulation   Every transaction conducted during training is an exact simulation of a live transaction. Training of this type ensures that fear caused by novelty diminishes into familiarity and routine by the time go-live day arrives. In this case, familiarity does *not* breed contempt; instead, it breeds confidence and extreme productivity. Routine ensures accuracy.

When the SAP system is live, VR Three remains in the background as a help tool. If difficulties are encountered later, VR Three can easily be accessed. Simulated practice and explanatory information at any stage dramatically reduce error rates and increase effectiveness.

Progress Analysis   VR Three has a statistical analysis tool that can monitor individual user progress during training. This allows precise validation of individual user capability before go-live day, which ensures optimum performance from day one.

Problem areas for individual users can easily be located. Dialog boxes, logic, guidance, and even conditional lessons can be added so that if inappropriate responses are given and help is deemed necessary, it can be delivered immediately.

Affordable Training   Developing customized lessons by using traditional classroom-based training methods is problematic, time-consuming, and expensive. VR Three reduces the drain on such resources. The system trains users in-house at their PCs. The extra costs of setting up classes, organizing external tutors, and traveling normally required for training courses are removed.

The precise nature of VR Three also ensures a greater return on investment. Training in an exact simulated environment is much more effective and successful than other forms of training.

Malleability   Business environments today tend to evolve continuously and rapidly. Configuration and design of any implementation may change at any period. There are also inevitable differences among the trainees' capabilities and needs. VR Three is not a rigid CBT system;

programs can be adapted, and all changes can be incorporated into the training quickly and simply.

The Three Components of VR Three

VR Three has three components for capturing screens, designing frames, and presenting training material.

VR Capture The VR Three screen-capture component has the unique capability to capture the major features of an SAP application screen and import the screen into a library file.

The screen-capture component runs nonintrusively behind an SAP application. It is a simple interactive process that allows you to scroll normally though an SAP application and to capture only those screens required for end-user training. A series of screens or an individual screen can be captured at any one point.

Constructing such complex screens from scratch would be extremely time-consuming. The capture process is a quick and simple way in which complex SAP screens, including the major SAP controls and the menu options, can be used in the training material.

The captured screens form the basis on which the training screens are built. Consequently, training materials exactly replicate the live screens and individual configuration of an SAP implementation.

VR Designer You can import captured screens from library files into VR Designer, where they appear as *frames*. Frames form the basic building blocks of lessons. Individual captured screens appear in VR Designer in their skeleton form, with little visual resemblance at this point to what was captured. As a frame, a captured screen is represented in code and resembles a series of fields. Every field that can exist in an SAP application can be seen; individual configuration is temporarily lost. Anything configurable in R/3 is configurable in VR Three. Codes can be simply deleted, so fields can be turned on and off without the need for a programmer. This allows for configuration of unique requirements and situations.

The Frame Designer enables you to use simple point-and-click techniques to build the captured screen into a lesson. Information boxes, scrolling text, pictures, icons, color, sound, action boxes, error messages, help boxes, and hot spots are some of the many controls that can be designed and included in a lesson. A time limit can be set for lesson completion. The statistical analysis tool can monitor the trainees' responses at a field or frame level allowing pass levels to be set. Pass levels can vary, depending on the importance of success in different tasks. The level of help offered by the system to trainees can be altered; VR Three can be configured to show and explain correct responses, or to continuously reset the screen until the correct response is given. Personal messages can be sent to a trainee who is highly successful during lesson time, and if desired, personal warnings can be sent to those who are less successful. PowerPoint and multimedia presentations can be included at various stages. Lessons can vary depending on the trainees' knowledge and confidence, or company expectations of the trainee; conditional lesson branching and lesson loops can be created for those requiring help in specific areas.

The Lesson Generator is a subcomponent of the Frame Designer. It is an essential stepping stone in moving from frame design to actual live presentation. You can call the Lesson Generator automatically from within the Frame Designer when required, and use it to define the relationship between the files. At this point, loops between frames can be integrated, and conditional lessons can be added. Because the frames are stored as independent units, there is no limit to the order in which they can appear, or to the conditions under which a frame will appear as a loop within a lesson. Frames created at a later time can easily be integrated into previously established lessons.

VR Presenter   The final component of VR Three, VR Presenter, enables training courses created in previous stages to be delivered to trainees.

VR Presenter is a small software package that is fully networkable. It is also small enough to be contained on a floppy disk. Trainees therefore can complete lessons wherever they desire: direct from a network in-house, at home, or anywhere from a laptop. Statistics can still be collected if training is running from a floppy disk.

At the lesson presentation stage, the screens return from their skeletal form to their actual go-live form. The lesson occurs as a live simulation, and the tasks completed during training are exactly what users will have to do when the system is live.

System Requirements

VR Three requires external software to work, as described in the following sections.

Screen Capture   The screen-capture component of VR Three must be implemented alongside an SAP application. It also requires

- Windows NT or Windows 95/98
- SAP Application software for Windows 95/98/NT
- SAP Automation (Intelligent Terminal) software
- SAP RFC software

The Frame Designer   The Frame Designer is not networked; it is a workstation application that needs to be run on a machine that meets the following minimum specifications:

- 486-66 MHz (although a Pentium 90 MHz is recommended)
- Graphics VGA/256 color
- 32MB RAM or greater (recommended)
- Microsoft Windows 3.0
- Microsoft mouse (or another compatible pointing device)

The Lesson Presenter   It is necessary to implement the Lesson Presenter at the lesson delivery sites. It is possible to run the Lesson Presenter as a workstation application or a networked application. In either case, the destined delivery machine should meet the following minimum specifications:

- 486DX2-66 MHz (although a Pentium 90 MHz is recommended)
- 32MB RAM or greater (recommended)
- Graphics VGA/256 color (ideally, the graphics support in the Lesson Presenter should be the same as the graphics support used in the Frame Designer to prevent picture degradation)
- Microsoft Windows 3.11
- Microsoft mouse (or other compatible pointing device)

CHAPTER 37

The Human Issues of SAP Implementation

In this chapter

The Effects of Major Change in an Organization

Behind the amazing feats of reengineering with SAP or any other similar system lies many a tale of human insecurity as the world goes topsy-turvy and of management resistance as the carpet starts to move under their feet.

Indeed, James Champy (co-author of *Reengineering the Corporation* and chairman of CSC Index, the management consultancy that pioneered the development and practice of reengineering) emphasizes in his follow-up book *Reengineering Management* that "the only way we're going to deliver on the full promise of reengineering is to start reengineering management—by reengineering ourselves."

This then is the final hurdle. The need to reassess how we as human beings operate as individuals and in groups, and evolve our learning and behaviors, if we are to willingly and wholeheartedly embrace the kind of change that SAP and its associated reengineering initiatives will bring in their wake.

N O T E   This chapter puts forward ideas that you can draw on to help your colleagues move through change successfully—even enthusiastically. It offers you some guidance on how to build and maintain the dedication of your colleagues through the process of rapid change and how best to provide them with the required support.

IS: Today's Number-One Change Agent

"Change is the only constant," said the Greek philosopher Heraclitus some 2,500 years ago, and the intervening years have not proven otherwise. Perhaps one of the most important recent changes as far as industry goes is a loss of confidence among workers in job security. Undoubtedly one major contributing factor to this loss is the automation of processes. The main contributor to automation has been the computerization of tasks that used to be performed manually.

Computers—or, rather, the applications that run on computers—have therefore been double-edged swords. Software programs are bringing changes in the way we all work—especially programs like SAP, which automates every fundamental process within a company. Indeed, SAP throws the past out the window. The implementation of SAP effectively forces a company to consider every aspect of its operation.

Today, organizations are striving to be customer-focused machines, and the implementation of new SAP systems is an important aid to making the necessary changes. But organizations are also repositories of people's hopes and aspirations and the stage on which they play out the major part of their lives. Changing a company's systems is akin to changing the plot and shifting the play's scenery and props while the play is in progress. It takes a dedicated actor to be able to give a good performance despite the changes. It also takes dedicated, well-guided, and well-supported people in a company to thrive through the distractions that any radical system changes entail.

But shouldn't people be used to change by now? What else can they expect? The sobering reality is that mankind's evolution is a slow process, and the human continuum leads us to expect at a fundamental level that tomorrow will be the same as today.

Viewed against this backdrop, SAP's implementation can be a potentially threatening event to some. People lose touch with the familiar, their usual work patterns, their colleagues, or a work area in which they feel proficient. In times of flux, people look for security, which usually comes from the familiar. Centuries ago, people found security among their own families and communities. As industrial growth led to the breakup of traditional communities, people transferred their handholds of security to their position in life—their job and their status within their company. Now it seems that the security of employment and status we have come to expect from the large companies (think of banks in particular) was only a passing phenomenon; there is no longer automatic security in employment.

This raises the question as to the role of management in all this change—particularly the responsibilities that the project management team has when, through implementing SAP, it may seem to be the cause of all this change.

Management's Role in Change

Management's role in change is simple: Create the highest rate of change that the organization and the people in it can stand. Then manage the transition.

This begs at least two questions:

- Change in what?
- How much change can your organization and people stand?

The answer to the first question is a strategic issue that only experts within your field of business can respond to. The answer to the second is open to response from any human, because we are all experienced at living through change.

Given this, you could do worse than ask your colleagues what helps them through change in general, and what in particular will help them through the process of change that implementing SAP entails. To find out their views, consider one-to-one interviews, group dialogs, surveys, or a combination of these methods. The answers you will get—and there is no mystery to this, because we all respond in a similar way—will include some of those listed in the following sections. But do not be seduced into relying on this list to the exclusion of finding out what is true for your colleagues; you will note that the first item on the list is also probably first in importance when it comes to help in riding the waves of change.

Consultation   You should ask the people affected by the changes for their views on the change process and get them to suggest ways in which change can be absorbed by the organization. Act on these suggestions, even if only to say why a suggestion will not be taken up. You will have much more success in getting your changes implemented if you work on getting everyone to understand the changes and let them feel as though they are a part of the change process.

Communication   People will begin grieving in anticipation of loss well before it happens, if in fact it does ever happen. This is purely a function of the human mind's tendency to throw up worst-case scenarios so that we are ready to survive them. The trouble is, we start taking evasive action in anticipation of a threat, and acting as if the threat were real. At this point, the rumor machine gets to work and begins an irrational pattern of fear.

In 1945, such fear caused thousands of Japanese civilians to throw themselves off the cliffs of "Suicide Island" in apprehension of the approaching U.S. Army. The same fear causes otherwise sane employees to ascribe agendas and motives to the perpetrators of change that are pure fiction. The human mind likes to know what is happening and more than likely will create meaning even if there is no basis for it. The antidote to this is to *communicate, communicate, and communicate.*

Job Security   People will worry about their job tenure, their future with the company, and maintaining their lifestyle. The only honest response may be that employment can no longer be guaranteed and that the best the company can do is to boost each person's "employability"— that is, to ensure that they have skills that will be sought after in tomorrow's job market, especially the company's internal job market. Companies that pride themselves on their loyalty to their staff might balk at the notion of offering "employability," with its connotation seemingly of preparing employees for redundancy. But it is important to note that equipping employees so that they can "surf the job market" is, especially in larger companies, a good way to add value to your staff that your company could use at some later date—and it is the accepted tool of succession planners. But if "employability" is not the word for you, choose another.

Change Management   Some employees will have a natural concern as to how they will cope with the new world, new systems, new people in their lives, and new, unfamiliar tasks. Those to whom such scenarios present little threat are those who have maintained the ability to learn, to create relationships, and to maintain a forward-looking attitude. But for every "around-the-world adventurer" who positively seeks out such experiences are 10 others for whom routine is the linchpin of their lives. It is the latter group that may need some handholding. Experience has shown that if their confidence in relationships to others can be boosted, their ability and willingness to learn and accept change follows closely behind (see "Maintaining Sound Relationships," later in this chapter).

As an individual moves through change, the responses that have helped with the change process are logged, stored in the person's memory, and are ready to be used again. In the same way, an organization can learn from experience and capture those change reflexes that have helped and those that haven't. Commonly, the human resource function will take it on itself to store this information, and it remains for the organization to draw on this fount of knowledge whenever change is in the offing—which, in Heraclitus' book, is all the time. In fact, the ability to successfully operate such a system lies at the heart of a company's claim to call itself a "learning organization." Consequently, it is incumbent on those leading change to ensure that the company's data bank is updated for the benefit of those who follow in their footsteps.

Overcoming the Barriers to Change

The biggest barrier to change is not lack of money, lack of ideas, or lack of market imperatives, but is most commonly the attitude that "if the system isn't broke, don't fix it."

Paradoxically, by this same token, the companies that are probably most at risk from change are those now most successful in terms of the bottom line. They are bringing in returns now for their stockholders, so there is every reason to maintain things as they are. Eventually, the "way things are done around here" becomes a creed and then simply the "way," as in the "IBM Way" or the "HP Way." IBM followed its own sweet "way" throughout the 1980s and far beyond its shelf life. The HP Way continues to bring success at the time of this writing. How is your company's "way" doing?

If you want to change your company's way of doing things (that you are reading this book suggests that you are serious about doing so), it will probably be easier if there are signs that your "way" is flawed—that the system is broken. If not, you have a major challenge, somewhat akin to those streetside doomsday soothsayers who receive no more than the lift of a wry eyebrow. Remember, by the time the car manufacturer Rover was taken in hand in the mid-1980s, the company had little reason to cling to historical ways of doing things. Rover was fed up with the tales of woe and was open to change. This is not the case with most companies.

So what message can you put on your "sandwich board" that will make a difference? Some ideas follow.

Case for Action   Come up with the secular version of "Ye shall all burn in hell!" In fact, people commonly talk about going around and lighting fires to encourage action, so the analogy is not so far-fetched. Your job is to stir up a bit of divine discomfort. How you do this will depend on the particular set of circumstances in which you find yourself. Use your team to help brainstorm ways of doing this. But make sure that if you are "setting fires," you have the metaphorical equivalent of those fire-escape signs of stick men running posted on every wall. In other words, avoid panic. Engender purposeful activity by pointing the way to safety. Do this by offering images of a more attractive future. If the word *vision* fits, use it—it's a term most people seem to understand. If you choose to use this tactic, however, remember that you need to consider the personalities of the individuals you are dealing with; some people will not react well (or will react in almost the opposite way you want) to this type of tactic.

Vision   At the same time you are building a case for action, rehearse some future scenarios with your team. Enlist outside expertise in the form of *futurists*—people who make a point of anticipating the future and among whom you may find some expertise specific to your industry. The best kind of vision is expressed in positive terms and does not exist by reference to the past.

Leverage   To change anything, it helps to know a bit about the system. An organization is a machine, and just as every mechanical engineer will rely on a knowledge of the system to tweak at just the right place, so you need to discover the points of leverage within your company where applying pressure will create the maximum effect. Knowing the system entails knowing whom to show your sandwich board to and knowing their agenda. How will your plans help them achieve their own? The synchronicity you create between your goals and those of the "movers and shakers" (that is, the department "barons") will determine the success you enjoy.

Managing Issues of Morale

Will the implementation of SAP mean downsizing, rightsizing, or just a plain old rationalization? Whatever the case, it is said that those made redundant are the "survivors" and those people who escape the cull are the "victims." The rationale is that depending on the way you have seen your colleagues treated, you are likely to fear for your own job after you witness a few layoffs. Morale can take a beating in such circumstances, and if it does, it can take a long time to restore that confidence.

Throughout history, when morale has taken a beating, lessons have been learned in how to restore it, and rather than reinvent the wheel, it pays to learn the lesson that worked so well the last time. In 1943, General William Slim took command of the 14th Army. The all-conquering Japanese had driven it out of Burma, and it now sat in India, licking its wounds. Slim identified his main problem—to restore the 14th Army's morale. But how was it to be done? In *Defeat into Victory,* he recollected how he thought through the problem:

> So when I took command, I sat quietly down to work out this business of morale. I came to certain conclusions, based not on any theory that I had studied, but on some experience and a good deal of hard thinking. It was on these conclusions that I set out consciously to raise the fighting spirit of my army.

> Morale is a state of mind. It is that intangible force which will move a whole group of men to give their last ounce to achieve something, without counting the cost to themselves; that makes them feel they are greater than themselves. If they are to feel that, their morale must, if it is to endure—and the essence of morale is that it should endure—have certain foundations.

> These foundations are spiritual, intellectual, and material, and that is the order of their importance. Spiritual first, because only spiritual foundations can stand real strain. Next intellectual, because men are swayed by reason as well as feeling. Material last—important but last—because the highest kinds of morale are often met when material conditions are lowest.

This example applies well to the change you are about to make in your corporate workplace. Although each worker's life is not at stake, major changes in the workplace can often be interpreted very personally. Some workers will interpret the changes as destroying their place in the corporation—or at least everything they have worked for in the past. Overcoming these preconceived notions is one of your biggest challenges.

I remember sitting in my office and tabulating these foundations of morale something like this:

Spiritual   Set a great and noble objective as the reason for your changes. The achievement of this objective must be vital.

To energize your employees, your method of achievement must be active and aggressive, not merely passive, defensive, or reactionary. You need to make sure that each person feels that what he is and what he does matters directly toward the attainment of the object.

Intellectual   The objective you are aiming at must be something that everyone believes can be obtained. It is impossible to build and sustain high morale for reaching an unobtainable goal.

You must also show employees that the restructured organization is an efficient one, and will be able to achieve the objective in the best way possible. Employees must have confidence in their leaders and know that whatever dangers and hardships they are called on to suffer will be respected and appreciated. Most employees will feel that they have quite a bit at stake in the current organization, so changes in that system are important.

Material   As already stated, employees are sacrificing a lot that was at stake in the previous system. They must feel that they will get a fair deal from the leadership and the new system so that they will not be worse off than they were before. You must convince the employees that they will be given all the materials they need to meet the objective—including the best working conditions possible.

Slim continues,

> It was one thing thus neatly to marshal my principles but quite another to develop them, apply them, and get them recognized by the whole army. We, my command-ers and I, talked to units, to collections of officers, to headquarters, to little groups of men, to individual soldiers casually met as we moved around.
>
> In my experience it is not so much asking men to fight or work with inadequate or obsolete equipment that lowers morale but the belief that those responsible are accepting such a state of affairs. If men realize that everyone above them and behind them is flat out to get the things required for them, they will do wonders.

Whatever the details of one's morale-boosting efforts, it seems that General Slim's integrated three-part approach is a sound template for commercial application. Indeed, such an approach is being rediscovered and used earnestly in industry today by leading corporate development strategists.

Demands on Management Time

When a change program gets under way, its demands on the finite resource of management attention begin to be felt, and something must give. Without exception, the extra workload and stress involved takes its toll on family life. Unless your company had the foresight to hire no one but recent college graduates, you and your colleagues by now have families who are at risk of paying part of the price of your company's new obsession.

So what to do? Here are some suggestions.

For Ambitious Careerists   Take some advice from a man who rose from merchant seaman to chairman of British Airways: "If there is a job to be done, you must get on and do it. If that means setting aside personal things, so be it." (Colin Marshall, April 1996)

For the Rest of Us   Our "personal things" are likely to include our friends, our spouses, and our children. Accept the inevitable and negotiates with them. Trade some lost evenings for a weekend of your undivided attention at Disney World, a Sunday picnic at a favorite location, a wild meal at Planet Hollywood, or a dinner for two at a romantic restaurant. Providing that all concerned feel they are not getting the worst of the deal, peace and harmony will reign. By the way, brush up on your negotiating skills.

As for ensuring that people have a balanced life—well, this relies on management's sensitivity in the way it delegates (or, rather, negotiates) tasks and the readiness of people to say "No" in the face of an unreasonable workload. Both behaviors will be a function of your company's culture, and your culture will be a function of historical accident or, if you are fortunate, of conscious and calculated activity.

Introducing New Ways of Operating

Why the need to operate in new ways? The answer must lie in the changing complexion of competition in the marketplace. For example, any manufacturer who is not facing the future head-on and actively considering the Far East as a source of competition or as a place to site its manufacturing operations must at least be nervously looking over its shoulder in that direction. Changes are on us of such magnitude that if we do not continuously seek new ways of operating, we will be consigned to the margins of the world markets.

The implementation of SAP certainly entails operating in a new way. The systems you have are deeply embedded in your current way of doing business. So to change one entails changing the other, and before you know it, you are reengineering the business from the ground up. If this is the direction your project takes, you must pause for thought. The clean-slate approach of business process reengineering is an attractive proposition. It has promised steep changes in business performance (see *Reengineering the Corporation,* by Mike Hammer and James Champy), and yet, by its practitioners' own admission, fewer than 30 percent of projects achieve the results they were intended to. The reason put forward is that business processes can be successfully reengineered only in tandem with the reengineering of management processes (*Reengineering Management,* by James Champy). But that's still not the end of the story. The master key to finding truly new ways of operating seems to lie outside the realm of processes altogether, and instead has its roots in the way people think and behave in groups—or, in the terminology of today, in the *operating state* of the group.

The operating state of an organization refers to its members' state of collective consciousness, their combined self-awareness, and by extension, their ability to initiate change from within. There are degrees of consciousness. Sleep is one level of consciousness; being awake is another level. Beyond this is the possibility of being awake to the extent to which one's surroundings are a reflection of oneself. Then beyond this lies the mastery of those skills needed to change one's surroundings through personal and organizational transformation. An organization's operating state refers to its ranking in this hierarchy of consciousness.

The condition of an organization's operating state matters because it determines how smart it will be in shaping its future. The good news is that an organization's operating state can be coached upward if its leaders and other movers and shakers within the organization are willing to acquire the "smart skills" needed. ("Smart skill" is a service mark of Harley Young, a UK-based management consultancy.) Such skills include the following:

- Conflict resolution
- Living in the question
- Listening for another's reality
- Transforming experience
- Straight talk
- "Save-as" thinking
- Context reframing

Managing Project Team and Staff Motivation

The ability to sustain motivation is the fundamental skill of any successful project manager. The degree of team and staff motivation you enjoy will, to a large extent, determine whether your implementation plan is completed on time, within budget, and to specification. The most important thing to realize, strange as it may seem, is that it is not up to you to motivate your team. If you have done your job of recruiting people to the team well, however, you will have taken on motivated people—that is, people who, given the chance, will do whatever they do to the best of their ability. (In fact, the idea that they need motivating is likely to seem patronizing to them.)

Your task (and it's a demanding one) is to give them the chance to provide the conditions within which they can exercise their skills. To do this, you must minimize those things that tend to demotivate, deflate morale, and get in the way of getting the job done. Your job is to remove obstructions from the path. The following sections give you some guidance on how to do this.

Maintaining Sound Relationships

The bedrock of success in any group endeavor is the creation and maintenance of sound (that is, open and respectful) relationships. Although Chapter 32, "Overview of SAP Implementations," relates the first steps in building sound relationships, this section is concerned with the attributes of sound relationships in business.

▶ **See** "Building Team Relationships," **p. 758**

In successful relationships, each party has to be at least

- **Authentic.** "Be yourself" is an overworked yet still valid entreaty. But it is easy to act natural when you are at ease; the difficulty is to be authentic when under pressure. This is particularly difficult for those in management who equate being a manager to being something different than who they really are. People who display leadership qualities are those who are at ease with themselves.

- **Flexible.** The opposite of *flexible* in this context is *wooden,* a word used to describe the kind of behavior that seems incapable of responding to events. It is important to be flexible or appropriate in your style if you are to build rapport with others. This does not mean being inauthentic; it simply involves showing the facets of your character. So you would respond differently to a judge in court than to a child in preschool. Both responses are equally authentic and appropriate to the situation. As project manager, you might need to show different facets of your management style in response to your different team members.

▪ **Attentive.** One story, passed down by Hsun Tzu (500 B.C.), chronicles the lives of some successful leaders, including a successful Chinese general. This warlord walked alongside his men, shared their living conditions, and knew their day-to-day concerns. The story tells of a mother bemoaning that this down-to-earth leader sucked poison from the leg of her son, who was one of his soldiers. Her cause for complaint was that the general had performed the same act of kindness several years earlier for her husband, who had then never left the general's side, eventually dying in battle.

Strong stuff, and yet Hsun Tzu's writings are to be found on the bookshelves amongst the more familiar management guides. Translate this into the modern idiom, and you will find yourself making time to be with your team members individually. Perhaps you will come in especially early, knowing that someone is in the office with whom you feel out of touch; perhaps you will use the pub as a forum for refreshing relationships—there are many ways of showing the attention that people warm to.

In every encounter, it will be your ability to listen to your team member's story, to acknowledge it sincerely, and to respond as if it were true (for, to them, it is true) that will make for a sound relationship.

▪ **Trustworthy.** The creation of *trust* derives from the willingness to speak the *truth*. The words have the same etymology. The *truth* in this connection is not some objective body of knowledge that has to be learned; instead, it refers to "what is so" for you—your truth. A person can always speak his truth, providing that he is aware of it. So the ability to be true depends on a degree of self-awareness and the courage to speak it.

In the workplace, this translates to your readiness to say how you feel about something, to declare what you think about some issue, and to go to the source of the problem if something is troubling you (the alternatives are to remain tightlipped, to gossip, or to play politics).

Trustworthiness is frequently put to the test in business when two or more people make an agreement. The most common agreement made is to meet on a certain date at a certain time. Someone who is habitually late might lose the trust of the others, his word will not be considered law, and this might have repercussions on how he is treated in general in the business.

▪ **Trusting.** This is the other side of the coin to being trustworthy. It demands an optimistic outlook and a willingness to be vulnerable to the extent that you are placing something of consequence in the hands of another. Sometimes you will be let down; more often, you will be rewarded by the extra effort people make to show that your trust has not been misplaced.

Establishing Strong Leadership

Given the basic operating principles of openness and respect, the foundation of strong leadership then rests on the ability to provide a clear brief at the outset and clear feedback during the course of the project.

Preparation for Briefing Team Members   Prepare the following information, which you will need at your fingertips when briefing your team members:

- Roles and areas of responsibility
- The minimum that each member will be held accountable for
- Command and communication lines relevant to them
- Facilities and resources available to do the job
- Information and reports that you require
- A schedule of individual progress meetings, training sessions, and project-appraisal meetings

Briefing Team Members   The context you set at the briefing meeting will color the relationship you have with your team members for the duration of your project. For this reason, it is vital to remember that all contexts work by common agreement. The degree to which contexts are set, understood, respected, and used will be the key to your success. With respect to each person reporting in to you, do the following:

1. Confirm the purpose and length of the meeting. Set the context for inviting this specific person to take on this particular task, showing that you know how it would fit in with his career plan.

2. Explain your role and your relationship with the person for the duration of the task. Outline in general terms how you operate, your values, and what you consider negotiable and not negotiable.

3. Explain your immediate goal relating to this brief and how it fits within the overall company objectives.

4. Explain the person's role, responsibilities, and reporting and communication lines.

5. Clarify the minimum performance level (what they are accountable for). This should be measurable; the more specific you are in terms of quantity and quality, the easier it will be for the person to understand and ultimately produce what is required.

6. List the resources and facilities available (that is, people, support, offices, and equipment).

7. Create a context for involvement and feedback.

8. Invite the person to take it on. Be prepared to negotiate. Treat your colleagues as though they are volunteers; people perform better when they act out of choice.

9. Arrange for the person to formulate a goal plan and to meet with you again to go through the plan, to agree to the nature and date of any reports you require, and to agree to the dates of checkpoints and progress meetings.

Offering Feedback   Feedback is traditionally saved up until the next scheduled performance review meeting, but this is most unsatisfactory. An appraisal system should not be used as a substitute for giving immediate feedback. Appraisal systems are a fallback position, a long stop to ensure that feedback is given at some time, even if it is six months too late.

Besides, working on a project team probably places you outside the official performance appraisal system. That's no loss, provided that when something needs saying within a relationship, you follow one of the two checklists described next.

The guidelines are very similar whether someone's impact on you is welcome or unwelcome. This is because the purpose in both cases is identical: to encourage what you feel is positive and productive behavior in this person and to keep your relationship fresh, alive, and vibrant.

It is important to let your current thoughts and feelings resulting from the person's behavior be your fuel when responding. If it is appropriate to respond at the moment of impact, express those thoughts and feelings. If it is not until later that you can speak your mind, express your thoughts and feelings as they are at that later moment. Don't try to recapture or fake the initial thoughts and feelings; they will probably have changed. Talk about them, if at all, as thoughts and feelings that you had.

Checklist for Welcome Behavior   Get in touch with how you feel now about this person's actions. Take no more than 30 seconds to

- Set a context for what you are about to say—include your own thoughts and feelings.
- Praise the behavior, not the person, using clear, concise, and specific ideas and let him know how you feel about his behavior.
- Reinforce the positive action—a "thank you" often is enough.
- Use physical contact (if appropriate) at any point to consolidate the relationship.

Checklist for Unwelcome Behavior   Get in touch with how you feel now in relationship to this person's actions. Take no more than 40 seconds to

- Set a context; include thoughts and feelings.
- Tell the person—with clear, specific, and concise ideas—what you think about the behavior, not the person, and let him know how you feel about the behavior. (Be real and let him have all your feelings straight, so you can let him off the hook!)
- Breathe and pause—to let him appreciate the impact it had on you, and for you to let go of that feeling.
- Reinforce positive behavior. Describe something he does or could do well. (Make it real and don't patronize him.)
- Ask a question to check his understanding of your point. This is not to invite a "reasonable" reply or excuse.
- Use physical contact (if appropriate) toward the end to consolidate the relationship.

Synthesizing a Desirable Future

People look for inspiration in their lives. In the Middle Ages, it was provided by the Church, which was then the dominant institution that strongly influenced the way people ran their lives. Later it was also provided by the military, which had grown steadily in influence (so the first son would join the army, the second the Church), and many companies were run (and still are) along military "orders are not to be questioned" lines.

Today, inspiration comes as well from our place of work. To many people, a career is the most important driving force, and the organizations to which we belong provide the vehicle for our aspirations.

Within this context, the implementation of SAP can be seen in two ways:

- To the project team charged with carrying it out, the implementation of SAP is a venture that will occupy their best efforts for quite some time. Team members will invest part of their dreams in what they do, so the project must be a worthy repository of their dreams. The project manager's role is to "synthesize" these dreams (that is, weave them into a shared vision of the future) and to articulate this vision in a meaningful way to the whole team.

- To the other employees who do not have a direct part in implementing SAP, it will likely represent a threat to their chosen vehicle and as such may be resisted—if not consciously, then certainly unconsciously. By way of forestalling such resistance, you must ensure that they too can appreciate the future being created.

Getting Stakeholder Support

Anyone who has a vested interest in the SAP project can be termed a *stakeholder.* So this will particularly include the following:

- Senior management
- Other employees
- Employees' families
- The local community
- Suppliers
- Customers
- Shareholders

Senior Management   One prime task of the project manager is to be familiar with the business case for implementing SAP. In the nature of things, especially in the fast-moving world of business, what seemed important yesterday does not seem as urgent today as the content of the last phone call. Thus, to maintain support for the SAP project, it's important at every opportunity to reiterate the business case to senior management and to stay alert to anything that may affect it and respond appropriately.

▶ **See** "What Should You Require of a Project Manager?" **p. 754**

Other Employees   Of course, it helps to have a mandate from employees to bring about necessary change. Mandates can be created by surveying staff members, customers, and suppliers, and then using those surveys as the basis for benchmarking the company against the competition or against the company's own aspirations. You then can use the results to reveal a performance gap for which the implementation of SAP may prove to be part of the solution.

In seeking backing for the project, pay particular attention to those people whose "empires" will be affected by the implementation of SAP. These may include

- Department heads
- IT personnel
- Secretarial and administration people

Employees' Families   Employees' families are a much-underrated constituency and one that deserves due attention. In as much as a person's job affects his lifestyle, the family bears the brunt of any changes. As always, the simple device of letting people know what is going on may elicit the understanding needed when it most counts. How you manage this communication depends very much on the relationship that exists between the company and employees' families.

The Local Community   How does your company affect the local community? How will the project you have in mind affect this impact? How can you ensure that the perception the community has of your company is positive? These are questions that need to be considered.

Suppliers   How will your plans affect your suppliers? To serve you well, they need to plan, so the earlier you can bring them into the loop, the better.

Customers   Customers are the arbiters of your success. Naturally, they need to be involved at every stage and even included as part of the project team. This is the group most free to vote with its feet, so leave no stone unturned in canvassing their views. Here are some methods to employ:

- Survey questionnaires
- Group dialogs
- One-to-one interviews

▶ **See** "Recruiting/Assembling the Right Team," **p. 758**

Shareholders   The shareholders are left until last because if you do right by the preceding groups, your success will be ensured and this group will be in clover.

Maintaining Robust Communication

In today's globalizing companies, the job of keeping people informed and including them in the decision-making process when necessary is becoming increasingly difficult. It is more than likely that you will have to rely on electronic communication as much as, if not more than, face-to-face communication. You might be accustomed to the new forms of communication, but others within your team might not be and will probably welcome some guidance on how to cope with the following:

- **Email.** Have a clear protocol as to who should have copies of email. Attach a status coding to each email so that the recipient can prioritize messages and therefore manage his time well. Use email in preference to the fax, because it is usually easier to handle at the other end—but check preferences first.

- **Voice mail.** Institute a similar protocol for voice mail. Keep messages short. Respond immediately, even if it is only to say that the message is being considered and you will get back by a certain date.

- **Telephone and videophone conferencing.** Already well in use, especially among larger companies, conferencing is acquiring a protocol along the lines explained in the following sections.

Preparing the Call   The chairperson (normally the person who calls the meeting) needs to be familiar with the correct procedures. The chairperson should do the following:

- Communicate the conference's objectives. Ensure that the purpose of the conference is known to and agreed to by all prospective participants.

- Establish the duration of the call, stipulating start and end times.

- When appropriate, circulate an agenda in advance and let individuals know whether any preparation is called for.

Starting the Call   The chairperson should

- Take a roll call. Clarify at the beginning of the call who is in attendance and who is acting as chairperson.

- Ensure that everyone's presence is acknowledged and that (for teleconferencing) each person says something to begin with so that voices can be recognized.

- Ensure that people who haven't met or spoken to each other before are formally introduced to each other and get a chance to say a few words to each other.

- Reestablish call parameters. Remind everyone of the purpose of the call and its duration.

- Remind participants of the appropriate ways of doing things—for example, to get everyone else's attention when they want to speak.

- Acknowledge that people may accidentally cut across each other.

- Check the level of preparation. Check that everyone has a copy of the agenda or, if the conference is less formal, that everyone is clear about the objectives that need to be addressed.

During the Call   All participants should

- **Ensure full participation.** Draw out all pertinent facts and opinions. Respond to sighs, hesitations, or any other subtle suggestions that somebody might have something else to say. This will help ensure that the more reserved participants get to contribute fully and that the medium is not "squashing" the message.

- **Sustain interest.** If there's a time delay, such as if you can't find the piece of paper you want to refer to, or anything else goes wrong or isn't going according to plan, make sure that you let the others know what's happening. As a general rule, always explicitly acknowledge the obvious.

■ **Acknowledge audibly.** If statements are met only by silence as people quietly nod or shake their heads, speakers might succumb to the urge to repeat themselves until they are convinced that the point has been taken.

■ **Encourage dialog.** Discussion can be helped along by the speaker seeking a direct response to the points being made via the use of an open question immediately afterward—for example, "I think we ought to do this, this, and this; what are your thoughts?" Even more direct, the speaker may request a response from a particular person—for example, "Jill, what do you think?"

■ **Stay on course.** If a point is raised that takes the conversation on a different tangent from the agenda at hand, intervene; acknowledge the point being discussed and ask whether it should be discussed in another forum or whether the existing agenda should be altered. Don't let themes carry on and then run out of time or allow other agenda points to be squashed.

The chairperson should watch the clock. Alert the others to the amount of time remaining to ensure that the call doesn't run over and that everyone gets their viewpoint across. If it appears as though the agenda will not be completed, signal your concern as far in advance as possible.

Addendum for Video Conferences Only   The chairperson should

■ **Check visibility.** Ensure at the beginning of the call that everyone can be seen, and if necessary, ask that the lighting be altered if it will help people's faces to be seen more clearly. It's a good idea to ensure that the remote camera is focused on the face of the person speaking.

■ **Check audibility.** Get both/all sides to check the sound levels for each individual at the beginning of the call so that people are aware in advance as to whether the microphone needs to be moved.

Some Tips on Motivation

There is no shortage of research into the roots of motivation. The difficulty is to extract something that makes absolute sense and is immediately transferable to the workplace. Of all the ideas that have passed over my desk in the last decade, just a few stand out.

The Hawthorne Findings   Once upon a time long ago, some tests were done in a U.S. factory. The management wanted to know how light levels affect productivity, so they began some scientific tests. First they raised the light level; production went up. Then they lowered the light level; production went up again. Then they lowered the light level still more; again, production went up. Baffled, they quizzed the employees about the effect of light levels on their work. The response? "To heck with the light, we just like the attention!"

Hygiene Factors Versus Motivational Factors   Abraham Maslow told us that there is a hierarchy of needs. It is only when we have our basic needs for air, water, food, and shelter handled that we turn our attention to higher needs such as the need for community, self-expression, and self-actualization. Nowadays, however, this message seems to be forgotten by managers as well as employees as each side searches for the Holy Grail: an amount of money destined to bestow ultimate happiness.

If only they had heeded Frederick Herzberg. In the 1950s, he proposed a simple model of human motivation that is particularly pertinent to these days of disposable income. He pointed out that, whereas food is important to life, there comes a time when increases in quantity bring diminishing returns. He distinguishes, for example, the ability to satisfy one's hunger (a "hygiene factor") from the ability to realize an important goal (a "motivational factor"). The full range of factors follows:

Hygiene Factors	Motivational Factors
Company policy and administration	Achievement
Supervision	Recognition
Salary	Nature of the task
Interpersonal relations	Responsibility
Working conditions	Advancement in ability/career

Of course, it is obvious that too much food loses its appeal after the second helping—but too much money? Too many holidays? Too large a car? Well, that depends.

The table suggests, and many would concur, that the factors on the left have the potential only to *demotivate* by their absence, but not to motivate by their presence. The factors on the right have the potential to motivate by their presence and a questionable ability to demotivate by their absence.

Managing Stress of the Project Team and Users

In the early 1990s, the National Association in the United Kingdom carried out a survey for Mental Health (Mind) of 109 British companies. The survey revealed that directors and managers believe that stress at work, heightened by the recession and fear of redundancy, causes them more apprehension than any personal difficulties. In January 1992, a leading Japanese newspaper conducted a poll and found that one in every two Japanese admitted to fears of becoming a victim of *karoshi* (death from stress or overwork). In Britain, the Health and Safety Commission attributes 40 percent of absenteeism to stress-related illnesses. And who knows how much "presenteeism" (unproductive busyness) is also due to stress? So what exactly is stress?

Stress: What Is It?

What actually happens in your body to cause stress? Stress is produced in response to your environment. When a stimulus from your environment registers on your eyes or ears, it travels to your thalamus and then to both your hippocampus and your auditory and visual cortices, where you attach meaning to the stimulus. If the stimulus is threatening, your brain tells your adrenal glands to produce epinephrine and norepinephrine (otherwise known as *noradrenalin)*, which gear up your body for an emergency. But because this is apt to be a long-winded process (since it involves thought), evolution has equipped you with a short circuit that cuts out your frontal lobes. This mechanism is designed to have you react first and ask questions later. So if you hear a low growl behind you, your involuntary reflex actions would be to prick up the hairs on the back of your neck, quicken your heart rate, and prepare for flight (or fight). All this happens in a second before your conscious mind has time to interrupt with the realization that it was merely a noise from the central heating.

Your emotional mind is the first to react and thus determines your response. What happens under stress is that the pattern of thought into which you slip triggers the same flight mechanism every time the thought surfaces. The body can take only so much of this and soon begins to creak at the seams, giving rise to the symptoms described in the following sections.

Recognizing the Symptoms of Stress

> I feel a sort of general nervousness, with a feeling that if anybody said or did something to upset me, I would be likely to erupt like a seething volcano. I have a couldn't-care-less attitude toward what other people think of me and a deep desire to be left alone. My self-confidence has been shattered, and I no longer feel capable of handling anything that is thrown at me. I have lost interest and enthusiasm. I feel disillusion, resentment and despair. A great lethargy and depression, like a dark cloud, hangs over my head, I feel squeezed dry.
>
> —From "Highly Stressed and Underperforming" in *Management Week,*
>   November 27, 1991

Desperate enough, you would think, but this litany of angst taken verbatim from a manager is just part of the whole story—namely, the internalized feelings or psychological symptoms. Another part is made up of the physiological symptoms. Stress suppresses the immune system by way of diverting resources to the (supposed) emergency at hand. The result: insomnia, aches, and pains—including migraines, arthritis, hair loss, weight loss or gain, shortness of breath and asthma, irritable bowel syndrome, peptic ulcers, heart disease, cold sores, and lingering colds and flu. And finally, there are the social symptoms: Sufferers become silent, cynical, and short-tempered—at home as well as at work. They can't enjoy others' success and may become increasingly dependent on alcohol or drugs. And as if this were not enough, sufferers become accident-prone.

 TIP   For a fuller list of the symptoms that can be caused by stress, I suggest *Emotional Intelligence,* by Daniel Goleman, who emphasizes that the research does not suggest that everyone who suffers stress goes on to develop a disease.

The only conclusion that follows from this analysis is that stress is severely toxic. The challenge is to recognize the earliest symptoms of stress before they multiply and cause irreversible damage. Theoretically, there is a simple way of doing so: Be alert to any feelings of hostility toward anyone within the working environment. If these feelings are not caught and dealt with early on, it is likely that they will gradually mutate into feelings of agitation, then despair, and finally numbness. That is, it is possible that the sufferer will, in the end, claim to be indifferent to the object of his initial hostility. From there, the route to acquiring the full range of symptoms can be short.

Notice the word *theoretically* in the preceding paragraph. Many people—including senior managers, successful or otherwise—have difficulty recognizing what they are feeling. Even feelings of hostility may go unnoticed or unremarked. The solution in this event is to provide education in emotional literacy (see "Management's Role in Alleviating Stress," later in this chapter).

Assuming, for the moment, an ability to recognize and articulate one's feelings, the primary contributors to a stress-free working life are the ability and willingness to do the following:

- **Accept responsibility for generating a particular feeling or set of feelings.** That is, it is not someone's behavior that makes you feel a certain way; instead, it is just the way you have learned to react in response to this kind of behavior.

- **Reexamine the thoughts that led to the feeling.** So if the thought was "So-and-so is ignoring me," recognize that your conclusion is no more than the result of your interpretation of someone's behavior. Consider alternative interpretations, such as "So-and-so is very self-preoccupied. Perhaps he is under pressure and needs some help. What can I do to help?"

If efforts to reinterpret the situation fail, check out your reality—your perception of what is really going on with the person in question. As soon as possible, seek out the object of your hostility (agitation, despair, and so on), and follow the guidelines set out earlier in "Offering Feedback." Note that this skill is included under the head "Establishing Strong Leadership." This doesn't mean that you have to be the person's "leader" to apply this skill; it simply means that within this relationship, you will be taking the lead and showing leadership qualities.

Is There a Right Amount of Stress?

No, not if stress is a result of an inability to cope with your environment. But what about the gap between your goals and the current reality? Surely this creates stress. Yes, perhaps it does, but if it does, it is to be redressed and not accepted as a condition of being in management.

Peter Senge, in his best-selling book *The Fifth Discipline,* sums up the difference between destructive stress and what he calls "creative tension," or the force that brings vision and reality together through the natural tendency of tension to seek resolution:

> The principle of creative tension is the central principle of personal mastery... Yet, it is widely misunderstood. For example, the very term "tension" suggests anxiety or stress. But creative tension doesn't feel any particular way. It is the force that comes into play at the moment when we acknowledge a vision that is at odds with reality.

How do you tell the difference between stress and creative tension? The former produces negative thoughts and feelings; the latter produces a rush of positive energy.

Management's Role in Alleviating Stress

There might not be a right amount of stress, but there is a right amount of creative tension. In General Slim's words (see the earlier section, "Managing Issues of Morale"), any person who takes on a goal "must be convinced that the object can be obtained; that it is not out of reach." Naturally, management has an important role to play in this.

So a balancing trick is involved. We each have a certain tolerance for taking on challenges. Some goals we are confident about achieving, and we talk of these as being within our *comfort zone*. Then there are goals that go beyond what we have achieved to date; these lie within our *stretch zone*. Finally, there are goals that are way in excess of what we consider reasonable, and here we enter our *panic zone*. If goals do not enter this final domain and appropriate support is given for activities within the stretch zone, stress should not be a problem. An athlete's training regime, for example, depends on staying within the stretch zone and consistently expanding the zone into new territory.

What can management do to alleviate stress? A number of tools are at your disposal.

Appraisal   It is important for a manager to consider each person on his team individually and how that person will react to the overall objective and his personal goals in particular. Research shows that a person's proneness to stress is programmed into his brain. Some people (approximately one-fifth of the population) have a neurochemistry that is far more sensitive than the average. As such, they are more prone to stress. Look out for the symptoms of stress (see the earlier section, "Recognizing the Symptoms of Stress"), and catch them early—if you can't preempt them—by getting to know your people well and fine-tuning your expectations to their individual abilities and aspirations.

Know the part you play in contributing to a stressful situation by providing the opportunity for at least two-way feedback, if not 360-degree feedback.

Empowerment   Studies of the British Civil Service show that the prevalence of stress within the lower ranks far exceeds that of the higher ranks. Part of the difference is attributed to those in the higher ranks having more control over their destiny and those below suffering from a lack of autonomy. Empowerment is a management tool that can be used by managers to delegate authority and by their reports to take on that authority.

Relationships   Maverick troubleshooters still, it seems, have their place. Brought in to rapidly strip out layers of management, they are "uncluttered" by relationships with their victims and can perform their duty to the shareholders with a clear conscience. But when the organization has to be rebuilt, it is time for the kind of management that coaxes the best out of people, puts emphasis on creating a strong matrix of relationships throughout the organization, and takes the necessary steps to build those relationships.

▶ See "Building Team Relationships," **p. 758**

Environment   There is an argument about how large a role genes play in determining your behavior versus how much your environment determines your behavior. But everyone is agreed on one thing: The environment has a part to play. From the ages of approximately 18 to 65, half of our waking life is spent within the work environment. The quality of our surroundings is determined by the *social architecture*—the effect that buildings and infrastructure have on people. Factors to consider include the following:

- **Location.** Is it at a site remote from town center amenities? Is there adequate transport to the amenities?
- **Outlook.** Is the area where the offices are situated uplifting to the human spirit or a cause for alarm? What alternatives are there?
- **Layout.** Are people kept apart or thrown together by the way the office is laid out? Are there common areas where people can congregate?
- **Facilities.** Are the basic requirements a person needs nearby—workstation, catering, drink machines, rest rooms, stationery, library, communications, car parking, child care, airport, and so on?
- **Lighting.** Natural daylight provides the best possible kind of light. Are you making the best of what's available?
- **Noise.** Machinery, lighting, water pipes, and air conditioning all conspire to produce a background drone that can induce a dream-like state of unreality. What can be done to stop it? Consider soundproofing and separating people from the things that cause noise. In the final analysis, should you move locations to a better-designed building?
- **Air.** Are you getting enough fresh air, or is it endlessly recirculated?

Coping with High Pressure

Of all the factors that help people cope with high pressure, quantity and quality of relationships must top the list.

By creating strong relationships and following through with the right actions, you should ensure that you and your colleagues

- Create a context for times of high pressure.
- Balance home and work life.
- Learn to say no.
- Delegate work that helps others enter their own stretch zone.
- Break down goals into achievable chunks.
- Learn to act on hostility before it declines into the lower energy emotions such as nervousness, despair, and apathy.
- Learn how to give feedback and receive it.

Personal Coaching and Other Remedies

There is a true story of a managing director who, while showing a prospective client around the offices, entered the marketing director's office only to find the blinds shut, the room in semidarkness, and the silhouette of someone lying flat out on the desk, apparently asleep. Quickly withdrawing, the embarrassed director blustered some excuse to his guest and moved on hurriedly. Later he reproached the marketing director for his behavior, to which the reply was, "My title is Creative Marketing Director. I think best with my eyes closed and my feet up. This is what you pay me for!"

Every manager needs some undisturbed time for thinking, and usually, our body clocks tell us exactly when the best time is. For some, it is the period as we sink into sleep; for others, it is the state of semisleep we enter before fully waking up; for the man in the story, it was the top end of the day. The ability to recognize the need for reflection, and to then reflect, is key to remaining beyond the grip of stress.

Here are some other sources of assistance:

- **One-to-one counseling.** There is a growing tendency among highfliers to seek out opportunities for personal coaching, tailored to their specific areas for improvement. Of those candidates who are encouraged by their manager or the Human Resources department to undertake personal counseling, by far the largest group consists of people who are stressed themselves or are causing stress among their colleagues.

- **Assertion training.** If steam builds up in a relationship and threatens to come to a head, there are ways that the relationship can be managed through to a point of satisfaction. The help of an experienced facilitator or qualified psychotherapist can alleviate stress using techniques borrowed from and initially proven in prisons, where tensions often need to be defused.

- **Hospitals.** Some institutions offer a wide range of services, including anxiety management, treatment for depression, relaxation therapy, assertiveness training, and psychotherapy. Some also run alcohol-treatment programs. Patients learn how to cope with their responses and reactions to external events by participating in various group and individual therapies.

- **Meditation.** Meditation involves practicing some mental exercises twice a day for 20 minutes (for example, yoga and the Alexander Technique). The effect is said to alleviate the symptoms of stress. One study showed that heart disease and diseases of the nervous system were reduced by 87 percent, and tumors were reduced by 55 percent. Recent medical studies in the U.S. have shown that prayer can have even more positive effects on patients.

- **Religion.** For many, religion is the first recourse if the going gets tough. If a person has a spiritual belief, there is much that his religion can do to help him through difficulties. Religious officials have more experience than most in counseling people through the depths of feeling, especially bereavement, and they can be a constant and reliable source of support.

CHAPTER 38

Managing the Change in Organization and Job Functions

In this chapter

Change: One of the Few Certainties in Business

The business world is changing at a far faster rate than ever. Organizational structures and methods, many of them dating back to World War I and earlier, have now been outgrown. More often than not, organizations are finding themselves obliged to alter direction, style, operations, and policies, usually in reaction to changes happening around them. In this respect, it is unusual for organizations to anticipate and preempt change.

New information technology—including SAP—is designed to help organizations cope with these structural and cultural changes. But for the new technology to reach optimum levels of effectiveness, the people using it have to change. The main emphasis in today's employment markets is on employability. In effect, this means that employees and job candidates must possess a number of relevant competencies and up-to-date skills. Whether people within organizations are to adapt to change by attitudinal shifts or by redirected training (or, more commonly, by combining the two), the complex question of how best to manage people within a changing organization first must be addressed.

Change, by its very nature, has an inherent tendency to destabilize what it affects. This destabilizing quality is especially evident to most of us when the affected entity is socioeconomic. Whether the entity is an organization, a social structure, or a personal relationship, even beneficial change can often be devastating to the old attitudes, forms, and norms of behavior. For this reason, while change is often welcomed verbally when proposed within an organization, the underlying unspoken reaction to its imminent arrival is more often one of alarm and mistrust.

Inside an organization, alarm and distrust can wreak havoc. That these emotions are normally entertained out of all proportion to the object of alarm and distrust is irrelevant. They cause far too much counterproductive damage, especially given their effect's necessary corollary: They tend to extend their effect to external factors, so external relations and operations are also adversely affected as a consequence.

The primary task of a change manager is to face up to and seek to calm these fears. Change must always be handled sensitively to secure its acceptance.

Change must be effectively—and positively—communicated. It must be communicated with great clarity. Its benefits must be outlined with enthusiasm; potential problems or obstacles in the way of its successful progress must be identified and solutions devised.

Major organizational change, which is just what you and your colleagues are undergoing as a result of installing SAP, is often mishandled. The consequence is decreased morale and efficiency, leading to decreased performance and results.

Managing Change

As you have seen indicated previously, most change is reactive. That is, the organization has to change for identifiable commercial, social, or legislative reasons—although, of course, change may be forced on an organization by external forces.

Whatever the reasons for change, management must always draw up a guidance program. The program should encourage those involved to take a proactive stance, thereby increasing its chances of success by means of ownership and opportunities for active contribution to the various processes entailed. Thus, the reasons for change should always be communicated comprehensively.

In the case of SAP implementation, many resulting changes will be immediately self-evident before implementation. SAP will provide solutions to questions raised across the entire spectrum of an organization's business needs. Restructuring your organization around information provision by means of new systems will affect all facets of your business. There will probably be an emphasis on aspects.

Management information and control systems that typically will be changed by SAP implementation include the following:

- Marketing and sales control—control of the processes whereby orders are obtained from customers and linked to requisitions

- Operations control—covering control of product and service outputs, quality and reliability, flexibility and responsiveness, timely delivery, facility capacity use, manpower efficiencies, and materials usage efficiencies

- Control of materials—procurement and availability

- Manpower control

- Facility control and maintenance

- Cost and revenue control (your budget)

- Control of debtors and creditors

- Control of capital expenditure and financing

You can expect an increased focus on the activity of specialists. General managerial, administrative, and support functions will probably be reduced after you introduce the SAP system. However, although the various administrative functions of the SAP system will deliver consistent quality, the completely successful deployment of these functions depends entirely on detailed, accurately drawn objectives. The applied systems you will be using are reliably excellent, but they need to be amply and expertly employed to ensure that they achieve excellence in practice.

The organizational change involved here, then, is all-embracing. However, it is important that the change program be flexible, as should the attitudes of those driving it, to account for any additional developments. There will be unpredictable events and results, which will often present themselves as opportunities for fine-tuning your change program or even for introducing further innovative progress. Be prepared for the unexpected.

Elements of Change in the SAP Program

The immediate issues raised during your implementation of SAP will cover areas such as amendments to job descriptions, changes to working practices, revisions to corporate organization charts, reorganization of office layouts, and relocation of staff (if necessary). With all of these, as much openness and honesty as possible will pay dividends in terms of morale and acceptance.

 TIP   Use these tasks as opportunities to "flatten out" the hierarchy and speed efficiency in communications and performance. The sooner everybody concerned understands his or her new role and is accustomed to a new theoretical or physical working environment, the better.

Operating teams are perfectly capable of writing their own job descriptions in close consultation with line management. Also, change teams, acting in collaboration with existing operating teams, can help to make the necessary amendments to their stated functions.

From the issues discussed earlier, it is obvious that a number of different departments will be actively liaising at the program planning stage. These will, of course, include the Personnel or Human Resources Department. You should make full use of the personnel management function to ensure that the following conditions and practices are well-established:

- You have an organizational structure that supports corporate and local strategies and gives a necessary focus (reinforcing the mission and related goals).
- Departments have a clear idea of their accountabilities, where there is no overlap in results. If this is the case, the accountabilities will be shared.
- Opinion surveys are carried out, and results are circulated to those concerned, leading to an action plan. Ideally, this should be done annually in every division and department.
- Organizational change is professionally managed, with a documented communication plan, full information describing the change(s), and answers to likely questions provided, where appropriate.
- Organizational charts are freely available and regularly updated.

The overall program, its nature, and steps must be made crystal clear to all concerned. The communication of the program, the reasons for it, and its proposed methodology must be clearly communicated: The keywords here are, as ever, *clarity* and *timeliness*. But before the change program is introduced, you should ensure that you have prepared the way for its acceptance.

Preparing the Way for Change in Your Organization

Most organizations are internally focused, many of them to a degree that allows for complacency. When changes occur in their markets, factors such as increased or new sources of competition can appear suddenly, finding an organization unprepared and sometimes inducing panic.

Clearly, such a state must be avoided. But how? Many successful organizations have a readiness for change incorporated into their everyday operations. These organizations have built in to their overall strategy an element of advantageous impatience. This means that they do not devote resources to resolving outdated issues or to solving outdated problems. Instead, these successful organizations devote their prime intellectual resources, with the necessary budgetary flexibility, to researching developments and seeking business opportunities. By using the SAP system, you will certainly find that you have more time to reflect on and devote to these considerations.

In many of the previously mentioned cases of successful organization change, that same successful embracing of change is initiated by two factors: the organization's vision and its mission. Perhaps your organization already has a vision and a mission statement. Installation of the SAP system may render them obsolete. Whether or not you have a corporate vision and mission, you will find it useful to investigate the possibility of devising ones that will help you manage change.

Your Organization's Vision

An organization's vision originates at the top or, at least, very close to the top. It is a matter of shared values and rests on considerable leadership qualities. It may exist independently of radical strategic redirection. Whatever its status, the vision must describe an organization's desired future state. It is a goal or series of goals that the organization must seek to achieve. Whether or not these goals are attained, the essential vision must not be lost or obscured. And of course, your organization's vision should be deployed to promote change.

Developing a vision allows you to think freely, without constraint. This is important, because you will need to look forward rather than be bound by the dictates of past conditions. Current limitations to your organization's freedom of action should not prevent you from envisaging any new strategic direction.

N O T E   Developing a vision for an organization means that you are not planning ahead, you are imagining ahead. You are thinking about what it is possible to achieve or what it is possible to become. If your organization's vision is wrong, change it accordingly.

You will find that the vision is fragile and tentative in the early stages. Thus, you and your colleagues will need to alter it, test it, and support your findings with data, if your vision is to become robust enough to withstand close and critical scrutiny. After all, the vision must be accepted throughout the organization.

For a vision to be effective—that is, accepted and adopted—senior management must demonstrate complete commitment to it, and convincingly.

When your vision is formulated correctly, you will be ready to present and promote it. Before you do so, prepare the ground:

■ Encourage the formation of discussion groups or forums, in which possible alternative developments are discussed at all levels within your organization. This will encourage employees to become accustomed to challenging current assumptions and methods. To do so, you must demonstrate that senior management is wholeheartedly committed to your new purpose.

■ Arrange informal meetings with staff members, where you can introduce the new thinking.

When you are ready to launch your vision, you will need to achieve the following in your presentation:

- It must be inspirational, motivating everybody to participate positively in your organization's new direction.
- It must give staff members a sense of purpose and direction, and demonstrate commitment from the top.
- It must be credible and feasible. Reaching far for the unattainable will demoralize your staff.
- It should give some indication of how the vision will be realized in practical terms.

It goes without saying (or should) that the successful launch of your vision will demand a high standard of presentation skills (refer to Chapter 35, "Managing Internal and External Communications," for some useful advice on this topic). Remember, you are effectively selling a concept that will take your organization forward in line with the increased technical and informational powers provided by SAP.

Your Organization's Mission

First, ask yourself the most basic questions, such as these:

- What business are we in?
- What business should we be in, in x years' time?

These questions might focus on how your company operates and how it should be operating, given SAP's implementation. Remember, you will need to project into the future, and it must be a desired and feasible future.

Given that senior management's primary responsibility is for performance and results, senior management should be posing questions to themselves, such as "What do we need to do to produce/improve on results?"

You should not ignore the possibility that your organization is doing a number of things correctly. In this case, you should also explore the question "Is there anywhere within our organization where we are doing x already?"

Your mission might be to practice what your organization is already preaching—perhaps, so far, unheard or unexecuted. Senior management will need to ask the following questions of line management and employees:

- What do we do that helps you produce the results that we all agree are our aims?
- What do we do that hampers your producing these desired results?

These questions should be answered as a primary task before formulating a mission statement or consequent strategy.

Your mission statement is your means of defining your organization's commercial rationale and identifying its markets and goals. You will need to ensure that your organization's mission serves as a focus of corporate cohesion; the values expressed are to be shared in pursuit of a common purpose. These values might include active qualities such as a stronger emphasis on service and customer care. Whatever your organization's set of values, care must be taken that the mission incorporates these values. Remember, you need everybody in the organization to adhere to certain standards and work to a common purpose.

Strategy goes hand in hand with your organization's mission. It is all very well to have a purpose, but you must have some idea of how that purpose will be achieved. Your strategy might identify new markets and how your organization will seek to establish a competitive edge in those markets.

Your mission must openly contain a message that challenges your staff. This might appear to be painfully obvious, but it is surprising how often managers fail in this vital respect. Your organization has good team members, and you want to keep them. Remember, people want to work for a dynamic, thriving organization—nobody wants to work for an ostrich.

Remember, too, that *purpose* and *strategy* are worthless words unless you put them into action.

Finally, your mission statement will fulfill its purpose of creating a coherent and cohesive sense of corporate direction only if you've identified the appropriate means and methods and requisite performance standards. When identified, these must be clearly communicated to your audience at the launch of your mission.

Further, mission-related change needs to be reinforced by actions aimed at bringing about change in operating behavior. Here, you will find that training focused on changing or adapting attitudes, beliefs, and behavior (as opposed to being solely focused on imparting information) is very effective. One objective is to help your organization become one that constantly learns, and hence constantly makes progress in line with social, economic, and market developments.

Change is more easily accepted when it is incorporated into an organizational structure based on updating and improving existing skills and acquiring new ones. In a plethora of systems and procedures designed to move products and services, it is easy to forget that the main resource of any business consists of its people.

Planning Your Change Management

After you clearly communicate the reasons for change, you must devote time and resources to ensuring that all stages of your change strategy implementation are agreed on and communicated.

Before the new strategy can be implemented, you need to agree on and plan the following:

- The program for change
- The identification of change agents—for example, in the case of drawing up new job descriptions, personnel management, line managers, and their teams
- Informing and consulting with those involved about the change process—establishing shared ownership and an atmosphere of active collaboration
- Identifying those who are unlikely to agree with the change program and persuading them of the benefits

Finally, if you need to set up a program of downsizing, adopt the following tactics:

- Proceed with great care, but announce your final plan openly.
- Wherever possible, seek voluntary layoffs, notably from among members of dissenting groups.
- Ensure that outplacement consulting services are available. Check these out first; use your networks to identify consultancies that will provide the quality service your organization gives, in this as in all other areas. These will serve to reduce stress among candidates for laying off and, as a result, among their colleagues.
- If valuable personnel members are lost to your organization because of insufficient work for them to do, take steps to remain in touch with these people. Such people often become consultants, and their services may well be called on by your organization in the future. New consultants often find, on leaving employment, that their first customer is their last (most recent) employer.

Remember, layoffs hurt but are rarely fatal. Most laid-off employees find work quickly after "Downsizing Day," and most of the rest succeed in finding employment during the course of the year following "D-Day."

Of course, significant and increasing numbers of laid-off employees opt to set up independently of an employer. This might mean setting up a consulting practice, a small business, or a franchise.

You must also bear in mind at this stage that it is always a mistake to try to change everything at once. Given the destabilizing effect of change noted at the beginning of this chapter, be aware that everybody needs some element of stability, however rudimentary that might be.

Change is best implemented progressively. So before you begin your implementation program, remember the following:

- Try to produce steady change.
- Management must avoid getting out of phase with the rest of the organization.
- Do not throw out perfectly good elements of your old systems that have historically encouraged success. Wait until these have been superseded.
- Avoid experimentation, especially when perceived as a fashionable, "academic" solution. Opt for the practical and feasible procedure every time.

You will find that the implementation program itself is best broken down logically into discrete components, such as these:

- Agree to the timescale(s).
- Agree to the overall goals.
- Agree to the strategy.
- Agree to the interventions to be used.
- Watch, observe, and record the change process.
- Evaluate the findings.

- Take corrective action.
- Identify and deal with any obstacles.
- Publish the success.

Agree to the Timescale

The change implementation program must have a definite starting point. The program is the responsibility of line managers. It must always be perceived as being owned by management; consultants are best deployed in planning and training for change, or in assisting with corporate communications and internal and external monitoring.

You will find that the shorter the agreed timescale for change in your organization, the more likely it is that the change will be contained and controlled. This means that the results will necessarily have a greater degree of predictability. Conversely, the longer the agreed timescale, the less predictable the results. However, bear in mind that a longer time frame, with less predictability, allows for increased opportunism.

Of course, you should agree to the timescale that suits your business: its size, scope, and current conditions. The SAP system assists you in determining the amount of time needed for streamlining business reengineering, for example.

Agree to the Overall Goals

The goals must be agreed on in advance and made public throughout the organization. These goals must be understood by all and achievable. See the earlier sections on vision and mission—the goals have already been devised. The two will act as mutual reinforcement. Certain therapeutic regimes that include more than one drug are said to be more powerful in their effects than a single drug used alone; the same is true of vision plus mission plus stated goals. When they are acting together, the combination is more effective than any one of them acting alone.

Your goals will be qualitative and quantitative. For example, when formulating a marketing strategy, you will be seeking to answer the following goal-related questions, among others. For qualitative, focus on the following:

- **Positioning.** How to achieve a stronger position in the marketplace and among competitors
- **Differentiation.** How your organization differs from others that offer similar products or services
- **Segmentation.** How to acquire increased knowledge of the demographics and qualitative characteristics of your market segments
- **Cultural.** How to improve the sense of identity, quality, and common purpose
- **Stylistic.** How to achieve an improved image for your organization that positively affects its culture
- **Functional.** What purpose(s) your organization fulfills beyond its own needs

For quantitative, focus on the following:

- Budget adequacy as well as constraints
- Costing methods and cost characteristics
- Price strategy
- Market share
- Growth rate

All these commercial elements will be familiar to you. They are not limited to a strategy confined to marketing; they apply to most corporate strategies.

The marketing strategy analogy holds true. Just consider how increasing segmentation in the market is a feature of the contemporary business world. The spread of increasingly demanding customers and increasingly sophisticated consumers serves to produce this effect, with an increasing overlap among the various segments and with products and services devised to meet their demands. SAP is designed to help you meet these and other functional demands and their allied activities.

Agree to the Strategy

The strategy of implementation now begs the question, "How are we going to produce/improve on results?" You need to consider this; you might find the following list of prompting questions useful (you can probably add to this list):

- Is the implementation plan going to be initiated entirely from the top, from senior management, or will it be generated via consultative processes from the lower levels within our organization? Or will it be a mixture of top-down and bottom-up? Whichever option you select, make sure that it is one that suits the style and culture of your organization.
- How do we consult with individuals, teams, departments, and so on?
- What are we offering our staff, and when do we need to know their responses?
- Will the change be made by division, by department, or at some other level?
- What degree of responsibility are we going to allow departmental managers in the decisions to be made?
- What methods of communication are we going to use to inform the staff of what is happening? Refer to Chapter 35, "Managing Internal and External Communications," for some tips on the best practice of internal communications.
- What external assistance will we be likely to require, and when?
- What training strategies are we going to use?
- How do we measure success?
- What will this cost, and who will monitor the budget? You must devise a way of drawing up a budget that takes into account the unpredictable, however anomalous this might seem. Change contingent on SAP implementation is cost-effective within a given term,

but the implementation of a change program should not itself be a matter for cost-cutting exercises.

Agree to the Interventions to Be Used

You will need to use some forms of intervention to coach and motivate those concerned, and drive the change through your organization. These processes must be understood by everybody concerned. You should also take care to avoid expressing these methods in terms your audience could perceive as manipulative. Examples of intervention procedures follow:

- Further training
- Time off for hours worked, where goals have been achieved
- Recognition events (informal celebratory gatherings)
- In-house promotion of information about the change program via, for example, dedicated newsletters or open access to change program rationale and process on CD-ROM

Watch, Observe, and Record the Change Process

You will find that follow-up and reinforcement are necessary to keep your change program on track. At all stages, you must be aware of levels of understanding, acceptance, and progress. Of course, you also must be able to monitor performance in terms of results.

Change agents in the front line must feel part of the change process for them to

- Feel in control of their element or elements of the program
- Maximize their contributions

Your change program should be flexible enough to allow for amendments by those driving it. Where possible, the work teams themselves should also observe and record the change process as it relates to them. These results should be fed back to senior management.

N O T E   Remember, no plan will be 100 percent accurate and successful. Just try to aim at a target as close as possible to that figure, and give yourself and your team(s) a suitably metaphorical pat on the back if you attain a 70 percent to 90 percent success rate. After all, you will be performing a delicate balancing act in managing change—balancing the demands of entrepreneurial and developmental opportunism with those of planning and control. It is not easy.

Evaluate the Findings

You will need to determine what has been done and what effect this is having on the organization and the business. You might find the following evaluation methods useful:

- Local meetings and site/division visits, held by senior management
- Discussion groups and invitations to analysts to review the organization and business post-change to provide helpful feedback
- Customer visits and seminars to monitor external effects

■ Brainstorming sessions among teams involved

■ Surveys by means of, for example, questionnaires (which may be transmitted via email)

 TIP You might also find that some people need to air complaints (which is often a function of human nature rather than poor change management). If this is the case, make time to allow people to complain. Do not let complaints fester; deal with them as quickly and as constructively as possible.

You will use these findings to adjust your change program accordingly, of course. Be prepared to change the change program. Remember, you have designed it to be as flexible as possible, because you are aware that change itself is not always entirely predictable.

However beneficial and positive your organizational change is, bear in mind that change is frequently perceived as (at best) unwelcome and unsettling, and (at worst) a threat to the security, stability, and livelihood of those on the receiving end. This constituent of change, allied with your preparedness to cope with unexpected developments, means you are likely to discover at times a need for corrective action.

Take Corrective Action

As you see in the preceding list, your change program feedback will often lead to further corrective action. You must ensure that such action is immediate and effective. You should also realize that when it is properly publicized, you must give explanations of why an action was necessary.

When possible, give feedback to corrective action teams, made up of those people doing the job where the problems are arising. When corrective action is taken, it might be necessary to rework the evaluation of findings to determine what effect the action has had.

NOTE Remember, timing is important and speed of response is of the essence, but make sure that you get your facts right. Do not be too quick to take corrective action. You should first ensure that the stated problem has not been exaggerated and is not the result of a lack of training or understanding. Do not allow yourself to be panicked into a fire-fighting mode; panic spreads faster through an organization than good news does, and the deleterious effects on morale are obvious. Poor morale always acts as a brake on the successful implementation of a change program. ■

Identify and Deal with the Obstacles

Any obstacles (and you will be living in a perfect corporate world if there are none) must be identified. These obstacles are often in the form of one or more of the following:

■ Lack of commitment from senior management (which you should have obviated by means of vision and mission formulation and acceptance).

■ Lack of involved responsibility—people waiting for somebody else to make decisions and make things happen.

■ Out-of-date working methods (which, for example, do not take into account the versatility and comprehensive nature of the SAP system).

- An inadequately trained workforce, unaware of the issues involved in the change program. Further training needs may be identified, and meeting them will prove invaluable in the medium-to-long term.

The communications strategy contained in your change program should enable you to cope successfully with most of these problems. Remember, regarding these obstacles as opportunities for further, tangible (and measurable) change will help greatly when you are incorporating them into the main body of your change program.

Publicize the Success

Your change program will not be just a matter of gaining commitment, promoting development, and overcoming obstacles—you will have successes to enjoy as well. These successes must be publicized, making their celebration as visible and enjoyable as possible. After all, you are promoting confidence and enthusiasm. You are also ensuring that the continuance of your change program is facilitated and that its future success has a firm foundation.

You will know what to publicize. This might include successes such as the following:

- Meeting a key date ahead of or on the date designated by the time plan
- Implementing a change within budget
- Establishing a successful new working method
- Achieving cost savings
- Receiving customer praise
- Receiving good, positive press coverage
- Increasing your customer base
- Launching a new product or service
- Realizing corrective action team results

You will certainly find that all the preceding, and more, will be possible with SAP. However, you will also be wondering how best to communicate your successes. You might do so via the following methods:

- Dedicated newsletters (produced in-house, exploiting your desktop publishing package to save costs)
- Articles in corporate publications
- Group meetings
- Two-way communication channels, inviting feedback and suggestions (a success might provide opportunities for further successes)
- Notice boards

Your celebration of success should never ignore the possibility of eliciting useful feedback. As previously suggested, opportunities can lead to further opportunities. You should be alert to this possibility and ensure that everybody knows that your program aims to build on success.

You will find, if you have not discovered this already, that publicizing success helps maintain impetus and morale. So remember to keep everybody informed. And remember to celebrate each success in a style appropriate to your organization.

Change is never easy, but when the correct balance between planning and control and openness to unforeseen opportunities is achieved, change is highly stimulating to growth and development. It is also a means of maintaining a sense of belonging and involvement among those engaged with implementing change and meeting its challenges. And that, of course, means everybody in your organization everywhere.

Beneficial organic change will affect those within and outside the bounds of your organization. Your customers and suppliers will also benefit, as will your shareholders and, in fact, all those with a stake in your organization.

Be sure to check their opinions to keep up the momentum of change and ensure that your direction is the right one for your organization.

Finally, here is a checklist of principal operative words and phrases:

Agreed-on aims	Control
Build on existing strengths	Corrective action
Collaboration	Flexibility
Commitment	High standards
Common cause	Openness to opportunity
Communication	Readiness to act
Consultation	Speed of response

SAP Employment Market

CHAPTER 39

Overview of the SAP Employment Market

In this chapter

Main Features of the SAP Employment Market

SAP has been a hugely successful phenomenon, and the SAP world has unique and attractive characteristics as an employment generator. It is also one that needs careful study if you want to get the best out of it, or to decide whether it's the right workplace for you. The earlier part of the book tells you about the product and how to implement it, but that's only half the story. If you're reading this book with a view to creating or developing a career in SAP, you need to know your way around the diverse environment that is the SAP world. To understand the SAP employment market, you need to know how SAP finds its way from factory to user, because this is central to the whole success of SAP, and also to the nature of the employment market it generates.

SAP is brought to users by an extended "virtual organization" of SAP AG and its subsidiaries, its network of business partners, independent consultancies, individuals, and the users' own IT departments. Partnering to market software is not unique to SAP, but SAP has been particularly successful at it, and partners have integrated their activities more than usual in IT distribution channels, without sacrificing their business independence. There can be little doubt that SAP's phenomenal success has been enabled by the success of the virtual working world that SAP has created, yet this working world is now generating problems of its own, as explained later.

The virtual organization has wider purposes than simply selling SAP products. It is also driven by the partners' need to sell services (as well as products sometimes). At base, it delivers solutions to the problems of business process reengineering, and the software suite that SAP produces is only one component of this. The people who identify the problems, propose solutions, and use the SAP software to implement them are also part of the salable product. They have to work in close concert in teams that span more than one employer, which dictates the need for many of the qualities demanded of the ideal SAP person.

The nature of the SAP user base also places special demands on SAP practitioners. Some 25 percent of the world's largest corporations use SAP (as of mid-1996), and they usually do so multinationally across multiple operations. The SAP employment market is founded on these "blue-chip" companies and the equally prestigious management consultancies that service them. This, along with the nature of the SAP product, creates a market for the highflying type of individual who is comfortable talking about big issues with big clients. It also means that systems are large and complex, and that project time scales are long.

SAP's big-company orientation has also had the happy (from the employee's viewpoint) effect of keeping salaries for SAP-skilled people at or near the top of the IT league. Someone with suitable IT skills and experience in installing packaged software or in business systems analysis can expect a salary premium of 25 percent or more by getting one year's SAP experience onto his or her résumé. People with senior project management experience may gain more than this, provided they can handle the cultural, logistical, and technical complexities of large, multinational projects.

The SAP world offers more than just high salaries (and indeed, it is highly suspicious of anyone who appears too interested in just the money). As IT becomes more and more pivotal to company operations, and a company's systems infrastructure becomes recognized as one of its most important assets, the route to the boardroom opens up for IT professionals, especially those who think strategically about its application to the company's business. No one is better placed to exploit this route to the top than experienced SAP consultants.

If travel is one of your career objectives, SAP will provide you with lots of opportunities to pursue it. Because many of the employers are multinational and the systems are rolled out across many subsidiaries, you can log many frequent-flier miles in many positions. You might find that to get the option of travel, however, you have to accept the obligation of it, and most people who think constant business travel is lots of fun haven't done too much of it.

In contrast, most people who have actually lived abroad for any length of time wouldn't swap the experience. You can really only experience a country by living in it, and the expatriate life has many merits. SAP, with its lengthy contracts and enough of a shortfall in skills to fuel international recruitment, offers the chance to get to know many fascinating parts of the world. But not all parts of the world are equally enjoyable, and if you want to travel, make sure that you want the lifestyle you are taking on, and not just the money.

The high salaries in the SAP world are not totally due to SAP's big company background. The laws of supply and demand also prevail, and demand outstrips supply in the SAP employment market. SAP's 62 percent global sales growth in 1997 crudely means the need for large numbers of new consulting and support resources. If you are looking to cross-train into SAP, be aware of the true nature of the supply and demand imbalance. There is a shortage of fully trained and competent SAP consultants, but no shortage of applicants to train in it.

Even for experienced SAP people, the demand is only for the best. The SAP world is a competitive one, in which your performance is visible and merit prevails. It is stimulating (unless you're bored by business systems). It is nonhierarchic, and you won't be deterred from taking the initiative by authority. But it is also demanding—of your technical skills, your commitment, and your personality.

As you will have gathered from the earlier chapters (if you didn't know already), the heart of the SAP product is a set of high-level building blocks and the means of configuring them to reengineer business processes. It is not a set of tools that you use after you have decided exactly what you want from the system, and then say, "Okay, now program that for me." The configuration process is inseparable from the whole process of defining strategies, analyzing business needs, and considering such issues as legacy systems and user interfacing. A pragmatic path has to be sought that optimizes the synergy between the users' needs and the functionality of SAP.

Most of the roles in the SAP world carry in their title the word "consultant," along with the area of specialty in the traditional management consultancy skills.

These skills are not what many people imagine them to be. They are not mostly about "being consulted" or cogitating and pontificating from your superior knowledge and thought processes. The first skill in management consultancy is the ability to sell yourself. People use management consultants to keep in step with the latest mainstream thinking, as a knowledge conduit, and as an insurance policy. They can get these benefits only from someone they trust and to whom they will listen.

This makes very little room for the pure technician, and it doesn't suit everybody. Many people in IT (almost all of them, to some extent) are fascinated by technology. You need to be fascinated by business and by people as well if you are to succeed in the SAP world.

If you're reading this as an aspiring entrant to the SAP world, you should be prepared to put some serious effort into it, and possibly lay a deeper plan than simply applying for SAP positions. SAP has lots of areas where requirements for other skills overlap or sit alongside the need for SAP skills. If you are skilled in UNIX or NT-based networks, for example, you have a much better chance of acceptance into an SAP user organization (present or prospective) that needs those skills if you don't emphasize your ambitions to cross-train into SAP when applying for a job. Be prepared to deliver productivity in your present area of expertise at first. Once you establish yourself as a valued employee, your prospects of getting cross-training are several hundred percent better than they are as an outside applicant.

SAP Market Facts and Figures

SAP is the fourth-largest software vendor in the world and is one of Europe's largest 100 companies (US$3.5 billion turnover in 1997). It has developed as a global phenomenon, providing very real international employment opportunities. It is the market leader in the client/server enterprise applications market, with an estimated 36 percent market share. SAP has in excess of 9,000 customers in more than 90 countries, with offices in more than 50 countries.

SAP is a German company that recognizes that its worldwide presence is crucial to its success, and its foreign sales contribute greatly to its earnings. The percentage of SAP profit resulting from foreign sales has always been high, and in 1997, it reached the massive proportion of 81 percent.

SAP's international presence is a key feature of both its sales and its employment patterns. Figure 39.1 shows the distribution of employees worldwide as of 1997. You can see that the majority of SAP employees are concentrated in Germany and the Americas, with Asia and the Pacific region ranking third in the distribution of employees worldwide. It is, however, the Asia/Pacific region that has been responsible for much of the recent growth in employee numbers. And this growth is a result of the SAP sales patterns.

There is, therefore, a dialectical relationship between sales patterns and international recruitment patterns. The areas in which SAP sales have been made require consultants. The concentration of sales dictates international recruitment possibilities. And dialectically, the sales are determined, to a degree, by the availability of SAP resources in the local areas.

So as well as being fundamental to its success, SAP's international presence provides the basis for the international employment opportunities. If global product sales continue to increase, it is likely that the aspiring globetrotter will always find SAP employment attractive.

Figure 39.2 shows SAP's installations by industry. These installations do not necessarily reflect the scale of usage, but they do provide an interesting guide to the industries that SAP services.

GURE 39.1

P has a presence in
ny countries of the
rld.

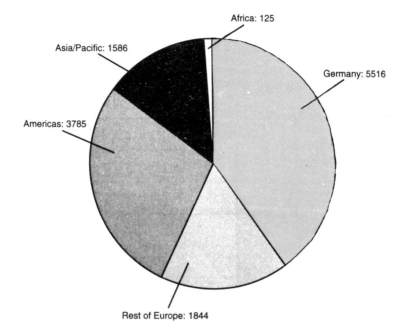

Africa: 125

Asia/Pacific: 1586

Germany: 5516

Americas: 3785

Rest of Europe: 1844

GURE 39.2

P R/3 is installed
th customers in many
ferent industries.

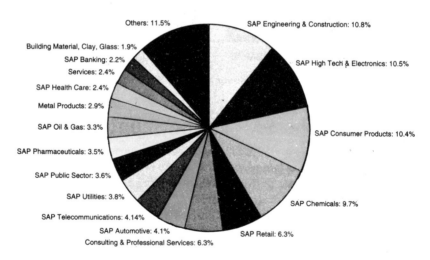

Others: 11.5%

SAP Engineering & Construction: 10.8%

Building Material, Clay, Glass: 1.9%

SAP Banking: 2.2%

Services: 2.4%

SAP High Tech & Electronics: 10.5%

SAP Health Care: 2.4%

Metal Products: 2.9%

SAP Oil & Gas: 3.3%

SAP Consumer Products: 10.4%

SAP Pharmaceuticals: 3.5%

SAP Public Sector: 3.6%

SAP Utilities: 3.8%

SAP Chemicals: 9.7%

SAP Telecommunications: 4.14%

SAP Automotive: 4.1%

SAP Retail: 6.3%

Consulting & Professional Services: 6.3%

As of 31 March '98 (Total: 11,803)
(Source SAP AG)

You can see SAP's market position in Figure 39.2. The entire market of client/server enterprise applications (now commonly referred to as *enterprise resource planning,* or ERP) is in high growth. Many factors together mean that SAP is unlikely to be surpassed by any of its competitors in the short to medium term. Because ERP systems involve major investments and have significant impact on the success of corporations, sales cycles can be long and investments are frequently written down over long periods of time. The ERP market is therefore at the opposite end of the spectrum compared to some commodity markets, where market positions can change rapidly. Figure 39.3 shows SAP's market domination with an estimated 36 percent market share; this compares with its nearest rival, Oracle Applications, at just 13 percent.

FIGURE 39.3

SAP's market share reached 36 percent in 1997.

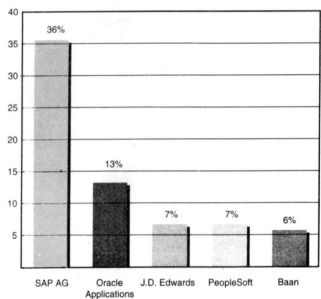

(Source: AMR, 1997 Estimated Market Share (January '98))

Growth in the SAP Employment Market

SAP revenue growth, which is public information, forms the underpinning for employment growth. SAP was formed in 1972 when the five founders—Dietmar Hopp, Hans-Werner Hector, Dr. Hasso Plattner, Dr. Klaus Tschira, and Klaus Wellenreuther—acquired the rights to a financial accounting package. Wellenreuther had developed this package originally (while an IBM employee) for Naturin, an IBM customer.

The founders, with their infant company, set about the design and implementation of a real-time finance system, based largely on Wellenreuther's experience in the application.

ICI became the first customer for this system, and as well as buying the package, it commissioned a suitable materials management system. This provided cash flow for the development of the FI system, as well as the nucleus of the MM standard package. The further development of MM was financed from sales of the FI package, and the show was on the road.

MM and FI formed the first modules of what was then called System R. Only after the successor versions R/2 and R/3 were introduced was System R renamed R/1.

As a mainframe product, SAP R/2 was very successful in Germany and made some inroads elsewhere, but it really took off in 1992 with the launch of R/3 as a UNIX client/server–based system. This was exactly the right time for such a product, and its combination of business process module orientation and client/server architecture was just what the large consultancies needed to implement the vision and to change what they were selling.

Since then, SAP has grown to be the world's fourth-largest software company (see Figures 39.4 through 39.6) and a huge success on the stock market. By the end of 1995, SAP and its business partners combined employed approximately 20,000 SAP consultants. The number today is significantly higher.

The company achieved around a 60 percent growth in revenue in 1997 to 1998 and is predicting a 40 percent growth in 1998. The German market is several years more mature than the rest of the world.

The effect this growth has had on employment growth is to some extent mitigated by the improved development tools, methodologies, and preconfigured solutions that SAP is producing, but the market will expand to accommodate their extra throughput while it remains resource-constrained. Also, remember that employment growth is partly a function of the installed base, which will continue to expand long after SAP sales performance levels off (as long as sales don't fall to zero).

Forecasts for the increase in SAP employment over the next year range from 20 percent as an overall figure to more than 100 percent from individual partners.

A view based on the consideration of everything in this book suggests that the number of SAP consultants worldwide will grow by at least 40 percent per year for the first couple of years from the end of 1998. You can see for yourself how accurate this prediction proves to be, because SAP regularly publishes the figures.

FIGURE 39.4
The growth of SAP sales has been rapid.

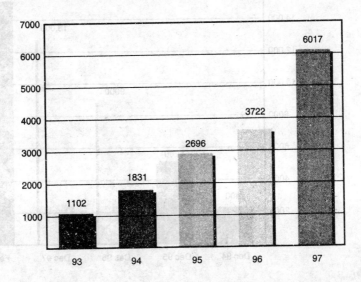

FIGURE 39.5
SAP profits show a
consistent rise.

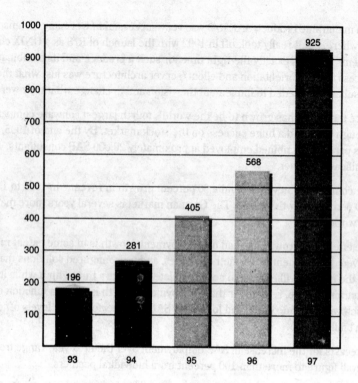

FIGURE 39.6
Since December 1994,
SAP installations (SAP
R/3) have grown
substantially.

No. of
Installations

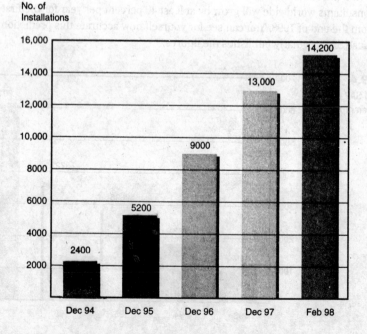

The American markets are growing rapidly, and the SAP Corporation is increasingly recognizing their significance as more of the group decisions and corporate initiatives are being driven by SAP America. Powerful and well-organized user groups are having a real impact on SAP's focus and developments. The diverse nature of the SAP market is affirmed by figures profiling the United States SAP customer base. In the U.S., a wide variety of businesses, both large-scale and small, uses the SAP products. Nearly half of SAP's U.S. customer base is made up of large-scale companies, with revenues between $250 million and $1.5 billion, while a further 33 percent of the customer base consists of smaller companies with revenues of less than $250 million.

SAP's client base is therefore not restricted to any one kind of company. This means that partial recessions in particular areas of the market won't greatly affect SAP's productivity. SAP's flexibility thus creates stability and ensures continued growth.

People often pose the same question for SAP employment as for many industry stars before it: When will the bubble burst? The answer is that it won't, because there is no bubble to burst. SAP is based solidly on the superiority of real-time processes in business, and SAP employment is based on understanding these processes. Although the demand is likely to remain, the high rates of pay cannot and will not continue. A large amount of the world's SAP consulting resource is overvalued. It is crazy that someone can go through a five-week SAP course, package himself as a consultant, and charge customers massive rates, unless he has some other impressive skill or experience that really adds value for the customer.

The client/server platform, although instrumental in SAP's phenomenal recent growth, is not crucial to its future. Indeed, it is arguable that if SAP saw a successor to client/server systems coming, it would profit hugely from it. Change is SAP's business.

Any real threat in the foreseeable future has to come from some competitor doing what SAP does, but better. In the long term, it would have to be something that makes SAP's concept of real-time processing for the back office and integrated business solutions obsolete.

This would have to be a fairly drastic change in the whole concept of business, backed up by some superior technology. If micromachines are forecast (as they are) to circumvent the long-intractable problem of turbulence on the airplane wing (among a host of other problems) by approaching it in a totally different way, why shouldn't the whole concept of business be changed with similar radicalism? Well, probably more for reasons of sociology, economics, and vested interest than anything technical.

All this says is that we'll be well into the realms of futurology before we can see a point for SAP careers to be under threat.

Growth is being fueled by a changing world of commerce. Business systems are playing an increasingly significant role in the success of organizations. Year-2000 computer problems are driving demands to huge levels, and the launch of the European Monetary Union is providing another reason for many companies to update their systems.

Employment Opportunities Generated by Market Growth

SAP's global success has translated into very real employment opportunities; employee numbers are rising constantly. Probably the greatest limiting factor to SAP's growth and success is the shortage of skilled resources to implement and support customers worldwide.

Within SAP itself, employee numbers have quadrupled since 1993. In 1997, there were approximately 12,900 SAP employees, comparing favorably to the approximately 3,700 employed in 1993. This boom is set to continue as SAP invests more and more capital in its employment programs. At the time of this writing, a new Training and Service Center is being developed close to SAP headquarters in Germany. Similarly, SAP (UK) has launched a recruitment drive aimed at recruiting 5,000 new SAP consultants into the UK market by the year 2000, not all employees of SAP (UK).

SAP investment in employment and training is mostly centered on its Research and Development section. Roughly 20 percent of SAP's annual revenues is invested in this section each year. It is SAP's commitment to research and development that ensures it maintains its status as the market leader in the ERP field. This, in turn, ensures the continuing prosperity of the SAP employment market.

Some commentators think that the need for human resources will ultimately be reduced because of this commitment to research and development.

New implementation tools, methodologies, and techniques are enabling swifter implementations, and the employee hours required for implementing and maintaining SAP will surely continue to fall. Progress is inevitable, and the SAP modules will be continually updated, requiring human resources, whether in technical, configuring, training, or supporting roles.

The development tools and Accelerated SAP methodology still require consultants to identify the particular needs of each end-user company. Because all end-user companies are unique, even within the same vertical market, customization will always be required and SAP consultants will always be needed.

Problems Created by High Market Growth

There are always two sides to the employment market: those employing and those seeking employment. For those seeking employment with the right skills, there could hardly be better times. The massive global demand for skilled resources has seen salaries rise to record levels. A skilled and experienced SAP consultant can take his pick of jobs; employers compete with each other to attract the best people. Employers are not only meeting the great difficulty of attracting the right employees but are having to face the continual threat of losing those they have to competitors prepared to offer more.

The following extract from a communication to a recruitment consultant from an experienced SAP consultant demonstrates the reality of market forces:

> I am not looking for a permanent position unless there is something very special on offer. As I mentioned to you before, I am getting excellent rates of pay and expenses. The SAP market is booming and I have freedom to pick and choose

projects. Please let me know what is so special in this offer, otherwise I don't see any benefit in proceeding.

Employers are having to pay out higher and higher sums to attract the experienced consultants. The point has been reached where no amount of money can fully satisfy the world's best SAP consultants. They want interesting projects with challenging work, and they are interested in quality of life. They want time to spend and enjoy the money they are earning.

Although SAP consultancies might have problems, it is the end users who are taking the brunt, in having to pay exorbitant fees for consultants. No doubt, many of them are distinctly unhappy about the current situation—something SAP itself is very aware of.

The poaching of employees out of SAP projects causes a huge amount of damage—intellectual knowledge is lost, disrupting projects with major cost implications.

In the demand vacuum, many employers are having to compromise on quality and take the best they can get.

In the long run, things will change, and they will change dramatically. Calls for the professionalization of the SAP employment market are being made and listened to. Initiatives that seek to stem the vicious Catch-22 situation of the shortage-of-skills cycle are being developed by many of the market players, including SAP itself. The market rates for consultants will not continue to skyrocket as they have been.

If you are professional-minded and willing to uphold quality standards, these changes shouldn't worry you. Remember the following factors:

- The employment market is changing.
- Employers don't like having to pay high salaries for inexperienced consultants.
- The employment market will become more professional.
- The top consultancy rates are likely to become higher, but the middle rates will remain the same or become lower.
- Willingness to uphold professional standards and to provide a quality service is what employers will be looking for in their SAP consultants of the future.
- Employers do not like having to pay what they might see as exorbitant fees, and when they are forced to pay high salaries, their expectations are also high.

Globalization of the SAP Employment Market

SAP has developed as a very international employment opportunity, which mirrors its global growth and installed customer base. Some of SAP's largest customers are huge multinational corporations looking to standardize their business systems and increase their global trade. The SAP world has developed an internationalist culture, with ample travel opportunities for those SAP practitioners looking to expand their horizons.

SAP has offices and partners in more than 50 countries, with customers using SAP systems in more than 90 countries. Around the world, there are at least 4,685 SAP installations (as of March 31, 1998).

Table 39.1 testifies to SAP's global market presence.

Table 39.1	SAP's Global Presence
Americas	
Argentina	Mexico
Brazil	Peru
Canada	United States
Chile	Venezuela
Colombia	
Europe	
Belgium	Khazakhstan
Bulgaria	Luxembourg
Croatia	Poland
Cyprus	Portugal
Czech Republic	Romania
Denmark	Russia
Finland	Slovak Republic
France	Spain
Greece	Sweden
Hungary	Switzerland
Ireland	Ukraine
Italy	United Kingdom
Africa	
South Africa	
Asia	
China/Hong Kong	Malaysia
India	Philippines
Indonesia	Singapore
Japan	Taiwan
Korea	Thailand
Australasia	
Australia	New Zealand

In percentile terms, the Asian and American installations have been growing the fastest. This is part of an underlying and perfectly normal pattern: Where there is more untapped potential, expansion is fastest.

If you look at the figures with even a rudimentary knowledge of geography (or the aid of an atlas) and of world economic trends, it is not difficult to see where the growth areas are going to be. All around the Pacific Rim, SAP will be growing fast for the next few years. The United States, the prime engine for this, is recruiting SAP expertise as fast as it can. The "tiger economies" of Southeast Asia have seen remarkable sales growth for SAP. The economic downturn will no doubt have an impact on sales in that region, but one might argue that when times are tough, the need to invest in technology that is going to bring business benefits could not be greater.

Singapore has built its success on the wholehearted and planned acceptance of high technology. It has strong ethnic and linguistic links with China and could be the catalyst that opens the emerging new-style economy of China to SAP.

Other areas where modern business economies are likely to develop fast are the former communist countries of Europe and the improving economies of South America.

SAP can be expected to flourish in these sorts of situations because it is an agent of change; more important, it is the agent of change of choice for multinational corporations. These multinationals are the main transferors of business practice to modernizing economies. Global economic trends—notably, the internationalization of business—have increased their influence enormously. Where they go, SAP goes.

In these emerging SAP markets, all sorts of infrastructure employment opportunities will open—in marketing, training, administration, and so on—within partners, service providers, and SAP subsidiaries themselves. But the largest and most critical requirement will be for the skilled SAP consultants and project managers who form the bulk of the SAP employment market anywhere.

Internationalist Culture

The globetrotting aspects of SAP employment have actually been less prevalent than you might expect, given its internationalism, but they are nonetheless exciting and are increasing. Apart from the routine "short-stay" business travel involved in working for international organizations, more substantial overseas relocation opportunities exist.

The internationalist culture growing around SAP has strong foundations:

- The large management consultancies that are partners with SAP have a long history of operating internationally and have propagated the SAP message worldwide.
- Similarly, the SAP platform and technology partners are some of the largest in the world and are very international in their outlook.
- The partnership approach that SAP has adopted has allowed it to expand worldwide very rapidly without prohibitive investment demands.

- The SAP culture of open communications and the transfer of knowledge and skills are highly palatable to operations thousands of miles from the home base.

- SAP has adopted English as its first language from its early days, despite its German origins, and English is the global language of commerce. SAP systems, however, have been translated into more than 20 languages, including Mandarin.

- International demand for SAP systems and the level of experience needed to implement them have meant that new markets have had to obtain this experience from more established markets, thus encouraging globalization of employment.

Building on these foundations, SAP has pursued an ethos that allows each SAP subsidiary to develop its own culture. Walldorf, Germany, for example, has a "techno-academic," almost campus-style culture, whereas Philadelphia prefers a more typical modern U.S. business culture.

The common denominator, to which all subsidiaries work, is to keep the structure nonhierarchic, nonbureaucratic, and very partner-oriented; and to espouse virtuality in building their operations. By *virtuality,* SAP means the facility for functional teams and organizations to be formed by people and resources working in partnerships but not necessarily employed or owned by the same company.

SAP is extending the internationalism of its operations wherever it is practicable, not just in the appointment of partners and the development of marketing subsidiaries, but also in the placement of strategic resources. Although currently, 95 percent of product development is done in Germany, this is changing. The United States is performing product development now, as is the United Kingdom, to a smaller extent; and some localized language versions of the product will be produced with local partners. *Industry Centers of Expertise* (ICOEs) are also strategic resources, and these are sited in far-flung locations. Worldwide special interest groups are encouraged and are not necessarily headquartered in Germany.

SAP has emphasized this trend by the recent restructuring of its alliance program management, which is absolutely critical to its partner-based marketing strategy. This will now be coordinated worldwide by SAP's global partner management group in the United States.

One of the group's first moves, aimed at generating add-on business for partners, was to propose a focus on rolling out existing SAP systems internationally. There are many clients with a large potential for this activity. Independently of SAP's own efforts, the recruitment industry is advertising very much on an international basis. In Europe, SAP ranks among the highest IT specialties in terms of the ratio of international appointments to local ones. This trend can be expected to continue, and as the United States gets its SAP numbers up, it can also expect a significant "brain drain" to the smaller SAP markets.

For the time being, however, the U.S. movement is mostly inward. The large U.S. consulting companies are offering high inducements to take people to the United States as well as to the Eastern Pacific. Contractors and employees moving to the United States can get good relocation perks as well as high earnings.

More of the international vacancies advertised are for consultants, module configurers, and project leaders than for ABAP programmers, although ABAP does feature to some extent.

Good SAP consultants gain a reputation internationally and can ply their skills in most parts of the world. Those who relocate regularly for the duration of projects can find themselves in a "global village" culture like those that arise in the oil industry, diplomacy, banking, and other international activities.

If you are looking to join this community and have the skills to contribute to it, you should consider your options carefully and plan to locate where you really want to go. Not all the locations you can end up in are exotic, and many are not suitable for taking families. On the other hand, expatriate life can enrich your life enormously. The key to success is to evaluate carefully the location and the culture. You don't have to go anywhere just for the money in SAP. The location is probably the most important part of your employment decision. Make sure that you have the full support of any partner you're taking, and expect it to be different from home. Expatriates who spend a lot of time whining about things the location lacks that they're used to at home are not usually happy or popular.

Those who take the trouble to adapt to "culture shock" and value what other societies can offer are usually very happy and only compromise their popularity when they get home by overdosing their friends with enthusiastic travelers' tales. ●

SAP Workplaces

An Overview of the SAP Working World Structure

SAP could never have reached its market position by simply selling the SAP software as a package and providing just routine technical support. The real salable product is an amalgam of the SAP core product and the consultancy and implementation services that together deliver the benefits of SAP systems to users.

Had SAP tried to provide all these essential value-added services itself, it wouldn't have been able to progress beyond the status of a consultant/implementer—with very good systems implementation technology, yet nonetheless constrained by people resources from achieving the kind of growth that has occurred.

It was when management consultancies found a strong affinity with the product—and saw it as a massive step forward in enabling technology for the vision and change management that is their prime offering—that the product really took off and burgeoned internationally. The marketing resources these consultancies have, in particular their access to top management in major end-user companies, were huge levers on the marketplace. Their position, at base, as suppliers of high-order people skills, meant that what was to SAP a potential problem was to them an opportunity—and vice versa. So a large industry has grown up around marketing and implementing SAP systems, without SAP having to face the investment and growing pains of trying to control it all directly.

SAP people like to refer to the whole infrastructure that creates, markets, and delivers SAP systems to users as the *virtual organization,* and this is quite an apt description.

The virtual organization involves many and various activities, and in the SAP world, the people who carry out these activities may be employed (or contracted) by SAP AG and its subsidiaries, partners of various types, and the end users themselves. These people often need to work in *virtual teams* that cross employer boundaries.

Many subsidiary virtual organizations form and reform, often at the project level, including some end-user personnel who are seconded into the SAP world only for the project's duration and will return to mainline business management roles after completion.

SAP software is realized on many platforms—database systems as well as operating systems and hardware platforms—by vendors with whom SAP has partnership agreements. SAP software also extends its capability by providing links with complementary software products—in some cases, along with partners. All this means that "ownership" of the virtual organization is further extended.

In this situation, cooperation—instead of hierarchy or proprietorship—rules. Cohesion is achieved through influence, quality control, shared aspirations, communication, and so on, instead of by command. This nonhierarchical, project-orientated approach is popular in many consultancy environments, and it suits the SAP world very well.

The organization as a whole exists to market solutions built from these component products and services:

- The SAP software
- Platform hardware and software
- Complementary products
- Consultancy and implementation services

These are brought together into working SAP solutions at the individual customer level. They can also be combined at levels that mediate between their individual "factories" and the individual customer. For example, at the industry sector level, a partner will create a value-added offering to target a vertical market sector.

The main lines show the flow in terms of product delivery. What motivates the parties is the common interest in delivering a product together, but the glue that holds the virtual organization together is more than that. These are some of the "binding agents":

- Business management
- Quality control
- Information flow
- Concerted marketing effort

SAP doesn't own the virtual organization in the way a single company owns its organization (nobody owns it in that sense), but SAP leads or at least influences it, and has the central role in cultivating these binding agents. (Partners, of course, lead other virtual organizations, which they drive, and in which SAP is only one contributor, but they aren't the topic here.)

Business Management

Business management is the main difference between the virtual organization and a "real" organization (that is, one owned by a single company). Within its owned organization, a company can command policies, actions, and priorities not only through its statutory rights to do so, but also through financial controls—it holds all the purse strings. SAP has no such control over its virtual organization, so its business management outside its own company walls is enforced by negotiation and contractual arrangements. This is no different from any other company that has marketing partners, but because the partners' value-added services are such a large and integral part of most SAP sales, the SAP partner program and the agreements it incorporates are absolutely central to its operation.

Quality Control

Quality control, extending beyond the core product to all the value-added elements, is a major feature for many multiowned virtual organizations, from IT marketing partner operations to franchised hotel and fast-food outlets, and it's also important for SAP. Here are the main planks in SAP's direct quality controls over the extended operation:

- The partner accreditation process, which accepts only partners who can meet and commit to maintaining SAP's quality standards.

- Customer satisfaction programs. End-user satisfaction is regularly monitored, and partners' performance in this respect is visible.

- The complementary solutions certification program, which is designed to ensure that third-party solutions interface properly with SAP.

- SAP consultant accreditation. This is a program that SAP is rolling out worldwide to accredit individual consultants within partner organizations.

Depending on your definition, you might include *quality improvement* within the term *quality control*. Here SAP's main policy is to seek improvement by encouraging the best practice and knowledge transfer, by providing conduits for open interchange of information, and also by providing a good example. SAP is unusual in its openness, and this has placed it in good stead.

Information Flow

SAP has been quick to espouse the "information superhighway" and delivers its SAP Infoline service via the World Wide Web, CompuServe, Lotus Notes, and The Microsoft Network. As well as disseminating SAP news and information, Infoline encourages discussion forums, provides a common medium for any participant in the SAP world to promote itself and share knowledge, and acts as a directory of sources of further information. You can learn a lot more about all these services, if you have access to email, by using the Internet email address **infoline@sap-ag.de.** Alternatively, you can access the SAP Web page at its URL: **www.sap.com.**

A growing range of *knowledgeware* and general information in multimedia format augments this online information.

For SAP users, the *Online Service System* (OSS) goes further. SAP introduced it into its R/3 Service System in 1994 and accepted the ten thousandth user of OSS in 1995. OSS provides SAP users with a problem management system with interactive facilities that assist in the whole area of support, commercial facilities (such as course registrations and ordering of documentation), and information.

SAP also engages fully in the traditional marketing communications activities. For example, it produces a very informative house magazine, which is recommended reading for anyone who wants to keep informed about the SAP world: SAP "INFO," around 60 pages, published quarterly and available from your nearest SAP subsidiary. SAP also participates in a full international program of events, seminars, conferences, and so on. And, it channels information through its marketing organization, focused in various ways—by product types, business sectors, and so on.

Good communications are crucial to the SAP operation, and none of the activities just described would unify the virtual organization as well as they do without the interpersonal communications skills that the SAP world consistently seeks in its recruits.

Concerted Marketing Effort

From SAP's own point of view, of course, the development of the extended virtual organization is in itself a major marketing effort, but SAP also has to lead the efforts to market the combined output of that organization.

SAP's primary role in this is to provide a broad framework of general marketing directions backed up by investment in strategic marketing resources and image creation. Partners add a lot of input to this process. SAP isn't the fount of all wisdom, and partner initiatives, stemming from their own experience, often determine strategic directions. SAP is the unifier and a major source, but not the sole source, of marketing creativity.

The drive toward industry-specific, or vertical marketing solutions, and the push into the volume market for mid-size and smaller companies are examples of major directional thrusts, each of which has many subsidiary threads.

The partner organizations take their cues from these general directions and build their own focuses to ride with the main thrusts and complement them.

Although SAP still handles some end users itself, partners provide the majority of the sales (as opposed to marketing) effort. SAP sales involve high-level decisions, and consultants are well-equipped to influence these. As an SAP alliance manager put it, "Senior executives don't buy products, they buy solutions."

So far, this chapter has basically focused on achieving marketing cohesion, and one factor you shouldn't ignore is the importance of the general spirit of cooperation that exists among SAP and its partners. The conduit provided by regular human contact and cooperation at the project level is a major factor in creating a cohesive marketing force from the virtual organization.

The structure of the SAP working world, then, is a nonhierarchical, virtual organization. People working in it need to be self-reliant types. It's been said that your boss can be defined as the person who approves your holidays and salary raises, but in many environments, he or she also manages the projects you are working on from month to month. This isn't true in much of the SAP virtual organization. Projects are often long and require a lot of commitment, and your project responsibilities are what you have to answer to.

The traditional boss is also a person you can use as a single source "supplier" to get things done or approved. In the virtual organization, there is often no one you can use as a one-stop shop in this way. You are expected to use initiative and find the people who can help you get the job done. That's one reason why good communications skills are so highly valued. It's also a reason why people with the right attributes find the SAP world so satisfying.

SAP: The Company

SAP's corporate structure is less important than how well it manages the aforementioned activities, because its policy isn't to overmanage the subsidiaries, but instead to put in place the standards and strategic policies, and then give the subsidiaries substantial autonomy to run the business within them.

Figure 40.1 shows the broad structure. The individual subsidiary shown is that of the UK, which is a good example because it's neither at the very top nor the bottom rank in importance, penetration, or potential. Structures vary from country to country, but most of the functions shown will appear in one guise or another in most subsidiaries.

FIGURE 40.1

The structure of a typical SAP subsidiary shows the roles it carries out and how people are organized to fulfill them.

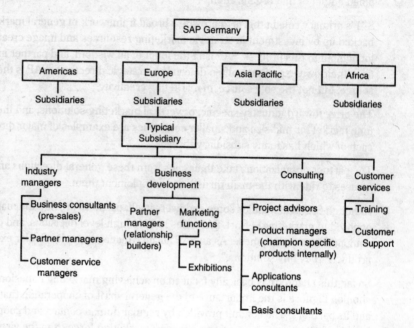

Bear in mind that the subsidiaries handle some direct end-user accounts as well as support partner activities. The consulting groups have a major role in this, although they also combine in virtual teams with partner consultants. The motivation behind direct sales is to meet customer preference for this, where it exists, and to keep in touch with the battlefront. SAP charges for its consultancy services, although the objective of the SAP consulting group isn't primarily to generate revenue from consulting, but instead to maximize product sales.

It's worth expanding a little on one or two of the roles within the consulting group:

- Project advisors act as customer service managers, but at the project rather than the account level.

- Product managers are experts in particular modules. They champion those modules internally and act as a conduit between SAP headquarters at Walldorf and the client on anything related to those modules.

- Application consultants are the largest group, accounting for some 40 percent of a subsidiary's headcount. The applications they specialize in are *horizontal* ones—that is, not so much industry-specific as function-specific, and they perform configurations to ensure that the required functionality is built in to end-user systems.

- BASIS consultants deal with the underlying systems components and tools. They are concerned with things such as datacoms, operating systems, databases, and ABAP programming.

If you are looking for employment opportunities in an SAP subsidiary, check out Appendix A, "Sample SAP-Related Job Descriptions," for several examples of role descriptions for the sorts of positions subsidiaries have. These will give you a good picture of the attributes required.

Essentially, SAP needs its own people to have all the SAP consultant skills in sufficient quantity to set the standards that it promotes among the partners. This applies both to technical expertise and interpersonal skills. In the early days, SAP consultants came out of the development team, and SAP will rarely employ anyone in a consulting role unless that person has good SAP experience. The ideal is that SAP people should be able to solve problems that have escalated from partner and end-user consultants. They should also be able to pass on their skills, so training abilities are desired.

The area in which SAP has found it beneficial to engage people from outside the SAP world is in marketing roles, where SAP has learned from the recruits as well as taught them.

SAP Business Partners

SAP has employed the partner program in the context of a global strategy (which has succeeded) aimed at making SAP the global market leader for standard applications. This has involved accreting a tremendous range of capability, quickly.

The program is founded on the philosophy that strategic alliances are a better way to develop and acquire new strengths than going it alone or buying up other companies. When individual companies bring their particular abilities into a partnership alliance, they get faster exploitation of the synergies without becoming wrapped up in the mechanics (or financial implications) of mergers, takeovers, and large-scale management change.

SAP believes that this approach can give a company a competitive edge. An essential precondition for success is, as expressed in its partner handbook, "the planned creation and development of a superior ability to cooperate in terms of a cooperative and dependable approach on the part of employees and an organizational structure that encourages cooperation."

The philosophy further says that to make this work, everyone involved must constantly seek ways to cooperate and think in terms of the collective benefits, rather than narrow partisan advantages. They must constantly strive to develop a mutual understanding of each other's situations and goals.

If this sounds like a string of platitudes, don't be misled. It's a very real policy that works. SAP must be at least a contender for the title "Most Effective Marketer Through Partnerships in the IT World." Although a lot of that success is due to having a product that partners want, SAP's approach to the partner relationship has also been crucial, and its consistent pursuit of cooperation and communication at the individual employee level is the cornerstone of that.

The partner program is organized, in broad terms, as shown in Figure 40.2. The relationship management aspects are handled via an alliance manager structure. This is headed in the USA by global alliance management, which manages the alliances with partners who have global logo status; it also directs the activities of the SAP regional and national alliance managers, who have direct "line responsibility" to the subsidiaries or regions where they are employed.

FIGURE 40.2

Global alliance management works through locally employed alliance management groups but directly manages the global logo partners.

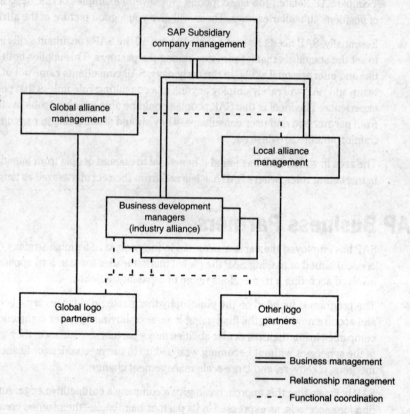

The relationship management aspects are substantial. Partner companies usually restructure their own organizations to best realize cooperative potential, and the contractual rights and obligations are intended to secure commitment to clear strategic goals understood by both parties, as well as operational ones, such as customer satisfaction.

As well as the alliance managers, partners have direct access to the industry-aligned business development managers, who are their first port of call to keep coordinated with, and informed on, the activities of other partners and SAP itself within given industry groupings. This is being instituted worldwide at the time of this writing, in line with the increasing verticalization of SAP's marketing.

The partner program has worked well so far for the partners and SAP alike. The partners have given SAP a better understanding of the "corporate change" market, market penetration and leverage, and extended resources. SAP has given consultants an enabling technology. Consultants sell "vision," and SAP is the enabling technology for realizing that vision, which is why the synergy between SAP and consultancy organizations is so strong. As SAP goes from strength to strength, and more end users become aware of its potential, it positively creates a demand for change (and therefore consultants) and helps to realize that change.

This provides the classic win/win scenario. SAP executives like to extend this and talk of a win/win/win philosophy. In other words, an arrangement has to benefit the customer, as well as SAP and the partner.

The main partner types in the SAP world are platform partners, technology partners, consulting partners, systems resellers, and complementary product partners.

Platform Partners

Platform partner relationships are in place with the major hardware vendors who implement some form of UNIX operating system, and some Windows NT specialists. AT&T, Bull Information Systems, Compaq, Data General, Digital Equipment Corporation, Hewlett-Packard, IBM, Sequent, Siemens Nixdorf Information Systems, and SUN are all SAP hardware platform partners.

The main requisite for platform partners is to obtain platform certification by SAP (or iXOS on SAP's behalf, in the case of NT systems), but in fact the level of cooperation runs far deeper than that.

SAP sets up joint R/3 competence centers with its platform partners, either in Walldorf or appropriate subsidiaries. These centers, apart from migrating R/3 to the vendors' platforms, provide a nerve center for cooperation across a wide spectrum of activity—marketing strategies, sales team activities, events, mutual training, and so on.

Some platform partners are also consulting, implementation, technology, and/or complementary products partners. IBM, for example, has accreditation in all categories.

Part of the attraction to SAP in forming these relationships is the access it gives SAP to the far larger national and international sales, distribution, and support networks that these hardware vendors have, compared to SAP. This may be an attraction to employees also. Something like 20 percent of SAP vacancies in some recruitment outfits emanate from hardware vendors.

If you are an SAP consultant seeking a change of environment, this is a fruitful area to consider. Virtually any of the whole range of SAP skills may find a home. If you are seeking to gain your first experience in SAP and finding it difficult, you may find that a platform supplier will open the door if you have experience that it wants in a technology other than SAP. The best route is to first get the platform partner to employ you, and then wait until you are entrenched and valued before trying to divert yourself into its SAP activities.

Technology Partners

Technology partners are mainly the big database players, along with a few hardware vendors. Partners include Apple Computer Inc., Hewlett-Packard, IBM, Informix, Intel, iXOS Software, Microsoft, Oracle, Platinum Technology, Siemens Nixdorf Information Systems, and Software AG.

Each technology partner agreement is based on an individual contract, and the focus is to exchange knowledge and engage in common activities to optimize the use of SAP and the partners' products together. These agreements secure essential technological underpinnings, such as databases and systems tools.

SAP-based activities in technology partners are more specialized and less wide-ranging than they are in platform partners.

They are nonetheless quite committed. Microsoft has had a strategic cooperation agreement with SAP since 1993. Windows NT is a strategic product for SAP, and it has signed an agreement with Microsoft to jointly develop Internet strategy. Oracle has been involved since the development of R/3 in 1987 and claims that SAP implementations are based up to 75 percent on Oracle. iXOS, as well as concerning itself with its imaging and archiving software, provides SAP with systems testing services, notably for the certification of Windows NT platforms.

As an employment prospect for the experienced SAP consultant with technical leanings who is ideally skilled in some other area of relevance, you might find a high premium on your ability to bring SAP into the particular fold of a technology partner. For the would-be SAP entrant, the story is much the same as it is with platform partners. You will need to have something to offer that meets a partner requirement, and use that as your ticket.

Consulting Partners

Consulting partners are also known as *logo partners*. The three levels are outlined in the following sections.

▶ See "Logo Partners," p. 1027

Global Logo Partners   A global logo partner operates the same way in all SAP geographical regions and maintains a consistent infrastructure for the support of globally active R/3 customers. The partner must qualify for regional logo partner status in at least two SAP regions, and SAP global alliance management, based in the USA, manages the global partnership.

Each global partner is entitled to use the logo "R/3 International Consulting Partner/Global."

Global logo partners include the major management consulting firms Andersen Consulting, Coopers & Lybrand, Ernst & Young, ICS (Deloitte & Touche Consulting Group), KPMG, and Price Waterhouse; as well as hardware vendors such as Digital Equipment, Hewlett-Packard, IBM, and IT specialists CSC, EDS, and Origin.

Regional Logo Partners   A regional logo partner operates mainly in one SAP geographic region and maintains a regional infrastructure that corresponds with its SAP activities. The partner must qualify for national partner status in a certain number of countries, which varies by region—for example, two countries in the Americas region, four countries in Asia, and so on. Alliance management at the regional level manages the partnership.

Each regional partner is entitled to use the logo "R/3 International Consulting Partner/Europe" (or "/Asia," "/Americas," "/Africa," as appropriate).

National Logo Partners   A national logo partner operates mainly in one country and has to meet the requirements of that country's SAP national cooperation agreement, which typically includes a satisfactory business plan, a minimum number of R/3 consultants, and a regular audit. The partnership is managed by the local SAP subsidiary, normally via the national alliance manager.

Each national partner is entitled to use the logo "R/3 Consulting Partner/France" (with the SAP national affiliation on the end).

The logo partners are a prime source of employment opportunity for those with the right skills and qualifications. Broadly speaking, there are two opportunity areas:

- Your career as a management consultant is more important than the SAP involvement. The large consultancies especially like to recruit and develop people with longer-term aims. This is discussed more in Chapter 42, "How to Find Employment Working with SAP," where the general message is to think management consultancy, not SAP, when approaching the global logo partners. Some national and regional logo partners are entirely dedicated to SAP, so you need to find out how much of an SAP specialist a partner is, and how much a management consultant, before deciding how promising they are for you and what your best line of attack is.

  Most logo partners have SAP training and induction programs, and this trend is growing, so the route is good for new SAP entrants with good management consultant attributes, especially if these are backed up by some sort of IT expertise.

- The second opportunity area with logo partners is for people with SAP skills to develop and widen their horizons. All logo partners will be interested in SAP experience.

A particular area that's likely to continue for some time is the drive by some global partners to recruit internationally to service the big SAP growth in the USA and the Pacific Rim. The urgency of this is overriding the general recruitment priorities described earlier, and they are usually looking for specific SAP skills to fill an immediate need. If you have these skills, they can provide the entry into an environment that can lead to broader opportunities.

If you are reading this outside the USA and want to work there, here is a generalized profile for SAP people recruited overseas into the USA for a "big six" consultancy. It's not "written in stone," and other international recruiters will vary a little, but it provides a rough score sheet to help you assess your prospects:

- **Age.** 28 to 35 is best. The large consultancies find it easier to induct younger people into their culture. Even within this range, if your age is near the top end, you will be required to have more experience, particularly in project or module leadership. If your age falls above the range, you will have to be exceptional, and there is a near ban on persons past their 40s.

- **Marital status.** Single people are generally preferred because of their greater flexibility when it comes to travel. If you are married or have other familial attachments, consider and be prepared to explain to the employer how they will deal with travel, any U.S. work interests, and so on.

- **SAP experience.** The consultancy firm for which this profile was prepared asked for a minimum of two years of hands-on implementation experience, as well as experience in configuring SAP in a relevant area. (Sales order management and distribution, financial, or manufacturing were the relevant areas in this consultancy's immediate needs.)

  You will need a sound understanding of the tables and transactions in your area of expertise, as well as a working knowledge of SAP module integration and the typical issues involved in interfacing with other systems.

  R/3 experience is highly desirable. People who have functioned in an SAP consulting role are preferable, because they understand the professional services role better. Working in a project rather than a transaction environment is preferred. People with SAP experience only from a user perspective normally lack the ability to configure the system and would have to provide evidence that they can do so.

- **SAP training.** You should have undertaken at least four SAP courses in your area of implementation experience.

- **Intelligence.** People of high intelligence (which as a rule of thumb can be taken as meaning an IQ within the top 10 percent of the population) are required. This is considered likely to enable you to quickly learn the client's situation, be analytical, take broad perspectives but also delve into detail, think on a conceptual level but understand the practical implications, have a questioning mind, and always be looking to do things better.

- **Interpersonal skills.** You should be a good listener, like to work with others, be able to build good relationships, be empathetic, and function well as part of a team.

- **Communication.** English-language skills are essential. Candidates must be able to understand and speak English well in a work environment. Equally important is that they can communicate ideas clearly and succinctly.

- **Motivation.** People who are enthusiastic, who take charge, have direction, plan and control their actions to meet deadlines, and in general are very results-oriented have a good opportunity.

The international recruitment drive is not only aimed at senior SAP consultants and project managers, but also targets people with more specific skills, such as applications engineers and module configurers.

Some logo partners are more specifically oriented toward IT and less toward general management consultancy. Indeed, as mentioned earlier, some are exclusively devoted to SAP.

These more IT-based partners, while still requiring the right personality type and the ability to deal with senior management concerns, tend to focus a little more on the traditional IT system house virtues. This extract from a job requirement statement is a good example. (The full version is in Appendix A, "Sample SAP-Related Job Descriptions.")

Candidates should have

- Worked in pre/post-sales support
- Implemented several large IT projects in commercial organizations
- Worked in consultancy or with a specialist software house
- Ideally trained in R/3, have R/2 experience, and/or have comparable product experience
- Extensive knowledge of the appropriate application area (in the case from which this example was extracted, appropriate areas were financial accounting systems, logistics/materials management, and/or manufacturing)
- Overall experience of large commercial implementations, which would be expected to extend over five years

Implementation Partners

Implementation partners sometimes are referred to as another case of consulting partners, and the cooperation agreement for implementation partners is regarded as the first step to becoming a logo partner.

The relationship doesn't include the intensive support and cooperation that logo partners enjoy, but it allows a consultancy firm to gain access to the SAP marketplace and the SAP-provided infrastructure (demonstration system, documentation, training facilities, and so on). The qualification process for a partner is less onerous, but the partner must maintain appropriate capabilities—for example, dedicated SAP consultants and demonstration capabilities.

You will find much the same employment opportunities in implementation partners as in logo partners, and some of them have put a lot of creativity into developing their SAP business.

R/3 System Resellers

System resellers engage in the promotion and sale of R/3 itself. They must develop value-added software themselves and have a product of their own that might be complementary to SAP R/3 or be replaceable by it. They also must have sales, consulting, training, and support resources in place before being accepted as an R/3 system reseller.

At the outset, resellers were restricted to a few companies, mostly operating in Germany and the immediate environs. By 1997, a global strategy was starting to emerge in countries such as the United Kingdom, where a number of resellers have been appointed with special skills in promising areas, notably manufacturing.

This development is worth watching as it advances globally, because it will open all kinds of new employment opportunities.

Complementary Product Suppliers

The design of the SAP R/3 system—its inherent modularity, and its position as the world's leading client/server product—makes it an attractive vehicle for many third-party software developers.

SAP has encouraged this by the interface technologies it has used in R/3: *Application Link Enabling* (ALE), *object linking and embedding* (OLE), *Remote Function Calls* (RFCs), and *open database connectivity* (ODBC).

SAP certifies third-party products for connection to its various R/3 interfaces, and these are categorized as the following (the SAP interfaces are in parentheses):

- Archive software/imaging software (SAP ArchiveLink *R*)
- *Computer-aided design* (CAD)
- *Electronic Data Interchange* (EDI) subsystems (WF-EDI)
- Plant Data Collection (PP-PDC)
- Product Data Management (CAD)
- Process Control Systems (PI-PCS)
- Machine Data Collection (PP-PDC)
- Laboratory Information Management Systems (QM-IDI)

Third-party solution providers with products in these categories that are either certified or awaiting certification are listed in Appendix E, "Complementary Solutions."

These are mostly in Germany, in line with SAP's history, but some are in the USA and the UK, and more are expected to come from these and other countries, in line with their present and future.

Some complementary solutions aren't subject to certification. These are primarily used with communications services. Both R/2 and R/3 systems allow access to these services directly from within the SAP system, and add-on product suppliers have developed in the following areas:

- Electronic mail
- Fax, telex, teletext
- Sending and receiving EDI documents
- Telephony

Again, you can find addresses for product suppliers in these categories in Appendix E, "Complementary Solutions."

As a source of employment, the complementary solutions providers as a group offer a tremendously wide scope, although individually they are often highly specialized. They offer a "bridging opportunity" for SAP-experienced people seeking to divert from the mainstream SAP world and advance up to another area of specialty, and also for SAP entrants to go the other way—using another skill to move into SAP.

Those people more interested in technicalities than using interpersonal and business skills will have a better chance of progression in a complementary solutions niche than in most places in the SAP world.

Ancillary Service Providers

Ancillary service providers are independent companies that provide support services to the SAP market that contribute to the "SAP Virtual World."

Employment Agencies/Recruitment Consultants

People are the most valuable resource in the SAP working world. It's therefore not surprising that there has been explosive growth in the number of firms specializing in recruiting contract and permanent SAP workers.

Documentation Specialists

Because each system is independently configured, there is a need to develop company-specific training and user documentation.

When the project teams have disbanded, the documentation produced offers a lasting record of what has been done and how the system should be used.

Because most companies implementing SAP will be operating a quality management program, there is frequently a need to update procedures, guidelines, roles, and responsibilities. There are also disaster recovery plans and other kinds of system documentation that need to be produced.

Human Issues Consultants

SAP is inextricably linked with *business process reengineering* (BPR) and change. Many human issues need to be addressed, from structuring the right project team to dealing with change, uncertainty, and stress. Human issues consultancy is a field of activity that is evolving as a specialist area within the management change activity. Human issues consultants help to identify potential problem areas related to psychological responses to change, and propose strategies for avoiding those problems. They also troubleshoot and offer counseling and reconciliation services when problems arise. The objective is to retain morale and team spirit through potentially testing times.

Good human issues consultants will be worth their fees many times over.

Security and Control Consultants

SAP security and control is a specialist area that requires specialist knowledge. Any software system has its own characteristics from the perspectives of data and systems security, and SAP security and control consultants need to know SAP well from these standpoints, as well as being experts in the general field of security and control. They also have to understand any special security and control considerations of the particular platform and complementary technologies that an individual client may be using.

Internal and External Communications Consultants

Communications form a vital element in the running of an SAP project and the managing of change in an organization.

Training Providers

Training is needed for project team members, management, and users alike. Some training is available off the shelf from SAP itself and other companies, but there is always a requirement for company-specific training.

Company-specific training for users generally is required over a very short period of time, when sufficient system development has been completed and before the go-live date.

Project Planning Consultants

SAP projects require the highest level of project management skills. The planning and control role is often best delegated to a well-focused professional team that can work with SAP's Project System as well as other project-management tools.

System Testing Consultants

Integrated and volume testing are the greatest indicators of project progress and readiness to go live. They create, however, a logistical nightmare, both in planning and execution. Some companies specialize in planning test programs and arranging the resourcing.

SAP Users

You can consider the end users as part of the SAP virtual organization because of the way they merge into virtual teams with SAP's and the partners' people.

End users employ a range of skills that extend farther down the scales into support roles and business analysis roles. These users also make more use of ABAP programmers than other parts of the SAP world, because ABAP is primarily used to make minor systems adjustments, instead of in the main installation phase of a project. End users also employ or contract higher-level SAP skills—from senior SAP consultants to configurers. This varies from user to user, some passing almost total responsibility to their SAP partner/installer, and others choosing to resource their own team, recruiting individual employees or contractors themselves.

There is usually a strong input, often including the project manager, from end users' own business management and IT teams. People seconded across to the SAP project are intended to return to the mainstream after the project is completed, and usually find that they have enhanced their career prospects because of their experience in the SAP world.

Some (usually from an IT background) don't return to their employer's mainstream, but instead divert to an SAP career—consultants and SAP itself recruit many of their people from end users. End user management finds this easier to bear when the defector goes to SAP itself or to the installing partner, because at least the person's knowledge isn't totally lost. Cases have occurred in which employers have deliberately encouraged SAP to recruit key people, as the lesser of two evils, knowing of the impending possibility of those people being recruited to work halfway across the globe.

If you are a systems person and your company is looking at installing SAP, you are in the right place at the right time.

If you have key project management or configuring skills in SAP, you can command a premium, in terms of cash or career progression, with installing end users.

If short-term cash is your goal, then contracting is probably the best answer, whether you organize it yourself or go through an agency. Employers can pay contractors what it's worth to the project, which they can't do with employees without upsetting corporate pay scales. Because SAP contracts can be so long, contractors have the chance to get the best of both worlds—getting paid for taking the freelance contractor's risk without actually taking much of a risk.

If you are more interested in building a career in management, you'll find it better to commit yourself to an employer. Not only will this give you the chance to use the project to lever yourself up the particular employer's management ladder, but it will also look much better on your résumé for future purposes.

Profile of the User Population: Who Uses SAP?

SAP's customers include many of the world's largest "blue-chip" organizations, among which it is the predominant standard application software. It now has started to make inroads into mid-size companies (roughly speaking, those with less than $100 million turnover). From its origins in the chemical industry, SAP has spread over a vast range of industries, as shown in Figure 39.2 in the preceding chapter.

▶ **See** "SAP Market Facts and Figures," **p. 904**

The figure shows the distribution of installations across industry sectors as of March 1998 based on SAP's published list of reference installations (after excluding partners and consultancies). Installations were spread across 53 countries all around the world.

Studying this figure will give you good insight as to the industries where you can find SAP employment.

Emerging User Marketplace: The Next Generation of Users

The two main market thrusts that will affect the customer base are

- The drive into mid-size and smaller companies
- Vertical marketing initiatives

These are discussed further in Chapter 43, "The Outlook for the SAP Employment Market," but it's worth mentioning here that SAP has currently earmarked banking, hospitals, the oil industry, retail, the public sector, publishers, and utilities for special attention. These are mostly areas where SAP already has a good foothold, and they are fairly broad areas.

Partners are picking up on the vertical market thrust and looking for niches in more specific areas, such as the beverage industry, estate administration, laboratory systems, and so on.

You can expect the next generation of users to be fewer in number and more specialized, and they won't expect to bear the extended installation times and costs that the giants have. You can also expect them to be engaging in intercompany systems access with the larger companies in their own vertical supply chain; many of these companies will already be using SAP. It may well be that this development, which combines elements of both the mid-size company and vertical marketing drives, will be a dominating feature of systems fashion in the next few years and will have a profound effect on the pattern of employment in SAP. ●

CHAPTER 41

Employment Opportunities Working with SAP

In this chapter

Special Skills and Experiences Required for Each SAP Function

Table 41.1 lays out the essential functions that have to take place in bringing SAP systems to customers, as well as some of the special skills these functions supply. The table uses a generalized set of function and skill descriptions so that it will be easily understood. You can use this table to map out the skills you have (or would like to develop), along with the various job titles and activity descriptions used by potential employers.

Table 41.1 Blank=Not Required, 1=Beginning, 2=Intermediate, and 3=Advanced					
Function Skills	Vertical Business Sector Knowledge	Business Function Knowledge	Special Knowledge of the Technology	Systems Analysis Skills	Program-ming
Developing the SAP Core Product	2	3	2	2	3
Extending Platforms and Interfaced Technologies			3	1	3
Extending the SAP Product with Solutions	3	2	1	3	3
Management Consulting	3	3	1	2	
Project Management	1	3	1	2	
Business Analysis	2	3	2	3	1
Fitting Business Needs with SAP	2	3	1	3	1
Modeling, Configuring, and Testing	2	3	2	1	1
ABAP Modifications	1	3	3	2	3
Installing "the User" (Documentation, Support, and Testing)	2	2	2	3	

Function Skills	Vertical Business Sector Knowledge	Business Function Knowledge	Special Knowledge of the Technology	Systems Analysis Skills	Programming
Ongoing Technical Support		2	3	1	2
Systems Administration and Management	2	2	2	2	1

The functions and skills mapped out in Table 41.1 are worth a little closer examination.

Functions: In Producing, Selling, Implementing, and Using SAP

Developing the SAP core product is the prime job of the development group at Walldorf, along with the smaller development group in the USA and other outposts. The core product includes the modules programmed in ABAP using the Development Workbench and the Workbench itself. Some localized foreign-language versions are being developed with "country partners"—for example, in Korea.

Extending Platforms and Interfaced Technology

SAP developers work with platform partners to port SAP onto new platforms and thereby add value in the shape of special platform benefits. Complementary solution providers create interfaces to SAP, which SAP tests and certifies, thus extending the SAP capability to embrace the special benefits of each complementary solution.

Extending the SAP Product with Solutions

SAP produces some vertical market modules—such as Industry Solutions, Oil, and R/3 Retail—as part of its development activities. In addition, some consultancy partners are adding value in the shape of vertical market solutions. This whole vertical market product is a growth area. Complementary solutions aren't usually vertical market solutions, but more technical ones, such as data storage or data communications systems. A company has to have a marketable solution in place before it will interest SAP, so to the complementary solution partner, it's more a case of adding SAP to the solution, rather than the solution to SAP, but it extends SAP's capability nonetheless.

Management Consultancy

SAP partners, especially the larger logo partners, are heavily centered on management consultancy. Their contribution in strategic vision, change management, and *business process reengineering* (BPR) is a significant part of the virtual organization's overall business. SAP subsidiaries also perform management consultancy for their direct accounts, and the Walldorf development team gets involved in this with German customers.

Project Management

All levels in the SAP supply chain may provide project management, from SAP itself through all partner types to the end user. End users may choose to appoint their own project manager and resource the project without handing over implementation responsibility to a partner.

Business Analysis

Here, *business analysis* means the analysis of business needs at the individual project or client level. (Elsewhere in the book, you will see discussions on the marketing role of "business analyst," which isn't quite the same thing. As a marketing role, business analysis is concerned with analyzing the needs of a whole marketplace.) All consultants—employed anywhere from Walldorf through the whole subsidiary, partner, and end-user chain—need to have some business analysis skills, and each project requires the skills to be in a pertinent industry.

Fitting Business Needs with SAP

This is an activity that demands a combination of SAP knowledge and business knowledge. It fits the business needs (identified by management consultancy and business analysis) with the configurability of SAP to arrive at an optimum solution. The optimum solution is one that gets as close as possible to the ideal working system for the user without imposing excessive or avoidable demands for customization of SAP modules.

Modeling, Configuring, and Testing

Configuring is the truly crucial skill, which can be acquired only by SAP training and experience. It's right on the critical path for SAP's business development. SAP is putting considerable investment into providing tools to lighten the task, but the complex nature of the product suite means that skilled configurers will always be in demand.

ABAP Modifications

ABAP programmers are often employed by end users directly. They are usually engaged in making minor modifications after implementation. (Most implementations are done without ABAP programming up front.) Less commonly, a substantial module modification will be specified at implementation time, requiring an ABAP design effort. Some partners do employ ABAP programmers and supply their services to clients for all purposes; this is also a fruitful area for contracting houses. ABAP development is also important for importing data from legacy systems.

Installing the User: Documentation, Training, and Support

Hardware and software don't make a working business system by themselves. The people who use the system, provide input, and operate it are important components, as are the surrounding manual systems that they use. Helping to train and support the users is often part and parcel of a systems analyst's work, but special roles may be created to handle these tasks in some companies.

Ongoing Technical Support

The implementing partner usually provides first-level technical support to the end user, who in turn receives second-level support from SAP. SAP provides first-level support to its direct end-user customers.

The SAP Walldorf development team gets involved in support, providing guidance on maintenance levels, release procedures, and so on; the support activity overlaps with marketing to some extent in the SAP subsidiaries.

Systems Administration and Management

End users normally keep responsibility for ongoing systems administration and management, and involve their mainstream management in the function (although they can also outsource the function from partners). From the users, a so-called *superuser* will often emerge, who understands how SAP "thinks" and knows how to get the best out of it; this superuser will also be able to ensure that it meshes with the surrounding procedures and objectives. This person can be very useful in making systems run smoothly and may progress into SAP consultancy.

Apart from the general ability to carry out the preceding functions, some special skills are required that cut across the functional lines.

In Table 41.1, these skills are grouped into broad skill types and cross-referenced to the main functions, according to the level of each skill required to effectively carry out the function. These skills are worth exploring a little further.

Skills Required to Perform Functions

Vertical business sector knowledge is needed at all levels, to a greater or lesser extent. SAP has developed by gaining practical field experience, taking it back up the supply chain, incorporating it into the product at "factory level" where possible, and distributing it with the product back down the supply chain. This practical field experience includes vertical market experience.

Business Function Knowledge (Module Application Knowledge)

Again, the need for this type of knowledge arises at all levels. The product is based on a defined set of business functions and the modules aligned with them. The remarks made on vertical business sector knowledge apply equally well here.

General Business Knowledge

Knowledge of business basics is very important for all who work with SAP. Practitioners should know why businesses exist, how they are structured, and how the various components of a business work together.

Special Knowledge of Other Technology

Apart from the platform technology development arena, a need for knowledge of particular technologies can arise at the individual project level, because of the variety of platform systems and interfaced systems that users may have. Where such a need does arise, end users and partners will both seek to recruit special technical skills. The job specifications in Appendix A, "Sample SAP-Related Job Descriptions," show examples of this need.

Systems Analysis Skills

These are the essential skills that interface user management—its operational objectives, constraints, and priorities—with SAP and the implementation process. Systems analysis skills are valuable in virtually all functional stages, but especially from the stage at which SAP implementation is agreed on.

Programming Skills

Skills in ABAP programming and analysis/design often are found in the same people. When this isn't the case, the analyst needs an appreciation of programming, and vice versa. But practical programming skills are only a strict necessity when the systems analysis yields a requirement for ABAP programming.

Each preceding skill type has many specialties—as many as there are permutations of vertical markets, business functions, other technologies, and areas of systems and programming experience.

Consultancy Skills

Consultancy skills are the general skills needed to operate effectively; they include knowledge of ethics and professional standards, legal obligations, communications skills, time management, and so on.

How SAP Partners Describe Their Services

Like the skills, the function titles in Table 41.1 are boiled down from the kaleidoscopic variety of descriptions the SAP world uses to describe its activities.

That boiling down makes analysis manageable but robs the descriptions of their variety and color. You can only get that by looking at examples. The following list shows a far from exhaustive sample of ways in which partners describe the SAP-related services they perform. Each partner will include anywhere from six to 20 or more of these service descriptions in its brochure. Looking at them all together, and mixing the superficial descriptions with the more detailed ones, gives a clearer picture of the activity spectrum and what the descriptions mean.

N O T E   Remember that service suppliers in the real world are more concerned with differentiating themselves, and suggesting special benefits of their particular offerings, than they are with fitting neatly into your paradigm. ▨

Here are some of the ways in which partners describe their SAP-related services:

- ABAP programming from customer specifications or as part of project
- Acting as either project manager or prime contractor
- Activity planning with date and effort control mechanisms
- Assessing migration impact
- Assuming full responsibility for R/3 projects and the integration of complementary products and services into a complete customer-specific solution
- BASIS consulting
- BPR consulting:
  - Defining specific improvement objectives
  - Redesigning business operations in ways to help achieve the objectives
  - Defining the new business processes to support new operations
  - Managing the implementation of the solution and driving this through into SAP implementation
  - Business change management consulting
  - Assessing degree of change requirement
  - Designing framework for change
  - Identifying components of change program
  - Developing detailed plans for change
  - Driving requirements of the SAP systems through into changes/enhancements
- Business operations analysis
- Business reengineering
- Business workgroup performance consulting:
  - Aligning workgroup process with business improvement objectives
  - Defining operation of workgroups to enable objectives to be met
  - Assessing information required, expertise of workgroup members, training, and tools needed
  - Planning and managing improvements
  - Software and technical training
  - Startup support

- Maintenance, fine-tuning
- Developing additional applications
- Help desk, FM (Financial Management) services

- Change management
- Client-specific module expansion/modification
- Concurrent transformation (synchronously reengineering your processes with SAP R/3 installation)
- Configuration design
- Configuration management
- Contingency planning and disaster recovery
- Conversions
- Customization
- Database workshops
- Data migration and coexistence management
- Data transfer or supply of interfaces to link up with remote systems
- Data warehouse consulting
- Database design and programming
- Designing and establishing new IT infrastructure
- Designing framework for change
- Developing individual applications with R/3
- Developing common standards and architecture for SAP projects
- Developing industry templates, prepackaged configurations, and tools
- *Electronic Data Interchange* (EDI) integration services
- Estimating implementation effort
- Evaluation consulting
- Hardware and network configuration, design, implementation, and management
- Hardware services
- Implementation
- Industry solutions
- Integration advocacy programs
- Integrating R/3 business processes
- Integrating with legacy systems
- Logical and physical database design
- Long-term support provision
- Managing backups, recovery, scheduling, and output for R/3 systems
- Migration change control

- Monitoring production environment
- Monitoring R/3 project status
- Performing needs analysis
- Network integration services
- Network security administration
- Optimizing balance between business/organization needs and R/3 functionality
- *Online Project Management System* (OPMS)
- Optimizing systems availability
- Performance analysis
- Performance optimization
- Planning, management, and implementation of migration tools
- Private on-site or remote lessons
- Process alignment
- Process improvement to an optimum
- Producing conversion and interface link programs for legacy systems
- Production hand over and training
- Project management
- Providing integrated performance support software environment
- Release upgrades
- Remote development facility linked to SAP R/3 Workbench
- Remote R/3 preventive maintenance and diagnosis
- SAP concepts Education Workshop
- Service-level agreements
- Software and technology selection
- Structured methodology
- Submitting backup/recovery concepts
- System and network management
- Systems cloning (for example, split R/3 for demerging companies)
- System configuration checking
- Systems integration
- Systems performance monitoring, control, and improvement
- Technology consultancy
- Training on EDI integration within SAP R/3
- Transfer of procedure models into prototypes
- Tuning guidance and implementation

- Tuning individual ABAP programs
- Tuning R/3 systems
- User and technical support and help desk
- Win NT Services

Even if you cannot really classify all the real-life descriptions, you'll find that just being aware of them helps when reading literature produced by SAP employers. You will be more comfortable with the terminology and better placed to investigate confidently.

To add further variety, some partners develop applications, development tools, or market platform and complementary products. Such partners have their own special product focuses, which aren't reflected in the previous function-based descriptions.

Both your employment prospects and your understanding of them will increase as you become more familiar with the terminology potential employers use.

To assess where the employment opportunities lie from your own perspective, you need to profile your experience in terms of the functions you can handle and the special skills you have (in terms of specific vertical markets, business processes, and so on—not just the general skill types). You must investigate where the employment market is generating jobs with a good match.

Of course, you don't need to seek a perfect match. You will probably want to extend your capabilities when making a job change, but you need to already have as many of the requirements as the employer can reasonably hope to get. Your best opportunities to develop often come not when you're changing employers, but instead through moving across your employer's spectrum of activities.

When pursuing a career in SAP, as in many other fields, remember that you have to constantly negotiate an unwritten compromise between your desire to develop your own capabilities and your employer's desire for productivity, which requires that you reuse your existing skills. How well you fare in this negotiation in large part determines the return you get on your efforts in your career. A negotiation is successful when both parties get a fair deal. If you remain focused on your own advancement and also address your employer's needs fairly, you will build a solid career and a good reputation.

Job Titles in the SAP World

The job title *consultant* appears in many SAP-world jobs, and different employers have different terminology. A cross-section of full role descriptions is available in Appendix A, which shows the requirements of applicants as well as the roles they are expected to carry out.

Appendix A includes a number of examples of positions in the SAP development group and SAP subsidiaries. These examples are worth reading if you aspire to the development, marketing, or special consulting roles that are particular to SAP itself.

But SAP itself isn't where most employment opportunities lie, so this section concentrates on job titles that occur more widely.

You will often see the title *SAP consultant*. This catchall title means many different things, and you have to look at the details to see what the job entails. This title usually means that SAP expertise (of whatever kind) is the prime requirement and is more important than industry or other ancillary knowledge.

Here are some examples of more specific job titles that occur in the SAP world—in recent advertisements and job descriptions—and what some of them mean (or at least have meant in example cases).

ABAP Programmer

In end users, the ABAP programming role involves mainly modifying systems that have been configured from SAP modules. A fairly major functional addition will be programmed only occasionally. ABAP is a high-level 4GL, so there isn't always a division of labor between programmer and analyst. (Although some companies still preserve the traditional programmer/analyst split, the trend with modern development tools is away from that distinction.) In SAP itself, of course, the development team uses ABAP for major module development tasks, and so do some developmental partners.

ABAP openings are very often associated with specific SAP modules, so knowledge of that particular module, or the application for which it is designed, is pertinent.

ABAP Designer

The more significant developments that take place in ABAP, whether in end users or elsewhere, must be designed to integrate with the rest of the system, as well as to provide the required functionality. ABAP designers are expected to have knowledge of ABAP programming, and engage in systems analysis and design at a bit more detailed level than SAP configurers, because although ABAP is a high-level "language," it is still a lower-level "language" than module configuration.

ABAP Developer

The title "ABAP Developer" often appears in advertisements; depending on the advertiser, it can mean programmers or designers or programmer/designers. The demarcation lines aren't always clear, and agencies that advertise usually have several positions to fill anyway. By using this catchall title, they can attract candidates for several of those positions.

Application Engineer

Partner employers have used the title "Application Engineer" to describe people who take their cues from the business requirements as defined by the R/3 implementation analysis, and use R/3 configuration tools to meet those requirements. They then may follow through to provide remote and on-site support to completed implementations.

BASIS Consultant

The title of "BASIS Consultant" is often suffixed with a vertical market specialty in advertisements (for example, "BASIS Consultant, Correction and Transport") and sometimes with a functional specialty (for example, "BASIS Consultant, Security/Support") or a platform technology skill (for example, "BASIS Consultant, HP-UX Support" or "BASIS Consultant, Oracle").

BASIS consultants engage in deep configuration and must understand the R/3 architecture and supporting BASIS technology.

Business Analyst

Typically, a business analyst has to define the needs of the business and understand its processes, interfacing management and user needs to the SAP capability. Depending on the other strengths in the employer's team, the business analyst might need a technical background (not always just in SAP, but sometimes in relevant technologies such as Oracle, Networking, UNIX, and so on).

Commercial Analyst

The term *commercial analyst* is synonymous with the term *systems analyst* (described later in this section), but it is particular to *commercial systems*. A commercial system can be any system concerned with transacting business. The term excludes systems for such purposes as technical design, process control, or scientific analysis. Depending on the organization, commercial systems can include financial systems.

Financial Analyst

The term *financial analyst* is synonymous with the term *systems analyst* (described later in this section), but it is particular to *financial systems*. Financial systems, depending on the organization, can include anything from investment management down through financial planning and accounting systems—and even billing, payment, and collection systems in some companies' terminology.

Industry Module Consultant

This title will include the particular industry module when it is advertised—for example, "IS-OIL Consultant" or "R/3 Retail Consultant." A module consultant configures the particular module and also needs the business and industry knowledge to discuss its benefits and limitations at the senior management level. In addition, he or she needs sufficient technical knowledge of the module, and of the integration issues surrounding it, to resolve problems.

Integration Manager

The title "Integration Manager" often implies duties very similar to those of module configurers (described later in this section). It doesn't always imply any extra responsibility for interfacing with other technologies.

Junior Module Consultant

Occasionally, the term *junior* appears in a title. This offers you the opportunity to get into that area to expand your general experience and possibly to gain your first SAP experience after training.

Management Information System (MIS) Manager

The position of MIS manager is of strategic importance to some end users, and this person often reports directly to the managing director. The role includes responsibility for strategy, budgets, vendor negotiations, resource allocation, project prioritization, performance and security issues, *service-level agreements* (SLAs), and the corporate interface. It's mentioned here because SAP experience is considered increasingly important in this role.

Module Configurer

The task of configuring SAP is never done in isolation from the exploration of needs, so the role of module configurer overlaps with business and systems analyst roles. As a typical example, one employer specifies module configurer responsibilities as "Working closely with clients to assess their requirements in finance, materials management, sales and distribution, production planning, and human resources."

Project Leader

An end user often will employ a project leader as the steward of its interests, appointing someone, usually from its existing staff, with more knowledge of the user's business than of SAP. Such a project leader would need to develop SAP knowledge, but would have more experienced SAP consultants available on the team.

Project Manager

The scope of a project manager depends entirely on the project, but many SAP projects are large and wide-ranging. (See "Senior Consultant/Analyst," later in this section; senior consultants are often de facto project managers.) The project leader role described in the preceding section can also be designated a project manager role by some end users.

R/3 Business Consultant

This title in consulting partnerships has been used to describe a consulting role with a high presales content in promoting R/3 (in one example specifically alongside Siemens Nixdorf's LIVE approach, but other consulting partnerships would have other value-added focuses). The job includes the typical pre- and post-sales support activities of an IT consulting partnership or specialist software house, and experience in these activities is as important as SAP knowledge.

SAP Analyst/Business Analyst

These titles have been used to describe a role that involves the capabilities of a business analyst, but with a greater orientation toward SAP. The person would be championing the use of SAP, advising on its functionality and configuration, and solving integration problems.

Senior Consultant/Analyst

How senior is "senior" depends a lot on the employer, and sometimes its pay-scale policies (it has to call you "senior" to justify what it has to pay in the SAP market). But usually these titles imply responsibility for coordinating SAP introduction across a wide range of functional areas and geographical locations, including other SAP consultant activities, and for integrating these into a cohesive strategy. A senior consultant in the SAP world is often in effect a project director.

Systems Analyst

The title "Systems Analyst" can stand alone or be incorporated into titles such as "Commercial Analyst" or "Financial Analyst," which specify the business process areas in which the analyst will work.

Systems analysts can expect to define processes and requirements, engage in detailed design, configure SAP systems, and follow through to perform documentation and user training. Some degree of project management is involved, as is planning and implementing systems cutover. Expertise in appropriate business areas is valued—sometimes to the extent that it will override a lack of SAP experience and provide an entry into SAP.

Technology Manager

This title designates the person responsible for international rollout of network technology, including R/3 systems. He or she manages the technical, installation, and testing aspects and interfaces with the application design team.

In addition to the titles (and their derivatives) described in this section, you will see advertised titles including the sort of special activities that are self-explanatory, such as security, auditing, and testing, which are performed around SAP systems.

The SAP world is unusual in the width of applications and ancillary technology knowledge that it embraces. This is because of its nature as a standard applications suite built on core business processes, plus the way in which a wide range of platform and technology partners has espoused it.

This chapter can only give you a feel for the SAP world's richly varied employment openings, especially the ones that crop up in this book. You can enhance this knowledge by looking at the job specification examples in Appendix A.

Again, if and when you start looking at the SAP job market in earnest, you can expect to come across many more job titles not covered here. But don't be fazed by that. These positions will boil down to something not too different from the titles described here.

What It Takes to Succeed: The Personal Attributes

Success is many things to many people. It's not anyone's place to tell you what you should want out of life, so this section addresses success only within the limited definition of achieving a *goal position*—a point where you have maximum career options.

The goal position is to achieve the status of "Senior Consultant/Analyst" described in the preceding section, with an international reputation for managing large and complex projects.

We're not saying that this should represent your life's ambitions, but only that from there, you're on your own. Options are open from there to climb on up the management ladder, go it alone, or simply enjoy a comfortable lifestyle.

You are in a position that many people would consider as having achieved success. Senior positions are now in your range, in consulting partnerships, large end-user organizations, or SAP itself. Beyond this point, you are dependent on your management skills. SAP experience will have helped you up the ladder, but it will not by itself take you much farther. You might—like many before you have done—choose to operate your own consulting partnership or "take the money" and go for the top-priced contracts that are available to you.

Before reaching that goal, there is a key switchpoint on your progression; it occurs when you have gained solid experience as an SAP consultant and are beginning to aspire to gain senior consultant experience. The switchpoint is a good time to consider widening your experience by moving across into another employer type—from end user to partner or SAP, or vice versa, or between SAP and partner.

To reach the goal, you obviously must have the basic qualifications to get started (see Chapter 42, "How to Find Employment Working with SAP"), and develop the skills to do the job along the way. But given these basics, excellence in certain personal attributes shows up time and time again as being what sets the high achievers apart in the SAP world:

- **Self-starter attributes.** As a self-starter, you will have initiative; enthusiasm; and the ability to organize yourself, plan and achieve your own goals, be proactive, and find better ways of doing things. This might seem paradoxical given the emphasis on teamwork, but it's not. A good team member is someone the other members can rely on.

- **Intellectual ability.** A high level of intelligence is indispensable to really succeed in the SAP world. The abilities to think broadly and conceptually while handling details well, as well as to merge an analytical approach with pragmatic realism, require high intelligence as a prerequisite.

- **Ability to work under pressure.** Deadlines are important in the SAP world, and delays are very expensive.

- **Interpersonal communications attributes.** These attributes include the ability and inclination to communicate openly and honestly; a generosity in sharing information and transferring knowledge; and the ability to communicate and make good relationships at all levels, be empathetic, be a good listener, and adopt team-building attitudes.

- **Credibility.** Communicating in a friendly way isn't enough by itself when large investments hang on your advice. You must also cultivate credibility. In part, this arises naturally from your work record, and also some people have a natural ability to inspire confidence. But good preparation and care with the acquisition and organization of facts will help you make the most of what you have with the hand you have been dealt.

- **Commitment.** Requirements for motivation, flexibility, and a willingness to travel are likely to place demands on your commitment if you want to excel.

■ **Leadership skills.** Leadership is the ability to motivate others and to get the best out of them. If you have the qualities mentioned so far, you are well on the way.

■ **Enterprise-wide business understanding.** This attribute includes knowing the logistics and culture of enterprise-wide software solutions, how and where integration and standardization should prevail over local priorities and vice versa, and the ability to coordinate projects across a wide range of activities and cultures.

■ **Vertical business sector understanding.** An in-depth knowledge of business issues in one or more vertical markets will help increase your breadth of vision, as well as your credibility and value.

These qualities create the team-building, wide-visioned managers, around whom successful project teams are created, whom are in such high demand in the SAP world.

Although this section isn't about specific SAP skills development, one point is worth mentioning. As you are making your way in the SAP world, you will have consistently wider options if you have the ability to configure SAP and understand its architecture thoroughly. You should take the opportunity to acquire this knowledge as early as possible.

You can cultivate some of the preceding attributes, whereas others aren't so easily acquired—you either have them ingrained from your infancy (and in part, some would say, your genes) or you don't. Take a realistic view of how well you match these attributes, and how much you can (or want to) change yourself to get these qualities. Then set your career goals accordingly. Don't be seduced by financial prospects into taking a route that's unsuitable for you.

Levels of Pay Working with SAP

SAP is in the premium-bearing band of IT employment. Comparing SAP positions with the general run of non-SAP ones (of similar seniority and skills requirement) shows that SAP confers a premium of the order of 25 percent. People skilled in its closest competitors—such as Oracle and PeopleSoft—also command premiums, as do some other software specialty areas that are in demand. But as of mid-1998, SAP heads the league.

The positions where SAP people enjoy the greatest salary premiums are at the top end. Those people with the capability to manage large multifaceted projects and who have several major projects on their résumé are most in demand; they are also least likely to have their premiums eroded by the improved systems development tools that SAP is turning out.

Configuration skills are also much sought after, but the general view in the recruitment and contracting market is that, although the jobs will last, the really heavy premiums for this skill will not. It's more possible to balance supply and demand in configuration by training and productivity tools than it is at a more senior level. Configuration skills will still remain highly valued, though, and in demand.

If your primary interest is in fast earnings, provided you are highly competent (whether or not you have yet reached "top-end" status), you will do best by contracting, either via a contracting agency or directly onto a project team. At the time of this writing, senior consultants who can place themselves directly can get rates as high as $8,000 a week, while those who go through an agency can command a salary of more than US$5,000 a week.

This is about twice the rate for permanent employees of a similar caliber (taking into account employee fringe benefits), and it represents the reward a contractor gets for taking risks. However, because SAP projects are so long and the demand is so high, the risks are minimal, and contracting is the way to the highest earnings in the shortest term.

Long-term earnings are a different matter. Contracting isn't the best way to climb the management ladder in a large company. Played for the long term, SAP offers a route into positions of strategic importance that can lead to the boardroom, where salaries, executive perks, and share option schemes may yield the sort of serious money that makes even SAP contracting rates look puny. To equal that by taking the contracting route means investing your extra early earnings wisely. If you are career planning for maximum overall financial benefit, you have some interesting comparative arithmetic to do.

Meanwhile, back to the present. Table 41.2 shows some examples of permanent positions being advertised internationally in mid-1996 (with all salaries translated to U.S. dollars). These were all advertised in the European computer press.

Table 41.2   Job Positions and Annual Salaries

Salary	Location	Position
$150,000	USA	Senior Consultant MM, SD
$150,000	Texas, USA	Project Manager
$140,000	USA	Project Manager
$125,000	London, UK	Senior Implementation Manager
$110,000	Singapore	Senior Consultant FI, CO
$60,000–$150,000	Europe	Implementation Specialists, Module Consultants, BASIS Consultants, and ABAP Analyst/Programmers
$95,000–$110,000	Australia/USA Sydney, Australia	R/3 Module Consultants
$45,000–$110,000	UK	SAP BPR Consultants
$45,000–$70,000	Australia	Module Consultants
$45,000–$85,000	USA	Implementation Consultants
$75,000	Europe	Project Manager
$75,000	UK	SAP Business Analyst

continues

Table 41.2	Continued	
Salary	**Location**	**Position**
$70,000–$75,000	UK	ABAP Developers
$70,000	USA	R/3 Module Configurer
$70,000	Germany	BASIS Consultant
$70,000	Saudi Arabia	BASIS Consultant
$62,000	London, UK	ABAP Programmer
$60,000	Germany	Project Manager
$60,000	South East Asia	Project Manager

These absolute figures will raise a smile, no doubt, in a few years, as the value of money changes. That's an occupational hazard of quoting the price of anything in a book, but for the time being, these examples give a fair picture of where SAP salaries sit. ●

How to Find Employment Working with SAP

Working with SAP

If you already have SAP experience, you know that you have many employment options. You are on the right side of a supply-and-demand imbalance, and your main concern will be making the best choices from the many open to you in order to direct your career toward achieving your life goals. This chapter may help in that process by widening your choices and suggesting some new avenues through which to exploit your advantage. It's potentially useful reading.

If, however, you are on the outside looking in, options aren't so plentiful, supply and demand doesn't work in your favor, and this chapter isn't merely useful but essential reading.

It can be frustrating to hear all this talk of shortfall, and then when you offer your services to help meet it, you find only closed doors. Why does this happen, and how can you get around it?

Well, there's bad news and good news. Let's get the bad news out of the way first.

Whereas for experienced SAP people there are more openings than there are qualified applicants, it's the other way around for new entrants to SAP. Supply and demand is against you.

A typical recruitment agency dealing in SAP jobs internationally reports that at least 50 percent of the overtures it receives for SAP employment are from people seeking to get their first SAP experience. This is true whether they are responding to advertised vacancies or making unsolicited inquiries. In contrast, less than 10 percent of the vacancies advertised are for new entrants to SAP. This is about par for the SAP recruitment world.

SAP itself receives thousands of unsolicited résumés. In Germany, as well as in the subsidiaries, these may outnumber vacancies by a factor of 20 to 1.

All this really means is that if you don't have SAP experience, the employers won't come looking for you because they don't need to, and they can afford to be selective when you go looking for them. It doesn't represent an insurmountable barrier, provided you have some useful expertise outside SAP (more on that later).

Console yourself, also, with the thought that the apparent "closed shop" that thwarts the inexperienced has always existed somewhere in computing (and indeed very many other careers). SAP is just today's prime example.

Also, isn't the fact that it's a privileged club at least part of your reason for wanting to join it? Certainly, it's the reason why the salary levels are so good, and Groucho Marx had a point in his oft-quoted assertion that "I wouldn't want to join any club that would have someone like me as a member."

So, on to the good news: However they do it, and wherever the new people come from, the fact is that the industry as a whole must train and accept more than 10,000 people per year worldwide as SAP consultants. No amount of movement by existing SAP people between employers can obscure that. In the USA alone, an estimated 3,000 new SAP consultants are coming onstream every year.

Given some of the developments in the marketplace, these figures might turn out to be gross underestimates.

The supply-and-demand situation looks likely to remain as it is for some years yet, with high premiums being paid to very experienced SAP people. At the same time, SAP is pressing on with lots of developments (discussed in Chapter 39, "Overview of the SAP Employment Market"). Many of these developments are designed to make installing SAP easier and, to some extent, reduce the need for manpower, but new departures always offer opportunities to the newcomer because the "sitting tenants" have less advantage—"everybody's a trainee."

The move into the market for smaller companies is proceeding rapidly, and these companies might provide a good route into SAP. The smaller companies simply cannot afford the huge budgets that the giants are spending on business systems reengineering, so they have to accept less-experienced people. SAP is moving toward more "load and go" type systems for this marketplace, and these should place less of a premium on experience.

Although SAP experience is considered vital, many other skills are involved in realizing SAP systems—that's the nature of the product. Knowledge of special application areas, business processes, platforms, and complementary technology all need to be welded to SAP skills in some part of the SAP activity spectrum. This provides many potential entry tickets. If you have some of these skills, you have something to bring to the party, and the right employer could consider it worth developing your SAP skills to complete the set.

Despite the premium being placed on experience, it's interesting that recruitment specialists, partners, and end users alike express the view that SAP knowledge isn't the most important predeterminant of success in implementing SAP projects. Some measure of it, of course, is essential, but the emphasis placed on other qualities, skills, and experience offers you, the novice, the chance to be a special candidate. Previous SAP experience isn't everything.

In summary, if you have something to contribute, don't be deterred by the SAP experience barrier. As an absolute fact, thousands of people are going to break through it in the next year. Some of them will do it by chance, by being in the right place at the right time. This chapter can help you do it by design.

Although there is competition for the openings, many of your competitors will take a passive approach—looking at advertisements, perhaps mailing their résumés to agencies or known employers. Few will mount a proactive, planned, and concerted campaign, and if you do so, you will have put yourself into a select group already.

The fact that it might take application and persistence to break into SAP isn't a reason to give up. The only reason for giving up is because a rational assessment has led you to believe that you will not succeed and be happy at it, once inside. This isn't the same thing as being deterred by the difficulty of getting there.

Self-Assessment: Know Your Realistic Options

The first two years of SAP experience will transform your prospects in the SAP world enormously, but what are your realistic options for getting that experience?

The answer to that will depend on a matching process between you, the individual, and the requirements of the various roles that can provide an entry.

Roles and Requirements

Let's consider the various roles in which it's possible to spend that vital first year. Those that exist in any real quantity can be grouped into four main categories:

- Management consultants
- Analysts/implementers/configurers
- Project managers
- ABAP programmers/developers

Other categories, such as trainers and salespeople, are on the borders of SAP specialization. A trainer might want to move into training in SAP, and it's not unheard of for trainers to move across into support and consultancy in most software environments, so there is no reason to suppose it will not happen in SAP. However, for the most part, trainers aren't assumed to be seeking an entry into a career based on their SAP skills.

Similarly, sales and marketing people don't rely primarily on their technical skills, and in any case, the role of the pure salesperson isn't central to the consultancy-centered process that sells SAP installations. Therefore, while there are important sales and marketing roles, notably in SAP subsidiaries and headquarters, these are rather special cases.

SAP acknowledges, however, that it has learned to be more commercial and sales-oriented by importing experienced marketers from backgrounds in major systems, large-scale software, and consultancy. If you are in this category, there will be opportunities around SAP; some examples of marketing job descriptions are included in Appendix A, "Sample SAP-Related Job Descriptions."

Greater opportunities could arise in the traditional sales executive role as penetration of smaller companies proceeds. It's arguable that the whole process will have to become a bit less wed to management consultancy and more like a typical solution sale if SAP is to realize its full potential with smaller companies.

That said, neither training nor sales and marketing roles are considered as a major category.

To reiterate, the four main categories you'll be looking at are management consultants, analyst/implementers, project managers, and ABAP programmers/developers.

For any of these roles, you will need to have something of an outgoing, confident personality and be good at teamwork and at organizing yourself to meet goals and deadlines. A glance through the sample job/role descriptions in Appendix A will show you how regularly such qualities are demanded, in one guise or another. Some of the roles described demand many more of these attributes than others, but all require a fair amount.

The nature of the SAP product means that it reaches out, communicates, and integrates, and the SAP world expects its people to do the same.

There is very limited scope for the backroom computer whiz who likes to withdraw into machines and technology. The SAP core product development team is the place that could most easily tolerate lack of personal communications skills in order to gain brilliance in software design. The recent advertisements on the Internet for developers in SAP's development team in Walldorf, Germany, place at least as much emphasis on technical skill as on personality, though they do stress the need to work cooperatively, and the general culture is one of easy communication. The difference, at least in some roles, is that the requirement to communicate with business management would be less than in most other places in the SAP world. The activity in core product development is tiny, though, compared to the vast opportunities out in the field, consulting on, designing, and implementing SAP systems.

Among end users, some need ABAP programmers simply to be good programmers, because these employers maintain the old distinction between analysts and programmers. But even there, if your aim is to progress from ABAP programming up any of the worthwhile career paths to which it could lead, you're going to need the typical SAP personality traits.

So if you lean toward the reclusive rather than the outgoing, however brilliant your technical ability, you might be better to apply it in some area other than SAP.

On the other hand, if you like personal responsibility, teamwork, and partnership better than hierarchical command structures, you are likely to fit in well and be happy working with SAP.

The second prerequisite quality is the ability to think logically, analytically, and constructively. In this regard, it's little different from working with other software, although SAP probably places a higher premium on the ability to take a broader perspective—to marshal high-level options—and puts less value on brilliant invention relative to many other software environments.

Given these two things—the right personality type and the right intellect—you have the ability to perform well in the SAP world, provided you can acquire the necessary training and experience.

To get that training and experience, you will almost certainly have to have some other advantages going for you. Some of these you either have or don't have; if you don't, there's not much you can do about it. Others you can cultivate if you really want to.

So much for the common prerequisites. What specific ones do you need in each category?

Management Consultants   The large management-consulting firms provide a major entry path to SAP for those who can meet their demanding standards. All these firms have a large commitment to developing people, in SAP as well as in other areas.

The policy of Andersen Consulting isn't to recruit in response to specific project demands. Instead, it has a supply side and a demand side, and the supply side tries to forecast and foresee demand, and develop capabilities to meet it. This is on a more strategic basis than simply meeting the needs of the moment. Andersen wants the people it recruits to have a career potential that goes well beyond the life span of the current SAP dominance.

The central message is that meeting the "Andersen profile" is much more important than SAP experience.

In the words of a senior manager, "People get too hung up on the dearth of SAP skills. The success of projects has a lot less to do with SAP skills than with project management skills. The most important skills are in handling big projects with complex structures, across multifarious cultures."

Andersen takes people at all ages, from their early twenties up. Basically, there are two types of intakes:

■ The fresh graduate (including those with minimal experience)

■ The experienced manager/consultant

There has been a shift in recent times toward the older, more experienced, recruit.

As a fresh graduate, you will need a degree with a good grade-point average (3.5 or higher, in U.S. terms), ideally with postgraduate qualifications. You also need the right personality type. An executive directly concerned with recruitment summed up this qualification in these terms:

■ Self-confident

■ Professional

■ Comfortable dealing with directors

■ Drive/motivation—a self-starter

You will need to pass muster on all these fronts. A combination of intellect and personality is required. A brilliant first-class degree holder will not be hired without the right personal attributes.

As an experienced manager/consultant, you will need an education similar to the fresh graduate, although the more advanced you are in your career, the less emphasis is placed on this. You also need the same personality type as for the fresh graduate, although there is more focus on relevance of skills and experience. "Cultural fit" is important, and you are most likely to have that fit if you have worked in another consulting firm or in management with a large "blue-chip" organization. Most important is very high attainment in these areas:

■ Business skills

■ Industry skills

■ Project/change/strategic management skills

■ Appropriate technology skills

Most experienced people taken are in their thirties, but they can be up to any age, provided they have commensurate experience. The older you are, the better experience you need.

If you are recruited as an experienced person, you have to be ready to be put out in front of clients and be useful to them very quickly.

The first-year induction process into the SAP team is to take a SAP course, and then work on a project either uncharged or at reduced rate (to the client). You will be on a team with experienced people and expected to pick up things quickly.

Andersen uses modern information tools to harness and disseminate experience. Lotus Notes, discussion databases, and expert networks are all used extensively.

Most of the considerations just described apply to all the leading management consulting firms and for lesser management consulting firms, unless they are totally focused on SAP.

These consulting firms represent a prime opportunity area for top-class entrants to SAP who are looking for a career rather than making "a quick buck" out of SAP, and these firms' stated policy isn't to evaluate purely on SAP experience.

Whether these firms can avoid having to chase ready-made SAP skills from time to time is another matter. Price Waterhouse, for example, has been mounting a massive campaign to recruit SAP expertise from around the world for the USA, and many consultants find that they need to fill gaps by using contractors. The general recruitment policy, nonetheless, provides a very good pathway into SAP.

Business Analysts/Implementers   This is a very large employment area in SAP. Opportunities exist with the implementation partners, contractors, and end users. Each would much prefer people experienced in SAP, but supply and demand dictates that some of them have to accept the training responsibility sometimes or leave jobs unfilled. For the partners and contractors, an unfilled post means a loss of profit; for the end user, it means worse—loss of development and gain of pain.

SAP itself, in its subsidiaries (from where the SAP product is sold and supported), isn't an employer of new-entrant SAP people. It has to have top-quality people to fulfill its role there. It's a great starting point for information (more on that later), but if you want to start out in SAP with the producer itself, then check out how you match the requirements of the development team, as described in "ABAP Programmers/Developers," later in this chapter.

A contracting agency will be more likely to help you break into SAP if you already have a good working relationship with it. Contracting houses are geared toward delivering people who are the finished article, immediately usable (that's why their clients use them), so developing people is a minority activity. Because of the extreme shortage of SAP people, however, some contracting houses have helped convert their existing contractors to SAP and may even help convert new applicants—but you will have to offer some other immediately usable skill. By looking at advertisements by contracting houses in the computer press, you can easily assess the skills in demand. A good background in client/server systems, UNIX, and *fourth-generation languages* (4GLs) is often cited as a key requirement. You should be prepared to accept a reduced rate while you learn SAP and find an agency.

The end-user route faces the problem of most large SAP users having employees of their own who they can retrain. This problem is exacerbated by the fact that business reengineering with SAP is likely to cost jobs in the user organization. To overcome this, you need to find the opportunity to match some special requirement that cannot be filled from inside.

End users will find, from time to time, that a particular skill is so important to SAP users that they will provide SAP training in order to get it. Sometimes the skill can be application- or industry-related, and sometimes it's in some other technology—specific operating system, database, or platform experience. The examples shown later in this chapter related to ABAP programmers are just as pertinent to analysts/implementers.

To break into SAP as an analyst/implementer, you will need to meet some general specifications. These are not hugely different from one type of employer to another. The specifications are described by various employers in different ways, and each has its own emphasis, but if you have the underlying personal qualities described earlier and score well on the following requirements, you'll be a good candidate:

- Experience in installing package-based solutions in a large commercial organization. This is a different process from designing systems from scratch.
- Demonstrable ability to think in depth about systems, their effect on the organization, and how they are integrated.
- Good analytical skills—the typical systems/business analyst skill set.
- Experience in client server systems (although there is still a lot of activity in R/2 systems, R/3 is where the growth is).

In addition, you will have a great advantage if you have a more specific hook on which to hang your application. This could be either one or both of the following:

- In-depth knowledge and working experience of a particular business application or process in which SAP may be applied.
- In-depth knowledge and working experience of a complementary technology—platform operating system, database, interfacing technology, and so on.

These criteria will have to match the specific needs of the particular employer. It's quite possible that you are interested in broadening your experience, but if you want to make the change to SAP, you'll find it much easier if you play to your strengths in other respects for the time being.

It's obvious from the preceding specifications that an analyst/implementer type of role in SAP isn't the best place to cut your teeth in computer systems. If you need to do that, and you don't qualify for the graduate entry points in development or management consultancy, the only way to do it with SAP is to get into a company—in a user role—that is using SAP.

In some cases, people who started off on the shop floor in quality control or in fairly routine clerical positions have become what one employer describes as "superusers"—people who understand how the system "thinks" and find their way around problems with it. From there they have obtained SAP training and gone on to a wider career as SAP consultants.

To be honest, though, they have usually been in the right place at the right time. Can this be achieved by design? It might be possible to engineer the situation if you are willing to do a lot of research and have a great deal of determination.

Project Managers   *Project manager* is a term that includes all very senior versions of analysts/implementers.

The "real diamonds," as one employer describes them, are people with good SAP experience and the ability to manage projects with a wide sweep, appreciating all the strategic possibilities and implications, as well as how business processes integrate to form the organization. These projects amount to reengineering the business, and the description "project manager" might not do these people justice.

These are the people who are attracting the large salaries (or fees, as the case may be), whether they are called senior consultants, project managers, or something else.

They probably have in their background most of the characteristics of the analyst/implementer, but have progressed beyond that level and have the full project management skill set.

Actual SAP experience isn't necessarily the most differentiating asset these people have. In other words, they are probably more different from an average SAP consultant than they are from an excellent non-SAP consultant/manager.

If you have demonstrated all the other assets described, except for SAP experience, then you will find that a move into SAP can be highly profitable. To get the first year's experience, you might have to take a drop in position, but probably not in earnings, and the rewards after the first year in SAP will be substantial.

All the employer options discussed for analyst/implementer are available to you, and similar considerations on the value of "relevant though non-SAP" experience apply.

Options described for management consultants may also be available to you, depending on whether you meet the educational requirements.

ABAP Programmers/Developers   At the peak of the pyramid for ABAP programmers/developers is SAP's own development team. This is mainly based in Germany, at Walldorf, near Heidelberg, but development activity is increasing in the USA, and a small amount is carried out in the UK. German language isn't a prerequisite, but English is; being multilingual will score points.

The development team provides the best opportunities for ambitious programmers/developers to get SAP experience; also, its activity areas and skill requirements provide a template for what to expect in the other parts of the SAP world.

The best way to keep in touch with this is via the Internet. SAP publishes a number of job opportunities there.

A cross-section of examples is included in Appendix A. Reading them will give you valuable insight into what employers are looking for and how you might fit, but these examples are only a cross-section. If you're looking seriously in that direction, watch that Internet space regularly.

Development is done by using ABAP/4 and development tools such as Active Data Dictionary, Screen Painter, and Dialog Manager.

Education is important, and good degrees are valued, but they aren't always absolutely essential. Here is a sampling of stipulations for different development jobs:

- First-class degree in computer science or business/economic studies with computing
- Good university degree in medicine/business, with computing, computer science mathematics, business/economics, or natural science

■ University degree

■ Information technology with business management, preferably a university or higher technical college degree

■ No education specified (for senior professionals in retail systems development)

SAP needs to bring in expertise from many different business areas, and very good experience in those areas can overcome shortcomings in formal education. The scope of SAP is vast and expanding. Applications and industry solutions currently enjoying attention follow:

■ Human resources

■ Payroll administration

■ Retail systems

■ Oil industry

■ Medical records

■ Retail systems

Forecasts show the utilities industry as a major growth area. Your own industry and application area, even if not among those mentioned, may very well be on the agenda in upcoming months.

Technical backgrounds that appear as requirements or "desirable extras" for SAP developers are equally varied. The following samples are culled from just the current batch of vacancies:

■ Programming skills, experience with PC applications

■ Basic professional experience in similar application area

■ C, 4GL programming, databases, PC software products

■ Database administration, preferably Oracle, system administration in UNIX

■ IBM 370 architecture, MVS, CICS, and VSAM in IBM 370 Assembler programming

■ Hands-on programming in C

■ In-depth technical knowledge of different UNIX systems (BSD and System V)

■ Excellent knowledge of the UNIX environment

■ Excellent knowledge of TCP/IP-based network programming

■ Experience in designing complex distributed software applications in C

■ Experience in development of error-tolerant software

■ Knowledge of current databases (for example, Oracle, Informix, Microsoft SQL Server)

■ Knowledge of Windows, Windows NT, Windows 95

■ Knowledge of C, C++, and particularly Visual Basic

■ Experience in Windows 6/32 bit environments, as well as OLE2 Automation and OCX

Any of the examples in Appendix A might ask for one or more of the preceding experience sets.

Outside SAP itself, the complementary or "interfaced" skills requirement is just as varied. There are numerous modules in SAP, and its range will be apparent from other parts of this book. Provided that you have some area of expertise, it's just a question of finding where your expertise is most needed. For ABAP programmers, the bulk of opportunities lie with contracting agencies and end users, so that's the place to look, even though both groups pose problems for the inexperienced.

Contractors' attitudes toward ABAP learners are much the same as for the inexperienced SAP analyst/implementer.

End users are important employers of ABAP programmers, because ABAP is mainly used for relatively minor modifications to systems that have been configured with very little use of ABAP. This tends to be the sort of work that goes on long after the project is "completed," as the system is "tweaked" to match user needs.

For the same reason, ABAP programming doesn't figure largely in the priorities of the partners who undertake implementations, so the partners aren't an opportunity area for the ABAP entrant.

Permanent Versus Contract Working

As a new entrant to the market, permanent employment is your only realistic option. As you get more experienced, the choice of moving to contracting becomes a possibility.

No doubt, you can earn considerably more as a contractor, but you earn only when you work—there is no holiday pay, sick pay, or fringe benefits. As a contractor, you have to run your own business, generate invoices for your services, chase payments, and so on.

Permanent Employment

As a permanent employee, you have increased security at face value, but less choice in your projects. Because of the shortage of candidates and the extreme fluidity of the SAP employment market, employers are now trying to lock in their employees to prevent them from leaving to work for someone else. Employers don't want to pay to train employees and then see them leave shortly afterward. Some employers stipulate that you must pay back the cost of training if you leave within a certain period; others require longer-than-average notice periods.

Contracting

In an ideal world, a contractor is meant to be the finished article, experienced and competent, who can deliver results from day one. Companies might pay a premium for such services, but they should have no training costs and expect productivity from day one. Reality is somewhat different now, because some relatively inexperienced consultants are leaving permanent employment for the high-earning contractor lifestyle. Customers often learn only too late about the poor knowledge and quality of work of some practitioners, by which time the contractor has moved on to a new lucrative contract using the credentials of his or her last contract. Clients are often unaware of the incompetence of some of the people whose services they use, leaving genuine contractors who have the knowledge and skill very frustrated. Customers would like to have meaningful standards and benchmarks by which they can judge people. The ASAP Institute is working toward the development of these.

To illustrate this point, ASAP received the following email recently:

To whom it may concern:

We wish to bring to your attention a UK based contractor by the name of XXXXXXXXX who trades through his own limited company, XXXXXXXXXXXXX.

The individual concerned is currently distributing his CV to various employment agencies throughout the UK. The technical knowledge and duration of experience he claims to have, however, is vastly overstated and is basically a complete fabrication with only the barest of facts.

We do not, of course, expect anyone to take this at face value and would urge that if you do receive any communication that you, at the very least, put him through some sort of technical interview. He basically memorizes buzzwords and glosses over or avoids the details when quizzed. Therefore, by asking probing questions relevant to the experience he claims to have, about exactly what something is, or how and why he would go about implementing a particular solution or strategy, we are confident that you will very quickly come to the same conclusion as us.

If you are wondering why we are going to all this effort then the answer is very simple. We are a group of contractors who are sick and tired of the number of cowboys trying to find their way into the SAP contracting market. It's not good for you and it's not good for people like us who depend on it to make a living.

One contractor described her choice of contracting enthusiastically: "I couldn't imagine working for a firm where someone was already planning what I was going to do next year and sorting out my pension." Contracting gives you the independence and ability to avoid this.

Independent consultants have to deal with all their own tax affairs, which can be quite daunting at first. You have to set yourself up as your own independent company and keep precise records of all your accounts and employment. However, most contractors have not experienced many difficulties in this respect.

There are several ways to find employment as a contractor. You can sell your services through a recruitment agency, or you can handle your own contracts. Using recruitment agencies can spare you the great deal of time and effort demanded by a job search. This is especially useful if you are already involved in an SAP project and cannot spare the time for the job search. These firms can do your marketing, introduce you to their clients, and help you secure your desired salary.

If you handle the contracts yourself, you will need to have a good network of contacts; it's helpful to keep one ear to the ground if you want to be aware of forthcoming employment. It can be difficult to get into the big SAP implementation sites, and a strong network of contacts is the best way to combat this. The advantage of marketing your services directly is that you don't have to share your wages with anyone else.

As far as the actual contracts are concerned, you can pick up their intricacies quite quickly. In fact, one contractor says the market is so buoyant at the moment that he doesn't need to draw up contracts at all. His services are in such demand that he doesn't need to safeguard his interests by a formal contract. This said, however, it's better to make sure that things are done properly. In this way, you can ensure that your fingers won't be burned.

Preparation to Gain a Foothold

Having decided that SAP might provide the right workplace for you, the next step is to prepare yourself to maximize your chances of finding the opening. Get the product right before you try to sell it, if you like to think of the exercise in marketing terms.

The main ways open to you to do this are training courses, self-development, and interview preparation.

SAP Training: Is It Worth Getting First, and How?

Some people in the industry express the view that training without experience is worthless, and certainly not worth buying with your own money.

A more measured view, and one shared by many employers of SAP skilled people, is that a training course is an advantage only if all other things are equal. In other words, when recruiting people without SAP experience, their general potential is more important than whether they've taken a course. In a tie-breaker situation, the course could make the difference.

Courses will rarely get you considered alongside experienced people for a position that requires experience, although some cultural differences exist from country to country. The highly qualification-oriented view in much of mainland Europe means that your SAP education carries greater weight there, and this is probably true in much of Asia; while in the United States and most of the English-speaking world, experience is valued more highly.

Wherever in the world you are looking for work, your course will be an asset of sorts. In most situations, you should approach the task of obtaining SAP employment as suggested for inexperienced people, regarding your SAP education as an advantage up that pathway, instead of as a ticket to the routes available to those with SAP experience.

Of course, you might have already taken a course, but if not, is it worth buying your own course?

The idea of buying your own course has become more acceptable. SAP has recently started an accreditation process that will maintain quality as more organizations acquire the capability to deliver SAP courses. These organizations and their courses are a far cry from some of the computer training courses that gave self-funded computer education a bad name in earlier times. You will be required to demonstrate prerequisite qualities before being accepted on them. To date, most of the people using these courses have been practicing computer consultants and contractors adding SAP to their capabilities.

But how valuable is having a course anyway, without the experience? One point about having an employer pay for your course is that you can be pretty sure he has plans to use your knowledge on a project.

The answer to this course decision depends on where you are coming from and where you are looking for the opening.

If you are in the graduate entry class, there isn't much point in buying an SAP course. The major consulting firms are more interested in your wider career potential than your usefulness in SAP; while SAP itself, in recruiting graduates for its development team, is looking for raw potential and excellence in computer science. Graduates from German universities are likely to have had some SAP education, as it happens, but SAP also recruits from outside Germany.

For the "man in the street" class (someone with little IT experience and not qualified for the graduate entry route), there are two major problems:

- You might not meet the prerequisites for the courses, or you could find it difficult to keep up because you don't have knowledge that the course assumes.
- Your path into SAP will be more tenuous, probably involving some time as a user, so there is a greater risk that you will gain little return on your investment in a course.

If you are absolutely sure that you have the basic attributes, coupled with the desire to break into SAP and a dogged determination to do so, and if you can easily afford the course, then consider buying one, but don't do so hoping that it will provide an automatic entry.

Along with the graduate entry class, the recruits the SAP world will most readily accept without SAP experience are those who match the specifications described earlier for analysts/implementers, project managers, and ABAP programmers. If you fall into one of these groups, then a course could be a good investment for you.

Anyone can buy a place on a standard SAP course from SAP itself, and third parties offer intensive courses for much less cost.

The best advice is to make sure that buying a course is part of a clear plan of marketing yourself, instead of a case of taking a hopeful leap before looking. Also, the workings of the accreditation program should be watched with interest. The effect the program has on the salability of training that does not offer accreditation, as well as the type of accreditation available to the private course purchaser, could be crucial.

Self-Development

You have taken at least one self-development step by reading this book. How far can you usefully go under your own steam?

As far as SAP skill experience is concerned, it is, like any technical subject, much easier to acquire by attending a course, and at some time you will need to do so. But if your strategy doesn't include buying a course, your goal has to be to get an employer to provide one. If you do so, you'll have killed two birds with one stone, because you will also be assured of the work experience to follow it.

However, it's possible to learn a great deal about SAP without taking a course. SAP, as a company, is very open with information.

You can't create experience out of thin air, but if you can't be experienced in an area, the next best thing is to be well-informed. Talking to people in SAP who come from a similar background to your own will help you build a special insight, but the main message is simply to start building your own knowledge base. Remember that any outstanding student gains most of his knowledge by self-organized reading, not by sitting in the classroom.

Think about the wider issues of corporate integration, and absorb the approach to it that SAP offers. Many recruiters say the essential skill is the ability to see the big picture. They say that it tends to dawn on SAP people after they've implemented one or two modules. You can develop that way of thinking about business processes by conscious application. There's nowhere anyone can go to really acquire the mindset that's any better than your self-training plan.

If you do this, then even if you never get involved with SAP, you'll still have gained knowledge that will stand you in good stead for your career in business and information technology.

But it might very well help you to get involved, because it will show that you have potential to develop, and that will help the employer to justify going to the trouble of training you.

Finally, don't forget the underlying attributes. Because the SAP world places a high premium on interpersonal communications and self-organizing skills, isn't it worth giving some thought to how you might develop these?

Personal presentation skills will most directly help you to get the job, as well as help you to do it. This is one area where you get the chance to give your prospective employer a sample of "the product." You don't have to tell them, you can show them.

Communicating well is something that some people do more naturally than others—that's undeniable. But at whatever level you start, it's possible to learn and improve. Trained salespeople and other professional communicators of all sorts know this.

Not everyone thinks that these personal communications qualities are vital in life, and throughout history, some people without them have been happy and successful and have enriched the world. In the SAP world, though, these qualities are important, and if you aren't totally happy with your mastery of them, consider what you can do about it.

Preparation for Interview

Whichever route you take to finding work in SAP, at some stage or another you are likely to be attending interviews. As a newcomer to SAP, you are in a highly competitive contest, and when the employer does the postinterview evaluation, the decision will often be more finely balanced than most interviewees ever realize. Even if you are an experienced SAP professional with a great deal of options, the job you most want is likely to be the one for which you have to stretch. In all cases, the edge you can get from good preparation is worth having.

There are more books on the subject of how to perform well at interviews than there are about SAP, and they can teach you—or at the very least remind you of—some basics that will increase your chances. These books represent a whole body of useful knowledge ignored by a large percentage of interviewees.

You should read at least one of these books, especially if you haven't been on the interview circuit recently. An hour or two browsing in your local library or bookstore is guaranteed to generate some useful thoughts. You could dismiss 90 percent of what you read as banal or inappropriate and still get very good value out of the exercise from the remaining 10 percent.

A couple of points are worth making directly here. Surprising though it is, many candidates show up at interviews with very little knowledge of the company they are looking to join. This gives an immediate advantage to anyone who has taken the trouble to do a little research. The more you can bone up on the company and its operations, the better, for a number of reasons.

An attribute probably overvalued by most interviewers is the ability to come up with good reasons for why you want to join the company. This ability might really prove no more than that you know how to prepare for interviews, but it leaves a strong impression on the interviewer. The research you do for this question might also help you decide whether you do indeed want to join that company.

If you are offering experience in a business process, industry application, or technology area, it will help your case if you have considered in advance how your experience might "map" across to the activities of the potential employer, especially one in which SAP is being applied.

Any common ground you can find between you and the employer, however irrelevant to the job, tends to "flag you up" in the interviewer's mind. You have a much better chance of finding such common ground if you've thought about it in advance.

The knowledge you have gained will enable you to ask informed questions, engage in intelligent discussion, and generally help make the interview flow. Of course, you should know not to use your knowledge to cut off, contradict, or otherwise embarrass the interviewer; or to unload your knowledge and tell the company how to run its business.

Many companies inviting you to an interview will send you some sort of information pack, and the main message is to study it thoroughly. But if you are taking the initiative and not applying for advertised positions, you might have to ask for a pack, or indeed you might have gotten it already as part of your "market research."

One source of information on the company's broad objectives and direction that you should always try to get is the annual report. This is usually available on request, along with an information pack from a press officer, corporate communications officer, or similar person.

Usually, you will not have to be very creative to get the information you need, but if you have to be, it is effort well spent.

Sources of Job Opportunities

Where to look for the most open doors, or at least the less-closed ones, is a question you will want to answer if you are seeking the quickest way into SAP.

Proceeding from the obvious to the not so obvious, this section takes a look at a number of sources from the viewpoint of the new entrant to SAP.

Advertised Vacancies

Earlier in this chapter, you learned that less than 10 percent of advertised SAP vacancies are open to people without SAP experience. Of course, this is much better than zero, so it's worth keeping a watch for these vacancies.

A perusal of such previous advertisements gives some picture of what to expect: Ads are usually for people with good computer experience in UNIX and C-based systems. Advertisers regard experience in installing package-based systems involving process change as a good advantage, and they also look for experience in the client's particular industry. Beyond that, experience in the particular hardware or operating system is a plus, and of course, advertisers often seek the more general systems analysis, implementation, and project management skills.

The clients are usually end users, and some are willing to provide training in return for the large savings in salary. Sometimes the clients have corporate pay scales that prevent them from paying more for experience, even if they would like to (say to their agencies), whereas others might be driven by the sheer unavailability of SAP-experienced people.

Leaving aside the major management consultancies, the partner consulting firms also intake and advertise for a small proportion of their SAP consultants as new entrants to SAP. These firms are driven by the need to build their organizations. Many large SAP contracts are perceived to be awaiting fulfillment, held up by the lack of resources to fulfill them within consulting partners.

The major management consultancies, SAP itself, and the contracting houses rarely advertise for new entrants to SAP.

Details and brief job requirements for some advertised positions that do not require SAP experience are included in Appendix A.

If you have taken an SAP course, you might have some success in applying for jobs for which minimal experience (say six months) is required. Certainly some people with one year's experience are going for, and getting, jobs where the advertiser stipulated two years, and people with six months' experience are picking up jobs for which one year was stipulated. Perhaps the syndrome might work back as far as the newly trained person getting a job advertised for someone with six months' experience.

Recruitment Agencies: Can They Help Proactively?

You can look at recruitment services as being broadly in two categories, although there is a fair degree of overlap:

- The project-based agency works closely with a client brief and mounts a campaign to solve a client recruitment requirement, usually with high-profile advertising. This type of agency usually offers executive search—*headhunting*—services.

- The database-oriented agency keeps large lists of candidates and frequently circulates to known recruiters details of candidates on file. They are a "matching" service, essentially.

Both types of agencies are really not geared toward doing a hard sell to help you into new areas. The database agencies will put out your résumé where they think there is a chance, but it will sit with a lot of other résumés from inexperienced people.

Some of the more project-oriented agencies, when asked how to get SAP training, advise applicants to talk to SAP, or approach end users directly and try to find those who would rather train than pay large premiums.

As a would-be entrant into a lucrative field, you have to accept that you will have a little self-marketing job to do. The recruitment industry is paid by the employers, not by you, and its job is to meet their objectives. Therefore, the agencies aren't geared toward doing a big selling job on your behalf. You are—or should be.

Contracting Houses

Contracting houses are only really interested in selling the finished article, although as discussed earlier, extreme supply and demand situations can cause them to be more developmental. Realistically, you'll have to work on building some confidence in your capability before a contracting agency is likely to help you develop into a new area as sought after as SAP. If you can do that, you certainly could help your case by thinking about the agency's problem, which is how to make sure it gets a return on its effort, and coming up with some concessions that might solve it. In other words, talk sensible business, and a deal might be possible.

Self-Marketing

If you really want to take control of your own destiny, the way forward is to devise and carry out your own marketing plan. You are a good product, in which you are an expert, so why not?

There are many ways of conducting a marketing campaign, and one of these, the "scatter-gun" approach (mailing out the same message to lots of people), is most used by job seekers. It's easy to produce vast quantities of résumé copies, and you only feel the pain of rejection at a distance. Unfortunately, it's the wrong technique for the purpose. Mailshots can be very effective for selling many similar articles to many similar buyers, but is that the kind of marketing you are engaged in?

Other kinds of marketing are more suitable to the "big game hunter"—someone who is trying to make only a small number of big and important sales. You are the ultimate big game hunter. You only need to make one sale in your whole campaign.

The technique recommended here is one with proven success in the "big game hunter" sort of marketing campaign. Start at those points where information is easiest to get, and from there, build as big a database of prospects as possible. SAP itself is a useful starting point, because the company is very open with its information. You will not find it difficult to compile a list of all the SAP users in your locale. Other useful starting points are employment agencies and contractors. This book provides you with lots of partner names. Don't forget to *network out* as you go along. In other words, ask any contact for other contacts.

The purpose at this stage is to find as many names as possible of companies involved with SAP in your area of interest. You are looking for market information, not direct openings. If you approach the exercise in research mode, you will gain far more from it.

Having widened out the prospect base, you now want to narrow it down by eliminating all but the most promising cases.

Before you start, devise a simple questionnaire that will remind you of the information you are seeking from each group. This should include information that identifies characteristics that match well with your *unique selling points* (USPs), as well as information that will help you prepare a sales call, including the name of the decision-maker on SAP recruitment.

Do as much of this narrowing down as possible by desk research and telephone contact with people other than those who will ultimately make the hiring decision. You should approach the decision-makers only when you are better armed.

After you narrow down the target group to prime prospects only, you can prepare your sales effort for each prospective employer individually, with a résumé that highlights experience relevant to that employer and a prepared approach.

At this stage, you are ready to contact the decision-makers in your target group. If you can, you want to talk to the "problem holder" rather than personnel managers. Call each of them, seeking an appointment to discuss how you could help him or her.

This is a plan that a professional salesperson might use to address the task, and there's no reason why you shouldn't be equally professional. A properly conducted, research-based self-marketing campaign not only gives you the best chance of finding the right opening, but it also makes you much more knowledgeable about the SAP world. This will increase your credibility and broaden your options throughout your career in SAP. ●

CHAPTER 43

The Outlook for the SAP Employment Market

In this chapter

Forming a View

Most independent forecasters paint a rosy picture for SAP in the foreseeable future, and this picture is echoed in the forecasts made by various parts of the SAP *virtual organization*—that is, SAP itself and its partners, some of which are drawn on here.

Although you might argue that the "SAP-interested" sources drawn on are not entirely unbiased, they are in fact among the most reliable. Why? Because they incorporate independent research, often from several research outfits, with their own unique, internal insights before they make their forecasts, and because they stake cash, effort, and "opportunity cost" on being right. Their money is where their judgment is.

Nonetheless, you will want to form your own view, which is ultimately the one you have to back with your own time and effort. Also, you might want to focus on your own special areas of interest within the overall SAP employment scene.

To do each of these things, you need to look at the factors that will drive or hold back growth—both the underlying factors and the initiatives under way or planned. These will dictate not only the amount of growth in SAP employment, but also the directions that growth will take.

Growth Forecasts and Indicators

The SAP group is predicting revenue growth of 40 percent for 1998.

Revenues are growing worldwide. The largest growth market is the Americas, which is assuming an increasingly powerful role within SAP AG.

SAP's revenue growth, of course, is not exactly mirrored by growth in SAP employment, and indeed SAP is at great pains to contain the need for SAP skills and prevent it from growing as fast as the product revenues. SAP is having some success at this with the introduction of various productivity tools and methodologies, but nonetheless, revenue growth is obviously a vital underpinning for employment growth.

Indications from various SAP statistics are that a 40 percent growth in revenues has incurred about a 30 percent growth in SAP's own head count, and SAP believes that it can improve revenue per employee further with the improved development tools it is rolling out. It also believes these tools will help partners meet the resource gap without massive expansion in employment. SAP sources forecast that the total number of SAP consultants required (in the virtual organization of SAP and partners combined) will increase by about 20 percent over the next 12 months.

Partners, in the main, make higher forecasts for SAP employment growth—or at least, each believes that it will grow faster than that.

Partners' forecasts more directly address personnel growth, because consulting is a large part (in some cases, the whole) of the salable product of most partners, whereas to SAP, the software sale is the goal. Although SAP charges for its consulting, it is not pursued primarily for profit but to enable sales of software.

The large consulting partners continue to build SAP expertise at an undiminished rate, while many of the smaller, more SAP-specialized consulting firms have quite specific plans and programs for the growth they anticipate.

You can keep up-to-date with partner activities very easily by accessing the Internet or asking your local SAP office for details of relevant publications.

Of course, end users are also employers of SAP skills. Their growth is likely to run alongside the growth of partner employees.

In summary, there is some divergence between the SAP view and that of the partners on the quantification of growth. Some may argue that the partners have their ears closer to the ground. Some perceive that a great many large SAP projects are waiting to be had, held up only by the lack of resources—that is, SAP-skilled people. In other words, whoever can put the team together can get the business. The view of some recruitment specialists, though, is that some big potential projects are being "double-counted" (or more than double) in these perceptions, because several partners are forecasting to win the same business.

It also is possible to argue that SAP is more aware than the partners of the impact of its productivity tools.

What is agreed all around is that growth will continue, and it seems likely that supply and demand will continue to favor the SAP-skilled employee, while SAP's efforts and those of its partners will prevent the balance from getting totally out of hand.

An Increasingly Customer-Driven Market

There can be little doubt that customers worldwide are becoming more demanding as *enterprise resource planning* (ERP) systems have become mainstream tools supporting the management of business processes.

Customers' expectations have risen, as has their influence in the SAP world. Not long ago, customers were implementing SAP to gain a competitive advantage—perhaps reducing their costs by 10 percent or improving their customer service. Now, in many industries, most of the leading companies have adopted SAP, gaining the same benefits. In some areas, the adoption of SAP has become a necessity just to keep up with competitors. The customers' focus is moving increasingly toward how to gain a competitive advantage and maximize the business benefits generated by using SAP. Customers are looking to implement SAP more quickly and cheaply and to use it in smarter ways to deliver tangible benefits. They are also realizing that SAP itself is just part of their enterprise transformation.

For years systems integration has reigned supreme in the SAP market. Knowledgeable business managers are now demanding business solutions.

The whole market centers on systems integration and implementation. All of SAP's training offerings are based on using, implementing, and maintaining the system. Certified SAP consultants only need to demonstrate that they have SAP systems knowledge. Customers need consultants with business knowledge, vertical market knowledge, functional knowledge, consultancy skills, and all the other skills and experience necessary to deliver business solutions. Consultants need to be able to integrate the systems with the company's vision and values, linking with real people in a real organization to deliver tangible benefits. The systems implementation is the easiest part of this process. Customers need meaningful standards and consulting resources that have the complete skills set to deliver their business solutions.

Some customers are dissatisfied with the market (not necessarily with SAP itself or its products), and rapid market growth is causing significant problems, not the least of which is the difficulty anyone has in controlling it. In the final analysis, the customer is king, and the market exists to serve the needs of the customer. Customers are now beginning to realize that they have real power, individually and collectively, and are beginning to use it.

Factors in the Supply-and-Demand Equation

As you learned earlier, it is a good idea to consider the underlying factors that will impact supply and demand before you arrive at a personal view of long-term SAP employment prospects.

To do this really means viewing the whole SAP marketing strategy and the market influences under which it has to operate. In the case of SAP, this is a very wide set of considerations, and it would be presumptuous to pronounce the "final word" on them in one small chapter here.

However, this chapter can look at some of the marketing considerations and the most vital planks in SAP's strategy from the standpoint of their effect on employment.

These are the main features you'll examine:

- **Market maturation.** Markets are said to mature as they approach saturation (roughly speaking, the point at which almost everybody who needs the product has bought it). Although the SAP marketplace is a long way from being mature, it is, like anything else, maturing all the time. The ratio of installed base to new installation potential increases with each sale that is made.

- **The volume market in mid- and small-size companies.** SAP has built its success mainly by selling to large and ultra-large companies. It now has definite strategies to increase its penetration of mid-size companies and possibly smaller than mid-size.

- **Vertical marketing moves.** A strong current thrust in SAP is toward industry-specific marketing and product development. This offers new and different ways of adding value to the product.

- **Expansion in the range of platforms and interfaced technology.** The range of platforms on which SAP can be installed is increasing all the time, giving new options for both downsizing and upsizing. The range of other software products with which SAP will work and communicate is also expanding.

- **New productivity tools for designers and implementers.** SAP has a number of developments designed to make installing SAP systems more efficient. These tools form a central part of its strategy for balancing supply and demand in the SAP skills market by keeping demand from getting out of hand.

- **Training initiatives.** Supply is critical in the supply-and-demand equation, of course; the key SAP strategy for the supply challenge is to improve it by developing training capacity internally and via partners.

- **Underlying market trends.** SAP, like every other company, depends on the infrastructure that the wider world provides. The SAP success phenomenon has occurred in large part as a result of being the right product for its time. Will times change, and if they do, how well-placed is SAP to adapt?

Each factor has an effect on the people requirement, in terms of both the overall quantity and the mix of skills required. These factors are worth looking at in a little more detail.

Market Maturation

A lot of steam is left in the SAP boiler, as evidenced by the forecasts from the SAP world and supported by judgment based on the underlying factors. Forecasts and judgments alike indicate that the market for SAP will be buoyant for several years to come. SAP skills will continue to be in demand to create brand-new SAP installations.

In this section, you'll look at what happens as the market matures, but nothing should be taken to indicate that maturation is imminent. The growth in new installations is forecast to proceed for years to come.

The demand from established users will eventually overtake that from new installers, though, as the market proceeds toward maturity and the percentile growth in new users slows down, so the ratio of existing to new customers will increase. Figure 43.1 illustrates this point.

SAP users continue to need SAP skills long after the initial implementation. That ongoing need generates employment not only with the end users, but also within partners and SAP itself.

SAP is expecting that partners will generate business from existing customers in the following areas:

- By providing increased functionality through installing additional modules, adding functionality within modules, and extending systems to include supplier and customer database interchange and interaction

- By extending the geographical reach of systems by rolling out into other countries and rolling out through other divisions

- By incorporating new technology, so that as new technologies become important, SAP systems are adapted to work with them and projects can migrate (currently, this means migrations from SAP R/2 to SAP R/3)

The secondary development areas listed are of most interest to the partners as a source of business from existing customers. Secondary developments of this sort will still require many of the skills used in initial systems implementation, although some activities place less emphasis on the wider skills of business process reengineering than do new implementations. Each opportunity area will demand a slightly different mix of skills, and there is clear potential for new specialization in the whole spectrum of add-on activities.

FIGURE 43.1

As market penetration proceeds, employment in existing SAP installations increases relative to employment in installing new SAP sites.

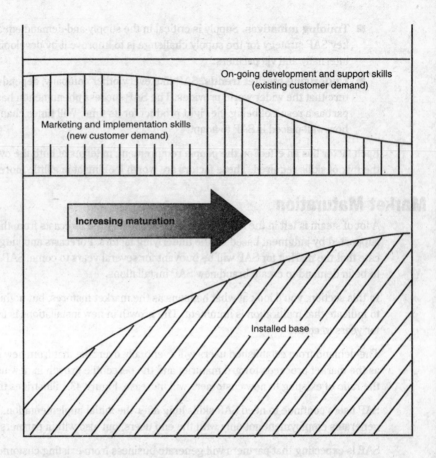

On-going development and support skills (existing customer demand)

Marketing and implementation skills (new customer demand)

Increasing maturation

Installed base

Unlike the partners, SAP itself does not always see special requirements as opportunity areas pure and simple. The company is finding that large customers are looking to SAP to provide more functionality and relieve the pressure on their own IT departments, and this places demands on SAP that can sometimes run counter to the needs of the mass market that it wants to address. Large customers will continue to demand the functionality, though, and this will sustain the need for SAP skills.

In both the partners and SAP itself, ongoing systems support roles will grow in number relative to developmental roles as the market matures, and will offer opportunities across a wide range of specialization. These support roles might diminish in status and benefits, however, as the trend toward remote and automated support continues.

End users, of course, are where the demand for ongoing SAP-skilled employment originates, and they will meet some of the demand by employing people directly. End users most frequently undertake with their own staff the following post–initial-implementation functions:

- User support (as opposed to specialized system support)
- Minor systems modifications, often carried out with ABAP/4
- Systems administration

Up to now, recruitment companies have reported slightly less demand for ABAP programmers than for SAP systems people, but the mix is likely to change as the market matures. ABAP programmers are likely to be needed for a longer period of time, because ABAP is mainly used for small-scale changes, which continue to take place long after implementation.

What you have been examining is essentially the market for SAP R/3, and it is still quite a young market. No one is anywhere near forecasting what its successor might be, but it is hard to think there will not be one when the SAP R/3 market matures. It is equally hard to believe that SAP R/3 skills will not be valuable in whatever migration process might take place then, just as SAP R/2 skills are valuable in a market dominated by SAP R/3.

Sooner or later, of course, even the most dominant software products may be overtaken by a competitor development, but the people who work with such overtaken products do not become immediately obsolete. Instead, they move gradually to being more of a niche resource, or they cross-train into some successor technology.

The SAP product, interfacing as it does with so many other technologies, is always likely to provide an escape route if you see yourself primarily as a systems technologist, even when the product passes its peak.

If you are (or become) one of the many SAP consultants who are essentially management, business process, or systems consultants that regard SAP as simply a tool, you have developed skills that you can apply with or without SAP. SAP skills might be what allowed you to progress and acquire those other skills, but you are not dependent on them, and certainly the large management consulting–based partners will seek to develop you as a more versatile resource than just an SAP specialist. You would be more at risk from any diminution in the whole management and computer consulting industry (unlikely though that may be) than from the demise of SAP as the industry darling.

The Volume Market in Mid- and Smaller-Size Companies

SAP has established some penetration in Germany and neighboring countries among what Germans refer to as the *Mittelstand*. This refers to a stratum of small- and medium-size businesses—component and subassembly suppliers, flooring and ceiling specialists, garden furniture and tools manufacturers, and a host of others, mainly in manufacturing, owner-managed, and fairly specialized and skills-based.

The *Mittelstand* is particularly strong because of Germany's localized banking support and other infrastructure factors, but it has its equivalents in mid-size businesses around the world.

To appreciate the potential in this industry stratum and the likely success of SAP's strategies, it is worth taking a brief look at the story so far.

The potential market worldwide among such companies is huge, and SAP's initial idea for addressing it was to develop a version of SAP that would be tailored specially for this marketplace.

Its early experiments in the United States were designed to establish the market requirements for this version, but yielded instead a rethink of that whole approach.

The exercise reminded SAP that mid-size companies are not really very different from large companies. They often need more functionality, rather than less, in each business process they operate. Being more specialized, they usually have fewer of these business processes, but it is not always easy to say which ones will not be used, and they will vary from industry to industry and, indeed, from company to company.

The upshot of this is that SAP has decided that it is not a practical proposition to write a special SAP version for smaller businesses. What a smaller company needs is the full-specification SAP with the capability to bypass the processes it does not use.

There is no major cost problem in delivering the whole system. From a pricing strategy point of view, the per-seat pricing policy that SAP adopts makes for a natural adjustment to the price, which runs roughly alongside the client's size and consequent capability to pay, without offending larger users. From a practical point of view, it actually costs SAP less to deliver the whole thing than to cut down the functionality. Also, very little additional *platform space* (computing and storage resources) is involved, because inactive SAP modules do not carry much of a penalty.

The real problem is how to save the user from grinding through myriad irrelevant options. That is the key to ease of use, and SAP has gone for *down-configuration* as its strategy for achieving it.

How well this works will be a major determinant of its success with the mid-size and smaller companies, and SAP has developed a concept for its realization, which it calls *configure to order* (in line with the assemble-to-order concept), within an overall strategy, which it calls *delta customizing*. You can learn more about the assistance this provides configurers in "New Productivity Tools for Designers and Implementers," later in this chapter.

Other moves—toward more vertical marketing and platform downsizing—will have important enabling roles in penetrating mid-size companies. They too are described later in this chapter.

The SAP attention to the mid-size company marketplace has stimulated activity from the partners. For example, Clarkson-Potomac has announced its intention to create a strong presence in the middle market. The company claims to have been working closely with SAP to prepare for this, and it has plans to add value in the area of easy configuration tools.

IBM sees one of its primary growth areas for SAP as being to roll out AS/400-based offerings to medium- and small-size customers.

The smaller, more SAP-specialized partners look likely to be better able to exploit the middle market than will the large Big Six type of operations, with their background in accountancy and management consulting. This is because the sales and installation process seems likely to become more like a typical software solution sale than it has been in selling to the large companies. New partner types are emerging, sometimes as distinct middle-market divisions within existing partner types.

The mix of skills and the total number of person-days required per seat to sell, design, and implement systems are going to change when each system contains fewer seats. Figure 43.2 shows the sort of effect to be expected.

FIGURE 43.2
As each system
contains fewer seats,
the profile of the
installation and support
effort changes.

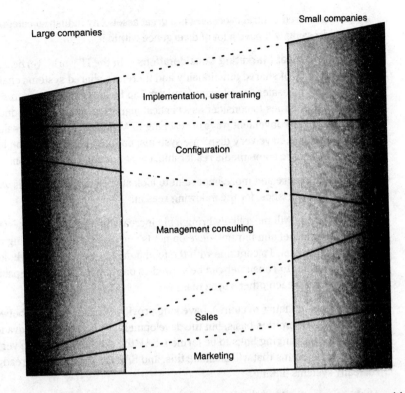

If this market continues to expand as expected, look for emerging employment opportunities not only in specialized configure-to-order skills, but also in sales roles traditionally associated with computer solutions and so far largely absent from the SAP world.

Vertical Marketing Moves

SAP has built a successful product by pinning down essential business processes and providing for them with real-time interaction between configurable modules that encapsulate "best practice."

These modules have always been to some extent aligned with industries—or at least with industry groups. The original SAP product sprang from the needs of supply chain–driven organizations, such as chemicals producers, and from the essential processes involved in meeting those demands.

This is not the same thing as producing a vertical market package. Off-the-shelf vertical market packages are largely the preserve of smaller specialist software houses. There are many thousands of these packages, most of which sell in only small numbers. I worked on a planned directory of vertical market packages in the '80s that was abandoned because the number of packages was so vast it was impossible to describe their features in enough detail to be useful.

SAP is not in the business of producing that kind of product, but it is moving more toward vertical marketing of the SAP product, where its architecture of configurability layered on top of well-engineered central processes is a great asset. Any industrial category big enough to be worth addressing will have a lot of divergence within it.

Underlying Vertical Marketing Considerations   In the IT world, vertical markets are often defined in terms of shared functionality and therefore shared systems characteristics—for example, all wholesalers or all manufacturers can be looked at as one, to some extent. But there are other issues to consider as a vertical marketer: As well as producing for the market, you want to have convenient ways of reaching it. Manufacturers, wholesalers, and retailers of food, for example, have very disparate systems, but they have a common interest in the food business and share some media readership, event attendance, and so on.

It is becoming more and more important to look at verticalization in this way, rather than by systems characteristics, for the following reason.

The next decade will most likely bring a big increase in intercompany systems access, fueled in part by the Internet and intranet developments and also by the expanding range of tools for linking applications. To continue with the food industry example, the whole process of getting food from farmer to consumer can be viewed as one supply chain, with participants along the route linked into each other's systems.

Some parts of industry, of course, have long provided shared systems between supplier and supplied on a committed basis, but the developments anticipated will advance the options and allow more free-ranging links to be formed. SAP the product provides a very good platform for building the systems that will facilitate this, and SAP the company is already promoting intercompany systems linking.

All this means that broadly based industry skilling is the key to successful vertical marketing in the SAP world. This requires elements of expertise in the marketplace, combined with an understanding of the business processes across several types of operations. This knowledge must be married to the capability to configure and modify SAP modules to produce industry solutions, modifiable at individual customer levels.

Only rarely will all these skills be found in the same person, but partner organizations will be building teams to incorporate them all. SAP itself will be a part of this, with its industry-skilled people involved in the kind of virtual teams that are central to the SAP partnership philosophy.

SAP Vertical Marketing Initiatives   SAP's industry-focused activity has the following two main threads:

- The partner program has been reorganized along industry-specific lines. In the SAP world, the partners are the most significant sales resource, so this is a highly significant move. The organization is described more fully in Chapter 40, "SAP Workplaces," but the key point here is that the pivotal interface between partners and SAP marketing resources becomes the *business development manager* (BDM), and BDMs are dedicated to particular industry groups. This means that the main marketing delineation for the virtual organization—the communications channels that extend through SAP resources and into partners' resources—is vertical.

- Both SAP and the partners are developing more industry-specific solutions.

SAP has earmarked a number of sectors for SAP product development attention, including the following:

Banks	Risk management, statutory reporting, controlling
Hospitals	Patient administration and accounting, hospital control systems
Insurance companies	Securities, loans, and real estate
Oil industry	Exploration, transport, distribution
Public sector	Financial budget planning and management
Publishers	Subscription management, advertising management
Retail	Product structure, distribution logistics, point of sales systems
Utilities	Device management, house connections, meter readings processing, billing

This list is expanding all the time, and other sectors are being singled out for marketing attention, often at individual SAP subsidiary—that is, country—levels. At the subsidiary level, it is likely to prove more flexible for the SAP marketing team to promote vertical value-added product development via the partners.

Partners are already promoting solutions in categories such as these:

- Airports
- Automobile industry and suppliers
- Banking and insurance
- Beverage industry
- Construction industry
- Energy supply
- Estate administration
- Export, shipping, and customs handling
- Financial services
- Hospital systems
- Laboratory and analytical systems
- Media management
- Mining industry
- Plant construction
- Production process data capture
- Transportation industry
- Warehousing, transportation, and storage

Verticality and Smaller Business Penetration   The term *vertical market* has become almost synonymous with *industry-specific marketing*. It was originally coined to describe markets that are, well, vertical. That is to say that you can move up and down the company size strata, and customers of all sizes can be fitted into the same category.

This feature applies to a greater or lesser extent in many of the SAP industry targets, and vertical focus will provide direction in the efforts to market to smaller companies. It is a way of relating SAP's experience in giant corporations to its target audience of smaller companies. Smaller companies specially value specific industry knowledge and experience.

After a partner uses this vertical market knowledge to penetrate the smaller company strata, horizontal marketing direction can be used to spread into other industry areas in that strata. Figure 43.3 illustrates this concept.

FIGURE 43.3

Vertical marketing provides a route into smaller companies for a supplier such as SAP, with its track record in larger companies.

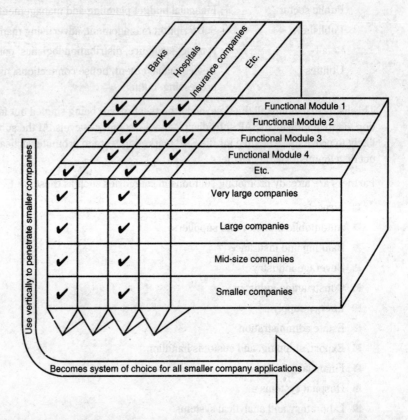

Because SAP has organized itself further toward industry-specific marketing, it is possible to forecast a massive proliferation of virtual teams marketing and delivering to vertical markets.

The SAP product has brought real-time processing to the back office, and it is hard to think of any industry where companies cannot benefit from the extra efficiency and responsiveness this can bring. But these companies have to be shown how SAP can do this for them, and they are most likely to be convinced by vertical marketing.

Partners will seek to gain an edge by differentiating themselves and exploiting any specific industrial expertise they have, new partners will enter the SAP arena specifically to exploit some vertical market strength, and SAP will reach out into ever more industries.

Expansion in the Range of Platforms and Interfaced Technology

Of all the factors that make an IT product successful, perhaps the most important historically has been to catch the right technology tide. SAP itself is an instance of that with SAP R/3, which was ideally positioned for the growth in client/server systems.

Today, many strands of technology are seeking to prosper in the client/server environment, and SAP needs to ensure that it covers any moves that technology fashion takes. It is very well-placed to do this, because its now-massive R&D capability, coupled with its capability to build partnership relationships, means that it can cover virtually all likely moves.

This capability to build partnerships is greatly assisted by the nature of the product, which provides a fount of applications solutions. Technology providers recognize that applications software is a key requirement to drive and facilitate sales of their products. Hence the major technology players need SAP just as much as SAP needs them.

This section gives you a few examples of the technologies that are now extending the SAP marketplace, as well as a little insight into SAP strategy, so that you can form your own view on their likely success and the impact on employment prospects.

Windows NT as a Platform   The most strategic direction that SAP has taken since the introduction of SAP R/3 is its adoption of Windows NT as a platform. The first SAP system on Windows NT went live at the Swiss company, Bally, in August 1994, and by October 1995, around 650 such installations were in place. The figure in 1998 is considerably higher.

The company now sees itself as having evolved from a mainframe-focused company to one with a primary focus on PC networks. Windows NT is a central feature in this change of focus. Here are a few of the reasons for this:

- Windows is the industry standard GUI. The vast majority of SAP R/3 users are familiar with it from their desktop systems and have developed Windows skills. With the server operating under Windows NT, these skills are exploited, and systems consistency produces efficiency in many areas.
- The consistency of the Windows user interface reduces training costs.
- SAP R/3 users on Windows NT have experienced substantial savings in cost of ownership per seat, compared with those running on UNIX servers.
- Windows NT provides an operating environment rich in the sort of services needed to build distributed and integrated computing environments.
- SAP regards Microsoft's *object linking and embedding* (OLE) as a key technology that allows customers to leverage their investment in desktop applications, such as Microsoft Office, when using SAP R/3.
- Windows NT is the fastest-growing operating system for the midrange and above server environment.

Joint developments between SAP and Microsoft continue unabated. For example, Microsoft's SQL Server 6.0 has recently been implemented primarily to target mid-size installations running in homogeneous client/server environments.

You can expect to see a continued expansion in the number of hardware platforms running SAP R/3 on Windows NT. iXOS Software GmbH has set up an SAP R/3 NTC Competence Center for SAP to run a certification program especially for Windows NT platforms. Products from companies such as AT&T, Compaq, Data General, Hewlett-Packard, IBM, Sequent, Siemens Nixdorf, and Zenith have already received this certification.

Windows NT client/server systems will often be wedded to other (notably UNIX-based) technologies. Data General, which is both a SAP platform partner and a Microsoft Solutions partner, was the first to combine a Windows NT–based operating environment with the choice of a Windows NT or UNIX database. This extended the benefits of Windows NT into enterprises with very large databases and user counts.

Data General's AViiON range can support Windows NT operating systems, and SAP R/3 can run under Windows NT while supporting databases on either Windows NT or DG/UX.

Major Platforms and Technology   The Windows NT thrust is additional to, rather than instead of, expansion in the UNIX world and beyond.

Release 4.0 of SAP R/3 is compatible with most of the leading hardware and operating systems, including Digital Alpha AXD and UNIX, IBM AS/400 and AIX, SNI SINIX, and SUN Solaris. It is also compatible with the leading database platforms, such as Informix, Oracle, and Adabas.

Its list of platform and technology partners alone assures it of a foothold in any major technology directions. These partners include the following:

Apple	Informix
AT&T	Intel
Compaq	iXOS Software
Data General	Microsoft
Digital Equipment	Oracle
Hewlett-Packard	Platinum Technology
Hitachi	Siemens Nixdorf
IBM	

Recent moves with IBM provide ample evidence that SAP intends to continue extending its capability with large systems. It has taken steps into the fast-growing world of scaleable parallel computing with the announcement that SAP will now operate on IBM's RS/6000 POWERParallel System (SP), using Oracle's parallel database, ORACLE 7 parallel server.

IBM also would reportedly like to see SAP R/3 running on its mainframe platforms, and it is looking at the possibilities of using the mainframe as a database server and possibly an applications server.

Complementary Technology   Less central to SAP's existence, but very important in its expanding influence and applicability, are the many third-party solutions that interface with SAP.

Many products are certified or awaiting certification under SAP's Complementary Software Program, in the following categories:

- Archive software/imaging software
- *Computer-aided design* (CAD)
- *Electronic Data Interchange* (EDI) subsystems
- Laboratory Information Management Systems
- *Plant Data Collection/Machine Data Collection* (PDC/MDC)
- Process control systems
- Product data management

Also, several categories of communications services are encouraged, though not certified.

Complementary solution providers are listed in Appendix E, "Complementary Solutions," along with their solutions. The *Complementary Software Program* (CSP) is expected to result in many more solutions being added over the next few years.

The technologies that develop around SAP will not only influence SAP's continuing success but will also extend the width of skills involved in the SAP world. A glance at the small sample of job specifications in Appendix A illustrates how different technology skills are welcomed into the SAP camp.

Opportunities to use experience in complementary and platform technology alongside SAP skills (or as a ticket to get an opening into SAP) exist at all levels—not just with SAP itself and the technology and platform partners, but also with the other partners and end users who are implementing systems that combine SAP with these technologies.

New Productivity Tools for Designers and Implementers

Independent industry analysts' ratings of SAP for ease of implementation and flexibility are in sharp contrast to their rating of the product generally. Its capability to deliver and support a full range of modern client/server applications, for example, puts SAP well ahead of the field, whereas it has been rated near the bottom of the league for ease of implementation.

This means that there is a lot of room here for improvement, which SAP has already started with the release of SAP R/3 4.0 and plans to continue. Ease of implementation will be a focus for its advertising as it seeks to redress this perceived weakness, and the words are being backed up by action. SAP spends around $1 million per day on R&D, and a substantial part of this is going into productivity tools for systems designers and implementers.

No one is yet putting firm figures on the impact this will have on SAP employment, but it is a central part of SAP's strategy and will certainly have some effect in mitigating demand.

Bear in mind, though, that in many installations, much of the project time attributed to SAP implementation and customizing is in fact spent on redefining customer requirements, which are often ill-documented and unclear. Improved implementation tools will not greatly impact the consulting business time that goes into this area.

Some of the initiatives taken by SAP to ease implementation will affect employment qualitatively as well as quantitatively. Skills in using the new tools will become important, and some configuration skills will become, while not exactly redundant, at least at less of a premium.

It is worth understanding the following main areas of focus in recent improvements.

SAP has significantly improved the productivity of the ABAP/4 Development Workbench through

- Simplified database analyses
- Simplified dictionary maintenance
- Integration of the data-modeler
- Repository Information System—a central storage system for all development objects that describes the application
- Open repository interface
- Enhancements to the SAP GUI
- *Computer-aided test tools* (CATTs)

SAP R/3 Customizing tools have been considerably enhanced:

- A new procedure model is aimed at providing transparent management of the implementation process.
- The *Implementation Management Guide* (IMG), an interactive procedural model based on SAP R/3 implementation experience, will now provide project-specific views. You can determine the relevant functions from your business processes and make the necessary settings, guided by your own specific IMG with graphics support. The settings are automatically recorded ready to simplify production startup.
- *Applications Link Enabling* (ALE) functions are embedded in the Customizing facilities, making design, implementation, and maintenance of distributed applications simpler.
- Scenarios can be modeled with a methods-based procedure that maintains consistency and traps errors while obviating the need to perform myriad actions. The scenarios are transferred to implementations in the constituent systems.

The Business Engineering Workshop now enables SAP R/3 to be a true configure-to-order application suite:

- It includes a business process repository (which acts as a master blueprint for SAP R/3 system capabilities), graphical process models, and scenario-testing customizing tools.
- Once complete, the customer's unique "living" business process model can be stored in the Business Engineering Workshop and used to engineer ongoing changes.

The most important overall thrust is toward the concept that SAP calls *delta customizing*.

In delta customizing, all models—data, business, and process models alike—will be shipped along with the SAP system; SAP wants implementations to be based increasingly on these models. Figure 43.4 illustrates the process.

Delta customizing is a stripping-down process that can leave as little as a few percentages of the shipped system operative. Ideally, the system will guide the user through this, providing instructions each time he or she wants to activate a function.

FIGURE 43.4

In delta customizing, the whole SAP product is shipped, along with the tools that enable the customer to down-configure it.

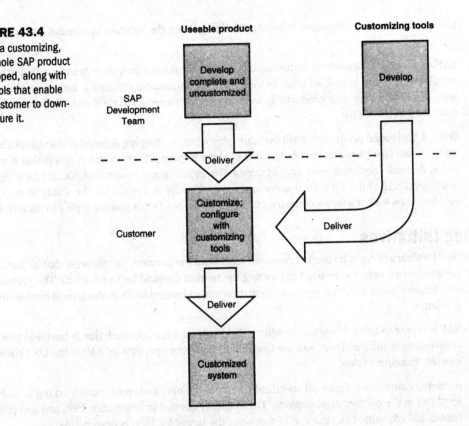

Dr. Hasso Plattner, SAP AG vice chairman, has characterized the ideal: being able to run a complete SAP R/3 system on a laptop and configure it in an airplane on the way to see a customer—and being able to add any function forgotten in a few minutes in the customer's office.

This capability to customize the system by computer-aided downsizing is expected to reduce consulting time significantly, because of the reduced need to pore over irrelevant documentation: You look only at the bits the system tells you to.

The delta customizing concept is not directed only at mid-size and smaller customers, but it has particular relevance for them.

SAP is working on a model designed to speed up implementation at these smaller customer sites. This model involves mapping out procedures for the first three weeks of implementation. SAP marries this approach to a sales concept tailored to the special needs of this marketplace. Paul Wahl, head of marketing at SAP AG, has said that the aim is to achieve more fast implementations and fewer customer-driven ones.

This lighter process will modify the increased demand for SAP employment as SAP surges in the mid-size and smaller market (discussed earlier in this chapter). Remember, though, this is largely a new market anyway, and is additional to growth in SAP's traditional large company marketplace, so this discussion talks about holding down the increase in demand rather than reducing it.

SAP's own efforts to improve implementation tools are not the only ones being made. Partners are always seeking to gain an edge by their ability to implement efficiently, and many of them have developed their own productivity tools, which are expected to yield reduced implementation times in the future.

Overall, increased productivity will certainly play a part in keeping demand within suppliable limits. It will also have an effect on the mix of skills required. One feature of this is that it will swing demand more and more toward personal-interfacing and business skills, and away from lower-level SAP skills. As tools become more user-friendly and powerful, the ability to work the tool becomes less of a factor compared to the knowledge of what you are trying to do with it.

Training Initiatives

SAP has learned from its market research (and from the partners themselves) that its partners have been resource-constrained in meeting the market demand for its products. The partners also require more business process orientation and enhanced skills in the area of module integration.

SAP is trying to solve this problem with a worldwide training approach that is business process–oriented and hands-on, and the Consultant Academy operated by SAP in the UK provides an early example of this.

Academy courses are designed specifically to meet the needs of consultants working in SAP itself and in the partner organizations. The academy opened in September 1995 and had processed 120 consultants by the end of that year; the target for 1998 is nearer 2,000.

The academy teaches the major building blocks and is much more process-oriented than the standard courses. It seeks to show consultants how to find their way around SAP, teaching them what they need to know and where to find what they do not know.

The three-week introductory course does not assume any SAP knowledge but requires a good background in business processes and IT. It is not suitable for new graduates with little or no business knowledge.

All SAP's own UK consultants and product managers will attend, and most are expected to teach at the academy, the principle being that "it takes a consultant to teach a consultant."

Participants are expected to carry on after the introductory course and take standard courses. These courses are more concerned with functional detail and less with cross-module integration than are the academy courses.

The academy approach is well-targeted and should help to induct into SAP more of the broad-reaching consultants with a good understanding of business processes that the SAP virtual organization needs.

If you meet that specification and want to use this route to induct into SAP, you will have to get into a partner organization first, because outside SAP employees, the scheme is open only to partners.

The initiatives SAP is taking are not limited to classroom training; SAP has a number of other strategies:

- An accreditation program—not dependent on attendance at SAP's own courses, but based on the ability to satisfy examination requirements—will enable SAP to exert quality control while allowing partners to expand their training activities.

- Knowledgeware, in the form of digestible chunks of information on CD-ROMs or other suitable media, will be increasingly produced as a cost-efficient way of reducing classroom time.

- Night schools for ABAP programming and links with universities are other ways in which at least some SAP subsidiaries will be seeking to boost training throughput.

Perhaps the most important of these strategies will be the accreditation program, which sends a signal to partners that they can engage much more heavily in training. SAP is giving positive encouragement to partners to do this, and there are signs from all around the partner spectrum that the challenge is being accepted.

IBM has declared one of its primary growth areas as leading the development of SAP education and training offerings.

Andersen Consulting was the first to acquire the right to deliver SAP's standard courses, but a growing number of other consultants are now looking to develop and train SAP skills. They are producing rational programs to induct people carefully into SAP, and that involves having the right framework to introduce them into projects with customer concurrence.

The overall drive to produce more SAP people will go a long way toward satisfying demand for people with some SAP skill. The senior people, around whom you can build a team and provide a framework for inducting SAP apprentices, will still command a premium that the training efforts will not affect for several years—until the new people become senior figures themselves.

Underlying Market Trends

If it is true that "no man is an island," it is even more true that no company is, and SAP's prospects depend on how well it adapts to its environment. You could divide the main underlying conditions that define SAP's wider environment into three main areas: technology, corporate practice, and socioeconomics. Trends in these areas are very much interwoven and interdependent, but the division provides a convenient way of looking at things.

Technology trends were touched on earlier in this chapter. Client/server systems growth has provided the main technology groundswell that SAP has exploited with SAP R/3. All forecasts are that the client/server market will continue to grow, and the convenience of the vehicle that it provides for many of the other technology trends means that it is very hard to see it failing to do so.

The other key trends are concerned with applications connectivity. The Internet will provide an increasing impetus to this, as will the many connectivity tools that are constantly being developed. SAP has a good foothold in this area, provided by the strategic relationships it has built with partners and complementary solution providers in the connectivity arena. SAP the product, of course, is well-placed to benefit from and contribute to the trend.

SAP is already taking some very positive steps in Internet use. It has developed information and support systems for access by the World Wide Web, CompuServe, and The Microsoft Network, as well as facilities within SAP R/3 to allow the development of intranet and intercompany systems directly from within SAP R/3 applications.

CPU and storage technology developments, unless of a profoundly revolutionary architecture, will not affect SAP's progress, because they provide a lower-level platform that will find a place regardless of the way in which they are configured into broader systems architectures.

It is hard, all in all, to see any serious threat from changes in underlying technology for the near- and medium-term future. The eventual threat to SAP is likely to come from directly competitive technology. SAP found a "better way to build a mousetrap," and the world beat a path to its door (well, nearly). Until someone finds a better way, SAP will predominate.

But changes in the underlying technology will offer new options, and it is when these occur that a competitor will have the best chance of creating an alternative to SAP that will oust it as the foremost applications solution. So it is worth keeping an eye on base technology developments, but not too anxiously.

Corporate practice has become much more internationalized, and multinational corporations have been very important to SAP's growth. All the signs are that this trend toward multinationalism will continue, and it favors SAP and its partners. Many international corporations, while extending geographically, want to reduce the diversity of their applications and espouse open systems. They also need their suppliers to have a global outlook, and most SAP partners are geared to service this need in one way or another. Not only will this trend help enhance the SAP employment outlook in general, but it will also maintain and extend the opportunities for travel and emigration in the SAP world.

Running almost parallel with SAP's history, socioeconomic conditions in much of the developed world have become more monetarist at the same time as unfettered free-marketing has been espoused. The effect of both together has been to cause companies to seek efficiency by reductionist means, such as the oft-heard retreat into "core business" and the plowing of investments into takeovers and mergers rather than organic development. This has caused a shedding of labor, which in theory should be available for use in new enterprises.

The investment community, however, in a monetarist world, has found that the opportunity to take up this spare labor and invest in it is a less-attractive prospect than the activity of stripping down businesses to shed the labor. Hence, much of the business process reengineering that SAP has been used to carry out has been concerned with reductionism.

It is not the purpose of this book to pass judgment on the economic value or social ethics of these forces. However, because the fashion (which is prevalent mainly where Western-style mobile capital controls events) will pass eventually, you should briefly look at the effect of that on the future of SAP.

There is no reason to think that any reversal of the trend will disadvantage SAP. SAP is an agent of change in business processes. It happens that the business changes during its lifetime have been reductionistic in the main and arguably short-term (ironically, given its German origins—Germany has a far more long-term investment structure than most countries in the West). However, SAP is equally well-equipped to help business creation when that once again becomes the prevalent driver of change.

Major Rewrite of SAP Core Code with Object-Oriented Codes

In mid-1998, SAP announced that it is rewriting the code of the R/3 system using object-oriented techniques. This is by far the most significant development since the launch of the R/3 system. For some time, commentators have been saying that object-oriented technology represents SAP's greatest threat.

The task of rewriting its software is massive, and the problems and risks that this exercise may involve should not be underestimated.

The upside however, is tremendous. The rewrite will enable SAP to split off pieces of code and sell them as standalone applications. It will also open up the code to third-party applications, which is part of SAP's strategy to expand its installed base beyond its users in Fortune 500 companies.

SAP plans to split off its analytical and supply-chain applications from its core ERP package. SAP is also looking to fight back against companies such as PeopleSoft, to which it has lost market share, with new human resources applications.

The following new object-oriented analytical and supply-chain applications are due for release by the end of 1998:

- Business Information Warehouse
- Advanced Planner and Optimizer
- Business-to-Business Procurement
- Maintenance, Repair, and Operation
- Strategic Enterprise Management

Sales Force Automation is due for release by the end of 1999.

The new applications will use middleware technology *Distributed Common Object Model* (DCOM), *Application Link Enabling* (ALE), and Object Request Broker architecture to link to third-party applications.

The object-oriented techniques should make it easier to coordinate different releases of SAP, which would bring huge benefits to customers who seem to be forever upgrading and overcoming resultant difficulties.

Summary of SAP Employment Outlook

SAP, and especially SAP R/3, is a product still on the rise, and employment prospects surrounding it look undiminished for a number of years to come.

These pages should have conveyed some idea of the rich tapestry of activities into which SAP is woven, and only if business and business technology bore you should you fail to be excited by the opportunities SAP offers.

Certainly very few people are bored by the prospect of high earnings, and the tales of huge contract fees and salaries for SAP consultants could very well be one of the reasons you are reading this book. Supply and demand will continue to favor the employee in the SAP world, although strenuous and promising efforts are being made to prevent staff shortages from hindering SAP's growth.

High short-term earnings should not be the overriding consideration, though. The SAP world is wary of consultants out to make a quick buck and is seeking to encourage people who have a genuine interest in what the product can do for business and an empathy with the SAP way of working. Many recruitment and contracting professionals forecast that the SAP jobs boom will last longer than the very high salaries.

SAP projects tend to be long, and this can provide security and job satisfaction, as well as lucrative assignments for contractors, but it cuts both ways, and locking yourself into a project for a number of years does not suit everyone.

If you are the sort of person the SAP world needs, then SAP will continue to provide a secure source of employment for many years and a first-rate platform for building a career in business and information management.

Trends in the SAP Employment Market

Some major trends will impact the SAP market over the next few years:

- The SAP market is still a young one, but as it matures, the number of installed systems increases relative to the number of new ones being sold, with a resultant change in the mix of implementation and support staff.

- SAP is actively seeking to market into much smaller companies than have been its target in the past. It is also engaging more heavily in vertical marketing.

- The range of platform and complementary product technology that sells along with SAP is increasing all the time and opening ever more bridges into SAP for people with skills in these areas.

- SAP is focusing greatly on making its development workbench tools easier to use. It expects this to help balance the supply-and-demand equation in SAP employment. It also changes the skill requirements for configurers.

- International recruitment is increasing as the emerging markets seek to recruit experienced people from the more established markets.

- SAP development tools continue to make the implementation process less complex. This will change the balance of implementation and support staff required at this stage.
- Platform and complementary technology is increasing. The technology that is growing up around SAP offers increasing employment opportunities.
- SAP AG is seeking increasing penetration of smaller companies and engaging in a vertical marketing strategy. This will add to the range of employment possibilities.
- Employers will seek to balance their interests before yours. This will change the nature of the SAP employment market.

44

The ASAP Institute and the ASAP Standards and Assessment Board

In this chapter

Solutions to Current Problems

Despite the numerous positive issues surrounding SAP, the following problems currently exist in the market:

- There is a skills shortage.
- The cost of consultancy is very high.
- The quality of consultancy received may not actually match the price paid.
- Current education and training is technically orientated and focuses on computer systems.
- Up-to-date business concepts are omitted from education.
- SAP is an international phenomenon, yet no common approach to training exists across international boundaries.

The consultancy market is changing. *Enterprise resource planning* (ERP) systems have moved from niche to mainstream, and a period of immense global growth has dawned. ERPsystems are now closely linked to the organization's performance and are therefore extremely important. Customers now want more than the software implementation skills that SAP certification indicates; they are looking for individuals who have a greater breadth of understanding and professionalism who can offer business solutions.

A new profession has arisen from this situation—the *ERP consultant*. Currently, good ERP consultants are in very high demand but are difficult to find. It is equally difficult to assess the competence and value of individual consultants. Globally, a lack of standards and training exists in the vital nonsystems areas of enterprise transformation. As a result, customers are becoming frustrated and are looking for assistance.

At the launch of the ASAP Institute in July 1998, one SAP project manager made a passionate plea for skilled consultants with wider knowledge bases, to whom simple professional practices such as etiquette and ethics were second nature. He had interviewed SAP consultants who specialize in the Financial and Controlling modules, yet have no understanding of basic bookkeeping. The same manager asked the question, "What is a consultant?" "Ask five different people," he told the crowd, "and you get five different answers."

The authors of this book launched the ASAP Institute to address such problems.

History of the ASAP Institute

The ASAP Institute was founded in December 1997.

The formal launch of the ASAP Institute was hosted by SAP (UK) at its new head office in Feltham, near London, England, in June 1998.

Senior managers from SAP and a number of SAP's competitor companies, customers, business executives, functional managers, trainers, and industry practitioners attended the launch. Attendees came from the USA, Europe, and South Africa, as well as the UK.

ASAP Institute Mission Statement

The mission of the ASAP Institute is to set and maintain standards of professionalism and effectiveness for those working within the field of Enterprise Transformation, where ERP-Integrated Business Systems are used as the driving force.

The Institute will support the interests of both existing and potential end-user customers within the market, as well as the interests of its members; all aspire to raise the level of professionalism available to them.

The Institute primarily wants to achieve the outcomes required by end-user customers. The Institute will set standards of professionalism that will reflect the best practices and highest levels of performance considered "effective" by the end-user companies. The Institute will support the achievement of these standards by consultants through accreditation of performance at various levels, and the provision of relevant quality training. The Institute's additional role is to help members in their working lives; it will achieve this through career development.

ASAP Institute Characteristics

The characteristics of the ASAP Institute follow:

- The Institute runs independently of any ERP vendor.
- Accreditation will have relevance for all ERP systems professions, including SAP.
- The operation is global. Membership is available to professionals anywhere in the world.
- An independent Advisory Council will drive the Institute. Fundamental to the council will be a vision of high ideals for the ERP market and consideration for the requirements and desires of end-user customers.

Training

The Institute offers a comprehensive range of programs for people working in enterprise transformation. It addresses issues from specialist systems knowledge through to the development of personal skills. A structured framework of progressive learning and career development within the ERP market is available.

The Institute is developing training courses in the following areas:

- Industry/vertical markets
- General business knowledge/value chain processes
- Functional knowledge
- ERP overview/enterprise transformation/strategy
- Professional skills
- Project management
- Training
- System

Constitution and Organization of the ASAP Institute

An Executive Committee governs the ASAP Institute. It is supported by an Advisory Council consisting of primarily end-user customers and representatives from all sectors of the enterprise transformation market who together create and approve standards.

Institute activities include technical seminars, tailored training programs, professional accreditation, conferences, and setting and maintaining the standards of provision within the marketplace.

The Institute operates globally, using modern technology to deliver effective services to its members. Membership is open to the following:

- Business executives, directors of major organizations
- Senior functional managers—for example, accounting managers, human resources managers, purchasing managers
- Business consultants—for example, management consultants, change managers, business process reengineering consultants, strategy consultants
- Systems consultants—for example, configurers, programmers, technical personnel
- Trainers

The Institute will have three main categories of members:

- Student members
- Associate members
- Full members

The ASAP Standards and Assessment Board: An Overview

The ASAP Standards and Assessment Board has been formed to administer standards and manage the assessment of ASAP Institute members.

Assessments are competency-based. There is no prerequisite to attend or complete ASAP Institute courses.

The assessments are likely to incorporate certification offered by ERP software vendors. The intention is for ASAP certification to be complementary to and not competing with that offered by software vendors, whose certification currently relates to just software knowledge and technical skills.

ASAP Institute certification will assist customers and consultants. Customers will have the power to select consultants whose skills, knowledge, and ability have been proven. For the first time, customers will be able to accurately attribute value to individuals and see through the fog that exists in the market.

Consultants with genuine skills, knowledge, and ability will be able to differentiate themselves from those without these attributes. The result of the standards and assessments should be to create career paths. Individuals will be able to develop themselves along desired routes and add value to their remuneration based on the value they add to customers.

Contact Details

For membership, training, and assessment inquiries; or to apply to join the Advisory Council (if you are a senior manager in an end-user company), contact the following:

Country	Telephone	Fax
UK	+44 (0)1491 414411	+44 (0)1491 414412
USA	(212) 253 4180	(212) 253 4180
Australia	+61 (0) 2 9475 0551	+61 (0) 2 9475 0551
Belgium	+32 (0) 2 706 50 04	+32 (0) 2 706 50 04
South Africa	Contact UK for Johannesburg office details	

Email: **institute@asap-consultancy.co.uk**

Web site: **http://www.asap-consultancy.co.uk/**

Appendixes

Sample SAP-Related Job Descriptions

Looking at Real-Life Examples

This appendix lists real-life examples of descriptions published inside companies or prepared for recruitment companies. In some cases, where the employer wants to preserve anonymity, examples have been edited slightly, but only enough to satisfy employers' wants; the substance is unaltered. The descriptions are grouped according to these criteria:

- Jobs carried out in SAP subsidiaries
- Examples of SAP-related jobs advertised on the Internet, which include several in the SAP development team
- Job descriptions from SAP business partners
- Job descriptions of positions with end users

Description of Jobs Carried Out in SAP Subsidiaries

Although the structure of jobs in SAP subsidiaries and SAP partners is changing and varies according to a company's history and work areas, certain key positions will be recognized, even if they have a "local" title.

Account Executive (Customer Support Manager)

Scope:

- Responsible for the measurement of customer satisfaction by being the principal point of contact throughout the time that the organization remains a customer.
- Develops ongoing business within the account by proactively anticipating customer needs and applying SAP solutions to meet these needs.
- Maintains multiple customer relationships simultaneously within one or several vertical market sectors.

Experience:

- Implementing enterprise-wide software solutions.
- Fundamental understanding of business issues within appropriate market sectors.
- Track record of empathizing with customer to achieve results and the management of long-term customer relationships.

Functional knowledge:

- Expert in relationship building.
- Proficiently applies a logical methodology to servicing a customer's requirements.
- Acts as a liaison between partners and SAP to ensure customer satisfaction.
- Monitors customer satisfaction regularly.

Product knowledge:

- A high-level understanding of the functionality of the product suite.
- An understanding of the integration and implementation issues involved.

Industry knowledge:

- An understanding of current and future business issues within one or more vertical markets.
- Credibility within the vertical market as an expert.

Business vertical or technological knowledge:

- A broad, high-level understanding of all applications in the current product suite.
- A high-level understanding of the business issues within the application areas.

Assignment management:

- Plans, schedules, and manages to achieve the measurement of customer satisfaction.
- Acts as a liaison internally to inform the appropriate bodies on the state of customer satisfaction within their accounts.
- Maintains and develops contacts with key influencers and decision-makers.

Leadership/teamwork:

- Assumes overall responsibility for customer.
- Acts as a role model and mentor.
- Influences the direction and effectiveness of the organization in achieving the highest levels of customer service.
- Conducts timely and effective administrative duties associated with a key role within the organization.
- Develops and maintains good working relationships within SAP and with partners.

Communication:

- Can communicate at all levels within a customer organization/SAP and with partners.
- Skilled at written and oral communication.
- Open, honest, and credible.

Training:

- Acts as an internal educator for business issues relating to customers and vertical markets.

Business development:

- Quickly establishes good relationships with customers, based on credibility.
- Identifies, qualifies, and develops opportunities for further business within account.

- Ensures that he or she knows, understands, and can actively promote new product developments.
- Maintains a complete and concise record of SAP and customer relationships.
- Understands and actively sells SAP UK and SAP AG Services, SAP Partner philosophy, and SAP Implementation strategy.

Alliance Partner Manager

Scope:

- Leads, develops, and manages partner relationships to ensure company and customer satisfaction and to generate revenue targets.

Experience:

- Building and developing client/partner relationships.
- Developing informal networks.
- Developing third-party relationships to achieve customer satisfaction and revenue targets.

Functional knowledge:

- Recognized as a central point of contact for issues relating to partner management.
- Assists in the implementation of "partner academy" initiative and ancillary partner training.
- Champions partners internally within the organizations, particularly with the vertical market teams.

Product knowledge:

- A high level of understanding of the functionality of the product suite.
- An understanding of the integration and implementation issues related to the product suite.

Industry knowledge:

- An understanding of current and future business issues within the IT market.

Business vertical or technological knowledge:

- A high-level understanding of all applications in the current product suite.
- A high-level understanding of business issues related to the application area.

Assignment management:

- Plans, schedules, and manages to achieve customer and partner satisfaction.
- Acts as internal liaison to champion appropriate partners.
- Maintains and develops contact with key influencers and decision-makers.

■ Maintains timely and critical partner information to position partners within SAP and customers' organizations.

Leadership/teamwork:

■ Assumes responsibility for the partners.

■ Acts as a role model and mentor.

■ Influences the climate of the organization in terms of new incentives relating to partner management.

■ Performs administrative duties associated with the role.

■ Develops and maintains good working relationships with appropriate internal agencies.

Communication:

■ Can communicate at all levels with a partner organization.

■ Skilled at written and oral communication.

■ Helps internal organization to be informed of developments with the partner community.

Training:

■ Acts as mentor.

Business development:

■ Positions SAP with the partner community to achieve maximum advantage.

■ Generates a positive image for the product suite.

■ Coordinates SAP's Sales and Marketing function, developing partner relationships in specific vertical account sections.

Business Consultant

Scope:

■ Presents a business-focused SAP solution to prospective customers by using in-depth knowledge of one or more vertical markets, and is instrumental within the industry team in facilitating the sale.

■ To be seen internally and externally as a vertical market center of exchange.

Experience:

■ Competent at providing an integrated system solution within a business context.

■ Experience in the ways of doing business within the appropriate vertical.

Functional knowledge:

■ Can proficiently demonstrate the SAP business solution to provide a formal response to the prospective customer's business needs.

■ Understands and contributes to relevant aspects of the sales cycle.

■ Understands customer motives and buying criteria.

Product knowledge:

- Sound working knowledge of one area of the product suite.
- A broad knowledge of all other areas.
- An in-depth understanding of implementation issues.

Industry knowledge:

- An in-depth understanding of all business aspects pertaining to a vertical market.
- The ability to apply this knowledge in other areas.
- To be seen as an industry "guru."
- Keeps abreast of competitor activity within vertical market.

Assignment management:

- As part of an industry team, employs flexible and adaptable strategies in providing business solutions.
- Understands the sales cycle as a broad framework within which to work.
- Works quickly to establish the customer's business needs.
- Can work on multiple assignments.

Leadership/teamwork:

- Acts as a role model and mentor.
- Influences other areas of the organization.
- Conducts administrative duties associated with a leadership role.
- Develops and maintains strong working relationships with the leadership team.
- Transfers business knowledge to others.

Communication:

- Effectively communicates with prospects at all levels, orally and in writing.
- Effectively communicates with team members and other units within SAP.
- Actively supports the maintenance or development of prospect/customer relationships.
- Provides feedback to other parts of the SAP organization.

Training:

- Acts as a mentor and coach for other employees.

Business development:

- Quickly establishes good relationships with prospects based on credibility.
- Takes a pivotal role in bringing a prospect to a close.
- Is viewed as a specialist by the customer within the appropriate market sector.

Consultant

Scope:

- Leads consulting assignments to support customers in the implementation of an SAP solution to satisfy a business need.

Experience:

- Evidence of having the ability to implement a standard application software-based, business-oriented solution within a project environment.

Functional knowledge:

- Can apply a logical methodology for the collection and analysis of business or technical issues.
- Leads or advises on the processes needed to implement solutions.
- Can gain customer's agreement on outcomes and deliver results.

Product knowledge:

- Requires in-depth knowledge of at least one area of the product suite.
- Has a broad knowledge of other areas.
- Understands the integration issues related to the product's implementation.
- Can align product's functionality with complex business needs.

Industry knowledge:

- Requires knowledge of one or more business sectors.
- Can align business issues within a sector to the product's functionality.

Business vertical or technological knowledge:

- Has an in-depth knowledge of one or more specific applications areas, or a broad knowledge of technology.

Assignment management:

- Leads, plans, schedules, and manages assignments, using established processes.
- Establishes requirements for assignments.
- Can work on multiple assignments.

Leadership/teamwork:

- Makes decisions with minimal direction.
- Acts as a mentor.
- Transfers industry product and technical knowledge to others.
- Develops a working relationship with multiple levels within SAP.

Communication:

- Effectively communicates with consulting team members and other units within SAP.
- Effectively communicates with customers at multiple levels.
- Supports the maintenance or development of customer relationships.
- Develops and assists in making customer presentations.

Training:

- Participates in the development and teaching of product-related training course.

Business development:

- Assists in scoping assignments.
- Identifies opportunities for additional business.
- Participates in the sale of consulting services to potential customers.

Industry Manager (Sales)

Scope:

- To achieve the sales and support revenue target for the industry sector.
- To achieve customer satisfaction and referenceability by working as a team player.

Experience:

- A track record of selling integrated software solutions.
- A broad knowledge of IT-related business issues within nominated industry sector.

Functional knowledge:

- A fundamental knowledge of the sales cycle.
- Understand buying motives at high levels within customer organization.

Product knowledge:

- Must have a broad, high-level overview and understanding of the business impact of the product's functionality.
- Understand related implementation issues.

Industry knowledge:

- An in-depth knowledge of business issues relating to one or more vertical markets.

Business vertical or technological knowledge:

- A broad, high-level overview of all applications within the knowledge product suite.

Assignment management:

- Leads, plans, schedules, and manages prospects and internal staff to convert prospects to customers.
- Can flexibly approach each customer's issues.

Leadership/teamwork:

- Sets the lead in getting maximum use from the team to obtain commitment to the plan and achieve results.
- Conducts administrative duties relating to role.

Communication:

- Develops and cultivates prospect relationships at all levels.
- Effectively communicates with prospects at all levels orally and in writing.
- Effectively communicates with team members and other units within SAP.
- Provides feedback to other parts of the SAP organization.

Training:

- Acts as a mentor and coach.

Business development:

- Quickly establishes good relationships with prospects based on personal credibility.
- Responsible for closing sales.

Instructor

Scope:

- Responsible for maintaining the quality of training systems and documentation and for giving courses in one or more application areas.

Experience:

- Consistent high performance as a dedicated software systems trainer.
- Training or implementing some or all aspects of the product suite.

Functional knowledge:

- Can proficiently train in one or more aspects of the product suite.
- Can develop course material to meet new and existing functionality.
- Can take a consulting role on certain product implementations.

Product knowledge:

- An in-depth knowledge of one of the product suites.
- A broad knowledge in other areas.
- Understands the integration issues related to product implementation.

Industry knowledge:

- A broad, high-level understanding of the business issues within the markets in which we operate.

Business vertical or technological knowledge:

- An in-depth knowledge of one or more specific applications areas, or a broad knowledge of technology.

Assignment management:

- Plans, schedules, and manages issues as they arrive, to achieve customer satisfaction.
- Can multitask.

Leadership/teamwork:

- Ensures that decisions are made by using the best information available to the team.
- Networks within the training team and with other areas of the organization.

Communication:

- Effectively communicates with customers, team members, and other areas of the organization.
- Has highly developed presentation skills.
- Supports the maintenance or development of customer relationships.
- Acts as a liaison with SAP AG trainers/course developers.

Training:

- Acts as a center of excellence for training issues.
- Delivers training courses to achieve customer satisfaction.
- High standard of training delivery based on own credibility.

Business development:

- Quickly establishes good rapport with customers.
- Instrumental in achieving add-on business by ensuring customer satisfaction.
- Understands the services of other SAP departments and actively sells them.
- Understands and actively sells the SAP Partner philosophy.
- Understands and actively sells the SAP Implementation approach.
- Sells training services.

Product Manager

Scope:

- Is seen as a product center of excellence.
- Is the single point of contact for all issues related to a specific area of the product suite.
- Leads multiple or complex assignments to support customers in the implementation of an SAP solution to satisfy a business need.

Experience:

- Extensive reputation for product knowledge.
- Has proven ability to implement standard application software based on business solutions within complex project environments.

Functional knowledge:

- Proficiently applies a logical methodology for the collection and analysis of issues related to the product suite.
- Leads or advises on the development of programs that implement solutions.
- Can gain others' agreement on outcomes and deliver results.

Product knowledge:

- Is recognized as a center of expertise for one area of the product suite.
- Has in-depth knowledge of other areas that directly affect product expertise.
- Has in-depth understanding of integration issues related to product implementation.
- Can align product's functionality with complex business needs.
- Can facilitate communication between business and technical experts.

Industry knowledge:

- Requires knowledge of one or more business sectors.
- Can align business issues within a sector to the product's functionality.

Business vertical or technological knowledge:

- Has an in-depth knowledge of one or more specific application areas, or a broad knowledge of more technical issues.

Assignment management:

- Leads, plans, schedules, and manages multiple or complex assignments, using established processes.
- Establishes requirements for assignments.
- Acts as a liaison internally to champion the product.

Leadership/teamwork:

- Acts as a role model and mentor.
- Influences the strategic direction of the group.
- Conducts administrative duties associated with a leadership role.
- Develops and maintains a strong working relationship with the leadership and development teams.

Communication:

- Develops and cultivates customer relationships at senior and executive levels.

- Effectively communicates with consulting team members and other units within SAP, and facilitates information flow from SAP AG.
- Supports the maintenance or development of customer relationships.
- Develops and assists in making customer presentations.

Training:

- Participates in the development and teaching of product-related training courses.

Business development:

- Assists in scoping assignments.
- Identifies opportunities for additional business.
- Participates in the sale of consulting services to potential customers.
- Acts as a liaison with research and development teams to ensure that they're aware of how the products could better suit the requirements of potential customers.

Remote Consultant

Scope:

- To provide first-line applications support to customers in specified application areas.

Experience:

- Evidence of being able to provide applications support to customers within a remote services environment.

Functional knowledge:

- Proficiently applies a logical methodology to the collection, analysis, and solution of customer problems and support issues.
- A fundamental commitment to customer satisfaction.

Product knowledge:

- Requires an in-depth knowledge of at least one area of the product suite.
- Has broad knowledge of other areas.
- Understands integration issues related to product implementation.

Industry knowledge:

- A broad, high-level understanding of the business issues within the markets in which we operate.

Business vertical or technological knowledge:

- An in-depth knowledge of one or more specific applications or of one or more technology (BASIS) areas.

Assignment management:

- Plans, schedules, and manages issues as they arrive, to achieve a satisfied customer.
- Can work on multiple issues.

Leadership/teamwork:

- Makes decisions with minimal direction.
- Networks within the Remote Consulting team and with other areas of the SAP organization.

Communication:

- Effectively communicates with customers, team members, and other areas of the SAP organization.
- Supports the maintenance or development of customer relationships.

Training:

- Acts as a coach to customers within a specialized area of expertise.
- Responsible for keeping their knowledge up-to-date and relevant.

Business development:

- Quickly establishes credibility with the customer.
- Instrumental in achieving add-on business by ensuring customer satisfaction.

Senior Consultant

Scope:

- Leads multiple or complex assignments to support customers in the implementation of an SAP solution to satisfy a business need.

Experience:

- Has proven ability to implement standard application software-based business solutions within complex project environments.
- Extensive reputation for product knowledge.

Functional knowledge:

- Proven ability to apply logical methodology for the collection and analysis of issues related to the product suite.
- Leads or advises on the processes needed to implement solutions.
- Ability to gain others' agreement on outcomes and deliver results.
- Leads a team to deliver results.

Product knowledge:

- Has an in-depth knowledge of multiple areas within the product suite.
- Understands in-depth the integration issues related to product implementation.
- Can align product's functionality with complex business needs.
- Can facilitate communication between business and technical experts.

Industry knowledge:

- Requires knowledge of one or more business sectors.
- Can align business issues within a sector to the product's functionality.

Business vertical or technological knowledge:

- Has an in-depth knowledge of one or more specific applications areas and a broad knowledge of more technical issues.

Assignment management:

- Leads, plans, schedules, and manages multiple or complex assignments by using established processes.
- Establishes requirements for assignments.

Leadership/teamwork:

- Acts as a role model and mentor.
- Influences the strategic direction of the group.
- Conducts administrative duties associated with a leadership role.
- Develops and maintains strong working relationships with the leadership and development teams.

Communication:

- Develops and cultivates customer relationships at senior and executive levels.
- Effectively communicates with consulting team members and other units within SAP.
- Supports the maintenance or development of customer relationships.
- Develops and assists in making customer presentations.

Training:

- Participates in the development and teaching of product-related training courses.

Business development:

- Assists in scoping assignments.
- Identifies opportunities for additional business.
- Participates in the sale of consulting services to potential customers.

Senior Remote Consultant

Scope:

- To provide first-line applications support to customers in specified application areas.

Experience:

- Evidence of having the ability to provide applications support to customers within a remote services environment.

Functional knowledge:

- Proficiently applies a logical methodology to the collection, analysis, and solution of customer problems and support issues.
- A fundamental commitment to customer satisfaction.

Product knowledge:

- Is an expert in one area of the product suite to the highest level.
- Has a broad knowledge in other areas.
- Understands integration issues related to product implementation.

Industry knowledge:

- Has a broad, high-level understanding of the business issues within the markets in which we operate.

Business vertical or technological knowledge:

- Has an in-depth knowledge of one or more specific applications or of one or more technology (BASIS) areas.

Assignment management:

- Plans, schedules, and manages issues as they arrive, to achieve a satisfied customer.
- Can work on multiple issues.

Leadership/teamwork:

- Ensures that decisions are made by using the best information available to the team.
- Networks within the remote consulting team and with other areas of the SAP organization.

Communication:

- Effectively communicates with customers, team members, and other areas of the SAP organization.
- Supports the maintenance or development of customer relationships.

Training:

- Coaches customers within a specialized area of expertise.
- Responsible for keeping knowledge up-to-date and relevant.
- Responsible for mentoring and nurturing new staff.

Business development:

- Quickly establishes credibility with the customer.
- Instrumental in achieving add-on business by ensuring customer satisfaction.

Sample SAP-Related Job Descriptions Advertised on the Internet

Advertisements for jobs tend to carry titles designed to attract suitable applicants. The title might not be the most apt name for what the position entails, however.

SAP Development Team

A team engaged in developing standard business process software might be part of the SAP corporation, or it might be located in one of the partner organizations that can provide particular industrial or commercial expertise. In either case, the software will have to receive SAP Certification after formal testing before it can be released for use in an SAP R/3 implementation. Both development team types will therefore be working toward the same standards.

SAP R/3 Installation Tools Developer   The software logistics department develops tools and technologies for managing the SAP R/3 system internally (source code control and transport systems) and implementing the system at the customer site (installation, upgrade).

The R3INST tool is now being used to support the installation of distributed SAP R/3 system configurations on eight different UNIX platforms with four different relational database systems and on Windows NT with three different relational database systems.

Our small development team is seeking a new member, whose main area of responsibility will be maintaining and enhancing the R3INST tool.

Our requirements:

- In-depth technical knowledge of different UNIX systems (BSD and System V).
- Hands-on programming experience in C.
- Knowledge of database systems would be an asset.
- Good command of English.
- Can work in a team, communications skills.
- Commitment and flexibility.

Senior SAP R/3 Software Developer to Enhance the Error Tolerance of SAP's R/3 BASIS Software

Your duties will include:

- Highly responsible tasks in the design and implementation of SAP R/3 BASIS software.
- Analyzing the error-tolerance of SAP R/3 BASIS software and developing a concept to increase SAP R/3 System availability.

You will have:

- Experience in designing complex distributed software applications in C.
- Excellent knowledge of the UNIX environment.
- Excellent knowledge of TCP/IP-based network programming.
- A university degree.
- At least three years of relevant work experience.
- Experience in the development of error-tolerant software would be an advantage.
- Preferably some knowledge of current databases (such as Oracle, Informix, Microsoft SQL Server).
- A good knowledge of English.

SAP R/3 Software Developer

Your duties will include:

- Cooperation in the design and implementation of SAP R/3 BASIS software.
- Providing support in analyzing the error tolerance of SAP R/3 BASIS software and developing a concept to increase SAP R/3 System availability.

You will have:

- Experience in designing complex distributed software applications in C.
- Excellent knowledge of TCP/IP-based network programming.
- A university degree.
- Experience in the development of error-tolerant software would be an advantage.
- Knowledge of current databases (such as Oracle, Informix, Microsoft SQL Server) would be an advantage.
- A good knowledge of English.

ISS Internal Service Systems   Your duties will include developing in the internal information systems area.

We expect:

- Knowledge of Windows, Windows NT, Windows 95.
- General experience with PCs.
- Knowledge of the programming languages C, C++, and particularly of Visual Basic.

- Experience in working in Windows 6/32-bit environments as well as in OLE 2 Automation and OCX.
- General understanding of relational databases.
- Flexibility, motivation, and the ability to cope with stress.
- Creativity.
- A sound knowledge of written and spoken English.
- Communications and teamwork skills.

We offer:

- A challenging, rewarding position in a leading-edge company at a time of global expansion.
- A pleasant working environment in a young team.
- Personal and professional development in our ongoing internal training program.
- An excellent compensation package.

Software Developers: HR-Human Resource Systems, International Developments   Our software developers are based at our Development Center in Walldorf, near Heidelberg, Germany. They work with our own development tools, such as ABAP/4 (fourth-generation programming language), Active Data Dictionary, Screen Painter, and Dialog Manager.

Your tasks:

- As a member of an international team, you will develop and enhance the national versions of our HR products for the European market.
- Coordinating the international functionality of our HR module and communicating with our international subsidiaries and customers is an important aspect of the work.

We require:

- A first-class university degree, preferably in computer sciences or business studies/economics with computing.
- Excellent programming skills.
- Knowledge of German isn't essential; however, fluent English is essential. Knowledge of other languages would be an advantage.
- A strong interest in the practical application of business concepts.
- Capability for interdisciplinary and intercultural work and above-average motivation and commitment.
- Willingness to work abroad.

We offer:

- Ongoing challenges in one of the world's leading technology enterprises that is continuously expanding.
- Stimulating working atmosphere in a young team.

- A program of continuous personal development and subject-related training.
- Generous benefits.

Software Developers: HR-Human Resource Systems, Personnel Administration and Payroll   Our software developers are based at our Development Center in Walldorf, near Heidelberg, Germany. They work with our own development tools, such as ABAP/4 (fourth-generation programming language), Active Data Dictionary, Screen Painter, and Dialog Manager.

Your responsibilities:

- You will work in an international team on important, challenging tasks in the areas of Personnel Administration and Payroll.
- You and your colleagues will create HR-oriented concepts in coordination with our international subsidiaries and customers and implement these with state-of-the-art software technology.

We expect:

- An excellent university or higher college degree, preferably in the areas of information management, economic science, mathematics, or physics.
- Very good programming knowledge.
- Fluent English knowledge; other languages are advantageous.
- A keen interest in the productive implementation of business concepts.
- The ability to work in an interdisciplinary and multicultural team and to offer above-average commitment.

We offer:

- Ongoing challenges in one of the world's leading technology enterprises that is continuously expanding.
- Stimulating working atmosphere in a young team.
- A program of continuous personal development and subject-related training.
- Generous benefits.

Product Developers: Patient Management/Accounting (IS-H) Module   The IS-H module has been on the market for two years and constitutes the core of our SAP R/3 Hospital Information System, which has been installed at more than 80 hospitals in Germany, Austria, and the Netherlands.

Our current development focus is on meeting and keeping up-to-date with our German customers' requirements, in accordance with German healthcare legislation, and on the continuing internationalization of this product.

We require:

- A good university degree in medicine/business with computing, computer science, mathematics, business/economics, or natural sciences.

- A keen interest in translating hospital-specific requirements into an IT solution.
- Programming skills, experience in PC applications.
- A sound knowledge of English and German.
- Basic professional experience in a similar area, if possible.
- The successful candidate will be able to work in a team and in a variety of disciplines, above-average commitment and motivation, excellent communications skills, and a strong commitment to customer satisfaction.

We offer:

- Ongoing challenges in one of the world's leading technology enterprises that is continuously expanding.
- Stimulating working atmosphere as part of a young team.
- A program of continuous personal development and subject-related training.
- A broad range of benefits.

Software Developer: SAP R/3 IS-Oil

Job description:

- Development of business application software using the SAP Development Workbench for the SAP R/3 IS-Oil Industry Solution in cooperation with international oil companies.
- Performance of tasks in the following software development phases: concept, design, implementation, quality assurance, and software maintenance.
- Use of methods for object-oriented analysis of business processes in the oil industry supply chain.
- Implementation of functions in SAP R/2 technology.
- Use of SAP tools and methods for software quality assurance.

Requirements:

- Training/Education: Information technology with business management, preferably a university or higher technical college degree.
- Practical experience: 4GL programming, databases, PC software products, teamwork.
- Additional knowledge: English, experience in customer relations.
- Personal qualities: Reliable, can work under pressure, analytical approach.

Development of SAP R/3 IS-Oil

Your duties will include:

- Handling of software logistics for the decentralized IS-Oil development.
- Coordination of the operation of SAP R/3 development systems with the computer center and the database group.
- Installation of SAP R/3 maintenance levels in IS-Oil development.
- Managing projects for software assembly and delivery.

- Coordination of cooperation with the Software Factory.
- Technical creation of maintenance levels, advance corrections, and releases.
- Take on the remote support and help desk of customers who are installing IS-Oil or maintenance levels.

We expect:

- Database administration, preferably ORACLE, system administration in UNIX environments, C programming.
- Ideally, SAP R/3 system administration, service experience, problem analysis.
- English language ability.
- Experience in customer relations.

Software Developer: SAP R/2 IS-Oil

Job description:

- Development and maintenance of business application software for the SAP R/2 IS-Oil Industry Solution in cooperation with international oil companies.
- Performance of activities in the following software development phases: concept, design, implementation, quality assurance, and software maintenance.
- Design of software functions for the supply chain.
- Implementation of functions in SAP R/2 technology.
- Use of SAP tools and methods for software quality assurance.

Requirements:

- Training: Information technology with business management, preferably a university or higher technical college degree.
- Practical experience: Preferably, experience with SAP R/2 BASIS and RM or RV.
- Additional knowledge: English and customer relations.
- Personal qualities: Reliable, can work under pressure, analytical approach. Willingness to work in a mainframe environment.

Development: SAP R/2 IS-Oil

Your duties will include:

- Handling software logistics for the decentralized IS-Oil development.
- Coordination of the operation of SAP R/2 development systems with the computer center and the database group.
- Installation of SAP R/2 maintenance levels in IS-Oil development.
- Managing projects for software assembly and delivery.
- Coordinating cooperation with SAP R/2 Services.
- Technical creation of maintenance levels, advance corrections, and releases.

■ Taking on the remote support and help desk of customers installing IS-*Oil* or maintenance levels.

We expect:

■ IBM 370 architecture, MVS, CICS, and VSAM in IBM 370 Assembler *programming.*

■ Ideally, SAP R/2 system administration, service experience, *problem* analysis.

■ English language ability.

■ Experience in customer relations.

SAP R/3 Retail   SAP R/3 Retail is an Industry Solution within SAP R/3, tailored to the requirements of the retail sector. The project offers a number of sections, such as application development, documentation, sales, consultancy, and implementation. SAP R/3 Retail has met with tremendous response from the market, because it offers a *full-fledged* business solution for all the different retail formats and gives retailers unprecedented global networking ability supported by a powerful central information system. Each installation requires innovative, proactive thinking and provides enormous scope for direct personal involvement.

Duties Profile 1   Senior professionals with specific skills in the development of retail systems and in other project areas to actively support our development team. Familiarity with topics such as ECR, EDI, EPOS, store management, merchandise planning, and retail information systems. Successful candidates will have proven track records as consultants to the major players in the retail sector and will be able to communicate at the senior management and departmental management level.

■ High degree of flexibility

■ Profound understanding of international relations

■ Willingness to travel

■ Knowledge of foreign languages

Duties Profile 2   Top retail graduates from international business schools and universities. Familiarity with topics such as ECR, EDI, EPOS, store management, merchandise planning, and retail information systems. Detailed knowledge in specific areas of the retail trade would be welcome.

■ High degree of flexibility

■ Profound understanding of international relations

■ Willingness to travel

■ Knowledge of foreign languages

Documentation Developer

Your responsibilities:

■ Create excellent documentation on the BASIS system software of SAP's R/3 client/server system, in written and multimedia form.

Priorities:

- User-friendly documentation for end users.
- Real-world documentation of system administration and system programming tasks.

Our requirements:

- Must be able to present complex information clearly and concisely.
- Must be a self-starter with a commitment to quality and innovation in the presentation of information.

The following qualifications are helpful:

- Experience in documentation development in technical areas such as programming and system or database management.
- Experience or education in programming, information management, or management; and operation of modern information systems.
- Experience with multimedia.
- Experience with authoring tools.

Documentation Developer: Banking Sector

Your duties will include:

- You will create user documentation for application software in the banking sector in cooperation with the development team.
- You will participate in creating a process-oriented online help system.

We expect:

- Practical experience in creating documentation or in basic programming, as well as knowledge of business administration.
- A basic knowledge of data processing.
- Knowledge of the banking sector; previous bank employment experience is desirable.
- Ability to turn complicated information into clear and understandable information for the end user.
- Experience in WinWord, Excel, and PowerPoint.
- Good written and spoken English.

Logo Partners

The term *logo partner* tends to be used for associated companies that have been given permission to use their SAP connection as a selling point and therefore as a reference when recruiting.

SAP Consultant with "Big Six" Management Consultancy Position is based in the United States, but consultants must be prepared to travel extensively.

Experience:

- Candidates should have a minimum of two years of experience in implementing SAP systems; SAP R/3 experience is highly desirable.

Experience should include one or more of the following areas:

- Financial applications
- Distribution and sales order management
- Manufacturing

Candidates should have in their area of proficiency:

- A good understanding of business processes
- Experience in configuring SAP to meet corporate needs
- A good understanding of the transactions and tables
- A sound working knowledge of issues regarding SAP module integration and interfacing with other systems

It's advantageous if:

- You're experienced in a consulting role within a project environment
- You have a good background in technology

SAP training:

- A minimum of four SAP courses should have been taken.

Personal attributes:

- Highly intelligent—in the top 10 percent of the population. You should have good analytical skills, be able to think broadly and conceptually but also handle detail well, and understand practical considerations.
- Good interpersonal skills—can work well with others, be empathetic, and build good relationships.
- A questioning mind, with the desire to do things better.
- Enthusiasm and ability to plan and control actions to achieve results, meet deadlines, and provide direction.
- The ability to communicate ideas and facts clearly and succinctly in English.

Jobs with SAP Business Partners

The following is a job with consultancy partners.

SAP R/3 Business Consultant

Duties and responsibilities:

- A presales role; works closely with the SAP R/3 sales team promoting our approach to implementation with a strong emphasis on implementation analysis. Must be able to present and demonstrate the specific implementation philosophy as well as SAP R/3 functionality. You would then be responsible for conducting the implementation analysis—evaluating the technical configuration aspects and the economics of the SAP R/3 project.

Ideal experience:

- Worked in pre/post-sales support.
- Implemented several large IT projects in commercial organizations.
- Worked in consulting or with a specialist software house.
- Ideally, have trained in SAP R/3, have SAP R/2 experience, or have comparable product experience.
- Have extensive knowledge of financial accounting systems, logistics/materials management, or manufacturing.
- The overall experience of large commercial implementations would be expected to extend over five years.

Personal attributes:

- Can present an experienced professional image to prospects and customers.
- Can discuss intelligently and provide consulting on all aspects of corporate business with senior managers in large companies.
- Highly developed presentation skills, and experience in using them in a presales environment.
- Self-starter.

Implementation Partner

The following are jobs with an implementation partner.

Application Engineers

Duties and responsibilities:

- Use the SAP R/3 configuration tools to meet the requirements as defined and interpreted by the SAP R/3 implementation analysis, and follow through to provide remote and on-site support to completed implementations.

Experience required in:

- Business analysis in an IT environment
- Implementing large projects in commercial organizations, preferably in finance, materials management, sales and distribution, or production

- Working either in an IT supplier/software house environment, or in a large commercial organization's IT department
- Overall experience in analyzing requirements and implementing IT-based business solutions in large commercial organizations should extend over 10 years

Personal attributes:

- The personality type required can interface at senior levels in the organization and be a dynamic self-starter.

Module Configurers for International Projects

Duties and responsibilities:

- Working closely with clients to assess their requirements in finance, materials management, sales and distribution, production planning, and human resources.

Requirements:

- Minimum one year's experience with SAP.
- Good degree.
- Excellent interpersonal and presentation skills.

Descriptions of Jobs with End Users

The following is a job with an end user.

Commercial Analyst

Position not requiring SAP experience. Reports to MIS manager.

Responsible for:

- All aspects of commercial systems development based on SAP software modules.

Specific responsibilities:

- Acquire SAP skills by attending formal courses and by working with a team of SAP consultants.
- Communicate with all levels of management and staff.
- Establish and manage project plans and budgets.
- Define the scope and requirements of new developments.
- Carry out detailed system design and write specifications.
- Configure SAP and document the configuration.
- Train users at all levels.
- Test new developments.
- Plan and implement the cutover to new systems.

Experience:

- Sound experience in commercial business systems in appropriate areas (logistics, sales, and marketing).
- IT background.

Key skills/attributes:

- Proactive, self-motivated with the ability to motivate others.
- Outgoing personality with well-developed communications skills.
- Potential to assume a management role as the MIS department expands.

Financial Analyst

Position not requiring SAP experience. Reports to European MIS manager.

Responsible for:

- All aspects of financial systems development based on SAP software modules.

Specific responsibilities:

- Acquire SAP skills by attending formal courses and by working with a team of SAP consultants.
- Communicate with all levels of management and staff.
- Establish and manage project plans and budgets.
- Define the scope and requirements of new developments.
- Carry out detailed system design and write specifications.
- Configure SAP and document the configuration.
- Train users at all levels.
- Test new developments.
- Plan and implement the cutover to new systems.

Experience:

- Sound experience with financial business systems in appropriate areas.
- IT background.

Key skills/attributes:

- Proactive and self-motivated, with the ability to motivate others.
- Outgoing personality with well-developed communications skills.
- Potential to assume a management role as the MIS department expands.

Systems Analyst

This position does not require SAP experience.

The opportunity:

- The position offers the satisfaction of solving problems, taking projects from early investigation of user needs right through to implementation. It also offers the opportunity to develop new skills working with modern IT tools. Systems analysts can readily transfer to other business functions for career development.

Responsibilities:

- Develop personal SAP knowledge and skills through formal courses and informal induction and training.
- Help user departments to assess business needs.
- Develop SAP-based business systems designs for new applications, and act as a liaison to user departments and IT functions throughout their implementation.
- Conduct feasibility studies into new applications.
- Provide support and training to users of existing SAP and legacy systems. Resolve problems and develop systems enhancements.

Background required:

- A wide variety of backgrounds can provide the business experience required, including finance, manufacturing, and marketing.

Attributes required:

- An analytical approach to problem-solving, coupled with the ability to conceptualize systems.
- The ability to relate to user needs and problems.
- Awareness of business issues.

Project Leader

This position does not require previous SAP experience.

The opportunity:

- The position offers the opportunity to develop systems awareness, as well as team-working, leadership, and project-management skills. Project leaders can subsequently pursue careers in information systems or return to mainstream positions within their functional area.

Responsibilities:

- Analyze business processes and procedures with a view to computerizing them.
- Develop personal SAP knowledge and skills through formal courses and informal induction and training.

- Provide a link between user and IT personnel, translating user requirements into logical, well-defined steps.
- Develop, implement, and test systems to meet changing business requirements.

Background required:

- It's likely, but not absolutely required, that project leaders will be recruited internally, and will have a good understanding of the user department to which the project pertains.

Attributes required:

- An analytical approach to problem solving, coupled with the ability to conceptualize systems.
- The ability to apply patience and logical thought to complex problems.
- Awareness of business issues concerning the specific area of business to which the project pertains.

SAP Business Analyst

Responsibilities:

- Support an international SAP R/3 implementation and rollout.
- Provide business analysis consulting.
- Identify and champion appropriate use of SAP R/3 to meet changing business requirements.
- Provide consulting on SAP functionality and configuration.
- Identify, specify, and design interface solutions between SAP R/3 and legacy systems, providing business analysis in this area.
- Specify and apply suitable testing and quality monitoring procedures, and assume responsibility for the quality of developed solutions.
- Maintain quality and efficiency by applying prescribed policies and standards.

Education and experience required:

- Degree level or equivalent in computer science or a business systems-related subject.
- At least three years' experience in systems development, using structured methods and CASE tools.
- At least two years' systems experience in a supply-chain or manufacturing environment.
- At least two years' hands-on experience with SAP (R/3 or R/2).

Other requirements:

- Good communications and interpersonal skills.
- Good organizational skills, with the determination and dedication to meet objectives and get the job done.
- A customer-focused, service attitude.

SAP Analyst

Prime responsibilities:

- Analyze business requirements for an Information System, and produce an agreed-on and documented set of user requirements from it.

- Determine SAP's fitness level with the preceding needs, configure the SAP system to fulfill them, and make alternative recommendations where appropriate.

- Produce system documentation, and assist in the production of user documentation.

- Provide training and support for users of the system, and for other SAP-based systems.

Requirements:

- Educated to degree level or equivalent.

- A minimum of two years' experience in an IT environment.

- Working knowledge of SAP.

- Good interpersonal and communications skills, preferably gained within an IT context and involving contact with all personnel levels.

- An appreciation of the relevant business processes; experience in them would be an advantage.

MIS Manager

Reports to managing director.

Responsible for:

- Overall UK and European IT strategy and budgets. All accounting and logistics systems are to be upgraded with SAP R/3. Sales force automation is to be undertaken, and Windows technology is to be introduced.

Specific responsibilities:

- Vendor negotiations, resource allocation, project prioritization, performance and security issues, *service level agreements* (SLAs), and the corporate interface.

Experience:

- Appropriate management experience, preferably involving an SAP project.

Key skills/attributes:

- Financial, budgetary, and management skills, and ability to communicate plans and objectives at board level.

Example Request for Quotation of SAP Services

In this appendix

Structure of Request for Quotation

DREAMCAR OF SOUTH AFRICA
REQUEST FOR QUOTATION
FOR THE PROVISION OF A
COMPUTING INFRASTRUCTURE TO SUPPORT SAP R/3

This Request for Quotation (RFQ) is structured in three parts.

Part A - The Quotation Process

The introduction and purpose of this document, confidentiality, and the offer conditions

The selection process including the quotation return date, the contact persons, and the selection criteria

An introduction to the company, including an overview of the current technology

The scope of this RFQ

An outline of the required structure and format of your offer response

Part B - The Quotation Contents

Detail of the required structure and format of your offer response (that is, the questions that you, the supplier, are requested to answer)

Part C - Technical Requirement Specifications

An introduction into the technical requirements

Key users and business volumes

Benchmarking procedures and acceptance tests

All supplier response documentation packs must be compiled in the required format and sequence for ease of reference and analysis

Part A - The Quotation Process

Introduction - Purpose of Document

100   This document is a formal Request for Quotation (RFQ) for the supply and installation of a new computer (server) environment to support the SAP R/3 package at Dreamcar of South Africa (DCSA).

101   This RFQ describes the system for which hardware, system software, and other services are required and sets out the details to be included in your quotation. The technical requirements and reply format of this RFQ are not open to negotiations, but the final extent and content of the contractual arrangements between the selected supplier and DCSA will be negotiated.

Confidentiality

102   This RFQ, its technical requirements, and any related documents, information, and discussions are to remain strictly confidential and must not be communicated to anyone not directly involved in the preparation of your quotation.

103   No information may be provided to any third party or publicized unless specifically authorized by DCSA.

Conditions of Request for Quotation

104   In issuing the RFQ, there is no implied obligation on DCSA to procure any of the systems being proposed.

105   Any statement made by a supplier in its quotation concerning equipment, software, performance, and costs will be considered to form part of any contract that may be entered into in the event that DCSA enters into such contract with such supplier.

106   Suppliers should respond on the basis of being appointed to design, purchase, deliver, implement, and commission the specified configuration. Any limitations of responsibility that suppliers want to negotiate should be clearly stated.

107   Suppliers should respond on the basis that this will be a fixed-price contract. Prices should be given for all the hardware, software, consultancy, ancillary items, and continuing support necessary to meet DCSA requirements. Suppliers should state the length of time for which the prices quoted will remain valid.

108   This RFQ is issued on the understanding that suppliers will not levy a charge for the quotation preparation, or for arranging and conducting reference site visits and benchmark demonstrations and other related activities.

109   No additional charges or levies will be entertained unless by prior negotiation and written authorization from DCSA.

110   Suppliers must be prepared to:

- Answer any questions relating to their quotation and provide additional information as requested
- Make a formal presentation of their quotation
- Give a benchmark demonstration of their proposed solution
- Nominate relevant reference sites for DCSA staff to contact or to visit

111   The issues relating to a breach of the contractual obligations on the part of the supplier will be discussed, negotiated, and finalized at the time DCSA enters into an agreement with the preferred supplier. These issues will cover the following:

- Technical faults in the delivered system
- Inability to meet preagreed deadlines

- Inability to rectify system hardware and software errors
- The supplier will be appointed on DCSA's standard terms and conditions applicable to the goods and services purchased and/or manufactured and installed
- A performance guarantee equal to the contract sum will be required

112   Should the supplier not conform to these requests, Dreamcar of South Africa will not accept the participation of your company in the quoting process.

Quotation Return Date

200   Three copies of your quotation should be delivered by hand or by courier to DCSA by not later than 10 a.m. on _____ 1999. Your quotation will not be assessed if it is delivered after this date and time.

The copies of the quotation must be addressed to:

Mr. John Wilkinson
Purchasing Officer
Purchasing Department
Dreamcar of South Africa
Golden Road
Johannesburg

Please note that telefaxed documentations are not accepted.

Contact Persons

201   Any technical queries relating to this RFQ should be addressed to any of the following DCSA officials.

Name	Telephone Number	Telefax Number
Peter Mall	011 112-5558	011 134-5421
Gavin Rink	011 112-4728	011 345-5421

202   Any commercial queries relating to this RFQ should be addressed to any of the following DCSA officials.

Name	Telephone Number	Telefax Number
Mike Brent	011 456-5036	011 345-5521

Selection Criteria

203   The following criteria will be used to evaluate a supplier's response and it is advisable that these issues receive due attention during the process of quotation preparation. These criteria, if specifically addressed by a supplier, should appear in the relevant sections of the quotation format in Part B:

- The closeness of fit of the proposed solution to the technical specification
- The reliability and performance of the hardware and software as demonstrated by a proven track record at other customer sites
- The field upgradability and scalability of proposed hardware (including CPU, disk storage, memory)
- The experience, track record, and organizational characteristics of the supplier's own organization
- The support capability of the supplier's organization (including, for example, installation assistance, technical support, user training, and continuing hardware and software maintenance)
- The cost of equipment, implementation, installation, and continuing support
- The time scales required for the complete installation
- The financial stability of the supplier
- Level of confidence in the supplier's quotation (e.g., depth of understanding shown, quality of staff, and abilities)
- Strategic positioning and strength of the supplier in the server/mid-range computing market
- Successfully completed site(s)

Business and Information Technology Overview

Company Background

300   Dreamcar of South Africa, a wholly owned subsidiary of Dreamcar AG, is predominantly a motor vehicle manufacturer, producing some 70,000 passenger and light commercial vehicles for the local market.

301   It is managed by an executive committee consisting of six directors and a chairman of the board. Reporting to them is a team of approximately 100 managers. The company employs about 6,600 people in one main production plant in Johannesburg and a number of supporting plants in the Johannesburg and Johannesburg districts. There is also a Parts and Accessories warehouse located in Germiston.

302   Dreamcar of South Africa supports approximately 200 franchise dealerships throughout South Africa, Botswana, Swaziland, and Namibia. This support structure comprises regional offices in Johannesburg, Cape Town, Durban, and Bloemfontein.

303   Dreamcar of South Africa intends to replace its predominantly legacy systems as part of its IT modernization strategy. The international VW-Group is currently considering the adoption of SAP as the preferred application systems package with a view to standardizing the process throughout all subsidiaries.

304   Thus, in line with VW international policy, DCSA is compelled to adopt SAP R/3 for the administrative sector and will therefore implement the Finance, Human Resources, and

Purchasing (Non-Production) in the immediate future. In the medium- to long-term, the scope of the project will extend to Sales and Distribution, Materials Management, and Production Planning.

Technical Overview

305   Dreamcar of South Africa is currently running its systems on a combination of processing platforms:

- IBM 3090 running MVS
- HITACHI 7/90 running VM
- IBM RS/6000's running AIX v4—Catia and Racking Store
- PCs (386-Pentium) running SCO UNIX—Racking Store, Vehicle Tracking
- PCs (286-386) running DOS—Companywide
- PCs (486-Pentium) running DOS and Windows 3.11—Companywide
- File servers running Novell—Companywide

306   DCSA have recognized that there are significant opportunities to reduce the technical complexity of the current technology architecture. Most of the platforms are located in Johannesburg, with a few file servers and PCs distributed nationwide. All of the technical support staff is located in Johannesburg. DCSA relies mainly on in-house support structures.

307   The Local Area Network (LAN) comprises a fiber-optic backbone, connecting a variation of thick, UTP, and predominantly thin cable. We run at 10 Mbps throughout the LAN and will soon be upgrading the backbone to 100 Mbps. We use the IPX/SPX and TCP/IP protocols, with the intention of using only TCP/IP in the future. Currently we are using Novell file servers and these will be replaced with Windows NT. This project will begin in the next few months.

RFQ Scope

401   The scope of this RFQ covers the detailed technical design, a proven benchmark test from your Competency Center, and the delivery and installation of the processing platforms, complete with associated software and network connections that will support the SAP R/3 application system implementation. This project will be completed when the processing platforms have been successfully commissioned, linked to the network, and the DCSA staff has been trained to a competent level. In delivering this package, you should take into account the following major assumptions:

- SAP R/3 is the application package of choice
- Oracle or DB2 is the relational database management system
- Both the Data Center and the Disaster Recovery site will be situated at Dreamcar of South Africa's Main Plant in Johannesburg
- UNIX or Windows NT is the operating system

- Standard network protocol is TCP/IP
- The processing platform and any associated software must successfully integrate to the current LAN
- The technical configuration must be demonstrated and support the performance requirements
- Conform to the high-level design, which is defined in detail in Part C

402   The installation of all of the users' PCs, together with the SAP "Presentation Layer," will be the responsibility of the supplier. DCSA will be responsible for the procurement of the PCs and will ensure that all software will be preloaded.

Form of Response

500   A supplier who intends to prepare and submit a quotation in terms of this RFQ is required to first complete and return to DCSA the Intention to Quote Form no later than one week before the due date of the RFQ. This form, duly completed and signed, may be forwarded by hand or fax or prepaid mail to the street, fax, or mail addresses furnished on the form. The onus is on the sender to ensure that this Intention to Quote Form is duly received by DCSA. Noncompliance with this requirement will lead to the exclusion by DCSA of a quotation submitted by such supplier.

501   The supplier should then respond to the RFQ in the following structure and format as more fully outlined under Part B:

General

Section 1 - Summary of Quotation
Section 2 - Supplier Profile

Hardware & System Infrastructure

Section 3 - Hardware
Section 4 - System Software

Maintenance and Support

Section 5 - Hardware Warranty, Maintenance and Support
Section 6 - Software Maintenance and Support

Implementation

Section 7 - Implementation Plans

Finance

Section 8 - Summary of Costs

502   Appendixes to be provided by a supplier include:

Appendix I   Quotation Overview
Appendix II   Supplier's Profile

Appendix III	Hardware Quotation
Appendix IV	Sizing Rationale
Appendix V	Hardware and Software Maintenance Contracts
Appendix VI	Implementation Plan
Appendix VII	Curricula Vitae of Team Members
Appendix VIII	Supplier's Annual Report
Appendix IX	Summary of Costs
Appendix X	Details of partnerships or associations formed for the purposes of this RFQ

503   Part B of this RFQ describes the structure, format, and content of the Suppliers quotation, using the structure described as "Form of Response." More-detailed information will be referenced in Part C of this document. Each question posed in the RFQ should be answered in full—an incomplete response to any question will imply a negative answer from the supplier.

Part B - Quotation Contents

Section 1 - Summary of Quotation

Please provide as part of Appendix I a summary of your quotation, including:

101   A high-level diagram and description of your proposed solution.

102   A high-level implementation plan.

103   The main advantages and special features of your proposed solution.

104   A summary of the costs in the following format, including any assumptions on exchange rates:

CAPITAL COSTS

Hardware	xxx xxx.xx
Software	xxx xxx.xx
Implementation	xxx xxx.xx
Training	xxx xxx.xx
Total (Capital)	xxx xxx.xx

CONTINUING COSTS

Software	xxx xxx.xx
License Fees	xxx xxx.xx
Support	xxx xxx.xx
Total (Continuing)	xxx xxx.xx

105   A brief statement of your capabilities and the main reasons why you believe that DCSA should accept your quotation.

106   A statement accepting the terms and conditions detailed in this Request for Quotation.

Section 2 - Supplier Profile

Organization RFQ Example:Supplier Profile:Organization

Please provide as part of Appendix II the following information.

201   Background information on your organization:

- Your company's legal status, the name of the holding company (if a subsidiary), international offices, alliances
- The date your company or office was established in South Africa
- The number and locations of your sites/offices
- The total number of staff employed worldwide by your company currently and for the last two years
- A copy of your latest annual report (this to be included as Appendix VIII)

202   What are the main business activities of your company? Please provide a breakdown of the extent of revenue from each of these activities.

203   Please give an indication of your company's likely future growth and business direction.

204   Please give the total number of staff employed currently and for each of the last two years, in South Africa, and neighboring countries, stating for each location:

- Total number of staff
- Sales staff
- Administration staff
- Development staff
- Implementation staff
- Support staff for the proposed software and hardware
- Management staff
- Other (please specify)

205   Please explain the business and legal relationships between all the suppliers in your quotation (e.g., between yourselves and any subcontractors).

206   Please provide details of any past and pending legal actions or claims against your company.

Experience

207   Please outline your company's experience in:

■ Proposed hardware and operating system software

■ Target application environment (SAP R/3)

208   What are the total number of staff members currently working on the technical configuration and what are their roles (technical, support)?

209   What is the average length of experience of the installation and support staff on the proposed technical configuration?

Reference Sites

210   Please provide details of appropriate reference sites for the proposed system (in South Africa and abroad). For each, please detail:

■ The name, address, and telephone number of the company

■ The name and title of a contact

■ The scope and length of involvement with the reference site

Section 3 - Hardware

Hardware Components

300   In Appendix III, please provide:

■ A detailed design of the proposed hardware configuration

■ A detailed list of all system components including:

Memory

Storage devices

Workstations

Printers

■ For each component, please specify:

Original manufacturer and model number

Rated speeds, capacity, and modes of operation

Number of components proposed

Lead-time for delivery

Cost of the component

Any plans to extend the range of components with target availability dates

Warranty periods (where applicable)

■ Details on any limitations on the hardware used (e.g., connectivity protocols, maximum number of lines, maximum number and types of workstations)

Environment Requirements

301   Also include in Appendix III full details of the recommended environmental conditions for the hardware, to include:

- Air conditioning
- Floor space requirements
- Cabling requirements
- Main stabilizers
- Ancillary equipment

Hardware Sizing

302   Please detail in Appendix IV the rationale used for your hardware sizing exercise.

Upgradability

303   Please supply details of the hardware upgrade path for the proposed configuration.

Back-Up Facilities

304   Describe any back-up facilities available in the event of a disaster at the primary site including:

- Availability of back-up equipment
- Availability of alternative sites
- Details of any disaster recovery plans available with yourselves, the supplier, or any third party
- Costs for the recovery services

Fault Tolerance and Resilience

305   In connection with fault tolerance and resilience, please outline:

- All hardware modules that are fault-tolerant
- All hardware components that are hot-swappable
- Describe the software (if any) that supports the fault-tolerant hardware
- Whether full "English" error condition messages are produced on a console
- Describe the resilience features of all your proposed hardware components

306   What facilities exist for regenerating the system in the event of a system failure. Please specify the following:

- Minimum time to restart system
- Procedures for warm and cold start
- Procedures for reloading data

Section 4 - System Software

400   Please provide for each system proposed, full details of all system software. The system software described should comply with all technical requirements as described in Part C. The system software must include:

- Operating system
- Ancillary utilities to support SAP R/3 environment. These utilities must cater to the following functions:

    Access protection

    Data integrity

    Backup and recovery of data

    Performance monitoring

Software Description

401   For each of the preceding specified software please provide:

- An outline description of the software
- Main function supported by the software
- Any proposed customization required to meet DCSA's needs

Software History

- Original date and authorship
- Place of origin of the software
- Brief supplier profile (for any third-party software)
- Date and version number of the last major rewrite or revision
- Major developments planned for the next 12 months including a description of the additional features and the planned release date

Software Licenses

- Terms of the software license and such license period
- License fees and charges in the stated currency
- Software warranties specific to South Africa

Section 5 - Hardware Warranty, Maintenance, and Support

500   Describe the legal relationship between yourselves and any third party made responsible for maintenance and support and your interpretation of the legal relationship between DCSA and these parties.

501 Please provide full details of the hardware warranties provided.

502 Please specify the cost and types of hardware maintenance that are available:

- Preventative
- Fix on failure
- Repair on site
- Replace with new

503 Please provide as Appendix V a standard copy of your proposed hardware maintenance contract.

504 What are the standard hours of service for onsite support?

505 With the location of the data center being in Johannesburg, what are the guarantees and average response times to hardware failure:

- During standard hours?
- Outside standard hours?

506 What are the procedures for hardware fault reporting?

507 Where is the support center located?

508 What help desk facilities are provided?

509 Please specify the number and experience of support staff.

510 How is the maintenance charge calculated?

511 Indicate your anticipated time during which these maintenance charges would remain fixed.

512. Indicate an estimated annual increase that could potentially be submitted for consideration.

513 In your experience, please specify the number and caliber of DCSA staff required to manage the proposed hardware and software. Briefly describe each position.

514 Please describe any services you have to offer in the form of facilities management including:

- Location
- Service description
- Cost
- Loan system facilities in the event of malfunctioning equipment

515 For each component in your proposed solution, please specify:

- Spare parts that will be held in Johannesburg
- Spare parts not held in Johannesburg and their guaranteed delivery time
- The expected MTBF (Mean Time Between Failures) giving the source of your data

516   Please calculate the expected MTBF for the total system solution, providing the method used for calculation.

Section 6 - Software Maintenance and Support

Your responses to this section should be included as Appendix V.

600   Describe the legal relationship between yourselves and any third party made responsible for system software, maintenance, and support and your interpretation of the legal relationship between DCSA and these parties.

601   Please provide (as part of Appendix V) a standard copy of your proposed software maintenance contract. Please note that the terms, conditions and time frames of software maintenance and support will be negotiated at the time DCSA enters into an agreement with the preferred supplier.

602   What are the standard hours of service for software support?

603   What is the procedure for fault reporting?

604   Given that Johannesburg is the location, what are the guaranteed and average response times to software failure on the central development system:

- During standard hours?
- Outside standard hours?

605   Where is the support center located?

606   What help desk facilities are provided?

607   Please specify the number and experience of support staff.

608   Describe your policy for the maintenance and support of your proposed software and system software upgrades.

609   How is the maintenance charge calculated, if any?

610   Indicate your anticipated time during which these maintenance charges would remain fixed.

611   Indicate an estimated annual increase that could potentially be submitted for consideration.

Section 7 - Implementation Plans

Your responses to this section should be included as Appendix VI.

Implementation

700   Please confirm that you will take total responsibility for the implementation of the proposed solution.

701 Please provide a detailed implementation plan specifying the following activities:

- System installation and customization
- Site preparation
- Training
- Delivery of equipment
- User procedures
- System data preparation/initialization
- Acceptance testing

702 For each of the preceding activities, please show:

- The key tasks to be undertaken
- Total-man-day effort
- Total-man-day effort by type (e.g., project manager, analyst, programmer, and so on) for:
  Supplier staff
  DCSA staff
  Elapsed time
  All major dependencies between activities

703 Please outline any dependencies on third-party suppliers (e.g., for equipment, supplies, and key dates for delivery).

704 Please indicate any external events that could cause delay.

705 Please specify the level of contingency you have assumed in your plans.

706 Please confirm that the implementation cost is included in the contract price. If not, please specify the additional cost (travel and accommodation expenses).

Project Organization

707 Describe reporting procedures you will adopt to report to DCSA.

708 Provide details on the timing and frequency of meetings.

709 Describe any project planning and control methodologies/tools you intend to use.

710 Please specify the configuration control and quality control procedures that will be used during the project.

Project Staffing

711 Outline the proposed team structure, including client staff.

712 Outline the project responsibilities of all team members.

713 Where will the project team be located?

714   What will the availability of team members be during the assignment, expressed as number of days per week throughout the course of the project?

715   What are your standard charge rates for different grades?

716   What are the project charge rates for all team members?

717   Please provide as part of Appendix VII curricula vitae of key team members.

Training

718   Please describe the training courses that would be appropriate to DCSA. For each course, please specify:

- The level of staff at which the course is aimed (i.e., operator, technician, and so on).
- The course format (i.e., workshop, presentation).
- The numbers permitted on the course.

719   Where is training provided (i.e., onsite, offsite venue)?

720   How much of this training is included in the contract price and what is additional?

721   What training literature will be made available to DCSA? What is included in the contract price and what is additional?

Documentation

722   Please describe what documentation (i.e., user, operational, technical, etc.) will be made available to DCSA. For each type, please specify:

- Format
- Scope and content
- What is included in fixed price and what is additional
- Media
- Which recognized standards the document conforms to, and for which regulatory authority
- Cost, if appropriate

Section 8 - Summary of Costs

Your responses to this section should be included as part of Appendix IX.

800   Please specify costs as detailed in the following, indicating percentage in foreign currency where applicable and exchange rate assumption.

801   Please state the period for which this quotation and the costs quoted are valid.

802   The summary of costs must be presented in the format as shown at the end of this section.

Capital Costs

803   For the proposed hardware configuration, please provide summary information for each of the following capital costs:

- Each item of equipment for the central hardware (e.g., processor, disk storage, tapes, and so on) and the total cost for all central site equipment
- Each item of communications and network equipment, and the total cost for the entire communications configuration (LAN card and so on)
- Each peripheral item (console, workstations, printers) and the total cost for all peripheral items regarding servers
- Any other hardware costs not itemized previously (e.g., any extra charges for delivery, shipping, transport, insurance, warranty, installation, commissioning)
- Summary of total cost

You must list these costs in the format shown in the example at the end of this section.

804   Please state your policy on when hardware costs are payable to you.

805   Please provide details for each of the following software capital costs:

- Operating system software licenses
- Each item of customization showing the cost and effort required (if any)
- Ancillary software licenses
- The charge for all documentation
- Any other software capital costs payable but not itemized previously
- Summary of total cost

You must list these costs in the example format shown at the end of this section.

806   Please state your policy on when the software license costs are payable to you.

807   Please outline the installation costs of your proposed system. Please outline for each of the following categories the costs, type of staff proposed, and number of days required for:

- Assistance with testing
- Training
- Site planning
- Project management

Continuing Costs

808   Please provide details for each of the following hardware continuing costs:

- Summary total cost
- Each item of equipment for the central hardware
- Each item of communications and network equipment
- The total continuing costs for peripheral devices (consoles, printers, and so on)
- Any other hardware maintenance costs not included in the preceding

You must list these costs in the format shown in the example for continuing costs at the end of this section.

809   Please state clearly the warranty and the basis of this warranty available on each item of hardware in the proposed system. (e.g., carry-in, parts only, labor and parts, fix onsite, and so on)

810   For all continuing hardware maintenance costs, please indicate your proposed due dates for payment.

811   Please provide details for each of the following software continuing costs:

- Systems software (operating system)
- Ancillary software
- Operating licenses (e.g., if there are remote site copies of software)
- Any other continuing software costs not included previously.

You must list these costs in the format shown in the example for continuing costs at the end of this section.

811   Please state clearly the warranty and the basis of this warranty available on all software in the proposed system.

812   For all continuing software maintenance costs, please indicate your proposed due dates for payment.

813   Please ensure that all costs are quoted on a uniform basis throughout your offer response (for example, monthly or annually).

814   Example for capital cost.

CAPITAL COSTS		Costs	Costs	Costs
HARDWARE	Central Hardware		xxx xxx.xx	
	Item 1 (DB Server)	xxx xxx.xx		
	Item 2 (App Server)	xxx xxx.xx		
	Item 3	xxx xxx.xx		
	Communications/Networks		xxx xxx.xx	
	Item 1 (modem)	xxx xxx.xx		
	Item 2 (LAN Card)	xxx xxx.xx		
	Item 3	xxx xxx.xx		

CAPITAL COSTS		Costs	Costs	Costs
	Peripheral Items		xxx xxx.xx	
	Item 1 (laser printer)	xxx xxx.xx		
	Item 2	xxx xxx.xx		
	Delivery/installation and other		xxx xxx.xx	
	Item 1	xxx xxx.xx		
	Item 2	xxx xxx.xx		
	TOTAL		(Hardware)	xxx xxx.xx
SOFTWARE	Operating System Software		xxx xxx.xx	
	Package 1	xxx xxx.xx		
	Package 2	xxx xxx.xx		
	Ancillary Software		xxx xxx.xx	
	Package 1	xxx xxx.xx		
	Package 2	xxx xxx.xx		
	Documentation		xxx xxx.xx	
	Item 1	xxx xxx.xx		
	Item 2	xxx xxx.xx		
	Other		xxx xxx.xx	
	Item 1	xxx xxx.xx		
	Item 2	xxx xxx.xx		
	TOTAL		(Software)	xxx xxx.xx
INSTALLATION	Acceptance Testing	xxx xxx.xx		
	Training	xxx xxx.xx		
	Cabling installation	xxx xxx.xx		
	Site Planning	xxx xxx.xx		
	Project Management	xxx xxx.xx		
	Travel and Accommodation	xxx xxx.xx		
	Other	xxx xxx.xx		
	TOTAL		(Installation)	xxx xxx.xx
	TOTAL CAPITAL			xxx xxx.xx

CONTINUING COSTS		Costs	Costs	Costs
HARDWARE	Central Hardware		xxx xxx.xx	
	Item 1 (DB Server)	xxx xxx.xx		
	Item 2 (App Server)	xxx xxx.xx		
	Item 3	xxx.xxx.xx		

continues

continued

CONTINUING COSTS		Costs	Costs	Costs
	Communications/Networks		xxx xxx.xx	
	Item 1 (modem)	xxx xxx.xx		
	Item 2 (LAN Card)	xxx xxx.xx		
	Item 3	xxx xxx.xx		
	Peripheral Items		xxx xxx.xx	
	Item 1 (laser printer)	xxx xxx.xx		
	Item 2	xxx xxx.xx		
	Other		xxx xxx.xx	
	Item 1	xxx xxx.xx		
	Item 2	xxx xxx.xx		
	TOTAL		(Hardware)	xxx xxx.xx
SOFTWARE	Operating System Software		xxx xxx.xx	
	Package 1	xxx xxx.xx		
	Package 2	xxx xxx.xx		
	Ancillary Software		xxx xxx.xx	
	Package 1	xxx xxx.xx		
	Package 2	xxx xxx.xx		
	Other		xxx xxx.xx	
	Item 1	xxx xxx.xx		
	Item 2	xxx xxx.xx		
	TOTAL		(Software)	xxx xxx.xx
	TOTAL CONTINUING COSTS			xxx xxx.xx

Part C - Technical Requirements Specification

Introduction

100   Part C of this RFQ specifies the technical requirements that must be satisfied by your proposed solution. Key transaction figures are provided to enable you to size your solution. Also contained is a high-level configuration to guide your detailed design. The viability of the design must be proven by your conformance to the benchmarking procedures, as defined in Part C.

Key User and Business Volumes

200   Appendix B contains the current key transaction volumes for each SAP module. The table contains an average month's transactions. These transactions are taken from the existing systems and reflect the current business operation. It is estimated that the business transactions will grow at an annual rate of approximately 10 percent.

More importantly, it is expected that demand for SAP services will expand well beyond the Finance and Human Resource areas to Material Management, and Sales and Distribution. While you are not expected to size your solution for these additional components, your solution should have sufficient inherent scalability to grow significantly beyond the proposed installation.

201 Appendix B shows the current number of users by business units. These are total users, not concurrent users. For the purposes of memory sizing, you should treat these as concurrently logged-in users but not necessarily active users. These figures should be used as a guide for your design.

202 The system must store up to two years of history except for the HR module where 10 years history is required.

High-Level Design

300 This design has three key features, described in the following, to provide high availability, disaster recovery, and commonality of disk systems.

301 The technical architecture will be a three-tier client server distributed system. It will have a main "productive" data server with a "backup" data server that will also serve as the development system. A third machine will be configured as a "Central" SAP R/3 system, and it will be used as a test system. It will reside in the "main" computer center.

302 DCSA has two computer rooms, separated by 500 meters. It is intended that the data server reside in the newer, "main" computer center and the backup/development system reside in the "old" computer center. The disc system must also be partitioned between the two computer centers. The objectives are twofold:

■ Allow quick restart in the event of computer failure.

■ Allow processing to carry on in the alternative site should one of the sites be destroyed by a disaster.

303 Both computer centers are powered by UPS systems.

304 The system will be connected to the SAP Early Watch service.

305 DCSA supports three different types of computing platform, each with its own disk storage systems (file servers, mid-range computers, and IBM mainframe computers). It is intended to replace the three disparate disk systems with a single, uniform system. The chosen disk system must be capable of supporting all three platforms and be fault-tolerant.

306 While the immediate goal of the disk subsystem is to support SAP R/3, it will in the future be expanded to support the file servers and the IBM host mainframes.

307 Please produce a detailed design and associated costing for your proposed system setup. Identify any operating assumptions in your response.

308 In the design, provide a detailed response to the benchmarking procedures of the proposed system.

Timing Requirements

400   The following timing requirements are essential for a successful implementation of the SAP R/3 product at Dreamcar of South Africa:

■ A Development/Training environment by September 1, 1997

■ A Production and Test environment by December 1, 1997

Technical Requirements

500   All requirements to be satisfied by the system are listed in Appendix D. The requirements are shown as a set of tables.

501   List in a table format, as shown in Appendix D, all proposed components and indicate on the right side the degree to which the components satisfy the requirements.

502   Following are the priority ratings for the requirements:

■ E—Essential requirements that must be satisfied

■ R—Requirements that should be satisfied, exceptional conditions may warrant exclusion

■ D—Desirable requirements, the obligation to satisfy them is optional

503   You, the supplier, should indicate your proposed component's ability to satisfy each requirement as follows:

■ F—System will fully satisfy the requirement

■ P—System will partially satisfy the requirement

■ X—System will not satisfy the component

504   You should also indicate the level of customization you will need to do to enable your system to satisfy each requirement.

■ N—No customization required

■ C—Some customization required

■ MC—Major customization required

505   You are reminded that completion of the table in this document represents merely a summary of your response to the technical requirements. Please ensure that you have specified your proposed solution in detail as requested in Part B of this RFQ.

Supplier and Support Requirements

600   All of the supplier profile and support requirements are listed in Appendix F. The requirements are shown as a set of tables.

601   List in a table format, as shown in Appendix F, the degree to which your company will satisfy the requirements.

602   Following are the priority ratings for the requirements:

■ E—Essential requirements that must be satisfied

■ R—Requirements that should be satisfied, exceptional conditions may warrant exclusion

■ D—Desirable requirements, the obligation to satisfy them is optional

603   You, the supplier, should indicate your ability to satisfy each as follows:

■ F—Supplier can satisfy the requirements completely

■ P—Supplier can satisfy the requirement

■ X—Supplier cannot satisfy the requirement

604   You should also indicate the degree to which your organization would need to change (locally, nationally, and internationally) to satisfy each requirement.

■ N—No changes required

■ C—Some changes required

■ MC—Major changes required

605   You are reminded that completion of the table in this document represents merely a summary of your response to the technical requirements. Please ensure that you have specified your proposed solution in detail as requested in Part B of this RFQ.

Benchmarking and Acceptance Tests

700   Please submit details of any previous benchmarks performed by using the same or similar configuration of SAP R/3, your hardware, and operating system.

701   Please submit for each machine in your configuration the following benchmark data:

■ TPC-A

■ TPC-C

■ TPC-D

702   Please submit the following data for your proposed configuration:

■ SAP's throughput

■ Number of benchmark SD users at 60 percent processor utilization.

703   Submit in detail your calculations and rationale for arriving at your proposed sizing configuration.

704   Before your quotation can be accepted, you will be required to formally demonstrate the capabilities of your proposed solution. This demonstration may be conducted at any one of your competency centers.

705   Please confirm your willingness to formally demonstrate the capabilities of your configuration once your solution has been short-listed.

(Note: Copyright of this section remains with Dr. Max Nyiri.)

SAP Glossary of Terms and Concepts

ABAP Objects   An object-orientated language for developing business applications compatible with R/3 and ABAP/4.

ABAP/4   Advanced Business Application Programming/4, a fourth-generation language in which SAP R/3 application software is written. It has been developed by SAP.

ABAP/4 Data Dictionary   Store of metadata that contains descriptions of tables, data elements, domains, and views.

ABAP/4 Native SQL   A method for accessing a specific database by using its proprietary commands to implement Structured Query Language.

ABAP/4 Open SQL   A portable method for accessing all supported databases by Structured Query Language commands.

ABAP/4 Query   A user tool for generating special report programs without requiring any knowledge of ABAP/4.

ABAP/4 Repository   Store for all objects managed by the ABAP/4 Development Workbench.

ABAP/4 Repository Information System   Navigation aid for the ABAP/4 Repository.

ABAP/4 Workbench   Development environment that contains all the necessary tools for creating and maintaining business applications within the R/3 system.

ABAP/4 Workbench Organizer   A software development project management tool that is an integral component of the ABAP/4 Development Workbench.

ABC analysis   Analysis of materials (for example) can be conducted according to several criteria, such as importance or consumption value:

- Important part or a material with high consumption value
- Less-important part or material with medium consumption value
- Relatively unimportant part or material with low consumption value

account assignment element   Work breakdown structure element to which actual or commitment postings can be made.

active R/3 repository   The directory now in operational use that contains descriptions of all of an enterprise's application data and its interrelationships, including how the data is used in programs and screen forms. During ABAP/4 program development, a separate development repository directory is maintained for versions of the program components undergoing development or modification.

activity (controlling)   Internal or external physical measure of the activity output of a cost center according to activity type.

activity (project system)   An instruction to perform a task within a network in a set period of time. Work, general costs, or external processing can be associated with it.

activity input   Transaction to plan the secondary cost quantities on a receiver cost center that uses activity from a sender cost center.

Activity logs   Records of all activities in the SAP R/3 system for each transaction and each user.

activity type   Classification of an activity and the data structure—for example, number of units produced, hours, machine times, and production times.

actual costs   All the costs accruing to an object in a period.

ALE   See *Application Link Enabling (ALE)*.

allocation group   Defines which orders within one controlling area are to be settled together:

- By settlement timing—monthly, weekly, and so on
- By order types—repair, capital spending, and so on
- By settlement receivers—cost center, GL account

allocation receiver   Object to which the costs of a cost center or order are allocated.

API   See *Application Programming Interface (API)*.

Application Link Enabling (ALE)   An SAP method for using documents to carry messages that control distributed applications while maintaining integration and consistency of business data and processes across many systems.

capitalized profit   Calculated in results analysis by subtracting the capitalized costs from the value of the inventory from which revenue can be generated.

cardinality   The number of lines in a dependent table to which the table under consideration, in principle, can or must relate. A line in a table may be related to another dependent line in a cardinality of one-to-one correspondence. The relationship may be one-to-many if there can be several dependent lines for any referenced line.

CCMS   Acronym for *Computing Center Management System*.

characteristic   A property of an object, such as length, color, or weight, used to describe and distinguish the object. Characteristics are also used to differentiate data objects in a database.

CIM   Acronym for *Computer Integrated Manufacturing*.

classification   When an object is assigned to a class, values for the object are assigned to characteristics belonging to the class.

client   The highest level in SAP R/3. The data of one client cannot be accessed by another client. There are often a training client and a testing client, in addition to the client code that represents your group or corporate identity and under which the SAP system runs normal business. Some data is managed at the client level, because everyone in the corporate group of companies will want to refer to exactly the same information and be certain that it has been maintained as up-to-date and correct. Vendor addresses are an example of data managed at the client level.

client caches   Work areas set up in the database application servers for data that is frequently accessed by the client's applications.

collective invoice   A billing document for several deliveries to one customer that's initiated by the vendor at the end of a billing period.

company code   A unit within a client that maintains accounting balances independently and creates the legally required balance sheet and the profit-and-loss statement.

compiler   A tool that translates source code statements written in a general programming language into statements written in a machine-oriented programming language.

condition   A data element, term, or rule that defines prices, taxes, and output according to user-defined criteria.

condition record   A data record that stores a condition and perhaps refers to condition supplements. Condition records can include prices, discounts and surcharges, taxes, and output.

consignment stock   A particular inventory made available by the vendor that's stored on the purchaser's premises but remains the vendor's property until withdrawn from stores for use or transferred to the purchaser's own valuated stock.

contact person   A person at the customer location who deals with the vendor's sales or marketing department.

contingency order A results analysis object on which the costs of complaints are collected. Reserves are created by results analysis for the expected cost of complaints and are drawn from as costs are incurred.

contract A long-term agreement with a vendor that's fulfilled by individual release orders, which are initiated according to customer requirements.

control indicator Determines, in cost accounting, which application components are active, how certain data is stored, and what types of validation are to take place.

control key Determines how an activity or activity element is to be processed in operations such as orders, costings, and capacity planning.

controlling area An area within an organization that shares a cost accounting configuration (normally the same as company code). For cross-company cost accounting, one controlling area may be assigned to multiple company codes of one organization.

controlling area currency Default currency in cost accounting objects, cost centers, orders, and so on.

controlling functions Financial controlling, investment controlling, cost and profitability controlling.

controlling tasks Planning, monitoring, reporting, advising, and informing.

conversion Translation from one data format to another—for example, from decimal to binary code.

cost center Place in which costs are incurred. A unit within a company distinguished by area of responsibility, location, or accounting method.

cost component A group of cost origins.

cost component layout (product cost accounting and cost center accounting) A technical term that indicates how the results of a product cost estimate are saved. Assigns cost elements to cost components and determines the following:

- How the costs for raw materials, finished products, and semifinished products are rolled up in a multilevel assembly structure
- Which portion of the costs is treated as fixed costs
- Which costs are treated as the costs of goods manufactured
- Which are sales and administration costs
- Which are the costs of goods sold

cost element Mandatory criterion for classifying costs arising in a company code, including these:

- Direct cost elements for goods and services procured externally
- Indirect (internal activity) cost elements

Direct cost elements are maintained in the General Ledger master records. Indirect cost elements have no counterpart in the financial accounts and are maintained exclusively in cost accounting.

cost element group   A group of cost elements used to select records and to define lines and columns in reports. These elements can be used for planning purposes.

cost element planning   Planning primary and secondary costs on a cost center, order, or project.

cost element type   Classification of cost elements by uses or origin—for example, material cost elements, settlement cost elements for orders, or cost elements for internal cost allocations.

cost object   An account assignment term for individual cost objects to which actual data—such as costs, budgets, and sales revenues—can be assigned. The object can consist of individual products, such as product groups, or local situations based on classification criteria, such as shop floor areas.

cost object hierarchy   Structure of cost objects as nodes to which actual data can be assigned.

cost origin   A logical category to which costs can be assigned. Activity types and cost elements are cost origins.

cost planning   Planning the costs to be incurred during a transaction.

cost planning type   A technical term that indicates the purpose of a cost planning method—for example,

- Rough planning—estimating costs to be incurred for an order or for an element in a work breakdown structure
- Cost element planning
- Unit costing

cost-of-sales accounting   Form of results analysis. Sales deductions and unit costs are assigned to the sales transaction.

costing   Calculating total production costs of individual product units, which may be a piece, a batch, a lot, or an order, for example. Costing may also take place on the provision of services.

costing type   Technical term used to control unit costing and product costing. The costing type determines the following:

- For which reference object a costing may be used
- Which costing object will be updated
- How the key of the costing file is made up
- Which costing application can use this costing type

costing variants   Technical term to determine criteria for a cost estimate. The main costing variants follow:

- Costing type
- Valuation variant
- Organizational level
- Quantity structure determination, which includes the date control parameter

costing version   Technical term that determines the quantity structure when cost estimates are created. When production alternatives exist, there can be more than one product cost estimate for a material. Cost estimates with different production alternatives are given different version numbers.

CPI-C   Acronym for *Common Programming Interface-Communications*. A set of standardized definitions for communications between programs.

credit memo request   Reference document for creating a credit memo. If a customer applies for a credit memo, the sales department initiates a credit memo request, which is blocked until it's checked. The credit memo block is removed if the request is approved.

customer billing document   Statement of payment due as a result of the business transaction referred to in the document.

customer credit group   A group of customers defined by industry sector, by country, or by any characteristic useful for credit management. Credit representatives can generate reports for statistical analysis and retrieve information such as credit holds for processing using customer credit groups.

customer delivery   A collection of sales products delivered together.

customer group   A set of customers specified in any way for the purpose of statistical reporting or other management tasks.

customer hierarchy   A method of representing complex customer structures, such as a buying group. Pricing and other information that's valid for all members of a customer hierarchy can be stored in the master record.

customer inquiry   Request from a customer to a sales organization for a price and availability check of in-hand inventory.

customer material information record   A collection of information and references to be used in specifying material for a particular customer.

customer quotation   An offer submitted by a sales organization to a customer for the delivery of goods or the provision of services according to fixed terms.

Customizing   An SAP tool, provided as part of the R/3 system, consisting of two components: implementation guides and customizing menus and their associated functions. It doesn't change the program coding. This tool provides support for all activities necessary for the following:

- Initial configuration of the SAP system before going into production
- Adjustment of the system during production
- Implementation of additional SAP applications

data element of a field   A description of the contents of a record or field in terms of their business significance.

database interface   A work area to receive data from ABAP/4 Data Dictionary tables and from which any changed data can be passed to the database.

date of next credit review   This date can be entered manually. It is used to trigger an automatic credit review that issues a warning or a block if anyone attempts to process a sales order after that date.

DBMS   Acronym for *database management system*, a software system used to set up and maintain a database. It includes SQL facilities.

DDL   Acronym for *Data Definition Language*, which is used to define database objects under the DBMS.

debit memo request   A document created because of a discrepancy in the price or quantity, or as a result of a customer complaint. The debit memo request has to be approved before a debit memo can be created.

decentralized shipping   Round-the-clock shipment processing that is independent of the host computer. The following functions can be included:

- Copying data from the central Sales and Distribution system
- Shipping processing in the decentralized Shipping system
- Confirmation of goods issued on the goods issue date to the central Sales and Distribution system

delivering plant   Storage plant from which customer goods are to be delivered.

delivery   An SD-Sales and Distribution document for processing a delivery of goods that stores information needed for the following tasks: planning material requirements, picking, creating shipping documents, creating shipping units, transportation, and billing.

delivery due list   A work list that serves as the basis for creating deliveries. This list includes all sales orders and scheduling agreements that are due for delivery within a specified period.

delivery scheduling   The result of determining all dates relevant for shipping the goods referred to in a goods issue note. The system determines when the delivery plant must start picking and packing activities to ensure that the requested loading date is met.

delta management   System of transferring only data that has changed when using *Remote Function Calls* (RFCs).

dialog module   A group of dialog steps in a program.

direct costs   Costs directly and fully identifiable with a reference object according to the costs-by-cause principle.

distribution (controlling)   A business transaction used to allocate primary costs. The original cost element is retained on the receiver cost center. Information on the sender and the receiver is documented in the cost accounting document.

distribution channel   An organizational unit that determines how a product reaches customers. This channel indicates how a company generates business and which organizations are involved in distribution activities.

distribution key   Contains rules on how the costs are to be distributed. It is used for the following:

- Planning to spread costs over the planning period
- Assessment
- Distribution of direct costs in order to divide the costs of a sender cost center among the receivers

division   An organizational unit set up to supervise distribution and to monitor the profitability of a particular product. Customer-specific arrangements such as partial deliveries, prices, or terms of payment can be defined for each division.

DLL   Acronym for *dynamic link library,* which is integral to the runtime functioning of the Windows architecture.

DMS   See *Document Management System (DMS).*

document   A printable record of a business transaction in Sales and Distribution processing. There are three kinds of printed documents in SD: sales documents, shipping documents, and billing documents.

document date   Date on which the sales document becomes valid for SD processing. The document date is different for each document in a sales sequence. In the quotation, the document date is the date from which the quotation is valid; in the order, it is the date from which the agreement becomes binding. For example, the order-creation date can vary from the date on which the agreement in the order becomes binding. In such a case, the agreement date is taken as the document date.

document flow   A stored representation of the sequence of documents necessary for one particular business transaction. For example, a particular document flow could be defined as a quotation, a sales order, a delivery, and an invoice.

Document Management System (DMS)   Supports the management of documents across and within applications. Status and version can be controlled. Documents can be linked to objects such as material master records. DMS documents can be retrieved by the Classification system and archived optically.

domain   A description of the technical attributes of a table field, such as the type, format, length, and value range. Several fields with the same technical attributes can refer to the same domain.

dynamic credit limit check with credit horizon   The credit exposure of a customer is split into a *static* part and a *dynamic* part. The static part includes open items, open billing, and delivery values; the dynamic part is the open order value, which includes all orders that aren't yet delivered or are only partially delivered. The value is calculated on the shipping date and stored in an information structure using a time period that you specify (days, weeks, or months). When you define a credit check, you can specify a particular horizon date in the future by indicating a number of these time periods. When evaluating credit, the system has to ignore all open orders that are due for delivery after the horizon date. The sum of the static and dynamic parts of the credit check cannot exceed the credit limit you've set for the credit horizon time period.

dynpro   A *dynamic program* that controls the screen and its associated validation and processing logic to control exactly one dialog step.

EBCDIC   Acronym for *Extended Binary-Coded Decimal Interchange Code.*

EDI   Acronym for *Electronic Data Interchange,* a standardized scheme for exchanging business data between different systems via defined business documents such as invoices and orders.

enqueue service   An R/3 system mechanism for the management of locks on business objects throughout client/server environments. The enqueue service can withhold the updating of a business object master until all related messages among different application servers are processed.

entity   The smallest possible collection of data that makes sense from a business viewpoint and is represented in the R/3 system.

Entity Relationship Model   Entities can be linked by logical relationships with business significance. Entities and their interrelations can be used to build static models of the enterprise, which in turn are portrayed in the respective computer application with its tables.

Environment Analyzer   A help program that lists the development objects that belong together and the boundaries between development classes.

EPC   See *event-driven process chain (EPC).*

equivalence number   A specification of how any given value is to be distributed to the different receiving objects.

event (reference model)   A status that has business relevance. It can trigger an SAP system function or can be the result of such a function.

event (workflow management)   A collection of attributes of objects that describes the change in an object's state.

event-driven process chain (EPC)   Describes the chronological and logical relationships of functions of the R/3 system and business system statuses that initialize the functions or are generated as a result of function execution.

external activities   Nonstock components and/or activities in a production order that are produced or performed outside the company.

external credit data   Credit data about a customer from external sources, such as the Dun and Bradstreet data that's standard for SAP R/3. You refer to the D&B credit information number (DUNs number) that identifies the customer and append the D&B indicator and rating. You can also enter the date when you last acquired this data.

float   Period of time that allows you to start a network or activity at a later date without incurring a scheduling delay.

follow-up costs   Incurred after the actual manufacturing process has been completed—for example, costs of rework and warranties.

forecasting   An estimate of future values based on historical data. An SD forecast is carried out using a model that you can select or allow the system to select automatically after conducting a "best-fit" analysis.

foreign key   Defines a relationship between two tables by assigning fields of one table (the foreign key table) to the primary key fields of another table (the check table).

forward scheduling   A way of scheduling a network, starting from the basic start date and adding durations to determine the earliest start and finish dates for successive activities.

free float   Time in which an activity can be shifted into the future without affecting the earliest start date of the following activity or the end date of the project. Must not be less than zero or greater than the total float.

function module   A program module that has a clearly defined interface and can be used in several programs. The function module library manages all function modules and provides search facilities in the development environment.

function-oriented cost accounting   Assigning costs to a business function for the purpose of analysis.

general costs activity   General costs incurred during the lifetime of a project are planned via this type of activity in a network. Examples of such planned costs are insurance, travel, consulting fees, and royalties.

goods issue   The decrease of warehouse inventory resulting from a withdrawal of material or a delivery to a customer.

goods issue document   A statement that verifies goods movement and contains information for follow-up tasks. A corresponding material document is initiated for the subsequent outflow of material with the goods issue document in the delivery. The material document contains one or more items and can be printed as a goods issue slip for the actual physical movement of goods.

GUI Acronym for *graphical user interface*. The SAP GUI gives users an ergonomic and attractive means of controlling and using business software.

hypertext Online documentation set up like a network, with active references pointing to additional text and graphics.

IDoc *Intermediate document.* The SAP R/3 system EDI interface and the ALE program link enabling both use standardized intermediate documents to communicate.

IMG *Implementation Management Guide,* a component of the SAP R/3 system that provides detailed steps for configuring and setting the applications.

imputed costs These costs don't represent operational expenditures or correspond to expenditures in either content or timing (for example, depreciation and interest).

Incompletion log A list that indicates what information is missing in a sales document. You can set up conditions to specify the information that has to be included in a document.

indirect costs Costs for which one single receiving object can't be directly and fully identified according to the cost-by-cause-principle—for example, indirect expenses such as building insurance, indirect labor costs such as supervisor wages, or indirect materials costs such as coolant cleaning materials.

initial cost split Cost component split for raw materials procurement, showing details such as purchase price, freight charges, insurance contributions, and administration costs.

inquiry A request from a customer to a sales organization for a price and on-hand availability.

inventory from which revenue can be generated The revenue expected in view of costs already incurred can be divided into capitalized costs and capitalized profits. It's calculated as calculated revenue minus actual revenue. Results analysis calculates the inventory for profit orders.

invoice Sales and Distribution document used to charge a customer for a delivery of goods or for services rendered.

invoice date Date on which a delivery is due for settlement. In some firms, invoices are processed periodically. All deliveries that become due at the same time can be combined and settled in a collective invoice. As soon as the next billing date determined by the calendar is reached, the orders and deliveries are included in the billing due list and can be billed.

invoice list Method of billing by combining all billing documents for a specific period for a particular payer. Additional discounts, such as factoring discounts, can be granted based on the total value of an invoice list. The list may include individual and collective documents.

invoice split Creation of several billing documents from one reference document, such as an order or delivery. The split may be based on materials, for example.

item Element of a document that carries information on the goods to be delivered or the services to be rendered.

item category   An indicator that defines the characteristics of a document item. The categories for items kept in inventory, value items, and text items are predefined. The item category controls the following tasks: pricing, billing, delivery processing, stock posting, and transfer of requirements.

job order cost accounting   Instrument for the detailed planning and controlling of costs. Used when collecting, analyzing, and allocating the costs incurred for the internal production of noncapitalized goods.

joint products   Made in the same manufacturing process.

Kerberos   A technique for checking user authorizations across open distributed systems.

library network   A generic network structure that many projects can use. Used in a project system for repetitive processes or for process planning.

line item   Display of posting according to activity and document number.

loading date   Date by which goods must be ready to be loaded and the vehicles required to transport them must be available.

loading group   A key that identifies the equipment needed to load the goods. For example, "crane or forklift truck" could be defined as a loading group.

loading point   Place within a shipping point where goods are loaded.

logical database   A set of predefined paths for accessing the tables in a specific database system. Once defined and coded, they can be used by any report program.

logical system   A system on which applications integrated on a common data basis run. In SAP terms, this is a client in a database.

loop   Circular path through activities and their relationships.

lot-size variance   Variances between the fixed planned costs and the fixed allocated actual costs, which occur because part of the total cost for an order or a cost object doesn't change with output quantity changes. For example, setup costs that don't change, no matter how often the operation is carried out.

LU6.2   IBM networking protocol used by the SAP R/3 system to communicate with mainframe computers.

LUW   Acronym for *logical unit of work,* an elementary processing step that's part of an SAP transaction. An LUW is either executed entirely or not at all. In particular, database access is always accomplished by separate LUWs, each of which is terminated when the database is updated or when the COMMIT WORK command is entered.

make-to-order production   Type of production in which a product is generally manufactured only once and to a customer order.

MAPI   Acronym for *Messaging Application Programming Interface,* which is part of the Microsoft *Windows Open Service Architecture* (WOSA).

master data   Data relating to individual objects; remains unchanged for a long time.

match code   An index key code attached to the original data that can be used to perform quick interactive searches for this data.

material   A product, substance, or commodity that is bought or sold commercially or is used, consumed, or created in production. A material master record can also represent a service.

material availability date   The date on which a material has to be available. On the material availability date, the vendor has to start the activities relevant for delivery, such as picking and packing the goods. The material availability date should allow time for the goods to be completely prepared by the loading date.

material determination   The process of conducting an automatic search for a material master record during the creation of SD documents using a key instead of the actual material number. The key can be a customer-specific material number or the *European Article Number* (EAN) of the material.

material exclusion   A restriction that automatically prevents the sale of specific materials to a particular customer.

material listing   A restriction that controls the sale of specific materials to a customer. Customers can buy only materials included in the material listing assigned to them. The system doesn't allow you to enter a sales document for particular customer materials that aren't included in the material listing.

material requirements planning   Generic term for activities involved in creating a production schedule or a procurement plan for the materials in a plant, company, or company group. A set of techniques that uses *bills of material* (BoMs), inventory data, and the master production schedule to calculate requirements for materials.

material substitution   Automatic replacement by another material for technical reasons or during a sales promotion.

material type   An indicator that subdivides materials into groups (such as raw materials, semifinished materials, and operating supplies) and determines the user screen sequence, the numbering in the material master records, the type of inventory management, and the account determination.

maximum document value   A specific value that the sales order or delivery cannot exceed. The value is defined in the credit check and is stored in the currency of the credit control area. Checking is initiated by a risk category defined specifically for new customers if a credit limit hasn't yet been specified.

maximum number of dunning levels allowed   The customer's dunning level cannot exceed this specified maximum.

measuring point   Physical or logical place at which a status is described—for example, the temperature inside a reactor or the speed of revolution of a windspeed measuring wheel.

menu painter   An R/3 system tool for developing standardized menus, function keys, and pushbuttons in accord with the SAP Style Guide.

metadata   Information about data structures used in a program. Examples of metadata are table and field definitions, domains, and descriptions of relationships between tables.

milestone   An operation or task that also confirms the completion of processing of previous tasks. When you confirm a milestone, the system traces back through its component operations to confirm their completion also.

mode   A user interface window in which an activity can be conducted in parallel with other open modes.

modified standard cost estimate   A costing type. Uses the quantity structure that changed during the planning period to calculate the cost of goods manufactured for a product.

moving average price (MAP)   Value of the material divided by the quantity in stock. Changes automatically after each goods movement or invoice entry.

network   In SAP R/3, an activity-on-node structure containing instructions on how specifically to carry out activities, in a specific order, and in a specific time period. Made from activities and relationships.

network type   Distinguishes networks by their usage. The network type controls costing variants for plan, target, and actual costs; order type; number ranges; open items; status profile; and authorizations.

object currency   The currency of the controlling area is the default currency of a cost accounting object, such as cost center, order, and so on.

object dependency   Product variants may entail certain combinations of parts and exclude other combinations. If the customer chooses one variant, certain options may not be available for technical or commercial reasons. These reciprocal relationships are represented in the system by object dependency. A special editor is provided in the Classification system to maintain the object dependency for characteristics and the characteristic values. You can also store object dependency in a *bill of material* (BoM); the system uses this information during BoM explosion. Object dependency controls whether all possible components are taken into account in materials planning.

object master data   Information stored in order to produce variants for a standard product. Bills of material list the parts needed, and routings store instructions for combining the individual parts.

object master data and object dependency   Master records for the manufacture of products with many variants. Information on the objects involved and their interrelationships is stored as object master data and object dependency.

object overview   Customized list of data and line display layout—for example, routings, inspection plans, maintenance tasks, and networks.

ODBC Acronym for *open database connectivity,* a Microsoft standard based on SQL Access Group definitions for table-oriented data access.

oldest open item The oldest open item cannot be more than a specified number of days overdue.

OLE Acronym for *object linking and embedding,* a Microsoft technology that enables the connection and incorporation of objects across many programs or files.

one-time customer A collective customer master record used to process transactions involving any customer who's not a regular customer. If a transaction is entered for a one-time customer, the customer data must be entered manually.

open item A contractual or scheduled commitment that is not yet reflected in Financial Accounting but will lead to actual expenditures in the future. Open item management provides for early recording and analyzing for cost and financial effects.

operating concern An organizational unit to which one or more controlling areas and company codes can be assigned. Certain criteria and value fields are valid for a specific operating concern. The criteria define business segments, and the value fields then are updated for these objects.

operating level The planned or actual performance of a cost center for a period—for example, output quantity, production time, and machine hours.

operating rate Ratio of actual to planned operating level. Measures the effective utilization of a cost center or activity.

operating resources Personnel and material necessary to carry out a project; can be used once or many times. Defined in value or quantity units. Planned for a period or a point in time. Includes, for example, materials, machines, labor, tools, jigs, fixtures, external services, and work centers.

operational area A technical term used to signify a logical subdivision of a company for accounting or operational reasons and therefore indicated in the EDM-Enterprise Data Model. An operation area is an organizational unit within logistics that subdivides a maintenance site plant according to the responsibility for maintenance.

operations layout A list, sorted by operations, of costing results from product costing and final costing.

order Instrument for planning and controlling costs. Describes the work to be done in a company in terms of which task is to be carried out and when, what is needed to carry out this task, and how the costs are to be settled.

order category The SAP application to which the order belongs—SD, for example.

order combination A combination of complete sales orders, of individual order items from different sales orders, or of partial deliveries of individual order items in a delivery. Order combination in a delivery is possible only when you authorize it for customers in the customer master record or when you manually authorize it for individual sales orders in the sales order document header.

order group   Technical term for grouping orders into hierarchies. Use to create reports on several orders, to combine orders, and to create order hierarchy.

order hierarchy   Grouping of orders for processing at the same time as in order planning and order reporting.

order phase   System control instrument for the order master data. Allows and prohibits operations on orders, depending on the phase or stage: opened, released, completed, or closed.

order/project results analysis   Periodic valuation of long-term orders and projects. The o/p results analysis evaluates the ratio between costs and a measure of an order's progress toward completion, such as revenue or the quantity produced. The results analysis data includes costs of sales, capitalized costs or work in progress, capitalized profits, reserves for unrealized costs, reserves for the costs of complaints and commissions, and reserves for imminent loss.

order settlement   Complete or partial crediting of an order. The costs accrued to an order are debited to one or more receivers belonging to Financial or Cost Accounting.

order status   Instrument to control whether an order can be planned or posted to. Reflects the operational progress—the order phase. Determines whether planning documents are created during cost element planning; the transactions allowed at the moment (phase), such as planning, posting actual costs, and so on; and when an order can be flagged for deletion.

order summarization   Allows you to summarize data by putting orders into hierarchies. Also lets you analyze order costs at a higher level.

order type   Differentiates orders according to their purpose, such as repair, maintenance, marketing, or capital expenditure.

outline agreement   Generic term for contracts and scheduling agreements. The outline agreement is a long-term agreement with the vendor involving delivery of products or rendering of services according to specified requirements. These requirements are valid for a limited time period, a defined total purchase quantity, or a specified total purchase value. A further transaction determines when deliveries and services take place.

output   Information sent to the customer by various media, such as mail, EDI, or fax. Examples of output are printed quotations or order confirmations, order confirmations sent by EDI, and shipping notifications sent by fax.

overall network   The network resulting from the relationships among all existing networks.

overdue open items   The relationship between the total value of open items that are more than a specified time overdue and the customer balance cannot exceed a specified percentage.

overhead   Total cost of indirect expenses, indirect labor, and indirect materials (indirect costs). Allocated to cost objects by means of overhead rates.

overhead cost management   The entirety of cost accounting activities for planning and controlling indirect costs: responsibility-oriented overhead cost management by cost centers, and decision-oriented overhead cost management by action-oriented objects, which are orders and projects.

overhead costing   Most common method in product cost accounting. Assigns the direct costs to the cost object and applies the indirect (overhead) costs to the cost object in proportion to the direct costs, expressed as a percentage rate.

overhead group   Key that groups materials to which the same overheads are applied.

PA settlement structure   Settles costs incurred on a sender to various business segments, depending on the cost element. The *profitability analysis* (PA) settlement structure is a combination of assignments of cost element groups to profitability segments.

partial delivery   A quantity of goods received that is smaller than the quantity ordered, after making allowance for the underdelivery tolerance.

partial payment   Payment that only partially settles the outstanding invoice amount.

partial quantity   Quantity of a product that deviates from the standard packaging quantity. In the warehouse management system, bin quantities containing less than the standard pallet load defined in the material master are regarded as partial pallet quantities.

partner   An individual within or outside your organization who is of commercial interest and can be contacted in the course of a business transaction. A partner can be a person or a legal entity.

payer   Person or company that settles the bill for a delivery of goods or for services rendered. The payer is not necessarily the bill-to party.

period accounting   One basis for profitability analysis. Costs are identified in the period in which they occur, regardless of the period in which the corresponding revenue occurs.

pick/pack time   Time needed to assign goods to a delivery and to pick and pack them. The pick/pack time depends on the loading point, the route, and the weight group of the sales order.

picking   The process of issuing and grouping certain products from the warehouse on the basis of goods requirements from the sales or production department. Picking can take place with transfer orders or picking lists. The procedure distinguishes between picking from fixed storage bins and random picking.

plan version   Control parameters for comparative analyses in planning in cost accounting. The plan version determines whether planning changes are documented, whether a beginning balance is to be generated, and whether the planning data of another version can be copied or referenced.

planned activity   The planned cost center activity required to meet the demand, measured in the corresponding physical or technical units.

planned delivery time   Number of days required to procure the material via external procurement.

planning   Assigning estimates of the costs of all activities required to carry out the business of an organizational unit over the planning period.

planning document   Line item for documenting planning changes.

planning element   *Work breakdown structure* (WBS) element on which cost planning can be carried out.

plant   The main organizational entity for production planning and control. MRP and Inventory Maintenance are often conducted at the plant level.

pooled table   A database table used to store control data, such as program parameters, or temporary data. Several pooled tables can be combined to form a table pool, which corresponds to a physical table on the database.

price difference account   Used to record price differences for materials managed under standard prices, or differences between purchase order and billing prices.

price group   Grouping of customers for pricing purposes.

price variance   Occurs if planned costs are evaluated in one way and actual costs in another. The planned standard rates for activities might change in the meantime, for example. Can also be the result of exchange-rate fluctuations.

pricing element   A factor that contributes to pricing. Any of the following can be identified as pricing elements: price, discount, surcharge, freight, and tax.

pricing procedure   Definition of the conditions permitted for a particular document and the sequence in which the system takes these conditions into account during pricing.

pricing scale   Scale within a condition record where prices, discounts, or surcharges are defined for different customer order quantities or values.

pricing type   Controls whether prices are copied from a reference document to a new document or are recalculated in the new document.

primary cost planning   By values and as quantities.

primary costs   Incurred due to the consumption of goods and services supplied to the company from outside. Costs for input factors and resources procured externally—for example, bought-in parts, raw materials, supplies, and services.

process manufacturing   A production type; continuous manufacturing process from raw materials to finished product.

product costing   A tool for planning costs and setting prices. It calculates the cost of goods manufactured and of goods sold for each product unit, using the data in the PP-Production Planning module. Product costing based on bills of material and routings is used for calculating production costs of an assembly, with alternatives for showing the costs of semifinished products; and for detailed estimates of the cost components down to their lowest production level.

product proposal   Product groupings, combinations, and quantities frequently ordered. You can save time by referring to and copying from product proposals. You can also define a product proposal for a particular customer. The system automatically enters the customer-specific product proposal when you create an order for this particular customer.

production costs, total The costs of finished products bought for resale, or the costs of goods manufactured, plus sales overhead, special direct costs of sales, and administration overhead.

production cycle A manufacturing process in which the output of the final manufacturing level (or part of it) becomes input for lower manufacturing levels of the same process (recycle).

production order For the production department to produce a material. It contains operations, material components, production resources and tools, and costing data.

production resources and tools (PRTs) Needed for carrying out operations at work centers; assigned to activities for which they are necessary for execution. Stored as material master, equipment master, and document master data. PRTs include job instructions, tools, test equipment, numerically controlled programs, drawings, and machinery and fixtures.

profit center Area of responsibility for which an independent operating profit is calculated; responsible for its own profitability. Separate divisional result is calculated.

profit order An order in which the planned revenue is greater than the planned costs. Results analysis uses the profit percentage rate of a profit order to calculate the inventory from which revenue can be generated, and to calculate the cost of sales.

profit percentage rate Planned revenue divided by planned costs of an order.

profitability analysis In SAP R/3, analysis by cost-of-sales approach or period accounting.

project definition Framework laid down for all objects created within a project. The data, such as dates and organizational data, is binding for the entire project.

project management An organizational structure created just for the life of the project, to be responsible for planning, controlling, and monitoring of the project.

project structure All significant relationships among the elements in a project.

project type Capital spending or customer project, for example.

PRT See *production resources and tools (PRTs)*.

Q-API Acronym for *Queue Application Programming Interface*. Supports asynchronous communication among applications of different systems by using managed queues or waiting lines.

quantity structure The quantity-related basis for calculating costs. The bill of material and routing form the quantity structure for product costing and the preliminary costing of a production order.

quantity variance Difference between target costs and actual costs, which results from the difference between planned and actual quantities of goods or activities used. For example, more raw materials from stock for a production order, or fewer activities from a cost center than were planned for.

rate of capacity utilization Ratio of output to capacity. Fixed costs can be divided into used capacity costs and idle time costs.

realized loss   Usage of reserves for imminent loss by results analysis. Loss can be realized when actual costs are incurred or when revenue is received. Results analysis realizes loss as the difference between the actual costs and the calculated revenue, or between the calculated costs and the actual revenue:

- Actual costs minus calculated revenue
- Calculated costs minus actual revenue

rebate   Price discount that a vendor pays to a customer after the sale. The amount of the rebate usually depends on the total invoiced sales that the customer achieves within a specified time period.

rebate agreement   Agreement between a vendor and a customer regarding the granting of rebates. A rebate agreement contains relevant information, such as the rebate basis, rebate amount, rebate recipient, and validity period.

reference date   Used to determine the start and finish dates of suboperations, as well as usage dates for production resources/tools. You can enter time intervals for reference dates, or a reference date can be a point of time within an activity—for example, the start date.

reference document   Document from which data is copied into another document.

relationship (project system)   Link between start and finish points of two activities in a network or library network. The relationship types in R/3 follow:

- SS-Start-Start
- FF-Finish-Finish
- SF-Start-Finish
- FS-Finish-Start

Remote Function Call (RFC)   A protocol, written in ABAP/4, for accessing function modules in other computers. RFC-SDK is a kit for integrating PC applications so that they can access SAP R/3 functions.

Remote Procedure Call (RPC)   A protocol for accessing procedures residing in other computers from C programming environments. Corresponds to *Remote Function Call (RFC)*.

repetitive manufacturing   A production type. Many similar products are manufactured together or one after another. In R/3, bills of materials and routings are created for each product.

reserves for costs of complaints and sales deductions   Inventory can't be created for certain costs—for example, costs arising under warranties or because of sales deductions. For such costs, results analysis creates reserves equal to the planned costs. These reserves are used when (and if) actual costs are incurred.

reserves for imminent loss   Results analysis creates reserves equal to the planned loss. These reserves are reduced as (and if) this loss is realized.

reserves for unrealized costs   Calculated in results analysis by subtracting the actual costs from the cost of sales.

resource-usage variance   Occurs if the used resource is different from the planned one—for example, the actual raw material used is different from the planned raw material.

results analysis   Periodic valuation of long-term orders. Results analysis compares the calculated and actual costs of an order as it progresses toward completion. It calculates inventory (if actual costs are greater than calculated costs) or reserves (if actual costs are less than calculated costs). The data calculated during results analysis is stored in the form of cost of sales, capitalized costs, capitalized profit, reserves for unrealized costs, reserves for costs of complaints and commissions, and reserves for imminent loss.

results analysis account   A General Ledger account that records the figures calculated during results analysis.

results analysis data   Analysis of work in progress and capitalized costs, reserves, and cost of sales.

results analysis key   Determines whether results analysis is revenue-based, quantity-based, or manual; the basis on which it is carried out (planned or actual results); how profits are to be realized; and whether to split inventory, reserves, and cost of sales.

results analysis version   Describes the business purpose for which results analysis was carried out. Determines, for example,

- Whether in accordance with German and American law
- For financial accounting purposes
- For profitability analysis
- Which results analysis accounts the results are posted to
- How the life cycle of an object will be broken down into open and closed periods

returnable packaging   Packaging material or transportation device used to store or transport goods. The returnable packaging is delivered to the customer along with the goods and has to be returned to the vendor afterward; if it isn't returned, the customer incurs a charge.

returns   Return of goods by customers. Returns are planned by means of a returns order. A receipt of returns records the arrival of goods, which then are posted to inventory.

revenue   The operational output valued at market price in the corresponding currency and sales quantity unit:

$$\text{Quantity} \times \text{Revenue} = \text{Sales}$$

revenue account determination   Notifies the revenue accounts to which prices, discounts, and surcharges are to be posted. The system uses predefined conditions to determine the appropriate accounts.

RFC   See *Remote Function Call (RFC)*.

risk category   Enables the credit manager to classify customers according to commercial risk. Along with the document type, the risk category helps to determine which kind of credit check the system automatically carries out. For example, you might decide to carry out stringent checks at order receipt for high-risk customers but waive a credit check for customers with an acceptable payment history.

RPC   See *Remote Procedure Call (RPC)*.

sales activity   A data record that contains information on customer interaction, including sales calls, telephone calls, conferences, and presentations.

Sales and Distribution document   A document that represents a business transaction in the SD module. SD documents include sales documents, shipping documents, and billing documents.

sales and operations planning (SOP)   The creation and maintenance of a meaningful sales plan and corresponding operations plan that includes a forecast of future customer demand.

sales area   An organizational unit responsible for three facets: sales-related aspect (sales organization), customer-related aspect (distribution channel), and product-related aspect (division).

sales document   A document that represents a business transaction in the sales department. Sales documents include inquiry; quotation; sales order; outline agreements such as contracts and scheduling agreements; and returns, credit, and debit requests.

sales document type   Indicators used to control processing of various SD documents by allowing the system to process different kinds of business transactions, such as standard orders and credit memo requests, in different ways.

sales order   Contractual arrangement between a sales organization and a sold-to party concerning goods to be delivered or services to be rendered. Also, an SAP Document that contains information about prices, quantities, and dates.

sales organization   The division or other organizational unit responsible for negotiating sales and distributing products and services. Sales organizations may be assigned to market subdivisions by geographical or industrial criteria. Each sales transaction is carried out by one sales organization.

sales plan   The overall level of sales, usually stated as the monthly rate of sales per product group or product family. The plan is expressed in units identical to the operations plan for planning purposes and represents a commitment by sales and marketing management to take all reasonable steps necessary to achieve actual customer orders that add up to the sales forecast.

sales unit   Unit of measure in which a product is sold. If several alternative sales units of measure have been defined for one product, conversion factors are applied by the system to convert them to the base unit of measurement.

schedule line A subdivision, according to date and quantity, of an item in a sales document. If the total quantity of an item can be delivered only in partial deliveries, the system creates schedule lines corresponding to each partial delivery and determines the appropriate quantities and delivery dates for each schedule line.

scheduling, network Determines earliest and latest start dates for activities and calculates the required capacity, as well as floats.

scheduling agreement A type of long-term outline agreement, with a vendor or customer that defines the creation and continuous updating of schedules. Schedules specify timing of partial deliveries for each item in schedule lines.

screen painter An ABAP/4 Development Workbench tool that can be used to create, modify, display, and delete dynpros.

secondary cost element Cost centers require services from other cost centers of their own to produce activity. These are secondary costs. Planned assessment is used to plan the secondary cost quantities; activity input is used to plan the secondary cost values.

settlement parameters Control data required for order settlement: allocation group, settlement cost element, and settlement receiver.

settlement rule Consists of the sender and the settlement distribution rule, which includes the settlement receiving accounts, the distribution factor, the settlement type, and the validity period.

ship-to party Person or company that receives goods. The ship-to party isn't necessarily the sold-to party, the bill-to party, or the payer.

shipping conditions A statement of the general strategy for shipping goods to a customer. If one of the shipping conditions states that goods must arrive at the customer location as soon as possible, the system automatically suggests the shipping point and route that will deliver the goods the fastest.

shipping document A document that defines a shipping transaction. SD shipping documents include delivery, material document containing goods issue information, and grouped deliveries.

shipping material Material used for packing and transporting products. Shipping material includes crates, pallets, or containers. A shipping unit master record normally specifies a shipping material.

shipping point Location that carries out shipping activities, such as a mail department or rail depot. Each delivery is processed by one shipping point.

shipping type An indicator that shows which means and mode of transport are used to carry out a shipment of goods.

shipping unit Combination of products packed together in a shipping material at a particular time. Shipping units may contain delivery items or items that are themselves shipping units.

simultaneous costing   Process that displays the actual costs incurred to date for such things as an order. The process describes all costings of an order in the SAP system, including order settlement. These costings come in the form of preliminary costings and actual costings. The values then can be analyzed in final analysis.

sold-to party   Person or company that places an order for goods or services. The sold-to party can also perform the functions of the payer, bill-to party, or ship-to party.

spooling   Buffered relaying of information to output media, across multiple computers, if necessary.

SQL   Acronym for *Structured Query Language*, defined by the *American National Standards Institute* (ANSI) as a fourth-generation language for defining and manipulating data.

standard cost estimate   Calculates the standard price for semifinished and finished products. Relevant to the valuation of materials with standard price control. Usually created once for all products at the beginning of the fiscal year or a new season. The most important type of costing in product costing. The basis for profit planning or variance-oriented product cost controlling.

standard hierarchy   Tree structure for classifying all data objects of one type. For example, the cost centers belonging to a company from a cost accounting point of view are represented by a standard hierarchy copied from the R/3 Reference Model and then customized.

standard price   Constant price with which a material is evaluated, without taking into account goods movements and invoices. For semifinished and finished products calculated in product costing.

static credit limit check   The customer's credit exposure cannot exceed the established credit limit. The *credit exposure* is the total combined value of open sales documents, open delivery documents, open billing documents, and open items in accounts receivable. The *open order value* is the value of the order items that haven't yet been delivered. The *open delivery value* is the value of the delivery items that haven't yet been invoiced. The *open invoice value* is the value of the billing document items that haven't yet been forwarded to accounting. The *open items* represent documents that have been forwarded to accounting but aren't yet settled by the customer.

status   Order items with the item category code TAK are made to order and have an object status that passes through the following phases:

- **1 Released.** The system sets this status automatically when the item is created to indicate that production can be initiated.

- **2 Revenue posted.** The system sets this status automatically, as soon as revenue is posted for an item for the first time.

- **3 Fully invoiced.** This status must be set manually, as soon as all revenues are posted for the item. After this status is set, no more revenues can be posted.

- **4 Completed.** This status must be set manually when the procedure is completed. If this status is set, no further costs can be posted.

stock   A materials management term for part of a company's current assets also known as *inventory*. Stock refers to the quantities of raw materials, operating supplies, semifinished products, finished products, and goods on hand in the company's stores or warehouse facilities.

stock transfer   The removal of materials from storage at one location and their transfer to and placement into storage at another. Stock transfers can occur either within a single plant or between two different plants. The removal of inventory from storage at the first location and its placement into storage at the other can be posted in the system in one or two steps.

Style Guide   A collection of the SAP design standards for uniform design and consistent operation routines for SAP applications.

subitem   An item in a sales document that refers to a higher-level item. Services and rebates in kind can be entered as subitems belonging to main items.

summarization object   An object containing data calculated during order summarization, project summarization, or the summarization of a cost object hierarchy. A summarization object can contain the costs incurred for all orders of a specific type, for example, and a specific responsible cost center.

surcharge   Supplement, usually as a percentage, used to apply overhead in absorption costing.

target costs   Calculated using the planned costs, along with the following:

- The planned activities divided by the actual activities (for cost centers)
- The planned quantities divided by the actual quantities of goods manufactured (for orders)

target document   A document to which the data from a reference document is copied.

tax category   A code that identifies the condition that the system is to use to determine country-specific taxes automatically during pricing.

tax classification   Specification of the method for calculating the tax liability of the customer based on the tax structure of the customer's country.

task list type   Distinguishes task lists according to their functionality. In production planning task lists, for example, a distinction is drawn between routings and reference operation sets.

TCP/IP   Acronym for *Transmission Control Protocol/Internet Protocol,* the standard network protocol for open systems.

text   A system function that provides a note pad where you can store any related text about the current customer. The system indicates in the credit management status screen whether any text is already available about this customer.

text type   A classification for various texts that users can define in master records or in documents. Text types include sales texts, shipping texts, and internal notes.

third-party business transaction   Commerce in which goods or services are delivered directly from vendor to customer.

time interval   Time period between at least two activities linked in a relationship. The relationship type determines how start and finish times are used in the calculation.

total float   Time that an activity can be shifted out into the future starting from its earliest dates without affecting the latest dates of its successors or the latest finish date of the network.

transaction   The series of related work steps required to perform a specific task on a business data processing system. One or more screens may be required. From the user's viewpoint, it represents a self-contained unit. In terms of dialog programming, it is a complex object that consists of a module pool, screens, and so on and is called with a transaction code.

transaction currency   Currency in which the actual business transaction is carried out.

transportation lead time   Time needed to organize the transportation of goods. For example, the interval between the booking of the freight space (transportation scheduling date) and the loading of the goods onto the means of transport (loading date) is called transportation lead time. The transportation lead time may depend on the route.

transportation planning date   The date when the organization of goods transport must begin. The transportation planning date must be selected early enough so that the transport means are available on the loading date to load the goods.

transportation scheduling   Determination of all dates relevant for transportation, based on the delivery date. The system determines when transport activities must start to ensure that the requested delivery date is met.

transportation zone   The zone in which the ship-to party is located. The system uses zones to help determine the route. Transportation zones can be defined according to postal or ZIP code areas, or according to the territory conveniently covered by the means of transport.

unit costing   Method of costing where bills of material and routings aren't used. Used to determine planned costs for assemblies or to support detailed planning of cost accounting objects, such as cost centers or orders.

unit of measure   A standard measurement recognized by the SAP R/3 system. Base unit of measure, unit of entry, unit of issue, order unit, sales unit, and weight group are examples of units of measure. *Grouping,* used in delivery processing, refers to the weight of a convenient quantity of a material. The weight group is one factor the system uses to determine the route. It's also used in delivery scheduling to determine the pick/pack time.

usage variance   Difference between planned and actual costs, caused by higher usage of material, time, and so on.

user exit   An interface provided by an SAP R/3 application that allows the user company to insert into a standard R/3 component a call to an additional ABAP/4 program that will be integrated with the rest of the application.

user-defined field types   A classification code used to interpret the meaning of a user-defined field. For example, a user may designate a specific field as one of the following types:

- General field of 20 characters to be used for codes or text
- Quantity fields with a unit
- Value fields with a unit
- Date fields
- Check boxes

user-defined fields Entry fields that can be freely defined for an activity or a work breakdown structure element (Project System) or an operation (Production Planning).

valuation date Date on which materials and internal and external activities are evaluated in a costing.

valuation variant Determines how the resources used, the external activities, and the overheads are to be valued in a costing (that is, at what prices).

variance category Distinguishes variances according to their causes:

Input	Price and usage variances
Yield	Scrap, mix variances, labor efficiency variances, schedule variances
Allocation	Fixed-cost variances, overabsorption variances, underabsorption variances

variance key Controls how variances are calculated. Assigning a variance key to an object determines, for example, whether variances are calculated for the object by period or for the life of the object, which may be a cost center, an order, or a cost object ID.

variance version Specifies the basis for the calculation of variances:

- How the target costs are calculated
- Which actual data is compared with the target costs
- Which variance categories are calculated

view A relational method used to generate a cross-section of data stored in a database. A virtual table defined in the ABAP/4 Dictionary can define a view by specifying how and what will be selected from whichever tables are targeted.

volume variance Cost difference between the fixed costs estimated for the products based on standard capacity and the allocated fixed costs that are either too low or too high due to operating either below or above capacity.

WBS See *work breakdown structure (WBS)*.

WBS element A concrete task or a partial task that can be subdivided.

work breakdown structure (WBS) A model of a project that represents the hierarchy of actions and activities to be carried out on a project. Can be displayed according to phase, function, or object.

work in progress Unfinished products, the costs of which are calculated by subtracting the costs of the order that have already been settled from the actual costs incurred for the order or by evaluating the yield confirmed to date.

work order Generic term for the following order types: production order, process order, maintenance order, inspection order, and network.

work process An SAP R/3 system task that can be assigned independently to, for example, a dedicated application server—for example, dialog processing, updating a database from change documents, background processing, spooling, lock management.

workflow management Tool for automatic transaction processing used in a specific business environment.

Migrating from SAP R/2 to SAP R/3

In this appendix

R/2 and R/3 systems can link in many ways to suit your company's needs and your progress in the evolution of your computer support installation. Chapter 6, "Optimizing Business Processing," discusses improving your business computing facilities by developing new programs. Some of these programs may be directed at forging automatic links with systems, such as databases, that your company has been using for some time and that probably contain valuable data and perhaps specific procedures unique to your particular business.

This appendix concentrates on situations in which some of your existing installations are SAP systems that will be improved by being moved to a different hardware configuration (referred to as *migration)* or by acquiring new releases of the SAP software. The third possibility is to have an SAP system operating in the position of a satellite system that communicates with the central host system whenever necessary. The satellite system usually can continue functioning on its own between the occasions when it links up to the central or "hub" system. This arrangement is discussed in Chapter 3, "Exploring R/3 Architecture."

A standalone mainframe system will use a release of the R/2 system. Client/server installations will use R/3 for best results. Systems using R/2 may be linked to R/3 systems permanently, or the linkage may be used as a transition stage in the process of migrating completely to an R/3 installation.

SAP Release and Migration Tools

It is SAP's policy to provide tools to support each update of your system, whether it be a full migration to a different host or an update occasioned by the purchase of a new release of existing software. The release and migration tools, although different in scope, provide the same basic support to the user organization:

- Information on the new functions and facilities available when the update is completed
- Update to the R/2 or R/3 Reference Model, which includes the additional functions
- Support for using the updated Reference Model to design any modifications to your business procedures in order to best use the new functions
- Support for establishing trials where necessary of the new functions

Migrating Data and Functions from SAP R/2 to SAP R/3

The SAP modules of standard business software are designed to accommodate the widest possible variety of user organizations and an extensive range of hardware and software systems. For example, the SAP R/2 system was developed in the context of mainframe architectures, which were integrated with server systems for specific purposes, such as database management. This can be said to be a relatively homogeneous environment.

By contrast, the thrust of SAP R/3 system design and development is toward heterogeneous architectures with multiple layers of client/server configurations that can take advantage of the rapid but uneven developments by the vendors of low-cost equipment and operating systems for tasks such as user interface and database management. With the improvement of communications facilities, the development of worldwide business systems has progressed considerably.

Many companies will want to take advantage of their archived business information and the most recent transaction data when they install new equipment or software components, and when a complete business process reengineering project is being conducted. The objective is to transfer data and perhaps customized business functions to the new SAP R/3 system installation or application module.

Migration Data Objects

The SAP R/3 system focuses on the handling of structured data objects that may be of any complexity and yet be accessed as single entities. With such techniques, the SAP R/3 system generates its power and flexibility without excessive annexation of computing resources. The SAP R/2 system does not manipulate data objects in the same manner; it relies on access to fields and tables of fields.

The migration process must allow the information in the SAP R/2 tables to be rebuilt into the structures of the SAP R/3 system. In effect, what is migrated are migration objects that make sense in the business context and are named accordingly. They have to be unloaded from the SAP R/2 database, transferred to the SAP R/3 database, and made available to the SAP R/3 system as a whole.

Special Migration Functions

The data in the SAP R/2 system is exported as *Database Decimal Interchange Code* (DDIC) structures that contain the data objects in *Extended Binary-Coded Decimal Interchange Code* (EBCDIC) format, which has to be converted to ASCII. The programs to create the export structures are automatically generated in the SAP R/2 system in real time. Similarly, the SAP R/3 system generates import programs to receive and integrate the structures and their data objects. All the customers' conversion rules and their program logic are integrated into the import programs.

Linked System Windows

The *Common User Access* (CUA) graphical interface is available in both SAP R/2 and R/3. Separate windows at the user interface can independently display the progress of functions in both systems and from any integrated PC systems that are running. Windows, SF/Motif, and Presentation Manager are included in the list of front-end systems that can be used to display essentially the same screens and conduct the relevant dialog activities.

Varieties of Migration Strategy

Although the "big bang" creation of a totally new business process support system is a feasible project, it is by no means the only option. Coexistence among some or all legacy system hardware and software components can be brokered in many ways, ranging from the evolution of peripheral SAP R/3 system functionality to a complete redesign and fresh implementation of what must be regarded as a new business entity.

SAP R/3 System Satellites

The increasing range of independent systems that can be managed by program-to-program communications allows the use of specialized and optimized systems for the business functions that might otherwise co-opt excessive amounts of shared computer resources. The same style of configuration can be adopted to carry out a flexible migration strategy among the various SAP R/2 and R/3 system possibilities.

The satellite systems, for example, can introduce new SAP applications, hosted from the start by an SAP R/3 system. This way, users can gain experience on the route to a future total SAP R/3 system solution.

SAP R/3 system satellites have successfully supported the following functional areas to a central SAP R/2 system host:

- Application-neutral servers, which perform particular functions, such as optical archiving of mass data and documents
- Consolidation of financial statements from corporate cost centers
- Cash and capital fund management through the treasury workstation
- Executive information system services
- Time management of decentralized personnel
- Decentralized production control and quality assurance
- Managing dispersed warehouses
- Decentralized shipping control
- Industry solutions, which entail specialized satellites in banks, hospitals, and insurance companies, for example

Key Date Total Migration

On a planned key date, your entire business operation can be migrated to the SAP R/3 system environment, perhaps leaving a few independent database servers, running now as satellites.

One Company Code Structure at a Time

It might be that your corporation has acquired a number of subsidiaries that are not all at the same stage in the evolution of their data-processing facilities. The SAP systems can support the integration of heterogeneous systems in which each company code is supported by a different computer configuration. Each may choose to migrate to an integrated SAP R/3 system at different times. The functions of legal consolidation and enterprise management in general can continue without interruption as the waves of migration occur.

Full SAP R/3 Business Process Reengineering with Minor Migrations

You might decide that your business deserves a thorough overhaul in terms of its data processing and, hence, management functions. Tools to support this are described in Chapter 6, "Optimizing Business Processing." Some important data should be migrated to the SAP R/3 environment when the design of the new system has been established.

Application Link Enabling with R/3 System Logistics Modules

An important type of satellite configuration can be seen in connection with applications in the Logistics group. The following systems can be controlled and accessed by using the *Application Link Enabling* (ALE) technology:

- DASS manufacturing control station
- DASS-QSS quality control station
- DISS maintenance control station
- Decentralized LVS inventory management system
- Cross-platform *computer-aided design* (CAD) interactive interface

Coexistence and Linkage Scenarios

The trend for coexistence is supported by a wide range of linkage programs that use the standard business functions with specialized ABAP/4 program elements to provide whatever links are required to make possible continuous business development without loss of effectiveness as new technology is introduced. Wherever possible, these linkage scenarios are executed in the SAP R/3 system environment, where they can be automatically integrated and will benefit from enhancements to this system.

Special Migration Provisions

Although you might need to migrate data, you will not need to migrate functionality in some circumstances.

Superior SAP R/3 Modules

In most cases, it is not common to use migration for the logic of SAP R/2 systems for which fully developed SAP R/3 applications exist. The following are examples:

- RV-Pricing
- RM-Plant Maintenance
- RM-Production Orders
- RK-Orders/Projects/Profit Analysis
- RP-Human Resources Management

Specialized System Enhancements

Full migration is not indicated if your system has already been extensively specialized by a standard modification package. The following are examples:

- IS-OIL, Industry Solution for the petroleum industry
- RIVA
- RV-CPG, Sales and Distribution central processing
- RV-Export
- RV-Transport
- RV-Steel Trading

Migration Alternatives for SAP R/2 Prior to Release 5.0

A number of options are available if Releases 4.3 and 4.4 require migration:

- Upgrade the SAP R/2 system to Release 5.0 and apply the standard package for migration from Release 5.0 to the SAP R/3 system.
- Commission a specific enhancement to the standard migration package to take account of your SAP R/2 system Release 4.3 and 4.4 modules.
- Redesign your system in SAP R/3. Historical data and document data will not be transferred, but minor amounts of master data can be migrated in batch mode.

The standard migration package will not carry out conversion of customer-developed ABAP/4 programs, because changes in the logical database and the field names will not necessarily be correctly migrated.

Many SAP R/2 reports developed specifically for customer installations are not necessary under the SAP R/3 system, because of the highly flexible reporting systems built in. There is no reason to have them transferred.

The standard migration package includes migration programs, planning advice, and a handbook to highlight the differences between SAP R/2 and SAP R/3—particularly the organizational structure changes, which make for better mapping of your company onto the SAP R/3 Enterprise Data Models.

Migration Project Steps

The data migration element of an SAP R/3 system implementation is best carried out under the control of a project plan. The following steps are indicated:

1. Arrange for the personnel to become familiar with the SAP R/3 system.
2. Define the data migration strategy.

3. Establish a formal SAP R/3 system implementation project with the data migration phase included.

4. Rework the functions and processes that exist in the SAP R/2 system so that they will take advantage of the enhancements of the SAP R/3 system.

5. Completely customize the target SAP R/3 system prototype.

6. Install the mechanisms by which high-speed file transfer can occur between the SAP R/2 system mainframe and the SAP R/3 system—*File Transfer Protocol* (FTP), for example.

7. Carry out data migration tests and verify the transfers.

8. Conduct large-scale volume tests for data conversion.

9. Plan and optimize the schedule for closing the production system and transferring the data.

10. Run the SAP R/3 system live in the productive situation.

The task force needed to carry out such a migration project will depend on the complexity and extent of the changes envisioned. In most instances where a substantial SAP system is already in operation, system enhancements will be related to existing components, and the pilot project team will want to refer to the relevant Reference Model to see just how well the new requirements can be met by using the existing software installation. Three key experts are needed:

- A specialist in the business requirement
- A specialist in the existing software installation and its development potential
- A specialist who can see how the system can be best developed by installing and configuring the products available, whether they are SAP or from other suppliers

A pilot scheme can include several independent modules that are under separate development teams but working under a strict management regime so that unnecessary work is avoided.

Many organizations will want to minimize downtime on their productive capacities. Their preference therefore will tend to be toward the establishment of a satellite configuration for the new module that can coexist with the established arrangements until the case for full integration is demonstrated. ●

Complementary Solutions

Extending R/3 with the *Complementary Software Program* (CSP)

SAP has encouraged third-party software developers to interface with SAP and thus extend the R/3 suite's functionality. The technologies used in R/3 help make this possible—technologies such as *Application Link Enabling* (ALE), *object linking and embedding* (OLE), *Remote Function Calls* (RFCs), and *open database connectivity* (ODBC). You can get a fuller appreciation of the place complementary solutions providers occupy in the SAP world in Chapter 43, "The Outlook for the SAP Employment Market." These companies are of special interest to people seeking to "bridge" into SAP work on the strength of a particular technology expertise.

SAP operates a certification program to ensure that complementary products interface properly with SAP, although it doesn't evaluate other aspects of complementary solution software. The complementary software program has extended so rapidly that an up-to-date listing of products is best obtained from the SAP AG Web site **(http://www.sap.com).** Some of the function types available as certified and validated third-party modules compatible with R/3 follow:

Advertising data collection	Interface generation
ALE converters	Job scheduling
Bar-code and radio-frequency devices	Laboratory information management
Business Information Warehouse	Message handling
Collections and deductions	Mobile data entry
Component and supplier management	Modeling software
Computer-aided design	Network security
Credit card handling	Output management
Credit management	Payment Card Interface
Data migration	Plant data collection
Database backup	Point-of-sale
Demand planning	Process control systems
Demand resource planning	Product data management
Development tools	Production optimization
Document management systems	Project systems
Electronic banking	Quality inspection
Electronic commerce	Retail - Additional Printing
Electronic Data Interchange subsystems	Sales and use tax
	SAPScript - Raw Data Interface
Export invoices	System management statistics
Fax and email	Test tools
Form printing	Time and attendance
Geographic information systems	Transportation optimization
GUI-Builder for Executive Information System	Treasury management
	Warehouse control
Health insurance settlement	Web Development tool
Imaging software, optical archives	Weighing instruments

Bibliography

Books

Authorizations Made Easy by SAP Technology Inc.

Champy, James. *Reengineering Management.* Harper Collins.

Coleman, Daniel. *Emotional Intelligence.* Bloomsbury.

Curran, Tom, and Peter Zencke. "Business Process Reengineering—Trend, Reality, or Vision." In SAP AG (ed.), *SAPinfo—Business Reengineering.* Walldorf: 1995.

Davis, Alan M. *Software Requirements—Objects, Functions, and States.* PTR Prentice Hall: 1993.

Department of Trade and Industry (U.K.). *A Code of Practice For Information Security Management.*

Ernst & Young. A 1990 U.K. study by Ernst & Young reported that only two out of the 86 organizations surveyed had IT and business strategies aligned.

Ernst & Young. *Audit Control and Security Features of SAP R/3.*

Fritz, Franz-Josef. "Workflow Implementation Based on the R/3 Reference Model." In SAP AG (ed.), *SAPinfo—Business Reengineering.* Walldorf: 1995.

Gray, John. *Men Are From Mars, Women Are From Venus.* Thorsons.

Hammer, M., and James Champy. *Reengineering the Corporation.* New York: Nicholas Brealey, 1993.

Herzberg, F., et al. *The Motivation to Work.* John Wiley & Sons.

Hewson, Wendy. *The Impact of Computerised Sales and Marketing Systems in the U.K.* Hewson Consulting Group: 1994.

Huck, V.; H.P. Müller; and H.J. Uhink. "Costs Slashed by Business Process Reengineering." In SAP AG (ed.), *SAPinfo—Business Reengineering.* Walldorf: 1995.

Keller, G. "A Strategic Challenge." In SAP AG (ed.), *SAPinfo—Business Reengineering.* Walldorf: 1995.

———. "Transparent Design of Business Process with 'Event-Controlled Process Chains' (EPC)." In SAP AG (ed.), *SAPinfo—Business Reengineering.* Walldorf: 1994.

Keller, G., and S. Meinhardt. "'SAP R/3 Analyzer'—Business Process Reengineering Based on the R/3 Reference Model." In SAP AG (ed.), *SAP Information.* Walldorf: 1994.

———. "'SAP R/3 Analyzer'—A Computer-Assisted Consultancy Tool for Introducing SAP." In SAP AG (ed.), *SAP Information,* Issue 38/39. Walldorf: 1993.

Meinhardt, S. "Interesting Ways to Optimize Business Processes." In SAP AG (ed.), *SAPinfo—Business Reengineering.* Walldorf: 1994.

———. "Process-Oriented Implementation of R/3." In SAP AG (ed.), *SAPinfo—Business Reengineering.* Walldorf: 1995.

Popp, Karl. "Business Process Reengineering with the R/3 Reference Model." In SAP AG (ed.), *SAPinfo—Business Engineering*. Walldorf: 1995.

Strassmann, Paul. *The Business Value of Computers*. The Information Economics Press.

————. *The Impact of Sales and Marketing Systems in the U.K.*

Teufel, T., and F. Ertl. "Process-Oriented Implementation with R/3 Analyzer." In SAP AG (ed.), *SAPinfo—Business Reengineering*. Walldorf: 1995.

Tschira, K., and P. Zencke. "Business Process Optimization with the SAP R/3 System." In SAP AG (ed.), *SAPinfo—Business Reengineering*. Walldorf: 1994.

CD-ROM

R/3 System Online Documentation (CD-ROM)

SAP Training Course Material

BC010 SAP Architecture

BC110 R/3 Correction and Transport System

CA010 SAP Authorization Concept

Index